Less	Equals	Less personal outlays			Equals	Percentage of disposable personal income			Gross national product		Disposable personal income		
(15)	(16)	(17)	(18)	(19)	(20)	Personal outlays							
						(21)	(22)	(23)	(24)	(25)	(26)	(27)	
Personal tax and nontax payments	Disposable personal income	Total	Personal consumption expenditures	Interest paid by consumers	Personal saving	Total	Personal consumption expenditures	Personal saving	Current prices	1972 prices	Current prices	1972 prices	
Billions of dollars						Percent			Per-capita dollars	Billions of dollars	Per-capita dollars	Billions of dollars	
2.5	74.5	71.1	69.9	0.9	3.4	95.4	93.8	4.6	734	268	605	203	1930
1.9	58.5	56.4	55.7	0.5	2.0	96.3	95.2	3.7	566	247	459	194	1935
2.6	75.3	72.0	71.0	0.8	3.4	95.5	94.2	4.5	754	344	570	244	1940
20.8	149.1	120.4	119.5	0.5	28.7	80.8	80.1	19.2	1,514	560	1,066	338	1945
20.6	206.6	194.7	192.0	2.3	11.9	94.2	92.9	5.8	1,887	534	1,362	362	1950
35.4	275.0	258.5	253.7	4.4	16.4	94.0	92.3	6.0	2,416	657	1,664	426	1955
50.4	352.0	332.3	324.9	7.0	19.7	94.4	92.3	5.6	2,800	737	1,947	489	1960
52.1	365.8	342.7	335.0	7.3	23.0	93.7	91.6	6.3	2,847	756	1,991	503	1961
56.8	386.8	363.5	355.2	7.8	23.3	94.0	91.8	6.0	3,020	800	2,073	524	1962
60.3	405.9	384.0	374.6	8.8	21.9	94.6	92.3	5.4	3,140	832	2,144	542	1963
58.6	440.6	411.0	400.5	9.9	29.6	93.3	90.9	6.7	3,309	876	2,296	580	1964
64.9	475.8	442.1	430.4	11.1	33.7	92.9	90.5	7.1	3,536	929	2,448	616	1965
74.5	513.7	477.7	465.1	12.0	36.0	93.0	90.5	7.0	3,822	984	2,613	646	1966
82.1	547.9	503.6	490.3	12.5	44.3	91.9	89.5	8.1	3,999	1,011	2,757	673	1967
97.2	593.4	551.5	536.9	13.8	41.9	92.9	90.5	7.1	4,317	1,058	2,956	701	1968
115.7	638.9	598.3	581.8	15.6	40.6	93.6	91.1	6.4	4,615	1,087	3,152	722	1969
115.8	695.3	639.5	621.7	16.7	55.8	92.0	89.4	8.0	4,795	1,085	3,390	751	1970
116.7	751.8	691.1	672.2	17.7	60.7	91.9	89.4	8.1	5,136	1,122	3,620	779	1971
141.0	810.3	757.7	737.1	19.5	52.6	93.5	91.0	6.5	5,607	1,185	3,860	810	1972
150.7	914.5	835.5	812.0	22.3	79.0	91.4	88.8	8.6	6,210	1,255	4,315	865	1973
170.2	998.3	913.2	888.1	24.1	85.1	91.5	89.0	8.5	6,666	1,248	4,667	858	1974
168.9	1,096.1	1,001.8	976.4	24.4	94.3	91.4	89.1	8.6	7,238	1,231	5,075	875	1975
196.8	1,194.4	1,111.9	1,084.3	26.7	82.5	93.1	90.8	6.9	7,991	1,298	5,477	904	1976
226.5	1,314.0	1,236.0	1,204.4	30.7	78.0	94.1	91.7	5.9	8,839	1,369	5,972	940	1977
258.8	1,474.0	1,384.6	1,346.5	37.4	89.4	93.9	91.3	6.1	9,668	1,439	6,609	983	1978
302.0	1,650.2	1,553.5	1,507.2	45.5	96.7	94.1	91.3	5.9	10,724	1,479	7,333	1,012	1979
336.5	1,828.9	1,718.7	1,668.1	49.6	110.2	94.0	91.2	6.0	11,544	1,475	8,022	1,027	1980
387.7	2,041.7	1,904.3	1,849.1	54.4	137.4	93.3	90.6		12,861	1,512	8,878	1,042	1981
404.1	2,180.5	2,044.5	1,984.9	58.5	136.0	93.8	91.0		13,228	1,480	9,401	1,054	1982
404.2	2,340.1	2,222.0	2,155.9	65.1	118.1	95.0	92.1		14,064	1,534	9,957	1,088	1983
435.1	2,578.1	2,421.2	2,342.3	77.7	156.9	93.9	90.9		15,447	1,639	10,878	1,156	1984

Contemporary Economics

SIXTH EDITION

Milton H. Spencer
Wayne State University

Worth Publishers, Inc.

Contemporary Economics, Sixth Edition

Copyright © 1971, 1974, 1977, 1980, 1983, 1986 by Milton H. Spencer

All rights reserved

Printed in the United States of America

Library of Congress Catalog Card No. 85-51294

ISBN: 0-87901-297-8

First printing, January 1986

Editor: Rosalind Lippel

Production: José Fonfrias

Design: Malcolm Grear Designers

Composition: Progressive Typographers

Printing and binding: Von Hoffmann Press, Inc.

Worth Publishers, Inc.

33 Irving Place

New York, New York 10003

To the students:

Forsan et haec olim
meminisse iuvabit*

VIRGIL, *AENEID*, BOOK 1

* Perhaps some day it will be pleasant
to remember even this

Preface

I hear and I forget
I see and I remember
I do and I understand
    Confucius

As a professor who has also been a consultant to domestic and foreign corporations and governments, it has been my experience that the most effective and interesting way of learning economics is by "doing" it. It has also been my experience that a sound understanding of basic theory is necessary for the intelligent application of economics. Accordingly, an introductory text in the subject should, in my judgment, provide students with the fundamental theory needed to do three things:

1. Understand matters of public policy

2. Evaluate conflicting opinions

3. Arrive at informed conclusions

This book seeks to achieve these objectives in a number of ways. To an extent not found in other texts, this one abounds with recent news articles, real-world examples, current issues, case studies, and practical problems. Most important, these motivating features are provided *without sacrificing basic theory*. As a result, the book enables students to become deeply *involved* in the learning process by "practicing" economics instead of merely hearing about it in lectures and seeing it in a text.

What's New in the Sixth Edition?

One of the notable features of this edition is that it is considerably shorter than the previous one. This has been accomplished by substantially pruning, rewriting, and recasting nearly 50 percent of the book. Topics that have declined in relative importance have been dropped and much new material has been added — thanks to the suggestions of numerous users. The result is a text that is as modern as today's journals and as current as today's news.

Here is a summary of the *major* changes in this edition:

The Private Sector (Chapter 3) After a discussion of the reasons for disparities in personal income distribution, the difficulties of measuring disparities are explained. Emphasis is placed on understanding the factual errors of omission and comission that are often encountered in reports concerning income distribution. The end of the chapter contains a unique class-participation problem in which a Lorenz curve and a Gini coefficient of inequality are derived for the class's distribution of cash on hand. The problem, which can be done in about 15 minutes, is current, practical, and highly motivating.

The Public Sector (Chapter 4) A thoroughly revised discussion of externalities is provided, including explanations of how they can be redressed through market and nonmarket methods. New supply-and-demand models illustrating spillovers are included. The diagrams are integrated in a way that makes the basic concepts exceptionally understandable and teachable.

Economic Instability: Business Cycles, Unemployment, and Inflation (Chapter 6) The Department of Labor's seven measures of unemployment are illustrated and explained. The new definitions of full employment, natural employment, and natural unemployment are discussed. In accordance with today's views, emphasis is placed on understanding and estimating the GNP gap.

The Self-Correcting Economy: Introduction to Classical Economics (Chapter 7) This new chapter introduces the necessary micro foundations of today's macro theory and policy. Classical views of the economy's markets are explained and illustrated with demand-and-supply models. These provide a basis for formulating the aggregate-demand/aggregate-supply model that is refined and extended in later chapters.

Income and Employment Determination: The Income-Expenditure and Income-Price Models (Chapter 9) After learning about the classical and Keynesian theories of instability, this chapter compares and contrasts the two views. Two approaches—the income-price (aggregate-demand/aggregate-supply) and income-expenditure (Keynesian-cross) models—are used consistently to illustrate fundamental ideas. The two models are

then integrated to provide a unified illustration of recessionary and inflationary gaps.

Fiscal Policy and the National Debt (Chapter 10) Both the income-expenditure and income-price models are employed to analyze fiscal-policy principles and issues. A substantially revised and simplified explanation of the balanced-budget multiplier is provided. Today's fiscal-policy controversies, including the inflation and interest-rate issues, are given major attention.

Money, Financial Markets, and the Banking System (Chapter 11) The changing nature of the financial system and the important role of financial (money and capital) markets are emphasized. The "crisis of confidence" in the banking system is also discussed, and some recent bank failures are examined.

Banking Institutions: Money Creation and Portfolio Management (Chapter 12) A concise explanation of bank legislation since 1980, a self-explanatory consolidated balance sheet of all U.S. banks, and a revised demonstration of credit creation in terms of uniform transaction accounts are provided. In addition, the money multiplier, as distinguished from the deposit multiplier, is explained and illustrated. The importance of each is discussed in the context of today's monetary thinking.

Central Banking: Monetary Policy (Chapter 13) A self-explanatory consolidated balance sheet of the 12 Federal Reserve Banks provides a new starting point for the discussion of central-bank monetary policy.

Macroeconomic Equilibrium (Chapter 14) This chapter has been revised to include a more concise discussion of interest-rate theory, classical and Keynesian interpretations, the Fisher effect, and an enlarged schematic outline of the Keynesian model.

Monetarism and the New Classical Economics: Changing Ideas (Chapter 15) The section on monetarism has been substantially shortened and rewritten. It now serves as a "preface" to new-classical economics and the theory of rational expectations. The coverage of this topic is comprehensive and thoroughly modern. Several novel diagrams and illustrations provide interesting pedagogical vehicles that instructors will find extremely useful.

Understanding Macroeconomic Issues (Chapter 16) Today's inflation and unemployment issues are addressed, using the tools provided in previous chapters. Up-to-date data on the Phillips curve are presented, as well as analyses of current major public-policy issues.

The Open Economy: International Trade and International Finance (Chapters 17 and 18) These two chapters provide a comprehensive survey of modern international economics. Several supply-and-demand models illustrate tariffs, import quotas, and exchange-rate appreciation/depreciation in interesting and novel ways. A comprehensive and self-explanatory balance-of-payments statement makes it easy for students to understand, and for instructors to teach, this important but difficult topic.

Supply, Demand, and Elasticity (Chapter 19) Two news articles illustrate important principles that are developed in the chapter. One article, a debate on the minimum wage, focuses on the impact of minimum-wage legislation on the youth market. The other discusses the U.S. wool subsidy and its role in the economy.

Costs of Production (Chapter 21) An account of Ford Motor Company's experience with an iron-casting plant in Flat Rock, Michigan, provides an interesting example of "economies of scale run amok."

Our Farm Problem (Chapter 22 Supplement) Rapid changes occurring in agriculture, especially the effects of the trend toward fewer and larger farms, are pointed out. An unusual set of tables and graphs provides a comprehensive view of the present state of American agriculture.

Monopoly Behavior (Chapter 23) Many people are surprised to learn that there are several dozen *private* prisons in the United States. A debate over privatization of the prison system provides an interesting case study of government monopoly.

Imperfect Competition (Chapter 24) McDonald's, Burger King, Wendy's—these and other fast-food enterprises illustrate monopolistic competition in action. Similarly, price wars in the airline industry demonstrate oligopoly behavior, as do threats of price cuts by some OPEC members. These and other practical applications of imperfect competition enliven this chapter.

Determination of Factor Prices (Chapter 26) Bilateral monopolies are of theoretical interest but are difficult to illustrate with real-world examples. This chapter presents a revised theoretical model as well as a full-page discussion of the conflict between the Baseball Players Association and team owners.

Stability, General Equilibrium, and Welfare Economics (Chapter 27) The September 1985 issue of the *American Economic Review* carried a lead article on some economic aspects of animal behavior. In the previous (1982) edition of this book, the ongoing nature of that research was described. Now, in the sixth edition, the remarkable findings of the article's authors are elaborated in a fascinating boxed essay on "Rat Economics."

Industrial Organization (Chapter 28) This new chapter provides a comprehensive survey of the field. It is organized in terms of structure, conduct, and performance—the basic themes of modern industrial organization theory.

Antitrust Policy (Chapter 29) Almost entirely reorganized and rewritten, this chapter provides a fresh look at the antitrust problem. The exposition is thoroughly modern with numerous brief sketches of landmark antitrust cases extending up to the 1980s. The chapter concludes with a discussion of the "new" antitrust.

Human Resources (Chapter 30) This new chapter covers labor economics and related topics. Labor markets, sex discrimination, comparable-worth issues, and the "new" industrial relations are only a few of the modern problems discussed. The exposition throughout deals with today's labor-economics principles and controversies.

Social Problems (Chapter 31) The discussion of social security has been thoroughly revised and updated to reflect today's problems. A new section on the economics of crime has been added, and the discussion of pollution has been revised with emphasis on policy alternatives.

The Less Developed Countries (Chapter 32) This chapter, which has been shortened, places greater emphasis on development strategies. An interesting section on the newly developing countries of the Pacific Rim is included.

Marxism and Socialism (Chapter 33) This chapter has been substantially shortened by eliminating the discussion of alternative socialist theories. The chapter focuses on Marxism, traditional socialism, democratic socialism, and modern market socialism in Eastern Europe and China.

Economic Planning (Chapter 34) The length of this chapter has been greatly reduced. Attention is focused on Soviet planning and on market socialism in China and Eastern Europe.

Special Features

News Articles, Issues, and Cases Most chapters contain recent news articles that apply the principles being addressed, and a number of chapters contain controversial Issues or Cases. These brief topical essays focus on real-world situations that allow students to apply concepts learned in the chapter. Many of these essays contain thought-provoking questions for discussion, while others require graphing or problem solving.

Leaders in Economics As in previous editions, there are several brief essays on the work of important economists, past and present. These essays focus on the subject's main ideas and contributions as they relate to the topics discussed in the chapter.

Chapter Supplements An optional supplement on indifference curves follows Chapter 22, and one on our farm problem follows Chapter 20. They may be omitted without affecting the continuity of the text.

Dictionary of Economic Terms and Concepts All technical terms and concepts are defined in the text where they are first discussed. In addition, all of these (and many others) are included in an extensive Dictionary at the back of the book. The Dictionary has been revised and expanded since the last edition, and it now contains approximately 1,000 entries. It will serve as a convenient reference for this course and also for other courses students will take in economics and business.

Study Guide and Teaching Aids

The following supplements to *Contemporary Economics* are also available.

Study Guide The *Study Guide*, by Muriel W. Converse (University of Michigan), makes use of several pedagogical methods to help students learn the material covered in the text and to provide them with an opportunity to test their mastery of each topic. The *Study Guide* is written to be useful to *all* students, from those who are having difficulty (who may need to spend more time with it) to those who learn things quickly (who may be primarily concerned with self-testing to assure complete comprehension).

Instructor's Manual The *Instructor's Manual* contains an outline and learning objectives for each chapter. Suggested answers to all of the chapter-end questions in the text are included, as well as a good deal of supplementary material. For example, additional news articles that instructors may want to distribute to their students have been included here.

Transparencies Key charts, graphs, and diagrams from the text are available on acetate transparencies for use in lectures on overhead projectors.

Test Bank and Computerized Test-Generation System In this edition of the *Test Bank,* many new questions have been added to reflect the content and organizational changes in the text. Approximately 2,000 five-choice multiple-choice questions and more than 300 true–false questions are included. Most of the questions emphasize theory and applications, while others test for knowledge of important facts. Fourteen ready-made model examinations are provided at the back of the *Test Bank.*

For those who adopt the book, the questions in the *Test Bank* are available on diskettes (for use on an Apple II+/IIe/IIc or an IBM PC) or on a mainframe tape, either of which can be used to generate examinations. Instructors can add their own questions, edit the existing questions, and print out as many as four different versions of an exam.

Acknowledgments

It is a pleasure to acknowledge the help and cooperation I have received in the preparation of this book.

A general expression of thanks goes to Muriel Converse. She is not only the author of the accompanying *Study Guide* but also my severest critic. Her demanding standards have made the book much better than it might otherwise have been.

William Bowen of *Fortune* magazine read the entire manuscript and made good use of his wide experience and his impressive power of logic in editing it with great skill.

Julie Hearshen-Miller typed a substantial portion of the manuscript and was helpful in many other ways.

Over the life of this book, I have benefited greatly from the criticisms and suggestions of hundreds of dedicated teachers. I cannot list them all here, nor can I list all of my students who have also helped to shape and improve the book. But I am grateful for the many suggestions, over the years, from so many people. I do want to mention and thank those who reviewed substantial portions of this edition and shared their classroom experiences with me:

John Andrulis, WESTERN NEW ENGLAND COLLEGE

Carl J. Austermiller, OAKLAND COMMUNITY COLLEGE — FARMINGTON

Andrew H. Barnett, AUBURN UNIVERSITY

George S. Bohler, FLORIDA JUNIOR COLLEGE — NORTH CAMPUS

James H. Breece, UNIVERSITY OF MAINE — ORONO

C. Ann Brink, PALOMAR COLLEGE

Lillian Broner, OAKLAND COMMUNITY COLLEGE

Yung-Ping Chen, THE AMERICAN COLLEGE

Don L. Coursey, UNIVERSITY OF WYOMING

Elizabeth Crowell, UNIVERSITY OF MICHIGAN — DEARBORN

Carl Davidson, MICHIGAN STATE UNIVERSITY

Philip Duriez, UNIVERSITY OF TEXAS AT EL PASO

Ann Garrison, UNIVERSITY OF NORTHERN COLORADO

Douglas F. Greer, SAN JOSE STATE UNIVERSITY

Martin D. Haney, PORTLAND COMMUNITY COLLEGE

Curtis Harvey, UNIVERSITY OF KENTUCKY

James B. Heisler, HOPE COLLEGE

Roy B. Helfgott, NEW JERSEY INSTITUTE OF TECHNOLOGY

Peter Hofer, METROPOLITAN STATE COLLEGE

Alexander B. Holmes, UNIVERSITY OF OKLAHOMA

Jack Inch, OAKLAND COMMUNITY COLLEGE — FARMINGTON

Jack Klauser, CHAMINADE UNIVERSITY OF HONOLULU

James V. Koch, BALL STATE UNIVERSITY

S. N. Koenigsberg, SAN FRANCISCO STATE UNIVERSITY

Thomas Kompas, IOWA STATE UNIVERSITY

Keith R. Leeseberg, MANATEE JUNIOR COLLEGE

Dona K. Lehr, UNIVERSITY OF ALASKA—
ANCHORAGE

Kenneth Long, NEW RIVER COMMUNITY COLLEGE

Marjorie F. Mabrey, DELAWARE COUNTY
COMMUNITY COLLEGE

John Martin, BARUCH COLLEGE

Bruce McCrea, LANSING COMMUNITY COLLEGE

Starr McMullen, OREGON STATE UNIVERSITY

Mary Helen McSweeney, BARUCH COLLEGE

Gary A. Moore, STATE UNIVERSITY OF NEW YORK—
GENESEO

H. Richard Moss, RICKS COLLEGE

Pearse E. Nolan, EL PASO COMMUNITY COLLEGE

Emlyn A. Norman, TEXAS SOUTHERN UNIVERSITY

Kent W. Olson, OKLAHOMA STATE UNIVERSITY

Edward S. Phillips, SHEPHERD COLLEGE

Donald I. Price, LAMAR UNIVERSITY

Willard W. Radell, Jr., INDIANA UNIVERSITY OF
PENNSYLVANIA

William Schaffer, GEORGIA INSTITUTE OF
TECHNOLOGY

David E. Spencer, BRIGHAM YOUNG UNIVERSITY

Gary L. Thiege, CITY COLLEGE OF SAN FRANCISCO

Michael B. Vaughan, WEBER STATE COLLEGE

Walter J. Wessels, NORTH CAROLINA STATE
UNIVERSITY

Helen L. Youngelson, PORTLAND STATE UNIVERSITY

Joseph A. Ziegler, UNIVERSITY OF ARKANSAS

Contents

Suggested Outlines for One-Semester Courses

● = Recommended chapters.   ○ = Optional chapters, time permitting.

Contents in Brief

Contents

Contemporary Economics

Part 1

Overview: Our Economic System

Introduction

Economics is exciting and important. Anyone who thinks otherwise has failed to realize that economic ideas and practices have moved people to rebellion, and nations to war. Many of the great issues that confront us today — among them unemployment, inflation, poverty, discrimination, and ecological decay — have economic roots. In order to diagnose and remedy these ailments, we must first understand their complex nature.

What Is Economics About?

Anyone beginning the study of a subject likes to have a concise description of its nature and content. Here is a modern definition of economics — one you will use frequently:

Economics is a social science concerned chiefly with the way society employs its limited resources, which have alternative uses, to produce goods and services for present and future consumption.

In other words, economics explains how human and material resources are used to provide people with things they want. By *resources*, economists mean anything that can be used to produce goods or services. This includes human resources, such as hours of labor or a particular skill, and material resources, such as machinery, oil, or land. Another way of putting it is that *economics is concerned with the production and delivery of a standard of living*.

The definition of economics above needs some amplification.

First, why is economics a *social* science? Because it deals with the interactions of people (in particular, their interactions as they buy, sell, produce, and consume). Other social sciences, such as psychology and sociology, also deal with human interactions—sometimes even economic interactions. But in economics, as you will see, the problems studied are approached from a special standpoint and with special tools.

Second, what does it mean to say that resources are limited? Simply that, taken together, people in any society want more goods and services than it is possible to produce. Human and material resources are scarce when compared with people's wants—even in a relatively rich country such as ours. Therefore it is important for any society to use resources effectively. Economics is concerned both with choices regarding the use of resources and with the forces that determine the choices.

Finally, what does it mean to say that resources have alternative uses? Only this: That just as you cannot at the same time both read at home and go to the movies, so any resource that is being fully used for one purpose is not available to be used for another purpose. If a society decides, for example, to allocate more resources to the construction of highways, it will have fewer resources available for the construction of buildings. If it decides to allocate more resources to the production of military goods, it will have fewer resources available for the production of consumer goods. Can you think of some other examples?

Of course, every society operates according to its own rules and regulations. These determine the ways in which resources are used. A society's laws, customs, and practices, and their relationships to its business firms, households, and government, constitute that society's **economic system.** Today, the two major types of economic systems are capitalism

and socialism. The nature of these "isms," and of modern variants of them, will concern us frequently in this book.

"Micro" and "Macro"

Beginning courses in economics are traditionally divided into two components: microeconomics and macroeconomics. They contain some differences in viewpoint as well as some similarities.

Microeconomics is concerned with the specific parts or economic units that make up an economic system and with the relationships between those parts. In microeconomics, emphasis is placed on understanding the behavior of individual firms, industries, and households and the ways in which such entities interact.

Macroeconomics is concerned with the economy as a whole, or with large segments of it. Macroeconomics focuses on such problems as the rate of unemployment, the changing level of prices, the nation's total output of goods and services, and the ways in which government raises and spends money.

Here is a convenient way of thinking about the differences and similarities between "micro" and "macro:"

> Microeconomics looks at the trees, while macroeconomics looks at the forest. Both "macro" and "micro" aim at the construction of theories and the formulation of policies—activities that are the heart of economics.

Working with Theories and Models

Economists, like other scientists, study problems by observing the world and collecting appropriate data. The purpose of this is to discover relationships between events or between quantities called *variables.* For example, economists may study the relationship between the price of automobiles and the amount of automobiles purchased. From such a study, it may be possible to determine how changes in the price affect the quantities purchased. Ultimately, it may be possible to offer a good explanation for the relationship.

At one time, an explanation of a relationship between variables was called a *hypothesis* if there was no evidence to support it, a *theory* if there was some evidence, and a *law* or *principle* if it was certain. Scientists no longer emphasize these distinctions. They know that no hypothesis can be made about a subject of which one is completely ignorant. They know also that no scientific law is ever certain. Consequently, modern scientists tend to use the terms "theory," "law," and "principle" more or less interchangeably.

A theory may be stated in the form of a **model.** This is a representation of the essential features of a theory or of a real-world situation. A model may be expressed in the form of words, diagrams, tables of data, graphs, mathematical equations, or combinations of these. Generally, a model is easier to manipulate than the reality it represents because only the relevant properties of the reality are included. A road map, for example, is a model. Unlike some other maps, which are also models, a road map does not show vegetation or climatic variation because these are not relevant to its purposes. But a road map will serve better than any other type of map to guide you across the country.

A theory or model usually fits the observed facts only approximately. It might have to be revised or even discarded as time passes and the facts themselves change. In recent years, some economic theories have been revised and have replaced older ones to provide better explanations of today's problems.

Common Fallacies in Reasoning

Like physicists and chemists, economists try to use observed, verifiable facts as steppingstones to an understanding of how their portion of the world works. But physicists and chemists can usually discover rather quickly when they are in error. Typically, an experiment goes wrong; perhaps it causes an explosion. Economists, on the other hand, may labor for years under misapprehensions and may advocate policies that affect thousands or even millions of people. Consequently, it is important to discern at the outset whether economic arguments are rational. One way of doing this is to examine them carefully with the help of formal logic.

In common usage, the word *fallacy* denotes any mistaken idea or false belief. In a stricter sense, a fallacy is an error in reasoning or argument. This is what you should look for when you analyze economic ideas. Of course, an argument may be so obviously incorrect that it deceives nobody. For our purposes, however, we shall reserve the word *fallacy* for certain types of reasoning that, although incorrect, are nevertheless persuasive—a dangerous combination. Here are some typical fallacies of economic thinking. Understanding them will help you to pinpoint errors in other people's reasoning as well as in your own.

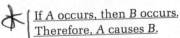

Fallacy of False Cause

Every science tries to discover cause-and-effect relationships. The fallacy of false cause, or ***post hoc fallacy,*** is often encountered in such efforts. (The latter name comes from the Latin expression *post hoc ergo propter hoc,* which means "after this, therefore because of this.") This fallacy is committed when a person mistakenly assumes that, because one event follows another or both events occur simultaneously, one is the cause and the other the effect.

It is common for a fallacy of false cause to be expressed in the form of an "if–then" argument:

If *A* occurs, then *B* occurs.
Therefore, *A* causes *B.*

Is this sufficient reason for concluding that *A* causes *B*? Not necessarily. There are other possible explanations:

- *B* may occur by chance.
- *B* may be caused by factors other than *A* (or by a third factor that is a common cause of both *A* and *B*).
- *B* may cause *A.*

Economics in the News

At Harvard at Least, Economics Was Never as Popular As It Is Now

Students' Interest in Money Offsets The Dismal Image

By Lindley H. Clark Jr. and Alfred L. Malabre Jr.

CAMBRIDGE, Mass.—Here are Harvard, the dismal science rides high. A procession of erroneous forecasts and theories that seem to work only on the blackboard may have soured business planners on economics. But no such disaffection is apparent among students here.

By the standards of this 348-year-old institution, this popularity isn't of long standing. As recently as the early 1970s, economics ran a feeble sixth, far behind such majors as government, history, English and psychology-social relations, the front-runner. But now economics claims over 600 undergraduates, and no other major comes close.

More attuned to marketplace practicalities than their predecessors of a dozen years ago, Harvard undergraduates, including an increasing number of women, are taking economics as a springboard to jobs as investment bankers and corporate managers.

Some possibilities are illustrated in the following examples:

Example 1 Company *X* hired a new sales manager, and the firm's sales soared during the ensuing year.
Therefore, the growth in sales was due to the new sales manager.

This argument, consisting of both the statement and the conclusion, is obviously a false cause or *post hoc* fallacy. It fails to point out that, although some of the growth in sales may be due to the manager's efforts, much or even most of it may be the result of other factors. These may be lower prices for the company's products, higher incomes of buyers, or an increase in the number of buyers in the market.

Example 2 The severity of hay fever varies inversely with the price of corn. That is, the lower the price of corn, the greater the severity of hay fever, and vice versa.
Therefore, corn prices affect hay fever.

It is true that the price of corn and the severity of hay fever are inversely related. But the fact is that ragweed is a cause of hay fever. The summer conditions that produce an abundance of ragweed—high temperatures and adequate rainfall—also produce an abundance of corn. This usually results in lower corn prices. Thus, it may *seem* as if corn prices affect hay fever. In reality, these factors are independent of each other, and a third factor is operating that is a common cause of both.

Fallacies of Composition and Division

Two additional fallacies are often encountered in economic arguments. The ***fallacy of composition*** occurs when one reasons that what is true of the parts of something is also necessarily true of the whole of it. The ***fallacy of division*** occurs when one contends that something that is true of the whole is also necessarily true of its parts taken separately.

The following true statements from economics illustrate these common fallacies:

- It may be desirable for a family to increase its savings by cutting down on its consumption expenditures. If all families do this, however, spending in the economy may decline. If this happens, firms will lay off workers, the level of total income will fall, and families will find themselves saving less rather than more.

- If the prices in a specific industry were to increase tomorrow by x percent, the firms in that industry would probably experience an increase in profits. But if the prices of all goods and services throughout the economy were to increase tomorrow by x percent, no firms would experience an increase in profits.

- Economic policies that may be wise for a *nation* are not necessarily wise for an *individual*, and vice versa.

The fallacies of composition and division are thus particularly relevant to the study of microeconomics and macroeconomics.

The fallacy of composition warns us that what is true of the parts is not necessarily true of the whole. Thus, generalizations of a microeconomic nature may not always be applicable to a macroeconomic problem. The fallacy of division warns us that what is true of the whole is not necessarily true of the parts. Thus, generalizations of a macroeconomic nature may not always be applicable to a microeconomic problem.

These ideas may seem obvious. However, the fallacies can be remarkably subtle when they occur in discussions of actual economic problems.

What You Have Learned

1. Economics is a *social* science. It deals with aspects of human behavior—particularly how people earn a living and how societies produce goods and services.

2. Like all sciences, social or physical, economics uses theories and models to represent reality. However, a model is a simplified version of reality. As such, it may need to be adjusted or even abandoned as facts change or as new facts come to light.

3. Many types of fallacies can be committed in economic reasoning. Perhaps the most common are the fallacy of false cause and the fallacies of composition and division.

Terms and Concepts To Review

economics
economic system
microeconomics
macroeconomics
variables
model
fallacy of composition
fallacy of division

Know these terms

For Discussion

1. "Everyone knows that the United States is one of the richest countries in the world. Therefore, economics as it is defined may be correct for poor countries, but certainly not for America, where the problem is one of abundance, not scarcity." True or false? Explain.

2. Senator Jason is campaigning for a tax reduction. He argues that tax cuts in other major industrial nations have stimulated their rapid economic growth. Senator Blaine replies that what happens in nations thousands of miles away is no guide to what will happen here. Do you agree with Senator Blaine? Why or why not?

Identify at least one fallacy in each of the following:

3. "All rich nations have steel industries. Therefore, the surest way for a poor nation to become rich is to develop its own steel industry."

4. "The students who do best in economics have some working experience. Therefore, the surest way to receive a good grade in this course is to go out and get a job."

5. "To press forward with a properly ordered wage structure in each industry is the first condition for curbing competitive bargaining; but there is no reason why the process should stop there. What is good for each industry can hardly be bad for the economy as a whole."

 Twentieth Century Socialism, 1956, p. 74

6. "Each person's happiness is a good to that person, and the general happiness, therefore, a good to the aggregate of all persons."

 John Stuart Mill, *Utilitarianism, 1863*

7. In a capitalist system, each manufacturing plant is free to set its own price on the product it produces. Therefore, there can't be anything wrong with all manufacturers getting together to agree on the prices of the products they produce.

8. Economics textbooks usually are long and dull, so we can't expect this one to be short and interesting.

9. "Roger Babson was best known for his predictions of the stock market. He once wrote an article in which he contended that gravity affects weather and crops, crops influence business, and business affects elections. He supported his thesis with an analysis of 27 presidential elections [covering a period of more than 100 years]. In

75 percent of the cases, he said, the party in power remained in power when weather and business were good, and was voted out when weather and business were bad."

Martin Gardner,
Fads and Fallacies in the Name of Science, 1957, p. 97

Working with Graphs

Economic ideas are often expressed by means of models. One common way of presenting a model is in the form of a line graph. Such a graph shows relationships between variables—that is, how one quantity varies in relation to another. The procedure for making line graphs is illustrated in the following paragraphs and in Figures (a) through (f).

In Figure (a), a common sheet of graph paper is shown. Two intersecting straight lines at right angles to each other are drawn on the graph paper. The horizontal line is called the x axis, the vertical line the y axis, and the point of intersection the origin. The two lines divide the graph into four parts called quadrants. These quadrants are identified by starting with the upper right-hand corner and numbering them counterclockwise. Observe that positive numbers on the x axis are to the right of the origin and negative numbers are to the left. Positive numbers on the y axis are above the origin, and negative numbers are below. For brevity, we write the coordinates of a point in the form (x,y), where x is the value on the x axis and y is the value on the y axis. These procedures for labeling and numbering are used in all branches of science.

Using this information, you can locate any point on the graph with two numbers—one for x and one for y—in much the same way as you would locate a ship at sea by its latitude and longitude. The two numbers are called the coordinates of the point. Thus, the coordinates of point A are (3,5), those of point B are (5,2), and those of point C are (4,0). The horizontal, or x, coordinate is always stated first and the vertical, or y, coordinate second. Can you give the coordinates of the remaining points?

Graphs such as these are used to show how one quantity varies in relation to another. In Figure (b), for example, the values of x and y are plotted from the data in the accompanying table. First, the points representing each pair of values of x and y are located and marked. The points are then connected with a smooth curve, in this case a straight line. Because the line slopes upward from left to right, the two variables are said to be *directly* related. Thus, as x increases, y increases; as x decreases, y decreases. In contrast, the line in Figure (c) slopes downward from left to right. Therefore, the two variables are said to be *inversely* related. Thus, as x increases, y decreases; as x decreases, y increases.

In economics, the lines plotted usually fall entirely in the first quadrant. This is because the data on which the lines are based are positive, although there are important exceptions. Sometimes two or more lines are plotted on the same graph in order to examine the relationships between them, as in Figure (d). In order to distinguish between the lines, they may be labeled with different letters, such as S and D. In the accompanying table, each P_S value refers to the S curve, and each P_D value refers to the D curve. Can you read the coordinates of the points determining these lines? Try filling in the table.

Different scales and labels may be used on the horizontal and vertical axes, to suit the particular purpose of the graph. An example of this is shown in Figure (e). The vertical axis in this graph shows P, the price in dollars of a particular bond. The horizontal axis shows t, the time in number of years after the bond was purchased. The curve shows the relationship between these two variables—that is, what happened to the price, P, of a bond t years after it was purchased. For example, at $t = 0$, $P = $1,204$; and at $t = 2$ years, $P = $1,190$. Can you fill in the table? Where necessary, try to estimate the numbers from the graph.

Finally, Figure (f) shows the unit costs, C, that a certain firm experiences as a result of producing different quantities, Q, of a commodity. You should be able to fill in the table from the graph.

x	-3	-2	-1	0	1	2	3	4
y	-2	-1	0	1	2	3	4	5

x	-3	-2	-1	0	1	2	3	4
y	5	4	3	2	1	0	-1	-2

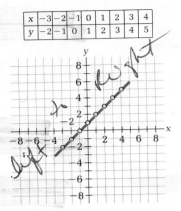

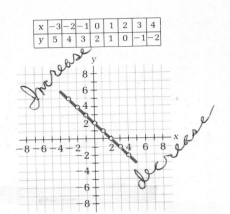

Figure (a): The two intersecting straight lines divide the graph into four quadrants, which are numbered counterclockwise. Positive values are measured to the right along the x axis and upward along the y axis. Negative values are measured to the left along the x axis and downward along the y axis. Any point on the graph can be located by its coordinates.

Figure (b): A line that slopes upward from left to right exhibits a direct relation between the two variables. As one variable increases, so does the other; as one decreases, so does the other.

Figure (c): A line that slopes downward from left to right exhibits an inverse relation between the two variables. As one variable increases, the other decreases; as one decreases, the other increases.

x	2	3	4	5	6
Ps	3	4	5	6	7
Pd	7	6	5	4	3

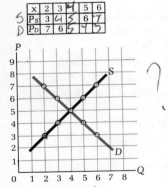

t	0	4	8	12	16
P					

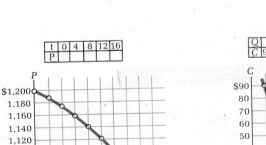

Q	1	2	3	4	5	6	7
C	90	60	30	20	30	60	90

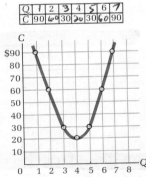

Figure (d): Two or more lines may be drawn on the same graph in order to study the relationships between them. Can you complete the table from the graph?

Figure (e): Scales should be chosen and axes labeled in the manner that best suits a particular problem. Can you use the graph to estimate the missing numbers in the table?

Figure (f): The points should be connected with care because the resulting curve may be quite pronounced. Can you fill in the table from the graph?

Exercises in Graphing

For exercises 1–3, sketch the graphs of the following relationships:

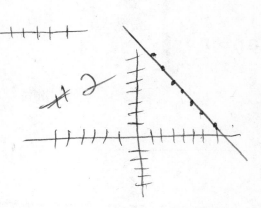

1.

x	1	2	3	4	5	6	7	8
y	1	2	3	4	5	6	7	8

2.

x	1	2	3	4	5	6	7
y	7	6	5	4	3	2	1

3.

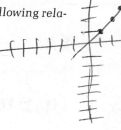

x	−2	0	2	4
y	−8	−4	0	4

4. Sketch the following data on the same graph. Estimate the coordinates of the point of intersection of the two lines.

x	1	2	3	4
y	2	3	4	5

x	1	2	3	4
y	5	4	3	2

5. Sketch the graph of hog prices as a function of time:

time (t)	0	1	2	3	4	5	6	7	8
hog prices (P)	8	33	40	35	24	13	8	15	40

Chapter 1

Our Mixed Economy: Resources, Goals, and Institutions

Learning Guide

Watch for answers to these important questions

What are the resources of our economic system?   What kinds of payments are made for their use?

What goals do we want our economy to achieve?   Can we trade various goals against one another?   Are there costs of doing so?

Why is our economic system called "capitalistic"? What social, political, and economic institutions constitute the basis of capitalism?   How can we depict the flow of goods and resources in a capitalistic system?

This evening, it would be nice if you could (1) read this chapter, (2) do all your other course assignments, (3) earn some money, (4) engage in some pleasant recreational activity, and (5) relax and enjoy a leisurely dinner at the best restaurant in town. But you cannot do all these things.   You will have to give up one or more of them because you are faced with limitations of time and (possibly) of money. Economic systems also face limitations.   They are limitations of the human and nonhuman resources needed to produce goods and services.   This chapter describes the nature of those limitations and the ways in which an economy adjusts to them.

Factors of Production: Resources of Our Economic System

Every economic system has various resources at its disposal to produce goods and services.   These resources are of two broad types:

Material Resources   These include such things as natural resources, raw materials, machinery and equipment, buildings, and transportation and communication facilities.

Human Resources   These consist of the productive physical and mental abilities of people.

As you learn more about economics, you will find this classification of resources to be too general for some practical applications. Economists therefore divide property resources into two subcategories, "land" and "capital," and human resources into two subcategories, "labor" and "entrepreneurship." These four types of resources are known as the ***factors of production.*** They are the basic ingredients, or "inputs," that are used to produce "outputs."

Land   ~~PROPERTY RESOURCE~~

The term ***land,*** in economics, means all nonhuman or "natural" resources, such as land itself, mineral deposits, timber, and water. Land thus consists of all the natural physical stuff on which any civilization must be built.

You may be surprised to learn that many countries, even some of the poorest, have vast quantities of untapped natural resources. This is true because world demand for those resources is not sufficient to make their extraction profitable with existing technology. When these conditions change, as they often do, a country's natural resources may take on new economic significance.

Because of this, a nation's "stock" of natural resources should not be thought of as a fixed physical quantity. Instead, it should be viewed as a variable one whose size is determined by changing economic and technological conditions. The United States, for example, has large untapped reservoirs of oil and natural gas. However, these resources will not be extracted until higher prices resulting from increased demand, or lower costs resulting from technological advances, make their extraction profitable.

Capital   ~~PROPERTY RESOURCE~~

People in business use the term "capital" differently from the way it is used by economists. In economics, ***capital*** may be defined as a produced means of further production. What "produced"

means here is that capital is created by human resources working with material resources. Thus timber is considered to be land, but lumber is capital. In this sense, capital means *capital goods or investment goods,* the things that are used by business. Other examples are tools, machinery and equipment, factory buildings, freight cars, and office furniture. Capital is thus an economic resource that can be used to help produce consumer goods and services, such as food, cars, clothing, and health care.

It is important to note that capital, to the economist, means *physical* capital (goods used in production) and not *financial* capital (money). Businesspeople, *but not economists,* generally use the term "capital" to mean money—the funds used to purchase capital goods and to finance the operation of a business. For the economy as a whole, however, money is not a productive resource. If it were, nations could become rich simply by printing money. Money's chief function is to facilitate the exchange of goods and services. Money therefore serves as a "lubricant" rather than a factor of production within the economic system.

Labor   ~~HUMAN RESOURCE~~

To make land and capital productive requires ***labor,*** the efforts or activities of people hired to assist in the production of goods and services. In this sense, labor refers not to the workers themselves but to the service they provide by working.

In a broader sense, however, "labor" also means the services of everyone who works for a living. We often refer to the labor force of a nation—that is, all the people above a certain age who have jobs or are seeking jobs. The meaning of "labor force" and the notion of labor as a factor of production are different concepts in economics. The distinction between the two is generally clear from the context.

Entrepreneurship   → ~~HUMAN RESOURCE~~

For production of goods or services, the three factors described above must be organized and combined.

~~Human Resource~~

This is where **entrepreneurship** (sometimes called "ownership") enters the picture. Entrepreneurs recognize the opportunities to be gained from production. The entrepreneur assembles the factors of production, raises the necessary money, organizes the management, makes the basic business policy decisions, and reaps the gains of success or the losses of failure. Some entrepreneurs act as their own managers; others hire people to serve as managers. But, regardless of who acts as manager, the *entrepreneurial function* is necessary.

Something to Think About

Is there such a thing as "human" capital? Are scientists, engineers, teachers, doctors, lawyers, and skilled workers, for example, part of society's capital? What criteria would you use when deciding whether something is qualified to be called capital?

Returns to Owners of Resources

In a capitalistic system, the factors of production are privately owned. In other types of economic systems, one or more of the factors of production might be owned by government. There is never enough land, capital, labor, or entrepreneurship to produce enough goods and services to satisfy everyone. Therefore, in a capitalistic system, the owners of these factors can command a price for them in the market.

Those who supply land receive a payment called rent. Those who supply financial capital, the money that business firms borrow for the purchase of physical capital, receive a return called *interest*. Workers who sell their labor receive a payment called *wages*, which includes salaries, commissions, and the like. Finally, those who perform the entrepreneurial function receive, or at least hope for, *profits*.

The yearly sum of rent, interest, wages, and profits for a country is the total annual income earned by all resource owners. This total is called **national income.** A summary of these ideas is presented in Exhibit 1.

Exhibit 1
Classifying the Factors of Production

Resource or factor of production	Description	Payment
Land	Natural resources (e.g., land itself, including minerals, water, timber)	Rent
Capital	Produced resources (e.g., tools, factories, machines)	Interest
Labor	Physical and mental efforts (e.g., hired workers and professionals)	Wages
Entrepreneurship	Ownership function (e.g., organizing and financial risk taking)	Profit
Annual total		National income

Specialization and Division of Labor

Although the factors of production are grouped into four broad classes, there is generally a considerable degree of specialization within each class. Machines, for example, are designed to do specific jobs, and people are often trained to perform specific tasks.

Technically, **specialization** is the division of productive activities among people and regions with the result that no one person or area is self-sufficient. Specialization by workers is sometimes called **division of labor.** The result of specialization is an enormous gain in productivity, such as output per worker.

These ideas have been fundamental to economic thinking for well over 200 years. They were first expressed in 1776 by Adam Smith, a Scottish philosopher who was the founder of modern economics. To generalize from Smith, specialization and division of labor increase production because they:

- Allow for the development and refinement of skills.
- Eliminate the waste of time that is entailed in going from one job to another.

Economics in the News

On Campuses, Making Dean's List Comes Second to Making a Profit

By Karen Blumenthal

DALLAS—Students talk of painting yachts, delivering birthday cakes or selling underwear emblazoned with school crests. "It's become fashionable on campus to be 19 and say, 'I have my own company,'" says Verne Harnish, national director of the Association of Collegiate Entrepreneurs.

Many collegiate entrepreneurs market to the customers whose needs they know best: their fellow students. At the University of Texas, for instance, men try to wow that special date by sending her flowers in advance. So junior Steve Schaffer decided to buy long-stem roses wholesale and deliver them.

With lower overhead, he markets the posies for about ⅓ the price of the flower shops, sells about 25 dozen before each big dance and sees a nice profit.

Two freshmen at the University of California-Santa Barbara learned a business lesson, when they decided to put on dances for students too young for the local discos. They spent more than $1,000 up front, printing invitations, renting a roller-skating rink and buying roses for the ladies. Only 350 students showed up. They were left with a loss and a lot of roses.

Some businesses that begin with only modest aspirations have become grand enterprises. Another U.C.-Santa Barbara student, Dan Bienenfeld, borrowed $2,000 from his father to produce a calendar. It was to feature photos of some of the good-looking men about campus, an imitation of a popular calendar created by University of Southern California students. He grossed $10,000. [Then] he aimed higher, taking on two partners and finding an investor to put up $80,000.

Calendar sales [eventually] hit $200,000 and College Look Inc., as it's now called, has added lines of posters, gift-wrap and a teddy-bear that sings "Love Me Tender" when hugged. Sales are expected to reach $3 million. "We've hit the home run," says 22-year-old Chip Conk, an original pinup boy and now one of the partners. "Now we just have to run the bases."

– Simplify human tasks, thus permitting the introduction of laborsaving machines.

Of course, specialization has its shortcomings. A repetitive, boring job can dull a worker's mind and can become little more than a naked means of subsistence. Accordingly, many companies continually seek ways to improve the quality of working life. In numerous manufacturing firms, for instance, assembly-line workers are being given larger shares of responsibility in the management of their work. And participatory decision making between workers and managers, once considered textbook theory, is becoming much more of a reality.

Goals of Our Economic System: What Do We Want to Accomplish?

When we refer to the economy as a "system," we imply that it has a purpose and that there is order in its structure. What are the purposes of our economic system? What do we want our economy to do?

Every society seeks to attain certain objectives. Four goals that are fundamental to all economic systems, capitalistic as well as socialistic, are efficiency, equity, stability, and growth. The meanings of these terms are worth examining because they are universal standards used for judging economic practices and policies.

Efficiency: Full Employment of Resources

Because every society possesses only limited amounts of the various factors of production, it is important to use them efficiently. What does this mean? In general, efficiency is the best use of available resources to attain a desired result. It is important to distinguish between two kinds of efficiency—technical and economic.

Two Types of Efficiency

Technical Efficiency

Engineers measure physical efficiency by the ratio of physical output to physical input. The greater the ratio, the greater the physical efficiency. If a motor, for example, uses 100 units of energy input to produce 75 units of energy output, the motor is said to be 75 percent efficient. If the motor produces 80 units of energy output for 100 units of energy input, the motor is 80 percent efficient.

A firm, an industry, or an entire economy is said to have achieved *technical efficiency* when it is producing maximum output by making the fullest possible utilization of available inputs. The available resources are then said to be *fully employed* in the most effective way. Therefore, no change in the combination of inputs can be made that will increase the output of one product of the system without decreasing the output of another.

This idea can be illustrated with an example. Suppose a farmer growing as much corn as possible with the available quantities of labor, capital, and land has achieved technical efficiency. Under these circumstances, it will be impossible for the farmer to transfer some resources out of corn production and into wheat production without decreasing the farm's output of corn. Can you give a similar example for a manufacturing firm? For the producer of a service?

The concept of technical efficiency can be broadened from simple production systems to more complex ones, such as firms, industries, or the entire economy. An economic system, for example, is technically efficient if every producing unit in the system has attained technical efficiency—the greatest possible ratio of physical output to available physical input. No change in the combination of society's resources can then be made that will increase the output of one product without decreasing the output of another.

Economic (Allocative) Efficiency

Suppose a society has achieved technical efficiency and is making full use of its available resources. Would you give high marks to such a society if families who wanted a larger apartment had to wait ten

years before one became available? Would you think the economy efficient if people who wanted to buy meat for dinner were required to spend all afternoon waiting in line outside the meat market? Most people would agree that an economic system ought to deliver the goods and services that people want and are able to pay for.

A standard that is useful in determining the success of an economy is *economic,* or *allocative, efficiency.* An economy is said to have achieved economic (allocative) efficiency when it is producing that combination of goods and services that people prefer, given their incomes. No change can then be made in the combination of resources or output that will make someone better off without making someone else worse off—each in their own estimation.

Because technical and economic efficiency are important concepts, it is useful to look at the relation between them:

1. A society that has achieved technical efficiency is making full use of its available resources. But the society is not *economically* efficient unless it is producing the goods that people prefer to purchase with their existing incomes.

2. A society that has achieved economic efficiency has also achieved technical efficiency. That is, the society is not only producing the largest possible output with the available resources but also satisfying consumer preferences. Economic efficiency is thus a general concept that includes technical efficiency.

Equity: Fairness or Economic Justice

Consideration of economic efficiency does not address the question of how a society's goods are shared. This is a matter of *income distribution*. It concerns the division of a society's output (that is, the income or value of what society earns from production) among its members. Because income distribution deals with the matter of who gets how much, it raises fundamental issues of equity, or justice. One of the major goals of our society is to achieve an equitable distribution of income. It is important to note that equitable means "*fair*" or "*just,*" *not* "equal."

Equity is both a philosophical concept and an economic goal. There is no scientific way of concluding that one distribution of income is fair and therefore "good" while another is unfair and therefore "bad." For example, in the United States a neurosurgeon may earn twenty times as much as a schoolteacher; in Britain, four times as much; in Israel, twice as much; and in Cuba, an even smaller ratio. Which ratio is considered equitable depends on society's prevailing rules or standards of income distribution. You will learn about such standards in later chapters.

Stability: Steady Average Price Level

A third economic goal of every society is to achieve stability of prices. This does not mean that *all* prices should be stable. That would be impossible in a society in which people are free to make economic decisions. However, it means that the general or average level of prices should be reasonably stable. This goal is important because the costs to society of a sharply rising average price level — inflation — are serious and pervasive.

Inflation does harm in various ways. It impairs efficiency by lowering incentives to produce. It redistributes income arbitrarily and inequitably by reducing many people's purchasing power by disproportionate amounts. Further, it greatly weakens the nation's ability to compete in world markets when prices at home rise faster than those in other countries with which we trade.

Growth: Rising Output per Person

A fourth economic goal of every society is economic growth. By this is meant an increase in the quantity of goods and services produced per person — in other words, a rising standard of living.

Economic growth is related to the goals of stability, efficiency, and equity. By maintaining stability, an economy avoids substantial price fluctuations and is better able to encourage efficiency — continuous full employment of available resources. This, in turn, leads to a robust volume of economic activity and to steady economic growth. As a result, living standards are enhanced for all income groups in society because all of them benefit even if each receives a constant proportion of an expanding economic pie.

Striving for A Mix of Goals

The goals of efficiency, equity, stability, and growth seem reasonable enough. However, their realization may involve certain sacrifices — for the following two reasons.

Free Choice Versus Governmental Direction

In a democracy, there is a close connection between political freedom and economic freedom. Citizens vote for legislators who influence government policy. Consumers choose the goods they want. Workers select their occupations. And holders of wealth employ their assets as they see fit. Government, of course, may impose certain restrictions that it believes are in the public's interest (or in the interest of some large voting bloc or effective pressure group). Also, social or racial discrimination may deprive some people of equal opportunities. Nevertheless, *freedom of choice is an ideal of our political and economic system.*

Unfortunately, freedom of choice may not always lead to efficiency, equity, stability, and growth. When it does not, a society may be inclined to rely heavily on governmental direction and control to try to achieve these goals. This could cause some loss of political and economic freedoms.

Conflicting Goals

A second reason why sacrifices may be necessary is that goals can conflict with each other. For example, efficiency can conflict with stability if a high level of employment exerts upward pressure on prices. Similarly, economic growth can conflict with equity if a rising volume of output benefits some groups much more than others.

Where such conflicts occur, government may try, through legislation or regulation, to promote the desirable goals while minimizing the undesirable consequences. But even if such efforts achieve their declared objectives, they are likely to entail some costs. For instance, legislation that establishes a ceiling for wages and prices may very well succeed in curbing inflation. However it will also limit freedom of choice for consumers, workers, and business-people alike.

Conclusion: Decisions Involve Trade-Offs

As these considerations indicate, every decision entails a choice between alternatives. If the choices are to be made rationally, we must understand the trade-offs. A trade-off is the cost of choosing one objective over another, or of formulating compromises between them. Thus, an overall problem faced by every society is to establish a proper mix of goals. In doing so, a society — or a person, for that matter — cannot avoid trade-offs.

> The goals of nations vary according to their political as well as their economic philosophies. For example, the Soviet Union and some other Eastern bloc countries have striven for a high level of military preparedness along with rapid economic growth. As a result, they have sacrificed much political and economic freedom. Democratic capitalistic countries, such as the United States, Canada, Japan, and many Western European nations, have tried to achieve somewhat different goals. They have sought higher levels of efficiency and growth (and in some cases national defense) without sacrificing political and economic freedom.

Scarcity: A Fact of Life

In economics, *scarcity* is the name of the game and *economizing* is the way it is played. Every society must face a fundamental economic challenge. How can limited resources best be used to satisfy unlimited wants? This is the problem of scarcity.

For most people, scarcity is a fact of life. Most of the things they want and need are **economic goods,** in that they have a price. In this sense, they differ from **free goods,** for which the market price is zero. But even "free goods" may be scarce in some circumstances. Hawaiian sunshine and surf are free to residents of Hawaii, but not to tourists who must expend time, effort, and money to get there. The fish in a mountain lake may be free goods, but in a city they are economic goods.

These considerations suggest an important law:

> **Law of Scarcity** Economic resources are scarce. There are never enough at any given time to produce all the things that people want. Scarce resources can be increased, if at all, only through effort or sacrifice.

Scarcity of resources is what forces people in every economic activity to make choices. A decision to produce one thing frequently implies a decision to produce less of certain other things. All societies face the basic problem of deciding what they are willing to sacrifice to get the things they want. *This is the central problem of economics.*

> Economics is fundamentally concerned with choices about the use of resources. Problems of choice arise when there are alternative ways of achieving a given objective. Economics develops criteria that define the conditions for making the best use of resources. These criteria can be used as guidelines for formulating and evaluating public policy.

The Great Questions: What? How? For Whom?

It is the task of an economic system to combine efficiently its *resources*, *wants*, and *technologies*. To do so, it must answer three fundamental and interdependent questions.

What Goods and Services Should Society Produce — and in What Quantities?

How should a society's scarce resources be allocated? Should some of them be taken out of the production of consumer goods (food, clothing, automobiles, and appliances) and put into the production of capital goods (tools, machines, tractors, and factories)? Would the reverse be better? For instance, by enlarging its proportion of capital goods now, the economy will be able to produce more consumer goods in the future. It is necessary, then, to decide how much consumption should be sacrificed today to provide for increased output of consumer goods later.

A related question is: *How much* of each good will society produce? How many automobiles? How much food and clothing? How many tractors, factories, and so on? The values and priorities involved in making such decisions are extremely complex. Nevertheless, in answering this question, society is again choosing between present and future satisfactions. It is making a trade-off between the amount of consumption to be sacrificed today and the prospect of increased consumption at a later time.

How Should Resources Be Organized for Production?

Most goods can be produced in more than one way by using resources in different quantities and combinations. In the early days of the United States, for example, land was in abundant supply and labor was not. Therefore, labor was the limiting factor in producing agricultural commodities. In parts of the Far East, by contrast, land is relatively more scarce than labor. Consequently, large quantities of labor are applied to limited amounts of arable land.

Similarly, it is often possible to vary the combinations of resources in manufacturing. Automobiles, for example, can be produced from different combinations of such materials as steel, aluminum, or fiber glass, as well as with different combinations of labor and capital. Any society, therefore, decides how it will *organize* its scarce resources in order to use them efficiently.

For Whom Shall the Goods Be Produced?

Who is to receive what share of the economic pie? This question is of enormous significance — for two reasons:

1. An economic system is often judged by the way in which it distributes its goods and services.

2. The pattern of distribution determines our individual standards of living.

The three great questions — *what, how,* and *for whom* — are fundamental in all societies. Each society meets these challenges in different ways.

At one extreme is a **command economy.** This is one in which an authoritarian government exercises primary control over decisions concerning what and how much to produce. The Soviet Union and some other socialist nations are examples of countries with predominately command economies. At the other extreme is the **market economy.** In such an economy, questions concerning what and how much to produce are decided in an open market through competitive forces of supply and demand. The market economy embodies the idea of "pure" capitalism, also called "theoretical capitalism." It is an extremely useful model of what would happen in the absence of governmental direction. (The model's uses are examined in later chapters.) It is important to note, however, that no countries with pure market economies exist.

Between the two extremes of a command economy and a market economy is the **mixed economy.** Here economic questions are decided partly by the workings of a free market and partly by governmental authority. Most of the developed nations fall into this category. However, they vary in the degree of reliance they place on market mechanisms.

Society's Production Possibilities

Even a wealthy society cannot escape the need for economizing. The problem of economizing is complex, and we must simplify it in order to focus on the basic concepts involved.

We may begin by constructing a model of the economizing process for a hypothetical society. The model is based on four simplifying assumptions:

1. **Two Goods** *The economy produces only agricultural products, such as crops and livestock, and capital goods, such as machines and factories.* This

assumption permits us to derive principles for a simple economy.   These principles are also applicable
to a complex economy producing many goods.

2. Common Resources   *The same resources can be
used to produce either or both of the two classes of
goods and can be shifted freely between them.*   This
means that labor and other factors of production can
be used to produce either food or machines, or different combinations of both.

3. Fixed Conditions   *The supply of resources and
the state of technological knowledge are fixed.*   This
is an appropriate assumption for the short run.   In
the long run, of course, the supply of resources and

the level of technological knowledge are expand-
able.

4. Full Employment   *Society's available resources
are working in the most (technically) efficient way.*
It follows from this assumption that in the short run
the economy may be able to increase the production
of one class of goods by taking resources away from
the production of another class of goods.   However,
the economy cannot increase the production of *both*
classes of goods because there are no excess resources available.

   The model is depicted, in both tabular and
graphic form, in Exhibit 2.   The table is called a
production-possibilities   schedule.   Notice   that

Exhibit 2
Society's Production-Possibilities Curve:
Achieving Technical Efficiency

A society that is producing a combination of goods on
its production-possibilities curve has achieved technical efficiency.   This means that the society has attained the largest possible output with available
inputs.   Therefore, no change in the combination of
inputs can be made that will increase the output of one
product without decreasing the output of another.
   However, the society will not have achieved economic efficiency unless it is producing the combination of goods that people prefer to purchase with their
existing incomes.

(NOTE When   sketching   a   production-possibilities
curve freehand, you should draw it smooth.   A smooth
curve is an idealization or model of a real situation and
is easier to interpret than a jagged line.)

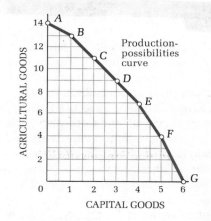

Production-Possibilities Schedule

Production alternatives	Capital goods production	Agricultural goods production	Sacrifice of agricultural goods for capital goods
A	0	14	−1
B	1	13	−2
C	2	11	−2
D	3	9	−2
E	4	7	−3
F	5	4	−4
G	6	0	

under production alternative A, the society would be devoting all its resources to the production of agricultural goods. It would thus be producing 14 units of agricultural goods and zero units of capital goods.

At the other extreme, alternative G, the society would be putting all its resources into the production of capital goods. It would then be producing six units of capital goods and zero units of agricultural goods.

Realistically, a society operates somewhere between these extremes. If a society tries to increase its production of capital goods by choosing among alternatives B, C, D, and so on, it must *sacrifice* some agricultural goods. The amount of sacrifice for each production alternative is shown by the negative numbers in the fourth column of the table. The negative numbers represent the amount of agricultural goods the economy must give up to acquire one more unit of capital goods. Note that these negative numbers grow larger as the society moves from zero production of capital goods toward zero production of agricultural goods.

The information in the production-possibilities schedule can be transferred directly to the accompanying graph. The units of capital goods are scaled on the horizontal axis and those for agricultural goods on the vertical axis. The line that connects the various production alternatives A through G is called a ***production-possibilities curve.*** It indicates all possible combinations of maximum total output for the society it represents.

Law of Increasing Costs

Why does an increasing amount of one good have to be sacrificed to obtain each additional unit of the other? The answer is that the economy's factors of production are not all equally suitable for producing the two types of goods. Fertile land, for example, is more suitable for crops than for factories, and unskilled farm workers are more adaptable to agriculture than to manufacturing. Even though an economy's resources may be substitutable within wide limits for given production purposes, the resources are relatively more efficient in some uses than in others. Thus, as society tries to increase its production of capital goods, it must take increasing amounts of resources out of agriculture.

These points suggest the operation of an important law.

Law of Increasing Costs As a society increases production of one good, it must sacrifice increasing amounts of an alternative good to produce each additional unit. The real cost of acquiring either good, therefore, is not the money that must be spent for it. The real cost is the *amount* of the *alternative* good that must be sacrificed. Increasing costs are reflected in the shape of the production-possibilities curve, which is bowed outward.

Conclusion: The Idea of Opportunity Cost

The concept of a production-possibilities curve and the associated law of increasing costs point to a fundamental idea in economics. Because resources are scarce, the extent to which they are used for one purpose necessarily precludes their use for another. The alternative opportunity that is sacrificed is therefore the cost of their use.

Consider an example from your own experience. The more hours you devote to your schoolwork each day, the fewer hours you have available for other purposes. Therefore, the cost to you of allocating more hours to your studies is measured by the value of the time you are giving up. This value may consist of the income you could have earned from a job or even the pleasure you would have derived from additional hours of recreation.

In economics, we give a special name to this idea:

The value of the benefit that is forgone by choosing one alternative rather than another is called ***opportunity cost.*** This concept is also known as "alternative cost." It is measured by what an economic entity — such as a society, a business, a household, or a person — is not doing but could be doing. *The opportunity cost of any decision is thus the value of the sacrificed alternative.*

Some applications of production-possibilities curves are presented in Box 1.

Box 1
Applications of Production-Possibilities Curves

Production-possibilities curves can be used to depict several interesting situations.

Effect of Resource Underutilization

An economy that underutilizes its resources is producing at some point, such as *U*, inside its production-possibilities curve. This is shown in Figure (*a*). Three of the moves that it can make to get back on the curve are to produce more capital goods (*horizontal arrow*), more consumer goods (*vertical arrow*), or more of both (*diagonal arrow*).

Economic Growth

Increases in resources or improvements in technology will shift an economy's production-possibilities curve outward from the origin, as indicated in Figure (*b*). The resulting expansion represents *economic growth*—a higher level of real output per capita. Note from Figures (*c*) and (*d*) that the new curve need not necessarily be "parallel" to the old one. Changes in resources or in technology may be such as to bring about a greater increase in one type of output than in another.

Present Goods Versus Future Goods

A society that allocates more resources in the present to the production of capital goods than to consumer goods will have more of both kinds of goods in the future. In other words, the society will experience more economic growth. This is because consumer goods are used to satisfy present wants, whereas capital goods are used to satisfy future wants.

Figures (*e*) and (*f*) show how the degree of outward shift of a society's future production-possibilities curve is affected by whether it chooses to be at point *A* (emphasizing consumer goods) or at point *A'* (emphasizing capital goods) on its present curve. Note that the outward shift of the curve in Figure (*f*) is greater than that in Figure (*e*).

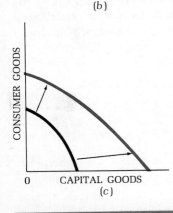

(a)

New curve

Economic growth

C

Old Curve

D

A   B

0   CAPITAL GOODS
(b)

If a new curve developed then there is economic growth

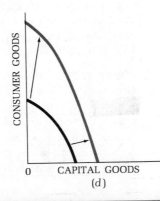

(c)

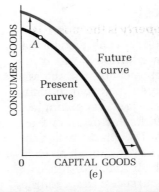

A

Future curve

Present curve

(e)

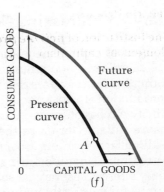

Future curve

Present curve

A'

(f)

Capitalism and Our Mixed Economy

The economic system of our nation and of many other countries of the Western world is commonly known as "capitalism," "free enterprise," or "private enterprise." What does this mean?

Capitalism is a system of economic organization characterized by private ownership of the factors of production and their operation for profit under predominantly competitive conditions.

On what theoretical foundations does capitalism rest? Is our economy typical of theoretical (or pure) capitalism? The answers are best understood in terms of the institutions of our economic system.

Institutions of Capitalism

If you take a course in sociology, you will learn that social systems are often characterized by their *institutions*. These may be defined as those traditions, beliefs, and practices that are well established and widely held to be fundamental parts of a culture. Because capitalism is a type of social system — or more precisely, a type of *socioeconomic system* — it has its own particular institutions. The following are those on which a pure capitalistic system rests.

Private Property

The institution of *private property* is the most basic element of capitalism. It assures each person the right to acquire economic goods and resources by legitimate means, to enter into contracts concerning their use, and to dispose of them as he or she wishes.

This concept of private property was set forth in the writings of the late-seventeenth-century English philosopher John Locke. He justified private ownership and control of property as a "natural right" independent of the power of the state. This right, he maintained, provides maximum benefits for society as a whole. (In contrast, socialist views

prevailing since the nineteenth century have held that private property is a means of exploiting the working class.)

The granting of property rights fulfills three important economic functions:

1. It provides people with personal incentives to make the most productive use of their assets.

2. It strongly influences the distribution of wealth and income by allowing people to accumulate assets and to pass them on to others at the time of death.

3. It makes possible a high degree of exchange, because people must have property rights before those rights can be transferred.

The social and economic consequences of these functions, as you will see, have been instrumental in the development of capitalism.

Self-Interest — The "Invisible Hand"

In 1776, the Scottish professor of philosophy, Adam Smith, published *The Wealth of Nations*. In this book, the first systematic study of capitalism, Smith described his principle of the *"invisible hand."* This principle states that each person, pursuing his or her self-interest without interference by government, will be led, as if by an invisible hand, to achieve the best good for society. In Smith's words:

> An individual neither intends to promote the public interest, nor knows he is promoting it. . . . He intends only his own gain, and he is led by an invisible hand to promote an end which was no part of his intention. . . . It is not from the benevolence of the butcher, the brewer, or the baker that we expect our dinner, but from their regard to their self-interest. We address ourselves not to their humanity, but to their self-love, and never talk to them of our necessities, but of their advantages.

Self-interest drives people to action, but alone it is not enough. People must understand the effects of their decisions and their actions on their economic well-being. They must think rationally if they are to make the right decisions.

Because of this, economists long ago introduced the concept of *economic man*. This notion holds

economic man

that each person in a capitalistic society is motivated by economic forces. In other words, each person will always attempt to obtain the greatest amount of satisfaction for the least amount of sacrifice or cost. These satisfactions may take the form of greater profits for a businessperson, higher wages or more leisure time for a worker, and greater pleasure from goods purchased for a consumer.

Of course, these assumptions are not entirely realistic. People may be motivated by forces other than self-interest. Nevertheless, the idea of economic man does serve as a reasonable approximation of the prevailing pattern of economic behavior in a capitalistic society. And in economics, as in other social sciences, reasonable approximations are often the best that can be made.

Economic Individualism — Laissez-Faire *leave us alone*

In the late seventeenth century, Louis XIV reigned as King of France. His finance minister, Jean Baptiste Colbert, asked a manufacturer by the name of Legendre how the government might help business. Legendre's reply was *"laissez nous faire"* (leave us alone). The expression became a watchword and motto of capitalism.

Today we interpret *laissez-faire* to mean that absence of government intervention leads to economic individualism and economic freedom. Under laissez-faire conditions, people's economic activities are their own private affairs. As consumers, they are free to spend their incomes as they choose. As producers, they are free to purchase the economic resources they desire and to use these resources as they wish.

In reality, economic freedom is almost always subject to restraints imposed by society for the protection and general welfare of its citizens. Prohibitions against force and fraud are examples. Can you give some others? Can you explain why such restraints are necessary?

Competition and Free Markets

Capitalism operates under conditions of *competition.* This means that there is rivalry among sellers of similar goods to attract customers and among

buyers to secure the goods that are wanted. There is rivalry among workers to obtain jobs and among employers to obtain workers. There is also rivalry among buyers and sellers of resources to transact business on the best terms that each can get from the other.

Theoretical capitalism is often described as a free-market system. Competition and free markets are closely related. In their most complete or purest form, free markets have two characteristics:

1. There are a large number of buyers and sellers, each with a small enough share of the total business so that no individual can affect the market price of the good.

2. Buyers and sellers are unencumbered by economic or institutional restrictions, and they possess full knowledge of market prices and alternatives. As a result, they enter or leave markets as they see fit.

Under such circumstances, the market price of a particular good is established by the interacting forces of demand and supply. Each buyer and each seller, acting in his or her own best interest as an economic being, decides whether or not to transact business at the going price. No individual has control over the price because no one buyer or seller is large enough to exert any perceptible influence in the market.

In the real world, competition does not exist in this pure form. However, there are markets in which it is approximated in varing degrees. The closest we get to a pure free market is in organized exchanges such as the Chicago Board of Trade and the New York Cotton Exchange. These markets, which are open to all buyers and sellers, deal in such standardized commodities as soybeans, grains, basic metals, and cotton. Markets of this type are studied in considerable detail in microeconomics.

To summarize:

A free market performs a number of important functions. Among them:

— It establishes competitive prices both for consumer goods and for the factors of production.

— It encourages the efficient use of economic resources.

Free markets may fail to perform these functions if there is a growth of monopolistic or restrictive practices. When this occurs, society (through government) will frequently intervene in the market to regulate such practices. Much of economics is concerned with whether such intervention is warranted, or whether other means can be found to resolve the problem.

The Price System

Who tells workers where to work or what occupations to choose? Who declares how many cars should be produced and how many homes should be built? Who specifies the predominant style of women's dresses or men's suits?

The greater the degree of competition, the more these matters will be decided impersonally and automatically by the **price system** or the *market system*. This may be viewed as a system of rewards and penalties. Rewards include profits for firms and people who succeed. Penalties include losses, or possibly bankruptcy, for those who fail. The price system is fundamental to the traditional concept of capitalism.

The price system basically operates on the principle that everything that is exchanged — every good, every service, and every resource — has its price. In a free market with many buyers and sellers, the prices of these things reflect the quantities that sellers make available and the quantities that buyers wish to purchase.

Thus, if buyers want to purchase more of a certain good than suppliers have available, its price will rise. This will encourage suppliers to produce and sell more of it. On the other hand, if buyers want to purchase less of a certain good than suppliers are prepared to sell, its price will fall. This will encourage buyers to purchase more of it.

This interaction between sellers and buyers in a competitive market, and the resulting changes in prices, are what most people refer to by the familiar phrase "supply and demand." However, care must be exercised in using this expression. As you will soon discover, it has a much more precise meaning than is at first apparent.

Government: Rule-Maker, Protector, Umpire

Capitalism has strong political as well as economic implications. According to the doctrine of laissez-faire, as popularized by Adam Smith in *The Wealth of Nations*, the functions of government in a capitalistic system are clearly identified. They include maintaining order, defining property rights, enforcing contracts, promoting competition, and defending the realm. They also include issuing money, prescribing standards of weights and measures, raising funds to meet operating expenses, and adjudicating disputes over the interpretation of the rules.

Government, in Smith's view, is thus essential to the existence of capitalism. When society's economic, social, or political values are violated, government, usually through its system of law, takes corrective action. When personal freedoms conflict, one individual's freedom must be limited so that another's may be preserved. In theoretical capitalism, government fulfills the roles of rule-maker, protector, and umpire. Government does this, *in theory*, by imposing only those restrictions on personal freedoms that are necessary to protect the well-being of society and by reconciling conflicts of values resulting from the free exercise of property rights.

Conclusion: Our Mixed Economy

Are these functions of government fulfilled in our economy? The answer is neither completely positive nor completely negative. Over the years, our economy has become increasingly complicated and the role of government has expanded.

Through the use of legislation of various types, government has come to play a significant role as a protector and regulator of certain groups within the economy. For example:

Government has tried to promote the interests of agriculture, labor, and the consumer. It has controlled competition among such regulated industries as domestic transportation, communication, and power. It has sought to maintain effective competition in the unregulated industries that constitute the bulk of the business sector. Government

Economics

Brown Brothers

Adam Smith
1723–1790
*Founder of Economics and
Apostle of Economic Liberalism*

The year 1776 was marked by two great events in the struggle for emancipation. In North America, representatives of the British colonies adopted the Declaration of Independence—an eloquent statement setting forth a doctrine of political freedom. In Europe, a former Scottish professor of philosophy at the University of Glasgow published a monumental book entitled *An Inquiry into the Nature and Causes of the Wealth of Nations*. Usually known simply as *The Wealth of Nations,* it is an eloquent statement expounding a doctrine of economic freedom. Both the Declaration of Independence and *The Wealth of Nations* stand as milestones in the Age of Enlightenment and Liberalism that blossomed during the eighteenth century.

Free Markets
The book earned Smith the epithet "founder of economics" because it was the first complete and systematic study of the subject. Smith argued that individuals know best what is good for them. If unrestricted by government controls or private monopolies, people will be motivated by the quest for profit to turn out the goods and services that society wants. Consequently, through free trade and free markets, self-interest will be harnessed to the common good.

Permanent Legacy
Through his approach to economic questions and his organization of the science, Smith cast a mold for the main body of nineteenth-century economic thought. His views on public policy, which became the semiofficial doctrine of the British government, left their imprint on parliamentary debates and governmental reports. For these reasons, and because of his enormous influence upon succeeding generations of scholars, Smith's unique position in the history of economic thought is forever ensured.

Classical Liberalism
Reading *The Wealth of Nations* today, one can see why the influence of this book reached out beyond the borders of economics. Like the Bible, Smith's treatise contains familiar concepts and well-worn truths on almost every page. As a result, "the shy and absent-minded scholar," as Smith was affectionately called, became the apostle of classical economic liberalism—meaning laissez-faire in his time. Today we tend to refer to such ideas as "conservatism."

has tried to keep the economy's total production and spending at a high level to achieve the long-run objectives of economic efficiency and growth.

These activities of government are discussed and evaluated in many places throughout this book. At present, it is sufficient to note that historical trends suggest the following conclusion:

Our economy is neither a pure market economy nor a pure command economy. It is a mixed but capitalistically oriented economy in which both private individuals and government exercise their economic influence in the marketplace. All countries today that call their economic systems "capitalistic" are actually mixed, capitalistically oriented economies.

The Circular Flow of Economic Activity

How does a capitalistic system make products available to households and resources available to businesses? The answer is summarized in a simplified way in Exhibit 3. This model, the **circular flow of** **economic activity,** assumes that the total economy is divided into two sectors: households and businesses. The model shows how the two sectors meet each other in two sets of markets: the product markets and the resource markets.

In the **product markets,** households buy the goods and services that businesses sell. Payments for these goods and services are represented by con-

---

Exhibit 3
The Circular Flow of Economic Activity

look at class note

In this highly simplified model of an economy, households and businesses are linked through two markets:

1. the product markets, where goods and services are exchanged;

2. the resource markets, where the factors of production are exchanged.

Questions of *what* and *how* to produce are answered in these markets. Note that households act as buyers in the product markets and as sellers in the resource markets. The reverse is true of businesses. Observe also that the outer loop shows physical flows in one direction, and the inner loop shows money flows in the opposite direction.

(NOTE The question, For *whom?* is not directly apparent in this diagram. The answer depends on factor prices, which are determined in the resource markets, and on other considerations.)

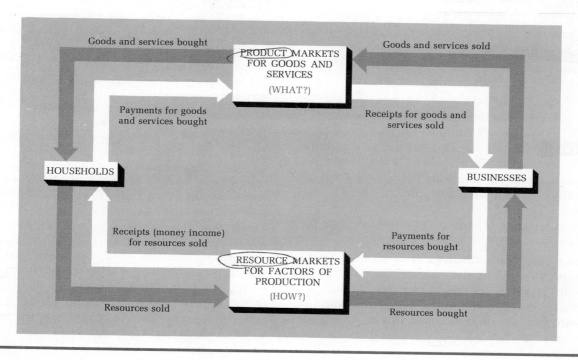

sumption expenditures that become the receipts of businesses. In the *resource markets,* businesses buy the factors of production that households sell. Payments for these factors of production are costs that become the money incomes of households.

All these transactions are accomplished in free markets by a price system that registers the wishes of buyers and sellers. In this system the product markets are the places where businesses decide *what* to produce, whereas the resource markets are the places where businesses decide *how* to produce.

One other feature of the diagram should be noted. The outer loop portrays the physical flow of goods and resources in one direction. The inner loop shows the corresponding flow of money in the opposite direction.

Limitations of Circular-Flow

The circular-flow model is a simplified representation of an economic system. The chief function of the model is to illustrate several important economic relations. But, like any model, it is an abstraction from reality and therefore depicts only certain essential features. Among them:

- **Macroeconomic relations** The model says nothing about the behavior of individual buyers and sellers. Nor does it show how they react to determine prices and quantities in the product and resource markets. Hence, it is a *macroeconomic* rather than a microeconomic model.

- **Stable flow** The model assumes a steady, rather than a fluctuating, circular flow. It does not disclose the effects of variations in the flow on the economy's production and employment of resources. Therefore, it says nothing about recession and inflation, which are problems of continuing concern.

Despite these shortcomings, the circular-flow concept provides many useful insights. They will become increasingly apparent as we seek to amplify the underlying implications and ideas of the model in order to gain a better understanding of our modern mixed economy.

Summary

What You Have Learned

1. A society's resources are the ingredients of its production. The four classes of resources—labor, land, capital, and entrepreneurship—are commonly referred to as the factors of production. The returns received by the owners of these resources are wages, rent, interest, and profits.

2. Every economic system seeks to attain certain objectives. The chief ones are (a) *efficiency* in the use of scarce resources, (b) *equity* in the distribution of income, (c) *stability* of prices, and (d) *growth* of real output per capita. In democratic capitalistic countries, these goals are sought within a framework of political and economic freedoms. These societies vary, however, in the priorities they place on economic goals and the sacrifices to be made in attaining them.

3. All societies are faced with the problem of scarcity because they have limited resources and apparently unlimited wants. Therefore, most economic problems are aspects of the three big questions that every society must answer: *What* to produce—and in what quantities? *How* to produce? *For whom* to produce? The methods by which these questions are answered differ in mixed and in command economies.

4. In an economy characterized by technical efficiency (that is, by full employment of available resources), any increase in the output of some goods and services causes a reduction in the output of others. With given resources and technology, the production choices open to an economy can be summarized by its production-possibilities curve. The shape of this curve reflects the operation of the law of increasing costs. These costs are measured by their opportunity costs, the value of the sacrificed alternatives.

5. Capitalism is a type of economic organization in which the means of production and distribution are privately owned and used for private gain. All capitalistic countries today are, in varying degrees, "mixed" economies.

6. Pure capitalism rests on a foundation of certain socioeconomic institutions. These include private property, self-interest, economic individualism or laissez-faire, competition, and the price system.

7. The circular-flow model is a simplified representation of our economy. It focuses on aggregate relationships by depicting the streams of money, goods, and resources that link major sectors and markets.

Definitions for flash cards

Terms and Concepts To Review

factors of production
land
capital
labor
entrepreneurship
division of labor
efficiency
income distribution
equity
economic goods
free goods
law of scarcity
command economy
market economy
mixed economy
production-possibilities
  curve

law of increasing costs
opportunity cost
capitalism
institutions
private property
"invisible hand"
economic man
laissez-faire
competition
price system
circular flow of
  economic activity
product markets
resource markets

For Discussion

1. Would entrepreneurship exist in a purely communistic society in which all citizens live and work by the motto; "From each according to his ability, to each according to his needs"?

2. "No one in a rich society has to starve or go naked. Therefore, it is incorrect to say that scarcity pervades our economy. Because enough food and clothing are available to dress and feed everyone, these goods are not scarce." True or false? Explain.

3. It is sometimes asserted that the act of exchange does not *create* wealth because it merely results in a redistribution of goods already in existence. Evaluate this argument.

4. Denmark produces some of the world's best butter. Yet most Danish butter producers use margarine in their homes instead of butter. Does this make sense? Explain.

5. "Money is a resource because a person who has it can put it to productive use. The same is true of a nation's money." Do you agree?

6. The question, *For whom shall goods be produced?* is concerned with distributing total output among the members of society. Can you suggest at least three different criteria or rules for deciding who gets how much? Which criterion is best?

7. A conventional production-possibilitie[s]
[il]lustrates the law of increasing costs. Can yo[u]
that illustrate (a) constant costs and (b) dec[...]
Define the meaning of each case.

8. Suppose that an economy produces only agricultural goods and capital goods. Using production-possibilities curves, illustrate the effect of a new capital-goods invention, assuming that it has *no direct impact* on agriculture (although it may have some indirect effects). Describe the possible adjustment paths that society may take as a result of the invention.

9. Distinguish between the concepts of *capital* and *capitalism.*

10. The "profit motive" is sometimes said to be one of the most fundamental features of capitalism. (a) What do you suppose is meant by the "profit motive"? (b) Why wasn't it explicitly listed in this chapter as one of the pillars of capitalism?

11. (a) "In a free competitive economy, the consumer is king." What does this mean? (b) "The producer, not the consumer, is king. After all, the producer is the one who advertises. Therefore, the producer is the one who creates wants and thereby influences what consumers will purchase." True or false? Explain.

12. "A shortcoming of a capitalistic society, as compared with a collectivist or socialistic one, is that people are not compensated in proportion to the usefulness and difficulty of their work." True or false? Explain.

13. If no pure market economy exists and no pure command economy exists, why does economics, which purports to be a science and to deal with reality, bother with these concepts?

Chapter 2

The Laws of Supply and Demand: The Price System in a Pure Market Economy

Learning Guide

Watch for answers to these important questions

What are the "laws" of supply and demand? How do they affect the prices you pay for the things you buy?

What is a market economy? Why do we study it? How is a market economy related to a price system?

Are there advantages to a market economy? Disadvantages? How well does such an economy answer the questions, *What? How?* and *For whom?*

A parrot could answer many important economic questions correctly with just three simple words, *supply and demand.* Here are a few examples.

Question Why are Rembrandts expensive while water is cheap—especially since everyone needs water more than Rembrandts?

Answer Supply and demand.

Question Why is the cost of medical care rising faster than prices generally?

Answer Supply and demand.

Question Why are some luxury apartments vacant while there is a shortage of low-cost housing?

Answer Supply and demand.

Question Why do the prices of some commodities fluctuate while the prices of others remain stable?

Answer Supply and demand.

Such simple answers to complex questions are not very illuminating. Nevertheless, it is true that much of economics is largely concerned with supply and demand. In this chapter, therefore, you will discover more about them and the conditions that affect them.

What Do We Mean by Demand?

In economics, demand has a special meaning:

> **Demand** is a relation showing the various amounts of a commodity that buyers would be willing and able to purchase at alternative prices during a given time period, all other things remaining the same.

The commodity can be anything—pizzas, shoes, television sets, haircuts, labor time, computers, or any other good or service bought by consumers, businesses, or government agencies. The definition assumes that demand means *both* the desire to buy and the ability to pay. Either of these taken separately is of no significance in the marketplace.

Thus, if you want a steak but cannot pay for it—or if you can pay for a steak but prefer to buy pizza—you exercise no economic influence in the market for steaks. But if you have both the desire and the ability to pay for steak, these together will affect your demand for the product.

Demand Schedules and Demand Curves

Suppose that you are a merchant dealing in grain—for example, wheat, corn, barley, or oats. What is your demand for a specific commodity, such as wheat?

According to the definition of demand, you must first ask, "At what prices?" Within a given period, you would be inclined to buy more wheat at a lower price than you would at a higher one. In view of this, you could prepare a hypothetical list of the number of bushels of wheat you would buy at different prices during a particular period of time. The period could be of any length—a day, a week, a month, or more. During this period, *your income and the prices of other commodities are assumed to remain the same.*

Exhibit 1 shows such a list, which economists call a *demand schedule.* This schedule represents your demand for wheat over the price range shown. Thus, at $5 per bushel, you would buy 5 bushels per

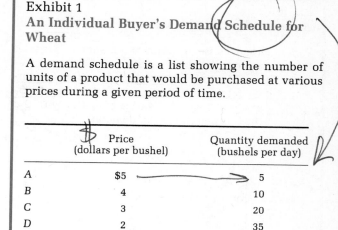

Exhibit 1
An Individual Buyer's Demand Schedule for Wheat

A demand schedule is a list showing the number of units of a product that would be purchased at various prices during a given period of time.

	Price (dollars per bushel)	Quantity demanded (bushels per day)
A	$5	5
B	4	10
C	3	20
D	2	35
E	1	60

as the Price goes up the DEMAND is low

day. At $4 per bushel, you would buy 10 bushels per day. And so on. You could make the schedule more detailed if you wanted to by extending the price scale upward and by quoting the prices in dollars and cents instead of just dollars. But such detail is not necessary. As you will see, the schedule already gives you the highlights of your demand for wheat.

The information in the demand schedule can easily be presented in graphic form. The graphing process is done in three steps.

Step 1 Draw the vertical and horizontal axes of the graph and put the labels on both axes as shown in Exhibit 2. The starting point or origin of the chart is always the lower left-hand corner, labeled *0* (zero).

Step 2 Plot the corresponding prices and quantities with dots. Then label them with the appropriate letters (*A, B, C, D,* and *E*) from the demand schedule in Exhibit 1. The letters help you to identify the points. (After you gain some experience in graphing, you can do without the letters.)

The Law of Demand

A look at the demand curve in Exhibit 2 will reveal its most fundamental property. *The curve slopes downward from left to right.* This characteristic illustrates the law of demand. The law applies to virtually all goods: wheat, houses, cars, books, stereo records, or practically anything you care to name. Here is a definition:

> **Law of Demand** The quantity demanded of a good varies inversely with its price, assuming that other things that may affect demand remain the same. The most important of these are the buyer's income and the prices of related goods.

(NOTE In the definition, "inversely" means that when the price of a good decreases, the corresponding quantity demanded increases. Also, when the price increases, the quantity demanded decreases.)

Why does the law of demand operate as it does?

1. If the price of a good decreases, you can *afford* to buy more of it if your income, tastes, and the prices of other goods remain the same. For instance, if you like steak but find it too expensive to buy frequently, a lower price might induce you to buy it more often.

2. When the price of a product is reduced, you may buy more of it because it becomes a better bargain relative to other goods. Again, this is based on the assumption that your income, your tastes, and the prices of other goods remain constant. Thus, if the price of steak falls, you might buy more steak and fewer substitutes, such as hamburger or hot dogs. If the price of steak rises, however, you would tend to buy less steak and more substitutes.

3. Finally, the downward-sloping demand curve tells you that you would be willing to pay a relatively high price for a small amount of something. However, the more you have of it —other things remaining the same —the less you would care to pay for one more unit. Why? *Because each extra unit gives you less additional satisfaction* or "utility" *than the previous unit gave you.*

Exhibit 2
An Individual Buyer's Demand Curve for Wheat

A demand curve is the graph of a demand schedule. Each point along the curve represents a different price-quantity combination. A demand curve slopes downward from left to right, reflecting the fact that the quantity of a product demanded varies inversely with the price. This is called the *law of demand.*

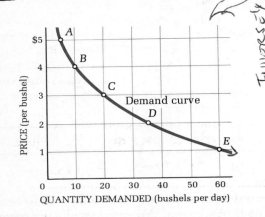

Step 3 Connect the points with a smooth curve.

You have just drawn a ***demand curve.*** It is the graphic equivalent of the demand schedule in Exhibit 1. The advantage of the curve is that it enables you to "see" the relation between price and quantity demanded. You can also read off the values at a glance.

For instance, point *C* represents 20 bushels of wheat demanded per day at a price of $3 per bushel. Would you agree that, at $1.50 per bushel, the quantity demanded is 45 bushels per day? Can you verify that, if the quantity demanded is 35 bushels per day, the highest price you would be willing to pay (called the ***demand price***) is $2 per bushel? Can you think of why we use an agricultural product as an example rather than a manufactured product? Box 1 provides an answer.

Box 1
Why Wheat?

Why use wheat as an example in explaining demand schedules and demand curves? Why not use a familiar consumer product, such as cars or television sets?

The answer is that we want to show how the price is established for a uniform or standardized product in a highly competitive market. Such a market is characterized by a great many buyers and sellers, each acting independently according to his or her best interests. This type of situation will result in a *single market price* for the product at any given time. Clearly, autos and television sets do not meet these requirements, for at least three reasons: **1.** Autos and TV sets are produced by a relatively small number of sellers. **2.** The products are not standardized, being differentiated by brand name, model, year, style, color, and so on. **3.** The products are characterized by different prices rather than by a single price. These conditions are true in varying degrees for nearly all the products we buy every day.

On the other hand, such products as wheat, as well as the other commodities shown on the list below, approximate the requirements of the model rather closely. Any one of them may be used to illustrate the "pure" operation of supply and demand. Prices of these commodities, which are bought and sold in national and international markets, are quoted daily in many newspapers. Note how drastically commodity prices can change in a year. Here, cocoa, rye, soybean oil, and cotton more than doubled. Even a period of a few days can bring sharp price changes — look at barley.

Commodities: Cash Prices at National Markets (final quotations)

	Monday	Friday	Year ago		Monday	Friday	Year ago
Foods				Miscellaneous			
Flour, hard winter, per cwt.	$11.90	$12.00	$ 8.50	Cottonseed oil, per lb.	$ 0.19	$ 0.18	$ 0.10
Coffee, Santos 4s, per lb.	.80	.76	.65	Soybean oil, per lb.	.19	.19	.09
Cocoa, Accra, per lb.	.77	.79	.37	Peanut oil, per lb.	.24	.21	.17
Sugar, raw, per lb.	.11	.10	.09	Cotton, 1 in., per lb.	.72	.71	.29
Butter, fresh, per lb.	.74	.75	.69	Print cloth, 64 × 60, 45 in., per yd.	.50	.51	.23
Eggs, per doz.	.64	.66	.39	Steel scrap, per ton	90.00	91.00	98.23
Broilers, dressed "A," per lb.	.36	.39	.28	Lead, per lb.	.16	.16	.14
Grains and feeds				Zinc, per lb.	.20	.20	.18
Pepper, black, per lb.	.59	.58	.45				
Wheat, No. 2, per bu.	4.50	4.92	3.40				
Oats, No. 1, per bu.	1.40	1.36	.85				
Rye, No. 2, per bu.	2.45	2.48	1.15				
Barley, per bu.	3.80	2.90	1.65				

For example, however crazy you are about ice-cream sundaes, there is a limit to the number you can eat in any given period. After the first few sundaes, you would probably lose your appetite for more.

No matter how much you like a product, your demand curve will slope downward for the three sets of reasons given above. Do people in business usually act as if they believed in the existence of a law of (downward-sloping) demand? Evidently, they do. Why else would they advertise bargains that encourage people to buy more goods at lower prices?

Market Demand Is the Sum of Individual Demands

If you were the only buyer of wheat in the market, your demand schedule would also be the demand schedule for the entire market. In reality there are many buyers. The total market demand schedule is obtained by adding up the quantities demanded by all buyers at each price. Exhibit 3 shows how this is done. This example is based on the assumption that there are only three buyers—X, Y, and Z. However, the example can easily be expanded to include as many buyers as you wish.

Exhibit 3
Market Demand for Wheat, Assuming Three Buyers

The total market demand is obtained by summing all the quantities demanded by individual buyers at each price.

Price (dollars per bushel)	Quantity demanded (bushels per day)							Total market demand per day
	buyer X		buyer Y		buyer Z			
$5	0	+	15	+	20	=		35
4	9	+	20	+	26	=		55
3	22	+	27	+	33	=		82
2	42	+	38	+	43	=		123
1	80	+	65	+	60	=		205

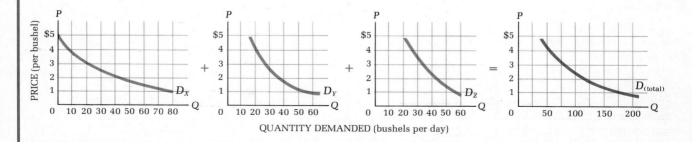

What Do We Mean by Supply?

You now have a basic understanding of demand and the behavior of buyers.   The other half of the picture is supply and the behavior of sellers.   Like demand, the term supply has a special meaning in economics.

> **Supply** is a relation showing the various amounts of a commodity that sellers would be willing and able to make available for sale at alternative prices during a given time period, all other things remaining the same.

Compare this definition of supply with the definition of demand given near the beginning of this chapter.   Note the similarities.   Are there any differences?

Supply Schedules and Supply Curves

Each seller in the market has a **supply schedule** for a product, just as each buyer has a demand schedule.   Thus, if you were a wheat farmer, Exhibit 4 might represent your individual supply schedule for wheat.   This schedule indicates that, at a price of $1 per bushel, you would not be willing to supply any wheat at all.   At a price of $2 per bushel, you would be willing to supply 21 bushels of wheat per day; and so on.   Plotting these data on a chart gives the **supply curve** shown in Exhibit 5.   What is your estimate of the quantity supplied at a price of $2.50 per unit?   What is the *least price*, approximately, that will persuade you to supply 40 bushels per day?

In economics, the "least price" is more often called the **supply price.**   This is the price necessary to call forth a given quantity.   What do you estimate the supply price to be for 25 bushels per day? $2.50

An example of the supply schedules for three individual producers, A, B, and C, is presented in Exhibit 6.   When the data are plotted, they yield the corresponding supply curves shown on the graphs.   Note that the total market supply schedule is obtained by adding up the quantities supplied by all sellers at each market price.   How does this compare with the way in which the total market demand schedule was derived earlier?

Exhibit 4
An Individual Seller's Supply Schedule for Wheat

A supply schedule is a list showing the number of units of a product that sellers would be willing and able to make available for sale at various prices during a given period of time.

	Price (dollars per bushel)	Quantity supplied (bushels per day)
A'	$5	50
B'	4	42
C'	3	33
D'	2	21
E'	1	0

Exhibit 5
An Individual Seller's Supply Curve for Wheat

A supply curve is the graph of a supply schedule.   Each point along the curve represents a different price-quantity combination.   A supply curve slopes upward from left to right, reflecting the fact that the quantity of a product supplied varies directly with the price.   This is called the *law of supply.*

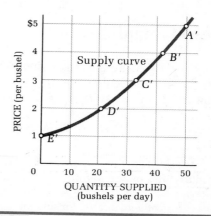

Exhibit 6
Market Supply of Wheat, Assuming Three Sellers

The total market supply of wheat is obtained by summing all the quantities supplied by individual sellers at each price.

Price (dollars) per bushel)	Quantity supplied (bushels per day) seller A		seller B		seller C		Total market supply per day
$5	52	+	56	+	60	=	168
4	46	+	49	+	50	=	145
3	36	+	42	+	40	=	118
2	26	+	28	+	26	=	80
1	0	+	15	+	10	=	25

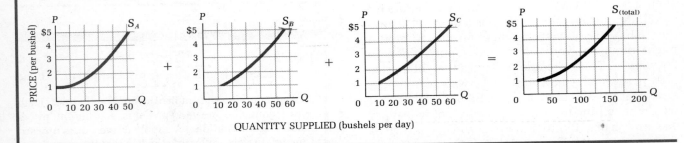

QUANTITY SUPPLIED (bushels per day)

The Law of Supply

The supply curve as drawn has a distinguishing feature. Unlike the demand curve, the supply curve slopes *upward* from left to right. This feature reflects the law of supply:

> **Law of Supply**   The quantity of a commodity supplied usually varies |*directly*| with its price, assuming that all other factors that may determine supply remain the same. (NOTE As used here, "directly" means that the quantity produced and offered for sale increases as the price of the product rises, and decrease as the price falls.)

Note that the direct relation between quantity and price is *usually* true, but not always. The reasons for exceptions are examined in the study of microeconomics.

Just as buyer behavior determines the law of demand, so seller behavior determines the law of supply. Say you are a farmer cultivating both wheat and corn. If the price of wheat were to rise relative to the price of corn, you would make greater profits by shifting your limited resources — fertilizer, land, labor, machinery, and so on—out of corn production and into wheat production. If the price of wheat were to rise high enough, you would even find it worthwhile to grow wheat on land on which you had previously grown nothing. Prices, in other words, affect producers' decisions concerning *what* and *how much* to produce.

Supply and Demand Together Make a Market

The concepts of supply and demand must be united in order to provide an explanation of how prices are determined in competitive markets.

A market exists whenever and wherever one or more buyers and sellers can negotiate for goods or services and thereby participate in determining their prices. A market, therefore, can be anywhere —on a street corner, on the other side of the world, or as close as the nearest telephone. Competitive markets consist of buyers and sellers so numerous that no single one can influence the market price by deciding to buy or not to buy, to sell or not to sell.

Buyers and Sellers in the Marketplace

By using the *total* demand and supply information derived in Exhibits 3 and 6, we can discover how the market price of a product and the quantity bought and sold are determined. The total market demand and supply schedules and their corresponding curves are reproduced in Exhibit 7. Note that the curves, labeled *D* and *S*, are identical with the total market curves that were graphed in Exhibits 3 and 6. The only difference is that both curves are now plotted in the same figure so that their interactions can be studied.

Observe that the supply and demand curves intersect at an **equilibrium** point. A dictionary will tell you that "equilibrium" is a state of balance between opposing forces. Let us see what this means in Exhibit 7.

Exhibit 7

Equilibrium Price and Equilibrium Quantity for Wheat

The intersection of the supply and demand curves determines the equilibrium price and the equilibrium quantity. Thus:

— At any price above the equilibrium price, the quantity supplied exceeds the quantity demanded and the price tends to fall.

— At any price below the equilibrium price, the quantity demanded exceeds the quantity supplied and the price tends to rise.

— At the equilibrium price, the quantity supplied precisely equals the quantity demanded, and hence there is no tendency for the price to change.

Price (dollars per bushel)	Total market supply (bushels per day)	Total market demand (bushels per day)
$5	168	35
4	145	55
3	118	82
2	80	123
1	25	205

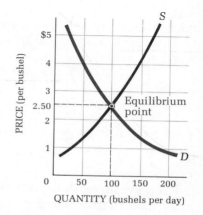

QUANTITY (bushels per day)

At any price above $2.50 per bushel, the quantity supplied exceeds the quantity demanded. For example, at a price of $5 per bushel, the quantity supplied is 168 bushels per day, and the quantity demanded is 35 bushels per day. This means that, at the price of $5 per bushel, there is a **surplus** of $168 - 35 = 133$ bushels per day. Because sellers have made more wheat available than buyers want, sellers will compete with one another to dispose of their product and will thereby drive the price down.

At any price below $2.50 per bushel, the quantity demanded exceeds the quantity supplied. At $1 a bushel, for example, the quantity demanded is 205 bushels per day and the quantity supplied is 25 bushels per day. At this price, there is a **shortage** of $205 - 25 = 180$ bushels per day. Because buyers want more wheat than sellers will make available at this price, buyers will compete with one another to acquire the product and will thereby drive the price up.

At a price of $2.50 per bushel, the quantity demanded just equals the quantity supplied, 100 bushels per day. At this price there will be no surpluses or shortages. We refer to this price as the **equilibrium price** and to the corresponding quantity as the **equilibrium quantity.**

When the quantity demanded equals the quantity supplied, the market is in a state of *equilibrium*. The price of the product and the corresponding quantities bought and sold are "in balance." That is, they have no tendency to change as a result of the opposing forces of demand and supply. On the other hand, when the quantities demanded and supplied at a given price are unequal or "out of balance," prices and quantities will be changing. Then the market is in a state of **disequilibrium.**

Two Kinds of Changes Involving Demand

Demand and supply curves have practical uses. You can employ them to answer many fundamental questions in economics. However, before doing so, it is important to note that there may be two kinds of

changes involving demand. One is "a change in the quantity demanded," which is reflected in a movement *along the demand curve.* The other kind is "a change in demand," which is reflected in a movement of the demand curve itself.

Changes in the Quantity Demanded

Take another look at Exhibit 2. According to the law of demand, a downhill movement along the curve in the general direction $A, B, C, \ldots$ signifies an increase in the quantity demanded as the price is reduced. On the other hand, an upward movement along the curve in the general direction $E, D, C, \ldots$ signifies a decrease in the quantity demanded as the price is raised. Any such movement along the curve, whether downward or upward, is called a **change in the quantity demanded.** Note that this expression refers to changes in the quantities purchased by buyers in response to *changes in price.*

Changes in Demand

The law of demand says that the quantity of a good demanded varies inversely with its price, assuming that all other things remain the same. What are these "all other things"? What happens if they do not remain the same?

Among the "all other things" that will influence the demand for a good are (1) buyers' money incomes, (2) prices of related goods, and (3) nonmonetary factors. These demand determinants are not measured on the axes of the graph and hence are assumed to be constant when you draw a demand curve. Therefore, a change in any one of them will cause a shift of the demand curve to a new position. When this happens, we say that there has been a **change in demand.** The change may be either an increase or a decrease.

- An increase in demand can be visualized on a graph as a shift of the demand curve to the right. This is shown in Exhibit 8. The shift takes place from the old demand curve D to the new demand curve D'.

Exhibit 8
Increase in Demand

An increase in demand can be represented by a shift of the demand curve to the right. At any given price, people are now willing to buy more than they were willing to buy before.

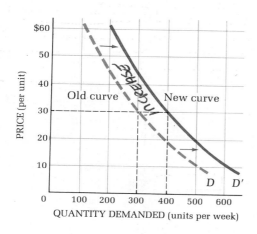

QUANTITY DEMANDED (units per week)

Exhibit 9
Decrease in Demand

A decrease in demand can be represented by a shift of the demand curve to the left. At any given price, people are now willing to buy less than they were willing to buy before.

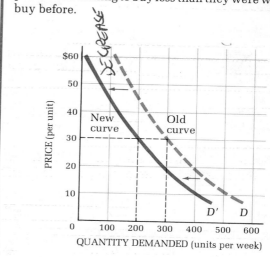

QUANTITY DEMANDED (units per week)

What does this increase in demand tell you? It shows that, *at any given price, buyers are now willing to purchase more than they were willing to purchase before.* For example, the new curve indicates that, at a price of $30 per unit, buyers were previously willing to purchase 300 units per week. Now, after the increase in demand, they are willing to buy 400 units per week at the same price of $30 per unit.

A decrease in demand can be visualized as a shift of the demand curve to the left, as shown in Exhibit 9. This time the graph illustrates that, *at any given price, buyers are now willing to purchase less than they were willing to purchase before.* Thus, at $30 per unit, people were previously willing to buy 300 units per week. Now, after the decrease in demand, they are willing to buy only 200 units per week at the same price of $30 per unit.

Test Yourself

An increase in demand also means that for any given quantity demanded, buyers are *now willing to pay a higher price* per unit than they were willing to pay before.

1. Can you define a decrease in demand in a parallel way?

2. Look at Exhibit 8. What is your estimate of the highest price per unit that buyers were willing to pay for 300 units per week, before and after the increase in demand?

3. Look at Exhibit 9. What is your estimate of the highest price per unit that buyers were willing to pay for 200 units per week, before and after the decrease in demand?

4. Can you think of some actual examples that illustrate these ideas?

How do changes in the demand determinants mentioned above (buyers' incomes, prices of related goods, and nonmonetary factors) bring about a change in demand? In other words, how do the changes cause a shift of the demand curve to the right or to the left?

Buyers' Incomes

The demand for most goods varies directly with buyers' incomes. This means the demand curves shift to the right when incomes rise and to the left when incomes fall. Goods whose demand curves behave in this way are known as *superior goods,* or more popularly as *normal goods.* They are called this because they represent the "normal" situation. Examples include most food, clothing, cars, and appliances, and other items that people typically buy.

For some goods, however, changes in consumption (prices remaining constant) vary inversely with changes in income over a certain range of income. Such goods are called *inferior goods.* Typical examples are bread, potatoes, beans, and used clothing, all of which are *relatively* inexpensive and are therefore bought in quantity by low-income families. As their incomes rise, these families can afford to buy goods of better quality. Thus, they spend less on bread and potatoes and more on fruits and vegetables, less on beans and more on meat and fish, less on used clothing and more on new clothing.

Prices of Related Goods

The demand for any good is also affected by the prices of related goods. The strength of this relation depends on the extent to which consumers regard the products as competitive with, or complementary to, each other.

Some products are *substitute goods*—they are competitive with each other. The more people consume of one, the less they consume of another. An increase in the price of one leads to an increase in the demand for the other. Similarly, a decrease in the price of one leads to a decrease in the demand

for the other. For example, if the price of Coca-Cola increases, cola drinkers will buy less Coca-Cola and more Pepsi-Cola. The market demand curve for Pepsi-Cola will therefore shift to the right. On the other hand, if the price of Coca-Cola decreases, people will be inclined to buy more Coca-Cola and less Pepsi-Cola. Then the market demand curve for Pepsi-Cola will shift to the left. What other substitute goods can you think of?

Some products are *complementary goods.* The more people consume of one complementary good, the more they consume of the other. An increase in the price of one leads to a decrease in the demand for the other. Conversely, a decrease in the price of one leads to an increase in the demand for the other. For example, if the price of cameras increases, people will buy fewer cameras—and less film. The market demand curve for film will shift to the left.

Products that are neither substitutes nor complements are unrelated. The consumption of one does not affect the consumption of the other. Therefore, a change in the price of one does not cause a change in the demand for the other. Some examples are salt and pencils, chewing gum and paper clips, thumbtacks and mustard.

But if a buyer's expenditure on a particular kind of good absorbs a considerable proportion of his or her budget, a change in its price may affect the buyer's demand for another product. This may be true even if the latter product is neither competitive with nor complementary to the former. One example is housing and entertainment. Can you give some other examples?

To generalize thus far:

If buyers' incomes remain constant, the market demand curve for a product will move in the same direction as a change in the price of its substitute. Conversely, the market demand curve for a product will move in the direction opposite from a change in the price of its complement. This means that, for substitute products, the relation between a change in the price of one commodity and the resulting change in demand for the other is *direct.* For complementary products, the relation is *inverse.*

COKE + PEPSI

Expectations Buyers' *expectations* of incomes and prices can also influence their demands for goods and services. If buyers expect higher incomes or higher prices in the near future, larger quantities of goods may be bought in anticipation of the increases. This causes the demand curves for those goods to shift to the right. On the other hand, if buyers expect lower incomes or lower prices, smaller quantities of goods and services may be bought. This causes their demand curves to shift to the left. For these reasons, economists who are engaged in economic forecasting often try to incorporate the effects of buyers' expectations in the predictive models that are constructed.

Nonmonetary Factors

Many factors other than prices and incomes influence the demands for goods. These factors include all nonmonetary determinants of demand, such as the age, occupation, sex, race, religion, education, and tastes of consumers, as well as their number. Changes in these factors can affect the preferences of actual and potential consumers. However, economists customarily assume that, for large numbers of consumers, these nonmonetary factors are stable —for two reasons:

1. They vary widely among people so their effects in the market tend to cancel out.
2. They change slowly over time because they are primarily the result of demographic characteristics and cultural traditions.

Therefore, economists analyze short-run changes in demand in terms of prices and incomes.

An Important Distinction

You have learned that demand can be represented by a schedule or curve that reflects buyers' behavior at the time. If the demand curve does not shift, a change in price leads to a *change in the quantity demanded*, not to a change in demand. This means that there has been either an increase in the quantity demanded, as represented by a movement downward along the curve, or a decrease in the quantity demanded, as represented by a movement upward along the curve. The change is due to either a decease or an increase in the price of the product (while all other demand determinants remain the same).

A *change in demand* means that the schedule itself has changed. The demand curve has shifted either to the right, if there has been an increase in demand, or to the left, if there has been a decrease in demand. The shift is due to a change in any of the demand determinants that were assumed to remain constant when the curve was initially drawn.

It is easy to commit errors in economic reasoning by failing to understand the important distinction between a change in the quantity demanded and a change in demand.

Test Yourself

Which of the following involve a change in the quantity demanded and which involve a change in demand?

1. People buy more bathing suits in the summer than in the winter. *demanded (quantity)*
2. Consumer incomes fall and the number of automobiles purchased declines. *demand*
3. Honda reduces the prices of its motorcycles by 10 percent and sales of Honda motorcycles increase. *demanded*
4. State College raises its tuition and student enrollments fall off. *demanded*

Two Kinds of Changes Involving Supply

As with demand, so too with supply, two types of changes may occur. One is called "a change in the quantity supplied;" the other is called "a change in supply." On the basis of what you now know about the theory of demand, can you guess the meanings of these two concepts before they are explained?

Changes in the Quantity Supplied

Look back at Exhibit 5.   According to the law of supply, an upward movement along the curve signifies an increase in the quantity supplied as the price is raised.   On the other hand, a downward movement along the curve signifies a decrease in the quantity supplied as the price is reduced.   Any such movement along the curve, whether upward or downward, is called a ***change in the quantity supplied.***   Note that such movements are due exclusively to a change in price.

Changes in Supply

The law of supply says that the quantity supplied of a product usually varies directly with its price, assuming that all other things remain the same.   The "other things" that may have an influence in determining supply are (1) resource prices or the costs of the factors of production, (2) prices of other goods, and (3) nonmonetary factors.   If any of these factors change, a new relation is established between price and quantity offered.   On a graph, this is shown by a shift of the supply curve to a new position, representing a ***change in supply.***

- An increase in supply is a shift of the supply curve to the right, as shown in Exhibit 10.   *At any given price, sellers are now willing to supply more than they were willing to supply before.*   For example, at a price of $30 per unit, sellers were previously willing to supply a total of 300 units per week. Now, after the increase in supply, they are willing to sell a total of 400 units per week at the same price of $30 per unit.

- A decrease in supply is represented by a shift of the supply curve to the left, as shown in Exhibit 11.   *At any given price, sellers are now willing to supply less than they were willing to supply before.*   For example, they were previously willing to supply a total of 300 units per week at a price of $30 per unit.   Now, after the decrease in supply, they are willing to sell a total of 200 units per week at the same price of $30 per unit.

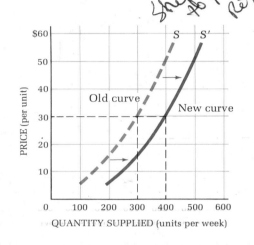

Exhibit 10
Increase in Supply

An increase in supply can be represented by a shift of the supply curve to the right.   At any given price, sellers are now willing to supply more than they were willing to supply before.

How will a change in any of the supply determinants listed above (resource prices, prices of other goods, and nonmonetary factors) bring about a change in supply?

Resource Prices

Ordinarily, a decrease in resource prices (such as costs of materials) in a particular industry will reduce production costs and thus raise the potential for profits.   Firms will then be likely to increase their output in order to capture more of these potential profits.   This action will shift the total market supply curve to the right.   Conversely, an increase in resource prices (such as wages) would tend to have the opposite effect, because it raises production costs and decreases profits.   This encourages businesses in that industry to reduce their output. The market supply curve thus shifts to the left.

Exhibit 11
Decrease in Supply

A decrease in supply can be represented by a shift of the supply curve to the left. At any given price, sellers are now willing to supply less than they were willing to supply before.

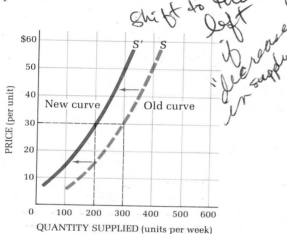

shift to the left
"decrease in supply"

prices for their goods in the future and, therefore, to earn higher profits. Other producers may decide to increase their current output because they expect to get lower prices for their goods in the future.

Nonmonetary Factors

Various factors other than prices can affect the supply of a commodity. The most important are the state of technology and the number of sellers in the market. For example, the adoption of a new production method or a new machine can reduce the need for labor. This may improve efficiency and increase supply, shifting the market supply curve to the right. On the other hand, a decline in efficiency as a result of a failure to modernize can have the opposite effect. Similarly, an increase in the number of sellers in the market will result in a rightward shift of the market supply curve. A decrease in the number of sellers will cause a leftward shift of the curve.

Summing up: Another Important Distinction

You have seen that supply can be represented by a schedule or curve that reflects sellers' attitudes at the time. If the supply curve does not shift, a change in price leads to a *change in the quantity supplied*, not to a change in supply. An increase in the quantity supplied is indicated by a movement upward along the curve. Similarly, a decrease in the quantity supplied is indicated by a movement downward along the curve.

A *change in supply* means that the schedule itself has changed. That is, the curve has shifted to the right if there has been an increase in supply or to the left if there has been a decrease in supply. The shift is the result of a change in any of the supply determinants that were assumed to remain constant when the curve was initially drawn.

As with demand, so with supply: you have to understand this important distinction to avoid errors in economic reasoning.

Prices of Related Goods

Business firms produce goods to earn profits. Changes in the relative prices of goods may change the relative profitabilities of those goods. This brings about changes in their respective supply curves. For instance, if the price of wheat increases relative to the price of corn, farmers may find it more profitable to transfer some land and other resources out of corn production and into wheat production. This would shift the market supply curve of corn to the left and the market supply curve of wheat to the right.

Expectations Of course, suppliers' *expectations* of prices will also influence their supply decisions. Some producers may decide to hold back on their current output because they expect to get higher

Economics in the News

All the Tea in China: Price Soars by 400%

PEKING, May 14 (AP) — The price of tea in China has soared up to 400 percent this year because an abnormally cold and rainy spring seriously cut production, the Government reported today.

The official New China News Agency said tea bushes in Zhejiang and Anhui Provinces, the country's main producing regions, sprouted late because of the weather, and picking was delayed.

Test Yourself

An increase in supply also means that, for any given quantity supplied, sellers are now willing to accept a *lower price* per unit than before.

1. Define a decrease in supply in a parallel way.

2. Look back at Exhibit 10. What is your estimate of the lowest price per unit that sellers were willing to accept for a supply of 300 units per week, before the increase in supply? After the increase in supply?

3. Look at Exhibit 11. What is your estimate of the lowest price per unit that sellers were willing to accept for a supply of 200 units per week, before the decrease in supply? After the decrease in supply?

Combined Changes in Demand and Supply

Demand and supply curves rarely remain fixed for very long. This is because the factors determining them, such as buyers' incomes, resource costs, or the prices of related products, are continually changing. These changes cause the curves to shift. Because we are interested in learning about the behavior of prices and quantities in competitive markets, we must be able to analyze such shifts to evaluate their effects.

What happens when a demand or supply curve moves to a new position? The answer is that there may also be a change in the equilibrium price, the equilibrium quantity, or both. Some examples are presented in Exhibit 12, with the arrows indicating the directions of change.

Note that, in each of Figures (a) through (d) of Exhibit 12, one of the curves shifted while the other remained unchanged. The effects on the equilibrium price and quantity in each case are depicted by the arrows. In Figure (a), an increase in demand resulted in an increase in both the equilibrium price and the equilibrium quantity. The opposite occurred in Figure (b) as a result of a decrease in demand. In Figure (c), on the other hand, an increase in supply resulted in a decrease in the equilibrium price and an increase in the equilibrium quantity. The opposite occurred in Figure (d) as a result of a decrease in supply.

Can you explain, using similar terms, what happened in Figures (e) and (f)?

You can see by now that supply and demand curves are often drawn as straight lines. Even when they are, we still refer to them as supply and demand curves.

The Market Economy: Is It "Good" or "Bad"?

In a competitive market, prices are determined solely by the free play of supply and demand. An economy characterized entirely by such markets would be a **pure market economy,** sometimes called a "competitive economy." The two expressions are often used interchangeably. They represent the "pure" model of capitalism.

What are the desirable features of such an economy? Does it have shortcomings? Is it realistic as a description of the capitalistic system? Answers to these questions can be expressed within the familiar framework of our society's four basic economic goals: efficiency, equity, stability, and growth.

Exhibit 12
Changes in Demand and Supply

Shifts in the demand or supply curves will cause changes in equilibrium price, equilibrium quantity, or both.

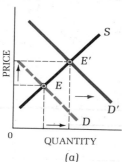

Increase in demand, supply remains constant

(a)

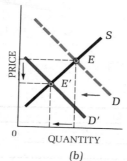

Decrease in demand, supply remains constant

(b)

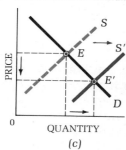

Increase in supply, demand remains constant

(c)

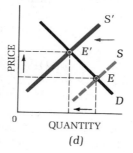

Decrease in supply, demand remains constant

(d)

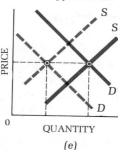

What happened here?

(e)

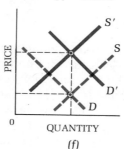

What happened here?

(f)

Efficiency

In a competitive economy there is ***consumer sovereignty***. That is, consumers "vote" by offering more dollars for products in greater demand and fewer dollars for products in lesser demand. In this way, consumers cause shifts in demand curves. How do producers respond to these changes in demand? In general:

> In a pure market economy, resources will be used as efficiently as possible. This is true to the extent that supply and demand reflect all costs and benefits of production and consumption. The efficient use of resources occurs because firms in each industry compete for the dollar "votes" of consumers. As a result:
>
> 1. Each firm, and the economy as a whole, achieves technical efficiency by making the fullest utilization of available inputs.
>
> 2. The economy also achieves economic efficiency by fulfilling consumer preferences, producing the combination of goods that people are willing and able to purchase with their incomes.

In other words, a pure market economy achieves maximum output at the lowest prices consistent with existing costs, technology, and incomes. What is most important, perhaps, is that these results are realized without direct intervention by government. Indeed, they come about through the free interactions of market supply and demand forces. These forces, like Adam Smith's "invisible hand," guide the allocation of society's resources to their most efficient uses.

Equity

A second feature of a pure market economy is that it distributes income in proportion to each person's contribution to production. If Smith adds twice as much to the value of total output as Johnson does, then competition among employers and among suppliers of resources will tend to see to it that Smith earns twice as much as Johnson.

The reason for this is not hard to see. No employer will pay either Smith or Johnson more than the value that each contributes. And neither Smith nor Johnson need accept less. Why? Because in a competitive economy there would always be some other employer who would find it profitable to pay them what they are worth. The result is that the "invisible hand" of competition — the forces of supply and demand — guide Smith and Johnson into the occupations that each performs best. In more general terms:

In a pure market economy, the factors of production tend to move into their most remunerative employments. This ensures that the entire income of society is distributed to the owners of resources in proportion to their contribution to the economy's total output.

Can we conclude in any *scientific* way that this method of apportioning society's income is fair or equitable? Not really. Equity considerations are based on value judgments of right and wrong, good and bad. In such matters, your own opinion is not necessarily better or worse than someone else's. However, we will examine this matter in considerable detail at later points.

Stability and Growth

There are two other important features of a pure market economy. The first concerns fluctuations in prices, output, and employment, or the problem of economic *stability*. The second concerns the expansion of real output, or economic *growth*.

1. *A pure market economy maintains a level of total spending sufficient to sustain full employment (or full utilization) of society's available resources.*
   Of course, innovations and changes in production methods may cause lapses from full employment. However, such lapses tend to be temporary. Because of the competitive nature of both the product market and the resource market, the supplies of and demands for goods and the factors of production adjust quickly to changing economic conditions. As a result, the economy's output and employment tend to remain relatively

stable while prices fluctuate around a long-run level corresponding to full employment.

2. *Part of the income received by the household sector is spent for consumption. The remaining portion is borrowed by the business sector for investment in new production techniques, new plant and equipment, and the like.*
   As a consequence, a society's stock of capital increases, and the production-possibilities curve shifts outward to the right. This means, as you have already learned, that the society produces larger quantities of goods — that is, it experiences economic growth.

To summarize:

With respect to stability and growth, a pure market economy has the following characteristics:

1. Prices fluctuate relatively more than output and employment to accommodate short-run changes in the supplies of and the demands for goods and resources.
2. Economic growth takes place in response to innovations by entrepreneurs that seek new and better ways of improving production methods.

These are among the more important features of a pure market economy. Their implications will become more apparent in later chapters as you learn about the achievements and failures of modern capitalism. Meanwhile, some further aspects of a pure market economy are pointed out in Box 2.

Some Real-World Imperfections

A pure market economy is the prototype of theoretical capitalism. But no real-world economy can be considered a pure market economy. The ways in which modern, mixed capitalistic economies differ from the model are many and various. Although a pure market economy may achieve a high score when judged by the standards of efficiency, equity, stability, and growth, the report card on our own capitalistic system would be far less glowing. De-

Box 2
Freedom and Power

A pure market economy is the prototype of capitalism. As such, it has the advantage of combining maximum economic freedom with minimum concentration of economic power—for two reasons:

1. Private Property and Economic Freedom

Freedom of enterprise is an extension of the institution of private property. Private property is the most fundamental characteristic of a capitalistic system and hence, of a pure market economy. Freedom of enterprise means that owners of resources are free to employ them where and how they see fit. The owners are subject only to the minimal governmental restraints needed to protect the welfare of society. Unlike a command economy, therefore, a pure market economy has no central authority that decides *what, how,* and *for whom* economic resources should be used. Instead, these decisions are made individually by producers seeking to earn profits by allocating resources according to the ways in which consumers freely register their preferences through the price system.

2. Dispersion of Economic Power

Economic power exists when a single buyer or seller can exert an influence on the market price of a good or resource. The fragmentation of economic power is an integral feature of a pure market economy and is closely related to economic freedom. Theoretically, economic power does not exist in a highly competitive system. This is because the market price of a commodity is established by the bids and offers of numerous buyers and sellers. An individual buyer or seller can either accept or reject the going price but cannot influence it. Each is a passive participant whose presence or absence in the market has no influence on the economic process because each is an insignificant part of it.

fenders of real-world capitalism, critics charge, mislead people by attributing to it the virtues of a pure market economy. Some of the more important criticisms may be described briefly.

Market Imperfections and Frictions

The market may not work as neatly in the real world as the theoretical model suggests. Imperfections and frictions, such as imperfect knowledge, resource immobility, and barriers to entering markets, impede the smooth functioning of the system.

For example, buyers and sellers of goods and resources do not usually have complete information about alternative prices, working conditions, and the like. Unemployed people frequently must be retrained before they can qualify for new jobs. And even when they are retrained, they may not be willing to bear the economic or psychic costs of moving long distances to accept employment.

Economics in the News

Elementary Exercise in Noontime Economics

By Marvin Phaup

Parents who think their children don't understand the real world of business may be mistaken. Many school children have experienced the frustration of fraud, regulation, supply disruptions, "foreign" competition, and price instability. Many also share an appreciation of the gains afforded by the opportunity to trade. This understanding often stems from their experience in the school lunchroom.

First indications that our fifth-grader was enjoying the gains from trade appeared last September in requests for packed lunch items he would not ordinarily eat: fruit cocktail and chocolate pudding in easy-open cans. The mystery was soon solved: "I just want the stuff I can get the best trades for." As details emerged, it became obvious that the lunchroom at Drew—a public elementary school—had a lot in common with some better known markets and that the students had

already acquired a substantial knowledge of both.

Features of the Drew Lunch Market

The 100 students in grades five and six have lunch together at about 10 large tables. Most bring their lunch from home and purchase milk. A "hot," usually tepid, lunch is also served. Trading begins almost as soon as students reach their tables and continues until the day's fixed stock of goods is consumed.

Two types of trade are regarded as "bad": fraud and disequilibrium transactions. Fraud usually involves misrepresentation: half-full milk cartons and empty gum wrappers described as full weight. A variety of means have been adopted by students for dealing with swindlers. These include social derision, demands for close pre-sale inspection and a refusal to deal with "bad traders."

Lunchroom prices fluctuate in a predictable manner. In November 1984, the appearance of a citrus canker in Florida sharply reduced the supply of oranges in stores. The relative price of oranges in the lunchroom soared. Student traders cater-

ing to the sweets and desserts market, however, have seen the demand for and price of their offerings significantly reduced by the introduction of substitutes, milkshakes and ice cream sold by cafeteria staff. Prices sometimes reach zero. Free goods deemed to have no trading value are disposed of by declaring the item "up for grabs," meaning that it belongs to the first claimant.

Student Policy Views

Students had no trouble describing the usefulness of their market as a means of reallocating lunch items more closely in accord with wants. They concluded that both parties gain in a voluntary exchange.

For a variety of good reasons, lunchroom trading is bound to remain a semiclandestine, "imperfect" activity. Where it exists, however, it is a good candidate for educational use as an introduction to such topics as opportunity cost, supply, demand, the gains from trade and regulation. And when you complain about "that jungle out there," your kids may know exactly what you mean.

Similarly, entrepreneurs and workers are often prevented from entering new industries because they lack the capital or the special know-how required. Or perhaps they cannot overcome monopolistic barriers, such as patent rights and apprenticeship requirements, that protect various business firms and unions from increased competition.

These and other obstacles retard the rate at which the factors of production shift out of declining industries and into expanding ones. As a result, imbalances in the form of shortages and surpluses arise in various product and resource markets. In a pure market economy, these imbalances would not occur—or, if they did, they would be short-lived.

Economic Inequity

In a market economy, incomes tend to be proportional to people's contributions to production. As we have seen, if Smith adds twice as much to the value of total output as Johnson does, then Smith's income will tend to be twice that of Johnson's.

This economic inequality can be further magnified by the right of inheritance. This fundamental institution of capitalism permits the accumulation of wealth within families. Such disparities in income and wealth can lead to economic and social inequities that are not based on people's contributions.

Technology and Large-Scale Production

The model of a pure market economy assumes that each industry comprises numerous small firms. Yet modern technology dictates that in many industries, such as automobiles and steel, firms must be very large if they are to make use of the most efficient means of production. In such industries, a few large firms are dominant.

"Externalities"

Another criticism is that the market system fails to reflect all the costs associated with production and consumption. As a result, there are side effects, or "externalities." For example, production of some goods, such as steel, rubber, and chemicals, pollutes the environment and so contributes to *social costs*. Other goods, such as education, sanitation services, and park facilities, add to community satisfactions and so contribute to *social benefits*.

These externalities may not always be fully reflected in the prices of commodities. To the extent that they are not, supply and demand curves fail to show *all* the costs and benefits of production. As a result, either too much or too little is produced, and resources are misallocated. You will learn more about this in later chapters.

Relevant Even If Not Realistic

For these reasons, the model of a pure market economy does not convey a true picture of the way in which the price system operates in a modern capitalistic society. Nevertheless, as you will see later, the pure market model developed in this chapter provides a useful framework for evaluating the performance of a capitalistic system. Hence, the model is relevant, if not always realistic.

What You Have Learned

1. The purpose of studying supply and demand is to learn how a competitive or pure market economy works.

2. *Demand* is a relation between the price of a commodity and the quantity of it that buyers are willing and able to purchase at a given time. Other things affecting demand, such as buyers' income, prices of related goods, buyers' expectations of future incomes and prices, and various nonmonetary factors, are assumed to remain the same. The law of demand states that the relation between price and quantity demanded is *inverse*—as the price rises, less is demanded. Demand curves slope downward from left to right.

3. *Supply* is a relation between the price of a commodity and the quantity of it that sellers are willing and able to sell at a given time. Other things affecting supply, such as resource costs, prices of related goods in production, suppliers' expectations of future costs and prices, and various nonmonetary factors, are assumed to remain the same. The law of supply states that the relation between price and quantity supplied is usually *direct*—as the price rises, more is supplied. Supply curves typically slope upward from left to right.

4. The intersection of a market demand curve with a market supply curve shows the equilibrium price and the equilibrium quantity of a commodity. Demand or supply curves may shift either left or right as a result of changes in any of the determinants assumed to remain constant when the curves were drawn.

5. Movements along supply and demand curves result from changes in the price of the commodity while the other underlying determinants of demand and supply remain constant. Such movements are called either a change in the quantity demanded or a change in the quantity supplied. The distinction is important.

6. In the real world, demand and supply curves are always shifting. A change in demand or a change in supply may result in a new equilibrium price, a new equilibrium quantity, or both, depending on the relative shifts of the curves.

7. A market economy is highly competitive. Prices and quantities are determined by numerous buyers and sellers through the free operation of supply and demand. Organized commodity markets, such as the New York Mercantile Exchange, the London Cotton Exchange, or the Chicago Board of Trade, typify highly competitive markets. However, most of the markets in our economy differ from such competitive markets to varying degrees.

Terms and Concepts To Review

demand
demand schedule
demand curve
demand price
law of demand
supply
supply schedule
supply curve
supply price
law of supply
equilibrium
surplus
shortage
equilibrium price
equilibrium quantity

disequilibrium
change in quantity
  demanded
change in demand
normal goods
inferior goods
substitute goods
complementary goods
change in quantity
  supplied
change in supply
pure market economy
consumer sovereignty
externalities

For Discussion

In the following problems, use graphs whenever possible to verify your answer.

1. Do the numerical quantities of a demand schedule describe buyers' behavior? If not, what is the fundamental property of a demand schedule?

2. Evaluate the following editorial comments on the basis of what you know about the meaning of demand and scarcity in economics. (HINT How meaningful are the italicized words?)

Our community *needs* more schools and better teachers; after all, what could be more *critical* than the education of our children as future citizens?
    Lynwood *Times*

The health of our citizens is uppermost in our minds. Ever since the rate of garbage pick-up in our northwest suburbs deteriorated to its present deplorable levels, it has been evident that our *shortage* of collection facilities has reached *emergency* proportions.
    Lexington *Daily Explicit*

3. Some people would buy more of a good (such as jewelry or furs) at a high price than at a low price. This results in an upward-sloping "demand" curve. Would such a curve be an exception to the law of demand? Explain.

4. What would happen to the market demand curve for steak as a result of each of the following: (a) an increase in the average level of income; (b) an increase in the number of families; (c) a successful advertising campaign for veal and pork; (d) an increase in the prices of veal and pork; (e) a decrease in the prices of veal and pork?

5. What would happen to the demand for Pepsi-Cola if the price of Coca-Cola were doubled? Why would it happen?

6. Determine the effect on the supply of office buildings if each of the following happened: (a) the price of land rose; (b) the price of steel fell; (c) the price of cement fell; (d) a new and faster method of construction were adopted; (e) the number of firms that build offices declined; (f) rents for office buildings were expected to decline.

7. Analyze the following:
   (a) What would happen to the equilibrium price and equilibrium quantity of butter if the price of margarine rose substantially? (b) What would happen if there were an increase in the cost of producing butter?

8. "Wheat is wheat. Therefore, the price of wheat at any given time should be the same in Chicago as it is in Kansas City." Do you agree? Explain.

9. In organized commodity markets, buyers often become sellers and sellers often become buyers, depending on the price of the good. Examine the following schedule for five people, A, B, C, D, and E.

Price (dollars per unit)	Quantities that people will buy (+) or sell (−) at each market price				
	A	B	C	D	E
$1	+6	+5	+3	+8	−2
2	+3	+4	+2	+7	−5
3	0	+3	+1	+6	−8
4	−2	+2	0	+5	−10
5	−2	−3	−1	+4	−10
6	−4	−5	−2	+3	−11
7	−5	−6	−3	+2	−12

(a) Draw the market supply and demand curves, and estimate the equilibrium price and quantity.
(b) Show the effects on the supply and demand curves if C drops out of the market.

Chapter 3

The Private Sector — Households and Businesses: Income and Industrial Structure

Learning guide

Watch for answers to these important questions

What is meant by "income distribution"? Are there patterns or trends that enable us to compare the shares of income that different people receive?

How is income inequality measured? Why does income inequality exist? Are incomes more nearly equal today than they were several decades ago?

What standards exist for judging how income should be distributed? Is it possible to judge the fairness of such standards? Is there a "best" distribution of income for society?

How are businesses organized in our economy? Are some businesses too big? How big is big?

Our mixed economy is like a three-legged stool. One leg represents households, the second businesses, and the third, government. The first two, which constitute the ***private sector*** of the economy, are explored in this chapter. The third is the ***public sector,*** which is the subject of the next and several subsequent chapters.

You and I are part of the household segment of the private sector. So too are some 80 million families. Households are the ultimate suppliers of the economy's inputs of human resources and the major purchasers of its outputs of goods and services. Businesses, of which there are more than 15 million, including farmers and professional people, make up the second major group within the private sector. This group accounts for most of the society's production of goods and services.

Households: Income, Wealth, and Equity

In the United States, concern with the distribution of income and wealth is as old as the nation itself. Alexander Hamilton believed that liberty without inequality of property ownership is impossible because the inequality "would unavoidably result from the very liberty itself." Thomas Jefferson re-marked that the perpetuation of wealth through in-heritance "sometimes does injury to the morals of youth by rendering them independent of, and diso-bedient to, their parents." And James Madison supported legislation that "would reduce extreme income and wealth toward a state of mediocrity and raise extreme indigence toward a state of comfort."

What constitutes an equitable or fair distribution of income and wealth among people? This ques-tion has been debated for centuries by economists, politicians, and social critics. It is a problem of fun-damental importance that deserves our attention.

A Look at the Facts

Many people believe that income and wealth in our economy have been distributed inequitably and that this maldistribution is one of the fundamental social problems of our time. This belief is not new. It has been widely held (although its popularity has shown cyclical swings) since the early nineteenth century. Whether it is correct is a question we shall try to answer here and in later chapters.

To begin with, let us examine the facts. This is not easy, because there are different concepts of income and wealth. To most of us, income is sim-ply money that people receive from various sources. Wealth is the value of the goods and prop-erty that people own. But a significant part of many people's income consists of more than wages and salaries. Income also includes money and non-money benefits that are never reported to the tax authorities or to census takers. A similar problem affects the reporting of wealth. As a result, no gov-ernment or private source provides complete and accurate information about the distribution of in-come and wealth.

With these deficiencies in mind, we can turn our attention to the available facts. First, however, we need two definitions:

Income is the gain derived from the use of human or material resources. It is a flow of dollars per unit of time. Thus, wages or salary is an example of income.

Wealth is anything that has value because it is capa-ble of producing income even if it has to be sold to do so. Thus, your car, stereo, stocks, bonds, house, or any other things of value you may own are examples of wealth. Wealth is a stock or accumulation of value, as distinct from a flow of income.

Functional Income Distribution

The study of income distribution is customarily di-vided into two parts—"functional income distribu-tion" and "personal income distribution."

Functional income distribution refers to the in-come payments made to the owners of the four fac-tors of production. The four factors, you will recall, are labor, land, capital, and entrepreneurship. The kinds of payments made to the owners of these fac-tors are wages, rent, interest, and profit. Their an-nual sum is a measure of the nation's earnings, and hence is called *national income*.

Exhibit 1 shows the shares of national income going to each class of resource owners. These pro-portions change very little from one year to the next. Therefore, it is more instructive to convey the highlights of the information over intervals of several years, as has been done in the graphs.

The titles in the exhibit are those used by the U.S. Department of Commerce. This agency compiles the data shown in the graphs. It should be noted that the classification "proprietors' income" in Fig-ure (b) consists of both the wages earned by self-em-ployed people and the profits of unincorporated businesses. For purposes of description, this classi-fication is shown separately here. But for purposes of analysis, it could be eliminated by allocating it to the other related class of income payments, "com-pensation of employees," in Figure (a). This would leave Exhibit 1 showing the four familiar classes of income payments: wages, rent, interest, and profit.

Compensation of Employees This category of in-come payments, shown in Figure (a), represents wages. It constitutes by far the largest share of na-tional income—approximately 75 percent. The proportion has expanded steadily over the years, reflecting the growing importance of paid employ-ment as the main source of people's income.

Exhibit 1

Functional Distribution of National Income in the United States

(decade averages; payments are shown as percentages of national income)

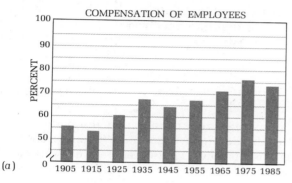

(a)

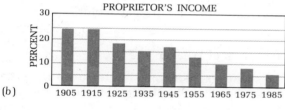

(b)

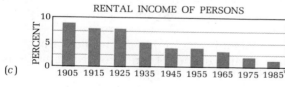

(c)

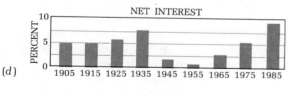

(d)

(e)

* Estimated

Source: U.S. Department of Commerce.

Proprietors' Income   This class of payments, illustrated in Figure (b), has declined to about six percent of national income. The reason is that corporations have grown rapidly in importance during this century. As a result, they long ago replaced proprietorship as the economically dominant form of business organization and as a significant source of people's income.

Rental Income of Persons   This component, shown in Figure (c), has been decreasing steadily for decades. Its share is now less than two percent of national income. One of the major reasons for the decline is that corporations, rather than individuals, have become the chief owners of rental property. Therefore, corporations are receiving an increasing proportion of rental income. This income becomes part of the gross income of corporations. After their expenses are deducted, their rental income ends up as part of corporate profits. These are shown in Figure (e).

Net Interest   This item, illustrated in Figure (d), is the difference between what the business sector pays in interest and what it takes in. Stated differently, it is the interest income that the nonbusiness sector (mostly households) receives on its loans to the business sector. For example, if you buy a Ford Motor Company bond, you are lending the company money for which it pays you interest. Net interest is thus the business sector's total interest payments to other sectors minus their total interest payments to the business sector. The trend of net interest payments is strongly affected by monetary and credit conditions. These are matters of fundamental concern in macroeconomics.

Corporate Profits   This component of national income, shown in Figure (e), is what is "left over." It is a residual representing a reward for entrepreneurship (that is, for organizing and risk taking) after other income payments, which are largely contractual, have been made. Compared with the other payments, therefore, corporate profits are the most variable. They exhibit the greatest period-to-period fluctuations when measured in terms of percentage changes.

To summarize:

> Functional income distribution refers to the allocation of national income among the classes of resource owners. Over the long run, compensation of employees averages about 75 percent of national income. Proprietors' income, rental income of persons, and net interest each average less than 10 percent. Corporate profits, which are the most variable because they are noncontractual, tend to average about 10 percent.

Personal Income Distribution

How are personal incomes distributed in the United States? What percentage of families is rich and what percentage is poor? This is the problem of *personal income distribution* — the allocation of income among people.

Exhibit 2 shows the relative share of total money income *before taxes* received by each fifth and the top 5 percent of all families in the United States. This table reveals three long-run characteristics:

1. The income received by the lowest one-fifth of families has averaged slightly more than 5 per-

---

Exhibit 2
Percentages of Aggregate Income (Total Money Income Before Taxes) Received by Each One-Fifth and the Top 5 Percent of Families*

Income rank	1950	1960	1970	1980
Lowest fifth	4.5	4.8	5.4	5.1
Second fifth	11.9	12.2	12.2	11.8
Middle fifth	17.4	17.8	17.8	17.5
Fourth fifth	23.6	24.0	23.8	24.2
Highest fifth	42.7	41.3	40.9	41.5
Top 5%	17.3	15.9	15.6	15.7
Ratio of top 5% to lowest fifth	3.8	3.3	2.9	3.1

* Because figures are rounded, the sum of the five fifths in each column may not add to 100.

Source: U.S. Department of Commerce.

---

cent of total money income. (Money income is distinguished from in-kind income, such as food stamps, subsidized housing, and subsidized medical care.) The income received by the highest one-fifth has averaged more than 40 percent of total money income. This represents a long-run ratio of approximately 8:1.

2. The ratio of the share received by the top 5 percent to the share received by the lowest 20 percent has declined substantially since 1950. However, the former is still roughly three times as large as the latter.

3. The entire distribution has remained remarkably stable.

Many observers believe that the pattern of income distribution will continue to remain about the same as it is now. Therefore, the equity question of whether or not incomes should be more nearly equal is a matter of continuing debate. The issues will be taken up later in the chapter.

Distribution of Wealth

The distribution of income has to do with who *gets* how much. The distribution of wealth has to do with who *has* how much. As you will recall, wealth consists of assets that are capable of producing income — either while they are owned or when they are sold. Examples of wealth are stocks, bonds, savings accounts, land, houses, and automobiles. Unfortunately, facts and figures about the distribution of wealth are limited and are not published periodically. As a result, we must rely on estimates from infrequent studies and reports.

Exhibit 3 shows that the wealthiest 1 percent of families in the United States own 25 percent of the total wealth. In fact, this top 1 percent owns about as much wealth as the lowest 80 percent of families. The wealthiest one-fifth owns approximately three times as much wealth as the lowest four-fifths.

The concentration of wealth is thus considerably greater than the concentration of income. Further, the concentration of income-producing wealth is even more pronounced. The top one-fifth owns the great bulk of stocks and bonds (not shown in the table). It is important to note, however, that this

Exhibit 3
Percentage of Total Wealth Held by Each One-Fifth, the Top 5 Percent, and the Top 1 Percent of Families

Wealth rank	1984
Lowest fifth	Less than 1%
Second fifth	2
Third fifth	5
Fourth fifth	17
Highest fifth	75
Top 5 percent	41
Top 1 percent	25

Source: Author's estimates from Internal Revenue Service data, U.S. Treasury.

Exhibit 4
Illustrating Inequality with a Lorenz Diagram

Percentage of Aggregate Money Income (Before Taxes) Received by Each One-Fifth of Families

Income rank	1980
Lowest fifth	5%
Second fifth	12
Middle fifth	18
Fourth fifth	24
Highest fifth	42

Source: U.S. Department of Commerce.

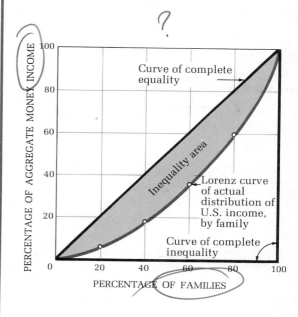

refers to direct holdings of securities. Indirectly, a large and growing proportion of the population owns stocks and bonds through retirement and pension funds, which invest heavily in such securities.

Measuring Inequality and Explaining the Facts

How can we illustrate and measure inequalities in the distribution of income and wealth? The most commonly used device is a type of graph called a *Lorenz diagram.* Such a graph is shown in Exhibit 4. Both the table and the graph show what percentage of people, ranked from the poorest to the richest, received what percentage of the nation's total income in a given year.

The graph is constructed by laying off on the horizontal axis the number of income recipients—not in absolute terms but in percentages. Families, rather than individuals, are usually represented. The point marked 20 denotes the lowest 20 percent of the families; the point marked 40, the lowest 40 percent; and so on. The vertical axis measures percentages of total money income. Both axes have

You can use the data from the table to construct a *Lorenz curve.* This curve shows the extent of departure between an equal distribution of income and the actual distribution of income.

From the curved line showing actual distribution, can you estimate the percentage of income received by the lowest 20 percent of families? The lowest 40 percent? 60 percent? 80 percent? 100 percent? Check your estimates against the data in the table to see if you are correct.

the same length and equal scales. Therefore, a diagonal line beginning at *0* and sloping upward from left to right at a 45° angle represents the curve of complete equality.

Along this diagonal line of equal distribution, 20 percent of the families would receive 20 percent of total income. Similarly, 40 percent of the families would receive 40 percent of total income, and so on. This line is compared with the curve of actual distribution—called a ***Lorenz curve***—derived from the data in the table. The area between the diagonal line of equal income distribution and the curved line of actual income distribution reflects the degree of income inequality. Thus, the more the curved line is bowed away from the diagonal, the greater is the inequality of income distribution.

How does the distribution of income compare with the distribution of wealth? The answer, given in terms of two Lorenz curves, is shown in Exhibit 5.

Why Are Some People Rich and Others Poor?

What factors account for differences in income among households? There are many reasons. Among them:

1. Differences in Wealth   Wealth is a significant source of income. Therefore, it appears obvious that a widely skewed (asymmetric) distribution of wealth is a major cause of income inequality.

2. Differences in Earning Ability and Opportunity   People differ widely in education, intelligence, skill, motivation, energy, and talent. These differences translate into differences in earning ability. There are, moreover, differences in the opportunities that are available to people. Many people face job barriers because of their age, sex, or race. Legislation has made these barriers less formidable, but they are still responsible for some of the inequality in income distribution.

3. Differences in Resource Mobility   The factors responsible for differences in earning ability and opportunity also make for differences in resource mobility. Many people, for example, are prevented by a lack of information or a lack of financial means

How close you are to job opportunities

Exhibit 5
Lorenz Curves of Income and Wealth Distribution

The distribution of wealth is considerably more unequal than the distribution of income. Inequality of wealth is both a cause and an effect of income inequality. High income leads to higher savings, which make possible further accumulation of wealth. This in turn begets still higher income.

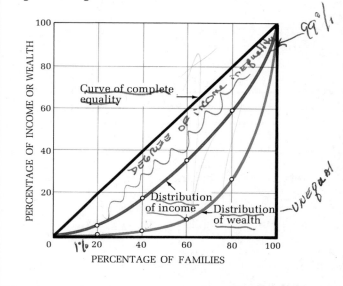

from moving into higher-paying occupations or locations. Consequently, low incomes and even extensive poverty may persist for years in some regions. This is true in certain parts of the United States, where sharecroppers, migratory farm workers, and some factory laborers are able at best to earn only a substandard living.

4. Differences in Luck   A person born into a favorable environment and provided with opportunities to develop inherited potentials stands a greater chance of earning a higher income than one not so fortunate. This has been borne out by sociological studies of "vertical mobility"—the climb up the socioeconomic ladder.

At Right place and Right Time

5. Differences in Age Young people who have recently entered the job market, and old people who have left it, have significantly lower incomes than those in midcareer.

INVESTED IN SELF

6. Differences in Human-Capital Investment
Some people make heavier investments in their future earning capacity than do others. Sales clerks, for instance, may begin earning income immediately after graduating from high school. Most professionals, on the other hand, must spend many additional years in training. They often do this by living on borrowed funds. But in the long run they realize higher financial rewards for their investment of time and effort. *EnGoing to College*

7. Differences in Risk, Uncertainty, and Security
Some occupations are more risky, and some have more uncertain futures, than others. These differences are reflected in earnings. Many people prefer security, in return for lower incomes, in the less risky and more certain fields of employment. For example, employees in relatively stable industries, such as civil service and banking, generally earn less than their counterparts in more unstable industries, such as manufacturing. Admittedly, lower incomes in some stable industries may be partly offset by nonmonetary factors, such as longer vacations, shorter working hours, and better fringe benefits. But the fact remains that coal miners earn more than road-construction workers, and window washers in skyscrapers earn more than dish washers in restaurants. Similarly, college professors earn less (but probably live longer) than corporate executives. Clearly, the clash between risk, uncertainty, and security reveals itself in many ways.

These and other factors affecting people's incomes help explain why a Lorenz curve will always show some degree of inequality.

Measuring Inequality

Social scientists often express the precise degree of income inequality in terms of the *Gini coefficient of inequality* (named after Corrodo Gini, an early-twentieth-century Italian statistician). Look again at the Lorenz diagram in Exhibit 4. The Gini coeffi-

cient may be defined as the numerical value of the area between the Lorenz curve and the diagonal line divided by the numerical value of the entire area beneath the diagonal line. In simplest terms, the Gini coefficient is the ratio of the inequality area to the entire triangular area under the diagonal:

$$\text{Gini coefficient of inequality} = \frac{\text{inequality area}}{\text{triangular area}}$$

The value of the ratio may therefore vary from 0 to 1. As incomes become more equal, the inequality area narrows relative to the triangular area under the diagonal. Thus, the Gini coefficient approaches zero. At zero there is no inequality—that is, all incomes are equal. As incomes become more unequal, the inequality area widens relative to the triangular area. Consequently, the Gini coefficient approaches 1. But the coefficient for any real-world society is always less than 1. A coefficient of 1 would indicate complete inequality, with one family getting all the income and the rest getting none.

Has the degree of income inequality become greater or less over the years? In 1950, the Gini coefficient of inequality for the U.S. was .38. Since then, the Gini coefficient of inequality has shown a gradual downward trend, decreasing to about .35 at present. The degree of income inequality has thus declined slightly since the middle of this century.

Evaluating the Data: The Trouble With Lorenz Curves

As you have seen, income inequality is typically measured by a table of income distribution or by a Lorenz curve. The curve, of course, is derived directly from the table. The data in the table consist of what the U.S. Census Bureau (which compiles the figures) calls "money income."

Do money-income data reveal all of the facts about income inequality? The answer is *no*—for several reasons:

1. Money Income is Before-Tax Income : It includes both personal income taxes and social security taxes. Payment of these taxes reduces income available for spending.

Economics in the News

Coming Soon: 1 Million Millionaires

Special for USA TODAY

ATLANTA—The USA soon will have 1 million millionaires, with the South having the biggest share, a researcher said Tuesday.

Dr. Thomas Stanley of Georgia State University, who has studied millionaires since 1973, reported:

- There were 832,602 millionaires in 1984 and will be 1 million by 1987.

- California has the most millionaires, 114,427; Vermont has the fewest, 1,031.

- The South has 30.6 percent; Northeast, 24.1 percent; Midwest, 23.1 percent; and West 22.1 percent.

Stanley said he found:

- Millionaires emphasize minimizing taxes, providing financial protection for their family and assuring their children's college education.

- Most have money tied up in real estate and companies. "I have to borrow money to eat lunch," one said.

- The average millionaire is 57; 85 percent have a college degree, 20 percent are retired, 70 percent are self-employed.

"I think it's neat, the South is flying," Stanley said. "You're losing a lot of talent from the Northeast."

2. Money-Income Data Exclude Subsidies and Tax Advantages Many low-income families benefit from food stamps, low-cost housing, government rent supplements, and free medical care. Many middle- and upper-income families benefit from company-subsidized expense accounts and fringe benefits, and from favorable tax treatment of certain income and expenses. Because of these factors, money income and *equivalent spending income* can differ widely within income groups.

3. Money-Income Data Do Not Reflect Differences in Family Size A given amount of income can go further in a small family than in a large one. As a result, small families with low income may sometimes be better off than large families with greater income, depending on their relative *per capita* spendable income.

4. Money-Income Data Reflect Current Earnings, Not Lifetime Earnings The income of a schoolteacher and a professional athlete may be about the same over the course of their lifetimes. But the schoolteacher's income will be spread over a period of forty years, whereas most of the athlete's income will be realized in less than ten years. In any given year, therefore, the two incomes are likely to be highly unequal.

5. Money-Income Data Are Not Adjusted for Age Differences Among Income Groups To a large extent, income inequalities at any given time result from differences in the age and, therefore, in the earning power of the people in question. We do not ordinarily expect young people who have recently entered the job market, or old people who have left it, to have incomes as high as people in midcareer. The money-income data, however, do not distinguish incomes by ages, and therefore reflect the inequalities across all ages.

Conclusion: Be Wary of the "Facts"

Studies of income inequality are published frequently, and their results are reported in the news media. The studies are conducted by economists employed in universities, research organizations, and government departments. Sometimes these experts conclude that inequality has increased. At other times they conclude that it has decreased. Which conclusion is correct?

It is essential to keep in mind that studies of income inequality are always based on very limited information. No one really knows how certain factors such as subsidies, taxes, family size, and age differences affect inequality between income groups. Consequently, *judgments regarding changes in income inequality should always be regarded with skepticism.*

> Income-inequality studies always fall short of accounting for all of the relevant facts. Because of this, conclusions based on such studies are likely either to overstate or to understate the true extent of income inequality. To be meaningful, estimates of income inequality should always be accompanied by explanations of the factors that have been allowed for, and the factors that have been neglected, in the measurement of income.

The Ethics of Distribution

The seventeenth-century English philosopher and essayist Francis Bacon remarked: "Money is like manure; not good except it be spread." But what criteria can be used for deciding how best to spread money? In other words, who should get how much? This is the age-old problem of economic justice.

The problem can have no completely satisfactory solution because justice in any form is at best a tolerable accommodation of the conflicting interests of society. Nevertheless, a number of distributive standards have been proposed over the long history of discussions on the subject. Most of these standards derive from one of three criteria:

1. Distribution based on productive contribution.

2. Distribution based on needs.

3. Distribution based on equality.

Contributive Standard

Most people would agree that a person should be paid what he or she deserves to be paid. This criterion, which fundamentally hinges on *merit*, represents one of the oldest concepts of justice.

Merit, however, is difficult to define and impossible to measure. How can we decide, in a manner acceptable to everyone, what each person merits or deserves? Surely, responsibility in a job is not the criterion, because air-traffic controllers earn far less than heart surgeons but hold more lives in their hands. Nor are years of formal education a criterion; many plumbers are more highly paid than schoolteachers. Certainly, the difficulty of a job is not the criterion, because difficulty depends on individual aptitudes and interests. Many more people can master advanced mathematics than can run a mile in six minutes. Almost all other standards of merit lead to similar contradictions. However, there is one measure of merit that is unique to capitalism:

> The criterion of distribution in a capitalist society can be expressed by the phrase, "To each according to what he or she produces." This may be called a *contributive standard* because it is based on the principle of payment according to contribution.

How is one's productive contribution measured? The most objective measure is the value placed upon it in a free market. Here the prices of the factors of production are established by the interactions of supply and demand. The contribution to the total product made by a particular factor of production and the payment received for the contribution can then be measured. This is done by multiplying the price per unit of the factor by the number of units supplied. Thus, under these conditions, if the market price of your labor is $6 per hour and you work 2,000 hours each year, your contribution to the total product and the payment you receive are both equal to $12,000. Much more is involved in determining factor contributions and payments than is implied by this example. Nevertheless, the illustration emphasizes an important principle:

> In a capitalistic or market economy, the payment received for a factor of production is the measure of its worth. This payment, which reflects the value of the factor's contribution to the total product, is determined by the impersonal pressure of market forces—not by the judgment of a central authority.

Of course, society also recognizes obligations to its nonproducers. These include the aged, the disabled, the very young, the involuntarily unemployed, and so on. As a result, society employs some noncontributive criteria for apportioning income. But the contributive standard is the dominant one in our economy.

Needs Standard

The distributive principle of capitalism, as we have seen, can be expressed by the phrase, "To each according to what he or she produces." In contrast, the distributive principle of pure communism may be described by the expression, "To each according to his or her needs."

It is interesting to note that the *needs standard* is not a distributive principle of communist philosophy only. This standard serves also as the criterion of distribution within most families. Further, in time of war or other emergency, some form of needs standard is adopted by all kinds of governments as a basis for rationing a severely limited supply of goods.

Distribution according to need has wide appeal. Upon close examination, however, its implementation poses two major difficulties.

1. No impersonal mechanism exists for measuring need. Thus, decisions to allocate goods according to need—whether such decisions are made within a family or on a national scale—must be based on someone's personal judgment.

2. Even if individual needs could be measured accurately, it is likely that the implementation of a needs standard would not precisely utilize the economy's entire output. There would be either shortages or surpluses, depending on whether the sum of needs was greater or less than the total product. (For example, people may "need" more cars than are produced, or the society may produce more cars than are "needed.") This is less likely to occur when output is distributed according to the contributive criterion of capitalism. Under such a system, market mechanisms tend to equate the incomes people receive with the value of what they contribute.

Equality Standard

A third criterion of distribution, proposed as far back as biblical times, is the *equality standard*. It is expressed most simply by the phrase, "To each equally."

The equality standard disregards the *inequality* of people's contributions. In view of this, is it a just standard? It may be considered so only if we assume that all individuals are alike in the *added* satisfaction or utility they receive from an extra dollar of income. In reality, an additional dollar of income may provide a greater gain in utility to some people than to others. In that case, justice is more properly served by distributing most of any increase in society's income to those who will enjoy it more.

However, there is no conclusive evidence that people are either alike or unlike in the satisfactions they derive from additional income. Therefore, the equalitarians (also called "egalitarians") argue that, because we cannot prove that people are unlike, we should assume that they are alike and distribute all incomes equally.

This conclusion, regardless of how plausible it may seem, illustrates a logical fallacy in reasoning. The fallacy is what philosophers call "argument from ignorance." It is committed whenever someone argues that a proposition is true simply because it has not been proved false, or that it is false because it has not been proved true.

In terms of the equality standard, this implies that we should go beyond the stage of theorizing about individual utilities and consider instead some of the realistic effects of an equality standard. Among the most important are the "motivational" ones:

> An equal distribution of income would eliminate the incentive of rewards. There would be no economic motivation for people to develop or apply their skills, or to use economic resources efficiently, because there would be no commensurate return. The result would be declining economic progress and probable stagnation.

This argument assumes, of course, that economic progress attributable to inequality and material rewards is desirable. Some critics think it is not. We discuss this issue in later chapters.

Conclusion: An "Optimal" Distribution?

The preceding arguments raise the question of whether there is some "ideal" degree of income inequality—a distribution that is not too extreme either way. What can be said about this hypothesis?

In a society characterized by a very unequal distribution of income, the economic surplus or savings of the rich minority can finance investment in capital. The result is material and cultural advancement. This was true of such ancient civilizations as Egypt, Greece, and Rome. Their economies were based on slavery—the most unequal distributive system of all. But as a result, they were able to produce magnificent art, architecture, and other cultural achievements.

On the other hand, in a society whose limited income is distributed equally, virtually all income is likely to be spent on basic consumption goods. This leaves little if any savings with which to acquire capital goods. (Here we meet the familiar production-possibilities concept of earlier chapters. It involves the notion that every society makes choices between the proportions of consumption goods and capital goods it wishes to have.) Such a society, because of its equalitarian distributive policy, would tend to remain poor.

Every society seeks the best compromise—the "optimum"—between two extremes of income distribution. One of these is substantial inequality. The other is complete equality. But each society's concept of the optimum depends on the society's goals and institutions. Therefore there is no objective way of determining that a particular distribution of income is either "good" or "bad."

Businesses—Organization and Size

Business decisions and policies influence the nature, structure, and goals of our society. This makes the motives and actions of business firms the subject of ceaseless scrutiny and debate.

How are business firms organized? Why are some of them large and some small? Before we go on to answer these questions, a definition of a business firm will be helpful:

A *firm* is a business organization that brings together and coordinates the factors of production—capital, land, labor, and entrepreneurship—for the purpose of supplying goods or services.

Business firms may be classified in various ways. One way is to group them according to their products. Firms that turn out similar or identical products are said to be in the same *industry.* Thus, General Motors and Ford Motor Company are in the automobile industry. But General Motors also produces trucks, buses, and diesel locomotives, among other things. Therefore, it would be correct to say that General Motors is also in the truck industry, the bus industry, and the diesel locomotive industry. Indeed, most large companies make more than one product. Can you name at least five industries in which General Electric is an important producer?

Another method of classifying firms is by their legal form of organization. Three types of organizations are particularly common: the individual proprietorship, the partnership, and the corporation. More than 75 percent of all firms in the United States are proprietorships, about 10 percent are partnerships, and the remainder are corporations. Although the proportion of corporations is relatively small, this form of business organization accounts for most of our economy's total output.

The Proprietorship

The simplest, oldest, and most common form of business is the *proprietorship.* This is a firm in which the owner (proprietor) is solely responsible for the activities and liabilities of the business. Most of the firms you see every day, such as bakeries, barber shops, beauty salons, restaurants, gas stations, and radio and TV repair shops, are proprietorships. Why are proprietorships so common? Because they are relatively easy to establish. They usually do not require special business skills, experience, or large amounts of capital (although there are some exceptions). But proprietorships have some disadvantages too. They tend to lack stability and permanence, it is difficult for them to raise funds for expansion, and their owners are personally liable for all debts of the business.

The Partnership

A partnership is simply a modified version of a proprietorship. That is, a *partnership* is an association of two or more people to carry on, as co-owners, a business for profit. A partnership has the same kinds of advantages and disadvantages as a proprietorship—but on a somewhat different scale. For example, partners can pool their funds to establish a business and they can combine their talents to manage it. However, they are jointly and personally liable for all debts of the business.

The Corporation

The third form of business organization, and the most important from an economic standpoint, is the corporation. Here is a definition that will be amplified in the following paragraphs:

A *corporation* is an association of stockholders (owners) created under law but regarded by the courts as an artificial person existing only in the contemplation of law. The chief economic characteristics of a corporation are (1) the limited liability of its stockholders, (2) stability and permanence, and (3) the ability to accumulate large sums of capital through the sale of stocks and bonds.

Some of the ideas behind this definition may already be familiar to you. For example:

The ownership of a corporation is divided into units represented by shares of *stock.* A stockholder who owns 100 shares of stock in a corporation has twice as much "ownership" as a stockholder with only 50 shares. Stockholders may participate in the profits of the corporation by receiving *dividends* in the form of a certain amount of money per share. If the corporation does not earn a profit, there may be no dividends.

One of the distinguishing features of a corporation is the *limited liability* of its stockholders. The owners of a proprietorship or partnership can be held personally liable for the debts of the business. However, stockholders in corporations cannot be held liable for any of the firm's debts. For almost all practical purposes, the most that stockholders can lose if the business goes bankrupt is the money they paid for their stock.

The corporation has durability. Stockholders may come and go, but the corporation itself lives on. Indeed, some corporations in existence today were originally chartered hundreds of years ago.

This permanence enhances the ability of corporations to finance their operations. They can raise large amounts of capital by selling stocks and bonds to the public. (*Bonds* are promises to pay a certain sum of money, called "principal," a year or more in the future, plus interest at specified dates in the interim. Bonds may be thought of as *long-term* IOUs, in comparison to short-term IOUs that pay principal and interest in less than a year.)

Stockholders elect a board of directors, which is responsible for the management of the corporation. Each stockholder gets one vote for each share of stock owned. Some stockholders may thus elect themselves to the board if they own enough shares or if they can get the support of enough other stockholders. In large corporations, the board employs executives to manage the company and to report back to the board. In many corporations, one or more officers also serves as members of the board.

Business Size and Problems of Bigness

Most corporations in the United States are "small." Their assets (cash, buildings, equipment, inventories, and so forth) total less than a few hundred thousand, or perhaps up to a few million, dollars each. At the other extreme are corporations whose total assets run into tens of billions, and whose annual net profits after taxes exceed $1 billion. Some of these large corporations employ hundreds of thousands of workers and distribute profits to hundreds of thousands, or even millions, of stockholders. Together these companies control a large share of the nation's income-producing wealth. The names of most of the large corporations in the United States are already familiar to you. In fact, you are probably a customer for many of their products. Several of these firms are listed in Exhibit 6.

How big is big? By way of comparison, the annual sales of each of the companies shown in Exhibit 6 often ranks with the value of output produced by such countries as Argentina, Belgium, Colombia, and Denmark. And, like a number of other U.S. corporations, each of those in Exhibit 6 has annual sales far exceeding, by many billions of dollars, the combined total outputs of several dozen other nations.

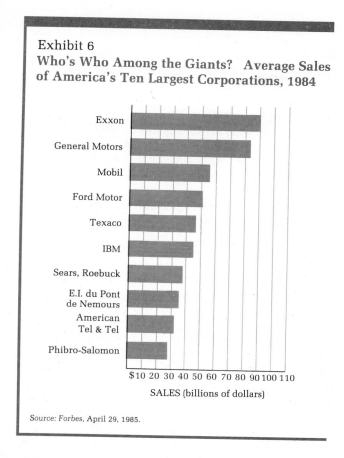

Exhibit 6
Who's Who Among the Giants? Average Sales of America's Ten Largest Corporations, 1984

SALES (billions of dollars)

Source: *Forbes*, April 29, 1985.

Is Bigness a Curse or a Blessing?

Is it "good" or "bad" to have an economy in which some major industries are dominated by a few giant corporations? Are such companies as Exxon in the petroleum industry, General Motors in automobiles, and AT&T in electronic communications beneficial or harmful? Would we be better off if we had an economy whose industries were composed of many small firms in active competition?

There are no simple answers. Nevertheless, the issues concern two fundamental problems of business size that affect all of us:

1. Stockholders Are Not Managers
A striking feature of most large corporations is the **separation of ownership and control.** This means that the stockholders own the business and the hired managers

control it. Most of the stockholders are usually interested only in their investment and not in who manages the corporation. Consequently, a corporation's board of directors and officers may be able, once in power, to represent their own interests more consistently than those of the company and its stockholders. To some extent, government regulations and laws have reduced the magnitude of this problem. But the difficulty still exists in varying degrees and will probably never be eliminated completely.

2. Market Domination
Important industries dominated by a few large companies include aluminum, telephone equipment, aircraft engines, and cigarettes. The giants in these industries exercise varying degrees of power over the markets in which they deal. This *may* have several implications for such firms. For instance:

- They *may* be able to charge prices higher than would be charged were the industries more competitive.
- They *may* not improve their efficiency and productivity as much as they would were they subject to greater competition.
- They *may* have the power to influence some of the legislators and federal agencies responsible for regulating them.

While recognizing these negative possibilities, we should also take note of some positive considerations. The productive resources and scientific know-how of many of today's corporate giants are vital to the country in peace as well as war. As some of the harshest critics of big business have acknowledged, these companies have been instrumental in providing us with the standard of living we now possess.

Conclusion: Free Markets for Greater Efficiency

In light of these considerations, we cannot state without qualification that big business is either "good" or "bad" for society. There are important advantages, as well as disadvantages, to large corporations, as you will see in some later chapters. Meanwhile, the following points should be kept in mind.

The task of a modern capitalist society is not to make a choice between large firms and small ones. Both types are here to stay. The practical problem is to find ways of making the free market work to improve the efficiency of businesses in general, both large and small. In this way, firms will utilize their resources more fully for the benefit of society.

What You Have Learned

1. Income and wealth are among the chief measures of society's well-being. Their distribution within society and the forces determining their distribution are of central concern.

2. The Lorenz diagram and the corresponding Gini coefficient are the most commonly used devices for measuring inequality. But they are only as reliable as the data on which they are based. Therefore, the data should always be analyzed with a critical eye.

3. There are many reasons for income inequality. Among the more important are differences in such factors as wealth, earning ability and opportunity, resource mobility, luck, age, human-capital investment, and occupational risk.

4. The degree of income inequality among income groups is affected by such factors as subsidies, taxes, and

How and Why Do Firms Become Big?

A business may expand through internal growth by plowing most of its profits back into the business. Or it can sell securities, such as stocks and bonds, to the public. In this way, it acquires the funds it needs to pay for new equipment, research, and product development.

A classic example of both types of growth is the Ford Motor Company. Founded as a privately (mostly family) held corporation, its stock became available to the public after several decades of operation.

A firm may also expand by combining or merging with others. This has been the most common method of growth in American industry. Indeed, many of our largest firms achieved their present huge size through "marriages" with others.

Firms may combine with other firms in the same or in related types of activity for various reasons. One of them might be to improve efficiency by gaining economies in production or distribution. Other reasons might be to regularize supplies, or to round out a product line. Thus, some container manufacturers make cardboard boxes, tin cans, glass jars, and plastic bottles. Some automobile producers also own rubber companies, iron mines, and steel mills.

Many companies have grown by combining with firms in unrelated activities. This may reflect various goals on the part of the acquiring company. Among these are the desire to spread risks and to find investments for idle capital funds. Other objectives may be to add products that can be sold with the firm's merchandising knowledge and skills or simply to gain greater economic power on a broader front.

age differences. The net effects on inequality of some of these factors is not known with any degree of certainty. Therefore, any statements about increases or decreases in income inequality should always be regarded with some skepticism.

5. Ethical criteria exist for allocating income. Three major ones are (a) productive contribution, (b) needs, and (c) equality. The first is the primary standard of distribution in capitalistic economies. The second and third criteria are philosophical goals of pure communistic and of egalitarian societies—neither of which exist anywhere on a national scale.

6. Economic history indicates that the higher a nation's real income per capita, the more that nation tends to progress toward greater income equality. This is because only a rich nation can generate the savings needed to assist its poor. That is why low-income nations tend to have the most unequal distributions of income.

7. The business sector of the economy consists primarily of proprietorships, partnerships, and corporations. The number of proprietorships greatly exceeds the number of partnerships and corporations. However, corporations produce by far the largest proportion of the nation's goods and services. One reason is that corporations can raise large sums of money to finance expansion.

8. The consequences of bigness are mixed. On the one hand, it has resulted in increased market power for the largest firms in many industries. On the other hand, the largest firms have also been significantly responsible for some of the major advances in our standard of living and in our military preparedness.

Terms and Concepts To Review

private sector	firm
public sector	industry
income	proprietorship
wealth	partnership
functional income	corporation
distribution	stock
national income	dividend
personal income	limited liability
distribution	bond
Lorenz diagram	separation of ownership
Gini coefficient of	and control
inequality	

For Discussion

1. What are the chief causes of income inequality among households? Would it be better if all incomes were equal? Explain.

2. Is it a necessary condition of capitalism that some people be rich and others be poor? Is it morally right for the government to tax the incomes of the rich and redistribute them to the poor? Defend your answer.

3. We cannot distribute goods according to people's needs because we do not know how to determine those needs. Therefore, why not solve the problem by (a) distributing *incomes* according to needs, and (b) permitting goods to be allocated through the price system, thereby preserving freedom of consumer choice?

4. "The principle of payment according to one's contribution to production (that is, the contributive standard) assures that people get what they deserve. Therefore, it is more democratic than payment based on needs or on equality." Do you agree? Explain.

5. "If payments to individuals are based on needs or on equality, some people are bound to be exploited for the benefit of others." Is this statement true? What does "exploitation" mean? Explain.

6. "In a democracy, we do not allocate political votes in proportion to one's intelligence and ability to use them. Instead, everyone gets an equal vote. Therefore, the same should be true of dollar votes (income); everyone's should be equal." Do you agree?

7. "The value of a culture is measured by its peak accomplishments, not by its average level of achievement. Thus, a society of mud huts and one great cathedral is better than a society of stone huts and no cathedral. To put it differently, it is by the quality of its saints and heroes, not its common people, and by its masterpieces, not its domestic utensils, that a culture should be judged." What implications does this have for income distribution?

8. An eminent political scientist, Robert A. Dahl of Yale University, has challenged the assumption that stockholders should control the direction of a company. "I can discover absolutely no moral or political basis," he says, "for such a special right. Why investors and not consumers, workers, or, for that matter, the general public?" What implications does this statement have for the future of capitalism?

9. Can you suggest some advantages and disadvantages of "big" business?

How To Calculate Your Class's Gini Coefficient

The Lorenz curve and the Gini coefficient are usually employed to express the degree of income inequality among families. But you can use these concepts to calculate the degree of *cash* inequality among the students in your class. Here is how to do it.

Step 1 Each student counts the cash in his or her possession, writes the amount on a slip of paper, and submits it to the instructor.

Step 2 The instructor may now ask a few students (depending on the size of the class) to analyze and tabulate the results. These are entered in columns (2) and (3) of the accompanying illustrative table. (The resulting table may be reproduced on the board so everyone can see it.) For illustrative purposes, it will be assumed that the class holds a total of $100, as you can verify by adding up the numbers in column (2).

Step 3 Complete columns (4) and (5) of the table. Then enter the letters *A* through *F* as shown in column (6).

Step 4 Construct a Lorenz diagram. *Connect the points with straight lines—not with a curved line.* (Straight lines will enable you to use a simple geometric approach that yields accurate results.) Note that, in this example, the lowest 20 percent of the students are holding 5 percent of the cash; label this point *B* on the Lorenz curve. The lowest 40 percent are holding 15 percent of the cash; label this point *C* on the curve. And so on.

Step 5 Decide how you will calculate the Gini coefficient of inequality. In order to do this, you must determine the inequality area. This is easily done by subtracting the entire area under the Lorenz curve from the large triangular area *AFG*. Here is the way to attack the problem:

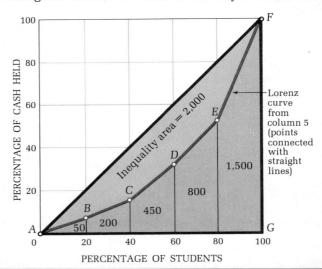

(1) Percent of students	(2) Cash held	(3) Percent of cash held	(4) Cumulative percent of students	(5) Cumulative percent of cash held	(6) Point on Lorenz curve
0	$ 0	0%	0%	0%	A
Lowest fifth	5	5	20	5	B
Second fifth	10	10	40	15	C
Third fifth	15	15	60	30	D
Fourth fifth	20	20	80	50	E
Highest fifth	50	50	100	100	F

First, note that the area under the Lorenz curve is equal to the sum of the separate triangular and trapezoidal areas beneath it. (A trapezoid is a four-sided figure with two parallel and two nonparallel sides.)

Second, to perform the necessary calculations, make use of the fact that the area A in terms of the base b and height h is found as follows:

$$\text{for a triangle: } A = \tfrac{1}{2}bh$$
$$\text{for a trapezoid: } A = \tfrac{1}{2}b(h_1 + h_2)$$

where h_1 and h_2 represent the heights of the left and right vertical sides.

Step 6 Now calculate the Gini coefficient of inequality, as follows:

(a) Calculate the total triangular area beneath the diagonal (i.e., the area of triangle AFG).

Total area beneath the diagonal: $\tfrac{1}{2} \times 100 \times 100 = 5{,}000$.

(b) Calculate the sum of the areas under the Lorenz curve (i.e., the sum of the small triangular area under AB and the four remaining trapezoidal areas under $BCDEF$).

Area beneath the Lorenz curve: $50 + 200 + 450 + 800 + 1{,}500 = 3{,}000$.

(c) Subtract the answer in step (b) from the answer in step (a).

Area between diagonal and Lorenz curve: $5{,}000 - 3{,}000 = 2{,}000$.

(d) Express the result as a fraction of the total area in step (a).

Gini coefficient of inequality: $2{,}000/5{,}000 = 0.40$.

Chapter 4

The Public Sector — Government: Public Choice and Taxation

Learning Guide

Watch for answers to these important questions

What is the role of government in our economy? How do we distinguish between the different types of goods that government provides?

Can government provide goods efficiently? What concepts can help us to analyze and evaluate the provision of goods by the public sector?

How does the government raise money? How does it spend money? What methods can be used to achieve greater efficiency in budgeting?

What is the nature of our tax system? What principles are used to evaluate particular taxes and their effects?

One of the most remarkable trends in contemporary history has been the growth in the importance of government in economic life. As measured by government purchases of goods and services, the public sector bought 10 percent of the nation's total output in 1930. By 1960, this figure had risen to 20 percent. Today the public sector purchases close to 25 percent of the nation's total output. These facts raise many questions concerning the economic functions of government in our mixed economy. This chapter examines a few of the more important ones and provides some basic tools for understanding them.

Any serious discussion of government is bound to raise questions about taxes. Taxes, you may recall from your study of history, have been a major cause of wars and revolutions. Moreover, in our society today, taxes affect economic activity in many different ways.

When we speak of government, we ordinarily mean the federal government. But this chapter will also say some things about government at the state level and the local level. The local level includes counties, cities, villages, townships, school districts, and so on.

Economic Scope and Functions of Government

For centuries, political scholars have theorized about the purposes and functions of government. In *The Wealth of Nations*, Adam Smith said that government's role should be limited to national defense, the administration of justice, the facilitation of commerce, and the provision of certain public works. Many social scientists today would agree with Smith, although some might add a few items to his list. For present purposes, the economic role of government can be considered to consist of two broad functions: (1) the promotion and regulation of the private sector, and (2) the provision of social goods.

Promotion and Regulation of the Private Sector *Business + Households*

Government promotes and regulates the private sector in many ways. Sometimes it does this to the net advantage, and sometimes to the net disadvantage, of society as a whole. A complete analysis of the public sector's economic functions is impossible here. However, <u>six</u> major activities can be identified.

Providing a Stable Economic Environment

Government facilitates orderly exchanges. It does this by defining property rights, upholding contracts, adjudicating disputes, setting standards for weights and measures, enforcing law and order, and maintaining a monetary system. These conditions are so fundamental to organized society that they existed even in the most ancient civilizations. The Code of Hammurabi (circa 2100 B.C.), and the later laws of ancient Egypt and Rome, are examples. They went into considerable detail in defining property rights and related matters pertaining to commerce.

Protecting the Public Welfare

Government establishes health and safety standards in industry and regulates minimum wages for certain classes of workers. It also provides old-age, disability, sickness, and unemployment benefits for those who qualify. Of course, these social welfare measures are enacted primarily for humanitarian reasons. Nevertheless, some of the measures may be tacit admissions that the private sector has failed to fulfill human wants in a manner that society regards as equitable.

Granting Economic Privileges

Through selective subsidies, tariffs, taxes, and other legal provisions, government favors particular consumers, industries, unions, and other segments of the economy. This elaborate network of privileges and controls results as much from political pressures as from economic logic. To a large extent, therefore, government privileges cause reduced efficiencies, higher prices, and misallocations of society's resources.

Maintaining Competition

Specific laws forbid unregulated monopolies and unfair trade and labor practices. If government enforces these laws vigorously, it helps ensure the perpetuation of a strong private sector.

Encouraging Efficiency, Equity, Stability, and Growth

Through appropriate tax, expenditure, and regulatory policies, government seeks to attain certain objectives. These include high employment, an equitable distribution of income, stable prices, and a steady rate of economic growth. The government's efforts are not always successful, however, for political reasons as well as for economic ones. Much of the study of economics is concerned with learning to understand these reasons.

This brief sketch of the economic activities of government leads to an important observation:

The promotional and regulatory activities of government are complex and widespread. Ostensibly, some of these activities are undertaken to correct for market failures. That is, they address the inability of the private sector, if left to itself, to achieve the goals of efficiency, equity, stability, and growth to the degree that society seeks. However, as you will see, the extent to which government activities contribute to the realization of these goals is often debatable.

Provision of Social Goods

All economic systems are concerned with the three fundamental questions: *What* will be produced? *How* will it be produced? and *Who* will receive the final output? In mixed capitalistic economies such as ours, these questions are answered primarily by the market system. But, if certain types of goods and services are not adequately provided by a free market, supplying them usually becomes a function of government. We refer to such products as *social goods.* For present purposes, they may be classified into two groups—public goods and merit goods.

Public Goods

Public goods are sometimes called "collective" goods. Examples include national defense, street lighting, disease control, the administration of justice through the courts, air-traffic control, and public safety. An essential characteristic of public goods is that you cannot be excluded from receiving their benefits, regardless of whether or not you pay for them. Every person in the nation or community benefits equally from national defense, street lighting, and other public goods, even those who pay no taxes.

Public goods can thus be distinguished from nonpublic goods. These consist of private goods (such as food, clothing, services, and so on) that people buy in the market and certain social goods, known as merit goods, which are described below. Someone who does not pay for nonpublic goods can con-

ceivably be excluded from using them. Therefore:

The distinction between public and nonpublic goods rests on what is called the *exclusion principle.* According to this principle, a good is nonpublic if someone who does not pay can be excluded from its use. Otherwise, it is a public good.

Merit (Quasi-Public) Goods

Public goods are not the only products that government provides. It also provides *merit goods,* because it deems them meritorious, or intrinsically worthy, of production. Merit goods (also called "quasi-public goods") share, to different degrees, some of the properties of both public and private goods. Some examples of merit goods, provided by the federal and state governments, are parks, public housing, and public hospitals. Local governments may supply such merit goods as municipal libraries, tennis courts, golf courses, and museums.

In contrast to public goods, merit goods are subject to the exclusion principle, *even though the principle may not always be invoked.* Therefore, merit goods are not (pure) public goods. People could be charged for the use of merit goods instead of being given them "free" or at reduced prices. As you will see, this raises interesting questions about efficiency and equity, problems that are among the fundamental concerns of economics.

Conclusion: Achieving Efficiency Through the Market

Throughout the nation's history, government has served as a rescuer, subsidizer, owner, and regulator of special interests. It has financed roads and canals, subsidized industries, sheltered workers, protected consumers and businesses, stabilized credit, refereed competition, and regulated markets.

Government has also become the chief producer of social goods, both public and merit goods. Everyone receives the benefits of the former. The benefits of the latter are widely available and, in most cases, are provided at reduced prices. How does this affect the allocation of such goods?

In a free market, prices perform the allocative function. A resource is always allocated to its highest-valued use, as determined by the prices that buyers offer. But the situation is different with most social goods. Because many are made available "free" or at reduced prices, it is impossible to know the value people place on the goods. How, then, should government decide *what* and *how much* to produce?

A reasonable answer to this question is that government should seek ways of making more effective use of market mechanisms in its pricing practices. This can be done through the use of special taxes, grants, and pricing strategies designed to test the demand for social goods. In this way, as you will see below, officials can be guided in learning how to improve efficiency in the provision of these goods. Equally important, legislators can consider whether certain social goods might better be provided through the private sector.

Something to Think About

Garbage collection is a public good in some communities, a merit good in others, and a private good in others. Can you suggest examples of social goods that could be financed entirely by user fees and charges? Can you think of social goods that could be privatized—that is, provided by the private sector? Why might this be desirable?

Economics in the News

When Public Services Go Private

Taxpayers Save 20% or More by Using Contractors to Provide Government Services

by Jeremy Main

OLD BUT STILL hotly controversial, the idea of letting private industry do more of government's work has caught fire in the 1980s. Pressed by tax revolts and spending limits, federal and local officials are buying more and more services from corporations. They have accumulated enough evidence lately to evaluate the risks and rewards. What they find is impressive. Turning government work over to business can cut costs 20% or more—often much more—without loss of quality.

Private industry has always provided services such as garbage collection and road mending in many places. Not only are governments now contracting for more of these traditional services, such as public transportation, but they are also finding new functions to put out to bid. At some small airports the Federal Aviation Administration no longer staffs control towers. The FAA provides funds and local authorities hire entrepreneurs to control air traffic. Los Angeles County and New York City have turned public golf courses over to private operators.

Government is starting to reach far beyond contracting for services by looking to private industry to finance, design, build, and run public facilities from waste-water treatment plants to prisons.

The limits of how much of its functions government can pass to profit-seeking companies aren't visible yet. Most authorities would balk at turning police and fire departments over to the private sector, yet Scottsdale, Arizona, has an excellent for-profit fire department. It grew out of a private fire-protection service that existed before the town was incorporated.

Implicit Privatization

Even where no policy to contract services exists, a kind of privatization may occur. In a sense the country's police are being privatized. Because Americans feel the need for greater protection, the number of private guards has grown much faster since 1970 than the number of publicly sworn law enforcement officers. The mail is also being privatized as users grow fed up with the plodding U.S. Postal Service and turn to more efficient and reliable commerical couriers, such as Federal Express and Airborne Freight.

In theory, since the public sector doesn't have to make a profit or pay taxes and can generally borrow money more cheaply than the rest of us, government should be able to underbid the private sector. But it doesn't work that way. The bracing winds of competition more than make up for the built-in advantages of government.

Spillovers, Market Failure, and Public Choice

Many social goods (as well as private goods) create "fallout" effects, or spillovers. These are external benefits or costs for which no compensation is made. Spillovers are also called **externalities.**

For example, in the public sector, air-traffic control at busy airports reduces noise for some nearby residents while increasing it for others. This is an unpaid-for benefit to the former and an uncompensated "cost" to the latter. In the private sector, similarly, a factory may provide income and employment to a community while polluting its environment. Thus, spillover benefits and costs exist with some private goods as well as with some social goods.

Spillovers are a cause of **market failure.** That is, they prevent a competitive free market from allocating resources efficiently. As you will recall from your study of supply and demand, resource misallocation occurs if a good's costs and/or benefits are not fully reflected by its equilibrium price. When that happens, it is because the good's supply-and-demand curves do not incorporate the full value of society's sacrifices and preferences. The values that are not incorporated are what have been called "externalities" or "spillovers." Their existence accounts for the failure of competitive free markets to provide outputs that are socially ideal.

Redressing Spillovers

What can be done to correct for the effects of spillovers? Because they result from private-sector market failure, corrective action to eliminate or offset them can come only from government. Two major approaches may be considered:

1. Market Measures: Internalizing the Externalities

One way of reducing spillovers is to look for ways to incorporate them in a good's market-supply and market-demand curves. This approach is illustrated in Exhibit 1.

In Figure (a), any point on the normal market-demand curve D expresses the **demand price.** This is the highest price that buyers are willing to pay for a given quantity of the good. The demand curve thus reflects only private benefits to buyers, not spillover benefits to nonbuyers or to society.

Similarly, any point on the normal market-supply curve S expresses the **supply price.** This is the least price necessary to bring forth a given output. That is, it is the lowest price that sellers are willing to accept in order to supply a given quantity of the good. The supply curve thus reflects only private costs to producers, not spillover costs to anyone else.

The diagram assumes that *all* benefits and costs are incorporated in the demand and supply curves —there are no spillovers. Accordingly, the equilibrium quantity at Q is socially ideal because it represents an optimum allocation of society's resources. On the other hand, if all benefits and costs are not included in the supply and demand curves, then spillovers exist. The equilibrium quantity is not socially ideal. In that case, government can undertake two sets of policy measures to correct the situation.

Internalizing Spillover Costs by Incorporating them in the Market Supply Curve The effect of this approach is shown in Figure (b). It illustrates the case of an industry that pollutes its environment, thereby externalizing some costs of production to others. As a result, the supply curve S is "too low" because it does not include *all* of the costs of producing the product. Because of this, the equilibrium quantity is at Q' rather than at Q.

One measure that government can adopt to correct the situation is to require sellers to pay a **specific tax.** This is a per-unit payment on a good. That is, sellers would pay the tax T on each unit of the good produced. This would increase its costs of production by the amount of the tax, causing the supply curve to shift from S to S'. If the tax is large enough, it can compensate for any spillover costs that were not included in the original supply curve. The tax will thus reduce output from the

Exhibit 1
Spillover Effects in a Competitive Market

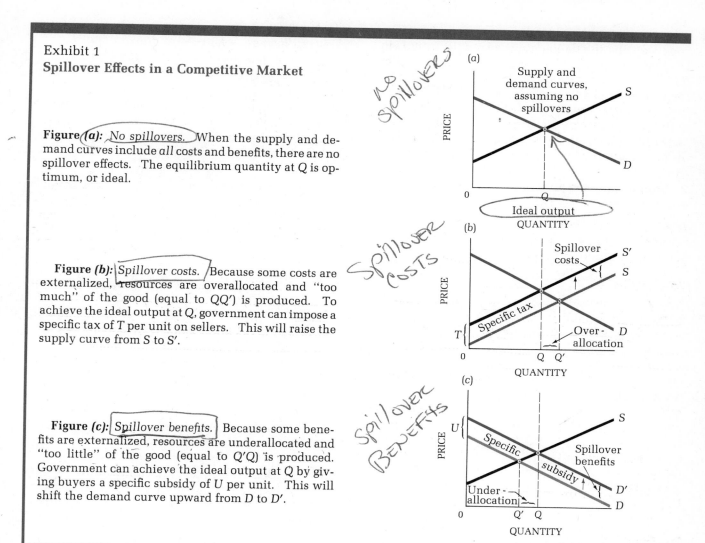

Figure (a): _No spillovers._ When the supply and demand curves include _all_ costs and benefits, there are no spillover effects. The equilibrium quantity at Q is optimum, or ideal.

Figure (b): Spillover costs. Because some costs are externalized, resources are overallocated and "too much" of the good (equal to QQ') is produced. To achieve the ideal output at Q, government can impose a specific tax of T per unit on sellers. This will raise the supply curve from S to S'.

Figure (c): Spillover benefits. Because some benefits are externalized, resources are underallocated and "too little" of the good (equal to $Q'Q$) is produced. Government can achieve the ideal output at Q by giving buyers a specific subsidy of U per unit. This will shift the demand curve upward from D to D'.

level at Q' to the socially optimum level at Q. (_Question:_ Can you show how the ideal output may also be achieved by imposing a specific tax on buyers?)

Internalizing Spillover Benefits by Incorporating them in the Market Demand Curve The effect of this approach is shown in Figure (c). It illustrates the case of an industry, such as private higher education, that externalizes some benefits by providing

society with a more informed and concerned citizenry. As a result, the demand curve D is "too low" because it does not include _all_ of the benefits obtained from the product. Because of this, the equilibrium quantity is at Q' rather than at Q.

To correct this, government can bring about an increased output of the product by giving buyers a **specific subsidy.** This is a per-unit grant on a commodity. As shown in the diagram, buyers would receive the subsidy U on each unit of the good purchased. This would increase the consumption of the good, causing the demand curve to shift from D to D'. If the subsidy is large enough, it can compensate for any spillover benefits that were not included in the original demand curve. Thus, the subsidy will increase output from the level at Q' to the socially optimum level at Q. (*Question:* Can you demonstrate that government can also achieve the ideal output by granting a specific subsidy to sellers?)

2. Nonmarket Measures: Government Regulation and Provision

In addition to the foregoing market devices, government can employ various nonmarket measures to influence output and resource allocation. This is accomplished by enacting appropriate legislation. For instance:

Through government regulation the outputs of some products (and by-products) for which spillovers are deemed to be undesirable can be reduced. Examples are industrial-waste disposal, smoke emission, and water pollution. In terms of Figure (b), the purpose of such regulation is to shift the supply curve *upward* to achieve results similar to those attained by market measures (such as taxing sellers.)

Through government provision the output of some goods for which spillovers are deemed to be desirable can be enlarged. You will recall that when government makes available such products, they are called "merit goods." Examples include public recreation, public safety, and public higher education. In terms of Figure (c), the purpose of such provision is to shift the supply curve *downward*, to achieve the same ideal output attained by market measures (such as subsidizing buyers).

Thus, government regulation and provision by their very nature, focus on influencing the supply of goods, not the demand for them.

Conclusion: Efficiency and Public Choice

The foregoing analysis enables us to arrive at three important generalizations:

1. As shown in Figure (b), a competitive free market *overallocates* resources to the production of a good that has spillover costs. Consequently "too much" of the good is produced relative to its ideal output.

2. As shown in Figure (c), a competitive free market *underallocates* resources to the production of a good that has spillover benefits. Because of this, "too little" of the good is produced relative to its ideal output.

3. Government alters the outputs of many goods that have spillover costs and benefits. The alterations are accomplished both by market mechanisms such as taxes and subsidies, and by nonmarket mechanisms such as regulation and provision.

The analysis of spillover costs and benefits is part of a larger branch of economics known as **public choice.** This may be defined as the study of nonmarket collective decision making, or the application of economics to political science. Public choice seeks to develop ways of improving efficiency in the public sector — in the provision of social goods.

> Under pressure to provide social goods, the public sector continually seeks better ways of allocating scarce resources. Sophisticated applications of market and nonmarket mechanisms can be helpful for this purpose. The mechanisms can be used to reduce spillovers in the private sector, thereby improving its efficiency and releasing resources for more effective use in the public sector.

Public Budgeting: Tools for Collective Decision Making

In the past few decades, the public sector has been characterized by a remarkable growth of expenditures at all levels of government — federal, state, and local. This means that a rising volume of the nation's output is being allocated by collective (rather than private) decision making. Four major

Exhibit 2
Growth of Government Expenditures

The size of the public sector, measured by government expenditures, has expanded rapidly.

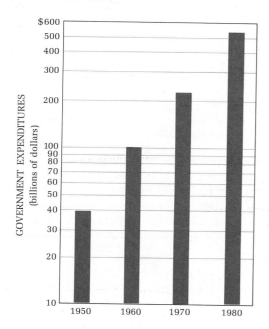

(NOTE The vertical axis of this graph is a logarithmic scale. On this type of scale, *equal distances represent equal percentage changes*. Thus, the changes from 10 to 20, 20 to 40, 100 to 200, 200 to 400, and so on, all equal 100 percent. Therefore they are represented by equal vertical distances on the graph. This facilitates comparisons of *percentage* changes over time.

Source: U.S. Department of Commerce.

social goods, including education, transportation, social security, housing, and consumer protection.

National Defense A large part of the increase in federal spending can be attributed to expenditures on defense-related activities. These include both military personnel and military equipment.

Interest on the Federal Debt The last few decades have witnessed a huge rise in the interest payments made on our growing national debt. (The national debt is also called the public debt or the government debt.)

Lagging Productivity of Government Employees Productivity in the delivery of government services has lagged far behind rising costs. Government has found that the salaries and fringe benefits it pays its employees are growing faster than the efficiency of the services they perform.

As you might guess, any discussion of public-sector expenditures is bound to raise questions about public-sector revenues. The methods used by governments to manage their revenues and expenditures constitute what is known as "public budgeting." Exhibit 3 describes and illustrates some trends of government budgets.

Budgeting for a government, like budgeting for a family, is an activity dealing with hopes and daydreams as well as hard facts. What is a *budget?* It is an itemized estimate of expected revenues and expenditures for a given period in the future. The federal budget covers a fiscal year. (A fiscal year is any 12-month period for which a business, government, or other organization plans the use of its revenues.) The budgets of some state and local governments cover a fiscal period that is longer than a year (typically two years).

You will often hear people complain of waste in government spending. Can financial controls be developed to reduce public-sector inefficiencies? Two scientific techniques for improved budgeting have come to be extensively used at certain levels of government. The two techniques are:

1. Planning-program-budgeting systems.
2. Benefit-cost analyses.

reasons for the growth of government spending may be given. The long-run trends can be seen in Exhibit 2.

Increased Demand for Social Goods and Services
The public sector has increased its expenditures on

Exhibit 3
Federal, State, and Local Budgets: What Happens to Your Tax Dollars?

(a) FEDERAL BUDGET RECEIPTS AND OUTLAYS: 1960–1985

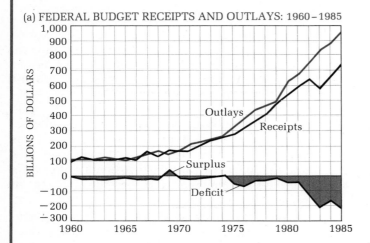

(b) ANNUAL FEDERAL BUDGET: 1985

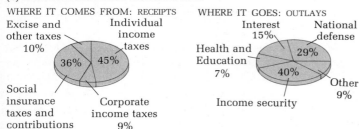

WHERE IT COMES FROM: RECEIPTS
Excise and other taxes 10%
Individual income taxes 45%
36%
Social insurance taxes and contributions
Corporate income taxes 9%

WHERE IT GOES: OUTLAYS
Interest 15%
National defense 29%
Health and Education 7%
40%
Other 9%
Income security

(c) STATE AND LOCAL GOVERNMENT BUDGETS: 1985

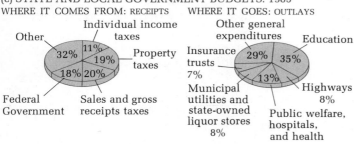

WHERE IT COMES FROM: RECEIPTS
Other 32%
Individual income taxes 11%
19%
Property taxes
18% 20%
Federal Government
Sales and gross receipts taxes

WHERE IT GOES: OUTLAYS
Other general expenditures 29%
Education 35%
Insurance trusts 7%
13%
Municipal utilities and state-owned liquor stores 8%
Highways 8%
Public welfare, hospitals, and health

Figure (a): The government's total revenues and expenditures for any given year are rarely equal. When they are, the budget is said to be *balanced*. When total revenues exceed total expenditures in any given year, the budget is said to have a *surplus*. When total revenues are less than total expenditures, the budget is said to have a *deficit*.

Figure (b): For the federal government, *income taxes*, both individual and corporate, constitute the largest source of receipts. *Income security* payments, including social security benefits, unemployment compensation, public assistance (welfare), and federal employment retirement and disability benefits, constitute the largest category of outlays.

Figure (c): For state and local governments combined, *property taxes* (on land, buildings, etc.) and *sales taxes* make up the chief sources of tax income. *Education* is the largest category of expenditure.

Figure (d): Over the long run, state and local governments have received a rising percentage share of total tax revenues. In contrast, the federal government has received a declining percentage share. These trends reflect the need of state and local governments to finance their growing public functions.

(d) PER CAPITA TAX REVENUE, BY LEVEL OF GOVERNMENT

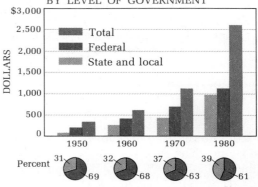

Source: U.S. Department of Commerce.

KNOW THIS

Planning-Program-Budgeting Systems (PPBS)

A budget is a financial road map. It tells you where revenues are expected to come from and where expenditures are expected to go. Most traditional budgets are simply "administrative" budgets. They classify expected money inflows and outflows by administrative units (such as departments or agencies) or by activities (describing the work to be performed). Administrative budgets do not ordinarily explain *why* or *how* the funds are to be coordinated to fulfill objectives.

A budget that is designed to avoid this shortcoming is a "program budget." It is part of a larger complex called a *planning-program-budgeting system (PPBS).* This may be defined as a method of revenue and expenditure management based on:

BASED ON

1. Determination of goals.
2. Assessment of their relative importance.
3. Allocation of those resources needed to attain the goals at least cost.

Thus, PPBS is a budgetary method that relates expenditures to specific goals or programs. This is done so that the costs of achieving a particular goal can be identified, measured, planned, and controlled. You can best appreciate the difference between an administrative budget and a program budget by comparing the two tables in Exhibit 4.

In many government departments in which PPBS has been adopted, it has improved budgeting efficiency. However, it has also been found to have some important limitations. In particular:

Outputs are usually in the form of indivisible services, which are therefore difficult to measure. For example, neither the quantity nor the quality of most governmentally provided social goods—such as education, health care, police protection, space exploration, and so on—can be broken down and measured in precise units. As a result, the establishment of budgetary goals and priorities is generally based on value judgments rather than on scientific determinations.

Exhibit 4
Alternative Budget Structures for the U.S. Coast Guard

In an *administrative budget*, funds are allocated by administrative agencies and by activities. In a *program budget*, funds are allocated for the purpose of attaining certain objectives, or for undertaking specific programs. The totals in both budgets may be the same, but the ways in which the expenditures are broken down are quite different. As explained in the text, a program budget is part of a larger planning and control system.

Administrative budget (allocation by administrative agencies and activities)	Amount
General funds: finance division	
Operating expenses	x
Retired pay	x
Reserve training	x
Activities funds: departments	
Vessel operations	x
Aviation operations	x
Training and recruiting	x
Administration	x
Other expenses	x
Total	x

Program budget (allocation by specific objectives and programs)	Amount
Search and rescue	x
Navigational aids	x
Law enforcement	x
Military readiness	x
Merchant Marine safety	x
Oceanography projects	x
Supporting services	x
Total	x

Despite this shortcoming, PPBS is a useful tool for facilitating overall budgetary decision making. However, when specific alternatives must be evaluated to determine whether certain large-scale projects and expenditures should be undertaken, a more scientific approach is needed.

Benefit-Cost Analysis

A scientific approach to government budgeting and financial planning is ***benefit-cost analysis.*** This is a method of comparing alternative investment projects or spending programs to help determine which should be undertaken. Benefit-cost analysis can also be used for personal financial planning. For example, if you are thinking of buying a house, a car, or even a vacation, benefit-cost analysis can help you make the choice that gives you the greatest value for your dollar.

In general terms, a typical governmental benefit-cost study consists of three steps.

Step 1: Determine Benefits   Identify the future advantages or benefits that will accrue to society as a result of the project. Then express the value of these benefits in today's dollars. For example, if the project is a program for flood control in an agricultural area, how much will be saved through reduction of damage to crops, homes, and recreational facilities?

Step 2: Determine Costs   Identify the sacrifices, or *opportunity* costs, that will be incurred as a result of the project. In other words, what benefits will people have to forgo because money is being used for, say, a flood-control project rather than a job-training program?

Step 3: Determine the Benefit/Cost Ratio   Divide the total dollar benefits by the total dollar costs. As an illustration, suppose the benefits equal $11 billion and the costs equal $10 billion. Then the ratio of benefits to costs is:

$$\frac{\text{Benefits}}{\text{Costs}} = \frac{\$11}{\$10} = 1.1$$

If no other project being considered by the government has a higher ratio, then this project, among all those under consideration, would result in the most efficient expenditure of public funds. Why? Because it would produce the largest value of benefits per dollar of costs.

Some Difficulties

This simple example conveys some of the basic ideas, but not the real difficulties, of conducting an actual benefit-cost analysis. Most of the difficulties fall into two categories — constraints and measurement.

Constraints   Government agencies are not always free to select the most socially desirable projects — the ones with the highest benefit/cost ratios. The reason is that they are subject to various administrative, financial, and legal constraints. For example, certain projects may be unable to attract enough qualified supervisors. The budgets for financing particular projects may be inadequate. And there may exist laws (such as zoning laws) that prohibit the use of particular resources for certain projects.

Measurement   It is rarely possible to measure all the benefits and costs of a government spending program. This is because most projects have many secondary and intangible impacts. For example, how can we measure the value of a new educational program to a community, or the value of an antipollution program on the quality of life? Similarly, how can we fully measure the opportunity costs of such programs? Because of such problems, economists conducting benefit-cost studies are often compelled either to make rough estimates of certain benefits and costs or to omit them entirely.

Despite limited applications, benefit-cost analysis has certain fundamental advantages:

In a conventional budgeting system, funds tend to be allocated according to expected "needs" or "requirements." Little or no effort is made to establish, in any precise way, how those needs or requirements are determined and whether they are worth the costs. In a benefit-cost budgeting system, each expenditure is compared with the benefit it will produce. The expenditure is not undertaken unless its value is at least equaled by the value of its benefit. Resources are thus allocated more efficiently—through explicit comparisons of benefits and costs rather than suppositions about "needs" or "requirements."

Our Tax System

Government budgets deal not only with expenditures but also with revenues. Governments raise revenues through taxation. In view of this, we must ask: What is the nature of our tax system?

A *tax* is a compulsory payment to government. You will often hear it said that certain taxes are "good" and others are "bad." What do such statements mean?

The results of any tax are judged in terms of its effects on the economy's four major goals:

Efficiency — full use of society's available resources to produce goods and services.

Equity — a distribution of income and wealth that society regards as fair. *(Equitable distribution of income + wealth)*

Stability — the avoidance of substantial inflations or deflations. *(Increases + decreases in price.)*

Growth — a rising level of output, making possible gains in living standards for all members of society. *(per capita)*

Taxes can be levied and classified in many ways. In our own country and in many other nations, there are three principal types of taxes:

1. Taxes on income
   (a) Personal income taxes.
   (b) Corporate income taxes.

2. Taxes on wealth (including its ownership and transfer)
   (a) Property taxes.
   (b) Death (estate and inheritance) and gift taxes.
3. Taxes on activities (consumption, production, employment, and so forth)
   (a) Sales and excise taxes.
   (b) Social security taxes.

Various other less important kinds of taxes exist, but nearly all can be placed in one of these three main categories.

Taxes on Income

Income taxes are based on net income—what remains after certain items are deducted from gross income. The items that can be deducted and the tax rates that are applied are specified by law.

Personal Income Tax

In poetry, spring is a time when a young person's fancy turns to thoughts of love. But in economics, spring is a much more mundane and certainly less romantic period. It is the season when millions of Americans begin to sort their previous year's income and expense records. As shown in Exhibit 5, this is the first step in determining your personal income tax.

In calculating this tax, you are allowed to take specific types of deductions and exemptions. Some deductions that may be made (within limits) from your income are donations to your alma mater and to various other nonprofit organizations. You may also deduct some payments for doctor's bills, x rays, and taxes paid to state and local governments; interest paid on loans; and various other outlays. In addition, exemptions are permitted for support of yourself, your family, and your dependents. In this way, the government acknowledges that larger families require more funds than smaller ones do to meet their living costs.

Exhibit 5
Logical Structure of the Federal Personal Income Tax

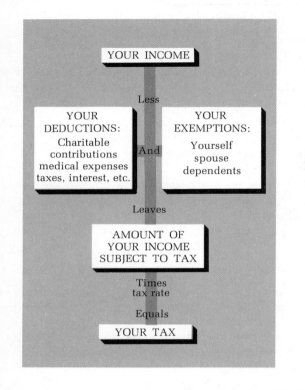

Columns (1), (2), (3), and (4)   As the level of total taxable income increases, the amount of each increase is called "marginal income". The average tax rate, which is established by government, tells you what percentage of total taxable income is paid in taxes. This amount is shown in column (4).

Column (5)   "Marginal tax" is the additional tax paid as a result of an increase in total taxable income.

Column (6)   This tells you the *percentage* of each increase in total taxable income that is paid out in taxes. The distinction between the **average tax rate** in column (3) and the **marginal tax rate** in column (6) is thus shown by the formulas:

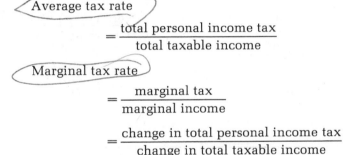

$$\text{Average tax rate} = \frac{\text{total personal income tax}}{\text{total taxable income}}$$

$$\text{Marginal tax rate} = \frac{\text{marginal tax}}{\text{marginal income}}$$

$$= \frac{\text{change in total personal income tax}}{\text{change in total taxable income}}$$

After studying these formulas and the table, you can see why two controversial aspects of the personal income tax are especially worth noting:

Incentives   The marginal tax-rate schedule in column (6) of the table shows the percentage of tax paid on each gain in income. The steepness of this schedule may therefore have serious economic consequences. Rates must be high enough at all income levels to yield the desired amounts of revenues. However, rates that are too high at the upper income levels may discourage investment and risk taking. Rates that are too high at the lower levels may reduce the incentive for taking on overtime work or second jobs. In view of this, is there a "best" or optimum tax-rate schedule for the econ-

The amount of income tax you must pay at a given income level depends on several things. These include whether you are single or married and what the particular tax rates happen to be at the time. A typical tax-rate schedule is shown in Exhibit 6. The rates are usually revised by the government every few years. Nevertheless, certain principles underlying a tax-rate schedule never change. For example, in terms of Exhibit 6, note the following relationships between the columns:

Exhibit 6
Personal Income Tax Schedule
(hypothetical data)

The income taxes people pay are determined from government tax schedules such as the one shown here.

In comparing columns (3) and (6), note that the marginal tax rate in going from one income level to the next is always higher than the average tax rate at either income level. Observe also that, according to the marginal tax-rate schedule, you can never find yourself worse off by making an extra dollar. No matter how high your total taxable income may be, you would still be able to keep some percentage of every additional dollar you earned.

Although this is not an actual tax schedule, the basic ideas and relations conveyed are reasonably representative of one.

(1) Total taxable annual income	(2) Marginal income [change in col. (1)]	(3) Average tax rate	(4) Total personal income tax (3) × (1)	(5) Marginal tax [change in col. (4)]	(6) Marginal tax rate (5) ÷ (2)
$ 5,000		5%	$ 250		
	$5,000			$ 750	15%
10,000		10	1,000		
	5,000			950	19
15,000		13	1,950		
	5,000			1,250	25
20,000		16	3,200		
	5,000			1,550	31
25,000		19	4,750		
	5,000			1,850	37
30,000		22	6,600		
	10,000			4,600	46
40,000		28	11,200		
	15,000			7,500	50
55,000		34	18,700		
	20,000			10,000	50
75,000		38	23,700		

omy as a whole? There probably is. But it changes with different needs and conditions, reflecting political as well as economic circumstances of the times.

Loopholes Legal methods of *tax avoidance* enable many taxpayers to reduce their average rates. This is because our tax system contains dozens of legal "loopholes" which permit relative tax advantages for people in almost every income class. For example, certain income receipts are exempt, and certain interest payments are deductible for income-tax purposes. Although changes in the tax laws have, over the years, closed many loopholes, it is not likely that they will ever be entirely eliminated. (By contrast, illegal methods of escaping taxes, such as lying or cheating about income or expenses, come under the general heading of *tax evasion.*)

Economics in the News

Reagan's Second Step Toward A Free-Market Economy

By Norman Jonas

President Reagan has boldly proclaimed that his new tax-reform plan represents a second American Revolution. The phrase has a fine ring, but it's not exactly right. More accurately, the plan is a continuation of Reagan's own revolution begun in 1981, when he set out to reverse 50 years of government growth and attempted to revitalize the U.S. economy with his huge tax cuts. Reagan is simply being Reagan.

As in 1981, the President is proposing a sharp reduction in personal income tax rates in the belief that lower marginal rates will increase incentives for work, saving, and investment. Unlike 1981, this package contains, at least on paper, a wide array of loop-hole-closing measures that would offset the revenue cost of the rate cuts — a belated rec-

ognition that the White House and Congress shrank the government's base of taxable income dangerously four years ago. But again, Reagan's implicit agenda remains: Cut back the size and influence of government by putting the tax-gobbling monster on a rigid diet.

Since the Reagan plan would neither raise nor lower revenues for Washington, the purpose of this package is to move the antigovernment campaign down a level and try to shrink the capacity of state and local governments to spend and tax. The deductibility of state and local income, retail, real estate, and personal property taxes from federally taxable income, a part of the code since 1913, cost the Treasury Dept. nearly $30 billion in lost revenues in fiscal 1984. By ending those deductions, Reagan could force high-tax states to shave taxes to stay competitive with their neighbors and, as a result, lower their spending on education, social programs, and other services.

Business Week, June 17, 1985, p. 131.

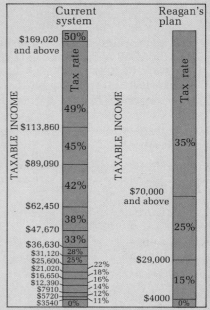

HOW TAX BRACKETS WOULD CHANGE FOR INDIVIDUALS

Source: USN & WR — Basic data: U.S. Dept. of the Treasury *U.S. News & World Report*, June 10, 1985.

Nearly all taxpayers, rich and poor alike, benefit from tax loopholes of one form or another. However, the greatest share of benefits from tax loopholes goes to taxpayers with above-average incomes. Although many people do not realize it, this group also pays more than half the total personal income tax bill.

Corporate Income Tax

One of the federal government's important sources of revenue is the corporate income tax. (Many

states also tax corporate incomes, but at lower rates.) The corporate income tax is based on profit — the difference between a company's total income and its total expenses. The tax rate has varied over the years. During recent decades, it has averaged somewhat less than 50 percent.

The corporate income tax raises some important issues. Among them:

- Some authorities argue that lower rates would leave corporations with more funds to use for expanding their operations, thereby creating more jobs. Others, however, contend that the rates should be higher, enabling government to reduce other taxes, especially personal income taxes.

- There is considerable controversy over who ultimately bears the burden of the corporate income tax. Some economists believe that the tax is shifted "forward" to consumers in the form of higher prices. Others contend that much of the tax is shifted "backwards" to resource owners in the form of lower wages, rents, etc. Still other authorities believe that the tax is borne by the owners (stockholders) of the corporation because the tax is imposed on corporate profit.

- The tax involves a form of **double taxation.** The corporation pays a tax on its profits, and the stockholder pays a personal income tax on the dividends received from those profits. Therefore, it is often argued that the tax is inequitable.

There are no simple resolutions for these controversial issues. Each has valid aspects that are subject to frequent debate.

The remaining two categories that make up the structure of the American tax system—taxes on wealth and taxes on activities—can be sketched briefly.

Taxes on Wealth

Property taxes are levied primarily on land and buildings to help pay for public services. The taxes vary from low rates in some rural areas to high rates in localities with expensive public services.

Death taxes are levied, at the time of death, on estates by the federal government and on inheritances by some state governments. An estate is the value of everything that someone owns; an inheritance is an amount that someone receives. Like income taxes, death taxes exempt small estates and inheritances but tax the unexempt portions at progressive rates. Many wealthy people might try to avoid these taxes by distributing most of their property before death. Therefore, **gift taxes** are imposed on the transfer of assets beyond certain values. However, various legal devices, most notably trust funds, have enabled many people to lighten the burden of these taxes.

Taxes on Activities

Sales taxes are imposed by many state and local governments. These taxes are flat percentage levies on the retail prices of goods. In some states or cities, food, medicine, and certain services are exempt from sales taxes. In other places, they are not. The federal government imposes no general sales tax on the final sale of goods. However, it does impose special sales taxes, called **excise taxes,** on the manufacture, sale, or consumption of liquor, tobacco products, gasoline, and certain other goods.

Social security taxes are federal payroll taxes on wages and salaries. The taxes finance our compulsory social insurance program covering old-age and unemployment benefits. The taxes are imposed both on employees and on employers and are based on the incomes of the former. After a person has earned a certain amount each year, his or her income above that level is exempt from the tax.

Theories of Taxation

The power to tax is not only the power to destroy but also the power to keep alive.

So stated the U.S. Supreme Court in a famous case in 1899. Today hardly anyone would disagree. Because the power to tax is so weighty a matter, economists have developed several broad standards for judging the merits of a tax:

1. Equity Tax burdens should be distributed justly.

2. Efficiency, Stability, and Growth A tax should contribute toward improving resource allocation, economic stabilization, and growth in the total output of goods and services.

3. Enforceability A tax should be adequate for its purpose and acceptable to the public, or else it will be impossible to enforce.

These criteria are simple and persuasive. But implementation, especially of equity, has caused much controversy. Let us see why.

Principles of Tax Equity

A good tax system should be fair. If people believe it is unfair—that too many loopholes benefit some people and not others—taxpayers' morale and the effectiveness of the tax system will deteriorate. Therefore, two standards of tax equity have evolved over the years.

Horizontal Equity "Equals should be treated equally." This means that people who are economically equal should bear equal tax burdens. That is, if people have the same income, wealth, or other taxpaying ability, they should pay the same amount of tax.

Vertical Equity "Unequals should be treated unequally." This means that people who are economically unequal should bear equal tax *burdens*. That is, people with different incomes, wealth, or other taxpaying abilities should pay different amounts of tax so that everyone sacrifices equally.

Horizontal and vertical equity are standards for judging the fairness of a tax. Efforts to apply them have resulted in two fundamental principles of taxation—the benefit principle and the ability-to-pay principle.

Benefit Principle

The **benefit principle** holds that people should be taxed according to the benefits they receive. For example, the tax you pay on gasoline reflects the benefit you receive from driving on public roads. The more you drive, the more gasoline you use and the more taxes you pay. These tax revenues are typically set aside for financing highway construction and maintenance. Similarly, local governments pay for at least part of the construction of streets and sewers by taxing those residents who benefit directly from them.

What is wrong with the benefit principle as a general guide for taxation? There are two major difficulties:

- Relatively few publicly provided goods and services exist for which all benefits can be readily determined. For many goods and services, the benefits would be impossible to determine. The entire nation benefits from social goods, such as public education, health and sanitation facilities, police and fire protection, and national defense. How can we decide which groups should pay the taxes for these things and which should not?

- Those who receive certain benefits may not be able to pay for them. For instance, it would be impossible to finance public welfare aid or unemployment compensation by taxing the recipients.

Ability-to-Pay Principle

The **ability-to-pay principle** states that the fairest tax is one that is based on the ability of the taxpayer to pay it, regardless of any benefit derived from the tax. Therefore, the more wealth a person has or the higher his or her income, the higher the tax rate should be. This is based on the assumption that each dollar of taxes paid by a rich person "hurts" less than each dollar paid by a poor one. The personal income tax in the United States is structured on this principle.

There are two major difficulties in the use of this principle as a general guide for taxation:

- Ability to pay is a debatable concept—difficult to determine and impossible to measure. How can we really *know* that an additional thousand dollars a year in income means less to a rich person than to a poor person? The concept involves psychological and philosophical issues that economics is not equipped to explore.

- Even if we *assume* that certain taxes should be based on ability to pay, how can we distinguish between degrees of ability among different individuals? You may feel that a person who earns $50,000 a year is able to pay a higher tax rate than someone who earns $25,000. But *how much* higher? There is no simple answer, and no answer that is unarguably "just."

Real-World Compromises

As a result of these difficulties, it has become necessary to adopt methods of implementing the benefit and ability principles. The methods may not always be ideal, but they have proven to be practical.

Thus three major classes of tax rates—proportional, progressive, and regressive—have evolved over the years. These types of rates differ from each other according to the way in which the amount of the tax is related to the tax base. This is the item being taxed. Examples are the value of property (in the case of a property tax), income (in the case of an income tax), and the value of goods sold (in the case of a sales tax). When the total tax is divided by the tax base, the resulting figure, expressed as a percentage, is called the *tax rate.* Thus, a $10 tax on a tax base of $100 represents a tax rate of 10 percent. It follows that the tax base times the tax rate equals the tax yield to the government. This principle applies to all types of taxes.

Proportional Tax

A *proportional tax* is one whose percentage rate *remains constant* as the tax base increases. Consequently, the amount of the tax paid is proportional to the tax base. The property tax is an example. If the tax rate is constant at 5 percent, someone who owns property valued at $10,000 pays $500 in taxes. Someone who owns property valued at $100,000 pays $5,000 in taxes.

Progressive Tax

A *progressive tax* is one whose percentage rate *increases* as the tax base increases. In the United States, the federal personal income tax is the best example. The tax is graduated so that, theoretically, a person with a higher income pays a greater percentage in tax than a person with a lower income. We say "theoretically" because in reality certain loopholes in the tax structure reduce the progressive effect of the tax.

Regressive Tax

A *regressive tax* is one whose percentage rate *decreases* as the tax base increases. In this narrow, technical sense, there is no regressive tax in the United States. In practice, however, the term "regressive" is applied to any tax that takes a larger share of income from the low-income taxpayer than from the high-income taxpayer. Most proportional taxes, such as sales taxes, are considered to have regressive effects. For instance, a 6 percent sales tax is the same rate for everyone, rich and poor alike. But people with smaller incomes spend a larger percentage of their incomes. Therefore the sales taxes they pay are a greater proportion of their incomes.

To summarize:

In the narrow, technical sense, definitions of proportional, progressive, and regressive taxes are expressed in terms of their actual tax bases. These are the things that are taxed, such as income, property, or value of goods sold. For *equity* purposes, however, the base chosen for reference is always income—regardless of the actual tax base.

The distinctions between the three types of tax rates are illustrated with brief explanations in Exhibit 7.

How do the foregoing principles and compromises apply to our tax system? Some of our taxes tend to lean more toward the benefit principle and others more toward ability to pay. Social security, license, and gasoline taxes are some examples of the former; income, estate, and inheritance taxes are illustrative of the latter.

We can find examples of progressive, regressive, and proportional taxes in our tax system. Income and death taxes are progressive in both the technical sense and the equity sense because their percentage rates increase with the tax base. Property, general sales, and excise taxes are proportional in their technical structure because their rates are a constant percentage of the tax base. But these taxes tend to have regressive effects from an equity standpoint when related to the *incomes* of the taxpayers.

Exhibit 7
Proportional, Progressive, and Regressive Tax-Rate Structures in Equity Terms
(hypothetical data)

In equity terms, the structure of a tax is *always* evaluated by comparing the tax rate to the taxpayer's income—regardless of the actual tax base to which the tax is applied.

Figure *(a):* Proportional tax. The tax takes the same percentage of income from high-income taxpayers as from low-income taxpayers. In this example, the tax is 40 percent of a $10,000 income, 40 percent of a $20,000 income, and so on.

Figure *(b):* Progressive tax. The tax takes a larger percentage of income from high-income taxpayers than from low-income taxpayers. In this example, the tax is 10 percent of a $10,000 income, 20 percent of a $20,000 income, and so on.

Figure *(c):* Regressive tax. The tax takes a smaller percentage of income from high-income taxpayers than from low-income taxpayers. In this example, the tax is 60 percent of a $10,000 income, 50 percent of a $20,000 income, and so on.

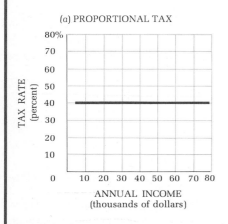

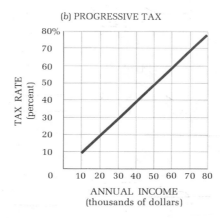

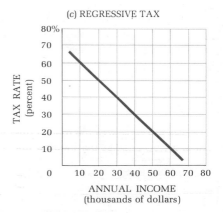

Tax Shifting and Incidence: Direct and Indirect Taxes

Surprisingly enough, the person or business firm upon whom a tax is initially imposed does not always bear its burden. For instance, a company may be able to *shift* all or part of a tax "forward" to its customers by charging them higher prices for its goods. Or it may be able to shift a tax "backward" to the owners of its factors of production by paying them less for their materials and services. When a tax has been shifted, its burden or *incidence* is on someone else. In this connection, it is convenient to classify taxes into two categories: direct and indirect.

Direct Taxes These taxes are not shifted; their burden is borne by the persons or firms originally taxed. Typical examples are personal income taxes, social security taxes paid by employees, most property taxes (excluding rental and business property), and death taxes. Taxes on corporate income are often considered to be only partly direct. Can you suggest why?

Indirect Taxes   These include all taxes that can be shifted either partly or entirely to payers other than the person or firm originally taxed.   The most familiar example is the sales tax.   Contrary to popular belief, this tax is imposed on sellers, not buyers. Sellers, however, typically shift the tax burden to buyers.   Other examples of indirect taxes are excise taxes, taxes on business and rental property, social security taxes paid by employers, and most corporate income taxes.

In what direction will a tax be shifted, assuming that it is shifted at all?   This is a thorny problem in economic theory, and the experts do not always agree.

In general:

Most taxes are like an increased cost to the taxpayer. Each taxpayer will try to pass them on to someone else.   When an indirect tax is imposed, it tends—like lightning or water—to follow the path of least resistance through the markets in which the taxpayer deals.   That is, the taxpayer tries to shift the tax by altering prices, inputs, or outputs according to the least degree of opposition encountered.

Economics in the News

Simplifying Taxes

Flat Rates: Postcard Returns

"Disgraceful."   "Unduly complicated."   "Too many exceptions and special provisions."   "Encourages evasion."   "Discourages productive activity."

These are typical of the many criticisms levied against our income-tax system.   What can be done to correct it?   The obvious answer is simplification.   But although numerous critics have voiced this opinion, relatively few have offered a comprehensive approach to reform.   Two who have are Robert E. Hall and Alvin Rabushka, economists at Stanford University.   Their simple income-tax system for both individuals and businesses rests on four principles:

1. All income is taxed only once, as close as possible to its source

2. All types of income are taxed at the same percentage rate—called a "flat" rate

3. Low-income households pay no taxes

4. Tax returns are simple enough to fit on a postcard or on a single page.

Individual Tax
The proposed tax return for individuals looks very much like the one in the accompanying illustration.   Several features of the form should be noted:

First, the only income that is taxed is individual compensation (lines 1 through 3).   This is broadly defined as anything of value received by workers from employers.   It consists of wages and salaries, the market value of fringe benefits, and contributions to pension plans.   Thus, income in the form of interest, dividends, and capital gains (profits) from the sale of assets are not taxed.   This is because, as shown below, they are taxed only once, at the source.

Second, deductions for personal allowances, including marital status and number of dependents (lines 4 through 7) are provided.   Note that no other expenses, not even interest paid, can be deducted.

Third, the tax rate (line 9) is a proportional tax.   It takes the same percentage of compensation from high-compensation taxpayers as from low-compensation taxpayers.

Business Tax
The proposed tax on business income would apply to all types of businesses.   These include proprietorships, partnerships, corporations, professions, rentals, and royalties. The base for the tax would be simply gross revenue minus the sum of four classes of expenditures:

1. Cost of goods sold

2. Compensation paid to employees

3. Other direct costs

4. Cost of plant and equipment

Notice that no deductions would be permitted for interest paid or for depreciation.   Expenditures on capital goods would be deducted entirely in the year in which they are incurred.   The tax rate, which would be the same as the one for individuals, would be applied to the resulting tax base.

Economics in the News *(continued)*

Favorable Consequences

What are the advantages of the simplified tax system?

− It would raise about the same amount of revenue as the current combination of personal and corporate income taxes.

− It would encourage taxpayers to spend less time looking for tax shelters and concentrate instead on earning higher incomes.

− It would provide greater incentives to work, save, and invest because low marginal tax rates would leave taxpayers with more after-tax income.

− It would save numerous hours of unpaid bookkeeping that people incur each year in preparing their tax records.

Form 000A	Individual Compensation Tax		19____

Your first name & initial (plus spouse if joint)		Last Name	Your Social Sec. No.
Address			Spouse's Social Sec. No.
City, State & Zip		Your Occupation	
		Spouse's Occupation	

1 Compensation (including fringe benefits) reported by employer................	1	
2 Other wage income, including pensions paid directly by employer.............	2	
3 Total compensation (line 1 plus line 2)	3	
4 Personal allowance		
(a) ☐ $7,000 for married filing jointly..........................	4a	
(b) ☐ $4,000 for single............................	4b	
(c) ☐ $5,000 for single head of household....................	4c	
5 Number of dependents, not including spouse....................	5	
6 Personal allowances for dependents (line 5 multiplied by $700)..........	6	
7 Total personal allowances (line 4 plus line 6).....................	7	
8 Taxable compensation (line 3 less line 7)......................	8	
9 Tax (20% of line 8).........................	9	
10 Tax withheld by employer........................	10	
11 Tax due (line 9 less line 10, if positive)...................	11	
12 Refund due (line 10 less line 9, if positive).................	12	

Source: Adapted with changes from Robert E. Hall and Alvin Rabushka, "A Proposal to Simplify our Tax System." *The Wall Street Journal*, December 10, 1981.

What You Have Learned

1. The economic role of government may be considered to consist of two broad functions: (a) promotion and regulation of the private sector and (b) provision of social goods.

2. Government promotes and regulates the private sector in many ways. For example, it
   (a) tries to provide a stable economic environment,
   (b) performs social welfare activities,
   (c) grants economic privileges,
   (d) seeks to maintain competition,
   (e) tries to promote high employment, and
   (f) redistributes income.

3. Government provides social goods, which consist of public goods and merit goods. Public goods are those not subject to the exclusion principle. Examples are national defense, street lighting, and disease control. Merit goods are subject to the exclusion principle even though the principle is not always invoked. Examples are municipal libraries, national parks, and public hospitals.

4. Many social goods create "spillovers"—externalities in the form of benefits or costs. Methods for redressing spillovers consist of (a) internalization of costs and benefits and (b) government regulation and provision. When properly implemented by government, these methods can contribute toward improving economic efficiency.

5. The last several decades have witnessed a remarkable growth of expenditures at all levels of government. This has been due primarily to (a) increased demand for collective goods and services, (b) increased expenditures for national defense, (c) increased interest on the national debt, and (d) lagging productivity.

6. In the federal budget, income taxes, both individual and corporate, are the chief source of revenue. The main expenditure items are income security payments and national defense. In state and local budgets, the chief sources of revenue are property taxes and sales taxes. The main expenditure items are education (especially schools) and public welfare and health.

7. Two related approaches to scientific budgeting are planning-program-budgeting systems (PPBS) and benefit-

Relative worth of the program

cost analysis. The former method emphasizes revenue and expenditure planning based on identifiable objectives. The latter focuses on the relative worth of a program, project, or other economic activity.

8. Our economy's tax structure consists of taxes on income, taxes on wealth, and taxes on activities. A chief requirement of a good tax system is that it be fair. Accepted standards of fairness are horizontal equity and vertical equity. Two principles of taxation that seek to apply these standards are the benefit principle and the ability-to-pay principle. However, these principles are often difficult to apply. In practice, we find some taxes that are proportional, some that are progressive, and some that are regressive.

9. Those upon whom a tax is levied are sometimes able to shift it forward or backward through changes in prices, inputs, or outputs. Thus, the burden or incidence of the tax falls on someone else. Such taxes are called indirect, as contrasted with direct taxes, which cannot be shifted.

Terms and Concepts to Review

social goods
public goods
exclusion principle
merit goods
public choice
demand price
supply price
specific tax
specific subsidy
planning-program-
  budgeting system
  (PPBS)
benefit-cost analysis
double taxation

property tax
death tax
sales tax
excise tax
horizontal equity
vertical equity
benefit principle
ability-to-pay principle
proportional tax
progressive tax
regressive tax
direct tax
indirect tax

Know all definitions

For Discussion

1. Public goods are not subject to the exclusion principle. How, then, do you explain the fact that some public goods are nevertheless provided by the private sector? Give some examples.

2. Spillover benefits and costs can be redressed in different ways. One approach was illustrated in this chapter with supply and demand curves. Using a similar approach, demonstrate the following propositions:

(a) Spillover costs can be corrected by imposing a specific tax on buyers.
(b) Spillover benefits can be corrected by granting a specific subsidy to sellers.

Do you see any equity implications in these approaches?

3. What are PPBS's major problems in our system of government? How does benefit-cost analysis relate to PPBS?

4. Can you explain the formal definition of benefit-cost analysis given in the Dictionary at the back of the book? In particular, what does the word "discounted" in the definition mean?

5. How can the costs of benefits provided by the government sector be reduced?

6. Some economists and legislators contend that the present federal income tax reaches too far down into low-income brackets. Assume that you disagree with this contention, and offer arguments to defend your position.

7. If you were considering taking on an extra part-time job, would you base the decision on your average tax rate or on your marginal tax rate? Why?

8. The ability-to-pay principle of taxation may also be called the "equal-sacrifice principle." Can you explain why?

9. How can a market-oriented economy such as ours justify the large expenditures made by government on free public education?

10. Is the desire to maximize net social benefit a goal useful only to capitalistic economies, or does it apply to socialistic economies, too?

11. If you were advising a legislator on whether the government should spend an additional $2 billion on space exploration as opposed to public transportation, what approach would you use? What difficulties would you expect to encounter?

12. When the private costs of a decision are equal to its social costs, *all* the costs are borne by the decision maker. Do you agree? Explain.

13. What is wrong with using figures showing expenditures by government as a measure of the importance of government in our society?

Part 2

National Income, Employment, and Fiscal Policy

Chapter 5

National Income and Wealth: Measuring the Nation's Economic Health

Learning Guide

Watch for answers to these important questions

How do we judge the nation's economic health? Are statistical measures available for evaluating the economy's overall performance?

What sorts of difficulties are encountered in estimating gross national product? Does it reflect society's well-being?

What is the relation between the economy's output and its income? Is the flow of expenditures on output equal to the flow of payments for income?

How does the value of the nation's output relate to the money that households actually have available for spending? Of what practical use is this information?

People are becoming increasingly concerned with their physical health. They are paying closer attention to their weight, pulse rate, blood pressure, and other measures of physical well-being. The same is true for those who are concerned with the nation's economic health. They are paying closer attention than ever before to statistical measures of the nation's output, unemployment rate, and prices. That is all to the good, for it helps make the public more aware of the nation's economic well-being.

The economy's level of activity—its state of health—is expressed in the form of data and graphs. These are published by the federal government and by various public and private organizations. Since the early 1930s, the U.S. Department of Commerce has been the nation's principal bookkeeper. It has been responsible for developing the majority of measures used to depict the economy's overall performance. Among the chief measures of economic performance are those known as "national income statistics." In this chapter, you will learn about the most important types of national income statistics.

Gross National Product: The Broadest Measure of a Nation's Output

The most comprehensive measure of a nation's economic activity, and the one referred to most frequently in newspapers and magazines, is **gross national product** (GNP). It is always stated in money terms, representing the total value of a nation's final output for the year. More precisely:

GNP is the total market value of all final goods and services produced by an economy during a year.

Calculating and Interpreting GNP

The items that make up GNP range from apples and automobiles to zinc and zippers. However, because you cannot add these diverse items, you must first state them in terms of their monetary values. Then, when you add x dollars' worth of automobiles to y dollars' worth of oranges to z dollars' worth of doctors' services, and so on, you arrive at a total dollar figure. If you do this for all final goods and services produced in the economy during any given year, the result is GNP. And if you repeat this process for several years, the different GNPs can be compared. In that way, you may be able to tell whether there has been a long-run growth or decline in the economy.

However, there are several pitfalls to avoid.

Watch Out for Price Changes

If the prices of goods and services change from one year to the next, the GNP may also change — even if there has been no change in physical output. For instance, if apples cost 20 cents each this year, five apples will have a market value of $1.00. But next year, if the price rises to 30 cents each, five apples will have a market value of $1.50.

This poses a problem: How can we tell whether the variations in GNP are due to differences in prices or to differences in *real output* — that is, output unaffected by price changes? The answer is shown in Exhibit 1. Observe that GNP is expressed in two ways. One is in *current dollars,* reflecting actual prices as they existed each year. This is often referred to as *nominal* GNP. The other is in *constant dollars,* reflecting the actual prices of a previous year, or the average of actual prices in some previous period. GNP expressed in constant dollars is often referred to as *real GNP.*

The use of constant dollars is a way of compensating for the distorting effects of inflation — the long-run upward trend of prices. This is accomplished by a reversing process of **deflation.** You can get an idea of how this is done by studying Exhibit 2.

Avoid Double Counting

Note that the definition of GNP covers only *final* goods and services purchased. These are distin-

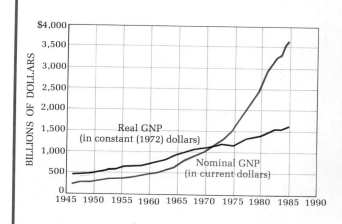

Exhibit 1
Gross National Product
(in current and in constant dollars)

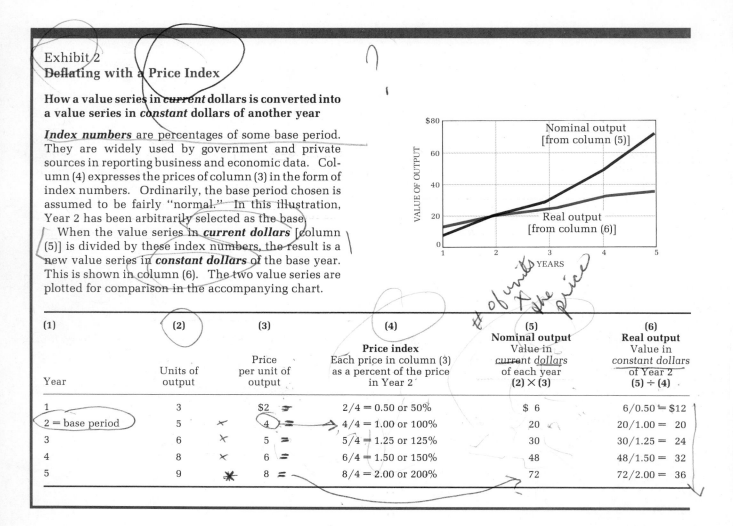

Exhibit 2
Deflating with a Price Index

How a value series in *current* dollars is converted into a value series in *constant* dollars of another year

Index numbers are percentages of some base period. They are widely used by government and private sources in reporting business and economic data. Column (4) expresses the prices of column (3) in the form of index numbers. Ordinarily, the base period chosen is assumed to be fairly "normal." In this illustration, Year 2 has been arbitrarily selected as the base.

When the value series in ***current dollars*** [column (5)] is divided by these index numbers, the result is a new value series in ***constant dollars*** of the base year. This is shown in column (6). The two value series are plotted for comparison in the accompanying chart.

(1) Year	(2) Units of output	(3) Price per unit of output	(4) Price index Each price in column (3) as a percent of the price in Year 2	(5) Nominal output Value in current *dollars* of each year (2) × (3)	(6) Real output Value in constant *dollars* of Year 2 (5) ÷ (4)
1	3	$2	2/4 = 0.50 or 50%	$ 6	6/0.50 = $12
2 = base period	5	4	4/4 = 1.00 or 100%	20	20/1.00 = 20
3	6	5	5/4 = 1.25 or 125%	30	30/1.25 = 24
4	8	6	6/4 = 1.50 or 150%	48	48/1.50 = 32
5	9	8	8/4 = 2.00 or 200%	72	72/2.00 = 36

guished from *intermediate* goods and services, which enter into the production of final commodities. For example, if you purchase a new automobile this year, it is a final good. However, the materials of which the automobile was made, such as steel, engine, tires, and paint, are intermediate goods. Because the values of final goods include the values of all intermediate goods, only final goods are included in calculating the GNP. If you allow intermediate goods to enter the picture, you will commit the cardinal sin of *double counting*—or even triple and quadruple counting.

Exhibit 3 illustrates this with the example of the production of a loaf of bread. As you can see, the "total sales values" at the bottom of column (2) include the sales values at all the intermediate stages. This, of course, is an incorrect statement of the actual value of the product. However, the sales value of the final product, or the total ***value added*** for all the stages of production, given in column (3), shows the true value of the total output. It also shows the total income—the sum of wages, rent, interest, and profit—derived from the production process.

Exhibit 3
Sales Values and Value Added at Each Stage of Producing a Loaf of Bread

Stage 1 A farmer purchases 4 cents worth of seed and fertilizer, which he applies to his land.

Stage 2 The farmer grows wheat, harvests it, and sells it to a miller for 28 cents. The farmer has thereby added 24 cents worth of value. His factors of production then receive this 24 cents in the form of income: wages, rent, interest, and profit.

Stage 3 The miller, after purchasing the wheat for 28 cents, adds 20 cents worth of value by milling the wheat into flour. The miller's factors of production receive this 20 cents as income: wages, rent, interest, and profit.

Stage 4 The baking company buys the flour from the miller for 48 cents, then adds 40 cents worth of value to it by baking it into bread. This 40 cents becomes factor incomes in the form of wages, rent, interest, and profit.

Stage 5 The retailer buys the bread from the baker for 88 cents and sells it to you, the final user, for $1.20. The retailer has thus added 32 cents in value, which, again, shows up as factor incomes in the form of wages, rent, interest, and profit.

Note that the value of the final product, $1.20, equals the sum of the values added.

(1) Stages of production	(2) Sales values (dollars per loaf)	(3) Value added (= income payments: wages, rent, interest, profit) (dollars per loaf)
Stage 1: Fertilizer, seed, etc.	$ .04	$ .04
Stage 2: Wheat growing	.28	.24
Stage 3: Flour milling	.48	.20
Stage 4: Bread baking	.88	.40
Stage 5: Bread retailer, final value	1.20	.32
Total sales values	$2.88	
Total value added (= total income)		$1.20

We can summarize with an important principle:

GNP may be calculated by totaling either the market values of all final goods and services or the values added at all stages of production. The values added are equal to the sum of all incomes—wages, rent, interest, and profit—generated from production.

Include Productive Activities, Exclude Nonproductive

The purpose of deriving GNP is to develop a measure of the economy's total output, based on the market values of final goods and services produced. Thus, even if all these market values are estimated, some *productive* activities do not show up in the market. The value of these activities should nevertheless be included in GNP. There are also some *nonproductive* activities that do appear in the market but should be excluded from GNP.

Here are some examples of productive nonmarket activities:

PRODUCTIVE NONMARKET

"Rent" of Owner-Occupied Homes The rent that people pay to landlords enters into GNP. However, the majority of dwellings in the United States are owner-occupied. The rental value of this housing — the rent that people "save" by living in their own homes — may be thought of as the value of shelter produced. This value is assumed to be the same amount that individual homeowners would receive if they became landlords and rented out their homes to others. Hence, this amount is included in GNP.

Farm Consumption of Home-Grown Food The value of food that people buy is included in GNP. But the value of food that farmers grow and consume themselves is also a part of the nation's productive output and is therefore included in GNP.

Some productive nonmarket activities never enter into GNP because their values either are too difficult to estimate or involve complex definitional issues. These include such activities as the labor of a do-it-yourselfer who performs his or her own repairs and maintenance around the house. Similar activities are the productive services of homemakers in their capacities as cooks, housekeepers, tutors, dieticians, chauffeurs, and so on, for which no salaries are received.

Here are some examples of nonproductive market activities:

Transfer Payments Government and businesses often shift funds within or between sectors of the economy with no corresponding contribution to current production. Such shifts of funds are called *transfer payments.* Because these payments are not made for current output, they are excluded from GNP. Some examples of government transfer payments are social security benefits, unemployment compensation, and welfare payments. Some examples of business transfer payments are charitable contributions, allowance for bad debts, and interest payments from one firm to another.

Securities Transactions When you buy or sell stocks or bonds, you exchange one form of asset for another — either money for securities or securities for money. These financial transfers add nothing to current production and therefore are excluded from GNP. (However, broker commissions on security transactions are included in GNP, because brokers perform a productive service by bringing buyers and sellers together.)

Sales of Used Goods Billions of dollars are paid each year for used automobiles, houses, machines, factory buildings, and so on. But these goods are omitted from the calculation of current GNP because each was counted as part of the GNP in the year in which it was sold new. (As with brokers, however, the value added by dealers in used-merchandise transactions is included in current GNP.)

Is GNP a Measure of Society's Well-Being?

GNP is a comprehensive indicator of the economy's output. However, it is an imperfect measure of society's well-being. To begin with, it reveals nothing about these important developments that have occurred during this century:

- The growth of leisure time — that is, the substantial reduction in the workweek that has taken place.
- The improved quality and variety of goods and services that the economy produces.
- The growth of total output relative to the population.

The long-run trends of these variables have been rising. As a result, our society is much better off materially than the GNP figures indicate.

Gross National "Disproduct"; Inclusions and Exclusions

Another reason GNP cannot be taken as a reliable index of social benefits is that it makes no distinction between the useful and the frivolous. It embraces everything from the cost of hospital care to the wages of belly dancers. For example, it includes cloth coats for people as well as mink coats for dogs, and life-saving antibiotics as well as useless patent medicines.   Further, there is no measure of the amount of "disproduct," or *social cost*, that results from producing the GNP.   Some illustrations:

- The cost of air and water pollution is a disproduct of the nation's factories.
- The cost of treating lung-cancer victims is a disproduct of cigarette production.
- The cost of geriatric medicine is a disproduct of good medical care in the earlier years, which results in increased longevity.
- The cost of commuter transportation is a disproduct of living in the suburbs.
- The cost of aspirin for headaches resulting from TV commercials is a disproduct of advertising.

Can you suggest some more examples?

If this process were carried through our whole product list, the sum would be **gross national disproduct.**   And if the total were then set against the aggregate of production as measured by GNP, the difference might serve as a valuable statistical estimate of what the economy has accomplished.

Unfortunately, however, the estimate would be far from complete as a "social indicator," or index of social welfare.   Because GNP measures the market value of final goods and services, it can only reflect the amount of money that society exchanges for goods and services.   As a result, many important activities that affect our standard of living are excluded from the calculation of GNP.   For example, some things that are excluded—and related things that are included—are:

- The nonpaid value of homemakers' services—but not the salaries paid to housekeepers.
- The benefits received from public goods—but not the costs of providing them.
- The environmental pollution arising from production—but not the money spent to clean it up.
- The social value of education—but not the expenditures incurred in acquiring it.
- The rising level of crime—but not the funds allocated to fight it.

Conclusion: GNP and Social Welfare

Because of the many inclusions and exclusions involved in calculating GNP, some economists have expressed interest in devising a better measure of the economy's true output.   Such a measure would indicate *social welfare* rather than just the market value of final goods and services.

Would it be possible to transform GNP into a general measure of social welfare?   Probably not.

"Social welfare" is a multidimensional concept.   It has many deep economic and psychological implications which make precise definition, let alone measurement, impossible.

Something to Think About

1. Would it be better to produce wool suits and vaccines instead of mink coats and patent medicines?   Would the nation thereby move closer to "worthwhile" national goals?   Worthwhile according to whom?

2. Does the GNP of an advanced, interdependent economy necessarily contain a considerable amount of disproduct compared to that of a relatively simple economic system?

3. Are the costs of the disproducts of our economy borne in the present or in the future?

Two Ways of Looking at GNP

Because GNP is the market value of the nation's output of final goods and services, it can be expressed conceptually by the simple diagram in Exhibit 4.   Equivalently, it can be expressed by the following fundamental identity, which says that the *total amount spent* equals the *total amount received*:

$$\left.\begin{array}{l}\text{total flow of}\\\text{expenditures}\\\text{on final output}\end{array}\right\}\ \text{GNP} \Leftrightarrow \text{GNI}\ \left\{\begin{array}{l}\text{total flow of}\\\text{income from}\\\text{final output}\end{array}\right.$$

The left side of the identity (or the upper pipeline in Exhibit 4) shows GNP as a sum of household sector expenditures on business-sector output. The right side (or lower pipeline) shows **gross national income** (GNI) as a sum of incomes resulting from values added at each stage of production. GNI in this example is the sum of wages, rent, interest, and profit earned in the production of GNP. Therefore, GNI is equal to GNP.

This diagram illustrates a *simple* circular-flow system consisting of only two sectors. It provides a "first look" at the relation between an economy's output and its income. A more elaborate model, consisting of four sectors, is necessary for understanding the underlying forces at work. Such a model is presented in Exhibit 5.

GNP from the Expenditure Viewpoint: A Flow-of-Product Approach

On the left side of the table in Exhibit 5, the economy is divided into four major sectors: household, government, business, and foreign. These are the major markets for the output of the economy. In any one year, the total expenditures of these sectors constitute the nation's GNP. An historical record of these expenditures is presented in the first several columns of the front endpapers (the inside front cover) of this book. Note that the sum of the four expenditure columns for any given year equals GNP. Let us see what can be said about the meaning of these four categories.

Personal Consumption Expenditures

Frequently referred to as "consumption expenditures" or simply "consumption," this category consists of expenditures on consumer goods and services. Some examples are food, clothing, appliances, automobiles, medical care, and recreation.

Government Purchases of Goods and Services

The items in this category are purchased by all levels of government. They include guided missiles, school buildings, fire engines, pencils, and the services of clerks, administrators, and all other government employees. However, recall that transfer payments, which are a significant portion of government expenditures, are omitted because they do not represent part of current output of goods and services.

Exhibit 4
Gross National Product = Gross National Income
(a two-sector model — without a government or foreign sector)

A simplified circular-flow model can be used to illustrate the fundamental principle that gross national product and gross national income are actually two sides of the same coin. *The nation's flow of output in the upper pipeline equals the nation's flow of income in the lower pipeline.* Profit is the residual or "balancing item" that brings this equality about. Can you explain why? How is the model affected if profits are positive? Zero? Negative (i.e., losses)?

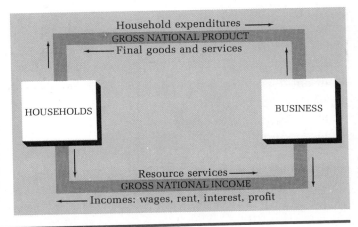

Exhibit 5
Gross National Product = Gross National Income (1984)
(a four-sector model, in billions of dollars)

The data for measuring the nation's total output can be estimated from two points of view:

- The expenditure side—showing the value of goods and services produced and/or purchased by each sector.
- The income side—showing the payments made and/or received in producing those goods and services.

The expenditure side is divided into four sectors—household, government, business, and foreign. These represent the major markets for the output of the economy. The sum of their expenditures on final products (output) constitutes GNP. The income side summarizes the costs incurred or payments made by business firms to produce final products. These costs are wages, rent, interest, profit, indirect business taxes, and capital consumption allowances or depreciation. Their sum equals *GNI*.

Can you explain why it must be true that, for any given period, GNP = *GNI*? What is the meaning of the expression "national income at factor cost"? Why is profit listed as a "cost"?

Expenditure viewpoint: flow of product	Output	Income viewpoint: flow of costs	Income
Household sector		National income (at factor cost)	
Personal consumption expenditures	$2399	Wages	$2386
+		Rent	64
Government sector		Interest	297
Government purchases of goods and services	783	Profit	289
+		+	
Business sector		Nonincome (expense) items	
Gross private domestic investment	636	Indirect business taxes	314
+		Capital consumption allowance (depreciation)	413
Foreign sector		Adjustment*	−102
Net exports of goods and services	−64		
Adjustment*	−93		
	GNP $3661 =		GNI $3661

* Necessary because data in the table are from preliminary government estimates.

Gross Private Domestic Investment

This category includes total investment spending by business firms. The term "investment" has two meanings: (1) In everyday language, a person makes an investment when buying stocks, bonds, or other properties with the intention of receiving an income or making a profit. (2) In economics, ***investment*** means additions to, or replacement of, physical productive assets. Thus, investment represents spending by business firms on new job-creating and income-producing goods. Such expenditures contribute to GNP. Therefore, this concept of investment is the one that concerns us in this book.

Investment goods fall into two broad classes:

1. New capital goods, such as machines, factories, offices, and residences, including apartment houses and owner-occupied homes. (Owner-occupied homes are included because they could just as well be rented out to yield incomes to their owners, as do apartment houses.) Recall that, when a firm buys a used machine or an existing factory, it merely exchanges money assets for physical assets. The purchase itself creates no additional GNP. But, when a firm buys new machines or new buildings, it creates jobs and incomes for steelworkers, carpenters, bricklayers, and other workers, thereby contributing to the nation's GNP.

2. Increases in inventories (including raw materials, supplies, and finished goods on hand). These are as much a part of a business firm's physical capital as are plant and equipment. Thus, the market values of any additions to inventories are part of the current flow of product that makes up GNP. In contrast, any declines in inventories are reductions from the flow of product that makes up GNP.

In the process of producing goods during any given year, some existing plant and equipment is used up, or **depreciated.** Therefore, a part of the year's gross private domestic investment goes to replace it. Any amount left over, called **net private domestic investment,** represents a net addition to the total stock of capital. For example, suppose

gross private domestic investment = $400 billion
replacement for depreciation = $300 billion

then:

net private domestic investment = $100 billion

You can see from this that an economy will tend to grow, remain static, or decline according to one of three possibilities:

1. Gross Investment Exceeds Depreciation When this happens, net investment is positive. The economy is thus adding to its capital stock and expanding its productive base.

2. Gross Investment Equals Depreciation In this case, net investment is zero. The economy is merely replacing its capital stock and is neither expanding nor contracting its productive base.

3. Gross Investment is Less Than Depreciation If this occurs, net investment is negative. The economy is thus diminishing, or **disinvesting,** its capital stock and is thereby contracting its productive base.
To summarize:

The term **investment** refers to spending by business firms on job-creating and income-producing goods. It consists of replacements or additions to the nation's stock of capital, including its plant, equipment, and inventories—that is, its nonhuman productive assets.

Net Exports

Some domestic expenditures are made to purchase foreign goods. These are our imports. Some foreign expenditures are made to purchase domestic goods. These are our exports. To measure GNP in terms of total expenditures, we must include the value of exported goods and services. This is because the value of our exports represents the amount that foreigners spent on purchasing some of our total output. Then we subtract the value of imported goods and services from our total expenditures, because we are interested only in measuring the value of domestic output. In performing these adjustments it is simpler to combine the separate figures for exports and imports into a single figure called net exports, according to the formula

net exports = total exports − total imports

Thus, if a nation's total exports in any given year amount to $350 billion, and its total imports are $330 billion, its net exports of $20 billion are part of that year's GNP. (Look back at Exhibit 5.) Of course, the country's imports may exceed its exports in any particular year. In that case, net exports will be negative and will reduce GNP. If you have any doubts about this, look again at Exhibit 5 and note the effect on GNP if net exports are negative.

GNP from the <u>Income</u> Viewpoint: A F<u>low-of-Costs Approach</u>

Now turn your attention to the right side of the table in Exhibit 5.   This shows a second method of calculating GNP.   It is expressed in terms of the flow of costs or payments that businesses incur as a result of production.   The sum of these payments consti-tutes *gross national income (GNI)*.   However, only the first four items — wages, rent, interest, and profit — represent incomes paid to the owners of the factors of production for their contribution to the nation's output.   The remaining two types of payments — indirect business taxes and capital consumption allowance (depreciation) — do not.   Let us see why.

4 items that constitute GNI

Wages

The broad category of **wages** embraces all forms of remuneration for work.   Thus it includes not only wages but also executive salaries and bonuses, commissions, payments in kind, incentive payments, tips, and fringe benefits.   It also includes earnings received by owners of unincorporated businesses, such as proprietorships and partnerships.

Rent

Income earned by persons for the use of their real property, such as a house, store, or farm, is **rent**.   This category also includes the estimated rental value of owner-occupied nonfarm dwellings and royalties received by persons from patents, copyrights, and rights to natural resources.

Interest

Interest is expressed in net rather than gross terms.   It represents the business sector's total interest payments to other sectors minus their total interest payments to the business sector.   All other types of interest payments are considered "unproductive."   (Examples are interest payments between individuals, between businesses, and be-

tween government and individuals.)   Therefore, they are omitted from this classification.

Profit

Profit consists of corporate profits before payments of corporate income taxes or disbursements of dividends to stockholders.   Profits of unincorporated businesses are not counted here because they were already included as part of wages.

The sum of wages, rent, interest, and profit is called **national income (at factor cost)**.   It consists of the payments that business firms make to the owners of the factors of production in return for the services provided by those factors.

The two remaining components of gross national income are indirect business taxes and capital consumption allowances (depreciation).   Because these two items are not payments to the owners of productive resources, their inclusion in GNI requires some explanation.

Indirect Business Taxes

Indirect business taxes consist primarily of sales, excise, and real property taxes incurred by businesses.   You will recall that an indirect business tax is actually "paid" — that is, turned over to the government — by the business firm on which the tax is imposed.   Therefore, the tax is regarded as a business expense — the same as wages and other costs.   This is true even though the real burden of the tax may be borne by the firm's customers in the form of higher prices.   (Keep in mind that *all* of a firm's costs are ultimately borne by its customers in the form of prices paid.)   Because the tax is viewed as a business expense, it is included in *GNI* as a cost item.

To put it somewhat differently, indirect business taxes tend to be passed on or shifted "forward" by business firms to buyers.   (This is why they are called "indirect," in contrast to *direct* taxes, such as personal income taxes, which are not shifted.)   Sales taxes are typical.   If you live in a state or city that has a 5 percent general sales tax and you buy a product whose price is $1, your total *expenditure* is actually $1.05. Of this, $1 goes to pay incomes — the wages, rent, interest, and profit — earned for making the product. The remaining 5 cents goes to the local government, which has not contributed directly to production. It follows, therefore, that indirect business taxes cause the expenditure side of GNP to be greater than the income side. In view of this, indirect business taxes must be added to total incomes (or subtracted from GNP) if GNI is to equal GNP.

Capital Consumption Allowance (Depreciation)

In the process of producing GNP, some decline in the value of existing physical capital occurs as a result of wear and tear, obsolescence, and accidental loss. To reflect this decline, firms count as part of their costs a *capital consumption allowance* — or simply "depreciation." The allowance consists primarily of depreciation on business plant and equipment and on owner-occupied dwellings. For purposes of national-income accounting, depreciation may be thought of as the portion of the current year's GNP that goes to replace the physical capital "consumed" or used up in production.

Depreciation is thus the difference between gross and net private domestic investment, as already explained. *If there were no such thing as depreciation, and if the government returned all indirect business taxes to households, the nation's income from production would be identical to its output.* However, because depreciation is a reality, it causes the income side of GNP to be less than the expenditure side. Therefore, depreciation must be added to total incomes (or subtracted from GNP) if GNI is to equal GNP.

To summarize:

Indirect business taxes and depreciation are treated as *costs* by business firms. Therefore, they charge higher prices for their goods in order to cover these costs. It follows that these expense items must be added to the other expense items (wages, rent, interest, and profit) in order for the total expenditures on GNP to equal the total payments expended in producing it.

Four Other Concepts, All Related

What relation exists between the value of the nation's output and the money that households actually have available for spending? We may arrive at the answer by examining the items listed in the nation's income statement shown in Exhibit 6.

Gross National Product to Net National Product

Gross national product (GNP) is the total market value of the economy's annual output of final goods and services. It is also the economy's gross national income. But, as you know, this figure does not equal the actual dollar incomes available to households. To arrive at a closer measure of the dollars received by individuals, we must subtract the proportion that was spent to replace used up capital goods. This is the *capital consumption allowance* (or depreciation) figure. The number that results is net national product, or simply NNP.

Net National Product to National Income

Net national product (NNP) measures the total sales value of goods and services available for society's consumption and for adding to its stock of capital equipment. As such, NNP may be thought of as "national income at market prices."

But NNP still does not represent the dollars people actually had available to spend. This is because NNP is overstated by the amount of indirect business taxes — such as sales taxes. For purposes of national income accounting, the taxes are assumed to be shifted forward by sellers to consumers in the form of higher prices. Therefore, the sum of all indirect business taxes must be deducted from NNP in order to arrive at a more accurate estimate of the dollars available to people for actual spending. This deduction results in national income (at factor cost).

[handwritten: # KNOW SET UP]

Exhibit 6
The Nation's Income Statement: Gross National Product and Related Accounts
(billions of dollars)

Can you fill in the figures for the most recent year? See the endpapers in the front of the book.

[handwritten: # DON'T put GNP as Gross National Product]

	19__
Gross national product (GNP)	$_____
Minus: Capital consumption allowance (depreciation)	_____
Equals: Net national product (NNP)	_____
Minus: Indirect business taxes	_____
Equals: National income (NI)	_____
Minus: Income earned but not received *[handwritten: equals]*	_____
1. Corporate income taxes	_____
2. Undistributed corporate profits *[handwritten: 3 categories]*	_____
3. Social insurance contributions	_____
Plus: Income received but not earned	_____
Transfer payments *[handwritten: → move from one sector to the other]*	_____
Equals: Personal income (PI)	_____
Minus: Personal taxes	_____
Equals: Disposable personal income (DPI)	_____
Out of which come:	
Personal consumption expenditures *[handwritten: spend]*	_____
Personal savings *[handwritten: save]*	_____

[handwritten: # DOES NOT REPRESENT THE dollars that people actually had available for spending]

National Income to Personal Income

National income (NI) is the total of all incomes earned by the factors of production. Thus, NI is the sum of wages, rent, interest, and profit earned by the suppliers of labor, land, capital, and entrepreneurship. Does NI represent the dollars that people actually had available for spending? Once again, the answer is no. Some people earned income they did not receive; others received income they did not earn.

[handwritten margin note: income earned but not received]

For example, the stockholders in a corporation are its owners and hence earn the corporation's profits. However, stockholders do not receive all the profits, for two reasons. Some profits are paid to the government in the form of corporation income taxes. Some profits are also plowed back into the business for future expansion instead of being distributed to stockholders as dividends. Likewise, social security contributions are taken out of workers' current earnings, and thus they are also part of income earned but not received.

[handwritten margin note: income received but not earned]

As for income received but not earned, the major items are transfer payments. These are merely shifts of funds within the economy — primarily from the government sector to households — for reasons other than current production.

To measure the dollars people actually had available for spending, we therefore adjust the NI in two ways.

1. Subtract income earned but not received.
2. Add income received but not earned.

These two steps result in a figure called personal income.

✳ Personal Income to Disposable Personal Income

Personal income (PI) is the total received by persons from all sources. It is the dollars that you and I receive for the various ways in which we contribute to GNP. Does PI measure the dollars actually available to people for spending? The answer is still no, because out of personal income people must first pay their personal taxes. This amount must therefore be deducted from PI, leaving a figure called **disposable personal income (DPI).** It is this amount that people actually have available for spending. As you can see from the front endpapers of this book, the great bulk of DPI goes for personal consumption, while the rest is saved.

Thus, there are five measures of income and output for the economy:

World Wide Photos

Simon Kuznets
1901–1985

UPI/Bettmann Newsphotos

Sir Richard Stone
1913–

Today, such widely employed concepts as gross national product and disposable personal income are essential yardsticks of economic performance. But they came into extensive use only a few decades ago, largely as a result of the efforts of two men. One was Simon Kuznets, at that time an economist at the National Bureau of Economic Research, a prominent private research organization. The other was Richard Stone, who was serving as a research assistant in economics at England's Cambridge University.

Kuznets: Father of National Income Accounting

More than anyone else, Kuznets pioneered the development of national-income data. When the nation plunged into the Great Depression of the early 1930s, the amount of factual information available was, said Kuznets, "a scandal. No one knew what was happening. The data available then were neither fish nor flesh nor even red herring."

It remained for Kuznets to point out the kind of information that was needed. When the Senate ordered official national-income estimates, the Department of Commerce turned to the National Bureau of Economic Research for assistance. The young Kuznets went to Washington as a consultant, lecturing government economists and statisticians on his concepts. On January 4, 1934, a Senate document was published that contained the country's first national-income figures. They covered the period 1929 to 1932. This was the beginning of one of the most significant advances in the history of economics. The measurement of GNP and related concepts was not fully developed by the Department of Commerce until the 1940s. Although the technical structure of GNP is quite different from that of Kuznets's original conception, he is still recognized as the person most responsible for its statistical formulation.

Stone: International Systematizer

It remained for another young scholar to provide a national-income accounting system that other countries could adopt. That person was Richard Stone. During the early 1940s (the World War II period), he worked as a research assistant to the British economist John Maynard Keynes, whose ideas were revolutionizing the way people thought about economic problems. Stone helped prepare a statistically-based profile of the British economy that enabled the country's leaders to assess its resources with far greater accuracy than had been possible before.

After the war, Stone headed a United Nations project that developed a standard national-income accounting model for other countries. Today more than 100 nations follow these guidelines, making international comparisons possible.

Many Honors

To a degree rarely equaled by other economists, both Kuznets and Stone have demonstrated an ability to analyze and structure huge masses of data. From these, they were able to draw many provocative hypotheses about long-term economic change.

Kuznets's and Stone's lifeworks have been crowned with honors. Among them have been the Nobel prize. It was awarded to Kuznets in 1971 when he was 70, and to Stone in 1984 when he was 71.

- Gross national product.
- Net national product.
- National income.
- Personal income.
- Disposable personal income—or, simply, disposable income.

These measures are closely interrelated, can be derived from one another, and tend approximately to parallel one another over time. In many macroeconomic discussions (except those involving specific accounting practices as described in this chapter), *economists loosely use the term "national income" or simply "income" to represent all five terms.* A complete income-flow model is shown in Exhibit 7.

Wealth of a Nation: How Much Is America Worth?

If you wanted to buy the United States—its land, buildings, machines, people's personal belongings, government property, everything—what would you have to pay? In 1776 the answer was $3.7 billion; in 1986 it was $10 trillion. In the year 2000, according to trends in recent decades, the figure is likely to be about $20 trillion.

This sum includes only physical wealth—wealth consisting of tangible assets. Such items as cash, corporate stocks and bonds, and savings and checking accounts are excluded because they represent intangible assets—claims against physical wealth.

Exhibit 7
The Flow of National Income and Related Concepts

Can you fill in the data for the most recent year? See the front endpapers.

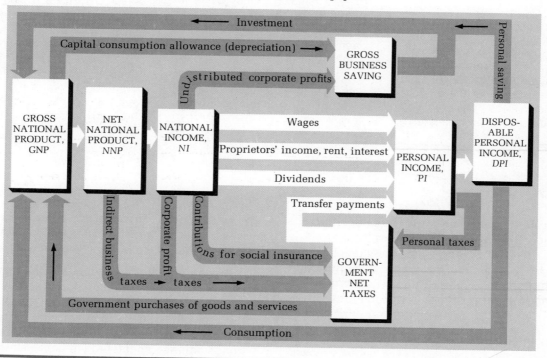

The Underground Economy

Take the Money and Skip the Taxes

Fred Henderson owns his own Jeep and snowplow, earns enough during the winter months to cover an entire year's college expenses, and files no income tax return. Janet Brennan works full time as a waitress, files an annual income tax return, but generally declares only about 50 percent of her tips as income. Dr. S. J. Jackson, a physician, exchanges medical care for car maintenance services with a patient who is an automobile mechanic; as a result, no money passes between them.

Although the names in these scenarios are fictitious, the cases are not. They illustrate some of the activities that take place in the underground economy. This is a segment of the private sector in which transactions go unreported to government agencies, especially to the Internal Revenue Service.

The results are by no means trivial. Some experts estimate that the amount of unreported income each year equals as much as 25 percent of actual GNP, and that the percentage may be growing. Further, most of this income derives from legal activities, not from illegal ones like prostitution, gambling, or drugs.

Some Implications

If the estimate is correct, or even if the true figure is only half as much, the income that goes unrecorded and untaxed amounts to hundreds of billions of dollars annually. The implications for economic policy are staggering. They indicate that, if the subterranean economy is large and growing, the nation's economic health is quite different from what the official figures indicate. For example:

- Actual national output is significantly higher than the official GNP data suggest. Therefore, the nation's rate of economic growth is higher than is generally believed.

- The unemployment rate is much lower than is generally believed. According to some estimates, many more people, perhaps a third of those listed as unemployed, are actually working full time and earn-

ing incomes that are either unreported or underreported.

- Taxes on unreported income are lost to the government. In any given year, this loss in tax revenues could be enough to erase a large portion of the deficit in the federal budget.

Because of these and other considerations, government officials are seeking ways to reduce the scope of the underground economy.

Experiences Overseas

Unfortunately, the task is not easy, as the experiences of other advanced countries bear out. Subterranean economies have thrived much longer and are considerably more extensive in western Europe than in the United States. A major reason is the high tax rates in these countries. When taxes rise sharply with increases in income, the pressure on people to seek ways of escaping taxes— through illegal means, if necessary — becomes pronounced. As a result, without major tax reductions, a growing proportion of the world's economies will continue to go underground.

What kinds of items enter into the calculation of a nation's wealth? You can get an idea by examining Exhibit 8. This illustrates a balance-sheet form for the country as a whole. When used in conjunction with the nation's income statement shown in Exhibit 6, two important types of information are revealed:

The nation's balance sheet shows the country's financial position on a given date. The nation's income statement shows the country's output and income for a given period. Therefore, the balance sheet is like a "snapshot" of the nation's financial status, whereas the income statement is like a "motion picture."

As you may know, business firms regularly prepare balance sheets and income statements. These terms are defined *for businesses* in the Dictionary at the back of the book. You will find it instructive to compare these definitions with the concepts of *national* balance sheets and income statements explained in this chapter.

Exhibit 8
The Nation's Balance Sheet

Assets are what we own; *liabilities* are what we owe; *net worth* is the difference between the two. Can you explain why liabilities owed to domestic residents are the same as intangible assets?

	19__
Assets	
Tangible	
Buildings and other structures	$x
Land	x
Durable goods, equipment, and inventories	x
Intangible	
Currency and checking accounts	x
Other bank deposits and shares	x
Insurance and pension reserves	x
Credit, securities, and other claims	x
Total assets	$x
Liabilities	
To domestic residents (= intangible assets)	x
To foreigners	x
Total liabilities	$x
Net worth (or net national wealth)	
Total assets less total liabilities	$x

3. The items that make up the nation's income accounts are GNP, *NNP*, *NI*, *PI*, and *DPI*. All five measures are closely related and can be derived from one another. They are among the most important measures of our economy's performance. In economic discussions (except those involving accounting practices) we often refer to all five measures as "national income" or simply "income."

4. The financial status of a nation is reflected by its income statement, showing gross national product and related accounts. Financial status is also reflected by a nation's balance sheet, showing assets, liabilities, and net worth. Taken together, these financial statements provide an overall picture of the economy's income and wealth.

Terms and Concepts To Review

gross national product
real output
current dollars
constant dollars
deflation
index numbers
value added
transfer payments
gross national income
investment
inventory

depreciation
disinvestment
national income (at
   factor cost)
capital consumption
   allowance
net national product
personal income
disposable personal
   income

What You Have Learned

1. GNP, the basic and most comprehensive measure of a nation's output, represents the total market value of all final goods and services produced during a year.

Some pitfalls to avoid in calculating GNP include (a) failing to take the effects of price changes into account, (b) double (actually multiple) counting, and (c) the inclusion of nonproductive transactions.

2. From the expenditure standpoint, GNP is the sum of personal consumption expenditures, government purchases of goods and services, investment, and net exports. GNP can be viewed from the income standpoint as gross national income (*GNI*) or the sum of wages, rent, interest, and profit, plus two nonincome business expense items: indirect business taxes and depreciation.

For Discussion

1. Suppose that a nation's GNP increased from $100 billion to $200 billion. What has happened to its *real* GNP during that period if
   (a) Prices remained the same?
   (b) Prices doubled?
   (c) Prices tripled from their constant level in (a)?
   (d) Prices fell by 50 percent of their constant level in (a)?

2. What happens when you "deflate" a *rising* current-dollar series, as in Exhibit 1? Obviously, the constant-dollar series lies below the current-dollar series for all years after the base year, and above it for all years prior to the base year. What would happen if you deflated a current-dollar series that was *declining* rather than one that was rising? Explain your answer.

3. Why is "value added" a logically correct method of measuring the nation's output?

4. The level of inventories serves as a "balancing" item between sales to final users and current production. True or false? Can sales to final users exceed current production? Can sales be less than current production? Explain your answers in terms of changes in inventories and their effects on GNP.

5. How is the growth or decline of an economy related to its net investment? Do you think an economy's percentage growth or decline is related to its percentage change in net investment? Explain.

6. What is the effect on national income if you (a) marry your housekeeper; (b) take an unpaid vacation? Is there any effect on social welfare (that is, well-being) from either act?

7. Which of the following is included, and which is not included, in calculating GNP?

(a) One hundred shares of General Motors stock purchased this week on the New York Stock Exchange.
(b) Wages paid to teachers.
(c) A student's income from a part-time job.
(d) A student's income from a full-time summer job.
(e) The value of a bookcase built by a do-it-yourselfer.
(f) The purchase of a used car.
(g) A monthly rent of $800 that a homeowner "saves" by living in his or her own home instead of renting it out to a tenant.

8. Each year the total amount of dollar payments by checks and cash far exceeds — by many billions of dollars — the GNP. If GNP is the market value of the economy's final output, how can this huge difference exist?

9. Gross business saving represents that part of business income that is available for various forms of investment. Examine the following hypothetical data (in billions of dollars):

Corporate profits	$90
Corporate income taxes	43
Dividends to stockholders	25
Retained profits	22
Depreciation	75

(a) How much is gross business saving? Show your method of calculation.
(b) Of what significance is depreciation in your calculation?
(c) Can gross business saving be larger than corporate profits *before* taxes and dividends? Can it be smaller? Explain.

10. Examine the following hypothetical data (all in billions of dollars) for a particular year:

(1) Gross private domestic investment	$180
(2) Contributions for social insurance	25
(3) Interest paid by consumers	9
(4) Personal consumption expenditures	600
(5) Transfer payments	60
(6) Undistributed corporate profits	45
(7) Indirect business taxes	75
(8) Net exports of goods and services	5
(9) Capital consumption allowance	60
(10) Government purchases of goods and services	175
(11) Corporate income taxes	70
(12) Personal tax and nontax payments	90

On the basis of these data, calculate (a) gross national product; (b) net national product; (c) national income; (d) personal income; (e) disposable income. (SUGGESTION You will find the front endpapers helpful.)

11. Examine the following hypothetical data (all in billions of dollars) for a particular year:

(1) Indirect business taxes	$ 90
(2) Corporate profits before taxes	150
(3) Capital consumption allowance	90
(4) Compensation of employees	675
(5) Undistributed corporate profits	60
(6) Proprietors' income	120
(7) Contributions for social insurance	40
(8) Corporate income taxes	70
(9) Net interest	15
(10) Transfer payments	80
(11) Personal tax and nontax payments	$105
(12) Rental incomes	45
(13) Personal consumption expenditures	750

On the basis of these data, calculate the five types of national income discussed in this chapter. (HINT Do not try to calculate GNP first.)

12. A country's gross national product rose from $285 billion in 1970 to $504 billion in 1980. During the same period, the country's Consumer Price Index (1982 = 100) rose from 72.1 to 88.7

(a) What was the percentage increase of nominal GNP over the decade?
(b) By how much did average prices, measured by the Consumer Price Index, rise over the decade?
(c) How would you calculate GNP for 1970 and for 1980, expressed in 1982 dollars?
(d) Is the percentage change of GNP in constant dollars greater or less than the percentage change in current dollars? Show your calculations.

13. Convert personal consumption expenditures into 1977 dollars for the years shown in the following table. What is the economic significance of your calculations?

Year	Personal consumption expenditures (regional data, billions of dollars)	Consumer Price Index (1977 = 100)
1970	$325.2	88.7
1975	432.8	94.5
1980	445.6	104.2
1985	532.2	114.4

14. Which measure of national income best tells you:
   (a) The amount by which the economy's production exceeds the capital equipment used up in producing it?
   (b) The amount of income available to consumers for spending?
   (c) The market value of commodities produced for final use?
   (d) The amount of income available to people for government taxation?
   (e) The incomes earned by resource owners engaged in production?
Which measure of national income is best?

yr. dollars
of inflation
caused

Economic Instability: Business Cycles, Unemployment, and Inflation

Fluctuations in general economic activity

Learning Guide

Watch for answers to these important questions

What is the nature of the fluctuations in general economic activity that are commonly referred to as "business cycles"? Why do these fluctuations occur? Can they be forecast?

Why is unemployment a problem of continuous concern in our economy? What are some of the causes of unemployment?

What is inflation? How does it affect each of us? Why is it important for our economy to achieve greater price stability?

Fluctuations in economic activity—or "business cycles," as they are frequently called—have been a recurrent plague for mixed economies. Inflation and unemployment are the costs of that plague— costs we have paid throughout a large part of our history.

This chapter examines the nature and interrelations of business cycles, unemployment, and inflation. Once we understand the characteristics of these problems, we can look at ways of trying to deal with them.

Essentially, as you will learn, our government tries to keep all three problems at bay simultaneously. However, our nation's policy makers are not consistently successful. Both the problems and their solutions continue to be subjects of controversy.

1) Recurrent
2) Irregular
tend to occur
in income, output,
employment,
prices
They demonstrate changes
the rates of growth

Business Cycles — A Long History of Fluctuations

What are business cycles? You can get a preliminary idea by looking at the historical picture in Exhibit 1. You can see that, although we no longer

Exhibit 1
How Do Business Cycles Look?

An Historical Picture of American Business Cycles
Fluctuations are recurrent but not periodic. That is, the peaks and troughs do not occur at regular intervals.

According to the definition of business cycles, fluctuations may occur in production, prices, income, employment, or in any other chronological series of economic data. Such series are called *time series*. In order to measure business cycles for the economy as a whole it is necessary to combine many different time series into a single index of business activity. Then, if the value of the index for each year is expressed as a percentage of the long-term "average" or trend, the resulting data when graphed would resemble the fluctuations in the chart.

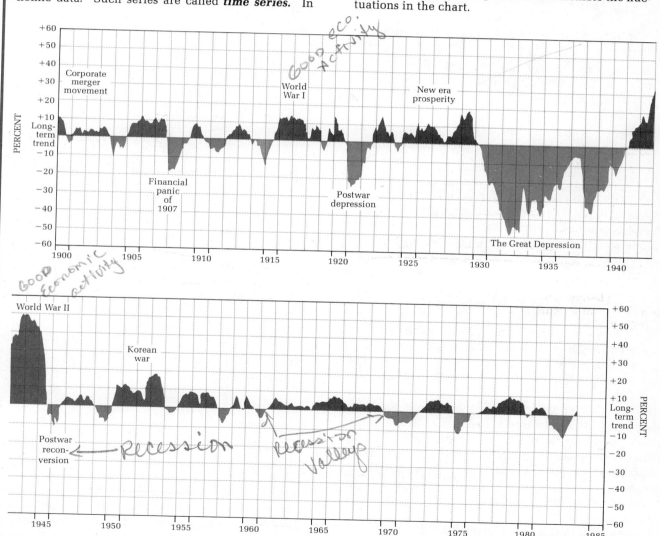

Aggregate demand

have the frequent booms and busts that characterized the economy prior to World War II, we still have fluctuations in business activity. The following modern definition of business cycles is appropriate:

> **Business cycles** are fluctuations in general economic activity. The fluctuations are recurrent but nonperiodic (that is, irregular). They occur in such aggregate variables as income, employment, and prices, most of which move at about the same time in the same direction but at different rates.

It is important to note what the definition *excludes:*

- Business cycles are not **seasonal fluctuations,** such as the upswing in retail sales that occurs each year during the Christmas and Easter periods.
- Business cycles are not **secular trends,** such as the long-run growth or decline that characterizes practically all economic data over a long period of years.

Note that, since World War II, extreme prosperities and depressions are no longer common. Therefore, economists customarily classify business cycles as either recoveries or recessions, depending on whether they are above the long-term trend or below it.

Some Facts About Business Cycles

Economists who have analyzed business cycles have learned a great deal about them, from studies going back to the nineteenth century. One striking set of observations concerns the different behavior of "hard goods" and "soft goods" industries. Over the course of a business cycle, the durable-goods (or hard-goods) industries tend to experience relatively wide fluctuations in output and employment and relatively small fluctuations in prices. The nondurable-goods (or soft-goods) industries tend to experience relatively wide fluctuations in prices and relatively small fluctuations in output and employment.

These observations can be attributed primarily to two factors: durability and competition.

Durability

Durable goods—precisely because they are durable—do not have to be replaced at a particular time. They can be repaired and made to last longer, if necessary. What effect does this have on businesses that buy such capital goods as iron and steel, cement, and machine tools? What effect does it have on consumers, who purchase such durable goods as automobiles, furniture, and appliances? In a recession or depression, total demand for the economy's output is often low. Business managers thus find themselves with excess production capacity. Therefore, they see little chance of profiting from investment in capital goods. Likewise, consumers find that they can get along with their existing cars and other durable goods, and so they decide to postpone buying new ones. As a result, the "hard-goods" industries experience relatively sharp decreases in demand.

During recovery and prosperity, the opposite is true. Aggregate demand is high, and business executives and consumers are ready to replace, as well as add to, their existing stocks of capital and durable goods. The hard-goods industries, therefore, experience relatively sharp increases in demand.

This is less true, however, of the purchase of nondurables and semidurables—the so-called "soft goods." Examples include fresh food, some clothing, and certain services. Their purchase is not as readily postponable. Therefore, the change in demand for them over the course of a business cycle tends to be much less pronounced.

Some comparisons between income and consumer spending are shown in Exhibit 2. Note the relatively wider fluctuations for durable goods than for nondurable goods.

Competition

The degree of competition in an industry is often influenced by the number of its sellers. This usually has a bearing on the way in which the industry adjusts its prices and outputs in response to changes in demand. For example, how does a fall in aggregate demand affect hard-goods producers as compared to soft-goods producers?

Exhibit 2
Consumer Spending Relative to Income

Consumer spending fluctuates with income over the years. But expenditures for durable goods fluctuate much more widely relative to income than expenditures for nondurable goods.

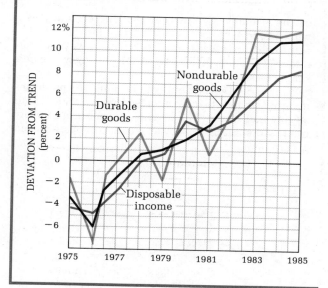

Many durable-goods industries tend to be characterized by relatively small numbers of dominant sellers. The aluminum, locomotive, aircraft-engine, and telephone-equipment industries, among others, are typical. The "big three" or "big four" producers in these industries control a large proportion of the total output of their product. Consequently, they can influence the prices they charge and can follow relatively stable pricing policies despite fluctuations in sales. As a result, when they are confronted with a decline in aggregate demand, they try to reduce costs and maintain profit margins by cutting back on production and jobs. Eventually, if market sluggishness continues, some hard-pressed firms may seek to reduce their inventories by cutting prices. But even then, price decreases are likely to be small relative to the declines in output and employment.

The opposite tends to occur in industries producing nondurable and semidurable goods. Examples are ladies' dresses, men's suits, millinery, and toilet preparations. In these industries, unlike most durable-goods industries, a considerable number of sellers are usually competing in the same market. Each firm, therefore, is likely to have too small a share of the market to ignore the importance of price reduction as a means of countering a decrease in demand. Consequently, when aggregate demand falls, firms in such industries tend to reduce their prices while holding output and employment relatively steady. To summarize:

Two factors—durability and competition—help account for different degrees of price and output changes when aggregate demand declines. During a recession, for example, we first hear about production cutbacks and layoffs in such industries as automobiles and steel—not in food processing or textiles. The latter industries may also reduce their output and employment, but for them the *percentage* decreases are usually much smaller.

Tracking the Economy

Which way is the economy heading? Are business conditions going to improve during the coming months? Or will production and employment continue at their present levels?

These are the kinds of questions that economists (and other people) often ask. Their answers are often obtained from statistical indexes, called *time series,* because they are expressed chronologically. Among those time series that are used to monitor the nation's health are gross national product, employment, housing starts, consumer prices, and retail sales. Hundreds of other indexes are also closely watched. Some of the more important ones are shown in the front and back endpapers of this book.

The time series that are continuously scrutinized are obviously too numerous to list. However, many of them can be classified into one of three categories:

Time Series

Coincident Indicators   These time series tend to move approximately in phase with the aggregate economy and therefore are measures of current economic activity. *Examples:* GNP, industrial production, retail sales.

Leading Indicators   These time series tend to move ahead of aggregate economic activity, producing peaks and troughs before the economy as a whole. *Examples:* New orders for plant and equipment, new building permits, stock-market prices.

Lagging Indicators   These time series tend to trail behind aggregate economic activity. *Examples:* Business loans outstanding, manufacturing and trade inventories, unit labor costs.

The trouble with all three types of indicators (especially with leading indicators) is that they often give false signals by temporarily reversing their upward or downward direction. This, of course, impairs their usefulness for interpreting and forecasting economic trends. You can appreciate this by examining the graphs in Exhibit 3 and their explanations.

Conclusion: The Trade-off Between Stability and Freedom

Some people contend that the business cycle could readily be cured if only certain fundamental adjustments were made. This belief is especially popular during economic recessions. "Find a proper balance between wages and prices." "Improve labor-management relations." "Reform our tax system." If these and other measures were adopted, it is said, economic instability would be eliminated.

Unfortunately, such beliefs are false. Even if these desirable objectives could be achieved, we would still experience economic fluctuations. The reasons are not difficult to see:

Business cycles are an inherent characteristic of mixed economies. This is because households, which express their demands for goods and services in the marketplace, are not the same as the businesses that seek to

Exhibit 3
Forecasting with Economic Indicators: Computer, Crystal Ball, or Tea Leaves?

Ideally, the three types of indicators might look like the theoretical ones shown in the figure. They illustrate distinct leads and lags, in terms of the peaks and troughs. The shaded area is a reference range. It covers a temporary downturn for the economy as a whole, represented by the coincident indicator.

In reality, the leads and lags are not always so definite or consistent. If they were, forecasting would be a simple task.

The U.S. Department of Commerce publishes monthly composite indexes of leading, coincident, and lagging indicators. The leading indicators are widely used as forecasting tools by economists in business and government.

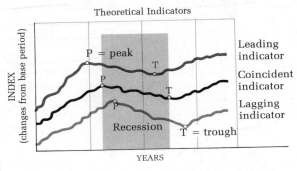

Theoretical Indicators

fulfill those demands. *Each group is composed of different people with different motivations.* Consequently, the economic actions of the two groups— their decisions to spend or not to spend—generally differ. The result is that waves of economic activity are always being created.

In view of this, you will find that eliminating instability is not one of the goals of macroeconomics. That would be impossible in our type of economy. Instead, a chief goal is to *reduce* instability without sacrificing our capitalistic institutions and freedoms. At least to some extent, *there is a trade-off between stability and freedom.*

Economics in the News

Unemployment and Inflation Hurt

Together They Can Be Devastating

Recessions accompanied by rapidly rising prices affect people in more ways than business balance sheets can ever show. This is clear from several sociological studies concerned with the effects of unemployment and rising prices on human interactions.

Some of the results of these studies are summarized below:

— A one-percentage-point rise in unemployment causes about 37,000 deaths over a six-year period. One reason is that when people's health insurance runs out, they postpone visits to the doctor. In addition, they eat poorly and turn to alcohol and drugs as stress increases; some even resort to crime as a way to survive.

— During high inflationary periods, too, many otherwise law-abiding citizens may resort to larceny and fraud. This can take the form of passing bad checks, embezzling funds, shoplifting, and cheating on taxes.

Sociological studies such as these drive home an important point. They remind us that the costs to society of unemployment and inflation are much greater than is suggested by the percentages and dollar figures reported by the government.

Unemployment

You will often hear it said that one of our primary national objectives is to maintain the economy's resources at a "full" or "high" level of employment. What do these terms mean?

Before this question can be answered, it is necessary to understand some basic terms and concepts that are part of the language of modern economics.

The first is the **labor force.** It is defined as all people 16 years of age or older who are employed, plus all those unemployed who are actively seeking work. The *total* labor force includes those in the armed services as well as those in the civilian labor force. However, only the civilian labor force is of interest to us here, because this is the segment that experiences unemployment.

The number of people who are unemployed and actively seeking work is determined through a monthly survey conducted by the U.S. Department of Labor. This number divided by the civilian labor force is the official *unemployment rate.*

$$\frac{\text{\# people unemployed}}{\text{Civilian labor force}} = U Rate$$

Types of Unemployment

The Department of Labor encounters certain difficulties in trying to measure unemployment. The circumstances and conditions of unemployment vary widely among individuals. Accordingly, distinctions are made between different kinds of unemployment.

Frictional (Transitional) Unemployment

A certain amount of unemployment, which is of a short-run nature and is characteristic of a dynamic economy, may be called *frictional unemployment.* It exists because of "frictions" in the economic system resulting from imperfect labor mobility, imperfect knowledge of job opportunities, and the economy's inability to match people with jobs instantly and smoothly. Typically, frictional unemployment consists of people temporarily out of work because they are between jobs or in the process of changing jobs. It is possible to reduce frictional unemployment by improving labor mobility and knowledge. But in a society that values freedom frictional unemployment cannot be completely eliminated. Efforts to do so would greatly reduce people's freedom to change jobs. In view of the nature of frictional unemployment, an equally suitable and more descriptive name for it might be *transitional unemployment.*

Cyclical Unemployment

In mixed economies such as ours, a major type of unemployment has been *cyclical unemployment.* This type of unemployment is a result of business recessions and depressions. Obviously, society would like to reduce cyclical unemployment as much as possible. However, this would involve conquering the business cycle. Although substantial progress in this direction has been made in recent decades, cyclical unemployment continues to be one of our economy's most serious problems. Therefore, it is a topic of major importance in subsequent chapters.

results from economic instability

Structural (Mismatch) Unemployment

Unlike cyclical unemployment, which results from economic instability, *structural unemployment* arises from deep-rooted conditions and changes in the economy. Two major groups of people make up the structurally unemployed.

One group consists of the *hard-core unemployed.* These are people who lack the education and skills needed in today's complex economy and who are often the victims of discrimination. This group is composed mainly of minorities: blacks, Puerto Ricans, Mexicans, the "too young," the "too old," high-school dropouts, and the permanently displaced victims of technological change.

The other group is completely different. This group consists of skilled workers, college graduates, and professionals whose talents have been made obsolete by changes in technology, markets, or national-defense priorities. Many mathematicians, physicists, chemists, artists, musicians, and other people whose specialized skills or training are not always in strong demand find themselves in this group.

Structural unemployment thus exists because the location and skill requirements of job openings do not always match the location and skills of unemployed workers. Therefore, a more descriptive name for structural unemployment is *mismatch unemployment.*

Measuring Unemployment: Who Are the Unemployed?

The accuracy of unemployment figures is always subject to attack, especially when the figures are high. Critics point out that the overall unemployment rate may at times be either overstated or understated because of the inclusion or exclusion of three categories of workers:

1. **The Marginally Employed** The jobless total is swollen by the inclusion of many people, among them some homemakers and students, who may be only marginally dependent on regular paychecks.

2. **Discouraged Workers** The unemployment total is understated by the failure to include "the hidden unemployed."—discouraged people who have given up trying to find work.

3. **The Partially Employed** The published unemployment statistics do not reflect the fact that many jobholders work only part-time because they cannot find full-time jobs.

With overstatement here and understatement there, unemployment data are always somewhat ambiguous. Because of this, perhaps the chief value of such data lies in what they reveal about the *direction* in which unemployment is changing.

Employment Ratio: A Different Measure

The shortcomings of the unemployment rate have led many economists to advocate a measure called the *employment ratio.* This is the percentage of the working-age population that is employed.

The advantage of the employment ratio (compared to the unemployment rate) is that it focuses on the number of jobs actually held by people while ignoring those people who are entering and leaving the labor force. Thus, if businesses hire more workers, the employment ratio goes up. Meanwhile, the unemployment rate may remain constant or even rise, because it is dependent on the size of the labor force rather than on the size of the working-age population.

Of course, the employment ratio is affected by the number of part-time workers and by various other factors. These also influence the unemployment rate. But, when the proper statistical adjustments are made, economists agree that the employment ratio turns out to be a much better indicator of the economy's health.

Despite its advantages, the employment ratio cannot serve as the government's official measure unless Washington approves it. That will not happen until Congress decides to legislate the change.

Exhibit 4 reflects some further difficulties encountered when measuring unemployment.

Exhibit 4
Measuring Unemployment: Seven Different Concepts

Difficulties encountered when measuring unemployment

How should unemployment be measured? The answer depends on how the concept is defined. The U.S. Department of Labor, which compiles the unemployment data, publishes seven different measures, ranging from the narrowest to the broadest. In the accompanying chart, the narrowest, U_1, consists of those people unemployed for 15 weeks or more. The broadest, U_7, includes *all* types of unemployed—full-time, part-time, and so on. As a rule, all seven types tend to move up and down approximately together.

There is thus no single "true" measure of unemployment. There are different measures, reflecting different judgements about the economic and psychological hardship caused by unemployment.

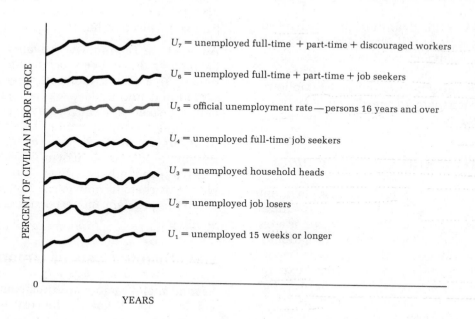

U_7 = unemployed full-time + part-time + discouraged workers

U_6 = unemployed full-time + part-time + job seekers

U_5 = official unemployment rate—persons 16 years and over

U_4 = unemployed full-time job seekers

U_3 = unemployed household heads

U_2 = unemployed job losers

U_1 = unemployed 15 weeks or longer

PERCENT OF CIVILIAN LABOR FORCE

YEARS

Full Employment and "Natural" Unemployment

Ideally, the economy should maintain a high level of employment. But how high is high? There is no simple answer. As you learned above, cyclical and structural unemployment stem from different causes. Therefore, government measures aimed at reducing one kind of unemployment may not work very effectively at reducing the other. Besides, as you will discover in later chapters, some government policies that seek to raise the level of employment can create serious inflationary pressures, causing the average price level to rise.

To help deal with these problems, economists use a concept called *full employment.* It is the level of employment at which two conditions prevail:

1. Everyone who wants to work is working, except for those who are frictionally and structurally unemployed

2. The average price level is stable, neither increasing nor decreasing

You can see from this definition that, when the economy is operating at full employment, there is no cyclical unemployment. However, frictional and structural unemployment exist. Together these comprise *natural unemployment.* It follows that the expression *natural employment* may be used as another name for full employment.

Causes of Structural Unemployment

As you have learned, structural unemployment exists because of a failure to match job openings with unemployed workers. This can occur as a result of changes in technology, markets, or national-defense priorities. Because of the growing importance of structural unemployment, some experts predict that it may exceed 10 percent of the labor force by the end of the century. They base their beliefs on three major trends.

Changing Composition of the Labor Force The proportion of secondary income earners (especially part-time job holders) in the labor force has been increasing relative to the proportion of primary bread-winners. Because most secondary income earners are less skilled and less experienced, the percentage of unemployed within these groups is usually relatively high. In some years, the figures are as high as 20 or 30 percent. Thus the growing importance of secondary income earners within the labor force helps to boost the hourly unemployment rate.

Rising Minimum Wage According to many studies, continued increases in the minimum wage will intensify unemployment. Such increases eliminate jobs that are not productive enough to be done at the legal minimum wage. Many unskilled, low-paying occupations that could be held by teenagers will not be, simply because employers will find it unprofitable to pay the minimum wage. These jobs, therefore, will not be done unless cheaper methods can be found to do them. Various studies conducted by economists in universities and the U.S. Department of Labor support this view. The studies show that teenage unemployment rates are very low or virtually nonexistent in many industrial countries that have no minimum-wage laws.

Advances in Technology Advances in science and technology have been occurring at very rapid rates. As a result, increasing proportions of unskilled and untrained workers have been permanently displaced. This aggravates the problem of structural unemployment. The trend will continue unless methods are developed—through training programs, employer subsidies and tax incentives, and other devices—to absorb the displaced workers in new jobs. You will learn more about this problem and its possible solutions in later chapters.

Conclusion: Costs of Unemployment

Several major factors are thus contributing to unemployment. What are the costs to society?

Society suffers a social cost of unemployment. This consists of what the nation forgoes and never gets back. The loss includes not only consumer goods and capital goods that society fails to produce, but deterioration of human capital resulting from the loss of skills. The cost also includes the human misery, deprivation, and social and political unrest brought on by large-scale unemployment.

The costs of unemployment are matters of deep and general concern. Although all of the costs cannot be measured, an important step toward doing so is explained in Exhibit 5.

Exhibit 5
Estimating the Economic Cost of Unemployment: The GNP Gap

How much output does society lose from unemployment? You can obtain a rough estimate by calculating the GNP gap. This is the difference, in any given year, between potential GNP and actual GNP. Potential GNP is the output that would occur at full employment. For example, suppose that full employment exists when 95 percent of the civilian labor force is working. Then potential GNP can be derived from the following formula:

$$\text{potential GNP} = \frac{\begin{array}{c}\text{hours worked}\\\text{by all persons}\\\text{at full employment}\end{array}}{\begin{array}{c}\text{actual hours worked}\\\text{by all persons}\end{array}} \times \left(\begin{array}{c}\text{actual}\\\text{GNP}\end{array}\right)$$

$$= \frac{\left(\begin{array}{c}95\% \text{ of}\\\text{civilian}\\\text{labor force}\end{array}\right)\left(\begin{array}{c}\text{average}\\\text{weekly}\\\text{hours} \times 52\end{array}\right)}{\left(\begin{array}{c}\text{actual}\\\text{employment}\end{array}\right)\left(\begin{array}{c}\text{average}\\\text{weekly}\\\text{hours} \times 52\end{array}\right)} \times \left(\begin{array}{c}\text{actual}\\\text{GNP}\end{array}\right)$$

Notice that two of the factors, *average weekly hours times 52*, cancel out. This leaves the formula:

$$\text{potential GNP} = \frac{\begin{array}{c}95\% \text{ of civilian}\\\text{labor force}\end{array}}{\text{actual employment}} \times \left(\begin{array}{c}\text{actual}\\\text{GNP}\end{array}\right)$$

Here is an illustration of the calculation:
Suppose that in a given year, the civilian labor force was 100 million, actual employment was 92 million, and actual GNP was $2,100 billion. Applying the formula,

$$\begin{aligned}\text{potential GNP} &= \frac{95 \text{ million}}{92 \text{ million}} \times (\$2,100 \text{ billion})\\ &= 1.03 \times (\$2,100 \text{ billion})\\ &= \$2,163 \text{ billion}\end{aligned}$$

The GNP gap in any given year is then the difference between potential GNP and actual GNP:

$$GNP \text{ gap} = potential\ GNP - actual\ GNP$$

Using the above example,

$$\begin{aligned}GNP \text{ gap} &= \$2,163\ billion - \$2,100\ billion\\ &= \$63\ billion\end{aligned}$$

The chart provides a hypothetical illustration of the GNP gap over a period of years. Can you construct a chart from actual data covering the most recent ten years? All the information you need is available in the front and back endpapers of this book.

Question How might actual GNP sometimes exceed potential GNP?

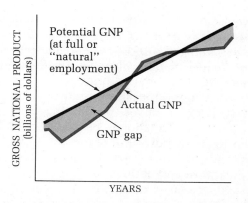

Renewed Effort for Subminimum Wage

The President again is urging Congress to enact a three-year, temporary summer-work program that would allow employers to hire teenagers at $2.50 an hour—well below the current legal-minimum wage of $3.35.

Supporters include many Republicans and conservative Democrats, along with the National Conference of Black Mayors and various business groups. The program, they estimate, would create some 400,000 jobs, mostly for minority youths among whom joblessness is about 45 percent.

Opposed are labor leaders and many Democrats who argue that employers would be tempted to hire youths at low wages to replace higher-paid adults. Black members of Congress and others reject the proposal as demeaning to minorities.

Although the administration vows to push the proposal—as it has every year since 1981—opponents appear to have the upper hand in both houses.

Reprinted from *U.S. News & World Report*, June 3, 1985. Copyright 1985, U.S. News & World Report, Inc.

Inflation

What is it that erodes the purchasing power of the dollar, acts as a hidden tax, and contributes to economic instability? Answer: Inflation. *Inflation* is a rise in the general price level (or the average level of prices) of all goods and services. The purchasing power of a unit of money (such as the dollar) varies inversely with the general price level. For example, if prices double, purchasing power decreases by one-half; if price halves, purchasing power doubles. Therefore, inflation is also a reduction in the purchasing power of a unit of money.

Does inflation mean that all prices rise? Clearly not. In almost any period of inflation, some prices rise, some are fairly constant, and some even fall.

However, the "average" level of prices—the *general price level*—rises.

Types of Inflation: Is Our Nation Inflation-Prone?

Different explanations for inflation have been given from time to time. Here are the more common types you are likely to encounter in the news media and should know something about. Note that some of them may be overlapping in their causes and effects.

Demand-Pull Inflation

The traditional type of inflation is known as *demand-pull inflation.* It takes place when total expenditures for goods are rising while the available quantity of goods is not growing fast enough to meet the demand. Goods may be in short supply because resources are already fully utilized or because production cannot be increased rapidly. As a result, the general level of prices begins to rise. This is the market's way of responding to a situation sometimes described as "too much money chasing too few goods."

Cost-Push (Market-Power) Inflation

A second type of inflation is *cost-push inflation.* It occurs when prices increase because factor payments to one or more groups of resource owners rise faster than productivity. Typical forms of cost-push inflation are "wage-push," "profit-push," and "commodity inflation."

Wage-Push Inflation This occurs when strong labor unions manage to force wage increases in excess of productivity gains. Unit costs of production are thereby raised, exerting pressure on sellers to increase prices in order to maintain profit margins.

Profit-Push Inflation This occurs when sellers try to increase profits by raising prices rather than by reducing costs through improved efficiency. Such efforts may not always be successful. Nevertheless, rising prices prompt workers and other factor owners to "catch up" by seeking higher resource payments. That increases unit costs of production and stimulates inflation.

Commodity Inflation   This occurs when prices of material inputs rise sufficiently to cause significant increases in costs of production. Firms are prompted to respond by raising the prices of finished goods. In the 1970s, for example, inflation in the U.S. and abroad was worsened by commodity inflation resulting from rising costs of energy and raw materials.

These types of cost-push inflation suggest the following:

> Cost-push inflation is usually attributable to "market power." This is the degree of discretion that those who control resources, such as unions or firms, have in setting wages and prices. Market power is generally stronger in prosperity periods because labor is in relatively short supply and consumers are less sensitive to price increases. Conversely, market power tends to be weaker in recession periods, for the opposite reasons. Because of the existence of market power, our society may frequently be vulnerable to some degree of cost-push inflation.

Inflations in our economy have resulted at various times from demand-pull as well as from cost-push factors. These forces have been at work in different degrees. This has led many observers to conclude that our nation is inflation-prone or that it has a built-in inflationary bias. Some of the implications of this will be examined shortly.

Who Loses from Inflation? Who Gains?

Does inflation impose a burden on all of us? Not necessarily. The effects of inflation are not distributed equally. Most people suffer from it, but others sometimes benefit.

To see why this is so, we must understand the difference between two kinds of income:

1. Nominal or Money Income   This is the amount of money received for work done.

2. Real Income   This is the purchasing power of nominal income as measured by the quantity of goods and services that it can buy.

Clearly, your nominal income may be quite different from your real income. The latter is determined not only by your nominal income but also by the prices of the things you purchase. In view of this, let us see how inflation can affect people in *real* terms.

If the rate of inflation were fairly steady, it would be easier for people to plan for it. They could do this by *anticipating* future increases in the average prices of goods and services. Then they could adjust their *present* earning, buying, borrowing, and lending activities in such ways as to offset the expected depreciation of the dollar. However, if they failed to forecast the rate of inflation correctly, they might inadvertently transfer some of their wealth to other groups in society.

As an illustration, suppose that you lend someone $100 for one year. If you expect the general price level to remain stable, and if you want to earn a real return (in terms of constant purchasing power) of 5 percent, you will charge 5 percent interest on the loan. Assume, however, that you expect the average level of prices to rise by 10 percent. In that case, you should charge about 15 percent interest on the loan. Of this, 5 percent represents a real return and 10 percent represents compensation for your loss in purchasing power due to inflation.

Suppose that a year elapses and the borrower pays you what is owed, but the rise in prices has been greater than you anticipated. Are you better or worse off? Obviously, the repaid loan plus interest has not provided full compensation for your decreased purchasing power. Hence, your change in real wealth is less than you anticipated. You have suffered a loss from inflation. The borrower, on the other hand, has repaid the loan in terms of less purchasing power than was originally borrowed. The

Economics in the News

What Is Hyperinflation?

The 100 Quintillion Note

The governments of certain countries, among them Argentina and Brazil, often turn out paper money as if it were confetti. The result is that their economies frequently experience annual inflationary rates of several hundred percent. That, as far as anyone is concerned, is hyperinflation.

But these are not the worst hyperinflations in history. That distinction belongs to the financial debacles that took place in Germany in the 1920s and in Hungary after World War II (1945).

Germany in 1923 suffered 4 *trillion* percent inflation. During that hectic period, Germans literally took their weekly wages home in wheelbarrows full of money. And the wheelbarrows were often worth more than all the currency inside.

Hungary holds the alltime inflation record. In 1946 that country suffered a 5 *quadrillion* percent inflation. It was brought on by the issuance of 100 quintillion pengo notes. That's 100 followed by 18 zeros.

Hungarian inflation currency. A 100 quintillion pengo note, 1946; highest denomination note issued in the history of currency. (100,000,000,000,000,000,000)

Courtesy: Chase Manhattan Bank, Museum of Monies of the World.

borrower has thus experienced an increase in wealth—a gain from inflation. On the whole, therefore, there has been a redistribution of wealth—in this case from you to the borrower—because of your failure to predict inflation correctly.

Conversely, if the rise in prices has been less than you anticipated, you are better off. You will experience an increase in wealth—a redistribution from the borrower to you. Can you explain why?

To generalize:

People who do not predict inflation correctly are unable to adjust their economic behavior to compensate for it. As a result, some people experience gains while others experience losses. *The net outcome is a redistribution of wealth between debtors and creditors.* The redistribution is not on the basis of income levels, number of dependents, or other socially acceptable economic criteria. Instead, *the redistribution is haphazard and inequitable in a manner unrelated to society's objectives.*

Measuring Inflation: The Declining Value of Money

Everyone is aware that many things cost more today than they did a few years ago. It is plain enough that the trend of prices has been upward. By how much? You can gain some idea from the graphs in Exhibit 6, showing important price indexes.

The Consumer Price Index (CPI) is an average of the prices of various goods and services commonly purchased by families in urban areas. Generally referred to as a "cost-of-living index," the CPI is published monthly by the Bureau of Labor Statistics of the U.S. Department of Labor.

The Producer Price Index (PPI) is an average of selected items priced in wholesale markets. The items whose prices go into the index include raw materials, semifinished products, and finished goods. The PPI, like the CPI, is also published monthly by the Department of Labor.

You have probably heard it said that the dollar today is worth only 60 cents, or 50 cents, or perhaps

Exhibit 6
Price Indexes (1967 = 100)

The Consumer Price Index and the Producer Price Index are prepared by the U.S. Department of Labor. They are the most widely used measures of inflationary price trends in our economy. Can you project the indexes to the year 2000? What are you assuming when you make such projections?

Technical Note: The vertical axis of this figure is scaled logarithmically. This facilitates comparison of relative (percentage) changes in the graphs. To understand why, look up the meaning of *logarithmic scale* in the Dictionary at the back of the book.

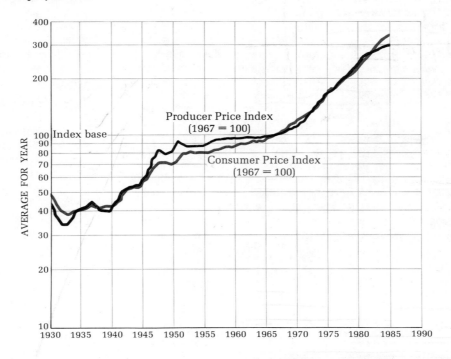

Source: U.S. Department of Labor.

even less. Such statements try to convey the idea that today's dollar buys only a fraction of what a dollar bought during some period in the past. What fraction? It depends on which past period you choose as a reference point. The decline in the purchasing power of the dollar is much greater during high inflationary years than during low ones.

The most widely used measure of the general price level is the Consumer Price Index. It tells you the average level of prices in a given year as a percentage of the average level of prices in some other year, called the "base year." For the base year, of course, the average is 100 percent of itself. In any given year, the average may be greater than, equal to, or less than 100 percent. Whichever it is will depend upon whether the average level of prices has risen, remained constant, or fallen in relation to the base year.

Economics in the News

From High Unemployment to a Labor Shortage?

Carey W. English and Maureen Walsh

How far can the unemployment rate drop before the country faces labor shortages, pressure for higher wages and a resurgence of inflation?

That point, termed "full" employment by economists, will be reached if the civilian unemployment rate drops into the 6 to 6.5 percent zone.

Economists generally consider 6 to 6.5 percent to be the nation's long-term, underlying jobless rate, below which it is difficult to reduce unemployment without causing inflationary pressures.

It is also the level at which every person who can reasonably be expected to hold a job has one, and only those with little education, training or work skills are jobless.

Changing Work Force

In the 1950s, a jobless rate between 4 and 4.5 percent was considered full employment. Over the years, economists say, this threshold has risen, mainly because of demographic shifts in the nation's work force.

The most significant of these involved the huge influx into the labor market of young people—the post-World War II "baby boom" generation—and women in general, both of whom typically have higher-than-average unemployment rates. Their rates are higher because they tend to leave and re-enter the labor force more frequently and change jobs more often than do adult men.

Experts also believe that unemployment benefits, while important to jobless workers, raise the unemployment rate associated with full employment. They do this by reducing the economic cost of the job search and encouraging workers to remain unemployed while seeking the best possible job offer.

Also contributing to a higher threshold is wage rigidity. A number of studies indicate that wages have become less flexible in the postwar period as workers resisted pay cuts more vigorously. As a result, employers faced with changing demands for their goods have tended to lay off workers instead of cutting costs by reducing wages.

These structural upheavals in the economy explain in large part why, since World War II, each major recession has tended to leave the U.S. with successively higher levels of unemployment during recoveries.

Inflation Fears

The big worry among experts is that, as labor markets tighten, employers will increase wages to compete for workers. With production bottlenecks occurring, prices will be bid up.

Thus, analysts say, 6 percent or lower unemployment puts the economy in danger of overheating.

Exhibit 7
Measuring the Value of the Dollar

(1) Year	(2) CPI	(3) Reciprocal		(4) Value of dollar
1 (base)	100	1 ÷ 1.00	=	$1.00
2	125	1 ÷ 1.25	=	0.80
3	87	1 ÷ 0.87	=	1.15

[handwritten: Deflation   More value for your Dollar]

Exhibit 7 illustrates this. Look at the hypothetical data shown in the first two columns. Suppose we arbitrarily select Year 1 as the base year. This means that the CPI for that year equals 100.

Note that the CPI in Year 2 was 125 percent of its value in Year 1. This tells you that the average level of prices was 25 percent higher in Year 2 than in the base year. In Year 3, the CPI was 87 percent of its value in Year 1. That is, the average level of prices was 13 percent lower in Year 3 than in the base year.

With the use of this information, the value or purchasing power of the dollar is calculated in the third

Exhibit 8
Tracking Inflation: Consumer Prices and the Value of Money

The Consumer Price Index (CPI) is an average of the prices of various goods and services commonly purchased by families in urban areas. The reciprocal of the CPI thus provides a measure of the value, or purchasing power, of the dollar.

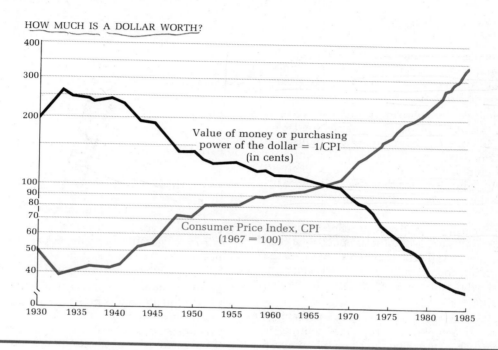

HOW MUCH IS A DOLLAR WORTH?

Value of money or purchasing power of the dollar = 1/CPI (in cents)

Consumer Price Index, CPI (1967 = 100)

column. You do this by expressing the CPI in decimal form and taking its reciprocal. (The reciprocal of a number is 1 divided by that number.) The answer for each year is given in the fourth column.

The actual CPI is shown in the back endpapers of this book. From these data, the linked performances of the CPI and the value of money are graphed in Exhibit 8.

Conclusion: The Need for Price Stability

The term "inflation" means rising prices. However, it is important to remember that not *all* prices rise at the same rate. Nor does the average price level rise at a steady pace. As a result, inflation tends to be erratic and incorrectly anticipated. Among those households that underestimate inflation, it creates more losers than winners. But even if households could anticipate inflation correctly, they would still lose wealth to the extent that they held money during periods of rising prices. Of course, most households do. Consequently:

Inflation results in inequities caused by haphazard redistributions of wealth.

As you will learn in later chapters, inflation also has adverse effects on the economy's efficiency and growth. For these reasons, much of macroeconomics is concerned with understanding the causes of inflation and with formulating policies for achieving price stability.

What You Have Learned

1. Mixed economies suffer from recurrent but nonperiodic fluctuations in economic activity known as business cycles. The four phases of such cycles are prosperity, recession, depression, and recovery.

2. Industries in the economy react to business cycles in different ways. Most durable-goods industries tend to be less competitive than nondurable-goods industries. Therefore, they experience relatively wide fluctuations in output and employment. The opposite is likely to occur in many nondurble-goods industries. In these industries, prices fluctuate more than output and employment.

3. The economy's health, or illness, is reflected by economic indicators. Hundreds of these are published each month by government and private sources. Many of the indicators are closely monitored by economists and business executives who are interested in interpreting and forecasting business activity.

4. The unemployment rate is expressed as a percentage of the labor force. Unemployment rates may continue to rise in future years because of (a) the changing composition of the labor force, (b) a rising level of minimum-wage rates, and (c) advances in technology.

5. Inflation is a rise in the general price level. Looked at another way, it is a reduction in the purchasing power of a unit of money. Inflations are commonly attributed to demand-pull or cost-push forces. In general, inflation tends to redistribute wealth haphazardly without regard to social goals. It also impairs a nation's efficiency and growth.

6. Many observers believe that virtually all mixed economies, including our own, have an "inflationary bias." This means they are inflation-prone. Therefore, a desirable social objective is not only to reduce inflation, but to make it less erratic. People would then be better able to adjust to inflation by altering their asset and liability holdings, thereby minimizing adverse redistributive effects.

Terms and Concepts to Review

Know these ✓

business cycles	inflation
seasonal fluctuations	trend
time series	general price level
labor force	demand-pull inflation
unemployment rate	cost-push inflation
frictional	Consumer Price Index
unemployment	Producer Price Index
cyclical unemployment	nominal income
structural	real income
unemployment	
employment ratio	
involuntary	
unemployment	

For Discussion

1. If business cycles were recurrent and periodic, would they be easily predictable? Why? What, precisely, would you be able to predict about them?

2. Suppose you were to compare two industries, automobiles and agricultural products, over the course of a business cycle. Which would be more stable with respect to (a) output and employment and (b) prices? Explain why.

3. It is customary to remove both the seasonal and long-term trend influences from time-series data before undertaking an analysis of cyclical forces. Although there are no unusual controversies concerning removal of the seasonal factor, there is considerable disagreement among economists over removal of the trend. Can you suggest why?

4. Can you explain how the interaction of changes in consumption and investment may cause business cycles?

5. What do you suppose are some of the chief difficulties in using leading indicators for forecasting purposes?

6. Is an increasing level of aggregate demand likely to cure the problems of cyclical unemployment and structural unemployment—without encouraging inflation? Explain.

7. Is it better to have full employment with mild inflation or moderate unemployment with no inflation? Explain.

8. "Because of the changing composition of the labor force, a single measure of full employment proves to be an inadequate goal." In view of this statement, what alternatives can you suggest? Discuss.

Economics in the News

Unemployment or Underemployment? They're Not the Same

If you get a college degree and end up working as an office clerk, are you unemployed? The answer, of course, is no. However, you may be "underemployed."

Underemployment (also called disguised employment) is a condition that exists when employed resources are not being used in their most efficient ways. This happens when individuals are employed below their training or capabilities.

Underemployment is an interesting problem that raises some thought-provoking questions. For example:

1. If a scientist who is unable to find work in the field of science takes a job as a taxi driver, should his or her unused scientific skills be counted as unemployed? If so, then the taxi-driving skills should not be counted as employed. Otherwise, the same individual would be counted as two people—an unemployed scientist and an employed taxi driver.

2. Is a taxi-driving scientist an economic loss to society? Apparently not—from a *social* viewpoint. The fact that the scientist was able to get a job as a taxi driver rather than as a scientist indicates that society valued the services of an additional taxi driver more highly than the services of an additional scientist.

In view of this, perhaps the taxi-driving scientist should not be classified as underemployed. What do you think?

show, with supply and demand curves, how minimum-wage legislation results in unemployment? What market solution can you suggest to increase employment among low-skilled members of the labor force?

11. "Reduce working hours. Spread the work. That's the way to solve the unemployment problem." So say many critics, union leaders, and social reformers. They argue for a reduction in working time—with *no loss of pay*—as a cure for unemployment. Do you agree with them?

12. Examine the news article "Unemployment or Underemployment? They're Not the Same." What differences do you see between unemployment and underemployment?

9. It is often said that our economy has a built-in inflationary bias and is inflation-prone. Can you give reasons to account for this statement?

10. Minimum-wage legislation, despite its good intention, has been called "the most racially discriminating law on the books." Can you explain why? Can you

Chapter 7

The Self-Correcting Economy: Introduction to Classical Economics

Learning Guide

Watch for answers to these important questions

What is classical economics? How do classical economists explain the operation of our economic system?

Why is the flexibility of prices and wages central to classical economics? Can a model be developed to explain the relationships between prices and the levels of output and employment?

What conclusions does classical economics provide concerning the effects of government economic policies?

In our mixed economy, the makers of economic policies face an awesome task. They must try to maintain a high level of employment. At the same time, they must try to restrain upward pressures on prices. These are the problems of unemployment and inflation. In a broader sense, as you already know, they are the fundamental problems of efficiency and stability. Both are at the heart of modern macroeconomics.

How do economists view these problems? You can best appreciate the answer by examining the classical foundations of modern macroeconomics. These, as you have already learned, were built by Adam Smith and refined by his followers. Their ideas, extending from the late eighteenth century to the present, constitute what is known as "classical economics." As you will see, classical economics includes some microeconomic as well as macroeconomic principles.

Essentials of the Classical Theory

In the early nineteenth century, a French economist, Jean Baptiste Say, wrote:

. . . a product is no sooner created than it, from that instant, offers a market for other products to the full extent of its own value . . . Thus, the mere circumstance of the creation of one product immediately opens a market for other products.

This conclusion has come to be known as *Say's Law.* But the idea has been expressed more pointedly by David Ricardo, a British contemporary of Say, an advisor to Parliament, and a great pioneer in economic thought:

supply creates its own demand.

No man produces but with a view to consume or sell, and he never sells but with an intention to purchase some other commodity which may be immediately useful to him or which may contribute to future production. By producing, then, he necessarily becomes either the consumer of his own goods, or the purchaser and consumer of the goods of some other person.

Say's Law—whether as originally expressed by Say or as restated by Ricardo—amounts to saying that *supply creates its own demand.* This means that the income a person receives from production is spent to purchase goods produced by others. For the economy as a whole, therefore, total income equals total production, or what is the same thing, aggregate expenditure equals aggregate output. Consequently, any addition to output generates an equal addition to income, which in turn is spent on the added output.

$AD = AS$

It follows from Say's Law that firms will always find it profitable to hire unemployed resources up to the point of full employment. This is true provided that the owners of unemployed resources are willing to be paid no more than their physical productivities justify. If this condition is granted, there can be no prolonged period of unemployment—for two reasons:

— Workers and other resource suppliers will be receiving what they are worth, as measured by the value of their contribution to production.

— The additional income earned from increased production will be spent on purchasing the additional output.

The economy, therefore, is self-correcting.

This belief was central to classical economic thought of the nineteenth and early twentieth centuries. It is a belief that is widely held with varying degrees of conviction today. In view of this, what does the classical model really tell us? What are its implications for our economic system?

The classical model assumes the operation of a free-enterprise, highly competitive economic system. This is a system in which there are many buyers and sellers, both in product markets and in resource markets. It is also a system in which all prices are flexible so that they can quickly adjust upward or downward to changing supplies and demands in the marketplace. In this type of economic system, the product and resource markets will *automatically* adjust to full-employment levels as if guided by an "invisible hand." This is because *aggregate expenditure equals aggregate income or output.* Let us examine this idea more closely.

$GNP = GNI$ Sum

Aggregate Expenditure = Aggregate Income or Output

AGGREGATE DEMAND = Aggregate Supply

You have learned that an economy's aggregate output (GNP) equals its aggregate income (GNI). But the classicists argued that the purpose of earning income is to spend it on output. Hence, the level of aggregate expenditure on all goods and services *always* equals the level of aggregate income or output.

This does not mean that oversupply of some particular items cannot occur. Unprofitable overproduction of specific commodities can and does occur when business managers misjudge the markets for their goods. But these errors are temporary and are corrected as entrepreneurs shift resources out of production of less profitable commodities into production of more profitable ones. What is impossible, according to the classical view, is general overproduction, or a deficiency in *aggregate expenditure.*

But what if households choose to *save* a portion of their income—that is, not to spend it all on goods and services? Will these savings represent a withdrawal or "leakage" of funds from the economy's circular flow of income and expenditure? Will aggregate expenditure then fall below aggregate income or output, resulting in excess production, increasing unemployment, and decreasing incomes? The classical economists' answer is no, because *all savings by households are invested by businesses.* Let us see why.

All Savings Are Invested

Say's Law tells us that total spending will always be high enough to maintain full employment. The reason, according to the classicists, is not hard to see. If some people save part of their income, there will always be businesses that will borrow those savings and pay a price for them called **interest.** The businesses will invest this borrowed money in capital goods in order to carry on profitable produc-

tion. Saving by households, therefore, leads directly to spending by businesses on capital or investment goods. Thus, aggregate income is always spent. Part of it is spent by households for consumption and part of it is spent by businesses for investment.

What mechanism ensures that all money saved is invested at full employment? The classicists' answer is interest, which they view as a reward for saving. That is, interest is a price that businesses pay households to persuade them to consume less in the present so that they can consume more at a later date. Current interest rates are determined in the economy's financial markets, collectively called the "loanable funds" market. In this market, households' supply of savings interacts with businesses' demand for them.

This is illustrated in Figure (a) of Exhibit 1. Note that the quantity of loanable funds is measured on

Exhibit 1
Markets in the Classical Theory of Income and Employment: Some Microeconomic Foundations

The classical model rests on certain microeconomic foundations. It assumes that all markets are competitive and all resources mobile. Therefore, prices and quantities are flexible. That is, they adjust automatically to their full-employment equilibrium levels

through the free play of market forces. (You should recall from your study of supply and demand that the intersection of the S and D curves determines the equilibrium price and quantity.)

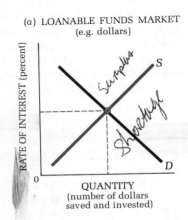

(a) LOANABLE FUNDS MARKET
(e.g. dollars)

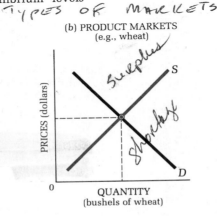

(b) PRODUCT MARKETS
(e.g., wheat)

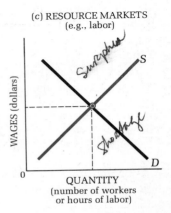

(c) RESOURCE MARKETS
(e.g., labor)

Everything adjusts to full employment

the horizontal axis and the interest rate (which is always expressed as a percentage) is measured on the vertical. The model is based on the classical assumption that no household will save (and thereby forgo the pleasure of spending) unless it is offered interest in return. Also, no business will borrow (and thereby pay interest) unless it plans to invest. Therefore, a flexible interest rate assures that every dollar saved by households will be borrowed and invested by businesses. This *automatically* ensures the maintenance of a full-employment level of aggregate spending.

Prices and Wages Are Flexible

But suppose some unemployment *did* develop, causing a decline in aggregate income or purchasing power. Would such a situation be more than temporary? The classicists answered no, because *prices and wages are flexible*. In classical theory, prices in all markets—the loanable funds market, the product markets, and the resource markets—are assumed to move freely. Therefore, they *automatically* adjust to their individual full-employment equilibrium levels.

These ideas are shown in all three diagrams of Exhibit 1:

1. As you can see, if the price in any of the three markets is below its particular equilibrium level, the quantity demanded will exceed the quantity supplied. Competition among buyers (demanders) in that market will therefore drive the price up.

2. If the price in any market is above its equilibrium level, the quantity supplied will exceed the quantity demanded. Competition between sellers (suppliers) in that market will therefore drive the price down.

3. At the equilibrium price in each market, the quantity that sellers want to sell is equal to the quantity that buyers want to buy. At these prices, *there are no shortages and no surpluses* in any of the product, resource, or loanable funds markets. Accordingly, there must be full employment and full production throughout the economy.

Classical Conclusion: Capitalism Is a Self-Correcting Economic System

To Full Employment

In the classical economists' view it follows that a capitalistic economic system will tend *automatically* toward its full- or natural-employment level through the free operation of the price system. (You will recall from the previous chapter that *full employment* and *natural employment* mean the same thing.) Therefore, the functions of government, as Adam Smith emphasized, should be limited to national defense, the administration of justice, the facilitation of commerce, and the provision of certain public works. Adherence to such a policy would establish laissez-faire (freedom from government intervention) as the watchword of capitalism. It would place government in an economically neutral position, leaving the economy to allocate its resources optimally as if guided by an "invisible hand." To summarize:

Classical economics emphasizes people's self-interest and the operation of universal economic laws. These tend automatically to guide the economy toward full-employment or natural-employment equilibrium if the government adheres to a policy of laissez-faire or non-interventionism. Among the chief early proponents of classical economics were Adam Smith (1723–1790), Jean Baptiste Say (1767–1832), and David Ricardo (1772–1823).

The Income-Price Model

The foregoing macroeconomic concepts of aggregate income and the level of employment made use of some microeconomic ideas. These include the behavior of the particular markets shown in Exhibit 1 and an explanation of the forces at work in those markets to establish equilibrium.

Because we are concerned with macroeconomics, it is useful to formulate these ideas in terms of a more "general" model. Such a model, which may be called an *income-price model*, relates the economy's real aggregate output, GNP, to the average

Leaders in Economics

Dictionaire de l'Economie Politique, Paris

Adam Smith

Dictionaire de l'Economie Politique, Paris

Jean Baptiste Say (1767 – 1832)

Brown Brothers

Thomas Malthus (1766 – 1834)

The Classical Economists: Adam Smith's "Children"

"I am a beau only to my books," remarked Adam Smith. Little did the shy, absent-minded scholar suspect that, though he would never marry and (as far as history knows) never have any love affairs, his offspring would include numerous "children" and "grandchildren."

Smith's masterwork, *The Wealth of Nations* (1776), marked the beginning of *classical economics*. This body of thought dominated the Western world during the nineteenth and early twentieth centuries. Classical economists typically emphasized people's self-interest and the operation of universal economic laws. These laws tend automatically to guide the economy toward full-employment equilibrium if the government adheres to a policy of laissez-faire.

During the nineteenth century these ideas, initiated by Adam Smith, were refined and expanded by many of his "children." Four are especially worthy of mention because of their prominence.

Jean Baptiste Say

"Supply creates its own demand." This was the famous Law of Markets expounded by the French economist Jean Baptiste Say in his *Treatise on Political Economy* (1803). This work was the first popular and systematic presentation of Adam Smith's ideas. As a result, it established Say as one of the leading economists of the early nineteenth century.

Say's Law became central to classical economic thinking. In modern language the Law meant that the level of aggregate output (GNP) always equaled the level of aggregate income (*GNI*). This income enabled society to buy the output produced. Therefore, general overproduction of goods (due to a deficiency in aggregate spending) was impossible.

But what if businesses misjudged the markets for their goods? In that case, the classicists contended, unprofitable overproduction of specific commodities could and would occur. But such errors would be temporary and would be corrected as entrepreneurs strove to fulfill consumers' preferences by shifting resources out of the production of unprofitable goods and into the production of profitable ones.

Thomas Malthus

As the eighteenth century drew to a close, England found itself facing grave social problems. Among them were widespread poverty, the growth of urban slums, and severe unemployment. These social problems resulted from economic dislocations caused by years of war with France. In addition, the factory system of production had begun and was displacing numerous workers.

It fell to a hitherto unknown English clergyman, Thomas Robert Malthus, to explain these problems. In his famous *Essay on Population* (1803), he expounded the belief that population tended to outrun the food supply. The result would be bare subsistence for the laboring class.

Historical Pictures Service

David Ricardo (1722–1823)

Brown Brothers

John Stuart Mill (1806–1873)

This prophecy has become a stark reality in many of the overcrowded poor countries of the world.

Malthus also contributed significantly to economic thought, anticipating certain concepts that became important in twentieth-century thinking. In his *Principles of Political Economy* (1820), he developed the concept of "effective demand," which he defined as the level of demand necessary to maintain full production. If effective demand fell short, he said, overproduction would result. Malthus thus disagreed with Say on the Law of Markets.

David Ricardo

Generally considered to be the greatest of the classical economists, David Ricardo was the first to view the economy as an analytical model. That is, he saw the economic system as an elaborate mechanism with interrelated parts. His task was to study the system and to discover the laws that determine its behavior. In so doing, Ricardo formulated

theories of value, wages, rent, and profit. These theories, although not entirely original, were for the first time stated completely, authoritatively, and systematically. Portions of them became the basis of many subsequent writings by later scholars. Some of Ricardo's ideas still remain pillars of economics.

Ricardo, an English businessman rather than an academician, wrote a number of brilliant papers. His ideas were largely incorporated in his work *Principles of Political Economy and Taxation* (1817). The book was an immediate success, and it attracted many disciples. As a result, Ricardo's influence became pervasive and lasting. Indeed, Ricardian economics became a synonym for classical political economy (or "classical economics," as we call it today). Fifty years were to pass before that influence waned.

Like his predecessors, Ricardo was mainly concerned with the forces that determine the production of an economy's wealth and its distribution among the various classes of so-

ciety. He also made major policy recommendations to Parliament concerning the dominant social and economic problems of his day.

John Stuart Mill

Known equally well as a political philosopher and as an economist, the Englishman John Stuart Mill was the last of the major "mainstream" classical economists. His great two-volume treatise *Principles of Political Economy* (1848) was a masterful synthesis of classical ideas. The book became a standard text in economics for several decades. Numerous students in Europe and America learned about economics from this basic work. So, too, did a number of American presidents—including Abraham Lincoln—although they did not always correctly apply the principles they learned.

Mill's major objective was economic reform. Although he believed in laissez-faire, he went beyond the "natural law of political economy." He did so by advocating worker education, democratic producer cooperatives, taxation of unearned gains from land, redistribution of wealth, shorter working days, improvements in working conditions, and government control of monopoly. These measures, Mill felt, would ensure workers the benefits of their contributions to production without violating the "immortal principles" of economics.

It is easy to see why contemporaries of Mill often labeled him a socialist. But he believed too strongly in individual freedom to advocate major government involvement in the economy. By today's standards, Mill probably would be classified as a moderate conservative.

price level measured by a price index. The relationship consists of two curves—an aggregate demand curve and an aggregate supply curve. Because of this, the income-price model may also be called an aggregate demand/aggregate supply model.

(INCOME - PRICE Model)

The Aggregate Demand Curve

The first step in developing an income-price model is to formulate an *aggregate demand* (AD) curve. This is done in Exhibit 2. Note that real GNP is

measured on the horizontal axis. The average price level, expressed as a price index, is measured on the vertical.

How is the AD curve interpreted? It discloses the *total value of real aggregate output that all sectors of the economy are willing to purchase at various average price levels*. As you can see, the curve is downward sloping. This tells you that the public will spend more on real output at a lower average price level than at a higher one. There are two reasons:

1. **Real-Balance Effect** At any given time the public is holding a certain amount of cash balances with which to buy goods and services. The real value or purchasing power of these balances varies inversely with the average price level. That is, at lower prices people's cash balances can buy more; at higher prices their cash balances can buy less. Therefore, changes in the average price level affect people's *real* cash balances, and hence total spending. This idea is called the ***real-balance effect***. (It is also sometimes called the ***Pigou effect,*** after Arthur Pigou, an early twentieth century British economist who formulated the concept.)

2. **Interest-Rate Effect** The public borrows money to finance its purchases of houses, cars, factories, machines, and many other goods. Interest rates, which may be viewed as the costs of borrowing money, tend to vary directly with the average price level. Two examples illustrate the reasons for this:

   – When prices decline, people's *real* cash balances increase. This reduces the public's demand for credit—and therefore interest rates. Spending thus becomes less costly, thereby increasing the amount of consumption and investment demand by households and businesses.

   – When prices rise, the opposite occurs. People's *real* cash balances decline, so the public borrows more funds in order to finance purchases. As a result, the demand for credit increases, causing interest rates to rise. Spending thus becomes more costly, thereby decreasing the amount of consumption and investment demand by households and businesses.

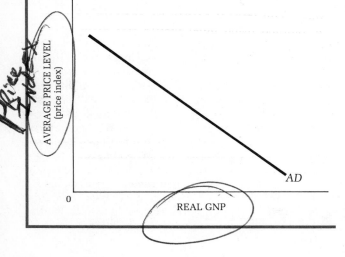

Exhibit 2
The Aggregate Demand Curve

The aggregate demand (AD) curve is downward-sloping. This means that the public will spend more on real GNP at a lower average price level than at a higher one. The reason for this inverse relation is explained by two factors:

Real-Balance Effect At lower average prices, the purchasing power or *real* value of people's cash balances is greater.   INVERSE RELATIONSHIP

Interest-Rate Effect When prices decline, interest rates tend to decline too, thereby stimulating total spending.   DIRECT RELATIONSHIP

The ways in which changes in the price level affect interest rates, which in turn affect total spending, is called the **interest-rate effect.** (It is also sometimes called the **Keynes effect,** after John Maynard Keynes, a distinguished British economist of the 1920s and 1930s.)

Like most relationships in economics, these assume that all other things remain the same. In the case of both the real-balance and the interest-rate effects, one of the most important of the "all other things" is the public's cash balances. That is, both effects assume that the amount of money held by the public—the supply of money in the economy—remains constant.

The Aggregate Supply Curve

An aggregate demand curve comprises only half of an income-price model. The other half consists of an **aggregate supply** (AS) curve. This is illustrated in Exhibit 3. The curve shows the amount of real aggregate output, that is, real GNP, that will be made available at various average price levels.

You cannot help but notice that the curve is a vertical line. It characterizes two propositions of classical economics that you have already learned:

1. The economy operates at the full- or natural-employment level. The volume of output produced at this level is the economy's potential output, also called **potential real GNP.**

2. The average price level is flexible. Output is independent of prices, as indicated by the fact that the same potential real GNP is produced at a relatively low price level as at a relatively high one.

Conclusion: Today's Classical Views

The aggregate demand and the aggregate supply curves can now be graphed on the same chart. This is done in Exhibit 4. As you can see, the intersection of the two curves determines an equilibrium full- or natural-employment level of real GNP and a corresponding equilibrium average-price level at P.

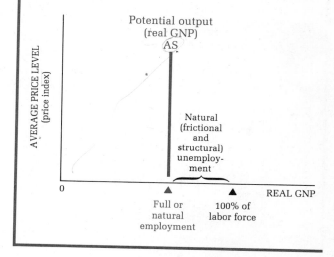

Exhibit 3
The Aggregate Supply Curve

In classical theory, the aggregate supply curve is a vertical line at the full- or natural-employment level. This is because prices and wages are flexible, adjusting freely to changes in one another. Therefore, firms produce the same potential real GNP at higher price levels as at lower ones.

Suppose aggregate demand should now increase from AD to AD'. This might happen, for example, if the amount of money in the economy were increased, leaving people with larger cash balances to spend. The impact would be entirely on prices. The average price level would rise from P to P' without having any effect on output and employment.

The reverse, of course, would occur if the amount of money in the economy were decreased. People would have smaller cash balances available to spend, so the aggregate demand curve would decrease. The average price level would thus decline without affecting output and employment.

What does this imply with respect to the classical ideas expressed earlier? Modern classicists, like their early predecessors, believe that the economy is self-correcting. This means that, in terms of the

SKIP

Exhibit 4
Aggregate Demand and Aggregate Supply

Classicists believe that the aggregate supply curve is a
vertical line at the potential output level.   Therefore,
any change in aggregate demand, such as a change from
AD to AD', causes the average price level to change
from P to P', without affecting production and employment. In more general terms, *classical theory contends
that the price level fluctuates while the full-employment level of real output tends to remain stable.*

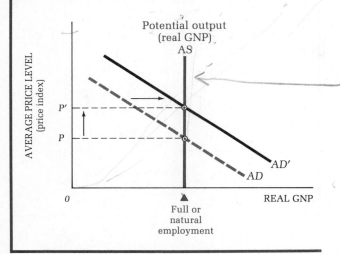

Does this mean that government should do nothing about trying to cure the ills of unemployment
and inflation?   There is considerable disagreement
on this question.   As you will learn in the next several chapters, it is at the heart of modern macroeconomics.

What You Have Learned

1. Classical economics is a body of ideas that began with
Adam Smith.   Although these ideas have undergone
much refinement and extension, the essence of classical
macroeconomics is the belief that *the economy is self-correcting.*

2. A fundamental assumption of classical economics is
that prices and wages are flexible.   The full-employment
level of real output tends to remain stable while the average price level fluctuates in response to changing market
conditions.

3. Because classicists believe that the economy is self-
correcting, they contend that government policies aimed
at stimulating employment or curbing inflation may actually do more harm than good.   Such policies, they contend, can disrupt the economy, impeding its "natural"
tendency to achieve efficiency, stability, and a steady rate
of growth.

income-price model, *output and employment are
always moving toward their natural level while
prices are adjusting quickly to changing market
conditions.*   In other words, aggregate demand and
aggregate supply are always tending toward equality at the economy's potential-real-GNP level.

This analysis has important implications for government policy makers:

Today's classical economists believe that deliberate
government policies designed to stimulate employment or to hold down prices tend to impede rather than
facilitate the economy's self-correcting adjustment
process.   Modern classicists conclude, therefore, that
such policies are likely to reduce rather than improve
the economy's efficiency, stability, and rate of economic growth.

Terms and Concepts to Review

Say's Law
interest
full (or natural)
   employment
aggregate demand

real-balance effect
interest-rate effect
aggregate supply
potential real GNP

For Discussion

1. Does Say's Law apply to *individual* goods?   Explain.

2. Why do people save?   Why do businesses invest?

3. "During a recession, a firm will probably increase its
sales if it cuts its prices, and it will reduce its costs if it cuts
its wages.   It follows that the whole economy will be better off if all firms do this."   True or false?   Comment.

4. Review the definition of aggregate demand. Assuming that all other things remain the same, how would each of the following affect (shift) the curve:
(a) Increase in household-sector spending
(b) Reduction in personal income taxes
(c) Decrease in interest rates
(d) Decrease in business-sector investment spending

5. How would your answers to question 5 affect the average price level?

6. Classical economists believe that *markets clear* very quickly. What do you think this means?

7. If the aggregate supply curve were upward sloping but not vertical, would this affect the classical theory? Explain.

8. In reality, is it possible for both output and employment to deviate from their natural levels? What does this suggest about the slope of the aggregate supply curve?

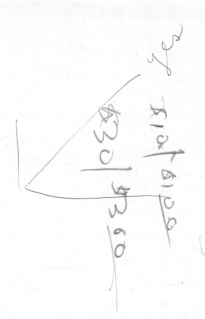

Chapter 8

What Causes Unemployment? Introduction to Keynesian Economics

Learning Guide

Watch for answers to these important questions

Can our mixed economy achieve and maintain economic efficiency, that is, *full employment* of resources?

What happened during the 1930s to change the thinking of most economists? How did developments since then contribute to the formulation of new ideas for studying today's economic problems?

In modern macroeconomics, what basic variables are used for analyzing the central problems of efficiency, stability, and growth? What are the relationships between these variables?

With perfectly free competition . . . there will always be a strong tendency toward full employment. The implication is that such unemployment as exists at any time is due wholly to the fact that frictional resistances (caused by monopolistic unions and firms maintaining rigid wages and prices) prevent the appropriate wage and price adjustments from being made instantaneously.

So wrote the English classical economist Arthur C. Pigou, in a book entitled *The Theory of Unemployment* (1933). Pigou was interpreting economic conditions of the 1930s — a decade in which the world was caught in the throes of a deep depression. Commonly referred to as the Great Depression, it was the longest and most painful economic setback of modern history.

For example, at the bottom of the business cycle in 1933, unemployment in the United States reached almost 13 million, approximately 25 percent of the labor force. For the remainder of the decade, it never dropped below 8 million, or 14 percent of the labor force. Comparable rates of unemployment existed in the United Kingdom and other European countries during this period.

Such severe unemployment was obviously contrary to classical thinking. As a result, many economists were inclined to explain the situation away by saying that it was the "world" and not the theory that was at fault. A flexible wage and price policy, Pigou and other classical economists contended, "would abolish fluctuations of employment entirely." In America, many orthodox economists added the proviso that the government under President Franklin Delano Roosevelt's administration should also stop interfering with the free operation of the markets through its extensive regulatory legislation and activities.

In response to this widespread view, and to Pigou's book in particular, an eminent British scholar named John Maynard Keynes (pronounced "canes") stepped into the picture. In 1936 he published a treatise entitled *The General Theory of Employment, Interest and Money.* In this landmark book, Keynes strongly criticized the classical theory and formulated a theory of his own. This new theory soon revolutionized economic thinking and became a foundation for the study of macroeconomics.

Much of modern macroeconomic theory is rooted in the work done by Keynes. In addition, a good deal of non-Keynesian thinking has been integrated into today's macroeconomics. As a result, many controversial economic issues you read and hear about — including taxes, inflation, unemployment, interest rates, and so forth — are analyzed within the framework of modern macroeconomic theory.

The remainder of this chapter deals with the basic macroeconomic relationships that Keynes and later economists developed. Subsequent chapters will bring the relationships together and build upon them with certain non-Keynesian ideas. The result will be a comprehensive view of macroeconomics as it exists today.

Essentials of the Keynesian Theory

How does Keynesian macroeconomic theory contrast with the classical theory? We may answer by formulating several propositions showing how Keynes responded to the classicists' arguments.

Aggregate Expenditure May Not Equal Full-Employment Aggregate Income

Keynesian theory rejects the classical notion that aggregate expenditure always equals full-employment aggregate income. Nor does Keynesian theory accept the contention that the economic system automatically tends towards its full-employment equilibrium level. Indeed, Keynesian theory demonstrates that the economic system may be in equilibrium at *less* than full employment and *may remain so indefinitely.*

Changes in aggregate expenditure play a critical role in Keynesian theory. An economy may be operating at a level equal to or below full employment. If the economy experiences a drop in aggregate expenditure, there will be a consequent decline in real output and resource use. If the economy experiences an increase in aggregate expenditure, there will be a consequent rise in real output and resource use. And if aggregate expenditure continues to increase above full-employment levels, the result will be rising prices without any corresponding increase in real output and resource use.

Savers and Investors Are Different People with Different Motivations

An important feature of the Keynesian theory concerns the roles of saving and investment.

Keynes pointed out that, in a primitive economy, saving and investing are undertaken largely by the same groups for the same reasons. But in an advanced economy, *saving and investing are undertaken by different groups for different reasons.*

In our own economy, for example, households such as yours and mine may save for any of several reasons. Among them: to purchase a new car, to finance an education, to make a down payment on a house, or to pay for a vacation. Households may also save to provide for future security, to amass an estate that can be passed on to future generations, or to buy stocks and bonds for income or future profit.

And, of course, many households may save simply to accumulate funds without a specific purpose in mind.

Business firms save when they retain part of their net profits instead of distributing them to stockholders. Their reasons for saving, however, are different from those of households. Businesses usually save in order to invest in plant, equipment, and inventories; they may also borrow for the same purposes. In any case, they invest primarily on the basis of the rate of profit they anticipate.

Savers and investors, in other words, are different people with different motivations. Most of the economy's saving is done by households, whereas its investment is done primarily by businesses on the basis of profit expectations. The amount businesses want to invest fluctuates widely from year to year and is not likely to equal the amount households want to save. The interest rate, therefore, is not a mechanism that brings about the equality of saving and investment at full employment, as the classicists assumed.

Prices and Wages Are Not Flexible

Do prices and wages exhibit the flexibility the classicists assumed? Keynes's answer was no. Our economy is characterized by big unions and big businesses, and there is great resistance to reductions in prices and wages. We often hear of prices and wages going up, but we do not often hear of them going down.

Nevertheless, let us assume for the moment that wages and prices are flexible and that the fall in wages during a period of unemployment is greater than the fall in prices. This is what the classical economists postulated. If the wage decreases (relative to prices) are experienced by one firm only, its profits will increase and it will be encouraged to expand its production and employment. But if wage decreases (in relation to prices) are experienced by *all* firms in the economy, **real wages** (that is, money wages relative to the general price level) or general purchasing power will decline. The result is likely to be a further reduction in output and employment instead of the reverse.

To summarize:

A reduction in *real* wages within a single firm is not likely to affect the overall demand for that firm's product. However, it cannot be assumed that a general reduction in *real* wages of *all* workers throughout the economy will have no effect on aggregate demand.

Keynesian Conclusion: Laissez-Faire Cannot Ensure Full Employment

In contrast to the classicists, Keynes put forward these ideas:

A modern capitalistic economy is not self-correcting. It provides no *automatic* tendency toward full employment. The levels of aggregate output and employment are determined by the level of aggregate expenditure, and there is no assurance that aggregate expenditure will always equal full-employment aggregate income. As aggregate expenditure increases, so do aggregate output and employment—up to the level of full employment.

Many economists since Keynes have subscribed to these beliefs. In view of this, what does the Keynesian theory say about the nature of **aggregate expenditure?** This, as you will see, consists of the sum of desired or *planned* spending that will be undertaken at each aggregate-income level by all sectors of the economy.

Consumption Expenditure

The household sector spends its income on consumer goods and services. Such spending, called simply **consumption,** is by far the largest component of aggregate expenditure. What factors determine consumption?

Take your own case. What determines the amount your family spends on goods and services? You can probably think of many factors. First and foremost is your family's disposable income—the amount it has left after paying personal taxes.

Factors affecting family consumption expenditure

The situation is much the same with other families. Disposable income is usually the single most important factor affecting a family's consumption expenditures. Other conditions, such as the family's previous income levels, its expectations of future income, its expectations of future prices, the size of the family, and the ages of its members, will also have some influence.

The Propensity to Consume

No two families spend their incomes in exactly the same way. However, the relation between a family's disposable income and its consumption expenditures can be illustrated by the schedule in the first two columns of Exhibit 1. Observe from the subtitle of the table that *prices are assumed constant*. This enables you to compare the family's spending with its real (rather than nominal) income. The difference between disposable income and consumption is shown in column (3). Notice that, as disposable income increases, consumption increases and so does saving.

The consumption and saving data are graphed in Exhibit 2. Let us consider the upper figure first. Note that consumption expenditures are measured on the vertical axis and disposable income on the

Exhibit 1

A Family's Consumption and Saving Schedule
(annual data in constant dollars, i.e., prices are assumed constant)

As disposable income increases, so do savings and consumption

This table illustrates the relationship between consumption and income. The figures show that, as the family's disposable income increases, the amount it spends on consumption and the amount it saves also increase. The meanings of the various columns are explained in the text.

(1) Disposable income (after taxes), DI	(2) Consumption, C	(3) Saving, S (1)−(2)	(4) Average propensity to consume, APC (2)÷(1)	(5) Average propensity to save, APS (3)÷(1)	(6) Marginal propensity to consume, MPC Change in (2) / Change in (1)	(7) Marginal propensity to save, MPS Change in (3) / Change in (1)
$ 8,000	$ 9,200	−$1,200	1.15	−0.15		
10,000	10,600	− 600	1.06	−0.06	0.70	0.30
12,000	12,000	0	1.00	0.00	0.70	0.30
14,000	13,400	600	0.96	0.04	0.70	0.30
16,000	14,800	1,200	0.93	0.07	0.70	0.30
18,000	16,200	1,800	0.90	0.10	0.70	0.30
20,000	17,600	2,400	0.88	0.12	0.70	0.30
22,000	19,000	3,000	0.86	0.14	0.70	0.30
24,000	20,400	3,600	0.85	0.15	0.70	0.30

Exhibit 2
A Family's Consumption and Saving in Relation to Income
(annual data in constant dollars)

The vertical distances show how much will be consumed and saved at each income level, according to the figures in Exhibit 1. For example, at an income of $22,000, the amount spent on consumption is $19,000 and the amount saved is $3,000.

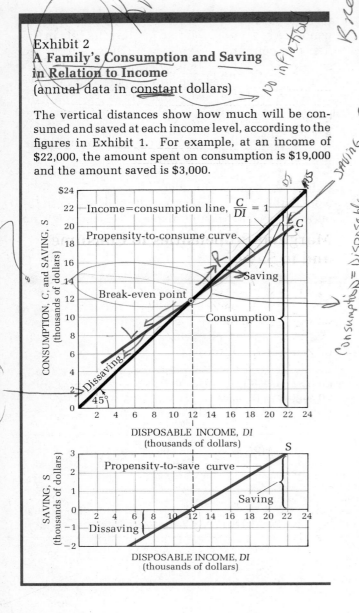

DISPOSABLE INCOME, *DI*
(thousands of dollars)

DISPOSABLE INCOME, *DI*
(thousands of dollars)

horizontal. Observe also that both axes are drawn to the same scale. Therefore, the 45-degree diagonal is a line along which consumption *C* is 100 percent of disposable income *DI*. That is, the ratio $C/DI = 1$.

The consumption curve *C* is the graph of the data in columns (1) and (2) of the table. The intersection

of this curve with the diagonal line is the "break-even point." This is the point at which a family's consumption exactly equals its disposable income. At this level the family is just getting by, neither borrowing nor saving.

To the right of the break-even point, the family is consuming less than its income. The vertical distance between the consumption line and the diagonal represents *saving*. To the left of the break-even point the family is consuming more than its disposable income. The difference is called *dissaving*. How does a family dissave or live beyond its means? Either by spending its previous savings, by borrowing, or by receiving gifts from others (that is, by being subsidized).

Here are some important ideas to remember:

The level of consumption depends on the level of income (that is, disposable income). As income increases, consumption increases, but not as fast as income. This relation between consumption and income is called the *propensity to consume,* or the *consumption function.* The word "function" is used here in its mathematical sense. It means a quantity whose value depends on the value of another quantity. (For example, we say that the amount of consumption depends on, or is a function of, the level of income.)

Note that the consumption curve *C* is the family's propensity-to-consume curve. It assumes that, apart from income, *all other factors that may affect consumption remain constant.* What are these "all other" factors? Among those consumption determinants mentioned above, the family's previous income levels, its expectations of future income, and its expectations of future prices, are the most important. This is because these factors are the ones that change most often in the relative short run.

The Propensity to Save

You know that saving is the difference between income and consumption. You also know that consumption depends on income. Therefore, you may correctly conclude that saving depends on income.

(Keep in mind that the term "income" as used here means *disposable income*.)

Let us look again at the table in Exhibit 1. The data on saving in column (3), taken together with the data in column (1), are shown in the graph in the lower panel of Exhibit 2. Here, disposable income is again measured on the horizontal axis, but saving alone is now scaled vertically. The saving curve S depicts the vertical differences between the diagonal line and the consumption curve in the upper chart. As you can see:

The level of saving depends on the level of income. This relation between saving and income is called the *propensity to save,* or the *saving function.*

Thus, the saving curve S is the propensity-to-save-curve.

Average Propensities to Consume and to Save

What will the family's *average* consumption be? What will be its *average* amount of saving? The answers are given in columns (4) and (5) of Exhibit 1.

The *average propensity to consume* (APC) is simply the ratio of consumption to income:

$$APC = \frac{consumption}{income}$$

The APC tells you the proportion of each income level that the family will spend on consumption. Similarly, the *average propensity to save* (APS) is the ratio of saving to income. The APS tells you the proportion of each income level that the family will save:

$$APS = \frac{saving}{income}$$

For example, at an income level of $20,000, the family will spend 88 cents of each dollar, or a total of $17,600. It will save 12 cents of each dollar, or a

total of $2,400. In other words, the family will spend 88 percent of its income and save 12 percent.

Note that as income increases, APC decreases. Therefore, APS increases because both must total 1 (or 100 percent) at each income level. What can you learn from the fact that APC declines with rising incomes? Basically, this tendency confirms the everyday observation that the rich save a larger proportion of their incomes than the poor. You probably would have guessed this without looking at the figures in the table. Nevertheless, they help to fix this important idea more firmly in your mind.

Marginal Propensities to Consume and to Save

You will see later that it is important to know both the amount of each *extra* dollar of income that a family will spend on consumption and the amount it will save. These amounts are shown in columns (6) and (7) of Exhibit 1.

The *marginal propensity to consume* (MPC) is the change in consumption resulting from a unit change in income. As you can see from the table, the formula for calculating MPC is

$$MPC = \frac{change\ in\ consumption}{change\ in\ income}$$

The MPC tells you the *fraction of each extra dollar* of *income that goes into consumption.* An MPC of 0.70, for instance, means that 70 percent of any *increase* in income will be spent on consumption.

The *marginal propensity to save* (MPS) is the change in saving resulting from a unit change in income:

$$MPS = \frac{change\ in\ saving}{change\ in\ income}$$

The MPS tells you the *fraction of each extra dollar* of *income that goes into saving.* An MPS of 0.30, for example, means that 30 percent of any *increase* in income will be saved.

Economics in the News

Should You Save?

A Formula Can Help To Decide

People save for a variety of reasons. One is the belief that today's saving will result in tomorrow's greater purchasing power. That belief may not always be true, however, depending on tax rates and inflation.

One way to decide for yourself is with the following formula:

Savings growth rate =

$$\left[1 + \frac{\text{interest rate}}{\text{on savings}} \left(1 - \frac{\text{marginal}}{\text{tax rate}} \right) - \frac{\text{expected}}{\text{inflation rate}} \right]^{\text{years of saving}}$$

For example, suppose you are in a 20% marginal tax bracket and are thinking of buying a four-year savings certificate that pays 10%. If you expect an average annual inflation rate of 6%, the formula becomes:

Savings growth rate = $[1 + .1(1 - .2) - .06]^4 = 1.08$

You will thus come out ahead by saving. Each dollar you save will grow by 8 cents after allowing for taxes and inflation.

But if you are in a marginal tax bracket of 40% and you forecast 12% inflation, you get this result:

Savings growth rate = $[1 + .1(1 - .4) - .12]^4 = 0.78$

In this case you will come out a loser by saving. Each dollar you save will leave you with 78 cents after allowing for taxes and inflation.

What is the difference between APC and MPC? What is the difference between APS and MPS? At any given level of income, the APC relates total consumption to total income. On the other hand, the MPC relates a change in the amount of consumption to a change in the amount of income. The "average" may thus be quite different from the "marginal," as you can see from the table in Exhibit 1. The same kind of reasoning applies to the difference between APS and MPS. The "average" and the "marginal" tell you distinctly different things.

Note from the table, however, that just as APC and APS must always total 1 (or 100 percent) at any level of income, MPC and MPS must always total 1 (or 100 percent) for each change in income.

The MPC and MPS are of great practical value. For example, suppose that the nation is in recession and the MPC for the economy as a whole is 0.70. This means that, to increase the volume of consumption by $700 million in order to move the economy closer to full employment, the level of aggregate disposable income must be raised by $1 billion. As shown in later chapters, government may adopt various economic measures in an effort to achieve such a goal.

"Marginals" Are Slopes

By now you have probably recognized an important feature of MPC. Because it is the change in total consumption resulting from a unit change in income, it measures the **slope** (steepness) of the consumption function or line. The slope of any straight line is defined as the number of units it changes vertically for each unit of change horizontally. Thus, in Exhibit 3 the line rises 4 units on the vertical axis for a run of 6 units on the horizontal. Therefore, the slope, which is measured by the rise over the run, is ⅔.

Similarly, the MPS measures the slope of the saving line. You should be able to verify that the slope of a straight line is the same at every point. This is why the table in Exhibit 1 shows all values of MPC as equal and all values of MPS as equal. This is, the consumption and saving functions in this example are each straight lines.

Two Kinds of Changes Involving Consumption

The consumption function (propensity-to-consume curve) expresses a relation between consumption expenditures and income. Your understanding of this concept can serve as a basis for distinguishing between two kinds of variations in consumption.

[handwritten: Know]
[handwritten: Know]
[handwritten: No flation]

Exhibit 3
Slope of a Line

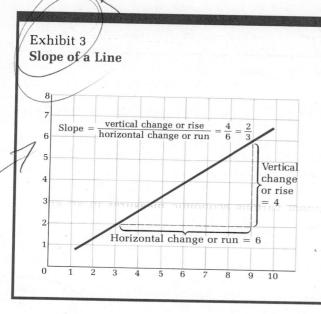

Slope = $\dfrac{\text{vertical change or rise}}{\text{horizontal change or run}} = \dfrac{4}{6} = \dfrac{2}{3}$

Vertical change or rise = 4

Horizontal change or run = 6

Exhibit 4
Changes in the Amounts Consumed and Saved
(variables are in constant dollars)

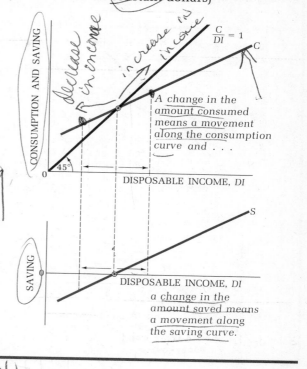

[handwritten: decrease in income]
[handwritten: increase in income]

$\dfrac{C}{DI} = 1$

A change in the amount consumed means a movement along the consumption curve and . . .

DISPOSABLE INCOME, DI

DISPOSABLE INCOME, DI

a change in the amount saved means a movement along the saving curve.

One is called a change in the amount consumed. The other is a change in consumption.

Change in the Amount Consumed

Examine the figures in Exhibit 4. In the upper figure, any movement along the consumption curve represents a **change in the amount consumed.** The change will consist of an increase in the amount consumed if income rises and a decrease in the amount consumed if income falls. This is indicated by the vertical dashed lines. Thus:

- A movement to the right always signifies an increase in income and hence a movement upward along the existing C curve.

- A movement to the left indicates a decrease in income and therefore a movement downward along the existing C curve.

Note also in the lower figure that saving, like consumption, varies directly with income. Therefore, a change in the amount saved — either an increase or a decrease — occurs for the same reason as a change in the amount consumed. The reason, of course, is a change in income.

Change in Consumption

A second type of movement, shown in Exhibit 5, is a **change in consumption.** This may take the form of an increase in consumption, whereby the curve shifts to a higher level. Or it may take the form of a decrease in consumption, shown by a shift of the curve to a lower level. An increase in consumption from curve C to curve C′ means that, at any given level of income, people are now willing to consume more and save less than before. What does a decrease from curve C to curve C″ mean?

As with supply and demand curves, the consumption curve may shift as a result of a change in any one of the "all other" things that were assumed to remain constant when the curve was initially

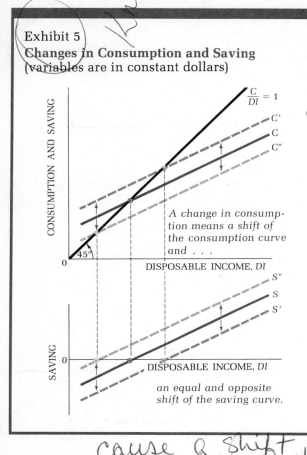

Know

Business

Exhibit 5
Changes in Consumption and Saving
(variables are in constant dollars)

A change in consumption means a shift of the consumption curve and . . .

an equal and opposite shift of the saving curve.

cause a shift in the curve

factors that cause a shift in curve

drawn. What are these factors? Some of the more important ones are these:

1. Expectations of future prices and incomes.
2. The volume of liquid assets (for example, currency, stocks, or bonds) owned by a household.
3. Credit conditions—ease of borrowing money.
4. Anticipation of product shortages (resulting, for example, from a war or a strike).

An increase in any one of these factors (and several others that you may be able to think of) can cause an increase in consumption and shift the curve upward. Likewise, a decrease in any one can cause a decrease in consumption and shift the curve downward. Because these factors do not usually re-

main constant for very long, the *true* consumption function for the economy is likely to vary over a period of time.

Private Investment Expenditure

"The economy turns on capital investment; capital investment turns on confidence; confidence turns on certainty; and certainty turns on predictability." These words, spoken by a major corporation president, suggest that investment is of critical importance to our economy.

Investment, in this context, means spending by business firms on physical capital, such as additions to plant, equipment, and inventories. As you know, the private sector's consumption expenditure and investment expenditure are the two major components of aggregate expenditure. Therefore, having studied consumption, we must now turn our attention to understanding investment.

If you were in business, what would determine your decision to invest? The fundamental answer, of course, is your profit expectation. If you think a new machine would add sufficiently to your profit, you will try to purchase it. If you believe that an additional wing on your factory would yield greater profits, you will try to build it.

In the business world, the money you get back each year from an investment, in relation to the dollars invested, is called the *rate of return*. It is always expressed as a percentage. Thus, if you buy land for $1,000 and rent it out for $100 a year, the annual rate of return on your investment is 10 percent:

Formula

$$\text{rate of return} = \frac{\text{annual receipts}}{\text{investment}} = \frac{\$100}{\$1,000} = 0.10, \text{ or } 10\%$$

Understanding the *MEI*

The rate of return measures the profitability of an existing investment. More often, we want to know whether an *additional* (or "marginal") investment should be undertaken. The measure that businesses use for determining this is called, by economists, the "marginal efficiency of investment."

The **marginal efficiency of investment (MEI)** is the expected rate of return over cost of an *additional* unit of a capital good. Thus, you might have an MEI or expected rate of return of 25 percent for one type of investment, 15 percent for another, and so on.

You can gain a better understanding of the MEI by studying its graph in Figure (a) of Exhibit 6. The figure shows that, at any given time, a business firm is faced with a number of investment opportunities. These may include renovating its existing plant, purchasing new machines, acquiring additional power facilities, or installing a computer system. Each project competes for a firm's limited funds. However, some projects are expected to be more profitable — that is, to have a higher rate of return (or MEI) — than others. In view of this, which projects should management select? Or, to put it differently, how much investment expenditure should management undertake?

The first step in answering this question is to imagine that the managers of a firm rank alternative investment projects in decreasing order of their MEIs. In Figure (a), each project's cost and corresponding MEI are shown. The most attractive investment open to the firm is the renovation of its plant at a cost of $2 million. For this, the firm anticipates a rate of return, or MEI, of 27 percent, which is read from the vertical axis. The next most profitable investment is the addition of a new wing to its factory at a cost of $1 million, for which the MEI is 20 percent. Each remaining investment project is interpreted in a similar manner. If we assume that the risks of loss associated with these investments are the same, the descending order of MEIs suggests two things:

1. Fewer investment opportunities are available to a firm at higher rates of return than at lower ones. For example, it is harder to find investments yielding 25 percent than to find investments yielding 10 percent.

2. A firm will tend to choose those investment projects that have the highest MEIs. Therefore, a project with a higher anticipated rate of return over cost is likely to be selected over a project with a lower one.

Cost of Funds: The Rate of Interest

Once the MEI (or rate of return) on an investment is estimated, the next step is to establish the cost of funds needed to finance the investment. Only then can you decide if the investment is worth undertaking.

The cost of funds needed to finance an investment is expressed as a percentage. Thus, if a business firm borrows money for investment and agrees to pay an annual interest charge of, say, 10 percent, then that is the firm's cost of funds. Alternatively, if the firm uses its own money instead of borrowing, the interest return sacrificed by not lending the money in the financial markets (through the purchase of bonds or other securities) may be thought of as the company's cost of funds. This cost, of course, is the **opportunity cost** of the funds. In any case:

The MEI and the cost of funds are each quoted as percentages. Therefore, they can be easily compared. This makes it possible to determine the amount of investment that will take place.

The *MEI* and the Interest Rate

How much investment will the firm undertake? To answer this, we must understand that at any given time there is an interest rate in the market that represents the current cost of funds to the firm. We will assume that this interest rate or cost of funds is the same whether the firm borrows the money or uses its own. It follows that a higher interest cost will mean a lower expected return and therefore a smaller volume of investment. Conversely, a lower interest cost will mean a higher expected return and hence a larger volume of investment. In general terms, we may conclude:

Exhibit 6
Investment Demand in the Private Sector

Figure (a): The solid stepped line is an individual firm's *MEI* (or rate-of-return) curve. It shows the amount of investment the firm will make at various interest rates or costs of funds at any given time. The *MEI* curve is thus the firm's demand curve for investment. There are many such stepped curves at any given time, one for each firm in the economy.

Figure (b): The *MEI* curve for all firms is a smooth line obtained by summing individual *MEI* curves. It shows the total amount of private-sector investment that will be made at various interest rates or costs of funds. The *MEI* curve in this chart is thus the economy's aggregate demand curve D_I for investment. Therefore, the horizontal axis in this figure, in contrast to the one in Figure (a), measures *billions* of constant dollars.

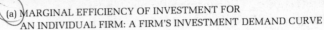
(a) MARGINAL EFFICIENCY OF INVESTMENT FOR AN INDIVIDUAL FIRM: A FIRM'S INVESTMENT DEMAND CURVE

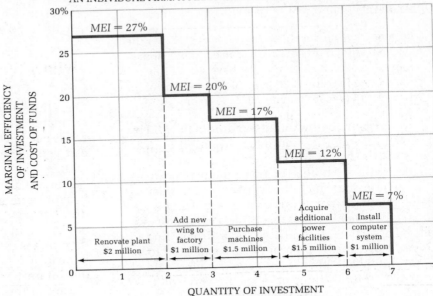

(b) MARGINAL EFFICIENCY OF INVESTMENT FOR ALL FIRMS: THE PRIVATE SECTOR'S INVESTMENT DEMAND CURVE D_I

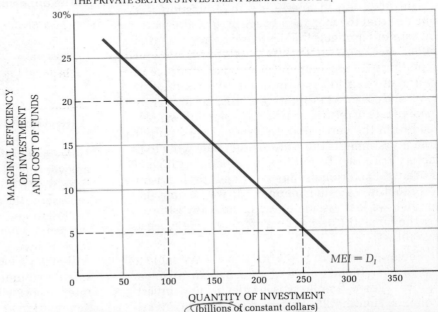

Investment by a firm occurs when the *MEI* (expected rate of return) on an addition to investment exceeds the rate of interest or cost of funds that is incurred in making the investment.

For example, look again at Figure (*a*) of Exhibit 6. The graph tells you that, at an interest cost (shown on the vertical axis) of, say, 13 percent, this particular firm would demand $4.5 million for investment. Of this amount, $2 million would be spent on renovating its plant in anticipation of a return or *MEI* of 27 percent. In addition, $1 million would be allocated to a new wing for its factory for an expected *MEI* of 20 percent. Finally, $1.5 million would be used to buy new machines in anticipation of an *MEI* of 17 percent. If the interest cost should fall to 6 percent, the firm will demand an *additional* $2.5 million, or a *total* of $7 million. The extra amount would be invested in the next two projects—power facilities and a computer system. In general, therefore, *the total amount of investment funds demanded by the firm depends on its* MEI *relative to the interest rate or cost of funds.*

This analysis leads to two important principles. *At any given time:*

— A demand curve relates the quantities of a commodity that buyers would be willing and able to purchase at various prices. For business investments, the prices are interest rates (costs of funds) to business firms. Hence, the *MEI* curve shows the amounts of investment that a firm would be willing and able to undertake at various interest rates. This is illustrated by the solid irregular line in Figure (*a*) of Exhibit 6. It follows that *a firm's* MEI *curve is its demand curve for investment.*

— Each firm's own *MEI* curve is based on its particular investment needs and expectations. If the individual *MEI* curves of businesses are summed, we get the *MEI* curve for all firms in the economy. Because there are numerous firms, the irregularities disappear, giving a smooth continuous line like the one in Figure (*b*) of Exhibit 6. The *aggregate* MEI *curve depicts total private investment demand at different rates of interest.* For example, at an interest rate of 20 percent, the amount of private-sector investment would be $100 billion. If the interest rate fell to 5 percent, the amount of private-sector investment would increase to $250 billion.

Determinants of the *MEI*: Shifts of the Curve

The *MEI* curve, or D_I curve, is an investment demand curve. Therefore, like any demand curve, it may shift to the right or left as the result of a change in one or more of the factors that determine it. At least four factors are particularly important:

1. **Expected Product Demand**   To businesses, the *expected* net return on an investment will depend largely on the demand that is anticipated for the product produced by the investment. For example, if you are a shoe manufacturer, your expected *MEI* for shoe machinery will be influenced by your anticipated demand for shoes. Similarly, for the economy as a whole, the expected return on new investment will be influenced by business executives' anticipations of total spending on the products of businesses.

2. **Technology and Innovation**   Advances in technology and the introduction of new products often require the construction of new plants or the installation of new equipment. This stimulates the demand for additional capital.

3. **Cost of New Capital Goods**   Changes in the cost of new plant or equipment affect business firms' demand for them. Thus, a rise in the cost of new capital goods shifts the *MEI* curve to the left (decrease in demand). A fall in cost shifts the curve to the right (increase in demand).

4. **Corporate Income Tax Rates**   Businesses are interested in expected rates of return on investment expenditures *after* allowances for corporation income taxes. Hence, an increase in the tax rates, other things being equal, shifts the *MEI* curve to the

left (decrease in demand). A decrease in the tax rates shifts the curve to the right (increase in demand).

These, as well as other economic and psychological conditions, affect businesses' expected rates of return on investment. Because one or more of these factors is always changing, the *MEI* curve is continually shifting either to the right or to the left. As a result, the level of private investment in the economy fluctuates widely over the years, as shown in Exhibit 7.

Exhibit 7

The Instability of Private Investment (data in constant dollars)

The *MEI* curve is continually shifting, owing to changes in the factors that determine it. As a result, private investment spending fluctuates widely over the years.

Note that changes in GNP are closely related to changes in investment.

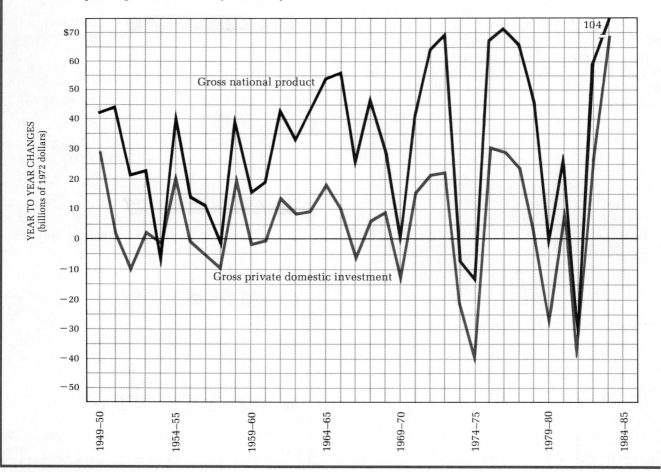

ASK NANCY

In Keynesian theory, fluctuation in private investment is the single most important cause of fluctuations in income and employment. This, in turn, is the major reason for periods of prosperity and recession.

Government Expenditure and Net Foreign Expenditure

The remaining components of aggregate expenditure stem from government and from international sources.

Government expenditure, which consists of public investment spending, depends to a large extent on public needs. These include such things as highways, schools, welfare benefits, and defense requirements. The volume of government expenditure is independent of profit expectations and, beyond the minimum levels required by society, is determined at will by government. No scientific law or guiding set of principles exists to predict changes in the level of public investment.

Net foreign expenditure, which is the difference between our exports and our imports, is another factor affecting aggregate expenditure. In the next several chapters, attention will be focused entirely on domestic factors affecting the economy. Therefore, the influence of net foreign expenditure on the nation's income and employment will be set aside for the time being.

Ignore for now

Skip

Conclusion: Reviewing the Basic Relationships

You now have the basic building blocks necessary for understanding much of modern macroeconomic theory. This theory will be developed in greater detail in the following chapters. In the meantime, you can test your knowledge of the fundamental relationships explained thus far by making sure that you understand the equations presented in Exhibit 8.

Exhibit 8
Some Key Relations in Macroeconomic Theory

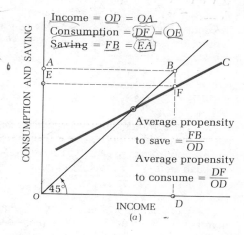

Income = OD = OA
Consumption = DF = OE
Saving = FB = EA

Average propensity to save = $\dfrac{FB}{OD}$

Average propensity to consume = $\dfrac{DF}{OD}$

(a)

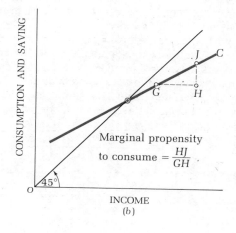

Marginal propensity to consume = $\dfrac{HJ}{GH}$

(b)

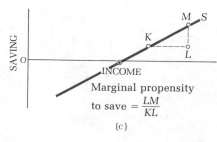

Marginal propensity to save = $\dfrac{LM}{KL}$

(c)

Review these

Economics in the News

Why All Those Jobs Still Go Begging

Many Companies Are Finding It Difficult to Fill Payroll Vacancies Despite the Large Pool of Unemployed Workers

With more than 8 million people unemployed in this country, employers should have little trouble finding workers. Right?

Wrong. Even in communities with relatively high jobless rates, positions paying anything from the $3.35 hourly minimum wage to $40,000 or $50,000 a year in fields such as fast food, construction and high tech are going begging, sometimes for months at a time.

Despite a slew of roadside "Help Wanted" signs, newspaper and radio advertisements and intensive talent searches by private and government employment agencies, many employers report meeting frustration when they attempt to fill vacancies.

Why, when millions are looking for work, is recruiting so difficult? Often, say employment experts, noncompetitive pay is to blame. Another major reason can be a poor match between the skills needed for the job and the training of the unemployed. In some cases, a long commute or unreliable travel connections via public transportation discourage a worker from taking a job.

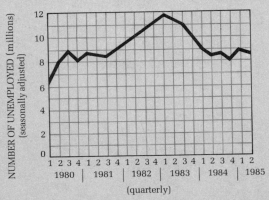

Reprinted from *U.S. News & World Report,* July 8, 1985. Copyright 1985, U.S. News & World Report, Inc.

What You Have Learned

1. The Keynesian theory of income and employment is rooted in several fundamental ideas. Among them:

— Aggregate expenditure may be greater than, equal to, or less than full-employment aggregate income.

— The interest rate may fail to equate households' intended saving and businesses' intended investment, because these are done by different people for different purposes.

— Most prices and wages are not flexible. This is especially true on the down side—because of
(a) resistance by large businesses and unions and
(b) minimum-wage legislation and other institutional forces.

For these reasons, the economy may not necessarily adjust itself to full-employment equilibrium.

2. The propensity to consume, or the consumption function, expresses a relationship between consumption and income. The relationship is such that, as income increases, consumption increases, but not as fast as income.

3. At any given level of income, the average propensity to consume (APC) is the proportion of income spent on consumption. Similarly, the average propensity to save is the proportion of income saved. Therefore, $APC + APS = 1$ (or 100 percent). Out of any given increase in income, the marginal propensity to consume (MPC) is the proportion of the increase spent on consumption. Similarly, the marginal propensity to save is the proportion of the increase saved. Hence, $MPC + MPS = 1$ (or 100 percent).

4. A *change in the amount consumed* means a movement along the consumption curve as a result a change in income. A *change in consumption* means a shift of the entire consumption curve to a new level. This occurs because of a change in one or more of the "all other" things that are assumed to be constant when the curve is initially drawn. These factors include expectations of future prices and income, the volume of liquid assets owned by households, credit conditions (ease of borrowing money), and anticipation of product shortages.

5. Investment expenditure, like consumption and saving, is a major variable in income and employment determination. The expected rate of return on an additional unit of investment is called the *marginal efficiency of investment (MEI)*. Investment occurs when the *MEI* ex-

Leaders in Economics

UPI/Bettmann Newsphotos

John Maynard Keynes
1883 – 1946
Founder of a "Revolution"

"You have to know that I believe myself to be writing a book on economic theory which will largely revolutionize . . . the way the world thinks about economic problems." So wrote John Maynard Keynes to the Irish wit and author George Bernard Shaw in 1935.

Keynes was right. He did indeed write a book that revolutionized economic thinking. As a result, he became recognized as one of the most brilliant and influential economists of all time. In fact, as one who helped shape the thinking of future generations of scholars, Keynes ranks with Adam Smith and Karl Marx.

Unconventional Ideas

Keynes's best known work, *The General Theory of Employment, Interest and Money* (1936), is one of the most influential books ever written in economics. Here Keynes made it clear that he was departing significantly from traditional economic theory. This theory held that there is a natural tendency for the economy to reach equilibrium at full employment. Indeed, Keynes showed that equilibrium can be reached at a level of output less than full employment.

Because of this, Keynes advocated reduction in the bank interest rate to stimulate business borrowing for investment. He also believed in progressive income taxation to make incomes more equal and thereby increase the *percentage* of aggregate income that people spend on consumption. And he argued for government investment spending through public works projects when private investment expenditures fall off. Today, as you will see in the following chapters, these and several related ideas are part of a larger family of concepts that make up macroeconomic theory and policy.

---

ceeds the rate of interest or the cost of funds that is incurred in making the investment.

6. Private investment spending depends on the profit expectations of businesses. These expectations are determined by such factors as expected product demand, the rate of technology and innovation, cost of new capital goods, and corporate income-tax rates. For these reasons, private investment tends to be highly volatile over the years and is the major cause of fluctuations in economic activity.

Terms and Concepts to Review

aggregate expenditure
consumption
saving
dissaving
propensity to consume

propensity to save
average propensity to consume
average propensity to save

marginal propensity to consume
marginal propensity to save
slope
change in amount consumed

change in consumption
investment
marginal efficiency of investment

For Discussion

1. In the field of marketing, a concept called *Engel's Laws* is often used. Look up the meaning of this idea in the Dictionary at the back of the book. Then express Engel's Laws in terms of the average propensity to consume (*APC*).

2. Why does the *APC* differ from the *MPC*? Why does the *APS* differ from the *MPS*?

3. What factors other than income are likely to be most important in determining consumption?

4. Complete the following table on the assumption that 50 percent of any increase in income is spent on consumption. Sketch the graphs of consumption and saving. Label all curves.

DI	C	S	APC	APS	MPC	MPS
$100	$150	-50	150/100		.5	.5
200	200	0	200/200			
300	250	50				
400	300	100				
500	350	150				
600	400	200				

5. Would you expect expenditures on consumer durable goods to fluctuate more widely than expenditures on consumer nondurable goods? Explain your answer.

6. What would be the effect on aggregate consumption if social-welfare expenditures on public hospitals, parks, medical care, and so on were financed entirely by our progressive income tax system? Does it make any difference if there are tax loopholes?

7. How would you distinguish between a "change in the amount invested" and a "change in investment"?

Chapter 9

Income and Employment Determination: The Income-Expenditure and Income-Price Models

Learning Guide

Watch for answers to these important questions

How do we distinguish between the income-expenditure model and the income-price model? What do these models do?

How do changes in investment relate to the level of income? What is this relationship called? What, essentially, does the relationship show?

What is meant by inflationary and recessionary gaps? How are they defined? How are they illustrated graphically?

Scientists in all fields try to identify important variables and to discover relationships between them. In macroeconomics, as you have already learned, the important variables include consumption, saving, investment, income, and employment. How do relationships between these variables help us to understand the economy as a whole?

In order to answer this question, it is necessary to distinguish between two kinds of models that are used in this and in subsequent chapters:

Income-Expenditure Model This relates the economy's real aggregate income (or output) to the public's total spending on goods and services. The model assumes that the *average price level remains constant*. The income-expenditure model may also be called the *aggregate output/aggregate expenditure* model.

Income-Price Model This relates the economy's real aggregate income (or output) to the average price level. The model assumes that the *average price level varies*. The income-price model may also be called the *aggregate demand/aggregate supply* model. (As you will recall, this model was used to illustrate the classical theory of income and employment determination.)

Both models can help us interpret many current macroeconomic problems and policies.

The Income-Expenditure Model

The income-expenditure model shows how consumption, saving, and investment interact to determine the overall level of income and employment. This is the basic model that Keynes's followers developed in an effort to explain the workings of the modern economy.

The model is "basic" in that it focuses on the barest essentials. That is, it covers only the household and business sectors while omitting, for the time being, the public and foreign sectors. With this model, you can learn how the simplest system works before additional factors are introduced to

make the model more representative of the real world.

Structure of the Model

The table in Exhibit 1 shows values of the relevant variables. Because a stable price level, or constant dollars, is assumed (as indicated in the subtitle), all dollar figures are in *real*, not nominal, terms.

Note from columns (1) and (2) that the amount of employment depends on GNP. Higher levels of output result in higher levels of employment because, as you have already learned, more people are employed to produce the increased output.

Consumption and saving, shown in columns (3) and (4), vary directly with GNP — which is the same as aggregate income. (Remember from your study of national income accounting that gross national product equals gross national income.) Note from

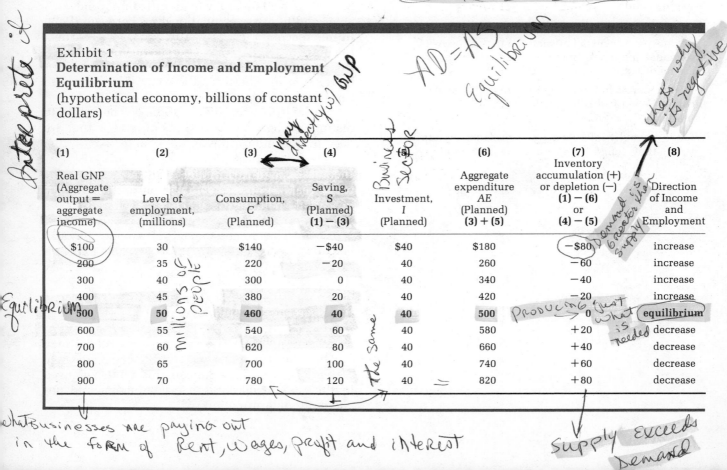

Exhibit 1
Determination of Income and Employment Equilibrium
(hypothetical economy, billions of constant dollars)

(1) Real GNP (Aggregate output = aggregate income)	(2) Level of employment, (millions)	(3) Consumption, C (Planned)	(4) Saving, S (Planned) (1) − (3)	(5) Investment, I (Planned)	(6) Aggregate expenditure AE (Planned) (3) + (5)	(7) Inventory accumulation (+) or depletion (−) (1) − (6) or (4) − (5)	(8) Direction of Income and Employment
$100	30	$140	−$40	$40	$180	−$80	increase
200	35	220	−20	40	260	−60	increase
300	40	300	0	40	340	−40	increase
400	45	380	20	40	420	−20	increase
500	50	460	40	40	500	0	equilibrium
600	55	540	60	40	580	+20	decrease
700	60	620	80	40	660	+40	decrease
800	65	700	100	40	740	+60	decrease
900	70	780	120	40	820	+80	decrease

the column headings that consumption and saving are the amounts that households *plan* (or *intend*) to consume and save at each income level.

The amount of investment spending by the business sector, column (5), is also planned. For reasons that are explained shortly, although investment spending fluctuates widely over time, it is assumed to be *independent* of GNP. Therefore, investment spending (= $40 billion) is constant in relation to GNP.

Column (6), aggregate expenditure, is simply the total amount of spending on consumption and investment planned by all sectors of the economy.

The difference between aggregate output and aggregate expenditure is the economy's change in inventory, shown in column (7). (Note that the change in inventory is also the difference between saving and investment.) As explained below, the inventory level tends toward equilibrium. (That is, it tends toward zero *unplanned* or undesired accumulation or depletion.) When the equilibrium inventory level is reached, income and employment shown in column (8) are also in equilibrium. This means there is no tendency for them to change.

Against this background, you can turn your attention to Exhibit 2. This shows the graphs of the data from the table in Exhibit 1. Some important features of the graphs in Exhibit 2 should be noted:

Figure (a) depicts both aggregate expenditure and aggregate output. The graph of **aggregate expenditure,** *AE,* shows the amount that households and businesses *plan* to spend for consumption and investment (measured on the vertical axis) at each level of aggregate output or income (real GNP) measured on the horizontal axis.

Because the scales on both axes are the same, the 45° line serves as a reference line. At each point along the line, aggregate expenditure equals aggregate output, *AO.* That is, *AE/AO* = 1 (or 100 percent). Therefore, the line is labeled **aggregate output,** *AO,* and used below as a basis for comparison with the *planned AE* line.

Figures (a) and (b) show that the graphs of consumption and saving vary directly with income. This is what you would expect from your knowledge of the propensities to consume and to save.

Figure (b) also depicts the graph of investment—a horizontal line. Why is investment ($40 billion) the same at all levels of aggregate output? As emphasized in the previous chapter:

> The investment plans of businesses depend on the marginal efficiency of investment (*MEI*) relative to the interest rate. The *MEI* is affected by such factors as expected product demand, the rate of technology and innovation, the cost of new capital goods, and corporate income tax rates. Therefore, the level of investment that businesses *plan* or intend to undertake can be assumed to remain constant in relation to aggregate output. The level of investment, however, varies widely from year to year, as you have already learned.

The Equilibrium Level of Income and Employment

You now have the information needed to interpret the model. The question to be answered is: What will be the equilibrium levels of aggregate income and employment—and why? In other words, where will the level of aggregate output and the corresponding level of employment finally settle? As you can see, there are two parts to the question.

1. Look again at the table in Exhibit 1. It shows that, at the equilibrium level of aggregate output, in column (1), consumers in column (3) are buying just the amount they want to buy. In addition, businesses are holding the precise level of inventory they desire. Therefore, businesses are neither accumulating nor depleting their stock of goods and have no incentive to change their level of production. As a result, there are no changes in inventory in column (7). That is, the difference between aggregate output and aggregate expenditure (or between planned saving and planned investment), is zero.

The equilibrium points *E* in the two figures in Exhibit 2 depict these notions graphically. Note the vertical dashed line connecting them. It shows that, in this hypothetical economy, equilibrium occurs at an aggregate output level of $500 billion and an employment level of 50 million persons.

The *what* part of the question above has thus been answered. The next part concerns *why.*

2. Why do aggregate income and employment tend toward equilibrium? As a start toward an answer, ask yourself what happens when they are not in equilibrium. There are two possibilities:

(a) Suppose that GNP is greater than $500 billion — say $600 billion. This means that businesses are paying $600 billion in the form of wages, rent, interest, and profit, which are incomes to factor owners. (Remember that GNP = GNI). At the same time, the corresponding level of planned expenditures, $C + I$, is $580 billion. The consequences can be seen both from the table in Exhibit 1 and from the graphs in Exhibit 2. Thus:

— In Figure (*a*), the amount that businesses produce ($600 billion) is greater than the amount that households and businesses together want to buy ($580 billion).

— In Figure (*b*), the amount that households plan to save ($60 billion) is greater than the amount that businesses plan to invest ($40 billion).

For both reasons, businesses find their sales to be less than anticipated. This imbalance causes firms to accumulate inventories beyond desired levels, so managers cut back on production and lay off workers. As a result, aggregate output, income, and employment decrease toward their equilibrium levels, as shown by the arrows in the figures.

(b) Conversely, suppose that GNP is less than $500 billion — say $400 billion. In that case, the reverse process occurs. Stated briefly: In Figure (*a*), households' and businesses' planned aggregate expenditure *exceeds* aggregate output; in Figure (*b*), businesses' planned investment *exceeds* households' planned saving. Households and businesses together are buying goods at a faster rate than firms are producing them. As a result, business inventories are being depleted — they are falling below desired levels. Managers then seek to expand production and to hire more workers. This causes aggregate output, income, and employment to increase toward their equilib-

rium levels, as indicated by the arrows in the figures.

Thus, three fundamental conclusions may be drawn from this model:

1. Income and employment tend toward an equilibrium level at which aggregate output equals aggregate expenditure and planned saving equals planned investment.

2. The movement toward equilibrium takes place as businesses seek to adjust their inventories to desired levels.

3. Equilibrium can occur at any level of employment, not necessarily at full employment.

Injections and Withdrawals: The "Bathtub Theorem"

You can gain further understanding of these ideas by thinking of them in terms of a physical analogy.

For example, suppose that we use the notions of "injections" and "withdrawals" to account for expansions and contractions in the economy's circular flow of income. These terms can be defined in the following way.

Injections These are expenditures that are not dependent on income. Investment expenditures are an example. (So too are government expenditures and exports, which you will be learning about in subsequent chapters.) The effect of injections is to increase aggregate expenditure and thus to raise the economy's level of income and employment.

Withdrawals These are "leakages" from total income. Saving is an example. (Some other examples you will be learning about in later chapters are taxes and imports.) The effect of withdrawals is to decrease aggregate expenditure and thus to reduce the economy's level of income and employment.

The significance of these terms can be visualized by referring back to Figure (*a*) in Exhibit 2. Injections may be represented by investment (*I*), and withdrawals or leakages may be represented by

Exhibit 2

Determination of Income and Employment Equilibrium (based on data in Exhibit 1)

Figure (a)   Figure (b)

At the equilibrium point E:

Aggregate output equals aggregate expenditure (AO = AE) ↗   and   Saving equals investment (S = I) ↘

To the right of E:

Aggregate output exceeds aggregate expenditure (AO > AE) ↗   and   Saving exceeds investment (S > I)

To the left of E:

Aggregate expenditure exceeds aggregate output (AE > AO) ↗   and   Investment exceeds saving (I > S)

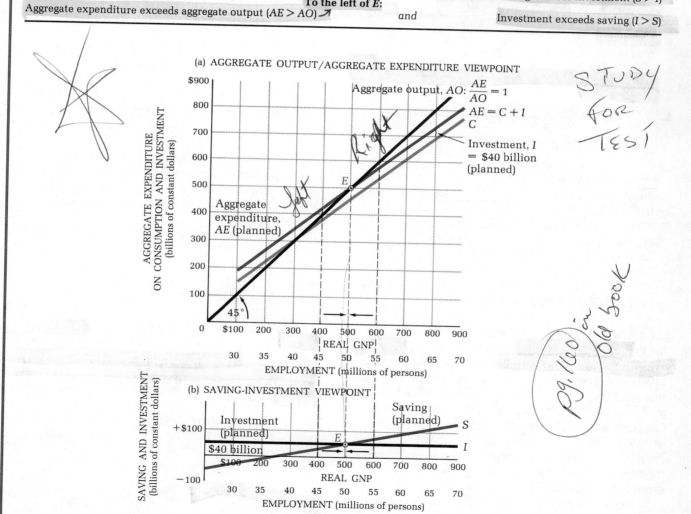

(a) AGGREGATE OUTPUT/AGGREGATE EXPENDITURE VIEWPOINT

(b) SAVING-INVESTMENT VIEWPOINT

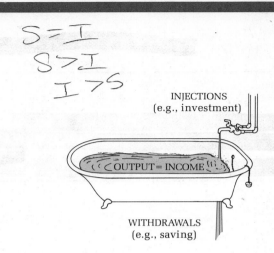

Exhibit 3
Injections and Withdrawals: The "Bathtub Theorem"

This diagram helps you visualize the effects of investment and saving on the economy's level of income.

Investment may be thought of as an injection into the income stream. Saving may be thought of as a withdrawal. If the investment inflow exceeds the saving outflow, the level in the tub will rise. If the saving outflow exceeds the investment inflow, the level in the tub will fall. However, the water in the bathtub can be in equilibrium at *any* level as long as the investment inflow equals the saving outflow. In other words, *at any given level of output or of income, investment equals saving.*

INJECTIONS
(e.g., investment)

OUTPUT = INCOME

WITHDRAWALS
(e.g., saving)

saving (S). As you have already learned, equilibrium will occur where $I = S$. This is the level of income and employment at which injections and withdrawals are equal.

We can now illustrate these ideas by means of the **"bathtub theorem"** explained in Exhibit 3.

The Income-Price Model

As you have learned, the income-expenditure or basic Keynesian model studied thus far assumes that *prices remain constant.* During many periods of history, including the 1930's when Keynes formulated his theory, this assumption was reasonable. In recent decades, however, periods of rapidly rising prices have been common. Because of this, it is necessary to see how the effects of price-level changes can be incorporated into an alternative type of macroeconomic model. This new model may be called an "income-price model."

You are already familiar with the income-price model from your earlier study of classical economic theory. Its main features can be summarized briefly with the help of the diagrams in Exhibit 4.

To begin with, note that the average price level in the two charts is measured on the vertical axis and the level of real GNP is measured on the horizontal axis. (The amount of employment corresponding to each level of real GNP is also measured on the horizontal axis, but it is *implied* rather than explicitly indicated.)

Shapes of the Curves

Observe that, in both diagrams, the **aggregate demand** *(AD)* curve is downward-sloping. (You will recall that aggregate demand is the total value of real aggregate output that all sectors of the economy are willing to purchase at various average price levels.) The downward-sloping curve tells you that the public will buy more real output at a lower average price level than at a higher one. The reasons, which you learned when you studied the classical theory, may be summarized briefly:

Real-Balance Effect At lower average prices, the purchasing power or *real* value of people's cash balances is greater. Therefore, people can buy more goods with their cash balances.

Increase in √

Exhibit 4
Equilibrium in the Income-Price Model

In the short run, as shown in Figure (a), the AS curve is upward-sloping. This means that rising prices bring forth higher levels of real output and employment.

In the long run, as shown in Figure (b), the AS curve is vertical. This means (as in classical theory) that the price level can fluctuate while real output and employment remain stable at their full or natural levels.

The equilibrium price level at P, as shown in both diagrams, is determined by the intersection of the AD and AS curves.

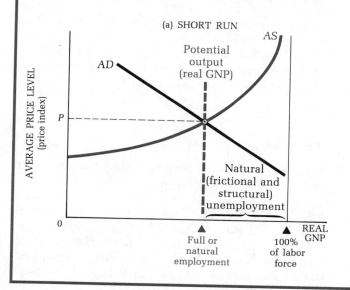

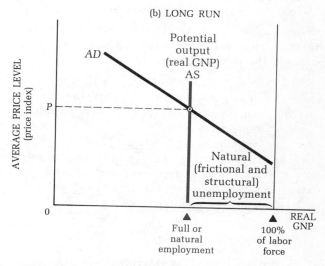

Interest-Rate Effect When prices decline, interest rates tend to decline too. Therefore, people can buy more goods because borrowing costs are lower.

The second important feature of the diagrams is the **aggregate supply** (AS) curve. It shows the total value of real aggregate output that will be made available at various average price levels. Note that the curve in Figure (a) has three important characteristics:

1. *It is upward-sloping.* The curve tells you that, up to a point, businesses will supply larger volumes of output at higher prices than at lower ones. This is because most wages and certain other production costs are set by contracts, and hence do not increase immediately in response to a rising price level. Therefore, higher prices mean wider profit margins, which give producers incentive to increase output.

2. *It rises more quickly as the full-employment level of real output is approached.* The curve becomes steeper because, as increasing quantities of the economy's resources are utilized, labor and other inputs become scarcer. Less efficient resources are thus brought into use. Therefore, greater increases in prices relative to costs are needed to bring forth additional increments of output.

3. *It continues rising after the full-employment level of real output is reached.* The curve extends beyond the vertical line representing the econ-

omy's **potential real GNP.** This, you will recall, is defined as the level of real output that exists at **full employment** — that is, when there is only natural (frictional and structural) unemployment. For example, if full employment exists when 95% of the labor force is employed, then the remaining 5% constitutes natural (frictional and structural) unemployment. Steep increases in prices are therefore necessary to call forth the additional output needed to absorb this remaining pool of unemployed resources.

You can now understand the distinction between the short-run and the long-run aggregate supply curves in the two diagrams:

In the short run, rising prices bring forth higher levels of real output and employment. Therefore, the upward-sloping AS curve in Figure (a) is a *short-run aggregate supply curve.*

In the long run, the economy produces its potential output or real GNP regardless of the average price level. (This, you will recall, accords with the classical view.) Therefore, the vertical AS curve in Figure (b) is a *long-run aggregate supply curve.*

Equilibrium Possibilities

When the AD and AS curves are combined, their intersection determines both the equilibrium output and price levels. In the long run, as shown in Figure (b), the economy's equilibrium output will be at the full- or natural-employment level and the corresponding equilibrium price level will be at P.

In the short run, as shown in Figure (a), the equilibrium output *may* occur at the full- or natural-employment level. However, it may also occur at a lower or higher level, and hence at a correspondingly lower or higher price level, depending on where the AD and AS curves intersect. You will see the consequences of such possibilities later in the chapter.

How does the income-price model compare with Keynesian views of equilibrium? Before answering, you should recall that Keynes formulated his

ideas during the Great Depression of the 1930s. He was concerned about the high rate of unemployment, and he was impatient with the classical contention that the economy would adjust to full employment in the long run. What was needed, he said, was a short-run theory because, in his words, "*in the long run we are all dead.*"

Keynes did not use graphs when he constructed his theory. Graphic models, such as the income-expenditure model, were formulated in later years (1940s) by other economists. The two income-price models in Exhibit 5 are of more recent vintage. These models, depicting both strict and modified Keynesian views, provide us with an opportunity to interpret Keynesian ideas from a modern vantage point.

Strict Keynesian View

Keynes would have assumed that the aggregate supply curve could be depicted as a reverse L-shaped curve. This is the situation shown in Figure (a) of Exhibit 5. The reason for the assumption is that, at any output short of full employment, the economy has unemployed resources. Therefore, as aggregate demand increases from AD_0 to AD_1, producers can expand real output to the full-employment level. Within this range of output, competitive pressures remain strong enough to keep the average price level at P.

But what happens if the aggregate demand curve increases beyond AD_1, say, to AD_2? The result will be pure inflation — an increase in the price level to P' without any increase in output. Keynes reasoned that, once the economy is operating at full employment, further increases in aggregate demand can result only in higher prices, not in additional production and jobs. This view of the nature of inflation accorded with that held by the classical economists in Keynes's time.

Modified Keynesian View

One of the shortcomings of this strict Keynesian view is its failure to deal with the simultaneous

Exhibit 5
Keynesian Equilibrium

Keynes did not use graphs when he formulated his theory of macroeconomics more than 50 years ago. However, these Keynesian interpretations of equilibrium illustrate some of his ideas.

Figure (a): Strict Keynesian View Keynes would have viewed the AS curve in terms of a horizontal and a vertical range — a reverse L-shape. Increases in aggregate demand from AD_0 to AD_1 result in *noninflationary* expansions in real output and employment because there are unemployed resources available. Once full employment is reached, an increase in aggregate demand to AD_2 results in pure inflation because prices

rise without any expansion in real output or in employment.

Figure (b): Modified Keynesian View This revised version introduces an "intermediate range" for the AS curve. Although the economy's aggregate demand and aggregate supply curves have shifted frequently over the long run, they have generally intersected in this middle range. This helps explain why our nation has often experienced irregular rates of inflation along with expansions in real output, while employment has remained less than "full."

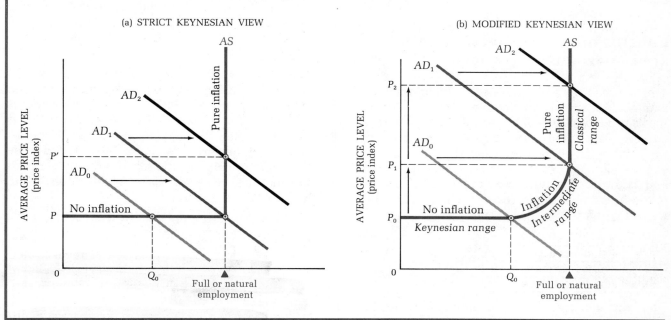

(a) STRICT KEYNESIAN VIEW

(b) MODIFIED KEYNESIAN VIEW

occurrence of inflation *and* high (but not full) employment. This is a condition that our economy has often experienced in the last several decades. Accordingly, Figure (b) provides a modified version of the Keynesian view by incorporating two features:

- *Revised aggregate supply curve* The AS curve is divided into three "ranges." The Keynesian

range (no inflation) and the classical range (pure inflation) are based on the previous diagram and have already been explained.

- *Intermediate range* In this stage, increases in aggregate demand from AD_0 to AD_1 will stimulate increases in output. The reason is the same as that for the upward-sloping AS curve that you studied previously. That is, in this stage prices are rising faster than firms' production costs because much of the latter (especially wages) are fixed periodically by contractual agreements. As less efficient resources are brought into use, the AS curve becomes steeper. Therefore, further increases in aggregate demand cause the average price level to rise faster than real output.

Summarizing these ideas:

In the *Keynesian range*, the average price level remains constant while the volume of real output can vary. In the *intermediate range*, both the average price level and the volume of real output can vary. In the *classical range*, the average price level can vary but not the volume of real output.

Conclusion: Short-Run Determinants are Important

You can see from this analysis that unemployment and inflation are related problems. They arise from the *relative* positions of the economy's *AD* and *AS* curves. Depending on the shapes of the curves and the point at which they intersect, the economy will experience some combination of unemployment and inflation. The outcome can be a misallocation of resources, resulting in losses of efficiency, stability and growth. Because of this:

It is important to know the factors that influence aggregate demand and aggregate supply. Once the factors are known, we can better evaluate government policies aimed at reducing unemployment and inflation.

As you will learn, most of the factors affecting aggregate demand and aggregate supply are short-run, not long-run in nature. This suggests that the following quotation is as significant today as when it was first written more than half a century ago:

But the *long run* is a misleading guide to current affairs. *In the long run we are all dead.* Economists set themselves too easy, too useless a task if in tempestuous seasons they can only tell us that when the storm is long past the ocean is flat again.
—John Maynard Keynes

The Multiplier Principle

One of the most significant factors affecting aggregate demand, and therefore the economy's level of income, is the amount of investment. You already know that an increase in investment can cause an increase in income. Likewise, a decrease in investment can cause a decrease in income. What you may not know is that *investment spending may have an amplifying effect on economic activity:*

An increase in investment may cause a magnified increase in income and output. Similarly, a decrease in investment may cause a magnified decrease in income and output. The amount by which a change in investment is multiplied to produce an ultimate change in income and output is called the **multiplier.** (Keep in mind that the variables, such as investment, income, and others mentioned below, are assumed to be expressed in *real*, not nominal, terms.)

For instance, if a permanent increase in investment of $5 billion per year causes an increase in income and output of $10 billion, the multiplier is 2. If, instead, the increase in income and output is $15 billion, the multiplier is 3. How does the multiplier principle work? It can be illustrated in three ways: numerically, in the form of a table; graphically, in the form of a diagram; and algebraically, in the form of an equation.

In order to understand the illustrations, you must recall two important concepts that you learned in the previous chapter:

1. The *marginal propensity to consume (MPC)* is the fraction of each additional dollar of income that is spent on consumption.
2. The *marginal propensity to save (MPS)* is the fraction of each additional dollar of income that is saved.

You will now see how these two fundamental ideas, when applied to the multiplier principle, can be put to use. To begin with, it will first be assumed that the *average price level remains constant.* This assumption will then be dropped and a new illustration showing the effect of a *varying* price level will be presented.

Numerical Illustration

Suppose that businesses decide to spend $5 billion more per year on construction of new plants and equipment. This means that unemployed workers, materials suppliers, and so on, will be hired for the construction. If we assume that they have an MPC of ⅘ and hence an MPS of ⅕, they will tend to spend four-fifths and save one-fifth of any additional income they receive.

The ultimate effect on income is illustrated in Exhibit 6. In the first round of expenditures, the increase in investment of $5 billion becomes increased income to the owners of the newly hired resources. Because their MPC is ⅘ and their MPS is ⅕, they utilize 80 percent, or $4 billion, for increased consumption and 20 percent, or $1 billion, for increased saving.

In round 2, when the four-fifths is spent on consumption, firms find their sales increasing and their inventories decreasing. Therefore, firms hire more resources in order to increase their production, thereby creating $4 billion of income for the owners of the resources. These income recipients then utilize four-fifths, or $3.2 billion, for increased consumption and one-fifth, or $0.8 billion, for increased saving.

In round 3 and in each subsequent round, the process is repeated. Four-fifths of each increase in income is spent in the following round and is thereby added to the economy's previous gain in income.

Thus, a permanent increase in investment of $5 billion in round 1 has brought about an ultimate increase in income of $25 billion. The multiplier is therefore 5. This overall increase in income consists of a $20 billion increase in consumption plus a $5 billion increase in saving. The total saving increase is always the amount of the original investment, as you can verify from the table.

Note from the table that the greatest increases in income occur during the first few rounds. After that, however, the income effects tend to fade away gradually—like the ripples produced by a stone dropped into a pond.

Exhibit 6
The Multiplier Illustrated Numerically
(all data in billions of constant dollars)

$$MPC = ⅘$$
$$MPS = ⅕$$
$$\text{multiplier} = 5$$

Expenditure rounds	Increase in income	Increase in consumption, MPC = ⅘	Increase in saving, MPS = ⅕
1 increase in investment = $5 billion	$ 5.00	$ 4.00	$1.00
2	4.00	3.20	0.80
3	3.20	2.56	0.64
4	2.56	2.05	0.51
5	2.05	1.64	0.41
6	1.64	1.31	0.33
All other rounds	6.55	5.24	1.31
Total	$25.00	$20.00	$5.00

Graphic Illustration

Exhibit 7 represents the same multiplier concept graphically. It shows how an increase in investment, represented by an upward shift of the $C + I$ curve in Figure (a), or by an upward shift of the I curve in Figure (b), causes a magnified increase in output. As before, the diagrams are based on the assumption that the MPC is ⅘ and the MPS is ⅕. That is, the aggregate expenditure curve has a slope of ⅘ and the saving curve has a slope of ⅕.

Point E in both diagrams represents the initial equilibrium level at which aggregate expenditure equals aggregate output and saving equals investment. Point E' in both diagrams defines a new equilibrium resulting from an increase in investment.

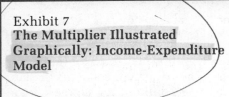

Exhibit 7
The Multiplier Illustrated
Graphically: Income-Expenditure
Model

$MPC = \frac{4}{5}$
$MPS = \frac{1}{5}$
multiplier = 5

Figure (a): An increase in the level of investment by \$5 billion causes an increase in the level of income, or NNP, by \$25 billion.   Hence, the multiplier is 5.

Figure (b): What happens to income, or NNP, if investment falls back to \$40 billion?   To \$35 billion?

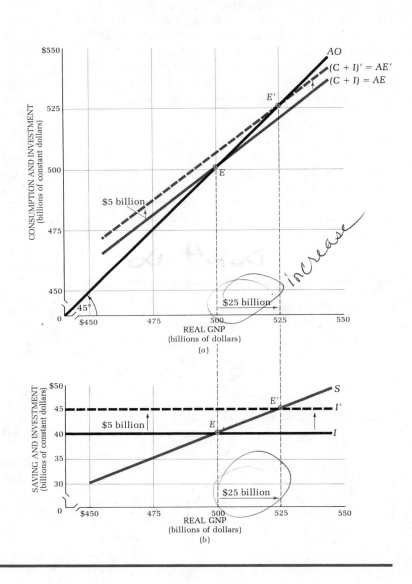

Note from the description accompanying the diagrams that the increase in income is a *multiple* of the increase in investment. The multiplier, as you can see, is 5.

Can you also see that the multiplier works in reverse? For example, what happens to income if investment falls back to its initial level? What happens if investment falls below its initial level?

Algebraic Illustration

The tabular and graphic illustrations of the multiplier demonstrate that the increase in income is related to the marginal propensities to consume and to save. For example, you have already learned from the study of the consumption function that

$$MPC + MPS = 1$$

Therefore,

$$MPS = 1 - MPC$$

From the previous illustrations, you know that MPC is $\frac{4}{5}$ and MPS is $\frac{1}{5}$.

Therefore, you can easily verify that

$$\text{multiplier} = \frac{1}{\frac{1}{5}} = \frac{1}{1 - \frac{4}{5}} = 5$$

This is the same value of the multiplier obtained previously in the numerical and graphic illustrations.

These ideas have been stated in the form of a specific example. They can now be expressed in a general formula:

$$\text{multiplier} = \frac{1}{MPS} = \frac{1}{1 - MPC}$$

This means that, if you know either the MPC or the MPS, you can determine the multiplier immediately. (This is what was done above to determine a multiplier of 5.) Then, once you know the value of the multiplier, you can predict the ultimate change in income that may result from a change in investment by the formula:

$$\text{multiplier} \times \text{change in investment} = \text{change in income}$$

The same formula applies to a decrease as well as an increase in investment. Go back and check it out in the illustrations above, just to make sure that you see how it works.

Notice that *the multiplier is the reciprocal of the MPS.* (The reciprocal of a number is 1 divided by that number.) Thus, the lower the *MPS*, the less withdrawal or "leakage" into extra saving that occurs at each round of income and the greater the *MPC*. Therefore, the greater the value of the multiplier. Conversely, the greater the *MPS*, the lower the *MPC*. Therefore, the lower the value of the multiplier.

To summarize:

The *multiplier* principle states that changes in investment can bring about magnified changes in income. This idea is expressed by the equation: multiplier × change in investment = change in income. The formula for the multiplier coefficient is thus

$$\text{multiplier} = \frac{\text{change in income}}{\text{change in investment}}$$

$$= \frac{1}{MPS} = \frac{1}{1 - MPC}$$

where *MPS* stands for the marginal propensity to save and *MPC* for the marginal propensity to consume. (NOTE This multiplier is also sometimes called the *simple multiplier*, the *expenditure multiplier*, or the *investment multiplier*. These names are used to distinguish it from other multipliers in economics.)

What Happens When the Price Level Varies?

Until now, the explanation of the multiplier principle has been based on the assumption that the *average price level remains constant*. That is, the analysis was done in terms of an *income-expenditure* model, like the one shown earlier in Exhibit 7. What happens if this assumption is relaxed?

The answer is shown in terms of an *income-price* model in Exhibit 8. Note that the equilibrium point at E_0 results from the intersection of the aggregate supply curve AS and the initial aggregate demand curve, AD_0. This equilibrium point denotes an income level of $500 billion and a price level of P_0.

Exhibit 8
The Multiplier Effect When the Price Level Varies: Income-Price Model

An increase in aggregate expenditure of $5 billion (shown previously in Exhibit 7) shifts the aggregate demand curve in this diagram from AD_0 to AD_1. This increases real income by $20 billion — a multiplier of 4 — and the price level by an assumed 20 percent. If the price level had remained constant at P_0, the AS curve would have been the horizontal dashed-and-dotted line from P_0 to E_0'. The increase in real income would have been $25 billion, a multiplier of 5. Thus:

When the price level rises, part of the multiplier's effect is lost through higher prices, and only part is left to increase real income. In this example, a 20 percent increase in prices resulted in a 20 percent smaller multiplier (4 instead of 5). It also resulted in a 20 percent smaller increase in real income ($520 billion instead of $525 billion).

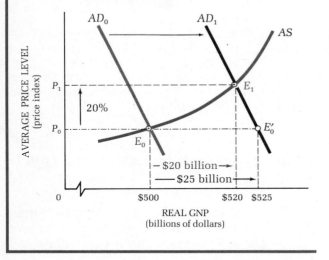

Let us now assume the same $5 billion increase in aggregate expenditure that was employed in Exhibit 7. The effect of this increased expenditure is to shift the aggregate demand curve to the right from AD_0 to AD_1. The equilibrium point, therefore, changes from E_0 to E_1. This new equilibrium point denotes an income level of $520 billion and a price

level of P_1. The gain in real income is thus $20 billion, and hence the multiplier is 4.

What would have happened if the price level had remained constant at P_0? In that case, the new equilibrium point would have been at E_0'. (In other words, the aggregate supply curve, as in the strict Keynesian view presented earlier, would have been the horizontal dashed-and-dotted line extending from P_0 to E_0'.) Therefore, the equilibrium income would have been $525 billion. Thus, an increase in aggregate expenditure of $5 billion would have resulted in an increase in real income of $25 billion. The multiplier, therefore, would have been 5 — the same as in the income-expenditure model of Exhibit 7.

This example has assumed that the increase in the price level from P_0 to P_1 was 20 percent. (In reality, the amount of the increase will depend on the *slopes* of the AD and AS curves.) Because of this, the size of the multiplier was 20 percent less (4 instead of 5) than it would have been if the price level had remained constant. Similarly, the increase in real income was 20 percent less ($520 billion as compared to $525 billion) than would have been realized if the price level had remained constant.

Conclusion: Different-Sized Multipliers

The multiplier principle is of fundamental importance in macroeconomics. The larger the multiplier, the greater the amount by which an increase in aggregate expenditure results in an increase in aggregate income. However, the size of the multiplier will be affected by the *change* in the average price level. Thus:

If the aggregate supply curve is upward-sloping, an increase in aggregate demand causes the average price level to rise. As a result, the size of the multiplier is smaller than it would be if the average price level remained constant. This is because part of the multiplier's effect is lost through higher prices, and only part is left to increase real income.

Economics in the News

Search for a Miracle Cure

An Economist Touts Profit Sharing as a Prescription for Prosperity

—*By Charles P. Alexander*
Reported by Gisela Bolte/Washington and Rosemary Byrnes/New York

M.I.T. Economist Martin Weitzman may at first appear to be his profession's version of a snake-oil salesman. In his new book *The Share Economy* (Harvard; $15), Weitzman claims to have found a cure-all that will end both unemployment and inflation. The trick, he says, is for U.S. industry to abandon the practice of paying fixed wages and adopt a scheme that would compensate workers in relation to their employers' revenues or profits.

Suppose, says Weitzman, that workers agreed to accept a share of the company's revenues or profits —two-thirds, for example—as compensation in lieu of set wages. That money would be divided among all employees. When revenues dipped during a slump, workers' income would drop accordingly, and the firm could then reduce prices to revive sales. Because all the workers take a temporary cut, no one

would have to be laid off. The burden of the recession would be shared by the entire work force.

Weitzman contends that even in good times, fixed wages are a barrier to increased employment. Companies today are afraid to hire too many new employees because they do not want to be stuck with them when the economy turns down. But in a share system, says Weitzman, the company would have more incentive to hire new employees. The workers would be there to help when business is good, but they would not be a drag on earnings when it is bad because the employees' average pay would fall along with revenues. Workers might be willing to take a pay cut in exchange for job security. "Firms ever hungry for labor," writes the economist, would be "always on the prowl—cruising around like vacuum cleaners on wheels, searching in nooks and crannies for extra workers."

The major practical problem with Weitzman's plan is that it is not attractive to workers with seniority who are in little danger of being laid off during a recession. Many of them would undoubtedly make less money in a share economy than they do now. For that reason, labor unions are decidedly cool toward the pro-

posal. Says Murray Seeger, director of information for the AFL-CIO: "This scheme would continue the suppression of workers' earnings." Weitzman says the Government would have to lead the way in overcoming worker opposition. He suggests that employees who accept a share plan be given income tax breaks similar to the preferential treatment of capital gains.

Some businessmen also dispute Weitzman's reasoning. They argue that companies cannot add employees unless demand for their products increases.

Many economists praise the theoretical elegance of Weitzman's plan, but doubt that it could be put into practice any time soon, if at all. Says David Glasner, a senior fellow at the Manhattan Institute for Policy Research: "Workers simply prefer having a known wage rate and do not want to take the risk of a variable income." Contends Melvin Reder, a professor of urban and labor economics at the University of Chicago's Graduate School of Business: "Weitzman's proposal is like the advice of a philosopher to a King, not to a President and Congress in a democratic society."

On the basis of this conclusion, you should be able to demonstrate, by sketching your own graphs, the following proposition:

> *The change in the price level, and therefore the size of the multiplier, will be determined by the steepness (slopes) of the AD and AS curves.*

Inflationary and Recessionary Gaps

You have now reached a point where the foregoing theoretical models can be put to use in analyzing such important macroeconomic problems as unem-

Exhibit 9
Inflationary and Recessionary Gaps

Inflationary and recessionary gaps are always measured with reference either to full (natural) employment or to potential output.   These are corresponding concepts, as you can see from the graphs.   The gaps can be shown in two ways:

1. In terms of total spending (measured on the vertical axis) in the income-expenditure model.

2. In terms of real output (measured on the horizontal axis) in the income-price model.

INCOME-EXPENDITURE MODEL

INCOME-PRICE MODEL

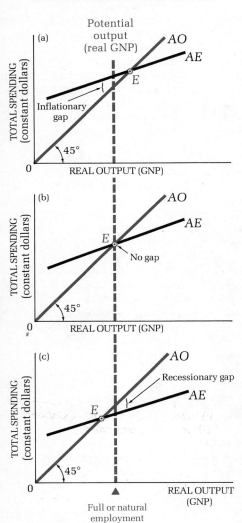

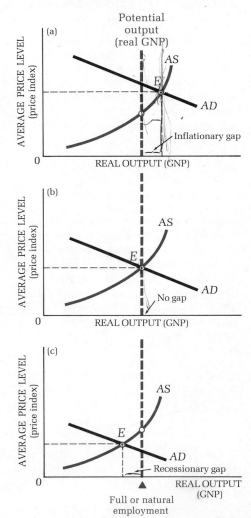

Figure *(a):* Inflationary Gap
(Left) Aggregate expenditure exceeds aggregate output at the full-employment level.
(Right) Actual output exceeds potential output at the equilibrium price level.

Figure *(b):* No Gap   *(Left)* Aggregate expenditure equals aggregate output at the full-employment level.
(Right) Actual output equals potential output at the equilibrium price level.

Figure *(c):* Recessionary Gap
(Left) Aggregate expenditure is less than aggregate output at the full-employment level.
(Right) Actual output is less than potential output at the equilibrium price level.

ployment and inflation. But before doing that, you will find it helpful to formulate the problems in terms of both the income-expenditure and income-price models.

The type of formulation needed is shown in Exhibit 9. This exhibit illustrates what may be called inflationary and recessionary gaps. These are defined in terms of *total spending* (measured on the vertical axis) in the income-expenditure model. In contrast, they are defined in terms of *real output* —that is, real GNP (measured on the horizontal axis)—in the income-price model. The figures illustrate three possibilities:

Inflationary Gap: Figure *(a)* An inflationary gap occurs in the income-expenditure model when, on the vertical axis, aggregate expenditure (AE) exceeds aggregate output (AO) at the full-employment level. It also occurs in the income-price model when, on the horizontal axis, actual output exceeds potential output at the equilibrium price level.

No Gap: Figure *(b)* This pleasant state of affairs is realized in the income-expenditure model when, on the vertical axis, aggregate expenditure (AE) equals aggregate output (AO) at the full-employment level. It is also realized in the income-price model when, on the horizontal axis, actual output equals potential output at the equilibrium price level.

Equilibrium is greated

Recessionary Gap: Figure *(c)* A recessionary gap occurs in the income-expenditure model when, on the vertical axis, aggregate expenditure (AE) is less than aggregate output (AO) at the full-employment level. It also occurs in the income-price model when, on the horizontal axis, actual output is less than potential output at the equilibrium price level.

Note from these explanations that inflationary and recessionary gaps are always defined with reference either to full (natural) employment or to potential output. Both are corresponding concepts, as you can see from the graphs.

Conclusion: Closing the Gaps

At any given time, the economy may not be at full- or natural-employment equilibrium. Economists view this as a short-run phenomenon. It evidences either of two conditions:

1. An inflationary gap, creating upward pressure on prices.

2. A recessionary gap, resulting in cyclical unemployment.

To avoid these possibilities, and to try to correct them if they occur, government has come to play an important role in modern macroeconomics.

In an effort to close inflationary and deflationary gaps, government adopts various types of measures. Some are designed to shift aggregate demand while others are intended to shift aggregate supply. The extent to which government policies are successful is a subject of continual debate. As a result, such policies are among the most controversial issues of our time.

Fiscal Policy
Inflation: promote higher taxes
Recession: decrea taxes

What You Have Learned

1. Real GNP and the level of employment tend toward equilibrium. In the income-expenditure model, equilibrium occurs where aggregate output equals aggregate expenditure and planned saving equals planned investment. The movement toward equilibrium occurs as businesses seek to adjust unplanned inventory accumulations or depletions. At any given time, the location of the equilibrium point may or may not correspond to full (natural) employment.

2. Investment spending may be thought of as an injection into the economy's circular flow of income; saving may be thought of as a withdrawal. Disparities between the "inflow" of investment and the "outflow" of saving will cause the economy's level of income to rise or fall. However, at any given level of income, the investment inflow equals the saving outflow.

3. In the income-price model, the downward-sloping aggregate demand curve and upward-sloping aggregate supply curve determine an equilibrium output and price level. At any given time, the location of the equilibrium

point may or may not correspond to full (natural) employment.

4. Any increase (or decrease) in investment can cause a multiple expansion (or contraction) of real income. Any changes in consumption (or saving) can similarly produce multiple effects on real income. All such effects are called *multiplier effects*. The simple multiplier is also called the investment multiplier. It shows the extent to which changes in investment may cause magnified changes in real income. The multiplier is equal to the reciprocal of the marginal propensity to save.

5. The multiplier will be smaller if prices vary than if they are constant. This is because a rising price level dissipates part of the multiplier's effect through higher prices. As a result, only a portion of the multiplier is left to increase real income.

6. Inflationary and recessionary gaps arise because of disparities between aggregate expenditure and aggregate output, and between actual output and potential output, at full employment. These gaps raise the question whether government policies can be designed to close the gaps.

Terms and Concepts to Review

aggregate expenditure
aggregate output
"bathtub theorem"
aggregate demand
real-balance effect
interest-rate effect

aggregate supply
potential real GNP
full employment
multiplier
inflationary gap
recessionary gap

For Discussion

1. Complete the following table for a hypothetical economy. (All figures are in billions of constant dollars.)

Real GNP	C	S	I	APC	APS	MPC	MPS
$100	$125		$25				
$200	200						
300							
400							
500							

Assume that the consumption function is a straight line and that investment is constant at all levels of income.

(a) From the data in the table, draw a graph of the consumption function and of the consumption-plus-investment function. Underneath this graph, draw a graph of the saving and investment curves. Then connect the two sets of break-even points with vertical dashed lines.
(b) Has there been a multiplier effect as a result of the inclusion of investment? If yes, by how much? What is the numerical value of the multiplier?
(c) What is the equilibrium level of income and output before and after the inclusion of investment?
(d) What will income be if investment increases by $10 billion?
(e) What will happen in your answer to (d) if the price level rises by 25 percent? Explain the reason for your answer.

2. How does the size of the multiplier vary with MPC? How does it vary with MPS? Explain why, without using any equations. How does the size of the multiplier vary with changes in the price level?

3. Thrift may be desirable for an individual, but it *may* cause a recession if practiced by everyone. Why?

4. A student remarked to his instructor: "First you say that saving and investment are almost never really equal. Then you say they are always really equal. Why don't you economists make up your minds?" Can you help the student out of his muddle? SUGGESTION Use the "bathtub theorem" to explain your answer.

5. Suppose your consumption C is related to your disposable income DI by the equation

$$C = 120 + 0.60\,DI$$

(a) What will be the amount of consumption at an income level of 100?
(b) How much income is required to support a consumption level of 420?
(c) What will be the amount of consumption if income is taxed 100 percent? How can consumption be financed under such circumstances?
(d) What is the value of your MPC? What is the value of your MPS?
(e) Prepare your personal consumption and saving schedule, and graph the consumption and saving functions for income levels from DI = 100 to DI = 500. What is your equilibrium level of income?

6. If the previous problem were for an entire economy, and if planned investment were 50, what would be the equation for aggregate demand? Draw the aggregate demand curve and investment curve on your graphs. Can you estimate the equilibrium level of income from your graphs?

7. (Advanced Problem) Refer to your graphs from the previous problem.

(a) At a realized income of 500, how much is unplanned investment? How much is realized investment? Is this an equilibrium situation? Explain.

(b) At a realized income of 400, how much is unplanned investment? How much is realized investment? Is this an equilibrium situation? Explain.

(c) At the realized-income levels in (a) and (b), does saving equal investment? Explain.

8. Can you suggest at least one method that government might employ in an effort to close inflationary and recessionary gaps?

Chapter 10

Fiscal Policy and the National Debt

[handwritten: Refer to old economics text]

Learning Guide

Watch for answers to these important questions

How is Keynesian economics applied to the problem of reducing unemployment? In what ways do government spending and taxing policies affect the levels of output and employment?

What is the balanced-budget multiplier? What lesson does it teach us? Does it always work as expected?

How does fiscal policy operate?

Has discretionary fiscal policy been successful in achieving its economic goals?

What are the burdens of a national debt? Are there some practical guidelines for managing it?

[handwritten marginal notes: inflationary + recessionary gaps / Tries to fix inflationary + recessionary gaps]

[handwritten left margin notes: ① Increase Spending / ② Decrease Taxes of Fed./Decrease Recession goal / ③ Combination to Close / B/D]

How does macroeconomics explain the existence of inflationary and recessionary gaps? The answer, you will recall, was given near the end of the previous chapter. The gaps occur when, at the full-employment level of output, there are disparities between aggregate expenditure and aggregate output, or between aggregate demand and aggregate supply.

How does macroeconomics seek to remedy these conditions? Through the use of what is known as *fiscal policy*, government applies measures whose aim is to achieve full utilization of available resources at stable prices.

In other words, *fiscal policy deals with the deliberate exercise of the government's power to tax and spend for the purpose of closing recessionary and inflationary gaps.* We will be concerned with fiscal policy in this chapter and in several later ones.

Bringing in Government

The economic role of government is always controversial. Should taxes be raised or lowered? Should government spending be increased or reduced? These are among the fundamental issues of fiscal policy. In this chapter, both the income-expenditure and the income-price models are enlarged to include the role of government.

Income-Expenditure Model: Constant Price Level

In the previous chapter you learned that, in the income-expenditure model, prices are assumed to remain constant. Aggregate expenditure and aggregate output are then compared to total spending in order to identify recessionary and inflationary gaps. This approach, as you will now see, makes it possible to formulate useful fiscal-policy tools. We can begin by demonstrating the first of two propositions:

PROPOSITION 1:
Increased government spending raises aggregate expenditure; decreased spending lowers it.

Government fiscal policy affects the income-expenditure model through two major variables—taxes and spending. Let us assume for the moment that *taxes are held constant.* Then government spending (G) on goods and services becomes a net addition to total spending or aggregate expenditure (AE). That is, government spending supplements household consumption expenditures (C) and business investment expenditures (I).

This is illustrated in the hypothetical case of Exhibit 1, Figure (a). The C + I + G curve shows total spending at each level of real GNP. The new equilibrium point at which aggregate expenditure AE equals aggregate output AO occurs at E. The corresponding information in terms of saving and investment is given in Figure (b). Observe that the upward-sloping line now represents saving plus taxes (S + T). This is because taxes, like saving, denote a portion of income not spent on consumption.

Notice in Figure (a) that the AE curve includes a certain amount of government spending. However, the equilibrium GNP of $600 billion is still short of the $700 billion needed to reach the full (natural) employment level of output. Full or natural employment can be achieved only if the aggregate expenditure curve is raised high enough to close the recessionary gap. This can come about through an increase in any of the components of AE—namely, C, I, or G. If we assume that C and I remain constant, an increase in G by the amount G' will close the recessionary gap by raising the aggregate expenditure curve from AE to AE'.

Multiplier Effect

Note that an increase in government expenditure, with taxes held constant, has a multiplier effect on GNP just as does an increase in private investment expenditure. As you can see in the assumptions accompanying the diagram, the multiplier is 5. Therefore, an increase in aggregate expenditure of $20 billion, from C + I + G to C + I + G + G', increases GNP by $100 billion. We can infer from this that a rise in government expenditure has the same multiplier effect on GNP as a rise in consumer expenditure or a rise in investment expenditure. This is because a rise in government expenditure (i.e., government purchases of goods and services) increases the sales and profits of firms that sell to the government. This, in turn, leads to further increases in output throughout the economy. Because of this, the multiplier in Exhibit 1 may be called an **expenditure multiplier.** Thus:

Increased government spending can raise the level of aggregate expenditure from an unemployment to a full-employment level. (So too can increased consumption and investment spending.) However, any additional spending that raises aggregate expenditure above full-employment levels will be inflationary.

Against this background, you can now appreciate the meaning of the second proposition.

PROPOSITION 2:
Increased taxes reduces aggregate expenditure; decreased taxes raise it. ~Spending~

What happens to the equilibrium level of GNP when government spending is constant and taxes vary? You can answer this question in terms of the diagram in Exhibit 2. The C curve, as always, is

Exhibit 1
Effect of Increased Government Spending on Gross National Product

Assumptions: $MPC = \frac{4}{5}$ and $MPS = \frac{1}{5}$; therefore:

$$\text{expenditure multiplier} = \frac{1}{1 - \frac{4}{5}} = \frac{1}{\frac{1}{5}} = 5$$

multiplier

Figure (a): Increased government spending by the amount G' raises aggregate expenditure from AE to AE'. This produces a multiplier effect on GNP. Because the multiplier is 5, increased government spend-

ing of $20 billion increases GNP by $5 \times \$20$ billion = $100 billion: from $600 billion to $700 billion. This closes the recessionary gap.

Figure (b): The multiplier effect of increased government spending G' can also be seen in terms of a saving–investment diagram. A $20 billion increase in government spending raises the equilibrium GNP by 5 times the increase in spending: from $600 billion to $700 billion, an expansion of $100 billion.

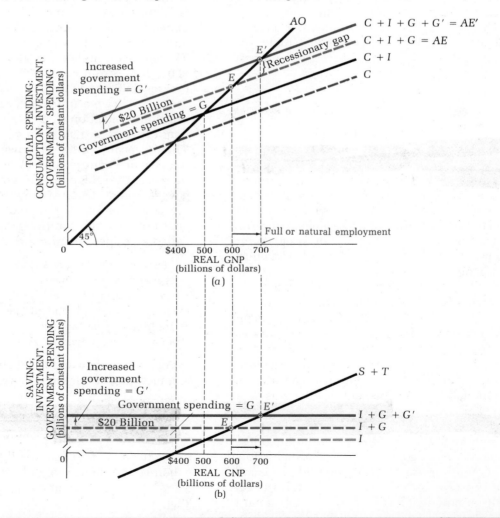

Exhibit 2
Effect of Increased Taxes on Consumption and on GNP

Assumptions: (1) MPC = ⅘ and MPS = ⅕; therefore, expenditure multiplier = 5.   (2) T = tax increase of $20 billion.

As a result of the tax increase, the consumption curve shifts downward from C to C', and hence the equilibrium point changes from E to E'. The amount of change equals $MPC \times T$. Thus, because MPC = ⅘ and the tax increase is $20 billion, the C curve shifts downward by ⅘ × $20 billion = $16 billion.

However, because the expenditure multiplier is 5, GNP on the horizontal axis decreases by a multiple of the decrease in spending—by 5 × $16 billion = $80 billion. Note too that, although the decrease in GNP is equal to 5 times the $16 billion decrease in spending, it is equal to 4 times the $20 billion increase in taxes. The number 4 may therefore be called the *tax multiplier*.

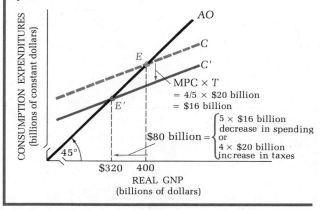

drawn on the assumption that consumption expenditures depend on income while *all other factors that may affect consumption remain constant*. A change in any of these "all other" factors will cause the consumption curve to shift.

Thus, suppose a net increase in personal income taxes *(T)* of $20 billion is imposed on consumers. The results may be analyzed in two steps:

Step 1 The first effect of the $20 billion increase in taxes is to reduce people's disposable income by

$20 billion. Therefore, the consumption curve in Exhibit 2 shifts downward from C to C'. However, because *consumption depends on income* and the MPC is ⅘, consumption expenditures decrease by ⅘ of $20 billion = $16 billion. Thus, as you can see, the *decrease in consumption, measured by the amount of downward shift of the curve*, equals $MPC \times T$.

Step 2 What will be the effect of the increased taxes on GNP? Because the expenditure multiplier is 5, a decrease in consumption expenditures of $16 billion will reduce GNP by 5 × $16 billion = $80 billion. Equivalently, because taxes have increased by $20 billion, GNP will be reduced by a multiple of that amount, namely, 4 × $20 billion = $80 billion. This is shown in the diagram, where the equilibrium GNP changes from E at $400 billion to E' at $320 billion, a decrease of $80 billion.

As you might expect, a decrease in taxes of $20 billion would have had the opposite effect. Such a decrease would have stimulated consumer spending, raised aggregate expenditure, and thereby—according to theory—increased GNP by $80 billion.

The Balanced Budget Multiplier

Suppose that we now allow government spending, G, and taxes, T, to vary simultaneously. For instance, what will be the effect if G and T are both increased simultaneously by the same amount—in our example, by $20 billion?

- By itself, the increase in G would raise GNP by 5 × $20 billion = $100 billion. In general, the multiple by which an increase in total spending, by raising aggregate expenditure, may be expected to expand GNP is called the **expenditure multiplier** (M_E). In this example, M_E has a numerical value of 5.

- By itself, the increase in T would lower GNP by 4 × $20 billion = $80 billion. In general, the multiple by which an increase in personal income taxes, by lowering aggregate expenditure, may be expected to contract GNP is called the **tax multiplier** (M_T). In this example, M_T has a numerical value of 4.

— Therefore, the net effect of *equal* increases in G and T together will be to increase GNP by $1 \times \$20$ billion = $20 billion, which is the amount of the initial increment. In general, the multiple by which equal changes in government spending and taxes affect changes in GNP is called the **balanced-budget multiplier** (M_B). In this example, M_B has a numerical value of 1.

The reason for this result is that the $20 billion increases in G and T are precisely equal, but their effects are opposite. The two multiplier processes thus cancel each other out—except on the first round, when the full amount of G ($20 billion) is added to GNP. This is why the *net* multiplier effect of equal increases in G and T is 5 — 4 = 1.

We can now summarize all of the foregoing ideas in this way:

If G and T are increased (or decreased) simultaneously by equal amounts, GNP will be increased (or decreased) by the same amount. For example, a simultaneous increase in G and T by $20 billion will raise GNP by $1 \times \$20$ billion = $20 billion. Similarly, a simultaneous decrease by $20 billion will lower GNP by $1 \times$ $20 billion = $20 billion. Thus, the numerical value of the expenditure multiplier, M_E, minus the numerical value of the tax multiplier, M_T, is called the *balanced-budget multiplier*, M_B. In general, it is always true that, *if prices remain constant, $M_B = M_E - M_T = 1$.*

Income-Price Model: Varying Price Level

In reality, of course, prices are not likely to remain constant. Because of this, it often proves useful to employ the income-price model instead of the income-expenditure model to evaluate fiscal-policy actions. As you will recall, the income-price model allows the price level to vary. Recessionary and inflationary gaps are then analyzed in terms of aggregate demand and aggregate supply.

Exhibit 3 shows how government spending and taxing policies can be used to close recessionary and inflationary gaps. The diagrams illustrate what

Exhibit 3
Fiscal Policies for Closing Recessionary and Inflationary Gaps

To close a recessionary or an inflationary gap, government uses fiscal policies in order to shift the *AD* curve.

Figure (a): Closing a Recessionary Gap An increase in government demand, a decrease in individual or in corporate income taxes, or some combination of both will shift aggregate demand from *AD* to *AD′*. The average price level will also rise, from *P* to *P′*.

Figure (b): Closing an Inflationary Gap A decrease in government demand, an increase in individual or in corporate income taxes, or some combination of both will shift aggregate demand from *AD* to *AD′*. The average price level will also decline, from *P* to *P′*.

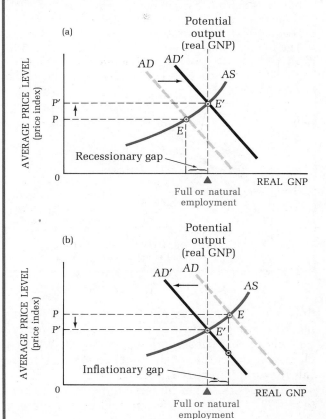

happens when fiscal policies are used to shift aggregate demand. This, you will recall, is the sum of consumption demand, investment demand, and government demand at each average price level. Aggregate supply, on the other hand, is the value of real total output that will be made available at each average price level.

Figure (a) shows that, in trying to close a recessionary gap, government can adopt fiscal policies aimed at increasing aggregate demand. These would shift the curve from AD to AD'. Examples of such policies are increases in government demand (that is, government spending), decreases in personal and in corporate income taxes (in order to raise consumption and investment demand), or some combination of both. With the closing of the gap, the average price level would rise from P to P'.

Figure (b) shows how fiscal policies can be used to close an inflationary gap. These involve measures designed to decrease aggregate demand. For example, reductions in government demand, increases in personal and in corporate income taxes, or some combination of both, would shift the aggregate demand curve from AD to AD'. This would be accompanied by a decrease in the average price level from P to P'.

Conclusion: Need for Fiscal Understanding

In the income-expenditure model, prices are assumed to remain constant. Recessionary and inflationary gaps are closed by increasing or decreasing *aggregate expenditures* through various combinations of government spending and taxing.

In the income-price model, prices are permitted to vary. Recessionary and inflationary gaps are closed by increasing or decreasing *aggregate demand* through various combinations of government spending and taxing.

Which model is better for evaluating government spending and taxing programs? There is no simple answer because both models provide useful insights. Nevertheless:

Because it allows for changes in the price level, the income-price model is usually more suitable for judging the effects of fiscal policies in today's economy.

Unfortunately, however, the multiplier effects of changes in spending and taxing cannot be predicted precisely. Real-world economic conditions are too complex to be captured by a few simple formulas and diagrams. As a result, government fiscal policies are likely to overshoot or undershoot potential-output targets. To understand what is involved in trying to hit the targets, we now turn to the principles and problems that underlie the administration of fiscal policy.

Principles of Fiscal Policy

The foregoing analysis follows logically from Keynesian theory. The analysis suggests that fiscal policy offers a sure-fire means of stabilizing the economy at a high level of employment. By simply manipulating government spending (G) and taxing (T), it seems, Washington can greatly reduce the peaks and troughs of business cycles.

Most economists once held such beliefs with firm conviction. But since the mid 1970s when the United States experienced its worst recession in 30 years, these ideas have been regarded as somewhat naive. The reasons are best understood if we distinguish between so-called nondiscretionary and discretionary fiscal controls, so that their problems can be analyzed.

Nondiscretionary Controls: Automatic Fiscal Stabilizers

Some fiscal activity is *nondiscretionary*, meaning that it is neither deliberate nor planned by government. For example, significant changes in the levels of government spending and taxes occur automatically over the business cycle without any explicit decisions by the President or Congress.

In fact, the U.S. economy has certain "built-in" stabilizers called ***automatic fiscal stabilizers.***

They help cushion the economy against a recession by retarding a decline in aggregate income. They also help curb an inflation by retarding an increase in aggregate income. Automatic fiscal stabilizers thereby contribute to keeping the economic system in balance without human intervention or control, much as a thermostat helps to maintain an even temperature in a house.

Three stabilizers are particularly important:

Tax Receipts Income taxes are the largest source of revenue to the federal government. The tax rate that people pay on their incomes is progressive. Therefore, when aggregate income rises, there is a more than proportional increase in government tax receipts. This tends to restrain an economic boom. On the other hand, a declining aggregate income results in more than proportional decreases in government tax receipts. This tends to moderate an economic recession.

Unemployment Taxes and Benefits During times of prosperity and high employment, total tax receipts to finance the unemployment-insurance program exceed total benefits paid out. This creates a surplus, which has a dampening effect on the economy. During recession and unemployment, the reverse occurs. This creates a deficit, which has a stimulative effect on the economy.

Corporate Dividend Policy Corporations generally maintain fairly stable dividends in the short run. That is, their dividend payouts to stockholders do not fluctuate with each reported increase or decrease in profits. As a result, retained corporate earnings or undistributed profits, to the extent that they are saved and not invested, tend to have a stabilizing influence in expansionary and contractionary periods alike.

Exhibit 4 explains how automatic stabilizers tend to limit the peaks and troughs of business cycles. As you can see, because of our progressive tax structure, an increase or decrease in GNP can *automatically* push the budget toward a surplus or deficit.

Exhibit 4
Automatic Stabilizers

Suppose that government expenditures remain constant at all levels of the nation's output. As GNP rises or falls, the government's tax receipts increase or decrease correspondingly. Thus, starting with a balanced budget at an output of GNP_0:

— An increase in output from GNP_0 to GNP_1 causes tax receipts to rise. This *automatically* creates a budget surplus, which tends to dampen an economic expansion.

— A decrease in output from GNP_0 to GNP_2 causes tax receipts to decline. This *automatically* creates a budget deficit, which tends to soften an economic contraction.

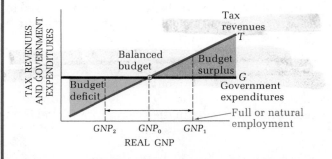

On the whole, the automatic stabilizers tend to reduce the severity of business cycles. Some studies suggest that all the automatic stabilizers acting together may reduce the amplitudes of cyclical swings by about one-third.

The automatic stabilizers are thus not a cure-all. They merely cut off some of the highs and lows of business cycles. What can be done to further reduce their intensity? Keynesian economics concludes that certain discretionary methods of fiscal policy are needed.

Discretionary Fiscal Policy

Not all fiscal activity occurs automatically. Some of it is *discretionary*, meaning that it is undertaken intentionally by Washington. This suggests the need for a fuller explanation of *fiscal policy.* It may be defined as deliberate spending and taxing actions by the government in order to achieve price stability, to help dampen the swings of business cycles, and to bring the nation's output and employment to desired levels.

Fiscal policy, as we know it today, is largely a direct result of Keynesian beliefs. These ideas hold that fiscal policies should differ over the course of a business cycle. Government spending and taxing policies designed to cure recession are not the same as those aimed at curbing inflation. For example:

During a recession, the goal is to raise aggregate demand to a full-employment level. Thus, an *expansionary* fiscal policy is needed to close the recessionary gap. This may require either an increase in G, a decrease in T, or some combination of both.

During a period of rapid inflation, the goal is to lower aggregate demand to the full-employment level. Therefore, a *contractionary* fiscal policy is needed to close the inflationary gap. This may necessitate either a decrease in G, an increase in T, or some combination of both.

Thus, the principal concerns of discretionary fiscal policy are the ways in which the federal government, *represented by the Treasury,* manages its budget. But these depend on the manner in which the government raises and spends money and on the economic consequences of such activities. Therefore, let us examine these activities.

Where the Money Comes From

In order to manage its budget, the government raises money in two ways — taxing and borrowing. Each of these has different effects on the economy.

Taxing

For purposes of fiscal policy, income taxes (rather than sales taxes, property taxes, or other kinds of taxes) are the most important by far. Changes in the rate structure of income taxes can affect both government revenues and the level of economic activity. The effect of a change in the rate structure depends on *both the MPCs and the MPSs of the income groups affected by the change.*

For instance, suppose tax rates are reduced for lower-income groups and raised for higher-income groups. There may be two possible consequences:

1. Lower-income groups have a relatively high MPC. Therefore, a tax-rate reduction for these groups is likely to stimulate their consumption spending.

2. Upper-income groups have a relatively high MPS. Therefore, a tax-rate increase for these groups may reduce their saving and, hence, the funds they make available for investment.

A change in income-tax rates of the type assumed would thus have definite effects on government tax revenues as well as on the levels of output and employment. On the other hand, a tax-rate change that put a heavier burden on lower-income groups and a lighter burden on higher-income groups could have other kinds of effects. Can you suggest some?

Borrowing

A second method by which the government can raise money is by borrowing. The government borrows when tax revenues are not high enough to cover expenditures. Borrowing, which is the means by which the government finances a deficit, consists of selling Treasury securities, such as bonds, to the public. This may have two consequences:

1. **Higher Interest Rates**   Treasury bonds compete with corporation bonds for investors' dollars. As a result, if all other things remain the same, heavy sales of bonds drive up interest rates. This is because both the Treasury and business borrowers find that they must offer higher interest rates to lenders in order to persuade them to purchase additional bonds.

2. **Crowding Out**   Because deficit spending, which is an expansionary fiscal policy, creates upward pressure on interest rates, it raises borrowing costs.

Economics in the News

Military Spending Lacks Its Usual Effects on Economy

By Peter T. Kilborn

WASHINGTON—Like so many other features of the economy these days, military spending no longer has the [expansionary] effect it used to. However much larger it is than in the past, it is not big enough to swing the whole economy. Services, such as banking, insurance, retailing and the like, represent about ⅔ of the overall economy and account for most economic growth.

One reason that the rise in military spending has not produced its usual effects is that the way the money is being spent has changed. In the Reagan Administration, a larger share has been destined for procurement of weapons and a lesser share for recruiting, wages, military bases and other support spending.

As a result, the rewards of military spending are more concentrated than in the past, bringing prosperity only to the geographical centers of military contracting. Michigan remains one of the nation's most depressed states, but Warren, Mich., where General Dynamics builds the Army's M-1 tank, is thriving.

The Pentagon has also contributed to the industrial renaissance of New England. With 6 percent of the population, the region now receives 12 percent of the procurement budget. (California is far and away the biggest beneficiary, however. The Pentagon reported that California received prime contracts worth $28.4 billion in 1984, nearly three times as much as New York, the No. 2 recipient. California's military payroll is also the nation's biggest.)

In only one area, the specialized job market, is the growth in nonwartime military spending behaving as it normally does. Pentagon contractors provide jobs, of course, but they use fewer and more highly skilled workers than the Government does when it undertakes other large programs, such as highway construction.

"A typical defense worker is a 48-year-old white male with an advanced degree or high technical skills," said Gordon Adams, a defense expert at the nonpartisan Center on Budget and Policy Priorities in Washington. "He's an unusual part of the work force."

Many businesses, of course, are not able to pay the higher costs. Consequently some private investment is reduced because numerous business firms are "crowded out" of the financial markets by government deficit spending.

Where the Money Goes

The second important aspect of discretionary fiscal policy has to do with the ways in which the government spends money. There are two forms that government spending may take: transfer payments and social-goods expenditures.

Transfer Payments

Transfer payments, you will recall, are expenditures within or between sectors of the economy for which there are no corresponding contributions to current production.

Certain types of transfer payments act as automatic stabilizers. For example, unemployment compensation rises and falls more or less inversely with the nation's income. Other transfer expenditures, such as veterans' benefits and interest payments on the national debt, are independent of the nation's income and do not have this automatic stabilizing characteristic.

Social-Goods Expenditures

A second outlet for government spending is *social goods.* These are products provided by the public sector because society believes that such goods are not provided in sufficient quantity by the private sector. Examples of social goods include national defense, highways, parks, public buildings, slum-clearance projects, and regional development. In addition, social-goods expenditures include money sometimes spent to create public-service employment in government agencies. The jobs may range from lawn mowing to social work, but the purpose is to provide temporary employment for people until they can find jobs in the private sector.

What are the economic effects of social-goods expenditures? On the whole, they can help stimulate the capital goods and construction industries, in which unemployment rates are usually among the highest. But they also give rise to fiscal policy problems that will be pointed out shortly.

Conclusion: Need for Budget Policies

The ways in which the federal government raises and spends money thus influence whether the federal budget will have a surplus or a deficit. How should these be managed?

A budget surplus means that the government has taken more money out of the economy in taxes than it has put back via spending. A surplus is therefore anti-inflationary. A budget deficit means that the government has put more money into the economy via spending than it has taken out in taxes. A deficit *may* therefore be inflationary. Whether it is or not depends (as will be shown) on how the deficit is financed, the use to which it is put, and the stage of the business cycle in which it is incurred.

Problems of Fiscal Policy

The foregoing fiscal-policy principles, as you have seen, provide two simple prescriptions:

1. To expand the economy, raise aggregate demand by decreasing taxes and increasing government expenditures.
2. To contract the economy, lower aggregate demand by increasing taxes and decreasing government expenditures.

In both cases, the expenditure and tax multipliers tell you how large the changes in spending must be to achieve full employment at stable prices.

How well do these principles of discretionary fiscal policy actually work? Because they require implementation by the federal government, many complicated economic and political issues arise. Several classes of difficulties may be identified.

Cyclical Forecasting and Policy Timing

The most difficult practical problems facing legislators concern (1) the forecasting of cyclical turning points and (2) the timing of countercyclical fiscal policies.

Forecasting Cyclical Turning Points

Substantial advances have taken place in economic model building over the years. Nevertheless, business-cycle forecasting remains an inexact science. Economists can usually explain reasonably well why past recessionary or inflationary trends have occurred and why present trends seem to be what they are. However, even economists working with elaborate computer models cannot predict with much accuracy or consistency the future turning points of business cycles. Yet these turning points—the peaks and troughs—must be forecast before attempts can be made to moderate their impact with appropriate fiscal policies.

Timing Countercyclical Policies

Appropriate timing of countercyclical fiscal policies is complicated by a variety of delays. Three types of delays are especially important.

Identification Lag It generally takes many months before a cyclical turning point can be identified. By that time a recession or inflation, or perhaps both, may be well underway.

Action Lag Even after a cyclical turning point has been identified, it takes many more months before Washington decides on what action is to be taken. The President, the President's advisers, and Congress are all involved in the time-consuming debates and compromises that major fiscal-policy decisions entail.

Multiplier Lag After government expenditure and tax policies are eventually implemented, additional months must pass for their effects to be realized. In fact, it may be necessary for a year or more to elapse before the successive multiplier rounds are completed and their full economic impact is felt.

What is the overall result of these lags? Various studies have concluded that the sum of all three factors usually delays the main impact of countercyclical fiscal policies by 2 to 3 years.

Unknown Multiplier Effects

A second source of difficulties with fiscal policy arises from the uncertain consequences of government spending and taxation. In reality, no one really knows the sizes, and therefore the effects, of *current* expenditure and tax multipliers. Among the main reasons for this are a lack of knowledge about (1) household *MPC*s and (2) the impact of business taxes on investment.

With respect to households, the expenditure and tax multipliers are usually calculated on the assumption that there is an "average" *MPC* for the entire household sector. This may be a vast oversimplification. In reality, the *MPC*s of households can differ widely according to their income levels, their tax brackets, and various other factors. This makes any estimates of the two multipliers very uncertain. As a result, any predictions based on them are open to considerable question.

With respect to businesses, economists are not at all sure how changes in corporate income-tax rates affect business investment. Does an additional dollar of corporate income tax reduce the amount of business investment by some fraction of a dollar? If so, by what fraction? The answers are unknown. However, it is known that at least three factors — taxes, investment, and corporate liquidity — are relevant to the question. In general, when corporations have abundant liquid assets (such as cash and marketable securities), they have more investable funds available relative to their investment opportunities. In such a case, an increase in corporate tax rates will have a smaller impact on investment spending than it will when corporations are relatively illiquid.

Restrictive Effects: Crowding Out

Some critics contend that one of the most serious consequences of discretionary fiscal policy concerns the problem of **crowding out.** This, it is argued, can occur when the federal government pursues an expansionary policy by borrowing heavily to finance expenditures.

For example, in order to cover its budget deficits, the Treasury borrows in the financial markets by selling debt securities, such as bonds. The Treasury thus competes with private borrowers in bidding for available funds. This causes interest rates — the prices of the funds — to rise. Private borrowers who are unable to pay the higher interest rates find themselves crowded out of the market. To the extent that private investment is decreased, the resulting negative multipliers will reduce the positive multipliers arising from the government's spending and tax policies.

The concept of crowding out has important financial implications. Therefore, it will be examined more closely after you have studied the nature of our banking system in subsequent chapters.

Public-Choice Problems: Political Business Cycles

In addition to the economic difficulties of implementing discretionary fiscal policies, there are political problems to overcome. These arise mainly from the nature of our democratic system. Because they deal with the interface between economics and political science, they come under the heading of what is known in both fields as "public choice."

One of the most significant public-choice problems concerns the way in which elected officials respond to their constituents. Political leaders know that voters are concerned with the *personal short-term effects* of economic policies. Therefore legislators seeking re-election will often adopt policies designed to achieve favorable short-term results, regardless of what the unfavorable long-term consequences may be.

Economics in the News

Why Public Works Don't Work

Can Government Make Jobs?

Many of the nation's roads, bridges, water systems and public housing facilities are inadequate and in disrepair. Why doesn't the government correct these deficiencies and reduce unemployment, too, by creating public-works programs?

This approach to reducing unemployment was advocated by Keynesians during the massive depression of the 1930s. It is also an approach that was used by President Roosevelt in that era. Since then, every presidential administration has considered, and several have passed, public-service jobs bills aimed at easing unemployment during recessions.

No Quick Fixes

Are public-works projects a real solution to the unemployment problem? Many experts answer *no* — for several reasons:

1. *Timing difficulties.* It usually takes about two years for public-works programs to get fully underway. By that time the recession may be over, so continued government expenditures on the projects will be procyclical rather than countercyclical.

2. *Capital intensiveness.* Most public-works expenditures pay for materials and equipment, not labor. A study by the government's Office of Management and Budget concluded that the typical public-works project expends less than 25 percent of its cost on direct employment.

3. *Matching problems.* The same OMB study also arrived at several other conclusions. These involve matching the right people with the right jobs in the right place. According to the OMB study:

- Because most jobs on public-works projects are skilled, very few of the unskilled unemployed are helped by the programs.

- There is little net job creation because federal public-works expenditures largely replace state-government expenditures for public works.

- Regional labor markets are adversely affected because sometimes jobs are created where they are not needed.

Quick-fix public-works programs are therefore not the answer. The failure of some political leaders to recognize this has often led to the adoption of the wrong short-term programs instead of the right long-term ones.

For example, it is not unusual for the government to follow conservative spending policies (aimed at curbing inflation) during the early years of an administration and liberal spending policies (intended to stimulate employment) in the later years, as election time draws closer. This has resulted in what economists and political scientists call a "political business cycle" — a type of instability caused by discretionary fiscal policies.

Conclusion: Some Successes and Failures

For these and other reasons, discretionary fiscal policy, which is a logical consequence of Keynesian economics, has been the subject of many critical evaluations. Two main conclusions, based on studies of recessions and inflations since the 1950s, may be summarized briefly.

First, attempts to curb recessions have had only limited success. Government taxation and spending programs designed to increase aggregate demand were generally adopted too late—usually after the worst of a recession was over—to be very effective. Nor have government spending programs succeeded in achieving sustained full employment. However, over the long run, transfer payments (particularly unemployment insurance, welfare assistance, and social-security benefits) have contributed to reducing the severity of business recessions. This is because transfer payments enable recipients to maintain higher levels of consumption expenditures than would be possible otherwise. As a result, the economy's aggregate demand curve is also higher.

Second, attempts to restrain inflation through discretionary fiscal policy have been less successful than measures aimed at curbing recession. A major reason for this is that inflation results primarily from *too much money chasing too few goods*. (This, as you will learn in the next several chapters, is a problem of *monetary policy*, not of fiscal policy.) In addition, political leaders are generally reluctant to increase income taxes sufficiently to pay for rising levels of government spending. For both reasons, the economy's aggregate demand curve has often shifted to the right at a faster rate than its aggregate supply curve. This has resulted in frequent increases in the average price level.

To conclude:

On the whole, the performance record of discretionary fiscal policies has been considerably less than ideal. These policies have been moderately better at limiting recessions than at curbing inflations. However, many experts believe that the economy's automatic fiscal stabilizers have played a *relatively* more important role than discretionary fiscal policies in helping to reduce the severity of business cycles.

Deficits and Debt

If you keep up with the news, you know that two topics that frequently receive national and even international attention are the government's budget deficit and the government's debt. What role does fiscal policy play in these matters? How do the size of the government's deficit and the size of its debt affect the economy?

Full-Employment (Structural) Budget

One of the most important concepts in modern fiscal policy is the "full-employment budget." Also known as the "structural budget," it is based on the fact that the actual federal budget reflects changes in the business cycle itself.

For example, during recession the government's tax receipts fall while the amount it pays in unemployment benefits rises. These help increase the federal-budget deficit. Conversely, during recovery the government's tax receipts increase while the amount paid in unemployment benefits declines. This helps generate a federal-budget surplus.

The underlying reasons for this are illustrated in Exhibit 5. Government spending and taxes, measured on the vertical axis, are related to real GNP, measured on the horizontal axis. The level of government spending (G) is given at 200. Increases in real GNP raise the government's tax receipts, so the tax-revenue line (T) is upward sloping.

Suppose the economy goes into a recession. If real GNP declines to 500, the actual budget deficit will increase to 100. This might suggest that the existing fiscal policy of taxing and spending is expansionary. In fact, however, the deficit exists because real output is too low to generate the tax revenues needed to cover government expenditures. If the economy had been producing at its potential-output level where real GNP equals 1,500, the *same fiscal policy* would have generated a full-employment-budget surplus of 100.

The *full-employment budget* (also called the *structural budget*) is an estimate of annual government expenditures and revenues that would occur at the level of potential real GNP—that is, at full employment. Any resulting surplus (or deficit) is called a full-employment surplus (or deficit).

Exhibit 5
Budget Deficits and Surpluses

At the recession output of 500, the actual-budget *deficit* is 100. But if the economy had been at its potential output of 1,500, the same fiscal (taxation and spending) policy would have produced a full-employment-budget *surplus* of 100. Thus the deficit *does not exist because of an expansionary fiscal policy. The deficit exists because, at the recession output, tax revenues shown by the T line are not high enough to cover government expenditures shown by the G line.* Therefore, the full-employment budget, not the actual budget, is the relevant one for judging the effects of discretionary fiscal policy.

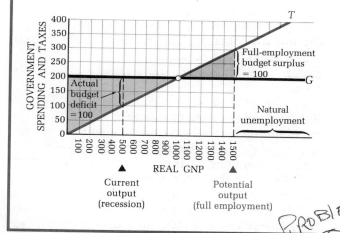

rate of "natural" unemployment. A figure of about 7 percent is believed by many economists and legislators to be realistic. This can produce a much smaller full-employment-budget surplus (or possibly even a full-employment-budget deficit), than figures of 5 or 6 percent, which some other economists and legislators think of as the natural rate of unemployment.

The Public Debt: Today's Issues

Over the past half a century, the number of budget deficits has far exceeded the number of surpluses. As a result, the government has accumulated a substantial national debt. The size of the national debt —also called the public debt and the government debt — has been the subject of a good deal of controversy and criticism. Before exploring the issues that are involved, you should examine the basic facts by studying the figures and the accompanying comments in Exhibit 6.

Is our present public debt too large? What are its economic consequences? These are the kinds of questions that thoughtful people ask. Some of the answers, as you will see, are contrary to what is widely believed.

Burdens on Future Generations

The advantage of the full-employment budget is that it eliminates changes in government revenues and expenditures that are due to cyclical forces. It therefore gives a truer picture of the direction of fiscal policy. But it also has political utility. In some years when the actual budget is running a deficit, the full-employment budget will show a surplus. This is one reason why many legislators favor it.

However, there is a catch. As you can see from Exhibit 5, any estimate of the full-employment budget depends in a critical way on the assumed

Many people argue that, when the government incurs long-term debt, it burdens future generations with the cost of today's policies. There is some merit to this argument, but several aspects of it should be examined.

To begin with, keep in mind that the basic idea of cost involves the idea of *sacrifice.* The real cost of something is not just the dollars you spend for it but the *opportunity cost* — the value of the alternative that you give up. In view of this, what are the real costs of public debt? The answer depends on whether the debt was incurred to cushion a recession or to help pay for war.

Exhibit 6
The Public Debt and Interest Payments

Figure (a): Sharp increases in the national debt have occurred at different times and for different reasons. The main causes of the increases have been the need to pay for national defense, other social goods, and income security benefits to the poor and the disabled.

Lagging productivity in the public sector has also contributed to the increasing costs of government.

Figure (b): The trend of a nation's debt relative to its income or GNP is a good indicator of its ability to carry that debt. Note that the long-run trend has been downward.

Figure (c): The chief burdens of a public debt are the annual interest payments. The long-run trend of these payments has been upward in recent decades.

Figure (d): The long-run trend of interest payments as a percentage of GNP has been rising since the 1960s. Note that the percentage is still relatively low.

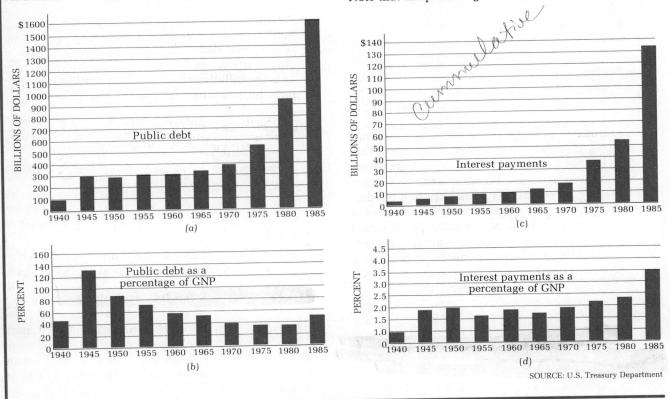

SOURCE: U.S. Treasury Department

Suppose the debt is increased by deficit spending during a period of unemployment. To the extent that resources that would otherwise have remained idle are thereby put to work, the increase in debt levies no real cost. That is, there is no added burden, either on the generation that incurs the debt or on future generations. Society has benefited from the greater output, and some of the output has added to the portion of the nation's capital stock that will be inherited by later generations.

The situation is somewhat different if debt is increased to help finance war. In that case, those people living during the war bear the heaviest sacrifice because they may go without some civilian goods in order to buy military ones. (Think in terms of the production-possibilities curve.) In addition, spending on war usually starves the nation of capital goods, which are not replaced as fast as they are used up. That burden, more than the burden of increased debt, may be the significant one borne by later generations.

External-Debt Burden: Do We "Owe It to Ourselves"?

In 1960, only about 5 percent of the national debt was owed to foreign creditors. In 1970, the figure was still less than 10 percent. In those days, therefore, it was generally accepted that the debt posed no particular burden because we "owed it to ourselves." That is, the debt was largely owed by the people of the United States to the people of the United States.

In 1985, approximately 15 percent of the national debt was owed to foreign creditors. Because of this trend, the assertion that we "owe it to ourselves" has become less valid than it once was.

Does a debt owed to foreigners impose a burden on our own and future generations? The answer is that it can. This is because we must pay interest without necessarily receiving corresponding benefits in return. The foreign bondholders may well spend their incomes in their own country rather than here. But even if they spend their interest income on the purchase of our goods, those goods are the *real* interest (sacrifice) we are paying for the loans. However, an exception can occur if the sums originally borrowed were spent here to buy capital goods and to create jobs. In that case, the resulting gains in current output may be large enough to cover most, if not all, of the interest and principal payments of the debt.

Inflationary Burden: Do Deficits Cause Rising Prices?

A rising public debt results from the tendency of the government to spend more money than it collects in tax revenues. Is this inflationary? The answer is not a mere *yes* or *no*. It depends on how the deficits are financed—that is, where the money comes from. There are two possibilities:

1. **Creating money** Government may simply create money to pay for the expenditures it incurs in excess of tax revenues. When this happens the inflationary impact is direct. The situation, as you have already learned, becomes one of *"too much money chasing too few goods"*.

2. **Borrowing** Government may borrow the money it needs to pay for its additional expenditures. Government borrows by selling Treasury bonds and other types of debt instruments to the public. Do the deficits that result from government borrowing cause interest rates to rise? Are the deficits inflationary? Despite conflicting opinions, here is what the evidence shows:

Deficits are simply the accounting result of comparing revenues with expenditures. Therefore, deficits by themselves exercise no active role in the economy—they are not fiscal agents. Government spending and taxing are fiscal agents.

There is no established relationship between deficits and the direction of interest rates or the rate of inflation. The economy has experienced deficits of all sizes during all phases of the business cycle without any consistent influence on interest rates or on the price level.

If you read or listen to the news, you know that these conclusions involve some of the most controversial macroeconomic issues of our time. Therefore, they must be examined more closely. However, this cannot be done until we have studied the nature of our financial system—which is the subject of the next several chapters.

Conclusion: Practical Debt-Management Guidelines

On the basis of these arguments, should the public debt be allowed to grow without limit? There is no simple answer. However, certain principles of debt

Do Budget Deficits Really Matter?

Even Conservatives Disagree

Time was when almost all conservative economists spoke with one voice about the dangers of large government deficits. That is no longer true. While many conservative experts still warn of the perils of heavy federal borrowing, many others contend that the fears voiced have no basis in fact or economic analysis.

Here are some recent viewpoints from three prominent conservative economists. Each has served as chairman of the President's Council of Economic Advisers:

If federal borrowing continues at high levels, economic growth will slow down and the economy will stagnate. Ultimately, "the game would have to end, because confidence in the ability of society to service such mounting debt loans would crack and interest rates would soar. . . . The whole thing would seem laughable if it wasn't so damn, deadly serious."

Murray Weidenbaum, Professor of Economics, Washington University

"The primary long-term effect of deficits is to reduce the rate of capital formation. Government borrowing crowds out private borrowing and causes a lower rate of investment. The lower rate of capital formation hurts productivity, decreases growth, limits the rise in real incomes, and weakens our international competitiveness."

Martin Feldstein, Professor of Economics, Harvard University

"The country has been told for years that budget deficits cause inflation. Analysis and experience have shown that not to be necessarily true. The antideficit cause has been weakened by the false argument. Now the country is being told that the economy cannot recover if deficits are so high. The country may discover that isn't true either."

Herbert Stein, Professor of Economics, University of Virginia

management have been proposed by various authorities. The principles assume that the government's ability to meet its payments of interest and principal is determined by the taxpaying capacity of the nation. This, in turn, depends on the growth of aggregate income, GNP. Therefore:

According to some experts, there need be no adverse consequences of an indefinitely large public debt, provided that:

1. The public debt does not, over the long run, grow faster than GNP. That is, the public debt as a percentage of GNP should not rise for a prolonged period.

2. Interest payments on the debt are a relatively small percentage of GNP.

3. The debt is incurred for constructive purposes and is financed by noninflationary means.

Looking back at Exhibit 6, can you judge the extent to which the guidelines have been followed?

What You Have Learned

1. Fiscal policy is an outgrowth of Keynesian economics. The goal of modern fiscal policy is to achieve economic efficiency and stability. Fiscal-policy actions are usually best analyzed in terms of the income-price model. However, the income-expenditure model is also useful for certain purposes.

2. According to fiscal-policy theory, government spending and tax policies can be used to alter aggregate demand in order to close inflationary or recessionary gaps. For example, an increase in government spending, with individual income taxes held constant, will raise aggregate demand. An increase in those taxes, with government spending held constant, will reduce aggregate demand. And a simultaneous and equal change in government spending and individual income taxes will alter real GNP by the amount of the change. This is because of the operation of the balanced-budget multiplier principle.

3. Fiscal policy may be nondiscretionary or discretionary. Nondiscretionary fiscal policy is "passive." It relies on automatic or built-in stabilizers to keep the economy on course. Discretionary fiscal policy is "active." It involves conscious changes in government spending and

taxation to create expansionary or contractionary effects. Modern fiscal policy embraces some degree of both kinds of policies.

4. The implementation of discretionary fiscal policies poses several difficulties. They include:

(a) business-cycle forecasting and policy timing

(b) the lack of knowledge of multiplier effects

(c) such adverse fiscal-policy consequences as "crowding out"

(d) such public-choice problems as the creation of "political business cycles"

Because of these difficulties, fiscal policy has experienced failures as well as limited successes.

5. The full-employment budget (also called the "structural budget") is an estimate of government expenditures and tax revenues at the level of potential real GNP—that is, at full employment. Because this budget eliminates changes in government expenditures and revenues that are due to cyclical factors, it gives a truer picture of the direction of fiscal policy than does the actual budget.

6. The real burdens of a large public debt depend on several factors. Among them:

(a) whether it is externally held

(b) whether it causes inflation because it is financed by creating money instead of by borrowing

7. A large public debt may have adverse psychological consequences. However, its principal and interest must be assessed in relation to GNP and to the growth of the economy as a whole before a meaningful evaluation can be made.

Terms and Concepts to Review

expenditure multiplier   fiscal policy
tax multiplier   crowding out
balanced-budget   full-employment budget
  multiplier
automatic fiscal
  stabilizers

For Discussion

1. Assume that the economy is in recession, the *MPC* is ½, and an increase of $100 billion in output is needed to achieve full employment. Then, using diagrams if necessary, and assuming that private investment is constant, answer the following questions:

(a) How much should government spending be increased to achieve full employment?

(b) What would happen if taxes were reduced by $10 billion? Is this enough to restore full employment? If not, how much of a tax reduction is needed?

(c) What would be the effect of a simultaneous increase in government spending and taxes of $50 billion? Of a simultaneous decrease of $50 billion? Explain why. Would the situation be different in the case of a simultaneous increase in G and T under full employment? Explain.

2. What are our chief automatic stabilizers, and how do they operate?

3. The ways in which government raises and spends money can affect the economy's performance. What are the government's sources of revenue and its outlets for expenditures? Which are expansionary? Which are contractionary?

4. In view of the difficulties of applying fiscal policies, it has been suggested that a law involving an automatic tax-rate formula be enacted. In this way, tax rates could be tied to GNP and perhaps to other measures, and they would vary automatically when these measures changed by given percentages. What are some of the chief advantages of such a proposal?

5. "Some increases in government expenditures, such as those for health, education, and welfare, are inflationary, whereas other government expenditures, such as those incurred for national defense and public works, are not." Do you agree? What central questions must be considered to determine whether some government expenditures are more inflationary than others?

6. Evaluate the following argument about the public debt: "No individual or family would be wise to continue accumulating indebtedness indefinitely, for eventually all debts must either be paid or repudiated. It follows that this fundamental principle applies equally well to nations. As Adam Smith himself said, 'What is prudence in the conduct of every private family can scarce be folly in that of a great kingdom.'"

7. "A federal deficit crowds out private investment." Is this statement likely to be true during a deep recession? During a period of full employment?

8. "The size of the *externally* held national debt as a percentage of GNP is a more meaningful statistic than the size of the *domestically* held national debt as a percentage of GNP. The same is true of interest payments on the national debt." Do you agree?

Part 3

Monetary Economics and Macroeconomic Equilibrium

Chapter 11

Money, Financial Markets, and the Banking System

Learning Guide

Watch for answers to these important questions

What is money? What forms does it take? How is it defined and measured?

What types of credit (or debt) instruments are used as money? In what markets are these instruments exchanged? What economic functions do these markets perform?

What are financial intermediaries? Why do they exist? What economic functions do they perform?

What is the Federal Reserve System? Why was it created? What are its objectives?

What is money? Most people want it, but few can define it. The average person will probably say: "It's cash, and whatever you've got in the bank." An economist may describe money in terms of its four basic functions—the needs it fulfills in every society:

1. **A medium of exchange**—money used as a means of payment for things.

2. **A measure of value**—money used to express the prices of things.

3. **A standard of deferred payment**—money borrowed or loaned, until it is repaid in the future with interest.

4. **A store of value**—money saved so that it can be spent in the future.

But money and credit—which is an "extension" of money—are even more important than these functions indicate. For money and credit have a direct influence on the level of economic activity. Some economists argue that the supply of money is the chief determinant of the economy's health.

The reason for this is not hard to see. A monetary system's primary task is to provide society with an adequate supply of money that is widely acceptable. The long history of money shows that this is no easy task. As a result, there has been a continuous evolution of monetary systems designed to achieve this objective.

What does it mean to say that the supply of money must be "adequate"? Interestingly enough, this question can be answered only in terms of the demand for money. Indeed, the demand for money poses the most fundamental problem faced by our monetary and banking system.

Defining and Measuring Money

If you think you know exactly what money is, you are way ahead of most economists. For economists are always in the midst of a painstaking search for "M"—an ideal measure of the quantity of money available in the United States.

Several measures of the quantity of money are currently in use. The four best-known of them are designated by the symbols M1, M2, M3, and L. Of these four measures, M1 is the narrowest, or least inclusive, and L is the broadest, or most inclusive.

M1: Narrow-Transactions Money, the Basic Money Supply

The most familiar form of money is that used by people for routine spending. This classification of money is M1. It may be called "narrow-transactions money," which means simply that it is readily spendable. Its main components are the currency in circulation plus checkable deposits—those on which checks can be written. M1 is also commonly referred to as the "basic money supply."

Roughly 30 percent of the money supply consists of paper money or *currency*—$1 bills, $5 bills, and so on. Coins, which are not part of currency, constitute less than 1 percent of the basic money supply. Because coins are interchangeable with currency, they are part of M1. However, since they are

a trivial component they are neglected in discussions of the money supply. So, too, are traveler's checks, which are also a very minor part of the money supply.

The chief remaining component of M1 is *checkable deposits.* If you write checks to pay for some of the things you buy, you may have one of several kinds of checkable deposits. It is helpful to distinguish between them. The most important kinds are demand deposits and savings-types of checking accounts.

If you have a *demand deposit* with a bank, it means that the bank promises to pay immediately an amount of money specified by you, the owner of the deposit. A demand deposit is thus a type of "checkbook money," because it permits transactions to be paid for by check rather than with currency. But unlike other checkable deposits, a demand deposit does not pay interest to its owner. Nevertheless, as you will see, demand deposits are an exceedingly important medium of exchange, because they are used primarily by business.

Other types of checkable deposits are actually savings-type checking accounts. There are two major types. *Negotiable-order-of-withdrawal (NOW)* accounts are essentially interest-bearing checking accounts available to individuals and to nonprofit organizations. They are offered by most banks, savings and loan associations, and other depository institutions. *Share-draft* accounts are basically the same as NOW accounts, but they are provided by credit unions. Summarizing:

The main components of M1 are currency and checkable deposits. Because checkable deposits are readily convertible into cash, M1 is frequently referred to as the "basic money supply."

M2: Medium-Range Money

M2 is a broader measure of money. It takes in M1 plus certain other assets. This enlarged category may be regarded as medium-range money. Among the components of M2 are savings deposits and certain short-term credit instruments.

Savings Deposits

Savings deposits come in different forms, such as passbook accounts, savings certificates, and certificates of deposit. All, however, are simply different kinds of time deposits.

A *time deposit* is money held in a depository-institution account of an individual or firm. Several types of time deposits have specified maturity dates, at which times the principal with accumulated interest becomes payable to the owner. For other kinds of time deposits, the depository institution may require advance notice of withdrawal. Only "small" denomination time deposits, defined as those under $100,000, are counted in M_2.

Repurchase Agreements (RPs)

Certain borrowers and lenders often make contracts involving the sale and buyback of short-term credit instruments. Such contracts are called *repurchase agreements* (RPs or "repos"). The borrower sells the securities to the lender and agrees to repurchase them on a later date at the same price plus interest.

RPs frequently arise when a borrower, such as a bank, is temporarily in need of funds. It may borrow from a corporation which has idle cash balances to lend. The bank borrows by contracting to sell to the corporation and subsequently repurchase some of its short-term government securities, such as U.S. Treasury bills. All banks hold government securities, including Treasury bills and bonds, in their portfolios as part of their income-earning assets. By selling some of these assets to the lending corporation, the bank acquires the temporary funds it needs. The corporation, of course, earns a return on what amounts to a secured loan to the bank. The terms of RPs may range from one day to several months. Those included in $M2$ are overnight RPs held by commercial banks.

Money-Market Mutual-Fund Shares

Also counted as part of $M2$ are shares in money-market mutual funds. The *money market* is where short-term credit instruments, such as U.S. Treasury bills, corporations' commercial paper or promissory notes, and other types of financial claims described later, are bought and sold. A mutual fund is an organization that pools people's money and uses it to buy securities, such as short-term credit instruments, stocks, and bonds. Putting the two terms together, a *money-market mutual fund* is one that buys money-market securities exclusively.

If you own shares (that is, a deposit account) in a money-market mutual fund, as do millions of individuals and corporations, you can write checks against your account. The minimum amount of the check must usually be $500. Therefore, an account of this type is like a checkable deposit included in $M1$, but it is somewhat more restrictive. Because of this, it is counted as part of $M2$.

The remaining component of $M2$ is dollar deposits held in banks outside the United States, mostly in Europe. These deposits are called *Eurodollars.* They are owned by American and foreign banks, corporations, and individuals. Eurodollars represent dollar obligations that are constantly being shifted from one country to another in search of the highest return. Because of their growing importance in our financial system, overnight Eurodollars held by residents of the U.S. are included in $M2$.

M3: Wide-Range Money

A still broader classification of money is called $M3$. It includes $M2$ plus these additional components:

- Large-denomination time deposits at all depository institutions. A large-denomination time deposit is defined as one of $100,000 or more.

- Term repurchase agreements. These are RPs arranged for as little as two days to as long as several months.

L: Liquid and Near-Liquid Assets

The broadest classification of money is symbolized L. It consists of the most liquid asset, cash, plus near-liquid assets—paper claims that are easily convertible to cash. The L classification thus includes M3 plus three additional types of assets:

- U.S. savings bonds and other government obligations, such as Treasury bills and Treasury bonds.

- Term Eurodollar deposits (that is, those with terms longer than one day) held by U.S. residents other than banks.

- Certain business obligations, such as commercial paper issued by major corporations and banker's acceptances (explained later in the chapter) issued by banks.

The foregoing ideas are summarized in Exhibit 1.

Conclusion: Money Is a Spectrum of Assets

Against this background, let us look again at the deceptively simple questions "What is money?" and "How is it measured?"

Currency and checkable deposits are readily convertible into one another. Together, they constitute money in the *narrow* sense.

In a broader sense, some other assets are also "money." But they are often called **near-moneys.** Their values are known in terms of money, and they can easily be converted into money, if this is desired. Some important examples are time deposits, such as savings certificates, and U.S. government short-term securities held by individuals and businesses. Other examples include the cash value of insurance policies, high-grade commercial paper, and similar near-liquid assets.

The concept of near-monies is important. For one thing, people who possess near-monies may feel wealthier than other people of the same income level who do not. Hence, people who hold near-monies are likely to have higher propensity-to-consume curves. This, as you already know, will affect the levels of income and employment for the economy as a whole.

So the answers to the questions "What is money?" and "How is it measured?" are by no means simple. Because there are different concepts of money, its definition and measurement are subject to controversy. The issues are examined in later chapters. Meanwhile, you will find it helpful to think about money in the following way:

> Money is more than just paper currency and coins. *Money is a spectrum of assets. It ranges from currency and checkable deposits through various types of time deposits to financial claims against businesses and the U.S. Treasury.*

Financial Markets

Who goeth a borrowing goeth a sorrowing.
  Benjamin Franklin

Let us all be happy and live within our means, even if we have to borrow the money to do it.
  Anonymous

One of the reasons why money is a complex concept is that it is closely related to credit (and debt). This is what you would expect, because credit replaces money, supplements money, and, in the final analysis, provides the base of the nation's money supply.

Credit and debt are the same thing looked at from two different sides. If I lend you money, my credit to you is the same as your debt to me. We can say, therefore, that the term **credit** implies a promise by one party to pay another for money borrowed or for goods or services received. Because of this, credit may be regarded as an extension of money.

A significant part of credit is that part represented by **credit instruments.** These are financial documents that serve either as promises to pay or as orders to pay. They provide the means by which funds are transferred from one party to another.

The most familiar example of a credit instrument is an ordinary **promissory note,** or simply a **note.** It is an "I.O.U."—a promise made by one party to pay another a specified sum of money by a given date, usually within a year. Such notes are issued by individuals, corporations, and government agencies. Firms make heavy use of notes to borrow

Exhibit 1
The Fed Is in the Counting House, Counting Up the Money Supply

"M1 is up 4 percent. M2 is up 2 percent. M3 is down 1 percent." This is the kind of information that is flashed weekly across the financial news wires. Every Thursday afternoon, most banks in the country tele-type their currency and deposit data to a federal communications station in Culpeper, Virginia. There the figures are collated and wired to Washington, where statisticians at the Federal Reserve System (the "Fed"), the nation's central bank, make the adjustments necessary to report the week's supply of money. The totals consist of various components, as the illustration shows.

Note from the percentage figures in the table that currency, demand deposits, and other checkable deposits as proportions of M1 have changed considerably over the years. In particular, the decline in demand deposits has been approximately offset by the gain in other checkable deposits.

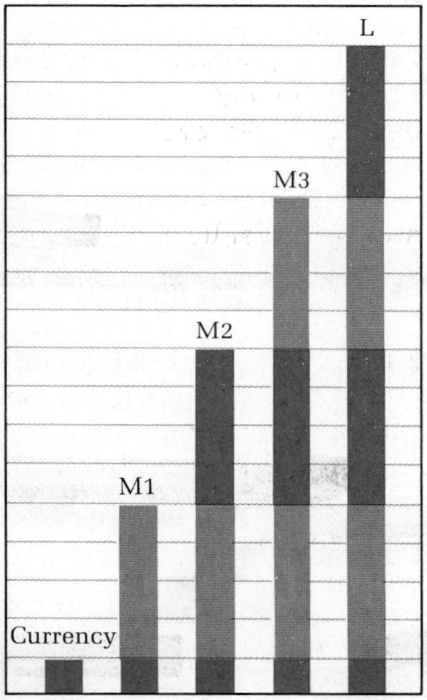

	Money-Supply Measures (Billions of dollars)		
	1975	1980	1984*
$L = M3$ + LIQUID AND NEAR-LIQUID ASSETS Treasury obligations, including bills and bonds. Term Eurodollars, high-grade commercial paper, and banker's acceptances.	1,368	$2,326	$3,490
$M3 = M2$ + WIDE-RANGE MONEY Large-denomination time deposits. Term repurchase agreements.	1,172	1,990	2,987
$M2 = M1$ + MEDIUM-RANGE MONEY Savings (time) deposits. Repurchase agreements (overnight). Money market mutual-fund shares. Eurodollars (overnight).	1,023	1,633	2,376
$M1$ = NARROW-TRANSACTIONS MONEY, BASIC MONEY SUPPLY	291	415	555
Traveler's checks	2	4	5
Other checkable deposits (NOW, share draft and other accounts)	1	27	143
Demand deposits	214	267	248
Currency	74	117	158

	Percentages of $M1$		
	1975	1980	1984*
Other checkable deposits	—	7%	45%
Demand deposits	74%	64	26
Currency	25	28	28

Source: Board of Governors of the Federal Reserve System. *Preliminary data.

working capital from banks at certain busy times of the year. The interest on such loans is a chief source of income for banks and certain other lending institutions.

Various other types of credit instruments are in use. The most important ones are traded in the nation's financial markets, whose components are the money market and the capital market. As you will see, both of these markets perform the important economic function of exchanging claims for liquidity. That is, *in the financial markets, organizations that have surplus funds can purchase claims against organizations that are in need of funds.*

TWO TYPES OF MARKETS

The Money Market

Markets exist for many types of credit instruments. As you have learned, a **money market** is a center where short-term credit instruments issued by banks, corporations, and governmental entities are bought and sold. A variety of credit instruments are traded in the money market. Among the most important are the following.

Important credit instruments

Treasury Bills

Each week, in order to help finance its operations, the U.S. Treasury issues marketable obligations known as *Treasury bills.* They come in minimum denominations of $10,000, and they usually mature in 3 months, 6 months, or 1 year. The Treasury sells the bills in weekly auctions at a discount from face value. This means that if you buy a 1-year Treasury bill today for $9,000, you will receive $10,000 at maturity—a rate of return of about 11%.

The money that the Treasury raises from the sale of its bills helps the federal government meet its operating expenses. These include the salaries of civil-service employees and armed-forces personnel, the costs of supplies for government offices, and numerous other things for which the government disburses money. In terms of dollar volume, Treasury bills are by far the dominant money-market instrument.

Other Instruments

All I.O.U.s

Government agencies, banks, and corporations sell a variety of other interest-earning money-market securities. The more important ones may be identified briefly.

Federal agency discount notes are sold by certain government agencies. Among them are the Federal Home Loan Bank, the Federal National Mortgage Association, and the Federal Farm Credit Bank System. The money raised by these agencies is used to provide mortgages and other types of loans.

Issued by Student Loan

Negotiable certificates of deposit (CDs) are large-denomination notes ($100,000 or more) issued by major banks. The banks sell these securities to corporations and large individual investors, who buy them for their interest payments. (As you may know, most banks also sell deposit or savings certificates for smaller investors. However, these are merely special types of time deposits. They are smaller in size and are not resalable, unlike negotiable CDs.)

Issued by Banks

Commercial paper consists of promissory notes, mostly in minimum denominations of $10,000, sold by several hundred major corporations. The most familiar example is GMAC paper, issued by General Motors Acceptance Corporation, to finance the purchase of General Motors cars.

Same as REPO

Issued by Companies

Banker's acceptances arise both in domestic trade and in international trade. In effect, a banker's acceptance (BA) is a bank-guaranteed "postdated check" written by one of its customers. If the bank stamps the check "accepted," it becomes a BA. This means that the bank assumes the customer's debt and guarantees payment on the postdated day. (The customer, of course, must eventually repay the bank the full amount plus interest.) In the interim, if the bank should need short-term funds, it can sell the check in the money market at a discount from face value.

Repurchase agreements, popularly known as RPs or "repos," constitute a kind of collateralized loan. As mentioned earlier in the chapter, in a repurchase agreement the borrower sells the lender a credit instrument, usually a government security. In addition, the borrower simultaneously agrees to buy the instrument back on a later date at the same price plus interest at a specified rate. The lender (investor) thus holds a security as collateral for a loan with a fixed maturity and a fixed interest rate. Banks, often in need of short-term funds, are major users of RPs. The RPs are sold to corporations and large individual customers who have surplus cash balances to lend.

Tax-exempt instruments are short-term obligations sold by some state and local governments and by local housing and urban-renewal agencies. They are issued in anticipation of future tax revenues. Banks are among the major purchasers of these instruments. One reason is that they are considered safer from default than some other money-market instruments. A second reason is that their interest payments are exempt from federal income tax.

Federal funds, unlike the credit instruments described so far, are not represented by paper claims that change hands in the money market. Instead, they are unsecured loans that banks and certain other depository institutions make to one another, usually overnight, out of their excess reserves. Federal funds are an integral part of the money market. The purchase and sale of such funds is limited to banks, savings institutions, and certain government agencies in need of very short-term liquidity.

The Capital Market

Besides the money market, the other important type of financial market is the **capital market.** This is where long-term financial instruments that mature in more than one year are bought and sold.

For example, bonds of various types are among the major credit instruments traded in the capital market. A **bond** is an agreement to pay a specified sum of money (called the principal) either at a future date or periodically over the course of a loan. During this time, interest at a fixed rate may be paid on certain dates. Bonds are issued by corporations (corporate bonds), state and local governments (municipal bonds), and the federal government (government bonds). Bonds are used for long-term financing.

Five major types of instruments are bought and sold in the capital market:

- U.S. government bonds—issued by the Treasury and by certain government agencies, such as the Federal National Mortgage Association, and the Federal Home Loan Bank.

- Municipal bonds—issued by state and local governments.

- Corporate bonds.

- Mortgages.

- Corporate stock.

The yields on these securities differ from one another at any given time. The differences reflect maturity dates, the stated interest rates on the securities, risk of default, tax treatment, and other factors.

In general, municipal bonds tend to have the lowest yields. This is because the interest received by purchasers of such bonds is exempt from federal income taxes. Therefore, these bonds can be sold at lower yields than comparable bonds issued by the Treasury or by corporations.

Long-term Treasury bonds generally have a lower yield than comparable corporate bonds. The reason is that Treasury bonds carry no risk of default. Yields on high-quality corporate bonds, in turn, are lower than those on mortgages, which cost more to administer and are not so easily marketed.

A comparison of interest yields for these different types of securities is shown in Exhibit 2.

Exhibit 2
Capital-Market Yields

Yields on securities tend to differ from one another at any given time. The differences depend on risk of default, maturity dates, tax considerations, and many other factors. Note that the various yields tend to rise and fall at about the same time.

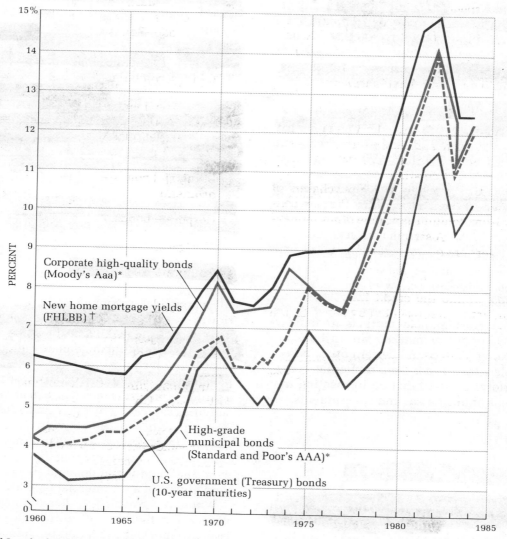

Corporate high-quality bonds (Moody's Aaa)*

New home mortgage yields (FHLBB) †

High-grade municipal bonds (Standard and Poor's AAA)*

U.S. government (Treasury) bonds (10-year maturities)

* Moody's and Standard & Poor's are private companies that rate the quality of bonds issued by corporations and government agencies. A rating of Aaa by Moody's or AAA by Standard & Poor's represents the highest quality—that is, the lowest risk of default.
† FHLBB stands for the Federal Home Loan Bank Board, a governmental agency.

Conclusion: Economic Functions of Financial Markets

The business and government sectors are continually seeking funds to finance production of goods and services. The acquisition of these funds is made possible through financial markets, namely the money market and the capital market. Taken together, these markets perform the task of transferring funds from lenders to borrowers. More specifically:

> The *financial markets* provide important economic functions:
>
> — The *money market* primarily enables firms and government entities (federal, state, and local) to obtain liquidity. This happens when these organizations borrow funds by selling short-term claims against themselves.
>
> — The *capital market* primarily facilitates the transfer of funds from savers to borrowers. This occurs when borrowing institutions acquire funds by selling long-term claims against themselves.
>
> To some extent, these functions overlap. In general, however, *the money and capital markets allocate financial resources between borrowers and lenders and between short-term and long-term uses.*

The world's largest financial markets are in New York City. Other major markets are in London, Paris, Hong Kong, Tokyo, and certain other cities. These markets attract funds from numerous countries and perform a vital function in meeting the financing needs of businesses and governments.

Financial Intermediaries

The institutions that serve the money and capital markets are known as *financial intermediaries.* These organizations constitute a connecting link between lenders and borrowers. How? By creating and issuing financial obligations or claims ("IOUs") against themselves in order to obtain funds with which to acquire profitable financial claims against others. In this and the next few chapters, you will learn how financial intermediaries do this.

A chief function of financial intermediaries, therefore, is to provide *liquidity.* This refers to the ease with which an asset can be converted into cash quickly without loss of value relative to its purchase price. Financial intermediaries also perform other important economic functions. They provide the economy with the money supply and with near-liquid assets. Financial intermediaries thus facilitate investment in plant, equipment, and inventories.

For our purposes, financial intermediaries may be divided into two broad classes: (1) commercial banks and (2) all other financial institutions. These include mutual savings banks, savings and loan associations, credit unions, insurance companies, private pension funds, finance companies, mortgage companies, and so on. As you will see, because these institutions deal in financial claims, *most of the activity of financial intermediaries consists of the wholesaling and/or retailing of funds.*

 # Commercial Banks

All banks deal in money and credit instruments. However, a *commercial bank* is the major type of bank engaged in making business loans by creating demand deposits. (Remember that a demand deposit is the technical term for a checkable deposit that does not pay interest to its owner.) In addition, a commercial bank may engage in many of the same activities carried on by other financial institutions. These activities include buying and selling money market instruments, taking savings accounts or time deposits, and providing life insurance. However, the handling of demand deposits is a fundamental part of a commercial bank's business.

When you establish a demand-deposit account with a commercial bank, the bank creates and issues a financial obligation or claim against itself. It does this by agreeing to honor your checks on demand up to the amount of the deposit.

When a bank accepts your savings or time deposit, it creates a claim against itself that is legally payable after a specified time. For example, although a bank rarely does so, it can legally require notice of intended withdrawal from a passbook savings deposit — usually 30 days or more. Hence, any time deposit, of which a passbook savings deposit is perhaps the most familiar type, may be thought of as a claim that carries a stipulated maturity date.

Other instruments representing time-deposit claims are savings bonds and savings certificates. However, none of these are as liquid as demand deposits.

Demand deposits are among the most liquid of all claims created and issued by financial intermediaries. This is because checks written against them are acceptable in exchange for currency. Therefore, demand deposits are included with currency as the *narrowest* measure of the basic money supply.

The role played by commercial banks in expanding and contracting demand deposits is of enormous importance in understanding how the economy works. Therefore, commercial banking will occupy a considerable part of our attention in this and in subsequent chapters.

Other Financial Intermediaries

Of course, other kinds of financial intermediaries seek to accommodate the particular needs and preferences of borrowers. Like commercial banks, these institutions create and issue claims against themselves in order to obtain funds with which to acquire profitable claims against others.

For example, mutual savings banks and savings and loan associations issue time-deposit claims. These claims are very much like those provided by commercial banks — except, in some cases, for differences in maturities and yields. The assets or claims against others that the issuing institutions acquire with the funds consist primarily of real-estate mortgages, corporate bonds, and government securities.

Likewise, credit unions issue savings-deposit claims to their members. The funds obtained are primarily to provide consumer loans. Insurance companies issue claims in the form of policies against themselves. Then they use most of the funds collected in premiums to purchase real-estate mortgages, corporate securities, and government bonds. In like manner, other financial intermediaries generate obligations against themselves in order to acquire funds with which to purchase profitable, but often less liquid, obligations against others.

Rules for Survival

As issuers of claims against themselves and as suppliers of funds to other sectors, financial intermediaries, especially banks, must strive to maintain their liquidity. They can do this by observing certain practical rules for survival. Two are especially important:

Rule 1: Lend Short and Borrow Long

Banks should make short-term loans, usually for less than a year. They should finance the loans by issuing claims against themselves for longer periods. This pattern, if followed, gives banks greater control over their short-term interest income while "locking in" their long-term interest expenses. In reality, banks sometimes find it more profitable to do the opposite — to "borrow short and lend long." During certain periods, for instance, some banks may have 10- to 20-year loans outstanding, often to African, Asian, and Latin American countries. However, the banks will be financing the loans with 90-day certificates of deposit, or with other short-term funds.

Rule 2: Spread Loans Widely

A second rule is to diversify loans among different types of borrowers. In this way, by not "putting all their eggs in one basket," banks can reduce the risks of borrowers defaulting on their loans. In practice, banks sometimes bend this rule in order to expand their loans. As a result, when an industry that has experienced much growth suddenly takes a turn for the worse, those banks that engaged too heavily in financing the industry's expansion are likely to participate in its decline.

Because the claims acquired by financial intermediaries are frequently less liquid than the claims they issue, it seems plausible that these intermediaries may sometimes find themselves temporarily illiquid. This means that they are unable to meet unexpected demands for payment out of their own assets. Situations of this type occurred frequently in American history. Sometimes they gave rise to financial crises or panics.

To help avoid financial crises, legislation designed to protect the public has been passed. It has provided insurance for bank deposits and set minimum financial requirements for banks, insurance companies, and certain other financial intermediaries. In addition, federally sponsored institutions have been created to provide liquidity to some financial intermediaries by lending to them or by purchasing assets from them. Notable among these have been special federal banks that supply funds to savings and loan associations and make intermediate-term loans to farmers. Most important for our purposes, however, have been the Federal Reserve Banks. They supply funds to depository institutions as one of the functions of the Federal Reserve System.

The Federal Reserve System

On December 23, 1913, President Woodrow Wilson signed the Federal Reserve Act. This created the Federal Reserve System, thus marking the beginning of a new era in American banking. Periodic money panics—"runs" on banks by depositors fearing that the banks were failing—had plagued the country for many years. Based on what was learned from the great panic of 1907, one of the worst in American history, the act was designed to end extreme variations in the money supply and thus avoid panics. It did contribute (along with other legislation described shortly) to improving stability of the banking system.

The Fed: Objectives, Organization, and Functions

The *Federal Reserve System*—often referred to as the Fed—is the nation's central bank. This means that, like other central banks throughout the world, the Federal Reserve regulates the flow of money and credit. That is its chief responsibility. It also performs many service functions for depository institutions, the Treasury, and the public. Broadly speaking, the Federal Reserve System seeks to provide monetary conditions favorable to the realization of four national objectives. These are: high employment, stable prices, steady economic growth, and a sound international financial position.

The Fed's form of organization is something like a pyramid, as illustrated in Exhibit 3. It consists of:

1. Member banks
2. Federal Reserve Banks
3. A Board of Governors
4. A Federal Open Market Committee
5. Other committees

Member Banks

At the base of the Federal Reserve pyramid are the System's *member banks.* All national banks (chartered by the federal government) must be members, and state banks (chartered by their respective states) may join if they meet certain requirements. Of some 14,000 commercial banks, fewer than 6,000 are members. However, these member banks are for the most part the larger banks in the country, holding the great bulk of all demand deposits.

Today the number of member banks relative to nonmember banks is not particularly significant.

Preventive for Money Panics: How the Federal Reserve System Came About

Brown Brothers

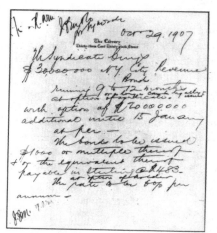

Brown Brothers

American banking history records a series of attempts to provide a currency that could expand or contract according to the demands of business. Theoretically, the ability of commercial banks, through the lending process, to expand or contract the amount of money available should have provided for the demands occasioned by changes in business activity.

Commercial banks, however, while they could expand credit, could not add to the amount of available currency. Inasmuch as bank depositors had a legal right to withdraw their money in the form of currency and coin, banks provided for ordinary withdrawals by retaining a part of their total deposits in the form of reserves. These reserves usually consisted of currency, coin, and deposits in other banks.

Money Panics

Occasionally there would be an extraordinary increase in demand by depositors for their money. This would result in a situation in which the available amount of currency and coin might not cover the reserves that the banks had set up. An unusual demand by depositors forced banks to exchange their assets, such as securities and deposits with other banks, for currency. An attempt by one bank to supply itself with currency by withdrawing its reserve balance from another all too frequently set up a "chain reaction," which resulted in a widespread shortage of currency among many banks.

Some banks were forced to close, although their assets could have been converted into currency if sufficient time had been allowed. Widespread bank closings resulting from unusual demands by depositors invariably brought on a period of economic depression. These unusual demands were called "money panics," and one that occurred in 1907 set into motion a thorough study of our nation's money system.

The congressional commission charged with this study found that almost all countries with a money supply that could be expanded or contracted to meet the needs of the depositors also had some form of central bank. This bank had the power to issue a currency that depositors would accept. As a result of this and other studies, Congress in 1913 passed the law that created the Federal Reserve System.

The money crisis of October 1907 brought thousands of nervous investors to New York City's Wall Street, the financial center of the world. On October 29, 1907, in the midst of the crisis, business buccaneer and financial tycoon John Pierpont Morgan wrote a personal guarantee on his library stationery to support the credit of New York City.

This is because legislation enacted in 1980 requires *all* depository institutions, members as well as non-members, to meet the same standards with respect to reserve requirements. In addition, all institutions can purchase, on equal terms, any of the System's services, such as check clearing and electronic transfer of funds. Therefore, although more than half the banks in the nation do not belong to the Federal Reserve System, this does not affect the System's ability to influence the economy by controlling the money supply.

Federal Reserve Banks

The country is divided into twelve Federal Reserve districts, each with a **Federal Reserve Bank.** There are also twenty-five Federal Reserve Bank branches serving areas within the districts. (See the map in Exhibit 3.)

Technically, each Federal Reserve Bank is owned by its member banks, which are the stockholders. But, unlike most private institutions, the Reserve Banks are operated in the public interest rather than for profit. However, they are, in fact, highly profitable because of the interest income they earn on the government securities that they own. After meeting their expenses, they pay a relatively small part of their earnings to the member banks as dividends, and return the major portion to the U.S. Treasury. Note that the district Federal Reserve Banks (and branches) constitute the second level of the pyramid.

Board of Governors

At the peak of the pyramid is the **Board of Governors** in Washington. It consists of seven members appointed by the President and confirmed by the Senate. Members are appointed for fourteen years, one term expiring every two years. This pattern reduces political influences on the Board—members do not come and go with every presidential election. The chairperson of the Board, who is also a member of the Board, is appointed by the President for a four-year term.

The Board of Governors supervises the Federal Reserve System and tries to see that it performs effectively. However, its primary function is to influence the amount of money and credit in the economy. The Board does this by engaging in certain special activities that are fully explained in subsequent chapters.

Federal Open Market Committee

The most important policy-making body within the System is the **Federal Open Market Committee.** This committee consists of twelve members—the seven members of the Board of Governors plus five Presidents of the major Federal Reserve Banks. The committee's chief function is to make policy for the System's purchase and sale of government and other securities in the open market in New York. Actual transactions are carried on by the so-called "Trading Desk" of the Federal Reserve Bank of New York.

Other Committees and Functions

Several other committees play a significant role in the Federal Reserve System's operations. One of these is the **Federal Advisory Council,** which advises the Board of Governors on important current developments.

To sum up:

The Federal Reserve System is the central banking system of the United States. *The primary purpose of the "Fed" is to regulate the flow of money and credit in order to promote efficiency, stability, and growth.* In addition, it provides a number of important services to the Treasury, the public, and depository institutions. These services include:

— Acting as fiscal agent for the Treasury.

— Operating a nationwide check "clearing-house."

— Providing for the electronic transfer of funds among depository institutions.

— Supplying coin and currency for circulation.

Exhibit 3
Organization and Map of the Federal Reserve System

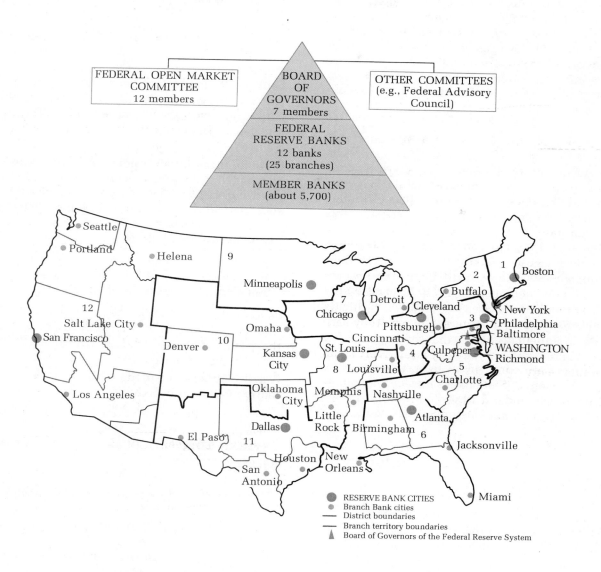

NOTE   Alaska is in the Seattle Branch territory and Hawaii is in the territory served by the Head Office of the Federal Reserve Bank of San Francisco.   Both are in the Twelfth District.

Organization of the Banking System

The banking system in the United States has an unusual structure, not found in any other country. Known as a **dual banking system,** this structure grew out of legislation passed during the 1860s, for the purpose of creating federally chartered banks. As a result, our banking system consists of two classes of commercial banks—national banks and state banks.

National Banks are commercial banks chartered by the federal government. Such banks are required to belong to the Federal Reserve System. About one-third of all commercial banks today are national banks; the rest are state banks. Although fewer in number, national banks hold considerably more than half the deposits of the banking system and are larger than most state banks. In case you are wondering how to tell the difference between a national bank and a state bank, the method is simple. A national bank is required to have either the word "national" in its title or the letters "N.A." (for *national association*) after its name. If it has neither, it is a state bank.

State Banks are commercial banks chartered by state governments. State banks may or may not be members of the Federal Reserve System. Today, only about 10 percent of state banks are members.

Banking Supervision: A Regulatory Thicket

Partly because of our dual banking system, which is rooted in U.S. political history, the nation's banks are regulated by several government agencies:

Comptroller of the Currency This federal entity, which is part of the Treasury Department, charters all national banks. It also oversees the operations both of national banks and of those state banks that are members of the Federal Reserve System.

Federal Reserve System The Fed exercises some degree of regulation over all banks, national as well as state. In addition, it exerts some control over thrift institutions, such as savings banks and savings and loan associations.

Federal Deposit Insurance Corporation (FDIC) This agency (described below) supervises the operations of all insured banks. These include national banks, state banks that belong to the Fed, and insured banks that do not. Only a small number of banks, however, are uninsured. The FDIC, therefore, has regulatory authority over almost all banks.

State Banking Commissions All fifty states exercise varying degrees of control over their state-chartered banks. The only banks not subject to state regulations are national banks. This is because they are federally chartered and hence subject to federal regulations.

> All banks in the United States are regulated by at least two government agencies, most are regulated by three, and many are regulated by four. As a result, there is considerable overlapping and conflicting supervisory responsibility among the regulatory agencies. This leads to much waste of resources and duplication of effort.

A partial illustration of the complex network of regulation is shown in Exhibit 4.

Deposit Insurance: Protecting Your Money

What happens to your money if a bank in which you have a deposit fails? Chances are you will be protected by insurance, provided by the **Federal Deposit Insurance Corporation** (FDIC). This government agency came into existence in 1934 when the country was in the throes of a major depression. More than 9,000 banks had failed during the years 1930–1933, leaving depositors unprotected. The FDIC was created to protect depositors and thereby help improve bank stability.

Exhibit 4
The Bank-Regulation Thicket

Bank regulatory agencies exchange some of their information and accept one another's audits for certain purposes. Nevertheless, duplication of efforts in the regulation of banking leads to much inefficiency and waste of resources.

This diagram illustrates only part of the regulatory maze. It includes only commercial banks and no other types of depository institutions, such as credit unions and savings and loan associations. These are regulated by the Fed and by agencies not shown.

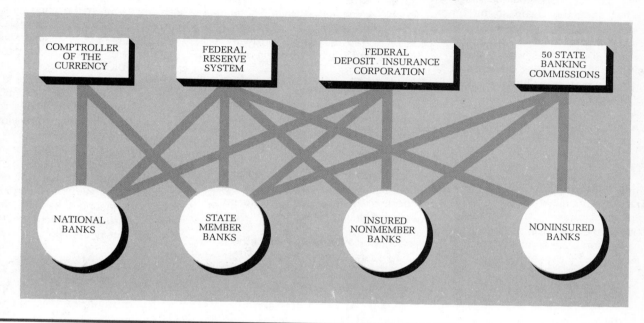

The main function of the FDIC is to insure deposits at commercial and savings banks. Each insured bank pays an annual premium equal to a fraction of 1 percent of its total deposits. In return, the FDIC insures each account up to $100,000 against loss due to bank failure. The FDIC also supervises insured banks and presides over the liquidation of banks that do fail. Two parallel agencies perform similar functions. One, the Federal Savings and Loan Insurance Corporation (FSLIC), insures deposits in savings and loan associations. The other, the National Credit Union Administration, provides deposit insurance for federally chartered credit unions.

All national banks must be insured by the Federal Deposit Insurance Corporation, and state banks may apply to the FDIC for insurance coverage if they wish. Since the late 1930s, practically all banks in the United States (more than 98 percent of them) have been covered by this insurance. Banks have therefore become much more stable than they were half a century ago, before the creation of government insurance. As a result, widespread runs on banks by panicky depositors seeking to withdraw their funds are no longer common. Nevertheless, a run will sometimes occur when a particular bank is believed to be in trouble.

Economics in the News

Banking Today: Is There a "Crisis of Confidence"?

Bankers are not supposed to be smart; they are supposed to be safe.

That statement used to be an axiom of banking. For about 50 years—from the early 1930s to the early 1980s—banks were viewed as the best places for people and businesses to keep money they could not afford to lose.

But that belief is no longer so strong. Depositors and investors see at least three major reasons for viewing the strength of our banking system with some skepticism.

Bank Failures

The conventional business of banks is to earn interest by lending money. But in their efforts to maximize profits, some banks have stretched themselves by extending risky loans for a chance at higher returns. Many of these loans have been to foreign governments whose economies are vulnerable to political unrest and to adverse changes in world economic conditions. Argentina, Brazil, Mexico, and some countries in Africa are notable examples. Result: The annual number of bank failures, due in part to defaults by large borrowers, has reached several dozen in some years since 1980.

High Interest Rates

When interest rates in the financial markets rise rapidly, many banks are caught in a two-way squeeze. They have to pay more on savings deposits while their interest income from loans does not rise as quickly. Consequently, earnings can suffer because expense outflows are not covered by income inflows.

Inadequate Deposit Insurance

The Federal Deposit Insurance Corporation was established in 1934 to provide protection for depositors. Some experts think that such protection encourages bank managers to take too many risks. Others question whether the amount of insurance premiums collected by the FDIC are sufficient to cover the huge losses that would occur if a large bank failure were to set off a chain reaction with other banks. Because of these concerns, the FDIC is experimenting with alternative types of insurance schemes. Among them: Deductible provisions as in automobile collision policies, and co-insurance provisions as in most health policies.

These problems account for the public's shaken confidence in the banking system. Until the problems are solved, depositors will continue to be skittish about keeping their money in a troubled bank, no matter how large it may be.

What You Have Learned

1. Money is a medium of exchange, a measure of value, a standard of deferred payments, and a store of value. The demand for money is the most fundamental problem of our monetary and banking system.

2. Money should be thought of as a spectrum of assets. "Narrow-transactions money," M1, is readily spendable money. It constitutes the basic money supply and consists primarily of currency and checkable deposits.

3. Broader measures than M1 are also in use. They include savings deposits, money-market mutual-fund shares, and various kinds of highly liquid assets referred to as near-monies.

4. The two major financial markets are the money market and the capital market. Short-term credit instruments are bought and sold in the former, long-term instruments in the latter. These markets thus perform the economic function of allocating financial resources between borrowers and lenders and between short-term and long-term uses.

5. Financial intermediaries, such as banks, insurance companies, credit unions, and other financial institutions, are connecting links between lenders and borrowers. They create and issue financial claims against themselves in order to acquire proceeds with which to purchase profitable financial claims against others. A large part of financial intermediaries' activities thus consist of the wholesaling and/or retailing of funds.

6. The Federal Reserve System is the central bank of the United States. It consists of about 5,700 member (commercial) banks scattered throughout the nation, 12 Federal Reserve Banks (plus 25 branches) located in various cities, and a seven-member Board of Governors appointed by the President and confirmed by the Senate. The function of the System is to foster a flow of credit that provides for stable prices, orderly economic growth, and strong international financial relationships.

7. The United States has a dual banking system consisting of national banks and state banks. Practically all banks are supervised by several government agencies. Almost all bank deposits (demand and time) are insured by the Federal Deposit Insurance Corporation (FDIC).

Terms and Concepts to Review

money	capital market
currency	bond
checkable deposit	financial markets
demand deposit	financial intermediaries
time deposit	commercial bank
repurchase agreement	Federal Reserve System
money market	member bank
Eurodollars	Federal Reserve Bank
near-monies	Board of Governors
credit	Federal Open Market
credit instrument	Committee
promissory note	Federal Advisory
Treasury bill	Council
negotiable certificate of	dual banking system
deposit	national bank
commercial paper	state bank
banker's acceptance	Federal Deposit
federal funds	Insurance Corporation

For Discussion

1. Which function of money is most important in today's society? Explain.

2. Which function does money perform least efficiently?

3. How would the functions of money be affected if the value of the dollar increased from year to year?

4. The more money you have, the richer you are. Similarly, the more money a nation has, the richer it is.

Therefore, nations can become rich simply by printing more money. Do you agree?

5. What economic reasons can you give for the existence of money markets?

6. Money-market instruments must possess certain characteristics in order to function *efficiently*. Can you think of three? What does "efficiently" mean in this case?

7. What economic reasons can you give for the existence of capital markets?

8. Capital markets have played an important role in our nation's growth. Can you explain why?

9. Financial intermediaries play a much more important role in today's economy than they did several decades ago. They are also more significant in the United States than in, say, African, Asian, or Latin American countries. Why?

10. Every nation has its own central bank. Why? What minimum functions does a central bank perform that a commercial bank does not?

Chapter 12

Banking Institutions: Money Creation and Portfolio Management

Learning Guide

Watch for answers to these important questions

How do we define money? What is the goldsmiths' principle and how does it relate to fractional-reserve banking?

Why is an individual bank in a banking system unable to lend more than its excess reserves? What would happen if it tried to do so?

Can the banking system as a whole lend more than its excess reserves? What is the deposit-expansion multiplier? The money multiplier? What do these multipliers tell you?

What goals do banks seek in the management of their portfolios? How do these goals impinge on one another?

How do banks allocate their funds among different classes of reserves? Which particular types of securities are likely to be found in a typical bank's portfolio?

The average person probably thinks of a bank as an institution in which to deposit money and from which to withdraw money. But banks are a good deal more than that. They play a fundamental role in the financial and monetary structure of our economy.

For example, banks engage in a varied assortment of financial activities. These activities include:

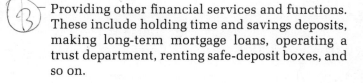

1. Dealing in money and credit instruments

2. Making business loans by creating checking deposits, and retiring loans when the deposits are repaid

3. Providing other financial services and functions. These include holding time and savings deposits, making long-term mortgage loans, operating a trust department, renting safe-deposit boxes, and so on.

The ways in which banks conduct most of these activities can have important effects on our economy. Therefore, the present chapter is concerned with examining the basic economic functions of today's banking institutions.

The Fundamental Principle of Deposit Banking

You have already learned that there are different measures of money, depending on what is included in its definition. For example, you will remember from the previous chapter that M1, the basic money supply, consists mainly of currency and checkable deposits. Thus we may say that for practical purposes

$$\text{money} = \text{currency} + \text{checkable deposits}$$

Checkable deposits, you will recall, are composed primarily of demand deposits, NOW accounts, and credit-union share accounts. Checkable deposits are also called **transaction deposits.**

Proportions of Currency and Checkable Deposits

Most of us are more familiar with currency than with checkable deposits. The amount of currency in circulation at any time is determined by the public—you and me and everyone else. This is because currency and checkable deposits are interchangeable. You will generally cash a check when you need currency and deposit currency in your checking account when you have more cash than you need.

Everyone behaves in much the same way. As a result, the public always holds the exact amount of cash that it wants, shifting its holdings back and forth between currency and checkable deposits. As you might expect, over the course of a year the economy holds a smaller proportion of M1 in currency than in checkable deposits. But at certain times of the year, such as Christmas and Easter, the proportion of currency in circulation increases significantly because people desire more cash for spending. After the holidays, the proportion of currency in circulation decreases significantly as businesses deposit their cash receipts in checking accounts.

The Goldsmiths' Principle

Because checkable deposits are by far the largest part of our money supply, it is important to know how they come into existence and what role they play.

The credit-creation process of deposit banking is based on the following fundamental principle:

> Not all of the customers of a bank will withdraw their funds at the same time. On any given day, some customers will decrease their deposits by withdrawing funds in the form of cash and checks drawn on the bank while others will increase their deposits by depositing funds in the form of cash and checks drawn on other banks. Under normal conditions, the volume of deposits and withdrawals will tend to be equal over a period of time.

This is a modernized version of what may be called the *goldsmiths' principle.* The principle was discovered centuries ago by the English precious-metal artisans, called goldsmiths. They found that, when people deposited gold for safekeeping, it was not usually necessary to store all the gold away. Instead, only a portion of it needed to be kept in reserve for those individuals who might want to withdraw their gold. The rest of it could be "put to work" earning interest by being loaned to others with the promise of repayment.

In a bank, of course, there is always the possibility that, during some periods, withdrawals will exceed deposits. To meet such contingencies, reserves equal to less than 5 percent of deposits are usually more than adequate. However, for legal reasons that will be explained shortly, the percentage of reserves that banks actually keep on hand is somewhat higher than 5 percent.

The Goldsmiths' Principle and Fractional Bank Reserves

The ways in which checkable deposits are expanded and contracted can best be illustrated in terms of changes in a bank's assets, liabilities, and net worth. These terms have special meanings.

For any economic entity such as an individual, household, or firm:

Assets are things of value that are owned — cash, property, and the rights to property.

Liabilities are monetary debts or things of value that are owed to creditors.

Net worth, or owners' equity, is the difference between assets and liabilities.

Thus, for any individual, household, or firm,

$$\text{assets} - \text{liabilities} = \text{net worth}$$

Therefore, it is also true that

$$\text{assets} = \text{liabilities} + \text{net worth}$$

As you will see shortly, the second equation is the form in which these concepts will be presented.

When these three classes of data are grouped together for analysis and interpretation, the financial statement on which they appear is called a *balance sheet.* For example, on a bank's balance sheet, the principal assets are loans and government securities; the principal liabilities are deposits.

As stated above, the English goldsmiths discovered by experience that they could run a banking business by maintaining a fractional — rather than a 100 percent — reserve in gold against their deposits. U.S. banks today also operate with fractional reserves, but not in gold. The law requires them to maintain fractional reserves of liquid assets against their deposit liabilities. There are three categories of reserves: legal, required, and excess. The first category includes the other two.

Legal reserves are assets that a bank or other depository institution (such as a savings and loan association or a credit union) may lawfully use as reserves against its deposit liabilities. For a member bank of the Federal Reserve System, legal reserves consist of currency held in the vaults of the bank — called *vault cash* — plus deposits held with the district Federal Reserve Bank. Any other highly liquid financial claims, such as government securities, are classified as *nonlegal* reserves. For a nonmember bank or other depository institution, legal reserves consist of vault cash plus deposits with the district Federal Reserve Bank or with an approved institution. The latter is any depository institution (such as a member bank) that holds a reserve balance with the Federal Reserve.

Required Reserves   are the minimum amount of legal reserves that a bank is required by law to keep behind its deposit liabilities. For example, if the required reserve ratio is 1:5, or 20 percent, a bank with checkable deposits of $1 million must hold at least $200,000 of required legal reserves.

Excess Reserves   are the amount of a bank's legal reserves over and above its required reserves. Excess reserves, as you will see, are the determinants of a bank's lending power.

It follows from these definitions that

$$\text{legal reserves} = \text{required reserves} + \text{excess reserves}$$

and therefore

$$\text{excess reserves} = \text{legal reserves} - \text{required reserves}$$

It further follows that any changes in either a bank's legal reserves or its required reserves will change its excess reserves. As you study the processes, illustrated below, by which banks expand and contract checkable deposits, you should keep in mind the simple equations above.

The preceding definition of legal reserves is a result of sweeping financial legislation passed in the 1980s. It made *all* depository institutions subject to uniform reserve requirements on similar classes of deposits. Prior to 1980, only member banks had to meet legal reserve requirements as defined above. Nonmember institutions were subject to less stringent and more heterogeneous requirements that varied by state. A fuller explanation of the legislation is provided in Box 1.

Box 1
Banking Legislation of the 1980s

The nation's financial system has undergone vast changes as a result of two major banking laws enacted in the early 1980s:

– Depository Institutions Deregulation and Monetary Control Act (1980)
– Depository Institutions Act (1982)

The second act was an extension of the first. Taken together, the two laws may be referred to as the ***Depository Institutions Acts*** of 1980, 1982. They provided primarily for the following:

– **Uniform Reserve Standards** All depository institutions must meet the same reserve requirements on similar types and sizes of deposits. (Prior to 1980, only member banks of the Federal Reserve System were subject to uniform reserve standards. Nonmember banks were subject to various standards depending on state requirements.)

– **Transaction Accounts** All depository institutions may hold interest-bearing checkable deposits, such as NOW accounts and credit-union share accounts. (Prior to 1980, the only type of transaction account was a demand-deposit account at a commercial bank.)

– **Federal Reserve Accessibility** All depository institutions that issue transaction accounts may borrow on equal terms from their Federal Reserve Banks. Depository institutions can also purchase the Fed's services, such as check clearing and electronic transfer of funds, if desired. (Prior to 1980, only member banks could apply for loans from the Fed; they could receive its services free.)

– **Thrift-Institution Banking Powers** Savings-and-loan associations and savings banks have limited authority to offer demand deposits and to make business loans. (Prior to 1982, only commercial banks could engage in such activities.)

– **Money-Market Deposit Accounts** Depository institutions can offer higher-yielding deposit accounts with limited checking privileges at money-market rates. (Prior to 1982, higher-yielding limited checking accounts were not permitted.)

The two acts contain many other technical provisions. But the main intent of the legislation can be summarized briefly:

The Depository Institutions Acts allowed banks to become more competitive by reducing the distinctions between them and the restrictions under which they operate.

Before we look at how banks expand and contract deposits, it will help to have an overall picture of their assets and liabilities. This is presented in the self-explanatory condensed balance sheet shown in Exhibit 1.

Exhibit 1
Consolidated Balance Sheet of
All Commercial Banks
December 31, 1985 (in billions)

(1) **ASSETS**	
(2) Vault cash (currency and coin)	$ 23.4
(3) Reserves with Federal Reserve Banks	19.7
(4) **Legal reserves: (2) + (3)**	33.1
These are assets that banks may lawfully use as reserves against their deposit liabilities.	
(5) Loans	1,149.3
Consists of the value of claims (or I.O.U.s) held by banks against borrowers.	
(6) U.S. Treasury and other securities	437.5
Includes mostly Treasury bills, Treasury notes, Treasury bonds, federal agency securities, municipal securities, and bankers' acceptances.	
(7) Other assets	450.
Includes cash items in process of collection, the value of bank premises, and other items.	
(8) **Total assets: (4) + (5) + (6) + (7)**	**$2,113.1**
(9) **LIABILITIES AND NET WORTH**	
(10) Transaction (checkable) deposits	$ 383.2
(11) Other liabilities	1,575.4
Includes savings deposits, time deposits, borrowings such as negotiable CDs issued by banks, and other items.	
(12) **Total liabilities: (10) + (11)**	1,958.6
(13) **Net worth: (8) − (12)**	154.5
This is the ownership interest of banks' stockholders.	
(14) **Total liabilities and net worth: (12) + (13)**	**$2,113.1**

Source: Board of Governors of the Federal Reserve System. Preliminary data.

Deposit Expansion by a Single Bank

The easiest way to understand the deposit-banking process is to examine the transactions of a single bank over successive stages. To keep the explanation from becoming unnecessarily complicated, two simplifying conditions will be introduced:

- **Uniform Transaction Deposits** Depository institutions are assumed to offer only one type of checkable deposit. In reality, as you know, several types of checkable deposits (also known as transaction deposits) are available.

- **Fixed Required-Reserve Ratio** A reserve requirement of 20 percent against deposits is assumed. (In reality, the average requirement for depository institutions as a whole is closer to 10 percent. However, rather than employing this figure in the following examples, it will be used instead for some of the problems at the end of the chapter.)

Stage 1 Let us begin by assuming that Bank A has the following simplified balance sheet:

Bank A: Balance Sheet
Stage 1: Initial Position

Assets			Liabilities and Net Worth	
Legal reserves		$ 5,000	Deposits	$20,000
Required	$4,000		Net worth	1,000
Excess	1,000			
Loans (Claims)		16,000		
		$21,000		$21,000

The first thing to notice is that the balance sheet "balances." That is, the totals always conform to the equation: assets = liabilities + net worth.

On the right side of the balance sheet, observe that deposits are a liability. This is because the bank is obligated to honor checks drawn by its depositors up to the amount shown.

On the left side, legal reserves (which consist of vault cash plus deposits with the district Federal Reserve Bank) are assets. Loans are also classified as assets because they represent financial claims held by the bank against borrowers. These claims (or accounts receivable) are usually in the form of promissory notes.

Return to the right side of the balance sheet. Observe that net worth is the difference between total assets and total liabilities. It is thus a "balancing item" representing stockholders' ownership in the bank.

Note also that, with $20,000 of deposits and a reserve requirement of 20 percent, required reserves (on the left side) are $4,000. Because legal reserves are $5,000, excess reserves are equal to $1,000.

Stage 2 Because the bank has $1,000 in excess reserves, it can make loans equal to this amount. Suppose you, a businessperson, borrow the funds and give the bank your promissory note in exchange. The bank then credits your account for $1,000. *Before* you write any checks, how does the bank's balance sheet look?

Bank A: Balance Sheet
Stage 2: After the bank grants a loan of $1,000
but before checks are written against it

Assets		Liabilities and Net Worth	
Legal reserves	$ 5,000	Deposits	$21,000
Loans (Claims)	17,000	Net worth	1,000
	$22,000		$22,000

As shown above, deposits have risen to $21,000. This reflects the bank's commitment (liability) to honor your checks up to $1,000. In addition, loans have increased to $17,000, reflecting the promissory note (asset) you gave the bank for $1,000. As a result of this transaction, *the bank has created $1,000 of new money.*

Stage 3 Of course, you can take your $1,000 out in currency if you wish. However, because you are in business, you will probably find it more convenient to write checks in order to pay your bills.

Suppose that you write a check for the full $1,000 and give it to a supplier from whom you purchased materials. The supplying company then deposits the check in its own bank, Bank B, which in turn presents it to Bank A for payment. The effect on Bank A, as shown in the following balance sheet, is to reduce its deposits to $20,000 and its legal reserves to $4,000. Note that required reserves are 20 percent of deposits, or $4,000—which equals the bank's legal reserves. The bank, in other words, no longer has excess reserves.

Bank A: Balance Sheet
Stage 3: Final Position

Assets			Liabilities and Net Worth	
Legal reserves		$ 4,000	Deposits	$20,000
Required	$4,000		Net worth	1,000
Excess	0			
Loans (Claims)		17,000		
		$21,000		$21,000

The foregoing analysis leads to an important conclusion:

No individual bank in a banking system can lend more than its excess reserves. In other words, when a bank's excess reserves are zero, it has no unused lending power. The bank, therefore, is "in equilibrium" or *fully loaned up.*

Of course, the supplier to whom you gave your $1,000 check might have had an account in Bank A instead of in Bank B. In that case, the *total* deposits of Bank A would have been unaffected. The bank, when processing the check, would simply have reduced your account by $1,000 and increased the supplier's account by the same amount. In the great majority of cases, however, this situation does not exist. Instead:

As a borrower writes checks against a deposit, his or her bank loses reserves and deposits to other banks within the banking system. Hence, a bank cannot afford to make loans in an amount greater than its excess reserves.

Deposit Expansion by the Banking System

Although a single bank cannot make loans totaling more than its excess reserves, the banking system can lend several times the amount. Thus, *what is true of the individual is not necessarily true of the whole.* Let us examine the reasons for this by continuing with the foregoing illustration. To keep matters simple, we will focus our attention on the relevant balance-sheet *changes* while disregarding all other items. As before, the reserve requirement is assumed to be 20 percent.

Stage 4   The $1,000 check you paid your supplier is deposited in the supplier's account in Bank B. Bank B's deposits increase by $1,000 and its legal reserves increase by $1,000 (after the check clears). Assuming that Bank B was fully loaned up prior to this transaction, it sets aside 20 percent or $200 in required reserves. Therefore it has 80 percent, or $800 in excess reserves.

Bank B
Stage 4: Bank B receives $1,000 deposit lost by Bank A

Assets		Liabilities	
Legal reserves	+$1,000	Deposits	+$1,000
Required	+$200		
Excess	+ 800		
	+$1,000		+$1,000

Stage 5   Bank B, of course, will try to lend $800 — an amount equal to its excess reserves. Assuming it grants such a loan, its balance sheet *before* any checks are written will show that deposits have risen from $1,000 to $1,800. Therefore, loans have increased by a corresponding amount. Thus:

Bank B
Stage 5: After Bank B grants a loan for $800 but before checks are written against it

Assets		Liabilities	
Legal reserves	+$1,000	Deposits	+$1,800
Loans (Claims)	+ 800		
	+$1,800		+$1,800

Stage 6   If we assume that the borrower writes a check for the entire amount of the loan, the check will be deposited by its recipient in Bank C. This will cause Bank B to lose $800 in deposits and (after the check clears) $800 of legal reserves to Bank C. This will then leave Bank B with the following net changes:

Bank B
Stage 6: After checks for $800 are written against Bank B

Assets		Liabilities	
Legal reserves (net change = +$1,000 −$800)	+$ 200	Deposits (net change = +$1,800 −$800)	+$1,000
Loans (Claims)	+ 800		
	+$1,000		+$1,000

Notice that the change in Bank B's legal reserves is equal to 20 percent of the change in its deposits. Therefore, its excess reserves are zero. Hence, Bank B is said to be "in equilibrium," or fully loaned up.

Stage 7   Bank C receives the $800 deposit that was lost by Bank B in Stage 6. Bank C thus gains (after the check clears) $800 in legal reserves. Assuming that Bank C had been fully loaned up, it then sets aside 20 percent of the deposit, or $160, as required reserves. Therefore, it has 80 percent, or $640, in excess reserves.

Bank C
Stage 7: Bank C receives $800 deposit lost by Bank B

Assets		Liabilities	
Legal reserves	+$800	Deposits	+$800
Required	+$160		
Excess	+ 640		
	+$800		+$800

Stage 8   Suppose that Bank C now grants a loan equal to the amount of its excess reserves. *Before* any checks are written, both its deposits and loans will have risen by $640.

Bank C

Stage 8: After Bank C grants a loan for $640 but before checks are written against it

Assets		Liabilities	
Legal reserves	+$ 800	Deposits	+$1,440
Loans (Claims)	+ 640		
	+$1,440		+$1,440

Stage 9 After the borrower writes a check against the loan and deposits the check in Bank D, deposits and legal reserves in Bank C go down by $640 (once the check clears). This leaves Bank C with the following net changes:

Bank C

Stage 9: After checks for $640 are written against Bank C

Assets		Liabilities	
Legal reserves (net change = +$800 −$640)	+$160	Deposits (net change = +$1,440 −$640)	+$800
Loans (Claims)	+ 640		
	+$800		+$800

Because the increase in Bank C's legal reserves is equal to 20 percent of the total increase in its deposits, its excess reserves are zero. The bank, therefore, is said to be "in equilibrium," or fully loaned up.

Stage 10 and Beyond You can see by now that a logical expansionary process is taking place. It is sufficient, therefore, to illustrate briefly a few further steps in the sequence. This can be done by noting the changes experienced by each bank on its partial balance sheet. As before, it is assumed that each bank is initially fully loaned up. (All data are rounded to the nearest dollar.)

Bank D

Assets		Liabilities	
Legal reserves	+$128	Deposits	+$640
Loans (Claims)	+ 512		
	+$640		+$640

Bank E

Assets		Liabilities	
Legal reserves	+$102	Deposits	+$512
Loans (Claims)	+ 410		
	+$512		+512

Bank F

Assets		Liabilities	
Legal reserves	+$ 82	Deposits	+$410
Loans (Claims)	+ 328		
	+$410		+$410

And so on.

The deposit-creation process thus continues until all excess reserves in the system are "used up." That is, until all legal reserves have become required reserves.

The process of deposit expansion is illustrated in Exhibit 2. As you can see, both the table and the graph depict the same ideas that were demonstrated above in terms of changes in banks' balance sheets.

The Deposit Multiplier

You may have noticed that the expansion in deposits by the banking system as a whole is influenced by the required reserve ratio. You can verify this from Exhibit 2 by demonstrating that the reciprocal of the required reserve ratio—that is, the number 1 divided by the required reserve ratio—gives what may be called the "deposit multiplier." Thus, letting r represent the required reserve ratio,

$$\text{deposit multiplier} = \frac{1}{\text{required reserve ratio}} = \frac{1}{r}$$

Hence, if you know the required reserve ratio, you can determine the deposit multiplier immediately. For instance, in our example, the required reserve ratio was 20 percent, or $\frac{1}{5}$. Therefore,

$$\text{deposit multiplier} = \frac{1}{\frac{1}{5}} = 5$$

Exhibit 2
Multiple Expansion of Checkable Deposits Through the Banking System

The table shows the cumulative expansion of checkable deposits in the banking system as a whole.   An initial deposit of $1,000 and a required reserve of 20 percent are assumed.   Data are rounded to the nearest dollar.

Note in column (2) that new deposits, which are banks' liabilities, are also equal to banks' new legal-reserve assets.   These increases are allocated partly to new required reserves in column (3) and partly to new excess reserves in column (4).

New excess reserves become new loans in the form of newly created money, which is deposited in banks.   Thus, the total of $4,000 created in column (4) is the same as the new deposit expansion created in column (2).   The deposit multiplier, therefore, based on the initial increase in excess reserves of $800, shown in column (4), is 5.   This is because 5 × $800 = $4,000.

If all banks in the system are aligned in decreasing order of new deposits created, the multiple-expansion process illustrated in the table can be depicted clearly in the form of a bar graph.

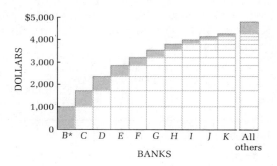

The Increase in a Bank's Deposit Liabilities Equals the Increase in Its Legal-Reserve Assets

(1) Banks	(2) New checkable deposits (=new legal reserves)	=	(3) New required reserves at 20%	+	(4) New excess reserves (=new loans) Newly created money	(5) Cumulative new deposits [from col. (2)]
B	$1,000 (initial*)		$ 200		$ 800	$1,000
C	800		160		640	1,800
D	640		128		512	2,440
E	512		102		410	2,952
F	410	new deposit expansion =$4,000	82		328	3,362
G	328		66		262	3,690
H	262		52		210	3,952
I	210		42		168	4,162
J	168		34		134	4,330
K	134		27		107	4,464
All other banks	536		107		429	5,000
Totals	$5,000		$1,000		$4,000	

* This deposit came from Bank A in Stage 4.

What does this mean? You will recall learning earlier in the chapter that *the increase in a bank's deposit liabilities is also equal to the increase in its legal-reserve assets.* Thus, in the table of Exhibit 2, new deposits and new legal reserves in column (2) are allocated to two components. One is new required reserves in column (3). The other is new excess reserves in column (4). When the new excess-reserve quantities are lent, they become newly created money that ends up as new deposits in column (2). The table thus illustrates two fundamental ideas:

— If the deposit multiplier is 5:

An initial excess reserve of $800, shown in column (4), results in a total of newly created money for the banking system as a whole of 5 × $800 = $4,000.

— The newly created money is in the form of a *net gain* in checkable deposits.

These ideas can be generalized and incorporated in a simple formula. Let *D* represent the change in checkable deposits for the banking system as a whole. Also, let *E* be the amount of excess reserves, and *r* the required reserve ratio. Then,

$$D = \text{deposit multiplier} \times E$$

That is,

$$D = \frac{1}{r} \times E$$

To illustrate, if r = 10 percent, or 1/10, the deposit multiplier is 10. Therefore, excess reserves *E* of $1,000 can result in a net increase in newly created money, in the form of checkable deposits, of as much as 10 × $1,000 = $10,000.

The following definition helps summarize the basic concept:

The **deposit multiplier** is the reciprocal of the required-reserve ratio. Its value determines the maximum *multiple* by which the banking system's deposits can expand as a result of an initial increase in excess reserves.

Three Real-World Factors

The principle of multiple expansion of bank deposits assumes that the banking system will produce a magnified expansion in deposits. The expansion may be 5:1 or some other ratio. The amount depends on the reserve requirement and the assumption that banks always make loans equal to the full amount of their excess reserves. Actually, this principle is modified in practice by at least three factors.

— **Leakage of Cash into Circulation** A business borrowing money from a bank may take part of it in cash. Or, someone who is paid a debt by check may "cash" some or all of it rather than deposit the entire amount. For these reasons, some money that would otherwise serve as excess reserves will tend to leak out of the banking system. This will leave less new reserves available for banks to lend.

— **Idle Excess Reserves** Banks do not always make loans equal to the full amount of their excess reserves. They may sometimes maintain idle excess reserves because they desire a "safety margin" or because they are unable to find suitable investments. Thus, if the reserve requirement were 20 percent, banks might at times choose to have available an average reserve of 25 percent. This, of course, would reduce the deposit-creating ability of the banking system from 5:1 to 4:1. It may also happen that businesses are not willing to borrow the banking system's entire excess reserves. That may be the case during a recession, for example, when business executives are gloomy about the future.

— **Transfer of Some Checkable Deposits to Time Deposits** It is unlikely that all newly created money will become checkable deposits, as the principle of multiple expansion assumes. Instead, the public will place some percentage of checkable deposits into higher-interest-paying time deposits. Some of these are subject to required reserves but certain others, such as long-term time deposits held by businesses, are not. Therefore, any transfer of funds from checkable deposits to *reservable* time deposits will leave a smaller volume of excess reserves available for the expansion of checkable deposits.

Conclusion: The Money Multiplier

Because the deposit-multiplier formula does not accurately fit the real world, we can make use of a more precise formula that expresses the money supply, M1, in relation to the **monetary base.** This is simply the sum of currency held by the public plus legal reserves. The monetary base may thus be thought of as "high-powered" money. It supports the money supply (M1) because our fractional-reserve banking system enables the system to *create* more money (through checkable deposits) than it holds in required reserves. Therefore, M1 is always some *multiple m* of the monetary base B. Thus:

$$M1 = mB$$

This formula may be called the **money multiplier.** It has several important aspects:

– **The Multiplier Is *m*** It can be derived from regularly published data for M1 and B. Thus, for example, if in a given year M1 is $700 billion and B is $300 billion, then $m = M1/B = \$700$ billion/$300 billion = 2.3. Over the long run, the value of m has ranged between 2 and 3.

– **The Multiplier *m* Is Not a Constant, but a Variable** It is affected by the same three factors described above that reduce the deposit multiplier. However, it is important to note that these factors affect B as well as m. That is:

The factors that influence the multiplier m also influence the monetary base B. This means that m and B are *not* independent of each other. Changes in one can cause changes in the other, and changes in either can affect M1.

Because of this, we must look at the ways in which certain banking practices can affect the components of the money-multiplier formula.

Managing a Bank's Portfolio

As a bank expands and contracts its deposits, it also acquires and disposes of income-earning (or interest-earning) assets. These assets make up what is known as the bank's *portfolio* — its security holdings. Income-earning assets — or simply earning assets — are of two types:

– Securities issued by the U.S. Treasury, federal agencies (such as the Federal National Mortgage Association and the Farm Credit Bureau, among others), and municipal governments.

– Financial obligations, such as promissory notes issued by borrowers, and corporate bonds.

A bank's earning assets are an important source of its income. The manner in which banks as a whole manage their portfolios, acquiring and disposing of earning assets as the need arises, can have important impacts throughout the financial markets and on the borrowing and expenditure practices of households and businesses. Let us see why.

Objectives: Liquidity, Profitability, and Safety

Imagine yourself responsible for managing a bank's portfolio. Because one of your major tasks is to acquire earning assets, the problem you continually face is to achieve a proper balance between liquidity, profitability, and safety. Let us look at what these terms mean.

Liquidity

Liquidity is a complex concept. For our purposes **liquidity** may be defined as the ease with which an asset can be converted into cash quickly without loss of value in relation to its purchase price.

Liquidity is a matter of degree. Money (that is, cash) is an asset that is perfectly liquid. It can be used as a medium of exchange, and it always retains the same value in terms of itself. A government obligation that is close to maturity is almost as liquid as money, because it can be readily sold for cash with little or no loss of value. On the other hand, a bank building is a relatively illiquid asset. It cannot easily be sold, and it may yield a loss when it is.

Profitability

Earning profits is a second goal in portfolio management. Profits consist of two parts. One is the difference between what you pay for an asset and what you realize when you redeem or sell it. The other is any returns you receive in the interim. Both parts are combined to provide a measure of profits.

For example, in the case of government bonds, which are a major form of earning assets for banks, the two parts are reflected by a single percentage figure called *yield to maturity.* A bond's yield to maturity may be 10 percent, 15 percent, or some other amount—and it will fluctuate according to market conditions. Portfolio managers, therefore, are continually changing the compositions of their earning assets. They do this by selling bonds and other securities that have lower yields in order to purchase those that have higher yields.

Safety

Maintaining safety is a third goal in bank portfolio management. Safety refers to the probability that the borrower will fulfill the contractual terms of an investment. In the case of a bond, for example, the main contractual terms are that the interest and principal payments will be made when due. Safety is a matter of degree. The safest of all financial obligations are Treasury securities—bills, notes, and bonds. This is because they are backed by the good faith and taxing power of the federal government. Bonds issued by many municipal governments also rank very high on the safety scale.

However, safety and liquidity do not always go together. Market prices of U.S. Treasury bonds, for example, may fluctuate substantially, thereby impairing their liquidity. But the safety of Treasury securities—that is, payment of interest and principal—is never in doubt.

The Conflict Between Liquidity and Profitability

The ideal bank portfolio is liquid, profitable, and safe. But it is impossible to maximize all three objectives.

A bank's most immediate obligation is to pay cash upon demand. The moment it is unable to make payments on a check, it must close its doors. Holding a certain portion of its assets in the form of vault cash helps a bank to meet its liquidity needs. But, because a bank's vault cash yields no return, there is a conflict between liquidity and profitability:

- Too large a proportion of a bank's assets in the form of cash provides greater liquidity but an unnecessary loss of income.

- Too small a proportion of a bank's assets in cash permits higher income from investment in earning assets, but at the risk of illiquidity and failure.

A portfolio manager has to strike a compromise between these two extremes. Moreover, the compromise must be achieved with a relatively high degree of safety. This is because banks are subject to many legal and conventional constraints that limit the types of earning assets they can acquire.

The nature of the conflict between liquidity and profitability is illustrated in Exhibit 3. The axes of the figure denote the two extreme alternatives. Keeping all the bank's funds in cash is represented by the vertical distance 0M. Investing all the bank's funds in earning assets is represented by the horizontal distance 0N. Neither of these extreme choices is acceptable. The former would leave the bank in too liquid a position to earn income. The latter would leave the bank completely illiquid and hence unable to pay cash on demand.

Exhibit 3
Investment-Possibilities Line

Each point along the line *MN* denotes a different combination of cash and earning assets. Thus, point *A* denotes *G* dollars of cash and *H* dollars of earning assets. Point B denotes *J* dollars of cash and *K* dollars of earning assets. The portfolio manager of a bank seeks to obtain an optimum combination of cash and earning assets (or liquidity and profitability). However, this objective is subject to various legal constraints designed to assure a high degree of safety.

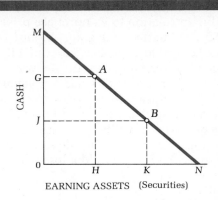

Suppose we now connect the two points. The resulting line *MN* shows all the combinations of cash and earning assets in which it is possible to invest the bank's funds. Therefore, it may be called an "investment-possibilities line." There is some point along the line—some combination of cash and earning assets—that is the optimum for a particular bank at a particular time. The challenge faced by every bank's portfolio manager is to find that point. This will provide the bank with the highest possible level of earnings consistent with liquidity and safety.

Priorities for Allocating Bank Funds

Because of the conflict between liquidity, profitability, and safety, priorities for allocating a bank's funds must be established. That is, criteria are needed for deciding how banks are to utilize their limited funds. Four classes of uses may be distinguished:

Primary Reserves: Liquid Assets

This category of assets receives the highest priority. It consists of a bank's legal reserves and the demand deposits it may have with other banks. In other words, a bank's primary reserves consist of *liquid assets*. They are instantly available to meet depositors' needs.

Secondary Reserves: Near-Liquid Assets

This category of assets, which receives the second highest priority, provides "protective investment." It is made up of *near-liquid earning assets*. Examples include such short-term financial obligations as Treasury bills, high-grade commercial paper (such as promissory notes issued by large corporations), and banker's acceptances. The main purpose of secondary reserves is to meet expected and more or less regular seasonal demands for liquidity. These demands typically occur during peak business periods such as Christmas and Easter.

Tertiary Reserves: Customer Loan Demands

The third priority in allocating a bank's funds is meeting business and consumer credit needs. This is the fundamental purpose for which a bank is created. By fulfilling this objective, a bank enhances its profits because interest rates on loans are usually higher than on securities. However, to some extent, this priority overlaps with the following one.

Residual Reserves: Investments for Income

The fourth priority concerns the use of a bank's funds after the three previous priorities have been satisfied. Thus, any funds that a bank has available after fulfilling the foregoing requirements are invested in long-term securities aimed at providing additional income. These investments, of course, are also subject to constraints of safety. Therefore, they consist primarily of government securities — notes and bonds — issued by federal, state, and local governments.

This order of priorities applies to all banks. However, the relative distribution of funds for these four purposes differs somewhat among individual banks. In general, the differences vary according to legal requirements, local business needs, and each bank's ability to balance the goals of liquidity, profitability, and safety.

Conclusion: Types of Bank Investments

The types of investment a bank can make are regulated by law. Therefore, three types of securities are likely to be found in a typical bank's portfolio:

1. U.S. Government Securities These consist of ***Treasury bills, Treasury notes,*** and ***Treasury bonds.*** All are readily marketable if the bank should wish to sell them, and they differ from each other in their periods of maturity. Those approaching maturity thus contribute greatly to satisfying the *near*-liquidity requirements of banks.

2. "Quasi-governmental" Securities These consist of notes and bonds issued by various agencies of the federal government. Examples, as mentioned earlier, are the Federal Home Loan Bank and the Federal National Mortgage Association.

3. Municipal Securities These are marketable financial obligations issued by state and local governments. Called simply ***municipals,*** they provide holders with interest income that is exempt from all federal income taxes. This is a major reason banks purchase them.

Leaders in Economics

UPI/Bettmann Newsphotos

James Tobin
1918 –
Portfolio Selection Theory

How do Washington's fiscal and monetary policies interact with business investment decisions?

This, in a broad sense, is a question that has occupied James Tobin's thought during much of his career. A professor emeritus at Yale University, he has published numerous studies that have sought to provide a link between abstract macroeconomic theory and the ways in which people and institutions behave.

An avid Keynesian, Tobin was an advisor to President Kennedy during the early 1960s. However, his best known work — and probably his most significant achievement — has been his development of "portfolio selection theory." The theory attempts to explain how people and institutions seek to obtain optimum combinations of risk, yield, and liquidity in their investment portfolios. Despite the complex mathematics involved, Tobin summarizes the theory simply as "not putting all your eggs in one basket."

The Swedish Royal Academy of Science, however, has not allowed Tobin's modesty to obscure his accomplishments. In 1981, the Academy awarded Tobin the Nobel Prize in recognition of his extraordinary contributions to economic science.

In general:

> Banks manage their portfolios by buying and selling earning assets in order to enhance profits. These actions influence both legal reserves and currency in circulation. Therefore, they affect the components of the money-multiplier formula and hence the level of economic activity.

What You Have Learned

1. Commercial banking rests on the goldsmiths' principle. This enables banks to maintain fractional reserves —rather than 100 percent reserves—against deposits, because not all customers will withdraw their funds at the same time. Hence, the banks can earn interest by making loans that equal the amount of their unused or excess reserves.

2. A single bank in a banking system cannot lend an amount that exceeds the amount of its excess reserves. When a bank's excess reserves are zero, it is said to be in equilibrium, or fully loaned up.

3. The banking system as a whole can expand deposits by a multiple of its excess reserves. This process is known as the principle of multiple expansion of bank deposits. It is of fundamental importance in banking.

4. The amount by which the banking system as a whole can expand deposits depends on the required reserve ratio and the initial amount of excess reserves. The required reserve ratio determines the deposit multiplier. This number, when multiplied by initial excess reserves, tells the maximum amount of expansion that can take place.

5. The deposit multiplier can be replaced by a broader measure—the money multiplier. This expresses the money supply (M1) as some multiple m of the monetary base B. Thus: $M1 = mB$.

6. The objectives of banks' portfolios are liquidity, profitability, and safety. Banks seek an optimum combination of cash and earning assets consistent with a high level of safety. Hence, they are largely limited to three major classes of investments: U.S. government securities, federal agency securities, and municipal securities. The way in which banks manage their portfolios of these securities affects the money multiplier and, therefore, the level of economic activity.

Terms and Concepts to Review

goldsmiths' principle	monetary base
assets	money multiplier
liabilities	liquidity
net worth	yield to maturity
balance sheet	primary reserves
legal reserves	secondary reserves
required reserves	Treasury bills
excess reserves	Treasury notes
multiple expansion of	Treasury bonds
bank deposits	municipals
deposit multiplier	

For Discussion

1. What is meant by "fractional-reserve banking"? How did it come into existence? Is it relevant today?

2. An individual bank cannot lend more than its excess reserves. Let us see why—by observing what would happen if it tried to do so.

Suppose that the reserve requirement is 20 percent, and Bank Z is holding:

Assets		Liabilities	
Vault cash	$ 50,000	Deposits	$200,000
Loans and			
other assets	160,000	Net worth	10,000
	$210,000		$210,000

(a) How much are Bank Z's excess reserves?
(b) The reserve requirement is assumed to be 20 percent, or ⅕. Show the effect on Bank Z's balance sheet after it expands its loans in a 5:1 ratio. What is the percentage of reserves to deposits?
(c) Suppose that borrowers write checks against their new deposits and the checks are deposited in other banks. Show the effect on Bank Z's balance sheet after all the checks are presented to it for payment. What has happened to the bank's reserves against deposits?
(d) What can Bank Z do to correct the situation? If it succeeds, how would its balance sheet look?
(e) What do you conclude from this exercise?

3. Suppose you borrow $1,000 in currency from Midwest Bank and give the bank your promissory note in return.
(a) Show the effects on the following balance sheets:

Your Balance Sheet

Change in Assets	Change in Liabilities and Net Worth

Midwest Bank's Balance Sheet

Change in Assets	Change in Liabilities and Net Worth

(b) Complete Balance Sheet 2 below.

Balance Sheet 1 — Midwest Bank
Before making $1,000 loan

Assets		Liabilities and Net Worth	
Cash	$ 3,000	Deposits	$20,000
Reserves	4,000	Other liabilities	25,000
Loans	15,000		
Other assets	50,000	Net worth	27,000
	$72,000		$72,000

Balance Sheet 2 — Midwest Bank
After $1,000 in cash is withdrawn by borrower

Assets		Liabilities and Net worth	
Cash	_____	Deposits	_____
Reserves	_____	Other liabilities	_____
Loans	_____		
Other assets	_____	Net worth	_____
	══════		══════

(c) How would Balance Sheet 2 be affected if you had written $1,000 in checks against your deposit instead of withdrawing the money in cash?

4. Some people argue that "loans create deposits," while others contend that "deposits permit loans." Which statement is correct? Which is likely to be defended by economists? By bankers? Explain.

5. Assume that the reserve requirement is 10 percent. There are no currency withdrawals. Bank A's partial balance sheet is as follows:

Bank A

Assets		Liabilities	
Legal reserves	$ 16	Deposits	$100
Loans	84		
	$100		$100

(a) How much can Bank A expand deposits? Explain.
(b) If all other banks are in equilibrium, how much can Bank B lend? How much can Bank C lend? What is the maximum for the whole banking system? Explain.

6. What is the deposit multiplier when (a) required reserves are 1 percent; (b) required reserves are 10 percent; (c) required reserves are 100 percent?

7. For Bank A, legal reserves are $1,000, required reserves are $800, and deposits are $8,000. All other banks are in equilibrium. By how much can the banking system expand its deposits?

8. Will the *actual* amount of deposit expansion by the banking system equal the *predicted* amount? Explain.

9. Fill in the gaps for the omitted banks in the following table, assuming a 15 percent reserve requirement against deposits. What basic principle does the table illustrate?

	Amount added to checking accounts (=legal reserves)	Excess reserves (=amount lent)	Required reserves
Bank 1	—	$10,000	—
Bank 2	$10,000	8,500	$ _____
. . .	. . .	. . .	. . .
Bank 11	2,315	1,968	347
. . .	. . .	. . .	. . .
. . .	. . .	. . .	. . .
. . .	. . .	. . .	. . .
. . .	. . .	. . .	. . .
Bank 20	537	457	80
All other banks			
Totals — all banks	$ _____	$ _____	$ _____

10. Why is the money-multiplier formula a better guide for judging deposit expansion than the deposit-multiplier formula?

Northfield Bank and Trust Co.:
Portfolio Management by
Linear Programming

One of the most challenging tasks faced by banks is the management of their portfolios. These consist of cash and earning assets. The latter include various types of financial claims — such as government securities, promissory notes issued by businesses, and other obligations. Banks continually change the composition of their portfolios, striving to achieve the best balance between three conflicting objectives: liquidity, profitability, and safety.

The method that many banks use to attain an optimally balanced portfolio involves a scientific technique known as linear programming. The theory underlying linear programming is mathematical, and its effective application usually requires the use of a computer. Nevertheless, you can gain some appreciation of the nature of linear programming from the following simplified example of an actual bank portfolio problem.

Investment-Possibilities Line

Northfield Bank and Trust Company has $100 million to allocate between two classes of assets — loans and securities. This task is represented in Figure (a) by the line AB, called an "investment-possibilities line." Each point along this line denotes a different possible combination of loans and securities totaling $100 million.

Figure (a): *Constraints and Feasibility.* Three intersecting straight lines establish the conditions of the bank's portfolio. The problem is to select the most profitable portfolio consisting of a combination of loans and securities. This combination is represented by a point somewhere in the feasible region.

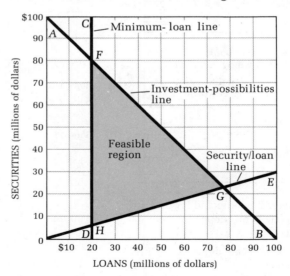

For example, at point A, the bank allocates $100 million to securities and nothing to loans. At point B, the bank allocates $100 million to loans and nothing to securities. At any point between A and B, the bank allocates some money to loans and some money to securities, the sum allocated to both equaling $100 million.

Of course, line *AB* represents the maximum attainable combinations of loans and securities totaling $100 million. If the bank decides to spend less than that amount, the combination chosen will be represented by a point to the left, or "inside," line *AB*.

Security/Loan Line

The bank seeks to obtain the most profitable combination of loans and securities. At the same time, it does not want to incur the risk of investing too much in one of these alternatives relative to the other. From experience the bank has concluded that a minimum ratio of $30 in negotiable securities to $100 in loans provides a satisfactory balance. Therefore, line *0E* represents what may be called a "security/loan line." Each point along this line denotes a different combination of loans and securities such that the volume of securities is always 30 percent of the volume of loans. For example, point *H* represents $20 million in loans and $6 million in securities. Point *E* represents $100 million in loans and $30 million in securities.

Minimum-Loan Line

Banks are in business to lend money. Although they also earn income from other sources, lending is their most important activity. Every bank, therefore, seeks to accommodate its principal customers by fulfilling their requests for loans. In the case of Northfield Bank and Trust, it has been found that customers' aggregate demand for loans totals at least $20 million for the period under consideration. This is shown by line *CD*, called a "minimum-loan line." Note that this line is vertical, intersecting the horizontal axis of the chart at $20 million. This means that the bank's portfolio cannot contain less than that amount in loans, irrespective of the amount allocated to securities.

The Feasible Region

You probably realize by now that the three lines defined above represent constraints. That is, the lines impose limiting conditions on the problem. For example, the investment-possibilities line tells you that the size of the portfolio is limited to a maximum of $100 million. The security/loan line tells you that the amount of money allocated to securities is limited to a minimum of 30 percent of the amount allocated to loans. And the minimum-loan line tells you that the amount allocated to loans must be at least $20 million.

(continued on next page)

Northfield Bank and Trust Co.:
Portfolio Management by
Linear Programming
(continued)

When these ideas are put together on the chart, we obtain the shaded area *FGH*. This area may be called the "feasible region" because it designates the field within which portfolio decisions can be made. Thus, any portfolio represented by a point outside the feasible region violates one or more of the constraints. Conversely, any portfolio represented by a point within the feasible region including any of its boundaries satisfies all the constraints. Therefore, the bank's portfolio will consist of some combination of loans and securities that can be represented by a point within the feasible region.

Income Line

To select the most profitable portfolio, the bank has to know the rate of return on loans and securities. These returns will vary according to market conditions. However, suppose that, for the present period, the bank is earning a 10-percent return on its loans and a 5-percent return on its securities. Then, the level of income that can be earned from the portfolio depends on the amounts allocated to loans and securities.

These ideas are depicted in Figure *(b)*. Each line, called an "income line," shows the amount of funds that must be allocated to loans and securities to earn a given income based on the above rates of return. At point *J*, for example, the bank allocates $20 million to securities. Assuming a 5-percent rate of return, this produces an income of $1 million. At point *K*, the bank allocates $10 million to loans. Assuming a 10-percent rate of return, this also yields an income of $1 million. Therefore, if we connect the two points, we get the income line *JK*. Each point along this line denotes a different allocation of funds to securities and to loans, the combined income from which totals $1 million.

In a similar manner, line *LM* is an income line representing $2 million. As you can see, therefore, the bank's income increases as the income line shifts outward from the origin of the chart.

The Optimum Portfolio

We now have the information needed to determine the bank's optimum portfolio. This is done by combining the essential ideas from the two previous charts, as shown in Figure *(c)*.

The bank's goal is to select an optimum portfolio—a combination of loans and securities that yields the highest income obtainable. As you have already learned, there are two considerations to keep in mind:

- The optimum portfolio will be represented by a point located somewhere within the feasible region.

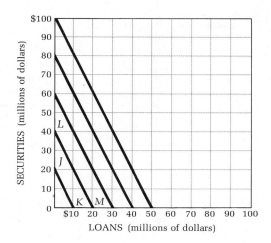

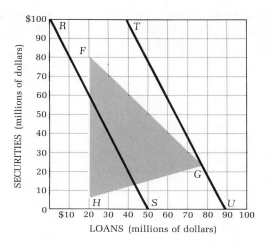

Figure *(b):* Income Lines. The downward-sloping lines are called "income lines." Each line shows the amount of funds that must be allocated to loans and securities to earn a given income, based on a 10-percent return on loans and a 5-percent return on securities.

Figure *(c):* The Optimum Portfolio. With the given constraints, the most profitable portfolio is determined by an income line *TU* that lies as far as possible to the right while still touching the feasible region. This occurs at point *G*. The optimum portfolio thus consists of $77 million in loans and $23 million in securities.

- The highest income obtainable will be represented by an income line that lies as far as possible to the right while still touching the feasible region.

Does the income line *RS* determine the optimum portfolio? Evidently not. Although the line contains points that are in the feasible region, none of these points represents the most profitable portfolio.

The income line *TU*, however, does determine the optimum portfolio. This line just touches the feasible region at point *G*. Therefore, the most profitable portfolio is the one indicated by this point. It represents a portfolio consisting of $77 million in loans and $23 million in securities.

What will be the bank's income from this portfolio? As stated earlier, the bank earns 10 percent on loans and 5 percent on securities. Therefore, earnings will be $7.7 million on loans and $1.15 million on securities, or a total of $8.85 million on the entire portfolio.

(continued on next page)

**Northfield Bank and Trust Co.:
Portfolio Management by
Linear Programming**
(continued)

Conclusion: A Practical Tool

Northfield Bank and Trust Co. is one of many banks that utilize linear programming as a management tool. In practice, banks' assets are broken down into detailed categories and grouped in various ways to achieve a balance between three conflicting objectives: liquidity, profitability, and safety. Numerous constraints are then introduced which set limits on the ways in which the variables in a problem may be combined to attain the optimum result. With the help of a computer, answers are thus obtained to complex problems that would otherwise be impossible to solve.

Questions

1. On the basis of what you have read, formulate a general definition of linear programming. In the light of your definition, can you suggest how a business firm might use linear programming to improve efficiency in production?

2. (a) What constraints does Northfield Bank and Trust Co. face in its efforts to attain an optimum portfolio? (b) Is the portfolio affected by a change in any of the constraints? Explain.

Chapter 13

Central Banking: Monetary Policy

Learning Guide

Watch for answers to these important questions

What is the meaning of monetary policy? What institution is responsible for conducting monetary policy?

How does the Federal Reserve influence economic activity? What tools are available to the Fed for controlling the money supply?

Which monetary policies are likely to result in higher and in lower interest rates? How do changes in interest rates affect business investment?

Do Treasury actions have an impact on monetary policy? What would happen to the banking system if the Treasury disbursed funds without concern for monetary influences?

What are the advantages and limitations of monetary policy as compared with fiscal policy?

FED RAISES RESERVE REQUIREMENTS
DISCOUNT RATE INCREASED BY FED
FED TO SELL U.S. SECURITIES

The financial press often contains headlines like these. They emphasize that the *Federal Reserve System* plays not one role but two.

First, it is a "banker's bank," performing for depository institutions much the same services that these institutions perform for the public.

Second, the Fed is the nation's monetary authority, exercising an important influence on economic and monetary policy.

You have already learned about the Fed's banking role. In this chapter you will look at the Fed's part in making and implementing economic decisions.

Essentially, the Fed can utilize five instruments to modify or even reverse the direction of the economy. They are (1) reserve ratios, (2) the discount rate, (3) open-market operations, (4) margin regulations, and (5) moral suasion. The first three are broad and extremely important controls because they influence the nation's money supply and the overall availability of credit. The fourth is a device used specifically to try to regulate the purchase of stock. The fifth is a psychological technique that relies on personal talk and public opinion. It is convenient, therefore, to classify the first three tools of monetary policy as "general," or major, controls and the remaining two as "selective," or minor, controls.

But first, what is meant by monetary policy? The following definition indicates the central concern of this chapter:

> *Monetary policy* is the deliberate exercise of the monetary authority's (the Fed's) power to induce expansions or contractions in the money supply. The principal purposes of monetary policy are to achieve price stability, to help dampen the swings of business cycles, and to help bring the nation's output and employment to desired levels.

Before beginning, it proves useful, as in the previous chapter, to understand the overall asset-and-liability structure of the institutions under discussion. Exhibit 1, therefore, provides a self-explanatory consolidated balance sheet for the nation's twelve Federal Reserve Banks.

Controlling of money supply

General (Major) Controls

Three types of general controls are available to the Federal Reserve for influencing the level of economic activity. These controls consist of (1) changes in bank reserve ratios, (2) changes in the discount rate, and (3) open-market operations. Let us see how each helps to shape the nation's monetary policy.

Changing Reserve Ratios

You already know that banks are required to maintain legal reserves against checkable deposit liabilities. Why? As you will see momentarily, it is primarily to provide the Fed with one of several mechanisms for controlling the money supply.

You also know that banks must maintain reserves equal to a minimum percentage of their deposits.

Exhibit 1

Consolidated Balance Sheet of Twelve Federal Reserve Banks

July 31, 1985 (in billions)

(1)	**ASSETS**	
(2)	Loans	$ 1.6
	Consists mainly of loans to depository institutions. Occasional loans to official government entities are also included.	
(3)	U.S. government securities	167.1
	Includes Treasury bills, Treasury notes, and Treasury bonds.	
(4)	Other securities	9.8
	Includes bankers' acceptances and debt instruments issued by federal agencies.	
(5)	**Total loans and securities: (2) + (3) + (4)**	**176.9**
(6)	Other assets	38.2
	Includes cash items in process of collection, the value of bank premises, and other items.	
(7)	**Total assets: (5) + (6)**	**$215.1**
(8)	**LIABILITIES AND NET WORTH**	
(9)	Federal Reserve Notes	$171.3
	This is paper money issued by the Federal Reserve System and used by the public.	
(10)	Depository institutions' reserves	26.3
	This is the part of legal reserves that depository institutions maintain with their Federal Reserve Banks.	
(11)	Other liabilities	13.4
	Consists of deposits held by the U.S. Treasury, foreign central banks, and other claims.	
(12)	**Total Liabilities: (9) + 10 + (11)**	**211.0**
(13)	**Net Worth**	**4.1**
	This is the ownership interest of the member banks because they are the stockholders of the Federal Reserve Banks.	
(14)	**Total liabilities & net worth: (12) + (13)**	**$215.1**

3 major controls

Source: Board of Governors of the Federal Reserve System.

The reserves may be held in the form of vault cash or as deposits with the local Federal Reserve Bank. The percentages of reserve requirements are graduated according to the size of banks' deposits. For the banking system as a whole, the average reserve requirement is approximately 10 percent.

The implications of this are readily apparent from the following partial balance sheets. (All data are in billions of dollars.) Thus, if the average required reserve ratio for all banks were 15 percent, $15 billion of reserves would be needed to support $100 billion of deposits:

All Banks

Assets		Liabilities	
Required reserves	$15	Deposits	$100
Excess reserves	0		
Legal reserves	$15		

But if the average required reserve ratio for all banks were reduced to 10 percent, the amount of required reserves would decline from $15 billion to $10 billion. This would make $5 billion of excess reserves available for lending.

All Banks

Assets		Liabilities	
Required reserves	$10	Deposits	$100
Excess reserves	5		
Legal reserves	$15		

The existence of excess reserves, as you already know, can lead to a *multiple expansion* of deposits for the banking system as a whole.

The reverse of this process is also true. For example, an increase in the average required reserve ratio from 10 percent to 15 percent would absorb the $5 billion of excess reserves. If banks were fully loaned up and had no excess reserves, an increase in the average required reserve ratio might lead them to sell some of their earning assets. In that way banks could raise the necessary funds to cover their reserve deficiency. This, as you have seen, causes a *multiple contraction* of deposits for the banking system as a whole.

Thus, changes in the required reserve ratio affect the economy as a whole in the following way:

A *decrease* in the required reserve ratio tends to be expansionary because it permits banks to enlarge the money supply. An *increase* is contractionary because it requires banks to reduce the money supply—depending on the degree to which they have excess reserves. The Federal Reserve System can thus affect the supply of money and the availability of bank credit. It can do this through its control over reserve ratios and, therefore, the volume of bank reserves.

The ability to alter the required reserve ratio is the Federal Reserve System's most powerful monetary tool. But it is a fairly blunt tool and is employed infrequently. Other instruments of control can be applied with greater flexibility and more refinement.

Changing the Discount Rate

Federal Reserve Banks can lend money at interest to depository institutions just as these depository institutions can lend money at interest to the public. Thus, it may be said that the Federal Reserve Banks are wholesalers of credit, while depository institutions are retailers. (Keep in mind that depository institutions and banks are essentially the same, for our purposes.)

No Federal Reserve policy tool is as well known or as poorly understood as the **discount rate.** In reality, it is simply the interest rate charged depository institutions on their loans from the Reserve Banks. However, it is called a "discount rate" because the interest on the loans is discounted or deducted from the loan when it is made, rather than added on when the loan is repaid.

When a bank borrows, it gives its own secured promissory note to the Federal Reserve Bank. The Reserve Bank then increases the borrowing bank's reserves by the appropriate number. Why would a bank want to borrow from the Fed? Usually, the bank wants to replenish its reserves, which may have been "used up" as the bank granted loans and purchased investments.

You can see, therefore, that the Federal Reserve's lending policy at the "discount window" (an expression widely used in banking circles) can be significant. It can affect not only banks' reserves but also credit conditions in the economy as a whole.

> The direct effect of changes in the discount rate is to raise or lower the price of admission to the discount window. An increase in the discount rate makes it more expensive for banks to borrow; a reduction has the opposite effect. Indirectly, increases in the discount rate are usually associated with a rise in market interest rates and a general tightening of credit. Decreases in the discount rate tend to be associated with a reduction in market interest rates and an overall easing of credit.

The discount rate was the preeminent tool of monetary policy in the early years of the Federal Reserve System. This has long since ceased to be the case. The major reason is that banks have alternative ways of obtaining liquidity. For example, they can replenish their reserves by selling earning assets or by borrowing from other banks rather than by seeking loans from the Federal Reserve.

Open-Market Operations

"The Fed is in." This expression, short for "The Fed is in the market," is heard frequently on Wall Street when the Federal Reserve Bank of New York buys or sells securities. Examples of such securities are Treasury bills, Treasury bonds, banker's acceptances, and repurchase agreements.

The Federal Reserve Bank of New York deals in these securities, sometimes as agent for the Federal Open Market Committee, or for the U.S. Treasury, or for other banks (as part of the services rendered by the Federal Reserve System). Such transactions are commonly referred to as **open-market operations.** They directly affect the volume of banks' legal reserves and hence the overall cost and availability of credit. In fact:

> Open-market operations are the Fed's most important monetary tool. They are used for day-to-day operations and for economic stabilization.

Here, essentially, is how open-market operations influence banks' legal reserves:

Buying Securities: Banks' Reserves Increase

When the Fed *buys* securities in the open market, banks' legal reserves are *increased* in two ways.

- If the Fed buys securities directly from banks, it pays by increasing the banks' reserves with the Federal Reserve Banks by the amount of the purchase.

- If the Fed buys securities from nonbanks (such as individuals or corporations), it pays with checks drawn on itself. The recipients of the checks then deposit them in their own banks, which, in turn, send the checks to the Federal Reserve Banks for collection. The Reserve Banks pay by increasing the reserves of the banks.

Selling Securities: Banks' Reserves Decrease

When the Fed *sells* securities in the open market, banks' legal reserves are thereby *decreased*:

- If the Fed sells securities directly to banks, the banks pay by reducing their reserves with the Federal Reserve Banks by the amount of the purchase.

- If the Fed sells securities to nonbanks, these individuals and corporations pay with checks drawn mainly on their own depository institutions. The Federal Reserve Banks collect on these checks by reducing the reserves of the depository institutions. These institutions, in turn, return the canceled checks to their depositors and reduce their deposit accounts accordingly.

Illustrations with Balance Sheets

You can gain a firmer grasp of these ideas by seeing them conveyed in terms of the following partial balance sheets. Keep in mind that the terms "bank" and "depository institution" mean the same thing, and are used interchangeably. (All data are in millions of dollars.)

Case 1

Suppose that the Federal Reserve Bank purchases $1 million worth of government securities in the open market. If the seller is a depository institution, the Reserve Bank pays the depository institution by increasing its reserve deposit:

Reserve Bank

Assets		Liabilities	
Government securities	+$1	Depository institution reserve deposits	+$1

Depository Institution (Bank)

Assets		Liabilities
Government securities	−$1	
Reserves with Federal Reserve Bank	+$1	

Case 2

If the seller is a nonbank — such as an individual or corporation — the check received in payment from the Federal Reserve Bank will most likely be deposited at the seller's depository institution. That bank, in turn, sends the check to the Reserve Bank for credit to its reserve account:

Reserve Bank

Assets		Liabilities	
Government securities	+$1	Depository institution reserve deposits	+$1

Depository Institution (Bank)

Assets		Liabilities	
Reserves with Federal Reserve Bank	+$1	Deposits	+$1

Note that the effect on the depository institution's reserves is the same in both cases. That is:

When the Fed purchases securities in the open market, the legal reserves of the depository institution are *increased*. The amount of the increase will be the value of the securities purchased by the Federal Reserve authorities.

Case 3

The opposite situation occurs when the Federal Reserve Bank sells $1 million of government securities in the open market. If the buyer is a depository institution, it acquires $1 million in government securities and loses $1 million of reserves:

Reserve Bank

Assets		Liabilities	
Government securities	−$1	Depository institution reserve deposits	−$1

Depository Institution (Bank)

Assets		Liabilities
Government securities	+$1	
Reserves with Federal Reserve Bank	−$1	

Case 4

If the buyer of the security is a nonbank, the Federal Reserve Bank receives payment with a check drawn on the buyer's depository institution. After the check "clears," that institution's deposit at the Reserve Bank and the buyer's deposit at the institution are both reduced by the value of the securities transacted:

Reserve Bank

Assets		Liabilities	
Government securities	−$1	Depository institution reserve deposits	−$1

Depository Institution (Bank)

Assets		Liabilities	
Reserves with Federal Reserve Bank	−$1	Deposits	−$1

Note that the ultimate effect is the same in cases 3 and 4. Thus:

When the Fed *sells* securities in the open market, the legal reserves of the bank are *reduced* by the value of the securities sold by the Federal Reserve Bank.

Economics in the News

Fed to Lower Margin Rules on Purchases of Securities from Current 50% Level

By Monica Langley

WASHINGTON — The Federal Reserve Board plans to lower the margin requirement, or credit limit, on purchases of securities. Since it was given responsibility for setting margin rules in 1934, the Fed generally has required margins of 50% – 70%, with its lowest margin level in history at 40%. Securities firms have predicted that cutting the margin requirement below 50% would create more business, particularly in a market rally.

The Securities and Exchange Act of 1934 directs the Federal Reserve to regulate credit purchases of certain securities: government securities are exempted. The law, passed in the wake of the 1929 stock market collapse and in the midst of the Great Depression, was intended not only to prevent credit from being diverted from commerce into stock market speculation, but also to protect unsophisticated investors and to prevent large price fluctuations in the stock market.

But a new Fed study concluded that the current, strict margin-lending requirements no longer are needed to meet any of these goals.

Recently, the Fed urged Congress to end its role in setting margin rules. It recommended that securities and commodity exchanges be allowed to establish their own credit requirements, subject to oversight by government regulators.

The Wall Street Journal, May 6, 1985, p. 8.

Open-market purchases of government securities are expansionary. They increase bank reserves and therefore permit a multiple growth of deposits. Conversely, open-market sales of government securities are contractionary. They reduce bank reserves and force a multiple decline of deposits.

Selective (Minor) Controls

In addition to its general (major) controls, the Federal Reserve can make use of certain selective (minor) tools. These, like the others, are designed to influence the level of economic activity. Among the principal selective controls available to the Fed are margin regulations and moral suasion.

Margin Regulations

The Federal Reserve Board is empowered to set the so-called **margin requirement.** This is the percentage down payment that must be made when someone borrows from a brokerage firm to finance purchases of stock. This power was granted by Congress during the early 1930s. In that era, the excessive use of credit to purchase stocks was believed to be a significant factor in the great stock-market crash of 1929.

Of course, the higher the margin requirement, the larger the proportion of a stock purchase that must be paid for in cash. Therefore:

An increase in margin requirements discourages stock-market speculation on borrowed credit. Conversely, a decrease in margin requirements may encourage purchases of stocks.

The margin requirement is altered infrequently because it is not as important as it once was. Nevertheless, it is a device for dampening or stimulating activity in the stock market. This, in turn, can affect the ability of firms to sell stocks in order to finance new investment.

Although these open-market operations have been illustrated for only one depository institution, the same ideas apply to all such institutions, i.e., *all banks* within the banking system. The overall economic effects of such transactions can therefore be summarized:

Threats

Moral Suasion

Of course, the Federal Reserve's Board of Governors can always exert pressure on bankers by using oral and written appeals to expand or restrict credit. This process, called *moral suasion,* does not compel compliance. Nevertheless, it has been successful on a number of occasions. During recessions, it has sometimes stimulated the expansion of credit by encouraging banks to lend more. During inflations, it has sometimes discouraged lending and restricted the expansion of credit. In a more general sense, the Federal Reserve exercises moral suasion every day when it advises individual member banks on ordinary loan policy.

Summarizing:

To be effective, all the foregoing methods of general and selective monetary control are coordinated by the Federal Reserve. Its goal is to promote economic growth and stability through management of the money supply. You can gain some appreciation of the Fed's task of coordination by examining Exhibit 2.

Exhibit 2
Flow of Federal Reserve Influence

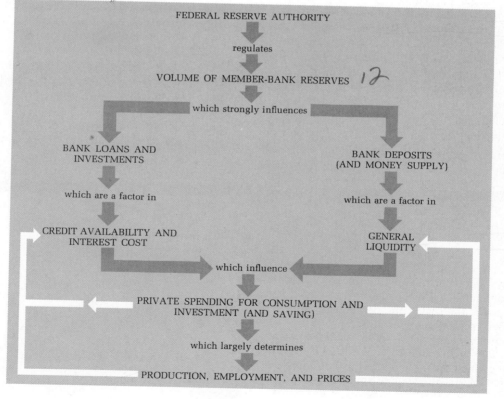

Source: Board of Governors of the Federal Reserve System.   Adapted.

Speculative => Very Risky

How Monetary Policy Affects Interest Rates and Business Investment

The tools of monetary policy are exceedingly important. Through the proper use of general and selective controls, the Fed can strongly influence the nation's level of economic activity.

Two of the Fed's tools—the discount rate and open-market operations—are especially significant because they are actively used and are closely connected with interest rates. You can see this connection by examining the relationship between the prices of bonds and their yields. Keep in mind that a bond, like any other credit instrument, is also a debt instrument. It is an asset to the party who owns it and a liability to the party who issues it.

If you buy a credit instrument, such as a bond, the effective percentage rate of return on the security is called the *yield.* Exhibit 3 shows the relationship between the market price and effective yield of a $100 bond. The bond matures one year hence and has a nominal interest rate of 8 percent. This means that it pays its holder an interest of $8 per annum. The chart shows that, if you could buy the bond in the market today for around $99, you would receive $100 upon maturity plus $8 in interest.

This is an effective yield of about 9 percent. On the other hand, if you bought the bond today at a market price of $101, you would still get $100 back at maturity (thereby losing $1 from your purchase price) plus $8 in interest. This makes an effective yield of about 7 percent. More broadly:

The price of a bond varies inversely with its yield. This is because the annual dollar payments received on a bond are a fixed amount. Therefore, the higher the market price of a bond, the lower its yield, and vice versa. This principle applies to all credit (or debt) instruments, not just to bonds.

Bank Portfolio Effects and Business Investment

What bearing does this inverse relationship have on longer-term interest rates? The answer can be understood in terms of the impacts of securities on banks' portfolios.

When the discount rate is increased, banks find it more costly to borrow from the Fed. Therefore, they may choose to replenish their reserves by selling some of their short-term securities instead. The increased sale of securities tends to lower security prices and raise their yields. These higher market

Exhibit 3
Bond Prices and Bond Yields Vary Inversely

A bond pays its owner a fixed amount of dollars annually. Therefore, the lower the price at which you can buy a bond, the higher the percentage return or *yield* you will receive, and vice versa.

This figure shows the price–yield relationship for a one-year $100 bond paying 8 percent (that is, $8) annually to its owner. As explained in the text, if you can buy the bond for $99, the yield to you will be approximately 9 percent. At $101, the yield will be approximately 7 percent.

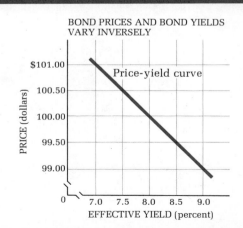

BOND PRICES AND BOND YIELDS VARY INVERSELY

Short-Term Rates Continue to Decline Amid Perception of Easier Fed Stance

By Edward P. Foldessy and Tom Herman

NEW YORK—Short-term interest rates continued to fall amid what many analysts say are signs that the Federal Reserve System is easing its credit hold in an effort to bolster the economy.

Rates plunged at yesterday's auction of Treasury bills to their lowest levels in more than two years.

Also falling sharply was the interest rate on federal funds, or reserves that banks lend one another.

Still, many analysts contend that it isn't clear whether the Fed has changed its credit policy. Even those who say the Fed has eased contend that yesterday's funds rate was much lower than Fed officials would like to see. They noted that the central bank moved to drain reserves through the temporary sale of U.S. government securities. When the Fed sells securities, it absorbs reserves because dealers draw on their bank accounts to pay for their purchases.

Mr. Kahan of Heinold Commodities said the Fed appears to be "setting the stage for a possible lowering" of the discount rate. But he said that a discount-rate cut would depend on how the economy performs this month. The discount rate is the fee the Fed charges on loans to banks and savings institutions.

The Wall Street Journal, April 23, 1985, p. 49.

Similar effects occur when the Fed, in order to dampen economic activity, sells securities in the open market. Examples are Treasury bills, repurchase agreements, and certain other short-term credit instruments that you have learned about. When the securities are sold by the Fed, their prices decline. Therefore, their yields increase. This raises short-term interest rates and puts upward pressure on long-term interest rates as well.

On the other hand, when the discount rate is lowered, banks are likely to maintain or even increase their borrowings because of cheaper rates. In addition, when the Fed tries to stimulate the economy by purchasing short-term securities in the open market, their prices are bid up. This reduces short-term interest rates, which, in turn, puts downward pressure on longer-term rates. The result is to encourage business investment by making it less costly.

Through its week-to-week open-market operations, the Fed exercises strong control over the money supply. This control is reinforced, from time to time, with changes in the discount rate and, on rare occasions, with changes in reserve requirements. In this way, by controlling the money supply the Fed plays a powerful role in influencing interest rates. But note this important point:

> Contrary to widespread popular opinion, *the Fed does not directly determine interest rates.* The Fed only determines the money supply. Interest rates are determined directly in the financial markets through the interactions of lenders (such as banks) and borrowers (such as businesses). These institutions interact as they respond to changes in the money supply, that is, to the Fed's monetary policies.

yields (that is, effective rates of interest on existing short-term securities) tend to push up longer-term market interest rates on new securities. Why? Because *all* securities compete for investors' dollars. The result of higher short-term and long-term interest rates is to discourage business investment.

Is Monetary Policy Really Useful?

How effective is monetary policy in influencing economic activity? As with other policy areas of economics, this is a subject of continual debate. The principal arguments for and against the usefulness of monetary policy can be outlined briefly.

Advantages of Monetary Policy

In evaluating the usefulness of monetary policy, it is often instructive to make comparisons with fiscal policy. As you have already learned, this is an alternative and sometimes complementary method of fighting inflation and unemployment. Thus the main advantages of monetary policy are these:

Nondiscriminatory (in Principle)

Monetary controls are ordinarily employed in a general way to influence the total volume of credit. The Fed is nondiscriminatory *in principle* with respect to the borrowers or activities that are to be encouraged or discouraged. Instead, the Fed leaves it to the market to discriminate. Thus, for example, home-construction, automobile, and major appliance industries feel the effects of tight credit more quickly than most other industries. This is because they are heavily dependent on the ability of buyers to borrow. Fiscal policy, on the other hand, involves changes in taxation and government spending. These changes can directly alter the composition of total production as well as its overall level.

Flexible in Application

Because the Board of Governors controls monetary policy, changes can be made quickly and smoothly without getting snarled in administrative red tape. By contrast, fiscal policy involves budgetary considerations of taxation and spending. On such matters, Congress usually deliberates for months before arriving at a decision.

Nonpolitical (in Principle)

Congress gave the Federal Reserve System political independence to ensure its effective performance. It provided fourteen-year terms of office for appointed Board members, made them ineligible for reappointment, and staggered their terms of office.

It also provided for the election of Reserve Bank presidents by their own boards of directors, subject to the approval of the Federal Reserve Board. As a result, although the institution is sometimes pressured by the White House, the Fed *can* nevertheless base its day-to-day decisions on economic rather than on political grounds. In contrast, fiscal policy is *always* strongly influenced by politics.

Limitations of Monetary Policy

Whereas the advantages of monetary policy are fairly general, most of its limitations arise out of specific situations and circumstances.

Incomplete Countercyclical Effectiveness

During an inflation, the Federal Reserve can use its instruments of control to choke off borrowing and to establish an effective tight-money (high-interest-rate) policy. But during a recession, even an easy-money (low-interest-rate) policy cannot ensure that businesspeople will want to borrow. If they regard the business outlook as poor, the increase in loans and spending will not be as large as needed for attainment of high employment. Further, during such periods there is the possibility that banks may be unwilling to lend when they have excess reserves. Thus, monetary policy is far more effective and more predictable as an anti-inflation instrument than as an antirecession instrument.

Cannot Correct Cost-Push or Profit-Push Inflation

Some observers contend that inflation often results from upward pressure on wages and prices. This pressure arises because of the monopolistic power that some large unions and business firms are able to exert in the market. If this argument is true, monetary policy can do little to correct the situation. At most, actions taken by the Federal Reserve may help dampen either a cost-push or profit-push inflation, but they will not eliminate either.

May Conflict with Treasury Objectives

Every debtor likes low interest rates. This is especially true of the U.S. Treasury, the biggest debtor of all. Because the Treasury is continually "refunding" maturing securities by selling new ones, it wants to keep the interest cost as low as possible. Indeed, a difference of one percentage point in the interest rate on government securities can cost the Treasury many billions of dollars annually.

Federal Reserve officials, on the other hand, regard high interest rates as an important anti-inflationary weapon. During strong inflationary periods, these two distinctly different goals can result in a policy conflict between the Treasury and the Fed. If in such periods the Fed, because of political pressure, compromises its objectives in order to accommodate the Treasury, the effectiveness of anti-inflationary monetary policies is reduced.

May Be Offset by Changes in the Velocity of Money

Discretionary monetary policy, as you have seen, requires that the Federal Reserve authorities follow a two-pronged approach:

– In prosperity, decrease the money supply to curb inflation.

– In recession, increase the money supply to stimulate recovery.

Unfortunately, the effectiveness of these actions may sometimes be at least partially reduced by opposite changes in the velocity, or turnover, of money. This is simply the average number of times per year that a dollar is spent.

As you might expect, the velocity of money is affected by the public's confidence in the future course of the economy. In prosperity, when people are optimistic, they tend to spend more freely. Hence, velocity may increase at a time when the money supply is being contracted. In recession, when people are pessimistic, they tend to curb their spending. Hence, velocity may decrease at a time when the money supply is being expanded.

Significant changes in the velocity of money can exert a substantial influence on the price level. How? By causing aggregate demand, and therefore prices, to rise when velocity increases and to decline when velocity decreases. As a result, *changes in velocity may offset, to some extent, the monetary authority's efforts to stabilize the economy by contracting or expanding the money supply.*

You will be learning much more about these concepts in the next several chapters.

Limited Fed Control over Lending

It is difficult for the Reserve authorities to exercise as much control over the total volume of lending as they would like. There are two reasons:

1. Nonbank Financial Intermediaries These nonbank lenders, such as insurance companies, finance companies, and credit unions, exercise an important influence on the financial market. They hold large volumes of savings, which they are continually trying to "put to work" by investing or lending to the public. This helps to offset restrictive monetary policies of the Reserve officials.

2. Money-Market Securities Substantial holdings of these short-term investments are in the hands of banks and business corporations. These organizations can sell the securities as needed to obtain additional cash.

Because both of these situations are largely outside the Fed's control, they tend to increase the velocity of money. This, in turn, can modify significantly the goals of monetary policies.

Forecasting and Timing Difficulties

You have learned that monetary policies can be implemented more quickly than fiscal policies. Despite this advantage, monetary policies suffer from some of the same kinds of forecasting and timing problems that beset fiscal policies. As a result, the

Is the Fed Too Independent?

Most people, if asked to name Washington's most powerful agency, would probably say the FBI or the CIA. In reality, the Federal Reserve Board has more influence.

The Fed's actions impact directly on such things as the interest rate charged on a bank loan, the ability of a potential home buyer to obtain a mortgage, and many other conditions affecting people's lives. Because the Fed's influence is so powerful and so extensive, critics keep raising the question of whether it is too independent.

When the Federal Reserve Board was created in 1913, no one perceived that it would some day exercise a powerful influence on government economic policy. In that pre-Keynesian era, the economic system was thought to be basically stable. Therefore, the Fed's primary purpose was to provide business with a proper supply of money. If that were done, it was believed, lapses from prosperity would be temporary, and the economy would automatically restore itself to full employment.

The Great Depression of the 1930s changed these beliefs. Legislation was passed that strengthened the Fed's economic powers substantially. The Federal Reserve Board was given complete control over open-market operations and was granted greater authority in setting reserve requirements.

This new independence has since been resented by many political leaders. One group argues that fiscal policy — government tax and expenditure actions — should take precedence over, and be accommodated by, the Fed's monetary policies. Another group believes that monetary policy should have priority over fiscal policy because the Fed's instruments of control are more powerful and faster acting. And some critics who subscribe to neither of these points of view contend that the Reserve Board's term of office should be changed to coincide with the President's. This would enable each President to choose a Board whose policies are consistent with the Administration's goals and policies.

These and related issues of Federal Reserve independence have been debated among political leaders for years. Whatever the outcome, it is likely to have profound economic effects on everyone's life.

Federal Reserve has often managed the money supply too erratically, thereby causing further instability. This has led to frequent criticisms of the Fed, and to proposed solutions ranging from its nationalization to its elimination.

Conclusion: Complex Issues

The Federal Reserve System seeks to provide the economy with the "right" quantity of money — enough to encourage steady growth, high employment, and stable prices. However, the task is a difficult and complex one. Because of this:

Monetary policy has shortcomings as well as benefits. The fact that there are more limitations than advantages should not lead you to believe that monetary policy is useless. It is a powerful force for stabilization and will continue to play an important role in the economy.

What You Have Learned

1. The chief responsibility of the central banking system is to regulate the supply of money and credit so as to promote economic stability and growth. The ways in which this responsibility is fulfilled determine our monetary policy.

2. The major instruments of monetary policy available to the Federal Reserve System are reserve requirements, the discount rate, and open-market operations. The minor ones include margin regulations and moral suasion, among others.

3. Monetary policy has important effects on interest rates and business investment. Through open-market operations and the discount rate, the Fed affects prices of credit instruments. These prices, in turn, affect interest rates. The interest rates, in turn, influence business investment decisions.

4. Monetary policy has advantages and limitations as a method of economic stabilization. Its chief advantages are that it is (a) nondiscriminatory, (b) flexible, and (c) nonpolitical (at least in principle). Its main limitations are these:

(a) it may be an incomplete countercyclical weapon
(b) it is relatively ineffective in combating inflationary forces caused by cost-push pressures
(c) it sometimes conflicts with Treasury goals
(d) it may be offset by changes in the velocity (rate of turnover) of money
(e) it lacks control of nonbank lending and credit operations
(f) it suffers somewhat from forecasting and timing difficulties

Despite these shortcomings, monetary control will continue to play an integral role in our general stabilization policy.

Terms and Concepts to Review

monetary policy	margin requirement
discount rate	moral suasion
open-market operations	yield

For Discussion

1. How do changes in reserve requirements, the discount rate, and margin requirements affect economic activity? Explain.

2. How do open-market operations work? When do they tend to be expansionary? Contractionary?

3. Suppose that the reserve requirement is 15 percent. If the Federal Reserve Bank purchases $1 million of government securities in the open market, a bank increases both its legal reserves and deposits by that amount. (Do you remember why?) Using the axes below, construct a bar graph showing the initial net new deposit and the *potential* cumulative expansion of bank deposits that may take place at each "round" of deposit creation. (SUGGESTION You may find it helpful to construct a table showing the multiple expansion of bank deposits. The table can then be used to sketch the graph.)

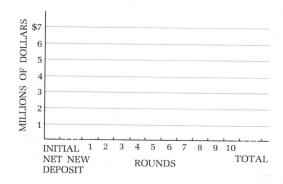

4. Suppose that the Treasury issues more paper currency than people want. (a) What will happen to bank reserves? (b) What can the Federal Reserve authorities do to offset the consequences?

5. Using two long "T-accounts" arranged side by side as shown, depict the positive (+) or negative (−) changes represented by each of the following transactions.

Federal Reserve Banks		Depository Institutions (Banks)	
Assets	Liabilities	Assets	Liabilities

(a) The Federal Reserve buys $100 of government securities from a dealer. The Fed pays the dealer with a check drawn on itself, which the dealer deposits in the bank.

(b) The bank sends the $100 check to the Federal Reserve, which credits the bank's reserve deposit.

(c) The Federal Reserve buys $100 of government securities from a bank and pays with a check on itself.

(d) The bank sends the $100 check to the Federal Reserve for credit to its account.

(e) The Federal Reserve lends $100 to a bank by discounting the latter's note.

(f) A depositor writes a check for $100 against a deposit and cashes it at his or her bank.

(g) A depositor adds $100 in currency to a deposit.

(h) The Treasury sells $100 of securities to the nonbanking public and deposits the checks it receives in its accounts at various banks. (NOTE To facilitate tax collections and revenue disbursements, the Treasury maintains a checking account in almost every bank in the country.)

(i) The Treasury transfers $100 of deposits from depository institutions (banks) in which it holds accounts to Federal Reserve Banks.

(j) The Treasury pays $100 for services by writing a check against its deposit at the Federal Reserve. (NOTE To facilitate the disbursement of government funds, the Treasury maintains a checking account at each of the Federal Reserve Banks.)

(k) The party to whom the check was paid deposits it. The bank sends the $100 check to the Federal Reserve for collection.

Chapter 14

Macroeconomic Equilibrium

Learning Guide

Watch for answers to these important questions

How does money affect output and prices? Is there a relationship between the quantity of money in circulation, its velocity or rate of turnover, and GNP?

What factors affect interest rates? How do changes in interest rates come about? How do these changes affect the volume of investment spending by businesses?

What basic relationships exist among the variables constituting the Keynesian model? How does a change in the money supply affect interest rates, investment expenditures, and hence aggregate demand?

The importance of money essentially flows from its being a link between the present and the future.

So wrote J. M. Keynes in *The General Theory of Employment, Interest and Money* in 1936. The following year he went on to say: "The possession of actual money lulls our disquietude; and the premium which we require to make us part with money is the measure of the degree of our disquietude."

The "link between the present and the future"—the "premium" to which Lord Keynes referred—is the rate of interest. This variable plays a strategic role in the explanation of income and employment determination. This fact was pointed out in earlier chapters but it must now be examined in closer detail.

To begin with, it is important to understand that a relationship exists between money and interest. In this chapter, you will learn how the rate of interest may be directly influenced by changes in the money supply. Once the relationship between money and interest is established, the Keynesian macroeconomic model of income determination will be complete. You will then see how the strategic variables in the model interrelate within the system as a whole.

Money Affects Output and Prices

You have already learned how the Federal Reserve can influence the level of economic activity by its discretionary actions. For example, to encourage economic expansion, the Fed can increase the supply of money by engaging in open-market purchases of government securities. To initiate economic contraction, the Fed can decrease the supply of money by undertaking open-market sales of government securities. (You will recall that the Fed can also vary reserve requirements and the discount rate to help achieve its goals, but it relies most heavily on open-market operations.) Thus, there is a direct relationship between the money supply and the level of economic activity. The relationship is such that changes in the former can produce similar changes in the latter.

Changes in the money supply may not only lead to changes in output. They can also lead to changes in the price level. This cause-and-effect relationship between changes in the money supply and changes in the price level was fundamental to classical economic thinking. But it was not stated with precision until the early 1900s. At that time, a distinguished American economist at Yale University, Irving Fisher (1867–1947), expressed the link between money and prices by means of an equation that soon became famous. A modernized version of that equation can be developed in the following way.

Equation of Exchange

You may not be able to see how fast individual dollars are spent. However, you can measure the average speed of money movements in the economy as a whole from a simple formula.

Let V stand for the **income velocity of money.** This is the average number of times per year each dollar is spent on purchasing the economy's annual flow of final goods and services — its GNP. Further, let M denote the nation's money supply. This is measured by the amount of money in the hands of the public. Then, the income velocity of money is

expressed by the formula

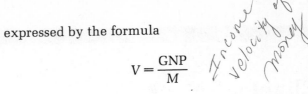

$$V = \frac{GNP}{M}$$

For example, suppose that in a certain year the GNP was $800 billion and the stock of money was $200 billion. Then V = $800/$200 = 4 per year for that year. In other words, each dollar must have been used an average of four times to purchase the economy's GNP.

The letter M in the equation above can, of course, be "transposed" to the left side. Then the equation becomes

$$MV = GNP$$

As you will recall, it is also true that gross national income (GNI) is equal to GNP. Therefore, MV is obviously the same as GNI.

Now suppose that we make the equation more refined by expressing GNP in terms of its component prices and quantities. Let P stand for the average price of final goods and services produced during the year and let Q represent the physical quantity of those goods and services. The value of final output is then price times quantity. That is, $GNP = P \times Q$. For example, GNP = average price of apples times number of apples, plus average price of haircuts times number of haircuts, plus . . . and so on for all final goods and services produced. The equation can therefore be written

$$MV = PQ$$

This is known as the **equation of exchange.** For example, imagine a highly simplified case in which the students in your class constitute an economy whose total supply of money, M, is $80. Further, assume that the class produces a quantity of output, Q, equal to 60 units of a good and that the average price, P, of this output is $4 per unit. Since $MV = PQ$,

$$V = \frac{PQ}{M} = \frac{(\$4)(60)}{\$80} = 3$$

So each dollar is spent an average of three times per year on the class's output.

> The equation of exchange is actually an identity. It states that the total amount of society's income *spent on* final goods and services, MV, is equal to the total amount of money *received* for society's final goods and services, PQ.

The equation $MV = PQ$ tells us that the given flow of money can be looked at from either the buyers' or the sellers' point of view. The aggregate flow is the same in either case. As in demand-and-supply analysis, the quantity of a commodity purchased is equal to the quantity sold.

The Quantity Theory of Money

What does the equation of exchange tell us about the role of money in influencing national income and expenditure? To answer this, we have to look more closely at how the equation works.

1. *Assume That V Remains Constant* This means that by controlling M we could control GNP. If M is increased, either P or Q or both will have to increase in order to maintain equality between the right and left sides of the equation. The changes in P or Q will depend on the state of the economy. In a period of recession, Q will tend to rise relatively more than P as unemployed resources are re-employed. In a period of relatively high employment, P will tend to rise more than Q as full utilization of resources is approached. What do you suppose would happen in a period of full employment?

2. *Assume That Both V and Q Remain Constant* This, in fact, is what the classical economists believed. They assumed that V was constant because it was determined by the long-run money-holding and money-spending habits of the public. These habits, the classicists argued, were fairly stable. Further, they assumed that Q was constant because the economy was always at, or at least rapidly tending toward, full employment. The classical economists thus concluded that *P depends directly on M.*

As a result, their theory has come to be known as the "quantity theory of money."

> *Quantity Theory of Money* The level of prices in the economy is directly proportional to the quantity of money in circulation. That is, a given percentage change in the stock of money will cause an equal percentage change in the price level in the same direction.

The quantity theory states, for example, that a 10 percent increase in M will cause a 10 percent increase in P. Likewise, a 5 percent decrease in M will cause a 5 percent decrease in P. In general, according to the quantity theory of money, changes in the price level are directly proportional to changes in the money supply.

What the Evidence Shows

How well does the quantity theory of money correspond with the facts? Can changes in M be used to predict changes in P?

In evaluating the theory, it is necessary to distinguish between long-term and short-term changes. The evidence, as history shows, consists of two major classes of findings.

1. During a number of long-run periods, changes in P have appeared to be closely tied to changes in M. For example, in the late sixteenth century, the Spanish importation of gold and silver from the New World caused major price increases in Europe. Likewise, the discovery of gold in the United States, Canada, and South Africa during the latter half of the nineteenth century brought sudden expansions in the money supply and rapidly rising prices in these countries. During more recent history, the excessive borrowing and printing of money by most countries has resulted in periods of upward-spiraling prices. In these and various other cases, prices have risen directly with increases in the quantity of money, without corresponding increases in output.

2. In the short run, V varies a good deal. However, its long-run trend has been steadily rising, as shown in Exhibit 1. And output, of course, may

Central Banking
Federal Reserve

Modernizing the Quantity Theory: The Importance of Velocity

Exhibit 1

Income Velocity of Money: $V = \dfrac{GNP}{M1}$

The income velocity of money (V) may fluctuate considerably within any given year. Its long-run trend, however, has been steadily upward. This graph shows the velocity of M1, which is the most widely used measure of the money supply.

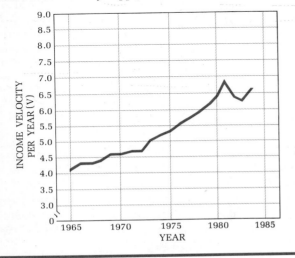

The quantity theory of money played a critical role in classical economic thinking. In recent decades, it has undergone substantial revision by various economists. Notable among them has been Nobel laureate Milton Friedman, Professor Emeritus of the University of Chicago.

The revised, or "modern," quantity theory retains much of the traditional doctrine but reorients it to emphasize the importance of V. For example, V is not assumed to remain constant as in the old theory but is believed instead to be influenced by certain specific factors. One of these (which, for the time being, may be expressed in general terms) is public confidence in the economy.

If people fear unemployment or are pessimistic about the future, they will tend to refrain from spending. This means that money will turn over more slowly. Therefore, its velocity will decline.

Conversely, if people are optimistic about the future, they will increase their spending. Money will thus turn over more quickly. Therefore, its velocity will rise.

Modern quantity theorists believe that, although V fluctuates over time, its range of short-run variation is limited. They also believe that, given sufficient knowledge, fluctuations in V are *predictable*. Therefore, the underlying determinant of GNP (or PQ in the equation of exchange) is still the quantity of money. This conclusion has important policy implications. To many economists, it suggests the following **money-supply rule:**

The central bank (that is, the Federal Reserve) should use its monetary policies—such as open-market operations and control over the discount rate and reserve requirements—in a consistent manner. That is, *it should provide a continuous expansion in the money supply at a rate sufficient to assure steady economic growth and full employment.* This rate should be 3 to 4 percent annually—the same as the long-run growth rate of the economy's real GNP. Failure to follow this money-supply rule, say modern quantity theorists, leads inevitably to economic instability.

Ex

Economic stability

Rule of Economic stability

also vary substantially from year to year. In addition, what might occur if P increases as a result of an increase in M? In that case, the rise in prices might encourage an increase in V as people spend money more quickly for fear of future price increases. If this happens, P is no longer merely a *passive* variable dependent on M. It is also a *causal* variable that can contribute to changes in other factors.

Thus:

Because of its complexities, the quantity theory of money has not yet proved suitable for predicting short-run changes in P from changes in M. But, as the evidence shows, the theory provides a useful guide for judging *the most likely influence* of monetary forces on changes in the general price level.

128
8 8

Leaders in Economics

Irving Fisher

1867–1947

Irving Fisher, a professor of economics at Yale University, was one of America's foremost economists prior to World War II. A mathematician and inventor as well as an economist, he was a profound scholar and a prolific writer. In addition to twenty-eight published books, he wrote dozens of articles in professional journals. Because of their high quality and enduring value, some of Fisher's publications are frequently referred to by scholars today.

Equation of Exchange

Among Fisher's major interests was the study of money and prices. In a book entitled *The Purchasing of Money* (1911), he stated the **equation of exchange**—which subsequently became known as the *Fisher equation*. A modernized version of the equation is

$$MV = PQ$$

Expressed in this way, the equation encompasses transactions for *final* goods, and thus uses readily available GNP data. (Such data did not exist in Fisher's time, causing him to use a less practical equation.)

Application

The equation explains a cause-and-effect relationship between the quantity of money and the price level. For example, Fisher assumed that the velocity of circulation (V) and the quantity of the final output (Q) tend to remain constant. Therefore, he concluded, if there is "a doubling in the quantity of money . . . it follows necessarily and mathematically that the level of prices must double." Or, in general, *"one of the normal effects of an increase in the quantity of money is an exactly proportional increase in the general level of prices."* From this it is evident, according to Fisher, that business cycles are not inherent in the economy. They are due largely to excessive expansions and contractions in the money supply—"especially in the form of bank loans." This conclusion, we shall see, has considerable acceptance today among many informed observers.

Does this mean that the use of diverse fiscal and monetary measures should be discarded in favor of a uniform, consistent policy that provides for steady growth in the money supply at an established rate? Many informed observers would answer *yes*. But many others believe that some sort of optimum fiscal–monetary mix would do better at providing economic stability at a high level of income and employment. However, the difficulties of attaining such a mix are considerable — for reasons that will become increasingly apparent.

Determination of the Interest Rate

Any study of money must inevitably lead to a discussion of the rate of interest and to an analysis of the forces determining it. This is a matter of great importance. As you will recall from the study of business-sector investment spending, businesses invest because they expect to earn profits. That is, they acquire capital goods only as long as the anticipated rate of return on an additional unit of investment — called the *marginal efficiency of investment* — exceeds the cost of money, or the rate of interest. But what determines the rate of interest? The answer, both from a classical and from a Keynesian point of view, completes the groundwork for understanding the essential features of the macroeconomy.

What determines the Rate of Interest

★ Classical Explanation: Fisher's Theory

People usually think of interest as a payment for the use of money. This interpretation is adequate for most purposes. To the classical economists, however, interest had a special and quite different meaning.

You will recall that, in a simplified circular-flow model, the total economy is divided into two parts — a household sector and a business sector. The household sector supplies the saving that the business sector borrows. The business sector uses the borrowed funds to invest in capital goods for the purpose of carrying on profitable production. Interest, therefore, is a price that businesses pay households to persuade the latter to consume less so that they can consume more at a later date.

i.e., In other words:

> Interest is a payment for "saving," for "abstinence" from consumption, or for overcoming people's preference for present as opposed to future consumption.

Why is interest necessary? The classicists believed that no household will save, and thereby forgo the pleasure of spending, unless it is offered interest in return. Likewise, no business will borrow, and thereby pay interest, without investing in profitable production. Saving, in classical theory, therefore leads *automatically* to spending on capital or investment goods. A flexible interest rate in the competitive financial markets (the money and capital markets) assures this. That is, the interest rate, determined by the free play of supply and demand, adjusts to the level where every dollar saved by households is borrowed and invested by businesses.

The Real Rate and the Market (Nominal) Rate

These ideas of classical economics were further developed in the early part of this century by Irving Fisher. The classical explanation of interest is also sometimes called the Fisher theory of interest. It rests fundamentally on a distinction between two interest rates: the real rate and the market (or nominal) rate.

The *real rate of interest* is the interest rate measured in terms of goods. That is, it is the rate that would prevail in the market if the general price level remained stable. Under such circumstances, suppose you lend a friend $100 today with the understanding that you will be repaid $105 one year from today. In that case you are giving up $100 worth of goods now for what you expect will be $105 worth of goods a year from now. The *real* rate of interest is therefore 5 percent.

According to the classicists, this rate is established by real economic forces of demand and supply. The "real demand" for funds by businesses is determined by the productivity (and therefore the profitability) of borrowed capital. The greater its productivity, the larger the amount of funds that businesses will want to borrow. The "real supply" of funds by households is determined by the willingness of consumers to abstain from present consumption. The greater their willingness, the larger the amount of funds that households will want to lend.

The *market rate of interest* is the actual or money rate that prevails in the market at any given time. (The market rate is thus another name for the nominal rate.) Unlike the real rate, which is not directly observable, the market rate is the one we actually see in the markets. This is because the market rate reflects the quantity of loans measured in units of money, not goods. Hence, it is the rate people ordinarily have in mind when they talk about "the" interest rate.

A crucial point in classical theory is that the real rate and the market rate usually are not equal. Only if borrowers and lenders expect the general price level (that is, the value of a unit of money) to remain constant will both rates be the same. This does not ordinarily happen. People are always expecting prices either to rise or to fall. Therefore, the market rate of interest will depart from the real rate, depending on either of two conditions:

Anticipated Inflation Suppose people believe that prices will rise—and hence that the purchasing power of a unit of money will decline. In that case, the market rate of interest will be higher than the real rate. For example, if lenders and borrowers expect the price level to rise 5 percent per year, the market rate of interest will tend to be the real rate plus 5 percent. This "inflation premium" is necessary to compensate lenders for their loss in purchasing power. At the same time, borrowers will be willing to pay the premium because they will be repaying their loans with money worth 5 percent less per year than the money they borrowed.

Anticipated Deflation Suppose people believe that prices will fall—and therefore that the purchasing power of a unit of money will rise. In that case, the market rate of interest will be below the real rate. The difference is a "deflation discount" (or *negative* inflation premium). This is necessary to compensate borrowers for their loss in purchasing power. At the same time, lenders will be willing to grant the discount because they will be repaid with money worth 5 percent more per year than the money they initially lent.

These ideas can be summarized briefly:

The market rate of interest may be greater than, equal to, or less than the real rate. The difference depends on whether households and businesses expect the general price level to rise, remain constant, or decline. Any differential between the market rate and the real rate represents either a premium or a discount. The differential is necessary to compensate lenders or borrowers for adverse changes in purchasing power resulting from anticipated inflation or deflation.

The determination of the market rate of interest is illustrated in Exhibit 2. The upward-sloping saving-supply curve S of households intersects the downward-sloping investment-demand curve D of businesses. This determines the equilibrium interest rate r on the vertical axis. As explained in the exhibit, the household sector *lends* loanable funds, or savings, and the business sector *borrows* them.

Exhibit 2
The Market Rate of Interest in Classical Theory

In the classical theory, the interest rate is the price paid for the use of *loanable funds*. This consists mainly of the amount of savings that the household sector will make available to the business sector at various rates of interest.

Like any other price, the interest rate rations the supply of a commodity—in this case, loanable funds—among those who want to use it. Only those business borrowers who are willing and able to pay the market interest rate can acquire the funds that are wanted. This rate is at r. In numerical terms, r might be 6 percent, 10 percent, or some other percentage.

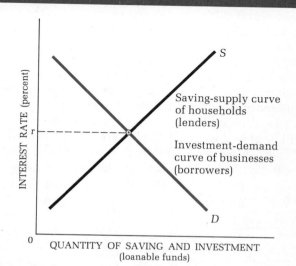

INTEREST RATE (percent)

S

Saving-supply curve of households (lenders)

r

Investment-demand curve of businesses (borrowers)

D

0   QUANTITY OF SAVING AND INVESTMENT
(loanable funds)

Deriving the Real Rate: A Modern View

This classical view of interest is held today by many informed observers. They believe that the interest rates you see quoted in the market contain an *inflation premium*. This premium reflects the public's beliefs about future prices. As a result, market interest rates and prices tend to move together.

On the basis of this idea, you can use classical theory to estimate the real interest rate from the following equation:

market interest rate
= real interest rate + inflation premium

Therefore, the real interest rate is equal to the market interest rate minus the inflation premium:

real interest rate
= market interest rate − inflation premium

To illustrate, here is how the real interest rate might be estimated.

First, in order to obtain a measure of the market interest rate, you should use the yield on 3-month Treasury bills. This is because these financial instruments provide a better combination of high marketability, short maturities, and zero default risk than any other securities. For this reason, their yield represents a "pure" rate of interest—the rate on a short-term riskless loan. The average annual yield on 3-month Treasury bills is shown in the back endpapers of this book.

Second, in order to obtain a measure of the inflation premium, you should estimate borrowers' and lenders' *expectations* of future prices. But expectations are subjective and changeable, so any estimate will be at best a reasonable "guess" based on recent trends. A rather simple approach that illustrates the basic idea can be accomplished in two steps.

Step 1 Choose a measure of the overall level of prices. One such measure, as you know, is the Consumer Price Index (CPI). However, there is an even broader indicator called the **Implicit Price Index** (IPI). Popularly known as "the GNP deflator," the IPI is the most comprehensive measure of the general price level available. Constructed by

Exhibit 3
Calculating the Inflation Premium

One possible estimate of the inflation premium is the *percentage change* in the general price level from the previous year to the current year. The real interest rate in column (5) will then reflect the observed market interest rate in column (4) *minus* the estimated inflation premium in column (3).

(1) Year	(2) General price level (Implicit Price Index, IPI)	(3) Estimated inflation premium (% change in IPI)	(4) Market interest rate (observed)	(5) Real interest rate (4) − (3)
1 (previous)	120			
2 (current)	126	5%	9%	4%

the U.S. Department of Commerce, the IPI consists of an average of the various price indexes used to deflate the components of GNP. The IPI is shown in the endpapers at the back of the book.

Step 2 Calculate the latest percentage change in the IPI to obtain the inflation premium in the current period. For example, suppose the IPI increased from 120 in Year 1 to 126 in Year 2, the current year. Then, as shown in Exhibit 3, the percentage change or inflation premium for the current year is $(126 - 120)/120 = 0.05$, or 5%. This procedure *assumes* that the inflation premium in the current year is best estimated by the percentage change in the general price level from the previous year. Of course, other assumptions could also be made. In fact, the inflation premium may depend on a number of factors, not just on the most recent percentage change in the general price level.

Once you have the necessary information, the formula is easily applied. For instance, if in the current year the market interest rate is, say, 9 percent and the inflation premium for the year (calculated as in step 2) is 5 percent, the real interest rate in the current year is 4 percent.

Prices and Interest Rates Move Together

Is the connection between prices and interest rates valid? There is strong evidence for believing that it is. Historically, market interest rates have risen when prices increased over a period and have declined when they decreased for some time. This indicates that high market interest rates reflect actual as well as expected inflation. Evidence of this can be seen in many nations. Countries that traditionally experience steep inflations generally have much higher market interest rates than countries whose price levels are relatively more stable.

This inflation-premium link between prices and interest rates suggests a way for the monetary authority (the Federal Reserve) to reduce interest rates. Classical economists contend that increases in the quantity of money result in "too much money chasing too few goods." Consequently, prices and interest rates rise. By reducing the rate of growth in the money supply, the monetary authority can retard inflation and bring about reductions in the market rate of interest. It is significant to note that practically all economists, classicists as well as nonclassicists, concur on this point.

Classical thinking went under major changes in the Great Depression

An Alternative Explanation: Keynes's Theory

As you have already learned, much of traditional economic thinking underwent major changes in the Great Depression of the 1930s. The person initially responsible for this restructuring of ideas was the British economist John Maynard Keynes. The revised theory, which Keynes called a "general theory," resulted in the birth of **Keynesian economics.** You will find it helpful to refresh your understanding of this term by looking it up in the Dictionary at the back of this book.

What did Keynes have to say about the role of the interest rate and the factors determining it? We already know part of the answer:

Capital spending or investment by businesses is the strategic determinant of the level of income and employment. Such spending is undertaken as long as the marginal efficiency of investment exceeds the rate of interest. Therefore, the rate of interest is crucial in relation to investment.

As for the factors determining the rate of interest, Keynes argued that the classical theory is correct for an economy that tends automatically toward full employment. His own theory, on the other hand, is more general because it applies to an economic system that may be in equilibrium at *less* than full employment.

Keynes and the Classicists

You can get a better understanding of these ideas by comparing some of Keynes's views with those of the classicists. For example, look again at the investment-demand curve illustrated earlier in Exhibit 2. This classical view shows the amount of capital spending that businesses are willing to undertake at each rate of interest (or cost of funds). This demand curve, therefore, is actually the same as the marginal-efficiency-of-investment (MEI) curve that you studied in earlier chapters as part of the Keynesian model. To refresh your understanding of this concept, look up the definition of "marginal efficiency of investment" in the Dictionary at the back of the book.

Although the classical economists' investment-demand curve is the same as Keynes's MEI curve, there is an important difference in the way they are viewed. This can be seen by comparing the two figures in Exhibit 4:

Classical View—Figure (a) The classicists regarded interest as a "price" that equates the demand for investment with the supply of saving at *full-employment.* It follows that a change in the business sector's demand curve for investment will result in a new equilibrium rate of interest. Thus, for example, a decrease in investment from D to D' will cause the interest rate to drop from r to r'. The economy will then adjust *automatically* to full employment at this new interest rate.

Exhibit 4
Effect of a Change in Investment

Investment spending on plant, equipment, and increases in inventory is undertaken by the business sector in anticipation of profits. The effects of a change in investment may differ according to the classical and Keynesian views.

Figure (a): Classical View A decrease in investment, say, from D to D', will cause the equilibrium rate of interest to decline from r to r'. The economy will adjust to full employment at this new rate of interest.

Figure (b): Keynesian View Aggregate expenditure AE consists of the sum of consumption spending C, investment spending I, and government spending G. A decrease in investment will cause AE to decline, say, to AE'. Hence, aggregate output will decline from N to N'. And, because employment depends on output, the level of employment will also decline.

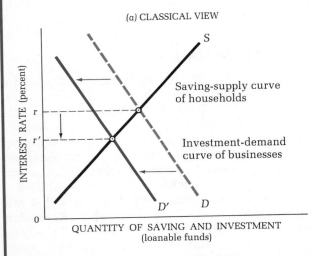

(a) CLASSICAL VIEW

Saving-supply curve of households

Investment-demand curve of businesses

INTEREST RATE (percent)

QUANTITY OF SAVING AND INVESTMENT
(loanable funds)

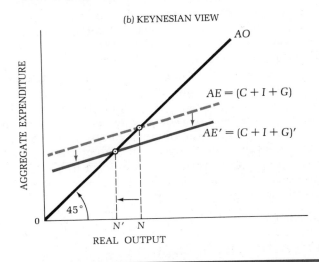

(b) KEYNESIAN VIEW

AGGREGATE EXPENDITURE

$AE = (C + I + G)$

$AE' = (C + I + G)'$

45°

REAL OUTPUT

Aggregate Expenditures $C + I + G$

Keynesian View—Figure (b) Unlike the classical approach, the Keynesian model utilizes the concept of aggregate expenditure, AE. You will recall that this includes the household sector's consumption expenditures, C, the business sector's investment expenditures, I, and the government sector's public expenditures, G. It follows that any decline in investment will result in a *decrease* in aggregate expenditure. Such changes, in turn, affect the level of output and employment. Thus, in the diagram, AE includes I. Therefore, a decrease in investment reduces AE to, say, AE'. This causes aggregate output to decline from N to N'. And, because employment depends on output, the level of employment (which varies directly with output) also declines.

According to Keynes, the classicists were wrong in assuming that a change in investment would affect only the interest rate, not the levels of output and employment.

Determining the Interest Rate

In contrast to the classical view, the Keynesian model emphasizes that the rate of interest is determined by the demand for, and supply of, money. This idea is illustrated in Exhibit 5. Observe that the quantity of money is measured on the horizontal axis and the interest rate is measured on the vertical. Also observe, from the subtitle of the diagram, that *the level of aggregate income is given*.

Exhibit 5
Determination of the Interest Rate in the Keynesian Model
(assuming a *given* level of aggregate income)

The demand for money varies *inversely* with the interest rate. The reason is that, at higher interest rates, people want to hold less money and more interest-earning securities (such as bonds and other debt instruments). At lower interest rates, the reverse is true. Therefore, the D_M curve is downward sloping.

The supply of money is determined by the Fed, through its reserve requirements, open-market operations, and discount-rate policy. At any given time the quantity of money in the economy is unrelated to the interest rate. Therefore, the S_M curve is a vertical line.

The intersection of the D_M and S_M curves determines the equilibrium rate of interest r.

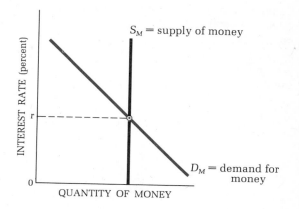

In the diagram, the demand curve D_M for money is downward sloping. This is because holding money entails an *opportunity cost* in terms of interest income foregone. Therefore, the public prefers to hold a smaller proportion of its assets in money (and hence a larger proportion in interest-earning securities) when interest rates are high. This preference, on the other hand, is reversed when interest rates are low. The public prefers to hold a larger proportion in money (and hence a smaller proportion in interest-earning securities). The public's desire to hold some of its assets in liquid form (that is, money) is called *liquidity preference.*

The supply-of-money curve S_M is determined by the monetary authority—the Fed. At any given time, this supply is simply the stock of money available. Therefore, the supply curve is a vertical line. It tells you that the quantity of money is unresponsive to changes in the interest rate.

You can now see what happens in the market when the demand for money interacts with the supply of money. A specific interest rate emerges: the equilibrium rate of interest r is determined by the intersection of the D_M and S_M curves.

Why Interest Rates Change

Like other demand and supply curves, those in Exhibit 5 assume that all other things affecting the demand for, and supply of, money remain constant. If one of the factors changes, the relevant demand or supply curve will shift. This will bring about a new equilibrium rate of interest as illustrated by the diagrams in Exhibit 6. For example:

Changes in Demand In Figure (a), if aggregate income rises, the quantity of money demanded for transactions purposes also rises. This causes an increase in the public's *liquidity preference*, or demand for money. The money-demand curve thus shifts to the right from D_M to D_M'. Therefore, the interest rate rises from r to r'. The opposite occurs if there is a decline in aggregate income. The public's liquidity preference decreases. Therefore, the money-demand curve shifts to the left, causing the interest rate to decline.

Changes in Supply In Figure (b), actions taken by the Fed can increase the supply of money. For example, by buying securities in the open market, or

Exhibit 6
Changes in Interest Rates

Changes in the demand for, or in the supply of, money cause changes in interest rates. For example:

Figure (a): An increase in the public's *liquidity preference* will increase its demand for money. The money-demand curve shifts to the right from D_M to D_M'. This causes the interest rate to rise from r to r'. A decrease

in the demand for money will have the opposite effect, causing the interest rate to decline.

Figure (b): An increase in the supply of money by the Fed will shift the money-supply curve to the right—from S_M to S_M'. This causes the interest rate to decline from r to r'. A decrease in the supply of money will have the opposite effect, causing the interest rate to rise.

(a) CHANGE IN DEMAND FOR MONEY

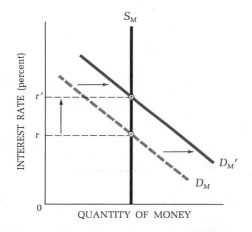

(b) CHANGE IN SUPPLY OF MONEY

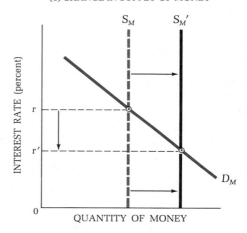

by lowering reserve requirements, or by reducing the discount rate, the Fed can "inject" reserves into the banking system. As banks' loans to the public (that is, checkable deposits) increase, the money-supply curve shifts to the right from S_M to S_M'. This lowers the interest rate from r to r'. The reverse occurs if the Fed reduces the supply of money. The money-supply curves shifts to the left, causing the interest rate to rise.

To summarize:

The public's desire to hold some of its assets in liquid form determines the demand for money, whereas the monetary authority determines the supply. The demand for and supply of money together determine the equilibrium rate of interest.

Practical Implications: Interest Rates and Business Investment

Of course, a theory that explains how interest rates are determined tells only half the story. The other half concerns the practical matter of how changes in interest rates affect business investment decisions. Before we move on to that important topic, it will help to review three fundamental concepts that you learned when you first studied the Keynesian model:

— Businesses base their investment decisions on anticipated profitability. Profitability is measured by the percentage rate of return on investment. The anticipated rate of return on an additional unit of investment is called the *marginal efficiency of investment (MEI)*.

– At any given time, each firm's *MEI* curve is its demand curve for investment. Like any demand curve, the *MEI* curve is downward-sloping. This tells you that the amount of investment spending a firm will undertake is greater at lower interest rates (costs of funds) than at higher rates.

– When all firms' anticipated rates of return are summed, the result obtained is an *MEI* curve for the business sector as a whole. This curve, like each firm's individual *MEI* curve, is downward sloping. It may be thought of as the *business sector's demand curve for investment.*

As you already know, *both the rate of return on investment and the interest rate are measured in percentage terms.* This makes it possible to link the financial market, where interest rates are determined, with the business sector, where investment decisions are made.

Exhibit 7 illustrates the linkage. In Figure (a), the equilibrium rate of interest r is determined by the intersection of the demand and supply curves of money. This rate is the cost of money capital to firms. Hence, in Figure (b), the amount of investment undertaken by the business sector at this rate of interest, shown by the aggregate *MEI* or *D_I* curve, is I.

Exhibit 7
The Interest Rate and Investment

In Figure (a), an increase in the money-supply curve from S_M to S_M' increases the quantity of money from Q to Q'. Therefore, the rate of interest drops from r to r'.

In Figure (b), the amount of investment thus increases from I to I'. This is because businesses invest to the point where the *MEI* equals the interest rate (or cost of money capital).

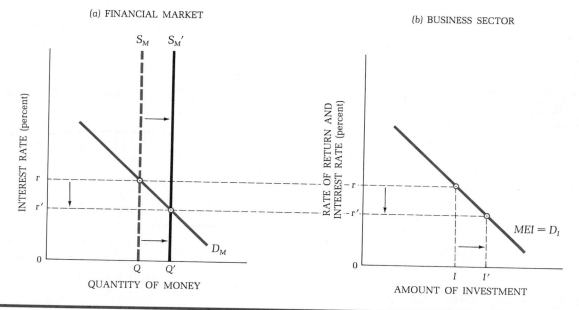

(a) FINANCIAL MARKET

(b) BUSINESS SECTOR

What happens if this volume of investment is insufficient to achieve full employment? In that case, according to the Keynesian model, the monetary authority can lower the rate of interest by increasing the money supply — say, from Q to Q'. Assuming that the D_M curve remains fixed, the equilibrium rate of interest will decline from r to r'. Accordingly, the amount of investment in Figure (b) will increase from I to I'. This increase in the amount of investment, as you know, will have a magnified effect on income, owing to the operation of the investment multiplier.

You can now see that the effectiveness of monetary policy for stimulating economic activity poses some challenging questions. For example:

— To what extent will the interest rate fall as a result of an increase in the money supply? The answer depends on the *relative steepness* of the D_M curve.

— To what extent will the amount of investment increase as a result of a decline in the interest rate? The answer depends on the *relative steepness* of the D_I (or *MEI*) curve.

— To what extent will income rise as a result of an increase in investment? The answer depends on the size of the investment multiplier.

You can verify these answers yourself by sketching some flatter and steeper curves and then noting the differences. As for the size of the investment multiplier, you will recall that it depends on the marginal propensity to consume or to save. This is because the investment multiplier, as you have learned, equals $1/(1 - MPC)$, or $1/MPS$.

Conclusion: Interest Rates a Continuing Concern

In the real world, fluctuations in interest rates occur frequently. This can affect the payments that businesses make on loans to purchase investment goods. It can also affect the payments that households make on loans to purchase cars, major appliances, and houses. Therefore, the role of interest rates in the economy is never a matter that is taken lightly. Indeed, it is a topic of continuing concern to everyone.

This suggests an important conclusion:

The mechanism that establishes equilibrium in the financial market is the rate of interest. The rate is affected by changes in the money supply, which, in turn, are controlled by the Federal Reserve. Because of their impact on interest rates and economic activity, the Fed's monetary policies are watched closely and reported upon almost daily in the news media.

Macroeconomic Equilibrium: Putting the Pieces Together

Our examination of the components of the macroeconomic theory of income determination, which we undertook at the beginning of Part 2, is now completed. (You will find it helpful to refer to the table of contents at the front of the book to get an overview of the material we have covered thus far.) We will now briefly review the major components of the theory. This will permit us to integrate certain fundamental relationships between a number of important variables.

Outline of the Keynesian Theory

A summary of the Keynesian theory of income determination is outlined in Exhibit 8. The relationships may be stated briefly in the form of several propositions:

— The level of aggregate income depends on consumption spending, investment spending, and government spending.

— **Consumption spending** This depends on the propensity to consume. It is expressed by a mathematical relationship between consumption and income, called the *consumption function*.

- The propensity to consume, or consumption function, determines both the average propensity to consume and the marginal propensity to consume. The latter, in turn, determines the investment multiplier, which is the reciprocal of the marginal propensity to save.
- **Investment spending** This depends on the marginal efficiency of investment relative to the rate of interest. The marginal efficiency of investment measures the expected rate of return on ad-

ditional capital expenditures. The rate of interest measures the cost of funds for financing those expenditures.
- The rate of interest is determined by the demand for money and the supply of money. The demand for money is a demand for liquidity preference. The supply of money is determined by the central bank's monetary policy. This depends mainly on reserve requirements, open-market operations, and the discount rate.

Exhibit 8
Outline of the Keynesian Theory of Income Determination

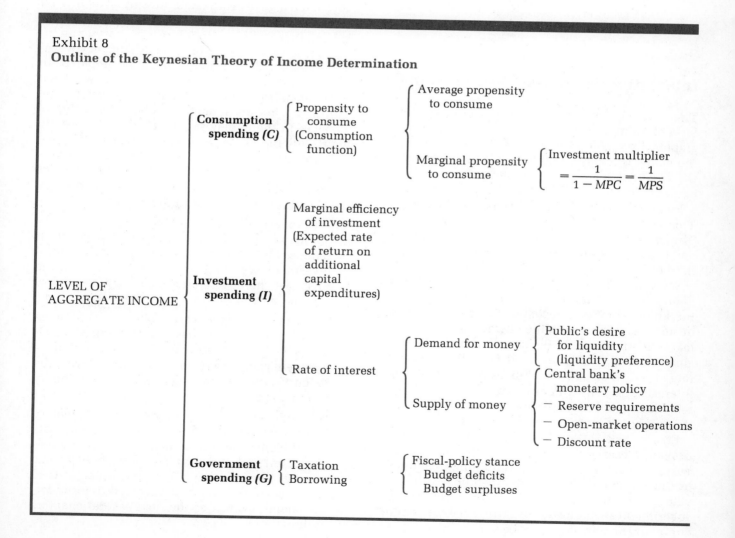

– **Government spending**   This is financed by taxation and borrowing. The ways in which these are combined determine the government's fiscal-policy stance. This is reflected in the size of budget deficits and surpluses.

These propositions contain only the main features of the theory. They do not express all the interrelations between the variables. Many of these interrelations were discussed in this and earlier chapters.

Integrating Some Basic Relationships

The Keynesian model can also be expressed in the form of an integrated set of relationships. This is graphically accomplished in Exhibit 9. Although the model is highly simplified, it contains many of the essential ideas of Keynesian macroeconomic equilibrium.

First, look at the financial market in Figure (a). This is where the rate of interest is determined. The intersection of the supply-of-money curve S_M and the demand-for-money curve D_M establish the market interest rate r.

Second, look at the business-sector diagram in Figure (b). The interest rate that was determined in the financial market becomes the cost of funds to businesses. As a result, the business sector undertakes investment up to the point at which the marginal efficiency of investment MEI (the expected rate of return on additional investment) equals the interest rate. The MEI curve is thus the business sector's demand curve for investment, D_I. Note that the amount of investment spending is I.

Finally, look at the total-economy diagram in Figure (c). Observe that investment spending by the business sector is added to consumption spending C by the household sector. Total spending by the private sector is thus $C + I = AE$. With the addition of government spending G, the aggregate expenditure curve for the total economy becomes AE'.

Conclusion: Putting Monetary Policy to Work

This Keynesian model of how an economy works has important implications for public policy. Let us consider some implications with regard to the two great, recurring problems of national economic policy — recession and inflation.

What happens if the equilibrium level of output — real GNP in Figure (c), Exhibit 9 — is either too low or too high to bring about full employment? As you learned when you first studied the Keynesian model, there will be either a recessionary or an inflationary gap. Fiscal policy, consisting of government spending and taxation, could be employed in an effort to close such gaps. But in light of what you have since learned about the banking system, you can now see how monetary policy, consisting of changes in the money supply, can also be used to help close recessionary and inflationary gaps.

For example, in terms of the graphs in Exhibit 9, expansionary and contractionary monetary policies have the following effects (which you should verify by sketching the changes in the curves):

– An expansionary monetary policy — a shift of the S_M curve to the right — has a stimulative effect. It reduces the interest rate, causing the amount of investment spending to increase. This raises the AE curve, thereby helping to close a recessionary gap that may exist.

– A contractionary monetary policy — a shift of the S_M curve to the left — has a dampening effect. It raises the interest rate, causing the amount of investment spending to decrease. This lowers the AE curve, thereby helping to close an inflationary gap that may exist.

Different combinations of fiscal and monetary policy exert different influences on the levels of aggregate income and employment. Which combination of fiscal and monetary policy is "best"? The answer to this question affects everyone. It is of continuing concern to those involved in formulating economic policy, as the next several chapters will show.

Exhibit 9
Simplified Keynesian Model of Income Determination

In Figure (a), the interest rate r is determined by the demand for money D_M and the supply of money S_M.

In Figure (b), the amount of investment spending I is determined by the marginal efficiency of investment MEI and the interest rate r.

In Figure (c), investment spending I is added to con-

sumption spending C to determine private-sector aggregate expenditure AE. This, plus the prevailing level of government spending G comprise the aggregate expenditure curve AE'. Note that the addition of government spending shifts the equilibrium point from E to E'.

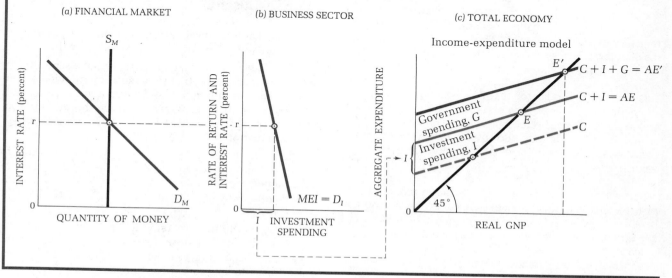

(a) FINANCIAL MARKET

(b) BUSINESS SECTOR

(c) TOTAL ECONOMY

Income-expenditure model

What You Have Learned

1. The equation of exchange is $MV = PQ$. It states, in effect, that the economy's gross income ($=MV$) is spent on purchasing the economy's final output of goods and services ($=PQ$). The equation is thus a truism or identity because it tells us that the same flow of money can be looked at either from buyers' or sellers' points of view.

2. The quantity theory of money was originally formulated by Irving Fisher. It assumes that the velocity of money and the volume of output are constant. Therefore, in terms of the equation of exchange, changes in the general price level are directly proportional to changes in the quantity of money.

3. Modern quantity theorists have extended Fisher's ideas. They take into account that the income velocity of

money fluctuates over time. But they believe that V's range of short-run variation is determined by the public's confidence in the economy. Therefore, modern quantity theorists focus much of their attention on the factors influencing velocity and on the role of the money supply as a determinant of GNP.

4. In classical theory, the market, or nominal, rate of interest is not necessarily the same as the real rate. The market rate will depart from the real rate if households and businesses expect the general price level to rise or decline. Any differential between the market rate and the real rate represents an "inflation premium." This may be either positive or negative. Its size represents the amount necessary to compensate lenders or borrowers for adverse changes in purchasing power resulting from anticipated inflation or deflation.

Economics in the News

Scrutinizing the Fed's Actions

If There's Smoke, There May Be Fire

NEW YORK—In the financial market, no activities are watched more closely than those of the Federal Reserve System. Weekly reports of increases or decreases in M1, the sum of currency and checkable deposits, cause money managers and financial analysts to scurry to their computers. The reason: to forecast the effects of changes in M1 on interest rates, demand for debt instruments, and other financial-market variables.

One important indicator that Fed watchers always examine is the interest rate on federal funds. These are excess reserves that banks lend one another, usually for a day or two. Borrowing banks may use these loans to make up a temporary shortage in their required reserves.

Changes in M1 and in the federal-funds rate can be signs of possible shifts in Federal Reserve monetary policies. As a money manager at one of the leading banks recently said, "No one who manages a portfolio can afford to overlook the Fed's behavior. To do so could be costly indeed. When you see smoke, it is wiser to investigate than to neglect."

5. The interest rate affects the business sector's decision to invest. The equilibrium rate of interest is determined by market forces of supply and demand between lenders and borrowers.

6. Monetary policy consists of changes in the money supply. Such changes can affect interest rates, business investment, and consequently the level of aggregate expenditure. Monetary policy can be a mechanism for helping to close recessionary and inflationary gaps.

Terms and Concepts to Review

income velocity of money	marginal efficiency of investment
equation of exchange	real rate of interest
quantity theory of money	market rate of interest
money-supply rule	inflation premium
interest	Implicit Price Index

For Discussion

1. What has been the long-run trend of the income velocity of money? Can you give the reasons for this trend?

2. Suppose that the Federal Reserve buys securities in the open market and that the securities are sold by nonbanks, such as individuals and corporations. As a result of this transaction alone, what will be the *initial* directions of change, if any, of M, P, Q, V (in that order), and MV in the equation $MV = PQ$? Explain.

3. In terms of the equation $MV = PQ$, what are likely to be the effects on P, Q, and PQ if there is a large increase in the money supply under conditions of (a) substantial unemployment, or (b) high or full employment? Explain your answer.

4. Suppose the interest rate on short-term loans is the same as that on long-term loans. What are the advantages and disadvantages to lenders of being in short-term as opposed to long-term investments?

5. "The classical theory holds that the equilibrium rate of interest equates the supply of, and demand for, *loanable funds*. The Keynesian theory holds that the equilibrium rate of interest equates the demand for, and supply of, *money*. What is the difference between these ideas? (SUGGESTION: Look up the meanings of *loanable funds theory of interest* and *liquidity preference theory of interest* in the Dictionary at the back of the book.)

6. Does the interest rate affect people's liquidity preferences? Explain.

7. If a reduction in the interest rate does not result in an expansion of investment, what might this suggest in terms of the Keynesian theory of interest?

8. Assume that the economy is in macroeconomic equilibrium.   What effect would each of the following
changes, considered separately and without regard to secondary results, have on income?   Explain why.

(a) Increase in the money supply.

(b) Increase in liquidity preference.

(c) Increase in the marginal efficiency of investment.

(d) Decrease in consumption.

In general terms, how would secondary effects have
influenced your answers?

Part 4

Macroeconomics Today: Ideas, Issues, and Policies

Chapter 15

Monetarism and the New Classical Economics: Changing Ideas

Learning Guide

Watch for answers to these important questions

What is monetarism? How does it relate to the classical quantity theory of money and the equation of exchange?

According to monetarist theory, what factors determine the public's demand for money? How do the public's expectations of inflation affect the velocity of money and the transmission process?

What fundamental assumptions underlie the new classical economics? Why does the new classical economics conclude that discretionary fiscal-monetary policies are ultimately ineffectual? Do monetarism and new-classicism share any common ground?

Is our economy inherently stable, or does it tend toward prolonged periods of unemployment and inflation? Keynesian macroeconomics, which has occupied most of your attention until now, has an answer to this question. As you know, Keynes's theory emphasizes the instability of private investment. The theory concludes that government intervention, through proper fiscal and monetary policies, is needed to maintain high levels of production and employment.

It is important to note that not all economists and political leaders subscribe to these policy prescriptions. Some of those who accept many underlying *principles* of Keynesian economics do not agree that the economy is inherently unstable. Therefore, they do not accept Keynesian *policy* conclusions which hold that active government fiscal and monetary intervention can reduce unemployment and inflation. Indeed, a large number of critics believe that government intervention can be a *cause* of instability rather than a cure.

These criticisms of Keynesian activist policies are expressed by those who subscribe to two schools of thought — *monetarism* and *new-classicism*. Along with *Keynesianism*, they are today's major contenders for the attention of policy makers in Washington.

Monetarism: Steady Monetary Growth Rate

As you can tell from its name, monetarism assigns a dominant role to the influence of money in the economy. Therefore, monetarism looks to Federal Reserve monetary policy as the chief factor affecting economic stability. You can best understand the implications of this by examining the main propositions of monetarism—the pillars on which it rests.

Origin: The Quantity Theory of Money

The beliefs of the monetarists stem from the ideas of the American classical economist Irving Fisher. These include the familiar quantity theory of money and the equation of exchange:

$$MV = PQ \quad \text{or equivalently} \quad MV = GNP$$

You will recall how Fisher and other classical economists interpreted the first equation. They believed that the velocity (V) of money was constant because it depended on the long-run spending habits of the public. These habits, the classicists contended, were fairly stable. They also assumed that the quantity (Q) of final output was constant because the economy was always either at full employment or at least tending toward it. Therefore, the classicists concluded, a given percentage change in the quantity of money (M) will cause an equal percentage change in the average level of prices (P) in the same direction.

Looking at the second equation, it follows that changes in the quantity of money will also cause changes in society's aggregate income, GNP. For example, because V is assumed to be constant, a 10 percent increase in M will cause a 10 percent increase in *nominal* GNP. This suggests the first proposition of monetarism:

Monetarists (like their classical predecessors) believe that changes in the quantity of money exert a dominant influence on changes in aggregate income.

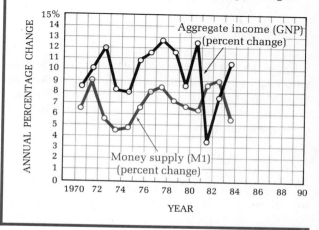

Exhibit 1
The Money Supply and Aggregate Income

Monetarists believe that changes in the monetary growth rate exert a powerful influence on changes in the growth rate of aggregate income. This graph indicates that there is a fairly close fit between the two variables—with changes in aggregate income, of course, responding somewhat later to changes in the money supply. Note that, in the graph, they are measured in terms of year-to-year percentage changes.

Some evidence of a significant long-run correlation between changes in the money supply and changes in aggregate income is shown in Exhibit 1.

Demand for Money

Although monetarism is rooted in the classical quantity theory of money and in the equation of exchange, it differs from them in certain important ways.

First, monetarists point out that people want money for what it will buy—its *real* purchasing power. Therefore, monetarists *redefine M* to represent the amount of money people want to hold in the form of real cash balances. This demand, they say, depends in a predictable way on two key variables — aggregate income and interest rates.

Money and Aggregate Income: Direct Relation

Monetarists believe that the public's demand for money—that is, real cash balances—varies *directly* with society's real income, GNP. This relation between money and income is easy to see when it is expressed in terms of a few symbols. For example, we can take the equation of exchange

$$MV = PQ$$

and rewrite it in terms of M:

$$M = \frac{PQ}{V} \quad \text{or equivalently} \quad M = \frac{1}{V}PQ$$

Expressed in this form, the equation on the right emphasizes the relation between the demand for money and the nation's income. To see why, suppose we let k stand for the ratio $1/V$. Then the right-hand equation becomes

$$M = kPQ$$

Of course, because PQ is the same as GNP, this equation can also be written

$$M = kGNP$$

What does this equation tell us? The answer can be expressed in words:

People want to hold an amount of money (M) equal to a fraction (k) of society's income $(PQ, \text{ or GNP})$. This is simply another way of saying that, in terms of constant dollars, the public's demand for *real cash balances* varies directly with society's *real income*.

This proposition is illustrated graphically in Exhibit 2. Note that the quantity of money is measured on the horizontal axis and society's aggregate income, GNP, is measured on the vertical. The figure conveys the following points:

1. At any given time, the public's demand for money, D_M, is equal to some fraction of GNP. For example, suppose the public's demand-for-

Exhibit 2
The Public's Demand for Money Depends on Aggregate Income (GNP)

At any given time, the public wishes to hold some fraction of its aggregate income (GNP) in the form of money. For example, it may wish to hold 10 percent, 20 percent, 50 percent, or some other percent of GNP as money. The public wants money (that is, cash balances) mainly for transaction purposes—to buy the GNP.

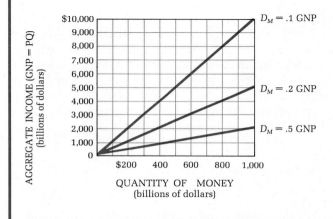

money curve is $D_M = .1GNP$. This means that people will want to hold 10 percent of GNP as money. Thus they will desire to hold $100 when GNP is $1,000, and $1,000 when GNP is $10,000. On the other hand, suppose the demand-for-money curve is $D_M = .5GNP$. Then people will desire to hold $500 when GNP is $1,000, and $1,000 when GNP is $2,000. As you can see, any other upward-sloping D_M line, such as $D_M = .2GNP$, is interpreted in a similar way.

2. The fraction of its income that the public wants to hold in the form of money is indicated by the *relative steepness* (slope) of the D_M curve. In general, the smaller the percentage of its income that the public will desire to hold as money, the greater the relative steepness of the curve.

What are the implications of this relationship? The answer is illustrated in Exhibit 3. Note that the quantity of money is again measured on the horizontal axis and society's aggregate income, GNP, on the vertical. As in the previous diagram, two important points are conveyed by this model:

1. The public's demand-for-money curve, D_M, represents some fraction, k, of society's aggregate income, GNP. Thus, $D_M = kGNP$. The supply-of-money curve, S_M, is a vertical line. This indicates that, at any given time, the quantity of money (determined by the Fed) is a fixed amount and is unresponsive to changes in aggregate income.

2. The equilibrium income at GNP_1 is determined by the intersection of the D_M and S_M curves. Suppose the Federal Reserve now decides to increase the supply of money from S_M to S_M'. This will produce an excess money supply in relation to what people want. They will therefore spend away the excess, which causes aggregate income to rise to the new equilibrium at GNP_2.

Money and Interest Rates: Inverse Relation

As you learned earlier, monetarists believe that a second major variable affecting the public's demand for money is the interest rate. (This view is also shared by many economists who are not monetarists.) The nature of the relationship, monetarists contend, is *inverse*. That is, people want to hold smaller cash balances when interest rates are high, and larger cash balances when interest rates are low.

The reason for this is not hard to see. Our economy is composed of decision-making units— individuals, households, and firms. These economic entities hold their wealth (that is, things of value) in the form of *portfolios of assets*. Examples are cash, property, and the rights to property. Thus, some of the things you might own, including both financial and nonfinancial assets, are money, stocks, bonds, a car, a house, furnishings, and perhaps a business. Because all of these items constitute wealth, each is, according to monetarists, a part of your portfolio.

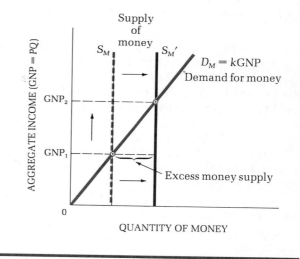

Exhibit 3
Money and Aggregate Income (GNP)

The public's demand for money (D_M) is equal to some fraction (k) of society's aggregate income (GNP). The supply of money (S_M) is determined by the Federal Reserve. Therefore, an increase in the supply of money from S_M to S_M' provides people with excess cash balances. These balances are then spent, which causes the equilibrium level of aggregate income to rise from GNP_1 to GNP_2.

How much of its portfolio will the public hold in the form of cash balances? The answer depends on how profitable it is to hold other assets, such as securities, property, and so on. For example, suppose there is a rise in the returns (measured by interest rates) on other assets. People will reduce their holdings of cash balances in order to take advantage of the higher returns available. The reverse, of course, occurs when the returns on other assets decline. In general, therefore, the public's demand for cash balances varies *inversely* with interest rates.

The foregoing explanation of the public's demand for money emphasizes the influence of two factors — aggregate income and interest rates. Summarizing the key ideas:

Monetarists believe that the public's demand for cash balances varies *directly* with aggregate income and *inversely* with interest rates. Under normal conditions the public's demand for cash balances tends to be stable in relation to those variables.

The Stability of Velocity

You know that, according to monetarist thinking, the amount of money people want to hold is equal to a constant fraction (k) of GNP. But, as you have already learned, k represents the ratio $1/V$. That is, $k = 1/V$. Therefore, because k is constant, V must also be constant in order for the equation to hold true. Further, if $k = 1/V$, then $V = 1/k$.

To illustrate these ideas, suppose that people want to hold 25 percent of their income in the form of cash balances. Then, $k = \frac{1}{4}$. And, since $V = 1/k$, $V = 4$. This means that each dollar is spent an average of four times during the year to purchase the economy's GNP.

Similarly, if people want to hold 20 percent of their income as cash, then $k = \frac{1}{5}$. Hence, $V = 5$. Each dollar is thus spent an average of five times per year.

As you can see, k is the reciprocal of V, V is the reciprocal of k, and both are constants. In view of this, what determines V?

In general, monetarists believe that the income velocity of money is stable. That is, although velocity can and does fluctuate over the years, it nevertheless bears a stable relationship to the variables that determine it. One of the chief determinants is the public's *expectations of inflation.* If people expect prices to rise, they will be inclined to spend more of their cash balances now. This will cause V to increase. Conversely, if people expect prices to decline, they will delay spending some of their cash balances. This will cause V to decrease. Thus:

Monetarists believe that changes in V vary in a stable and direct way with the public's inflationary expectations. That is, V increases when the public expects prices to rise, and decreases when the public expects prices to fall.

The Transmission Mechanism: Portfolio Adjustments

The foregoing ideas concerning the demand for money and its velocity of circulation can now be brought together. The linkage is what may be called the **transmission mechanism.** This is the process by which changes in the monetary growth rate bring about changes in people's spending behavior. The latter, in turn, affect prices, interest rates, and other economic variables.

The transmission mechanism, as the monetarists see it, may be thought of as a sequence of events:

First, decisions to increase or decrease the monetary growth rate are continually made by the Fed. These monetary-policy actions are aimed at achieving the goals of efficiency, stability, and growth. One of the most fundamental tenets of monetarism is the belief that the Fed fails to achieve these goals because its expansions and contractions of the monetary growth rate are *erratic.* As a result, monetarists argue, the Fed's actions often turn out to be a cause of inefficiency, instability, and inadequate growth.

Second, erratic changes in the monetary growth rate cause discrepancies between people's actual and desired real cash balances. To restore equilibrium, individuals adjust the composition of assets in their portfolios. For example, if a disequilibrium is caused by unexpected increases in the monetary growth rate, people reduce their excess cash balances by buying any of a wide range of other assets.

Third, individuals are always shifting their holdings of wealth between different assets in an effort to obtain satisfactory relative rates of return on their entire combination of assets. For example, if returns in the securities market are relatively higher than returns in the real-estate market, people will shift some of their funds out of buildings and land and into stocks and bonds. These reallocations of wealth are reflected by changes in the relative prices of assets as spending patterns shift over a wide range of goods and services.

Thus:

Monetarists believe that the transmission mechanism by which changes in the monetary growth rate cause changes in total spending is essentially a *portfolio-adjustment process*. Individuals are seen as disposing of their excess money balances over a broad spectrum of existing assets. These include stocks, bonds, consumer goods, and producer (capital) goods. As a result, the relative prices of these goods are always changing in response to shifts in people's spending patterns caused by fluctuations in monetary growth rates. The changes in prices, in turn, affect people's inflationary expectations, thereby influencing interest rates and the velocity of money.

This explanation is summarized by the diagram in Exhibit 4. It illustrates how most of today's monetarists would describe the transmission process.

Evidence and Policy Recommendations

Monetarists have always maintained that inflation is the result of "too much money chasing too few goods." Therefore, they conclude, *an acceleration in the monetary growth rate will produce an acceleration in the inflation rate at some later time.*

How much later? Monetarists' answers differ. However, their studies show that it can take anywhere from a few months to about two years, depending on other conditions. Perhaps the most important of these "other conditions" is the public's *expectations* of inflation. The role of expectations will be examined later in this chapter.

Exhibit 4
The Transmission Process: Monetarist View

There are several different monetarist explanations of the transmission process. This composite description fits most monetarists' views. However, differences of opinion exist as to the speed with which some of the variables in the boxes react to changes in the monetary growth rate.

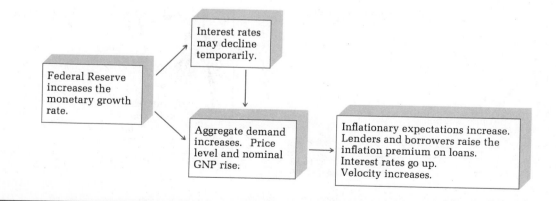

On the basis of what you now know about monetarism, it is appropriate to ask whether the main outcomes described by the transmission mechanism
actually occur.   Exhibit 5 suggests an answer.   Figure (a) shows that changes in the monetary growth
rate appear to influence the rate of price-level
changes about two years later.   Figure (b) illustrates
the idea that the rate of price-level changes affects
interest rates because lenders and borrowers attach
an inflation premium to loans.   These monetarist
views thus lead to a practical policy conclusion:

Monetarists contend that erratic changes in the growth
rate of the money supply cause economic instability.
Thus, they say, the Fed should adhere to a policy of
steady monetary expansion at a rate consistent with
the economy's long-run growth of real GNP—about 3
to 4 percent annually.   This would promote stability.
A faster rate of growth would cause inflation; a slower
rate would bring on recession.   This basic idea is called
the ***money-supply rule.***   It serves as a guide for Federal
Reserve monetary policy and as a basis for judging the
Fed's overall performance.

Exhibit 5
Tracking Economic Trends: The Fed
and Inflation

Monetarists contend that the Fed's monetary policies
are often destabilizing.   Erratic changes in the monetary growth rate cause fluctuations in the rate of price-
level changes.   These, in turn, cause the interest rate to
vary.

Figure (a):   This figure, say the monetarists, demonstrates the instability of the money supply, M1, and the
Consumer Price Index, CPI.   Both are measured in percentage changes.   The relationship shows that in-

creases in the monetary growth rate cause increases in
the inflation rate about two years later.

Figure (b):   Monetarists contend that interest rates respond to inflation.   Higher rates of inflation lead to
higher interest rates.   This is because lenders want to
be compensated for the purchasing power they expect
to lose due to inflation.   And borrowers are willing to
pay higher interest rates because they expect to be repaying their loans with cheaper dollars.

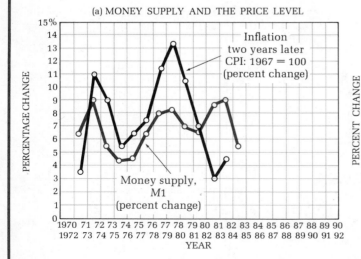

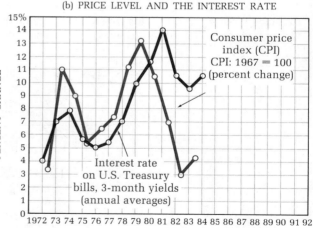

Some Agreements and Some Disagreements

The way in which the Fed manages the money supply can thus have important economic consequences. But experiences and research findings since about 1980 indicate that the consequences of monetary policy do not always accord with what the underlying theories predict. In certain ways this has helped to bring monetarists and Keynesians somewhat closer together on at least two fundamental points.

Transmission Mechanism

The transmission process, as monetarists see it, was illustrated earlier in Exhibit 4. Many of today's Keynesians are more or less in agreement with it. However, fundamental disagreements exist as to the speed with which certain variables in the boxes adjust to changes in the money supply. For example, monetarists believe that the price level responds relatively quickly—typically in about 18 to 24 months. (During periods of rapid inflation when inflationary expectations are high, such as existed in the late 1970s, the response time can be considerably shorter—perhaps a few months.) Keynesians contend that, under most normal circumstances, the full adjustment takes much longer—usually a number of years. Unfortunately, the statistical studies that have been done to test these beliefs are subject to different interpretations. Some of the studies support the monetarist contention while others give strength to the Keynesian case.

Velocity of Money

A somewhat similar situation exists with respect to the velocity of money. Most monetarists now believe that V is *relatively* (rather than almost rigidly) stable. They still think that changes in the money supply are likely to exert direct effects on the price level, but the relationship between money and prices is acknowledged to be looser than was once thought. Monetarists have thus moved somewhat closer to the Keynesian view which has always held that V is unstable. *To the extent that V is unstable, it is possible for changes in the money supply to be offset, at least partially, by opposite changes in V.*

Convergences of monetarist and Keynesian beliefs have not occurred in all areas. Indeed, there are portions of monetarism where the two points of view are far apart. For example, monetarists argue that the economy is inherently stable at a high level of employment unless disturbed by erratic monetary growth rates. Keynesians contend that, even with fairly stable monetary growth rates, inadequate business investment can cause the economy to become bogged down in prolonged periods of unemployment.

How do these differences of opinion affect judgments about the kinds of policies that should be emanating from Washington? As we proceed to answer this question, the following summary of monetarist and Keynesian attitudes toward public policy will prove useful:

- Monetarists believe that, if the money supply is expanded at a steady rate, the economy will rapidly absorb the adverse effects of normal economic disturbances. This will enable output to resume its long-run growth path. Therefore, no active stabilization policies should be undertaken. Indeed, such policies actually turn out to be *destabilizing*.

- Modern Keynesians contend that the economy does not readily revert back to its normal growth path when subjected to disturbances. Therefore, stabilization actions, consisting of appropriate fiscal-monetary policies, are needed to achieve and maintain full employment.

Rules or Discretion?

From what you now know, you will find it challenging to formulate your own brief definition of **monetarism.** To assist you, a comprehensive explanation is given in the Dictionary at the back of the book. You will note from this explanation that monetarism can be viewed in two ways:

1. As scientific analysis, it is a set of relationships between such variables as the demand for money, aggregate income, interest rates, and velocity.

2. As policy prescription, it is a course of behavior that monetarists think the Fed should follow in order to promote efficiency, stability, and growth.

Today the chief emphasis is on the implementation of policy. The question that monetarists ask is: *What sort of practices should the Fed adopt in order to replace the discretionary policies that it has employed in the past?* In their answer, monetarists prescribe several specific rules:

1. Provide an Optimum Monetary Growth Rate

The Fed should stabilize the expansion of the money supply at about 3 to 4 percent a year. This would "feed" money to the business sector at a rate consistent with the economy's long-run growth of GNP. When the monetary growth rate is much faster than this, as is often the case, it tends to be inflationary.

A rate of monetary expansion that is substantially greater than 3 to 4 percent annually should be reduced slowly. The reason is that a gradual reduction rather than a rapid one will permit a slower rate of business contraction. Therefore, it will be less destabilizing and will create less unemployment.

2. Do Not "Monetize" the Debt

You learned in earlier chapters that bond prices and interest rates are inversely related. Consequently, when the Treasury borrows heavily from the public by selling debt securities, their prices tend to decline and interest rates to rise.

High interest rates, in turn, may lead to **crowding out** of business investment and thereby bring on a recession. To reduce the chances of this happening, the Fed will often buy securities in the open market in order to maintain their prices and stabilize interest rates. But this action is inflationary —the same as printing money. Why? *Because open-market purchases of government securities increase banks' reserves.* This enables banks to expand loans (in the form of checkable deposits) and hence the money supply.

When the Fed buys securities in the open market, it thus *monetizes* some of the national debt by converting it into money. This policy, monetarists emphasize, should be avoided in order to reduce inflationary pressures. *The Fed should concentrate instead on stabilizing the monetary growth rate and not try to influence interest rates.*

3. Watch the Monetary Base, Not the Federal Funds Rate

Unfortunately, even if the Fed were to implement these rules, a difficulty would arise from the ambiguous notion of "money."

As you know, there are several different measures of money. The most important are M1 and M2. Which of these should the Fed try to stabilize? Many economists argue that for this purpose a narrower measure is needed. One that is usually recommended is called the "monetary base."

The sum of legal reserves and currency in circulation constitutes the **monetary base.** It may be called "high-powered" money because it supports the money supply (currency + checkable deposits). Because of our fractional-reserve banking system, the money supply is a multiple of the monetary base. Therefore, by controlling the monetary base, the Fed could exercise a stronger influence over the total monetary assets of the public.

According to critics, the Fed has often devoted too little effort to stabilizing the monetary base. Instead it has focused too much attention on influencing the **federal funds rate.** This is the interest rate at which banks borrow excess reserves from other banks' accounts at the Fed, usually overnight. Banks often borrow these reserves in order to keep their own required reserves from falling below the legal level. The Fed pays close attention to this interest rate. It is an indicator of what is happening to other short-term interest rates, because they all tend to move in the same direction as the federal funds rate.

Conclusion: Today's Conflicting Views

You have learned that, contrary to popular myth, the Fed cannot control interest rates. It can only control the supply of money, which, when combined with the public's demand for money, determines the level of interest rates in the market. Monetarists argue that frequent efforts by the Fed to influence interest rates (and perhaps other economic variables such as prices and GNP) by manipulating the monetary growth rate have been destabilizing and inflationary.

In view of this, why have the Federal Reserve authorities not adhered to monetarists' recommendations? The answer is that the Fed has not usually agreed with the recommendations.

According to the Fed, monetary policy cannot be based on a few simple guidelines. The economy is extremely complex, and conditions both at home and abroad are continually changing. Therefore, *discretionary policies, not fixed rules*, are necessary to achieve desirable levels of efficiency, stability, and growth. Of course, the monetarists' response to this argument is that the Fed's discretionary policies are precisely the *cause* of the trouble, not the cure.

You can now appreciate why it is true that today's monetary-policy dispute stems from several different points of view. They include those of strict monetarists, moderate monetarists, Keynesians, and even the Fed. The dispute focuses mainly on the *degree* of monetary management that is deemed advisable for achieving a healthy economy. Differences of opinion that exist thus remind us that economists are much like medical doctors. They often concur on the cause of an illness but they do not always agree on the best way to treat it.

Leaders in Economics

United Press International

Milton Friedman
1912 –
America's Best-Known Monetarist

A Nobel laureate (1976) and professor emeritus at the University of Chicago, Milton Friedman is perhaps best known for his approach to money and his unique position as America's leading monetarist. Using carefully documented research going back to the late nineteenth century, he argues that the crucial factor affecting economic trends has been the quantity of money, not government fiscal policy. Accordingly, he opposes the use of discretionary monetary policy by the Federal Reserve to achieve economic stability. Friedman advocates instead a **money-supply rule** —an expansion of the nation's money supply at a steady rate in accordance with the economy's growth and capacity to produce.

Friedman cites the past performance of the Fed as one of the major reasons for this view. Throughout its history, he says, the Fed has proclaimed that it was using its monetary powers to promote economic stability. But the record often shows the opposite. Despite the Fed's well-intentioned efforts, it has been a major cause of *instability* by causing the monetary growth rate to expand and contract erratically. Therefore, the urgent need is to prevent the Fed from being a source of economic disturbance.

Feasible Policy
Is the adoption of a money-supply rule technically feasible? Friedman claims that it is. Although he admits that the Fed could not achieve a precise rate of growth in the money supply from day to day or from week to week, it could come very close from month to month and from quarter to quarter. If and when it does, he says, it will provide a monetary climate favorable to economic stability and orderly growth. And that, Friedman concludes, is the most we can ask from monetary policy at our present state of knowledge.

Money's Role

Monetarists Succeed in Pushing Basic Ideas but Not Their Policies

Money Now Is Widely Seen As Having a Big Impact

By Lindley H. Clark Jr. and Laurie McGinley

The spread of monetarist ideas has sharply improved the odds that inflation will stay low, many economists believe. They give monetarists much of the credit for a fundamental shift in the balance of economic and political forces away from the pro-expansion, pro-inflation tendencies of the 1960s and 1970s.

Instead of being adopted wholesale, monetarist ideas have simply been added to the eclectic kettle of theories — Keynesian, neoKeynesian, supply side, rational expectationist, to name a few — that along with a hefty dollop of political expediency make up the mixed brew of economic policy in the U.S.

The total potion, however, is a lot less inflationary than before, and that is a major success, many economists argue. Here and abroad, they note, the need to curb money growth is now more firmly embedded in economic policy. The U.S., Britain,

West Germany, Switzerland, France, Italy, the Netherlands, Canada and Japan all announce some sort of money targets, a procedure unheard of 15 years ago.

Partial Success

That is only of moderate comfort to monetarists.

"It's widely accepted that you can't hold inflation down unless you hold down the money supply. Thirty years ago, people didn't agree with that," says Mr. Friedman, long the world's leading monetarist, who won the Nobel Prize in part for his studies on the relationship between money-stock growth and economic stability.

But, he complains, people still don't agree with the monetarists' principal recommendation: a requirement that the Fed produce slow, steady growth of the money supply at a set pace, year after year, regardless of fluctuations in prices, interest rates or employment.

To monetarists, a fixed rule is the only way to assure steady growth with stable prices because no one understands the economy well enough to adjust the rate of money growth appropriately for any given time. In fact, they contend, the Fed's efforts to "fine tune" the economy merely add to the financial markets' uncertainty, raise interest rates, destabilize prices and disrupt jobs.

But to other economists, even those who have accepted many other monetarist ideas, the fixed-rule prescription is like putting on a straitjacket before swimming the English Channel. Many economists believe that the Fed should be free to help the government fight recessions and the accompanying unemployment.

Because the Fed must react to unforeseen problems ranging from bank failures to international economic crises, Fed Chairman Paul Volcker contends, it would be "exceedingly dangerous and in fact practically impossible to eliminate substantial elements of discretion in the conduct of Federal Reserve policy."

Mr. Friedman insists that the Fed resists a fixed rule because of bureaucratic self-interest. "If the Fed gave up discretion," he asks, "would any poll show the chairman of the Fed as the second most important man in the country? The Fed would be a minor institution."

Mr. Friedman contends that the only way to get slow, steady growth in the money supply is to replace the Fed with a computer. On its own, he says, "the Fed never will become monetarist, and that's one forecast you won't prove wrong."

New-Classicism: The Self-Correcting Economy

The most extensive attack against Keynesian economics has come from the new classicists. Picking up with many monetarist ideas and conclusions, the new classicism (which has often been called "Monetarism II") contends that the economy adjusts automatically to full employment. Therefore, government policies designed to achieve full employment are ultimately ineffectual. This is because people learn to *expect* the policies and to respond *rationally* in such a way as to thwart them. The concept of "rational expectations" is thus fundamental to the new classicism.

Rational Expectations: What You Foresee Is What You Get

You can fool some of the people all of the time, and all of the people some of the time, but you cannot fool all of the people all of the time.
  Abraham Lincoln (1863)

Inflation does give a stimulus . . . when it starts from a condition that is noninflationary. But if the inflation continues, people get adjusted to it. Then, when they *expect* rising prices, the mere occurrence of what has been expected is no longer stimulating.
  Sir John R. Hicks (1967)

These quotations, the first by the sixteenth President of the United States and the second by a British economist and Nobel laureate, are more than 100 years apart. Yet they share the common recognition that much of economics involves predicting human behavior. Therefore, when goverment policy makers try to stabilize the economy, they must predict how people will respond.

But this appears to be impossible — according to the theory of rational expectations that underlies the new-classical economics. The theory holds that people form expectations about government fiscal-monetary policies on the basis of past experience, and then include these expectations in their economic decisions. Consequently, by the time the government's policies are initiated, the public has already acted on them, thereby offsetting the effects. As the quotation from Hicks implies, the only policy changes that can work are those that come as surprises, because they force people to revise their expectations.

Two examples will illustrate how the theory of rational expectations works.

1. If the economy is in recession, people will expect the Fed to take steps toward reducing interest rates. Businesses will therefore tend to defer investment expenditures on new plant and equipment until interest rates decline. This deferral worsens the recession. When the rates finally do come down, the lower cost of borrowing may stimulate a greater volume of investment than policy makers intended. The result will be more rather than less cyclical instability, caused by too much rather than too little government intervention.

2. From time to time, Washington proposes a reduction in corporate income taxes in order to spur business investment. According to the rational-expectations theory, such talks prompt executives to postpone many planned projects, waiting for the tax change to occur. When the change finally comes, capital spending may pick up — if a recession has not intervened.

Income-Price Model

You can gain a better understanding of these concepts by analyzing them within an aggregate-demand/aggregate-supply framework. This, of course, is the familiar income-price model studied in some earlier chapters. Exhibit 6, along with the following explanation, provides both a review and extension of important ideas.

The downward-sloping *AD* curve tells you that total spending on aggregate output, such as real GNP, will be greater at a lower average price level than at a higher one. This is due to the operation of

Exhibit 6
Income-Price Model

Potential real GNP is the output that occurs at full or natural employment. This corresponds to the equilibrium price level at *P*.

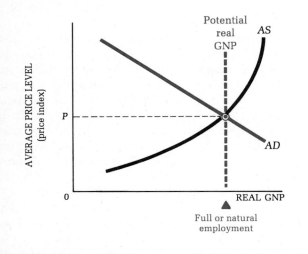

Changes in the Curves: Self-Correcting Adjustments

The aggregate demand and supply curves are drawn on the assumption that *all other things remain constant*. What are these things? A few of the more important ones may be listed separately for each curve:

Factors assumed constant for aggregate demand	Factors assumed constant for aggregate supply
1. Fiscal policy	1. Tax policies and government regulation
2. Monetary policy	2. Inflationary expectations
3. Inflationary expectations	3. Resource costs

two familiar concepts—the **real-balance effect** and the **interest-rate effect.** You can refresh your understanding of these ideas by looking them up in the Dictionary at the back of the book.

The upward-sloping *AS* curve associates a higher average price level with a larger volume of real output. One of the reasons, you will recall, is that most production costs (especially wages) do not increase immediately in response to rising prices. Therefore, in the short run a higher price level makes a larger volume of real output profitable.

The intersection of the *AD* and *AS* curves determines an equilibrium output and a corresponding equilibrium price level. In this case the equilibrium output occurs at full or natural employment, so the vertical dashed line represents the economy's potential real GNP. The corresponding equilibrium price level occurs at *P*.

In the real world these conditions frequently change, causing the curves to shift. For example:

− With respect to demand, expansionary fiscal or monetary policies will shift the *AD* curve to the *right*. So too will a rise in inflationary expectations because people will increase their current spending if they anticipate higher prices in the near future. On the other hand, contractionary fiscal or monetary policies or declines in inflationary expectations will shift the *AD* curve to the *left*.

− With respect to supply, decreases in taxes or in those government regulations that impose burdensome costs on business will shift the *AS* curve to the *right*. So too will a decline in inflationary expectations (because it encourages reduced wage demands by labor). And, of course, so too will a decline in the costs of resources (such as energy and other inputs used in production). On the other hand, increases in taxes, government regulations, inflationary expectations, or resource costs will shift the AS curve to the *left*.

What happens if the *AD* and *AS* curves do not intersect at full employment? The answer can be understood in terms of Exhibit 7:

Exhibit 7
Closing Recessionary and Inflationary Gaps: Self-Correcting Adjustments

Figure (a):   Recessionary Gap The equilibrium point at *a* occurs at less than full employment. This puts downward pressure on wages. Despite initial resistance by unemployed workers, they eventually accept wage cuts in order to get jobs. Reduced wages result in lower resource costs, causing the *AS* curve to shift to *AS'*. The recessionary gap thus closes as the economy moves along the adjustment path from *a* to *b*.

Figure (b):   Inflationary Gap The equilibrium point at *a* occurs at overfull employment. This puts upward pressure on wages, as workers seek increases in order to keep up with inflation. Resource costs therefore rise, causing the *AS* curve to shift to *AS'*. The inflationary gap thus closes as the economy moves along the adjustment path from *a* to *b*.

Thus, the vertical dashed line is the economy's ***long-run aggregate supply* (LRAS) *curve.***

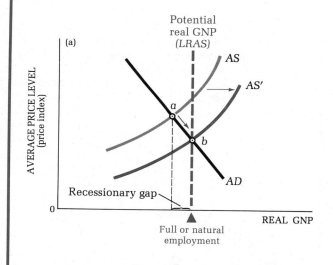

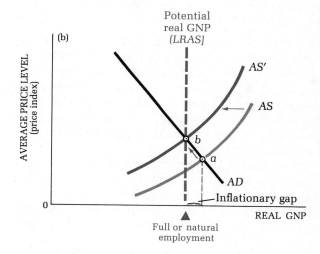

In Figure (a), the initial equilibrium occurs at point *a*, causing a recessionary gap. The resulting increase in unemployment puts downward pressure on wages. After some period of resistance, workers agree to accept wage cuts as a condition of employment. Reduced wages result in lower resource costs, causing the aggregate supply curve to shift rightward from *AS* to *AS'*. The economy thus adjusts *automatically* to full-employment equilibrium and to a *lower* price level as it moves along the adjustment path from *a* to *b*.

In Figure (b), the initial equilibrium occurs at point *a*, causing an inflationary gap. The resulting overfull employment puts upward pressure on wages as workers try to "catch up" with rising prices. Resource costs thus increase, causing the aggregate supply curve to shift leftward from *AS* to *AS'*. The economy adjusts *automatically* to full-employment equilibrium and to a *higher* price level as it moves along the adjustment path from *a* to *b*.

Thus, in the long run, real GNP equals the economy's full-employment or "natural" level of output. Therefore, the vertical potential-real-GNP line may be thought of as the economy's ***long-run aggregate supply*** (LRAS) ***curve.***

Experience shows that it may take a while for the economy's self-correcting mechanism to operate. Because of this, government often institutes policies aimed at hastening the adjustment to full-employment equilibrium. These actions, however, can be a serious cause of *instability*, as the following analyses of demand-side and supply-side inflation demonstrate.

Demand-Side Inflation: Counterclockwise Adjustment Path

The effect of demand-side inflation (also known as demand-pull inflation) can be seen in Exhibit 8. To begin with, the economy is assumed to be operating at less than full employment. Thus the intersection of the *AD* and *AS* curves occurs at point *a*. This results in a recessionary gap — an equilibrium price level at *P* and an equilibrium output and employment level at *Q*.

What happens if government adopts an expansionary fiscal-monetary policy aimed at closing the recessionary gap? The answer can be seen by tracing the adjustment path in the diagram through four stages:

Stage 1 The first effect of the government's expansionary policy is to provide people with more money to spend. Assuming the amount of fiscal-monetary stimulus is "just right," the aggregate demand curve shifts to the right from *AD* to *AD'*. A new equilibrium point is thus established at *b*. Along the adjustment path from *a* to *b*, the price level increases from *P* to *P'*. Simultaneously, output and employment rise from *Q* to the full- or natural-employment level. Thus, *the gain in production and employment is achieved at the cost of higher prices.*

Stage 2 If additional fiscal-monetary stimulus is provided, the aggregate demand curve will shift farther to the right — to *AD''*. This creates an inflationary gap. A new short-run equilibrium point is then established at *c*. Along the adjustment path

Exhibit 8
Demand-Side Inflation: Counterclockwise Adjustment Path

An expansionary fiscal-monetary policy can increase aggregate demand from *AD* to *AD'*. This will close the recessionary gap by raising the price level from *P* to *P'* and the output-employment level from *Q* to full (or natural) employment. The adjustment path thus goes from *a* to *b*.

Further fiscal-monetary stimulus will shift aggregate demand to *AD''*. Prices, output and employment will increase along the path from *b* to *c*, creating an inflationary gap. But with rising prices, resource costs also rise, causing aggregate supply to shift from *AS* to *AS'*. The adjustment path thus goes from *c* to *d*. The result is a new equilibrium at the same full-employment level but at a higher price level *P''*.

Note that the adjustment path runs *counterclockwise* from *a* to *b* to *c* to *d*.

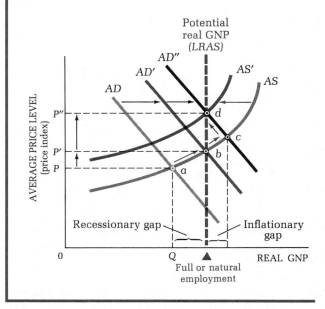

from *b* to *c*, prices are pulled up faster than production costs, especially wages. Business profits therefore rise, encouraging firms to increase production and to hire more workers. At point *c*, the employment rate reaches its highest level.

Stage 3 Workers now begin to realize that prices have been increasing faster than money wages, causing *real* wages to decline. Unions, therefore, negotiate higher money wages and this leads to higher resource costs for firms. The aggregate supply curve thus shifts from AS to AS', resulting in a new equilibrium at d. Along the adjustment path from c to d, production costs rise while business profitability and investment incentives decline. The employment rate thus starts decreasing while prices continue rising. At the equilibrium point d, the inflationary gap is closed and the economy is back to full or natural employment. At this point, the economy has also adjusted fully to the higher price level at P''. This means, for example, that money wages have "caught up" with prices so that real wages are constant.

Stage 4 and Beyond It is interesting to note that the equilibrium at d is stable — that is, has no tendency to change. However, it *can* change if government again employs stimulative fiscal-monetary measures. The economy would then follow a new inflation-employment adjustment path. But if people come to *expect* inflation, the adjustment path will be shortened. In the extreme, it will even be completely short-circuited. For example, if the inflation is fully anticipated, the price level would simply move "up" the potential-real-GNP line to a new and higher rate of inflation than exists at P''. The result would thus be a classical pure inflation, meaning that the price level would rise without any increase in output and employment.

As a final observation, note that the adjustment path from a to b to c to d proceeds in a *counterclockwise* direction. This is a characteristic of demand-side inflation.

Supply-Side Inflation: Clockwise Adjustment Path

The adjustment path under supply-side inflation (also known as cost-push inflation) follows a different route from that of demand-side inflation. You can readily see this by examining the following stages, based on Exhibit 9.

Exhibit 9
Supply-Side Inflation: Clockwise Adjustment Path

An increase in resource costs can shift the aggregate supply curve leftward from AS to AS'. The adjustment path from a to b leads to a higher price level and a decline in output and employment — a recessionary gap.

The higher level of unemployment creates downward pressure on wages. This eventually causes the aggregate supply curve to shift back to AS, thereby closing the recessionary gap. But before that happens, government may try to hasten the process with expansionary fiscal-monetary policies. This will shift the aggregate demand curve rightward from AD to AD', and the increase in aggregate demand will result in the higher price level at P'.

Note that the adjustment path runs *clockwise* from a to b (and from b to c if expansionary policies are employed).

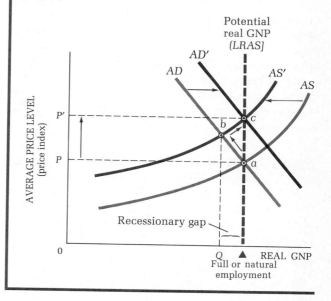

Stage 1 Suppose that an increase in resource costs (such as the cost of energy or of raw materials) shifts the supply curve to the left from AS to AS'. The short-run effect is a rise in prices accompanied by a

reduction in real output and employment along the adjustment path from a to b. At this point the economy is in equilibrium. If government does not try to stimulate the economy by adopting expansionary fiscal-monetary policies, the aggregate demand curve will remain where it is.

Stage 1′ The higher level of unemployment will put downward pressure on wages, thereby reducing business costs. This causes the aggregate supply curve to shift rightward to its original position, AS. In the process, prices decline while output and employment increase as the economy moves back along the adjustment path from b to a.

Stage 2 Of course, this reverse adjustment to full-employment equilibrium may occur very slowly. Workers do not accept wage reductions without resistance. Therefore, in order to hasten the closing of the recessionary gap, government may undertake expansionary fiscal-monetary policies while the aggregate supply curve is still at AS'. If government adopts such stimulative measures, the aggregate demand curve will shift from AD to AD'. This will create a new adjustment path from b to c. At point c, the economy is again at full-employment equilibrium, but the price level has risen to P'.

Stage 3 and Beyond It should be noted that the equilibrium at c is stable. However, a new event may occur that again shifts the aggregate supply curve to the left. If that happens, and government tries to close the recessionary gap with expansionary fiscal-monetary policies, the inflation scenario will repeat itself. Such policies will again cause the aggregate demand curve to shift to the right. This will lead to a new equilibrium at some higher point along the vertical potential-real-GNP line. Note, therefore, that the adjustment path from a to b (and from b to c if expansionary policies are employed) is *clockwise* in direction. This is a characteristic of supply-side inflation.

The case study in Exhibit 10 illustrates these concepts.

Exhibit 10
Demand-Side and Supply-Side Inflation: America's Inflationary Experiences

It is interesting to see how the foregoing ideas can be applied to the types of inflations that the United States has experienced in recent history. All of the data needed to prepare the accompanying graphs are provided in the front and back endpapers of the book. Note how the graphs are constructed:

Step 1 On the vertical axis, the average price level is measured by the Implicit Price Index, commonly known as the GNP deflator. On the horizontal axis, GNP is expressed as a proportion of potential GNP. This acknowledges the fact that the economy's *capacity* to produce (resulting from the growth of the labor force, capital investment, and other growth-determining factors) has expanded over the years.

Step 2 The calculation of potential GNP is accomplished by using the following simple formula that you learned in a previous chapter (Chapter 6) dealing with economic instability. If we *assume* that a 5 percent unemployment rate indicates full employment, then for any given year:

$$\text{potential GNP} = \frac{\substack{95\% \text{ of civilian} \\ \text{labor force}}}{\text{actual employment}} \times \substack{\text{actual} \\ \text{GNP}}$$

Step 3 When the points in the diagrams are connected, the results are as shown in the two graphs. Each point is identified by its own year. Brief interpretations of the graphs are provided alongside the diagrams.

Figure *(a):* The demand-side "counterclockwise" inflation of 1963–1972 was primarily the result of large government deficits accompanied by rapid expansions in the money supply. The deficits were incurred to finance President Johnson's domestic "War on Poverty" and a foreign war in Vietnam.

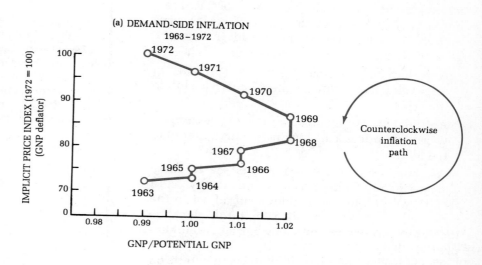

Figure *(b):* The supply-side "clockwise" inflation of 1973–1979 was due primarily to a series of rapid jumps in resource costs. These resulted partly from sharp increases in oil prices by most major oil-producing countries. They also resulted from several poor agricultural harvests in other parts of the world. This led to substantial exports of American food and fiber and, therefore, to higher domestic prices.

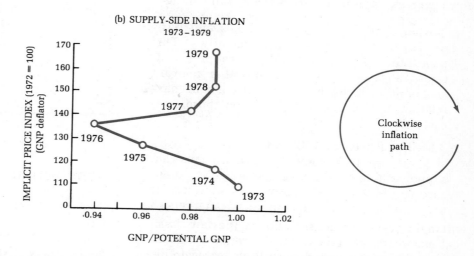

Underlying Assumptions

A fundamental feature of the new classical macroeconomics is the belief that *the economy is automatically self correcting*. This idea was illustrated earlier in Exhibit 7. As you saw there, *if the* AD *curve remains constant*, recessionary and inflationary gaps lead to predictable consequences:

- A recessionary gap creates downward pressure on wages and prices, causing the AS curve to shift to the right.

- An inflationary gap creates upward pressure on wages and prices, causing the AS curve to shift to the left.

As the new classical economists see it, these changes in the AS curve occur automatically. As a result, real output and employment adjust to the full-employment, or so-called "natural," level as indicated by the economy's long-run aggregate supply *(LRAS)* curve.

The new classical macroeconomics thus rests on two major assumptions:

1. **Rational Expectations** Individuals and businesses utilize information efficiently. This means that they analyze and forecast prices, interest rates, money supply, and other relevant economic variables, and then make benefit-maximizing market decisions based on those forecasts.

2. **Flexible Prices and Wages** Markets always allocate resources efficiently. This means that supply-and-demand forces operate so as to ensure equilibrium—the absence of shortages or surpluses—in the product and labor markets.

On the basis of these assumptions, the new classical economics contends that discretionary fiscal-monetary policies aimed at shifting aggregate demand ultimately prove ineffective. Because people are rational, they learn to *expect* government stabilization policies, and to act accordingly. As a result, discretionary policies only lead to higher rates of inflation while real output and employment continue to fluctuate randomly about the natural (full-employment) level. This is illustrated and explained further in Exhibit 11.

Exhibit 11
Economic Adjustments Under Rational Expectations

The economy is assumed to be in equilibrium at the full- or natural-employment level. If the Fed undertakes an expansionary monetary policy, people soon learn to *expect* prices to rise. Hence, the AD and AS curves shift upward, and the economy swiftly adjusts from point E to point E'. Thus, the monetary expansion has only increased prices, without affecting the natural rates of employment and real output.

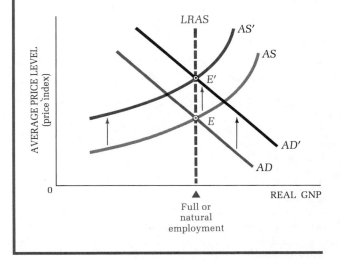

Conclusion: Minimize Uncertainty

Does the new classical economics, and the theory of rational expectations on which it rests, conclude that the only correct public policy should be no public policy? Not quite. Proponents contend that only *systematic* economic policy is impotent. Therefore, the only effective policy is balanced budgets and steady monetary expansion. This, proponents argue, will keep the economy on its stable long-run growth path.

The essential ideas of ***rational-expectations theory*** can be summarized in terms of three propositions.

1. Widely expected or *systematic* policy moves have no impact when made because they have already been incorporated into people's decisions.

2. The only policy moves that cause changes in people's behavior are the ones that are not expected — the *surprise* moves.

3. To ensure economic stability, government should choose the right policy and stick to it. This means that government should adhere to a policy of balanced budgets and a steady growth-rate of the money supply. Failure to do so will lead to public policies that are self-defeating and inflationary.

You can now see certain similarities in views between monetarism and new-classicism. For example, both theories end up with the same conclusion — the rejection of Keynesian interventionism. But the reasons differ:

- Monetarist theory contends that we do not know enough about the workings of the economy to stabilize it with discretionary fiscal-monetary policies.

- New-classicist theory holds that the public defeats discretionary policies because everyone expects them and therefore undertakes actions that thwart their effectiveness.

Both theories thus contend that government should adhere to steady, predictable fiscal-monetary policies in order to minimize uncertainty.

What You Have Learned

1. Monetarist beliefs are rooted in the classical quantity theory of money and the equation of exchange. However, monetarists reinterpret the quantity theory as a theory of the demand for real cash balances.

2. The demand for money — that is, real cash balances — depends mainly on aggregate income and on interest rates. The relationship between demand and aggregate income is *direct*; the relationship between demand and interest rates is *inverse*. Under normal conditions both relationships tend to be stable.

3. The velocity of money is strongly influenced by the public's expectations of inflation. Velocity increases when the public expects prices to rise, and decreases when the public expects prices to fall.

4. The transmission mechanism is viewed by monetarists as a portfolio adjustment process. That is, people spend their excess money balances on a wide range of both consumer and investment goods.

5. Monetarists believe that inflation is the result of "too much money chasing too few goods." Therefore, they argue, the Fed should expand the money supply at a steady 3 to 4 percent rate, corresponding to the nation's long-run growth of real GNP. By providing this optimum monetary growth rate and by not monetizing the debt, the Fed will ensure economic efficiency and price stability.

6. New-classical economics concludes that the economy is self-correcting. That is, the economy adjusts automatically to the full, or natural, level of employment.

7. According to new-classical beliefs, self-correction of the economy can occur in two ways. A recessionary gap creates unemployment, putting downward pressure on wages and hence on the aggregate supply curve. An inflationary gap causes overfull employment, putting upward pressure on wages and hence on the aggregate supply curve.

8. New-classical economics assumes rational expectations and flexible prices and wages. As a result, markets clear automatically. However, there is disagreement as to the speed of adjustment.

9. New-classical economists often agree that even an anticipated policy change can have a short-run impact. However, only policy *surprises* can have any lasting effects. But frequent surprises create instability and uncertainty. Therefore, government should adhere to stable, predictable policies in order to reduce uncertainty and ensure a steady high-employment growth rate.

Terms and Concepts to Review

transmission
  mechanism
monetarism
monetary base
federal funds rate

long-run aggregate
  supply curve
rational-expectations
  theory

For Discussion

Using graphs, demonstrate the propositions in questions 1 and 2. For convenience, assume that the aggregate supply curve is a straight line throughout its entire length.

Also, state whether the propositions are Keynesian or monetarist, and what they imply concerning the effectiveness of stabilization policies.

1. "Increases in aggregate demand have a greater effect on real output than on the price level."

2. "Increases in aggregate demand have a greater effect on the price level than on real output."

3. The velocity of money varies directly with interest rates. Can you explain why? (Think in terms of opportunity cost and the effects of inflation.)

4. Erratic growth of the money supply is worse than rapid but steady growth. Can you explain why?

5. If the money supply increased at a steady rate of about 4 percent a year, would business cycles still occur? How would monetarists and new-classicists answer this question?

6. There is a close relationship between GNP and the money supply. Can you offer an explanation as to why either one may be the cause of the other?

7. Which is more important, the size of the nation's budgetary deficit or the deficit's rate of growth? Assume that the deficits are monetized by the Fed.

8. Is it possible for Keynesians, monetarists, and new-classicists to agree on public policy even though they disagree on certain fundamental matters of theory?

9. "Government budgetary deficits are not necessarily a cause of inflation. It depends on how they are financed." Explain.

10. "The Fed cannot simultaneously control both the money supply and interest rates." Is this statement true? Explain.

Chapter 16

Understanding Macroeconomic Issues

Learning Guide

Watch for answers to these important questions

Unemployment and inflation are the chief macroeconomic problems of our time. What is the relationship between these two phenomena?

How do new-classicists and Keynesians view the unemployment-inflation relationship? Are these views consistent, or are they fundamentally different?

What is supply-side economics? How does it differ from demand-side economics? Do these differences contain implications for policy purposes?

What is stagflation? What are some of the proposals and policies that economists and political leaders have advanced for overcoming it?

The fault, dear Brutus, is not in our stars, but in ourselves.

William Shakespeare

Should the federal government serve as the balance wheel of the economy? Can Washington adopt measures that will encourage production and employment without exerting upward pressure on prices?

These questions, and the answers they entail, are fundamental to macroeconomics. Unfortunately, the answers tend to be elusive because the implications of the questions are complex, and our understanding of them frequently changes.

Accordingly, new policies for coping with unemployment and inflation are continually being proposed by economists and political leaders. What sorts of policies are these? Can they accomplish what they are designed to do? These are the fundamental questions that this chapter seeks to answer.

Unemployment and Inflation: Phillips-Curve Analysis

For many years, the major macroeconomic problems facing our own and most other mixed economies have been *unemployment* and *inflation*. Evidence that they have been major problems can be seen in the data in the back endpapers of this book. Since the early 1970s, unemployment has usually exceeded 5 percent of the labor force, while the price level has often advanced by 6 percent to 10 percent annually.

Many economists believe that there is a relationship between inflation and unemployment and that it can be expressed by a *Phillips curve*. This idea is named after A.W. Phillips, a British economist who proposed it several decades ago.

The relationship is illustrated in Exhibit 1. It emphasizes the notion that there can be only one Phillips curve for the economy at any given time. Let us see why.

Observed Phillips Curves

In Exhibit 1, the percentage of unemployment is measured on the horizontal axis. The rate of inflation—the annual percentage change in the price level—is measured on the vertical. The Phillips curve labeled PC_1 depicts the statisticial relationship between unemployment and inflation that existed in the Keynesian Kennedy-Johnson years of the 1960s. The curve can be thought of as an "average" of the cluster of dots that it represents. Each point on the curve designates a specific combination of unemployment and inflation. The point labeled *A*, for instance, represents an unemployment rate of 5 percent and an inflation rate of 3 percent.

What happens if there is a shift—for reasons to be explained shortly—from PC_1 to PC_2? This, in fact, is what happened in the early 1970s—in the Nixon years. As a result, a given point on this higher curve denotes *at least* as much of one variable plus more of the other. For example, point *B* represents the same unemployment rate as point *A* (5 percent), but a higher inflation rate (6 percent). Point *D*, on the other hand, represents the same inflation rate as point *A* (3 percent), but a higher unemployment rate (6½ percent). The same notion applies to any other point you may choose. Any point on curve PC_2

Exhibit 1
A Curve Named Phillips: Different Ones at Different Times

A Phillips curve (*PC*) depicts a statistical relationship between unemployment and inflation. Each curve is an "average" of the cluster of dots that it represents. Points (such as *A*) along a lower curve denote smaller combinations of unemployment and inflation than corresponding points (such as *B* and *D*) along a higher curve. Therefore, lower curves are better than higher ones.

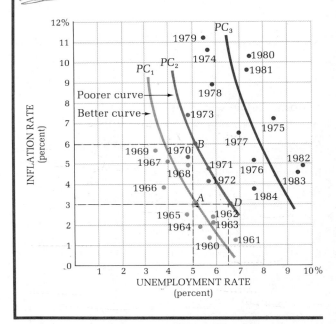

between *B* and *D*, however, represents a higher rate of *both* unemployment and inflation as compared with point *A* on curve PC_1. These ideas suggest that lower Phillips curves are "better" and higher ones are "poorer" for the economy as a whole.

The Phillips curve, of course, has not stood still. It shifted again to PC_3 during the Carter and Reagan years, reflecting a different statistical relationship between unemployment and inflation.

You can now see why a Phillips curve can be defined in the following way:

A *Phillips curve* represents a statistical relationship between unemployment and inflation. Every point on the curve denotes a different combination of unemployment and inflation. A movement along the curve measures the change in one of these associated with a change in the other.

Why has the Phillips curve shifted over time? The answer can be given in terms of two sets of explanations—new-classical and Keynesian.

New-Classical Explanation *of the shift in the Phillips curve*

As you will recall, Keynesian economics was born during the depression of the 1930s. Keynes's ideas led most economists and political leaders to believe that the economy could be "fine tuned." That is, government could select a target rate of employment and, with predominant emphasis on fiscal (rather than monetary) policies achieve it. Of course, if the target chosen was too high, the economy might experience moderate inflation. But some Keynesians thought that even this undesirable effect could be reduced if the government adopted legislation designed to restrain increases in prices and wages.

These beliefs dominated economic thinking until the 1970's. In that period, Keynesian ideas became the subject of increasing criticism as the combination of inflation and unemployment reached unprecedented heights. New-classical economists, including many monetarists, argued that the practice of setting a numerical target for employment (or unemployment) should be discarded. Instead the Fed should stabilize the price level by maintaining a steady rate of monetary expansion and allow the market to determine the "*natural*" or lowest percentage of unemployment that is sustainable. *new-classical ideas*

The basic idea is illustrated in the Phillips-curve model of Exhibit 2. The model rests on the assumption that *a separate Phillips curve is associated with each expected rate of inflation.* Because the

Exhibit 2
New-Classical Analysis: Phillips-Curve Model

Expansionary monetary policies cause the Phillips curve to shift as the public comes to expect higher rates of inflation. In the short run, there may be a limited trade-off between unemployment and inflation as the economy moves along an adjustment path (such as the path from *a* to *b*). But in the long run the economy is self-correcting, returning to its natural rate of unemployment and a higher inflation rate (such as the path from *b* to *c*). To reduce the inflation rate, the Fed would have to contract the monetary growth rate in order to lower the Phillips curve. The economy would then move *down* an adjustment path (such as *cfa*).

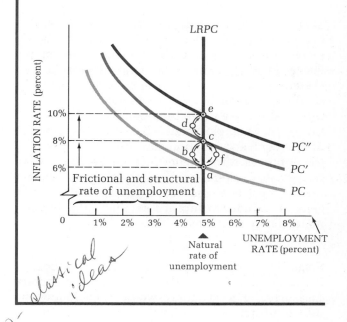

economy, as you will see, always tends toward the natural rate of unemployment, the vertical line is simply a long-run Phillips curve (*LRPC*). To understand why, we can examine the inflation-unemployment adjustment path that results from an *unexpected* increase in the monetary growth rate.

Stage 1 The economy is assumed to be at point *a*, representing a hypothetical natural unemployment rate of 5 percent and an inflation rate of 6 percent. The Phillips curve associated with this inflation rate is *PC*. As you learned when you studied the income-price model, an unexpected expansion in the monetary growth rate causes the aggregate demand curve to shift to the right. (You should sketch your own income-price diagram with *AD* and *AS* curves to illustrate this). In Exhibit 2, therefore, the unemployment rate decreases and the inflation rate rises as these variables move along the adjustment path from *a* to *b*. At point *b*, the unemployment rate reaches its lowest level. Meanwhile, the public's *expectation* of higher inflation causes the Phillips curve to shift to *PC'*.

Stage 2 Wages and other resource costs, which have been lagging behind inflation, are now adjusted upward. This causes the aggregate supply curve in the income-price model (which you sketched in Stage 1 above) to shift to the left. In Exhibit 2, therefore, the unemployment rate and the inflation rate move from point *b* to point *c*. At this point, unemployment is back to its natural rate of 5 percent, and inflation, now fully anticipated by the public, is at the higher rate of 8 percent. With respect to workers, nominal wages have "caught up" with prices so that real wages are constant. In general, the equilibrium at *c* is stable — that is, it has no tendency to change.

Stage 3 Of course, the equilibrium *can* change if the Fed employs further stimulative monetary measures. The economy would then follow the inflation-unemployment path shown by the curved line *cde*.

How does the economy get back to point *a*? To simplify the answer, let us assume that the economy is at *c*. If the Fed ends monetary stimulation, aggregate demand (in the income-price model that you sketched in Stage 1 above) declines relative to aggregate supply. As a result, the inflation rate declines and the unemployment rate at first increases,

then decreases, following the path *cfa*. At point *a*, the economy is again in stable equilibrium, this time at the same 5 percent natural rate of unemployment and at a 6 percent inflation rate.

Against this background, you can appreciate the meaning of the natural rate of unemployment. To begin with, let us *assume* that full employment exists when 95 percent of the labor force is employed. Then that is the natural rate of employment. Looking at Exhibit 2:

> The **natural rate of unemployment** is the percentage of unemployment (including frictional and structural) that is consistent with full employment and a stable rate of inflation. (A stable rate of inflation is one that is neither increasing nor decreasing, such as 6 percent, 8 percent, or 10 percent in the diagram.)

You can now see why the vertical line *LRPC* in the figure is a **long-run Phillips curve.** It relates different rates of inflation to a constant natural rate of unemployment. This concept suggests two ideas:

— In the short run, expansionary monetary policies aimed at reducing unemployment are virtually certain to create inflationary pressures. These occur as the economy moves (along an adjustment path) from one point on the *LRPC* curve to a higher one.

— In the long run, attempts to reduce unemployment through expansionary monetary policies will be unsuccessful, and will only lead to more inflation. Thus, *there is at best only a short-run, not a long-run, tradeoff between unemployment and inflation.*

Summarizing:

> New-classical economists attribute shifts in the Phillips curve to *changing inflationary expectations.* These are caused by fluctuations in aggregate demand resulting from the Fed's erratic monetary policies. Because the economy is self-correcting, it adjusts in the long run to its natural rate of unemployment and to some stable rate of inflation. However, the latter may change if the Fed's policies result in significant changes in the monetary growth rate.

Review Income-price model

Keynesian Explanation

Today's Keynesian economists agree with the new-classical contention that shifts in the Phillips curve are caused by fluctuations in aggregate demand. But they also believe that Phillips-curve shifts are caused by fluctuations in aggregate supply. These result from changes in three sets of factors: resource costs, the economy's competitive structure, and government fiscal policies.

Changes in resource costs occur when raw-materials prices, wage rates, and other factors affecting the production expenses of the business sector are altered. A notable example of this occurred during the late 1970s, when world oil prices escalated, causing the aggregate supply curve to shift to the left. This resulted both in a higher inflation rate and in a higher Phillips curve, as you saw earlier in Exhibit 1.

Similarly, changes in the economy's competitive structure have a direct effect on the aggregate supply curve. In general, an increase in competition leads to improvements in efficiency. The aggregate supply curve shifts to the right, thereby lowering prices, inflationary expectations, and the Phillips curve. A decrease in competition has the opposite effects, thereby raising the Phillips curve. There is evidence that, since the early 1980s, greater pressure from foreign competition has often contributed significantly to lowering both inflationary expectations and the Phillips curve.

Finally, changes in components of fiscal policy, including tax rates, business subsidies, and transfer payments, can cause the aggregate supply curve to shift. For example, executives view most business taxes as costs. Therefore, an increase in tax rates may shift the aggregate supply curve to the left and a decrease may shift it to the right. Such shifts affect inflation rates and, therefore, inflationary expectations and the Phillips curve.

It is important to note that new-classical economists do not deny the validity of these Keynesian arguments. As implied above, however, they believe that erratic monetary policy is the main cause of *continued* inflation and instability.

Conclusion: Today's Phillips Curve

The Phillips curve was initially conceived in the 1960s. At that time it was widely believed that a reasonable trade-off existed between unemployment and inflation. This meant that fiscal and monetary policies could be used to bring about significant reductions in unemployment, but only at the expense of somewhat higher rates of inflation. Conversely, reductions in inflation could be achieved only at the cost of significant increases in unemployment.

Subsequent experience has shown these beliefs to be in need of modification. Thus:

> There is considerable evidence to indicate that, if a trade-off exists between unemployment and inflation, it is a costly one. This is because the long-run Phillips curve (see PC_3 in Exhibit 1) is relatively steep. Therefore, in the long run, expansionary monetary policies aimed at reducing unemployment are very likely to create strong inflationary pressures without achieving substantial gains in employment.

Supply-Side Economics

> The encouragement of mere consumption is no benefit to commerce, for production alone furnishes the means for consumption. Thus, it is the aim of good government to stimulate production, of bad government to encourage consumption.
> Jean Baptiste Say (1803)

If Say, one of the early classical economists, were alive today, he would have some definite suggestions for improving the unemployment-inflation relationship. He would argue, for example, that in order to shift the Phillips curve to the left, policies are needed to shift the aggregate supply curve to the right. This means, in effect, that a distinction can be made between a demand-side and a supply-side view of the economy.

Demand-side economics prescribes measures and policies to regulate purchasing power. Keynesian economics, because it focuses on fiscal and monetary policies to control aggregate demand, may be characterized as demand-side economics. ***Supply-side economics*** prescribes measures and policies to stimulate production. Some of the most fundamental supply-side policies are those that make use of *incentives*. For example, reductions in marginal tax rates—the taxes paid on the last increment of wages, interest, and dividends—provide incentives to work, save, and invest.

Supply-side economics is thus a reconsideration of the ramifications of *Say's Law*—the proposition that "supply creates its own demand." You can appreciate the significance of this by examining the major pillars on which supply-side economics rests. These include:

1. Rejection of Keynesian demand-management policies.
2. Tax reduction to stimulate production.
3. Nonmonetization of government deficits.
4. Deregulation of industries and markets.

Rejection of Keynesian Demand-Management Policies

Supply-side economists point out that the Keynesian model provides an *underconsumption* explanation of recessions. That is, Keynesian theory attributes unemployment to insufficient aggregate demand, resulting in a recessionary gap. Therefore, to restore full employment, government policy should aim at stimulating aggregate demand. As you know, Keynesian demand-management policies are implemented through changes in the money supply and in taxes, among other things. Rejecting such policies, supply-siders argue as follows:

1. Experience shows that the Fed is unable to achieve economic stability by manipulating the money supply. Therefore, it should give up trying to do so. Instead it should adopt measures that will ensure a steady monetary growth rate and, as a result, stable prices.

2. Whenever people's incentives to produce are stifled, any form of demand stimulation will lead to inflation. Policies should therefore be formulated to increase the supply of goods by encouraging increases in *productivity*.

3. Contrary to Keynesian belief, not all income-tax cuts are the same. Only those that emphasize reductions in *marginal* (rather than average or total) tax rates provide maximum incentives to work, save, and invest. This is because marginal tax rates affect people's willingness to undertake *additional* work, saving, and investment.

4. Contrary to Keynesian belief, an increase in government spending is not likely to have the same effect as a reduction in taxes. A reduction in taxes, if properly designed, can exert a substantial impact on *incentives* to produce. An increase in government spending, on the other hand, absorbs resources from the private sector and thus expands the size of government relative to business.

Summarizing these ideas:

Supply-side economics stands in sharp contrast with Keynesian demand-side economics. The principal supply-side prescription is (a) tight monetary control to curb inflation and (b) tax reduction to encourage greater output. It is especially important to reduce marginal tax rates on personal income (to encourage work and saving incentives) and business income (to encourage investment incentives). This is because the goal is to stimulate aggregate *supply* rather than aggregate demand.

Tax Cuts to Stimulate Production

Exorbitant taxes destroy industry by producing despair. An attentive legislature will observe the point when the revenue decreases and the prejudice begins.
David Hume (1756)

High taxes, sometimes by diminishing the consumption of the taxed commodities and sometimes by encouraging smuggling, afford a smaller revenue to government than what might be drawn from more moderate taxes.
Adam Smith (1776)

Exhibit 3
Dr. Laffer's Famous Curve

"Except for the optimum rate, there are always two tax rates that yield the same revenues." So says economic consultant and former professor Arthur Laffer, whose curve has received a great deal of attention from many legislators and economists.

Figure (a): The "Laffer curve" is one of the pillars of supply-side economics. Basically, it says that, if marginal tax rates are in the "normal" range, increases in the rates will yield more tax revenues. But if marginal tax rates are in the "prohibitive" range, *decreases* in the rates will actually produce more revenues by stimulating incentives to work, save, and invest.

Figure (b): In reality a Laffer curve of some kind may exist. However, neither the optimum tax rate nor the true shape of the curve is known. For instance, curve A and curve B are two of many possible shapes. Consequently, in order to maximize revenues, the present tax rate, r, must be either decreased or increased, depending on whether curve A or curve B is correct. On the other hand, reducing tax deductions and closing tax loopholes could shift the curve upward to C. This curve yields higher revenues at *all* tax rates between the extremes of zero and 100 percent.

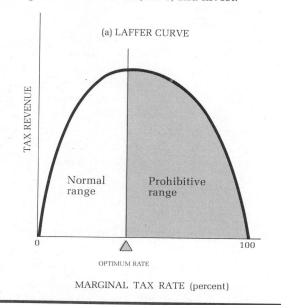

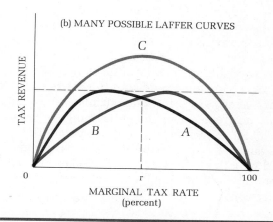

Hume was an eighteenth-century philosopher. Smith was the founder of modern economics. Both understood human nature as it relates to taxation and spending.

For instance, they would have agreed with the idea underlying Figure (a) of Exhibit 3. The diagram, called a ***Laffer curve,*** expresses a relationship between tax revenues and the marginal tax rate—the rate on the last few dollars of income. The relationship shows that, as the tax rate increases from zero to 100 percent, government revenues from taxation correspondingly rise from zero to some maximum level and then decline to zero. Thus, the optimum tax rate—the one that produces the largest revenue—is somewhere between the two extremes.

An important feature of the curve is that it covers both a "normal" range and a "prohibitive" range. In the normal range, a higher tax rate brings higher revenues. In the prohibitive range, the tax rate is so high that it impairs incentives. Therefore, a tax *cut* would actually increase revenues by spurring the incentive to work and invest.

These considerations lead to the following conclusion:

Supply-siders contend that, if *marginal* tax rates are in the prohibitive range, they should be cut. This action would make working, saving, and investing more rewarding, thereby stimulating economic activity. The result would be greater economic growth and employment, leading to higher, not lower, tax revenues.

The Laffer curve is an interesting idea. But no one knows where the optimum point is located or even what the true shape of the curve is. This can pose difficulties for public policy.

For example, in Figure (b) of Exhibit 3, the actual Laffer curve might be either curve A or curve B. If the present tax rate is r and the goal is to maximize revenues, tax rates should be *decreased* if A is the correct curve and *increased* if B is correct. Alternatively, revising the tax laws to reduce deductions and close loopholes could shift the entire curve to a higher level—say, C. Along curve C, revenues would be greater over the entire range of tax rates (except, of course, at zero and 100 percent).

Because of such possibilities, it is easy to understand why the Laffer curve, which has been a fundamental part of supply-side economics, is also highly controversial.

Depreciation Reform

Policies concerning tax reduction are closely related to those concerning depreciation. What is *depreciation*? It is the decline in the value of a fixed asset, such as plant or equipment, due either to wear and tear or to obsolescence resulting from the development of new and better techniques.

Companies treat depreciation as a cost. That is, the tax laws allow firms to deduct from their income

each year a certain amount of depreciation on buildings, machines, vehicles, and other capital goods as a cost of doing business.

For example, suppose that a firm owns a building that cost $1 million. If the tax laws require the firm to "write off" the building over 20 years, the firm could deduct from its income $50,000 a year as a depreciation expense. If the tax laws allow the firm to accelerate depreciation over 10 years, however, it could deduct $100,000 a year.

Obviously, the more a firm can deduct each year for depreciation, the smaller will be its profit and, therefore, the less it will pay in income taxes. The same is true for other firms. Therefore:

Laws permitting accelerated depreciation—that is, faster write-offs of plant and equipment—can be an important part of a tax-reduction policy. Accelerated depreciation gives firms a greater incentive to undertake new investment in order to replace existing capital equipment. However, accelerated depreciation also (1) reduces tax revenues to the Treasury and (2) benefits capital-intensive firms while neglecting labor-intensive ones. (Examples of the latter are firms that specialize in high technology, research, and development.) Because of this, there is always controversy over any proposal that involves changes in depreciation rates.

Nonmonetization of Government Deficits

Supply-siders recognize that, in the short run, a reduction in marginal tax rates may result in increased budget deficits until the positive effects of the tax cuts take hold. Are the rising budget deficits likely to be inflationary? The answer, say the supply-siders, depends on how the Federal Reserve reacts.

As you will recall, the Treasury incurs a budget deficit by spending more than it collects in taxes. It finances the excess spending (that is, gets funds to cover it) by selling debt instruments (such as Treasury bills and Treasury bonds) to the public. The increased supply of debt instruments on the market causes their prices to decline and, therefore, interest rates to rise. (Remember that prices of debt instruments and interest rates are inversely related.) As a result, many would-be borrowers that cannot afford to borrow at higher interest rates may be forced out of the financial markets—a process known as **crowding out.**

What can the Fed do when it sees interest rates rising and fears the possibility of recession? It may engage in open-market purchases of Treasury securities in an effort to bid up their prices and bring interest rates down. This action, of course, enlarges banks' reserves. As a result, banks seek to expand their lending, thereby increasing checkable deposits and hence the money supply. Thus, through its purchase of Treasury securities in the open market, the Fed *monetizes* the Treasury's deficits by making them part of the money supply. (As you will recall from earlier chapters, the term "monetize" means to convert into money.)

Supply-siders thus conclude that rising deficits are not by themselves inflationary. This is because they represent transfers of purchasing power from the public to the Treasury with no net increases in total spending. However, if the Fed monetizes the Treasury's deficits, the results will be inflationary because *monetization transforms the deficits into money.*

Supply-side ideas provide an interesting contrast to Keynesian ideas:

— According to Keynesian policy, a budget deficit resulting from a tax cut without a spending cut creates a fiscal stimulus. This becomes even more pronounced when the Fed monetizes the deficit.

— According to supply-side policy, a deficit is not inflationary unless monetized by the Fed. *The purpose of a tax cut is to improve production incentives, not to provide a fiscal stimulus. Therefore, a deficit resulting from a tax cut should not be monetized.*

Does this mean that mounting deficits are harmless as long as they are not monetized? Supply-siders answer *no.* They emphasize an important point:

> Cutbacks in government spending are desirable because they permit reduction in taxes. This encourages the increase in private savings resulting from tax reduction to flow into private investment. Otherwise, the increased savings may be used to purchase Treasury securities, thereby financing the growth of government spending.

Deregulation of Industries and Markets

There are literally millions of federal and state laws, rules, and specifications that must be complied with in the process of producing the nation's GNP. These laws pertain to occupational safety and health, consumer products, foods, drugs, cosmetics, transportation, energy production, finance, marketing, and many other things.

For example, the production and sale of an ordinary cheeseburger involves more than 40,000 regulations. These range from numerous laws controlling the feeding and slaughtering of cattle and the processing of meat to detailed specifications of the fat content of the meat and cheese, the chemical composition of the bun, the texture and freshness of the lettuce, tomatoes, and pickles, and the color and density of the ketchup and mayonnaise. It has been estimated that all the rules and regulations together may add as much as 20 percent to the price you pay for a cheeseburger.

Many regulations impose heavy burdens on large and small businesses, discourage productivity, and contribute to inefficiency. It is easy to see, therefore, why the desire for substantial deregulation is strong among a wide spectrum of economists and political leaders, not just supply-siders.

A number of deregulatory measures have been adopted since the late 1970s. Nevertheless, numerous economists and political leaders agree that a great deal more needs to be done to promote greater efficiency in the nation's industries and markets.

Despite Forecasts, Revenues Are Down

Verdict on the "Supply-Side" Tax Cut

By Joseph J. Minarik

A recent survey by the Internal Revenue Service seems to show that upper-income people are shouldering more of the tax load than they did before 1981, when tax rates were slashed across the board. In 1981, people with at least $100,000 of income paid 15.2 percent of the total tax take; the recent I.R.S. figures for 1983 show that people with incomes of at least $100,000 paid 20 percent—4.8 percentage points more.

This news has been heralded by some as an indication that "supply-side economics" is working—that rich people are earning more money and, despite the lower tax rates, paying more in taxes. Perhaps we really can grow out of that budget deficit, as President Reagan once insisted. But don't count on it . . .

. . . Since the 1981 tax cuts, total revenues from the individual income tax have fallen for two years in a row—from $284.1 billion in 1981, to $277.6 billion in 1982, to $276.1 billion in 1983. This is the first time revenues have fallen for two consecutive years since the late 1940's. The drop certainly wasn't part of the supply-side script; the Administration predicted that revenues would increase by about $30 billion between 1981 and 1983.

Does this make the Reagan tax cuts a failure? Not necessarily. In the long term, lower tax rates could change taxpayers' work and saving habits, leading to a stronger economy. But until people fully adjust their behavior to the new incentive, tax revenues will be down, swelling the budget deficit. The national debt will continue to grow—saddling us with an enormous interest burden, keeping interest rates up and the dollar strong, and handicapping American businesses that compete in world markets.

Low tax rates are certainly preferable to high ones, all else equal. But all else isn't equal. The tax-rate cuts are primarily responsible for our large budget deficits—leaving the economic outlook at least as uncertain as the meaning of tax share statistics.

Conclusion: Different Emphasis

It is interesting to note that these and other supply-side beliefs are not new. Many of them were expressed by Keynes and others as long ago as the 1930s. Further, they have been adopted and implemented in varying degrees since President Reagan took office in 1981. Thus:

> It would be a mistake to conclude that supply-side and demand-side views are the result of opposing theories. Indeed, policies aimed at improving incentives to invest and produce are measures that demand-siders as well as supply-siders have always supported. In a larger sense, therefore, supply-side economics is not so much a rejection of Keynesian economics as a necessary reminder of its limitations and a different emphasis on some of its ideas.

Curing Recurrent Stagflation: Market Policies

For many years, a chief macroeconomic problem facing our own and most other mixed economies has been *recurring periods of stagflation*. As the name suggests, **stagflation** is a combination of two words—"stagnation" and "inflation." Stagnation is a condition resulting from slow economic growth and high unemployment. Inflation, of course, means rising prices.

What measures should Washington consider for curing recurrent stagflation? In general, all anti-stagflation policies can be classified in either of two categories—market and nonmarket. Market policies, which will be considered first, seek to minimize if not avoid the bureaucracy of complex regulations that usually arises when nonmarket measures are employed.

Monetary and Fiscal Guidelines

Most authorities agree that both fiscal and monetary actions affect the level of economic activity. Although there are differences of opinion about their relative importance, neither policy can be pursued effectively to the exclusion of the other.

The reason is not hard to see. When unemployment rises to undesirable levels, government spending is often increased in order to stimulate the economy. To keep a lid on interest rates, the monetary authority expands the money supply. This may succeed in reducing interest rates for a while. But it also promotes further inflation, causing subsequent upward pressure on interest rates. The process thus continues until government budgetary and monetary policies are revised in an effort to check inflation. Then the economy enters a recession and the cycle starts over again.

This scenario, more or less, has been a fairly typical pattern for several decades. If it is to be avoided in the future, measures are needed to ensure greater control over monetary and fiscal policies. This is part of a larger goal of limiting the size of government. An expanding federal deficit, for example, may be an indication that government is growing. If it grows faster than the national economy, command over resources is shifted from the private sector to the public sector.

What can be done to avoid this possibility? Four major monetary and fiscal guidelines aimed at curing stagflation have been proposed.

Stabilize Monetary Growth

Practically all experts agree that steady, as opposed to erratic, monetary expansion is a first step toward achieving stability. Many of them maintain that, if the monetary growth rate is excessive, it should be reduced gradually until it equals the expected long-run growth rate of the economy—approximately 3

to 4 percent annually. As you will recall, this prescription is the familiar *money-supply rule*. By adhering to a policy of gradual rather than sudden monetary reduction, government can minimize the possibility of causing economic disturbances.

Balance the Federal Budget Annually

This frequently heard proposal is often advocated as a constitutional amendment. The intention is to eliminate budget deficits, but not necessarily budget surpluses. If the proposal were adopted, it would prevent the use of government deficit spending, unless approved by a specified majority of Congress. Consequently, monetary policy would become the key means of achieving economic stability.

Limit Federal Spending

A constitutional amendment that would place an upper limit on federal spending has often been proposed. This measure would limit federal spending to a certain percentage of GNP. Figures ranging from 18 to 21 percent, which are somewhat less than historical trends, are typically suggested. Of course, a spending limit is concerned only with the level of spending, not with budget balance or with the relationship between spending and revenues. Therefore, passage of the measure would not necessarily eliminate deficits or surpluses. On the other hand, it would restrict the activities of government and weaken its ability to utilize antirecessionary fiscal policy. Thus it might lead government to adopt less desirable alternatives, such as increased regulations and controls.

Limit Federal Revenues

Another measure sometimes advocated as a constitutional amendment is to restrict federal tax revenues to some percentage of GNP. This form of revenue limit would not eliminate deficits or surpluses because it would deal with the level of revenues, not with spending or the budget balance. Further, it would restrict somewhat the activities of government and reduce its ability to use antirecessionary fiscal policy. However, it would not encourage increased regulations and controls because tax incentives and additional spending to increase GNP could be employed when deemed necessary.

You can see from this analysis that guidelines of any type have certain disadvantages as well as advantages.

Employment Programs: Putting People to Work

Our economy faces an awesome challenge. Each year it must generate many millions of new jobs. That is what is needed to keep the unemployment rate at a socially acceptable level.

How can the task be accomplished? Many specific proposals have been offered. They range from the conservative position advocating a hands-off government policy to the liberal view that government should become more deeply involved. Most of the proposed measures can be grouped into either of two approaches: (1) public employment and (2) employment-training policies and employment subsidies (vouchers).

Public Employment

There is a need for people to clean up parks, assist in hospitals, perform routine tasks in municipal buildings, and fill other types of public-service jobs. Therefore, a direct way to reduce unemployment is for Washington to appropriate in advance the necessary funds for public employment. Then, when unemployment reaches a certain critical level — say, 8 percent — the money could be used to put unemployed people to work.

This statement is correct as far as it goes. However, it considers only the direct effects of a public-employment program. The indirect ones, which can be considerable, arise from the ways in which the program may be financed. These will be discussed shortly.

Employment-Training Policies and Employment Subsidies

A second approach to dealing with unemployment is through *employment-training policies.* These are deliberate efforts undertaken in the private and public sectors to help people develop and use their capacities as actual or potential members of the labor force. Employment-training policies have been financed largely by government. Such policies aim at improving job skills, thereby enhancing worker motivation and mobility.

Somewhat related to employment-training policies as a means of reducing unemployment are employment subsidies. These are grants given to employers who hire and train unemployed people. One way of implementing subsidies would be for government to issue vouchers to the unemployed and unskilled. Those who find jobs at the minimum wage would give the voucher to their employer, who would present it to the government for redemption. The redemption value might be, say, 40 percent of the minimum wage. The employer would then be required to spend the payment on training the new workers.

Rifle or Shotgun Approach?

Critics contend that most employment programs are simply disguised "make-work" schemes. To some extent this may be true. However, careful design of employment programs can greatly reduce, if not eliminate, inefficiency and waste.

For example, government can formulate selective programs focusing on unemployment problems among particular age groups and industries. Several European countries, among them Sweden and the Netherlands, have followed this course, making effective use of *selective* labor-market techniques. These include free training programs, progressive incentive payments, and relocation grants for people willing to work in certain occupations and regions. These countries have also made some use of public-employment programs for people unable to find work in the open market. For the most part, however, a rifle approach that targets on specific problems, rather than an indiscriminate shotgun approach, has proved to be the most effective way of attacking unemployment.

Conclusion: Need for Better Employment Programs

What are the economic consequences of employment programs? Historically, they have tended to be inflationary because they have been financed by expansionary fiscal-monetary measures. Oftentimes, they have also been poorly administered. Nevertheless, well-designed programs, especially employment-training programs, yield two major benefits.

1. They lower the cost to employers of hiring workers who might otherwise remain unemployed because of their low productivity.

2. They make it possible for young people to be employed and trained for higher-paying jobs.

In view of this, what practical conclusions can we formulate about the desirability of employment-training policies?

A comprehensive employment-training strategy would be difficult and expensive to establish. But the alternative should be recognized. Government now spends many billions of dollars annually on unemployment insurance and welfare benefits. Most of the funds produce neither new jobs nor additional output. The money could be used instead to put people to work.

10 STEPS improving

Productivity: Steps Toward Improving Efficiency

Productivity is the output of goods and services obtained from a given amount of the factors of production. A rise in productivity means that the economy is getting more output, and therefore more real income, from its productive resources. A decline in productivity means the opposite. Productivity is thus a measure of an economy's technical efficiency. It follows that increases in productivity

make higher living standards possible. Without such increases, efforts to provide more goods and services per capita must inevitably produce inflationary pressures.

Comparisons and Trends

Although every nation recognizes the importance of achieving high rates of productivity growth, not all are able to do so. There are numerous reasons for this, and the reasons differ from country to country. In the United States, for example, management blames unions for establishing make-work rules and wasteful labor practices. Unions, on the other hand, blame management for its indifference toward, and callous disregard of, labor's needs. And both blame government for failing to adopt legislation that would be conducive to stimulating greater production.

In recent history, America's stagflation has often been accompanied by productivity growth rates that are among the lowest of the major industrial nations. Some interesting comparisons and trends are shown in Exhibit 4.

Causes of the Poor Performance

What are the reasons for prolonged periods of relatively low productivity growth that America has experienced? Experts offer a number of explanations, but four are especially important:

Inadequate Investment Private-sector expenditures on new plant and equipment have not increased rapidly enough to sustain a high rate of growth of real output. Corporate executives attribute the main causes of sluggish investment to lack of confidence engendered by large government deficits, high business taxes, and erratic inflation.

Excessive Regulations Government rules have required firms to spend large amounts of money on expensive health, safety, and environmental-protection equipment. Regardless of their worthiness, these expenditures have left firms with less to spend

Exhibit 4
Comparisons of Productivity

America's gains in productivity have, at times, lagged far behind those of some other industrial nations.

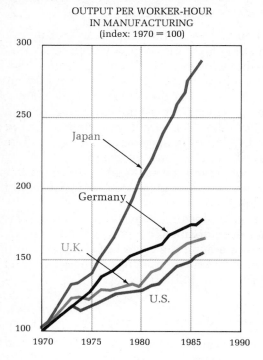

OUTPUT PER WORKER-HOUR
IN MANUFACTURING
(index: 1970 = 100)

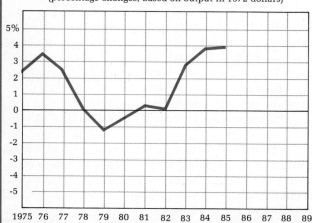

OUTPUT PER HOUR OF ALL PERSONS,
BUSINESS SECTOR
(percentage changes, based on output in 1972 dollars)

on modernizing and expanding their productive facilities. Moreover, compliance with government regulations—preparing required reports, for example—can entail substantial costs apart from the costs of equipment.

Increased Services   The economy's service sector has grown so much that it now accounts for more than 50 percent of GNP. Because it is usually harder to increase the productivity of a service worker (such as a barber, a police officer, a teacher, or a lawyer) than it is to increase that of an assembly-line worker, significant gains in productivity have become more difficult to attain.

Protected Inefficiencies   Import quotas, tariffs, subsidies, and occasional loan guarantees to failing firms are measures that have been used by government to support and protect weak firms. Many have thus been preserved, or allowed to die slowly, and this has retarded the flow of their resources into high-productivity occupations.

Work Incentives: What Can We Learn from Japan?

What can be done to improve the nation's productive efficiency and thereby achieve larger output from our resources? Many of the answers have already been given. They include revision of the fiscal-monetary mix, broad-scale tax reductions, effective employment-training policies, and special tax incentives. Adoption of these measures on a systematic basis would go a long way toward improving efficiency and stability.

But there is more that can be done. Most experts agree that one of the surest ways of improving productivity is through the use of *incentives*. Without them, workers will not be motivated to fulfill more than their minimum job requirements.

No country has had more success with incentive systems than Japan. There are several reasons for this. Among them:

Lifetime Employment   Many Japanese workers are guaranteed a job until retirement age. The introduction of new labor-saving machinery, therefore,

Economics in the News

Good News Ahead for Productivity

By Sylvia Nasar

After languishing during the 1970s, U.S. productivity has come alive and started kicking.

Scarcely any economic development could have happier effects. Growth in productivity makes the country more competitive in world markets and better able to sustain vigorous, noninflationary expansion. Over the long haul it's the only way to raise living standards. Productivity in the U.S. is still the highest in the world, but other countries are catching up.

Examined separately, the basic factors underlying productivity growth underscore the case for optimism.

▶ THE LABOR FORCE   Growth will slow to 1.6% a year.   And the young, inexperienced workers of the last decade are becoming the mature, experienced workers of the Eighties.   The only negative is that average education, one factor in productivity, has already leveled out.

▶ CAPITAL PER WORKER   Higher rates of investment will expand capacity rapidly and speed the spread of new technology.   Investment in plant and equipment is up 28% from its recession low, and has recently been running at more than 12% of GNP.   That's way above the average for the Seventies and close to the peaks of the mid-1960s.

▶ RESEARCH AND DEVELOPMENT   Private and public R&D spending has rebounded to 2.7% of GNP, close to its 1968 peak.   Com-

panies are also likely to get more bang from their R&D bucks than they did in the 1970s, when they spent a lot to offset rising energy costs and meet new regulations.   The payoff will show up later in the decade.

Based partly on these developments, most economists argue that the trend of productivity growth in the nonfarm business sector has shifted from less than 1% into the 1.5% to 2% range.   Reaching 2% would bring the U.S. back to the average of the past century.

Fortune, December 10, 1984, © 1984 by Time, Inc. All rights reserved.

---

is not a threat to them.   The worker will simply be assigned to a different job within the company if his or her job is eliminated for any reason.

People-Related Wage Rates   Wage rates are assigned to the individual rather than to the job.   Bonuses consist of money, prizes (such as gifts or extra vacation days), and praise.   They are based on increases both in productivity and in corporate profitability.

Labor-Saving Initiatives   Workers are encouraged to seek ways of reducing the amount of labor used in production.   Teams of workers meet periodically to discuss methods of increasing efficiency and improving their company's products.

In contrast, most American workers view labor-saving machinery as a potential threat to employ-

ment.   They may be aware that gains in productivity can lead to higher wages, but they perceive the connection between the two as loose and remote. Consequently, American workers often have little incentive to increase productivity.   Indeed, they have frequently looked for ways to curb productivity by resisting technical change, imposing restrictive work rules, and limiting the introduction of innovations.   Accordingly:

Investment in new plant and equipment is a necessary but not a sufficient condition for achieving substantial gains in technical efficiency.   If America is to achieve a substantial improvement in long-term productivity growth, it will have to devise new incentive systems for labor and management.   *Only when workers expect to benefit from change, not to be penalized by it, will they be eager to support it.*

There is growing evidence that this principle is gaining increasing acceptance in modern labor–management relations.

NOT MARKET

Curing Recurrent Stagflation: Can Nonmarket Measures Work?

The various policies described thus far work directly through the market to slow down inflation or speed up economic growth. As a result, these measures do not tend to limit our economic freedoms. Certain other policies, however, replace the operation of the market with laws and regulations. These not only limit personal choices but often reduce them. The chief examples of such nonmarket measures are (1) wage–price controls and (2) economic planning.

Wage–Price Controls: Incomes Policies

One way in which government can try to deal with inflation is to impose wage and price controls. Measures of this type provide examples of what is known as *incomes policies.* These are laws aimed at curbing inflation by establishing conditions under which businesses' production costs (especially wages), prices, and profits may be allowed to increase. As you might expect, incomes policies in general, and wage–price controls in particular, are the subject of frequent debate.

Arguments Against Wage–Price Controls

Those who oppose government wage and price controls believe they have a number of undesirable effects:

Misallocation of Resources   Under a system of controls, resource and product prices are determined by governmental rules or orders. Buyers' and sellers' responses to the free-market forces of supply and demand are thus replaced by government edicts. The wage–price structure becomes frozen. This impairs the ability of producers to respond to changes in tastes and technology, as would happen if markets were unregulated. As a result, resources are misallocated and economic efficiency is impaired.

Reduction of Productivity   Controls put a lid on wages and prices, keeping them from rising to their free-market levels. This diminishes productivity in several ways. Among them:

1. Millions of working hours in government and industry are wasted on administering controls.

2. To the extent that wage increases are restrained, workers' incentives are reduced and employers are prevented from paying more for the high-quality workers that are wanted.

3. If ceilings are imposed on profit margins, as they were during some previous periods of control, businesses lose much of their incentive to improve efficiency. The reason is that profits above the ceiling are taxed at prohibitive rates. To keep profits below the ceiling, firms may use funds in frivolous ways — spending lavishly on advertising and promotion, buying corporate jets, providing generous expense accounts for executives, and so on.

Institutionalization of Inflation   Wage and price controls provide at best only a temporary palliative for inflation. They do not get at the root causes. Those causes are found, as you have already learned, primarily in monetary policies. But they are also found in the monopoly power wielded by large firms and trade unions and in government legislation that establishes minimum wages, subsidies, tariffs, and import quotas. These restrictive elements interfere with the effective functioning of a free market. Therefore, public policy should be directed toward eliminating them in order to help achieve price stability.

The Case for Controls

On the other side of the fence, most advocates of wage and price controls are generally sympathetic with the competitive market philosophy. However, they believe that the inflationary bias has become entrenched by our failure to reduce the power of monopolistic elements, represented by large corporations and unions, within the economy. As a result, they believe, it is unrealistic to assume that these elements, which are now deeply embedded, will ever be significantly reduced. Therefore, the choice is not between free markets or public controls; it is between free markets and *some degree* of public controls. As many advocates of controls contend:

> Less than half the economy's private sector is responsive to reasonably competitive market forces. Within the remainder of the private sector, prices are essentially set by the great corporations. It follows that public controls can be confined to the less competitive segment, where market power is greatest. They are not needed in the more competitive segment, where the market still functions.

As it happens, there is no strong evidence to support this point of view. As a result, critics have proposed other approaches—among them economic planning—as a way of reducing unemployment and inflation.

Economic Planning

Another method of trying to cope with unemployment and inflation is economic planning. It may be—and often is—employed in conjunction with wage–price controls. Hence, the two approaches should not necessarily be thought of as mutually exclusive.

> An ***economic plan*** is a detailed method, formulated beforehand, for achieving specific economic objectives. The plan governs the activities and interrelations of those economic institutions—firms, households, and governments—that have an influence on the desired outcome.

To repeat, the purpose of economic planning is to achieve certain objectives. Those who advocate national economic planning believe that a federal agency should be established to perform the task—both for government activities and for the private sector's actions. The government planning board would thus be directly involved in dealing with the three fundamental questions of every economic system. These questions, you recall, are *what* to produce, *how* to produce, and *for whom*.

As you would expect, there is much controversy over the desirability of planning. Proponents contend that the government's central planning board would act purely in an *advisory* capacity to major industries and government agencies. The board would merely point out long-run goals or targets and suggest how they might be realized. Opponents of planning disagree strongly. They offer such arguments as the following:

– Planning would create a new federal bureaucracy to administer economic activity. The free market—and with it consumer sovereignty—would be replaced by governmental authority and coercion.

– The government's planning office might come to be dominated by special interests—perhaps by the major corporations whose activities are planned. This possibility is evidenced by the fact that many government regulatory agencies have long been influenced by the industries that are regulated. Collaboration and collusion between big business and government might thus be promoted rather than discouraged.

– There is no evidence that government is more adept at planning than private industry is. On the other hand, there is considerable evidence, based on experiences in some mixed economies, that government involvement in economic planning may seriously impair economic efficiency, price stability, and growth.

For these and other reasons, controversies over economic planning arise from time to time, especially during periods of rapid inflation and/or high unemployment. As a result, you are likely to read and hear about the issues in the news media.

Economics in the News

UC Students Outdo Reagan Experts on Economy

By Carla Marinucci

BERKELEY—If Ronald Reagan, Congress and the Federal Reserve Bank would step aside, the national economy might be run better by a group of first-year economics students at the University of California at Berkeley.

Using a computer model that let them play at running economic policy, the 330 students collectively were able to significantly lower taxes, cut the federal deficit, reduce unemployment and still maintain government services.

Why were students able to make substantial improvements with serious problems that are still dogging Reagan and Co.?

"It is a reasonable question," concedes Jeff Frankle, senior staff economist with the President's Council of Economic Advisers in Washington, D.C. "Part of the answer is that the world is always easier in models than in reality."

"The fact that a group of college students taking their first course in macroeconomics on the average did better than Ronald Reagan, Fed Chairman Paul Volcker, and the Congress is amusing—if not politically significant," said William Dickens, the assistant professor of economics who developed the experiment.

Dickens designed the complex computer model so that if the class had made the same policy decisions as President Reagan and other leaders, the model would have produced the same results as the real economy did from 1981–83, the period the class studied.

Students were split up in 15 teams, each one developing tax rates, levels of government spending, and money supply growth rates.

The surprising contrasts between the outcomes resulted from their different approaches to managing the economy. While the students' major priority was to lower unemployment, the Reagan administration concentrated first on cutting inflation, Dickens said.

The study showed that if the nation's economy had been run by the Cal students, there would have been a nearly 2 percent drop in unemployment, a trimming of the federal deficit by $60 billion, and an almost 3 percent increase in the gross national product.

The students' policies would have raised business investment by 7.5 percent, and increased housing investment by 9.5 percent. . . . Americans would have had $176 more each in personal income to spend—the result of lower taxes.

For all this improvement, the nation would have seen "a small increase" in inflation, about 2.3 percent annually, Dickens said.

Economist Frankle said that Cal students didn't have to contend with the key factor that greatly influences the nation's top economic decision makers—politics.

Students "may decide to do things, like cutting government spending, that may not be politically feasible," he said. The nation's top economic advisers "aren't always free to do what they would like."

But Dickens said that, if anything, his economic model "leans toward the conservative monetarist view" and was based on the most widely held belief about how the economy operates.

"During the time when the students were running the economy, they did much better than I expected," he said. "Not a single section of my class came up with higher unemployment than Reagan did."

Collin Cooper, a 19-year-old Cal economics major who worked on the model, said, "Yeah, it was great to do better than Reagan. But one thing we really learned was that you can't manipulate the economy."

"Our feeling was that it was better to have a job and higher prices, than have no job at all and lower prices," said Cooper.

How Reagan, Students Did

Area of economy	Reagan/Volcker	UC students
Unemployment	10.02%	7.99%
Gross Nat'l. Product (in current dollars)	$3,121 billion	$3,185 billion
Business investment (in current dollars)	$348.8 billion	$374.6 billion
Housing investment	$102.3 billion	$111.7 billion
Federal deficit	$124 billion	$82 billion
Inflation (median)	4.78%	7.11%

Examiner chart

The San Francisco Examiner, May 31, 1984.

Conclusion: Economics, Politics, and Rationality

Stagflation has been a recurring macroeconomic problem. To help overcome it, numerous policy proposals have been made. Those explained in this chapter are among the most important.

Most of these proposals have been tried, in varying degrees, during recent history. For example, since the early 1970s the nation has experimented with wage–price controls, wage-and-price guidelines, tax reduction, public-employment schemes, employment-training policies, and economic planning. These programs usually attack the symptoms of stagflation rather than the cause.

Stagflation is caused mainly by improper fiscal and monetary policies and by insufficient incentives to produce. These conditions lead to greater economic uncertainty, reduced private investment, and slower economic growth. Therefore, policies that fail to recognize the real causes of stagflation will not be successful in curing it.

Today these beliefs are held by practically all informed observers. But, unfortunately, there is no consistent agreement on what constitutes the "right" fiscal-monetary mix or the "right" combination of incentives. However, there is substantial agreement that, at the very least, a reasonably steady expansion of the money supply and a continuous reduction in budget deficits are necessary to promote greater long-run stability.

Despite this understanding, it is characteristic of our type of democracy that political considerations often outweigh economic logic. Few political leaders are willing to risk their careers on policies designed to curb inflation at the cost of increased joblessness. Consequently, policy makers have often found that budget deficits accompanied by rapid monetary expansion is an expedient short-term means of combatting unemployment.

Until Congress develops some rational rules for relating government spending to revenues, large deficits and erratic fluctuations in the money supply will continue to plague the economy.

What You Have Learned

1. Economists have observed a statistical relationship between unemployment and inflation. The relationship, expressed by a Phillips curve, is inverse.

2. There may be a limited trade-off between unemployment and inflation. If so, the Phillips curve will be downward sloping. However, evidence shows that the long-run Phillips curve is relatively steep. Therefore, the trade-off is quite costly in that small reductions in the unemployment rate are achieved at the expense of large increases in the inflation rate.

3. New-classical economists believe that the main cause of shifts in the Phillips curve is changes in aggregate demand brought about by erratic monetary policy. Keynesians believe that shifts in aggregate supply, caused by changes in fiscal policy and fluctuating resource costs, are also important in affecting the Phillips curve.

4. To the extent that the economy is self-correcting, recessionary and inflationary gaps exert pressures that cause the economy to adjust *automatically* to its natural (full-employment) rate. New-classical economists believe that the adjustment always occurs quickly. Keynesians believe that the adjustment may often occur slowly.

5. Supply-side economics emphasizes the adoption of government policies aimed at stimulating production and investment. Examples of such policies are reductions in marginal tax rates, nonmonetization of government deficits, and deregulation of industries and markets.

6. Economists have proposed a number of market measures for curing stagflation. Among them:

   (a) *Fiscal and monetary policies*. These seek to stabilize the growth of the money supply and also help establish closer ties among government tax revenues, government spending, and the nation's income.
   (b) *Employment programs*. These are comprehensive policies designed to promote the employment of the unemployed and the training of people for higher-paying jobs.
   (c) *Productivity improvement*. These are measures designed to stimulate investment in physical and human capital.

7. In addition to the market measures for curing stagflation, some observers have proposed two major nonmarket policies:

   (a) *Wage–price controls: incomes policies*. These are laws aimed at curbing inflation by establishing limits within which businesses' production costs, prices, and profits may be allowed to increase.

(b) *Economic planning.* This is a program for achieving specific economic goals through a comprehensive plan that embraces the activities of households, firms, and government.

8. Nearly all of the foregoing proposals have been tried in varying degrees since the early 1970s. However, because stagflation is fundamentally caused by an improper mix of government fiscal and monetary policies, these are the activities that must ultimately be modified. Otherwise, any other measures can yield only temporary benefits at best and may even be harmful in the long run.

Terms and Concepts to Review

Phillips curve	crowding out
natural unemployment	depreciation
rate	money-supply rule
long-run Phillips curve	employment-training
demand-side economics	policies
supply-side economics	incomes policies
Laffer curve	economic plan

For Discussion

1. "Phillips curves are Phillips curves, regardless of whether they are short-run or long-run." Do you agree?

2. What legislative and fiscal actions can you recommend to *improve* the economy's Phillips curve? Before answering, explain precisely what is meant by "improve."

3. If everyone had complete knowledge of market prices and if labor were perfectly mobile, what would the short-run Phillips curve look like?

4. Many economists want to limit government spending by tying it to some percentage of tax revenues. For example, spending might be limited to, say, 103 percent of tax revenues. (a) What is the reason for allowing spending to exceed revenues? (b) Why not set the figure at 100 percent or even less? (c) Can we limit government spending by putting a ceiling on taxes?

5. Tax reduction is often seen as a device to stimulate demand. But it can also stimulate supply. Can you explain how?

6. "Indexation of the income tax and of government bonds would lower the Treasury's tax revenues. This reduction in the benefits that government receives from inflation would stimulate incentives to curb inflation." Explain this statement. How does government benefit from inflation? (Before answering this question, look up the meaning of **indexation** in the Dictionary at the back of the book.)

7. (a) Can you give at least two arguments against indexation and (b) two rebuttals in favor? (c) What are your conclusions?

8. How would the position or location of our economy's short-run Phillips curve be affected by each of the following? Explain your answers.

(a) A reduction in tariffs.

(b) A decrease in import quotas.

(c) A new law making labor unions illegal.

(d) A merger of the largest firm in each major industry (for example, automobiles, oil refining, and so on) with the second largest firm in its industry.

(e) A new law prohibiting any firm's sales from exceeding 50 percent of its industry's sales.

(f) Significant advances made in automation throughout most of industry.

9. Some people contend: "Inflation promotes growth and diminishes unemployment. We must recognize that the costs of inflaton are much less than the costs of avoiding it. Therefore, we should accept inflaton and learn to live with it. This can be done by recognizing that it is easier to compensate the victims of inflation than the casualties of recession." What specific compensatory measures can you propose to make inflation less painful and less inequitable? Discuss.

Economics in the News

A Theory of Deficits

Some economists have worked out a theory which attempts to find the optimal combination of deficits and taxation necessary to finance a given pattern of government spending plans. The theory of optimal deficits rests on two pillars: first, the proposition that government debt is neutral, and second, the theory of efficient taxation.

Debt Neutrality

The proposition that debt is neutral recognizes that government spending must be paid for and suggests that government debt is nothing more than a means of substituting future taxation for current taxation. If people are rational, they realize that real deficits today imply higher taxes in the future. Knowing that higher future taxes will reduce their future after-tax income, people will save more when there is a deficit to maintain a constant level of consumption. In other words, people base their consumption plans on the present value of their after-tax income. Suppose the government were to reduce taxes by $1 billion today, issue a bond (that is, run a deficit) worth $1 billion bearing an interest rate of, say, 6 percent, and announce that it will raise taxes by $1.06 billion next year to pay the debt plus interest. Then rational taxpayers would save the $1 billion from the deficit caused by the tax cut, invest it in a bond earning 6 percent, and use the principal and interest from the bond to pay off the tax increase in the following year. By acting in this way, they are better off than not saving the $1 billion today and having to consume $1.6 billion less the next year when taxes are raised. Deficits (surpluses) raise (reduce) savings, dollar for dollar, according to the theory of debt neutrality.

When debt is neutral, deficits do not raise interest rates, crowd out borrowers, reduce investment, appreciate the dollar on foreign exchange markets, or cause inflation, because deficits automatically generate enough extra savings to fund the deficit.

Principles of Efficient Taxation

Deficits redistribute the tax burden from year to year. But is there a unique pattern of taxes better than any other? If all taxes were lump-sum (fixed amounts) in nature, then as long as debt is neutral it would not matter how or when the government ran deficits. But what if taxes are not lump-sum, but instead are proportional to income? This is where the theory of efficient taxation plays a role. As long as debt is neutral, the only consideration necessary in setting the level of deficits is the goal of minimizing the deadweight loss due to taxation. Efficient taxation requires that tax rates be set so that they are *expected* to remain constant, given forecasts of future GNP and government spending. If new information is obtained, the tax rate must be revised to reflect the new information. The new tax rate must be set such that, once again, the expected tax remains constant in the future. (More technically, the tax rate follows a random walk.) If tax rates are set efficiently, then the deficits that result are "efficient" deficits.

From Brian Horrigan, "Sizing Up the Deficit: An Efficient Tax Perspective," *Business Review,* Federal Reserve Bank of Philadelphia, May/June 1984.

Chapter 17

The Open Economy: International Trade

Learning Guide

Watch for answers to these important questions

Why do nations trade?

What is meant by "comparative advantage"? How do a country's terms of trade differ from its gains from trade?

What is the foreign-trade multiplier? How is it affected by the marginal propensity to save? The marginal propensity to import?

How are import quotas and tariffs used to restrain trade? What are their consequences?

What arguments are commonly heard in defense of import protection? Are these arguments valid?

The study of economics would be incomplete without an understanding of our nation's role in the world economy. Until now we have neglected this consideration by assuming that ours is a "closed" economy, insulated from the economies of other nations. It is time to broaden this outlook by recognizing that we live in an "open" economy. This means that many of our nation's economic actions affect other countries and are affected by them.

The study of the world economy is known as "international economics." It is one of the oldest branches of economics. As you will recall from your study of history, many wars have been fought over international economic issues.

International economics embraces two broad areas of interest:

1. International trade — the commerce of nations.
2. International finance — the payments of nations.

This chapter surveys the major economic principles and ideas underlying international trade. It then shows you how to apply these concepts to analyze and interpret many practical international economic problems. These problems, you will find, are the kinds you read and hear about almost every day in the news media.

Why Trade?

World trade has been gaining increasing significance among nations. You can see the growing importance of trade for the United States by noting the trend shown in Exhibit 1.

The graph shows that, until the 1960s, the dollar sum of U.S. imports and exports was less than 10 percent of GNP. By 1970 the proportion had climbed to more than 12 percent. Within a decade the figure approximately doubled, reaching 25 percent in 1980. During the 1990s, according to some experts, the proportion will range between 30 and 40 percent. And after the year 2000, it may be even greater. These sharp increases reflect the growing economic interdependence between the United States and other countries.

Why do nations trade? Why, for example, does not the United States produce all of the cars, motorcycles, electronic goods, and cameras that it wants so that Americans would not have to buy these products from Japan? In return, why does not Japan produce all of the food, machinery, transportation equipment, and chemicals that it wants so that the Japanese would not have to buy these goods from the United States?

Exhibit 1
The U.S. Economy and Foreign Trade

International trade has assumed an increasingly important role in the economy of the United States in recent decades. The sum of imports and exports as a percentage of GNP will probably continued to grow in future years.

What the U.S. Buys		What the U.S. Sells	
	1984		1984
Major products imported by the U.S.		*Major products exported by the U.S.*	
Oil and gas	$62 billion	Machinery	$41 billion
Machinery	41	Grain and cereal	16
Automobiles	30	Office equipment	15
Telecommunications	16	Aircraft	11
Clothes	15	Chemicals	10
Office equipment	11	Professional tools	10
Iron and steel	11	Soybeans	6
Chemicals	8	Automobiles	5
Metal goods	6	Coal	5
Paper	6	Synthetics, plastics	4
Total	$206 billion	**Total**	$127 billion

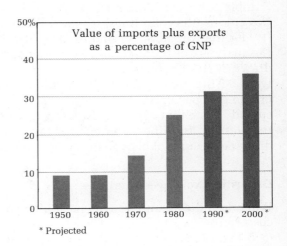

Value of imports plus exports as a percentage of GNP

* Projected

Source: U.S. Department of Commerce.

The answer is that nations have different quantities and qualities of economic resources and different ways of combining them. As a result, each country can produce certain goods more efficiently, or at relatively lower costs, than others.

This idea can be stated somewhat differently. Imagine a world consisting of only two countries, each producing the same two goods. Under such circumstances, the alternative or **opportunity cost** to each country of producing more of one good is the amount of the second good that must be sacrificed. In view of this, which of the two goods should the countries produce?

The answer is that each should **specialize.** How? By producing the good with the lower opportunity cost and trading with the other country for the good with the higher opportunity cost. In that way, the combined output of both goods will actually be larger, and each country will get more of them than it would if it tried to be self-sufficient by producing both.

Specialization and Trade

These concepts can be illustrated by an example. Exhibit 2 shows hypothetical production-possibilities curves (the solid lines) for meat (M) and wine (W) for the United States and France. To simplify the analysis, the production-possibilities curves are drawn as straight lines instead of being bowed outward. This means that *constant* rather than increasing opportunity costs of production are assumed. Note that opportunity cost is measured by the *slope* of the line—the change in the vertical distance per unit of change in the horizontal.

Domestic-Exchange Equations

What does the assumption of constant opportunity costs imply?

In Figure *(a)*, any point along the United States' production-possibilities curve reveals a different output combination of meat and wine. For instance, point A denotes an output of 60M and 0W; point B, an output of 40M and 10W; point C, an output of 20M and 20W; and point D, an output of 0M and 30W. In general, at any point along its production-possibilities curve, the United States must sacrifice meat for wine at the rate of 20M to 10W. This is equivalent to a rate of 2M to 1W. The opportunity cost of the two products is therefore 2$M = 1W$.

In Figure *(b)*, on the other hand, France's production-possibilities curve reveals a different opportunity cost for the two products. For example, in order to go from point E to point F, France must sacrifice 10 units of meat to gain 30 units of wine. Similarly, a movement from F to G entails sacrificing another 10M for an additional 30W. In order to go from G to H, the sacrifice is again the same. Therefore, the rate of sacrifice in France is 10M to 30W. This is the same, of course, as a rate of 1M to 3W, or ⅓M to 1W. The opportunity cost of the two products is therefore ⅓$M = 1W$.

Opportunity costs in the United States and France thus determine each country's domestic-exchange equation. The equation expresses each country's opportunity costs—the rate at which either commodity can be "exchanged" for the other. The two equations are therefore:

United States:
    $2M = 1W$ or equivalently $1M = \frac{1}{2}W$

France:
    $\frac{1}{3}M = 1W$ or equivalently $1M = 3W$

You can now see two facts that are evident from these equations:

1. Wine is more expensive in the United States than in France. In the United States, it costs 2M to acquire 1W whereas in France it costs only ⅓M to acquire 1W.

2. Meat is less expensive in the United States than in France. In the United States, 1M can be acquired for only ½W, whereas in France 1M can be acquired only at the higher cost of 3W.

Exhibit 2
Production and Trading Possibilities: Terms of Trade and Gains from Trade

For each country, the opportunity cost (or domestic-exchange equation) for meat and wine is represented by the slope of the production-possibilities curve. The **terms of trade,** on the other hand, are represented by the slope of the trade-possibilities curve. Each country, by specializing in production of the good with the lowest opportunity cost and then trading, can end up with more of both goods than it would if it produced them both itself.

For example, suppose that each country tried to be self-sufficient. In Figure (a), the United States might produce a combination of meat and wine represented by point C. In Figure (b), France might produce a com-

bination shown by point F. By specializing and trading, however, the United States could end up with the products at point I, and France with those at point J. The net benefit or increase in consumption for each country thus represents its **gains from trade.** These are shown by the shaded areas. Thus, for the United States, the gains are 10 units of meat and 10 units of wine. For France, the gains are 10 units of meat and 30 units of wine.

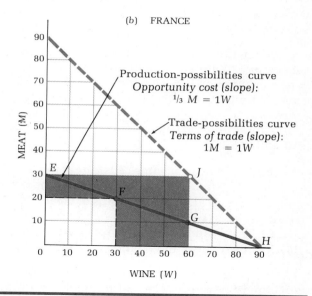

Because of these cost relationships, it can be said that France has a comparative advantage in wine production and that the United States has a comparative advantage in meat production.

That is:

Given any two products, a country has a *comparative advantage* in the product with the lower opportunity cost.

Specialization and the Gains from Trade

If the two countries were self-sufficient, each would produce its own meat and wine. The amounts produced in each country would depend on consumer preferences as reflected through the price system. For example, the United States might produce at point *C*, representing 20 units of meat and 20 units of wine. France, on the other hand, might produce at point *F*, representing 20 units of meat and 30 units of wine.

Suppose, however, that each country were to specialize by producing the product in which it has a comparative advantage and then were to trade with the other. In that case, the United States would allocate all of its resources to meat and none to wine, producing at point *A* (60M and 0W). Likewise, France would allocate all of its resources to wine and none to meat, producing at point *H* (90W and 0M). By trading, each country could then end up with more meat and more wine, as represented perhaps by points *I* and *J*.

Thus:

— At point *I*, the United States consumes 30 units of meat and 30 units of wine. This is greater than the consumption level at point *C* (20 units of meat and 20 units of wine), which existed before trade was undertaken. For the United States, therefore, the *gains from trade* are 10 units of meat and 10 units of wine.

— At point *J*, France consumes 30 units of meat and 60 units of wine. This is greater than the consumption level at point *F* (20 units of meat and 30 units of wine), which existed before trading began. For France, the *gains from trade* amount to 10 units of meat and 30 units of wine.

In other words, through specialization and trade, the United States produces 60 units of meat and France produces 90 units of wine. The United States then exports 30 units of meat to France, and France exports 30 units of wine to the United States. As a result, both countries end up with more meat and more wine than they would if each tried to be self-sufficient in both products.

Summarizing:

By specializing in the good in which it has a comparative advantage, each nation is able to produce enough of the good so that it can exchange some of it for the other. Both nations thus obtain **gains from trade**. These are the net benefits or increases in goods that a country receives as a result of trading with others.

Comparative Advantage

You can now appreciate the meaning of the familiar expression, "it pays to specialize." This idea refers to the *relative* benefit of producing one good instead of another. The concept can be expressed as a law — one of the oldest in economics.

Law of Comparative Advantage A basis for trade exists when each of two nations, both capable of producing the same two goods, specializes in producing the one that is *relatively* cheaper for it to produce. This is the good in which the country has a lower opportunity cost — a comparative advantage. The two countries can then have more of both goods by engaging in trade. This is a general principle applicable not only to nations but also to regions and even to individuals.

The law of comparative advantage accounts for the benefits that nations receive from engaging in trade. Therefore, as you will see shortly, the law also accounts for the costs that nations incur when they erect barriers to trade.

Terms of Trade

When two parties engage in a transaction, the sacrifice that each makes to obtain something from the other is called the "terms of trade." For example, in order to buy this textbook, you might have had to give up five visits to the movies. Your terms of trade, therefore, are 5 movies = 1 book. On the other hand, if you bought four fewer pizzas in order to accumulate enough money to purchase this book, your terms of trade are 4 pizzas = 1 book. The **terms of trade** for a given transaction equal the number of units of goods that must be given up for one unit of goods received by each party to the transaction.

Using these ideas, what are the terms of trade for meat and wine between the United States and France? To begin with, you have already learned that the domestic exchange equations are:

$$\text{United States:} \quad 2M = 1W$$
$$\text{France:} \quad \tfrac{1}{3}M = 1W$$

In Exhibit 2, of course, these equations simply represent the *slopes* of the production-possibilities curves (solid lines). They express the sacrifice of one good for the other that each country incurs if it chooses to produce both commodities.

On the other hand, the terms of trade (dashed lines) express the actual exchange rate between the two countries' goods. The *slopes* of the lines for both countries, as you can see from the figures, are given by $1M = 1W$. These lines may therefore be called **trade-possibilities curves.**

Limits of the Terms of Trade

Keeping these facts in mind, you can now see the importance of the following proposition and the examples illustrating it:

The terms of trade must fall somewhere between the two domestic-exchange equations, or slopes, in order for both countries to experience gains from trade. Otherwise, one of the countries will not find it advantageous to trade.

Two examples illustrate why this is true.

Example 1 Suppose the terms of trade are $3M = 1W$. Trade would then be advantageous to France but not to the United States. Why? Because, by specializing and trading, France could import 3 units of meat in return for exporting 1 unit of wine. This is a better value than obtaining only ⅓ unit of meat for 1 unit of wine by producing both commodities domestically.

The United States, on the other hand, would have to export 3 units of meat in order to import 1 unit of wine. This is more expensive than producing both commodities domestically at a cost of only 2 units of meat for 1 unit of wine.

Example 2 Suppose the terms of trade are ⅓$M = 1W$. In that case, trade would be advantageous to the United States but not to France. The United States, by specializing and trading, could export ⅓ unit of meat in order to import 1 unit of wine. This is cheaper than producing both products domestically at a cost of 2 units of meat for 1 unit of wine.

France, however, would have to export 1 unit of wine in order to import ⅓ unit of meat. This is not as good a value as producing both commodities domestically at a cost of 1 unit of wine for ⅓ unit of meat.

Thus, international trade will not occur in either of these examples because only one country would experience gains from trade. However, if the terms of trade fall *between* the two domestic-exchange equations, as does $1M = 1W$, trade will occur because both countries will be able to realize gains.

What determines the terms of trade? In general:

The terms of trade for nations' goods are determined in world markets by international forces of supply and demand. The larger the overall global demand for a product relative to its supply, the higher its price — or terms of trade — in relation to other goods. Conversely, the smaller the overall global demand for a good, the lower its price — or terms of trade — relative to other goods. However, *the terms of trade must lie within the range of the nations' domestic-exchange equations in order for trade to occur.*

Increasing Costs and Incomplete Specialization

You can see from the foregoing analysis why nations find it profitable to trade. *A basis for trade exists when there are differences in opportunity costs between countries.* Thus, with respect to the United States and France, the difference in the opportunity costs of producing meat and wine reflects the different slopes of their production-possibilities curves.

In view of this, what would happen if the curves bowed outward? This, as you will recall from your first study of production-possibilities curves near the beginning of the book, is the typical situation. It means that costs are *increasing* rather than constant because resources are not perfectly substitutable between alternative uses.

In other words, as each country expands production of its specialty, its opportunity cost (sacrifice) in terms of the alternative good rises. A point can eventually be reached at which the two opportunity costs are equal. When that happens, the basis for trade, and hence the need for further specialization, is eliminated. Thus:

When increasing costs result in equal opportunity costs between countries, there are two effects:

1. *Incomplete specialization.* Both countries stop short of complete specialization because further increases in specialization cease to be economic.

2. *Reduced trade.* Each country continues to produce both products—its specialty as well as some of its nonspecialty. Although trade is still carried on, its total volume is less than it would be if costs were constant.

The Foreign-Trade Multiplier

International trade can therefore affect the level of a nation's income and employment. Indeed, international trade can have a *multiplier* effect on these variables. It will help you to see why if you refresh your understanding of some fundamental concepts.

First, recall from your earlier study of macroeconomic equilibrium the meanings of the terms "injections" and "withdrawals." These ideas, you will remember, were illustrated with a model called the **"bathtub theorem."** The model is reproduced in Exhibit 3, but the inflows and outflows are now represented by export income and import payments.

Summarizing the concepts briefly:

— *Injections* are expenditures that expand the nation's circular flow of income, thus raising the level of water in the tub. Examples are investment spending, government spending, and exports (that is, foreign spending for domestic goods).

— *Withdrawals* are "leakages" that contract the nation's circular flow of income, thus lowering the level of water in the tub. Examples are saving, taxes, and imports (that is, domestic spending for foreign goods).

Second, a distinction must be made between "closed" and "open" economies. A closed economy is one that is not engaged in international trade. This is the type of economy that occupies our attention throughout most of macroeconomics. In contrast, an open economy is one that is engaged in international trade. This is the type of economy that concerns us in this chapter.

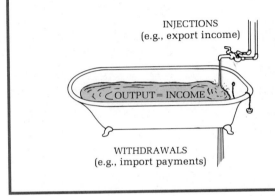

Exhibit 3
Injections and Withdrawals: The "Bathtub Theorem" in an Open Economy

Exports may be thought of as an injection into the income stream; imports may be thought of as a withdrawal. Hence, the water in the bathtub can be in equilibrium at *any* level as long as the inflow equals the outflow. If the inflow exceeds the outflow, the level in the tub will rise. If the outflow exceeds the inflow, the level in the tub will fall.

Open-Economy Model

Against this background, how does international trade affect the level of a nation's income and employment? It will be easier to answer this question if we simplify it. We can do this by making two assumptions about the determinants of a nation's imports (M) and exports (X).

1. *Imports depend on the level of income.* As the nation's income increases, so do domestic expenditures on imports of foreign cars, electronics products, steel, and other goods. We can thus define the **marginal propensity to import,** MPM, as the change in imports resulting from a unit change in income:

$$MPM = \frac{\text{change in imports}}{\text{change in income}}$$

The MPM *is thus the fraction of each additional dollar of income that is spent on imports.*

2. *Exports* are independent of the domestic level of income. That is, the dollar volume of exports is assumed to depend on the level of income in the importing country, not the exporting one.

The difference between a country's total exports and its total imports is its *net exports (X_N)*. Thus:

$$X_N = X - M$$

Obviously, X_N may be positive, zero, or negative, according to whether the country's total exports are greater than, equal to, or less than its total imports.

Three Possibilities for Net Exports

With these ideas in mind, take a look at Exhibit 4. The AE_0 curve represents aggregate expenditure in a closed economy. Note that the intersection of AE_0 with aggregate output, AO, determines an equilibrium level of real GNP at $600 billion.

If the economy is now opened to trade, one of three possibilities may occur:

1. Neutral Effect: Net Exports Equal Zero ($X_N = 0$) and GNP Does Not Change   If exports equal imports, net exports are zero. This signifies that the export "injection" into the economy's circular flow

---

Exhibit 4

Aggregate Expenditure and the Foreign-Trade Multiplier

An open economy engages in international trade. Therefore, its aggregate expenditure, AE, curves are not as steep as the AE_0 curve for a closed economy. The reason is that, in an open economy, a part of each increase in income is spent on imports instead of on domestic goods. Therefore, the MPC is lower.

The lower MPC (and, thus, the higher MPS) reduces the size of the multiplier, as explained in the text.

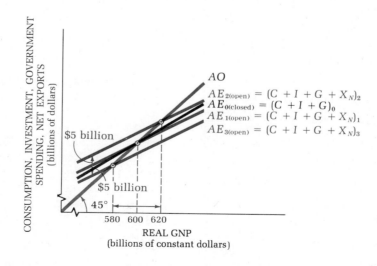

of income has been exactly offset by the import "withdrawal" or "leakage." In terms of the bathtub theorem, therefore, the level of water in the tub, representing GNP, remains the same.

The aggregate expenditure curve, AE_0, may shift to AE_1. This new curve is less steep than the previous one because the AE_1 curve reflects the fact that some goods are now being purchased from abroad. Therefore, the slope or MPC of AE_1—the expenditure on *domestically* produced goods—is smaller. This is because *part of each increase in income is spent on imports rather than on domestic goods.* Thus, spending on imports or foreign GNP is assumed to be a substitute for spending on domestic GNP.

2. Expansionary Effect: Net Exports are Positive ($X_N > 0$) and GNP Rises   If exports are larger than imports, net exports are positive. This causes the aggregate expenditure curve to rise, say, to AE_2, signifying an "injection" into the nation's circular flow of income. In terms of the bathtub theorem, the water (GNP) in the tub rises to a new and higher level.

3. Contractionary Effect: Net Exports are Negative ($X_N < 0$) and GNP Falls   If exports are less than imports, net exports are negative. This causes the aggregate expenditure curve to decline, perhaps to AE_3, signifying a "withdrawal" or "leakage" from the nation's circular flow of income. Therefore, the level of water (GNP) in the tub declines.

Summarizing:

International trade may have a neutral, expansionary, or contractionary effect on an economy's output and income. The effect of international trade on a country's GNP is neutral if net exports are zero, expansionary if net exports are positive, and contractionary if net exports are negative.

Multiplier Effect

If you look again at Exhibit 4, you can see how a change in net exports can have a multiplier effect on GNP. First, however, it will help you to review certain fundamental concepts concerning the multiplier principle that you learned when you first studied the notion of macroeconomic equilibrium in a closed economy.

Closed Economy   Assuming there are no taxes, how is an increase in society's income allocated? In a closed economy, you will recall, part of the increased income is spent on domestic goods and the rest of the increase is saved. Thus, $MPC + MPS = 1$. Further, the simple multiplier (also called the investment multiplier) equals the reciprocal of the MPS—that is, $1/MPS$. The MPS, of course, is the fraction of any increase in income that "leaks" into saving. Therefore, the multiplier may be thought of as the *reciprocal of the leakage.*

Open Economy   In contrast to a closed economy, an open economy (assuming again that there are no taxes) may allocate any increase in income to a third spending alternative—imports. Therefore, $MPC + MPS + MPM = 1$. The MPM is the fraction of any increase in income that "leaks" into imports. This suggests the existence of a foreign-trade multiplier, which, like the simple multiplier for a closed economy, is the *reciprocal of the leakage.* But the leakage now includes imports as well as saving. Thus:

$$\text{foreign-trade multiplier} = \frac{1}{MPS + MPM} = \frac{1}{\text{leakage}}$$

This means, for example, that, if the MPS is 0.20 and the MPM is 0.05, the total leakage is 0.25. Therefore, the foreign-trade multiplier is $1/0.25 = 4$. In contrast, the simple multiplier (for a closed economy) is $1/0.20 = 5$.

What do these numbers imply? In terms of Exhibit 4, a change in the open economy's aggregate expenditure curve of $5 billion, *whether due to a change in investment or to a change in net exports,* changes GNP by 4 times that amount, or by $20 billion. In a closed economy, on the other hand, the same change in aggregate expenditure (due, of course, to a change in investment) would have resulted in a change in GNP of $25 billion. The difference, as you have already learned, is due to a lower *MPC* in the open economy. This is because part of any increase in income is spent on imports, leaving a smaller portion to be spent on domestic goods.

To summarize:

The *foreign-trade multiplier* is a principle that states that fluctuations in net exports (= exports − imports) can generate magnified variations in aggregate income. In general, an increase in net exports tends to raise domestic income — the same as an increase in net investment expenditures would. But the increased income also induces some imports, or "leakages." These reduce the full multiplier effect on income that would exist if imports remained constant.

The Case for Free Trade

The study of international trade is one of the oldest branches of economics. Adam Smith, in *The Wealth of Nations*, devoted considerable attention to the subject.

Among the concepts Adam Smith emphasized was that each country has different quantities and qualities of resources. These differences enable each country to produce at least one low-cost product it can sell to others. It behooves nations to specialize in what they can produce most efficiently, and to engage in free (that is, unrestricted) trade. In that way, all countries can share in the gains from trade.

Absolute Advantage

This principle subsequently became known as the *law of absolute advantage.* It states that a basis for trade exists when one nation is more efficient than another in producing a good that the other wants. Each country can then specialize in producing the good it can produce most efficiently. By trading, nations can acquire one another's goods more cheaply than they can if they produce the same goods at home.

This law accounts for much of the world's trade. For example, Brazil has an absolute advantage over the United States in the production of coffee. However, the United States has an absolute advantage over Brazil in the production of computers. Therefore, Brazil finds it advantageous to specialize in coffee and the United States finds it advantageous to specialize in computers. By trading, Brazil gets computers more cheaply and the United States gets coffee more cheaply than if each produces both products itself.

Similar illustrations can be given with many other goods. For instance: French perfume and Arabian oil; Bolivian tin and Peruvian cotton; Florida oranges and Nebraska wheat. Can you think of other examples?

Comparative Advantage

But what if a country can produce *two* goods, such as meat and wine, more cheaply than another country? Is there still a basis for trade in those goods between the two countries? This question was asked by the English economist David Ricardo in *The Principles of Political Economy and Taxation* (1815). Ricardo's answer was *yes,* and his brilliant reasoning helped to establish him as the greatest of the classical economists.

Ricardo showed that, even if one country has an absolute advantage in the production of two products, it is the *relative* advantage — the *comparative* rather than absolute advantage — that counts. Ricardo proved this by demonstrating that it pays for each country to specialize in producing the good in which it has the greatest "degree" of advantage. The two countries can then trade for the alternative good.

The law of comparative advantage accounts for the logic of international trade, and it underlies the meat-and-wine example used earlier. Thus, because the United States had a comparative advantage in meat and France had one in wine, it paid for them to specialize and trade. More meat and wine were thereby consumed by the two countries than if each tried to produce both goods.

Can you think of similar illustrations for individuals? For example, if you were a doctor as well as an expert gardener, you might nevertheless employ a gardener who is less competent than yourself. Why? Because you could be more productive (and thus earn more income) as a doctor than as a gardener. Similarly, if you were a lawyer as well as a good typist, you would probably find it more profitable to hire a typist — even one who is less proficient than you.

Conclusion: The Argument for Free Trade

However, suppose a law prohibited you from hiring a gardener (or a typist), so that you were compelled to do the gardening (or typing) yourself. In that case, you would be less efficient as a doctor (or as a lawyer).

The same principle applies to countries. Through specialization and free or unrestricted trade, nations achieve a more efficient allocation of world resources. As a result, all nations end up with more goods, and hence with a higher standard of living, than if they imposed legislation restricting free trade.

The effect of free trade on nations is the same as the effect of increases in resources or improvements in technology. That is, the effect on nations is the same as if they experienced outward shifts of their production-possibilities curves. Thus, legislation that restricts free trade also reduces nations' standards of living.

Free Trade Versus Import Protection

You have just learned that the law of comparative advantage demonstrates a fundamental principle. *By engaging in free trade, nations make more efficient use of the world's scarce resources, thereby raising standards of living.*

This principle is universally acknowledged. Despite this fact, all nations impose import restrictions of one form or another to protect some of their domestic industries. The restrictions may be of several types:

Tariffs   These are customs duties or taxes imposed by a government on the importation of a good. Tariffs may be (1) specific, in the form of a tax per unit of the commodity, or (2) ad valorem, based on the value of the commodity.

Import Quotas   These are laws that limit the number of units of a commodity that may be imported during a specified period. An import quota (often simply referred to as a "quota") is thus an example of a nontariff barrier to free trade.

Nontariff Barriers   These are any laws or regulations, other than tariffs, that nations impose in order to restrict imports. For instance, to "protect the health and safety" of their citizens, many countries establish higher standards of quality for various kinds of imported goods than for similar goods produced domestically. Food products and automobiles provide typical examples. Nontariff barriers (other than import quotas) are direct but subtle protective devices that are never publicly stated as such. Hence they have become a major form of trade protection and are used to different degrees by nearly all countries.

Analyzing Quotas and Tariffs

The economic effects of quotas and tariffs can be examined more closely within the framework of a supply-and-demand model. Such a model is presented in Exhibit 5. To simplify the analysis, the model is based on two assumptions:

1. There are only two countries in the world, the United States and Britain.

2. Each country produces and consumes a product such as wool sweaters.

Exhibit 5
Quotas and Tariffs at Work

If there were no trade between the two countries, the market price of a sweater would be $90 in the United States and $30 in Britain.

But if unrestricted trade is permitted, the United States and British markets will automatically adjust to a *single* "world" price of $50 per sweater. At this price, the United States will import, and Britain will export, 400,000 sweaters. The two markets will be in equilibrium because there will be no excess quantities demanded or supplied—no "shortages" or "surpluses."

If the United States imposes an import quota of 200,000 sweaters, the price will rise to $70. Correspondingly, the price in Britain will decline to $40 in order that British exports of 200,000 sweaters precisely equal American imports. Thus, the two markets will again be in equilibrium, but not at a single world price.

The United States could achieve the same results by imposing a tariff of $30 per sweater. The U.S. price would then rise by $20 and the British price would decline by $10, resulting in a *price differential* of $30.

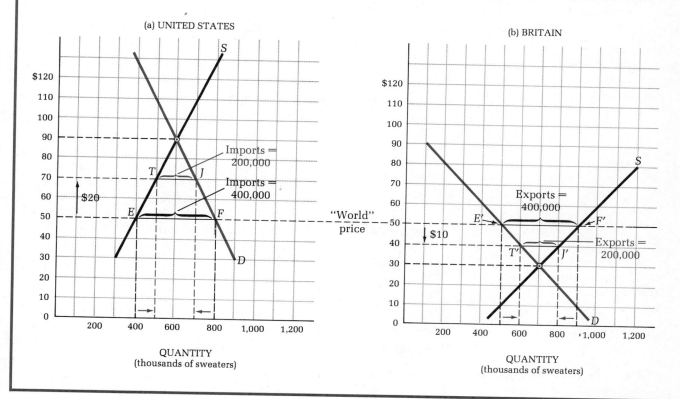

(a) UNITED STATES

(b) BRITAIN

QUANTITY
(thousands of sweaters)

Therefore, each country's supply and demand for the good is reflected by its own supply and demand curves.

What will be the "world" equilibrium price of wool sweaters under these circumstances? The answer is best understood if we first conduct the analysis under conditions of free trade and then under restricted trade.

Nontariff Barriers: When Is a Salami a Bologna?

In France, it is illegal to advertise whiskey and gin—allegedly because they are bad for the health. Without the pressures of advertising, the French tend to drink domestic wines and brandies instead of importing scotch and gin.

Similar restrictions on trade exist in other countries. The United States, for example, prohibits the importation of French candies—on the ground that their colorants are unsafe. Japan prohibits the exportation of calculators containing integrated circuits made in other countries. And the Netherlands prohibits exports of pharmaceuticals not manufactured by members of a Dutch trade association.

Especially interesting is the question: When is a sausage not a sausage? The not-so-simple answer is: When it is exported and bumps into another country's definition of a sausage. The definition may be expressed in terms of size, shape, casing, color, the mix of ingredients, and, in some instances, the number of links per string. Anything that does not conform to a particular country's definition of a sausage is ruled a nonsausage and may not be imported.

No less interesting are the difficulties involved in defining an importable cow. The classic nontariff barrier was a provision of a German tariff law of 1902. This granddaddy of nontariff barriers was designed to exclude Dutch and Russian cattle competitive with German types but to allow importation of Swiss cattle. It did so with a definition that gave an extra-low duty rate to *"large dappled mountain cattle or brown cattle reared at a spot 300 meters above sea level and which have at least one month's grazing at a spot at least 800 meters above sea level."*

The old German law, while not mentioning any country, achieved its aim with what amounted to a description of Swiss cattle-raising practices. Modern nontariff barriers, however, are not so diplomatic. The catalog of such barriers seems infinite, and as more is found out about them, almost every country, including the United States, is seen to be an offender.

Free Trade

If we assume that trade is unrestricted between the two countries, the world equilibrium price will settle at $50. The reason is that, *only* at this price, United States' excess quantity demanded EF (a "shortage") precisely equals Britain's excess quantity supplied E'F' (a "surplus"). To make up these differences, the United States imports, and Britain exports, 400 thousand sweaters. The world market is thus in equilibrium. At any other *single* world price, as you can easily verify, there can be no equilibrium, because a shortage in one country is not offset by a surplus in the other.

It is important to note how the $50 world price compares with the domestic price that would exist in each country if there were no trade. In the United States the domestic price would have been $90; in Britain it would have been $30.

Restricted Trade

Suppose the United States imposes a quota that limits the importation of sweaters to a maximum of 200,000. This will make the excess quantity demanded in the United States equal to TJ, at a price of $70 per sweater. The corresponding excess quantity supplied in Britain will be T'J', at a price of $40 per sweater. This means that the United States will import, and Britain will export, 200,000 sweaters. The two markets will thus be in equilibrium but at different prices.

What are the economic consequences of the quota? Some of the more important results may be noted:

1. The equilibrium price in the importing country is higher, and the equilibrium price in the exporting country is lower, than the single world equilibrium price that would result in the absence of quotas.

2. Both countries experience a decline in trade—in this example, 200,000 sweaters.

3. American producers benefit from the quota by increasing their production from 400,000 sweaters to 500,000. British consumers also ben-

efit by increasing their consumption from 500,000 sweaters to 600,000. Conversely, the quota penalizes American consumers by reducing their consumption from 800,000 sweaters to 700,000. It also penalizes British producers by reducing their production from 900,000 sweaters to 800,000.

4. The same results could have been achieved if the United States imposed a tariff of $30 per sweater. In order for American imports to equal British exports, the market price in the United States would rise to $70 and the market price in Britain would decline to $40. The *price differential* of $30, the amount of the tariff, would thus be shared by both countries.

These results suggest a surprising conclusion:

The economic consequences of import restrictions are to a large extent the same as those resulting from an *increase in transportation costs.* Such costs raise prices in the importing country and reduce the volume of goods consumed. Therefore, anyone who argues in favor of imposing a quota or tariff on a good in order to protect it from foreign competition should, in order to be logically consistent, also argue in favor of *increasing the cost of transporting the good.*

Visible and Invisible Effects

If the world's political leaders know that free trade leads to greater efficiency, why do they impose protective trade restrictions? The most common reason among many of the advanced countries is obvious: *In the industries affected, imports cause unemployment.* For example, the American automobile and steel industries, as well as their suppliers, have suffered substantial increases in unemployment due partly to the importation of foreign cars and steel.

But these are the visible effects. There are also invisible effects that rational policymaking must take into account.

1. Imports Create Jobs It is not usually obvious that imports provide a significant source of new jobs. These occur in those industries producing the exports that foreigners buy with the money earned from our imports. Some major American exporting industries include those producing various kinds of agricultural, mineral, fuel, chemical, and manufactured goods.

2. Protection Reduces Exports It follows that the volume of our exports suffers from import restrictions. By making it harder for foreigners to sell to us, we reduce their income and therefore their ability to buy our goods. As a result, although we may be reducing unemployment in our protected industries, we may also be increasing it in our exporting industries.

3. Protection Reduces Consumer Choice Import restrictions narrow the range of choices available to consumers. They are denied the privilege of purchasing what they believe is the best product for their money. Instead, they are required to pay higher prices either for similar products or for what they regard as less desirable products.

4. Protection Reduces Competition Import restrictions limit competition from foreign producers. This permits protected domestic industries to become less efficient and perhaps to gain more monopolistic control over their markets. It is interesting to note that, in the opinion of many experts, unrestricted trade is a far more effective means of promoting competition and efficiency than the federal antitrust (antimonopoly) laws designed for those purposes.

Unemployment and Trade-Adjustment Assistance

It is logical to conclude, therefore, that nations will experience the greatest gains from trade by engaging in free trade. In that way, countries will produce and exchange those goods in which there are the greatest comparative advantages.

What happens to American workers who become unemployed due to increased foreign competition? In most cases they become eligible for gov-

Stop Sign

An End to Auto Import Quotas

When it comes to world trade, temporary can mean a long time. Four years ago, Japanese automakers "voluntarily" agreed to limit exports to the U.S. . . . The restrictions, of course, were not really voluntary, since the Japanese firms acted only to stop the U.S. Congress from imposing even tougher controls. The restraints were twice extended for a year. . . .

The Japanese companies actually [did] well under the restrictions. Since they could export only a limited number of autos, they began shipping more expensive premium models rather than small economy ones. In addition, Japanese firms could raise prices on their small cars because they were often in short supply. If there were no restraints, one U.S. study said, the average Japanese car would have cost $1,300 less in 1984.

Thanks in part to less Japanese competition, Detroit's automakers climbed out of the grim trough of recession. They earned profits of $9.8 billion in 1984, vs. a loss of $4.2 billion in 1980. Last year the carmakers' sales rebounded to 7.9 million cars, vs. a paltry 5.7 million in 1982. In his announcement, the President complimented Detroit's automakers on their "improved performance." Allowing the Japanese controls to come off seemed to make no sense to most Detroit auto executives. Said Chrysler Chairman Lee Iacocca: "This is a sad day for America — for American workers and American jobs."

Time, March 11, 1985, copyright 1985, Time Inc. All rights reserved. Reprinted by permission from TIME.

ernmentally financed trade-adjustment assistance. This consists of extended unemployment compensation, job retraining programs, and moving allowances to help cover the costs of re-employment in distant locations. Unfortunately, the various assistance programs have frequently been poorly managed and inadequately funded. However, this is a criticism of governmental administrative failures, not of free trade.

Conclusion: Tariffs Preferred to Quotas

Despite the universally acknowledged benefits of unrestricted trade, it is likely that nations will always employ certain forms of protection. This is done for political as well as economic reasons. In democratic countries, it is also done because of enormous pressures exerted by special-interest groups that benefit from protection. That being the case, which type of protection is economically preferable — quotas or tariffs?

With respect to quotas, there are two facts to consider:

1. A quota limits the domestic availability of a good. This drives up its price, thus enhancing profits for domestic and foreign producers.

2. A quota requires importers to apply for government licenses. These are usually granted in proportion to the applicant's past sales (not to mention political connections) or some other arbitrary standard unrelated to costs, efficiency, or any other meaningful economic criterion.

With respect to tariffs, there are also two facts to consider:

1. A tariff is a tax on imports. This raises the price of a good and reduces quantity demanded. But a tariff does not discriminate against exporters, so the more efficient ones may still be able to penetrate the protected market.

2. A tariff yields tax revenues to the government. The benefits of these revenues are distributed in one form or another to various groups in society.

Because of these considerations, quotas are a socially worse form of import protection than tariffs.

Import quotas and tariffs both entail economic costs. Quotas stifle competition, create vested interests in quota allocation, and are discriminatory in their effects. Alternatively, tariffs distort relative prices, but nevertheless permit market forces to allocate society's resources. Thus, if some degree of trade protection is desired for whatever reason, the country would be better off with tariffs than with import quotas.

Arguments for Protection

The law of comparative advantage and the economic benefits of free trade have never been successfully refuted, despite many heroic attempts to do so. Nevertheless, efforts by special-interest groups to obtain import protection are common. American history is replete with long and eloquent pleas by business executives, union representatives, and political leaders contending that theirs is a "different" situation requiring special consideration. Most of these arguments for protection can be grouped into one of the following categories:

1. Infant-industry argument.
2. National-security argument.
3. Wage-protection argument.
4. Employment-protection argument.

You will see below that there are flaws in all these arguments. But before you read on, you should understand the following fundamental point:

We can sell abroad only if we buy abroad. When the U. S. imports from foreign countries, those countries earn thereby most of the dollars they need to purchase American exports. In general, *exports are the cost of trade and imports are the return from trade*, not the other way around. Over the long run, a nation must export (sacrifice goods) in order to import (acquire goods).

Infant-Industry Argument

Should a nation pass legislation to protect its growing "infant industries" from foreign competition?

An **infant industry** is an underdeveloped industry that may not be able to survive competition from abroad. The infant-industry argument for protection says that such industries should be shielded temporarily with high tariffs or quotas. The protection is needed until the industries develop technological efficiency and economies of scale that will enable them to compete with foreign industries.

This type of plea was the basis on which tariffs were established for a number of industries during the nineteenth and twentieth centuries. But economists have come to recognize three major points regarding this argument:

1. Tariffs or other protective devices become the vested interests of particular business and political groups. When that happens, protective measures become extremely difficult to eliminate.

2. Some protected industries never grow out of the "infant" stage. That is, they never become able to compete effectively with more mature industries in other countries.

3. An increase in tariffs or quotas results in higher prices to domestic consumers. Therefore, if an industry must be shielded from foreign competition, a subsidy would be more desirable because it tends to increase output as well as to reduce costs and prices. Moreover, a subsidy is visible and must be voted periodically by Congress. This makes it easier to eliminate when it has outlived its intended function.

National-Security Argument

Some years ago the chairman of the board of the U.S. Steel Corporation asked a congressional committee: "Can we be assured of the strong industrial base in steel we need for modern defense if one-quarter or more of the steel we require were imported from countries lying uncomfortably close to the Soviet Union?"

This quotation provides an illustration of the "national-security argument" for protection. The argument is based on the assumption that a nation should be as self-sufficient as possible in the production of goods needed for war and defense.

On the face of it, this plea for protection seems persuasive. On closer examination, however, the following criticisms become apparent:

1. It is primarily a military argument rather than an economic one. Therefore, it should be decided by the proper military experts without the distorting influence of people who have a direct business interest in the outcome. Those with a knowledge of economics can help by pointing out

Who Will Be the Sacrificial Lamb?

Despite all the economic arguments that can be presented in favor of free trade, many prominent people, including some business executives, labor leaders, and politicians, continue to plead for protection. For example:

"Are we now to tell the typical shoe worker, aged 50, that he must cheerfully surrender his job to a 12-year-old girl in Taiwan or a peasant working behind his cottage in Spain? Can we make him whole by offering him a course in bricklaying or bus driving? He will not buy it. And neither, we think, will the nation."

George O. Fecteau, President
United Shoe Workers of America

"Thousands of our members have become sacrificial lambs on the altar of foreign trade. The flood of foreign-made tires is being felt by our members in that segment of the rubber industry. If nothing is done to check this trend, thousands of tire plant jobs will be eliminated. We cannot and will not stand still for this. Our people don't want to hear ideological phrases of the learned economists' theories on free trade. What all our members really want is a steady job."

Peter Bommarito, President
United Rubber Workers

"South African ferrochrome producers, using predatory prices, are destroying producers in a drive to control U.S. supply of this critical material. Without import relief, there would then be nothing to prevent a South African ferrochrome cartel from extracting monopoly prices or withholding supply from U.S. steel producers and thus substantially disrupting this essential industry."

A. D. Gate
Committee of Producers of High Carbon
Ferrochrome, Washington, D.C.

the costs of protection in terms of resource misallocation and a reduced standard of living.

2. Many industries are important, in one way or another, to defense or national security and could qualify equally well for increased protection.

3. As pointed out in the discussion of the infant-industry argument, a subsidy is preferable to a tariff or quota if some form of shielding is necessary.

Wage-Protection Argument

Because wages in the United States are higher than in most other nations, some people argue that tariffs or quotas are needed to protect American workers from the products of cheap labor abroad. Three criticisms and qualifications of the wage-protection argument are particularly important:

"Comparative advantage [says] let each country produce what they make best and we have unlimited free trade and the end result is prices are cheaper and everybody's life is better.   There is one catch.   If the comparative advantage is that some countries work children, have no minimum wage, no 40-hour workweek, no other protections, no free unions, then obviously they have an advantage of exploitation and it should not be subsidized by the workers of this country.   In fact, it ought to be opposed."

Edmund G. Brown, Jr.
Former Governor, State of California

AP/Wide World Photo

1. As you know, labor is not the only resource entering into production.   It is a resource that is combined with varying quantities of capital and land.   Because of this, products may often be characterized as *labor-intensive*, *capital-intensive*, or *land-intensive*, depending on the relative proportions of resources that are employed in production.

2. Other things being equal, low-wage countries will have an advantage over high-wage countries *only* in trading products that are labor-intensive. These are goods for which wages are a relatively large proportion of total costs.   In such cases, high-wage countries may be better off not competing with low-wage countries in trading these products.

Economics in the News

U.S. Consumer Is Seen as Big Loser In New Restraints on Imported Steel

By Thomas F. O'Boyle

Economists call it protectionism, but U.S. consumers might wonder who is being protected. Now the Reagan administration has added the ailing domestic steel industry to its protected list.

Critics say that such protection, which begins this year and runs until 1990, effectively sanctions a global steel cartel—a network of trade restraints that will increase prices for U.S. consumers.

Consumers will see it in higher sticker prices for automobiles and appliances; businesses, in the raw steel they buy to fabricate myriad products. A preliminary Congressional Budget Office estimate predicts that steel prices will be about 7% higher over the five-year life of the restraints than they would be otherwise, which translates to about a $50 tax on the average car. The total cost to the economy is potentially enormous: The budget office puts the price tag at $18 billion over five years.

Under the relief plan, the U.S. steel market has been carved up, with each of seven large steelmaking nations getting an allocated slice of the pie. That, combined with an existing curb on Common Market steel and an informal commitment from the Canadians, will cut finished steel imports about 30% to a targeted 18.5% share of the U.S. market from the current 25.4% share.

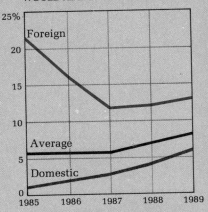

WHAT REAGAN'S TRADE POLICY WOULD ADD TO STEEL PRICES

Source: Congressional Budget Office estimates

3. Even where labor-intensive products are concerned, however, high-wage countries may be able to compete effectively with low-wage countries if labor productivity in the former is high enough to compensate for lower wage levels in the latter.

Employment-Protection Argument

Supporters of trade protection often argue that tariffs or quotas are desirable because they reduce imports. This leads to higher levels of production, employment, and income in domestic industries.

Is this a valid plea for protection? Like the previous arguments, it may seem persuasive, but the following considerations should be kept in mind:

1. Any benefits in the form of higher income and employment, if they occur, are not likely to last long. The history of tariffs and quotas shows that nations tend to retaliate with their own protective measures, leaving all sides worse off than before.

2. Tariffs and quotas tend to result in higher prices, thus penalizing domestic consumers while benefiting inefficient domestic producers. This encourages a movement of resources out of more efficient industries into less efficient (protected) ones, thereby raising costs and reducing comparative advantage.

3. In international trade, goods pay for goods. Hence a nation that exports must also import. Protective measures tend to impede this and, therefore, to limit rather than to encourage higher real income and employment in the long run.

Conclusion: Fundamental Principle

The most frequently heard argument for quotas and tariffs is that they *"protect American workers from the products of cheap labor abroad."* Is the argument valid?

If foreign countries can sell textiles, or steel, or computer memory chips, or any other products more cheaply than U.S. manufacturers can, that will mean fewer jobs in those American industries. But it will also mean more jobs in other industries. Which ones? Those that can now export goods to the countries that are spending their dollar earnings to buy American products. Therefore, quotas and tariffs do not protect American jobs. They only protect *some* jobs by preventing the growth of others that would emerge in a free (unprotected) market.

In view of this, you can see why the following principle of international trade is fundamental:

You and I sell ("export") our labor in order to earn income with which to buy ("import") the goods we want. Similarly, nations export in order to earn income with which to buy the imports they want. Thus, just as you and I work in order to consume, nations export in order to import — *not the other way around!*

What You Have Learned

1. By engaging in free or unrestricted trade, nations receive the greatest gains from trade. These gains are measured by the increases in goods that a country receives as a result of trading with others.

2. Trade involves sacrifice. A nation must give up some goods in order to receive others. These sacrifices are the terms of trade, and they are measured by the slope of a trade-possibilities curve.

3. A basis for trade exists when there are differences in opportunity costs between countries. Therefore, when few differences exist, there will be incomplete international specialization and hence a reduced volume of world trade.

4. Fluctuations in net exports — the difference between exports and imports — can generate magnified variations in national income. This proposition is demonstrated by the foreign-trade multiplier.

5. The law of comparative advantage is among the oldest principles of economics. The law shows why it pays for each nation to specialize in producing the goods in which it has the greatest *relative* advantage. Then, by trading with others, nations can have more goods than if each nation tried to be self-sufficient.

6. Despite the mutual benefits of free trade, nations have instituted various forms of protection. Common instruments of protection consist of tariffs, import quotas, and other nontariff barriers.

7. Many arguments may be advanced in favor of protection. Most, however, involve serious flaws. In general, if some form of protection is to be imposed, a tariff is less objectionable on economic grounds than an import quota.

Terms and Concepts to Review

opportunity cost
specialization
terms of trade
gains from trade
trade-possibilities curve
"bathtub theorem"
marginal propensity to import
foreign-trade multiplier

law of absolute advantage
law of comparative advantage
tariff
import quota
nontariff barrier
infant industry

For Discussion

1. Suppose that, with the same resources, the United States can produce either 40 cars or 40 tons of food per unit of time. With the same resources, Japan can produce either 60 cars or 20 tons of food in the same time. Assume that both countries have constant costs of production (their production-possibilities curves are straight lines).

(a) Using graph paper, plot the production-possibilities curves on separate graphs. To facilitate uniformity for classroom discussion, use the vertical axes for cars and the horizontal axes for food. Label the axes and curves.

(b) What is each country's domestic-exchange ratio? Are there any comparative advantages? Explain.

(c) Suppose that each country is self-sufficient. Then the United States might produce, say, 30 cars and 10 tons of food. Japan, on the other hand, might produce, say, 15 cars and 15 tons of food. On your respective graphs, label these points A and A'.

(d) If the United States and Japan each specialize and trade, what combinations of goods will each produce? Label the points B and B', respectively.

(e) Suppose the United States and Japan trade 20 tons of food for 40 cars. What combinations of goods will each country consume? Label these points E and E' on the countries' trade-possibilities curves. What are the gains from trade for each country and for the two countries together?

(f) Explain the gains from trade in terms of the slopes of the production-possibilities curves and the trade-possibilities curves. Label these curves along with their slopes.

2. Assume the following conditions:

— GNP is below its full-employment level.

— Exports (X) equal imports (M).

— MPS = 0 and MPM = 0.1.

Suppose that X, which is independent of GNP, rises by $100 and remains at its new higher level.

(a) What is the size of the foreign-trade multiplier (K)?

(b) Will the increase in X affect GNP? If so, by how much?

(c) What will happen to M?

(d) Describe in words, rather than equations, the nature of the income-adjustment process.

(e) What would have been the effect if GNP had initially been at its full-employment level?

3. Referring to problem 2, suppose that MPS = 0.15.

(a) Calculate the size of K.

(b) Calculate the increase in GNP.

(c) Calculate the increase in M.

(d) Is the income adjustment complete? Explain.

4. The Constitution of the United States (Article 1, Sec. 10) states: "No State shall, without the consent of the Congress, lay any imposts or duties on imports or exports, except what may be absolutely necessary for executing its inspection laws." Do you think the Founding Fathers were wise to pass this law? What would happen to the American standard of living if each state were allowed to impose protective barriers to trade?

5. "If you believe in the free movement of goods between nations, you should logically believe in the free movement of people, too. This means that cheap foreign labor should be admitted to the United States, even if it results in the displacement of American labor." Do you agree? Explain your answer.

6. An editorial in the Washington Inquirer stated that: "The United States should develop a large shipbuilding industry. Such an industry would provide more jobs and higher incomes for workers. Moreover, the ships could be used for passenger and cargo service in peacetime, and could be quickly converted for military purposes in case of war. In view of these advantages, it would be wise for the U.S. government to protect the domestic shipbuilding industry from foreign competition until it can grow to a stronger competitive position." Do you agree with this editorial? Explain.

7. Abraham Lincoln is reputed to have remarked: "I don't know much about the tariff. But I do know that when I buy a coat from England, I have the coat and England has the money. But when I buy a coat in America, I have the coat and America has the money." Can you show that Lincoln was correct only in the first sentence of his remark?

Chapter 18

The Open Economy: International Finance

Learning Guide

Watch for answers to these important questions

What is the balance of payments? Why do nations prepare balance-of-payments statements?

Where is foreign exchange bought and sold? What determines the price of foreign exchange?

Why must fixed exchange rates result either in overvalued or undervalued currencies? Why do nations today engage in managed floating?

The study of international economics deals not only with the flow of goods between nations but also with the flow of money. This involves the area of international finance, a vast and complex subject. You can gain some appreciation of its nature by examining two of its main components — the balance of payments and the foreign-exchange market.

The Balance of Payments

Most countries publish a periodic financial report called the **balance of payments.** This is a statement of the money value of all transactions between a nation and the rest of the world during a given period, such as a year. These transactions may consist of imports and exports of goods and services and movements of short-term and long-term investments, gifts, currency, and gold. The transactions can be classified into several categories, of which the two broadest are the current account and the capital account.

The balance of payments for the United States is shown in Exhibit 1. Note that the monetary results of transactions are recorded either as debits (—) or as credits (+). A **debit** is any transaction that results in

Exhibit 1
U.S. Balance of Payments, 1984 — Summary of International Transactions (billions of dollars)*

Debits (−), money outflows.
Credits (+), money inflows.

(1) CURRENT-ACCOUNT TRANSACTIONS

(2) Merchandise exported $220.2

(3) Merchandise imported .... −370.2

(4) Balance on merchandise trade: (2) + (3) .... **−150.0**

(5) Services exported 148.6

(6) Services imported .... −74.2

(7) Balance on services: (5) + (6) **74.4**

Services exported (+) include: travel expenditures by foreigners here (which is the same as "scenery exported by the U.S."), interest and dividends received from abroad, banking and insurance services rendered to foreigners by domestic financial institutions, and expenditures by foreign governments here.

Services imported (−) include the opposite, such as travel expenditures by Americans abroad (i.e., "scenery imported by the U.S."), interest and dividends paid to foreigners, and so on. .... **−75.6**

(8) Balance on goods and services: (4) + (7) .... **−12.4**

(9) Unilateral transfers, net
These are "one-way" gifts and grants involving no return commitments or claims. Money outflows (−) consist of U.S. private remittances sent abroad plus U.S. government military and nonmilitary grants to other countries. Money inflows (+) are the opposite. The net result (i.e., balance) has generally been negative. .... **−88.0**

(10) Balance on current account: (8) + (9) ....

(11) CAPITAL-ACCOUNT TRANSACTIONS .... −2.2

(12) U.S. official reserve assets abroad, net
Includes major currencies, gold, and other internationally accepted reserve assets. They are held at the International Monetary Fund, an arm of the United Nations. The assets are owned by the central bank of the United States, the Federal Reserve System. They are used for settling accounts with the central banks of other countries, such as the Bank of England, the Bank of Japan, etc. .... −4.9

(13) U.S. government assets abroad, other than (12), net
Includes U.S. government loans and other long-term claims, less repayments. .... −12.5

(14) U.S. private assets abroad, net
Includes direct investment by U.S. individuals and companies in foreign property and securities, plus other financial claims. .... **−19.6**

(15) U.S. assets abroad, net: (12) + (13) + (14)
NOTE: Increases in U.S. assets abroad are money outflows (−). Decreases are money inflows (+). 5.4

(16) Foreign official assets in the U.S., net
Includes U.S. Treasury securities and other official claims against the U.S. government held by foreigners. 95.7

(17) Other foreign assets in the U.S., net
Includes direct investment by foreigners in U.S. property and securities, plus other financial claims. **101.1**

(18) Foreign assets in the U.S., net: (16) + (17)
NOTE: Increases in foreign assets in the U.S. are money inflows (+). Decreases are money outflows (−). .... **−81.5**

(19) Balance on capital account: (15) + (18) .... −6.5

(20) Balance on current and capital accounts: (10) + (19)
This line would equal zero if there were no omissions in the data, as explained below for line (21). 6.5

(21) Statistical discrepancy
Includes omissions (which may be quite large) that arise because the balance of payments summarizes millions of individual recorded international transactions only — not unrecorded ones. Hence, complete accuracy is impossible. Note that the statistical discrepancy, which is simply the number on line (20) with the sign reversed, serves as a balancing item. It assures that the balance shown on line (22) below is zero — i.e., that the balance of payments balances. .... $ 0.0

(22) Overall balance (20) + (21)

* Preliminary data

Source: U.S. Department of Commerce.

a flow of money out of the country. A *credit* is any transaction that results in a flow of money into the country. Thus, an import is a debit and an export is a credit.

The balance-of-payments statement is easy to comprehend. By reading each line and the accompanying explanations, you will understand how the various items are obtained. If you do that now, the following additional comments will prove helpful.

Line (4) This discloses what is popularly known as the *balance of trade.* It is that part of a nation's balance of payments dealing with merchandise imports and exports. You will sometimes hear it said that a nation has either a "favorable" or an "unfavorable" balance of trade. Such a statement depends on whether the value of the country's merchandise exports is greater or less than the value of its merchandise imports. In reality, however, as you will discover shortly, the statement is misleading. It neglects the fact that other items in a nation's balance of payments will necessarily offset a surplus or deficit in the balance of trade.

Line (10) This reflects the net effect of all short-term transactions. The number may be either positive or negative, disclosing how much money the United States received from, or paid to, the rest of the world.

Line (19) This reflects the net effect of all long-term transactions. Here, too, the number can be either positive or negative.

Line (20) This is where the current and capital accounts are combined into a single number. If the number is positive, it means that the value of what the nation sold to the rest of the world, such as goods, services, securities, or other assets, exceeded the value of what it purchased. If the number is negative, the value of what the nation bought from abroad exceeded the value of what it sold.

Lines (21) and (22) Finally, these entries show you why the balance of payments always balances in *an*

accounting sense. That is, the sum of debits equals the sum of credits because of the principle of double-entry bookkeeping. As you can see from the explanation accompanying line (21), the statistical discrepancy assures that the overall balance on line (22) is zero.

The Foreign-Exchange Market

It is impossible to use the information provided in the balance of payments without an understanding of *foreign exchange.* This consists of instruments used for making international payments. Examples of these instruments include currency, checks, drafts, and bills of exchange (which are orders to pay currency). Foreign exchange is bought and sold in a world market called the "foreign-exchange market."

Thus, if you take a trip to France, you will have to sell some dollars to buy French francs. The francs are needed in order to pay for lodging, food, and anything else you purchase while you are in France. If you travel from France to Italy, you can buy Italian lire with any francs or dollars you may have. And if you go from Italy to Britain, you can purchase British pounds with francs, lire, or dollars.

The same principle applies to any country you visit. You can always buy one currency with another.

Graphic Illustration

The market for a currency, like the market for wheat, copper, and other raw-material commodities, can be represented by an ordinary supply-and-demand model. The reason is easy to see.

1. There are numerous participants in the market for each currency. Most of the participants are banks and other dealers who buy and sell currencies on their own behalf as well as for their customers. These include importers, exporters, multinational corporations, tourists, and so forth.

2. The product, whether it be dollars, francs, lire, or pounds, is standardized. Therefore, like raw-material commodities, buyers and sellers of currencies are concerned only with their prices.

3. The market participants' knowledge of currency prices is "perfect." This means that buyers and sellers are completely informed about bids and offers throughout the world, because information is transmitted immediately by telex and telephone.

Because of these conditions, the determination of a currency's price, such as the U.S. dollar price of Japanese yen (¥), can be illustrated as in Exhibit 2. Thus, in Figure (a), the demand curve for yen is downward-sloping, indicating that buyers will purchase more yen at lower prices than at higher ones. The supply curve is upward-sloping, signifying that sellers will offer more yen at higher prices than at lower ones.

> At any given time, the demand curve for yen represents *"dollars looking for yen"* and the supply curve of yen represents *"yen looking for dollars."* The equilibrium price of yen is determined by the intersection of the two curves. In the figure, this price is $1 = ¥200.

Shifts of the Curves: Causes and Effects

As with all supply-and-demand models, certain factors are assumed to be constant when the curves are drawn. A change in one or more of these factors may cause a change in demand or in supply — *a shift of the curves.* The result may be a new equilibrium price, a new equilibrium quantity, or both, as you learned when you first studied supply and demand.

Which factors are assumed to be constant? There are many, but three are especially important: (1) relative real income levels, (2) relative price levels, and (3) relative interest rates.

Exhibit 2
The Foreign-Exchange Market: Dollar Prices of Japanese Yen

Equilibrium prices and quantities are determined by the interactions of supply and demand.

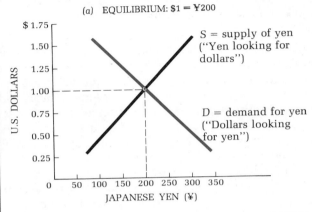

(a) EQUILIBRIUM: $1 = ¥200

S = supply of yen ("Yen looking for dollars")

D = demand for yen ("Dollars looking for yen")

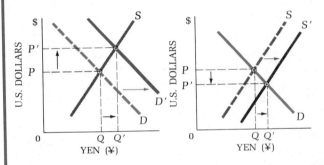

(b) INCREASE IN DEMAND

(c) INCREASE IN SUPPLY

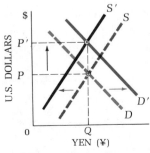

(d) INCREASE IN DEMAND DECREASE IN SUPPLY

1. Relative Real Income Levels

Suppose that the level of real income in the United States rises in relation to that of the "rest of the world"—specifically, Japan. This enables Americans to purchase more Japanese-made products: Hondas, Sonys, steel, "scenery" (that is, trips to Japan), and so on. The result will be an increase in "dollars looking for yen," causing the demand for yen to increase. In Figure (b), the curve shifts from D to D', leading to a higher equilibrium price and a larger equilibrium quantity of yen. The yen thus *appreciates*, or increases in value, relative to the dollar. This, of course, is equivalent to saying that the dollar *depreciates* relative to the yen.

Conversely, if Japan's real income rises in relation to that of the United States, the supply curve of yen will shift to the right. There will be an increase in "yen looking for dollars" as Japanese seek to buy more American goods. In Figure (c), the supply curve shifts from S to S, causing the equilibrium price of yen to decline and the equilibrium quantity to increase. The yen thus *depreciates* relative to the dollar, which means that the dollar *appreciates* relative to the yen.

2. Relative Price Levels

How do changes in each country's general price level affect foreign-exchange rates? Because the effects are slightly more complicated, it helps to analyze them in two steps.

Step 1 If inflation in the United States is higher than it is in Japan, many Japanese products (such as cars and televisions) will be cheaper than similar American products. In Figure (d), therefore, the demand for yen increases from D to D' as Americans substitute more of these Japanese goods for American goods.

Step 2 Because these Japanese goods are cheaper than their American substitutes, some Japanese buyers will switch from American goods to their own domestic goods. In Figure (d), the supply curve shifts from S to S' because there are fewer "yen

looking for dollars." The result is a higher equilibrium price of the yen—an *appreciation* of the yen—and hence a *depreciation* of the dollar. What about the equilibrium quantity? This may remain the same or it may change, depending on the relative shifts of the curves.

3. Relative Interest Rates

Government economic (fiscal and monetary) policies may cause interest rates to be higher in the United States than in Japan. The Japanese, therefore, may decide to increase their supply of "yen looking for dollars" in order to purchase American interest-earning securities. In Figure (c), the price of the yen will fall in terms of the dollar. That is, the yen will *depreciate* and the dollar will *appreciate*.

Various other conditions can affect foreign-exchange rates. Economic and political policies in each country and expectations about future developments are some of the factors that may play a role. However, relative income-level, price-level, and interest-rate changes are of major importance, as you will see shortly.

Conclusion: Important Ideas and Potential Problems

In the world of international finance, two concepts are of fundamental importance. One of these is the balance of payments; the other is the foreign-exchange market.

The balance of payments discloses the inflows and outflows of money that a nation experiences during a given period. These flows result from the purchase and sale of goods, services, securities, and other assets, and from gifts and grants. In general, a nation's balance of payments is affected by the price of its currency relative to others in the foreign-exchange market.

The foreign-exchange market is a world market in which various nations' currencies (and certain other financial claims) are bought and sold. In an unregulated foreign-exchange market—one in

The Mighty Dollar

Beware of Its Short-Term Benefits

By Jerry J. Jasinowski

Much has been written about how the overvalued dollar and the resultant trade deficit hold down the cost of living for both industrial and domestic consumers of imported goods—and force companies to become more efficient in order to survive in the competition with less expensive imports. But that highlights only one side of the story. The other side is the cost to exporters and to the economy in general of a dollar that is at least 35 percent higher than normal market.

If the United States Government does not move to correct these market distortions, industry will be forced to live with an overvalued dollar for the foreseeable future. How does industry cope and at what loss to the nation?

In some cases, industry is trying to cope by shifting more and more of its production, design and marketing activities abroad. This allows United States companies to fill export orders from foreign plants, rather than those in this country, but at a loss to the communities and employees where the plants are located.

But despite using these strategies to try to claw their way out from under the crushing weight of an over-valued dollar, American companies are still losing the competitive game. Great efforts have been made to modernize, to economize through drastic reductions of office and production staffs, and to out-source—not only capital equipment, but also assemblies and components. But the successes are few.

A ''leaner, meaner'' industrial sector has ways of coping with the high dollar, but these techniques mean a huge trade deficit, slower economic growth, lower domestic employment and increased reliance on foreign debt. Lower inflation benefits cannot be permanently paid for at these costs.

The New York Times, January 13, 1985, © 1985 by The New York Times Company. Reprinted by permission.

which governments do not interfere—equilibrium prices and quantities are determined by the forces of supply and demand. When the price of one currency rises relative to the price of another, the more valuable currency is said to *appreciate* and the less valuable one is said to *depreciate*. It follows that changes in exchange rates affect the prices that domestic buyers pay for foreign goods as well as the prices that foreign buyers pay for domestic goods.

In general:

An *appreciation* of a nation's currency makes its exports dearer and its imports cheaper. A *depreciation* does the opposite: It makes a country's exports cheaper and its imports dearer. Thus, changes in exchange rates may substantially influence a country's balance of payments. This can create fundamental policy problems of deep concern to the community of nations.

Flexible Versus Fixed Exchange Rates

One of the fundamental financial problems facing an open economy concerns its balance-of-payments adjustments to surpluses and deficits. How do adjustments in the balance of payments take place? The answer depends on whether foreign-exchange rates are flexible or fixed.

Flexible (Floating) Exchange Rates

Flexible exchange rates are also called floating exchange rates. They are simply exchange rates that are free to fluctuate in response to market forces of supply and demand.

Exhibit 3 provides an illustration in terms of U.S. dollars and British pounds (£). Suppose that the equilibrium exchange rate is $2 = £1 and the equilibrium quantity is £300 million. If U.S. imports from Britain now increase, the demand curve for pounds will shift to the right from D to D'. The pound will thus *appreciate* to $3 = £1, and the dollar will therefore *depreciate*.

Exhibit 3

The Foreign-Exchange Market: Undervaluing the British Pound; Overvaluing the American Dollar

An increase in the demand for pounds from D to D' raises their free-market equilibrium price from $2 = £1 to $3 = £1.

In order to hold down (undervalue) the price of a pound to $2, the Bank of England can increase the supply of pounds. The bank does this by printing and selling the amount EF (=£200 million) in the foreign-exchange market, thus shifting the supply curve from S to S'. Britain will thereby receive $400 million.

D = Demand for pounds: "Dollars looking for pounds"
S = Supply of pounds: "Pounds looking for dollars"

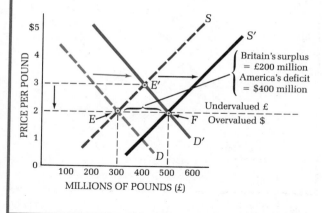

What will be the economic effects? Because the pound is now more expensive, American imports of British goods, as well as American investments in Britain, will decline. Also, because the dollar is now cheaper, British imports of American goods, and British investments in America, will rise. Therefore, at the new equilibrium price of $3 per pound, any disequilibrium (either a deficit or a surplus) in either country's balance of payments will be *automatically* corrected. This automatic correction, it should be emphasized, will always occur under a system of flexible exchange rates.

Fixed Exchange Rates

Despite the advantage of automatic balance-of-payments adjustment under a system of flexible exchange rates, many countries have often maintained fixed exchange rates. Under a system of fixed exchange rates, a country's currency may be either undervalued or overvalued in relation to its free-market price. This can result in a prolonged *economic* disequilibrium in a country's balance of payments even though the statement always balances in an accounting sense.

Undervaluation

An undervalued currency is one whose price is held *below* the price that would exist in a free market. This makes the currency cheaper, thereby encouraging exports. It also makes other currencies dearer, thereby discouraging imports.

For example, look again at Exhibit 3. Suppose Britain wants to offset the increase in demand by keeping the price of the pound at $2. This is easily done. Britain's central bank, the Bank of England, can increase the supply of pounds in the foreign-exchange market simply by printing and selling an amount equal to the excess demand EF (=£200 million). This action will have several effects:

1. Exports and Imports Because the pound is now undervalued in terms of the dollar, British goods will be cheaper for Americans to buy. However, the dollar is now overvalued in terms of the pound. Therefore, American goods will be more costly for Britons to buy. Thus, undervaluation of the pound relative to the dollar encourages British exports and discourages British imports.

2. Terms of Trade Britain's terms of trade with the United States will worsen. That is, Britain will have to export more units of goods (such as textiles) for each unit of goods imported (such as food). On the other hand, the United States' terms of trade with Britain will improve. This is because the United States will have to export fewer units of goods for each unit of goods imported.

3. Balance of Payments Because of the undervalued pound, Britain will experience a surplus in its balance of payments with the U.S. And in turn, because of the overvalued dollar, the U.S. will experience a deficit in its balance of payments with Britain. As shown in Exhibit 3, the amount of the surplus or deficit is EF = £200 = $400 million.

Overvaluation

An overvalued currency is one whose price is held *above* the price that would exist in a free market. This makes the currency dearer, thereby discouraging exports. It also makes other currencies cheaper, thereby encouraging imports.

Intentional overvaluation may be as common as intentional undervaluation. For example, some of the less-developed oil-exporting nations have at various times overvalued their currencies. The purpose was to use the money (such as dollars, yen, and marks) earned from oil exports to more developed countries, where demand for oil was relatively strong, to pay for imports of technology, capital, and other goods from those countries.

How does overvaluation work? For illustrative purposes, look at Exhibit 4. It shows the free market equilibrium price of pounds in terms of dollars at $3 = £1. What would happen if Britain were to fix the exchange rate at $4 = £1? The Bank of England would then have to buy up the excess supply of pounds — equal to the amount GH = £200 = $800 million. This would shift the demand curve to the right from D to D'. The Bank could make these purchases only as long as it had enough dollars, gold, or other internationally acceptable reserve assets with which to buy the pounds. Once the assets were spent, the demand curve would shift back. The price of pounds would thus fall to the free-market level of $3 per pound, unless other countries were willing to lend additional reserves to the Bank in order to sustain the demand curve at D'.

What would be the results of an overvalued pound? The effects would be the opposite of those for an undervalued one. Try listing the various effects to make sure you understand them.

Exhibit 4

The Foreign-Exchange Market: Overvaluing the British Pound; Undervaluing the American Dollar

Suppose the free-market equilibrium price of British pounds is $3 = £1. In order to raise (overvalue) the price of a pound to $4, the Bank of England can increase the demand for pounds. The bank does this by buying up the amount GH (=£200 million) in the foreign-exchange market, thus shifting the demand curve from D to D'. Britain will thereby spend $800 million.

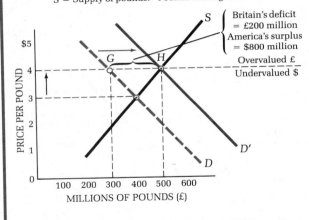

D = Demand for pounds: "Dollars looking for pounds"
S = Supply of pounds: "Pounds looking for dollars"

Britain's deficit = £200 million
America's surplus = $800 million
Overvalued £
Undervalued $

PRICE PER POUND

MILLIONS OF POUNDS (£)

Managed or "Dirty" Floating

It is obviously easier for a country to maintain an undervalued currency than an overvalued one. Undervaluation requires the nation's central bank simply to continue printing and selling its own currency. Overvaluation, on the other hand, requires the central bank to continue receiving an inflow of internationally acceptable reserve assets sufficient to buy its own excess currency in the foreign-exchange market.

Are today's foreign-exchange rates flexible or are they fixed? The answer is that they are some of both. Many nations' central banks intervene in the foreign-exchange market to prevent unwanted fluctuations beyond a few percentage points. This is called "managed" or "dirty" floating. Both terms are commonly used.

Countries engaged in managed floating thus incur, at least partially, a major benefit of flexible rates—namely, automatic balance-of-payments adjustments. At the same time, by keeping foreign-exchange-rate fluctuations within a relatively narrow range, these countries also realize, at least partially, two of the chief advantages of fixed exchange rates: reduced uncertainty and stable terms of trade.

Reduced Uncertainty   Fixed exchange rates can encourage international trade and investment. If you are an importer or an exporter, for example, you like to know that the prices at which you do business today will yield an anticipated rate of profit in the coming months. If exchange rates fluctuate, you may realize unexpected losses (as well as gains) when merchandise is paid for upon delivery—say, 30 or 60 days later. The same principle applies whether you are a long-term foreign investor or the president of a multinational corporation. Your objective is to earn future profits on your investment abroad. You do not want to incur the *additional* risk of fluctuations in the foreign-exchange rate when you eventually convert your foreign profits into dollars in order to "bring them home."

Stable Terms of Trade   A nation's terms of trade tend to vary directly with the international value of its currency. For example, a decrease in the value of the pound will encourage British exports while discouraging imports. Britain will thus give up more units of goods to other countries for each unit of goods imported from them. Of course, an increase in the value of the pound will have the opposite effect. Managed floating, therefore, helps countries to stabilize their terms of trade rather than allowing them to vary substantially. Thus:

In the opinion of many experts, a system of managed exchange rates combines the advantages of flexible and fixed rates. However, the validity of this conclusion depends on (1) the range of exchange-rate fluctuations that countries permit and (2) the frequency of their intervention.

Conclusion: Today's Problems and Policies

Today's international economic system is often characterized by varying degrees of managed exchange rates. However, like all supply and demand curves, those in the foreign-exchange market frequently shift. As a result, the currencies of some countries become overvalued, causing balance-of-payments deficits. The currencies of other countries become undervalued, causing balance-of-payments surpluses. Eventually realignments of exchange rates take place. These occur in one of two ways:

1. Devaluation   This is an official (government) act that makes the price of a country's currency cheaper in terms of other currencies. History shows that a country whose currency is intentionally significantly overvalued will eventually be forced to devalue it in order to reduce a persistent balance-of-payments deficit.

2. Revaluation   This, the opposite of devaluation, serves to appreciate (rather than depreciate) a country's currency in the foreign-exchange market. History shows that a country whose currency is intentionally undervalued is not particularly prone to revalue it in order to reduce a persistent balance-of-payments surplus.

Evidently, devaluation and revaluation are not *lasting* corrective measures. To achieve such corrections, nations must adopt appropriate long-term policies. Three that can be employed are (1) fiscal and monetary policies, (2) trade controls, and (3) exchange controls.

Fiscal and Monetary Policies

Government actions pertaining to taxing, spending, and growth of the money supply are known as fiscal and monetary policies. Depending on the ways in which these policies are used, they can have either contractionary or expansionary effects. How might a nation employ fiscal and monetary policies to correct either a deficit or a surplus in its balance of payments?

Deficit Nation: Contractionary Policies   A *deficit* nation can lower the price of its overvalued currency by pursuing contractionary fiscal and monetary policies. By reducing its prices at home relative to those in surplus nations, the deficit nation will discourage imports and encourage exports. However, contractionary fiscal and monetary policies will also cause increased unemployment at home. The deficit nation will thus be sacrificing domestic employment stability for balance-of-payments equilibrium.

Surplus Nation: Expansionary Policies   A *surplus* nation can raise the price of its undervalued currency by pursuing expansionary fiscal and monetary policies. If prices in the surplus nation rise faster than those in deficit nations, imports will be encouraged and exports will be discouraged. However, the surplus nation will then be sacrificing domestic price stability in order to reduce other countries' deficits. This, of course, is not something that the surplus nation is likely to do.

Thus:

A nation's balance of payments is affected by its fiscal and monetary policies. The use of these policies to achieve balance-of-payments equilibrium entails a sacrifice of some domestic stability. This is a trade-off that countries are usually reluctant to make.

Trade Controls

A second approach to reducing payments imbalances is through trade controls. A deficit nation can contract imports by imposing tariffs, quotas, and other trade barriers. It can also try to expand exports by subsidizing the industries it wants to encourage and by providing them with special tax benefits.

All countries, to varying degrees, engage in such policies. Their effects, of course, are obvious. Because they impede the operation of the law of comparative advantage, they misallocate resources. As a result, efficiency is impaired and the volume of world trade is reduced.

Exchange Controls

Finally, nations can reduce imbalances, or at least manage them more effectively, through exchange controls. These are commonly utilized by command economies. They require exporters to sell their foreign exchange to the government, which then uses the scarce funds to purchase needed imports. These may include such staple goods as foods, raw materials, and capital goods deemed necessary for economic growth. As a general rule, the scarce funds are not likely to be used for such "luxury" goods as imported sports cars, audio-video equipment, and liquors.

As with trade controls, exchange controls misallocate resources and therefore contract the volume of world trade. In addition, they severely reduce consumer choice and hence are likely to encourage the growth of black (illegal) markets. For these reasons, exchange controls are not commonly employed by market-oriented economies, except perhaps in wartime emergencies.

In conclusion:

International economic policies are strongly influenced by economic and noneconomic (including political and military) considerations. Because of this, all nations, in varying degrees, impose trade restrictions and engage in managed floating. As a result, most political leaders are continually seeking to establish a set of workable rules for improving the efficiency of the international economic system.

Economics in the News

The Age of the Megadollar

The U.S. currency upsets world markets and defies attempts to knock it down.

For a brief moment last week, it looked like the megadollar was finally beginning its long-anticipated decline. On Monday the U.S. dollar staged an unprecedented advance, reaching record levels against most major foreign currencies.

The central banks spent an estimated $4 billion trying to drive the dollar down, yet by the close of trading Friday, it had regained some of its losses. Moreover, there was no indication that intervention would

continue—and no guarantee that it would be effective if it did. As much as $200 billion can change hands in a day, and in Europe only West Germany's Bundesbank has substantial dollar reserves. (The Fed made only token dollar sales, holding to its long-standing policy of nonintervention.)

The reasons for the strength of the dollar are by now familiar. With its robust growth, low inflation and relatively high interest rates, the U.S. economy offers investors the greatest potential returns.

As long as those fundamentals remain intact, a rapid reversal is unlikely. In fact, many analysts believe that even completely opposite economic developments will tend to strengthen the dollar. For example,

many European and Japanese officials say that the best way to lower the dollar is by cutting the U.S. budget deficit, which would presumably lead to lower U.S. interest rates. Yet others contend such a move, by improving the prospects for sustained growth, would only strengthen the dollar.

Eric Gelman, Madlyn Resener, Fred Coleman, Ronald Henkoff, Rich Thomas, David Lewis, *Newsweek*, March 11, 1985, Copyright 1985, by Newsweek Inc. All Rights Reserved. Reprinted by permission.

AS THE DOLLAR ROLLS ALONG . . .

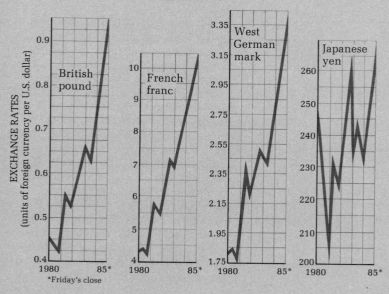

*Friday's close

PRODUCTS POUR IN FROM ABROAD; EXPORTS LAG

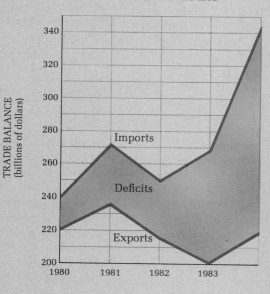

What You Have Learned

1. The study of international finance is concerned with the payments of nations. Such payments are reported in a country's balance of payments, a periodic financial report.

2. The balance of payments summarizes all of a country's recorded money inflows and outflows resulting from international transactions, public and private.

3. Adjustments in the balance of payments take place through the foreign-exchange market, where currencies are bought and sold. The prices of currencies are determined by international forces of supply and demand. Consequently, the currencies of nations may appreciate or depreciate relative to one another in the foreign-exchange market.

4. Flexible exchange rates permit automatic adjustments to balance-of-payments equilibrium. Nevertheless, most countries today adhere to managed exchange rates in order to keep currency fluctuations within a fairly narrow range. Under such circumstances, balance-of-payments adjustments to equilibrium may not occur automatically.

5. Because of trade restrictions and managed exchange rates, resources are misallocated and world trade is reduced. Consequently, most political leaders are continually seeking workable rules for improving the efficiency of the international economic system.

Terms and Concepts to Review

balance of payments   foreign exchange
debit   devaluation
credit   revaluation
balance of trade

For Discussion

1. What are the sources of demand for foreign exchange? What are the sources of supply?

2. State whether each of the following transactions is a debit or a credit on the U.S. balance of payments.
   (a) An American firm imports $100,000 worth of French perfume.

(b) An American tourist flies via British Airways from New York to London.
(c) A British tourist flies via Pan American Airlines from London to New York.
(d) A British tourist flies via Pan American Airlines from New York to London.
(e) An American buys stock in a Swiss corporation.
(f) An American sells stock in a German corporation.
(g) The Federal Reserve Bank of New York reduces it debt to the Bank of Japan.

3. In a free market, if the dollar rate of exchange for French francs rises, what happens to the French rate of exchange for dollars? Explain.

4. How does each of the following transactions affect the supply of money in the United States?
   (a) The United States sells Chevrolets to England.
   (b) France sells perfume to the United States.
   (c) An American tourist visits Japan.
   (d) A Japanese tourist visits the United States.

5. From an *accounting* point of view, can there be a net positive or net negative balance in the balance of payments? What about an "economic" point of view?

6. Why do nations engage in managed floating?

7. **How Does "the" Foreign-Exchange Market Operate?**

It is generally not possible to go to a specific building and "see" the market where prices of foreign exchange are determined. With few exceptions, the vast bulk of foreign exchange business is done over the telephone between specialist divisions of major banks. Foreign exchange dealers in each bank usually operate from one room; each dealer has several telephones and is surrounded by video screens and news tapes. Typically, each dealer specializes in one or a small number of markets (such as sterling/dollar or deutschemark/dollar). Trades are conducted with other dealers who represent banks around the world. These dealers typically deal regularly with one another and are thus able to make firm commitments by word of mouth.

Only the head or regional offices of the larger banks actively deal in foreign exchange. The largest of these banks are known as "market makers" since they stand ready to buy or sell any of the major currencies on a more or less continuous basis. Unusually large transactions, however, will only be accommodated by market makers on more favorable terms. In such cases, foreign exchange brokers may be used as middlemen to find a taker or takers for the deal.   Brokers (of which there are four major firms and a handful of smaller ones) do not trade on their own account, but specialize in setting up large foreign exchange transactions in return for a commission (typically 0.03 cents or less on the sterling spread).

Most small banks and local offices of major banks do not deal directly in the interbank foreign exchange market.   Rather they typically will have a credit line with a large bank or their head office.   Transactions will thus involve an extra step.   The customer deals with a local bank, which in turn deals with a major bank or head office.   The interbank foreign exchange market exists between the major banks either directly or indirectly via a broker.

From K. Alec Chrystal, "A Guide to Foreign Exchange Markets," *Review*, Federal Reserve Bank of St. Louis, March 1984.

"If a foreign-exchange market did not exist, it would be necessary to create one."   Do you agree?

Part 5

Using Supply and Demand: The Laws of Production and Cost

Chapter 19

Working with Supply, Demand, and Elasticity: Some Practical Applications

Learning Guide

Watch for answers to these important questions

What is elasticity? How is it measured? What factors determine elasticity?

How can basic supply-and-demand models be used to explain such concepts as shortages and surpluses? What are the effects of taxes and subsidies on the prices and quantities of goods?

What is the income elasticity of demand? What is the cross elasticity of demand? Can they be applied to practical problems?

What assumptions underlie the use of supply-and-demand models? In what way does the price system serve as a rationing or allocative mechanism?

Is there a distinction between pure and applied science? In answer to this question, the nineteenth-century French scientist Louis Pasteur replied:

> No, a thousand times no. There does not exist a category of science to which one can give the name applied science. There are only science and the applications of science, bound together as the fruit to the tree which bears it.

Supply and demand can be viewed in much the same way. You are already familiar with the "pure" side of the subject from your study of it early in this book. Now you can explore the "applied" aspects of supply and demand by taking up some interesting problems. When you complete this chapter, you will probably agree with Pasteur that the principles and applications of supply and demand, like those of any science, are indeed "bound together as the fruit to the tree."

Before going on, take a few moments to review the basic concepts of supply and demand presented in Exhibit 1.

Exhibit 1
Brief Review of Supply and Demand

Figure (a): The *law of demand* states that the quantity demanded of a good varies inversely with its price. In other words, people will buy more of a good at a lower price than at a higher price.

Figure (b): The *law of supply* states that the quantity supplied of a good usually varies directly with its price. In other words, sellers are willing to supply larger quantities at higher prices than at lower prices.

Figure (c): When demand and supply curves are graphed, their intersection indicates the equilibrium market price and quantity. At any price above this equilibrium level, the quantity supplied will exceed the quantity demanded, thereby driving the price down. At any price below the equilibrium level, the quantity demanded will exceed the quantity supplied, thereby driving the price up. At the equilibrium level there are no product surpluses or shortages, and thus the market is precisely cleared.

Figures (d) and (e): A *change in demand* or a *change in supply* is represented by a shift of the curve to a new position. Such shifts may occur as a result of changes in any of the factors assumed to be constant when the curves were initially drawn. In the case of demand, these factors include buyer incomes, tastes, expectations, the prices of related goods, and the number of buyers in the market. In the case of supply, they are resource costs, technology, sellers' expectations, the prices of other goods, and the number of sellers in the market. Changes or shifts in demand or supply may bring about new equilibrium prices and quantities.

Figures (f) and (g): If the demand curve remains fixed, a movement along the curve from one point to another denotes a *change in the quantity demanded.* Likewise, if the supply curve remains fixed, a movement along the curve denotes a *change in the quantity supplied.* Such changes are always associated with changes in price.

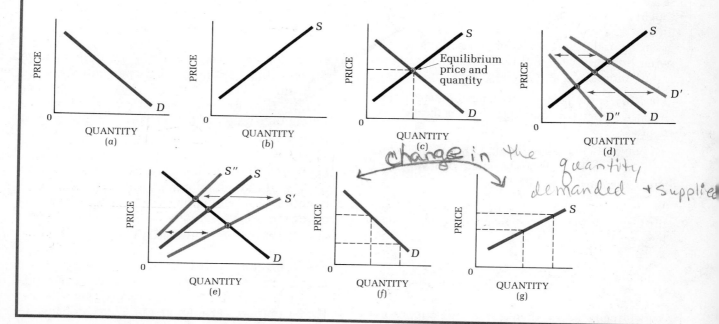

The Concept of Elasticity: Responsiveness to Changes in Price

✗ test ✗

You know from Exhibit 1 that the relationship between the price and quantity of a good is *causal*. For instance, a rise in price will cause a decrease in the quantity demanded and an increase in the quantity supplied. A fall in price will produce the opposite effects—an increase in the quantity demanded and a decrease in the quantity supplied.

But by *how much* will a change in price affect the quantities supplied or demanded? The answer depends on the particular good. There is a big difference, for example, between a commodity such as salt and a commodity such as vacation trips. In the case of salt, the quantity demanded varies relatively little with changes in price. In the case of vacation trips, however, changes in price may cause relatively large changes in the quantity demanded.

One way to gain an understanding of this idea is to use a concept called "elasticity." Elasticity may be thought of as the *responsiveness* of a change in one variable to a change in another, with responsiveness measured in percentage changes. Thus, the following interpretive definition of *elasticity* can be used to understand and explain its meaning:

> *Elasticity* is the percentage change in quantity (demanded or supplied) resulting from a 1 percent change in price.

The following mathematical definition of elasticity can be used to calculate elasticities of supply or demand, as illustrated later:

> *Elasticity* is the ratio of the percentage change in quantity (demanded or supplied) to the percentage change in price:

$$E = \frac{\% \Delta Q}{\% \Delta P}$$

$$\text{elasticity} = \frac{\text{percentage change in quantity}}{\text{percentage change in price}}$$

You already know that the law of supply expresses a *direct* relation between price and quantity supplied. Therefore, the coefficient you get when you calculate supply elasticity will be positive. On the other hand, the law of demand expresses an *inverse* relation between price and quantity demanded. Therefore, the coefficient of demand elasticity will be negative. In practice, however, it is customary to disregard the negative sign and express all elasticities as if they were either positive or zero.

Visualizing Elasticities from Graphs

Exhibit 2 illustrates five types of elasticity—that is, five different degrees of responsiveness. Study these diagrams and the following definitions carefully.

$E = \infty$

(1) **Figure (a): Perfectly Elastic** An infinitesimally small percentage change in price results in an infinitely large percentage change in the quantity demanded or supplied. The numerical elasticity is infinite. Thus, a change in price from P_1 to P_2 produces a change in quantity demanded or supplied from zero to a positive amount. In terms of percentages, this is an "infinite" change.

(2) **Figure (b): Relatively Elastic** A given percentage change in price results in a larger percentage change in quantity. The numerical elasticity is greater than 1. Thus, a change in price from P_1 to P_2 causes a more than proportionate change in quantity from Q_1 to Q_2. $E > 1$

$E = 1$

(3) **Figure (c): Unit Elastic** A given percentage change in price results in an equal percentage change in quantity. The numerical elasticity is 1. Thus, a change in price from P_1 to P_2 causes an equal proportionate change in quantity from Q_1 to Q_2. $E = 1$

(4) **Figure (d): Relatively Inelastic** A given percentage change in price results in a smaller percentage change in quantity. The numerical elasticity is less than 1 (but greater than zero). Thus, a change in price from P_1 to P_2 causes a less than proportionate change in quantity from Q_1 to Q_2.

$E < 1$

Exhibit 2
Five Types of Elasticity

Elasticity is a measure of the *responsiveness* of a change in quantity to a change in price. The changes can be visualized from the graphs, showing five different degrees of responsiveness for demand (D) and for supply (S).

Note that E = numerical elasticity (that is, negative signs are disregarded). Therefore, an elasticity coefficient will always be either a positive number or zero, but never a negative number. (The symbol < means "less than"; the symbol > means "greater than.")

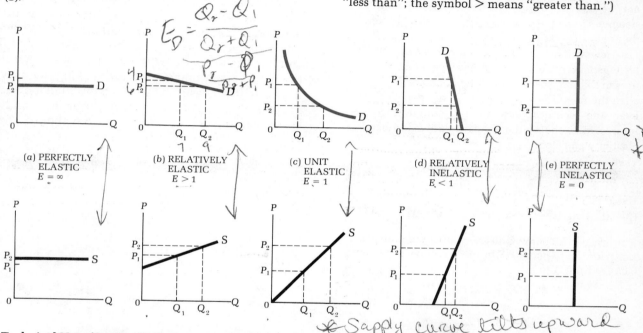

$$E_D = \frac{Q_r - Q_1}{Q_r + Q_1} \div \frac{P_1 - P}{P_2 + P_1}$$

(a) PERFECTLY
ELASTIC
E = ∞

(b) RELATIVELY
ELASTIC
E > 1

(c) UNIT
ELASTIC
E = 1

(d) RELATIVELY
INELASTIC
E < 1

(e) PERFECTLY
INELASTIC
E = 0

Technical Note (Optional) If you are mathematically inclined, you may be able to see that the slope and elasticity of a curve would be the same if the *logarithms* of price and quantity were plotted in the figures. Or, equivalently, the slope and elasticity of a curve would be the same if the curve were plotted on a special type of graph paper whose vertical and horizontal axes were

both scaled in *logarithms*. The reason for this is that, on a logarithmic scale, equal distances represent equal proportional (or *relative*) changes. Because elasticity is nothing more than a measure of relative change, the slope of a straight line on logarithmic scales is the same as its elasticity. It is an interesting exercise to prove these ideas algebraically.

Figure *(e)*: Perfectly Inelastic A given percentage change in price results in no change in quantity. The numerical elasticity is zero. Therefore, a change in price from P_1 to P_2 causes no change in quantity.

There is an easy way to remember the charts in

Exhibit 2. Think of them as the frames of a motion picture. For both supply and demand, the curve in the first "frame" is in a horizontal position. In successive frames, the demand curve gradually tilts downward while the supply curve tilts upward until both curves end up in a vertical position.

Do the five different definitions of elasticity in Exhibit 2 sound intuitively reasonable? They should. After all, elasticity is nothing more than the "stretch" in quantity compared with the "stretch" in price, with both stretches being measured in percentages.

Caution Do not confuse elasticity with slope. They are not the same. The slope of a curve at any point is its steepness (or flatness) at that point. A straight line has the same slope at every point, but not necessarily the same elasticity. Therefore, *you cannot always infer the elasticity of a curve from its slope alone.* The figures in Exhibit 2 are merely intended to help you visualize the five different types of elasticity. (See, however, the technical note in the exhibit if you are interested in the mathematical relationship between elasticity and slope.)

Measuring Elasticity

A hypothetical demand curve is shown in Exhibit 3. Our objective is to estimate the elasticity of demand for this curve. We may begin by choosing two points near the ends of the line. The points chosen are A and B, because they are conveniently located on at least one of the grid lines. We calculate the elasticity for the segment AB as follows:

To begin with, how does the change in quantity demanded compare with the change in price over this segment? Disregard for the time being the calculations accompanying the figure. Observe from the figure alone that a movement along the curve from A to B is measured by two changes: an increase in quantity from 20 bushels to 80 bushels and a corresponding decrease in price from about $52 to about $17. An increase in quantity of 60 bushels is

---

Exhibit 3
Calculating the Elasticity of Demand

The procedures below illustrate the calculation of elasticity for the segment AB in the accompanying figure.
Change from A to B:

At A: $Q_1 = 20$, $P_1 = 52$
At B: $Q_2 = 80$, $P_2 = 17$

$$E_D = \frac{\dfrac{Q_2 - Q_1}{Q_2 + Q_1}}{\dfrac{P_2 - P_1}{P_2 + P_1}} = \frac{\dfrac{80 - 20}{80 + 20}}{\dfrac{17 - 52}{17 + 52}}$$

$$= \frac{0.60}{-0.51} = -1.2, \text{ or } 1.2 \text{ numerically}$$

Change from B to A:

At B: $Q_1 = 80$, $P_1 = 17$
At A: $Q_2 = 20$, $P_2 = 52$

$$E_D = \frac{\dfrac{Q_2 - Q_1}{Q_2 + Q_1}}{\dfrac{P_2 - P_1}{P_2 + P_1}} = \frac{\dfrac{20 - 80}{20 + 80}}{\dfrac{52 - 17}{52 + 17}}$$

$$= \frac{-0.60}{0.51} = -1.2, \text{ or } 1.2 \text{ numerically}$$

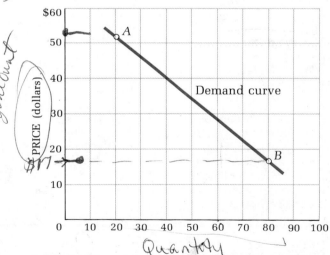

Interpretation A 1 percent change in price results in a 1.2 percent change in quantity demanded. (Similarly, a 10 percent change in price results in a 12 percent change in quantity demanded.) Because the change in quantity demanded is more than proportional to the change in price, demand is said to be relatively elastic.

thus associated with a decrease in price of $35. The change in quantity per unit change in price, therefore, is $60/(-35) = -1.72$, or 1.72 if the sign is disregarded.

Is this the elasticity of demand? The answer is *no*, because the result is obviously affected by the units in which the quantities and prices are measured. The solution would have been different, for example, if quantities had been expressed in millions of bushels or if prices had been expressed in British pounds or in French francs. Accordingly, a measure of elasticity is needed that is unaffected by the units in which the data are quoted. That is, what is needed is a *coefficient of elasticity*.

The Coefficient of Elasticity

You will recall from the definition of elasticity that its measurement is simply the percentage change in quantity divided by the percentage change in price. The most common method of measuring these percentage changes is to divide the observed change in quantity by the average of the two quantities, and the observed change in price by the average of the two prices. This enables us to express the definition by the formula

$$\text{elasticity} = \frac{\text{percentage change in quantity}}{\text{percentage change in price}}$$

$$= \frac{\dfrac{\text{change in quantity}}{\text{average quantity}}}{\dfrac{\text{change in price}}{\text{average price}}}$$

You can use this formula in calculating the elasticity of demand in Exhibit 3. In doing so, substitute the letters P for price and Q for quantity in the formula and attach subscripts to the letters so that you do not mix up your Ps and Qs. Thus, let

Q_1 = old quantity, or quantity before change
Q_2 = new quantity, or quantity after change
P_1 = old price, or price before change
P_2 = new price, or price after change

The formula for elasticity of demand E_D is then expressed as follows:

$$E_D = \frac{\dfrac{Q_2 - Q_1}{(Q_2 + Q_1)/2}}{\dfrac{P_2 - P_1}{(P_2 + P_1)/2}}$$

$$= \frac{\dfrac{Q_2 - Q_1}{Q_2 + Q_1}}{\dfrac{P_2 - P_1}{P_2 + P_1}}$$

Notice, from the first part of the equation, that the average quantity is the sum of the two quantities divided by 2 and the average price is the sum of the two prices divided by 2. These 2s then cancel out, leaving the complex fraction at the end.

An application of the formula for elasticity of demand is illustrated by the equations in Exhibit 3. Observe that the same result is obtained whether the change is from A to B or from B to A. This is an important advantage, because many practical situations arise in which we know only two prices and two quantities without knowing which price and quantity came first.

Example The Savemore Paint Company sold an average of 300 gallons of paint per week at $10 per gallon and 500 gallons of paint per week at $8 per gallon. What is the elasticity of demand for their paint?

The answer is -2.25, or 2.25 numerically, regardless of the values you choose for your initial price and quantity. Work it out both ways and see for yourself. How do you interpret this answer? What would you expect the percentage change in quantity to be if the price were to change by 10 percent? (HINT Refer back to Exhibit 3.)

What about elasticity of supply E_S? Do we measure it in the same way? The answer is *yes*. We also use the same formula. However, we let Q_1 and Q_2 stand for the quantities supplied before and after the change and P_1 and P_2 represent the corresponding prices.

Test Yourself

1. Suppose that you calculate the elasticity of supply for a certain commodity to be 2.8. This means that a 1 percent increase in the price of the product will result in a 2.8 percent increase in the quantity supplied.

   (a) What would a 1 percent decrease in the price mean?

   (b) A 10 percent increase in the price?

   (c) A 10 percent decrease in the price?

2. If you estimate the elasticity of demand for a certain product to be −0.5, this means that a 1 percent increase in the price of the commodity will result in a *decrease* in the quantity demanded of ½ of 1 percent.

   (a) What would a 1 percent decrease in the price mean?

   (b) A 10 percent increase in the price?

   (c) A 10 percent decrease in the price?

3. Instead of measuring elasticity in terms of relative amounts or percentages, why not measure it in terms of actual amounts? For example, suppose that you wanted to know which has the greater influence on quantity demanded—a reduction of $100 per carat in the price of diamonds or a reduction of $1 per bushel in the price of wheat.

   (a) Would you express the price and quantity changes in terms of actual amounts or in terms of percentages?

   (b) Suppose that you chose to express the changes in terms of actual amounts. Would you be able to compare carats and bushels in order to tell which was more affected by the changes in price?

Elasticity of Demand and Total Revenue

In many practical situations involving the study of demand, economists find it convenient to have a simple guide for judging whether demand is elastic or inelastic. An easy method that can be used for this purpose is to compare the change in the price of the commodity with the corresponding change in the seller's gross receipts. These receipts are custo-marily called "total revenue." It is important to keep in mind that a seller's total revenue (abbreviated TR) is equal to price (P) per unit times the quantity (Q) of units sold. That is, $TR = P \times Q$. Thus, if a necktie manufacturer charges $10 per tie and sells 1,000 ties, the total revenue is $10,000.

Exhibit 4 illustrates the relation between demand elasticity and total revenue. These charts are similar to three of the five types of demand elasticities described in Exhibit 2.

Relatively Elastic Demand

Exhibit 4, Figure (a), illustrates a relatively elastic demand curve. Suppose that the price is at P, which is represented by the distance 0P. Then the corresponding quantity demanded is at M, measured by the distance 0M. The seller's total revenue is therefore price times quantity, or $0P \times 0M$. This is also the area of the rectangle 0PSM, because the area of *any* rectangle is the base × height.

Suppose that the selling firm lowers its price to 0T. The quantity demanded then increases to 0N. The seller's new total revenue is again equal to price times quantity, or the area of the rectangle 0TVN. This new rectangle is larger in area than the old one. That is, as a result of a price reduction, the seller has lost a relatively small amount of total revenue represented by the rectangle TPSU. The seller has also gained a larger amount of total revenue represented by the rectangle MUVN. Because the gain exceeds the loss, the seller's final total revenue is larger after the price reduction than before.

What happens if price increases, say from 0T to 0P? The result is exactly the opposite. Total revenue declines from 0TVN to 0PSM. In other words, the large loss more than offsets the small gain.

The relationship between changes in price and changes in total revenue can be readily explained in terms of elasticity. When demand is relatively elastic:

1. A given percentage decrease in price is more than offset by a corresponding percentage increase in quantity demanded. Therefore, total revenue rises.

2. A given percentage increase in price is more than offset by a corresponding percentage decrease in quantity demanded. Therefore, total revenue falls.

Exhibit 4
Demand Elasticity and Total Revenue

[handwritten: Relation Between]

A seller's total revenue is equal to the price per unit multiplied by the number of units sold. Therefore, total revenue in all three figures can be measured by the rectangular area under the demand curve. Thus, at a price equal to the distance 0P, quantity demanded is represented by the distance 0M. Therefore, total revenue is the area of the rectangle 0PSM. At a price of 0T, quantity demanded is 0N. Therefore, total revenue is the area of the rectangle 0TVN. By comparing the rectangular areas before and after a price change, you can tell whether the elasticity of the demand curve is greater than, equal to, or less than 1.

The comparisons are explained in the following descriptions:

Figure (a): Relatively Elastic When demand is relatively elastic, a decrease in price results in an increase in total revenue. Rectangle 0TVN is larger than rectangle 0PSM. Conversely, an increase in price results in a decrease in total revenue.

Figure (b): Unit Elastic When demand is unit elastic, a decrease or increase in price results in the same total revenue. Rectangle 0TVN is the same size (has the same area) as rectangle 0PSM.

Figure (c): Relatively Inelastic When demand is relatively inelastic, a decrease in price results in a decrease in total revenue. Rectangle 0TVN is smaller than rectangle 0PSM. Similarly, an increase in price results in an increase in total revenue.

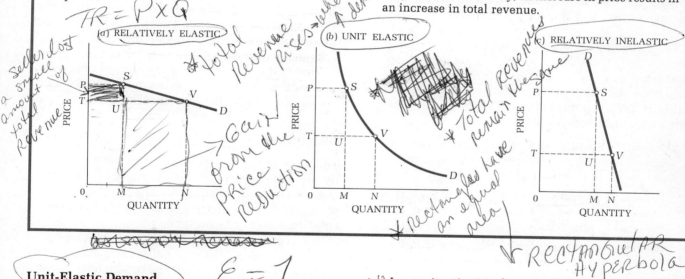

(a) RELATIVELY ELASTIC   (b) UNIT ELASTIC   (c) RELATIVELY INELASTIC)

Unit-Elastic Demand

[handwritten: E = 1]

A second type of situation is illustrated in Exhibit 4, Figure (b). Here demand is unit elastic. At a price of 0P, the quantity demanded is 0M. Hence, the seller's total revenue is the area of the rectangle 0PSM. On the other hand, at a price of 0T, the quantity demanded is 0N. Therefore, the seller's total revenue is the area of the rectangle 0TVN.

It is interesting to note that the rectangles are equal in area. That is, 0PSM = 0TVN. This suggests an important principle:

In any situation involving a unit-elastic demand curve, the rectangular areas associated with each corresponding price and quantity are always equal. This means that a given percentage decrease (or increase) in price is exactly offset by an equal percentage increase (or decrease) in quantity demanded. Consequently, the total revenues remain the same.

This principle helps to explain why a unit-elastic demand curve has such a special shape. It is the only type of mathematical curve (called a "rectangular hyperbola") that permits percentage changes in price to be exactly offset by equal percentage changes in quantity demanded. As a result, the elasticity remains equal to 1 and hence the total revenue stays constant.

Relatively Inelastic Demand

What happens in the case of a relatively inelastic demand, as in Exhibit 4, Figure (c)? The relationships are obvious. When price is reduced from $0P$ to $0T$, total revenue decreases from $0PSM$ to $0TVN$. Clearly, the percentage decrease in price more than offsets the percentage increase in quantity demanded. This causes total revenue to fall. The opposite occurs in the case of a price increase, say from $0T$ to $0P$. Total revenue rises because the percentage increase in price more than offsets the percentage decrease in quantity demanded.

The foregoing ideas are helpful for analyzing and predicting the effects of price changes on sellers' total revenues. You will encounter many practical situations in which such predictions are a useful guide to policy formulation. The basic concepts can be summarized briefly:

The relationship between price and total revenue depends on whether the elasticity of demand is greater than 1, equal to 1, or less than 1.

- If demand is relatively elastic (greater than 1), a change in price causes a change in total revenue in the *opposite* direction.
- If demand is unit elastic (equal to 1), a change in price causes *no* change in total revenue.
- If demand is relatively inelastic (less than 1), a change in price causes a change in total revenue in the *same* direction.

How well do you understand these basic ideas? You can judge for yourself by answering several relevant questions.

Some Practical Applications

1. Public transit systems often raise their rates to offset increased costs. Some of these systems find that their gross incomes decline in the first few weeks after the rate increase, and then rise. What does this suggest about the elasticity of demand for these services?

2. A country's currency may decline in value and therefore become cheaper for foreigners to buy. When this happens, the country may experience both (a) an increase in exports and (b) an influx of tourists. How would you interpret these occurrences?

3. If your college football stadium is drawing less-than-capacity crowds, under what conditions might a price increase be desirable? A price decrease? No change in price?

What Determines Elasticity?

Once you have learned how to calculate elasticity, you have mastered only half the job. The other half is to understand the factors that determine elasticity so that you can put this important concept to use. What makes some demand or supply curves elastic and others inelastic? The answers involve three key words—substitutes, inexpensiveness, and time.

Substitutes

The most important determinant of demand elasticity and supply elasticity is the number and closeness of available substitutes. That is, the elasticity of demand for a product depends on the ease of substitution in consumption.

For example, if a product has good substitutes, and if the prices of these substitutes remain the same, a rise in the price of the product will divert consumer expenditures away from the product and over to the substitutes. A fall in the product's price will swing consumer expenditures away from the substitutes and back to the product. Thus, the demand for the product tends to be elastic.

On the other hand, if good substitutes for a product are not available, consumers will not respond significantly to changes in its price. Thus, the demand for the product tends to be inelastic.

The same principle can be applied to the elasticity of supply. This depends on the ease of substitution of resources used in production.

For example, suppose the resources (such as labor and capital) that are used in the production of a certain product can easily be increased by hiring similar resources away from other activities. Then, if the price of the product rises relative to its costs of production, producers will find it profitable to produce more of it. They may do this by hiring *substitutable* resources away from other occupations, thereby increasing the output of the product.

Conversely, if the price of a product falls relative to its costs, its profitability will decline. Some of the resources engaged in producing the good may shift into other activities, thereby decreasing the output of the product.

In both instances, supply tends to be elastic because of the *ease of substitution* of the resources — that is, the ease with which they can be transferred from one activity to another. On the other hand, if it is difficult for resources to enter or leave a particular use or occupation, the supply curve will tend to be inelastic.

Inexpensiveness

The more inexpensive a product — that is, the smaller the fraction of their total expenditures consumers allocate for it — the more inelastic the demand for it tends to be. For example, the demand for salt, matches, and toothpicks tends to be relatively inelastic because these products account for a relatively small part of consumers' total expenditures.

Time

Elasticities of demand and supply for a given product tend to increase over *time*. That is, elasticities tend to be greater in the long run than in the short run, because buyers and sellers have more time to adjust to changes in price by turning to substitutes. Demands for certain products may tend to become more elastic as buyers develop new tastes and habits of consumption. Supplies of certain products may tend to become more elastic as sellers find alternative resources for producing those products.

You may think of exceptions to some of these principles. This is true of almost any principle in economics. However, there is ample evidence to indicate that the principles work in most cases.

Models of Supply and Demand

After studying supply and demand, we can apply its principles to the solution of many practical problems. Some are illustrated here in the form of real-world models involving government price fixing, taxes, and subsidies.

Price Fixing by Law

Government sometimes interferes with the normal operation of supply and demand by establishing a price that is either lower or higher than the price would be in an unregulated market. For example, price ceilings have been placed on many consumer goods during war or other critical inflationary periods to keep prices from going "too" high. Price floors have been used to keep the hourly wages (labor prices) of many workers from going "too" low. What are some of the economic effects of these legally established prices?

Price Ceilings Cause Shortages

An example of a price ceiling is provided by rent control on apartments, which has been instituted in some parts of the country. The nature of such a price ceiling is illustrated by the normal supply and demand curves in Exhibit 5. The equilibrium price that would be established in the market if there were no outside interference would be at P, represented by the distance $0P (= NP')$. The equilibrium quantity would be at N, represented by the distance $0N$.

What happens if the government regards the equilibrium price as too high? In that case, the government might establish a ceiling price, making it illegal to sell the product at any price higher than the price at H. The result will be a ***shortage*** equal to the amount RL, because this represents the excess of quantity demanded over quantity supplied at the ceiling price.

When this situation occurs, the limited amount of the product, equal to the distance $0R$, will be snatched up by the early buyers. This will leave nothing for later customers who want to buy a

Exhibit 5
Price Ceilings Result in Shortages

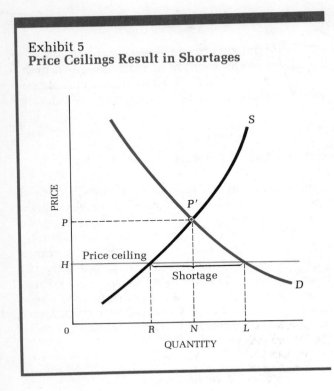

Exhibit 6
Price Floors Result in Product Surpluses

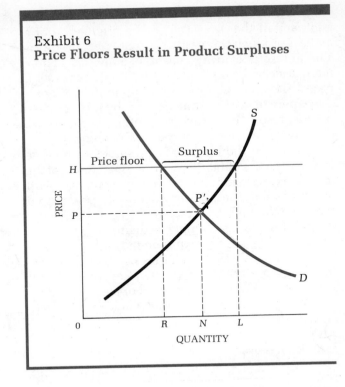

quantity of the product equal to the amount RL at the ceiling price.   The government, therefore, may find it necessary to introduce some form of *rationing* as an equitable method of allocating the limited good among all the buyers who want it.

Price Floors Cause Surpluses

Price floors, which are the opposite of price ceilings, are designed to prevent a price from falling below a specified level.   Although price ceilings have typically been a wartime phenomenon (with some exceptions), price floors have played a continuing role in our daily lives.   Two types have been particularly common: agricultural price supports and minimum-wage legislation.

The effects of these price floors are illustrated in the general model of Exhibit 6. The equilibrium price and quantity that would emerge from an unregulated market are at P and N, respectively.   But now the price at H represents a government-imposed price floor.   At this price the quantity supplied will exceed the quantity demanded, resulting in a *surplus* of the amount RL.

What can be done about this surplus?   In agriculture, where price floors for certain commodities have been employed during some periods, surpluses have been a recurrent phenomenon.   As a result, government at various times has sought to cope with the situation in three major ways:

Restrict Supply   Acreage allotments have been imposed on farmers, limiting the amount of land they can use to grow certain agricultural commodities.   (This has had the effect of shifting the supply curve to the left.)

Stimulate Demand   Research into new uses for agricultural products has been encouraged. (This has had the effect of shifting the demand curve to the right.)

Economics in the News

A Debate on the Minimum Wage: Does $3.35 Price the Young Out of the Job Market?

WASHINGTON—President Reagan sent to Congress a bill that calls for a minimum wage of $2.50 an hour for workers 16 to 19 years of age, instead of the $3.35-an-hour minimum that now applies to all workers. Labor Department officials predict that the new wage scale, which would be effective for three summers, would induce businesses to create as many as 400,000 jobs, an estimate the plan's opponents vigorously dispute.

Kenneth B. Noble, a Washington correspondent of *The Times,* asked two experts—Christopher C. Quarles 3d, a special assistant to the Secretary of Labor, and Jessica Smith, chairman of Frontlash, a youth-organizing and lobbying arm of the A.F.L.-C.I.O.—to discuss the subminimum wage and its implications. Excerpts follow:

It Works Overseas

Christopher C. Quarles 3d

Question. What is the appeal of the youth subminimum wage? And how do we know it will work?
Answer. First, every Western European democracy, as well as Japan and Australia, has had a youth differential wage for at least the past 20 years. And those countries have accepted the youth differential as a method of increasing teenage employment opportunities.

As for our figures, they were arrived at by using academic studies conducted outside the Labor Department. For every increase in the minimum wage over the past 30 years, and particularly in the past 20 years, we've seen a measurable decrease in employment among teenagers.

Q. What prevents employers from substituting teenagers for current employees?
A. Because the proposal is for the summer only, it significantly decreases an employer's incentive to discharge current employees. For employers who violate the law, the penalties include fines of up to $10,000 and up to six months in jail.

Q. Some economists say that the bulk of the new jobs will go not to inner city youths, who need them most, but to middle-class suburban youngsters. They contend that jobs available to teenagers have been steadily shifting to the suburbs.
A. By and large, the further you get into the middle-class suburbs, the less you're going to find jobs for $3.35 an hour, particularly at the convenience or fast-out stores. Based on our projections, two-thirds of the 400,000 jobs are going to be outside of the food-and-beverage industry. You'll see the teenagers as movie ushers, delivery folks and workers at retail outlets.

Equal Work, Equal Pay

Jessica Smith

Question: Why is the minority unemployment rate, particularly among blacks, so high?
Answer. Simply because there are not enough community-based jobs in low-income neighborhoods; it's also because of discrimination in the workplace, and we don't have enough job-training placement programs in schools attended by inner-city youths. It's clear that a lot of young people do all they can to create work for themselves, but there just aren't enough jobs there. Also, they don't have the basic skills and discipline to find jobs.

Q. But won't the Administration's proposal be a step in the right direction?
A. No, we think it violates the principle of equal pay for equal work. And then, generally, businesses don't hire more young people than they can use, no matter what the wage costs are.

Q. Do you agree that sanctions prohibiting employers from substituting teenagers for current employees are tough enough?
A. No. Take, for instance, the employer presented with two individuals who come to interview for a job. One is 20 years old, which means that he would get $3.35. The other is 19 and could be hired at $2.50. It would be very hard to prove that the 19-year-old was hired because of the lower wage.

Buy up Surpluses   Certain agricultural commodities have been bought and stored by the government for future sale or disposal. (This has had mixed effects on the shifting of supply and demand curves, depending upon how the surpluses are managed.)

The government could have eliminated the surpluses by removing the price floor, thus allowing the price to settle at P. But that would have nullified the government's objective of raising farm prices in order to help farmers.

With respect to minimum wages, Exhibit 6 may be thought of as a model of the supply and demand for labor. Let the horizontal axis measure the quantity of labor in terms of hours of labor time, and let the vertical axis measure the price of labor in terms of dollars per hour. The surplus is then the volume of unemployment RL occurring at the minimum-wage level at H.

One way to reduce this labor surplus is to *lower* the hourly wage rate. What would this do to total payrolls if the demand for labor were relatively elastic? What would it do to them if the demand were relatively inelastic? Can you suggest other methods of reducing the unemployment surplus?

Effects of Specific Taxes and Subsidies

Supply and demand analysis can be helpful in solving problems involving certain kinds of commodity taxes and subsidies. As the following examples demonstrate, different degrees of elasticity affect in surprising ways the prices and quantities of some of the things we buy every day.

Specific Taxes

Suppose a *specific tax* is imposed on the sale of a good. That is, for each unit of a good sold a fixed amount of money is paid to the government. A specific tax is thus a *per-unit tax* that is independent of the price of the product. Some taxes on cigarettes and gasoline are of this kind.

How does a specific tax on a product affect its market prices and quantities? Is the *incidence*, or burden, of such a tax borne by those upon whom it is initially imposed, or is it *shifted* to others? These are practical questions that the analysis answers.

You can proceed by first examining the model in Exhibit 7, Figure (a). The curves D and S are the market demand and supply curves before the tax is

imposed. The equilibrium quantity is therefore at N; the equilibrium price is the distance NP.

Suppose that sellers are required to pay a tax of T per unit. The results of such a tax are these:

1. The supply curve shifts upward to the parallel position S', showing that less will be supplied at any given price. This is because the tax is an added cost to the producer at all levels of output. Hence, the **supply price**—the price necessary to call forth a given output—will be higher by the amount of the tax. For example, before the tax, consumers paid a price equal to NP to obtain the quantity at N. After the tax they must pay a price of NR to call forth the same quantity at N. When the selling firm receives NR, it will pay a tax of PR (=T) to the government, leaving itself with NP, the old price.

2. The tax will therefore cause the equilibrium point to shift from P to H. This movement will be associated with a decrease in quantity from 0N to 0L and an increase in price from NP to LH, where GH is the amount of the tax.

Importance of Elasticities

Are there any general principles that can tell us the extent to which prices and quantities will be altered as a result of the tax? Figures (b), (c), and (d) in Exhibit 7 will help answer this question.

In Figure (b), demand is perfectly elastic. That is, any increase in price will cause sales to drop to zero. Thus, the same price is maintained after the tax as before, but sellers compensate for the added cost of the tax by reducing their quantity. Consumers will get fewer units of the good, although they will continue to pay the same price per unit.

In Figure (c), the demand curve is perfectly inelastic. That is, no one will buy less of the product if the price is raised. Therefore, the entire burden of the tax is shifted forward from sellers to buyers in the form of a higher price, with no reduction in the equilibrium quantity.

In Figure (d), supply is perfectly elastic, and both price and quantity are affected as a result. The

Exhibit 7
Effects of Specific Taxes and Subsidies

Taxes will affect the equilibrium prices and quantities of commodities, depending on the relative elasticities of demand and supply. Subsidies have effects that are opposite to the effects of taxes, but their influence is also determined by the relative elasticities of demand and supply.

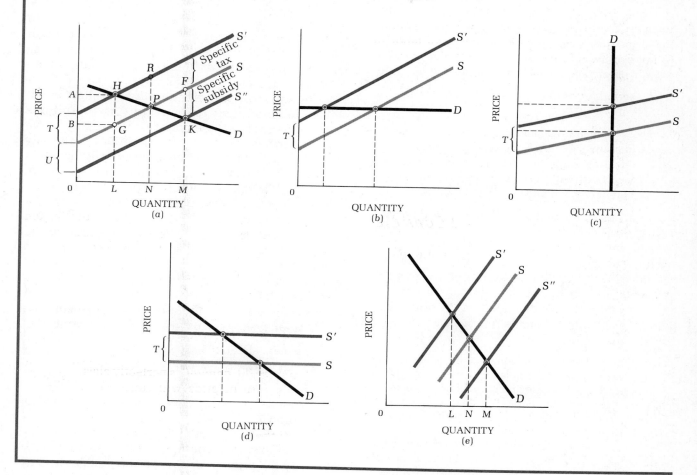

burden of the tax is shifted entirely to buyers, *and* the equilibrium quantity is reduced. Note how this compares with the case in Figure (c), in which only price is affected, not quantity. What would have happened in Figure (d) if the demand curve had been perfectly inelastic?

We can now establish two important principles:

— The more *inelastic* the demand and the supply of a commodity, the smaller will be the decline in output resulting from a given tax. [This is illustrated in Figure (e), where the letters have the same meaning as before. In this figure, both demand and supply are more inelastic than in (a). Therefore, a given amount of tax leads to a smaller decrease in supply.]

— The relative burden of a tax among buyers and sellers tends to follow the path of least resistance. That is, the tax is shifted in proportion to where the inelasticity is greatest.

The first principle leads to the following practical conclusion:

If government wants to minimize disruptions in production, industries whose goods are inelastic in demand and supply are better suited to specific taxation. This is because such industries suffer smaller contractions in output and hence in employment.

The second principle results in another useful conclusion:

In most supply-and-demand situations (except the extreme ones involving perfect elasticity or inelasticity), the tax will be shared by consumers and producers. The proportions will vary according to the relative elasticities of demand and supply.

From what you have learned, you should be able to illustrate both these propositions with supply and demand curves. Thus, as a result of the tax, the consumer's price will rise, but by less than the amount of the tax. Similarly, the producer's net price will fall, but by less than the amount of the tax. However, the *relative* changes in prices and quantities will depend on the *relative* elasticities of demand and supply.

NOTE   Exhibit 7 does not demonstrate the effect of a tax in the case of a perfectly inelastic supply curve. Can you illustrate such a case and explain it? Be careful; this is a tricky question. (HINT   If the supply curve is perfectly inelastic, can it shift as a result of the tax?) You will learn more about this problem in a subsequent chapter when you encounter a concept known as the "single tax." This idea once played an interesting role in American politics. In the meantime, see if you can work out the answer yourself.

Subsidies

A *subsidy* is a payment a government makes to businesses or households to achieve a particular purpose. The subsidy enables them to produce or consume a product in larger quantities or at lower prices than they would be able to otherwise. Government subsidies have been granted, and in some cases continue to be granted, to farmers, airlines, railroads, shipping companies, shipbuilding firms, low-income households, and certain other groups in the economy.

A *specific subsidy* is a per-unit subsidy on a commodity. It is thus the opposite of a specific tax. In fact, a specific subsidy can be thought of as a "negative" specific tax because the government is giving money to the seller or to the consumer rather than taking it away.

The effects of a specific subsidy on sellers are illustrated in Exhibit 7, Figure (a). As a result of a subsidy equal to the amount U, the supply curve shifts downward from its normal position S to the new position S''. This is because the subsidy is like a reduction in cost to the producer at all levels of output. Therefore, the supply price will be lower by the amount of the subsidy.

For instance, the subsidy causes the equilibrium point to shift from P to K. Hence, the equilibrium price decreases from NP to MK and the equilibrium output increases from $0N$ to $0M$. At this new and larger output, buyers will pay the price MK but sellers will receive the additional amount KF ($= U$). This is the amount of the subsidy per unit of output.

Our analysis leads us to an important principle:

The more elastic the supply and demand curves, the greater will be the expansion in output and the less will be the reduction in price resulting from a subsidy.

This can be verified by comparing Figures (a) and (e) in Exhibit 7.

The economic purposes of a subsidy are to reduce prices or to increase output. The latter objective is usually the primary one when the product is to be used wholly for domestic consumption. These ideas suggest a practical conclusion:

Subsidies to increase production work best if supply and demand for the products subsidized are relatively elastic. With such products, a given amount of subsidy leads to larger expansions in output and therefore in employment.

Economics in the News

A Subsidy Both Woolly-Headed and Mammoth

By James Bovard

The wool program is agricultural policy at its worst—ineffective, expensive and incorrigible. Since Congress began subsidizing sheep farmers after World War II to encourage the wool industry, production has fallen 75 percent, wool quality has slumped, and foreign producers have surpassed Americans in every measure.

One reason the program has so little effect is that wool is a byproduct of sheep production, providing only 20 percent to 30 percent of revenue. Sheep are raised primarily for their meat. A big increase in wool prices yields only a slight increase in sheep revenue. The General Accounting Office estimated in 1982 that the wool program has increased sheep production 6 percent to 13 percent.

Nor does the sheep farmer always benefit from raising more sheep. Because lamb and mutton prices are very elastic, a slight increase in supply often means a sizable drop in prices. The wool program, which works so hard to drive up the price for a sheep byproduct, probably drives down the price for the main product.

What would happen if the wool program were abolished tomorrow? Under the "Chicken Little" scenario offered by farm lobbyists, no more wool would be produced. But since the U.S. produces less than 2 percent of the world's wool, the loss wouldn't shake the pillars of commerce. Rather than getting almost all of their wool from overseas, U.S. consumers would get all of it from abroad. Many ranchers would, instead of raising sheep at a loss, raise cattle for a profit. The Pentagon could stockpile wool for less than the current program costs.

The wool program is the perfect example of our lethargic agricultural policies. It hasn't worked in the past, it isn't working now, and no one on Capitol Hill honestly expects it to work in the future.

Subsidies are also quite common in international trade. They occur when a government subsidizes a firm or even an entire industry to help it penetrate foreign markets at lower prices. For example, at various times Japan has been accused by its trading partners of subsidizing the production of automobiles, steel, electronic products, and cameras in order to encourage exports of these products.

Other Kinds of Elasticity and Their Uses

Early in this chapter you learned that elasticity is a measure of the responsiveness of changes in quantity (demanded or supplied) to changes in price. Actually, this kind of elasticity, called "price elasticity," is one of many kinds used in economics. However, it is the most common of all elasticity measures. Therefore, in any discussion of an economic or business problem, the term "elasticity" always means price elasticity unless otherwise indicated.

What are some other kinds of elasticity? Two that are especially useful are the income elasticity of demand and the cross elasticity of demand.

Income Elasticity of Demand

When you draw a demand curve that shows a relationship between price and quantity demanded, one of the things you assume to be constant is buyers' incomes. But if incomes change, the demand curve shifts—that is, there is a change in demand. How much of a change? The answer depends on the income elasticity of demand.

> The ***income elasticity of demand*** is the percentage change in the quantity purchased of a good resulting from a 1 percent change in income. This kind of elasticity thus measures the responsiveness of changes in demand to changes in income.

The method of measuring income elasticity is the same as that for measuring price elasticity. As you will recall, price elasticity is simply the ratio of the percentage change in quantity (demanded or supplied) to the percentage change in price. Similarly, the income elasticity of demand is the ratio of the percentage change in quantity purchased to the percentage change in income. Thus,

income elasticity of demand

$$= \frac{\text{percentage change in quantity purchased}}{\text{percentage change in income}}$$

It follows that the formula used for measuring income elasticity is the same as that for price elasticity — except for some differences in symbols. Thus, let

Q_1 = old quantity, or quantity purchased before the change in income

Q_2 = new quantity, or quantity purchased after the change in income

Y_1 = old income, or income before the change

Y_2 = new income, or income after the change

The formula for the income elasticity of demand is

$$_YE_D = \frac{\dfrac{Q_2 - Q_1}{Q_2 + Q_1}}{\dfrac{Y_2 - Y_1}{Y_2 + Y_1}}$$

NOTE Economists usually employ the letter Y to represent income because *I* is customarily used to represent investment.

Measurement and Interpretation

How is the income elasticity of demand interpreted? What are its uses?

It will help your understanding if you see how the income elasticity of demand is measured in a real-life situation. Exhibit 8 provides an example.

The data suggest that goods can be classified according to their income elasticity of demand. One such classification distinguishes between "superior" and "inferior" goods. (In this use, the word "goods" includes services.)

Exhibit 8
Measuring the Income Elasticity of Demand

Suppose that your monthly income, and some of the things you spend it on, are shown in the table. You can calculate your income elasticity of demand for each item quite easily. The following calculation, involving record albums, provides an example.

$$_YE_D = \frac{\dfrac{Q_2 - Q_1}{Q_2 + Q_1}}{\dfrac{Y_2 - Y_1}{Y_2 + Y_1}} = \frac{\dfrac{2 - 1}{2 + 1}}{\dfrac{\$1,500 - \$1,000}{\$1,500 + \$1,000}} = \frac{\dfrac{1}{3}}{\dfrac{1}{5}} = 1.67$$

You should verify the remaining elasticities shown in the table in the same way. For each good, be careful to pair Q_1 with Y_1 and Q_2 with Y_2, to avoid errors.

Item	Quantity purchased per month at \$1,000 income per month	Quantity purchased per month at \$1,500 income per month	Income elasticity of demand (calculated) $_YE_D$
Albums	1	2	1.67
Hamburgers	10	15	1.00
Magazines	4	5	0.56
Movies	3	3	0
Pizzas	4	3	−0.71

Superior Goods: $_YE_D > 0$ The income elasticity of demand for some goods is greater than zero. That is, the coefficient is positive. Such products are called **superior goods.** Consumption of these goods varies directly with money income, prices remaining constant. In the hypothetical illustration of Exhibit 8, record albums, hamburgers, and magazines are examples of superior goods. Each has an income elasticity of demand greater than zero. As you might expect, most goods are superior goods. That is, their consumption increases with income. Such goods are also called *normal goods*, because they represent the "normal" situation.

Superior goods can be subclassified in terms of income elasticity. If the income elasticity coefficient is greater than 1, the demand for the commodity is said to be income elastic. If the coefficient is less than 1 but greater than 0, the demand is said to be income inelastic. In Exhibit 8, record albums are income elastic while magazines are income inelastic. Hamburgers, being a borderline case, may be classified as income unit-elastic.

Inferior Goods: $_YE_D < 0$ The income elasticity of demand for some goods may be less than zero. That is, the coefficient may be negative. Such products are called ***inferior goods.*** Their consumption varies inversely with money income (prices remaining constant) over a certain range of income. Potatoes, used clothing, and other "cheap" commodities bought in relatively larger quantities by poorer families are examples. The consumption of these commodities declines in favor of fancier foods, new clothing, and the like as the incomes of low-income families rise. In the hypothetical example of Exhibit 8, pizza is an illustration of an inferior good. (Note that, unlike the price elasticity of demand studied earlier, the negative sign is not disregarded when reporting income elasticity of demand.)

Income elasticities of demand vary widely from product to product and from person to person. Indeed, a good that is superior for one individual may be inferior for another, and vice versa. Nevertheless, there are certain overall tendencies that can be observed.

Commodities that consumers regard as "necessities" tend to be income inelastic. Examples are food, fuel, utilities, and medical services. Commodities that consumers regard as "luxuries" tend to be income elastic. Examples are sports cars, furs, costly vacation trips, and expensive foods. Therefore, the income elasticity of demand provides an approximate guide for judging the importance of commodities to consumers.

Cross Elasticity of Demand   ~~Test~~

When you draw a demand curve, you assume that buyers' incomes and the prices of other goods remain constant. Of course, buyers' incomes may

vary. If they do, the resulting change in demand is measured by the income elasticity of demand. But what if prices of other goods vary? In that case, the resulting change in demand is measured by a new relationship—the cross elasticity of demand.

The ***cross elasticity of demand*** is the percentage change in the quantity purchased of a good resulting from a 1 percent change in the price of another good. This kind of elasticity thus measures the responsiveness of changes in the demand for one good to changes in the price of another.

Like every other kind of elasticity, the cross elasticity of demand is a ratio of two percentage changes. Its formula is the same as all other elasticity formulas, except for the choice of symbols. Thus, let

Q_{X1} = quantity purchased of product X before a change in the price of product Y

Q_{X2} = quantity purchased of product X after a change in the price of product Y

P_{Y1} = price of product Y before the change

P_{Y2} = price of product Y after the change

The cross elasticity of demand, $_+E_D$, is thus measured by the formula

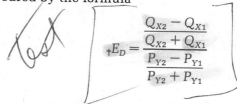

$$_+E_D = \frac{\dfrac{Q_{X2} - Q_{X1}}{Q_{X2} + Q_{X1}}}{\dfrac{P_{Y2} - P_{Y1}}{P_{Y2} + P_{Y1}}}$$

Measurement and Interpretation

Exhibit 9 shows three practical applications of this formula. The diagrams are derived from several recent business studies. As they show, the cross elasticities of demand for products will differ according to whether the products are substitutes, complements, or independent.

Substitutes: $_+E_D > 0$ Substitute goods are goods that compete with one another. The more you consume of one, the less you consume of the other. Examples are butter and margarine, coffee and tea, automobile and bus transportation.

*an increase in the cost of hot dogs will cause a decrease in the sale of buns.

*items that are usually bought together

Exhibit 9
Measuring the Cross Elasticity of Demand

Substitute Goods: In Figure (a), an increase in the price of Coca-Cola causes a *decrease in quantity demanded*. This, in turn, leads to an *increase in demand* for Pepsi-Cola, shown in Figure (b). Figure (c) estimates the cross elasticity of demand for Pepsi-Cola relative to the price of Coca-Cola.

Complementary Goods: In Figure (d), an increase in the price of shirts causes a *decrease in quantity demanded*. In Figure (e), therefore, there is a *decrease in demand* for ties as the curve shifts to the left. Figure (f) estimates the cross elasticity of demand for ties relative to the price of shirts.

Independent Goods: In Figure (g), changes in the price of lettuce have no effect on the demand for catsup, beer, or milk. Therefore, as shown in the graph, cross elasticities of demand for these products relative to the price of lettuce are zero.

CROSS elasticity of demand

*leftward shift of the Demand curve

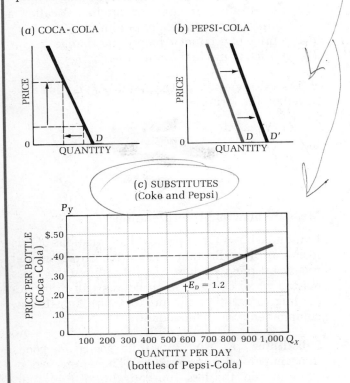

(a) COCA-COLA

(b) PEPSI-COLA

(c) SUBSTITUTES
(Coke and Pepsi)

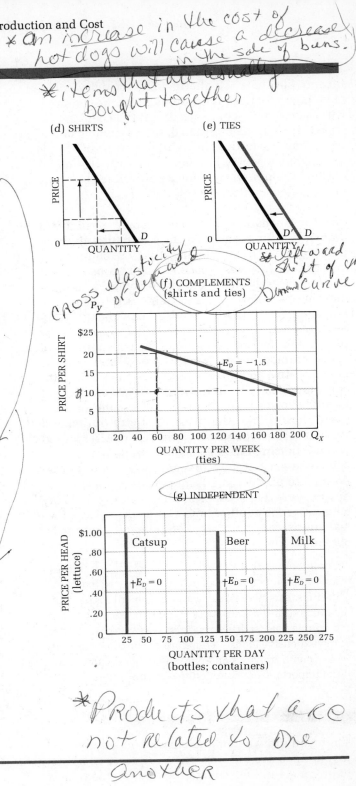

(d) SHIRTS

(e) TIES

(f) COMPLEMENTS
(shirts and ties)

(g) INDEPENDENT

*Products that are not related to one another

The cross elasticity of demand for substitute goods is significantly greater than zero. The coefficient is thus positive. The reason is that a price increase for one of the goods causes people to buy less of that good and more of the substitute. Hence, the quantity purchased of the substitute increases.

This idea is illustrated in Figures (a), (b), and (c) of Exhibit 9. Figure (a) shows a hypothetical demand curve for Coca-Cola. Similarly, Figure (b) shows a hypothetical demand curve for Pepsi-Cola.

What happens if there is an increase in the price of Coca-Cola? Obviously, less of it will be bought. There will be a *decrease in quantity demanded*, a movement "up" the curve. However, many people who previously bought Coca-Cola will now switch to Pepsi-Cola. As a result, there will be an *increase in demand* for Pepsi-Cola, shown as a shift of the demand curve to the right. Thus, the overall effect of an increase in the price of Coca-Cola is to reduce its sales while increasing the sales of Pepsi-Cola.

The opposite effects occur, of course, if there is a decrease in the price of Coca-Cola: The demand curve for Pepsi-Cola shifts to the left.

Figure (c) shows the actual consequences of changes in the price of Coca-Cola. These results are derived from a set of demand studies conducted for a chain of supermarkets. Note that higher prices of Coke result in increased purchases of Pepsi. Therefore, the cross elasticity of demand is positive. You should verify this result by applying the cross-elasticity formula to the data in the chart.

Complements: $_+E_D < 0$ Complementary goods are goods that "go together." The more you consume of one, the more you consume of the other. Examples are cameras and film, and gasoline and tires.

The cross elasticity of demand for complementary goods is significantly less than zero. The coefficient is therefore negative. The reason is that, as the price of a good increases, people buy less of it. Therefore they also buy less of the complementary goods. The opposite effects occur, of course, if the price of a good decreases.

These ideas can be seen in Figures (d), (e), and (f) of Exhibit 9. Figures (d) and (e) show hypothetical demand curves for shirts and ties. In Figure (d), an

increase in the price of shirts causes a *decrease in quantity demanded*. In Figure (e), therefore, there is a *decrease in demand* for ties, as shown by a leftward shift of the curve.

Some actual relationships, based on demand studies conducted for a department store, are shown in Figure (f). The downward-sloping curve tells you that the cross elasticity of demand must be negative. You should verify the estimate by applying the cross-elasticity formula to the data in the figure. (Note that, as with the income elasticity of demand, the negative sign is included when reporting the cross elasticity of demand.)

Independent: $_+E_D = 0$ Independent goods are unrelated. The consumption of one is not directly influenced by the consumption of the other. Consequently, changes in the price of one have no significant effect on quantities purchased of the other. The cross elasticity of demand is therefore zero.

An illustration of the cross elasticity of demand for independent goods is provided in Exhibit 9, Figure (g). Some examples of other pairs of independent or unrelated goods are pizza and jewelry, books and dishes, egg rolls and wristwatches.

Simple Rules to Remember

The following rules will help you remember these ideas:

The cross elasticity of demand provides a measure of *substitutability* between products. In general:

Goods whose cross elasticities of demand are significantly greater than zero may be thought of as "positive substitutes." (Examples are competing brands of goods in the same industry, such as soaps, toothpastes, and television sets.)

Goods whose cross elasticities of demand are approximately zero may be thought of as "weak substitutes" or "nonsubstitutes."

Goods whose cross elasticities of demand are significantly less than zero are complements. Such goods may be thought of as "negative substitutes."

[handwritten: coefficient is negative]

[handwritten: cross elasticities of demand < 0 = "Complements"]

The DuPont Cellophane Case: Using Cross Elasticity in the Courtroom

Every business firm would like to be a monopoly (the sole producer of a product) in order to have greater control over its prices and profits. But monopolies, if unregulated by government, could exploit their market power at the expense of the public. For this reason, government has enacted laws, called antitrust laws, that prohibit firms from obtaining or seeking a monopoly.

But What Is the Market?

In enforcing the laws, the government sometimes must specify the market for a particular product. This can be difficult. If substitution were not possible, every brand of every product would have a monopoly. If substitution were extremely easy, monopoly would be virtually nonexistent. The problem is to draw the proper boundaries — that is, to *define the relevant market.*

For example, are rugs, carpets, and linoleum sold in separate markets? Or are they all sold in the floor-covering market? Should toasters and blenders be classified in separate industries? Or are they both part of the electrical appliance industry?

The task of defining the relevant market has been undertaken by the courts in numerous cases. One of the most famous occurred in 1956. The E. I. DuPont Corporation, sole producer of cellophane, was charged by the U.S. Department of Justice with monopolizing the market. Was the company guilty or innocent? The answer depended on the definition of the market.

The government (that is, the Justice Department) argued that the relevant market was that for cellophane. Therefore DuPont clearly had a monopoly because it controlled the entire output of the product.

DuPont replied that the relevant market was that for flexible packaging materials. These included cellophane, waxed papers, parchment papers, aluminum foil, pliofilm, and glassine. In that market, cellophane accounted for only 18 percent of the total.

Substitutability to the Rescue

A Federal District court found in favor of DuPont. The case was appealed to the Supreme Court, and the lower court's verdict was upheld. Both courts agreed that "a relevant market exists when commodities are reasonably interchangeable by consumers for the same purposes."

Both courts also agreed that the relevant market determined the boundaries of the industry. According to the Supreme Court's majority opinion, "The cross elasticity of demand for cellophane was high and competition intense. . . . The relevant market, therefore, was not that for cellophane produced by the defendant . . . but for flexible packaging materials produced by various firms."

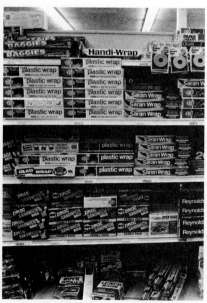

Robert Rattner

Flexible packaging materials: substitutes for cellophane.

Some Warning Notes on Assumptions

Before we conclude this study of supply and demand, it is important that you recognize certain assumptions that underlie the previous models. Two special assumptions are relevant to the kinds of models developed in this chapter. These serve as warnings about the limitations of the analysis.

Simplification Versus Complexity

Theoretical models of supply and demand make the simplifying assumption that economic actions—such as the imposition of price ceilings, price floors, taxes, or subsidies—can be analyzed in terms of economic considerations alone. These models thus neglect noneconomic factors. In reality, both types of conditions are usually at work.

Likewise, in analyzing the effects of taxes, subsidies, and so on, it must be remembered that conditions vary in the real world. Supply and demand curves are always changing over time as a result of changes in technology, tastes, and other factors ordinarily assumed constant. Complexities such as these must be introduced if the models are to be made more realistic.

Static Models Versus Dynamic Reality

Another important limitation of supply and demand models is that they are *static* rather than *dynamic*. Stated simply, a static model examines the effects of a change *after* it occurs. A dynamic model, however, examines the effects of a change *while* it is occurring. Thus, in a dynamic model, the influence of expectations by buyers or sellers would be recognized. This is because the process of moving toward an equilibrium might itself cause changes in the supply and demand curves.

As an example, a fall in the price of a good might prompt consumers to postpone their purchases of it in anticipation of further price decreases. This would cause a shift to the left of the demand curve. On the other hand, the supply curve of the good might shift to the right as suppliers sought to offset the future effects of the expected price drop by producing and selling more now at the higher price. Situations such as these continually occur in some markets (the stock market is an example) making it extremely difficult to predict future prices.

Fortunately, these limitations do not make static models too simple to be useful. They merely remind you that any model is a simplification of reality, and that care should be taken not to claim that a model is more than it really is.

Supply, Demand, and Price

You have learned how prices and quantities are determined under competitive market circumstances. It will be useful at this point to summarize what you know.

- Central to supply and demand is the idea that competition among many buyers and sellers will cause market prices and quantities to move toward equilibrium.

- Prices in a competitive market reflect the degree of *eagerness* of people to buy or sell. In such markets there will be a tendency for equilibrium prices to establish themselves automatically through the free operation of supply and demand.

- Once equilibrium prices are established, they will remain stable unless there are changes in the factors that determine supply and demand.

The third point requires some amplification. In reality, the equilibrium price is not likely to be the actual price that exists at any given instant. The forces that are at work to determine an equilibrium price are always changing, thus causing the equilibrium price to change. In view of this, it helps to distinguish between two kinds of price:

The **market price** is the actual price that prevails in a market at any particular moment. The **normal price** is the equilibrium price toward which the market price is always tending but may never reach. (Normal price may thus be viewed as a dynamic equilibrium price.)

& a target price

You can think of the market price as pursuing the normal price in much the same way as a guided missile pursues a moving target. The missile may never reach the target, just as the market price may never reach the dynamic equilibrium price. Yet the existence of a target is necessary to explain where the missile is heading, just as the concept of a normal (equilibrium) price is necessary to explain where the market price is heading.

Conclusion: The Price System As a Rationing (Allocative) Mechanism

We now come to one of the most significant ideas in the study of economics: *how the market system allocates scarce goods among competing buyers*.

You already know that scarcity — the inability of limited resources to produce all the goods and services that people want — is an economic fact of life. In a command economy some central authority — perhaps a king, a commissar, or a committee — decides the alternative uses to which these limited resources will be put. To a large extent the central authority may also ration the fruits among the members of society. In that way, a command economy answers three big questions: *what* to produce, *how* to produce, and *for whom* to produce.

In a pure market economy, on the other hand, these questions are answered by a competitive price system through the free operation of supply and demand. The concept, described in Exhibit 10, shows that the equilibrium price automatically admits certain buyers and sellers to the marketplace while simultaneously excluding others. The cost of admission to the market is the *demand price* for buyers and the *supply price* for sellers — two terms that are already familiar to you. The diagram and its accompanying description thus lead to the following conclusion:

A *price system* is a mechanism that allocates scarce goods and resources among competing uses. The price system accomplishes this by rationing goods among those buyers and sellers in the marketplace who are willing and able to deal at the market price.

Exhibit 10
How a Market Economy Rations (Allocates) Goods or Resources Among Buyers and Sellers

The equilibrium price serves as a highly selective filter. It admits to the market only those buyers whose demand price is greater than, or equal to, the equilibrium price and those sellers whose supply price is less than, or equal to, the equilibrium price. All buyers and sellers who are not able and willing to deal at the going price are excluded.

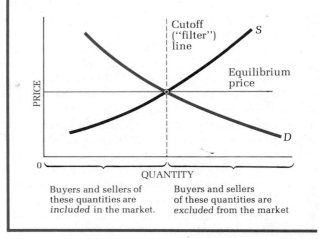

A price system in a competitive market allocates goods and resources through the free play of supply-and-demand forces. These, in turn, result from the interaction of many sellers and buyers. But what about "noncompetitive" price systems, in which buyers or sellers are relatively few? As you will see in later chapters, such systems result in pricing situations quite different from those that occur in the supply-and-demand models studied so far.

What You Have Learned

1. Elasticity is a basic concept in supply-and-demand analysis. It may be defined interpretively as the percentage change in quantity (demanded or supplied) result-

ing from a 1 percent change in price. Elasticity may also be defined mathematically as a ratio: elasticity = (percentage change in quantity)/(percentage change in price).

2. The coefficient of elasticity is commonly expressed in its absolute-value, or numerical form. This means that any minus signs are disregarded. There are five types of elasticity, ranging from zero to infinity:

perfect elasticity	$(E = \infty)$
relative elasticity	$(E > 1)$
unit elasticity	$(E = 1)$
relative inelasticity	$(E < 1)$
perfect inelasticity	$(E = 0)$

Know THESE TYPES of Elasticity

These five types of elasticity apply both to supply and to demand.

3. Because elasticity is a measure of relative changes, it may vary for each segment along a curve. The formula used for elasticity gives a type of "average" elasticity over an entire segment.

4. You can tell whether demand elasticity is greater or less than 1 by observing the effect of a price change on total revenue. If price and total revenue change in opposite directions, demand elasticity is greater than 1. If price and total revenue change in the same direction, demand elasticity is less than 1.

5. The availability of good product substitutes tends to make demand more elastic. Similarly, the availability of good resource substitutes tends to make supply more elastic. Goods that are relatively inexpensive tend to be more inelastic in demand. This is because they account for only a small part of the consumer's total expenditures.

6. Elasticities of demand and supply tend to be greater over longer periods of time. The reason is that buyers and sellers can eventually adjust to the use of substitutes.

7. Price ceilings are imposed to keep the market price of a commodity below its normal (free-market) equilibrium price. Price floors, on the other hand, are imposed to keep the market price of a commodity above its normal (free-market) equilibrium price. Price ceilings cause product shortages and may lead to rationing. Price floors cause product surpluses, which may require government action to absorb them.

8. Specific taxes tend to be shifted between buyers and sellers according to where the inelasticity is greatest. Industries whose goods are inelastic in demand and supply are better suited to commodity taxation because they suffer smaller contractions in output and hence in employment. However, industries whose goods are relatively elastic in demand and supply are better suited to subsidies because a given amount of subsidy leads to larger expansions in output and hence in employment.

9. The term "elasticity" always means price elasticity, unless otherwise indicated. In addition to price elasticity, two important kinds of elasticity are (a) the income elasticity of demand and (b) the cross elasticity of demand. The first measures the responsiveness of quantity purchased of a good to changes in income. The second measures the responsiveness of quantity purchased of a good to changes in the price of another good.

10. Some important points should be kept in mind in regard to supply-and-demand concepts:

(a) Simple supply-and-demand models do not take into account complex economic and noneconomic considerations, and they are static rather than dynamic.

(b) The competitive market is always tending toward the equilibrium price, but it may never reach that price because the underlying forces are always changing.

(c) In a market economy, the price system allocates goods and resources by rationing them among those buyers and sellers whose demand and supply prices are sufficient to admit them to the market.

Terms and Concepts To Review

elasticity	income elasticity of
shortage	demand
rationing	superior good
surplus	inferior good
specific tax	cross elasticity of
incidence	demand
supply price	market price
subsidy	normal price
specific subsidy	price system

For Discussion

1. Several studies have found that the overall demand for automobiles has an elasticity of about 1.3. (a) How do you interpret this coefficient? (b) After reading these studies, a Ford dealer cut prices by 10 percent and sold 22 percent more cars. What is the elasticity of demand in this case? Was the estimate of 1.3 incorrect? Explain.

2. Suppose that we are given the following demand schedule for a commodity:

		Price (cents)	Quantity demanded
A		20	50
B		15	100
C		10	200
D		5	400

(a) Calculate the elasticity between points A and B, B and C, C and D. (SUGGESTION Sketch the demand curve and label it with the points A, B, C, D in order to help you "see" what you are doing.)

(b) How will your results compare if you calculate the elasticity in reverse directions (that is, from B to A, C to B, and D to C)? Explain.

3. Fill in the blank cell in each of the following rows:

Price	Total revenue	Elasticity
increases	decrease	>1
decreases	decreases	<1, inelas
decreases	no change	unit
increase	increases	<1
raise	decreases	>1
increases	same	1

4. "At a given price ceiling or price floor, the size of a shortage or surplus varies directly with the elasticity of the demand and supply curves." Demonstrate this propostion graphically.

5. Many people criticize public transit systems (subways, buses, and so on) for being too crowded during rush hours. From what you know about the price system as a rationing mechanism, how would you correct the situation?

6. The R. H. Lacy Co., a department store, conducted a study of the demand for men's ties made from low-cost synthetic fibers. The store found that the average daily demand D in terms of price P is given by the equation $D = 60 - 5P$.

(a) How many ties per day can the store expect to sell at a price of $3 per tie?

(b) If the store wants to sell 20 ties per day, what price should it charge?

(c) What would the quantity demanded be if the store offered to give the ties away free?

(d) What is the highest price that anyone would be willing to pay for these ties?

(e) Plot the demand curve.

7. The demand D for sugar in the United States in terms of its price P was once estimated to be $D = 135 - 8P$. If this equation were valid today:

(a) How much would be demanded at a price of 10?

(b) What price would correspond to a quantity demanded of 95?

(c) How much would be demanded if sugar were free?

(d) What is the highest price anyone would pay?

8. The demand D for a certain product in terms of its price P is given by the equation $D = 3a - 3bP$, in which a and b are positive constants.

(a) Find the price if the quantity demanded is $a/2$.

(b) Find the quantity demanded at a price of $a/3b$.

(c) How much will the quantity demanded be if the product is free?

(d) What is the highest price anyone will pay for the good?

9. **Principles or Proverbs?** Many statements of an economic nature are accepted as principles when, in reality, they are hardly more than proverbs. The differences between the two are by no means trivial. For one thing, principles are never contradictory, whereas proverbs often are. (EXAMPLE "Look before you leap"; however, "He who hesitates is lost.") Statements such as the following are often heard. Are they principles or proverbs? Explain. Rephrase if necessary to improve the statement. Use examples.

(a) "Inexpensive products tend to have inelastic demands."

(b) "The demands of rich consumers are less elastic than the demands of poor consumers."

(c) "Products whose purchases are closely correlated with income are elastic in demand."

10. "Demand elasticity measures percentage changes in quantity demanded relative to percentage changes in price. It follows that, with 10 equal demanders for a product, the elasticity will be 10 times as great as it is for one." True or false? Explain.

11. "The elasticity of demand for a product usually increases with the length of time over which a price change persists. Thus, a 1 percent decrease in price may result at first in an increase in quantity demanded of less than 1 percent, but eventually the quantity may increase by 2 percent, 5 percent, or even more." True or false? Explain why.

12. Are the following statements true or false? Explain.
    (a) "For most consumers, the income elasticity of demand for restaurant meals is probably lower than the income elasticity of demand for ball-point pens."
    (b) "For some commodities, the price elasticity of demand may be greater than 1 (that is, relatively elastic) while the income elasticity of demand is negative."
    (c) "The cross elasticity of demand for commodity A relative to the price of commodity B may be quite different from the cross elasticity of demand for commodity B relative to the price of commodity A."

Chapter 20

Looking Behind the Demand Curve: Utility and Consumer Demand

Learning Guide

Watch for answers to these important questions

Why do demand curves slope downward?

What is the meaning of utility? How does it enter into the determination of consumer equilibrium?

How is consumer surplus identified and measured on a demand graph? How is it measured on a marginal-utility graph?

How do the shortcomings of utility theory relate to the law of demand? Is the law useless because of these shortcomings?

In economics, the term *demand*, with reference to market demand, has a specific meaning. Demand is a dependent relationship indicating the quantity of a particular commodity that will be purchased at various prices — other things remaining the same. This relationship, as you have seen, can be portrayed numerically in the form of a demand schedule or graphically in the form of a demand curve. (It can also be represented algebraically in the form of an equation, but this is not necessary for understanding the basic ideas.)

What are the underlying factors that account for the law of (downward-sloping) demand? This is a question we have not yet considered in much detail. To answer it more fully, we must turn our attention to the study of consumer behavior. This topic, which draws on psychology, has played an interesting and important role in the development of economic ideas.

Explaining Consumer Demand

Economists have long been interested in the factors that account for the shape of demand curves. One explanation of the downward slope is based on "common sense," by which we mean observation and intuition.   On the basis of our experience, it seems reasonable to expect that a reduction in the price of a product will enable a buyer to purchase more of it.   Conversely, an increase in the product's price will have the opposite effect.

A second explanation can be given in terms of what economists call "substitution effects" and "income effects."   Taken together, these effects explain how a price change influences a consumer's *willingness* and *ability* to buy.   Both effects assume that the consumer's nominal (or money) income, tastes, and the prices of other goods remain constant.

For example, if the price of a good you purchase declines, you may be willing to substitute more of that good for other products.   Therefore, the increase in quantity demanded of a good due to a decrease in its price can be explained in part by this **substitution effect.**

Of course, if the price of a good you buy decreases, you may not only purchase more of that good, but more of other goods too. The reason is that your *real* income — the quantity of goods you can buy with your nominal income — has risen.   Therefore, the increase in quantity demanded of a good due to a rise in a buyer's real income (resulting from a decrease in the price of a good) can be explained in part by this **income effect.**

The substitution effect thus helps account for a buyer's *willingness* to purchase more of a good when its price declines.   The income effect helps account for a buyer's *ability* to do so.   The two effects, taken together, explain why a demand curve slopes downward.

The Meaning of Utility

A third (and in some ways much more fundamental) explanation of the downward-sloping demand curve can be given in terms of utility.   **Utility** refers to the ability or power of a good or service to satisfy a want.   That is, the utility of a good or service is the satisfaction one receives from consuming it — whether it be a pizza, a pair of jeans, a vacation trip, or a stack of textbooks.

The concept of utility was employed by the classical economists of the eighteenth and early nineteenth centuries.   But the theory of utility as such did not come into full flower until the late nineteenth century, when it was formulated by certain neoclassical economists.   As you study the theory in the following paragraphs, be careful not to confuse "utility" with "usefulness."   At any given time, water may be much more useful than diamonds.   However, the utility of either one may be quite different for various individuals.

Total Utility and Marginal Utility

Although no one knows how to measure utility, it is interesting to *assume* that it can be measured.   Suppose, for example, that a "utility meter" could be strapped to your arm to measure the units of satisfaction, called *utils*, that you get from consuming a product.   This is the same idea as a doctor strapping a meter to your arm to measure your blood pressure.   What would such a utility meter reveal?

The answer is suggested by the data and curves in Exhibit 1.   The table and figures show the utils, or units of satisfaction, that you might experience from consuming some product.   This model assumes that your consumption is taking place at a *given period of time during which your tastes are constant.*   Otherwise, as you will soon see, it would make no sense to talk about the utility of different quantities of a product.

The exhibit illustrates the idea that 1 unit of the product (for example, ice-cream cones) yields a certain amount of total utility, 2 units yield a larger amount, 3 units still more, and so on.   Eventually, a level of intake is reached at which total utility is at a maximum.   The consumption of any additional units then results in a decline in total utility.   This can be clearly seen in the graph of total utility in the exhibit.   (The fact that the curve turns downward after the consumption of 7 ice-cream cones means that any more of them will make you sick.)

Exhibit 1
Total and Marginal Utility

The table and charts convey the same fundamental relations. That is, as consumption of the product is increased, both total utility and marginal utility rise to a maximum and then decline. The marginal-utility curve is more important, for it reflects the operation of *the law of diminishing marginal utility.* The vertical dashed line emphasizes the point that marginal utility equals zero when total utility is at a maximum.

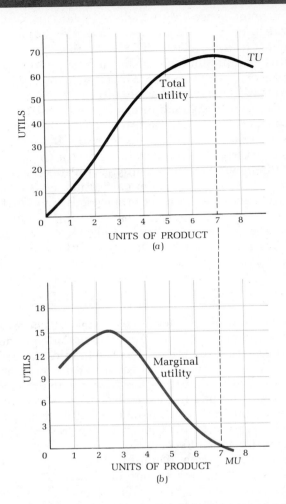

NOTE The marginal-utility curve is plotted to the *midpoints* of the integers on the horizontal axis. This is because marginal utility reflects the *change* in total utils from one unit of product to the next.

(1)	(2)	(3)
Units of product consumed	Total utility, TU	Marginal utility, MU **Change in (2)** / **Change in (1)**
0	0	
		10
1	10	
		14
2	24	
		15
3	39	
		13
4	52	
		9
5	61	
		3
6	64	
		1
7	65	
		−1
8	64	

Much more important than total utility is ***marginal utility.*** This is defined as the change in total utility resulting from a unit change in the quantity of the product consumed. As you can see from column (3) of the table, marginal utility may be measured by the equation

$$\text{marginal utility} = \frac{\text{change in total utility}}{\text{change in quantity consumed}}$$

Marginal utility is thus measured by the *ratio of change* in the two variables. This is emphasized by the way its values are recorded in column (3) of the table — a half-space between those shown for columns (1) and (2). Note that its graph is plotted in the same way — to the *midpoints* of the integers on the horizontal axis — as explained in the exhibit.

Observe from the figures in Exhibit 1 that the marginal-utility curve reaches a maximum and then turns downward while the total-utility curve is still rising. When the total-utility curve reaches its maximum height, the marginal-utility curve is at zero height. That is, the marginal-utility curve intersects the horizontal axis, as emphasized by the vertical dashed line. The reason for this relationship is a technical one that will be explained in a later chapter — after you have learned some more about "marginal" and "total" curves.

Law of (Eventually) Diminishing Marginal Utility

It is important to emphasize that, although marginal utility may at first increase, it must *eventually* decrease as more units of the product are consumed. What this means, for example, is that you might very well gain more satisfaction from the second unit (for example, a second slice of pizza) than you gained from the first. And you might even gain more from the third unit than from the second. However, you must eventually reach a point at which each successive unit gives you less gain in satisfaction than the previous one. This idea can be expressed more formally by the following important law:

> **Law of Diminishing Marginal Utility**   In a given period of time (during which tastes are assumed to remain constant), the consumption of a product may at first result in increasing gains in satisfaction (marginal utilities) per unit of the product consumed. However, a point will be reached beyond which the consumption of additional units of the product will result in decreasing gains in satisfaction (marginal utilities) per unit of the product consumed. This is the point of diminishing marginal utility.

As suggested by the word "diminishing" in this law, it is the *decreasing* part of the marginal-utility curve that is relevant. In effect, the law means that, on the downward side of the curve, the more you have of something, the less you care about one unit of it.

Consumer Equilibrium

How can the concepts of total and marginal utility be used to describe the economic theory of consumer behavior and the existence of downward-sloping demand curves? This is the question we set out to answer at the beginning of this chapter.

Imagine that you are a consumer with a given amount of money to spend on two commodities, A and B. Let us designate your marginal utility for product A as MU_A and the price of product A as P_A. Similarly, let your marginal utility for product B be represented by MU_B, and let the price of product B be represented by P_B.

Now, keep in mind that it is the *downward* side of a product's marginal-utility curve that is relevant. In view of this, how should you distribute your expenditures on these two products so as to maximize your total satisfaction or utility? The answer is that you must allocate your expenditures so that the marginal utility *per dollar* spent on the two commodities is equal. That is,

$$\frac{MU_A}{P_A} = \frac{MU_B}{P_B}$$

In other words, to achieve this result you will adjust the quantities you buy. For example, suppose that you have a combination of A and B such that the left-hand ratio is greater than the right-hand ratio. Then you can increase your total utility by giving up some of product B (thereby moving up on your MU curve of B) and buying more of product A (thereby moving down on your MU curve of A). It can be demonstrated that the gain will more than offset the loss.

To illustrate, suppose that you have a combination of products A and B such that

$$\frac{MU_A}{P_A} = 30 \text{ utils per dollar}$$

$$\frac{MU_B}{P_B} = 10 \text{ utils per dollar}$$

If you spend a dollar less on B, you will lose 10 utils. If you spend a dollar more on A, you will gain 30 utils. The transfer of a dollar from B to A will therefore result in a net gain of 20 utils. Hence, you will make the transfer. As the transfer proceeds, the marginal utility per dollar of B rises as the amount purchased decreases. At the same time, the marginal utility per dollar of A falls as the amount purchased increases. When the two ratios are equal — say, at 20 utils per dollar — there is no further gain by transferring expenditures from B to A. At this point your total utility is at a maximum.

But what about your *money*, which is being exchanged for these products? You can think of money (symbolized m) like any other commodity. That is, the marginal utility of money to you, the consumer, is represented by MU_m and its price by P_m. The foregoing marginal-utility equation, to be complete, should now be extended to read

$$\frac{MU_A}{P_A} = \frac{MU_B}{P_B}$$

$$= \frac{MU_m}{P_m}$$

Because the price of a dollar is \$1, the denominator in the last ratio may be omitted so that the equation becomes

$$\frac{MU_A}{P_A} = \frac{MU_B}{P_B}$$

$$= MU_m$$

This equation expresses your market equilibrium as a consumer. That is, the equation defines the conditions that exist when you have allocated your money and commodities, in the face of market prices, in such a way as to maximize your total utility. This equation is also equivalent to the following statement:

> For the consumer to be in equilibrium with respect to utilities and market prices, the last dollar spent on A must yield the same marginal utility per dollar's worth of A as the last dollar spent on B. This, in turn, must equal the marginal utility of money (per dollar of expenditure).

This principle can be extended to any number of commodities. The point is that, in order for you to be in equilibrium, your marginal utility per dollar of expenditure must be equal for all commodities, which, in turn, must equal your marginal utility for money. Otherwise, you will be able to increase your total utility by reshuffling your expenditures.

Marginal Utility and Demand Curves

We now wish to derive your consumer's demand curve for a specific commodity based on your utility data. The preceding equation says that, for any particular commodity, say commodity A,

$$\frac{MU_A}{P_A} = MU_m$$

If we "transpose" and solve for P_A, we get

$$P_A = \frac{MU_A}{MU_m}$$

Suppose that we now simplify by assuming that in the short run your marginal utility for money is a constant positive amount. For example, let us assume that MU_m is any positive number — say, 3. (The number itself makes no difference for our present purposes; any positive number can be chosen, as will be seen momentarily.) Your individual demand curve for commodity A can then be derived if your marginal-utility schedule is known.

Exhibit 2
Deriving a Consumer's Demand Curve for a Commodity, Based on Utility Data

The demand curve is graphed from columns (1) and (4) of the table. The curve will be negatively inclined regardless of the positive constant chosen for MU_m.

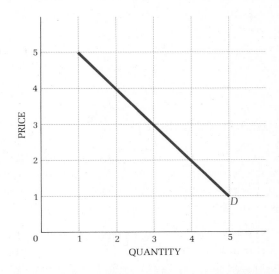

(1) Units of product, A (given)	(2) Marginal utility of money, MU_m (given)	(3) Marginal utility of product, MU_A (given)	(4) Price of product, P_A (3) ÷ (2)
1	3	15	5
2	3	12	4
3	3	9	3
4	3	6	2
5	3	3	1

This is illustrated in Exhibit 2, in which the price data in column (4) are obtained from the given information in the other columns. As you can see from the explanation in the exhibit, the demand curve represents the demand schedule from columns (1) and (4) of the table. This curve is downward (negatively) sloped, a fact that is not influenced by the constant positive value chosen for MU_m.

Some Applications of Utility Theory

The development of utility theory in general, and the concept of marginal utility in particular, permit us to interpret more precisely problems that would otherwise be handled in relatively crude ways.

For example, a question suggested earlier was, "Why is the price of water low and the price of diamonds high, especially since everyone needs water but no one really needs diamonds?" If we knew nothing about utility theory, the answer would be given simply in terms of "supply and demand." But we can go a step further. We can say that the marginal utility of water is ordinarily low because it is usually available in ample quantities. That is, the more we have of something, the less we care about *one* unit of it. Therefore, we do not usually hesitate to use the extra water we need to water our lawns and wash our cars. The marginal utility of diamonds, on the other hand, is relatively high and the availability of diamonds is extremely limited. Therefore, a single unit has considerable value. In a desert or on a battlefield, however, the circumstances might be exactly reversed. In those situations, we might be quite willing to trade a diamond for a pint of water, or perhaps a kingdom for a horse.

This suggests an interesting point:

For some products, total utility may be high while marginal utility is low or even zero. Examples include an urban freeway during off-peak hours, a fire department when there is no fire, and a doctor's service when there is no need for it.

Can you think of other illustrations?

Consumer's Surplus

A concept directly related to utility theory is **consumer's surplus.** In everyday language, a consumer's surplus is simply a bargain. In more formal terms, it may be defined as any payment made by a buyer that is less than the maximum he or she would have been willing to pay for the quantity of the commodity purchased. Consumer's surplus thus represents the difference between the buyer's **demand price** and the price actually paid.

The concept of consumer's surplus is illustrated in Exhibit 3. There the surplus is measured from a buyer's demand curve and marginal-utility curve. Both curves are based on the data given previously in Exhibit 2. In both cases, however, the curves have been extended to touch the axes. Notice that, although the curves appear to look alike, the scales on the vertical axes of the two figures are in different units.

In Figure (a), the demand curve tells us that, as a consumer, you would be willing to pay $2 for the fourth unit of the commodity. However, you would have been willing to pay more, if necessary, for the first, second, and third units. You therefore get a consumer's surplus — a net amount of "pure" satisfaction — by paying only $2 for each of the four units. Your total expenditure is therefore $8. This is the rectangular area (equal to base × height) shown in the diagram. Your consumer's surplus, which is the right-triangular area (equal to ½ base × height), also happens to be $8 in this case.

Exhibit 3
Measuring Consumer's Surplus from a Demand Curve and from a Marginal-Utility Curve

The rectangular and triangular areas, respectively, measure total expenditure and consumer's surplus. This is true whether they are measured in dollars, as in Figure (a), or in utils, as in Figure (b).

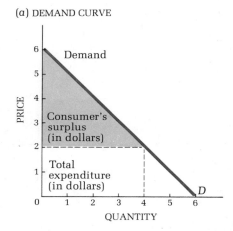

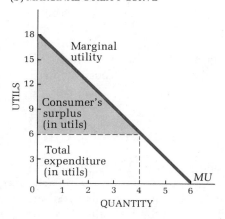

These two amounts, of course, need not always be the same, depending on the slope of the demand curve.

In Figure (b), we can calculate the same information in utils. Thus, your total expenditure *in utils* equals $4 \times 6 = 24$ utils. Likewise, your consumer's surplus *in utils* equals $(4 \times 12)/2 = 24$ utils. Suppose that we now invoke our earlier assumption that the marginal utility of money is equal to 3 utils per dollar. Then your total expenditure in dollars comes to $8, and your consumer's surplus in dollars also comes to $8. These amounts, of course, are the same as those calculated previously from the demand curve in Figure (a).

The concept of consumer's surplus has a long and interesting history. For our present purposes, it poses two important questions.

1. Because consumer's surplus represents the "extra" value of satisfaction to a buyer, could the government tax it away without affecting either the quantity purchased or its price?

2. Suppose that a seller could measure a buyer's demand curve. Would the seller then be able to capture the consumer's surplus? For instance, could the seller charge the highest possible price for the first unit, the next highest price for the second unit, and so on — instead of charging the *same* price per unit for *all* units?

The answer to these questions is *yes*. However, there are limitations and conditions. Some of these are indicated in the next section. Further exploration must wait until we have covered more ground in a later chapter.

Conclusion: Two Major Shortcomings of Utility Theory

As mentioned earlier, the theory of utility provides one of the more fundamental explanations of why a demand curve is downward-sloping. However, the theory suffers from serious shortcomings, at least two of which are especially important.

1. **Indivisibility of Products**   The theory assumes that commodities are sufficiently divisible to be consumed in small units — such as ice-cream cones, candy bars, or cups of coffee. In other words, marginal-utility theory refers to the consumption of successive units of the *same commodity within a given period of time while tastes remain constant.* But many products bought by consumers are large and indivisible and cannot be consumed in small, successive doses. For example, the ordinary consumer may buy one house or one piano in a lifetime, or a new car every several years.

2. **Immeasurability of Utility**   A more fundamental difficulty, as mentioned at the beginning of the chapter, is that no method has yet been devised for measuring a consumer's intensity of satisfaction. Utility cannot be measured in the same way we might measure the weight of an object in pounds or kilograms, or the distance between two points in miles or meters. In other words, we cannot measure utility in terms of *cardinal* numbers like 10, 23, 32.7, and so on, as the theory of utility assumes.

In view of the theory's rather tenuous assumptions, must we conclude that one of its most fundamental features — the law of diminishing marginal utility — is invalid? Most economists think not. They contend that the law of diminishing marginal utility is valid for the following reason.

Were it not for the law of diminishing marginal utility, we would spend all of our money on the one commodity that gave us the greatest gain in satisfaction (or marginal utility) relative to its price. We know, of course, that this does not actually happen. Therefore, even though there is no absolute measure of utility, the theory nevertheless permits the development of valid principles pertaining to consumer demand and equilibrium.

Leaders in Economics

Historical Pictures Service

William Stanley Jevons
1835–1882
Marginal-Utility Theorist and
Mathematical Economist

Brown Brothers

Thorstein Veblen
1857–1929
Great Iconoclast —
Institutionalist —
Antimarginalist

The English economist William Stanley Jevons is one of the towering figures in the development of economic thought. A trailbreaker in the application of mathematics to economics, he is best known as a leading contributor to marginal-utility analysis. A key passage of his book, *Theory of Political Economy* (1871), points out that exchange between two individuals will cease when "the ratio of exchange of any two commodities is . . . the reciprocal of the ratio of the final degrees of utility of the quantities of commodity available for consumption." Simply stated, this means that, *in equilibrium, marginal utilities will be proportional to prices.*

Jevons also did notable work in statistics and business forecasting. He formulated statistical correlations and forecasts of economic data that he sold to businesses — an idea that was at least 50 years ahead of its time.

Veblen: A Disturber of the Peace
The American economist Thorstein Veblen approached social problems in a very different way than Jevons did. Veblen belonged to what is known as the "institutionalist" school of economic thought. He believed that human behavior could best be understood by studying the history, practices, and customs of society.

Parodying the pseudoscientific style of some of the mathematical marginal-utility theorists of his time, he wrote:

What does all this signify? If we are getting restless under the taxonomy of a monocotyledonous wage doctrine and a cryptogamic theory of interest, with involute, loculicidal, tomentous and moni-liform variants, what is the cytoplasm, centrosome, or karyokinetic process to which we may turn, and in which we may find surcease from the metaphysics of normality and controlling principles?

No wonder Veblen was once referred to as "the archdisturber of the academic economist's peace of mind."

"Pecuniary Emulation"
Veblen wrote more than a dozen books, all of them controversial. In his first and best-known work, *The Theory of the Leisure Class* (1899, rev. 1918) he coined a famous phrase, ***conspicuous consumption.*** This meant the tendency of those in the upper income levels (that is, the "leisure class") to be concerned with impressing others through standards of living, taste, and dress — through what Veblen called "pecuniary emulation." This, Veblen argued, is a "commonly observed pattern of behavior" that is contrary to marginal-utility theory. In other words, conspicuous consumption clearly implies that people may sometimes buy more of a good at higher prices than at lower prices in order to impress others.

Throughout Veblen's writings there are predictions about the changing structure of society, many of which have materialized with impressive accuracy. There is little doubt that he was an extraordinary prophet of social and economic change.

What You Have Learned

1. The law of (downward-sloping) demand can be explained on the bases of observation and experience, substitution and income effects, or the theory of utility. Utility theory gives rise to the law of diminishing marginal utility—one of the most famous laws in economics.

2. The theory of utility shows how consumer equilibrium is obtained when the marginal utility per dollar of expenditure is equal for all commodities, including money. On the basis of this principle, a consumer's demand curve for a commodity can be derived and the concept of consumer's surplus can be demonstrated.

Terms and Concepts To Review

income effect
substitution effect
utility
marginal utility
law of diminishing
  marginal utility

consumer's surplus
demand price
conspicuous
  consumption

For Discussion

1. Assume that R is rich, that P is poor, and that both have the same marginal-utility-of-money curve (MU_m), as shown in the figure. Let R's income be equal to the distance 0R and P's income be equal to the distance 0P.

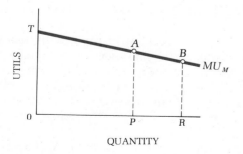

(a) What is R's marginal utility for money? What is P's?
(b) What is R's total utility for money? What is P's?

(c) If you could reallocate the total incomes of these two people, how would you do it so as to maximize their *combined* total utility for money? Illustrate on the figure.
(d) Which person would experience a loss in total utility for money as a result of this income reallocation? Which person would experience a gain?
(e) Is the *net* effect of income reallocation a gain or a loss in the total utility for money?
(f) Does this problem suggest any implications for society as a whole? Discuss.

2. "A proportional income tax is a fair tax because, other things being the same, people with equal incomes pay equal taxes and therefore make equal sacrifices." On the basis of this chapter, do you agree? Discuss.

(NOTE Look up the meaning of *proportional tax* in the Dictionary at the back of the book.)

3. Suppose that, after some minimum level of income is attained, each person's marginal utility of income changes in one of the following ways.
(a) It decreases at a rate *equal to* the percentage increase in income.
(b) It decreases at a rate *faster than* the percentage increase in income.
(c) It decreases at a rate *slower than* the percentage increase in income.

In a single figure, sketch the three curves depicting the conditions outlined above. Which type of taxation—progressive, proportional, or regressive—would you suggest in order to assure equal subjective sacrifice by taxpayers? Explain your answer. (NOTE Look up the meanings of *progressive tax, proportional tax,* and *regressive tax* in the Dictionary at the back of the book.)

4. Fill in the empty cells in the following table:

Total utility	Marginal utility
increasing at a constant rate	
	increasing
increasing at a decreasing rate	
	zero
decreasing	

Supplement

Indifference Curves

The law of diminishing marginal utility has long been used to explain the existence of downward-sloping demand curves. The chief difficulty with this explanation, as noted earlier, lies in our *inability to measure utility*. Unlike the weight of an object or the distance between two points, utility cannot be measured in terms of cardinal numbers. It was largely because of this shortcoming that economists devised an alternative approach for explaining demand phenomena. This approach makes use of a concept known as *indifference curves*.

The Price Line or Budget Line

Imagine that you are a consumer with $2 and that you are entering the market to spend your money on goods. You are confronted with two commodities, X and Y. The price of X is $2 per unit; the price of Y is $1 per unit. Thus, the price of X is twice the price of Y. Algebraically, if P denotes price, then $P_X = 2P_Y$.

You can spend your entire $2 on X, in which case you can buy only 1 unit and have nothing left to spend on Y. Or, you can spend your whole $2 on Y, in which case you can buy 2 units and have nothing left to spend on X. The table in Exhibit 1 shows a few of the combinations of X and Y that you can purchase with your $2. Of course, you can also purchase any other combination that will total $2.

The diagram in Exhibit 1 illustrates the same situation graphically. The vertical axis represents the various amounts of commodity Y that you can purchase, and the horizontal axis shows the corresponding amounts of X that can also be purchased.

The diagram shows that, if you spend your entire $2 on Y, you can purchase 2 units or an amount equal to the distance 0M. If you spend your $2 on X, you can purchase 1 unit or an amount equal to the distance 0N. If we connect these two points, the resulting line MN is called a "price line," or "budget line."

Just what does this price line tell us? It indicates all the possible combinations of X and Y that can be purchased for a total of $2, assuming that $P_X = \$2$ and $P_Y = \$1$. Thus, point Q shows that you can purchase 1 unit of Y and ½ unit of X for a total of $2. The same is true of any other point on the line MN. Notice, however, that, as we move along the line from M to N, more of X can be purchased and less of Y. This is just as we should expect. Out of any given money income, the more we spend on one commodity, the less we have to spend on other things. Thus:

A ***price line*** (or budget line) represents all the possible combinations of two commodities that a consumer can purchase at a particular time, given the market prices of the commodities and the consumer's money budget or income.

Many Possible Price Lines

Suppose now that you have $4 instead of only $2. Because you have twice as much money, you can buy twice as much of each commodity, provided that their prices do not change. Thus you can buy as much as 4Y or 2X, or any combination in between. In Exhibit 2, the line M'N' represents the new price line at a higher income or budget of $4 and MN represents the old price line at a lower income or budget of $2. Obviously, for every level of income there will be a different price line corresponding to that income level. If income rises, so does the price line; if income falls, the price line falls too. Because an infinite number of budgets or income levels are possible, an infinite number of price lines are possible.

Exhibit 1

A Consumer's Alternative Purchase Combinations

Assumptions: consumption budget = $2; price of X = $2; price of Y = $1.

The price line represents all the possible combinations of commodities X and Y that you the consumer can purchase at a particular time, given the market prices of the commodities and your money budget.

Purchase combinations	Units of X	Units of Y	Total amount spent
N	1	0	$2 + $0 = $2
Q	½	1	$1 + $1 = $2
M	0	2	$0 + $2 = $2

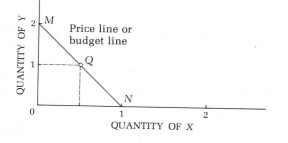

Exhibit 2
An Increase in the Price Line

An increase in your income shifts the price line outward, enabling you to buy more of X and Y at the given market prices.

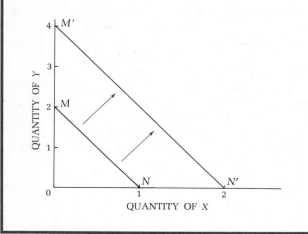

The Nature of Indifference Curves

If you are a consumer confronted with two commodities, X and Y, which of the many possible combinations will you purchase? This question may seem unanswerable, but if we proceed step by step, we can work out an answer to it.

For now, let us disregard the price relationships that were described earlier and pay attention solely to the satisfaction you would derive from possessing commodities X and Y. That is, let us forget for the moment that $P_X = \$2$ and $P_Y = \$1$ and that you have a given income.

We start by constructing an ***indifference schedule.*** This is a list showing the various combinations of two commodities that would be equally satisfactory to you at a given time. Column (1) of the table in Exhibit 3 is an example of a possible indifference schedule for two commodities X and Y.

In this column, each combination of X and Y is equally satisfactory to you. Thus, you would just as soon have combination 1, consisting of 60Y and 1X, as you would combination 2, consisting of 50Y and 2X, or combination 3, 41Y and 3X, and so on. This is true because each combination yields the same total satisfaction or utility. Hence, you are completely *indifferent* about which combination to choose because you prefer no particular combination. All combinations are equally desirable because they *all yield the same total utility.*

Now, there is an important thing to notice about an indifference schedule. Because each combination yields the same total utility, it follows that, if you were to increase your consumption or holdings of X by one unit at a time, you would have to decrease your consumption or holdings of Y by some amount in order that each successive combination would continue to yield the same total utility. For example, when you possess combination 1, 60Y and 1X, you derive a certain amount of total utility. If you were to possess 60Y and 2X, your total utility would be greater than the total utility of 60Y and 1X, because you would have the same amount of Y plus more of X. Therefore, in order to keep your total utility the same, you must give up a certain amount of Y for each unit increase in X. Column (1) in Exhibit 3 shows this relationship.

Marginal Rate of Substitution

Next, notice that, as you increase the amount of X you have, the amount of Y that you are willing to give up *decreases.* Thus, when you possess combination 1, 60Y and 1X, you are willing to give up 10 units of Y for 1 unit of X. This leaves you with 50Y and 2X, or combination 2. At this point, you are willing to give up only 9 units of Y for 1 more unit of X, which would leave you at combination 3. Column (2) indicates this relationship. It shows us the amount of Y you are willing to surrender for every unit increase in your X holdings so that the new combination yields you the same satisfaction as the previous one — that is, the same total utility.

Exhibit 3
A Consumer's Indifference Schedule, Indifference Curve, and Marginal Rate of Substitution

Each combination in column (1) yields the same total utility to you, the consumer. Hence, you are indifferent as to which combination you prefer.

In column (2), the marginal rate of substitution measures the amount of commodity Y you must give up in order to get 1 more unit of commodity X, and maintain the same total utility. The numerical value of this ratio decreases as additional units of X are acquired.

An ***indifference curve*** is a graph of an indifference schedule. Any point on the curve denotes a particular combination of commodities X and Y that yields the same total utility.

Note that, as X increases 1 unit at a time, the amount of Y that you are willing to give up decreases. This reflects a *decreasing* marginal rate of substitution of X for Y.

Combinations	(1) Indifference schedule	(2) Marginal rate of substitution of X for Y
1	60Y and 1X	
		10/1
2	50Y and 2X	
		9/1
3	41Y and 3X	
		8/1
4	33Y and 4X	
		7/1
5	26Y and 5X	
		6/1
6	20Y and 6X	
		5/1
7	15Y and 7X	
		4/1
8	11Y and 8X	
		3/1
9	8Y and 9X	
		2/1
10	6Y and 10X	
		1/1
11	5Y and 11X	

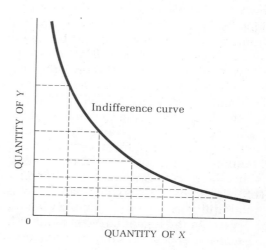

Indifference curve

QUANTITY OF Y

QUANTITY OF X

The rate at which the consumer is willing to substitute commodity X for commodity Y is called the ***marginal rate of substitution*** (MRS). It may be defined as the amount of change in the holdings of one commodity that will just offset a unit change in the holdings of another commodity, so that the consumer's total utility remains the same. Since the ratio of the change in Y to the change in X is negative (because the amount of one commodity decreases when the other increases), the MRS may be expressed by the formula:

$$MRS = -\frac{\text{change in } Y}{\text{change in } X}$$

As a general rule, the minus sign is understood and may be omitted.

Why does the MRS, as shown in column (2) of the table, decrease? You will remember that a demand curve slopes downward from left to right because the marginal utility of the commodity decreases as more of the commodity is consumed. (The more you have of something, the less you care about obtaining an additional unit of it.)

The concept of a decreasing *MRS* is similar to that of decreasing marginal utility. As *X increases* (one unit at a time), the marginal utility of *X decreases*. As *Y decreases*, the marginal utility of *Y increases*. Thus, the more you have of *X*, the less you want one more unit of it, and the less you have of *Y*, the less you are willing to give up one more unit of it. That is, the more of *Y* you have given up for *X*, the less of *Y* you are willing to give up for an additional unit of *X*.

Many Possible Indifference Curves

Suppose now that we were to plot the various combinations in the indifference schedule on a chart. The result would be a curve similar to the one in Exhibit 3. This curve is called an **indifference curve** because every point on it represents a particular combination of the two commodities *X* and *Y* that is equally satisfactory to you. That is, each point on the curve yields you the same total utility.

Just as it is possible to have an infinite number of price lines, so is it possible to have an infinite number of indifference curves. This is suggested in Exhibit 4, in which point *Q* represents a combination of 0*M* of *X* and 0*N* of *Y*. This combination yields the same total utility as any other combination on the same curve. On the higher curve at point *R*, however, the consumer possesses the same amount of *Y*, namely 0*N*, plus more of *X*, namely 0*M'*. Therefore, this combination must yield a higher total utility than any of the previous combinations to be found on curve 1.

If you now compare point *S* on the higher curve with point *Q* on the lower one, you will see that point *S* represents the same amount of *X* plus more of *Y*. Finally, if you pick any point between *S* and *R* on the higher curve, say point *T*, you will note that there is more of *both X* and *Y* than there is in the combination denoted by point *Q* on the lower curve.

These ideas suggest three important conclusions about indifference curves:

Exhibit 4
Two Indifference Curves

The higher a consumer's indifference curve, the greater the total utility. The points S and R, in comparison with the point Q, each represent as much of one commodity plus more of the other. Any point between S and R, such as T, represents more of *both* commodities. Although this figure depicts only two indifference curves, an infinite number of such curves exist for every consumer.

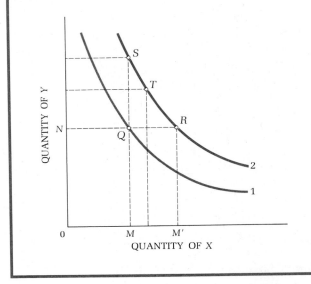

— The higher an indifference curve—that is, the farther it lies to the right—the greater the consumer's total utility. This is because any point on a higher curve will always denote *at least* the same amount of one commodity plus more of the other.

— A consumer will always try to be on the highest possible indifference curve. This is because it is assumed that the consumer will always try to maximize total utility.

— Each indifference curve represents a *different* level of total utility. Therefore, indifference curves can never intersect at any point.

The Equilibrium Combination

Now let us combine the concepts of price lines and indifference curves. Superimposing one diagram upon the other, we get a result such as the one depicted in Exhibit 5.

The price line *MN* shows the possible combinations of *X* and *Y* that could be purchased with given prices of *X* and *Y* at a given income. Each indifference curve, 1, 2, and 3, shows various combinations of *X* and *Y* that yield the same total utility along a given curve.

Given these price lines and indifference curves, precisely what combination of *X* and *Y* will be purchased? The answer is based on the following fundamental notions:

− The indifference curves represent the consumer's *subjective* valuations of *X* and *Y*. These valuations have no relationship to the *objective* facts that *X* and *Y* have certain prices and that the consumer has a certain money income to spend. These objective facts are shown by the price line.

− Subjectively, the consumer will try to be on the highest possible indifference curve. Objectively, this goal is limited by the price line. The problem, therefore, is to reconcile this difference.

Because the price line shows all the possible combinations of quantities of *X* and *Y* that can be purchased for a given money income, it follows that there will be only one point on the price line that will also be on the highest possible indifference curve. This is point *Q*, at which the price line is tangent to curve 2. Point *Q*, therefore, shows the particular quantities of *X* and *Y* that will be purchased, namely 0*L* units of *Y* and 0*P* units of *X*.

Thus, as a consumer, you would not want to be on curve 1, where you would purchase a combination determined by *D* or *E*, because your purchasing power (as determined by the price line) permits you to be on a higher indifference curve. The highest curve that you can be on and yet remain within your income is curve 2. And the only point at which the price line touches the highest indifference curve within your means is point *Q*. This

Exhibit 5
The Equilibrium-Purchase Combination

The tangency of the price line with an indifference curve determines the consumer's equilibrium-purchase combination. Thus, because the tangency is at point *Q*, you will buy 0*P* units of *X* and 0*L* units of *Y*.

A given price line may intersect any number of indifference curves, but it can be tangent to only one indifference curve.

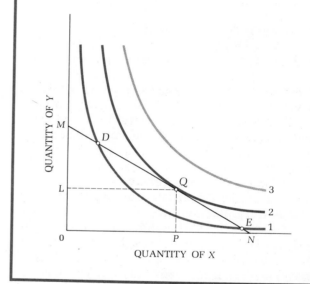

point, therefore, indicates the combination of *X* and *Y* that you will purchase at the prevailing prices, given your income.

Along an indifference curve without guidance from prices, you are in a position not unlike that of Buridan's ass. The ass (according to a story attributed to the fourteenth-century French philosopher Jean Buridan) stood equidistant between two equal bundles of hay and starved to death because it could not choose between them. Similarly:

All combinations on any one indifference curve are equally desirable. It is the point of tangency of an indifference curve with a price line that determines the equilibrium-purchase combination.

What Happens When Income Changes?

Suppose now that your income increases while the prices of X and Y remain the same. You would now purchase more of both X and Y. This condition is shown in Exhibit 6. The price line shifts to the right from MN to M'N' to M"N", indicating that a greater combination of both commodities can be purchased. At each new level of income, there is a tangency with a new and higher indifference curve. Connecting these points of tangency, we get the line QRS. Then, extending vertical and horizontal dashed lines from each of these points to the axes shows us by how much you increase your purchases of both X and Y as your income rises.

The line QRS may be called an **income-consumption curve** (ICC). It connects the tangency points of price lines and indifference curves by showing the amounts of two commodities that you will purchase if your income changes while their prices remain constant.

It is possible, however, that as your income increases, your consumption of one commodity may increase while your consumption of the other commodity decreases. This is shown in Exhibit 7. In Figure (a), as your income rises, your consumption of Y also rises, and, although your consumption of X at first increases, it gradually falls off. The opposite is illustrated in Figure (b). As your income rises, your consumption of both X and Y at first increases, however, at some point your consumption of Y decreases.

A good whose consumption varies inversely with money income (prices remaining constant) over a certain range of income is called an **inferior good.** Some classic examples of inferior goods are potatoes, lower-priced cuts of meat, used clothing, and other "cheap" commodities bought by low-income families. The consumption of these commodities by low-income families declines in favor of fancier foods, new clothing, and so on, as their incomes rise. It should be noted, however, that almost any

Exhibit 6
Income-Consumption Curve

An increase in income may increase your purchases of both X and Y. The line QRS connects the tangency points of price lines and indifference curves as your income increases. It is called an *income-consumption curve (ICC).*

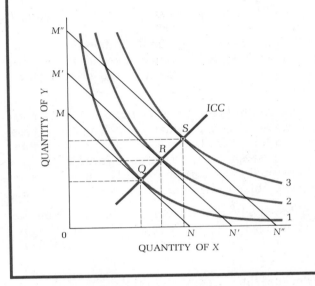

good may become "inferior" at some income level. For example, when a family steps up from a lower-priced to a higher-priced car because of an increase in income, the lower-priced car becomes an inferior good.

On the other hand, a good whose consumption varies directly with money income (prices remaining constant) is called a **superior good.** Most consumer goods are of this type. Superior goods are also sometimes called *normal goods* because they represent the "normal" situation. Examples include most foods, clothing, appliances, and other nondurable and durable items that people typically buy.

Exhibit 7
Superior and Inferior Goods

As your income increases, you may buy more of one commodity (a superior good) and less of another commodity (an inferior good).

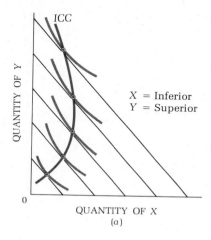

X = Inferior
Y = Superior

(a)

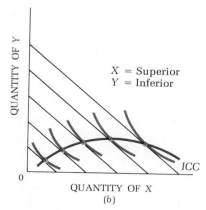

X = Superior
Y = Inferior

(b)

NOTE   The inferior good in each graph is inferior only over the range in which the income-consumption curve (*ICC*) has a negative slope. This occurs where the curve bends "backward" in Figure (*a*) and "downward" in Figure (*b*).

What Happens When Price Changes?

The previous case assumed that you, the consumer, had an increase in income while the prices of X and Y remained constant. Let us now assume that both your income and the price of Y remain constant while the price of X decreases. What happens?

The result is seen in Exhibit 8. The lower end of the price line shifts to the right from MN to MN' to MN''. This indicates that, as P_X falls, more of X can be purchased. The price line thus fans outward as a result of decreases in P_X.

We can work the same idea in the other direction by permitting the lower end of the price line to shift left. For instance, let us assume that the price line to begin with is MN''. Then suppose that the price

Exhibit 8
Price-Consumption Curve

With your income and the price of Y constant, decreases in the price of X result in your buying more of it. The line QRS connects the tangency points of price lines and indifference curves under these circumstances. It is called a *price-consumption curve (PCC)*.

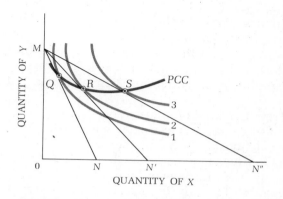

of X gradually rises while the price of Y and your income remain the same. As P_X rises, less of X can be bought, until finally the price of X is so high that it is not purchased at all. The price line then becomes the vertical line 0M, indicating that you spend your entire income on Y.

The line QRS in the diagram is thus a ***price-consumption curve*** (PCC). It connects the tangency points of price lines and indifference curves. The PCC curve thus shows the amounts of two commodities that you will purchase when your income and the price of one commodity remain constant while the price of the other commodity varies.

Deriving a Demand Curve

How do the principles of indifference curves and price lines relate to the law of demand? As you will recall, this is the question we started out to answer.

The answer is that these two principles together can be used to derive a *demand curve*. This is illustrated in Exhibit 9.

In Figure (a), the price line MN signifies an income of $10, with $P_Y = \$1$ and $P_X = \$2$. As a consumer, you can thus purchase either 10 units of Y, or 5 units of X, or various combinations in between. The tangency of the price line with your indifference curve, however, shows that you will maximize your total utility by purchasing 4 units of Y and 3 units of X.

Suppose now that the price of X falls to $1 while your income and the price of Y remain constant. The tangency of the new price line MN' with the higher indifference curve indicates that you will be in equilibrium by purchasing 3 units of Y and 7 units of X.

From this kind of information, you can derive a demand curve. For example, in Figure (b), you see the relationship between the price of X and the quantity demanded of X while all other things — namely, your income and the price of Y — remain the same. Thus, the dashed lines indicate that you will purchase 3 units of X at a price of $2 per unit and 7 units of X at a price of $1 per unit. Connecting these two points (as well as all the in-between points

that may be similarly derived), gives us the demand curve for X. Clearly, then, this curve obeys the law of demand. That is, the curve is downward-sloping — the lower the price, the greater the quantity demanded.

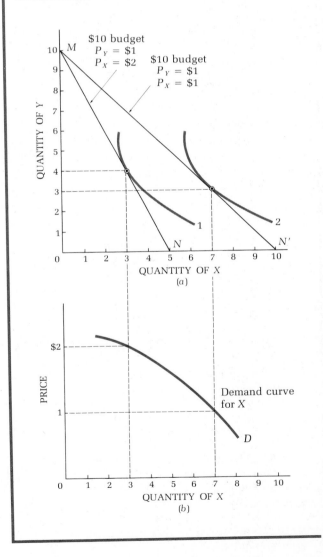

Exhibit 9
Derivation of a Demand Curve from Indifference Curves

Conclusion: Consumers' Preferences Tell the Story

The theory of indifference curves had its origins in the late nineteenth century and reached maturity in the 1930s. It marked a major advance in the history of economics, because it freed the concept of demand from a reliance on the older and controversial concept of utility.

You can easily see the reason for this. In the indifference-curve approach, it need only be assumed that, as a consumer, you are aware of your own preferences. That is, you know whether you prefer one combination of goods to another or whether you regard them as equivalent. You do not have to know by *how much* you prefer one good to another.

In the older approach to demand theory, the necessity of describing utility relationships in terms of *cardinal* numbers (1, 2, 3, and so on) was a serious shortcoming. In the newer approach based on indifference curves, this shortcoming is of no consequence. We need assume only an *ordinal* preference relationship (first, second, third, and so forth).

In short:

We can derive a downward-sloping demand curve directly from a consumer's indifference curves and price lines without using or even assuming a "law" of utility.

What You Have Learned

1. The theory of indifference curves relates *objective* facts determined by market prices and the consumer's income to the consumer's *subjective* valuations of commodities. The key mechanisms employed in the theory are price lines and indifference curves.

2. Through indifference-curve analysis, we can show how the consumption of goods changes when a buyer's income increases while prices are held constant. We can also illustrate how a buyer's consumption of a good changes when its price varies, while income and all other prices remain the same.

3. A consumer's demand curve can be derived directly from the tangency points of indifference curves and price lines. The law of demand can thus be established without reliance on the controversial theory of utility.

Terms and Concepts To Review

price line (budget line)
indifference schedule
marginal rate of
   substitution
indifference curve
income-consumption
   curve
inferior good
superior good
price-consumption
   curve

For Discussion

1. We have drawn indifference curves so that they are *convex* to the origin. What would it mean to draw an indifference curve that is *concave* to the origin? Would it make sense? Explain. (HINT Think in terms of the *MRS*.)

2. Draw a consumer's indifference curve that represents the situation that exists with each of the following combinations of commodities:
   (a) Two commodities that are perfect complements (that is, commodities that are used in 1 : 1 proportions, such as doors and doorknobs).
   (b) Two commodities that are perfect substitutes, such as nickels and dimes in the ratio 2 : 1.

3. Such commodities as diamonds and furs are sometimes cited as exceptions to the law of demand because some people will buy more of these at a higher price than at a lower price. Does this mean that the "demand" curve for these products is upward-sloping? Explain. (WARNING Be careful in your thinking. This is a much deeper question than is immediately apparent.)

4. In terms of indifference-curve analysis, what might be the effects of each of the following: (a) an increase in taxes; (b) an increase in the cost of living; (c) the expectation of inflation.

Chapter 21

Costs of Production

Learning Guide

Watch for answers to these important questions

What does the term "cost" mean? Is it employed in different senses? What specific meanings of cost are necessary for understanding production problems?

How are costs related to production? What relationships exist between the inputs and outputs of production?

How do we distinguish between short-run and long-run costs? How does this information help us understand the economic behavior of business firms?

According to a familiar saying, you have to spend money to make money. In the business world, this statement can be translated to mean that a company must be willing to incur costs if it is to receive revenues.

What do we mean by costs? The term is not as simple as most people think. Engineers, accountants, and economists are all concerned with the nature and behavior of costs, but they all deal with different cost concepts in solving different problems.

For example, suppose that you were the president of a corporation and were interested in constructing a new manufacturing plant. You might employ an industrial engineer to study the cost of designing the plant, and you might hire a cost accountant to classify and analyze production costs after the plant was in operation. You might also hire an economist to advise you as to how costs are related to production and profit.

Thus, analyses of costs by engineers, accountants, and economists may be done for very different purposes. This chapter explains the basic cost concepts and relationships that are of interest to economists.

What Do We Mean by "Cost"?

As long ago as 1923, a famous economist, J. M. Clark, wrote, "A class in economics would be a success if the students gained from it an understanding of the meaning of cost in all its many aspects." Clark was prompted to make this statement because the general concept of cost embraces a wide variety of specific concepts. However, one general meaning is common to all specific concepts of cost:

Cost is a sacrifice that must be made in order to do or to acquire something. The nature of the sacrifice may be tangible or intangible, objective or subjective. Also, it may take one or more of many forms, such as money, goods, leisure time, income, security, prestige, power, or pleasure.

Let us amplify this definition by describing and illustrating the notion of cost.

Outlay Costs Versus Opportunity (Alternative) Costs

To most of us, the concept of cost that readily comes to mind is what we may call *outlay costs*. These are the moneys expended in order to carry on a particular activity. Some examples of outlay costs to a business are wages and salaries of its employees and expenditures on plant and equipment. Other examples are payments for raw materials, power, light, and transportation; disbursements for rents, advertising, and insurance; and taxes paid to the government. Outlay costs are also frequently called *explicit costs, historical costs,* or *accounting costs.* This is because they are the objective and tangible expenses that an accountant records in the company's books.

Economists use a more basic concept of cost: *opportunity cost.* It is defined as the value of the benefit that is forgone by choosing one alternative rather than another. This is an extremely important concept because the true cost of any activity is measured by its opportunity cost, not by its outlay cost. How do you identify opportunity costs? By

making a comparison between the alternative that was chosen and the one that was rejected. Here are some examples:

— To a student, the cost of attending college full time includes more than the outlay costs for tuition and books. It also includes the opportunity cost of income forgone by not working full time.

— To a business firm, the cost of advertising includes more than its outlay costs for magazine space or television time. It also includes the opportunity cost of earnings sacrificed by not putting these funds to some other use. This might consist of the purchase of new equipment or the training of more salespeople.

— To a city, the cost of a public park includes more than the outlay costs for construction and maintenance. It also includes the opportunity cost of the tax revenues forgone by not zoning the land for residential, commercial, or industrial use.

You can probably think of other examples. It should be evident, however, why opportunity costs are often called "alternative costs."

The concept of opportunity cost arises whenever the inputs of any activity are scarce and have alternative uses. The real cost or sacrifice is then measured by the value of the forgone alternative. This principle applies at all levels of economic activity — macroeconomic as well as microeconomic.

For any economic entity — a society, a business, a household, or an individual — it is incorrect to confine the cost of an activity or a decision to what the entity is doing. *What the entity is not doing but could be doing is the correct cost consideration.*

What About Nonmonetary Alternatives?

The principle of opportunity cost raises some important questions. For example, is it not true that the alternative cost of a given action may often involve nonmonetary considerations, such as riskiness, working conditions, prestige, and similar factors? The answer is *yes.* This explains, to some extent, why window washers in skyscrapers earn more than dishwashers in restaurants. It helps explain why the prices of "glamour" securities in the stock market fluctuate much more widely than the share prices of relatively stable companies such as public utilities. And it also explains why some people may be willing to work for smaller returns in their own businesses, where they can be their own bosses, rather than for higher returns in other people's businesses.

The nonmonetary elements that help make the differences in resource allocation are often difficult to measure. But, in *principle*, the monetary returns plus or minus the various nonmonetary advantages and disadvantages determine the ways in which the owners of the factors of production put their human and material resources to use.

Economic Cost Includes Normal Profit

Once we recognize the existence of opportunity costs, it becomes apparent that there is a sharp distinction between costs in accounting and costs in economics. *Economic costs* are payments that must be made to persuade the owners of the factors of production to supply the factors for a particular activity. This definition emphasizes the fact that economic costs are supply prices or "bids" that buyers of resources must offer to attract the desired factor inputs.

Thus, a firm buys its resources, such as capital, land, and labor, in the open market. Expenditures for these resources are part of the firm's economic costs. These money outlays are the *explicit costs* that an accountant records in the company's books.

But there are other types of economic costs, called *implicit costs* because they are the costs of self-owned or self-employed resources that are not entered in a company's books of account. For example, if you own a business, including the building and its real estate, and if you manage the business yourself, part of your cost includes the following implicit items.

1. The *interest* *return* on your investment that you are forgoing by not putting your money into an alternative investment of equal risk.

2. The *rental* receipts that you are passing up by not renting the land and building to another firm.

3. The *wages* that you would earn if you could be hired to manage the same kind of business for someone else.

These implicit costs of ownership constitute what may be called ***normal profit.*** This is the least payment the owner of an enterprise would be willing to accept for performing the entrepreneurial function, including risk taking, management, and the like. Normal profit is thus part of a firm's total economic costs, because it is a payment that will keep the owner from withdrawing capital and managerial effort and putting them into some other alternative. Further, economic costs include both explicit costs and implicit costs, and implicit costs include normal profit. Therefore, any receipts that a firm may get over and above its economic costs represent ***economic*** or ***pure profit.*** These ideas are illustrated in Exhibit 1.

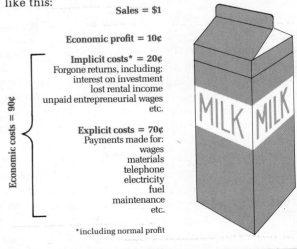

Exhibit 1
Economic Costs and Economic Profit

Suppose that you own your own business, including the building and its land. If you sell an item for $1, your economic costs and economic profit might look like this:

Sales = $1

Economic profit = 10¢

Implicit costs* = 20¢
Forgone returns, including:
interest on investment
lost rental income
unpaid entrepreneurial wages
etc.

Explicit costs = 70¢
Payments made for:
wages
materials
telephone
electricity
fuel
maintenance
etc.

Economic costs = 90¢

*including normal profit

Short Run and Long Run ~~Cost~~

Of course, the costs of resources are strongly influenced by the ways in which they are used. Because of this, any discussion of costs must include an explanation of two useful concepts—the short run and the long run. These refer not to clock or calendar time but to the time necessary for resources to adjust fully to new conditions. This is true regardless of how many weeks, months, or even years the adjustment may take.

At any given time, a firm has available a certain *capacity* to produce. This is determined by the quantity of the firm's equipment or the scale of its plant. If the firm experiences unexpected increases or decreases in the demand for its products, it can change its level of output by using existing plant and equipment either more or less intensively. But it cannot alter plant scale or production capacity with equal speed. Business firms do not put up new factories or discard old ones with every increase or decrease in demand, any more than colleges and universities erect new classroom buildings or abandon old ones with every rise or fall in enrollment.

This leads to an important distinction between the short run and the long run. The ***short run*** is a period in which a firm can vary its output through a more or less intensive use of its resources. However, it cannot vary its capacity because it has a fixed plant scale. The ***long run*** is a period long enough for a firm to enter or leave an industry or to vary its output by varying *all* its factors of production, including plant scale.

These concepts of the short run and the long run suggest a passage from Henry Wadsworth Longfellow's famous poem "The Day Is Done":

And the night shall be filled with music,
　And the cares that infest the day,
Shall fold their tents, like the Arabs,
　And as silently steal away.

In economics, business firms can depart like the Arabs to whom Longfellow referred. By our definition, however, businesses can do this *only* in the long run, not in the short run.

The Production Function

Every businessperson is well aware that costs of production depend on two things: the quantity of resources purchased and the prices paid for them. At this point, our concern is with the quantity purchased. Accordingly, it will be useful to analyze a concept known as the ***production function***. This is a relationship between the number of units of inputs that a firm employs and the corresponding units of output produced.

The Law of (Eventually) Diminishing Returns

You have probably heard of the *law of diminishing returns*. This law is as famous in economics as the law of universal gravitation is in physics. But in economics, just as in physics, you are not likely to have a precise understanding of the law without a basic course in the subject.

Exhibit 2 displays a production function based on only one variable input. The table and chart enable you to "see" the operation of the law of diminishing returns as well as to understand it in terms of the following definition.

Law of (Eventually) Diminishing Returns Assume that the state of technology is constant. Then, the addition of a variable factor of production, keeping the other factors of production fixed, will *eventually* yield diminishing marginal returns per unit of the variable factor added. (This law is also known by the more general name of the ***law of variable proportions***.)

The law of diminishing returns was discovered (by the English classical economist David Ricardo) in agriculture in 1815. Considered a heroic advance in the history of economic theory, the law is one of the most widely held and best-developed principles in economics. This is because it encompasses many kinds of production functions. These range from agriculture and automobiles through retailing and textiles to zinc and zippers. The law thus has enormous significance as well as generality.

Exhibit 2
Production Function

	(1)	(2)	(3)	(4)
				Marginal product, MP
	Units of variable factor, F	Total product, TP	Average product, AP (2) ÷ (1)	Change in (2) / Change in (1)
A	1	6	6	
				8
B	2	14	7	
				12
C	3	26	8.7	
				11
D	4	37	9.3	
				9
E	5	46	9.2	
				6
F	6	52	8.7	
				5
G	7	57	8.1	
				3
H	8	60	7.5	
				1
I	9	61	6.8	
				−3
J	10	58	5.8	

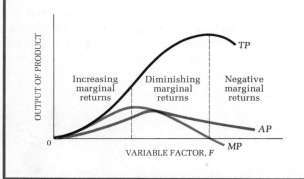

Two sets of features should be observed:

1. Note that columns (1) and (2) of Exhibit 2 are in general terms. In order to put them into specific terms, the variable input in column (1) of the table might represent pounds of fertilizer applied to an acre of land. Then the corresponding output in column (2) could be bushels of wheat. Or the variable input might be the number of workers on an assembly line in a factory and the output could be the number of units of the finished good produced. Practically any simple type of "input–output" relationship or production process could be used to illustrate the basic concepts.

2. The curves in the figure are actually "idealized" or smoothed-out versions of the data given in the table. This enables us to focus most of our attention on the graphs rather than on the numbers. Thus, the horizontal axis shows the variable factor from column (1) of the table, and the vertical axis represents the corresponding output from the remaining columns.

How Is the Law Interpreted?

The first thing you probably noticed in the figure in Exhibit 2 was the shape of the total product, or TP, curve. As the variable input increases from zero, the TP curve goes through three phases. At first it rises rapidly, then it tapers off until it reaches a maximum, and finally it declines.

These three phases are reflected by the **marginal product,** MP. This is defined as the change in total product resulting from a unit change in a variable input. Hence, marginal product can be calculated by the formula

$$MP = \frac{\text{change in total product}}{\text{change in variable input}}$$

You can verify these changes in MP from the table. **Average product,** AP, on the other hand, is simply the ratio of total product to the amount of variable input needed to produce that product:

$$AP = \frac{\text{total product}}{\text{variable input}}$$

For example, if Exhibit 2 is taken to represent the number of people working a given parcel of land in order to produce tomatoes, the results could be interpreted in the following way.

The efforts of the first person (whom we will call A), applied to the fixed amount of land, must be spread too thinly in covering all the land. Consequently, the total output is only 6 boxes of tomatoes. If a second person, B, is added who is *equally as efficient* as A, both persons can work the same amount of land and thereby increase total output to 14 boxes of tomatoes. The average output is then 7 boxes of tomatoes per person. However, the marginal product or gain in output is 8 boxes of tomatoes. Adding workers increases the total output. But, as you can see in Exhibit 2, a point is eventually reached at which there are so many workers that they get in each other's way and even trample the tomatoes. When this happens, the TP curve passes its maximum point and turns downward. When this occurs the gain in output or marginal product becomes negative.

Marginal Returns Are the Most Important

Note, therefore, that the MP curve at first rises and eventually begins to fall, even though *all the workers are equally efficient*. This is an extremely important idea. The reason the MP curve declines is not that the last person hired is less efficient than the previous one. It declines solely for quantitative reasons. That is, the MP curve declines because of the changing proportions of variable factors to fixed factors, while all qualitative considerations are assumed to remain equal. This is why the term "law of variable proportions" is more often employed than "law of diminishing returns."

Mathematically, of course, the MP curve is derived from changes in the TP curve. Indeed, the MP curve represents the *slope* of the TP curve. This is because the slope of any curve is the change in its vertical distance per unit of change in its horizontal distance. Thus, the fact that the TP curve first increases at an increasing rate and then at a decreasing rate is what causes the MP curve to rise to a maximum point and then fall. The resulting three phases — *increasing marginal returns, diminishing marginal returns,* and *negative marginal returns* — are labeled in the figure. It is to these phases — especially the first two — that the definition of the law of diminishing returns refers.

Because all three curves rise to a maximum and then decline, it can be said that *a law of diminishing returns applies to the total product, the average product, and the marginal product curves.* Indeed, from the time the law was initially formulated in 1815 until the late nineteenth century, it was often stated in general terms without distinguishing between total, average, and marginal returns. But it then came to be realized that *marginal* returns are of key importance for decisions involving changes in the quantities of input or output. This idea will become increasingly apparent in this and in subsequent chapters.

Short-Run Costs

You have seen that in the short run some resource inputs for a firm are variable while others are fixed. This is because it may be possible in a given production process to vary the number of unskilled workers, for example, or to draw down larger or smaller quantities of raw materials available in inventory. However, it may take considerable time to add a new wing to a plant or to have machines built to specification.

In view of this, what are the nature and behavior of a firm's costs in the short run? We shall answer this question by analyzing three families of cost concepts: *total cost, average cost,* and *marginal cost.*

Cost Schedules and Curves

The table in Exhibit 3 presents a company's cost schedule. It illustrates the relationship between quantities of output produced per day, as shown in column (1), and the various costs per day of producing these outputs, as shown in the remaining columns. The accompanying figures are graphs of the cost data presented in the table. Note that, as usual, output is measured on the horizontal axes and costs are measured on the vertical axes. Also, the graphs are idealized to show their interrelations more clearly.

Exhibit 3
Short-Run Cost Schedules and Curves for a Firm

(1) Quantity of output per day, Q	(2) Total fixed cost, TFC	(3) Total variable cost, TVC	(4) Total cost, TC (2) + (3)	(5) Average fixed cost, AFC (2) ÷ (1)	(6) Average variable cost, AVC (3) ÷ (1)	(7) Average total cost, ATC (4) ÷ (1) or (5) + (6)	(8) Marginal cost, MC Change in (4) Change in (1)
0	$25	$ 0	$ 25	$ —	$ —	$ —	$10
1	25	10	35	25.00	10.00	35.00	6
2	25	16	41	12.50	8.00	20.50	4
3	25	20	45	8.33	6.67	15.00	2
4	25	22	47	6.25	5.50	11.75	2
5	25	24	49	5.00	4.80	9.80	3
6	25	27	52	4.17	4.50	8.67	5
7	25	32	57	3.57	4.57	8.14	8
8	25	40	65	3.13	5.00	8.13	14
9	25	54	79	2.78	6.00	8.78	21
10	25	75	100	2.50	7.50	10.00	

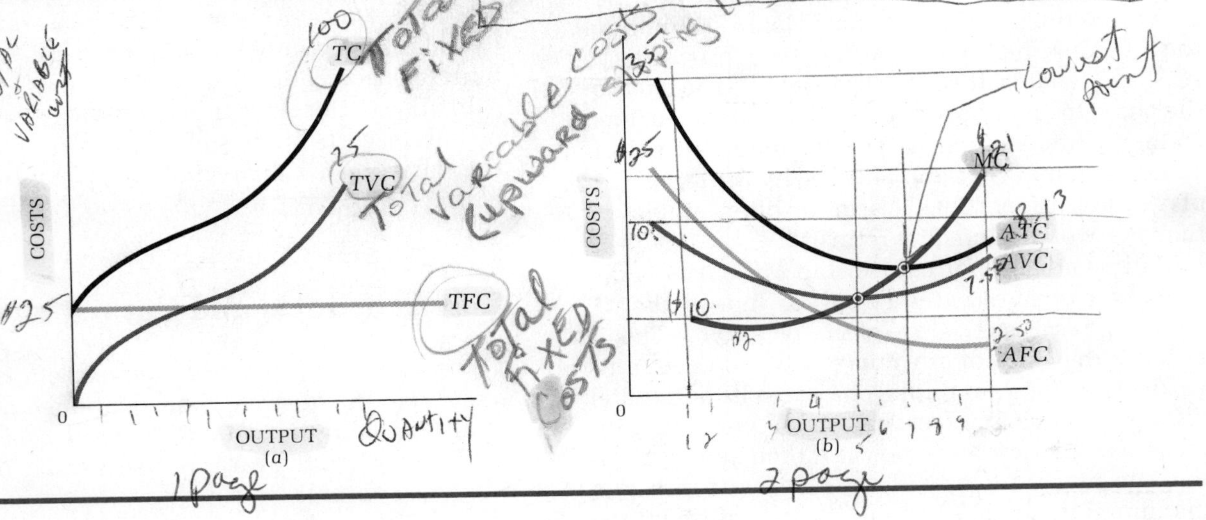

COSTS

TC

TVC

TFC

0   OUTPUT
(a)

COSTS

MC

ATC

AVC

AFC

0   OUTPUT
(b)

Our objective is to see how the different costs in Exhibit 3 are related to output. That is, we want to know how they do or do not vary with changes in output. Because the cost curves have a number of important properties, it is important to examine them closely. Remember that we are assuming that *a firm's total costs are its economic costs and hence include normal profit.*

The Family of Total Costs

The first class of costs to be considered is the "total" group shown in columns (2), (3), and (4) of the table.

Total Fixed Cost *TFC* in column (2) represents those costs that do not vary with output. Examples include rental payments, interest payments on debt, property taxes, and depreciation of plant and equipment. Also included are the wages and salaries of a skeleton staff that the firm would employ as long as it stayed in business—even if it produced nothing. The *TFC* figure is $25 at all levels of output in the table and hence appears as a horizontal line in Figure (a).

Total Variable Cost *TVC* in column (3) consists of those costs that vary directly with output. These costs rise as output increases over the full range of production. Examples are payments for materials, labor, fuel, and power. Note from Figure (a) that, as output increases, *TVC* increases first at a decreasing rate and then at an increasing rate. This reflects the operation of the law of diminishing (total) returns, as explained earlier.

Total Cost *TC* in column (4) represents the sum of total fixed cost and total variable cost. Thus, we have the basic equation

$$TC = TFC + TVC$$

This means that

$$TFC = TC - TVC$$

and

$$TVC = TC - TFC$$

You should also note from the table and Figure (a) that *TC* equals *TFC* at zero output. This is because there are no variable costs when there is no production. Observe too that the shape of the *TC* curve is the same as—or "parallel" to—the shape of the *TVC* curve. The only difference between them is

the constant vertical distance represented by *TFC*. In other words, because total fixed cost is constant, changes in total cost are due entirely to changes in total variable cost.

The Family of Average Costs

Columns (5), (6), and (7) give us three different types of average costs. These are represented by Figure (b), which accompanies the table.

Average Fixed Cost *AFC* is the ratio of total fixed cost to quantity produced:

$$AFC = \frac{TFC}{Q}$$

Note from Figure (b) that *AFC* continually decreases as output increases. This is because *TFC* in the foregoing equation is constant. Hence, increases in output will always reduce the value of the ratio.

Average Variable Cost *AVC* is the ratio of total variable cost to quantity produced:

$$AVC = \frac{TVC}{Q}$$

Notice that, as output increases, the *AVC* curve falls to a minimum point and then rises. The *AVC* curve thus reflects the operation of the law of diminishing (average) returns described earlier.

Average Total Cost *ATC* is the ratio of total cost to quantity:

$$ATC = \frac{TC}{Q}$$

Hence, it is also equal to the sum of *AFC* and *AVC*:

$$ATC = AFC + AVC$$

Of course, you can transpose the equation to express either *AFC* or *AVC* in terms of the other variables.

NOTE People in business often use the terms "unit cost" or "cost per unit" when they mean average *variable* cost. If you were a shirt manufacturer, for example, you might figure your cost per shirt to be $6 based on the cost of labor, materials, and other variable resources used. You would then set a "markup" price of perhaps an additional $6 per shirt to cover "overhead" or fixed costs. Economists, on the other hand, include fixed costs with total costs right from the outset. Hence, they use unit cost, or cost per unit, to mean average *total* cost.

Notice that the vertical distance between *ATC* and *AVC* diminishes as output increases. That is, *ATC* and *AVC* come progressively closer together. This is because the difference between them, *AFC*, continually decreases as output expands.

Marginal Cost

There is an important lesson to be learned from the table and charts of Exhibit 3. The lesson is that *total cost always increases as output increases.* That is, the more a firm produces, the greater its total cost of production. This is because increased production always requires the use of more materials, labor, power, and other variable resources. Only average costs — in particular *ATC* and *AVC* — decrease as output increases until some "optimum" or best level of production is reached. Thus, when you hear someone in business say that production needs to be increased in order to lower costs, that person is talking about unit costs — either *ATC* or *AVC* — not *TC* or *TVC*.

The fact that total cost changes with variations in production gives rise to an important cost concept called **marginal cost,** *MC*. It is defined as the change in total cost resulting from a unit change in output. The formula for determining marginal cost is thus similar to that for determining marginal product, except that "change in *TP*" becomes "change in *TC*;" and "change in variable input" becomes "change in output." Thus, marginal cost may be measured by the formula

$$MC = \frac{\text{change in } TC}{\text{change in } Q}$$

Of course, changes in *TC* are due to changes in *TVC*, because *TFC* remains constant as production varies. Hence, marginal cost can also be measured by dividing the change in *TVC* by the change in *Q*.

What does marginal cost really mean?

Mathematically, marginal cost represents the *slope* of the total cost curve (just as you saw earlier that marginal product represents the slope of the total product curve). Economically, it tells you, for any given output, the *additional* amount of cost a business firm would incur by increasing its output by one unit.

You will see later that, *for economic decisions involving changes in output, marginal cost is the single most important cost concept.*

The Average – Marginal Relationship

By this time you may have noticed an interesting geometric principle that characterizes all average and marginal curves. For convenience, Exhibit 4 groups the foregoing production curves and cost curves together, so that they may be examined simultaneously. However, we are interested for the moment only in the average and marginal curves, so these curves are shown separately below their corresponding total curves.

If you refer to these lower curves, you will note an important set of relationships.

1. When an average curve is rising, its corresponding marginal curve is above it.

2. When an average curve is falling, its corresponding marginal curve is below it.

3. When an average curve is neither rising nor falling, that is, is either at a maximum or at a minimum, its corresponding marginal curve intersects (is equal to) it.

This set of relationships constitutes what may be called the **average – marginal relationship.**

The sense behind the average – marginal relationship can be appreciated by a simple example. If to a class of students we add an extra, or "marginal," student whose age is above the average age of the class, the average will increase. If we add a student

Exhibit 4
The Average – Marginal Relationship and the Total – Marginal Relationship

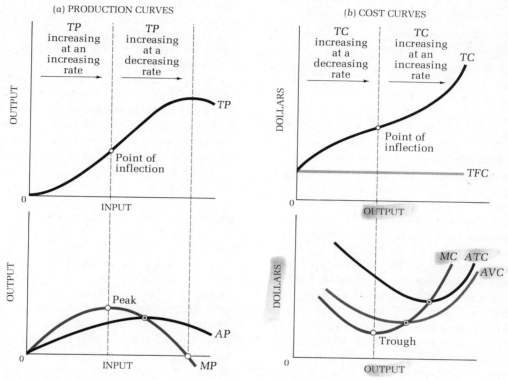

(a) PRODUCTION CURVES

TP increasing at an increasing rate →

TP increasing at a decreasing rate →

OUTPUT

TP

Point of inflection

0   INPUT

OUTPUT

Peak

AP

0   INPUT   MP

(b) COST CURVES

TC increasing at a decreasing rate →

TC increasing at an increasing rate →

DOLLARS

TC

Point of inflection

TFC

0   OUTPUT

DOLLARS

MC ATC
AVC

Trough

0   OUTPUT

whose age is below the average, the average will decrease. And if we add a student whose age is equal to the average, the average will remain the same.

Does the average – marginal relationship hold true for both the production-function and cost curves? The figures in Exhibit 4 indicate that it does. But in the production figure the marginal curve intersects the average curve at its maximum point, whereas in the cost figure the marginal curve intersects the two average curves at their minimum points.

In later chapters you will encounter other types of average and marginal curves, but the underlying geometric principle stated here characterizes them all.

The Total – Marginal Relationship

A geometric principle is also common to all total and marginal curves. It is based on the fact that every marginal curve is a graph of the *slope* of its corresponding total curve, as you have already seen.

If you refer again to Exhibit 4, this time to both the upper and lower figures, you will see an interesting relationship. This is emphasized by the vertical dashed lines. Thus:

1. When a total curve is increasing at an increasing rate, its corresponding marginal curve is rising.

2. When a total curve is increasing at a decreasing rate, its corresponding marginal curve is falling.

3. When a total curve is increasing at a zero rate, as occurs when it is at its maximum, its corresponding marginal curve is zero.

This set of relationships is called the **total–marginal relationship.**

Observe from the diagrams that the point at which the rate of change of the total curve changes direction is called the *point of inflection*. This point corresponds to either a peak or a trough in the marginal curve, as shown by the vertical dashed lines.

To avoid confusion, you might make note of an important aspect of the total–marginal relationship. It is not necessary to include the fact that when the total curve is falling—as in the case of the *TP* curve at its right end—the corresponding *MP* curve is negative. Although negative marginal curves may exist from a theoretical standpoint, they do not ordinarily have any economic significance. A rational employer, for example, will not knowingly hire so many units of an input as to yield the firm a negative marginal product.

As with the average–marginal relationship, there are several kinds of total–marginal relationships that you will encounter in later chapters. However, the underlying principle presented here characterizes them all.

Long-Run Costs

It was emphasized earlier that an important difference exists between the short run and the long run. In the *short run* a firm can vary its output but not its plant capacity. Thus, the firm will have some variable costs and some fixed costs. In the *long run* a firm can vary not only its output but also its plant capacity. That is, *in the long run all costs are variable.*

Of what practical value is this in the study of costs? The previous analysis of short-run costs reveals how a firm's costs will vary in response to output changes within a period short enough that the size of the plant remains fixed. If we now extend the logic one step further, we can develop a firm's *long-run cost curve*. This shows how costs vary with output in a period long enough for all resource inputs, including plant and equipment, to be freely variable in amount. Once the long-run cost curve is derived, the knowledge gained from it can be of use to businesses in determining the most economical size of a plant and its general operational standards.

Alternative Plant Sizes

Look at the problem in this way. Suppose that you were a manufacturer whose plant had gone through a series of additions and expansions over a period of years. For each plant size with its associated complement of equipment there would be a different production function and hence a different cost structure. Each of these cost structures would be represented by a different set of short-run cost curves of the type we have already studied. To illustrate, Exhibit 5, Figure (*a*), presents five short-run average total cost curves. Each curve, labeled ATC_1, ATC_2, and so on, represents one of five different plant sizes. Theoretically, there could be infinitely many such curves, one for each possible plant size.

These short-run curves can be looked at from still another point of view. Suppose that you were a manufacturer planning to construct and equip a plant for the production of a good. In that case, all your factors of production—and therefore all your costs—would be variable. Each possible plant size or "layout" would then be represented by a different cost structure, as illustrated by these short-run average total cost curves. As before, it should be borne in mind that from a theoretical standpoint

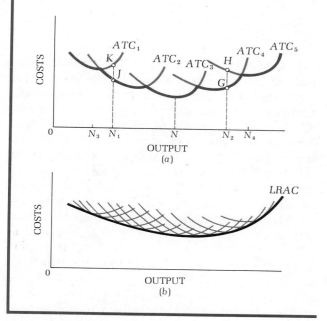

Exhibit 5

**Short-Run Average Total Cost Curves and the
Long-Run Average Cost (or Planning) Curve**

Figure (a): Each short-run plant size or "layout" represents a different plant-cost structure. The optimum level of output is at N. Theoretically, there may be infinitely many such curves, one for each possible plant size.

Figure (b): The planning curve, or long-run average cost curve, is tangent to all the short-run curves. But it can only be tangent to the minimum point of the *lowest* short-run curve. For every other short-run curve, the tangency occurs on either the declining or the rising side.

seems intuitively clear that the "optimum" output level is at N. Also, the lowest-cost or optimum-size plant for producing this output is represented by ATC_3. However, for all other levels of output two interesting principles exist — based on the assumption of infinitely many ATC curves:

— *At any output less than the optimum output at N, it pays better to "underuse" a larger plant than to "overuse" a smaller one.* For example, suppose that you want to produce the output at N_1. Obviously, it is cheaper to use the larger-scale plant ATC_2 at an average production cost of N_1J per unit than to use the smaller-scale plant ATC_1 at an average cost of N_1K per unit.

— *At any output greater than the optimum output at N, it pays better to "overuse" a smaller plant than to "underuse" a larger one.* For instance, suppose that you wish to produce the output at N_2. Clearly, it is cheaper to use the smaller-scale plant ATC_4 at an average cost of N_2G per unit than to use the larger-scale plant ATC_5 at an average cost of N_2H per unit.

It should be noted that these principles are true for *all* outputs — even for outputs like those at N_3 and N_4. Why? Because of the assumption that infinitely many ATC curves may be drawn. Therefore, you can sketch in the possible ATC curves for the outputs at N_3 and N_4 to demonstrate the validity of these concepts.

The Planning Curve

These principles suggest that the lower portions of the short-run average total cost curves are the only ones economically relevant to the selection of a particular plant. What would happen to these lower portions if, instead of having just five short-run curves, there were an infinitely large number of them, as was theoretically assumed? To find out, look at Figure (b) and the following explanation.

The heavy line, called a **planning curve,** is a **long-run average cost curve** (LRAC) that is tangent to each of the short-run average total cost curves from which it is derived. We have already noted

there can be infinitely many such curves, one for each possible layout.

Plant Utilization

Some important lessons may be learned from Figure (a). On the basis of the information presented, it

why the *LRAC* curve is called a "planning curve." When the plant is in the blueprint stage and all costs are variable, the *LRAC* curve tells you the average total cost of producing a given level of output. Thus, it can be thought of as a curve that shows what costs would be like at the present time for alternative outputs if different-size plants were built.

Economies and Diseconomies of Scale

These ideas give rise to an important question: What causes the *LRAC* curve (or the successive *ATC* curves of which it is composed) to decrease to a minimum and then rise? Or, to put the question in terms of real-world examples: Why are steel mills larger than machine shops? Why do some firms remain small while others become large?

The answers are based on what may be called *economies and diseconomies of scale.* These are simply decreases and increases in a firm's long-run average costs as the size of its plant is increased. Let us see why these decreases or increases occur.

Economies of Scale

Several factors may give rise to economies of scale —that is, to decreasing long-run average costs of production.

Greater Specialization of Resources   As a firm's scale of operation increases, its opportunities for specialization are enhanced. This is because a large-scale firm can divide the tasks and work to be done more easily than can a small-scale firm.

More Efficient Utilization of Equipment   In many industries, the technology of production is such that large units of expensive equipment must be used. The production of automobiles, steel, and refined petroleum are notable examples. In such industries, companies purchase whatever specialized equipment is necessary and try to use it efficiently by spreading the cost per unit over a sufficiently large volume of output. A small-scale firm cannot do these things.

Reduced Unit Costs of Inputs   A large-scale firm can buy its inputs—such as its raw materials—at a cheaper price per unit. This is because large firms buy in large quantities and can obtain discounts from their suppliers. And for certain types of equipment, the price per unit of capacity is often much less when larger sizes are purchased. Thus, the construction cost per square foot for a large factory is less than for a small one. The price per horsepower of electric induction motors varies inversely with the amount of horsepower.

Utilization of By-products   In certain industries, large-scale firms can make effective use of many by-products that would be wasted by a small firm. A typical example is the meat-packing industry. Here, major firms make glue, pharmaceuticals, fertilizer, and other products from the remains of animals.

Growth of Auxiliary Facilities   An expanding firm may benefit from, or encourage other firms to develop, ancillary facilities, such as warehousing, marketing, and transportation systems. These facilities save the growing firm considerable costs. For example, urban colleges and universities benefit from nearby public libraries and restaurants. Individual farms benefit from common irrigation and drainage ditches. Similarly, growing businesses often encourage the development of, and receive the benefit from, improved transportation facilities.

Diseconomies of Scale

At the same time that economies of scale are being realized, a point may be reached at which diseconomies of scale begin to exert a more-than-offsetting effect. As a result, the long-run average cost curve starts to rise, primarily for two reasons.

Limitation on Decision-Making Capacity of Management   As a firm becomes larger, heavier burdens are placed on management. Eventually, this resource input is overworked relative to the others, and "diminishing returns" to management set in.

Economics in the News

Ford Decides Bigness Isn't A Better Idea

By John Koten
Staff Reporter of THE WALL
STREET JOURNAL

FLAT ROCK, Mich.—In theory, every business believes in economies of scale. But as Ford Motor Co. has learned at an iron-casting plant here, theories don't always work the way they are supposed to.

When Ford erected a factory here [in 1971] to build engine blocks, it followed the principle that large-scale production could bring lower costs per unit of output. The company spent an estimated $200 million to construct a four-story-high plant big enough to enclose 72 football fields and designed exclusively to manufacture engine blocks in the fastest, most efficient way possible. The plant could turn out 500,000 tons of iron blocks a year. It was one of

Ford's largest and most economical facilities.

However, Ford announced plans to mothball the Flat Rock plant and lay off its 2,500 hourly employees. The company said that production of engine blocks will be moved to a much older plant in Cleveland. One of the reasons Ford officials gave for the decision: The Flat Rock plant is simply too big.

Too Highly Specialized

David L. Lewis, professor of business at the University of Michigan, says the Flat Rock factory is a case of "economies of scale run amok." The plant is a rare example of what can happen when a factory is too highly specialized, he says. "Flat Rock was efficient at producing what it was originally designed to make, but as soon as the product changed, the plant became outmoded by its own size. It was just too big to convert to other uses."

The casting plant originally was built to make V-8 engine blocks on

five ultra-high-speed production lines. The design worked well as long as strong demand for big engines kept the lines running at high capacity. Throughout most of the 1970s, the plant received high marks in Ford's internal cost studies.

But as cars started getting smaller and as fuel-efficient four and six-cylinder engines became more popular, the Flat Rock plant began to run into trouble, requiring large amounts of cash to retool its complicated and expensive machinery.

"When Flat Rock opened, it was hailed as a marvel. It was one of the most efficient plants of its kind in the world," says Prof. Lewis. "Its closing is a lesson in mass production. Sometimes you really can be too big."

Of course, management may be able to delegate authority to others, but ultimately decisions must emanate from a final center if there is to be uniformity in performance and policy. Even the modern principles of scientific management do not eliminate these diseconomies. At most, they may be postponed, or perhaps their seriousness may be lessened.

Competition for Resources Long-run average costs can rise as a growing firm increasingly bids labor or other resources away from other industries. This may raise the prices the firm pays for its inputs and cause increases in unit production costs.

Conclusion: Internal/External Classification *NO—omit*

These causes of increasing and decreasing returns to scale may be classified according to whether they are internal or external to the firm. The distinction is important, because the internal factors may be subject to a certain amount of managerial control, whereas the external factors are not. The following classification illustrates these ideas while summarizing important concepts.

Internal economies and diseconomies These are conditions that bring about decreases or increases

Exhibit 6
Three Typical Long-Run Average Cost Curves

The shapes of different firms' long-run average costs vary in different industries.

Figure (a): A situation in which economies of scale outweigh the diseconomies over a wide range of output. Examples are the aluminum, automobile, cement, and steel industries.

Figure (b): A situation in which diseconomies of scale set in quickly and many small firms exist side by side. Examples are the retailing, metal-fabrication, and publishing industries.

Figure (c): A situation in which economies of scale are either quickly exhausted and diseconomies take a long time coming, or else the economies and diseconomies tend to cancel each other out. Examples are the chemical, food-processing, furniture, and appliance industries.

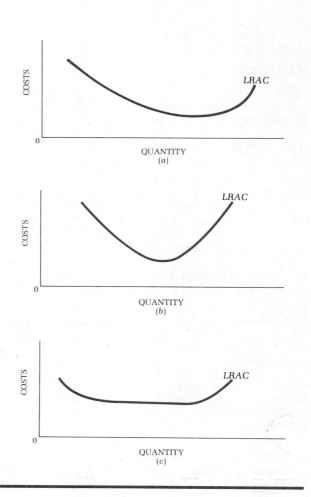

in a firm's long-run average costs as a result of size adjustments *within* the firm. They occur regardless of adjustments within the industry and are due mainly to physical economies or diseconomies. That is, reductions in long-run average costs occur largely because a greater division of productive factors becomes possible as size and output increase. On the other hand, increases in long-run average costs occur because of adverse or conflicting factor interaction between management and other resources.

External economies and diseconomies These are conditions that bring about decreases or increases in a firm's long-run average costs as a result of causes that are entirely *outside* the firm. The causes depend on adjustments of the industry and are related to the firm only to the extent that it is part of the industry.

On the basis of this distinction, you should be able to classify each of the various economies and diseconomies of scale listed in the two previous sections as either internal or external.

What Does the Evidence Show?

Do the long-run average cost curves of firms actually look like the ones shown earlier? Or do their shapes vary according to the economics of the industry in which they operate? The answer to both questions is yes.

In all industries, the long-run average cost curves of firms decline, reach a minimum, and eventually rise. However, some curves do so more quickly than others, depending on the particular industry and the types of economies and diseconomies that characterize it. Three basic variations are shown in Exhibit 6.

What You Have Learned

1. Cost is a sacrifice that must be made in order to do something or acquire something. The sacrifice may include monetary and nonmonetary elements.

2. Opportunity costs are critical in economics because they measure the value of a forgone alternative. Opportunity costs arise because resources are limited and have alternative uses.

3. Economic costs are payments that must be made to attract resources. Such costs include not only explicit costs or money expenditures for resources but also the implicit costs of self-owned or self-employed resources.

4. The law of diminishing returns—more accurately called the law of variable proportions—states what happens to output when a variable input is combined with fixed inputs. Although the law covers total, average, and marginal returns, the last is most important where changes in output are involved. Graphically, marginal product always intersects average product at its maximum point.

5. There are three families of costs: total, average, and marginal. The family of total costs consists of total fixed cost, which does not vary with output, and total variable cost, which increases as output increases. The family of average costs consists of average fixed cost, which is the ratio of total fixed cost to total output, and average variable cost, which is the ratio of total variable cost to total output. Marginal cost is a one-member family consisting of marginal cost alone. It is the change in total cost resulting from a unit change in output. Graphically, marginal cost always intersects average variable cost and average total cost at their minimum points.

6. The short run is a period long enough to vary output but not plant capacity. The long run is a period long enough to vary plant capacity. Therefore, in the short run some of a firm's costs are fixed and some are variable. But in the long run all of a firm's costs are variable because all its factors of production are variable.

7. The long-run average cost curve, or planning curve, tends to be U-shaped, reflecting first economies and then diseconomies of scale. Economies of scale result from greater specialization of resources, more efficient utilization of equipment, reduced unit costs of inputs, and fuller use of by-products. Diseconomies of scale arise mainly from the increasing complexities of management as a firm grows larger. Economies and diseconomies of scale can be classified as either internal or external to a firm.

8. The actual shape of a planning curve tends to vary among different industries. In heavy industries, such as autos and steel, internal economies extend over a wide range of output. Hence, such industries tend to have small numbers of large firms. In light industries, such as textiles and retailing, internal economies are exhausted rather quickly over a narrow range of output. Consequently, such industries tend to have large numbers of small firms.

Terms and Concepts To Review

cost
outlay costs
opportunity cost
economic costs
explicit costs
implicit costs
normal profit
economic (pure) profit
short run
long run
production function
law of diminishing returns (law of variable proportions)
marginal product
average product
total fixed cost
total variable cost

total cost
average fixed cost
average variable cost
average total cost
marginal cost
average–marginal relationship
total–marginal relationship
long-run average cost curve (planning curve)
economies and diseconomies of scale
internal economies and diseconomies of scale
external economies and diseconomies of scale

For Discussion

[handwritten: DUE NOV 6, 87 P.396 2 pages]

1. Complete the accompanying table, showing the cost schedule of a firm. Graph the family of total costs in one figure and all the remaining costs in another. (NOTE When you graph the marginal cost curve, plot each *MC* value to the midpoint between successive outputs. Thus, the first *MC* value in your figure corresponds to an output of 0.5, the second to 1.5, the third to 2.5, and so on.) Discuss the various curves in terms of their shape as influenced by the law of diminishing returns. (HINT Sketch the family of total costs on one figure and the family of average and marginal costs on a figure directly beneath it. Then see if you can draw a vertical dashed line through both figures such that the stage of increasing marginal returns is on the left side of the vertical line and the stage of decreasing marginal returns is on the right.) In your answer, account for the relative distances between *ATC* and *AVC* at different levels of output, and explain the reason for the intersection of *MC* with *ATC* and *AVC* at their minimum points.

[handwritten: P.396 2 pages]

2. Are opportunity costs entered in the accounting records of a firm? If so, what are the cost figures used for? If not, what good are they?

3. In estimating the annual cost of owning a fully paid-up $9,000 automobile, you might show the following cost entry on your books: "Interest on investment at 6 percent: $540." What would this mean? Explain.

4. Why do you suppose that some professors who could earn considerably more by working in industry continue to accept a lower salary by remaining in education?

5. "As a firm becomes larger and decision making becomes more complex, the long-run average cost curve turns upward. This is because the burden of administration becomes disproportionately greater and 'diminishing returns' to management set in." Would this statement be true of firms that are very well managed? Of what significance are technology, organizational structure, managerial ability, and similar factors?

6. The law of diminishing returns was originally intended to serve as an explanation of a historical process.

Cost Schedule of a Firm

[handwritten annotations across top: REFER TO PG. 406   2+3   2÷1   3÷1   4÷1 / 5+6   change in 4]

(1) Quantity of output	(2) Total fixed cost	(3) Total variable cost	(4) Total cost	(5) Average fixed cost	(6) Average variable cost	(7) Average total cost	(8) Marginal cost
0	$100	$ 0	$ 100	$ —	$ —	$ —	$ 40 .05
1	100	40	140	100	40	140	24 1.5
2	100	64	164	50	32	82	16 2.5
3	100	80	180	33.33	26.66	59.99	8 3.5
4	100	88	188	25	22	47	8 4.5
5	100	96	146	20	19.20	39.20	12 5.5
6	100	108	208	16.6	18	34.40	20 6.5
7	100	128	228	14.28	18.28	32.56	32 7.5
8	100	160	260	12.5	20.20	32.50	56 8.5
9	100	216	316	11.11	24	35.11	84 9.5
10	100	300	400	10	30	40	

In England, for example, as the population grew during the eighteenth and nineteenth centuries, it was predicted (by the early classical economist David Ricardo in 1815) that the marginal productivity of labor on land would decline. If this were true:

(a) What would happen to aggregate values of agricultural land?

(b) What would happen to total land rent as a percentage share of the nation's total income?

(c) What would happen to the price of food relative to nonfood goods?

(d) How would you answer these questions with respect to the United States during most of the nineteenth century?

7. What is the effect of a technological improvement on a company's production function?

8. "If it were not for the law of diminishing returns, it would be possible to grow all the world's food in a flowerpot." What does this statement mean?

9. The most common type of production function is one characterized by "constant returns to scale." This means that, if *all* inputs to a production process are increased in the same proportion, output is increased in that proportion. For example, if *all* inputs are expanded by 10 percent, output is expanded by 10 percent; if *all* inputs are doubled, output is doubled; and so on. In view of this, how do you account for the following situation?

(a) A suit-manufacturing firm doubled the size of its factory, the number of machines in it, the number of workers, and the quantity of materials employed. As a result, output increased from 200 to 420 suits per day. Is this an example of *increasing returns to scale*, that is, economies of large-scale production?

(b) The company then doubled the quantity of managers and found that output fell to 370 suits per day. What do you suppose might have happened?

10. **Physical-Growth Analogies of Returns to Scale**

(a) There is a relationship between the volume V and the surface area A of regular physical bodies. This relationship may be approximated by the "square-cube" law:

$$V = A^{3/2} = \sqrt{A^3}$$

For example, if the surface area of an object increases 4 times, its volume should increase about $\sqrt{4^3} = 8$ times.

Can you use this notion to explain why there are no small warm-blooded animals in the Antarctic or in the ocean? Can you use it to help explain why the largest insect is about as large as the smallest warm-blooded animal?

(b) There is often a tendency to think that constant returns to scale should be common in economic life. However, variable returns (both increasing and decreasing) are frequently encountered. For example, we should expect that, by doubling *all* inputs to a production process, we will double the output. Yet there are examples from nature to illustrate why this is not so. Therefore, if a house were scaled down so that it stood in the same proportion to a flea as it now stands to a person, the flea would be able to jump over the house. However, if a flea were scaled up to the size of a person, the flea would not be able to jump over the house. In fact, it could not jump at all because its legs would break. Can you explain why?

(c) What conclusions relevant to the size and growth of organizations can you draw from these notions? (HINT It has been said that some prehistoric monsters became extinct because they could not adjust to their changing environment. Why not?)

(d) Do you see any connection between question (a), question (b), question (c), and the following quotation?

There is a story of a man who thought of getting the economy of large-scale production in plowing, and built a plow three times as long, three times as wide, and three times as deep as the ordinary plow and harnessed six horses to pull it, instead of two. To his surprise, the plow refused to budge, and to his greater surprise it finally took fifty horses to move the refractory machine. In this case, the resistance, which is the thing he did not want, increased faster than the surface area of the earth plowed, which was the thing he did want. Furthermore, when he increased his power to overcome this resistance, he multiplied the number of his power units instead of their size, which eliminated all chance of saving there, and since his units were horses, the fifty could not pull together as well as two.

J.M. Clark,
Studies in the Economics of Overhead Costs, Chicago,
University of Chicago Press, 1923, p. 116

Sunshine Dairy Products Corporation: New-Plant Decisions

Sunshine Dairy Products Corporation is a leading producer of milk, ice cream, cheese, and other dairy products. After years of research, the company developed a very low calorie, low-cost, synthetic "ice cream." Extensive taste tests have indicated that this new ice cream tastes as good as any of the leading brands of regular ice cream. Accordingly, the management of the company has decided to produce and market the product on a test basis within one region of the country and to construct the necessary production facilities for that purpose.

The Sunshine Corporation conducted a market survey of the three largest population areas of the region. Results indicated that the company should package the product in liter-size containers, and that sales would average about 10,000, 5,000, and 2,500 liters per week in the three areas. The company's economic consultant suggested either of two alternatives with respect to the construction of ice-cream plants:

1. Construct a single plant equidistant between the three population areas, with a production capacity of 20,000 liters per week at a fixed cost of $5,000 per week and a variable cost of 70 cents per liter.

2. Construct three plants (one in each market area) with weekly capacities of 12,000, 6,000, and 3,000 liters, weekly fixed costs of $4,000, $3,000, and $2,000, and a variable cost of only 60 cents per liter (as a result of the reduction in shipping costs).

Questions

1. Assuming that the market survey is correct, which alternative should management select? At a price of $1.99 per liter, what would be the profit (or loss) per liter and in total?

2. If demand were to increase to production capacity, which alternative would be better?

3. Suppose that management selects the second alternative rather than the first and that demand is at the level of production capacity in all three markets. If the company wanted to make a profit of $1 per liter in each of the three markets, what price per liter would it have to charge in each of these markets? Can management be sure of realizing its expected profit? Explain why.

4. Instead of constructing a new plant, the management of Sunshine is contemplating the purchase of an existing plant. The following cost estimates were provided for the plant under consideration:

    (a) *ATC* of 5,000 liters is $12,600.

    (b) *AVC* of 4,000 liters is $10,000.

    (c) *TC* rises by $13,000 when production rises from 5,000 to 6,000 liters.

(d) *AFC* of 5,000 liters is $2,000.

(e) The increase in *TC* from producing nothing to producing 1,000 liters is $15,000.

(f) *TC* of 8,000 liters is $170,000.

(g) *TVC* increases by $25,000 when production rises from 6,000 to 7,000 liters.

(h) *AFC* plus *AVC* for 3,000 liters is $16,000.

(i) *ATC* falls by $6,000 when production increases from 1,000 to 2,000 liters.

On the basis of this information, complete the following cost schedule.

[HINT   First fill in all the data given in items (a) through (i).]

Cost Schedule of an Ice-Cream Plant

Output (thousands of liters per week)	Cost (thousands of dollars per week)						
	TFC	TVC	TC	AFC	AVC	ATC	MC
0	$ ___	$ ___	$ ___	$ ___	$ ___	$ ___	
1	___	___	___	___	___	___	$ ___
2	___	___	___	___	___	___	___
3	___	___	___	___	___	___	___
4	___	___	___	___	___	___	___
5	___	___	___	___	___	___	___
6	___	___	___	___	___	___	___
7	___	___	___	___	___	___	___
8	___	___	___	___	___	___	___

Part 6

The Economics of the Firm: How Are Prices and Outputs Determined?

Chapter 22

Perfect Competition: Criteria for Evaluating Competitive Behavior

Learning Guide

Watch for answers to these important questions

What is perfect competition? Why do we study it? Is it a fantasy or is it real?

What is the fundamental principle of profit maximization? Can it be explained in practical terms? How are supply curves derived from marginal cost curves?

What are the long-run equilibrium conditions of a firm in perfect competition? How does the adjustment to equilibrium come about? Why is $MC = P$ the condition of economic (or allocative) efficiency?

What are the favorable and unfavorable consequences of perfect competition? How are the consequences evaluated in terms of the economy's goals?

You know that economics is concerned with how society allocates its limited resources, which have alternative uses, to the production of goods and services. Economists have always been interested in how this can be accomplished with maximum efficiency—that is, with the least amount of waste. Hence, they have developed the theory of "perfect competition," also called "pure competition." The two terms may be regarded as synonymous. (However, a technical distinction that is sometimes made between them is explained in the Dictionary at the back of the book.) The theory underlies the operation of supply and demand that you studied in previous chapters. It attempts to explain how a "perfect" market economy or "pure" free-enterprise system tends to operate.

What Is Perfect Competition?

A scientist trying to describe a complicated problem starts by constructing a simplified picture of the situation—a *model*. In this chapter we shall develop a model or theory of perfect competition.

Let us begin with a definition.

Perfect (or **pure**) **competition** is the name given to an industry or market structure characterized by a large number of buyers and sellers all engaged in the purchase and sale of a homogeneous commodity. Each buyer or seller has perfect knowledge of market prices and quantities; there is no discrimination; and there is perfect mobility of resources.

The expression "perfect competition" can be used in discussing either an industry or a market. The distinction is always clear from the context in which the term is used. Now let us analyze each of the five essential conditions contained in the definition.

Large Numbers of Buyers and Sellers

What do we mean by a "large" number of buyers and sellers? Is 1,000 large and 999 small? To answer *yes* would be silly; the words "large" and "small" are relative rather than absolute. Therefore, the definition does not establish the size of a perfectly competitive market in terms of numbers. Instead, it uses the word "large" in a functional sense. "Large" means *large enough that no one buyer or seller can affect the market price by deciding to buy or not to buy, to sell or not to sell.* Whether it takes 1,000 or 1 million buyers or sellers is of no relevance. The only requirement is that the market price for any buyer or seller is *given*. The individual can accept the market price or reject the market price, but cannot alter it by going into or out of the market.

Homogeneous Commodity

This means that all units of the commodity that sellers make available are identical in the minds of buyers. The reason for this requirement, as will be shown later, is that buyers must be indifferent about which seller they deal with. They must be willing to purchase from the seller who offers the good at the lowest price.

Notice that we are referring to economic homogeneity, not physical homogeneity. Two sellers may be selling the same physical product, but buyers may be willing to pay more to seller A than to seller B. This may be so because seller A provides service with a smile, or offers the commodity in a more attractive package, or perhaps uses a brand name. In such cases, the two products are *not* economically homogeneous.

This point can be illustrated with a concrete example. Beet sugar and cane sugar are virtually identical for all practical purposes. That is, they look and taste the same. Yet, in some regions of the country, beet sugar sells for less than cane. Why? Because buyers do not think of them as the same. Instead, they believe that beet is somehow inferior to cane. And, because the law requires that a package of sugar must be labeled either "beet" or "cane," there sometimes is a price difference between them. In this case, the two products are physically homogeneous but economically heterogeneous. That is, they are similar but not identical. Can the same be said about butter and margarine? Two nickels and a dime? Are they homogeneous? Heterogeneous?

Perfect Knowledge of Market Prices and Quantities

The third condition—"perfect knowledge"—means that all buyers and sellers are completely aware of the prices and quantities at which transactions are taking place in the market. This permits buyers to compete with buyers, and sellers with sellers. For example, perfect knowledge does not exist if buyers do not know that sellers across the street are charging a lower price for a certain commodity. Likewise, perfect knowledge does not exist if sellers do not know that buyers across the street are offering a higher price for a certain product. In both instances, the buyers and sellers on one side of the street are not competing with the buyers and sellers on the other side. Hence, they are not even in the same market.

No Discrimination

This condition of no discrimination requires that buyers and sellers be willing to deal openly with one another. This means that they must be willing to buy and sell at the market price with any and all that may wish to do so. This condition also means that buyers and sellers must not offer or accept any special deals, discounts, or favors that are not available to everyone on equal terms. Discrimination therefore has an economic meaning, not just a social one.

Perfect Mobility of Resources

The condition of perfect resource mobility requires that there be no obstacles — economic, legal, technological, or others — to prevent firms or resources from entering or leaving the particular market or industry. Further, there must be no impediments to the purchase or sale of commodities. This means that firms, resources, and commodities can be shifted about swiftly and smoothly without friction. For example, the land, labor, capital, and entrepreneurship used in wheat production can be moved quickly and easily into corn production if it is more profitable. Similarly, potatoes stored in Idaho can be sold instantly in New York or in San Francisco if the price is right. In general, owners of resources and commodities are free and able to take advantage of the best market opportunities as they arise.

Is Perfect Competition a Fantasy?

Is the concept of perfect competition realistic or a fantasy? After all, no market or industry anywhere in the world exactly meets the five requirements just described. Should you infer, therefore, that the notion of perfect competition is "theoretical and impractical"?

The answer is *no*. As you shall see shortly, the concept of perfect competition is a *theoretical extreme* — like the concept of a perfect vacuum or the assumption of a frictionless state in physics.

For example, in elementary physics it is expressly assumed, in many problems of motion, that there is *no friction*. This assumption is made even though everyone knows that friction always exists in the real world. The assumption creates an idealized situation that permits simplification of a problem so that it may be analyzed. Similarly, the theory of perfect competition assumes a "frictionless" economic system in which the movement of goods and resources is unobstructed. Thus, like physics, economics uses idealized models in order to simplify and analyze specific problems.

But the model developed in this chapter, although it represents a theoretical extreme, is not completely unreal. Some markets do approach the conditions of perfect competition at least roughly, although none meets all the conditions precisely. The examples that come closest to the ideal are the organized commodity and stock exchanges in New York, Chicago, and many other cities, and, to a lesser extent, some industries producing standard raw materials. The approximation to perfect competition varies in these markets, but it is close enough to make the theory and conclusions of this chapter both meaningful and useful.

Costs, Revenues, and Profit Maximization in the Short Run

It follows from the explanation of perfect competition that the market price of a commodity under such circumstances would be established independently through the free operation of total supply and total demand. You have already seen how this happens. No individual buyer or seller can influence the price, yet the price emerges automatically as a reflection of the interaction of numerous buyers and sellers.

This leads to a vital question. How does a seller in perfect competition, faced with a market price over which he or she has no influence, decide how much of a commodity to produce? The answer to this question is one of the most fundamental principles of economics.

Total Cost and Total Revenue

To begin with, turn your attention to the table in Exhibit 1. This table gives the costs and revenues of an imaginary firm in perfect competition. The only costs shown are those needed for the present analysis.

Columns (1) and (2) represent familiar concepts, because they contain quantities produced and their corresponding levels of total cost. As always, total cost increases as the quantity increases.

Column (3) denotes *average revenue* (AR). This is the price per unit of output or, as you will see momentarily, the ratio of total revenue to quantity. In this case, the average revenue is $10 per unit. Thus, it is assumed that the price established in the market through the free interaction of supply and demand is $10. Hence, this is the price with which the firm is faced and over which it has no control.

Or, to put it somewhat differently, the firm finds that it can sell all the units it wants to at the market price P of $10.

Column (4), called *total revenue* (TR), is simply the price per unit times the number of units sold. Looking at the headings of columns (3) and (4) together, you will see that only the simplest arithmetic is needed to describe the connection between average revenue, total revenue, and price:

$$AR = \frac{TR}{Q} = \frac{P \times Q}{Q} = P$$

Finally, you can skip temporarily to column (8) of the table and examine *net revenue* or net profit — the difference between total revenue and total cost. Note that it is at first negative, but that it then rises to a peak of $15 at 8 units of output and falls thereafter.

me would be TC

Exhibit 1
Cost and Revenue Schedules of a Firm Under Perfect Competition

on test
KNOW THIS chart

(1)	(2)	(3)	(4)	(5)	(6)	(7)	(8)
		Price per unit, or average revenue, P = AR	Total revenue,	Average total cost,	Marginal cost, MC	Marginal revenue, MR	Net revenue,
Quantity per day, Q (given)	Total cost, TC (given)	(given)	TR (3) × (1)	ATC (2) ÷ (1)	Change in (2) / Change in (1)	Change in (4) / Change in (1)	NR (net profit) (4) − (2)
0	$ 25	$10	$ 0	$ —			−$25
1	35	10	10	35.00	$10	$10	− 25
2	41	10	20	20.50	6	10	− 21
3	45	10	30	15.00	4	10	− 15
4	47	10	40	11.75	2	10	− 7
5	49	10	50	9.80	2	10	1
6	52	10	60	8.67	3	10	8
7	57	10	70	8.14	5	10	13
8	65	10	80	8.13	8	10	15
9	79	10	90	8.78	14	10	11
10	100	10	100	10.00	21	10	0

← $10 →

FIXED COST

Graphic Illustration of Total Cost and Total Revenue

The TC and TR values are graphed in Figure (a) of Exhibit 2. The TC curve has a familiar shape, but note that the TR curve is a straight line. This reflects the fact, as stated earlier, that the firm receives the same price per unit for all the units it sells.

The points labeled B_1 and B_2 are called **break-even points.** They designate levels of output at which a firm's revenue equals its cost. Thus, the firm is neither gaining an economic profit nor incurring an economic loss. At any output between these two points, the firm's profit or net revenue is positive. At any output beyond the break-even points, it has a net loss (or negative net revenue) because its costs exceed its revenues.

Finally, it should be pointed out that net revenue, as represented by the vertical distance GH, is a maximum at 8 units of output. At this output, the slope of the total cost curve, as measured by the slope of the tangent at H, is equal to the slope of the total revenue curve. It is useful to focus a moment on this fundamental concept of slope:

> The slope (steepness) of a line is the change in its vertical distance per unit of change in its horizontal distance. The slope of a straight line (such as the TR curve) is the same at every point, but the slope of a curved line (like the TC curve) differs at every point. Geometrically, you can find the slope of a curve at a point by drawing a straight-line tangent to the curve at that point. The slope of the tangent will then be the slope of the curve at the point of tangency. As you will recall from elementary mathematics, parallel lines have equal slopes. Thus, the tangent at H is parallel to the TR curve.

This important concept is amplified further in the next section and in the descriptions in Exhibit 2.

Marginal Cost and Marginal Revenue

The use of total revenue and total cost is a valid and practical way to determine the most profitable level of output for a firm. However, this is not the method that economists usually employ. Economists prefer to use an approach that may seem a bit strange at first but that is actually much more useful for making decisions about whether to increase or decrease production.

Referring back to the table in Exhibit 1, observe that column (5) gives average total cost and column (6) presents marginal cost. Column (7), however, has a new term, **marginal revenue** (MR). This is defined as the change in total revenue resulting from a unit change in output. Therefore, the formula for measuring marginal revenue is

$$MR = \frac{\text{change in } TR}{\text{change in } Q}$$

Marginal revenue is thus exactly analogous to marginal cost.

What is the connection between slopes and "marginals"? As you know, the slope of a curve is the change in its vertical distance resulting from a unit change in its horizontal distance. Therefore, the following principle should now be clear:

> Marginal cost measures the slope of a total cost curve, and marginal revenue measures the slope of a total revenue curve.

Observe that the marginal revenue figures in column (7), namely $10, are precisely the same as the average revenue or price figures in column (3). Thus, MR = AR = P. This is no accident. If price remains constant while quantity increases, total revenue (which equals $P \times Q$) will have to increase by the amount of the price, and this amount of change will also be the same as marginal revenue. You can verify this relationship by experimenting with a few different numbers yourself.

Finally, note that columns (1) and (3) taken together constitute a demand schedule. This is because the two columns disclose the price per unit that buyers will pay (and the seller will receive) for various quantities of the commodity.

Now let us see how these data look in graphic form.

Exhibit 2

Cost and Revenue Curves of a Firm Under Perfect Competition*

Profit Maximization: Three Viewpoints

Figure (a): Total Curves   The most profitable level of output is determined where the difference between curves TR and TC, as represented by the distance GH, is greatest.   This occurs at an output of 8 units.   At this output, a tangent to the TC curve, such as the tangent at H, is parallel to the straight-line TR curve.   At smaller or larger outputs, such as 7 or 9 units, a tangent to the TC curve would not be parallel to the TR curve.

The break-even points are at B_1 and B_2, at which $TC = TR$.   The break-even outputs are thus 5 units and 10 units.

Figure (b): Marginal Curves   The most profitable level of output is the point at which $MC = MR$, as explained in the text.   This can also be seen by following the vertical dashed line downward at 8 units of output.

The break-even points are at B_1 and B_2, at which $ATC = AR$.

Figure (c): Net Revenue (net profit) Curve   The most profitable level of output is the point at which the net revenue curve NR ($= TR - TC$) is at a maximum.   The vertical dashed line at 8 units of output emphasizes these profit-maximizing principles in all three figures.

Technical Note (Optional)   You should recall from high-school mathematics that parallel lines have equal slopes.   Therefore, the most profitable output in the top figure is the one at which the *slope* (steepness) of the TC curve, measured by the slope of the straight-line tangent at H, equals the *slope* (steepness) of the TR curve.   In the middle figure, marginal cost is the graph of the *slope* of total cost and marginal revenue is the graph of the *slope* of total revenue.   Hence, at the level of maximum profit,

$$MC = MR$$

which is the same as saying that

$$\text{slope of } TC = \text{slope of } TR$$

* The curves have been smoothed to enhance readability, so at some points they may not correspond precisely to the data in the table.

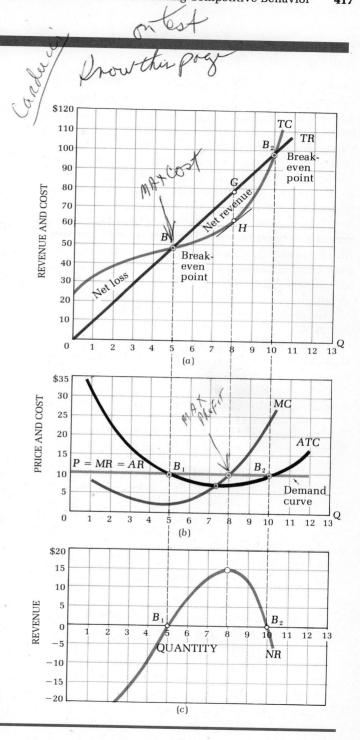

(a)

(b)

(c)

Graphic Illustration of Marginal Cost and Marginal Revenue

When the ATC, MC, and the MR = AR data are graphed, the results are as shown in Figure (b) of Exhibit 2. The first thing to notice is that the horizontal revenue line at the price of $10 is a demand curve based on columns (1) and (3) of the table in Exhibit 1. Indeed, it is a *perfectly elastic demand curve.* That means, in effect, that the firm cannot raise its price without losing all its sales. Note that the curve is labeled $P = MR = AR$, to emphasize the fact that it represents price, marginal revenue, and average revenue—all at the same time. However, this is a special property that exists only under perfect competition. As you will see in subsequent chapters dealing with other types of competition, a different situation arises when the demand curve slopes downward instead of being horizontal.

> NOTE For graphing purposes, recall from previous chapters that marginal values, in this case MC and MR, are plotted to the *midpoints* of the integers on the horizontal axis. This is because MC and MR reflect, respectively, the *change* in total cost and the *change* in total revenue resulting from a unit *change* in quantity. Notice also from the footnote in the exhibit that the curves have been smoothed. Therefore, some parts of the curves may differ slightly from the data in the table.

What is the firm's most profitable level of output? You already know that the answer is 8. But you can verify it further from Exhibit 2 by extending the vertical dashed line downward at 8 units of output. Figure (c) shows the graph of net revenue NR from column (8) of the table. The vertical dashed line at 8 units of output now enables you to focus on one of the most important principles in all of economics:

The most profitable level of output for a firm occurs where its MC = MR. [See Figure (b).] This is a *general* principle that applies under all types of competition. Under the special case of perfect competition it is also true that the most profitable level of output is the one at which $MC = MR = P = AR$, because the last three terms are one and the same. It is only at the output at which $MC = MR$ that a firm's net revenue, as measured by the difference between its total revenue and total cost, is greatest. [See Figures (a) and (c).]

This $MC = MR$ rule is of such great importance that it may appropriately be called the *fundamental principle of profit maximization.* You may also verify the principle from the table in Exhibit 1. For instance, look at the demarcated section at 8 units of output. It shows that, when NR reaches a maximum of $15, MC rises from $8 to $14 (thereby passing through $10) while MR remains constant at $10. Thus, at 8 units of output, $MC = MR = \$10$. The curves in Exhibit 2 reveal the relationships more clearly. You should study them and their accompanying explanations carefully.

Interpreting the $MC = MR$ Rule

The $MC = MR$ rule must be elaborated more fully. Why does the rule work as a guide for profit maximization? How does a firm react to the rule within the setting of a competitive market?

Part of the answer is given in Exhibit 3. In Figure (a), the market price at P and market output at N are determined by the intersection of the *total*-demand and *total*-supply curves, representing the interactions of many buyers and many sellers. In Figure (b), any individual seller finds that, by producing to the point at which $MC = MR$, the net revenue or profit is maximized. Also, under the conditions of perfect competition, the output measured by the distance 0J is an infinitesimal proportion of the industry's output measured in Figure (a) by the distance 0N. We may note the following important principle:

Under perfect competition, each seller faces a perfectly elastic demand curve at the market price—for two reasons:

1. Because the product is homogeneous, buyers will purchase the commodity from the seller who offers it at the lowest price.

2. Because only an infinitesimal part of the total market is supplied by each seller, *all* of that seller's output can be sold at the going market price. The seller cannot sell any output for more than that price and has no reason to sell any of it for less.

Exhibit 3
An Industry and a Firm in a Perfectly Competitive Market

KNOW/Test

Figure *(a)*: A Perfectly Competitive Market with Many Buyers and Sellers The market price at P and market output at N are determined by the intersection of the *total* market demand and supply curves. The total market demand curve is downward-sloping, because the quantity demanded will be greater at lower prices.

Figure *(b)*: A Typical Firm in a Perfectly Competitive Market Each firm is confronted with a perfectly elastic demand curve at the market price. This firm attains its most profitable output by producing at the point at which its MC = MR. Its output at J is an *infinitesimal fraction* of the industry's total output at N in Figure *(a)*.

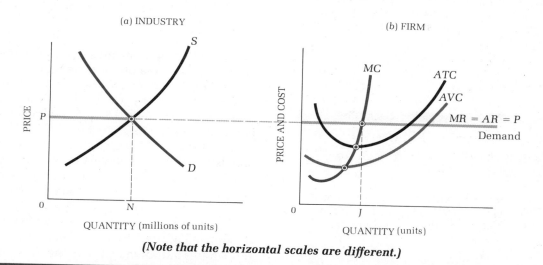

(Note that the horizontal scales are different.)

Thus, at any output less than the output at J, each 1-unit increase in output adds more to total revenue than it adds to total cost. That is, MR exceeds MC. Therefore, it pays to expand production. On the other hand, at any output greater than the output at J, each 1-unit decrease in output reduces total cost more than it reduces total revenue. That is, MC is greater than MR. Therefore, it pays to cut back production. Only at the point at which MC = MR do you find the most profitable output equal to the distance 0J. Hence, this MC = MR point may be called the seller's *equilibrium* position. It determines the profit-maximizing output that the firm will seek to achieve and maintain under the given market conditions and the company's existing cost curves.

This concept can be illustrated with a simple example. Suppose that you were a manufacturer of bicycles. You knew that by increasing your production by a specific amount you would raise your total revenue by $10,000 and your total cost by $8,000. In that case you would try to expand output and thereby increase net profit by $2,000. On the other hand, if you knew that by decreasing production by a given amount you would cut total cost by $15,000 and total revenue by $10,000, you would try to reduce output in order to increase net profit by $5,000. As a general rule, the only time you would not want to alter the production rate is when profits were already at a maximum. In that case the *changes* in TC and TR would be the same — which is the same as saying that MC would equal MR.

Analyzing Short-Run Equilibrium

What is the nature of the profit-maximizing or equilibrium position that the firm is trying to attain? Some of its important properties are illustrated by the figure in Exhibit 4.

First, note that the figure depicts the firm in short-run equilibrium. This means that, under the existing market conditions for the inputs the firm buys and the output it sells, and the given set of cost curves with which it operates, the most profitable output is at J. Why? Because at this output $MC = MR$ for this particular firm. You will see later that in the long run certain market conditions, as well as the seller's cost curves, are likely to change.

This will result in a different equilibrium position for the firm.

Next, you should verify that, at the most profitable level of output $0J$, the following geometric cost and revenue conditions exist.

- The average total cost of producing output $0J$ is represented by the vertical distance JK ($=0T$).
- The average revenue received from the sale of this output is the vertical distance JL ($=0U$).
- The difference between these two amounts, of course, is the net revenue per unit — that is, average net revenue — as represented by the vertical distance KL ($=TU$).

Thus, the total net revenue, which can be found by multiplying the net revenue per unit by the number of units, is the area of the rectangle $TULK$.

The same result can also be arrived at in a different way. The average revenue per unit (JL) times the number of units ($0J$) equals total revenue, which is the area of the large rectangle $0ULJ$. Similarly, average total cost (JK) times the number of units ($0J$) equals total cost or the area of the rectangle $0TKJ$. Therefore, when you subtract the total-cost rectangle from the total-revenue rectangle, the difference is the net-revenue rectangle $TULK$.

Finally, it is important to observe that profits are maximized at the output at which $MC = MR$, even though this output may be beyond the point of minimum average total cost. Profit, in other words, is *not* maximized at output $0R$, despite the lower average total cost of that output, namely RS. For by increasing output from $0R$ to $0J$, the seller increases the net-revenue rectangle from $GUHS$ to $TULK$. The rectangle thus gains the larger area $EHLK$ while losing the smaller area $GTES$. In general, the output at which the largest net-profit rectangle can be drawn is determined by the point L, at which $MC = MR$, and by the corresponding point K on the ATC curve. Or, to put it differently, it can be proved mathematically that any other net-profit rectangle must of necessity be smaller than the one determined by points K and L. But this is equivalent to saying that the net-revenue curve reaches a maximum at the output at which $MC = MR$, which you already know.

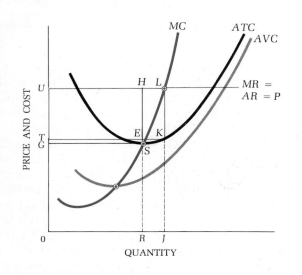

Exhibit 4
Profit Maximization in the Short Run for a Perfectly Competitive Firm

At the output at which a firm's $MC = MR$, the area of its net-revenue rectangle $TULK$ is greatest. This is the largest net-profit rectangle that can be drawn, given this firm's cost curves.

Deriving Supply Curves from Marginal-Cost Curves

(NO)

When you first studied the operation of supply and demand, you learned that a supply curve expresses a relation between the price of a product and the amount that sellers would be willing and able to produce at each price. You are now in a position to see how a perfectly competitive firm's supply curve is actually derived, based on what you know about the $MC = MR$ rule.

Suppose that a firm in perfect competition is represented by the cost curves shown in Exhibit 5. If the market price of the product is at P_1, the firm will produce an output at N_1, because this is determined by the point at which MC is equal to MR_1. If the price falls to P_2, the firm will reduce its output to N_2, following its marginal-cost curve. At a price of P_3 it will produce the amount N_3. However, because this price is tangent to the firm's average total-cost curve at its minimum, the firm will not be earning a positive net revenue. Rather, its net revenue will be zero. This means that the firm is only normally profitable, because *average total cost includes normal profit*. Thus:

A perfectly competitive firm maximizes its profit by always adjusting its output so that it follows the marginal-cost curve.

Exhibit 5
In Perfect Competition, a Firm's Supply Curve Is Its *MC* Curve Above Its *AVC*

The firm will always produce the quantity determined by the point at which $MC = MR$. Therefore, as the market price falls from P_1 to P_4, the firm reduces its output from N_1 to N_4, following its marginal cost curve. At P_4, the firm is just covering its average variable "out-of-pocket" costs and hence will remain in business in the short run. At a price below P_4, the firm will go out of business—as indicated by the shutdown point.

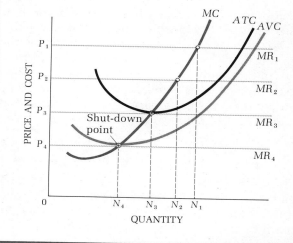

Minimizing Short-Run Losses

What will the firm do if the price falls below P_3, say, to P_4? The answer is the same as before. The firm will decrease its output following its marginal cost curve, thus producing the amount at N_4. At this output the firm's net revenue will be negative; but the firm will be *minimizing its losses*, for the following reason.

In the short run, the firm has certain fixed costs, such as rent, property taxes, and utilities. It must continue to pay these expenses as long as it remains in business, regardless of how much it produces. Therefore, as long as the firm can get a price that is

at least high enough to cover its average variable (or "out-of-pocket") costs, anything that it earns over and above this amount will go toward paying its fixed costs, which it is "stuck" with in any case.

As you can see, therefore, at any price above or equal to P_4, the firm will lose less in the short run by producing than by shutting down. But the firm will go out of business if the market price were to fall below the shut-down point shown in the figure. In the long run, on the other hand, the firm must receive a price at least high enough to cover all its costs, including a normal profit, if it is to stay in business. The firm must, in other words, cover its *ATC in the long run*.

We can now summarize these ideas in an important principle:

A perfectly competitive firm will produce the output determined by the point at which $MC = P (= MR)$. The firm will thus increase or decrease its output by following its marginal-cost curve. In this way the firm will maximize its profit (or minimize its loss).

This principle enables us to formulate two important propositions.

1. *A perfectly competitive firm's supply curve is the same as its marginal-cost curve above the level of average variable cost.*

The reason is that the MC curve tells you how many units of the good the firm will make available at various possible prices. This, however, is the meaning of a supply curve, as you will recall from your initial study of supply and demand. (You should refresh your understanding by looking up the definition of *supply curve* in the Dictionary at the back of the book.)

2. *The industry's supply curve is the horizontal sum of the firms' marginal-cost curves above their levels of average variable cost.*

In other words, you can derive a perfectly competitive industry's supply curve by summing the quantities that firms will make available at each price. This method, you should recall, was used to derive a total market supply curve when you first studied supply and demand earlier in this book. An explanation in terms of marginal cost curves is provided in Exhibit 6.

Long-Run Equilibrium of a Firm and an Industry

You have seen that, in the short run, a firm in a perfectly competitive industry may earn profits in excess of normal profits. Can this also happen in the long run? The answer is *no*. The conditions that are assumed in the definition of perfect competition prevent it from occurring. Let us see why.

An industry is said to be in *equilibrium* — that is, in a state of "balance" — when there is no tendency for it to contract or expand. This means that no firms in the industry are earning either below-normal or above-normal profits.

For instance, suppose some firms in the industry are earning less than their normal profit in the long run. Then by definition of normal profit their owners are receiving less than the least return they are willing to accept on the basis of their opportunity costs. The owners will therefore leave the industry, causing the industry supply curve to shift to the left and the market price to rise. The firms suffering the greatest losses will shut down first. The remaining firms will then become more profitable. This exodus of firms will continue until all firms in the industry are just normally profitable. When that happens, the industry will have no further tendency to contract.

The opposite situation occurs when some firms in the industry are earning more than normal profits. New firms will then be tempted to enter the industry to get a share of those profits. The industry will expand. That is, its total output will increase as the industry supply curve shifts to the right. At the same time, the market price will fall, making existing firms less profitable. This entry of new firms will continue until all firms in the industry are just normally profitable. At that point the industry will have no further tendency to expand.

Graphic Illustration of Long-Run Equilibrium

The final adjustment to long-run equilibrium for every firm in perfect competition can thus be illustrated by the curves in Exhibit 7. Each firm will have an average total cost curve and a corresponding marginal cost curve for each possible scale of plant. It follows that if some firms in the industry operate with optimum-size plants when the price is higher than the long-run equilibrium level at P, they will earn above-normal profits. This in turn will attract new firms into the industry. Market supply will increase, market price will fall, and su-

Exhibit 6
The Derivation of an Industry Supply Curve
From Firms' Marginal Cost Curves

In the industry diagram, equilibrium quantity and price are determined by the intersection of the supply curve S and the demand curve D. Thus the equilibrium quantity of Q units corresponds to the equilibrium price of $6 per unit.

Each firm in the industry produces to where its marginal cost equals price (MC = P). For example, Firm A produces J units and thus earns more than normal profit because the price is above ATC. Firm B produces L units and also earns more than normal profit. However, Firm B's net profit is not as high as Firm A's because Firm B is less efficient—its ATC curve is higher. Firm C is the least efficient; it produces N units and earns only a normal profit.

If the industry's demand curve decreases from D to D', the equilibrium quantity declines to R and the corresponding equilibrium price falls to $5. At this lower price, Firm A produces K units and earns a smaller net profit than before. Firm B produces M units and earns a normal profit. And Firm C produces T units, earning just enough to cover its AVC.

The accompanying table thus illustrates how the industry supply curve can be derived from the MC curves of firms. (Keep in mind that there are actually numerous firms in the industry, not just three. This is why the horizontal axes of the graphs are measured in different units.)

Market Price	Industry Quantity		Firm A Quantity		Firm B Quantity		Firm C Quantity
$6	Q	=	J	+	L	+	N
5	R	=	K	+	M	+	T

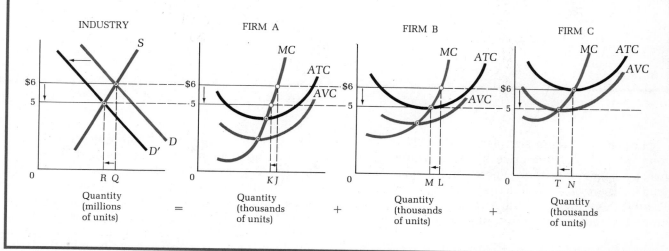

pernormal profits will disappear. Firms with plants that are larger or smaller than the optimum size will thus suffer losses, whereas those with optimum-size plants will earn normal profits.

Therefore:

In perfectly competitive industries, firms have no choice of whether to build large-scale or small-scale plants. Firms in these industries must eventually build optimum-size plants if they are to survive in the long run.

Exhibit 7
Long-Run Equilibrium for a Firm in Perfect Competition

At any given time, a firm may be represented by an *ATC* curve and a corresponding *MC* curve.

In the long run, competition will force each firm in the industry to end up with an optimum-size plant, such as ATC_3. At the optimum level of output for each firm, such as the output at N for this particular firm,

$$MC = P = MR = AR = ATC = LRAC$$

This equation defines the long-run conditions of equilibrium for every firm in a perfectly competitive market or industry.

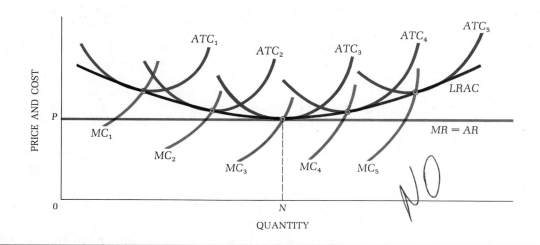

The firm's optimum-size plant is thus ATC_3. The long-run equilibrium price at P determines the firm's rate of output at N. These conditions are also true for every other firm in the industry. Although Exhibit 7 is a model of one firm, a similar diagram could be made for each firm in the industry.

The Long-Run Industry Supply Curve

We now know enough about the operation of supply and demand in competitive markets to introduce a new concept—the long-run supply curve of an industry. This curve may be constant, rising, or declining over an industry's range of output.

Each of the diagrams in Exhibit 8 represents the supply and demand situation for a different industry. We assume, in each case, that the industry is in equilibrium at point E. This represents the intersection of the industry's supply and demand curves, thus defining the industry's equilibrium price and output. Remember that the long-run supply curve of an industry is made up of the individual supply curves of all its sellers. The problem now is to examine the nature of each industry's long-run supply curve.

Referring to the three diagrams, suppose that there is an increase (shift) in demand from D to D'. If the costs of the firms in the industry remain the same, the equilibrium point shifts from E to E'. This

Exhibit 8
Long-Run Supply Curves for Constant-, Increasing-, and Decreasing-Cost Industries

The immediate effect of an increase in demand from D to D' is to change the industry's equilibrium from the long-run point E to the short-run point E'. At this higher price, new firms will find it profitable to enter the industry and the supply curve will shift to the right until it reaches S'. The industry's final equilibrium will thus settle at the long-run point E''. *The long-run industry supply curve S_L is therefore defined as the locus or "path" of the industry's long-run equilibrium points.*

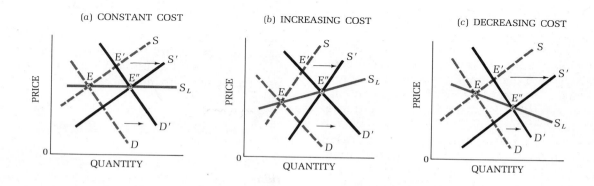

represents a higher market price and a larger market output than before. This expanded output occurs because firms that are already in the industry find it profitable to increase their production in response to the higher market price.

The equilibrium at E', however, is likely to be of relatively short duration. This is because the higher and more profitable price will soon attract new firms into the industry. As this happens, the supply curve of the industry will shift to the right and the market price will be driven down along the D' curve until it is no longer profitable for new firms to enter the industry. The supply curve will ultimately settle at S', and the final equilibrium will be at E'', where the new supply and demand curves intersect. The point E'' represents the *long-run equilibrium* position of the industry.

This analysis suggests an important principle.

If we connect each industry's initial and final long-run equilibrium points E and E'', we get the **long-run industry supply curve,** labeled S_L. This curve may be either horizontal, rising, or falling, depending on whether the industry is one of constant, increasing, or decreasing costs.

This principle requires an explanation of constant-cost, increasing-cost, and decreasing-cost industries.

Constant-Cost Industries

A ***constant-cost industry*** experiences no increases in resource prices or costs of production as new firms enter the industry. This tends to happen when an industry's demand for the resources it employs is an insignificant proportion of the total demand for those resources. In that case, new firms will be able to enter the industry and buy the labor, capital, and other inputs they need without bidding up the prices of these factors of production. The long-run industry supply curve will thus be perfectly elastic. Unspecialized resources (such as unskilled workers) that are in wide use by many industries are examples of such inputs. Janitors, retail-sales clerks, and office receptionists provide a few familiar illustrations.

Increasing-Cost Industries

An *increasing-cost industry* experiences rising resource prices and therefore increasing costs of production as new firms enter the industry. This happens because the industry's demand for resources is a significant proportion of the total demand. Therefore, any new firms must bid up the prices of the factors of production in order to acquire them from other firms. Specialized resources (such as skilled workers) provide examples of such inputs. Supplies of these resources are not readily expanded as the demand for them increases.

In general, increasing-cost industries are more common than constant-cost industries. This is especially true in our age of expanding technology, in which firms must make growing use of highly specialized resources. The computer, electronic, and aircraft industries are a few prominent examples of increasing-cost industries.

Decreasing-Cost Industries

A *decreasing-cost industry* experiences declining resource prices and therefore falling costs of production as new firms enter the industry and the industry expands. This, of course, is not as common as the two previous cases. However, it could exist for a while as a result of substantial external economies of scale, as you have already learned. Can you think of some examples?

Understanding Equilibrium

The concept of equilibrium is as fundamental in economics as it is in other sciences. It is important, therefore, to understand the meaning of equilibrium in the context in which it has been used here. Once you have achieved this understanding, you will be able to evaluate the social consequences of perfect competition — its effects on society as a whole.

The Equilibrium Conditions

Look back at Exhibit 7 and note carefully the properties that characterize a perfectly competitive firm in long-run equilibrium. As you can see, these properties may be described succinctly by the equations

$$MC = P = MR = AR = ATC = LRAC$$

These equations are called *equilibrium conditions.* They constitute a set of relationships that define the equilibrium position of an economic entity — in this case, a firm in perfect competition. In certain advanced courses in economic theory, other sets of equilibrium conditions are studied — not only for firms, but also for households, and even for entire economies.

Our purpose is to analyze and interpret the meaning of the foregoing equations. In so doing, we will see some important results of perfect competition. You may find it helpful to refer back to Exhibit 7 while reading the following explanation. Keep in mind that these characteristics apply to *every* firm in the industry.

1. *MC = P* This is an indicator of *economic efficiency.* It tells you that the additional cost of the resources used by the firm to produce the last unit of the product is just covered by the price that the firm receives. In other words, the value of the last unit of the good to the consumer (measured by the price he or she pays for the last unit, which is equal to the price paid for any other unit) is equal to the value of the resources used to produce that unit. Consequently:

At a level of output at which $MC = P$, the firm's resources are being allocated to the product in precise accordance with consumer preferences. At any smaller output, MC is less than P. Therefore, resources are being underallocated relative to consumer preferences. At any larger output, MC is greater than P. Therefore, resources are being overallocated relative to consumer preferences. The $MC = P$ condition is thus a *standard of economic (allocative) efficiency*. It measures the extent to which the firm is making full utilization of its resources to fulfill the preferences of consumers, given their incomes.

2. **$MC = MR$**   This tells you that the firm is maximizing its profits and there is no incentive for it to alter its output. The firm is thus in short-run (as well as long-run) equilibrium.

3. **$MR = AR \, (= P)$**   This means that the firm is selling in a perfectly competitive market. As we shall see in the following chapters, any other type of market situation results in a firm's marginal revenue always being less than its average revenue or demand price.

4. **$ATC = AR$**   This says that the firm is earning only normal profits. Thus, there is no incentive for other firms to enter or leave the industry.

5. **$MC = ATC$**   This indicates that the firm is operating at the minimum point on its average total cost curve. Hence, the firm is combining variable resources with its given plant so as to produce at the least cost per unit.

6. **$MC = ATC = LRAC$**   This means that the firm is producing the optimum output with the optimum-size plant. Thus, the firm is allocating *all* its resources in a *technically efficient* manner.

These equilibrium conditions are at the heart of microeconomics. Their implications and importance will become increasingly evident in the following pages and chapters.

Economic Goals: Efficiency, Equity, Stability, Growth

What are the economic consequences of perfect competition? That is, to what extent does perfect competition fulfill society's four economic goals — efficiency, equity, stability, and growth? One way to answer the question is to distinguish between the favorable and unfavorable features of a perfectly competitive system.

Favorable Features of Perfect Competition *(test)*

The equilibrium conditions listed above serve as a basis for describing the favorable features of an economic system composed entirely of perfectly competitive markets. Such a system would yield certain beneficial consequences in long-run equilibrium:

— Consumer preferences, as reflected in the marketplace, would be fulfilled with the largest amount of goods consistent with the minimum (average cost) prices and known production techniques of business firms.

— Society's resources would be allocated in the most efficient way, both within and between industries.

— Flexible factor and product prices would assure full employment of all resources.

— Competition among employers for factors and among factors for employment would cause factor owners to be paid their opportunity costs. These would be determined by the market value of the respective contributions to total output of each factor.

— With consumer incomes and tastes assumed to be constant, aggregate consumer satisfaction would be maximized because goods would be distributed among consumers according to their demands.

Unfavorable Features of Perfect Competition

Several undesirable consequences of a perfectly competitive price system were pointed out when we first studied the laws of supply and demand early in the book. At that time, you did not have a formal knowledge of the theory of perfect competition, nor did you know that it is the basis for supply-and-demand analysis. Now, however, you are in a better position to understand the shortcomings of perfect competition.

Incomplete Reflection of Consumer Desires

In a perfectly competitive system, sellers react only to those preferences that consumers register through their "dollar votes" in the marketplace. Consequently, this type of system does not measure the desire of consumers for "collective" or *public goods*, such as national defense, highways, parks, and unpolluted air and water.

Inadequate Reflection of Social Welfare

A chemical company disposes of its waste products in a nearby lake. A steel mill's smoke permeates the air of a neighboring city. A drive-in theater discharges its patrons onto a highway at the end of a movie. In each of these and many other situations, two types of costs, called "private costs" and "social costs," are involved.

Private costs are the dollar costs of performing a particular act. *Social costs,* which include private costs, also include spillovers or externalities. These are the reductions in incomes or benefits that accrue to society as a result of a particular act. In the examples above, spillovers would include the community's suffering due to water pollution, air pollution, and congested highways. Thus:

Social costs = private costs + spillover costs

A similar distinction can be made in terms of benefits. If you get a good education, this act will lead to *private benefits* for you in the form of higher income. However, society will also realize *social benefits* because you will (ideally) become a more enlightened and informed citizen. Life is full of other examples. If you maintain an attractive lawn, your neighbors will be pleased. If you bathe regularly, you are less likely to become a social outcast. Thus:

Social benefits = private benefits + spillover benefits

Of what significance are these distinctions between private and social benefits and costs? Competitive prices tend to reflect private costs and private benefits and may exclude some social costs and social benefits. Therefore, the equilibrium condition $MC = MR$ only guarantees maximum profit for a firm; it does not guarantee maximum welfare for society. To achieve the latter, the costs and benefits of production *to society* must be incorporated in firms' private costs and revenues. To the extent that they are not, the $MC = MR$ condition fails to reflect the full effect of production on social welfare.

Insufficient Incentives for Progress

A third major criticism frequently leveled against a perfectly competitive system is that it dampens incentives to innovate and therefore retards economic progress. This happens because the typical firm in perfect competition is relatively small. Therefore, it is not likely to have access to the considerable financial resources needed to support the research and development projects that often lead to major innovations. Even if a firm had the money to finance large-scale research, it would probably refrain from undertaking the needed capital investment. This is because the innovation, if successful, would be adopted quickly by competing firms.

Life Under Perfect Competition: On the Dull Side?

What would it be like to live in a perfectly competitive world? Most of us might find it monotonous.

Historical Pictures Service

Alfred Marshall
1842 – 1924
*Synthesizer and Pioneer in
Microeconomics*

In the last quarter of the nineteenth century, there arose in Europe and America a system of ideas known as *neoclassical* economics. One of the leaders of neoclassicism was Alfred Marshall, a British scholar whose landmark treatise, *Principles of Economics* (1890), will forever be regarded as a masterwork.

The book, which went through eight editions, was a leading text in economics for over forty years. Among the major contributions of this and other works by Marshall were the distinction between the short run and the long run, the extensive use of diagrams and models to describe economic behavior, and the equilibrium of price and output resulting from the interaction of supply and demand. Marshall also systematized the use of elasticity, the distinction between money cost and real cost, and many other ideas.

In short, almost everything we read today pertaining to supply and demand analysis, equilibrium, and related notions was originally formulated precisely and definitively by Marshall. Few students today realize or appreciate the significant role that Marshall's ideas play in their economics education.

Enduring Influence
By the time he retired from his professorship at England's Cambridge University, Marshall had trained several generations of eminent economists. These disciples went on to assume major positions in universities and government service. One of them was the famous British economist John Maynard Keynes whose ideas are studied in macroeconomics. Keynes referred to his former teacher as "a scientist . . . who, within his own field, was the greatest in the world in more than a hundred years."

For example:

Goods would be standardized in each industry and the range of consumer choices would be severely limited.

At the grocery store, bread would be just plain bread, and ketchup would likewise be just ketchup. The modern supermarket with its endless and colorful varieties of goods would cease to exist.

The choice of an automobile, like eggs in the dairy case, might be confined to "small," "medium," and "large." In all other respects, cars would be alike.

Because products in each industry would be homogeneous, there would clearly be no need for advertising (except perhaps for industry-wide or institutional advertising, such as "Eat more bread" or "Drink more milk"). Nor would there be any trademarks or brand names; and imaginative promotional campaigns, for good or evil, would be lost.

There would be no commercial television as we now know it, and newspapers and magazines (could they possibly be homogeneous?) would cost more. In a world of perfect competition, consumers would know their alternatives. Therefore, the only type of advertising needed would be the kind that informs rather than persuades. There would be no need for anything other than, perhaps, classified advertising and the Sears, Roebuck catalog.

Conclusion — And a Look Forward

Although a perfectly competitive economy would have various beneficial consequences, it would also have what many people would undoubtedly regard as undesirable features.

If the world of perfect competition is imaginary, why do we study it?   Does it have any practical value?   The answer is simple:

> We do not learn about perfect competition in the vain hope of making it a reality.   Instead, we study perfect competition because it provides us with standards for evaluating and improving the real world of imperfect competition, which we shall analyze later.

What You Have Learned

1.   A perfectly competitive industry or market is characterized by many buyers and sellers engaged in the purchase and sale of a homogeneous commodity.   Each buyer and seller has perfect knowledge of market prices and quantities, there is no discrimination, and there is perfect mobility of resources.   Perfect competition is thus a theoretical extreme rather than a real-world phenomenon, although some of its features are roughly approximated in the organized commodity and stock markets.

2.   In perfect competition, prices are established in the market through the interaction of many buyers and sellers.   Each firm thus finds itself faced with a market price over which it has no influence.   It cannot sell any of its output at a price that is the slightest bit above the market price.   Because it can sell its entire output at the market price, there is no inducement for it to sell at any lower price.

3.   In terms of costs and revenues, each firm's most profitable level of output is the one at which its marginal cost equals its marginal revenue.   This is the output at which the firm's total revenue minus its total cost is greatest.

4.   In perfect competition, a firm's supply curve is its marginal cost curve above the level of average variable cost.

The industry's short-run supply curve is thus derived by summing all the firm's marginal cost curves at each price above average variable cost.   In the short run, a firm will operate as long as the market price is at least equal to its average variable "out-of-pocket" costs.   This is because any price it gets over and above that will go to pay at least part of its fixed costs.   In the long run, however, the firm will have to receive a price high enough to cover all costs, including a normal profit, if it is to remain in business.

5.   In the long run, competition will force all firms to earn only normal profits and to operate with optimum-size plants.   When this occurs, the industry as well as all firms in it will be in long-run equilibrium, with no tendency to expand or contract.

6.   The industry's long-run supply curve connects all of its long-run supply-and-demand equilibrium points. The long-run supply curve may be constant, increasing, or decreasing.

7.   In long-run equilibrium, a perfectly competitive economy will have allocated its resources in the most efficient way so as to maximize consumer satisfactions.   This is assured by the equations

$$MC = P = MR = AR = ATC = LRAC$$

If these equations are analyzed separately, they tell us that firms are maximizing their profits and making the most efficient use of their resources, given the distribution of consumers' incomes and tastes.

8.   Among the favorable features of a perfectly competitive price system are the following:
(a) It fulfills consumer preferences with the largest amount of goods in the most efficient way.
(b) It allocates resources optimally and, as a result of flexible product and factor prices, encourages full employment of all resources.
(c) It provides for factor payments at their opportunity costs as determined by their respective marginal productivities.

Among the unfavorable features:
(a) It reflects consumer desires incompletely.
(b) It does not always reflect all social costs and social benefits.
(c) It provides insufficient incentives for economic progress.

Terms and Concepts To Review

perfect competition
average revenue
total revenue
net revenue
break-even point
marginal revenue
long-run industry
  supply curve
constant-cost industry

increasing-cost industry
decreasing-cost industry
equilibrium conditions
private costs
social costs
private benefits
social benefits

For Discussion

1. What is the "fundamental principle of profit maximization"? Explain. What special application of this rule applies to perfect competition? Why?

2. Is the price of a product determined by its cost of production, or is the cost of production determined by the price?

3. If new firms enter an industry, they will compete for factors of production and thereby raise the prices of those factors. How will this affect the cost curves of firms in the industry? Discuss.

4. "The farmer must receive a living price for milk." Discuss this statement in terms of what you have learned in this chapter.

5. If you owned a shoestore and the shoes you carried cost you $40 per pair, would you stay in business if the highest price you could get for them were $40 per pair? Explain your answer in terms of this chapter.

6. The long-run history of the automobile industry reveals an enormous growth of output and a substantial reduction in real (inflation-adjusted) prices. How do you account for this, since we have usually assumed that larger outputs come only from higher prices?

7. Insert words in the following sentences to make them true. Do not delete any words. Underline your inserted words.

    (a) A firm is in equilibrium when its costs and revenues are equal.

    (b) A perfectly competitive firm is in equilibrium when it is producing at its minimum average cost.

    (c) A perfectly competitive firm cannot earn supernormal profits.

    (d) A perfectly competitive firm's supply curve is its marginal curve.

8. What are the "equilibrium conditions" for a perfectly competitive industry in long-run equilibrium? Explain their meaning.

9. "It is an indictment of our economic system that our country can spend more on such unimportant things as cosmetics or liquor than it spends on education." Evaluate this statement.

Supplement

Our Farm Problem: A Case Study

American agriculture has staggered from crisis to crisis for more than a century. Although government has spent billions of dollars to alleviate farm problems, there have been no enduring economic solutions. Instead, politics has become intertwined with economics, resulting in public policies toward agriculture that have often impaired—rather than improved—the quest for efficiency, equity, stability, and growth.

We can best understand the nature of the so-called "farm problem" by examining the underlying economics of agriculture as a whole.

Economics of Agriculture

The problems that farmers have traditionally faced stem largely from four conditions that characterize the agriculture sector: (1) price and income inelasticities, (2) highly competitive structure, (3) rapid technological change, and (4) resource immobility. These conditions and the problems that arise from them are not unique to the United States. They are prevalent in agriculture in other advanced mixed economies as well.

Price and Income Inelasticities

The demand for most farm products, including foods and fibers, is largely unresponsive to changes in price. As a result, people usually do not buy much larger quantities of farm commodities when their prices fall or much smaller quantities when their prices rise. In more technical terms, this means that *the demand for most agricultural goods is relatively inelastic (unresponsive) with respect to changes in price.*

The supply of most agricultural goods, especially within a given year, *is also relatively inelastic.* It is not possible to increase production significantly in a single season. If prices are high, additional feed and fertilizer can be applied and land can be farmed more intensively. However, the industry's "plant"—the land itself—cannot be expanded very much.

Agricultural products tend also to be income-inelastic in demand. The ***income elasticity of demand*** is the percentage change in the quantity of a good purchased resulting from a 1 percent change in income. For practically all farm food products, this elasticity is less than 1.0—somewhere between 0.1 and 0.2. We may, therefore, expect a 10 percent rise in real disposable income per capita to cause only a 1 to 2 percent rise in the purchase of most agricultural food commodities.

Some Implications of Price and Income Inelasticities

Three important implications of these inelasticities should be noted.

1. Price inelasticities of demand and supply mean that small fluctuations in the output of farm products lead to large fluctuations in the prices of farm products.

2. Income inelasticity of demand means that total consumption of basic farm food products is limited largely by the rate of growth of total population. This characteristic holds in all wealthy nations. The proportion of any increase in income spent for food is always smaller in well-fed countries than in poorly fed ones.

3. As a result of both price and income inelasticities, increases in the rate of growth of farm production that exceed increases in the rate of growth of consumption will cause a downward trend in farm prices and in farmers' incomes. This has been the long-run trend in the United States. The effects are illustrated in Exhibit 1, which shows three variables:

   - An index of prices received by farmers for products sold.

   - An index of prices paid by farmers for products bought.

   - A parity ratio. This is simply an index of prices farmers receive divided by an index of prices paid. The parity ratio thus provides a measure of agriculture's economic well-being, as you will see shortly.

Note from Exhibit 1 that, since the 1940s, the long-run trend of the parity ratio has been downward. However, the well-being of farmers *as a group* cannot be judged from the parity ratio alone. There are three main reasons:

Unreported Income   A large proportion of farmers' incomes—as much as 30 percent, according to some government estimates—comes from cash sales that are never reported for income tax purposes. More conservative estimates place the figure at 15 percent.

Tax Benefits   Under our tax laws, farm firms receive special privileges that are not granted to other businesses.

Possible Capital Gains (or Losses)   Farm property values fluctuate over time. During periods of rising real estate values, some farmers may reap capital gains (profits) from the sale of their property. But when real estate values decline, capital losses can more than offset the advantages of unreported income and tax benefits.

Exhibit 1
How Well-off Are Farmers?

The long-run trend of the parity ratio, expressed in decade averages, reached a peak in the 1940s (during World War II). This was because American farmers had to supply domestic agricultural needs as well as those of war-torn countries. Since the 1940s, the long-run trend of the parity ratio has been downward.

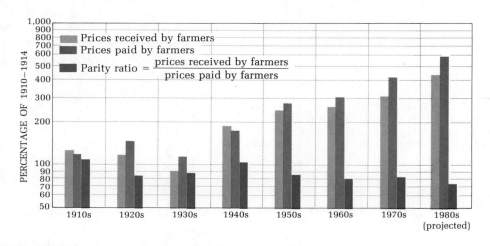

Highly Competitive Structure

In addition to price and income inelasticities, a second major characteristic of American agriculture is competition. Here, competition means three things:

1. There are many farms in the United States—more than 2 million. As a result, virtually no single farm can influence the market price by deciding to sell or not to sell.

   (NOTE We say "virtually" because today there are some large farms that can exert an influence on the market price of certain commodities. This has been true only since the 1960s.)

2. Agricultural products are homogeneous—at least within broad categories. Grains, for example, are not branded products, and hence cannot be identified with the farm from which they came. Milk, meat, and produce may carry the name of a store or processor, but not usually the name of the producer. Agricultural products within each class are therefore highly substitutable, and each farmer is faced with a perfectly elastic demand curve at the market price for the goods sold.

3. As with many areas of retailing, there are few non-capital barriers to entering the agricultural industry. No licenses, union membership, or formal education are required. Anyone who wants to farm, and has the necessary capital, can get into the business—at least on a relatively small scale. (Large-scale farming, on the other hand, requires a considerable amount of capital.)

Rapid Technological Change

American agriculture has made striking gains in productivity since 1930—greater gains, indeed, than were made in the previous two centuries.

What has been the nature of these advances? They have resulted from the introduction of new seeds, fertilizers, and pesticides; improved breeds of livestock and poultry; improved feeds for farm animals; and the mechanization and electrification of farming. These advances have gone hand-in-hand with the development of improved capital and credit facilities and with the emergence of more technically trained and educated farmers—most of them graduates of land-grant colleges. To a great extent, these gains have been fostered by government through special taxation and subsidization programs favorable to agriculture.

These changes have wrought profound social and economic effects, as illustrated in Exhibit 2. The

Exhibit 2
Farms and Farm Output

In the United States, over the long run, the farm population, the number of farms, and the labor input on farms have been decreasing. Simultaneously, the average size of farms, their total output, and their output per worker-hour have been increasing.

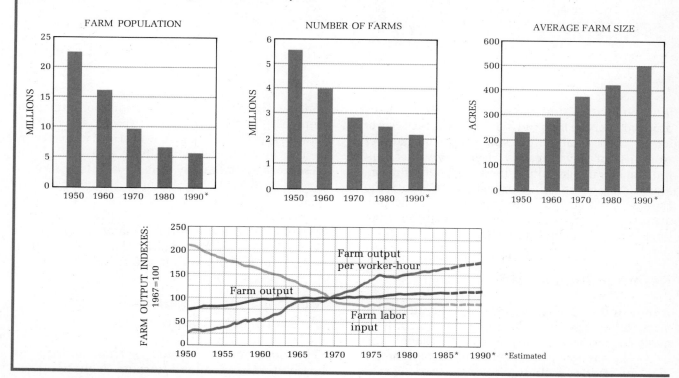

Farm Experts See a Future of Fewer and Larger Tracts

By William Robbins
Special to The New York Times

KANSAS CITY, Mo., Feb. 16 — Spreading hardship is speeding American agriculture toward a destiny of fewer and larger farms.

And while the result may be lower food costs, many of the country's more efficient farmers will be forced out of business, and the economic and social costs for rural communities are likely to be high.

These are the conclusions of some agricultural economists who are examining the mounting farm debt, rising costs and falling crop prices that are driving increasing numbers of growers out of business.

The number of farmers has gradually declined over the last 50 years, to about 2.37 million, from more than 6 million. And now most of them, about 1.7 million, produce very little.

The largest farms, about 25,000 or 1 percent, with sales above $500,000 a year, produce about 30 percent of all farm products in terms of cash volume and earn about half the profits. But among them only 14.6 percent, or about 3,650, are in the cash grain group, where most of the troubles have occurred.

With an outlook of larger and larger farms, more attention has focused on efficiency. As equipment has grown more advanced, studies have reflected continued increases in efficiency. Giant tractors on [large corporate] farms till vast acreages in less time than the smaller tractors more frequently used on smaller farms, and they work more hours than they could if run by a single family.

"Farming is a wonderfully, intrinsically good way of life for an individual," [said William Haw, president of huge National Farms, Inc.] "There will always be good intermediate farms, run by a farmer willing to settle for merely a living out of a tremendous investment. Because he's willing to settle for that, the largest operator is not going to be able to compete successfully with him."

farm population and the number of farms have dropped over the long run, while the average size of farms, their total output, and their output per worker-hour have steadily risen. However, improvements in agriculture have not been uniform. Many farmers are still poor because they lack the capital and knowledge to become efficient producers. This, as you will see, has been the traditional crux of the farm problem.

Resource Immobility

Although the number of farms and the number of farmworkers have been declining, there are still too many farmers on too many farms. Why should this be? Why has agriculture, which has experienced a long-run trend of declining prices and incomes relative to the rest of the economy, failed to reduce sufficiently its stock of human and nonhuman resources? Is not this failure contrary to what the laws of supply and demand would lead us to expect?

The fundamental difficulty is that agricultural resources are relatively immobile. Many farmers and farmworkers, for example, cannot use their skills in nonagricultural activities. Hence, they tend to remain in farming because it is the only type of work they know. Further, many of them prefer to make a modest living in rural areas rather than seek better-paying work in the cities.

Conclusion: Agriculture — A Declining Industry

The four major economic characteristics of agriculture — price and income inelasticities, a highly competitive structure, rapid technological change, and resource immobility—are universal in all developed countries. Such countries share a common pattern:

As an economy grows in wealth, it devotes less of its total resources to agriculture, and more to manufacturing and services.

The reason is simple. In technologically advanced societies, farmers can produce enough not only for themselves and their families but also for many other people. In less developed countries, on the other hand, nearly everyone is forced to farm. Productivity is so low that farmers have little left to sell after growing food and fibers to feed and clothe themselves and their families. The *relative* magnitude of the agriculture resource base is thus smaller in rich societies than in poor ones, and this base is being constantly "squeezed" as the society grows. Agriculture then becomes a declining industry in a growing economy, with the *proportion* of total resources employed in agriculture continually contracting.

Our Farm Policies

You can see from the information presented earlier in Exhibit 1, that for several decades, prices paid by farmers have been rising faster than prices received by farmers. As a result, since the late 1920s, government has employed policies designed to improve farmers' real incomes and to stabilize prices. Three alternative approaches that have constituted the core of our farm policy have been price supports, crop restrictions, and direct payments. All of these have long been used, separately or in combination, to reduce the effects of market adversities on farmers.

Price Supports

One way in which farmers can receive higher real incomes is for the government to maintain price supports for agricultural commodities. Such supports are, in reality, price "floors," established at levels above the prices that would prevail in free markets.

The basic idea is illustrated in Exhibit 3. The diagram shows a situation at harvest time. The demand curve D has a customary downward slope, whereas the supply curve S is vertical—*perfectly inelastic*. This indicates that the quantity supplied is fixed or unresponsive to changes in prices. The diagram demonstrates an important aspect of price supports:

Exhibit 3
Price-Support Policy

At harvest time, the quantity supplied is already determined. Therefore, the supply curve S is "fixed" or perfectly inelastic—unresponsive to changes in price—while the demand curve D is downward-sloping.

The diagram shows how a price-support plan establishes a price floor at some level above the free-market equilibrium price. Consumers pay and producers receive the higher parity-support price, and the resulting surplus is purchased and stored by the government.

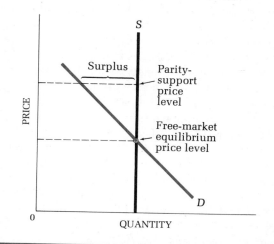

Under a price-support program, consumers do not pay, nor do producers receive, the lower free-market equilibrium price at which there are no surpluses or shortages. Instead, consumers pay and producers receive the higher "parity-support price." This results in a surplus of the commodity that government must purchase, store, and administer.

A price-support policy of this type has existed for a variety of farm products since the 1930s. The program has at times been terminated for certain products and then reinstated because of political pressures from farm groups. In general, price supports have involved two major problems — selecting parity prices and disposing of continually mounting commodity surpluses.

Selecting Parity Prices

There is a story of a farmer who was asked the meaning of parity. He replied: "If you could take a bushel of wheat to the market in 1912, sell it, and use the money to buy a shirt, then you ought to be able to do the same today. That's parity."

A dictionary will tell you that parity means the same thing as "equivalence." When applied to agriculture, a *parity price* is one that gives a commodity the same purchasing power, in terms of the goods that farmers buy, that it had in a previous base period. The period traditionally used has been 1910–1914 because it represents the "golden age of agriculture" — an era in which farmers prospered.

Over the years, the term "parity" also came to mean *parity ratio.* This, as you saw in Exhibit 1, is the ratio of prices received to prices paid by farmers. It serves as an economic indicator of agricultural well-being. The parity ratio, whose components are updated from time to time, is calculated by the Department of Agriculture and is often quoted in the news media. A parity ratio of 80, for example, might be interpreted to mean that the prices of farm products are 20 percent "too low." As a result, various farm programs are often proposed to raise farm commodity prices to 100 percent of parity, on the ground that this would restore the fair economic status of agriculture.

Surplus Disposal

A price-support policy has, at various times, resulted in the accumulation of huge surpluses by the government — billions of bushels of wheat, millions of tons of feed grain, and so on. The costs to taxpayers, including the costs of acquisition, transportation, storage, losses on sales, and interest on investment, have amounted to many billions of dollars. To alleviate the pressure, government has sought ways to reduce accumulated surpluses. The most common methods have been:

- Foreign dumping — the sale of foods and fibers abroad at much lower prices than at home.
- Domestic dumping — the free distribution of foods to poor families and to charitable institutions.
- Foreign aid — the donation of foods and fibers to countries in need.
- Waste and spoilage — the willful destruction, or neglect and consequent deterioration, of large quantities of agricultural commodities in order to keep them out of commercial markets.
- Industrial uses — the expenditure of much time and effort by government and businesses to find new industrial uses for food and fibers.

Have these methods of disposing of excess farm products been socially desirable? For the most part, they have not.

Informed observers generally agree that government has been inefficient in managing farm surpluses. Even foreign aid and domestic dumping, which may be desirable on humanitarian grounds, frequently have been poorly administered. These practices, it is contended, should be adopted on their own merits instead of being made incidental to the disposal of surpluses resulting from inappropriate farm policies.

Crop Restriction

A second way in which agricultural prices might be raised above free-market levels — and agricultural incomes thereby improved — is for government to legislate restrictions on farm production. In that way, society gets less output and consumers pay higher prices. However, farmers receive larger total revenues because the demand for most agricultural goods is relatively inelastic. The basic idea is explained and illustrated in Exhibit 4.

At various times since the depression of the 1930s, government has attempted several methods of output restriction. The most important have been acreage curtailment, marketing quotas, and land retirement.

Acreage Curtailment

When farm surpluses accumulated in the past, government frequently sought to limit production by curtailing the amount of acreage that could be planted in particular crops. Surprisingly, however, such policies generally failed to reduce output significantly and often even increased it. The reasons are not hard to find. When farmers are required to reduce their volume of acreage, they retire their poorest land and retain their best. They then cultivate the land more intensively by utilizing additional labor and capital. In this way, they increase their yields per acre and often maintain, if not expand, their total output.

Marketing Quotas

Because acreage curtailment generally has not reduced output, it has been suggested that marketing quotas based on physical units would be a better method of control. Each farmer would be given certificates permitting the sale of a certain number of units of a commodity at the support price. Any production in excess of these legal quotas would be subject to high taxes.

Such marketing quotas existed for tobacco, cotton, and potatoes during the early 1930s. Similar plans have subsequently been proposed for other commodities. Congress, however, has rejected the idea under the pressure of middle- and upper-income farm groups who would be made worse off under such a scheme.

Exhibit 4
Crop-Restriction Policy

If government requires farmers to curb output, the supply curve at harvest time is not the free-market curve S but the restricted curve S'. As a result:

Total output is at M rather than N.

Price is at J rather than H.

Farmers' total revenue (equal to price times quantity) is the area of the larger rectangle 0JKM rather than the small one 0HLN.

(NOTE Remember that the demand curve for most farm products is relatively inelastic. Therefore, higher prices result in larger total revenues. You can see that, by raising the price from H to J, the gain in total revenue, HJKR, more than offsets the loss, MRLN.)

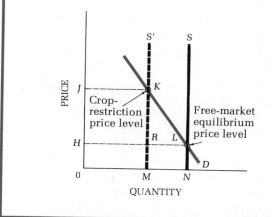

Land Retirement

Government has repeatedly tried, with little success, to reduce output by removing land from agricultural use. Unlike acreage curtailment, which may vary over the years, land retirement is usually fairly permanent. Many millions of acres of farm land have been retired as a result of the government purchasing or renting not only portions of farms but also entire farms.

Land retirement is convenient, it is cheaper than price supports, and it is easier to administer than production controls. However, it has had limited, and sometimes inverse, effects on output. This is because farmers usually sell or rent their poorest lands and increase their production on the superior land they retain. When the government retires land, therefore, it must do so on a scale large enough to avoid engaging in what would otherwise be a costly and largely self-defeating activity. Failure to do so will result in the government offering higher and higher purchase prices or rental fees in order to acquire the more productive land. The people who benefit from this government action are landowners, who are not usually farmers.

Direct Payments

A third way of protecting farmers from price declines while improving farm incomes is to adopt a system of **direct payments.** This plan would eliminate parity payments to farmers and allow the prices of agricultural products to be determined in a free market by supply and demand. Government would compensate farmers for the difference between the market price they receive and some higher target price established according to a selected base period in the past. The basic idea is illustrated and explained in Exhibit 5.

Direct payments are not a new idea. They were introduced on a significant scale in the 1950s and have been expanded and contracted since then for a variety of basic farm products.

Are Direct Payments Good or Bad?

Under a direct-payments plan, market prices adjust freely to whatever levels are necessary to move the entire supply into consumption. As a result, the plan has the following features.

On the positive side, the principal advantages are these:

- It does away with the cost of storage as well as the wastes of destruction and spoilage.

Exhibit 5
Direct-Payments Policy

This plan permits consumers to pay the lower free-market equilibrium price and producers to receive the higher support or target price set by the government. The difference between the two prices is the distance RT. This distance times the number of units RV equals the area of rectangle RTUV. This area represents the total subsidy or direct government payments to farmers.

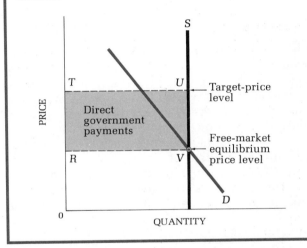

- It brings lower prices to consumers on the domestic market.

- It eliminates the pressure for export dumping at low prices and the resulting resentment of foreign governments, who want to protect their own farmers' incomes.

- It makes the farm subsidy visible, prompting Congress to debate it and vote on it periodically.

The principal disadvantages, on the other hand, are largely matters of costs. Direct payments are more costly to the government (and hence to the taxpayer) than price supports, because direct payments cover more commodities. These costs grow as production increases. Therefore, direct payments tend to lead to stricter production controls.

Land, for example, can still be taken out of crop production if the Secretary of Agriculture determines that farm output is likely to be excessive.

In general:

Under a system of direct payments, government subsidies to farmers are costly to taxpayers as long as free-market prices of farm commodities are below target prices. But if total (world) demand for farm goods increases to the point at which free-market prices are equal to or greater than target prices, no subsidies or direct payments are required. In that case, little land (if any) will be diverted from production, and the farm economy will be essentially a free-market economy.

In reality, total world demand for farm crops is rarely high enough for sufficiently long periods to eliminate *all* direct payments. As a result, subsidies to farmers, some of whom are quite rich, continue to be considerable.

Conclusion: Efficiency and Equity

The economics of agriculture is such that, in an advancing economy, the proportion of resources devoted to farming tends to decline. Although this has been the long-run trend, it has been retarded by our agricultural policies. These have inhibited rather than encouraged the orderly exodus of resources from the farm sector, thus impeding agriculture's adjustment to changing supply-and-demand conditions. The results have been distortions in the utilization of farm inputs and misallocations of productive resources — at considerable costs to society.

Our agricultural policies have also created inequities among farmers by doing relatively little to correct the fundamental problem of agricultural *poverty.* Despite the long-run decline in the farm population, a substantial proportion of the people living on farms may be classified as "poor." They are concentrated mostly in the South — particularly in the Appalachians and in the Mississippi Valley.

For these families, who consume most or all of what they produce, our farm policies have had relatively little effect. Instead, it is largely middle- and upper-income farmers — the ones who sell most of what they produce — who have benefited from government price- and income-support programs.

Despite these failings, our agricultural policies have been promoted as measures aimed at helping *all* farmers on the grounds that they are all poor. In reality, only *some* farmers are poor; others are actually quite well off. The latter, however, are the ones who dominate agricultural organizations and political-pressure groups. This helps explain why Congress has done little to correct the inequities that our farm policies have created.

Solution: Encourage Exodus

It is clear that new policies are needed to correct imbalances existing in the agricultural sector. The imbalances exist because of the need to *reduce the proportion of resources on farms.* Therefore:

Most experts agree that the solution to our farm problem is not to provide price supports or income-maintenance programs that keep agricultural resource owners where they are. *The solution is to encourage them to get out and relocate.* This requires that the patchwork of government subsidies and handouts be gradually eliminated, so that farmers can learn to respond to market conditions instead of government programs.

What You Have Learned

1. Agriculture in the United States is characterized by (a) products that are price-inelastic and income-inelastic in demand, (b) a highly competitive structure, (c) rapid technological change, and (d) resource immobility. These characteristics mean that small fluctuations in output lead to large fluctuations in prices. Further, as the economy grows, the proportion of its total resources that it devotes to agriculture declines and the proportion that it devotes to manufacturing and services increases.

Economics in the News

Farmers Up in Arms

From the cornfields of Iowa to the halls of Congress, angry and desperate food producers on the brink of bankruptcy are calling for help. Will the nation respond? What if it doesn't?
In one of the most massive and well-organized lobbying efforts since the height of protests against the Vietnam War, thousands of farmers, small-town bankers and other rural residents called for emergency funds to keep many among an estimated 430,000 financially desperate food producers from going under before spring-planting time.

Farmers and their backers complain that they are innocent victims of bad weather and of some misguided government policies that have resulted in high interest rates, low commodity prices and declining foreign sales. Opponents argue just as forcefully that the nation's other tax-payers are under no obligation to rescue farmers and lenders whose greed and inept business practices led them into overexpanding operations.

Many farmers compared their march on Washington to the outrage expressed by colonists before the Revolutionary War. Said South Dakota's Governor William Janklow: "If this were 200 years ago, the Potomac would be full of tea."

Reprinted from U.S. News & World Report, March 11, 1985. Copyright 1985, U.S. News & World Report, Inc.

WHAT THEY DO

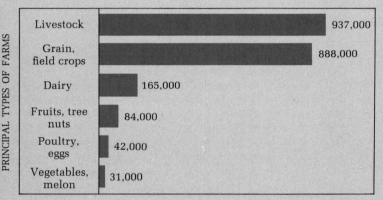

PRINCIPAL TYPES OF FARMS

Livestock	937,000
Grain, field crops	888,000
Dairy	165,000
Fruits, tree nuts	84,000
Poultry, eggs	42,000
Vegetables, melon	31,000

MANY SELL LITTLE

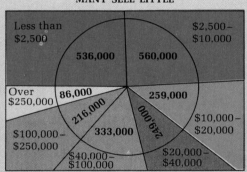

NUMBER OF FARMS IN 1982 WITH SALES TOTALING—

Less than $2,500 — 536,000
$2,500–$10,000 — 560,000
Over $250,000 — 86,000
$100,000–$250,000 — 216,000
249,000
$10,000–$20,000 — 259,000
$40,000–$100,000 — 333,000
$20,000–$40,000

A decade ago, 62% of farmers listed farming as their No. 1 job. The share at last count: 55%.

THE LAND THEY FARM

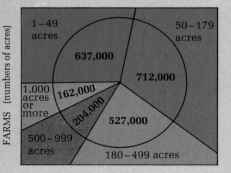

FARMS (numbers of acres)

1–49 acres — 637,000
50–179 acres — 712,000
1,000 acres or more — 162,000
204,000
500–999 acres
180–499 acres — 527,000

The average size is 440 acres.

THEY'RE SCARCER

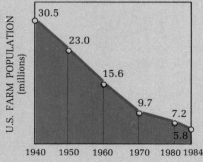

U.S. FARM POPULATION (millions)

Year	Population
1940	30.5
1950	23.0
1960	15.6
1970	9.7
1980	7.2
1984	5.8

Only 2.4% of America's people live on farms today, compared with 23% in 1940.

MOST ARE OVER 45

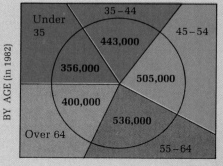

NUMBER OF FARMERS BY AGE (in 1982)

Under 35 — 356,000
35–44 — 443,000
45–54 — 505,000
Over 64 — 400,000
55–64 — 536,000

But the average age is dropping. In 1974, it was 51.7 years. Average at last count: 50.2.

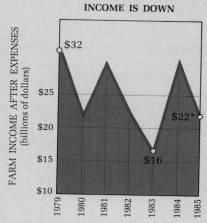

INCOME IS DOWN

FARM INCOME AFTER EXPENSES (billions of dollars)

$32
$25
$22*
$20
$16
$15
$10

1979 1980 1981 1982 1983 1984 1985

In inflation-adjusted dollars, farmers' 1985 net income is forecast at barely half of 1979's level.
*Estimated

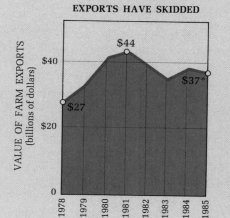

EXPORTS HAVE SKIDDED

VALUE OF FARM EXPORTS (billions of dollars)

$44
$40
$37*
$27
$20
0

1978 1979 1980 1981 1982 1983 1984 1985

This year's exports are forecast at 150 million metric tons, 14 million less than in 1980.
*Estimated

LAND IS WORTH LESS

AVERAGE VALUE PER ACRE (billions of dollars)

$795
$760
$720
$705*
$680
$640
$628
$600

1979 1980 1981 1982 1983 1984 1985

This means farmers have less collateral for vital loans.
*Estimated

AND DEBTS HAVE SOARED

FARM DEBTS AT START OF YEAR (billions of dollars)

$216
$212
$200
$150
$141
$100

1979 1980 1981 1982 1983 1984 1985

Debts now are falling slightly because farmers' borrowing power is decreasing.

Source: Farm-income figures for 1984 and 1985 are midpoints of ranges estimated by Agriculture Department. Land value estimate for 1985 is by US News and World Report Economic Unit.

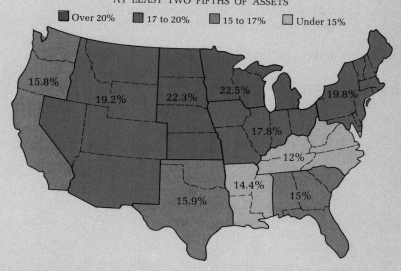

WHERE RED INK IS WORST
SHARE OF FARMERS WITH DEBTS EQUAL TO AT LEAST TWO FIFTHS OF ASSETS

■ Over 20%   ■ 17 to 20%   ■ 15 to 17%   ■ Under 15%

15.8%
19.2%
22.3%
22.5%
19.8%
17.8%
12%
15.9%
14.4%
15%

2. For many decades, prices paid by farmers have generally risen faster than prices received. As a result, since the late 1920s, government has employed various policies designed to improve farmers' real incomes and to stabilize prices. Three major policies that have long been in use, separately or in combination, are price supports, crop restrictions, and direct payments.

3. Our agricultural policies have had several adverse effects. Among them:
(a) The orderly exodus of resources out of agriculture has been hindered rather than helped. This has impeded the farm sector's adjustment to changing supply and demand conditions;
(b) The policies have created inequities. Middle- and upper-income farmers have been the chief beneficiaries, while poorer farmers have benefited little or not at all.

Society has thus borne the costs of policies that have proved to be inefficient and inequitable for agriculture as a whole.

4. Despite the world food shortages that occur from time to time, America's *long-run* agricultural problem is to reduce the proportion of resources on farms. This can best be done by subsidizing farmers to leave agriculture rather than paying them (through price supports or income-maintenance programs) to remain in it.

Terms and Concepts To Review

income elasticity of
   demand
parity price

parity ratio
direct payments

For Discussion

1. "The aggregate demand for agricultural products is relatively inelastic. Over the long run, aggregate demand has not increased as fast as aggregate supply. Hence, the pressure on prices has generally been downward." Illustrate this proposition graphically.

2. "Agricultural products are relatively inelastic in demand, whereas many manufactured goods are relatively elastic in demand. Therefore, a technological improvement in agriculture that results in a price reduction will bring about a decrease in the total revenue received by farmers. On the other hand, a technological improvement in manufacturing that results in a price reduction will often bring about an increase in the total revenue received by producers. This helps explain why agriculture must decline in a technologically advancing society." Illustrate this proposition with the use of demand curves.

3. "The demand for agricultural products is such that small increases in output resulting from improved technology result in relatively large decreases in price and income (that is, total revenue)." What type of elasticity is indicated in this statement? Illustrate your answer with a demand curve.

4. Which is likely to have the most favorable effect on agriculture as a whole: a 10 percent decrease in farm prices, a 10 percent increase in real disposable personal income, or a 10 percent increase in population? Explain.

5. "It is only humanitarian to help the poor. Therefore, we should help farmers because they are poor." Do you agree? Explain.

6. "The government should accumulate stockpiles of agricultural goods when crops are plentiful and sell the goods when crops are scarce. This would help stabilize farm prices and incomes without discouraging production." Discuss.

Chapter 23

Monopoly Behavior: The Other End of the Spectrum

Learning Guide

Watch for answers to these important questions

What is the meaning of monopoly? How does monopoly come about? Are there different types of monopolies?

How does a monopoly, seeking to maximize profit, determine its price and output? What fundamental rule of profit maximization does the monopoly follow?

What criticisms may be leveled against monopoly? How does monopoly behavior affect society's economic goals?

How is price discrimination defined? What conditions are necessary for effective price discrimination?

Market structures are usually classified into several categories. Each of these categories may be regarded as occupying a position along a spectrum. Up to now we have studied only the market structure called perfect competition, which may be visualized at the left end of the competitive spectrum:

Perfect competition	*Real world*	Pure monopoly

In this chapter you will turn your attention to the extreme opposite of perfect competition — pure monopoly. You will find that this type of market structure is, like perfect competition, a theoretical extreme and that it is virtually nonexistent in its pure (unregulated) form.

Does this mean that the study of monopoly is impractical, or even useless? The answer is *no*. The theory of monopoly provides many useful tools and concepts for understanding the behavior of actual business firms. Against this background, the next chapter will show how the features of perfect competition and monopoly can be combined. This will help to explain the competitive behavior of firms in the real world. For the time being, this "real" world is represented by the blank space in the spectrum above.

The Meaning of Monopoly

What is meant by the term *monopoly*? How do monopolies come into existence, and how do they survive? What is wrong with monopoly, and what can be done about it? The answers to these questions constitute the basic aspects of the study of monopoly.

What is Monopoly?

A *monopoly* is defined as a single firm producing a product for which there are no close substitutes. This means that no other firms produce a similar product. Hence, the monopoly firm constitutes the entire industry and is thus a "pure" monopoly. A buyer who wants this particular product must either buy it from the monopolist or do without it.

Pure monopolies are rare, but they do exist. The electric, gas, and water companies in your locality are good examples, because each produces a product for which there are no close substitutes.

Can a firm's degree of monopoly vary from one market to another? The answer is *yes*. For instance, the electric company has a monopoly in the production of electricity for lighting purposes. But for heating purposes, the company's electricity may compete with gas, coal, and fuel oil sold by other producers. An electric company may thus be a pure monopoly in the lighting market but a "partial" monopoly in the heating market. The latter is true in the sense that the company faces some degree of competition from sellers of reasonably adequate substitute goods. Similarly, railroads, bus companies, taxi companies, and airlines are not pure monopolies. But such firms are certainly partial monopolies, depending on the extent to which buyers can shift from one to another in meeting their transportation needs.

In view of this, most firms in our economy, as we shall see, may be characterized as "partial monopolies." In this chapter we shall develop a theory of pure monopoly. Many of its principles and conclusions, however, are applicable to partial monopolies as well.

Sources and Types of Monopoly

What are the origins of monopoly, and why do monopolies continue to exist? There are several possible explanations, all of which amount, in one form or another, to "obstacles to entry." These are economic, legal, or technical barriers that permit a firm to monopolize an industry and prevent new firms from entering. These obstacles give rise to the following common types of monopolies. The types are not mutually exclusive—that is, a monopoly firm may fall into more than one category.

Natural Monopoly

A *natural monopoly* is a firm that experiences increasing economies of scale—long-run decreasing average costs of production—over a wide range of output. This enables the firm to supply the entire market at a lower unit cost than two or more firms could do. Electric companies, gas companies, and railroads are classic examples of natural monopolies. The technology of these public utilities is such that, once the heavy fixed-cost facilities are established (such as power generators, gas transmission lines, or railroad tracks and terminals), additional customer service reduces average total costs over a wide range of output. This permits the operation of plants that are closer to optimum size, which lowers long-run average costs.

Legal and Government Monopolies

In some industries, unrestricted competition among firms may be deemed undesirable by society. In such cases, government grants one firm in an industry an exclusive right to operate—a status of *legal monopoly.* In return for this, government may also impose standards and requirements pertaining to the quantity and quality of output, geographic areas of operation, and the prices or rates that are charged. Investor-owned (as distinguished from governmentally owned) public utilities are typical examples of legal monopolies.

The justification of legal monopoly is based on judicial opinions handed down over many decades by the courts. These opinions have held that a "business affected with a public interest" may qualify as a public utility (and therefore a legal monopoly). This is because the welfare of the entire community is directly dependent on the manner in which the business is operated.

In some states the result of this vague definition has been the establishment of numerous types of businesses as public utilities. Some familiar examples are water, gas, electricity, telephone, and telegraph companies, as well as common carriers of all kinds. Other less familiar examples are bridges, warehouses, cemeteries, gristmills, sawmills, grain elevators, stockyards, hotels, docks, cotton gins, refrigeration plants, markets, and news services.

Whereas legal monopolies are privately owned but governmentally regulated, there are other monopolies that are both owned and regulated by the federal or local government. These are called ***government monopolies.*** Examples are the U.S. Postal Service, the water and sewer systems of almost all local municipalities, the electric power plants of many cities, and the central banks of most countries.

Strategic-Resource Monopoly

A firm that has gained control of an essential input to an important production process is said to have a ***strategic-resource monopoly.*** The possibility of this happening, however, is extremely remote. One of the very few examples is the International Nickel Company of Canada, which at one time owned almost the entire known world supply of nickel. Another illustration is the De Beers Company of South Africa, which once owned almost all of the world's diamond mines but today owns a substantially smaller share.

Patent Monopoly

A ***patent monopoly*** is a firm upon which government has conferred the exclusive right—through issuance of a patent—to make, use, or vend its own invention or discovery. A patent therefore enables a firm to profit from its invention while preventing its adoption by competitors. Several decades ago, the National Cash Register Company and the United Shoe Machinery Company each held a series of patents on their line of products. These patents enabled them to monopolize their respective industries for many years. Today, Apple, IBM, Kodak, and many other well-known firms have varying degrees of monopoly power through patent protection. Over the years, these companies have lost a good deal of their monopoly power, owing to product innovations by competitors.

As these examples suggest, a patent gives one an exclusive right to produce a specifically defined product, but it does not preclude others from producing a closely related substitute good. For example, Xerox Corporation has the exclusive right to produce copiers that function in a particular way, as described in the patents they hold. However, a number of other firms produce competing copying machines. Thus, though patents sometimes enable firms to establish pure monopolies, more often they provide only partial monopolies.

Price and Output Determination

You learned in the study of perfect competition that sellers in a perfectly competitive industry have no influence over the price at which they can sell their output. Each is faced with a perfectly elastic demand curve at the market price, and each maximizes profit by producing the output at which $MC = MR \ (= P)$.

A pure monopolist is in a different situation. Because the monopoly constitutes the entire industry, rather than just a small part of the industry, the monopolist can exercise complete control over the price at which output is sold. The monopolist will thus find that more of the product can be sold at a lower price than at a higher one. This means that the market demand curve for the product will be less than perfectly elastic. *The market demand curve will slope downward instead of being horizontal.* On the other hand, we may assume that the *shapes* (curvatures) of the monopoly's production function and cost curves are similar to those studied in previous chapters. This is because both the variable and fixed factors must be purchased in the input markets and then combined in order to produce a product. These activities are subject to the same laws of production and cost as those of any other seller.

Cost and Revenue Schedules

The cost and revenue data of a monopoly, illustrating the ideas discussed above, are shown in Exhibit 1. It should be apparent from this table that columns (1) and (2) actually compose the demand schedule facing the monopolist. Note that average revenue (=price) is inversely related to quantity.

This means that, in order to sell more units of a product, the monopolist must charge a lower price per unit for all units sold.

Because the average revenue or price varies inversely with quantity, total revenue rises to a maximum and then begins to fall. The changes in total revenue, as always, are reflected by marginal revenue [column (7)]. These figures turn out to be different from average revenue because of the changes in price.

The cost schedules in the table are those used in the previous chapter for a perfectly competitive firm. This is because, as already noted, we are assuming that the shapes or curvatures of the monopolist's cost curves are similar to those of any other seller. Besides, by using the same cost data, we shall be able to see more clearly that the chief dif-

Exhibit 1
Cost and Revenue Schedules of a Monopoly

(1) Quantity per day, Q (given)	(2) Average revenue or price, AR = P (given)	(3) Total revenue, TR (1) × (2)	(4) Total cost, TC	(5) Average total cost ATC (4) ÷ (1)	(6) Marginal cost, MC Change in (4) / Change in (1)	(7) Marginal revenue, MR Change in (3) / Change in (1)	(8) Net revenue, NR (net profit) (3) − (4)
0	$16	$ 0	$ 25	$ —			−$25
					$10	$15	
1	15	15	35	35.00			− 20
					6	13	
2	14	28	41	20.50			− 13
					4	11	
3	13	39	45	15.00			− 6
					2	9	
4	12	48	47	11.75			1
					2	7	
5	11	55	49	9.80			6
					3	5	
6	10	60	52	8.67			8
					5	3	
7	9	63	57	8.14			6
					8	1	
8	8	64	65	8.13			− 1
					14	−1	
9	7	63	79	8.78			− 16
					21	−3	
10	6	60	100	10.00			− 40

ferences between the two firms originate in the output market where goods are sold, rather than in the input market where factors are bought.

A look at the table shows that the fundamental principle of profit maximization still holds. The monopolist's most profitable level of output—the output at which net revenue or net profit [column (8)] is a maximum—is at 6 units, which is also where $MC = MR = \$4$. Why is this so? Because as you learned in the previous chapter, at any output less than this, the added cost of an additional unit is less than the added revenue. Therefore, it pays to increase production. At any output greater than this, the opposite is true. Only where $MC = MR$ is the firm's output at its most profitable level.

Looking at the Graphs

You can visualize these ideas more easily by examining the graphs of the cost and revenue schedules rather than the data. In Exhibit 2, the monopolist's total-revenue and total-cost curves are shown in Figure (a), the appropriate average and marginal curves in Figure (b), and the net-revenue curve in Figure (c). The vertical dashed line that passes through all three figures emphasizes the fact that, at the most profitable level of output:

1. $TR - TC$ is greatest.
2. $MC = MR$, since the tangents to TC and TR are parallel.
3. NR is greatest.   → net REVENUE

Note also in the middle figure that the average-revenue or demand curve facing the monopolist slopes downward, which was not the case for a perfectly competitive seller. As explained earlier, this means that, in order to sell more units of a product, the monopolist must charge a lower price per unit for *all* units sold. Since the AR curve is downward-sloping, the MR curve lies below the AR curve because of the ***average-marginal relationship,*** as you learned in a previous chapter. You can verify this for yourself by experimenting with a few prices and quantities on your own and then sketching their graphs.

Using the $MC = MR$ Principle

We must examine the profit-maximizing behavior of a monopoly more closely so that we are in a better position to evaluate the consequences of its actions. Let us therefore analyze its performance in terms of the fundamental $MC = MR$ principle, which is illustrated by the figures in Exhibit 3.

In Figure (a), the monopoly finds that the $MC = MR$ rule leads it to produce the output at N. At this output, the demand curve indicates that the highest price that can be charged is NG (=0P). Total profit, or net revenue, is thus the area of the shaded rectangle in the figure.

In Figure (b), the monopoly's costs are relatively high compared to its revenues. This may be due to an increase in the prices of the monopoly's factors of production (which causes its cost curves to shift upward), or to a decrease in demand for its output (which causes its revenue curves to shift downward), or to both. Thus, at the $MC = MR$ output, namely N, the corresponding price P is just high enough to yield a normal profit. Because the ATC curve is tangent to the AR curve at this output, the monopolist knows that any other level of production would yield losses because ATC would be greater than AR.

In Figure (c), the monopoly's ATC curve is everywhere higher than its AR curve. As before, this can be the result of an increase in costs, a decrease in demand, or both. Thus, at least for the short run, the $MC = MR$ rule prevails because the output N and the corresponding price P *will minimize losses.* That is, any other price and output will yield a larger loss area than the shaded rectangle in the figure.

You can see from these types of problems that it is essential to sketch correctly both average-revenue and marginal-revenue curves. Here is a convenient geometric rule to remember when the curves are straight lines (as they usually are):

An MR curve always bisects any horizontal line drawn from the vertical axis to the AR curve. Thus, in Figure (a), the distance PW = WG, and similarly for any other horizontal line that may be drawn.

Exhibit 2
Cost and Revenue Curves of a Monopoly

Profit Maximization: Three Viewpoints*

Figure (a): Total Curves The most profitable level of output is determined where the difference between the curves TR and TC, as represented by the distance *GH*, is greatest. This occurs at an output of 6 units. At this output, a tangent to the TR curve is parallel to a tangent to the TC curve, as at G and H. At smaller or larger outputs, such as 5 or 7 units, the tangents would not be parallel.

Figure (b): Marginal Curves The most profitable level of output is determined where $MC = MR$, as explained in the text. You can verify this by simply following the vertical dashed line downward at 6 units of output.

Figure (c): Net Revenue (net profit) Curve The most profitable level of output is determined where the net-revenue curve NR (= TR − TC) is at its highest point. The vertical dashed line emphasizes these profit-maximizing principles in all three figures.

TECHNICAL NOTE (OPTIONAL) If you like to think in geometric terms, remember that parallel lines have equal slopes or steepness. Hence, the most profitable output in the top chart is determined where the *slopes* of the TC and TR curves are equal, which is where the tangents are parallel. In the middle figure, marginal cost is the graph of the *slope* of total cost, and marginal revenue is the graph of the *slope* of total revenue. Therefore, it is true that, at the level of maximum profit,

$$MC = MR$$

or, equivalently,

$$\text{slope of } TC = \text{slope of } TR$$

NOTE For graphing purposes, you should recall from previous chapters that the MC and MR curves are plotted to the *midpoints* between the integers on the horizontal axis. This is because they reflect, respectively, the *change* in total cost and in total revenue resulting from a unit *change* in output.

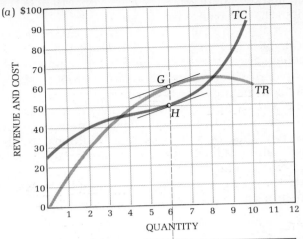

(a)

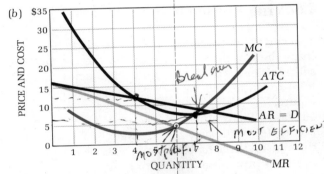

(b)

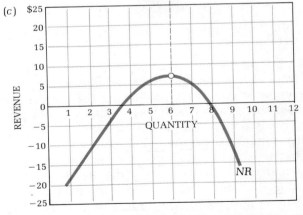

(c)

* The curves have been smoothed to enhance readability. As a result, the curves at some points may not correspond precisely to the data in the table.

Exhibit 3
Three Possible Profit Positions for a Monopolist

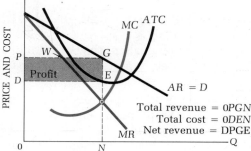

(a) MONOPOLIST EARNING A NET PROFIT

Total revenue = 0PGN
Total cost = 0DEN
Net revenue = DPGE

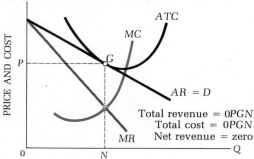

(b) MONOPOLIST EARNING A NORMAL PROFIT

Total revenue = 0PGN
Total cost = 0PGN
Net revenue = zero

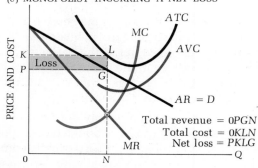

(c) MONOPOLIST INCURRING A NET LOSS

Total revenue = 0PGN
Total cost = 0KLN
Net loss = PKLG

This rule is based on a theorem that we shall not prove here. However, you can easily verify it for yourself by constructing your own tables and plotting the graphs. Actually, all that this rule means is that, *at any given price, an MR curve is twice as steep as (or has twice the slope of) its corresponding AR curve.*

Marginal Revenue Is Not Price; Marginal Cost Is Not Supply

You are now in a position to discover an important distinction between a monopoly firm and a perfectly competitive firm. When you studied the theory of perfect competition, you learned that the seller's marginal-revenue curve and average-revenue (=price) or demand curve were the same. You also learned that the marginal-cost curve was the supply curve above the level of average variable cost. Do these conditions also apply to a monopolist? The answer is *no*. You can verify this from the cost and revenue schedules shown earlier in Exhibit 1 and the figures in Exhibit 3.

When a seller's demand (AR) curve is downward-sloping:

— Marginal revenue falls faster than average revenue (=price) or demand. Thus, *marginal revenue is not price.*

— The most profitable level of output for the seller and the most profitable price that can be charged for that output are determined by MC = MR, not by MC = AR (=P). Thus, *marginal cost is not supply.*

The reasons for these differences between price and output determination by a monopolist as compared to a perfectly competitive seller are explained further in Exhibit 4. Each diagram compares a given MC curve of a monopolist with two arbitrarily different demand or AR curves and their corresponding MR curves. A study of these diagrams and the accompanying analysis leads to the conclusion that *a less than perfectly competitive firm has no supply curve.*

Exhibit 4
No Supply Curve for a Firm with a Downward-Sloping Demand Curve

For any given marginal-cost curve, the most profitable price and output depend on the firm's particular average-revenue curve and its corresponding marginal-revenue curve. Thus, in Figure (a), the single output at N corresponds to the two prices at P and at S. In Figure (b), the two outputs at N and at L correspond to the single price at K. This suggests the following principle:

A firm faced with a downward-sloping (or less than perfectly elastic) demand curve has no supply curve. This is because there is no single quantity that the firm will necessarily supply at a given price and no single price at which the firm will necessarily supply a given quantity.

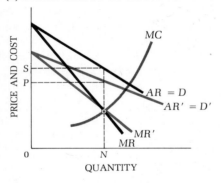

(a) SINGLE OUTPUT AT MULTIPLE PRICES

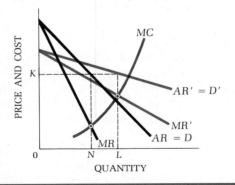

(b) MULTIPLE OUTPUTS AT A SINGLE PRICE

In view of this, is it possible to conclude that, strictly speaking, prices are determined by supply and demand *only* under perfect competition? You will have an opportunity to discuss this important question in a problem at the end of this chapter.

Do Monopolies Earn "Large" Profits?

You now know enough about the behavior of a monopoly to draw three important conclusions about monopoly pricing:

1. The price charged by an unregulated monopoly is not, as Adam Smith once remarked, "the highest which can be got." This fact may surprise many people. Instead, the monopoly's price is the highest that is consistent with maximizing profits. For instance, the monopoly of Exhibit 3, Figure (a), could produce somewhat less than N and charge a price higher than P. Then, as long as its ATC did not exceed its AR, the firm would still make a profit, but it obviously would not make the maximum profit possible.

2. A pure monopoly does not necessarily make "high" profits just because it is a monopoly. If its profits are relatively high, the monopoly may find that the owners of some of its factors of production, for example workers or landlords, will absorb part of the surplus by demanding larger payments. This will cause the monopoly's ATC curve to rise, possibly to the point at which the firm is earning a moderate profit or perhaps only a normal profit. This is shown in Exhibit 3, Figure (b).

3. In the short run, a monopoly may earn less than a normal profit and still remain in business. This is the situation depicted in Exhibit 3, Figure (c). In the long run, however, the monopoly would have to earn at least a normal profit to continue in operation, just like any other firm.

Thus, having a pure monopoly does not in itself assure extraordinary profit, although a monopoly is likely to be more profitable than a perfectly competitive firm. A monopolist is faced with certain market restraints that affect decisions about price and output. The ability of the monopolist to cope with these restraints will affect the profitability of the firm. By adhering to the $MC = MR$ principle, the monopolist will always maximize profits (or minimize losses). However, the $MC = MR$ principle in itself does not guarantee that those profits will be large (or that losses will be small).

What's Wrong with Monopoly?

You have probably heard that monopoly is "bad," but may not know exactly why. Now, however, on the basis of what you have learned from economic analysis, you can give some significant reasons.

Efficiency: It Misallocates Resources

The basic economic criticism of pure monopoly is this:

A monopoly adheres to the $MC = MR$ principle of profit maximization. Therefore, a monopoly misallocates society's resources by restricting output and charging a higher price than it would if it followed the $MC = P$ standard of perfect competition.

This basic criticism embodies the following fundamental ideas, all of which are best understood in terms of Exhibit 5.

Monopoly Price: $MC = MR$

In seeking to maximize profit, the monopoly produces the equilibrium output at Q and charges the equilibrium price QJ. The latter is called the **monopoly price** because it is determined by the intersection of the MC and MR curves. Note that this price is greater than the monopoly's marginal cost at that output. Therefore: *The value of the last unit to the marginal user (measured by the price he or she pays for the last unit, which is equal to the price paid for any other unit) is greater than the value of the*

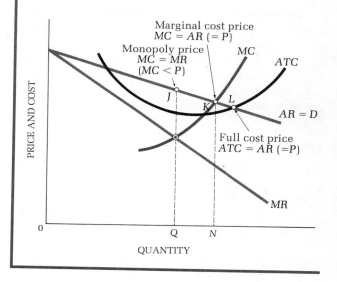

Exhibit 5
Price and Output Effects of Monopoly Behavior

The **monopoly price** at J maximizes the firm's profit. However, this price results in resource misallocation.

The **marginal-cost price** at K is the optimum price for society. However, this price is usually impossible to determine because marginal costs cannot ordinarily be estimated from a firm's accounting records.

The **full-cost** (or **average-cost**) **price** at L results in the largest output and lowest price consistent with earning a normal profit. Because average costs can be roughly estimated from a company's accounting records, the full-cost price is the one that government usually tries to impose on regulated monopolies.

resources used to produce that unit. In other words, because $MC < P$, society is not getting as much of the good as it wants in relation to the resources sacrificed to produce the good.

Marginal-Cost Price: $MC = AR (=P)$

If the monopoly followed the $MC = AR (=P)$ rule of perfect competition, it would produce the larger output at N and charge the lower price NK. The latter is called the ***marginal-cost price.*** It is the optimum price for society because at this price, the value of the last unit to the marginal user is equivalent to the value of the resources used to produce that unit. Therefore, society is getting as much of the good as it wants in relation to the resources sacrificed to produce it.

Technical Inefficiency

By adhering to the $MC = MR$ principle of profit maximization, the monopoly is technically inefficient. This is because it typically "underuses" the plant by producing on the declining side of the ATC curve. Because the entry of other firms into the industry is blocked, the monopoly can remain in this equilibrium position indefinitely. In contrast, you will recall that firms in perfect competition are technically efficient because they operate in the long run at the minimum point of their ATC curves. Thus, society's resources are ordinarily used less efficiently in monopoly markets than they are in perfectly competitive markets.

The Natural-Monopoly Case

Does this criticism mean that a monopoly produces less, and charges more, than a perfectly competitive industry with the same total demand curve? Not necessarily. In fact, the opposite may often be true.

In some industries, technology may widen the "spread" of the cost curves by bringing about increasing economies of scale over a broad range of output. If that happens, one firm may be able to supply the entire market at a lower unit cost (and perhaps at a lower price) than several. This, you will recall, is the basis of most natural monopolies, especially public utilities such as electric companies, gas companies, and railroads.

Full-Cost (Average-Cost) Price: $ATC = AR (= P)$

You can see from the foregoing analyses that an unregulated monopoly will seek to maximize its profits. This means that it will charge the so-called monopoly price determined by $MC = MR$. As a re-

sult, output will be smaller, and the price higher, than it would be if other pricing policies were followed.

Which policies? In most cases government agencies that regulate monopolies would like to require them to charge the marginal-cost price. In practice, however, marginal costs are ordinarily impossible to estimate from a firm's accounting records. Therefore, the price that regulatory agencies usually strive to impose is the ***full-cost*** (or ***average-cost***) ***price,*** which is shown in Exhibit 5. This price has two important characteristics:

1. It enables the firm to cover all its costs, both fixed and variable, and thus to earn a normal profit while producing the largest output consistent with that profit.

2. It is easier to determine than the marginal-cost price because average costs of production can be roughly estimated from a company's accounting records.

Equity: It Contributes to Income Inequality

A second criticism of monopoly is that it tends to create greater income inequality than would exist in a perfectly competitive economy. By restricting output and charging a higher price, the monopoly may make supernormal profits. These go to its owners or stockholders. These people thus benefit at the expense of the consumers and resource owners who make up the rest of society.

Growth: It Lacks Incentives for Innovation and Progress

A third major criticism is that a monopoly, unlike a perfectly competitive firm, is not under constant pressure to develop better methods of production. Therefore, its monopoly position may retard economic progress. This is because the obstacles to entry make the monopoly relatively secure. Competitive pressures that would otherwise stimulate innovation are absent for monopolies.

Public utilities—especially the railroads and telephone companies—are often cited as illustrations. At one time, critics contend, these monopolies intentionally retarded the development of new and improved products to avoid increasing the rate of obsolescence of their existing equipment. In addition, they were able to do this because of their protected status as legal monopolies. This protection, however, has been greatly reduced since the early 1980s. As a result, these firms have become more progressive and more innovative than they used to be.

Conclusion: What Can Be Done About Monopoly?

The general criticisms of monopoly are rooted in the fundamental notion of resource misallocation resulting from the restriction of output and higher prices. In view of this, what can be done about monopolies in our society? The four major possibilities for social policy are these:

1. Do Nothing   Sooner or later a monopoly that is not insulated by patents or other protective legislation is likely to see its position weakened. This will happen as new firms enter the industry in order to capture a share of the monopoly's market. The history of American business is replete with examples of companies that lost their dominant position as a result of competition from other firms, both domestic and foreign.

2. Break Monopolies Up into Competing Firms   In the United States and some other developed countries, *antitrust* legislation exists for dealing with monopolies by breaking them up into smaller firms. But the problems of implementing the laws are many and complex.

3. Tax Away All the Profits of Monopolies Above Their Normal Profits   If all of the excess profits of monopolies were taxed, their revenues could be distributed to the public through increased or improved government services. This would not drive monopolies out of business, because they would still be normally profitable. However, it would help to compensate society for some of the adverse consequences of resource misallocation brought about by monopolies.

4. Treat All Monopolies as Public Utilities   The outputs and prices of monopolies can be regulated by government agencies. The agencies could require monopolies to produce more and charge less than they would if they were completely free and unregulated. This, you have already learned, is the way in which legal monopolies are administered, as illustrated earlier in terms of the discussion of full-cost pricing.

Would the adoption of these policies "solve" the so-called monopoly problem? The answer is *no*.

No one of these approaches, nor any combination of them, would completely overcome the fundamental problem of resource misallocation. However, each would tend to reduce somewhat the adverse effects of misallocation.

Price Discrimination

Until now we have assumed that a monopoly sells its entire output at the *same* price per unit. However, a monopoly may sometimes find it more profitable to charge different prices instead of a single price for the units it sells. It is then engaging in what is known as price discrimination—one of the most interesting problems in the theory of monopoly.

Price discrimination may be defined as the practice of charging different prices to buyers for the same good. Hence, it is also sometimes called *differential pricing*. In general terms, price discrimination or differential pricing is a method that some sellers use to maximize profits by tailoring their prices to the specific purchasing situations of the buyers. The price may vary according to the amount purchased or according to the market in which the good is purchased.

Economics in the News

Breaking Up Government's Monopoly on Prison Cells

WASHINGTON—There are now about two dozen major correctional facilities under private ownership or operation. Martin Tolchin, a reporter in the Washington Bureau of *The New York Times,* asked two experts— James K. Stewart, director of the National Institute of Justice, the research arm of the Justice Department, and Mark A. Cunniff, executive director of the National Association of Criminal Justice Planners, which represents officials in 75 major urban areas—to discuss private prisons and their implications. Excerpts follow.

Cheaper, Better?

James K. Stewart

Question. What is the appeal of privately run prisons?

Answer. Construction of a typical prison takes about 7 or 8 years if we go through the political process. If built privately, it can be finished within a relatively short time, maybe 12 months. Second, we're very tight on public finances. Prisons cost about $100,000 a cell. The private sector, it has been suggested although not yet tested, can build and maintain a prison for about 10 to 15 percent—maybe 20 percent— less.

Q. How?

A. They *claim* that they don't have to pay the extraordinary retirement benefits of many public employees. They also believe that they

can act quickly, without a bidding process, so they can acquire property quicker and therefore save money.

Q. Are there other advantages?

A. The private sector seeks to have the people who are imprisoned actively employed, so they gain skills they can use later on. They can work for money, so they can provide restitution for victims. Some pay the institution for some of the cost of their incarceration as well as send money home.

Q. A corrections officer has a say in the length of prison terms, since he makes recommendations to parole boards, and he can deprive inmates of basic privileges or even put them in isolation wards. Should an employee of a private organization be able to do this?

A. The key is, are we providing adequate supervision? What we are doing is contracting with private groups, as many cities and states are doing to provide health care. The conflict comes if we delegate authority to a company and then don't watch it.

The use of force is something that bothers me, but in fact in our society we delegate it regularly to nongovernment entities—in the private security area in stores and banks, in hospitals and psychiatric wards.

The State's Role

Mark A. Cunniff

Question. Is there a conflict between the profit motive and the pursuit of justice?

Answer. The nature of the conflict has to do with the competing goals of criminal justice and correc-

tions. Criminal justice, despite what private contractors may maintain, is concerned with costs. But cost is not the sole concern of corrections.

When you bring in a private, for-profit firm—and since it is for-profit, its main goal is to make money— cost effectiveness and efficiency come to the fore. The main concern is how to turn a profit at the end of the year, and that means looking to cut costs. For a governmental entity, the driving force is the general welfare of the society.

Q. If prisons have been badly underfunded and have deteriorated, wouldn't privatization be a remedy?

A. Criminal justice has to compete with a lot of other functions government is trying to perform— roads, education, medical care— and legislators are very reluctant to make a decision that gets down to, "Yes, we're going to build an extra hundred prison beds, but in order to do that we're going to have to close down a school."

I am never going to argue against efficiency in the criminal justice system. I would welcome the private sector to come in, on a contractual basis, to consult with a department of corrections on how to manage resources. But efficiency is only one of the values we're dealing with in the administration of justice—fairness, propriety, equity under the law are others to consider.

"Tapping" The Demand Curve

An example of price discrimination occurs when a monopolist "taps" the demand curve of the buyer. This is done by charging the buyer higher prices for smaller quantities instead of a single price per unit for all units purchased. The monopolist may also charge different prices to different classes or groups of buyers.

For example, an electric company does not usually charge all buyers the same price per unit for electricity. Instead, it *segments* the total market — that is, divides it into homogeneous submarkets consisting, say, of residential users, commercial users, and industrial users. It then charges a different price to each class of user. In this way the company earns more money than it would if all users paid the same price. This concept is illustrated in Exhibit 6.

Assume that the AR curve is the demand curve of a single buyer or of a single homogeneous class of buyers. The monopoly may simply charge a price of P_4 per unit and sell N_4 units. In this case there is no discrimination, and the firm's total revenue is price times quantity, or the area of the rectangle $0P_4M_4N_4$.

However, the monopoly can enlarge total receipts considerably if it discriminates in price. Thus, it may charge a price of P_1 for the first N_1 units, giving it a total revenue of $0P_1M_1N_1$. Then it may lower the price to P_2 per unit and sell additional units equal to the distance N_1N_2. After that, it can lower the price to P_3 and sell additional units equal to the distance N_2N_3. Finally, it can lower the price to P_4, at which it sells further units equal to the distance N_3N_4. In this way the monopoly still ends up selling the same total number of units, namely N_4. However, its total revenue is now the entire shaded area instead of the area $0P_4M_4N_4$, which is what its revenue was when it charged a price of P_4 per unit without discrimination.

Exhibit 6
Price Discrimination Based on Quantity

A monopoly can charge a different price to the same buyer (or to the same homogeneous class of buyers) according to the quantity purchased. In that case, the total revenue will be larger (shown by the shaded areas) than it would be if the monopoly charged the same price per unit for all units purchased.

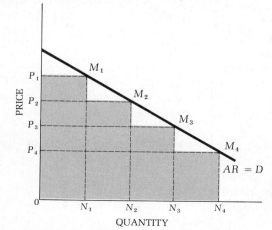

Dumping

Another form of price discrimination occurs when a monopolist sells the same product at different prices in different markets. This practice is known in international trade as *dumping*, but its underlying principles are equally applicable to domestic trade.

The basic concept is illustrated by the diagrams in Exhibit 7. As shown in Figures (*a*) and (*b*), a firm that has a monopoly in the domestic market will probably find that the demand for its product at home is more inelastic than the demand abroad. This is because foreign buyers have a greater number of alternative sources from which to purchase the product. Consequently, their demand for the monopolist's product is more elastic.

In Figure (*c*), the curve for the total marginal revenue of both markets, namely $MR_1 + MR_2$, may be obtained by summing the horizontal ordinates to the MR_1 and MR_2 curves in the other two graphs. In other words, by adding together the quantities in the domestic and foreign markets at each marginal revenue, the $MR_1 + MR_2$ curve in the total market can be derived.

Exhibit 7
Illustration of Dumping

To allocate the product between the domestic and foreign markets, the most profitable level of *total* output must be determined first. This is done in Figure (c). By adhering to the $MC = MR$ principle, the monopolist maximizes profit by allocating the total equilibrium output at N_3 among the two submarkets in Figures (a) and (b). The monopolist then charges a higher price in the domestic market because the demand elasticity is smaller (or the inelasticity is larger).

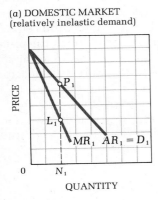

(a) DOMESTIC MARKET
(relatively inelastic demand)

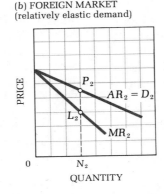

(b) FOREIGN MARKET
(relatively elastic demand)

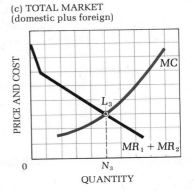

(c) TOTAL MARKET
(domestic plus foreign)

The most profitable level of *total* output must be determined first. This is done in Figure (c), in which the MC curve in the total market is the monopoly's marginal-cost curve. The firm's most profitable total output is at N_3 because this is where the marginal cost of the output equals the total marginal revenue.

It should be emphasized that only one marginal-cost curve is assumed to exist in this case, because it makes no difference to costs whether the product is sold at home or abroad. That is, the product is still the same, and the marginal cost is determined by the total output. Hence, for the output at N_3, the monopolist's marginal cost is equal to the distance N_3L_3. This in turn is equal to the distance N_1L_1 in the domestic market as well as to the distance N_2L_2 in the foreign market.

How will the monopolist divide total output among the two submarkets? What price will be charged in each market? The answers to these questions follow from the $MC = MR$ principle you have already learned. In order to maximize profit, the monopolist will sell N_1 units in the domestic market at the price N_1P_1 because this is where the marginal revenue in that market is equal to the marginal cost N_1L_1. Likewise, the monopolist will sell the remaining N_2 units in the foreign market at the price N_2P_2 because this is where the marginal revenue in that market equals the marginal cost N_2L_2.

There are many illustrations of dumping at both the domestic and international level. For example, some manufacturers of appliances and various other products sell part of their output to mail-order firms and department stores (such as Sears and Montgomery Ward) at lower prices under different brand names. Milk cooperatives frequently sell milk at a higher price to consumers and at a lower price to butter and cheese manufacturers. Tire manufacturers often sell identical tires under their own brand names in the domestic market and under different brand names through other marketing channels in both domestic and foreign markets. In each case, the seller earns a higher profit by making fuller utilization of plant capacity. However, this assumes that the extra or marginal cost of the additional output does not exceed the extra or marginal revenue.

The Conditions for Price Discrimination

Price discrimination is thus a practice of charging different prices to different segments of a market for the same good. Each segment represents a distinct market or submarket for the product. If you were a seller, what practical conditions would have to exist to enable you to practice price discrimination effectively? There are three: (1) multiple demand elasticities, (2) market segmentation, and (3) market sealing.

Multiple Demand Elasticities

There must be differences in demand elasticity among buyers, resulting from differences in income, location, available alternatives, tastes, or other factors. Otherwise, if the underlying conditions that normally determine demand elasticity are the same for all purchasers, the separate demand elasticities for each buyer or group of buyers will be approximately equal. In that case, a single rather than multiple price structure may be warranted.

Market Segmentation

A second condition for price discrimination is that the seller must be able to partition (segment) the total market. How? By segregating buyers into groups or submarkets according to elasticity.

Profits can then be enhanced by charging a different price in each submarket. There are many ways in which a total market can be effectively segmented into submarkets. For example:

Segmentation by Income A surgeon may charge a rich patient more than a poor patient for the same operation.

Segmentation by Quantity of Purchase A manufacturer may offer quantity discounts to large buyers.

Segmentation by Geographic Location A state university may charge out-of-state students a higher tuition than in-state residents.

Segmentation by Time A theater, tennis club, or telephone company may charge more at certain hours than at others. Similarly, a resort hotel, restaurant, or clothing store may charge higher prices during certain seasons of the year.

Segmentation by Brand Name The same product may be sold under different brand names at different prices.

Segmentation by Age An airline may charge less for children than for adults, despite equal costs of serving them.

Segmentation by race, religion, sex, and education provide still further opportunities for partitioning a market into relatively homogeneous subgroups. Can you suggest some examples?

Market Sealing

A third condition for price discrimination is that the seller must be able to seal the market. That is, the seller must be able to prevent — or natural circumstances must exist that will prevent — any significant resale of goods from the lower- to the higher-priced submarket. Any leakage in the form of resale by buyers between submarkets will, beyond minimum critical levels, tend to neutralize the effect of differential prices. The result will be to narrow the effective price structure so much that it approaches that of a single price to all buyers.

For example, a movie theater may use tickets of different colors for matinees and for evenings, or for children and for adults. In this way, it seals the segmented markets and prevents buyers from purchasing at the lower price and selling or using the product at the higher price. Similarly, some publishers of magazines, newspapers, and professional journals sell subscriptions to students at special rates. Of course, market sealing cannot always be complete. When it is not, a certain amount of leakage will occur between submarkets.

Is Price Discrimination Legal?

Price discrimination is a practical way for sellers to increase their profits. By identifying relevant demand elasticities and by effectively segmenting and sealing markets, firms can discover new and larger sources of profit.

However:

Certain types of price discrimination are expressly illegal under our antitrust laws. The legality of some other forms is not clearly defined, and those who practice these other forms of price discrimination may therefore be open to legal action by the government. As a consequence, sellers must be cautious about employing certain discriminatory pricing practices.

What You Have Learned

1. A monopoly is a single firm producing a product for which there are no close substitutes. Major types are natural monopolies, legal monopolies, government monopolies, strategic-resource monopolies, and patent monopolies.

2. The most profitable output of a monopoly is determined where its $MC = MR$. Unlike a firm in perfect competition, any firm faced with a downward-sloping demand curve is a partial monopoly. Such a firm finds that its marginal-revenue curve is not a demand curve and that its marginal-cost curve is not a supply curve.

3. The basic economic criticism of monopoly is that it misallocates resources. By adhering to the $MC = MR$ principle of profit maximization, a monopoly restricts output and charges a correspondingly higher price than it would if the $MC = P$ standard of perfect competition were followed. In addition, monopolies contribute to income inequality and they may lack incentives to be innovative and progressive. Four possible remedies are:

1. to do nothing

2. to tax away their supernormal profits

3. to break them up into competing firms

4. to regulate them as public utilities. If monopolies were regulated as public utilities, their rates would tend to accord with principles of full-cost pricing rather than monopoly pricing or marginal-cost pricing.

4. Price discrimination enlarges revenues by segmenting the market into submarkets. This enables sellers to charge different prices in each market according to relative demand elasticities. Markets may be segmented by income, brand names of products, locations of buyers, and various other criteria. Dumping is a typical form of price discrimination.

Terms and Concepts to Review

monopoly
natural monopoly
legal monopoly
government monopoly
strategic-resource monopoly
patent monopoly
average – marginal relationship
monopoly price
marginal-cost price
full-cost (average-cost) price
dumping

For Discussion

1. Evaluate the judicial definition that a monopoly is "a business affected with a public interest."

2. Answer *true* or *false*, and explain why:

(a) A monopoly is secure because, by controlling its price and output, it can guarantee a profit.

(b) A perfect monopoly is almost as unlikely as perfect competition.

(c) A monopoly's price is higher than a perfect competitor's price in the long run.

(d) A monopoly maximizes its profit by charging the highest price it can get.

3. "A monopoly is most likely to be successful when the demand for its product is relatively inelastic." True or false? (HINT Prove that a monopoly will never produce at an output at which the elasticity of demand is numerically less than 1. You can do this by first proving that, when marginal revenue is positive, the elasticity of demand is numerically greater than 1.)

4. What is the most profitable output for a monopolist faced with a unit-elastic demand curve throughout the entire length of the curve? (HINT What is the value of marginal revenue when demand is unit elastic?).

5. If the government wanted to extract the maximum revenue from a monopoly without driving it out of business, should the government tax profits or should it tax each unit of output? Explain.

6. "The prices of automobiles, TV sets, and corn flakes are each determined by supply and demand." Evaluate this statement in light of the fact that a less than perfectly competitive firm has no supply curve. What do "supply" and "demand" actually mean in this case?

7. Complete the table below, which shows cost and revenue data of a monopolist. Sketch the following curves on three separate figures, one beneath the other, as was done in this chapter:

(a) Total revenue and total cost.

(b) Marginal cost, average total cost, average revenue, and marginal revenue.

(c) Net revenue.

In the figures, draw vertical dashed lines showing the most profitable level of output and the two break-even points. (NOTE You will have to "project" the curves to obtain the second break-even point.) Label all the curves and explain their significance. Remember that marginal curves are plotted to the midpoints between the integers on the horizontal axis.

8. If you were an economic advisor to a monopoly, could you suggest ways in which the firm could engage in price discrimination by segmenting the market on the basis of (a) quantity, (b) geographic location, and (c) time?

Problem 7   Cost and Revenue Schedules of a Monopolist

(1) Quantity per day, Q	(2) Average revenue or price, AR = P	(3) Total revenue, TR	(7) Marginal revenue, MR	(4) Total cost, TC	(5) Average total cost, ATC	(6) Marginal cost, MC	(8) Net revenue (net profit), NR
0	$21	$ 0	$20	$22			$ -22
1	20	20	18	37	37	$15	-17
2	19	38	16	42	21	5	-14
3	18	54	14	45	15	3	+9
4	17	68	12	47	11.75	2	21
5	16	80	10	50	10	3	30
6	15	90	8	54	9	4	36
7	14	98	6	59	8.42	5	39
8	13	104	4	65	8.12	6	39
9	12	108	2	72	8	7	36
10	11	110	0	80	8	8	30
11	10	110	-2	89	8.09	9	21
12	9	108		99	8.25	10	9

9. Some critics have suggested that firms with strong monopoly power should be subsidized, or even governmentally owned, in order to have them adhere to a socially desirable pricing policy.   What do you think of this argument?   Be specific.

10. A monopoly firm's average revenue AR, in dollars, and total cost TC, in dollars, is given in terms of units of quantity q by the equations:

$$AR = 8 - q$$
$$TC = 2q + 5$$

Using elementary algebra only, verify each of the following:

(a) The firm's total revenue equation is $TR = 8q - q^2$
(b) The total revenue at $q = 3$ is $15
(c) The total revenue at $q = 4$ is $16
(d) The total revenue at $q = 5$ is $15
(e) The equation for average total cost is $ATC = 2 + 5/q$
(f) The equation for total fixed cost is $TFC = 5$
(g) The average fixed cost at $q = 5$ is $1
(h) The total variable cost at $q = 4$ is $8
(i) The price—(or vertical-axis) intercept of the demand curve is $8
(j) The break-even points occur at 1 unit and at 5 units of quantity
(k) The equation for net revenue NR (or net profit) is $NR = -q^2 + 6q - 5$
(l) The most profitable quantity is 3 units
(m) The most profitable price is $5 per unit
(n) Total revenue at the most profitable output is $15
(o) Total variable cost at the most profitable output is $6
(p) Total cost at the most profitable output is $11
(q) Net revenue (or net profit) at the most profitable output is $4

Chapter 24

The Real World of Imperfect Competition

Learning Guide

Watch for answers to these important questions

What types of market structures constitute imperfect competition?

What is monopolistic competition? Why is advertising a particularly important activity in monopolistic competition? What are the economic consequences of monopolistic competition?

What is oligopoly? How does oligopoly differ from monopolistic competition? What are the economic consequences of oligopoly?

Is it reasonable to assume that firms seek to maximize profit? Why does economic theory assume profit-maximizing behavior?

If the world of perfect competition is largely imaginary and the world of monopoly is relatively limited and regulated, what does the *real* world look like? We can answer this question by constructing models that come closer to approximating the kinds of markets in which most firms and industries in the economy operate. You will find that your knowledge of perfect competition and monopoly provides a basis for comparing and evaluating the consequences of these more realistic situations.

To give yourself a bird's-eye view of where you are and where you will be heading in this chapter, examine the following spectrum of market structures:

Perfect competition	Varying degrees of imperfect competition: monopolistic competition and oligopoly	Pure monopoly

You have already analyzed the cases of perfect competition and monopoly at the extreme ends of the spectrum. Now you will be turning your attention to the broad middle range in order to examine what is known as "imperfect competition." This includes market structures that are classified as "monopolistic competition" and "oligopoly." They combine, in various degrees, properties of both perfect competition and pure monopoly. You will find that these mixed structures characterize most of the markets in our economy.

Monopolistic Competition: Many Sellers, Similar Products

You know that a perfectly competitive market consists of many firms producing a homogeneous product. You also know that a monopolized market consists of one firm producing a unique product. Both kinds of markets are important for economic analysis. Some markets, such as those for many agricultural products and standardized raw materials, operate under conditions that exhibit certain characteristics of perfect competition. Organized commodity and stock exchanges operate under some of these conditions as well. Other markets, such as those for electric power and gas, have certain features of pure monopoly.

In reality, most of the nation's economic activity occurs under conditions of imperfect competition. This market structure consists of industries and markets that fall between the two extremes of perfect competition and pure monopoly. One such intermediate type that exists throughout the economy is called **monopolistic competition.** It may be defined as an industry or market characterized by (1) a large number of firms of different sizes producing heterogeneous (similar but not identical) products and (2) relatively easy entry for firms. This type of competition will be studied first. The other subcategory of imperfect competition, known as "oligopoly," is examined later in the chapter.

Product Differentiation Is a Key Factor

Does the term "monopolistic competition" contradict itself? How can a market be both monopolistic and competitive at the same time?

The answer is based on the fact that, in an industry characterized by monopolistic competition, the products of the firms in the industry are *differentiated*. But product differentiation, like beauty, is in the eye of the beholder. And, in economics, the beholder is always the buyer. Consequently, products may be differentiated by brand name, color of package, location of the seller, customer service, credit conditions, or the smile of the salesperson—even if the products themselves are physically the same. As a result, each firm has a partial monopoly of its own differentiated product.

Monopolistic competition is found in many industries. Retailing provides a good general illustration. Some more specific examples include the manufacture of clothing, household goods, shoes, and furniture. In some areas, the services provided by most barbers, doctors, and dentists are also good examples. In each of these industries the products sold are usually only moderately differentiated. This helps to explain why similar kinds of goods in monopolistic competition tend to have similar prices. In most markets, for example, the prices of haircuts are similar, as are the prices of appendectomies and the prices of dental fillings. In general, the less the degree of product differentiation in the minds of buyers, the less the disparity in prices.

Price and Output Determination

When we apply these ideas to the construction of a model, we find that the theory of monopolistic competition is as much a *theory of the firm* as it is a theory of market or industry behavior. Thus:

1. Because each seller has a partial monopoly due to product differentiation, there will be a separate AR or demand curve for each firm. These curves will be downward-sloping, indicating that a firm can raise prices to some degree without losing all of its sales.

2. You learned in the study of monopoly that a firm with a negatively inclined demand curve has no supply curve. This is because a given price may be associated with multiple outputs and a given output may be associated with multiple prices, depending on the position of the AR curve. Hence, there can be no industry supply curve. In

Exhibit 1
Firms in Monopolistic Competition

Firm *A* is earning above-normal profits, firm *B* only normal profits, and firm *C* below-normal profits. In the long run most firms in monopolistic competition will *tend* to be approximately normally profitable. However, there may be some exceptions due to locational factors or other special circumstances.

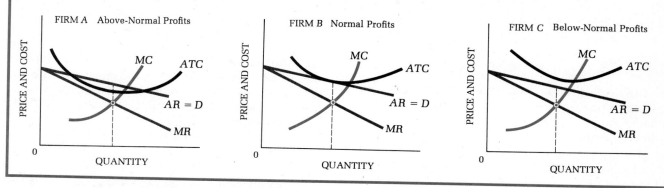

fact, because of product differentiation, the whole concept of an industry becomes somewhat cloudy and vague in monopolistic competition.

3. Because the products of competitors are close but not perfect substitutes, it can be assumed that their elasticities of demand are relatively high. (Examples include competing brands of soap, toothpaste, and soft drinks.) Indeed, the elasticity will vary inversely with the extent of product differentiation. And, of course, the less the degree of product differentiation and the greater the number of sellers, the closer the model will be to pure competition.

The *MC* = *MR* Principle Again

As always, to maximize profit, firms will seek to produce the quantity at which *MC* = *MR*. But this does not necessarily mean *all* firms that do so will be highly profitable. Because there are many firms in the industry and entry is relatively easy, some firms will earn only modest profits.

In the long run, however, there will be a *tendency* for most surviving firms to be close to normally profitable. Again, this is only a general tendency.

Profitability will depend on the degree of product differentiation and the number of firms. For example, a small retail store might continue to be considerably more than normally profitable because it happens to be in a particularly good location. On the other hand, a similar kind of store in a different location may continue to be considerably less than normally profitable. Why? Because the seller would prefer to be his or her "own boss"—despite the economic loss that may result—rather than hire out to do the same job at higher pay for someone else. Therefore, although most firms in a monopolistically competitive industry *tend* to earn approximately normal profits in the long run, some firms do not. These possibilities are illustrated and explained for the firms in Exhibit 1.

The Importance of Selling Costs

Because product differentiation plays a key role in monopolistic competition, many firms spend money on advertising, merchandising, sales promotion, public relations, and the like in order to increase their profits. Marketing expenditures of this type, which are aimed at adapting the buyer to the product, are termed **selling costs.** This distinguishes them from production costs, which are designed to adapt the product to the buyer. For purposes of analysis, economists generally view all sales outlays or selling costs as synonymous with advertising.

The seller in monopolistic competition who engages in advertising seeks to attain a delicate balance between commodity homogeneity and heterogeneity. To attract customers away from competitors, the seller must convey two ideas:

1. The firm's product is not sharply differentiated from competing products, so that buyers can contemplate purchasing the product instead of those of competitors.

2. The product is somehow superior to those of competitors.

Clearing Up a Misconception

These objectives of advertising account for an erroneous statement that is sometimes made about it. Marketing experts, for example, often contend that the seller's purpose in advertising is to make the demand curve more inelastic. This would allow a higher price to be charged for each unit sold.

If this statement were true, it would mean that the seller would prefer to be confronted with the demand curve D_1 in Exhibit 2 rather than D_2. Yet if output is most profitable beyond the level at N_1, say at N_2, then D_2 is clearly preferable to D_1. Why? Because it allows for sales at a higher price, even though D_2 is more elastic than D_1. On the other hand, if output is most profitable at N_3, then D_1 would be preferred to D_2. Therefore, the argument that advertising is desirable for the seller because it results in a more inelastic demand curve may be only partially true, and in many instances may be completely false.

The statement can be correctly reformulated by noting that what the seller really wants is not necessarily a more inelastic demand curve but rather a new and *higher* curve. This is illustrated by D_3. With this demand curve, the seller can charge a higher price per unit relative to either D_1 or D_2, regardless of the most profitable output volume indicated in the figure.

Is Advertising "Good" or "Bad"?

Advertising has been a subject of much debate among economists. The arguments have revolved around three major issues:

1. Information Versus Persuasion Those in favor of advertising argue that it educates and informs buyers about firms, products, and prices. Therefore, advertising tends to make markets more perfect than they otherwise would be. Those who oppose advertising reply that it seeks to persuade

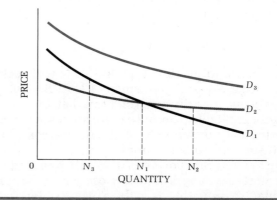

Exhibit 2
Advertising and Demand

The purpose of advertising is *not* to make the demand curve more inelastic so that a higher price can be charged. If that were the case, D_1 would be preferable to D_2. However, if N_2 is the most profitable volume of output, D_2 permits a higher price to be charged than D_1 does. The opposite is true if N_3 is the most profitable output. Thus:

The purpose of advertising is to shift the demand curve to a higher *level*, such as D_3. This permits a higher price to be charged for *any* volume of output.

buyers rather than to inform them, thereby creating wants that result in a distortion of "natural" preference patterns.

2. Competition Versus Concentration Defenders of advertising argue that it encourages competition. It does this by exposing consumers to competing products and enabling firms to gain market acceptance for new products more rapidly than they could without advertising. Critics of advertising contend that the opposite is true. Advertising, they say, facilitates the concentration of monopoly power because large firms can usually afford continuous heavy advertising, whereas small firms cannot.

3. Efficiency Versus Waste Proponents of advertising contend that it familiarizes consumers with products and thereby broadens the market for goods. This encourages not only further capital investment and employment but also large-scale operations that result in low-cost mass production. Critics of advertising reply that it encourages artificial product differentiation among goods that are physically similar and that advertising among competing firms tends to have a canceling effect. This duplication of effort results in a waste of resources, higher product costs, and higher prices. Consequently, any real economies of scale—if they exist—are lost through inefficiencies. This argument of efficiency versus waste is explained further in Exhibit 3.

These arguments indicate the fundamental nature of the controversy. Because both sides make persuasive points, the issues are not likely ever to be resolved.

Monopolistic Competition and Efficiency

From what we already know about the results of perfect competition and monopoly, the more relevant social effects of monopolistic competition may be stated briefly. Note that these effects pertain mainly to efficiency.

Exhibit 3
Advertising and Economies of Scale

Figure (a): In the short run, advertising raises a firm's average total cost curve by the advertising cost per unit. Thus, for the output at M, if the advertising cost per unit is DC, total advertising expenditures are equal to the area of the rectangle $ABCD$.

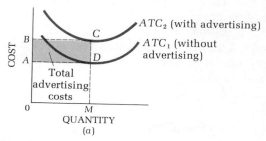

Figure (b): Advertising may also shift a firm's demand curve to the right and raise its long-run average costs. This, in turn, affects the firm's economies of scale. For example, suppose that without advertising the firm would have produced the output at J for a unit cost of JE. Then, as a result of advertising, there may be several possible effects:

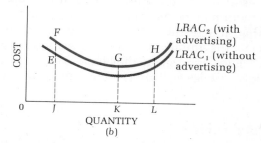

1. Advertising may give the firm economies of scale, enabling it to produce the larger output at K for the lower unit cost KG. This is true even though point G is on a higher $LRAC$ curve than point E.

2. Advertising may have a canceling effect, leaving output unchanged at J and simply increasing unit costs from JE to JF.

3. Advertising may cause diseconomies of scale, causing the firm to produce the output at L for unit costs of LH. This case is not very likely, however, since monopolistic competition results in firms of less than optimum size, as pointed out in the text.

Resource Misallocation

Monopolistically competitive firms determine their production volumes and prices by the $MC = MR$ rule of profit maximization. They therefore *misallocate resources* by restricting outputs and charging higher prices than they would if they adhered to the economically efficient $MC = P$ standard of perfect competition. Note that *this is the same basic criticism that was given for monopoly.* However, in the case of monopolistic competition, the extent of resource misallocation with its associated output restriction and higher prices will depend, in each industry, on the degree of product differentiation and the numer of sellers.

Nonprice Competition

A second consequence of monopolistic competition is that it encourages **nonprice competition.** This consists of methods of competition that do not involve changes in selling price. Examples include advertising, sales promotion, customer services, and product differentiation. Nonprice activities that result in greater innovation and product improvement may be desirable. However, to the extent that they result in higher production costs because of the duplication of resources, excessive style changes, and so on, they tend to cause technical inefficiencies and are therefore undesirable.

Wasteful Excesses

A third adverse consequence is that monopolistically competitive firms create what economists have called the *"wastes" of monopolistic competition.* This refers to the existence of "sick" or inefficient industries. These industries are characterized by chronic excess capacity resulting from too many sellers of differentiated products dividing up markets, operating inefficiently at outputs less than their minimum average costs, and charging higher prices. Examples abound in the retail trades, such as grocery stores, clothing shops, and restaurants. Other examples are found in the light manufacturing industries, such as textiles, shoes, and plastics.

Why do chronically inefficient industries of monopolistic competition continue to exist? There are several reasons. They include relatively low initial capital requirements, little need for financial or marketing knowledge, and the desire to own a business and "be your own boss." As a result, new firms enter the industry as fast as the unprofitable ones leave it, or even faster.

Conclusion: Hotelling's Paradox — More Is Less

Product differentiation is a fundamental characteristic of monopolistic competition. But the nature of the market is such that, in order for products to survive, they can be only minimally different.

For example, why do department stores in the same city usually tend to locate near each other? Why are banks, brokerage firms, and other financial institutions in New York City concentrated in the Wall Street area of lower Manhattan? Why is there a tendency for hotels and restaurants in the same market to offer, within the same price range, similar services and products? And why are there many similar kinds of breakfast cereals, frozen foods, canned goods, soft drinks, cosmetics, and liquor?

The answer to all of these questions is the same. It was demonstrated analytically as long ago as 1929 by a prominent American economist and statistician, Harold Hotelling.

Hotelling's Paradox: Principle of Minimum Differences In order to attract each other's customers, monopolistically competitive firms must make their products as similar to existing products as possible without destroying the differences. Therefore, as a type of market structure, monopolistic competition leads to maximum differentiation of products with minimum differences between them. (NOTE Because the theory of monopolistic competition had not yet been formally developed in 1929, Hotelling's model was based simply on what he called "industries composed of many firms and similar goods.")

Fast Food's Changing Landscape

It's a rough terrain for scores of chains. They must sell more than burgers now to prosper.

By N. R. Kleinfield

COLUMBUS, Ohio   The fast-food industry was born 30 years ago. But it is not an entirely merry 30th anniversary. The ominous news is, no matter how rapidly Americans demolish their meals, there are too many chains, too many similar dreams. "Everyone's jumping into new categories that are doomed to failure, because of the saturation," says Charles Bernstein, editor of Nation's Restaurant News. "How many gourmet hamburger chains are there room for? Probably one."

Michael Culp, a Prudential-Bache analyst who eats many fast-food meals in order to compute an edibility index, predicts unprecedented bloodletting in plastic America over the next two years. "There is a very serious long-term problem," he says. "It's called too much competition."

He and others envision slow but solid growth for the survivors—something like 10 percent a year. But they foresee a handful of powerhouses—the likes of McDonald's, Burger King, Wendy's, Kentucky Fried Chicken, Taco Bell, Pizza Hut—ruling America's roadsides, driving all but the sturdiest of the smaller combatants out of the game. Already the 10 biggest chains serve half of all superfast meals, and their shadows are lengthening over the industry.

Externalities

But the advent of fast food, perhaps, has also cheapened the look of cities and suburbs and corrupted the dining experience. Many argue that it has robbed hamlets of individuality and marred their esthetics, that it has wiped out the conviviality of dining and transformed it into a production-line experience in which the point is to get it done and done quickly.

Everything that can be said about fast food—the ups and the downs, the chicken and the baked potato—can be seen along the boulevards of any average-sized suburb or city just about anywhere in the United States.

The New York Times, April 14, 1985. Copyright © 1985 by the New York Times Company. Reprinted by permission.

Oligopoly: Competition Among the Few

When you drive a car, open a can of tuna fish, replace a light bulb, buy cigarettes, wash your hands with soap, purchase gasoline, type a term paper, or talk on a telephone, you are using products manufactured by oligopolistic industries. An **oligopoly** is an industry composed of a few firms. The industry produces either (1) a homogeneous product, in which case it is called *perfect oligopoly,* or (2) heterogeneous products, in which case it is called *imperfect oligopoly.* Oligopolistic industries are typically characterized by high obstacles to entry. These are usually in the form of substantial capital requirements, the need for technical know-how, patent rights, and the like.

Examples of perfect oligopoly are found primarily among producers of such industrial goods as aluminum, cement, copper, steel, and zinc. These goods are bought by other manufacturers who usually order them by specification. That is, the goods are ordered in a particular form, such as sheet steel, structural steel, or cold-rolled steel of a specific temper (i.e., hardness and plasticity). A specified type of steel is the same whether it is made by U.S. Steel, Bethlehem Steel, Republic Steel, or any other steel company.

Examples of imperfect oligopoly are found among producers of consumer goods. These include automobiles, cigarettes, gasoline, major appliances, soaps and detergents, television tubes, rubber tires, and typewriters.

In both perfect and imperfect oligopolies, the majority of sales go to the "big three" or the "big four" companies in each industry. Can you name the three or four leading firms in some of the oligopolistic industries mentioned above?

Some Characteristics of Oligopolies

In addition to low numbers of sellers, high obstacles to entry, and similar if not identical products, most oligopolistic industries tend to have several other characteristics in common.

Substantial Economies of Scale   Firms in oligopolies typically require large-scale production to obtain low unit costs. If total market demand is sufficient only to support a few large firms of optimum size, competition will ensure that only a few such firms survive.

Growth Through Merger   Many of the oligopolies that exist today have resulted from mergers of competing firms. In some cases, the mergers occurred as long ago as the late nineteenth or early twentieth centuries. In 1901, for example, the U.S. Steel Corporation was formed from a merger of eleven independent steel producers. The purpose, as in most mergers, was to gain a substantial increase in market share, greater economies of scale, larger buying power in the purchase of inputs, and various other advantages that smaller firms did not possess to the same extent.

Mutual Dependence   The low number of sellers in an oligopolistic industry makes it necessary for each seller to consider the reactions of competitors when setting a price. In this sense, the behavior of oligopolists in the marketplace may be somewhat similar to the behavior of players in such games of skill as chess, checkers, and bridge. In these games, the participants try to win by formulating strategies that recognize the possible responses of their opponents.

Price Rigidity and Nonprice Competition   Oligopolistic firms usually find it more comfortable to avoid price competition. These firms may prefer instead to engage in various forms of nonprice competition, such as advertising and customer service, in order to hold, if not increase, their market shares. Price reductions, when they occur, are sporadic. They usually come about only under severe pressures resulting from lessened demand or excessive inventories. These features give rise to a "live and let live" policy in many oligopolistic industries.

Price and Output Determination

With these characteristics as a background, how do oligopolistic firms determine their prices and outputs?

A number of different models may be used to portray various types of oligopolistic situations. One of the most interesting possibilities is demonstrated by the model in Exhibit 4. It illustrates what is commonly known as the **kinked demand curve.** This is a "bent" demand curve, accompanied by a corresponding discontinuous marginal-revenue curve, facing an oligopolistic seller.

Thus, suppose that an oligopoly's current price is at P and its output is at N. When contemplating a change in price, either up or down, the firm must consider how its rivals will react. Hence, management might visualize the firm's demand curve by reasoning in the following way:

If we reduce our price below the level at P, our competition will lose some of their customers to us and this will probably prompt them to match our price cut. Therefore, our sales will increase relatively little following the curve KD. On the other hand, if we increase our price above the level at P, our competitors probably won't match the increase and we'll lose some of our customers to them. Therefore, our sales will fall off rapidly along the curve KL.

In other words, *the kinked demand curve reflects the greater tendency of competitors to follow price reductions than price increases.* Price reductions take sales away from other firms and prompt them to cut prices in retaliation. Price increases do not usually invite such responses, because other firms

Exhibit 4
A Kinked Demand Curve Facing an Oligopolist

Given the kink at *K*, any price reduction below the level at *P* will increase sales slowly along *KD*. This is because other firms will probably match any price cuts.

A price increase above the level at *P* will reduce sales rapidly along *LK* because other firms will probably not match the price rise.

Because marginal cost can fluctuate widely between the points *G* and *H*, the equilibrium price at *P* and output at *N* tend to be stable. However, this model leaves some price uncertainty because it does not explain why the kink happens to occur at the point *K* rather than at some other point.

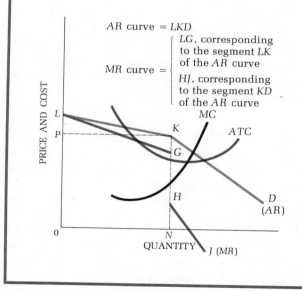

AR curve = *LKD*

MR curve = { *LG*, corresponding to the segment *LK* of the *AR* curve

HJ, corresponding to the segment *KD* of the *AR* curve

will take sales from the firm that raises its price. It follows that the more homogeneous or standardized the product, the sharper the kink. This is because customers will shift more readily and sellers will therefore react more quickly to changes in prices.

As you can see, the large discontinuity in the *MR* curve between the points *G* and *H* permits the *MC*

curve to fluctuate widely within this range. This helps explain why oligopolies exhibit a high degree of price stability. But there is also this seeming paradox:

> The kinked-demand-curve model leaves oligopolists with a considerable degree of price uncertainty. The model demonstrates that once the kink is *given*, the price at that point will tend to be stable. However, it does not say anything about *why* the kink happens to occur where it does instead of at some other point.

Some oligopolies have tried in various ways to reduce the state of uncertainty in which they operate. Two such methods have been collusion and price leadership.

Oligopolies in Collusion

Oligopolists in some industries have occasionally colluded. That is, they have gotten together and agreed on a single industry-wide price that they would all charge. This situation is most probable when the firms in the industry are faced with similar demands, as might occur in a case of perfect oligopoly. The result may then be much the same as in monopoly, except that there is more than one firm. Two interesting models, both illustrated in Exhibit 5, can be employed to demonstrate these possibilities.

Duopoly with Identical Costs

For simplicity, we will assume a case of perfect oligopoly, in which the industry consists of only two firms producing a standardized product. An industry composed of two sellers is also calld a ***duopoly***. It may be either a perfect or an imperfect duopoly, depending on whether the product is standardized or differentiated.

In Figure (*a*), we will further suppose that the products and the prices of the two firms are identical. Therefore, each firm will have a 50 percent chance of selling to any buyer. Hence *the market will be divided equally between the two companies.*

Exhibit 5
Price and Output Determination: Two Oligopolists — A Duopoly Model

In Figure (a), each firm maximizes its profits by adhering to the $MC = MR$ rule. Each firm thus produces an amount equal to N units and charges a price of P per unit. Both firms may also agree to stick to this rule at all times, thereby always charging a single, industry-wide price. This would assure price stability and leave the firms free to engage in nonprice competition.

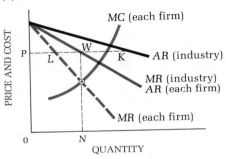

(a) IDENTICAL DEMANDS AND COSTS

In Figure (b), if each firm followed the $MC = MR$ rule, firm X, represented by MC_X, would prefer a price of P. Firm Y, represented by MC_Y, would prefer a price of P'. By colluding, both firms might agree on a price within this range. But through price leadership by firm X, which is the larger firm, firm Y may be willing to adopt firm X's price of P. This policy, like the previous one, would also assure price stability while permitting nonprice competition.

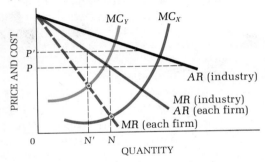

(b) IDENTICAL DEMANDS AND DIFFERENT COSTS

Of course, as is typically the case, the AR curve of the industry will be downward-sloping. At any given price such as the price at P, the quantity sold by each firm will be one-half the industry's total (because each firm is assumed to have 50 percent of the market). Also, you should recall a mathematical rule learned in the study of monopoly. *For all straight-line MR and AR curves, the marginal-revenue curve must bisect any horizontal line drawn from the vertical axis to the average-revenue curve.* Hence the AR curve of each firm corresponds to the MR curve of the industry, and so the distance PW is equal to the distance WK. Similarly, the MR curve of each firm is such that $PL = LW$.

If we assume that the two firms have identical marginal-cost curves, it follows that each firm will maximize its profits by following the $MC = MR$ rule. This means that each firm will produce N units of output and charge a price of P per unit. The two firms might also collude by agreeing not to deviate from the $MC = MR$ rule and to maintain a single-price policy even in the face of changing business conditions.

Duopoly with Different Costs

The identical demand conditions are also shown in Figure (b). Now, however, it is assumed that the two duopolists X and Y have different costs. Thus, duopolist X is a larger-capacity producer than duopolist Y because the marginal-cost curve of firm X, as represented by MC_X, is farther to the right than the marginal-cost curve of firm Y, as represented by MC_Y. This means that, for any given marginal cost, firm X can produce more than firm Y.

In this case, by following the $MC = MR$ rule, firm X will maximize its profit by producing N units and charging a price of P per unit. Firm Y will maximize its profit by producing N' units and charging a price of P' per unit.

The two firms are thus in conflict. If firm X charges its preferred lower price, firm Y *must* charge the same price or else lose sales. If firm Y charges its preferred higher price, firm X need not do the same, in which case firm Y will again suffer the consequences.

Economics in the News

American Airlines Slashes Fares on Many Routes; Industry Stock Prices Slip as Rival Carriers Follow

By Laurie P. Cohen
Staff Reporter of THE WALL STREET JOURNAL

DALLAS—American Airlines slashed certain fares on many routes, upsetting its competitors and sending airline stocks sharply lower.

American is offering new discount fares that would be about 70% below coach fares on more than 2,400 routes.

The new low fares aren't likely to be used by business travelers, who usually book trips less than thirty days in advance and pay full coach fares. They are aimed, American said, at encouraging more pleasure travel by people who might not have flown otherwise.

Competitors and analysts see American's strategy as an aggressive attempt to muscle weaker carriers out of its markets and fuel its own expansion. American, however, said its move was designed solely to generate new traffic.

The fare move by American, which it said would make it "fully competitive with anything being offered" by low-cost carriers, was immediately matched by several major competitors, including Chicago-based United Airlines, New York-based Trans World Airlines, Minneapolis-based Northwest Airlines, Atlanta-based Delta Air Lines, New York-based Pan American World Airways and Los Angeles-based Western Airlines. People Express said it wouldn't be matching the fares, which in some cases are lower than those already offered by the Newark, New Jersey-based discount carrier.

What will the two firms do? They might collude by agreeing on a single price for both, thereby avoiding an uncomfortable price war. The agreed-upon price may be at P, or at P', or at some price in between. And it may be a price that is profitable for both firms as long as each is earning at least normal profits.

In practice, a number of real-world factors can reduce the tendency toward collusion. They include:

- The antitrust laws (to be studied in a later chapter), which make such behavior illegal.

- A large number of firms in an industry—because the larger the number, the harder it may be for sellers to "get together."

- A wide range of product differentiation—because greater differentiation makes collusion more difficult.

Despite these obstacles to collusion, cases of it are often uncovered by the government.

Oligopolistic firms need not formally agree on a mutually satisfactory price, as concluded above with respect to Exhibit 5, Figure (b). It is possible instead that firm Y might accept a policy of **price leadership.** This is a situation in which all firms in an oligopolistic industry adhere, often tacitly and without formal agreement, to the pricing policies of one of its members. Usually, but not always, the price leader will be the largest firm in the industry, and other firms in the industry will simply go along with the leader.

Thus, in Figure (b) firm X, which is the largest of the two, would probably be the price leader. It could therefore set a price at P to maximize its own profit, and firm Y would follow the leader by charging the same price. This policy avoids unprofitable price wars, and it is not regarded as illegal by the courts unless it is proved to be the result of collusion or other monopolistic practices. It also leaves the price followers earning at least normal, although not maximum, profits. This explains why price leadership has at one time or another been a widespread practice in most oligopolistic industries. Examples include cigarettes, steel, farm equipment, newsprint, tin cans, lead, sulfur, and sugar.

Oligopoly and Efficiency

Oligopoly is a major form of market structure in our economy. What can be said about its social consequences? Unfortunately, the issues are extremely complex and the conclusions are by no means clear-cut. Nevertheless, several aspects of oligopoly are worth noting.

> The fundamental criticism of oligopoly, as a type of market structure, is the same as that of monopoly and monopolistic competition. Oligopoly misallocates resources by restricting output short of the point corresponding to $MC = P$.

With this basic criticism in mind, what are the consequences of oligopoly? A number of studies have come up with the following conclusions.

Concentration and Competition

Oligopolistic industries vary widely in the extent of their market dominance. The degree of market dominance is commonly measured by the **concentration ratio.** This is the percentage of an industry's output (such as sales or value of shipments) accounted for by its four largest firms. (More or fewer firms may be used to calculate a concentration ratio, but the four-firm ratio is the one most commonly employed.)

In some relatively concentrated oligopolistic industries, the "big four" firms are responsible for more than 80 percent of the industry's sales. Examples are the aluminum, flat glass, and breakfast-cereal industries. In a number of less concentrated oligopolistic industries, such as the construction equipment, television picture tube, and tire industries, the concentration ratios are considerably below 80 percent.

Are industries with high concentration ratios less competitive than industries with low ones? Not necessarily. A concentration ratio only provides an indication of market dominance by an industry's largest group of firms. It says nothing about the *intensity* of competition between firms or about the possibility that a high ratio may result from product innovation and low prices.

Economies of Scale and Lower Costs

As stated above, the basic criticism of oligopoly is output restriction and higher prices. Does this mean that a particular oligopoly produces less, or has higher unit costs and prices, than a perfectly competitive industry would have if it produced the same product?

Once again the answer is *not necessarily.* In some oligopolistic industries, technology may be such that economies of scale are very important, as they are in automobile and steel production. The firms in such industries achieve larger outputs and lower long-run unit costs than they would if their industries were perfectly competitive. An automobile manufacturer, for example, could not gain significant reductions in unit costs without the technology and economies of assembly-line mass production. These, in turn, would not be possible if the manufacturer were required to share the market with numerous competitors.

High Concentration and Lower, More Stable Prices

It has been traditionally assumed that large oligopolies are a chief cause of higher prices in high-concentration industries. It has also long been assumed that the largest firms in such industries are prone to increase their prices when economic conditions permit. Are these assumptions borne out by the facts? Several studies done by leading scholars have come up with two surprising sets of findings.

First, high concentration ratios may be a result of lower prices, not a cause of higher ones as has usually been believed. The reason is that in many oligopolistic industries, the largest firms are often the ones that gained their position by maintaining the lowest prices. In such industries, lower prices have actually been a *cause* of high concentration.

Second, the overall level of prices tends to be more stable in high-concentration industries than it does in low-concentration industries. Moreover, there is no evidence that the largest firms in high-concentration industries increase their prices more frequently than the largest firms in low-concentration industries.

Profitability and Economies of Scale

The relation between profitability and economies of scale has also been the subject of some investigations. The evidence indicates that, among large oligopolies, profitability is influenced more by economies of scale than by market power (that is, price-raising ability). Firms with substantial economies of scale and limited market power tend to be more profitable than firms with limited economies of scale and substantial market power.

Contestable Markets and Ease of Exit

An implicit requirement of perfect competition is ease of entry. This condition opens the market to competition, helping to assure efficiency. Does this mean that high-concentration industries with steep entry barriers cannot operate efficiently? The answer depends on the "contestability" of their markets.

A **contestable market** is one that is characterized by ease of exit — the ability to leave the market with little cost. Under such circumstances, companies already in the market are under pressure to maintain a low-price policy. This discourages outsiders from swooping in, capturing some of the industry's profits, and getting out quickly. Trucking and airlines provide good examples of contestable markets. Although the required investment in trucks and planes is high, these assets are both mobile and readily resalable.

Countervailing Power and Offsetting Influences

The economic influence of oligopoly may be somewhat offset by the growth of **countervailing power**. This term means that the growth of market power by one group may stimulate a reaction by another group on the other side of the market that offsets the influence of the first group. For instance, large labor unions have grown up to face oligopolistic industries across the bargaining table. Chain stores have emerged to deal with large processing and manufacturing firms. And the government has grown larger, partly in response to the growth of big business and big labor. Countervail-

ing power therefore has some favorable competitive effects within the economy. However, it is not equally effective in all oligopolistic industries.

Research and Development

Oligopolistic industries are more progressive in research and development (R&D) than perfectly competitive industries. The evidence shows, however, that oligopolistic industries tend to be considerably more progressive in development than in research. This is because it is usually more profitable to leave the job of product creation to independent inventors, research firms, and universities, so that limited funds can be used to finance product improvement and marketing.

Conclusion: Learning to Love Oligopolies

Oligopoly is subject to the same basic criticism as monopoly and monopolistic competition. The criticism is that it results in *resource misallocation* caused by output restriction and higher prices. However:

There is growing recognition that oligopolies are much more efficient than has been traditionally believed. Summarizing the major evidence from recent studies:

- High concentration ratios can result from innovation and low prices, and are not necessarily indicative of market power.

- Economies of scale play a more important role than market power in bringing about higher profitability, lower prices, and price stability.

- Contestable markets and countervailing power reduce the market independence of large oligopolies, while their R&D expenditures contribute significantly to our standard of living.

On the basis of these findings, there is considerable agreement that the offsetting benefits of oligopolies are much greater than has customarily been assumed.

Economics in the News

Crumbling Cartel
OPEC's Old Iron Grip On World's Oil Prices Becomes Ever Weaker

Yamani Concedes the Group No Longer Can Set Price

By Youssef M. Ibrahim
Staff Reporter of THE WALL STREET JOURNAL

After the days of luxury,
  we have become
A lamb in the midst of the jungle.
Like a gang, the wolves of the market
Swirl around us.

—Manel Saeed ai Otaiba,
Oil Minister,
United Arab Emirates

GENEVA, Switzerland—The Organization of Petroleum Exporting Countries has lost another round in the world-wide struggle over oil prices. The winners are the burgeoning free market in petroleum and oil consumers around the world.

Half to two-thirds of the oil sold globally every day is transferred at free-market prices that are at least $2 to $3 a barrel below OPEC's official benchmark price. And OPEC's share of the oil being sold in the non-Communist world has plunged to about one-third of the total volume from its 1979 high of about two-thirds.

A Dramatic Change

In OPEC's heyday, the oil ministers of its 13 member countries met twice a year for a day or so, dictated world oil prices and went home. Now, under pressure from the world oil markets, they are hurling accusations at each other and have been breaking agreements as fast as they make them. Mr. Yamani, the cartel's most powerful oil minister and its chief tactician [has conceded] that, a decade after seizing control of global oil markets, OPEC can't set prices any longer.

The worst damage to OPEC has been self-inflicted. As cartels go, OPEC has been a miserable flop.

Squeezed by falling demand and hard-pressed for cash, OPEC members began breaking ranks three years ago. Iran, Ecuador, the UAE, Qatar and Algeria, among others, instituted their own under-the-table discounts to sell oil below OPEC-mandated prices.

With little support forthcoming, most Saudi and industry sources say Saudi Arabia has nearly reached the limits of its patience and is ready to use what Saudis call "shock therapy": a price war that would shock everyone, from Britain and Norway to OPEC members, into returning to discipline. Such a policy option is being studied in earnest, by all accounts, in Riyadh, the Saudi capital.

Do Firms Really Maximize Profits?

The study of business behavior under imperfect competition is now completed. It is appropriate to ask: Do firms really strive to maximize profits as economic theory assumes? In other words, do managers actually behave the way the theory says they do, equating their MCs and MRs?

This question often comes up in discussions of politics, labor-management relations, and other matters of current social and economic interest. To arrive at an answer, we have to look closely at three classes of problems involving profit maximization. These are (1) definitional problems, (2) measurement problems, and (3) environmental problems.

Definitional Problems: Which Concept of Profit?

It is easy to define profit as total revenue minus total cost. But is this all there is to the concept of profit? The answer is not as simple as it may seem, because business executives do not always know whether they are seeking to maximize short-run profit or long-run profit. Nor do executives always view the approach to profit management in the same way. As a result of these *definitional* problems, it becomes difficult to state unequivocally that firms in the real world either do or do not strive to maximize their profits.

For example, firms frequently adopt policies that may reduce short-run profits but that are designed to establish a better long-run situation. Illustrations of this type of policy include (1) costly research and development programs for creating new products and new markets, and (2) employee benefits aimed at developing long-run loyalties. At the same time, these very same firms may exploit short-run market situations to the fullest advantage at the risk of adversely affecting their profitability in the long run.

Measurement Problems: Which Indicator of Profit?

The problems of defining the concept of profit are closely tied to the problems of measuring it. Economic theory assumes that businesses know their marginal costs and marginal revenues and can adjust their outputs to the most profitable levels — the levels at which $MC = MR$.

But in a dynamic economic environment, where changes in technology, tastes, and other underlying forces constantly influence costs and demands, a firm's executives cannot possibly have a precise understanding of how changes in output will affect costs and revenues. At best, executives may be able to gain a rough idea of costs at a few "typical" or standard volumes of output. But even this would be of relatively limited value as a guide to profit maximization in the manner described by economic theory.

As a result of these and other difficulties, business firms in imperfect competition do not, as economic theory assumes, set prices with full knowledge of their marginal costs and marginal revenues. Instead, managers establish prices on the basis of experience, trial and error, and the customs and practices of the industry of which they are a part. And

prices are not usually set with the direct objective of maximizing profits. Rather, pricing strategies often aim at attaining other objectives, including the following, which may (or may not) indirectly maximize profits:

- To achieve a certain target or percentage return on investment.

- To stabilize the firm's prices and outputs over a period of time long enough to permit effective planning of production and resource utilization.

- To achieve a certain target or percentage share of the market.

- To meet or match the prices of competitors.

None of these objectives is a substitute for profit maximization. All, however, influence a firm's net revenue, and all are usually easier for executives to use as practical guides for profit management and control. In studies of pricing practices of large corporations, it has been found that the first of the goals listed above is dominant, but that the others also play important roles.

Environmental Conditions: Reasons for Limiting Profits

A firm may actively avoid maximizing its short-run profits for long-run reasons. Four such practical long-run considerations may be noted as follows.

1. To Discourage Competitive Entry If a company has a moderately strong market position, management may prefer lower profits in order to discourage potential competitors from entering the industry. In this case a long-run price policy that is in line with the rest of the industry will be more advantageous to the firm than one that exploits current market conditions for immediate profit.

2. To Discourage Antitrust Investigation Profits are one of a number of criteria used by the government as evidence of firms' illegal monopolistic market control. This can seem somewhat paradoxical in view of the previous consideration. On the one hand, management may maintain lower profits in

Leaders in Economics

Harvard University News Office

Edward H. Chamberlin
1899–1967

Ramsey & Musprat

Joan Robinson
1903–1983

The theory of monopolistic competition had its origin in the early 1930s. Prior to that time there was only a theory of perfect competition and a theory of monopoly.

In the United States, the person responsible for the development of the theory was a professor at Harvard University, Edward Chamberlin. His distinguished treatise, *The*

Theory of Monopolistic Competition, was published in 1933.

In the same year, quite independently (the two were unknown to each other), an eminent economist at Cambridge University in England, Joan Robinson, published a volume entitled *The Economics of Imperfect Competition*. This book and Chamberlin's formed the basis of what we know today about economic behavior in monopolistically competitive markets.

Both authors stressed the joint influence of competitive and monopolistic elements in the determination of equilibrium. They pointed out that the distinguishing characteristics of imperfect markets are product differentiation and consumer preferences. In such markets, each firm is a "partial" monopoly, regardless of the number of competitors in its industry.

order to exclude competitors and thereby strengthen its monopoly control. Yet the federal government's prosecutors may sometimes consider high profits, not low profits, as one of several indexes of monopoly power.

3. To Restrain Union Demands Reducing the possibility of having to pay higher wages is another factor prompting management to restrain profits. This is particularly applicable in industries with strong labor unions. As long as the economy is prosperous and profits are rising, unions can more easily demand higher wages without inflicting damage on the firm. But if, in a recession, prices are falling faster than wages, the profit margin is squeezed at both ends. Those companies that

curbed wage increases in the beginning would then be in a better position to cope with changing market conditions.

4. To Maintain Consumer Goodwill Management may choose to limit profits in order to preserve good customer relations. Consumers frequently have their own ideas of "fair" prices, and some firms make conscious efforts to identify and adhere to those prices.

Conclusion: Maximize or "Satisfice"?

The profit problem is complex. This makes it extremely difficult to state unequivocally that firms in

UPI/Bettmann Newsphotos

Herbert A. Simon
1916 –

Decision Doctor's R$_X$: "Satisfice,"
Not Maximize

The Nobel Prize is not awarded in the fields of psychology, sociology, public administration, computer science, or applied mathematics. If the award were granted in any of these disciplines, Herbert Simon would be a strong prospect. Instead, the retired professor from Pittsburgh's Carnegie-Mellon University is a recipient of the 1978 Nobel Prize in Economic Science.

Decision Theorist

Simon, an authority on the mental processes of decision making, has criticized the traditional belief that firms seek to obtain maximum profits. In the modern corporation, he points out, decision making is diffused among many departments and individuals. This often leads to conflict and dissension, not harmony. Therefore, corporate policy makers are forced to make decisions without enough accurate information to maximize profits. As a result, they aim for "satisfactory" profits rather than maximum profits. They seek to *satisfice* rather than maximize.

Most economists have found it difficult to accept this view. They prefer to adhere to the traditional notion that firms seek to maximize profits. Otherwise, many of the conclusions and policy decisions that emerge from economists' models, both in industry and in government, would be difficult to justify.

---

imperfect competition do or do not seek to maximize profits. Perhaps in reality they do not seek to maximize but to **"satisfice."** What this means is that firms may often try to attain targets of satisfactory performance. These may include a specific rate of return on investment, a particular share of the market, or a defined average annual growth of sales.

However:

In economic theory, it is always *assumed* that the firm's underlying objective is to maximize profit. The reason is that this assumption, as already shown, enables us to evaluate the social performance of the firm as a resource allocator.

What You Have Learned

1. Monopolistic competition exists in industries characterized by many firms producing heterogeneous products. Product differentiation, which is largely a matter of buyers' perceptions, is thus a key factor among firms in such industries. Monopolistically competitive industries are a major segment of our economy.

2. The $MC = MR$ principle serves as a guide for profit maximization in monopolistic competition. Because there is reasonable freedom of entry, firms will *tend* to earn approximately normal profits in the long run, but there may be exceptions.

3. Advertising plays a major role in monopolistic competition because of the importance of product differentiation. The pros and cons of advertising have centered

around three major issues: information versus persuasion; competition versus concentration; efficiency versus waste.

4. Monopolistic competition is subject to the same basic criticism as monopoly: Resource misallocation resulting from output restriction and higher prices. This is due to adherence to the $MC = MR$ standard rather than the $MC = P$ standard of production and pricing. In addition, monopolistic competition encourages nonprice competition, which may or may not be undesirable, and it results in "wastes" as well as the perpetuation of industries that are overcrowded and inefficient.

5. Oligopolistic industries consist of several firms producing either homogeneous products (perfect oligopoly) or heterogeneous products (imperfect oligopoly). These industries play a major role in our economy. Oligopolistic firms usually tend to be characterized by substantial economies of scale, a history of growth through merger, mutual dependence, price rigidity, and nonprice competition.

6. The $MC = MR$ principle applies to oligopolistic firms that seek to maximize profit. In addition, each firm may see itself as being faced with a kinked demand curve, indicating that competitors will follow a price decrease by any one seller, but not a price increase.

7. The kinked demand curve results in a stable price, but it leaves the seller uncertain about the determination of the price. This has prompted oligopolists to reduce price uncertainty either by colluding with competitors or by accepting one of the competitors as a price leader and matching that firm's price.

8. Oligopolies are subject to the same basic criticism as monopolies: they result in resource misallocation caused by output restriction and higher prices. This is due to their adherence to the $MC = MR$ standard rather than the $MC = P$ standard of production and pricing. However, there is growing evidence that oligopolies are more efficient, and that their social costs are therefore less significant, than has been traditionally assumed.

9. It is difficult to state unequivocally that firms in imperfect competition either do or do not seek to maximize profits. In reality, it is quite likely that they strive to "satisfice" rather than to maximize. Nevertheless, the assumption of profit maximization is fundamental in microeconomic theory because it permits an evaluation of the social function of the firm as a resource allocator.

Terms and Concepts To Review

imperfect competition	kinked demand curve
monopolistic	duopoly
competition	price leadership
selling costs	concentration ratio
nonprice competition	contestable market
"wastes" of	countervailing power
monopolistic	"satisfice"
competition	
Hotelling's paradox	
oligopoly	

For Discussion

1. Firms in monopolistic competition tend to be only normally profitable in the long run. The same is true of firms in perfect competition. Therefore, why criticize monopolistic competition?

2. Why should firms in monopolistic competition spend so much money on advertising if much of it has canceling effects?

3. Is the kinked demand curve an objective fact of the marketplace, or is it a subjective phenomenon in the mind of each oligopolist? Explain.

4. Why is there a tendency toward some type of externally imposed price decision in oligopoly? What are some examples?

5. The need for self-protection is one reason often given for the rise of labor unions, consumer cooperatives, and agricultural cooperatives. Can you explain why in the light of this chapter?

6. One could easily argue that, because it is more *ethical* for people to cooperate than to compete, the same standard should apply to business firms. Do you agree?

7. "Economic theory is unrealistic because it assumes that firms seek to maximize profits. Yet we know that in reality this assumption is not a valid one." Evaluate this statement.

8. Are prices determined by costs of production or are costs of production determined by prices? Discuss. (SUGGESTION Think in terms of both perfect and imperfect competition.)

9. **Case Problem: Saturn Publishing Co.** Saturn Publishing Co. publishes two monthly magazines, called *Ac-*

tion and *Brisk.* The company charges the same price for both magazines, but the sales of *Brisk* are about twice those of *Action.* Both magazines are among the leaders in their field, with combined sales of 5 to 6 million copies per month. In this sales range, the marginal cost of producing the two magazines is practically constant. Further, it has been established, on the basis of previous pricing experiments in various markets, that the elasticity of demand is equal for the two magazines at the present price.

Recently, the president of the company posed the question of whether it is consistent with profit maximization for the two magazines to carry the same price. The sales manager replied that, in order for Saturn to maximize its profits, it ought to charge a higher price for *Brisk* than for *Action,* since demand is greater for the former.

The president has called you in as a consulting economist to settle the question. Both the president and the sales manager studied a considerable amount of economics while in college and both are fairly familiar with such concepts as average revenue, marginal revenue, and marginal cost. Can you provide them with an analytical (graphic) solution to the problem?

10. In the book publishing business, it is inherent in the royalty arrangement that the publisher's pricing policy results in an economic conflict between the author and the publisher. Thus, in the great majority of cases, the author's royalty is a percentage of the total revenue that the publisher receives on the sale of the book. The publisher, however, determines the price of the book (and also incurs all costs of manufacturing, promotion, and distribution). It follows that *the price that maximizes profit for the publisher is higher, and the output lower, than the price and output that maximize royalty payments for the author.* Why? Demonstrate this proposition graphically, using marginal analysis.

11. **Case Problem: Scrumptious Pizza Co.** Scrumptious Pizza Co. operates a chain of pizza parlors on a franchise basis. The company maintains a closely controlled, uniform set of production standards and selling prices as a condition for granting franchises. One of the unique features of Scrumptious pizzas is that they are made with a special blend of fine imported cheeses.

Recent cost increases of cheeses, dough, and other ingredients have made it necessary for the company to consider a revision of its pricing and product policies for all its franchises. Three alternatives have been proposed:

(a) Increase price by some specified percentage, but maintain quantity and quality.

(b) Reduce quantity by some specified percentage, but maintain price and quality.

(c) Reduce quality, but maintain price and quantity.

The company hired an economic consulting firm to estimate the effects on profits of each of these choices. In its report, the consulting firm submitted the following *payoff matrix.* This is a table showing the probable level of profit that will result from each alternative and its associated sales level.

Alternatives, profits, and probabilities	Average daily pizza sales			
	6,000	7,000	8,000	9,000
Alternative A				
Profit	$2,000	$2,800	$4,000	$4,200
Probability*	0.15	0.25	0.30	0.30
Alternative B				
Profit	$1,500	$3,000	$5,000	$5,100
Probability*	0.25	0.25	0.40	0.10
Alternative C				
Profit	$1,200	$2,500	$4,500	$4,800
Probability*	0.05	0.05	0.40	0.50

* The probability of an outcome is the likelihood of its occurrence. It can be expressed as a percentage by multiplying by 100.

For example, suppose that the company chooses alternative A and that its average daily sales are 6,000 pizzas. Then its *expected profit* on those sales will be 15 percent of $2,000, or $300. On the other hand, if its sales are 7,000, its expected profit will be 25 percent of $2,800, or $700. By extending this idea, you can see that the total expected profit of any alternative is simply the sum of the separate expected profits that comprise it. (Notice that for each alternative, the probabilities must add to 1.0, or 100 percent.)

(a) Which alternative should the company choose, assuming that it wants to maximize its profit?

(b) Which alternative should the company choose in order to maximize its sales?

(c) Is it possible to have a situation in which one alternative would maximize profit and another would maximize sales, or must the same alternative do both? Explain.

chapter 25

Hiring the Factors of Production: Marginal Productivity and Income Distribution

Learning Guide

Watch for answers to these important questions

What considerations determine a firm's decision to hire factors of production? Are there fundamental principles determining the price paid for a factor of production?

How do you distinguish between a change in demand for a factor of production and a change in the quantity demanded? What determines the former? What determines the latter? How do these affect the elasticity of demand?

What is the equilibrium condition, or equation, that expresses a firm's minimum cost in the input market? What is the equilibrium condition, or equation, for maximum profit?

How does the marginal-productivity theory serve as a guide for equitable income distribution in a pure capitalistic system? What are the difficulties of employing the theory for this purpose?

Until now we have focused on the behavior of firms in the *output* markets. We have done this by examining the principles of product pricing and production under the three main types of market conditions—perfect competition, monopoly, and imperfect competition.

But to produce their products, firms must buy factors of production. Therefore we must also examine the behavior of firms in the *input* markets. This chapter establishes microeconomic principles pertaining to the input side of the market rather than the output side. As you will soon see, the most interesting aspect of input principles is the way in which they parallel the principles that you learned about earlier. As a result, the various pieces will fit together like those of a large jigsaw puzzle.

The Marginal-Productivity Theory: How the Firm Buys Factors of Production

If you were a business executive, what principles would guide you in deciding how much of a resource you should purchase? After all, buying too little can be just as unprofitable as buying too much. A major problem facing a firm that wishes to maximize its profits is to utilize precisely the right combination of inputs. In order to do this, management must understand the nature of its demand for resources.

The demand for any resource is a ***derived demand.*** That is, the demand for a resource is based on what a particular factor of production contributes to the product for which it is used. For example, the demand for steel is derived in part from the demand for automobiles. The demand for land in the heart of a city is derived from the demand for the office buildings and stores that will be built upon it. The demand for college professors is derived mostly from the demand for education as measured by college enrollments. As a general rule, and as you will see shortly, the concept of derived demand embraces the following principles:

Other things being equal, the quantity of a factor of production that a firm demands will depend on three things:

1. The productivity of the factor.

2. The value or price of the product that the factor is used to make.

3. The price of the factor relative to the prices of other factors.

These principles make a good deal of practical sense. For instance, they tell you the following (all other things remaining constant):

1. An increase in the output of a factor of production relative to its input will result in an increase in the demand for that factor by the firms that use it.

2. If improvements in a product or reductions in its price create a greater demand for it, the need for the factors that produce or use that commodity will also increase. *Example:* computers and computer programmers.

3. If a factor of production becomes cheaper relative to other factors, the quantity of the lower-priced factor demanded will increase as producers begin to substitute it for the more expensive inputs. *Example:* labor-saving machinery relative to high-cost labor.

Physical Inputs, Outputs, and Revenues

The table in Exhibit 1 provides a more precise understanding of a firm's demand for an input. The first three columns illustrate the familiar law of variable proportions, which you learned in the study of production. They show how the total and marginal physical products change when a variable input such as labor is applied to fixed inputs such as land and capital.

The remaining columns of the table convert these physical data into revenues. In these columns, the assumption has been made that the firm is perfectly competitive in the sale of the product to which the variable factor is contributing. This is why the price of the product [column (4)] is assumed to be constant at $10 per unit.

The last two columns of the table are based upon the total revenue figures [column (5)]. They introduce two new terms. The first is ***marginal revenue product*** (MRP), defined as the change in total revenue resulting from a unit change in the variable input. The second is ***average revenue product*** (ARP), which is the ratio of total revenue to the quantity of the variable input employed.

Because the firm is operating under perfect competition in the input market, the supply of labor resources is so large that the firm cannot influence the price by buying or not buying. The firm can purchase as many units as it wants at the given price. Hence, *the marginal cost of the resource will be the same as its price.*

The Most Profitable Level of Input

When the revenue data from the table in Exhibit 1 are graphed, they yield the curves shown in the figures. In this case, because we want to relate the firm's revenues to the quantity of labor input, it is

Exhibit 1
Demand for a Resource by a Firm

(assuming perfect competition in the output market and perfect competition in the input market)

Figure (a): The most profitable input level occurs where the distance between the TR and TC curves is a maximum. This is where a tangent to the TR curve is parallel to the TC curve. (For example, at $20 per person, the most profitable input is 4 persons, because this is the input at which the tangent at D is parallel to the straight-line TC_1 curve.)

    Figure (b): By following the vertical dashed lines downward, you can see that the most profitable input also occurs where the marginal cost of the factor (MCF) or its price (P_F) equals its marginal-revenue product (MRP). Therefore, given the marginal costs or prices of the factors of production, the firm will maximize its profits by hiring each factor of production up to the point where its $MCF = P_F = MRP$. The firm's demand curve for an input is thus the MRP curve up to the maximum point on the ARP curve. As the price of the input falls, the firm hires more of it by following its MRP curve. (NOTE The MRP curve, like the marginal curves in previous chapters, is plotted to the midpoints between the integers on the horizontal axis. This is because the curve reflects the change in total revenue from one unit of input to the next.)

    (See also the technical note beneath the table.)

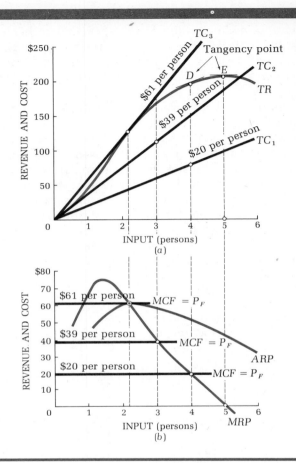

easier to plot the revenue curves against input rather than output on the horizontal axis. It also helps simplify matters a bit to assume, as stated in the footnote to column (1) of the table, that there are no fixed costs. That is, the firm's fixed factors of production are available free. This is not a realistic assumption, of course, but it is useful for getting to the heart of the matter. This assumption means that the firm's total variable costs are the same as its total costs. Therefore, the TC curve emanates from the origin of the figure rather than from a point higher up on the vertical axis.

What is the most profitable level of input for the firm? The answer depends on the *marginal cost of the input as compared with its marginal revenue product.* In other words, the answer depends on the amount each additional unit of the input adds to the firm's total cost as compared to the amount it adds to the firm's total revenue.

For example, Figure (a) shows that, when the marginal cost or price of labor is $20 per person, the most profitable input level is 4 persons. At this input the TC_1 curve in the figure is parallel to a tangent drawn to the TR curve at D. At the same time, Figure (b) shows that at this level of input the marginal cost of the factor (MCF), which is the same

(1) Units of variable factor, F (labor)*	(2) Total physical product, TPP	(3) Marginal physical product, MPP $\dfrac{\text{Change in (2)}}{\text{Change in (1)}}$	(4) Product price, P	(5) Total revenue, TR $(2) \times (4)$	(6) Marginal-revenue product, MRP $\dfrac{\text{Change in (5)}}{\text{Change in (1)}}$	(7) Average-revenue product, ARP $(5) \div (1)$
0	0		$10	$ 0		$?
		4			$40	
1	4		10	40		40.0
		8			80	
2	12		10	120		60.0
		5			50	
3	17		10	170		56.7
		3			30	
4	20		10	200		50.0
		1			10	
5	21		10	210		42.0
		−1			−10	
6	20		10	200		33.3

* Labor is assumed to be the only variable input. All other inputs are fixed and are available free. Therefore, total (labor) cost equals total variable cost.

TECHNICAL NOTE (OPTIONAL) Here is a simple explanation of the graphs in geometric terms. Each MCF curve in the lower figure is a graph of the *slope* of its corresponding TC curve in the upper figure. Likewise, the MRP curve in the lower figure is a graph of the *slope* of the TR curve in the upper figure. The input at which the slopes are equal (or at which a tangent in the upper figure is parallel to a TC curve) is the one at which net profit is maximized. You can verify these profit-maximizing principles by following the vertical dashed lines downward at each level of input.

as the price of the factor (P_F), is equal to its marginal revenue product MRP.

Similarly, at $39 per person, the firm's most profitable input is 3 persons. This is again determined in Figure (b), where $MCF = P_F = MRP$. On the other hand, if the factor were available free, the most profitable input level would be 5 persons, because the TC curve in Figure (a) would lie along the horizontal axis and would be parallel to a horizontal tangent drawn at the peak of the TR curve at E.

Finally, at $61 per person, the firm would just be covering its variable costs, because TC_3 is tangent to TR. Hence, the most profitable input would, theo-

retically, be 2.2 persons. This is again determined in Figure (b), where $MCF = P_F = MRP$. (NOTE If you dislike the idea of measuring "fractions of persons," you can think of the horizontal axis as being scaled in terms of hours of labor time instead of numbers of persons.)

Because the MCF or P_F line tells you the number of workers available to the firm at the particular wage, it is a *supply* curve of labor. The firm is thus faced with a horizontal supply curve of the factor in the input market just as it is faced with a horizontal demand curve for its product in the output market.

Two Important Principles

Two important principles follow directly from these marginal concepts. As you will see in the following paragraphs:

> When there is perfect competition in the input market, the marginal cost of an input will be the same as its price. Therefore:
>
> 1. The firm's demand curve for an input will be its MRP curve below the maximum point of its ARP.
>
> 2. The firm will maximize its profits by purchasing factors of production up to the point at which $MCF = P_F = MRP$.

By this time you may have noticed a certain symmetry between the input and output markets. For example, the two input propositions above are analogous to two output propositions that you learned a few chapters earlier in the study of perfect competition. As you will recall:

1. A perfectly competitive firm's MC curve is its supply curve above the minimum point on its AVC curve.

2. A perfectly competitive firm maximizes its profit by producing to the level at which its $MC = P = MR$.

In order to visualize the symmetry between the input market and the output market, try to imagine what the curves in Figure (b) of Exhibit 1 would look like if the diagram were flipped upside down on its horizontal axis. Or, if you have trouble visualizing this, try turning the book upside down and looking through the back of the page while holding it up to the light. You will see that the ARP and MRP curves resemble the AVC and MC curves of a firm in perfect competition. This suggests that there is a symmetry, in the theory of perfect competition, between the input market and the output market. *Indeed, the curves in one market are the reciprocals of the corresponding curves in the other market.*

In economic terms, why does the firm maximize its profit at the input level at which $MCF = P_F = MRP$? Because at any input less than this the added cost of an additional unit is less than the added revenue, so it pays to hire another unit. At any input greater than this, the opposite is true. Therefore, the fundamental principle of profit maximization—the $MC = MR$ rule, which you learned in previous chapters—applies here as well. In addition, a principle of fundamental importance can now be stated:

> In competitive input markets, the price paid to hire a factor of production will equal its marginal productivity. Therefore, the owners of each factor will be paid the value of what their factor contributes. This is called the ***marginal-productivity theory of income distribution.***

Demand for Inputs

You learned in the study of supply and demand that the market demand curve for a product is derived by summing the individual demand curves of all buyers in the market. A parallel situation exists in the market for inputs. Other things remaining the same, the market demand curve for a factor is derived by summing the individual demands or MRP curves of all firms in the market. Like any other demand curve, this aggregate MRP curve for a factor of production will be subject to two kinds of changes. One kind is *changes in demand*. The other is *changes in the quantity demanded*.

Changes in Demand

The market MRP curve for a given factor may shift from one position to another for several reasons:

- **A Change in Demand for the Final Product** For example, a change in demand for houses will affect the price of houses and may also change the demand for lumber, bricks, carpenters, and other resources.

- **A Change in Productivity** Improvements in the quantity and quality of the fixed factors of production will increase the productivity of the variable factor. Thus, workers who work with more and better machines are more productive than those who do not.

— **A Change in the Prices of Substitute or Complementary Factors** Some resources may be substitutable, some may be complementary, and some may be neither. Labor and machines provide typical examples of all three possibilities. Changes in the price of one relative to the other may encourage firms to use more or less of either or both. The choice depends on the proportions in which they must be used — such as the number of workers needed to operate a machine.

Changes in the Quantity Demanded: Elasticity of Demand for Factor Services

There are also conditions that will determine changes in the quantity demanded of a given factor. As you will recall, these changes represent movements along the curve due to a change in price. Hence, these movements reflect the sensitivity or elasticity of demand for the resource. What determines this elasticity?

— **The Rate of Decline of Marginal Physical Product** The rate at which the *MPP* curve declines as the variable factor is added to the fixed factors depends on the technological nature of the production process. The faster it declines, the more inelastic the resulting *MRP* curve will be and hence the less will be the change in the quantity of input demanded relative to a change in its price.

— **The Elasticity of Demand for the Final Product** The greater the elasticity of demand for the final product, the more elastic the demand for the factors used in making it. For instance, if the demand for a final product is relatively elastic, a small increase in its price will result in a more-than-proportional decrease in the purchase of it. This will cause a relatively large drop in the quantity demanded of the resources that are used to produce it.

— **The Proportion of the Factor's Cost Relative to Total Production Cost** The larger the cost of a factor of production relative to the total cost of the product, the more elastic the demand for the factor. For example, if labor costs are only 10 percent of the cost of a product, a 10 percent wage increase will raise production costs by 1 percent. Hence, the effect on the final price of the product should be small, and the quantity demanded of the factor should be relatively little affected. On the other hand, if labor costs are 90 percent of production costs, a 10 percent wage increase will have a more substantial impact on production costs as well as on final prices and sales. Therefore, the decrease in the quantity demanded of the factor is likely to be relatively large.

— **The Ease of Factor Substitutability** The greater the degree to which different factors can be substituted for one another in a given production process, the greater will be the elasticity of demand for any one of these factors. Thus, if copper, aluminum, and other light metals had equal conductive properties, the demand for each of them by the electrical industry would be highly elastic. But in fact copper is a superior conductor, and hence the demand for it is relatively inelastic within its typical price ranges.

The Optimum Allocation of Inputs

The foregoing principles apply to all factors of production that the firm may purchase. Let us assume that the firm is buying two factors of production, labor and capital, and that these factors are substitutable for one another. There are two questions to be answered:

1. What is the least-cost combination of factors needed to produce a given output?

2. Which combination of factors yields the largest profits to the firm?

The first question is concerned with cost minimization; the second is concerned with profit maximization.

Cost Minimization

If you were a manufacturer interested in producing a certain volume of output, in what proportion would you use the various inputs? The question is important because, although many different combinations will produce a given level of output, only one combination is cheapest. Clearly, the cheapest combination depends on the relative prices of the inputs. As a manager, therefore, you would adhere to the following fundamental principle:

Least-cost principle The least-cost combination of inputs is achieved when a dollar's worth of any input adds as much to total physical output as a dollar's worth of any other input.

To illustrate, suppose that you are buying only two factors of production, A and B, in a perfectly competitive market. Letting MPP_A represent the marginal physical product of A, and P_A the price of A, and similarly for factor B, the equation of minimum cost is

$$\frac{MPP_A}{P_A} = \frac{MPP_B}{P_B} \tag{1}$$

This indicates that, if the price of an input rises, you should use less of it, thereby increasing its marginal product. Simultaneously, you should use more of the other input, thereby decreasing its marginal product. As an example, suppose that P_A and P_B are each $1, and at some given volume of output,

$$MPP_A = 10 \text{ units}$$
$$MPP_B = 8 \text{ units}$$

Assuming that you want to minimize costs at the prescribed output level, you could proceed as follows:

1. Buy $1.00 less of B, thereby reducing production by 8 units.
2. Buy $0.80 more of A, thereby increasing production by 8 units (= ⅘ of the marginal product of a dollar's worth of A).
3. Save $0.20.

This example shows how you would go about minimizing total costs for a given volume of out-

put. Equation (1), of course, can be extended to include any number of inputs and corresponding prices. When all the ratios are equal, total costs are minimized at the established output volume. If a change should then occur in the price of one of the factors, the equality will no longer hold. This means that the cheaper factor will have to be substituted for more expensive ones until equality is restored. These ideas help explain why business firms are always seeking to change the composition of their inputs, replacing more costly ones (such as labor) with less costly ones (such as machines).

Profit Maximization

The second problem concerns the following question: Of all possible factor combinations, which one yields the largest profits for the firm? The answer has already been indicated, and it may now be expressed as a general principle:

Maximum-profit principle The most profitable combination of inputs is achieved by employing each factor of production up to the point at which the marginal cost of the factor is equal to its marginal revenue product.

This principle was demonstrated in Exhibit 1. When the firm is hiring a resource in a perfectly competitive market, it will employ further units of the resource as long as the MRP of the factor is greater than its price (or marginal cost). Why? Because each additional unit adds more to the firm's total revenue than to its total cost. Conversely, the firm will release some units of the resource if the MRP of the factor is less than its price. This is because each reduction of one unit of the input lowers the firm's total cost by more than it lowers total revenue.

These ideas can be summarized with a formula. You know that the firm will maximize profits by hiring units of factor A up to the point at which the marginal revenue product of that factor, MRP_A, is equal to its price, P_A:

$$MRP_A = P_A$$

If both sides of this equation are divided by P_A (or in

other words, if P_A is "transposed" to the left side), then

$$\frac{MRP_A}{P_A} = 1 \qquad (2)$$

Similarly, the firm will buy units of factor B up to the point at which the marginal-revenue product of that factor, MRP_B, is equal to its price P_B:

$$MRP_B = P_B$$

If you divide both sides by P_B (or transpose P_B to the left side),

$$\frac{MRP_B}{P_B} = 1 \qquad (3)$$

Because each of their ratios is each equal to 1, equations (2) and (3) can be expressed as a single equation for maximum-profit equilibrium:

$$\frac{MRP_A}{P_A} = \frac{MRP_B}{P_B} = 1 \qquad (4)$$

Equation (4), like equation (1) for least cost, can be extended to include any number of inputs and their corresponding prices. In general, equation (4) defines the profit-maximizing or equilibrium conditions of a firm in a perfectly competitive input market. It shows that:

The most profitable level of input for a firm in a perfectly competitive input market is attained when the firm earns the same increment in revenue *per dollar of outlay* from each of the factors that it hires, with each ratio equal to 1. That is, the firm hires each factor up to the point at which the marginal revenue product of the factor equals its price. You can think of the firm as juggling all its factors of production simultaneously until it achieves the desired equilibrium ratio.

Suppose, for example, that a firm is hiring two factors of production, labor L and capital C. If these factors are substitutable for one another, equation (4) says that the company will maximize profits in a perfectly competitive input market by hiring to the point at which

$$\frac{MRP_L}{P_L} = \frac{MRP_C}{P_C} = 1$$

What would happen if this equality did not occur? In other words, suppose the first ratio in this equation were greater than the second and the employment of capital were already in equilibrium at the point at which $MRP_C/P_C = 1$. Then the firm would be earning more of an increment in revenue on its labor relative to the price of labor than it would be earning on its capital relative to the price of capital. Graphically, this means that the firm would be to the *left* of its optimum input point for labor. Hence, it would pay to hire more workers, thereby reducing MRP_L until the ratios were equal.

Conversely, what would happen if the first ratio were less than the second? Graphically, this means that the firm would be to the *right* of its optimum input point for labor. Therefore, it would pay for the company to reduce its number of workers, thereby raising MRP_L until the ratios were again equal.

Marginal Productivity, Income Distribution, and Equity

You have seen that, when there is perfect competition in the input market, each firm will purchase factors of production up to the point at which the price or marginal cost of the factor is equal to its marginal-revenue productivity. This means that the owners of each factor will be paid a value equal to what their factor contributes to the national output. Stated differently, the owners of the factor will be paid what their factor is "worth." This concept, as you have learned, is known as the *marginal-productivity theory of income distribution.*

The theory itself was first introduced near the turn of the present century by a distinguished American economist, John Bates Clark. It was widely supported because it showed that a competitive (capitalistic) system distributed the national output in a socially "just" and "equitable" manner. Over the years, however, economists and social critics have pointed out three fundamental defects in this interpretation.

Leaders in Economics

Historical Pictures Service

John Bates Clark
1847 – 1938
Marginal-Productivity Theory

"It is the purpose of this work to show that the distribution of the income of society is controlled by a natural law. . . . This law, if it worked without friction, would give to every agent of production the amount of wealth which that agent creates."

In these words, J. B. Clark outlined the general plan for his book, *The Distribution of Wealth*, published in 1899. This was the first American work in pure economic theory. Prior to that time, American economists were generally interested in the socioeconomic problems of their period and in the achievement of social reforms. Clark's book was thus a landmark in economic theory.

Marginal Analysis
Clark showed that the level of pay for a firm's workers is determined by the productivity of the marginal worker. A firm, you will recall, will purchase labor up to the point where the cost of an additional unit is equal to what that unit adds to the firm's

revenues. The theoretical last person hired, in accord with this principle, is referred to as the "marginal worker."

Each unit of labor, Clark wrote, "is worth to its employer what the last unit produces. . . . The effective value of any unit of labor is always what the whole society with all its capital produces, minus what it would produce if that unit were to be taken away. This sets the universal standard of pay."

Clark's formulation of the marginal productivity theory, with its impeccable logic, became a standard of equity in economic discussions. It was widely employed by others to support the contention that a (perfectly competitive) capitalistic system distributes incomes in a "just" manner according to what each of the factors contributes.

In later decades, however, the development of the theory of imperfect competition and the growing power of labor unions made some of the unrealistic assumptions of Clark's theory more apparent.

Imperfect Markets   A large part of the market for inputs is imperfect rather than perfect. Thus, certain factors of production tend to be relatively immobile. In some markets there may be only one or a few firms buying inputs instead of a large number of firms. Further, union restrictions, patent controls, tariff barriers, and other limitations also create obstacles to the smoothly functioning input markets envisioned in the competitive model.

Complex Production Processes   Most production processes involve complex interrelations among inputs. Consequently, when a variety of factors are employed, it is usually impossible to divide the total output precisely into the amounts contributed by each class of factors, such as labor and capital.

Normative Versus Positive Standards   Such terms as "just" and "equitable" involve normative rather than positive concepts—what *ought* to be rather than what *is*. Their meanings may also vary from time to time and from place to place according to the customs and beliefs of society. Thus, in a philosophical sense, it is not necessarily "just" that a person who is twice as productive as another should be paid twice as much. It might be argued, for example, that it is "just" for a family of six to receive twice as much as a family of three—regardless of their relative productivities. In other words, the *normative* question of what constitutes a just distribution of income is quite different from the *positive* question of what specific steps can be taken to alter the distribution of income. The former is a philosophical question; the latter is an economic one.

It is appropriate to conclude with an important generalization:

The central idea of the marginal-productivity principle is that an employer will not pay more for a unit of input — whether it be a person, or an acre of land, or a dollar's worth of borrowed capital — than it is worth to the firm. The employer will continue to acquire an input as long as each unit purchased adds more to the firm's total revenue than it adds to its total cost. Because it is assumed that the units can be infinitesimally small, the net result is that the employer's profit is maximized at the point at which the added (or marginal) cost of the input equals its added (or marginal) revenue product.

In short, the marginal-productivity principle is correct in the sense that it can be deduced logically from given assumptions. However, it should be understood for what it is: *a guide for maximizing a firm's profits in the input market under prescribed market conditions.*

What You Have Learned

1. The marginal-productivity theory explains how a firm purchases its inputs in the factor market. In general, a firm's demand for any factor of production is a derived demand. It is based on the productivity of the factor, the price of the final product, and the price of the factor relative to the prices of other factors.

2. The aggregate *MRP* curve for a factor of production is determined by summing the individual *MRP* curves. Like any demand curve, the *MRP* curve is subject to changes in demand for a factor and to changes in the quantity demanded. The latter is based on a change in price and reflects the elasticity of demand for a factor.

3. The least-cost combination of factor inputs requires that the marginal physical product per dollar spent on every factor be equal. The maximum-profit combination of factor inputs requires that the marginal-revenue product per dollar spent on all factors be equal to 1. Both equilibrium conditions can be achieved simultaneously.

4. The marginal-productivity theory of income distribution is a guide for profit maximization in the input market. It cannot say what pattern of income distribution is

"just" or "equitable." That is a normative question based on philosophical rather than economic considerations.

Terms and Concepts To Review

derived demand
marginal-revenue
  product
average-revenue
  product

marginal-productivity
  theory of income
  distribution

For Discussion

1. What analogies do you see between a firm in the output market and a firm in the input market with respect to each of the following: (a) the profit-maximizing rule; (b) marginal cost and average variable cost, and (c) marginal-revenue product and average-revenue product.

2. Distinguish between a change in demand for an input and a change in the quantity demanded. What are the causes of each?

3. "The way to eliminate poverty and unemployment is through minimum-wage legislation. By raising the minimum wage, workers are given more purchasing power. This creates a greater demand for goods and services, thereby putting unemployed people to work." Evaluate this argument using the graphic tools employed in this chapter. (HINT There are *two* issues involved here. Can you identify them?)

4. "The marginal-productivity theory of income distribution is a *fair* theory because it demonstrates that each worker gets what he or she deserves." Evaluate.

5. "It is meaningless to say that the equilibrium factor price will equal the marginal-revenue product, since the latter varies with the number of factor units employed." Comment. Rephrase if necessary.

Chapter 26

Determination of Factor Prices

Learning Guide

Watch for answers to these important questions

Why are there different wage-determination models? Is any one of these models the appropriate one for today?

Is rent a cost or a surplus? How does rent arise?

How is the interest rate determined? What economic function does the interest rate perform?

How is profit determined? What economic function does profit perform?

About three-fourths of our nation's income consists of wages and salaries paid to workers. The rest of the economic pie is sliced into rent, interest, and profit. All four classes of income payments are made to resource owners who sell their factors of production — labor, land, capital, and entrepreneurship — in the economy's markets.

What determines the prices of the factors of production — the levels of wages, rent, interest, and profit? In this chapter we seek answers to these questions by deriving basic principles. You will find that many of the ideas from previous chapters are extremely important. Supply and demand, competition, market structures, cost and demand curves, and the like play an integral role in determining factor prices.

Certain other aspects of factor-price determination, however, are not so apparent. You will find that, although the theories of wages and rent are well established in modern economics, the theories of interest and profit involve some unsettled questions. These questions are the subject of more advanced discussions. We shall not delve into them in much detail, because our purpose at this time is to concentrate on the main features of the various theories rather than on the controversies that surround them.

Theory of Wages

Before analyzing the factors that determine wages, it helps to begin with some definitions.

Wages are the price paid for the use of labor. They are usually expressed as time rates, such as a certain amount per hour, day, or week. Less frequently, they are expressed as piece rates, such as a certain amount per unit of work performed or product produced.

Labor, as defined in economics, means all personal services, including the activities of wage-workers, professional people, and independent businesspeople. Thus, "laborers" are workers of any sort, whether they receive compensation in the form of hourly wages or in the form of annual salaries, bonuses, or commissions. Our interest in this chapter is in wages as defined above, especially in wages expressed as time rates.

Some Wage-Determination Models

How are wages determined in the market at any given time? The answer depends on the type of market model that is assumed to exist in a particular situation. There are several possibilities.

Competitive Model: Many Buyers, Many Sellers

Suppose that there are so many employers hiring a certain type of labor and so many employees selling it that no single employer or employee can influence the wage rate. We would then have a perfectly competitive model of wages, as shown in Exhibit 1.

In Figure (a) the downward-sloping market demand curve for this type of labor represents the sum of the individual *MRPs* (marginal revenue products) of the buyers. The upward-sloping market supply curve reflects the fact that, if these workers are already employed, the firms buying labor will have to offer higher wages to attract workers from other occupations and localities. The equilibrium wage at *W* and the equilibrium quantity at *M* are determined by the intersection of the labor supply and labor demand curves.

In Figure (b) the buying firm is faced with a perfectly elastic supply curve of labor at the market wage. This means that *the firm can buy all the labor it wants at the market wage but cannot buy any at a lower wage.* The horizontal supply curve represents the marginal cost or price of the factor (*MCF*), as you learned earlier in the study of marginal-productivity analysis. Since the firm's most profitable level of input is obtained by following the *MCF = MRP* rule, management will hire N units of labor at the corresponding market wage of W per unit.

What analogies do you see between this model and that of a perfectly competitive seller in the output market?

Exhibit 1
A Competitive Model of Wage Determination

In the perfectly competitive market of Figure (a), the wage at W and the corresponding quantity at M for a particular type of labor are determined through the free interaction of supply and demand. As a result, any firm in Figure (b) can buy all the labor it wants at the market wage. Therefore, the supply curve of this factor to any individual firm is perfectly elastic and is the same as the marginal cost of the factor. The firm's most profitable input at N and the corresponding wage at W are determined where the company's *MCF = MRP*.

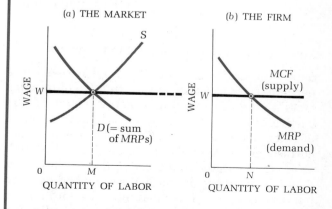

Monopsony Model: One Buyer, Many Sellers

A **monopsony** is a market structure consisting of a single buyer and many sellers of a good or service. Hence, it may be thought of as a "buyer's monopoly." (The term *monopsony* comes from the Greek *mono-*, "one," and *opsōnia*, "a buying.") An example would be a firm that is the sole employer in a company town, as has been the case in many mining communities. Similarly, in some farm areas a single food-processing plant dominates employment for many miles around.

A monopsony wage model is shown in Exhibit 2. Note from the second column of the table that the monopsonist must offer a higher wage rate or price per unit for *all* units in order to acquire more labor. (This is thus the "reverse" of the monopolist in the output market, who must charge a lower price per unit for *all* units in order to sell more products.) The result is that the marginal cost of labor will be greater than the average cost at each input, as shown in the figure.

The most profitable input level is determined, as always, by the location of the point at which *MCF* = *MRP*. Thus, the monopsonist will employ L units of labor and pay the lowest possible price for that quantity of labor, namely LT per unit. As a result, input, as compared to the amount at N, will be restricted. Further, the price per unit, as compared to the wage NW, will be lower than it would have been if the monopsonist were a perfectly competitive buyer in the input market.

What analogies do you see between this model and that of a pure monopolist in the output market?

Monopoly Model: One Seller, Many Buyers

Suppose a craft union of all skilled workers in a particular trade (such as printing or plumbing), faces a market consisting of many buyers of that particular skill. The craft union is then an example of a labor monopoly. What level of wages and what corresponding volume of labor output will result?

The model is illustrated in Exhibit 3. The curves S and D represent the normal supply and demand curves for labor in a free market. The equilibrium quantity of labor will be at N and the equilibrium

Exhibit 2
A Monopsony Model of Wage Determination

In order to acquire more labor, the monopsonist must offer a higher price per unit for all units hired. The average cost of labor will thus rise, and the marginal cost of labor will be different from the average cost.

The *MCF* curve lies above the average-cost curve *ACF*, which is also the labor-supply curve S. By hiring to the point at which *MCF* = *MRP*, the monopsony firm employs L units and pays the lowest price per unit consistent with that volume of input, namely LT.

The monopsony firm thus restricts its employment of resources and pays a lower price per unit of input *than it would if it were a perfectly competitive buyer in the factor market.*

Cost Schedule of Labor Factor

Units of labor factor, F	Average cost of labor factor (= wage rate or supply price of labor), ACF or S	Total cost of labor factor, TCF	Marginal cost of labor factor, MCF
1	$5	$ 5	
			$ 7
2	6	12	
			9
3	7	21	
			11
4	8	32	
			13
5	9	45	

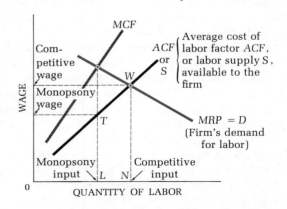

wage will be at W. A monopoly union, however, will seek to restrict the supply of its labor in order to attain a higher wage for its members. The union will thus shift the supply curve to the left from S to S'. This will reduce the equilibrium quantity of labor to the level at N' and raise the equilibrium wage to the level at W'.

This analysis helps explain why some labor unions, especially certain craft unions, have established long apprenticeship requirements, high initiation fees, and similar obstacles to entry. The same is true of certain professional associations in such fields as medicine, law, and engineering. Their motives, at least partly, have been to curb the supply of labor in the market and thus to boost wage rates. Of course, there are also unions that do not seek to maximize wages. They may try to maxi-

mize membership instead so that they can wield more market power. In order to portray such cases, the model in Exhibit 3 would have to be modified to reflect these objectives.

Bilateral Monopoly Model: One Buyer, One Seller

A **bilateral monopoly** is a market structure in which a monopsonist buys from a monopolist. The simplest version, which *combines the main features of the previous monopsony and monopoly models*, is shown in Exhibit 4.

Both the buyer and the seller are seeking to maximize their net benefits from the transaction. Therefore, let us assume that the two parties can agree on a given quantity to be exchanged, say the amount at M. It follows that the monopsonist will

---

Exhibit 3
A Monopoly Model of Wage Determination

A monopoly union, such as a craft union composed of skilled workers like plumbers or electricians, will behave like any monopolist. It will restrict the supply of labor in order to command a higher price or wage rate than could be commanded in a perfectly competitive market.

The curves S and D represent the free-market or unrestricted supply and demand curves. By restricting the supply of labor from S to S', the monopoly union reduces the equilibrium output from N to N' and raises the equilibrium wage from W to W'.

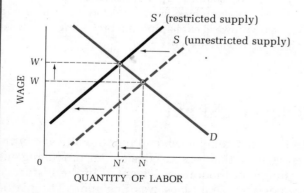

Exhibit 4
A Bilateral Monopoly Model of Wage Determination

In a bilateral monopoly, both parties may agree on some quantity, such as the amount at M. However, the theory does not predict the exact wage. At best, we can say that the price of labor will be somewhere between the monopsony's preferred wage at U and the monopoly's preferred wage at V.

If a wage of W is negotiated, it will be profitable for the employer to hire as many as N units of labor. Thus, a bilateral monopoly *may* achieve wage and employment levels that are closer to competitive standards than either a monopoly or a monopsony would.

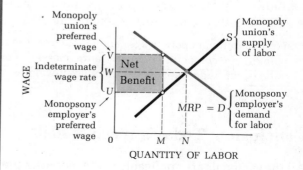

wish to purchase that quantity for the lower price at
U. On the other hand, the monopolist will want to
sell that quantity for the higher price at V. What
will be the transaction price?

Economists have never arrived at a solution to
this problem. Many years ago a fascinating series of
controlled experiments was conducted by an economist and a psychologist at Pennsylvania State University. In the experiments, numerous pairs of students participated in bargaining for money and
services in bilateral monopoly situations. Out of
these and other studies, there has emerged a fair
amount of agreement along the following lines:

1. It is not likely that both the quantity and wage
level will be uniquely determined in a bilateral
monopoly model. The reason is easy to see.
Suppose the two traders agree on a quantity, such
as M, that maximizes their *joint* net benefits.
Then, the lowest wage acceptable to the seller is
the wage at U. But this gives the whole net benefit (equal to the shaded area) to the buyer. Conversely, the highest wage acceptable to the buyer
— the wage at V—gives the whole net benefit to
the seller. Therefore, the actual wage cannot be
predicted.

2. The wage level will be somewhere between the
monopsonist's preferred rate at U and the monopolist's preferred rate at V. The precise level will
depend on the relative bargaining strength of the
two parties.

3. Suppose a wage level of approximately W is negotiated. Management will then find it profitable
to hire more workers—up to the amount at N.
This suggests an interesting conclusion.

In a bilateral monopoly, wages and employment *may*
approximate competitive levels more closely than
would occur under monopoly or monopsony alone.

Conclusion: Today's Wage Model

All these models are applicable to the modern economy. In the input markets, just as in the output

markets, there are *degrees* of competition and monopoly. Hence, these models, or modifications of
them, can be used to describe basic patterns of wage
determination. For example:

The majority of the American labor force is not
organized in any labor union. Among agricultural
and white-collar workers, for example, union
membership is relatively slight and the situation
conforms roughly to the competitive model. On
the other hand, in some of the service industries,
significant segments of the labor force are unorgan-
ized and relatively immobile for long periods.
Here, the monopsony model provides a good
approximation—with allowance for the legal minimum wage (which does not apply to many farmworkers).

What about the minority of the labor force that is
organized into unions? Here there are some industries, such as the garment and building trades, coal
mining, and stevedoring, in which the balance of
power has often been with the unions rather than
with the employers. The situation in those industries has at times approximated that of monopoly.
In much of manufacturing, transportation, and related sectors, strong unions often face strong employers or employers' associations, and the bilateral
monopoly model frequently applies. In these cases,
collective bargaining (negotiations between unions
and management) is the chief means of settling
issues. Thus:

A wide variety of situations exist in American labor
markets. No single model of wage determination can
be used to depict all types of conditions and circumstances. Nevertheless, each of the four models can go a
long way toward explaining and predicting the consequences of various outcomes.

Theory of Rent

In the early nineteenth century, a political controversy arose that was responsible for producing one
of the great theoretical advances in the history of
economics. The place was England. The period
was 1814–1816.

A Baseball Strike Is a Monopolists' Slugfest

by Susan Lee

Baseball is, as an economist would put it, a textbook illustration of a bilateral monopoly. And a strike is no more than the owners' monopsony power (that means a monopoly-buyer-of-labor, and I promise not to use the word again) pitted against the monopoly power of the players for the possession of the "scarcity rents" accruing from the teams themselves. To explain:

As a group, the owners are the sole employers of major-league baseball players; they could, and did, collude to limit the salaries and job mobility of those players. What were the hired hands to do? If they wanted to hit homers and be memorialized in candy bars (i.e., keep their jobs), they had to settle for a less-than-competitive wage. The hapless sluggers were faced with a take-it-or-leave-it wage, and til a few years ago, they took it.

But the players have a monopoly, too: Their organization, the Players Association, is a genteel name for a labor union that is the sole supplier of major-league-quality baseball players. And now that monopoly is refusing to supply the owners with sluggers or hurlers or fielders until the owners come to terms. In short, the players want the owners' monopoly to compete with itself for the players' services.

Back in 1976, the owners took the players' terms — sort of — and free-agent status got underway. Players whose contracts expired were free to sell their hitting or hurling to the highest bidder. Star players started shining in different cities in different uniforms — and salaries shot up.

The owners, feeling the squeeze from a monopoly other than their own, squawked about restoring "competitive balance." The players, enjoying the fruits of their own monopoly power, jawed about finally being paid a "just and reasonable wage."

The fans, however, started wondering where all the money was coming from to pay those multi-million-dollar contracts. Silly fans: It was coming from them, from something that accountants, believe it or not, call "goodwill." It came from their loyalty, their sense of baseball history and strong identification with the names of their teams.

For years the owners expropriated the "financial returns to goodwill" resulting from this kind of fan enthusiasm, this constancy that makes people willing to watch whichever nine guys run onto the field calling themselves the Padres, the Brewers or even, the Mets.

Until 1976, the monopolistic owners ate the full share of those big, juicy pies made from fans' ticket receipts, broadcasting rights and so forth. After 1976 and free agency, however, the players' monopoly started grabbing slices of the money pie. A strike, then, is just a tug-of-war between monopolists — and it is every bit as unseemly as these fights are.

For most of the previous century, from 1711 to 1794, the price of "corn" (the generic term in England for all grains) had been extremely stable. But between 1795 and 1800 the price tripled, and it continued to rise over most of the following two decades. Because grain was a primary source of food, the rise in price created great hardship and considerable political unrest. Many people starved, and employers reluctantly raised wages because of high food prices.

One group argued that the landlords were in a "conspiracy" to keep up corn prices by charging high rents to farmers. (Most of the corn was grown on rented land.) Another group, represented by the great English classical economist David Ricardo, argued exactly the opposite. Corn prices are high, said the "Ricardians," because of shortages resulting from the Napoleonic Wars in Europe (1804–1815). The high price of corn makes corn cultivation more profitable. This increases the demand for land and hence the price paid for the use of the land—namely, rent. If the price of corn fell, corn cultivation would become less profitable, and this would bring decreased rents. In Ricardo's own words:

> "Corn is not high because a rent is paid, but a rent is paid because corn is high." Ricardo meant that the price of land is determined by demand and supply, and that rent is *price-determined, not price-determining.*

Ricardo and his followers carried on a vigorous battle for the repeal of the English Corn Laws (tariffs) of 1815. Their goal was to bring more corn into the country, thereby increasing the supply and lowering the price.

The Meaning of Economic Rent

Ricardo's argument was based on three assumptions:

1. The amount of land available is fixed.
2. Land used for growing corn has no alternative uses.
3. A landlord would prefer to receive *any* payment for the use of land rather than to leave it idle and receive nothing.

In the language of modern economics, these statements mean that the *supply of land is perfectly inelastic,* as illustrated in Exhibit 5, Figure (a).

The intersection of the supply curve S with the demand curve D establishes the equilibrium quantity at N and the corresponding equilibrium price at P. It follows that this price (or rent) per unit of land must be a *surplus* to the landlord. This is because, rather than leave the land idle to grow weeds, the landlord would be willing to supply the same amount of land at a lower price. In fact, the landlord would accept *any* price, depending on where the demand curve intersects the supply curve. We call the resulting surplus "economic rent" and define it as follows:

> **Economic rent** is any payment made to the owner of a factor of production, in an industry in equilibrium, in excess of the factor's supply price or opportunity cost. That is, economic rent is a payment above the minimum amount necessary to keep that factor in its present occupation.

Note that this definition restricts the concept of economic rent to an *equilibrium* surplus. This is because the owners of some factors may receive surpluses while those factors are in a transitory stage from one equilibrium position to another. It is also because such surpluses may exist even in long-run equilibrium. It follows that the entire rectangular area in Figure (a), 0PRN, represents the total economic rent received by the landlord.

Originally, "rent" meant the payment made for the use of land. But economists eventually realized that the owners of any factor of production, not just the owners of land, may receive a surplus above the opportunity cost of that factor. Hence, they coined the expression "economic rent" to represent all such differentials. (Sometimes the term "producer's surplus" is used.)

Exhibit 5, Figure (b), is a hypothetical model of the supply and demand for bus drivers under perfect competition. According to the figure, a quantity of bus drivers equal to 0N would each receive a wage equal to 0P. But only for the Nth bus driver is this wage the supply price or opportunity cost. Each of the others that make up the amount equal to 0N would have been willing to work for less, as determined by the height of the segment KR of the supply curve. Therefore, all the other drivers are receiving a total economic rent equal to the triangle KPR. You should be able to see from both diagrams that an increase in demand from D to D′ will enlarge the amount of economic rent. On the other hand, a decrease in demand will reduce it.

Exhibit 5
The Determination of Rent

Figure (a): The landlord's opportunity cost is zero. Hence, the total amount received, the area 0PRN, represents economic rent. This is because the landlord would be willing to supply the same amount of land for any price (possibly even a zero price rather than letting it lie idle and grow weeds).

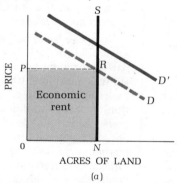

ACRES OF LAND

(a)

Figure (b): The total amount received by the bus drivers is the area 0PRN. But only the "Nth" driver is getting his or her exact opportunity cost. Those "to the left" are getting more than their opportunity costs, as shown by their total economic rent, the triangular area KPR.

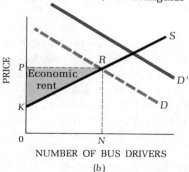

NUMBER OF BUS DRIVERS

(b)

This leads to an important conclusion:

Economic rent arises because the owners of the various units of a particular factor of production differ in the eagerness with which they are willing to supply those units. That is, the owners differ in their supply price. If all owners had equal supply prices, the supply curve would be perfectly elastic and there would be no economic rent.

Thus, in Exhibit 5, Figure (b), the area of economic rent would diminish to zero if the supply curve were to pivot on point R so as to approach the horizontal.

Economic rent is a concept similar to that of net revenue, inasmuch as both represent surpluses. The difference between them is merely a matter of reference. When the surplus is received by the owner of a factor of production, it is called economic rent. When the surplus is received by a firm, it is referred to as net revenue (or net profit).

Is Rent a Cost or a Surplus?

As Ricardo observed, units of land often have alternative uses and are of different quality. This explains why the demand for an acre of real estate in the heart of a city's business district may be quite different from the demand for an acre of farm land or an acre of desert land elsewhere in the country. These differences in demand also account for the differences in rent that are paid by the users of the land.

Are these rents a cost or a surplus? The answer depends on the point of view you take.

From the firm's viewpoint, rent is the price that must be paid to attract land from its alternative uses. Hence, rent is a *cost*. From the social viewpoint, rent is the value received for making available the land provided free by nature, regardless of the alternative uses to which the land is put and the rents that are paid. Hence, rent is a *surplus*.

The fallacy of composition thus plays a role in the interpretation of rent from the individual versus the social viewpoint.

Leaders in Economics

Henry George
1839–1897
A Single Tax on Land

A journalist and political aspirant with strong socialist leanings, Henry George was best known for his advocacy of a single tax on land. His ideas were fully elaborated in 1879 with the publication of his famous book, *Progress and Poverty*. Many millions of copies have been sold throughout the world, and it is undoubtedly the most successful popular economics book ever published.

Main Ideas

The central concept in George's writing is that poverty is caused by the monopolization of land by the few, who deprive the rest of the people of their birthright. Since land is endowed by nature, all rent on land is unearned surplus. The injustice to the landless grows when, as a result of natural progress, the value of land is augmented and rent increases correspondingly. The solution is the confiscation of rent by the government through a **single tax** on land. No other taxes would be necessary, according to George.

Great Debates

Famous economists, including Alfred Marshall and J. B. Clark, debated with Henry George over the single-tax issue. Their conclusions, and those of later economists, suggested that a land tax would probably have fewer adverse effects on the allocation of society's resources than other taxes. However, a single tax on land alone would have three major shortcomings:

1. It would not produce enough revenue to meet governments' needs.

2. It would be unjust. Surpluses (economic rent) may accrue to other resource owners besides landlords if the owners can gain monopolistic control over the sale of their resources in the marketplace.

3. It might be impossible to administer. The tax does not distinguish between land and capital—that is, between the proportion of rent that represents a surplus and the proportion that results from improvements made on the land.

George entered politics in 1886 as a candidate of the Labor and Socialist parties for mayor of New York City. He was enormously popular, and it took the maximum efforts of a coalition of parties to defeat him at the polls. Since his death in 1897, his beliefs have continued to be discussed, especially in some major cities where free public seminars on Henry George's ideas are often held.

Theory of Interest

If you incur a debt to buy a car or to pay your tuition, you must pay interest to the lender for the credit given you. Therefore, **interest** is defined as the price paid for the use of credit or loanable funds over a period of time.

Interest is always expressed as a percentage of the amount of the loan. Thus, an interest rate of 10 percent means that the borrower pays 10 cents interest per $1 borrowed per year, or $10 per $100 borrowed per year, and so on.

Interest is paid for the use of credit, which in turn is used to buy productive resources or capital goods. Therefore, you will often hear reference made to the interest on capital. What this really means, of course, is the interest on the value of the capital in which the investment was made.

In our economy there are many different interest rates on debt instruments of all types—notes, bonds, mortgages, and so on. The rates vary according to several factors:

Risk the chance of the borrower's defaulting on the loan.

Maturity the length of time over which the money is borrowed.

Liquidity the ease with which the creditor can convert the debt instrument into cash without loss of purchase price.

Competition the extent to which lenders compete for borrowers in particular money markets.

Other things being equal, interest rates will vary directly with the first two factors and inversely with the second two. If you are not sure why, imagine how these factors would affect the interest rate that you would charge if you were a banker making loans.

As a result of the wide structure of interest rates, economists find it convenient to talk about "the" rate of interest. By this they mean the theoretical **_pure interest rate_** on a riskless loan. This rate is best approximated by the interest on short-term negotiable government securities (such as 3-month Treasury bills).

Because the interest rate is the price of credit or loanable funds, we shall see shortly that it is determined by the interaction of demand and supply forces. But first, what are the sources of demand and supply?

Demand for Loanable Funds

You and I and people everywhere want credit. But from the economy's viewpoint we fall into three major groups: businesses, households, and government.

Business Sector

This is the largest source of demand for credit or loanable funds. Firms borrow because they want to purchase capital goods or build up inventories. A firm undertakes such purchases as long as it expects to receive a yield that exceeds the cost of its funds. The expected yield or rate of return on investment projects can be depicted by the marginal revenue product *(MRP)* curve of capital expressed in terms of percentages.

This is illustrated in Exhibit 6. You can see from the diagram that the *MRP* curve should be viewed as a *cumulative investment-demand curve*. It tells you, for example, that the firm can earn 18 percent on the first $200,000 of investment and 16 percent on the next $100,000. Therefore, it can earn *at least* 16 percent on the first $300,000. Similarly, it can earn *at least* 14 percent on the first $400,000 invested.

Of course, the rate of interest on borrowed funds is also expressed as a percentage. Therefore, *the points on the curve show the amount of investment the firm will undertake at various interest rates*. For example, at an interest rate on borrowed funds of 10 percent, the firm will demand $600,000 for investment. If the rate is lowered to 8 percent, the firm

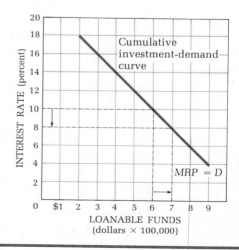

Exhibit 6
A Firm's Demand Curve for Loanable Funds

In a competitive market, the firm will demand loanable funds with which to purchase capital up to the point at which the *MRP* of capital equals the interest rate (or price). Thus, a decrease in the interest rate from 10 percent to 8 percent will increase the quantity of capital (or the amount of loanable funds) demanded from $600,000 to $700,000. (NOTE In macroeconomics, a firm's *MRP* curve of capital is called its marginal efficiency of investment, *MEI*.)

will increase the amount of funds demanded for investment to $700,000.

The diagram thus suggests a familiar marginal principle:

Under competitive conditions, a firm will demand loanable funds up to the point at which the marginal-revenue productivity of the capital purchased with those funds is equal to the interest rate (or price) that must be paid for the loan. *The MRP curve of capital is therefore the firm's demand curve for capital* (that is, loanable funds used to purchase capital).

Household Sector

This is the second major source of demand for loanable funds. Households borrow to buy automobiles, washing machines and other appliances, vacation trips, homes, etc. There is some limited evidence to suggest that the household demand curve for loanable funds is downward-sloping. This indicates that households will tend to borrow larger amounts of money at lower interest rates.

Public Sector

This is the third major source of demand for loanable funds. Governments at all levels — national, state, and local — borrow in order to finance national defense, highways, schools, welfare benefits, and so forth. The federal government, in particular, borrows in order to finance budget deficits. Therefore, we cannot assume that the federal government's demand for loanable funds depends on the interest rate. But there is ample evidence to support such an assumption about state and local governments. They tend to borrow more when interest rates are low than when rates are high.

Many studies point to the following conclusion:

For all three sources — businesses, households, and government — taken together, the total market demand curve for loanable funds is downward-sloping. In addition, various studies have concluded that the demand curve is probably relatively inelastic. Therefore, changes in the interest rate are likely to result in less-than-proportional changes in the quantity demanded of loanable funds.

Supply of Loanable Funds

We must now turn our attention to the supply side of the picture and ask: What are the main sources of credit or loanable funds?

Central Banking System

A country's central bank (the Federal Reserve System in the United States) exercises a great deal of influence over the supply of money and hence the supply of loanable funds. This influence is intertwined with government economic measures, including taxation and spending policies, for combating recessions and inflations.

Households and Businesses

These supply some loanable funds to the money market out of their savings. Household savings are that part of household income not spent on consumption. Business savings are mainly undistributed (plowed-back) profits and depreciation reserves (funds set aside for replacement of worn-out or obsolete physical capital). Most businesses reinvest their savings in new plant and equipment, but some savings find their way into the money market. In general, very little is known about the effects of interest rates on household and business saving, but the influences are believed to be slight.

Determination of the Interest Rate

The demand and supply forces generated by government, businesses, and households combine to determine the equilibrium interest rate in the market. This is shown by the familiar supply-and-demand diagram in Exhibit 7.

As mentioned above, the downward-sloping demand curve *at any given level of national income* reflects the willingness on the part of businesses to demand more funds for investment at a low interest rate than at a high interest rate. The upward-sloping supply curve, although it is based on much more complex and uncertain factors, *assumes* that household and business savers will make available some-

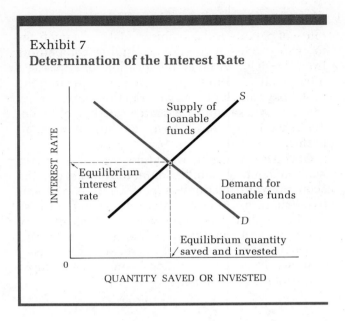

Exhibit 7
Determination of the Interest Rate

than the rate of interest — are undertaken.   Any project whose prospective yield is below the interest rate is dropped from consideration.   In this way the interest rate directs the growth of productive capacity.

Does the interest rate actually perform this function in our economic system?   For the most part the answer is *yes*, but there are some qualifications:

> The interest rate in our economy is not the sole mechanism for allocating scarce funds — for two reasons:
>
> 1. The government allocates some of the available capital to projects that it believes to be in the public interest, regardless of their financial profitability.
>
> 2. The unequal distribution of bargaining power among borrowers may enable many large firms to borrow on more favorable terms (at lower interest rates) than most small firms.   This is true even when the latter have relatively greater prospects for growth.

what larger quantities of loanable funds at a high interest rate than at a low one.

Actually, the determination of the interest rate has much deeper implications than is apparent from this simple supply-and-demand diagram.   Government monetary, taxation, and spending policies, as explained in macroeconomics, exercise a powerful influence on the forces that help determine the interest rate.   Nevertheless, you should now be able to formulate a definition of the **loanable funds theory of interest**.   (Compare your definition with the one in the Dictionary at the back of the book.)

Conclusion: The Allocating Function of Interest

Because the interest rate is a price, it performs the same rationing function as any other price.   *The interest rate allocates the economy's scarce supply of funds among those who are willing to pay for them.*

Thus, in a free market, only the most profitable investment projects — those projects whose expected return or productivity is equal to or greater

Theory of Profit

You have learned that **profit** or net revenue represents the difference between total revenue and total cost.   Profit is thus a *residual* or *surplus* over and above normal profit. It accrues to the entrepreneur after all costs, including explicit costs and implicit costs, have been deducted from total revenue. What does economic theory tell us about the determinants of profit?   What functions does profit perform?

The history of economics reveals a number of theories of how profits are derived.   Today, three are generally recognized as being particularly relevant:

1. Friction and monopoly theory.

2. Uncertainty theory.

3. Innovation theory.

This system of classification is not all-inclusive and any one of the theories may contain elements of the others.   The system merely emphasizes the main lines that have been followed in the course of thinking on the subject.

Friction and Monopoly Theory

By the end of the nineteenth century, the theory of a perfectly competitive economy was well on its way toward becoming a unified body of thought. Against this setting the noted American economist J. B. Clark (1847–1938) constructed a model of the economy that was intended to reconcile the static laws of theory with the dynamic world of fact.

According to Clark's "stationary" model (or the theory of perfect competition, as it is called today), the economy is characterized by a smooth and frictionless flow of resources. Theoretically, the system automatically clicks into equilibrium through the free play of market forces.

Of course, changes may occur that cause a temporary departure from equilibrium. But as long as resources are mobile and opportunities are equally accessible to all economic entities, the adjustment to change and a new equilibrium will be accomplished quickly and smoothly.

In this type of economic equilibrium all the owners of the factors of production would receive their opportunity costs. The revenues of each enterprise would exactly equal its costs (including the implicit wages and interest of the owner), and no economic surplus, or profit residual, could result.

In the real world, however, surpluses do occur. According to the theory, they can be attributed only to the frictions (or obstacles to resource mobility) and monopoly elements that actually characterize a dynamic economy. In the long run, according to the theory, the forces of competition would eliminate any surpluses. But in reality, the surpluses recur because new frictions and new monopoly elements continually arise. Therefore:

Profits are the result of institutional rigidities in the social and economic system that prevent the working out of competitive forces. To the extent that these rigidities cause profits, or surpluses, they are to the temporary advantage of the surplus recipient.

Many illustrations from real life substantiate the existence of friction and monopoly as a cause of economic surplus. The construction of military posts brings profit bonanzas to neighboring cities. Foreign crises often rescue domestic industries from losses due to excessive inventories. The existence of patents and franchises enables many firms to reap profits by legally excluding competitors from the field. A favorable location for a business often results in the value of the site exceeding the rental payment for it. In general, the control of any resource whose supply is scarce relative to the demand for it provides a basis for pure or windfall profits.

Of course, a surplus would not arise if resources were sufficiently mobile to enter the market or if the economy were frictionless (perfect) in its competitive structure. At best, any surpluses that did arise would be short-lived and would vanish entirely when the adjustments had time to exert their full effect in the market. But social processes—customs, laws, and traditions—make such rapid adjustments impossible.

Uncertainty Theory

The uncertainty theory of profit was introduced by Professor Frank Knight (1885–1972) of the University of Chicago. The theory, formulated in a remarkable doctoral thesis entitled *Risk, Uncertainty, and Profit* (1921), is rooted in a distinction between "risk" and "uncertainty."

The Meaning of Risk

Risk is defined as the quantitative measurement of the probability that a particular outcome, such as a gain or a loss, will occur. Because the distinguishing feature of risk is predictability, the firm can "insure" itself against expected losses by incorporating them in advance into its cost structure. This is true whether the risk is of an *intrafirm* or an *interfirm* nature.

Intrafirm Risk Such risk occurs when management can establish the probability of loss because the number of occurrences within the firm is large enough to be predicted with known error. For example, a factory may experience a loss of about 2 machine-hours out of every 100 machine-hours due to equipment breakdown. In this case, the cost of the production lost can be added to the cost of the production resulting from the remaining 98 machine-hours, and the profit rate can be altered by the revision in the cost structure. In other words, where the average expected loss for the company can be predicted for the coming period, the loss can be "self-insured"—the company can treat it as a cost of doing business. Therefore, no insurance from outside sources is necessary.

Thus, small-loan companies expect a certain percentage of defaults. Banks regularly charge off a portion of their loans as bad debts. And many companies institute self-insurance programs against risks for which they can prepare themselves through proper reserve accounting.

Interfirm Risk For some risks the number of observations or experiences is not large enough within any one firm for management to feel that it can predict the loss with reasonable confidence. However, when many firms are considered, the observations become numerous enough to exhibit the necessary stability for prediction.

Examples of such risks are losses caused by floods, storms, fires, or deaths. Because managers are unable to predict such losses for themselves, they are able to shift the burden of the risk to insurance companies who establish the probability of such losses based on a large number of cases. Although insurance companies cannot establish that a particular individual will die or that a specific building will burn, they can predict with small error what fraction of the population will die next year or how many buildings out of a given number will burn. Because a firm pays a risk premium for insurance, it treats this risk premium as a cost of doing business.

The Meaning of Uncertainty

Uncertainty is defined as a state of knowledge in which the probabilities of outcomes resulting from specific actions are not known and cannot be predicted. Unlike risk, uncertainty is a subjective phenomenon rather than an objective one. No two individuals who forecast a particular outcome based on given facts will necessarily arrive at the

same result. This is because there is not enough information on which to base a strong probability estimate.

Under conditions characterized by uncertainty, decision makers must make choices based on incomplete knowledge. They may do this by forming mental images of future outcomes that cannot be verified quantitatively. It follows from this that uncertainty, unlike risk, is not insurable and cannot be integrated within the firm's cost structure. At best, each manager may harbor his or her own subjective probability about a future outcome, but it is nothing more than a strong hunch. According to Knight's theory:

> The great majority of events in our society are unpredictable—they are uncertainties. *Profits are the rewards, and losses are the penalties, of bearing uncertainty.*

The uncertainty theory concludes that, in a market economy, entrepreneurs undertake an activity because they *expect*, but do not necessarily *receive*, profits. Like a dog chasing a rabbit, the expectation of gains is the incentive that keeps entrepreneurs running.

Innovation Theory

In the 1930s, one of the most distinguished economists of this century, Joseph Schumpeter, introduced a theory of business cycles based on innovations. This theory has often been extended to include the notion of innovation as a cause of profits.

An ***innovation,*** as economists define it, is "the setting up of a new production function." That is, an innovation is a new relation between the output and the various inputs (capital, land, labor, and entrepreneurship) in a production process.

Innovations may thus embrace such wide varieties of activities as the discovery of new markets, differentiation of products, or, more broadly, new ways of doing old things or different combinations of existing methods to accomplish new things. There is an important distinction between invention and innovation. Invention is the creation of something

Profits: How Much Is Too Little?

by David B. Tinnin

Dark suspicion of profit is an ancient turn of mind. Within Western culture there are deeply ingrained philosophical and religious misgivings about the morality of profits — most simply put, that to earn from the labors of another is an intrinsically evil form of extortion. . . .

However, as the era of capitalism dawned two centuries ago, the profit motive found an able defender. In *The Wealth of Nations,* Adam Smith argued that profits are the legitimate return for risk and effort and that the "Invisible Hand" of market forces would convert private greed into public benefits. A century later, Karl Marx was not so sure. Arguing the opposite view, he asserted that labor, not capital, was the essential ingredient that added value to goods or raw materials in the manufacturing process. Thus, in his view, profit was the "surplus value" that the capitalist unjustifiably tacked on to the real worth of the product. In the early part of the century, Bernard Shaw and his fellow Fabians contended that profits should be taxed into oblivion in order to create a new, socialist order. They believed that the profitless economy would function more effectively — and they were wrong. Since the onset of the Industrial Age 100 years ago, profits have proved to be indispensable to a prosperous economy.

In a capitalist economy, profit is, above all, the motivator. Without a hope of reasonable profit, no one would start a business, introduce a new product or service, or even continue producing an old one. And without the reality of profit, no business in the long run can keep itself alive — except by government subsidy, which has to be paid partly out of taxes levied on the profits of other businesses. . . .

Profit is also important as a measure of efficiency in industrial enterprises — a way of keeping economic score. Whether a business is well or badly run, whether investments are productive or misguided, whether the products are competitive and appealing — judging performance without reference to profits is like watching a baseball game where nobody bothers to count runs. . . .

It is time for a more sober analysis of profits and their importance as the engine of economic growth. It is a historic irony that in the U.S., the stronghold of world capitalism, so few citizens understand that profits provide the basis for the prosperity on which rests the well-being of both individuals and the nation.

new; innovation is the adaptation of an existing thing, such as an invention, to a new use. Many inventions never give rise to innovations.

Schumpeter's original purpose in propounding the innovation theory was to show how business cycles result from these disturbances and from successive adaptations to them by the business system. He began by assuming a stationary (perfectly competitive) system in equilibrium — in which all economic life is repetitive and goes on smoothly, without disturbance.

Into this system a shock — an innovation — is introduced by an entrepreneur who foresees the possibility of extra profit. The quietude and intricate balance of the system is then shattered as if the system had been invaded by a Hollywood-staged cattle stampede. The successful innovation causes hoards of businesspeople (followers rather than leaders) to flock into the new field by adopting the innovation, and these mass rushes create secondary waves of business activity.

When the disturbance has finally run its course, the system settles into equilibrium once again, only to be disturbed later by another innovation. Profit-making and economic activity are thus experienced as series of fits and starts (cycles) rather than as smooth and continuous progressions.

Functions of Profits

As mentioned earlier, there is no single "correct" theory of profit. All three theories contribute to explaining the cause of profit. They also help us understand the two major functions of profits in our economy:

1. Profits stimulate innovation by inducing business managers to undertake new ventures and to improve production methods.

2. To the extent that markets are free and competitive, the desire for profits induces business executives to allocate their resources efficiently in accordance with consumer preferences.

As a result of these functions, you can see that profits and the profit system account for a funda-mental distinction between capitalistic and socialistic systems. Indeed, as you will learn in a later chapter, attitudes toward profit are crucial in determining the economic success of any economic system.

What You Have Learned

1. Wages are determined in the market under different competitive conditions. Four models that explain most of the wage arrangements that exist in our economy are the competitive model, the monopsony model, the monopoly model, and the bilateral monopoly model.

2. Economic rent is a surplus that is price-determined, not price-determining. To an individual firm, rent is a cost of production just like any other cost. But to society, rent is a surplus that is received for making available nature's free land.

3. Interest is the price paid for the use of credit or loanable funds over a period of time. The interest rate is determined by the supply of, and the demand for, loanable funds, and can be influenced by government borrowing and by central-bank credit-creation policies. The chief function of the interest rate is to allocate scarce funds for alternative uses, thus directing the flow of capital.

4. Profit is a residual or surplus over and above all costs, including normal profit. It may result from frictions and monopoly elements in our economy, from uncertainty, and from innovations. There are two chief functions of profit. One function is to stimulate economic progress by inducing business managers to invest in plant and equipment. The other function is, to the extent that markets are competitive, to allocate resources in accordance with consumer preferences.

Terms and Concepts To Review

wages	single tax
labor	pure interest rate
monopsony	profit
bilateral monopoly	risk
economic rent	uncertainty
interest	innovation

For Discussion

1. The long-run trend of worker's real wages (purchasing power) has been upward, even though the supply of labor today is much larger than it was years ago. Can you suggest why?

2. Which wage-determination model best explains each of the following? Illustrate and explain each with an actual model. (a) The wages of file clerks and secretaries; (b) the wages of unskilled farmworkers; (c) the wages of typographers and stevedores.

3. A union official once advised the members of his union to ask for a 10 percent wage cut. Was he crazy? What economic factors might have prompted him to offer such advice?

4. "Wages are determined by the marginal productivity of labor, just as prices are determined by costs of production." True or false? Explain.

5. Do you see any similarity between the concept of economic rent received by the owners of a factor of production and net revenue received by a firm? Explain.

6. Henry George ran for mayor of New York in 1886. If you had been a voter at that time, how would you have reacted to his single-tax idea?

7. Money itself is not a resource, and it is unproductive. Why, then, should people be willing to pay a price in the form of interest in order to acquire it? What determines the interest rate that is paid? What functions does interest perform?

8. Classify each of the following as an interfirm or intrafirm risk: (a) glassware and china breakage in a restaurant; (b) egg breakage on a chicken farm; (c) absenteeism in a factory; (d) "acts of God" (cite examples).

9. (a) From a chicken farmer's standpoint, is the price of eggs (which is determined in competitive markets) a risk or an uncertainty? (b) Is the sale of next year's Chevrolets by General Motors a risk or an uncertainty? Why?

10. "Economic profits should be taxed away because they result from frictions and monopolistic influences." Evaluate.

Chapter 27

Stability, General Equilibrium, and Welfare Economics

Learning Guide

Watch for answers to these important questions

How do we distinguish between stable, unstable, and neutral equilibria? How do we distinguish between statics and dynamics?

What is the difference between partial equilibrium and general equilibrium? In what way is a general-equilibrium model a "system"?

What is welfare economics? How does it relate to the idea of Pareto optimality? What implications do these concepts have for efficiency and equity in a capitalistic system?

Equilibrium is a concept of fundamental importance, and we have already made considerable use of it. But what does "equilibrium" really mean? How significant is it in economic analysis?

Equilibrium was defined in earlier chapters as a state of balance between opposing forces. An object is in equilibrium when it is at rest. In effect it has no tendency to change its position because the forces acting upon it are offsetting each other. In economics, as we have seen, the "objects" may be prices, quantities, incomes, or other variables. You cannot consider a problem solved if, at the point you terminate your analysis, the variables that are germane to the particular problem are still changing. Only when the variables settle down to steady levels, or only when their future equilibrium positions can be predicted, can you consider the solution complete.

However, the study of equilibrium is not an end in itself. Economics is concerned with understanding the forces that can disturb an equilibrium and the policy measures that may have to be undertaken to restore it. These ideas will become more meaningful as we explore the ramifications of equilibrium in this chapter.

Stability of Equilibria

If the forces acting upon an object at rest suddenly change, the object may or may not have the ability to reestablish its position. If it does reestablish its position, the equilibrium is stable; if it does not, the equilibrium may be either unstable or neutral. Let us examine these ideas in both a physical and an economic context.

Exhibit 1 provides some examples of the stability of equilibria in terms of supply and demand curves.

Figure (a) illustrates a case of stable equilibrium. This represents the normal situation. In physical terms, it may be depicted by a cone resting on its base. In economic terms, it can be represented by the interaction of ordinary supply and demand curves. If the system is subjected to an external "shock" or disturbance sufficient to dislodge it from equilibrium, self-corrective forces will cause it to return to its initial position. If the price, for example, should for some reason rise above its equilibrium level at P, the quantity supplied of the product will exceed the quantity demanded, thereby driving the price down. If the price should fall below P, the quantity demanded will exceed the quantity supplied, thereby driving the price up.

Exhibit 1
Stable, Unstable, and Neutral Equilibria: Static Models

Figure (a): *Stable Equilibrium.* The equilibrium at P is stable — like a cone resting on its base. A "shock" sufficient to disturb the equilibrium brings into play self-corrective forces that automaticaly restore the initial position.

Figure (b): *Unstable Equilibrium.* The equilibrium at P is unstable — like a cone balanced on its vertex. If the equilibrium is disturbed, the system is forced away from its initial state. Thus, at any price higher than the level at P, the quantity demanded exceeds the quantity supplied, so the price continues to rise. At any price below the level at P, the reverse is true. Note, how-

ever, that the equilibrium at P would be stable if the downward-sloping supply curve cut the demand curve from above instead of from below. Can you illustrate and explain this?

Figures (c) and (d): *Neutral Equilibrium.* In Figure (c), any price equilibrium between P and P' is neutral. In Figure (d), any quantity equilibrium between Q and Q' is neutral. Within their neutral ranges, price and quantity are indeterminate; they may take on any values. Hence, the situation is analogous to a cone rolling on its side.

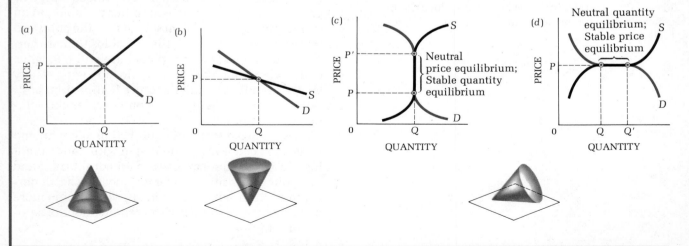

Although Figures (b) through (d) do not depict typical situations, they are useful for providing deeper insights into the concept of equilibrium.

Figure (b) presents a case of unstable equilibrium. A physical example is a cone balanced on its vertex. An economic example is one in which price is determined by the intersection of supply and demand but the supply curve is downward-sloping *and* cuts the demand curve from below. As you can see from the diagram, the system is in a delicate state of balance. That is, if the equilibrium is disturbed, the object will be forced away from its initial state.

As an example, suppose that for some reason the price rises above its equilibrium level. Then the quantity demanded will exceed the quantity supplied and the price will continue to rise. Conversely, if the price falls below its equilibrium level, the quantity supplied will exceed the quantity demanded and the price will continue to fall.

It is interesting to note that these conclusions would not hold if the downward-sloping supply curve cut the demand curve from *above* instead of from below. In that case the equilibrium would be stable. You should be able to demonstrate this by sketching the curves.

Figures (c) and (d) provide illustrations of neutral equilibrium. The physical situation can be depicted by a cone lying on its side. If the cone's equilibrium is disturbed, it simply "rolls" to some other neutral position. The analogous economic situation occurs in those ranges of price and quantity in which the supply and demand curves happen to coincide. Thus, in Figure (c), any price between P and P' is in neutral equilibrium—the price is "rolling" or indeterminate within this range. Similarly, in Figure (d), any quantity between Q and Q' is in neutral equilibrium—and therefore the precise quantity is indeterminate within this range.

Statics and Dynamics

The concepts of stable, unstable, and neutral equilibrium can also be depicted by the charts in Exhibit 2. Note from the titles of Exhibits 1 and 2 that Exhibit 1 consists of static models, whereas Exhibit 2 consists of dynamic ones. Let us examine these concepts more closely.

A **static model** is one in which economic phenomena are studied without reference to time—without reference to preceding or succeeding events. In a static model, time is not permitted to enter into the analysis in any manner that will affect the results. When we construct a static model, therefore, we are taking a "snapshot" and analyzing its essential features. Each of the diagrams in Exhibit 1, and most of the other theoretical situations and figures you have studied in this book, are static models.

Of course, in many practical situations, you want to analyze the effects of a change in one or more of the determining conditions in a static model. This method is known as **comparative statics.** It consists of comparing two "snapshots"—one taken before the change and one taken after. For example, when you analyzed supply and demand situations in previous chapters by comparing equilibrium prices and quantities before and after a shift in one or both of the curves, you were using comparative statics. Statics and comparative statics encompass most of the theory in this book—and by far the larger part of economic theory in general.

A **dynamic model** is one in which economic phenomena are studied by relating them to preceding or succeeding events. The influence of time is taken explicitly into account. Illustrations of dynamic models are shown in Exhibit 2. Each figure depicts a possible way in which price may behave in relation to its equilibrium level over a period of time. Each of these dynamic models is like a "motion picture," as distinguished from the "snapshot" of Exhibit 1.

Fluctuations in prices like those shown in Exhibit 2 do not continue in the same pattern indefinitely. Why? Because the underlying supply and demand curves that determine prices tend to change fairly frequently, so different patterns are generated. At any given moment the pattern may be tending toward stable, unstable, or neutral equilibrium. However, over a period of time, prices in most markets tend toward some stable equilibrium level.

Exhibit 2
Stable, Unstable, and Neutral Equilibria: Dynamic Models

Stable Equilibrium.   Price converges toward the equilibrium level at *P*.   Price may oscillate, or it may approach equilibrium from above or below.

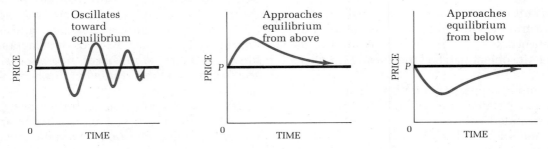

Unstable Equilibrium.   Price diverges from the equilibrium at *P*.   Price may oscillate, or it may "explode" upward or downward from the equilibrium level.

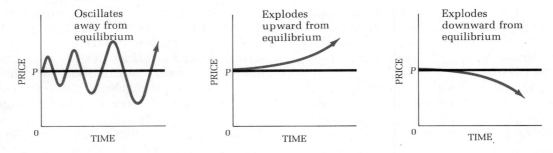

Neutral Equilibrium.   Price fluctuates around the equilibrium level at *P*.   Price has no permanent tendency to converge toward equilibrium or to diverge from it.

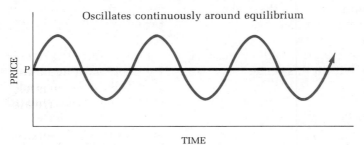

This suggests the following definition:

Stable equilibrium is a condition in which an object or system (such as a price, firm, industry, or market) in equilibrium, when subjected to a shock sufficient to disturb its position, returns toward its initial equilibrium as a result of self-restoring forces.

General Equilibrium: "Everything Depends on Everything Else"

There are various ways of thinking about equilibrium. For example, in the early part of this century, a famous American economist, Henry J. Davenport, investigated relationships between the prices of corn, pork, and land. He noted part of his conclusions in verse:

> The price of pig
> Is something big;
> Because its corn, you'll understand
> Is high-priced, too;
> Because it grew
> Upon the high-priced farming land.
> If you'd know why
> That land is high
> Consider this: its price is big
> Because it pays
> Thereon to raise
> The costly corn, the high-priced pig.

Long before Davenport observed connections between these three variables, a prominent French economist of the mid-nineteenth century, Frederic Bastiat, expressed amazement about the Paris of his day. Hundreds of thousands of people, he remarked, live in the city, yet each day a wide variety of goods and services are provided in approximately correct quantities without coordination or planning by any single agency. "Imagination," Bastiat wrote,

> is baffled when it tries to appreciate the vast multiplicity of commodities which must enter tomorrow to preserve the inhabitants from famine. Yet all sleep and

their slumbers are not disturbed for a single minute by the prospects of such a frightful catastrophe.

What Davenport and Bastiat (and many other observers as well) were commenting upon is the notion that a complex economy is a vast system of interrelated components—a system in which "everything depends on everything else." You can gain a better appreciation of this idea by examining some of the features of what is known as general-equilibrium theory.

Partial and General Equilibrium

Until now, almost all of our attention in microeconomics has been focused on "partial-equilibrium" theory, as distinguished from "general-equilibrium" theory. What do these terms mean?

Partial-equilibrium theory analyzes and develops models of a particular market on the assumption that other markets are in equilibrium. It thus ignores the interrelations of prices and quantities that may exist between markets.

For example, ordinary supply-and-demand analysis is normally of a partial-equilibrium nature. The reason is that it focuses on a single market while neglecting others. This method of investigation can be extremely useful for gaining a better understanding of how a market works. In particular, it is invaluable for analyzing the effects of such things as price control, rationing, minimum wages, and commodity taxes, as was done in earlier chapters. However, by ignoring the ramifications and repercussions of price and quantity changes that may occur in other markets, we are overlooking the possibility that such changes could have a significant influence on the market we are studying.

In view of this, it is necessary to think of the price system as an interrelated whole and to recognize that partial analyses can provide only approximations of a full explanation. This being the case, we need a "general" approach, which simultaneously takes into account all product and resource markets in the economy.

Leaders in Economics

Paul Samuelson is probably the world's most widely known economist. Several generations of college students in the U.S. and abroad took their first course in economics using his introductory textbook. Millions of readers of American and foreign newspapers and magazines have seen his articles on current economic policies. Professional economists throughout the world have studied, and have been stimulated toward further research by, the extraordinary range of his scientific work. This includes hundreds of profound papers and several books dealing with theoretical topics in many areas of economics.

Storehouse of Insights
In his *Foundations of Economic Analysis* (1947), which immediately established Samuelson's reputation as a highly creative economist, he presented a systematic analysis of static and dynamic economic theory. He described, in mathemat-ical form, the "state" of an economic system in equilibrium and the process or path of adjustment from one state to another. He then linked statics and dynamics by what he called the **correspondence princi- ple.** This is one of the most fundamental concepts in the *Foundations*. The proposition demonstrates that, before comparative statics (the comparison of equilibrium positions in static states) can be meaningful, it is first necessary to develop a dynamic analysis of stability.

In general, Paul Samuelson's scientific contributions—developed in precise mathematical rather than literary form—have greatly deepened our understanding of how the economic system works. He has shown the general applicability of the concept of maximization, subject to constraints, to many branches of economics. In recognition of his extraordinary contributions to economics, he became, in 1970, the first American to receive the Nobel Prize in Economic Science.

Paul Anthony Samuelson
1915–
America's First Nobel Laureate in Economic Science

General-equilibrium theory analyzes the interrelations between prices and quantities of goods and resources in different markets. It demonstrates the possibility of simultaneous equilibrium between all markets. Thus it views the economy as a system composed of interdependent parts.

In general-equilibrium theory, the structure of the economy is analyzed as a *system* of interrelated markets. The theory assumes that, if all participants are given such information as consumer demand schedules, resource supply schedules, production functions, and the demand for money for each particular market, equilibrium forces will cause all goods and resource prices to adjust themselves in a mutually consistent manner. The entire system can then settle down in a stable equilibrium of supply and demand.

However, any change in the determinants affecting the price and quantity of a good or resource can upset the entire system. This will have widespread repercussions on the equilibrium prices and quantities of all other goods and resources. Therefore, in the real world, there is often a significant degree of interdependence among various markets.

A General-Equilibrium Model: Two Commodities

A full explanation of general equilibrium requires considerable use of mathematics. However, many of the basic ideas can be conveyed without mathematics by a simple supply-and-demand analysis involving only two commodities—say, meat and fish.

In Exhibit 3, Figure (a), there is a market demand curve for meat, D_M, and a market supply curve for meat, S_M. Their intersection determines the equilibrium price of meat, P_M, and the equilibrium quantity of meat, Q_M. Similarly, in Figure (b), the intersection of the market demand and supply curves of fish, D_F and S_F, determines the equilibrium price of fish, P_F, and the equilibrium quantity of fish, Q_F.

Before we consider any changes in the curves, it is important to note some of the assumptions on which they rest. Basically, each curve in any one market is drawn on the assumption that the equilibrium price of the good in the other market remains constant. For example, in Figure (a) the demand curve for meat assumes that the price of fish in Figure (b) is at its equilibrium level P_F. Similarly, in Figure (b) the demand curve for fish assumes that the equilibrium price of meat in Figure (a) is at its equilibrium level P_M.

Exhibit 3
General Equilibrium—A Two-Commodity Model: Demand and Supply Curves for Meat and Fish

In Figure (a) the demand curve for meat D_M is drawn on the assumption that the equilibrium price of fish P_F in Figure (b) is given. Similarly, in Figure (b) the demand curve for fish D_F is drawn on the assumption that the equilibrium price of meat P_M in Figure (a) is given. The supply curves of meat S_M and of fish S_F are drawn under the same assumptions.

In Figure (a), suppose a specific tax of T per unit is imposed on meat sellers. The supply curve shifts from S_M to S'_M reflecting the cost increase. The equilibrium price of meat rises to P'_M and the equilibrium

quantity falls to Q'_M. Consumers, therefore, substitute fish for meat, causing the demand curve for fish in Figure (b) to shift to the right from D_F to D'_F. As a result, the equilibrium price of fish increases to P'_F and the equilibrium quantity to Q'_F.

In addition to these changes, some resources (not shown in the diagrams) are likely to move out of meat production and into fish production. This will cause the supply curves in both industries to shift. This process will continue until a new state of general equilibrium is reached.

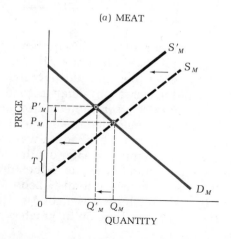

(a) MEAT

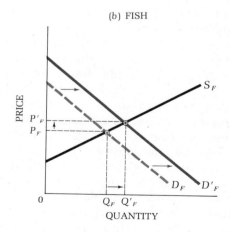

(b) FISH

Other assumptions not evident from the diagrams are also made. In particular, it is assumed that (1) consumer preferences for goods are given, (2) the stock of resources available for production is fixed, and (3) the techniques of production (the production functions for goods) are given. These conditions are among the basic determinants of the system being described. Therefore, a change in any one of them will disturb the existing equilibrium pattern.

Effect of a Specific Tax

Now suppose that government imposes a **specific tax** — a tax per unit of commodity — on sellers of meat. In Figure (a), if the tax is equal to T per unit, it will increase the cost to suppliers by shifting the supply curve from S_M to S'_M. This will cause the equilibrium price of meat to rise to P'_M and the equilibrium quantity to fall to Q'_M.

Because the price of meat compared with fish is now *relatively* higher than before the tax, consumers will substitute some fish for meat in their consumption patterns. This will cause an increase in the demand for fish — a shift of the demand curve in Figure (b) to the right from D_F to D'_F. Therefore the equilibrium price of fish will rise from P_F to P'_F and the equilibrium quantity will increase from Q_F to Q'_F. As a result of the tax, therefore, both the price of meat and the price of fish have risen. But the quantity of meat produced and consumed has decreased while the quantity of fish produced and consumed has increased.

Under normal circumstances, various other repercussions, not shown in the diagrams, will occur. For example, after the tax, fewer resources are needed to produce the smaller quantity of meat, while more resources are needed to produce the larger quantity of fish. Therefore, the price and employment of resources in meat production will decline. At the same time, the price and employment of resources in fish production will rise. As a result, some resources will move out of meat production and into fish production.

As these movements occur, the supply curves in the two industries will shift. This will cause mar-ket prices and quantities to change. In addition, the change in relative resource prices will cause shifts in the pattern of income distribution, and this will have further repercussions on the demand for the two commodities. This adjustment process will continue until the system is once again in general equilibrium.

Interdependence and the Circular Flow

The interdependence that exists between markets in the economy can be extended beyond what is shown in the model in Exhibit 3. However, the model would then be considerably more complicated. It is sufficient to convey the overall nature of the interrelations by means of a familiar circular-flow diagram. This is done in Exhibit 4.

The model is self-explanatory. Note that it lists the conditions that are assumed to be given or fixed in the household sector and in the business sector. The important thing to observe is that it emphasizes the *interdependence* between households, businesses, product markets, and factor markets.

The overall concept conveyed by the circular-flow model is that the quantities supplied and demanded for each product and for each factor of production must be equal. When this occurs, the economy is in a state of general equilibrium.

The earliest notion of general equilibrium was developed in the eighteenth century by a group of French economists called the **physiocrats.** Foremost among them was a physician named François Quesnay. In 1758, he presented a circular-flow model to depict what he called the "natural order" of an economic system. These ideas were subsequently developed in much greater depth and with mathematical precision in the late nineteenth century by a Swiss-French economist, Leon Walras (1834–1910). Although he was a college dropout, he nevertheless ranks as one of the greatest economists of all time.

Exhibit 4
Economic Interdependence—General Equilibrium and the Circular Flow

Households and businesses are linked through the product markets, where goods and services are exchanged, and through the resource markets, where the factors of production are exchanged.   The economy is in a state of general equilibrium when the quantities supplied and demanded of goods and services and of factors of production are equal.

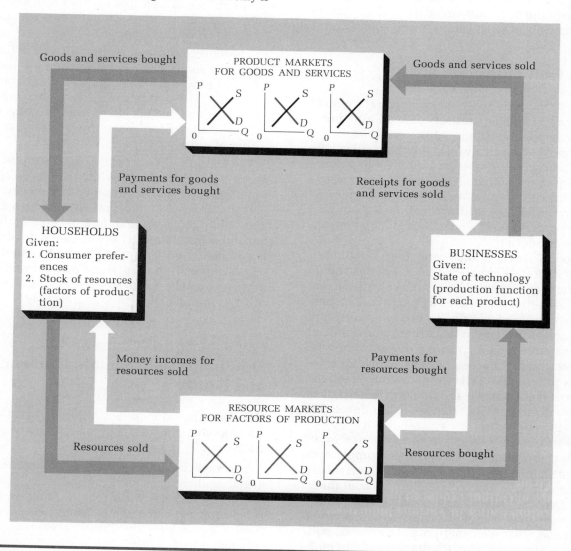

Welfare Economics

The concept of general equilibrium provides us with an overview of a perfectly competitive economy. But what are the main characteristics of such an economy? Is perfect competition "good" or "bad"? The answers to these questions provide some insights into what is known as **welfare economics.** This is a branch of economic theory concerned with the development of principles for maximizing society's satisfactions (that is, its social welfare).

Pareto Optimality

To begin with, what do we mean by social welfare? The concept cannot be precisely defined, and therefore it is impossible to measure. As a result, we cannot assert objectively that any particular economic situation represents greater or lesser welfare for society than another. One of the main reasons for this difficulty is that *we cannot make interpersonal comparisons of utility* or satisfactions. That is, the welfare of one person cannot be compared with that of another.

For example, as a rational consumer, I would feel better off if I could keep all my income so that I could spend more for consumption. But, as a good citizen, I might feel better off if I gave up part of my income (through taxes and charitable contributions) and thereby consumed less so that others who were not as fortunate as I could consume more. Similarly, some people argue that as a nation of consumers we are better off spending all our income on ourselves. Others contend that we should contribute part of our national income as foreign aid to less developed countries.

Therefore, even though we cannot make interpersonal comparisons of utility, such comparisons are made all the time. Indeed, it would be virtually impossible to have any social policy without them. Why? Because almost any social policy makes some people better off while making others worse off. Ideally, what we usually want are social policies that make some people better off *without making others worse off.* This involves what economists and other social scientists call "Pareto optimality."

Pareto optimality is a condition that exists in a social organization when no change can be implemented that will make someone better off without making someone else worse off—each in his or her own estimation.

This concept, named after a famous Italian-Swiss sociologist and economist, Vilfredo Pareto (1848–1923), leads to two important principles:

1. Any social action that benefits at least one person without harming someone else will clearly increase social welfare. Therefore, any such action should be undertaken.

2. The effect on social welfare of any action that benefits some while harming others—the *numbers* of people are immaterial—cannot be determined. The reason is that we cannot compare satisfactions and dissatisfactions among people. That is, *we cannot make interpersonal comparisons of utility.*

The first principle provides a useful guide for formulating public policies, while the second contains some interesting implications. The second principle tells us, for example, that, even though a particular policy (such as the imprisonment of criminals) benefits a large majority of the people while harming a small minority, we cannot be sure that adherence to it results in an increase in social welfare. At best we can only *assume* that it does, but we cannot prove it in any objective, scientific way.

General Equilibrium and Pareto Optimality — Economic Efficiency and Equity

What are the implications of Pareto optimality for an economic system? The answer can be stated in the form of a proposition:

When a perfectly competitive economy achieves a general equilibrium of prices and quantities, no economic entity (individual, household, or firm) can be made better off without some other entity being made worse off. The system has therefore attained a Pareto optimum—*an economically efficient allocation of resources.* (NOTE Certain qualifications to this statement are pointed out in the following sections.)

The proof of this proposition requires considerably more advanced economic theory than is covered in this book. However, you can appreciate the sense of the proposition on the basis of what was learned in previous chapters. For example, suppose that a perfectly competitive economy has settled down in general equilibrium. Keeping in mind the conditions that are "given"—namely, the pattern of consumer preferences, the stock of productive factors, and the state of technology—what are the main characteristics of the resulting state of balance?

Efficiency of Consumption in the Household Sector

In the household sector, each consuming unit spends its income on the goods and services it wants most, given the prices it must pay. Each consuming unit therefore allocates its income in such a way that it maximizes total utility or satisfactions. In terms of Pareto optimality, this means that society has achieved efficiency in consumption. This is because *no transfer of commodities can be made between any two consuming units that will make one consuming unit better off without making the other worse off.*

Efficiency of Production in the Business Sector

In the business sector, as you learned in the study of perfect competition, each firm in the long run ends up producing in the output market at the level of production at which certain efficiency conditions apply.

Among them:

$MC = P$ This means that the value of the last unit of the good to the consumer (measured by the price the consumer pays for the last unit, which is equal to the price paid for any other unit) is equal to the value of the resources used to produce that unit.

$MC = ATC = LRAC$ This means that the firm is producing the optimum output with the optimum-size plant. Therefore, it is allocating all its resources in a technically efficient manner.

Equity and Efficiency in the Economy

In the input markets, firms also achieve equilibrium by adhering to marginal principles. Thus, every firm hires each factor of production up to the point at which the marginal cost or price of the factor is equal to the value of what it contributes (its marginal revenue product). Each factor thus receives what it is "worth"—the value of what it contributes to total output—as determined in competitive markets by supply and demand. This, you recall, is the meaning of the **contributive standard**. It is the standard by which equity (economic justice) in the distribution of income is judged in a capitalistic system. To refresh your understanding of the concept, look up the meaning of *contributive standard* in the Dictionary at the back of the book.

Let us look again at the equilibrium conditions (equations) $MC = P$ and $MC = ATC = LRAC$. What do these equations mean? Basically they tell us that society has achieved **technical efficiency** in production by producing the largest possible volume of output with available resources. Thus, *no transfer of resources can be made between the production of any two goods that will increase the output of one good without decreasing the output of the other.* In other words, the economy is producing on its production-possibilities curve instead of at some point inside it. Therefore, there is full employment of all resources. Moreover, society has also achieved **economic efficiency** because the goods that are being produced are those that people want to buy with their available incomes.

General equilibrium and economic efficiency thus go hand in hand. It is particularly interesting to realize the remarkable way in which these end results come about:

All participants in the economy—consumers, businesspeople, resource owners—acting *independently* in their own self-interest and without direction from government, make millions of market decisions daily. These determine *what, how,* and *for whom* goods shall be produced. Yet the economic system, because it is perfectly competitive, is guided by Adam Smith's "invisible hand" toward general equilibrium and economic efficiency. This is an end result that, as Smith pointed out, is "no part of anyone's intention."

Implications for Social Welfare

Should we conclude from this that perfect competition leads to the best of all possible worlds? As pointed out earlier, when a perfectly competitive economy is in general equilibrium, it has attained a Pareto optimum. This is a situation in which no person can be made better off without someone else being made worse off, each in his or her own estimation. However, there are some qualifications. The more important ones have already been discussed in several earlier chapters. Therefore, it is sufficient to summarize them briefly at this time.

Social Costs and Social Benefits

Competitive prices tend to reflect private costs and private benefits, but they may exclude some social costs and social benefits. Environmental pollution arising from production is a typical example of a cost to society that may not be included in a manufacturer's private costs. Likewise, flood control and conservation practices undertaken by a seller provide illustrations of benefits that accrue to many people other than those who buy the producer's product. Therefore:

> To the extent that some social costs and benefits are not reflected in market prices, general equilibrium will fail to provide an optimum allocation of society's resources.

Income Distribution and Equity

In a system of perfect competition, the owners of each factor of production are paid according to the "contributive standard." That is, the owners of each factor are paid what their factor is "worth," as measured by what it contributes to total output. This is known as the **marginal-productivity theory of income distribution.**

According to this principle, a person who is twice as productive as another is paid twice as much. Whether or not this is a just or equitable standard of income distribution is a normative question rather than a positive one. Each society will answer the question for itself. Some might argue that the con-tributive standard takes too little account of poorer people's "needs." Therefore:

> To the extent that society regards the contributive standard as *unjust*, general equilibrium will *not* provide an equitable distribution of the economy's income.

Conclusion: Norms of Efficiency for Welfare Economics

You can now appreciate more fully the role played by modern welfare economics. In broad terms, welfare economics deals with the normative aspects of microeconomics. Welfare economics is concerned not with what the perfect world would look like but with the changes that may be undertaken to improve the well-being of consumers and producers in *today's* world. Welfare economics does this by providing us with a norm or standard expressed in terms of economic efficiency. This enables us to state unambiguously whether one equilibrium position is better or worse than another.

From what we now know about microeconomics, it is clear that perfect competition leads (with some qualifications) to an optimum allocation of society's resources. This is ensured by Smith's "invisible hand." Other types of market structures — such as unregulated monopoly, monopolistic competition, and oligopoly — do not achieve an optimum allocation. This suggests that the norm provided by welfare economics can serve as a guide for government intervention in markets. Intervention can occur through taxes, subsidies, direct regulation, or other means. The purpose of government intervention is to correct for costs and gains that result when the norm is violated. In other words:

> In markets in which supply and demand forces serve efficiently as mechanisms for allocating society's resources, no intervention by government is needed. But when markets fail to perform efficiently, certain types of intervention may be called for.

The nature and effects of various kinds of intervention pose many interesting problems that will occupy our attention in the following chapters.

Charles Phelps Cushing

Historical Picture Services

AP/Wide World Photos

Leon Walras
1834–1910

Vilfredo Pareto
1848–1923

Gerard Debreu
1921–

General Equilibrium and Welfare Economics

Leon Walras's fame rests on his formulation of the theory of general equilibrium, which he developed rigorously through the use of mathematics. He thus became one of the founders of mathematical economics, which has flourished to this day.

While serving as a professor at the University of Lausanne, Switzerland, Leon Walras (pronounced "valrah") published his great work, *Elements of Pure Economics* (1874). In this book he showed how a system of simultaneous equations could be used to describe an economy in general equilibrium. The "description," however, is determinate in a formal theoretical sense only. The necessary data cannot be obtained, and the number of simultaneous equations that would have to be

solved is virtually infinite. Nevertheless, this does not destroy the value of general-equilibrium theory. The virtue of the concept lies in the precise way in which it demonstrates the mutual interdependence of economic phenomena.

Walras was succeeded at Lausanne by Vilfredo Pareto, an Italian scholar.

In his major work, *Manual of Political Economy* (1909), Pareto, like Walras, formulated concepts of general equilibrium under static conditions. However, Pareto was also concerned with the problem of how to maximize total satisfactions in an economy. He developed the concept now commonly referred to as ***Pareto optimality***—a notion that is fundamental to modern welfare economics. In passing, it should be

noted that Pareto also made notable contributions to sociology. In fact, his reputation in that field is as strong as his reputation in economics.

Continuing Influence
Together, Walras and Pareto constitute what is known as the "Lausanne School" of economic thought. The influence of this school on subsequent writers—especially in mathematical economics, general-equilibrium theory, and welfare economics—has been enormous. Gerard Debreu is a contemporary scholar following in the Lausanne tradition. A mathematician and economist at the University of California, he was awarded the 1984 Nobel Prize in Economic Science for helping to "prove" the theory of general equilibrium.

Rat Economics

What motivates us? Psychologists often ask this question, and economists have been asking it too in recent years. Some economists, conducting experiments in the hope of finding answers, are getting results that support conclusions derived from many areas of economic theory.

Income Distribution

Two economists who have done pioneering work along such lines are Ray Battalio and John Kagel of Texas A&M University. In one of their studies, they set up a token economy in a women's ward of a state psychiatric hospital. Patients were paid tokens for performing various jobs, such as sweeping the floor, making the beds, and so on.

A remarkable result of the study was that the *pattern of earnings among the patients resembled the distribution of income in the United States as a whole.* For example, the highest fifth of the income earners at the hospital got 41% of all the earnings, compared with 42% for the highest fifth in the nation. The lowest fifth at the institution got 7%, compared with a little more than 5% for the country as a whole. Kagel and Battalio also came up with some fascinating findings in studies of mixed (male–female) token economies. In one of their studies they found that the median token income of women was 69% that of men. This compares with about 60% for the economy as a whole.

Income–Leisure Tradeoff

Do rising wages encourage workers to work harder, or do they work less hard as wages increase? The evidence indicates that, as wages rise, the work increases — but only up to a point. Thereafter, further increases in wages result in a reduction in work because workers are satisfied with what they are earning. This relationship gives rise to a "backward-bending labor supply curve," illustrating a tradeoff between income and leisure.

Kagel, Battalio, and several psychologists decided to test the income–leisure tradeoff under controlled laboratory conditions. The experimenters taught pigeons and rats in Skinner boxes (devised by Harvard psychologist B. F. Skinner) to peck at buttons and push levers in order to earn rewards of food. This research confirmed the existence of a backward-bending labor supply curve for the animals. As their wage rate (measured in terms of servings of food) went up, hungry pigeons and rats pecked and pushed harder and faster — but only up to a point. The point differed with each animal. But beyond their respective points, even though the animals were not satiated, their efforts slowed down as they traded off some work for more leisure.

Negative Income Tax

The research team also used Skinner boxes to investigate the effects of a negative income tax. Some economists and legislators have proposed this type of reverse income tax. It would provide government payments to poor people whose incomes are below a minimum level. As the recipients' income from work rises towards the minimum, the government's payments fall to zero. By programming the boxes to provide varying amounts of "free" food intermittently while the animals were working, the team observed several interesting results:

- The animals reduced their work effort approximately in proportion to the quantity of free food they received.

- Work reduction was relatively greater among the low-wage rats. These rats had to work longer for less food. High-wage rats seemed to enjoy working and reduced their efforts relatively less.

- Total income, both earned and free food, was less when free food was provided than when it was not.

Conclusion: Food for Thought

These studies have been criticized for being too simplistic. The experimenters disagree. They reply that economic theory often fails to predict the outcome of real-world policies. Theories, they argue, should be able to predict simple laboratory behavior before they are used as a basis for policy prescriptions.

What You Have Learned

1. The concept of equilibrium is of fundamental importance in economics. An equilibrium position may be stable, unstable, or neutral — in a static or in a dynamic sense.

2. A static model provides a "snapshot" of the essential features of an economic phenomenon at an instant in time, whereas a dynamic model provides a "motion picture" over a period of time. Although static analysis encompasses most of economic theory, many important problems cannot be analyzed without the use of dynamics.

3. General equilibrium, as distinguished from partial equilibrium, emphasizes the interdependence that exists between markets and sectors of the economy. The notion of general equilibrium can be depicted by a circular-flow diagram.

4. The concept of general equilibrium goes hand in hand with the science of welfare economics. The latter is concerned with the development of principles for maximizing social welfare. Thus, when a perfectly competitive economy achieves a general equilibrium of prices and quantities, it has attained a Pareto optimum — an efficient allocation of resources — and therefore has maximized social welfare. Some qualifications to this conclusion may be needed, however, depending on such factors as the inclusion of social costs and social benefits in firms' activities and the extent to which society regards the contributive standard of income distribution as inequitable.

Terms and Concepts To Review

equilibrium	physiocrats
static model	specific tax
comparative statics	welfare economics
dynamic model	Pareto optimality
stable equilibrium	contributive standard
partial-equilibrium theory	economic efficiency
general-equilibrium theory	marginal-productivity theory of income distribution
correspondence principle	

For Discussion

1. Which is more important — the stability of an equilibrium position or its "location"? Explain.

2. You have already learned the concepts of *demand price* and *supply price* in previous chapters. (To help your understanding, look up their meanings in the Dictionary at the back of the book.) Using these notions, and thinking in terms of supply and demand curves, formulate definitions of stable and unstable *quantity* equilibrium. (HINT You may find it helpful first to formulate definitions of stable and unstable *price* equilibrium in terms of quantity supplied and quantity demanded. Then use a parallel procedure to define stable and unstable quantity equilibrium in terms of demand price and supply price.)

3. In terms of supply and demand curves, can a price equilibrium be stable for an upward movement and unstable or neutral for a downward movement, and vice versa? Is the same true for a quantity equilibrium in terms of a leftward or rightward movement? Explain.

4. "If the world economy were perfectly competitive, a tariff (tax on imports) would result in a misallocation of resources and a reduction in net social welfare for the world community." Do you agree? Why?

5. Nations sometimes employ rationing as a means of distributing scarce goods. Usually, consumers are given ration coupons entitling them to purchase, say, 1 pound of meat and 1 pound of fish per week. In this way, an equal amount of each good is assigned to each consumer. Is this "fair"? Can you propose an alternative method of rationing that is more equitable?

6. It is contended by some social critics that, because we do not know the actual distribution of income that will maximize satisfaction, it must be assumed that an equal distribution of income out of any given level of national income would most likely maximize satisfaction. Evaluate this argument.

Part 7

Microeconomics Today: Ideas, Issues, and Policies

Chapter 28

Industrial Organization: Structure, Conduct, Performance

Learning Guide

Watch for answers to these important questions

What is industrial organization? Of what significance are market structure, conduct, and performance in the study of industrial organization?

How is market structure affected by such factors as seller concentration, product differentiation, and barriers to entry? Can the influences of these factors be measured?

How is market conduct affected by business pricing and competitive practices?

How is market performance affected by market structure and conduct? What are their impacts on efficiency, equity, stability, and growth?

When you studied microeconomic theory, you learned how firms allocate their resources under different types of market structures. These market structures, you will recall, were classified in the following way:

Perfect competition: Numerous sellers; standardized product.

Monopoly: One seller; unique product (that is, one that has no close substitutes).

Imperfect competition

(1) **Monopolistic competition:** Many sellers; differentiated products.

(2) **Oligopoly**

    (a) *Perfect oligopoly*: Few sellers; standardized products.

    (b) *Imperfect oligopoly*: Few sellers; differentiated products.

In this chapter, the role of markets as mechanisms for organizing firms' resources is explored. This is why the chapter is entitled *industrial organization.* It deals with a branch of applied microeconomics concerned with the ways in which firms direct their production activities in meeting consumer demands. The study of industrial organization may be pursued within a framework of three concepts:

1. *Market structure*—the types of competitive environments within which firms operate.

2. *Market conduct*—the practices and policies that firms adopt in their pursuit of profits.

3. *Market performance*—the effect of business behavior on the four economic goals: efficiency, equity, stability, and growth.

Market Structure

The structure of a market depends on the elements of which it is composed. Some of these are already familiar to you from your earlier study of the theoretical market structures outlined above. Now, however, the elements must be examined in somewhat closer detail. Among the more important are these:

1. Seller concentration
2. Product differentiation
3. Barriers to entry
4. Barriers to exit

Seller Concentration

The *number* of firms in a market is one of the factors determining market structure. So too is the *size* of firms in relation to one another. For example, in a market containing a few large firms, sellers may have a greater degree of monopoly power—an ability to influence market prices—than exists in a market containing many small firms.

It is useful to have some way of measuring the concentration of monopoly power in a particular market. Many measures, both theoretical and applied, have been devised for this purpose. Only a few, however, have had wide use because they are practical as well as easy to interpret.

Measures of Concentration

A measure that is extensively used by economists and government agencies to evaluate the monopoly power of a firm is ***market share.*** This is the percentage of an industry's output accounted for by an individual firm. For example, if 1,000 units of a good were sold in a particular year, and one firm in the industry sold 500 of those units, the firm's market share for that year would be 50 percent. In practice, market share is usually measured on the basis of sales. But other measures, such as value added at each stage of production or value of shipments, are also sometimes used.

In developed industrial societies such as ours, where many industries are dominated by a few large firms, it has proven useful to expand the concept of market share to a measure called ***concentration ratio.*** This is the percentage of an industry's output accounted for by its largest firms—typically, by its four largest. (Concentration ratios for larger numbers of firms are also somewhat common.) As in the measurement of market share, a concentration ratio is usually based on sales, value added, or value of shipments. Other measures of size, such as assets or employment, are also sometimes used. Concentration ratios in various industries in the United States are shown in Exhibit 1.

A second way of measuring the degree of concentration in a market is by use of the ***Herfindahl index*** (also called the *Herfindahl-Hirschman index*). It may be defined as the sum of the squares of the market shares for all the firms in an industry. (Measures of size other than market share, such as those mentioned above, may also be used.)

For example, suppose an industry contains four firms, each with the following market share:

Firm A: 70%

Firm B: 15

Firm C: 10

Firm D: 5

Exhibit 1
Concentration Ratios in Various Industries: Percentage of Output Produced by the Four Largest Firms

Industry	Value of shipments (percent of industry total)
High-Concentration Industries	80–100
Primary aluminum	
Cigarettes	
Aircraft engines and parts	
Metal containers	
Television broadcasting	
Medium-Concentration Industries	50–79
Photographic equipment	
Tires and inner tubes	
Aircraft	
Motor vehicles	
Industrial chemicals	
Low-Concentration Industries	Less than 50
Soap and detergents	
Electronic computing equipment	
Radio and television sets	
Construction machinery	
Toilet preparations	
Petroleum refining	
Pharmaceutical preparations	
Fluid milk	
Bottled and canned soft drinks	
Women's and misses' dresses	

Source: Bureau of the Census, U.S. Department of Commerce.

The Herfindahl index is calculated from the formula:

Herfindahl index

$$= \left(\begin{array}{c}\text{Firm A's}\\\text{market}\\\text{share}\end{array}\right)^2 + \left(\begin{array}{c}\text{Firm B's}\\\text{market}\\\text{share}\end{array}\right)^2 + \left(\begin{array}{c}\text{Firm C's}\\\text{market}\\\text{share}\end{array}\right)^2 + \left(\begin{array}{c}\text{Firm D's}\\\text{market}\\\text{share}\end{array}\right)^2$$

$$= (.70)^2 + (.15)^2 + (.10)^2 + (.05)^2$$
$$= 0.525$$

It is important to note that, because of the squaring process, the magnitude of the Herfindahl index is affected disproportionately more by large firms than by small ones. (For example, a 90 percent market share, when squared, equals 0.81. A 10 percent market share, when squared, equals 0.01.) Therefore, it is not necessary to know all of the market shares in an industry in order to estimate a Herfindahl index. The index can be closely approximated simply by using the market shares of the industry's largest firms.

How small or large can a Herfindahl index be? The answer depends upon the number and size of firms in an industry. In general:

— A Herfindahl index can range from 0 to 1. An index of 0 denotes pure competition — the absence of monopoly power. An index of 1 denotes pure monopoly — the absence of competition. An index between these limits denotes the degree of monopoly power.

— If all firms in a market are of *equal size*, the Herfindahl index equals the reciprocal of the number (N) of firms — that is, $1/N$. This is demonstrated in Exhibit 2.

Trends of Concentration

Various studies of concentration have been made from time to time. Have the long-run trends been rising, stable, or declining? This question can be answered by distinguishing between two kinds of concentration: (1) market or intraindustry concentration, and (2) aggregate or overall concentration.

Market (Intraindustry) Concentration Economists in universities and in government agencies who have studied the long-run trends of concentration have come up with mixed findings. However, a preponderance of the evidence suggests several broad conclusions:

1. In the manufacturing sector, market structures are characterized predominately by oligopoly and to a lesser extent by monopolistic competition. The overall pattern of concentration has exhibited two long-run trends:

   (a) A slight decrease for the period 1900 to 1950.

   (b) A moderate increase since 1950.

Exhibit 2
Herfindahl Indexes for Equal-Sized Firms

The Herfindahl index equals the reciprocal of the number (N) of *equal-sized* firms in an industry.

For example, in Industry I there is only one firm, so the index is 1. This denotes a case of pure monopoly. In Industry II there are two firms, so the index is ½. It

follows that in an industry composed of 1,000 firms, the index would be $\frac{1}{1,000}$. In general, as the number of firms becomes indefinitely large, the index approaches 0. This denotes a case of pure competition.

The Herfindahl index can thus range between 0 and 1.

Firms	Industry I $N = 1$ Market share	$\left(\dfrac{Market}{share}\right)^2$	Industry II $N = 2$ Market share	$\left(\dfrac{Market}{share}\right)^2$	Industry III $N = 3$ Market share	$\left(\dfrac{Market}{share}\right)^2$	Industry IV $N = 4$ Market share	$\left(\dfrac{Market}{share}\right)^2$
Firm A	1.00	1	0.50	0.25	0.333	0.1111	0.25	0.0625
Firm B			0.50	0.25	0.333	0.1111	0.25	0.0625
Firm C					0.333	0.1111	0.25	0.0625
Firm D							0.25	0.0625
Herfindahl index		1		0.50		0.3333		0.2500
1/N		1/1		1/2		1/3		1/4

2. In the nonmanufacturing sector, market structures range across the entire competitive spectrum. Thus:

(a) Agriculture, forestry, fisheries, and services have always been, and continue to be, strongly competitive.

(b) Retailing and finance are characterized predominantly by monopolistic competition, and to a lesser extent by weak oligopoly.

(c) Regulated industries such as electricity, gas, and public transportation have market structures that range from pure monopoly in local markets to strong oligopoly both in local and in national markets.

Aggregate (Overall) Concentration   A concept different from market concentration is aggregate concentration. This is the share of sales, assets, value added, profits, employment (or any other indicator of size) accounted for by the largest firms across

entire sectors or subsectors of the economy. The number of "largest firms" may range from a few dozen to several hundred depending on the size of the sector being measured. An ***aggregate-concentration ratio*** provides an indication of the relative size of firms within a large segment of the economy.

Various studies of aggregate concentration have been made from time to time. A synthesis of their findings reveals the following trends during the present half-century.

1. In the manufacturing sector, concentration among the largest 50, 100, 200, and 500 firms has increased substantially. To a large extent this is due to the fact that many large corporations today are "conglomerates," holding leadership positions in several industries rather than just one.

2. In the nonmanufacturing sector, concentration among the top 200 firms has increased moderately. The largest gains have occurred in retailing; the smallest, in public utilities.

Have these trends of concentration come about because of greater "monopolization" of the economy? The answer is not an unequivocal *yes* or *no*.

Firms in some industries may gain a high degree of concentration because of improvements in efficiency, product innovation, and lower prices. Therefore, it cannot be assumed from concentration figures alone that high concentration is the result of monopoly power.

Product Differentiation

Seller concentration is only one major aspect of market structure. Another is product differentiation. This, as you will recall from your study of monopolistic competition and oligopoly, can take many forms. Products can be differentiated by brand name, color of package, location of the seller,

customer service, credit conditions, or personality of the salesperson—even if the products themselves are physically the same. Product differentiation thus benefits buyers by providing them with a way to distinguish between competing goods on the basis of *nonprice* factors.

But product differentiation can also benefit sellers. How? By enabling them, through advertising, merchandising, or other nonprice marketing strategies, to shift the demand curves for their products to more favorable positions. This may enhance their market power by giving them greater control over price. Some possibilities can be explained in terms of Exhibit 3:

In Figure (a), a successful marketing strategy aimed at differentiating its product has shifted Firm X's demand curve to the right—from D to D'. As a result, Firm X can now sell more units at any given price. For example, it can sell 60 units instead of 40 units at $5 per unit. Of course, this increase in demand might have come at the expense of some

---

Exhibit 3
Changing a Demand Curve by Means of Product Differentiation

A firm adopts product-differentiation strategies in order to shift its demand curve to a more desirable position—one that provides *greater control over price.*

Figure (a): Through appropriate advertising or merchandising tactics, Firm X may manage to shift the demand curve from D to D'. This will enable Firm X to sell more units of its goods at any given price.

Figure (b): The increase in demand achieved by Firm X may come at the expense of a competitor, such as

Firm Y. This can be seen in the decrease in demand from D to D'.

Figure (c): Through product differentiation, Firm Z can manage to reduce the elasticity of demand for its product. Thus, along the new demand curve D', an increase in price from $4 to $5 per unit results in a larger total revenue than does the same increase in price along the old demand curve D. (Compare the total revenues at $4 and $5 along each demand curve.)

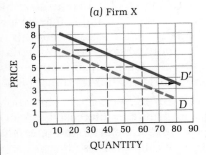

(a) Firm X

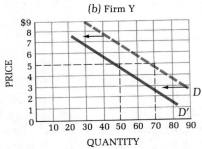

(b) Firm Y

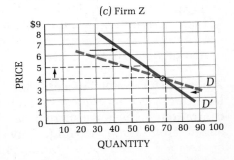

(c) Firm Z

competitors. Thus in Figure (b), Firm Y has experienced a decrease in demand from D to D'. Consequently, Firm Y can sell less at any given price — for example, 50 units instead of 70 units at $5 per unit.

In Figure (c), Firm Z's marketing strategy made the demand curve less elastic by shifting it from D to D'. Consequently, Firm Z is now able to increase its price, say, from $4 to $5, and thereby increases its total revenue. Can you see why? By way of comparison, how would the increase in price affect total revenue along curve D? Along curve D'?

Product differentiation thus provides a way for firms *within certain industries* to enhance their market control. In which industries? Mostly in consumer goods rather than in producer goods — for two reasons:

- **Heterogeneous Consumer Products** Consumer goods tend to be more diversified than producer goods (such as raw materials from agriculture, forestries, fisheries and mining).

- **Inferior Consumer Knowledge** Buyers of consumer goods are usually less informed about the products they purchase than are buyers of producer goods. Consumer-goods buyers therefore tend to be more susceptible to persuasive advertising appeals.

Barriers to Entry

A third element of market structure is barriers to entry. They are important because they are a source of market power. As you will see, just as seller concentration may disclose information about *actual* competition in a market, so barriers to entry may say something about *potential* competition. Three types of market barriers may be distinguished:

Cost Barriers Firms that are not in an industry must usually pay certain "admission charges" in order to enter it. These charges reflect the benefits accruing to firms that are already in the industry — that is, the benefits of their being established. For example, "inside" firms may possess certain advantages such as patents, specialized equipment, managerial expertise, and economies of scale. Therefore, "outside" firms, in order to enter an industry and compete effectively, must incur the costs necessary to acquire equivalent advantages.

Product-differentiation Barriers These are the advertising expenses that a firm entering an industry undertakes in order to convince buyers that its product differs from those of its competitors. Advertising can thus be a chief means of differentiating products. But it can also serve as a barrier to entry, depending on the user-turnover rate of goods in specific types of industries. For example:

Consumer Nondurable-goods Industries These tend to produce products with relatively high user-turnover rates. Examples are breakfast cereals, cigarettes, soap, and nonprescription drugs. Evidence shows that advertising is a significant barrier to entry in these industries.

Consumer Durable-goods Industries These tend to produce products with relatively low user-turnover rates — such as major appliances, cars, and furniture. Evidence indicates that in these industries, advertising is not a significant barrier to entry.

Legal Barriers The most important barrier to entry in many markets is government. Through various types of laws permitting zoning, patents, franchises, limited licensing, and so on, firms that would otherwise enter an industry are prevented from doing so. In numerous cities and states, for example, the number of taxis, liquor stores, taverns, hospitals, and various other businesses is strictly limited. The effect of this is to protect, at the expense of consumers, the market power of firms that are already in the industry.

Barriers to Exit

The barriers to leaving an industry are as important as the barriers to entering it. Firms that can leave an industry at little cost are said to be operating in a **contestable market.** This is one characterized by ease of exit. The airline and trucking industries are examples. Their principal assets—planes and trucks—though expensive, are both mobile and readily resalable. This encourages a greater "turnover" of firms in the industry and hence more rapid adjustments of output and prices to changing market conditions.

In contrast, industries with high exit barriers, due to heavy fixed costs of specialized plant and equipment, do not respond as quickly to changes in demand. Examples include the steel and cement industries. Their inflexibility results in prolonged periods of depressed prices and profits when market conditions become unfavorable. As you will see later in the chapter, this has sometimes caused competitors to engage in illegal conspiracies in an effort to raise prices and enhance profitability.

Conclusion: Stability and Interrelations

Market structure concerns the economic environment in which firms operate. Although many elements determine market structure, the most relevant are (1) seller concentration, (2) product differentiation, (3) barriers to entry, and (4) barriers to exit.

What can be said about the stability and interrelations of these elements? In general:

The determinants of market structure tend to remain stable for long periods of time. However, when one or more of the determinants do change, they tend to cause changes in the others. This alters the market structures within which firms operate, and their market conduct and performance.

Market Conduct

You have seen that the study of market structure is concerned with the competitive environments within which firms operate. We now turn our attention to an analysis of market conduct—the behavior of firms in the marketplace in their pursuit of

profits. For convenience, the market tactics that firms employ may be grouped into two categories:

1. Pricing practices and policies
2. Competitive practices and policies

This classification is most relevant to imperfect competition, particularly oligopoly. The reason is that firms in oligopolistic industries have the strongest tendency to be *mutually interdependent* — heavily influenced by one another's market behavior. This is why the study of market conduct in industrial organization is confined almost exclusively to oligopolistic practices and policies.

Pricing Practices and Policies

When you studied how prices and outputs are determined under perfect competition, you learned that the existence of flexible prices enables an economy to allocate its resources efficiently. When you studied how prices and outputs are determined under imperfect competition, you learned that the existence of stable prices reduces the uncertainty and costs of producers.

How much price flexibility (or price rigidity) actually exists in oligopolistic markets? The answer cannot be given in any precise way because oligopolistic industries exhibit many different forms of pricing behavior. A few of the more important may be identified briefly.

Administered Pricing

Models of oligopoly behavior were first formulated in the 1930s. Since that time, many economists have expounded a concept called **administered pricing.** According to this idea, oligopolistic firms control not only supply but also demand. Executives are therefore able to manage ("administer") their firms' prices instead of having to accept the determination of prices by the free interactions of market forces.

The administered-pricing doctrine employs either of two major theories to explain how oligopolies set prices. These are known as cost-plus pricing and target-return pricing.

Cost-plus Pricing This theory contends that, at a given level of output, a seller's price (P) is determined by adding a percentage markup to the direct cost (or average variable cost, AVC) of the product. Thus:

$$P = AVC + \% \text{ markup } (AVC)$$

For example, suppose that at a firm's planned level of production, its average variable cost is $40 per unit. If management believes that a 50% markup on AVC will maximize profit, it will charge a price of $60 per unit:

$$P = \$40 + .50(\$40) = \$60 \text{ per unit}$$

If management finds that this price is too high to maximize profit, it may decide to reduce the markup to, say, 20% of AVC. This results in a price of $48 per unit:

$$P = \$40 + .20(\$40) = \$48 \text{ per unit}$$

Among accountants and business managers, the markup percentage is known as the **contribution margin.** It represents that part of the price, above a firm's AVC, that contributes to the recovery of fixed costs or overhead and the earning of profit.

These examples show that cost-plus pricing is simple and practical. This explains why it is employed extensively by business firms. Because of its widespread use, several aspects of it are worth noting:

1. *The right markup can maximize profit.* As the above example suggests, firms can learn to set prices through trial and error. In this way, they can approximate the profit-maximizing price — the same price that is determined in microeconomic theory by $MC = MR$. Indeed, a number of studies have shown that many firms actually adhere to a practice of *flexible* markup pricing. That is, they adjust their prices from time to time to take advantage of "what the market will bear" or "to meet the competition."

2. *The markup percentage varies inversely with price elasticity.* To maximize profit, a firm will try to set a markup percentage that yields the largest possible contribution to overhead and profit. It follows that products with high price elasticities of demand are likely to have relatively lower markup percentages, and vice versa. The reason for this is that the price elasticity of demand for a good is strongly influenced by the availability of substitute goods. Thus, markup percentages on soft drinks, frozen foods, and most other grocery store items tend to be low while those on fancy foods, sports cars, and most other specialty items are usually quite high.

3. *List price tends to be stable with respect to output.* Once an oligopoly determines the most profitable markup, the list price is likely to remain stable. This is because the manufacturing processes of many oligopolies tend to be characterized by approximately constant returns to scale — a fairly flat *LRAC* curve — over a wide range of output. Therefore, although an oligopoly's *transactions* price may vary in response to competitors' practices in the marketplace, the *list* price tends to remain constant with respect to changes in the firm's level of production.

Target-return Pricing In administered-pricing doctrine, the alternative theory to cost-plus pricing is called **target-return pricing.** It assumes that firms set their prices so as to achieve a desired (targeted) percentage rate of return on stockholders' equity or ownership at the planned level of output. Thus the target return price (P) may be expressed as:

$$P = \frac{\% \text{ target return (stockholders' equity)}}{\text{planned output quantity, } Q} + AVC_Q$$

For example, suppose a firm plans to produce 10,000 units of output next year at an average variable cost of $80 per unit. If stockholders' equity is $5 million and the firm targets a 20 percent return, it will charge a price of $180 per unit:

$$P = \frac{.20(\$5,000,000)}{10,000} + \$80 = \frac{\$1,000,000}{10,000} + \$80$$
$$= \$180 \text{ per unit}$$

What are the economic implications of target-return pricing? As you can see from the equation, two are especially important:

1. *Price varies directly with average variable cost and inversely with the quantity produced.* For example, price will increase if *AVC* rises or if *Q* declines. This helps to explain why oligopolies often increase their prices in the face of rising costs and/or declining output.

2. *The theory assumes that the firm can sell its planned quantity of output at the target-return price.* To the extent that this is true, it is a factor which helps to explain why oligopolistic firms tend to resist price decreases, preferring instead to reduce output, in the face of declining demand.

Price Leadership

Administered pricing is one of several methods that some companies use to set prices. Another method is **price leadership.** It may be defined as adherence by firms in an oligopolistic industry, often tacitly and without formal agreement, to the pricing policies of one of its members. Frequently, but not always, the price leader will be the largest firm in the industry and other firms will simply go along with the leader by charging the same price.

Price leadership is thus somewhat of a paradox. On the one hand, it may be viewed as a type of noncompetitive behavior in which firms would rather match the leader's price than engage in uncomfortable price wars. On the other hand, it may be viewed as a type of competitive behavior in which *nonprice competition* — in the form of advertising, product differentiation, and customer service — replaces price competition as a means of attracting buyers. In either case, however, there are several important aspects of price leadership that should be understood:

1. *It reduces price flexibility.* Firms that depend on price leadership do not adjust their output to changing demand and cost conditions. Instead they adjust their output to meet the established price. This is usually a stable price that is in the best interests either of the price leader or of the industry.

2. *It is not necessarily the result of collusion.* Price leadership need not, and often does not, result from explicit agreements between competitors. (Such agreements are illegal and subject to civil and criminal penalties.) Instead it frequently arises "naturally" in many oligopolistic industries. Executives learn from experience that ruinous competition is easier to avoid as long as there are "live and let live" forms of nonprice competition that are available and effective.

3. *It is a symptom of market power.* Price leadership is not a cause of monopolization of markets. Rather it results from a type of market structure that provides some firms with enough power to *avoid* price competition if they choose to do so.

Price Discrimination

Administered pricing and price leadership are common pricing practices. Another is price discrimination. As you recall from your study of this subject in an earlier chapter, **price discrimination** is the practice by a seller of charging different prices to the same or to different buyers for the same good, without corresponding differences in cost. (It may also take the form of charging buyers the same prices despite differences in cost.)

This is a strict definition that is correct for theoretical purposes. In reality, however, price discrimination need not be limited to the same good. It can be applied to goods that are very similar — that is, differing only in color, labeling, or other minor factors. These surface differences may enable the seller to charge different prices for what customers perceive as different goods.

Competitive Practices and Policies

In addition to their own pricing and product policies, oligopolies may relate to one another through the marketplace. You can see how this might be done by examining several important competitive practices and policies. Among the most significant are those concerning (1) collusion, (2) monopolization, (3) mergers, and (4) trade practices.

Collusion

You learned in this and earlier chapters that oligopolies may have a tendency to avoid price competition. One way of doing so is by collusion. This occurs when two or more firms adopt a common course of action. The action may be explicit or tacit.

Explicit Collusion The most obvious way for firms to collude is by forming a *restrictive agreement.* This may be defined as a conspiracy of firms that results in a restraint of trade. ("Conspiracy," a term that comes from law, means an agreement between two or more parties to commit an illegal act.) A restrictive agreement is usually understood to involve a direct or indirect, explicit or implicit form of price fixing, output control, market sharing, or exclusion of competitors by boycotts or other coercive practices.

Tacit Collusion Firms in an industry may adopt similar patterns of behavior without necessarily engaging in explicit collusion. These patterns may be based on long-standing customs and practices. Price leadership provides a common example. As you learned earlier in this chapter, price leadership is the adherence by firms in an oligopolistic industry, often tacitly and without formal agreement, to the pricing policies of one of its members. It thus results in what the courts have termed ***conscious parallel action*** — meaning identical price behavior among competitors.

Monopolization

Collusion is one way for firms to avoid competition. Another is monopolization. A firm may become a monopoly in any of several ways. Among them:

− Driving competitors out of the market through price cutting, intimidation, or other coercive tactics

− Preventing competitors from entering the market through patent protection, ownership of a strategic resource used in production, or rapid internal growth

− Buying competitors by purchasing their stock

− Merging with competitors

As with certain kinds of collusion, some of these ways of achieving monopolization are illegal. However, all have been used at one time or another in the establishment of some of the nation's largest firms. As a result, these methods have played a very important role in America's economic history.

Mergers

Mergers among business firms have been especially significant in recent decades. A *merger* is an amalgamation of two or more firms under one ownership. It may result from one of three types of integration:

1. **Vertical Mergers** These unite firms engaged in different stages of production of the same or similar goods from raw materials to finished products. Such mergers may take the form of forward integration into buyer markets or backward integration into supplier markets. They may result in greater economies by combining different production stages and regularizing supplies, thereby increasing profit margins. *Example:* A clothing manufacturer merges with a chain of retail clothing stores and a textile plant.

2. **Horizontal Mergers** These unite firms producing similar products. The products may be close substitutes, like cement from different plants, or moderate substitutes, like tin cans and glass jars. The objective of such a merger is to round out a product line that is sold through the same distribution channels, thereby obtaining joint economies in sales and distribution efforts. The result may be an enhancement of market power.

3. **Conglomerate Mergers** These unite dissimilar firms producing unrelated products. Such mergers may reflect a desire by the acquiring company to spread risks, to find outlets for idle capital funds, or to add products that can be sold with the firm's merchandising knowledge and skills. They may also reflect a desire to gain greater economic power on a broader front.

Exhibit 4 shows some recent merger trends. Conglomerate mergers outweigh both horizontal or vertical mergers, whether measured by number of acquisitions or by value of assets.

Exhibit 4
The Merger Movement — Long-Run Trends
(latest data)

Conglomerate mergers have been more significant than either vertical or horizontal mergers — in number as well as in value of assets. One of several tidal waves of mergers occurred during the late 1960s. In that period many of today's well-known, diversified corporate giants were born.

ACQUISITIONS OF MANUFACTURING AND MINING FIRMS WITH ASSETS OF $10 MILLION OR MORE

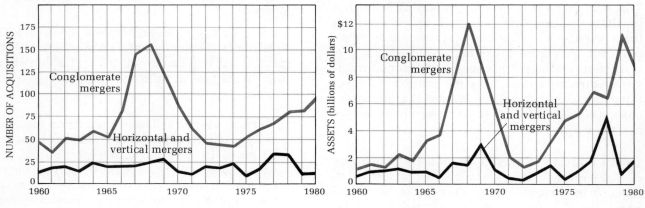

TOTAL ACQUISITIONS AND MERGERS

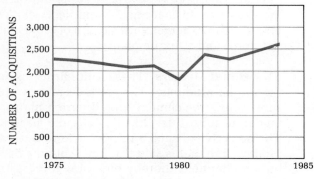
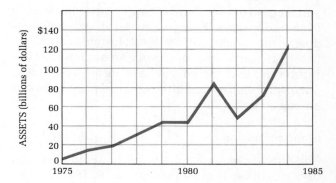

Source: Federal Trade Commission.

Reagan's Hands-Off Policy Is Working

By J. Paul McGrath

Today, our best economists recognize that mergers, acquisitions and joint ventures are essential to the nation's economic vitality—more so than ever before. Our economy operates at peak efficiency when productive assets are put to their highest and best use. A readily available merger market permits companies to dispose of businesses in which they are not prospering and to concentrate their efforts on businesses where they are more likely to succeed.

Just as important, mergers can make companies more efficient. A merger may produce greater economies of scale in production, distribution and marketing. An active merger market is a healthy threat to management that is incompetent or under-achieving. The market penalizes poor performance with a lower stock price, making the company a takeover candidate.

A free merger market is critical in a rapidly changing competitive environment. American industry cannot compete effectively with outmoded facilities and production techniques. Our "smokestack" industries (steel, aluminum, etc.) cannot survive without restructuring to close down less profitable capacity, shifting ownership of plants to insure more effective production patterns and combining know-how in joint ventures.

Price and supply shocks are forcing our energy companies, particularly oil companies, to realign to shed redundant overhead and rationalize marketing and exploration. Deregulation is pushing truckers, railroads, airlines and financial-services companies to fashion the lowest-cost, most service-oriented combination of assets. These and many other forces put pressure on companies to shed operations unrelated to their basic business so that they can focus on areas where they are most profitable.

Change is difficult to accept. We are more comfortable with what we have and what we know. If, however, we prevent our economy from adjusting to the shock waves of changing technology and international competition, we will suffer the unhealthiest kind of change.

The New York Times, May 19, 1985.

New Rules Breed Wasteful Mergers

By Herman Schwartz

Public policy is always fertile ground for irony. Today, for example, the economic landscape is strewn with merger fiascos, but current antitrust policy toward these combinations is increasingly lenient. "Economic efficiency" is now the "only goal" of merger policy, according to a former Justice Department official. As a result, the merger wave of the 1980's surges ahead, reaching a new peak with the Allied Corporation's $5 billion planned union with the Signal Companies, the largest industrial merger ever (outside the oil industry).

This preoccupation with economic efficiency ignores Congressional intent and judicial precedent. The legislative history of the antitrust laws contains almost no mention of efficiency, production or price. Rather, there is an insistent Jeffersonian concern for the small entrepreneur—for social, not economic reasons. Thus, the Supreme Court has always ruled that efficiencies cannot save an otherwise illegal merger.

Nevertheless, when the [Reagan] Administration took office, William F. Baxter, then the Assistant Attorney General in charge of antitrust, promptly redrew Federal guidelines to ease restrictions on mergers between competitors. The guidelines further legitimized virtually any "vertical" merger—between customer and suppliers—or between companies in neither a directly competitive nor supply relationship.

Obviously, many mergers don't sour. A large number do, however, because of communications problems, many-layered decision-making, management frictions, differing work styles and corporate cultures, labor problems, key personnel departures and more. One merger consultant estimated that 70 percent fail. Nevertheless, "economic efficiency" remains the antitrust lodestar.

The elevation of efficiency is just a fig leaf to cover a nakedly pro-business bias that appears not just in antitrust but also in tax, labor, safety, consumer protection, environmental and other areas. In antitrust matters, it makes for a policy that harms not only the country, but business itself.

Trade Practices

In addition to collusion, monopolization, and mergers, firms relate to one another in the marketplace through their trade practices. These embrace a wide variety of pricing and marketing policies that affect not only competing sellers, but also suppliers and customers. It is impossible to provide a complete list of trade practices, but a few questions concerning some major types will suggest the kinds of problems to which they give rise:

— Should price discrimination that consistently favors some customers (especially large ones), while possibly penalizing others, be permitted? If so, under what circumstances and conditions should this be allowed?

— Should government enact legislation aimed at promoting competition or at protecting competitors? How do these two goals differ? Can either one be achieved without the other?

— Should firms be permitted to establish either vertical or horizontal restrictions — that is, limitations on seller-buyer or seller-seller relationships? For example, is competition enhanced or reduced if manufacturers make price-fixing, exclusive dealing, territorial limitations, or patent-pooling agreements with other firms?

All of these as well as other types of trade practices have been common in American industry. Are all these practices legal? The answer is *no*. As with collusion, monopolization, and mergers, some types of trade practices are legal and some are not. Hence they must be judged with that consideration in mind when their effects on market performance are evaluated.

Conclusion: Common Behavioral Patterns

The study of market conduct is concerned with how firms behave in their pursuit of profits. There is much evidence that oligopolistic firms behave in a wide variety of ways with respect to their pricing, product, and competitive practices and policies.

Because competing firms in oligopolistic industries have a strong tendency to be mutually interdependent, they are heavily influenced by one another's market behavior. As a result, they respond in various ways to competitors' practices. These responses may take such common patterns as price leadership, tacit or explicit collusion, coercion and intimidation of competitors, monopolization, or mergers. Some of these types of market conduct are legal, and some are not. All have significant effects on market performance.

Market Performance

Having completed the study of market structure and market conduct, we now focus on the third component of industrial organization — market performance. The question to be answered is a familiar one. How do market structure and conduct affect the four fundamental goals — efficiency, equity, stability, and growth?

Efficiency

You know from your study of microeconomic theory that firms maximize their profits by producing the output, and charging the price, at which $MC = MR$. You also know that by adhering to the $MC = MR$ rule, firms faced with downward-sloping demand curves *misallocate resources*. This occurs because such firms restrict output (and charge higher prices) than if they adhered to a production and price rule determined by $MC = P$.

This is shown in Exhibit 5. The firm is faced with the downward-sloping demand or average revenue curve, AR, and the corresponding marginal revenue curve, MR. To simplify the analysis, the marginal cost curve MC is assumed to be a horizontal line over the range of output that concerns us, namely, JK.

The model can now be interpreted in three steps.

Step 1 In order to achieve economic efficiency, the firm should follow the $MC = P$ rule. This means that it should produce 60,000 units per day and charge the marginal-cost price of $30 per unit.

Exhibit 5
Measuring Deadweight Loss: The Cost of Inefficiency

What is the cost to society of a firm's resource misallocation, or inefficiency? The answer can be easily estimated if we assume that the firm's MC curve is horizontal over the relevant output range JK.

Thus, by adhering to the marginal-cost price or MC = P standard of perfect competition, the firm produces 60,000 units and charges $30 per unit. Resources are therefore allocated *efficiently* because society gets as much of the good as it wants in relation to the resources sacrificed to produce it.

By adhering to the monopoly price or MC = MR standard, the firm maximizes profit by producing 30,000 units and charging $60 per unit. Resources are thus allocated *inefficiently* because society does not get as much of the good as it wants in relation to the resources sacrificed to produce it.

The cost of this inefficiency to society—the value of output sacrificed—is called the **_deadweight loss._** It is measured by the area of triangle GHI. Thus: area = ½(base × height) = ½(30,000 units × $30) = $450,000 per day.

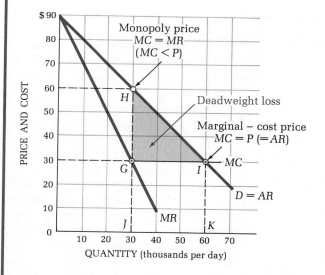

At this price, the value of the last unit to the marginal user (measured by the price paid for the last unit, which is the same price that is paid for any other unit) is equivalent to the value of the resources used to produce that unit. Therefore, society is getting as much of the good as it wants in relation to the resources sacrificed to produce it.

Step 2 In order to maximize profit, the firm will follow the MC = MR rule. This means that it will restrict output to 30,000 units and charge the monopoly price of $60 per unit. At this price, the value of the last unit to the marginal user is *greater* than the value of the resources used to produce that unit. Therefore, society is not getting as much of the good as it wants in relation to the resources sacrificed to produce it.

Step 3 How much does society lose as a result of this inefficiency? The answer is shown by the area of the triangle GHI. This represents what can be called the **_deadweight loss._** It may be defined as the loss in efficiency, measured by the value of output sacrificed, that society incurs as a result of firms practicing monopoly (MC = MR) rather than marginal-cost (MC = P) pricing. In dollar terms, since the area of a triangle is equal to ½ (base × height), the deadweight loss in the diagram is ½ (30,000 units × $30) = $450,000 per day.

Trends and Findings

What happens when the deadweight losses for particular industries are measured and combined to arrive at an estimate for the economy? A number of studies designed to answer this question have been done. Their conclusions, along with those of other economists who have examined the problem, may be noted:

1. Most studies have estimated the total deadweight loss to range between 1 percent and 5 percent of the economy's output—its gross national product, GNP. However, the majority of these studies are based on pre-1970 data. Since then, there has been a rapid growth of competition from abroad. Therefore, it is likely that studies based on more recent data would show a distinct downward trend of deadweight loss.

2. In some oligopolistic industries, high concentration ratios seem to be more the result of innovation, low prices, and economies of scale than of market power. Examples include the aluminum, computer, and telecommunications industries.

3. The existence of contestable markets reduces the market power of oligopolies. This, in turn, encourages increased research and development expenditures, leading to new and better products. The electronics and personal-computer industries provide two of many examples.

It may be concluded, therefore, that oligopolies do indeed misallocate resources to some extent. However, largely because of the above factors, many oligopolies are now more competitive than they once were. Therefore, their deadweight loss, in the opinion of many of today's experts, is probably much less, and their benefits to society much greater, than has traditionally been assumed.

Equity

There is evidence that high-concentration industries, which is where market power is greatest, contribute to inequality of income and wealth. This is based on studies which have concluded that excess profits — those above normal profits — of corporations average between 2 and 3 percent of GNP. The stockholders who benefit the most are those who hold the largest amounts of corporate stock — the wealthiest one-fifth of American families.

But this can easily be misinterpreted. The majority of corporate stocks is owned *directly* by a relatively small proportion of the population. However, a large and growing proportion, amounting to many millions of people, own huge quantities of stocks *indirectly*. Indirect ownership occurs through retirement and pension funds, which invest heavily in stocks. Therefore, the monopoly profits of American industry accrue directly and/or indirectly to a very large segment of society, not just to the well-off. Although this is not a defense of monopoly profit, it is a fact that should nevertheless be recognized when discussing the problem.

Stability

It has long been known that the overall level of prices is more stable in high-concentration industries than in low-concentration industries. This does not mean, however, that large firms encourage greater economic stability. Indeed, it has also long been known that firms possessing substantial market power actually tend to contribute to economic *instability* — for two reasons:

1. They raise prices more readily during inflationary periods because consumer resistance is not as strong.

2. They reduce output and employment during recessionary periods while holding prices relatively constant.

What is not known is the extent to which these practices exist among large firms. In general, *there is no strong evidence to show that these practices are more prevalent or pronounced among the largest firms in high-concentration industries than among the largest firms in low-concentration industries.*

Growth

Are oligopolies progressive in research and development (R&D) — and thereby important contributors to economic growth? The answer is somewhat surprising.

Movies and television to the contrary, many of the greatest inventions of this century were not made by white-coated scientists conducting experiments in gleaming laboratories of large corporations. Since 1900, independent inventors working alone or in universities or small research firms have produced most of the major inventions. Among them: air conditioning, automatic transmissions, power steering, cellophane, the cotton picker, the helicopter, the gyrocompass, the jet engine, quick-freezing, insulin, the continuous casting of steel, and the catalytic cracking of petroleum.

A relatively small proportion of the major inventions, including nylon, tetraethyl lead, the diesel electric locomotive, and transistors, were developed by large private organizations such as DuPont, General Motors, and Bell Laboratories. And in many oligopolistic industries, such as agricultural machinery, basic metals, and food products, relatively little has been spent on research.

Thus, for the most part, basic research is conducted mainly in academic institutions and private firms. However, the *development* part of R&D is the specialty of large industrial corporations. In fact, *the great bulk of R&D outlays is for development purposes.*

How does this contrast with research and development in agriculture, which serves as a rough approximation of perfect competition? In agriculture, R&D has been accomplished mainly with government support. Federal research laboratories, experiment stations, and land-grant colleges and universities have been responsible for most of the scientific advances that have made American agriculture extraordinarily productive.

Some long-run trends and policy implications of R&D outlays are indicated in Exhibit 6.

Conclusion: Oligopolies Today

Industrial organization is a branch of applied microeconomics. The purpose of industrial organization is to test certain hypotheses and conclusions of microeconomic theory. Particularly relevant are those focusing on the relationships among an industry's structure, conduct, and performance.

Industrial organization deals largely with the study of oligopoly. This is the most important type of market structure in our economy. Oligopolies misallocate resources to the extent that they do not adhere to the $MC = P$ standard of price and output determination. However, the extent of their inefficiency in *today's* world may be less than was generally believed in the past. A growing number of experts agree on at least three points:

1. *Market structure.* High concentration ratios do not necessarily reflect market power. They are often the result of innovative practices and low prices.

Exhibit 6
Encouraging More R&D

What can be done to promote more R&D, thereby stimulating innovation, productivity, and the nation's economic growth? Several measures have been proposed by various economists and legislators:

1. *Improve Taxation and Depreciation Benefits* Washington can broaden the tax incentives for corporate R&D spending. Also, depreciation allowances for special-purpose plant and equipment used in R&D can be liberalized.

2. *Reduce Excessive Regulations* Many government health, safety, and other regulations are viewed by business executives as too cumbersome and costly to meet. These regulations, if reduced and simplified, could stimulate corporate investment in R&D.

3. *Eliminate Antitrust Obstacles* At present, if a company gains a substantial share of a market because of an invention it has patented, it can be sued under the nation's antitrust laws for monopolizing the market. Several studies show that this factor has limited the willingness of firms to undertake heavy expenditures on R&D, especially those involving high-technology products.

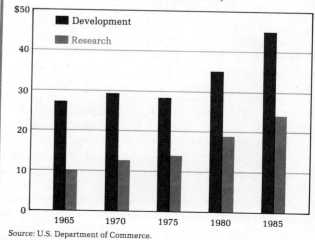

U.S. RESEARCH AND DEVELOPMENT EXPENDITURES
(billions of 1972 dollars)

Source: U.S. Department of Commerce.

2. *Market conduct.* Profits and prices are strongly influenced by factors other than market power. In modern industry, economies of scale, contestable markets, and competition from abroad are playing increasingly important roles in affecting firms' market behavior.

3. *Market performance.* Oligopolies today may be more efficient than has been traditionally believed. In addition, their R&D expenditures lead to social benefits (such as a rising standard of living) that help offset social costs arising from resource misallocation.

What You Have Learned

1. Market structure has to do with the types of competitive environments within which firms operate. These competitive environments are influenced by seller concentration, product differentiation, barriers to entry, and other factors.

2. Various methods exist for measuring seller concentration in a market. The most important ones, and those used most extensively by the government in its studies of market power, are the concentration ratio and the Herfindahl index.

3. Product differentiation, entry barriers, and exit barriers also affect an industry's market structure. When one or more of the determinants of market structure change, the impact on firms' market conduct and performance can be significant.

4. Market conduct is concerned with the policies that firms adopt in their pursuit of profits. The chief policies deal with pricing practices and competitive behavior.

5. The practices and policies adopted by oligopolistic firms is heavily influenced by competitors' mutual interdependency. This gives rise to different types of market strategies. Some examples: price leadership, collusion, monopolization, and mergers. All, of course, have significant impacts on firms' market performance.

6. Market performance concerns the effects of market structure and conduct on the economy's four goals — efficiency, equity, stability and growth. Many economists believe that because of the increasing importance of economies of scale, innovation, and the changing nature of competition (including competition from abroad), today's oligopolies make a more positive contribution to the economy than has been traditionally believed.

Terms and Concepts To Review

industrial organization
market share
concentration ratio
Herfindahl index
aggregate concentration ratio
contestable market
administered pricing

cost-plus pricing
contribution margin
target-return pricing
price discrimination
restrictive agreement
conscious parallel action
merger
deadweight loss

For Discussion

1. Industry A has three firms, each with one-third of the market. Industry B has one firm with 50 percent of the market, and five firms with 10 percent each. If there is no collusion, which industry is more competitive?

2. A U.S. senator introduced a bill that would break up a firm into smaller firms if either of the following occurred:
(a) The firm earns more than a 15 percent rate of profit during any five consecutive years.
(b) The industry in which the firm produces has a four-firm concentration ratio greater than 50.
Can you criticize this proposal?

3. "Large firms are more efficient than small ones. Therefore, small firms should be merged to become large firms." Do you agree? Explain.

4. Retail gasoline stations in the same market area often post the same price for gasoline. Is this the result of either tacit or explicit collusion?

5. Many corporations do not spend heavily on research because it is costly and the risks of failure are high. Should government insure corporations against such failures?

6. Is product differentiation wasteful? Would society be better off with only one of each product instead of many variations of the same product?

7. Before buying a new car, some consumers want more technical information about the product than the manufacturer provides. Should government require the manufacturer to provide such information? Should consumers have to purchase the information before buying a car? Is there such a thing as "too much" information?

8. Most empirical studies in industrial organization are based on very limited, and often "old" data. As a result, the conclusions of such studies may quickly become obsolete. Does this mean that such studies should not be done?

Chapter 29

Antitrust Policy: Business and Government

Learning Guide

Watch for answers to these important questions

Are big business and monopoly the same thing? What is the nature of the "monopoly problem"?

What are the nation's main antitrust laws? How are they enforced?

What has been the attitude of the courts toward restrictive agreements? Toward "good" monopolies and "bad" ones? Toward mergers, price discrimination, and market restraints?

Have the antitrust laws succeeded in attaining their objective? What criticisms have been leveled against them? What suggestions have been made to improve them?

More than two hundred years ago, Adam Smith remarked in a famous passage in *The Wealth of Nations:*

> People of the same trade seldom meet together, even for merriment and diversion, but the conversation ends in a conspiracy against the public, or in some contrivance to raise prices. It is impossible indeed to prevent such meetings, by any law which either could be executed, or would be consistent with liberty and justice. But though the law cannot hinder people of the same trade from sometimes assembling together, it ought to do nothing to facilitate such assemblies; much less to render them necessary.

According to Smith, competition in business is not a "natural" practice. Given the opportunity, business executives would prefer to seek ways of avoiding competition.

The history of American business suggests that this is indeed the case. As a result, the American government has, since the late nineteenth century, been engaged in constructing a body of laws and policies to assure that competition in our economy is at least maintained if not enhanced. This chapter sketches the main features of these laws, notes the ways in which they have been applied in major court cases, and evaluates the chief economic issues pertaining to problems of competition and monopoly in our society.

Big Business and the Monopoly Problem

In economic theory, a market is said to be monopolized when a single firm produces a product for which there are no close substitutes. This narrow definition is usually adequate for analyzing market structures. But when it comes to matters of public policy, economists, government officials, and judges in courts of law sometimes take a much broader view. They may regard a market as being monopolized if it is dominated by one or a few firms —that is, if it is "oligopolized."

In the American economy, the automobile, aluminum, chemical, and steel industries, as well as many others, provide notable examples of oligopoly. In each of these industries the sales of two, three, or four large firms account for a major share of the total market. This leaves a relatively minor share for smaller competitors to divide. According to this interpretation, such big businesses as General Motors, Aluminum Company of America (Alcoa), DuPont, U.S. Steel, and their chief competitors qualify as "monopolies."

The arguments for and against big-business monopolies have been debated for decades. Among the chief objections to monopolies are these:

- They maximize profit by restricting output and charging higher prices than they would if they were more competitive. Monopolies thereby misallocate resources and contribute to income inequality.

- They retard economic progress and technological advance because they are protected from the pressures of competition.

- They exert disproportionate influences at all levels of government, giving rise to an "indus-

trial-political complex" that favors big business at the expense of the rest of society.

Arguments in defense of big-business monopolies are these:

- Monopolies are effectively more competitive than the numbers of firms alone indicate. This is because there is rivalry among different products in specific markets (for example, aluminum versus copper, steel, and plastics). There is also countervailing power on the opposite side of the market exerted by labor unions and other monopolistic sellers of resources.

- Monopolies permit mass-production economies at lower unit costs and prices than would be possible with large numbers of small firms.

- Monopolies have the financial ability to support extensive research and development.

- Monopolies have the ethical and moral sense not to exploit their monopoly power.

To repeat:

The foregoing arguments are often applied to today's big businesses, which many people equate with "monopoly." This consideration should be kept in mind as you analyze the facts in each case before judging the merits of the arguments.

Reactions to Monopoly: The Antitrust Laws

During the last two decades of the nineteenth century, the American economy underwent an extraordinary transformation. The period 1879–1904 saw the first greater *merger movement* in American history. During these years, an unprecedented number of firms expanded by combining or merging with others, thereby forming new single-business units with huge investments, capacities, and outputs. These new business organizations were called monopolies or "trusts." In reaction to them and to subsequent economic developments,

Congress has passed a body of legislation known as the "antitrust laws."

The **antitrust laws** passed since 1890 commit the government to preventing monopoly and maintaining competition. There are also antitrust laws in almost every state in the country. But these are frequently ineffectual and erratically enforced. This is because states are powerless to control agreements or combinations in major industries whose activities extend into interstate commerce. Coupled with the states' relative lack of funds, this weakness has left the task of maintaining competition almost entirely to the federal government. Thus, it is the federal antitrust laws that will be of concern to us here. The main ones are the Sherman Antitrust Act, the Clayton Antitrust Act, the Federal Trade Commission Act, the Robinson–Patman Act, the Wheeler–Lea Act, and the Celler Antimerger Act.

The Sherman Antitrust Act (1890)

The **Sherman Antitrust Act** was the first attempt by the federal government to regulate the growth of monopoly. The provisions of the law were concise (probably too concise) and to the point. The act declared two things to be illegal:

1. Every contract, combination, or conspiracy in restraint of trade that occurs in interstate or foreign commerce.

2. Any monopolization or attempts to monopolize, or conspiracy with others in an attempt to monopolize, any portion of trade in interstate or foreign commerce.

Violations of the act were made punishable by fines, imprisonment, or both, and persons injured by violations could sue for triple damages.

The act was surrounded by a cloud of uncertainty because it failed to specify which kinds of actions were prohibited. Also, no special agency existed to enforce the law until 1903, when the Antitrust Division of the U.S. Department of Justice was established under an Assistant Attorney General.

The Clayton Antitrust Act and the Federal Trade Commission Act (1914)

In 1914, in order to put some teeth into the Sherman Antitrust Act, Congress passed both the Clayton Antitrust Act and the Federal Trade Commission Act. These were aimed at practices of **unfair competition,** defined as deceptive, dishonest, and injurious methods of competition. The **Clayton Antitrust Act** dealt with four specific areas: price discrimination, exclusive and tying contracts, intercorporate stockholdings, and interlocking directorates.

Price Discrimination   For sellers to discriminate in pricing by charging different prices to different buyers for the same good is *illegal*. However, such discrimination is permissible under certain circumstances:

1. If there are differences in the grade, quality, or quantity of the commodity sold.

2. If the lower prices make due allowances for cost differences in selling or transportation.

3. If the lower prices are offered in good faith to meet competition.

According to the law, illegality exists whenever instances of such discrimination "substantially lessen competition or tend to create a monopoly."

Exclusive and Tying Contracts   For sellers to lease, sell, or contract for the sale of commodities on condition that the lessee or purchaser not use or deal in the commodity of a competitor is *illegal* if such exclusive or tying contracts "substantially lessen competition or tend to create a monopoly."

Intercorporate Stockholdings   For corporations engaged in commerce to acquire the shares of a competing corporation, or the stocks of two or more corporations competing with each other, is *illegal* if such intercorporate stockholdings "substantially lessen competition or tend to create a monopoly."

Interlocking Directorates   For corporations engaged in commerce to have the same individual on

Alphabet of Joyous Trusts

Although the Sherman Antitrust Act was enacted in 1890, big businesses continued to monopolize certain industries. Consequently, popular resentment toward trusts became increasingly pronounced over the next several decades. The plethora of trusts that existed around the turn of the century prompted newspaper cartoonists to depict the more objectionable monopolies in sardonic ways.

The Granger Collection

two or more boards of directors is an interlocking directorate. Such directorships are *illegal* if the corporations compete with each other and if any one of them has capital, surplus, and undivided profits in excess of $1 million.

Thus:

> The Clayton Antitrust Act did not declare price discrimination, exclusive and tying contracts, and intercorporate stockholdings to be absolutely illegal. Rather, in the words of the law, they were unlawful only when their effects "may be to substantially lessen competition or tend to create a monopoly." On interlocking directorates, however, the law made no such qualification. The fact of the interlock itself is illegal, and the government need not find that the arrangement results in a reduction in competition.

The **Federal Trade Commission Act** served primarily as a general supplement to the Clayton Antitrust Act. It did this by stating broadly and simply that "unfair methods of competition in commerce are hereby declared unlawful." In addition, the Federal Trade Commission Act provided for the establishment of the **Federal Trade Commission** (FTC). This is a government agency that combats unfair competitive practices in commerce.

The FTC is also authorized under the act to safeguard the public. It does this by preventing the dissemination of false and misleading advertising of foods, drugs, cosmetics, and therapeutic devices used in the diagnosis, prevention, or treatment of disease. It thus supplements the activities of the Food and Drug Administration (FDA). This agency, established under the Food, Drug, and Cosmetic Act (1938), safeguards the public from adulteration and misbranding of foods, drugs, medical devices, and cosmetics moving in interstate commerce.

The Robinson–Patman Act (1936)

Frequently referred to as the "Chain Store Act," the *Robinson–Patman Act* deals with trade practices. It was passed for the purpose of protecting independent retailers and wholesalers, such as grocers and druggists. Protecting them from what? In the words of the law, from "unfair discriminations" by manufacturers, who might otherwise charge chain stores lower prices "because of their enormous purchasing power." The law was an outgrowth of the increasing competition faced by independents when chain stores and mass distributors developed during the 1920s.

Supporters of the bill contended that the lower prices charged by large organizations were attributable less to lower costs than to sheer weight of bargaining power. This enabled the large organizations to obtain unfair and unjustified concessions from their suppliers. The act was thus a response to the cries of independents who demanded that the freedom of suppliers to discriminate be more strictly limited.

The act, which amended the Clayton Antitrust Act, Section 2, relating to price discrimination, contained the following provisions:

Brokerage Fees

The payment of brokerage fees where no independent broker is employed is *illegal*. This was intended to eliminate the practice of some chains of demanding the regular brokerage fee as a discount when they purchased directly from manufacturers. The argument posed was that such chains obtained the discount by their sheer bargaining power and thereby gained an unfair advantage over smaller independents that had to use and pay for brokerage services.

Concessions

The making of concessions by sellers, such as manufacturers, to buyers, such as wholesalers and retailers, is *illegal* unless such concessions are made to all buyers on proportionally equal terms. This provision was aimed at preventing sellers from granting advertising and promotional allowances to large-scale buyers without making similar allowances to small competing buyers.

Discounts

Other forms of discrimination, such as quantity discounts, are *illegal* where they substantially lessen competition or tend to create a monopoly, either among sellers or among buyers. However, price discrimination is not illegal if the differences in prices make "due allowances" for differences in cost or if lower prices are offered "in good faith to meet an equally low price of a competitor." But even where discounts can be justified by lower costs, the FTC is empowered to fix quantity limits beyond which discounts may not be granted. It will do this if it believes that such discounts would be "unjustly discriminatory or promotive of monopoly in any line of commerce."

Predatory Behavior

Sellers are prohibited from preying upon one another. Thus it is *illegal* to charge lower prices in one locality than in another for the same goods or to sell at "unreasonably low prices" where either of these practices is aimed at "destroying competition or eliminating a competitor."

The Wheeler – Lea Act (1938)

An amendment to part of the Federal Trade Commission Act, the *Wheeler – Lea Act* was enacted for the purpose of providing consumers, rather than just business competitors, with protection against unfair practices. The act makes "unfair or deceptive acts or practices" *illegal* in interstate commerce. Thus, a consumer who may be injured by an unfair trade practice is, before the law, of equal concern with the merchant who may be injured by an unfair competitive practice. The act also defines "false advertising" as "an advertisement other than labeling which is misleading in a material respect." This definition applies to advertisements of foods, drugs, curative devices, and cosmetics.

The Celler Antimerger Act (1950)

The *Celler Antimerger Act* is an extension of Section 7 of the Clayton Antitrust Act relating to inter-corporate stockholdings. The Clayton Act, as stated ealier, made it illegal for corporations to acquire substantial amounts of the stock of competing corporations. But that law, the Federal Trade Commission argued, left a loophole through which monopolistic mergers could still be effected. A corporation could acquire the *assets* of a competing corporation, or it could first acquire *some* of the stock and, by voting or granting of proxies, acquire the assets.

The Celler Antimerger Act plugged the loophole in the Clayton Antitrust Act by making it illegal for a corporation to acquire the stock *or assets* of a competing corporation if such acquisitions "substantially lessen competition or tend to create a monopoly." Thus the Celler Antimerger Act could, depending on the circumstances, ban all types of mergers. These include:

1. **Horizontal Mergers** Plants producing similar products that are brought together under one ownership. (*Example*: the merging of two or more steel mills.)

2. **Vertical Mergers** Different stages of production that are integrated under one ownership. (*Example*: the acquisition of a steel mill by an automobile company.)

3. **Conglomerate or Circular Mergers** Unrelated product lines that are placed under one ownership. (*Example*: the purchase of a food-processing firm by a transportation company.)

These three types of mergers can be banned, provided the Commission can show that the effects may substantially lessen competition or tend to create a monopoly.

It should be noted, however, that the purpose of Congress in passing the Celler Antimerger Act was *maintenance of competition*. Accordingly, the act was intended to apply to mergers between large firms or between large and small firms. The Act was not designed to apply to mergers of small firms, which may be undertaken by such firms to strengthen their market position.

Enforcement of the Antitrust Laws

In general, the antitrust laws are applied on a *case-by-case* basis. That is, an order or decision resulting from an action is not applicable to all of industry, only to the defendants in the particular case. Cases may originate in the complaints of injured parties, in suggestions made by other government agencies, or in the research of the FTC or the Antitrust Division of the Department of Justice. Both of these agencies are responsible for enforcing the antitrust laws. However, most of the cases arise from complaints issued by injured parties.

The antitrust laws fix the responsibility for the behavior of a corporation on its officers and directors. These individuals can be subject to heavy fine or imprisonment for violating certain provisions of the laws. Business executives who do not want to risk violation of the law may present their proposed plans for mergers or possibly illegal practices to the Justice Department. If the plans appear to be legal, the Department may commit itself not to institute future criminal proceedings, but it will reserve the right to institute civil action if competition is later restrained. The purpose of a civil suit is not to punish but to restore competition by providing remedies. Typically, three classes of remedies are employed:

1. **Dissolution, Divestiture, or Divorcement** Examples include an order to dissolve a trade association or combination, to sell intercorporate stockholdings, or to dispose of ownership in other assets. The purpose of these actions is to break up a monopolistic organization into smaller and more competitive units.

2. **Injunction** This is a court order requiring that the defendant either refrain from certain business practices or perhaps take a particular action that will increase rather than reduce competition.

3. **Consent Decree** This is an agreement usually worked out between the defendant and the Justice Department without a court trial. The defendant in this instance does not admit guilt, but agrees nevertheless to abide by the rules of business behavior set down in the decree. This device is the chief instrument employed in the enforcement of the Sherman and Clayton Antitrust Acts.

Finally, the laws are also enforced through private suits by injured parties (individuals, corporations, or states), who may sue for treble damages including court costs. This approach to enforcement has become quite common.

Exemptions and Interpretations

As might be expected, a few industries and economic groups are exempt from antitrust laws. The most important of these are the transport industries and the labor unions. Transporters—including companies operating railroads, trucks, ships, and barges—are excluded because they are subject in varying degrees to the control of other regulatory agencies, such as the Interstate Commerce Commission. The exemption of labor unions was originally justified on the ground that they do not normally seek to monopolize markets or to engage in methods of unfair competition. They seek instead to protect and enhance the position of labor. However, labor unions may be subjected to antitrust prosecution if they combine with management to violate the antitrust laws.

To summarize:

1. The Sherman Antitrust Act (1890) forbids restraints of trade, monopoly, and attempts to monopolize.

2. The Clayton Antitrust Act (1914) forbids practices whose effects may be to lessen substantially the degree of competition or to tend to create a monopoly.

3. The Federal Trade Commission Act (1914) forbids unfair methods of competition.

A different kind of summary of the antitrust laws based on types of business activity is presented in Exhibit 1.

Exhibit 1
The Antitrust Laws in a Nutshell

The antitrust laws cover five major areas of business activity:

1. Restrictive Agreements It is *illegal*, without any qualification, to enter any type of agreement in restraint of trade (Sherman Antitrust Act, Sec. 1). This forbids attempts by firms to fix prices, allocate market territories, or organize boycotts.

2. Monopolization It is *illegal*, without any qualification, to monopolize, attempt to monopolize, or combine or conspire to monopolize trade (Sherman Antitrust Act, Sec. 2). This may also be interpreted to include "oligopolization" if a firm gains a large enough degree of control over a market.

3. Mergers Where the effect may be a substantial lessening of competition, it is *illegal* to:

(a) Acquire the stock of competing corporations (Clayton Antitrust Act, Sec. 7).

(b) Acquire the assets of competing corporations (Clayton Antitrust Act, Sec. 7, as amended by the Celler Antimerger Act in 1950).

4. Price Discrimination Where the effect may be a substantial lessening of competition, it is *illegal* to:

(a) Discriminate unjustifiably among purchasers (Clayton Antitrust Act, Sec. 2, as amended by the Robinson-Patman Act, Sec 1).

(b) Engage in particular forms of price discrimination (Robinson-Patman Act, Sec. 1 and 3).

5. Vertical (Supplier-customer) Restrictions Where the effect may be a substantial lessening of competition, it is *illegal* to engage in exclusive dealing arrangements, trying contracts, and similar practices (Clayton Antitrust Act, Sec. 3).

Also, it is *illegal*, regardless of the effect on competition, to use unfair methods of competition and unfair or deceptive acts or practices (Federal Trade Commission Act, Sec. 5, as amended by the Wheeler-Lea Act, Sec. 3). This forbids sellers from deceiving buyers through false or misleading advertising and claims.

Thus, the laws taken as a whole are intended not only to prevent the growth of monopoly but to maintain competition as well.

Experiences with Antitrust: Some Major Cases

Although Congress succeeded in passing the antitrust laws, it failed to define many of the essential terms. Instead, it left it to the courts to interpret in their own way the meaning of such concepts as "monopoly," "restraint of trade," "substantial lessening of competition," and "unfair competition." As a result, judicial interpretations have been crucial in determining the economic applications and effects of the antitrust laws. In view of this, it is useful to sketch briefly some major issues, court decisions, and trends that have emerged in the past few decades. This may be done within a framework of the five major areas of antitrust:

1. restrictive agreements and conspiracies

2. monopoly

3. mergers

4. price discrimination

5. vertical restrictions, or supplier-customer restraints

Restrictive Agreements and Conspiracies

The state of the law regarding restrictive agreements or conspiracies of virtually any type among competitors is reasonably clear, and the courts have almost always upheld the government in such cases.

In general, a **restrictive agreement** is defined by the government as a conspiracy that results in a restraint of trade among separate companies. It is usually understood to involve a direct or indirect, explicit or implicit form of price fixing, output control, market sharing, or exclusion of competitors by boycotts or other coercive practices. It makes no difference whether the agreement was accomplished through a formal organization such as a trade association, whether it was arrived at informally, or whether it was simply the result of "similar patterns of behavior." This expression, or the one used by the courts, **conscious parallel action,** means identical price behavior among competitors. Thus, the effects of market actions, more than the ways of conducting them, are judged.

Hundreds of antitrust cases illustrate this point. In recent decades, there are a few that stand as landmarks. Among them:

American Tobacco Case (1946)   The government charged that the "big three" cigarette producers — American, Liggett & Meyers, and R.J. Reynolds — exhibited striking uniformity in the prices they paid for tobacco and in the prices they charged for cigarettes. Although not one shred of evidence was produced to indicate that a common plan had even so much as been proposed, the Supreme Court declared that conspiracy "may be found in a course of dealings or other circumstances as well as in an exchange of words." Therefore, the companies were held in violation of the Sherman Antitrust Act.

Paramount Pictures Case (1948)   Five major integrated movie companies were charged with "parallel behavior" in the licensing of their copyrighted films to exhibitors. For example, the producers specified the same admission prices that theaters could charge, the same time intervals between reruns, and other identical conditions of exhibiting films. The Supreme Court ruled against the producers. A few years later, the producers also signed a consent decree agreeing to divest themselves of their theater holdings. Exhibition was thus divorced from production and distribution, and this resulted in more vigorous competition.

Topco Associates Case (1972)   Topco was a cooperative of about 25 small and medium-sized supermarket chains. It served as a purchasing agent for members and licensed them to sell Topco-brand merchandise within specified areas. The Supreme Court found the company guilty of violating the Sherman Antitrust Act, Section 1. Topco, the Court said, had engaged in a "horizontal restraint of trade by allocating markets among competitors at the same level of market activity."

Do the decisions in these and numerous other conspiracy cases mean that parallel action is always illegal? The answer is *not necessarily.* The court may take into account both legal and economic considerations.

From a legal point of view, parallel behavior may not be sufficient grounds for conspiracy. The test rests heavily on whether parallel behavior could reasonably have resulted from *independent* decisions, or whether it occurred because of explicit or even tacit collusion. If the court believes that the defendant acted independently, a conclusion of innocence may be reached. But from an economic point of view, the problem is whether an oligopolistic firm can really act independently in a market whose structure implies mutual interdependence.

Monopoly

In the real world, almost all firms have some degree of market power. Does this make them "monopolists"? Not according to the courts. They have focused attention mainly on *dominant* firms — those whose size relative to their market suggests that they have a strong degree of power. Some of the major cases have been these:

Standard Oil Case (1911)   The government accused Standard Oil of New Jersey (a huge holding company administered mainly by John D. Rockefeller), of violating Sections 1 and 2 of the Sherman Antitrust Act. The company controlled 90 percent of the oil-refining business. It was charged with monopolizing the market by buying out some competitors and by driving others out of business. The Supreme Court ordered the dissolution of Standard Oil into 34 separate companies. But it also introduced a new concept — the **rule of reason** — which stated that the mere size of a corporation is no offense. A firm, it said, must show "unreasonable" exertion of monopoly power to be held in violation of the law. The importance of this case is suggested by the attention it received in the news media, as shown in Exhibit 2.

Exhibit 2
The Rule of Reason

The Sherman Antitrust Act outlawed every contract, combination, and conspiracy in restraint of trade. In both the Standard Oil and the American Tobacco cases of 1911 — two of the most famous cases in the history of antitrust — the Supreme Court upheld the government. But the Court went on to write the "rule of reason" into law, contending that a distinction should be made between "good" trusts and "bad" trusts.

At the time of the antitrust suit in 1911, John D. Rockefeller was chairman of the board of Standard Oil Company of New Jersey. Largely under his guidance

the firm had become a huge holding company — a corporation that owned enough stock of other corporations to control them. By buying out many competitors and driving others out of the market, the Standard Oil "trust" had gained a 90 percent share of the oil-refining business.

As a result of the Supreme Court's dissolution order, Standard Oil Company of New Jersey was broken up into 34 separate companies. Many of them operate in different regions (although some no longer exist) as you may know if you have ever driven across the country.

The Chicago Daily Tribune

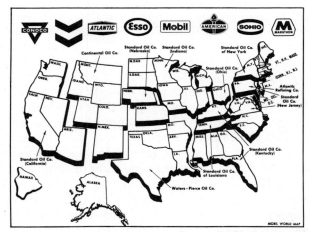

Courtesy of Mobil Oil Corporation

Alcoa Case (1945) This case against the Aluminum Company of America (Alcoa) reversed the rule of reason that courts had followed in various monopolization cases since the Standard Oil case in 1911. Judge Learned Hand of the Federal appellate court issued the decision. It was his opinion that:

– Even though Alcoa had gained monopoly power by growing with the market (that is, by reinvesting earnings rather than by combining with other companies), this behavior was illegal.

– The mere size of a firm is indeed an offense, for the power to abuse and the abuse of power cannot be separated.

– Alcoa's market share was 90 percent and that "is enough to constitute a monopoly; it is doubtful whether 60 or 64 percent would be enough; and certainly 33 percent is not."

– Prior to 1945, the good behavior of the company would have been an acceptable defense to the court. However, this is no longer valid, for "*Con-*

gress did not condone 'good' trusts and condemn 'bad' ones; it forbade all.''

It is easy to see why the Alcoa case ranks as a major milestone in the history of antitrust. It suggests that a monopoly firm *may* be held to be in violation of the law even if there is no proof that the firm intended to monopolize the market and even if the power to do so was lawfully acquired. It further implies that power may be condemned even if never abused, especially if it tends to limit or prevent access to the market by other firms.

Judge Hand's decision thus greatly tempered the rule-of-reason criterion. But as explained below, subsequent court decisions in other monopolization cases have softened his conclusions. Today the rule of reason is still an important criterion, but the rule has been broadened to include other considerations.

American Telephone & Telegraph Case (1982) In 1974 the Justice Department sued AT&T, charging the nation's largest communications company with monopolizing its market. The Department asked the court to separate Western Electric (AT&T's equipment manufacturing branch), the Long Lines (that is, long distance) Department, and the company's 23 local operating subsidiaries. A settlement with the government was reached in 1982. AT&T agreed to divest itself of its operating subsidiaries and of parts of Western Electric. In return, the Justice Department permitted AT&T to enter the fast-growing data communications market.

During the early 1980s, the government also dismissed charges against corporate defendants in several major antitrust suits. And in the federal courts, a string of decisions showed clearly that judicial attitudes toward monopolies were becoming more conciliatory. Thus:

Since about 1980, the judgement of monopoly has usually been based on factors comprising a new and broader "rule of reason." They include:

Efficiency A firm may achieve market dominance because of scale economies, and it may retain its dominant position because of superior performance.

Competition The availability of substitutes, from foreign as well as from domestic sources, can reflect the intensity of competition more accurately than the size of firms in the market.

Innovation A firm's ability to benefit the public by creating desirable products and selling them at attractive prices may be a major reason for its market entrenchment.

The third factor — innovation — is especially significant. It suggests that courts may presume legal almost any market conduct that monopolists claim would encourage innovation. The government would then be left with the burden of proving that the conduct in question did not benefit the public.

Mergers

One of the ways a firm can expand is to reinvest all or part of its earnings in additional plant, equipment, and personnel. Another way, much faster, is to acquire an established firm. This helps to explain why many companies have chosen to expand through mergers.

What is a **merger**? It is simply a joining of firms under one ownership. Three different types of mergers are illustrated by the following landmark cases.

Brown Shoe Case (1962) This involved a merger that was both vertical and horizontal. As you will recall:

A *vertical merger* unites firms in different stages of production of the same or similar goods. It may thus result in greater economies by combining separate production processes and regularizing supplies, thereby increasing profit margins. *Examples:* An automobile manufacturer merging with a steel producer; a supermarket chain merging with a food processing firm.

A *horizontal merger* unites firms producing similar products. The products may be close substitutes, like different brands of gasoline, or moderate substitutes, like waxed paper and aluminum foil.

The objective of such a merger is to round out a product line that is sold through the same distribution channels, thereby offering joint economies in sales and distribution efforts.

The Brown Shoe Company was the nation's fourth-largest shoe manufacturer. It had 4 percent of the industry's total sales, and it controlled a number of retail outlets besides. Seven years earlier, in 1955, Brown had merged with the G.R. Kinney Corporation. This company operated the nation's largest retail shoe chain, accounting for 1.2 percent of national shoe sales. It was also the nation's twelfth-largest shoe manufacturer.

Chief Justice Earl Warren spoke for the Court in ordering Brown to divest itself of Kinney. He noted that, despite the relatively small market shares involved, the merger was significant for two reasons:

1. The vertical aspect of the merger of Brown's manufacturing facilities with Kinney's retail outlets was "anticompetitive." That is, it would probably "foreclose competition from a substantial share of the markets for men's, women's, and children's shoes, without producing any countervailing competitive, economic, or social advantages."

2. The horizontal aspect of the merger — the marriage of Brown's retailing outlets with Kinney's outlets — involved a retail combination that could encompass the entire nation or a single metropolitan area. "The fact that two merging firms have competed directly on the horizontal level in but a fraction of the geographic markets in which either has operated does not, in itself, place their merger outside the scope of Section 7" of the Clayton Antitrust Act. The Court must recognize "Congress' desire to promote competition through the protection of viable, small, locally owned businesses."

Procter & Gamble – Clorox Case (1967) This was an example of a ***conglomerate merger.*** It united companies producing unrelated products. Such mergers may reflect a desire by the acquiring company to spread risks, to find outlets for idle capital funds, or to add products that can be sold with the firm's merchandising knowledge and skills. Alternatively, conglomerate mergers may simply reflect a desire of the acquiring firm to gain greater economic power on a broader front.

The P&G-Clorox case involved a conglomerate merger that had taken place between a major producer of a diversified line of soaps and the leading manufacturer of household bleach. When the Supreme Court ordered the dissolution of this marriage, it pointed out that a conglomerate merger is likely to be illegal if it combines two key features:

- *The acquired firm is a major factor in an oligopolistic industry.* In this instance, Clorox's sales were 48 percent of the national total, and the top four bleach producers had 80 percent of the market.

- *The acquiring company is in a closely related line.* Thus, P&G is in the detergent-soap-cleanser business, whereas Clorox sells bleach. Both companies sell low-cost, high-turnover household supplies to the same customers by the same marketing methods in grocery stores. In addition, both companies' products are largely "presold" through large-scale advertising and promotions.

In the opinion of the Supreme Court, these two factors resulted in a *significant lessening of competition.* Therefore, the merger was held to be illegal.

Today's Merger Guidelines

On the basis of these cases, you can see that mergers of all types raise difficult antitrust issues. This is because mergers can have adverse effects on competition in various ways. For example, mergers may:

- Reduce the number of firms capable of entering a particular market.

- Decrease the number of firms with the capability and incentive for competitive innovation.

- Increase the barriers to the entry of new firms in a particular market.

– Diminish the vigor of competition by increasing both actual and potential customer-supplier relationships among leading firms in a particular market.

Because of this, both the Department of Justice and the Federal Trade Commission watch mergers closely. However, since the late 1970s, they and the courts have recognized the increasing need of American business to be competitive in world markets. Unlike the previous era, therefore, the legality of any merger today is judged by its impact on the affected *industry's efficiency*. This is illustrated by the following guidelines.

Quantitative Guidelines Of the three kinds of mergers, horizontal types can cause the greatest increase in monopolization within an industry. The traditional way of measuring monopolization within an industry has been to add the **market shares**—the percentages of the industry's output —of the largest firms (usually the four largest). The resulting number, called a **concentration ratio,** discloses the degree of market dominance by the industry's major companies.

Various shortcomings of the concentration ratio have resulted in the government adopting an additional measure known as the **Herfindahl index** (also called the *Herfindahl-Hirschman index*). It is the sum of the squares of the market shares for all the firms in an industry. The calculations, based on the table in Exhibit 3, can be illustrated in two steps — before and after a merger:

Step 1 Before a merger occurs, the four-firm concentration ratio obtained from column (2) is: $.20 + .15 + .10 + .05 = .50$, or 50 percent. This places the industry in a relatively low-concentration category. The Herfindahl index is derived by squaring the market shares in column (3) and then totaling them, obtaining .0798. However, the government prefers to express the data without a decimal point. Accordingly, it moves the decimal point four places to the right (that is, multiplies the squared figures by 10,000) as shown in column (4). The resulting Herfindahl index H equals 798.

Step 2 Suppose Firm A acquires Firm C. This raises Firm A's market share to 30 percent, as shown in column (5). After squaring in column (6) and moving the decimal point four places to the right in column (7), the resulting Herfindahl index H equals 1198.

Is this merger likely to raise some antitrusters' eyebrows? Yes. Under guidelines used since the early 1980s, the government evaluates horizontal mergers according to their effect on Herfindahl indexes.

> Any horizontal merger that leaves the Herfindahl index at less than 1000 is unlikely to be challenged. (For comparison purposes it may be noted that an industry composed of 10 firms, each with a 10 percent market share, would have a Herfindahl index of 1000).
>
> Any horizontal merger is likely to be challenged if it *both* (a) results in a Herfindahl index of 1000 or more and (b) raises the index by 100 points or more.

The Herfindahl index thus plays an important role in today's antitrust policy. Several reasons for using it are explained in Exhibit 3. In addition, the government's classification of concentrated industries based on the index is illustrated with some examples in Exhibit 4.

Qualitative Guidelines In addition to the quantitative criteria for judging mergers, the government also considers several qualitative ones. These apply to all three types of mergers—horizontal, vertical, and conglomerate. Stated briefly, the qualitative factors include:

– *Barriers to entry*—the obstacles faced by potential competitors as a result of a merger.

– *Product homogeneity*—the extent to which consumer alternatives are reduced as a result of a merger.

– *Facilitation of collusion*—the chances that fewer firms in the industry, due to a merger, may be inclined to conspire against the public.

Exhibit 3
Judging Market Concentration with the Herfindahl Index

The Herfindahl index is derived by taking each firm's market share in column (2), squaring it as in column (3), and adding up the results. This gives an index of .0798. However, the government prefers to eliminate the decimal point by moving it four places to the right, that is, by multiplying the data by 10,000, as in column (4). The resulting Herfindahl index H is 798.

Note that as a result of the merger of Firms A and C, the index in column (7) rises to 1198. This is a cause for government concern because any index of 1000 or more is a sign that the industry may be too concentrated.

You can verify from columns (4) and (7) that the Herfindahl index has several useful properties:

1. Because of the squaring process, large firms affect the index disproportionately more than small ones.

Therefore, the index can be reasonably approximated by adding the squared market shares of the three or four largest firms.

2. You can calculate the increase in the index resulting from the merger by simply *multiplying the market shares (expressed as a percentage) of the merging firms and doubling the result.* Thus, the merger of Firms A and C increased the Herfindahl index by $(20 \times 10) \times 2 = 400$ points.

3. The index can be roughly related to the four-firm concentration ratio, C_4. Based on studies of various industries, the relationship is *approximately:*

$$C_4 = .025H + 25$$

This equation will produce an estimate of C_4 that is *usually* within 10 percent of the correct figure.

(1)	(2)	(3)	(4)	(5)	(6)	(7)
	Before Merger			After Firm A Acquires Firm C		
Companies	Market share	$\left(\begin{array}{c}\text{Market}\\\text{share}\end{array}\right)^2$	Col. (3) × 10,000	Market share	$\left(\begin{array}{c}\text{Market}\\\text{share}\end{array}\right)^2$	Col. (6) × 10,000
Firm A	0.20	.0400	400	0.30	.0900	900
Firm B	0.15	.0225	225	0.15	.0225	225
Firm C	0.10	.0100	100	—	—	—
Firm D	0.05	.0025	25	0.05	.0025	25
Firm E	0.03	.0009	9	0.03	.0009	9
Firm F	0.02	.0004	4	0.02	.0004	4
Others	0.45	.0035*	35	0.45	.0035*	35
	1.00	.0798	798 = H	1.00	.1198	1198 = H

* Estimated

In summary:

Barring any unusual effects that are likely to lead to future monopoly, any type of merger that is not anticompetitive is acceptable. In most cases, vertical and conglomerate mergers are less likely to be anticompetitive than horizontal mergers. However, because of the difficulty of judging "anticompetitiveness," the government uses both quantitative and qualitative guidelines in evaluating mergers.

Exhibit 4
**Classification of Industrial Concentration
Based on the Herfindahl Index, _H_**

**Unconcentrated industries (H < 1000)**
  Ready-mix concrete
  Specialty dies and tools
  Toilet preparations
  Women's and misses' dresses

_**Moderately concentrated industries (H = 1000
to 1800)**_
  Chemicals
  Copper
  Liquor
  Synthetic rubber

**Highly concentrated industries (H > 1800)**
  Cellulose synthetic fibers
  Light bulbs
  Motor vehicles
  Turbines

Price Discrimination

Why do many doctors, dentists and lawyers charge their clients different fees for the same services? Why do stores offer certain merchandise at quantity discounts? Why are long-distance telephone calls cheaper at night and on weekends than at other times?

The answers to these questions involve the problem of **_price discrimination._** As you will recall, this is the practice by a seller of charging different prices to the same or to different buyers for the same good, without corresponding differences in costs. (It may also take the form of charging buyers the same price despite corresponding differences in costs.)

Which concept of cost — average or marginal — is relevant for this definition? The answer is _marginal._ To illustrate, let P_A and P_B be the prices paid by customers A and B, and let MC_A and MC_B be the marginal costs of supplying them. If there is no

discrimination, each buyer will pay the marginal-cost price — the one at which $MC = P$. Thus:

$$MC_A = P_A \quad \text{and} \quad MC_B = P_B$$

This is equivalent to dividing each equation by its own P, obtaining

$$\frac{MC_A}{P_A} = 1 \quad \text{and} \quad \frac{MC_B}{P_B} = 1$$

In other words, the seller will _not_ be discriminating between buyers A and B so long as

$$\frac{MC_A}{P_A} = \frac{MC_B}{P_B} = 1$$

But what if the ratios are such that

$$\frac{MC_A}{P_A} \neq \frac{MC_B}{P_B} \neq 1$$

In this case, because the ratios do not equal 1, the seller will be discriminating between buyers A and B.

For convenience, you may find it helpful to _invert_ this equation so that it reads:

$$\frac{P_A}{MC_A} \neq \frac{P_B}{MC_B} \neq 1$$

This equation, of course, can be extended to include any number of buyers. Stated in words rather than in symbols the equation says:

> Price discrimination _in the economic sense_ exists so long as the price-cost difference (or ratio) is not the same for all buyers.

How does this economic meaning of price discrimination compare with its legal meaning? The Robinson-Patman Act, which amended Section 2 of the Clayton Act, provides the answer. The Act makes it illegal for a seller "_to discriminate in price between different purchasers of commodities of like_ *grade and quality . . . where the effect of such discrimination may be substantially to lessen competition or tend to create a monopoly in any line of commerce.*" Thus:

Price discrimination *in the legal sense* (based on the Robinson-Patman Act) exists so long as

$$P_A \neq P_B$$

and there is *substantial* injury to competition.

The legal meaning of price discrimination, in contrast to the economic one, is thus expressed in terms of *price differences* rather than in terms of *price-cost differences.*

Three Defenses

What defenses can a seller who is charged with price discrimination offer? The Robinson-Patman Act allows three:

1. Cost Defense   The seller must be able to show that differences in prices charged made "only due allowance" for differences in costs. In other words, the seller must be able to prove that economic discrimination did not occur.

2. Good Faith Defense   The seller must be able to show "that his lower price was made in good faith to meet the equally low price of a competitor." The seller, in other words, is permitted to match a competitor's price but not undercut it.

3. Insubstantial Injury Defense   The seller must be able to show that even though price discrimination was practiced, there was no *substantial* injury to competition. It is then up to the court to decide, on the basis of the evidence, whether or not the injury was "substantial."

The Robinson-Patman Act, as you learned earlier, was primarily designed to protect independent merchants, such as grocers and druggists, from the discriminatory practices of manufacturers. These producers often favored large chain-store buyers by charging them lower prices because of their greater purchasing power. However, the Act left considerable room for interpretation by the courts, as the following landmark cases indicate.

Morton Salt Case (1948)   The Morton Salt Company, a major producer, sold salt to grocery wholesalers, retailers, and other dealers on a volume-discount basis. Those buyers who purchased freight-carload quantities of salt within a period of 12 consecutive months paid significantly lower prices per case than those who did not. This pricing system, the FTC charged, discriminated against most retailers. The evidence showed that only a few large supermarket chains could purchase enough salt to obtain the discount. The Supreme Court sided with the government, stating:

1. Defendant's argument that its discount schedule was not discriminatory because it was "available to all on equal terms" is only of theoretical interest. In practice, the advantages were available only to large buyers.

2. The failure of the Federal Trade Commission to demonstrate that the defendant's discount schedule could not be justified on a cost basis is immaterial. *The burden of proof is on the defendant, not the plaintiff, to show that differences in prices make "only due allowance" for differences in costs.*

The Supreme Court concluded that there was sufficient injury to competition to find Morton's price schedule illegal. This decision gave the FTC virtually complete authority over firms' discount policies. It also made clear that the cost defense, which rests entirely on the defendant, is not a very practical one. It is usually impossible for firms to develop all the precise data needed to prove that their price differences make "only due allowance" for cost differences.

Utah Pie Case (1967)   This case raised some complex issues in price discrimination between competitors. The Utah Pie Company, a small Salt Lake City seller of frozen pies, sued three national competitors — Continental Baking, Carnation Milk, and Pet Milk. It accused them of injuring competition by cutting prices of their frozen pies below cost in the Salt Lake City market while maintaining prices elsewhere. The Supreme Court's decision went against the "big three" pie producers. Quoting from the Robinson-Patman Act, the court stated that Section 3 prohibits predatory behavior. That is, the Act forbids sales "at unreasonably low prices for the purpose of destroying competition or eliminating a competitor." However, the Court failed to state at what point a competitive price becomes "unreasonably low" or "predatory," or at what point a low price ceases to be desirable and becomes undesirable.

A&P Case (1979) The Robinson-Patman Act prohibits a buyer from knowingly inducing or receiving a discriminatory price. This provision of the law was considered by the Supreme Court in a 1979 case involving the A&P grocery chain and the Borden Company. A&P had informed Borden, a major milk producer, that its bid to supply private-label milk to A&P was unsuccessful. "Your bid is so far out of line it is not even funny. You are not even in the ball park," wrote an A&P executive to a Borden vice president. Borden responded with a much lower bid and was granted the contract—without knowing that its offer was $83,000 below the next lowest bid. When Borden discovered this, it complained to the FTC. The FTC then sued A&P for inducing a discriminatory price from Borden. A&P lost, but upon appeal, the Supreme Court decided against the government and in favor of A&P. It accepted the defendant's good-faith defense by noting that:

1. Borden had "acted in a reasonable and good-faith effort to meet its competition," and thus had not violated the Robinson-Patman Act. Therefore,

2. A&P could not be guilty of inducing an illegal discrimination and thereby violating the same Act.

Current Problems

On the basis of these cases, it is easy to see why the Robinson-Patman Act has been called ambiguous and inconsistent. Part of the reason has been summed up in a clever bit of verse:

> You're gouging on your prices if
> You charge more than the rest.
> But it's unfair competition
> If you think you can charge less.
> A second point that we would make
> To help avoid confusion:
> Don't try to charge the same amount
> That would be collusion!
> You must compete. But not too much,
> For if you do, you see,
> Then the market would be yours—
> And that's monopoly!
> —R.W. Grant, *Tom Smith and His Incredible Bread Machine.*

These ideas can be stated more generally in the form of two propositions:

1. The Robinson-Patman Act sometimes prohibits discrimination, sometimes permits it, and sometimes requires it.

The basis of this statement can be seen from several examples:

- The Act makes it illegal for sellers to discriminate among competing buyers—those in the same "line of commerce" such as grocers or druggists. However, it allows sellers to discriminate among noncompeting buyers and among consumers.

- The Act defines price differences that are unjustified by cost differences as discriminatory. But it permits sellers to charge identical prices where costs differ, which is also discriminatory.

- The Act permits the payment of brokerage fees where the services of independent brokers (such as food brokers) are utilized. However, it forces sellers to discriminate by denying brokers' commissions to buyers who perform their own brokerage services.

2. Both the Robinson-Patman Act and the courts have assumed that price differences that hurt competitors also hurt competition.

For example, in the Morton Salt case, competition was assumed to be lessened because smaller buyers could not take advantage of the seller's quantity discounts. In the Utah Pie case, the Supreme Court concerned itself with the effect of price competition on a single competitor in a particular market. And in many other cases, the courts have equated damage to competitors with damage to competition. They have thus placed greater emphasis on "protecting competition" than promoting it. To the extent that this attitude has preserved weak competitors, it has fostered inefficiency in the name of enhancing competition.

Suggested Reforms

It is apparent that the laws against price discrimination are not well coordinated with the other antitrust laws. What can be done about this? The answer, of course, is that the Robinson-Patman Act should be revised. Various studies have suggested three sets of reforms:

Price Discrimination This should be made unlawful only when it impairs the vigor of competition as a whole. Sporadic price discrimination undertaken to retain old customers as well as to attract new ones should be permitted, provided it extends over a broad market area.

Cost and Good-faith Defenses These should be liberalized and extended. Demonstrated savings based on reasonable cost data should be accepted, and price cutting to "beat" competition, not merely to meet it, should be allowed.

Brokerage Fees and Allowances These should be permitted for buyers who perform their own brokerage, merchandising, and promotional services. However, the payments should be some specified percentage of the cost of the services involved.

> Adoption of these reforms would go a long way toward reducing the current ambiguities and inconsistencies in the price-discrimination laws. The result would be a substantial improvement in economic efficiency, which is what Congress wanted to achieve when it initially passed the laws.

Vertical Restrictions: Supplier-Customer Restraints

Should a manufacturer, as a condition of selling to wholesalers and retailers, be allowed to prescribe the ways in which they conduct certain aspects of their businesses? This is the problem of vertical restrictions, a part of the antitrust laws dealing with supplier-customer restraints. The major types of restraints fall into three categories: vertical price fixing and refusal to deal; tying arrangements and exclusive dealing; and territorial restrictions.

Vertical Price Fixing and Refusal to Deal

Vertical price fixing is commonly known as *resale price maintenance* or *fair trade.* It is a practice whereby a manufacturer of a branded product sets the minimum (and sometimes the maximum) retail price at which that product can be sold. This eliminates price competition at the retail level.

Why might a manufacturer specify a minimum retail price for a product? There are several possible reasons:

− It may encourage retailers to "push" the product because the profit margin is stable and assured.

− It may help preserve the reputation of the product for those who associate quality and reliability with price.

− It may enhance the sale of products (such as major appliances) that require dealer installation or repairs, by assuring buyers of the services that go with the goods.

Vertical price fixing has a long and interesting legal history dating back to the early part of this century. Several landmark cases serve to illustrate the trend of judicial thinking on the subject.

Dr. Miles Case (1911) The Dr. Miles Medical Company produced proprietary drugs. It sold the drugs to wholesalers and retailers who agreed in writing to maintain the manufacturer's preset prices. The Supreme Court struck down these vertical restrictions, contending that a manufacturer who sells a good cannot continue to control it. Once title to a good passes to a buyer, so does the right to the disposition of that good.

Colgate Case (1919) Eight years after the Dr. Miles case, the Court established an exception to its rule. The case involved Colgate, a major producer of toothpaste and soap. The Court held that the company could announce the conditions under which it would deal — or refuse to deal — with others, and it could adhere to those conditions. *But it could not do more.* If it tried to formulate specific agreements with distributors regarding retail price policies, it would be violating the Sherman Antitrust Act.

During the 1930s most states, pressured by retail trade associations, passed resale price maintenance legislation under the euphemism of "fair trade." Congress helped out by enacting legislation exempting fair-trade agreements from the antitrust laws. But during the 1950s and 1960s, several distributors successfully contested fair trade in the courts. This gave rise to the growth of discounting and hence to the erosion of legislative support for resale price maintenance. In 1976, Congress repealed the federal statutes in recognition of the fact that the state laws had become largely ineffectual.

Only two remnants of fair trade remain. They are: (1) the practice by some manufacturers of announcing "suggested" retail prices and (2) the right of sellers to refuse to deal. The first is not legally enforceable and the second can be fulfilled only in the limited manner specified in the Colgate case.

Tying Arrangements and Exclusive Dealing

A seller may require the buyer to purchase one or more less-desired products as a condition for purchasing a desired product. This arrangement is called a **tying contract** or **tie-in sale.** The desired product is referred to as "tying" and the less desired as "tied-in." A good example of a tying arrangement occurred in the block-bookings of motion pictures. Movie theaters were once required to take a certain number of grade "B" films as a condition for obtaining grade "A" films. Similarly, in the early

years of television, RCA, Zenith, and other manufacturers required distributors to purchase a specified number of radios for each television set they ordered.

Why might a seller want to establish a tying arrangement? There a number of possible reasons:

1. *Obtain Leverage* The tying product may have a "strong" or relatively inelastic demand while the tied-in product has a "weak" or relatively elastic demand. The seller can therefore lever (or greatly boost) the sale of the weak product by tying it to the sale of the strong one.

2. *Facilitate Price Discrimination* Tying arrangements can achieve the same results as price discrimination, without the accompanying difficulties and risks. For example:

   (a) A tie-in contract may specify a particular combination of products, such as 1X and 1Y, or 1X and 2Y, etc. By selecting the best combination, the seller can realize a larger total revenue than if the two products were sold separately.

   (b) A tie-in sale can enable the seller to price the desired good according to the buyer's intensity of use. Both IBM and Xerox, for example, tied the sale of computer cards and copying paper to their main equipment. The tied-in products thus served a metering function, making it possible to *charge higher prices to heavier users.*

What has been the attitude of the courts with respect to tying contracts? Their decisions have generally been based on either of two criteria — *leverage* and *reasonableness.* For example:

International Salt Case (1947) This important case reflects the more typical way in which tying arrangements have been viewed by the courts. The courts have usually held that the leverage objective (explained above) does more than enhance the sale of a tied-in product. It also enables a firm that has substantial market power over a tying good to extend that power to the market for the tied-in good. This is what the court concluded in the case of International Salt Company, the nation's largest producer of salt for industrial uses. The firm was found guilty of injuring competition because it had tied the sale of its patented salt dispensing machines to the sale of its main product, salt. This, the Supreme Court said, prevented competing producers from selling salt to users of International Salt machines.

Jerrold Electronics Case (1960) Here the court ruled that "reasonableness" was an acceptable defense for a tying agreement. During the 1950s, Jerrold, the country's major producer of community antenna television systems, tied service contracts to the sale of its equipment. It argued that the antenna systems were "too delicate and sensitive," and the industry "too new with a highly uncertain future," for the company to risk its reputation by selling its equipment without service contracts. The federal district court, and ultimately the Supreme Court, accepted this defense. Jerrold was granted permission to engage in tying arrangements for a limited time—until the industry developed sturdier equipment and greater maturity.

Chicken Delight Case (1971) The courts have accepted the "reasonableness" defense in a few other instances. But not in the case of Chicken Delight. In order "to preserve its reputation," this fast-food franchise tried to tie the sale of its chicken and cookware to the sale of its franchises. The court prohibited the tie-ins on the grounds that the inputs were obtainable from other sources. Further, the court said, the franchiser could "maintain a consistency of reputation" for quality by establishing appropriate specifications.

Tying contracts are often related to exclusive dealing. This occurs when a manufacturer contracts with a distributor to be the sole supplier of a particular product or class of products. Standard Oil of California, for instance, was once the exclusive supplier, through a few distributors, of tires, batteries, and other auto accessories to several thousand Standard service stations in the western United States.

Exclusive dealing can provide advantages both to the manufacturer and to the distributor:

- The manufacturer may find it more efficient to deal with a few large distributors instead of many small ones.
- The distributor may realize savings by carrying lower inventories than would be required with many different brands of the same product.

The chief objection to exclusive dealing is that it reduces competition. This is because distributors and other suppliers are limited in the goods that can be brought to market. Therefore, consumer choice is curbed.

The courts, for the most part, have gone along with this view. Unless efficiency gains can be clearly demonstrated (which is usually difficult to do), and there is little or no evidence of intent or ability to "monopolize," exclusive-dealing arrangements are likely to be held illegal.

Thus, in general:

Both tying and exclusive dealing agreements are ordinarily regarded by the courts as anticompetitive. Tying contracts, courts have held, can enable a seller to gain monopolistic control over a tied-in good, and exclusive-dealing contracts are likely to curb competition. Therefore, only strong defenses of "reasonableness," demonstrated improvements in efficiency, and minimal adverse effects on competition persuade courts to permit such arrangements.

Territorial Restrictions

In some industries, producers provide their distributors with exclusive territories. Most automobile dealerships and fast-food outlets are typical examples. Such territorial restrictions usually give rise to two competitive consequences:

1. Reduction of Intrabrand Competition Manufacturers grant, and distributors accept, restricted territories in order to concentrate sales efforts on a specific product (or group of products) in a particular area. This leads to less competition in that product within that area. For example, General Motors reduces competition in the sale of Chevrolets by limiting the number of Chevrolet dealers in each territory.

Economics in the News

Department of Justice

STATEMENT OF
CHARLES F. RULE,
ACTING ASSISTANT ATTORNEY
GENERAL
ANTITRUST DIVISION,
BEFORE
THE
COMMITTEE ON THE JUDICIARY
UNITED STATES SENATE
CONCERNING
PROFESSIONAL SPORTS
ANTITRUST LEGISLATION
ON
JUNE 12, 1985

Mr. Chairman and members of the Committee:

I am pleased to be here today to present the views of the Department of Justice on S. 298, S. 259, S. 172 and S. 287, all of which address perceived problems common to professional sports leagues.

For the reasons that I will discuss in my testimony today, the Department opposes the enactment of any of these bills in their present form. All [of the bills] address professional sports franchise relocation. In addition, all of the bills except S. 298 would regulate franchise relocation by creating standards or criteria that would have to be met (to the satisfaction of either the courts or an arbitra-tion board) in order for a league-approved franchise relocation to be lawful.

The heavy-handed regulation contemplated by the bills runs counter to the laudatory trend toward deregulation in our economy generally. Our nation's fundamental economic policy is reliance on marketplace competition free from public and private restraints, rather than on unneeded state or federal regulation, to determine the location of businesses. Economic efficiency and consumer welfare are enhanced by allowing firms to locate where their costs are lowest and the demand for their products is greatest. The typical firm is free to relocate in order to reduce its costs (*e.g.,* wages, taxes, transportation) or to stimulate demand for its product. In general, Congress wisely has not interfered with market processes by regulating business relocation. By the same reasoning, government interference in the relocation of professional sports franchises also should be avoided.

In a free-market system, firms—not regulators or legislators—are generally considered the best judges of how and where their products are marketed. Congress does not mandate that steel manufacturers, for example, must open new plants in specific cities according to a specific schedule.

Professional sports have become so popular precisely because the entrepreneurs who own teams have been able to respond to market forces. Indeed, professional team sports in this country represent a triumph of capitalism. We would be unwise to ignore the importance of private economic decisionmaking in that success. But, the quasi-regulatory regimes that these bills would create would do just that. Moreover, they would provide a dangerous precedent for further, even more harmful, federal regulation of professional sports.

We believe that the interests of leagues in applying franchise relocation rules will nearly always coincide with the interests of consumer welfare. Because we cannot say that a narrowly-written and non-regulatory antitrust exemption for franchise relocation rules by itself would have a significantly adverse effect on our nation's competition policy, the Department would not oppose such an exemption. While the Department recommends against enactment of these bills in their present form, we would, of course, be happy to work with the Congress to develop legislation that avoids creating burdensome new regulatory schemes.

That concludes my prepared remarks, and I would be pleased to answer any questions the Committee might have.

2. Enhancement of Interbrand Competition   As a result of territorial restrictions, it is common to find different distributors selling competing brands of a product in the same area. This promotes competition between brands. For example, McDonald's, Burger King, Wendy's, etc., encourage competition with one another by curbing the number of their own outlets in a particular area.

What is the legal status of territorial restrictions? The answer is not always clear-cut.

> The courts have come down hard on *horizontal* territorial restrictions—such as the allocation of markets by competing sellers. (This is collusion.) But the courts' treatment of *vertical* territorial restrictions imposed by producers on their distributors has been less consistent. Nevertheless, territorial restrictions are likely to be permitted when it appears that the benefits to society of enhanced interbrand competition substantially offset the losses from reduced intrabrand competition.

Conclusion: Need for Reform

The antitrust laws have been in existence for many decades. Their purpose has been to improve efficiency through the maintenance, if not enhancement, of competition. Have they succeeded in this task? If not, are they an idea whose time has gone—and should they therefore be discarded?

Many economists and political leaders, liberals as well as conservatives, would answer *no* to the first question. Many others would answer *yes* to the second. They would contend that the fear of market concentration has been oversold. They would also argue that the benchmark or reference point of perfect competition is too removed from the real world of monopolistic competition and oligopoly.

Critics of the antitrust laws base their position on several arguments:

International Competition   Our economy is not as isolated from foreign competitors as it used to be. The automobile industry, the banking industry, the steel industry, and many others face much more foreign competition than they faced in the past.

Irrelevant "Relevant Markets"   Antitrusters have always been concerned with defining the relevant market for a monopolized product. For example, is cellophane a unique product, or is it competitive with other flexible wrapping materials, such as waxed paper, aluminum foil, plastic wrap, etc.? In today's economy, in which there are numerous substitutes for most products, monopolization of a "relevant market" is usually a meaningless concept.

Potential Competition and Contestable Markets   Most markets today are vulnerable to potential competitors. Many domestic and foreign firms are waiting in the wings with sufficient resources to take on a firm that is earning monopoly profits. Contestable markets—those characterized by ease of exit—create further pressure on existing firms to keep prices down.

Questionable Benefits of "Deconcentration"   When government succeeds in breaking up a large firm, the result may be more harmful than beneficial. One large IBM may be much better than four or five small ones, especially if the breakup sacrifices economies of scale. In such a case, foreign computer manufacturers would benefit the most.

Nonprice Competition   Antitrusters have traditionally looked more favorably on price competition than on nonprice competition. The latter consists of advertising, product differentiation, customer service, and other forms of competition that do not involve differences in selling price. However, there is no strong evidence that, when given the choice, the general public prefers price competition to nonprice competition. Therefore, some critics contend that both types of competition should be accepted as valid.

The "New" Antitrust

On the basis of such arguments as these, attitudes toward our antitrust laws are undergoing extensive reconsideration. As you have learned, the antitrust laws have had one major purpose—*to improve efficiency through promotion of competitive markets.*

But as stated above, many critics—liberal as well as conservative—contend that neither the laws nor the courts' interpretation of them have done this. Therefore, a number of experts argue for a "new" antitrust with three major features:

1. The use of productive (technical) efficiency as a practical guide for judging economic efficiency.

2. Strict prohibition of three types of behavior:

   (a) Restrictive agreements by competitors to fix prices or divide markets

   (b) Horizontal mergers that leave fewer than three significant rivals in the market

   (c) Predatory practices (not to be confused with hard competition) aimed at driving existing competitors from the market or at impeding the entry of new ones

3. Tolerance of all other practices, including vertical and conglomerate mergers, relatively small horizontal mergers, price discrimination over broad market areas, and vertical (supplier-customer) restraints.

Critics who favor the "new" antitrust argue that by adopting these policies, *the federal government would be promoting competition (and thereby encouraging efficiency) by putting greater reliance on the marketplace and less on the courts.*

It should be noted that this is only one of three points of view on this topic. A second holds that the antitrust laws, perhaps with some revision, should be enforced more vigorously. A third holds that the laws have been a failure and hence should be discarded—for either of two reasons:

1. To get government out of the private sector, thereby allowing the free market to operate.

2. To establish government ownership of large businesses, thus moving a step closer to socialism.

What You Have Learned

1. The antitrust laws are intended to curb monopoly and to promote efficiency by maintaining competition in the American economy. The chief antitrust laws are the Sherman Antitrust Act, the Clayton Antitrust Act, the Federal Trade Commission Act, the Robinson–Patman Act, the Wheeler–Lea Act, and the Celler Antimerger Act. Taken together and in a broad sense, they forbid restraint of trade, monopolization, price discrimination, and unfair competition. Major groups exempt from the antitrust laws are the regulated transport industries and labor unions.

2. Antitrust issues can usually be analyzed within a framework of five major topics. These are: (1) restrictive agreements and conspiracies; (2) monopoly; (3) mergers; (4) price discrimination; and (5) vertical restrictions, or supplier-customer restraints. Courts have ruled in all these areas, but issues remain unresolved.

3. Congress never defined many of the essential terms in the antitrust laws. The courts were left to interpret such concepts as "restraint of trade," "monopoly," "unfair competition," and "substantial lessening of competition." This has resulted in many inconsistent decisions, vague interpretations, and value judgments, all of which have served to reduce the effectiveness of antitrust policy.

4. Many critics contend that the antitrust laws have not succeeded in enhancing competition. Some of these critics argue in favor of placing greater reliance on the marketplace instead of the courts. Others contend that there should be greater government involvement in the management of large corporations.

Terms and Concepts To Review

antitrust laws
Sherman Antitrust Act
  (1890)
unfair competition
Clayton Antitrust Act
  (1914)
price discrimination
interlocking directorate
Federal Trade Com-
  mission Act (1914)
Federal Trade
  Commission
Robinson–Patman Act
  (1936)
Wheeler–Lea Act (1938)
Celler Antimerger Act
  (1950)

injunction
consent decree
restrictive agreement
conscious parallel action
rule of reason
merger
vertical merger
horizontal merger
conglomerate merger
market share
concentration ratio
Herfindahl index
resale price
  maintenance
tying contract

AP/Wide World Photos

John Kenneth Galbraith
1908 –
Painless Socialism

"Economics, as it is conventionally taught, is in part a system of belief designed less to reveal truth than to reassure its communicants about established social arrangements."

"Scientific truth in economics is not always what exists; often it is what can be handled by seemingly scientific methods."

These are typical of the criticisms John Kenneth Galbraith has leveled against traditional economic thinking. A retired Harvard professor, former ambassador to India (1961–1963), and a stimulating teacher as well as scholar, the 6-foot 8-inch iconoclast has devoted most of his professional career to assailing the conventional wisdom of economic

theories and policies. As a result, he has become a leading social critic, filling a position occupied by economist-sociologist Thorstein Veblen in the early decades of this century.

Capitalism's Failures
The modern industrial state, Galbraith argues, is not an economy of free enterprise or of consumer sovereignty. It is an economy dominated by a few hundred large corporations that are directly or indirectly dependent on government contracts. These corporations are governed not by stockholders but by a highly bureaucratic "technostructure" composed of the managerial and technological elite. This elite constitutes the corporate sector's "organized intelligence."

The goal of the technostructure is not to maximize profits, since these would not accrue to its members anyway, but to seek its own security and to produce the "minimum levels of earnings" necessary to assure corporate growth.

Systematic Bamboozlement
In striving for these goals, the technostructure is aided by government, fiscal, monetary, and welfare policies designed to assure an adequate level of aggregate demand. The cooperation between the technostructure and the state depends, of course, on the consent of the people. They are taught to believe, through "systematic public bamboozlement," that sustained economic growth and steadily rising incomes are *the* national goals.

But this process is self-defeating. As people become more educated, they begin to realize that the costs of their material gains are the sacrifices they must make of leisure, fellowship, cultural enrichment, and the like. In short, they must sacrifice

those ingredients that determine the quality of life.

Remedy: More Government
How to improve the quality of life? Galbraith's answer is that there must be a vast expansion of the public sector and greater emphasis on The Higher Things in Life. Otherwise, political forces must sooner or later arise that will seek to wrest the privilege of economic decision making away from the "corporate technostructure."

In short, what Galbraith advocates is closer ties between big corporations and government. At one extreme, these ties may consist of outright government ownership of large businesses. A more moderate solution might be some form of private-public partnership to ensure government involvement in business decisions. Either approach, according to Galbraith, would provide both a better response to the public's needs and desires and a painless transition to socialism.

For Discussion

1. "The rationale underlying restrictive agreements among competitors is based on the potential danger arising from the existence of the power of sellers to manipulate prices. Where this power does not exist, the laws pertaining to restrictive agreements are practically meaningless. Thus, there is no point in holding unlawful an agreement among competitors to fix prices, allocate customers, or control production, when the competitors involved are so small that they lack significant power to affect market prices." Evaluate this statement.

2. Suppose that tomorrow morning all grocers in Chicago, without previous public notice, were to raise their prices for milk by 3 cents per quart. Would this action prove the existence of an agreement or constitute an offense on the part of the grocers? What would your answer be if the automobile manufacturers without notice announced a 5 percent price increase next year on all new model cars? Explain.

3. If all the companies in an oligopolistic industry quote identical prices without prior agreement by following the prices of the industry leader, is this evidence of a combination or conspiracy?

4. In an industry characterized by price leadership without prior arrangement, is there likely to be a charge of combination or conspiracy leveled against that industry if: (a) prevailing prices are announced by the industry's trade association rather than by a leading firm; (b) all firms in the industry report their prices to their industry trade association; (c) all firms in the industry quote prices on a basing point system (that is, the delivered price is the leader's price plus rail freight from the leader's plant); (d) all firms follow the leader not only in price, but in product and sales policies as well? (These four questions should be answered as a group rather than individually.)

5. In the Columbia Steel case (1948), the Supreme Court said: "We do not undertake to prescribe any set of percentage figures by which to measure the reasonableness of a corporation's enlargement of its activities by the purchase of the assets of a competitor. The relative effect of percentage command of a market varies with the setting in which that factor is placed." Does this conflict with Judge Hand's statement in the Alcoa case? Explain.

6. "Since there are 'good' monopolies and 'bad' monopolies, a company should be judged by its total contribution to society—not by its market behavior alone." Do you agree? Explain.

7. "Many trustbusters and economists forget that con-

centration is a function of consumer sovereignty, and that the same consumers who make big businesses big can make them small or even wipe them out by simply refraining from the purchase of their products. This is a not-so-obvious principle of our free enterprise system which needs to be better understood." Do you agree? Discuss.

8. "To say that the degree of competition depends on the number of sellers in the marketplace is like saying that football is more competitive than tennis." Discuss. (HINT Can you describe different forms of competition, in addition to price competition, that exist in American industry?)

9. It is generally stated that growth, stability, and flexibility are three primary objectives of mergers.

(a) With respect to growth, it has been said that "a firm, like a tree, must either grow or die." Evaluate this statement.

(b) Why may instability be a motive for merger? Instability of what?

(c) What is meant by flexibility as a motive for merger? (HINT Compare *flexibility* with *vulnerability*.)

10. Section 7 of the Clayton Antitrust Act of 1914 and its amendment, the Celler Antimerger Act of 1950, states: "No corporation engaged in commerce shall acquire, directly or indirectly, the whole or any part of the stock or other share capital and no corporation subject to the jurisdiction of the Federal Trade Commission shall acquire the whole or any part of the assets of another corporation engaged also in commerce, where in any line of commerce in any section of the country, the effect of such acquisition may be substantially to lessen competition, or to tend to create a monopoly."

Assume that you are an economist for a large corporation and that you are asked to prepare a report on why this legislation should be repealed. What main points would you bring out in your argument?

11. Richard Posner, a professor, lawyer, and federal judge, has argued the following with respect to the Aluminum Company of America (Alcoa) Case of 1945:

This [Judge Hand's] theory of monopolization is a bad one because it encourages inefficient conduct. If a firm enjoys a monopoly position for many years, as did Alcoa, without engaging in any anticompetitive practices, there is a strong presumption that either a monopolistic organization of the market is the most efficient or that the monopolist is selling at the competitive price (perhaps because he really doesn't have any monopoly power). If in these circumstances the monopolist is told to let his market share decline or be punished under Section 2 [of the Sherman Act], he will raise his price and thereby encourage the expansion or entry of firms that may be less efficient; thus the consequences of his monopoly will be aggravated.

> Richard A. Posner, *Antitrust Law: An Economic Perspective*, University of Chicago Press, 1976.

Discuss this quotation. You may find it helpful to consider the following questions:

(a) Are the power to abuse and the abuse of power inseparable, as Judge Hand contended?

(b) Are small firms "better" than large ones, as Judge Hand claimed? How does the *efficiency* of small firms versus large firms affect your answer?

(c) Is the structure of a market more important than a firm's behavior in that market, as Judge Hand contended?

(d) Should Judge Hand have applied the rule of reason in the Alcoa case?

Chapter 30

Human Resources: Labor Markets, Discrimination, Unions

Learning Guide

Watch for answers to these important questions

What are the different concepts of the supply of labor? What are the different concepts of demand? How do these concepts provide a basis for labor market analysis?

How can supply-and-demand models be used to analyze policies affecting wages and employment? What types of labor-market imperfections limit the usefulness of these models? Are there policies for reducing these imperfections so as to improve the efficiency of labor markets?

Why does employment discrimination arise? What type of policies have been formulated to deal with it?

What is collective bargaining? How is the "new" industrial relations affecting unions and management? What is the economic impact of unions on wages, business efficiency, and inflation?

Workers constitute a large proportion of the nation's population and earn most of its income. (The balance is earned by owners of the other three factors of production—land, capital, and entrepreneurship.)

In this chapter you will learn about the role of labor in our economy. In a broader sense, you will learn how certain institutions and mechanisms in today's society help to shape the development and utilization of our nation's human resources.

The study of human-resource economics embraces many areas of interest. They may be grouped into three broad categories to form the framework of this chapter:

1. Labor-market analysis
2. Labor-market problems and policies
3. Unions and management: collective bargaining

Labor-Market Analysis

Employers and workers buy and sell labor services in a labor market. Because the services are usually difficult to quantify, they are typically measured either by number of workers or by hours of labor time. You can best gain an understanding of the labor market by examining these fundamental features:

- Supply of, and demand for, labor
- Wage determination and employment
- Labor-market imperfections

Supply of, and Demand for, Labor

The market for labor, like the market for any commodity, is affected by supply and demand forces. But there are a number of different concepts of labor supply and of labor demand that must be identified before you can understand the labor market itself.

Supply Concepts

When you encounter the term "labor supply" in the news media or in an economic discussion, it is likely to have one of three meanings:

Labor Force This concept of labor supply is simply the employable population. It is defined for measurement purposes as all people 16 years of age or older who are employed plus all those who are unemployed but actively seeking work.

Labor-force Participation Rate This is the percentage of the total population, or of one or more subgroups of the population, that is in the labor force. Subgroups are classified by race, sex, age, marital status, and other demographic characteristics. Thus, the percentage of the nation's white population that is in the labor force would be one type of labor force participation rate. The percentage of the nation's white males that is in the labor force would be another. The percentage of the nation's white males, ages 19 to 24, that is in the labor force would be still another. And so on. Some illustrations of labor force participation rates are shown in Exhibit 1.

Exhibit 1
Labor-Force Participation by Women

The participation rate of married women in the labor force has increased substantially in recent decades. Some major reasons:

Improved Marketability Changing social and cultural attitudes toward women have enabled them to advance their education and skills. This has made their talents more salable in the market.

More Service Occupations The economy is becoming less based on factories and more on services. This creates greater varieties of jobs for which women can compete.

Declining Family Size The average size of the family has declined since the 1960s. This has freed women to work outside the home.

Source: U.S. Department of Labor.   *Estimated

Labor-supply Curve A third concept of labor supply involves the relationship between wage rates and hours worked. The relationship can be illustrated graphically with supply curves. Two different types are shown in Exhibits 2 and 3.

Exhibit 2 depicts the supply curve of labor for a particular occupation. Notice that hours of labor

Exhibit 2
Supply Curve of Labor for a Particular Occupation

A long-run labor supply curve for a particular occupation is more responsive to changes in relative wage rates than a short-run curve. Note, however, that a long-run curve may still be relatively inelastic, as is S'. Or it may be relatively elastic, as is S". (You can judge the elasticity by comparing the increase in hours worked resulting from an increase in the relative wage rate.) The elasticity of the long-run curve will depend on the ease with which workers can enter the occupation and their willingness to do so.

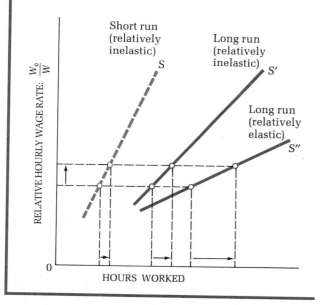

Exhibit 3
Backward-Bending Labor-Supply Curve

The graph shows that at relatively lower hourly wage levels such as $5, $10, etc., the relationship is *direct*. That is, the labor-supply curve slopes upward. At $25 per hour, this particular worker is willing to offer a maximum of 40 hours of work, resulting in an income of $1,000 per week. Beyond this point the relationship becomes *inverse*, or "backward bending." This is because the worker prefers additional leisure to additional income.

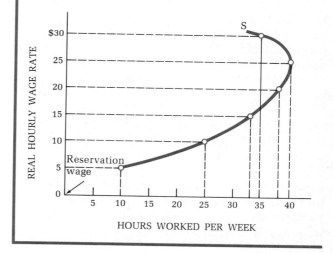

are measured on the horizontal axis and *relative* wage rates on the vertical. (The relative wage rate is the wage rate for a particular occupation W_0 divided by the economy's average wage rate W.) You can see that the upward-sloping supply curves obey the familiar law of supply. As the relative wage rate rises, so does the number of labor hours offered by workers.

Of course, some occupations require special

training. As a result, it may take some time before workers can respond to the higher relative wage rates. Therefore, as indicated in the exhibit, the short-run supply curve S is likely to be less elastic than a longer-run curve. That is, it is less responsive to changes in relative wage rates. Short or long run, the elasticity depends on the particular occupation and the ability and willingness of workers to enter it.

A different type of supply curve is shown in Exhibit 3. It illustrates a *possible* supply curve for an individual worker. In this case the real wage rate, that is, the hourly wage rate in terms of actual purchasing power, is now measured on the vertical axis. The resulting graph is called a ***backward-bending labor-supply curve.*** It has several interesting features:

Reservation Wage   No labor hours will be offered at a rate less than $5 per hour. This rate is often called the "reservation wage". At any wage rate below this, the worker places a higher value on leisure or "nonwork" than on the income that can be earned from working.

Substitution Effect   Beginning at $5 an hour, the worker is willing to trade some leisure for income. Thus, 10 hours of labor will be offered at $5 per hour, 25 hours at $10, 33 hours at $15, 38 hours at $20, and a maximum of 40 hours at $25. Up to this point, therefore, the relationship between wages and labor hours is *direct*. That is, the labor-supply curve slopes upward. It thus illustrates what may be called a "substitution effect" of work for leisure.

Income Effect   At a wage rate above $25 per hour, the relationship becomes *inverse* — the curve "bends backwards." This means that, at higher wage rates, the worker has enough income to buy more of everything, *including* leisure. Therefore, he or she is no longer willing to substitute additional work for some leisure. For example, if the hourly wage rate is $30, the worker will offer only 35 hours of labor for a weekly income of $1,050 (= $30 × 35). This compares with a weekly income of $1,000 that would be earned by working 40 hours at $25 per hour. The backward-bending portion of the curve illustrates what may be called an "income effect." It shows that at some high enough level of income, this worker will work fewer hours in order to enjoy more leisure.

What does this analysis imply for the economy as a whole?

You learned in your early study of supply and demand that a market supply curve represents the sum of individual supply curves. It follows that, if individuals have backward-bending labor-supply curves, then the *total* market supply curve of labor at any given time is also backward-bending.

Various studies have found that this is indeed the case. They have also concluded that the nation's average real hourly wage rate is on the backward-bending portion of the curve. Therefore:

A rise in real earnings, unless offset by other factors such as increases in labor-force participation rates, will result in a decline in total hours worked.

Demand Concepts

The suppliers of labor are, of course, workers. The demanders of labor are employers — the business firms that hire workers. The conditions that determine a firm's demand for labor are already familiar to you. They involve such notions as derived demand and demand elasticity — both of which you studied in some earlier chapters. A brief review of these concepts and the ways in which they affect the business firm's demand for labor will refresh your understanding of important ideas.

Derived Demand   You will recall that the demand for labor is derived from the demand for the products that workers help produce. Thus, if consumers' demand for goods increases, employers' demand for workers to produce those goods will also increase.

Elasticity of Demand for Labor   You will also recall that changes in wages affect the amount of labor that a firm employs. As a result, three major determinants of demand elasticity for labor may be identified:

Elasticity of Demand for the Product   The more elastic the demand for a good, the more elastic the derived demand for the labor used to produce it. For example, suppose the demand for a product is relatively elastic. Then an increase in its price will cause a more than proportional decrease in quantity demanded. Hence, there will also be a substantial decrease in the demand for labor used in making it. Of course, the opposite occurs when the demand for a good is relatively inelastic. Higher prices lead to less than proportional decreases in quantity demanded, and therefore to modest reductions in employment.

Percentage of Labor Costs to Total Costs The larger the proportion of labor costs to the total costs of producing a good, the more elastic the demand for the labor used to produce it. To illustrate, if labor costs in a firm are 30 percent of total costs, a 10 percent wage increase will raise total costs by 3 percent. This is likely to result in a relatively moderate decline in employment. But if labor costs in a firm are 90 percent of total costs, a 10 percent wage increase will raise total costs by 9 percent. This will probably result in a larger drop in employment.

Ease of Substituting Other Inputs for Labor The more easily a firm can replace labor with capital, the more elastic will be its demand for labor. For example, in many assembly-line production processes, an increase in wage rates causes substantial reductions in employment as firms find it less costly to substitute robots for workers.

Various other conditions can affect a firm's elasticity of demand for labor. However, the above factors are among the more important.

Wage Determination and Employment

Demand and supply may be thought of as the blades of a pair of scissors. Both blades are necessary to do the cutting—that is, to determine equilibrium wages and quantities. You can see why from the following illustrations of labor-market practices.

In a purely competitive labor market, wage and employment levels are determined by the free interaction of supply and demand. But in the world in which we live, some labor markets are not purely competitive. Deliberate policies are often adopted by unions, employers, or government to interfere with normal market operations. The reasons are best understood within the framework of certain supply-and-demand models.

Demand-Expansion Model

Exhibit 4 shows some familiar *S* and *D* curves. They relate the price of labor expressed in wages with the quantity of labor supplied and demanded.

Exhibit 4
Demand Expansion Model: Increase the Demand for Labor

Through featherbedding or other make-work practices, an organized group of workers may succeed in shifting the demand curve for its labor to the right. The shift from *D* to *D'* increases the equilibrium quantity of labor from 20,000 workers to 26,000, and the equilibrium wage rate from $10 per hour to $13.

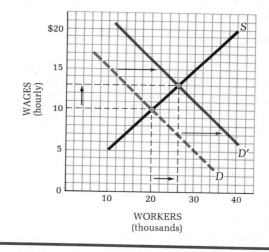

The model illustrates what happens when a union, professional association, or other group seeks to increase the demand for its members. That is, the group tries to shift the demand curve to the right, which would result in higher equilibrium wages and employment. In the diagram, the increase in demand from *D* to *D'* raises the wage rate from $10 per hour to $13 and the level of employment from 20,000 workers to 26,000.

The shift in demand is brought about by the use of ***featherbedding*** techniques. These are "make-work" rules or practices designed by unions to restrict output by artificially increasing the amount of labor or labor time employed on a particular job. For example, at various times in the past:

— The Painters' Union limited the width of brushes and the size of rollers.

- The Meat Cutters' Union required prewrapped meats to be rewrapped on the job.

- The Railroad Brotherhood demanded that railroads eliminate the use of radio telephones by crew and revert back to hand signals and lanterns. It also managed to maintain a "fireman" on diesel locomotives, which had no boiler fire.

- The American Medical Association and the American Dental Association prohibited anyone other than doctors and dentists from performing routine tests and health tasks.

Most featherbedding practices are imposed under the guise of promoting health or safety. In reality, however, featherbedding of any type is a market constraint usually undertaken either to enhance income or to protect the security of workers in a declining industry, or both. Whether used by unions or by professional associations, featherbedding ultimately results in higher prices to consumers and a misallocation of society's resources.

Supply-Limitation Model

An organized group of workers may succeed in limiting the supply of labor to a particular occupation. The effect is shown in Exhibit 5. The actual supply curve is S' instead of the free-market curve S. As a result, the equilibrium level of employment is 7,000 workers compared to the free-market level of 10,000. Correspondingly, the equilibrium wage is $26 per hour compared to the free-market rate of $20.

A number of methods can be used to limit the supply of labor to a particular occupation. For example:

- Certain **craft unions** composed of workers in particular trades, such as electricians and plumbers, have curbed the supply of labor in order to raise wages. The unions have done this by imposing high obstacles to entry. These include long apprenticeship requirements, high initiation fees, and closed membership periods for those seeking membership.

Exhibit 5
Supply-Limitation Model: Decrease the Supply of Labor

An organized group of workers, such as a craft union, may be able to reduce the number of people entering an occupation. The group will thereby shift its supply curve of labor to the left from S to S'. The equilibrium level of employment will thus decline from 10,000 workers to 7,000, and the equilibrium wage rate will rise from $20 per hour to $26.

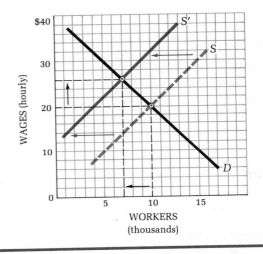

- Certain occupational groups have persuaded state legislatures to impose licensing requirements as a condition for entry. The granting of licenses, controlled by those already in the field, may be based on educational requirements, tests, a specified number of years of supervised experience, and personal interviews.

In addition to such specific labor-limiting practices, some unions have sought to restrict the overall supply of labor in the economy. They have done this by supporting legislation to (1) curb immigration, (2) shorten the workweek, and (3) assure compulsory retirement. (Of course, various special-interest groups besides unions have also supported

Featherbedding Versus Redundancy

To protect health or safety, certain production activities make intentional use of excess resources to accomplish a given task. The excess resources are called "redundancy factors," or simply "redundancies."

For example, hospitals require the presence of at least two surgeons for some kinds of major surgery. Commercial airlines assign a copilot to all flights. And fire and police departments often utilize backup crews when dealing with certain types of emergencies.

These examples of redundancy have the same effects as featherbedding. That is, they shift the demand curve for the particular type of labor to the right. But are they also examples of *featherbedding* as that term has been defined? When are featherbedding and redundancy the same, and when are they not?

---

these measures.) The model in Exhibit 5, therefore, applies to all such policies, because their effect is to shift the supply curve of labor to the left.

Industrial-Union Model

An ***industrial union*** consists solely of workers from a particular industry. Examples are a union of all workers in the automobile industry or a union of all workers in the steel industry. Such unions seek to organize on an industry-wide basis in order to impose a wage that is higher than the equilibrium wage.

Exhibit 6 illustrates this idea. The union is able to change the supply curve from its normal shape (which includes the dashed portion) to *WJS*. The equilibrium quantity of labor is thus reduced from 20,000 workers to 10,000. Correspondingly, the equilibrium wage is raised from $10 per hour to $15. Stated in somewhat different terms, the graph can be interpreted in the following way:

— At the union-imposed wage of *W* (= $15 per hour), the quantity of labor offered is *WJ* (= 30,000) workers. No labor is offered at less than this wage. In other words, the new supply curve *WJS* is perfectly elastic over the range *WJ*. This signifies that the industry can hire that much labor at the union wage.

Exhibit 6
Industrial-Union Model: Organize All Workers in an Industry

An industrial union covering all workers in an industry would seek a wage level, such as $15 per hour. This is above the equilibrium wage of $10 per hour. The supply curve of labor thus changes from its normal shape (which includes the dashed portion) to *WJS*. The equilibrium quantity, therefore, declines from 20,000 workers (represented by the distance 0N) to 10,000 (shown by the distance 0N').

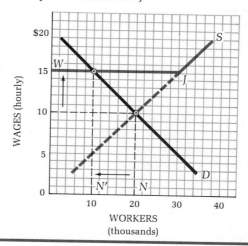

- If the industry wanted to hire more than WJ units of labor, it would have to offer a higher wage as shown by the JS portion of the supply curve. However, at higher wages the quantity of labor demanded by the industry decreases. Thus, only 10,000 workers (represented by the distance $0N'$) will be hired at the wage rate of $15 per hour imposed by the union.

Minimum-Wage Model

Unions are not the only groups in society that can affect wages and employment. Government can too. One of the ways it can do this is by imposing a minimum wage.

Minimum-wage legislation has a long history, both at home and abroad. The objectives of such legislation are:

1. To prevent firms from paying substandard wages when labor-market conditions enable them to do so.

2. To establish a wage floor representing some minimal level of living.

3. To increase purchasing power by raising the incomes of low-wage workers.

In the United States, the basic federal minimum-wage law is the *Fair Labor Standards Act* of 1938. Commonly called the Wages and Hours Law, the act has been amended from time to time. The purposes of the amendments have been to raise the statutory minimum wage and to provide coverage for additional categories of workers.

Analyzing the Effects of Minimum Wages   What are the economic consequences of minimum wages? Some of the answers are not certain because minimum wages have *many* effects and implications. You can gain some appreciation of these by examining the models in Exhibit 7.

In Industry A, the free-market equilibrium wage is at W and the corresponding equilibrium level of employment is at E. If society deems this wage rate to be "too low," it will support legislation to raise the rate to, say, W'. At this wage level, employers will want to hire the number of workers equal to the

distance $W'K$ ($= 0K'$). However, the number of workers that will offer their labor at this wage level is $W'L$ ($= 0L'$). The quantity of labor supplied thus exceeds the quantity demanded at the wage W'. Hence there is a surplus of labor—a pool of unemployed human resources—equal to the amount KL ($= K'L'$).

The same concepts are illustrated in the model of Industry B. However, the amount of labor surplus or unemployment is less in this industry. The reason is that the labor supply and labor demand curves are more inelastic than in Industry A.

It is interesting to note that the labor surplus consists of two types of unemployed people:

1. Those who were previously employed at a wage of W and have become unemployed at a wage of W'.

2. Those who were not previously in the labor force at the wage of W but have decided to enter it at the wage of W'.

Arguments Against Minimum Wages   You can readily see from the graphs that the higher the minimum wage, the greater the labor surplus. For example, if the minimum wage is raised above the level at W', the pool of unemployed (measured by the gap between quantity supplied and quantity demanded) will become larger.

On the basis of supply-and-demand analysis, opponents of minimum wages conclude that legally set wage floors cause unemployment. The workers who become unemployed are those whose productivities are not high enough to allow them to earn the legal minimum. As a result, they either remain permanently unemployed or seek work in low-wage marginal industries not covered by the minimum-wage laws. This depresses wages in those industries still further.

Arguments in Favor of Minimum Wages   In response, those who favor wider use of minimum wages offer arguments such as the following:

- The market for labor is not as competitive as the supply-and-demand models assume. Instead, employers have a high degree of market power in

Exhibit 7
Minimum-Wage Model: Raise Workers' Wages

In both diagrams, if the free-market wage rate at W is regarded by society as being "too low," government may raise it to the minimum rate at W'. At this higher wage rate there will be a labor surplus, or volume of unemployment, of KL (= $K'L'$). Minimum-wage legislation is thus a cause of unemployment. Note, however, that it is a more serious cause of unemployment in some industries (such as A) than in others (such as B). In general, *the more elastic the labor demand and labor supply curves in an industry, the greater the amount of unemployment that is caused by an increase in the minimum-wage rate.*

The people who are hurt by minimum-wage legislation are those who lack the skills and training to be hired at the legal wage. These are mostly young people, former homemakers entering the labor force after raising children, and members of some racial minority groups.

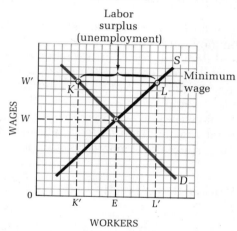

INDUSTRY *A*

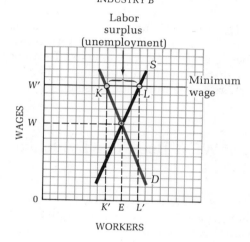

INDUSTRY *B*

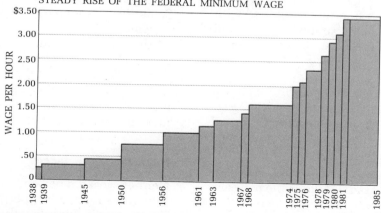

STEADY RISE OF THE FEDERAL MINIMUM WAGE

the hiring of resources. As a result, employers are able to exploit low-skilled workers by paying them less than their productivities warrant. Therefore, by raising minimum wages and by broadening coverage, government can reduce exploitation without causing unemployment.

— Increases in minimum wages raise consumer purchasing power as well as production costs. Low-income workers spend practically all of their increased wages, creating further increases in income and consumption for others. The resulting expansions in total demand more than offset the rise in production costs. This stimulates a higher level of employment rather than creating unemployment.

— Enforced higher wages encourage employers to develop better ways of utilizing their resources. This, in turn, leads to improvements in efficiency and results in benefits for everyone—business firms, workers, consumers, and society as a whole.

Conclusion: What Does The Evidence Show?

In view of what you have learned from the above analysis, what generalizations can be made about the relationship between minimum wages and unemployment? This question has been the subject of much research, both by government and by academic economists. Their findings, combined with what you already know about supply-and-demand analysis, can be summarized with four propositions:

1. *Unemployment exists when the quantity supplied of labor exceeds the quantity demanded at a given wage rate.* There would be no long-run unemployment if wage rates could adjust quickly, upward or downward, to changing market conditions.

2. *Minimum-wage legislation is a cause of unemployment.* Those people whose skills and experiences are insufficient to earn the minimum wage will be unemployed.

3. *How much unemployment minimum wages cause is not known.* The amounts can vary widely by industry, geographic area, and stage of the business cycle.

4. *Minimum-wage legislation helps raise incomes of some low-income workers.* However, the trade-off between the increase in income for some workers and the decrease in employment for others is not known.

The remainder of Exhibit 7 illustrates some further aspects of minimum wages.

Labor-Market Imperfections

The foregoing models of wage determination and employment disclose a great deal about supply-and-demand forces in the labor market. But the models are idealizations, or simplifications, of reality. In the real world, the labor market contains many complexities and imperfections. As a result, actual wage and employment levels may differ from what the models predict. What are some of the main sources of labor-market imperfections?

Worker Heterogeneity

Most workers do not sell homogeneous units of labor as the labor-market models assume. This is because people differ in both natural endowments and in the skills and experiences they have to offer. Some workers devote extra years to schooling and to specialized training. In return they earn higher lifetime incomes than those who never make the sacrifices needed to improve their qualifications. These efforts at job preparation and training are called "human capital investment." It helps explain some of the variations in wage and employment levels that exist in real-world labor markets.

Imperfect Knowledge

Neither workers nor employers have complete information about job opportunities and job seekers. Consequently, both search.

Worker Job Search   Those who are seeking employment weigh the benefits of looking for work against its costs.   The chief benefits are the additional, or perhaps better, job openings that may be discovered from further search.   The main costs are the sum of two types:

1. The direct expenses (such as traveling costs and the costs of meals away from home) that are incurred in looking for employment.

2. The opportunity cost of lost income from quitting a job in order to look for work, or from not taking jobs that are available.

As the job search continues, desirable new openings become harder to find.   Discouragement begins to set in as the marginal benefit of further search declines while the marginal cost rises.   When marginal benefit equals marginal cost, further search is no longer advantageous.   At that point the worker stops looking and accepts employment.

Employer Job Search   Employers adjust to limited labor-market information quite differently from workers.   Two types of management policies help explain why.

First, there is a trade-off between wage costs and search costs.   Other things remaining the same, firms that pay above-average wage rates soon become widely known.   These firms find that they can attract workers more easily and spend less on recruitment than firms that pay below-average wages.   This is one reason why wage and employment levels in actual labor markets may vary significantly from what theoretical labor-market models predict.

Second, many companies follow a policy of promotion from within.   Such firms place a minimum dependence on outside recruitment, preferring instead to create their own *internal labor markets.* Each firm's internal market contains its own rules governing job movement within the organization. To the extent that companies rely on such markets, they limit the ability of workers to move from one firm to another.   This impedes worker mobility and therefore reduces the efficiency of external labor markets.

Segmented Labor Markets

A third source of imperfection that tends to reduce the efficiency of labor markets lies in the structure of these markets.   Instead of being integrated into a unified whole as the theoretical models assume, real-world labor markets appear to be segmented. Each market has its own characteristics that help determine wage and/or employment levels.   Two types that are especially relevant today are the job-competition market and dual labor market.   Both types, proposed by various labor experts, are *hypotheses.*   They attempt to explain further how some modern labor markets operate.

Job-competition Market   This is a labor market in which the number and types of jobs are determined mainly by prevailing technology.   Workers compete with each other to fill particular job openings associated with existing plant and equipment.   (A factory, for example, needs a specific number of operators, maintenance people, supervisors, etc. to run its machines.)   Wages for these jobs are established largely by institutional and legislative conditions.   These include industry custom, union-management   contracts,   and   minimum-wage   laws. Market forces play a relatively minor role in affecting wages.   The function of job-competition markets, therefore, is to allocate workers to a given number of vacancies at prevailing, relatively fixed, wage rates.

Dual Labor Market   This is actually two distinct markets.   One is a primary labor market, in which jobs are characterized by relatively high wages, favorable working conditions, and employment stability.   The other is a secondary labor market, in which jobs, when they are available, pay relatively low wages, provide poor working conditions, and are highly unstable.   Both white-collar workers and blue-collar   workers,   many   of whom   are   union members, account for most of the participants in the primary market.   In contrast, the competitively "disadvantaged"—the unskilled, the undereducated, and the victims of racial prejudice—are confined to the secondary market.

It is important to note that the job-competition market and the dual labor market are not mutually exclusive. Indeed, there is evidence that both markets exist and that to some extent they overlap.

Conclusion: Supply-Side and Demand-Side Policies

Labor markets suffer from imperfections. As a result, they do not allocate human resources with maximum efficiency. Therefore, policies to improve the functioning of labor markets are needed.

For several decades, two broad approaches to improving labor-market efficiency have been followed:

1. **Supply-side Labor Policies**   These are aimed at improving the potential quality and marketability of human resources. Some major supply-side labor policies consist of programs in education, training, and the development of special skills.

2. **Demand-side Labor Policies**   These are designed to make fuller use of *existing* human resources. Important demand-side labor policies include public-sector employment programs, government-funded wage subsidies in the private sector, and measures to reduce discrimination in employment.

Labor-Market Policies and Problems

Supply-side and demand-side labor policies seek to improve people's employability. The need exists because workers differ in many ways, including aptitude, intelligence, physical appearance, race, sex, and various other human attributes. These differences give rise to two broad classes of labor-market policies and problems:

1. Human-resource development
2. Discrimination in employment

Human-Resource Development

The capital stock of a nation includes "the acquired and useful abilities of all the inhabitants or members of the society. An individual who acquires talents by study or by apprenticeship is putting capital into his person. Though to do so creates a certain expense, it repays that expense with a profit."

So wrote Adam Smith in *The Wealth of Nations* (1776). As he observed, investment in human resources yields benefits to the individual as well as to the nation. That is, it yields private as well as social returns. These returns are based on abilities and skills that are obtained from acquisition of knowledge.

Formal education, of course, is only one method of improving people's knowledge and skills. Other methods consist of various kinds of job training and work experience programs. All of them together constitute what may be called **human resource policies.** These may be defined as deliberate efforts undertaken in the private and public sectors to develop and use the capacities of human beings as actual or potential members of the labor force. Therefore, human resource policies are also known as **employment-training policies.**

Human resource policies have evolved during the past several decades. Funded largely by the federal government, they have consisted of programs intended to provide job training, work experience, and job-search assistance. Despite these laudable objectives, critics point out that the programs have suffered from several shortcomings:

– They have focused, often unsuccessfully, on upgrading workers from the secondary to the primary market, while failing to improve the quality of secondary employment.

– They have not succeeded in instilling disciplined work habits and a sense of job responsibility among trainees.

– They have often enlisted only the best prospects —those who have a reasonable chance of employment—while neglecting the worst cases.

– They have sometimes been managed inefficiently, and this has resulted in a great deal of waste.

These criticisms should not be interpreted to mean that human-resource policies have been a total failure. Many training programs have achieved remarkable successes. However, in the opinion of some critics, it is doubtful whether any human resource policy can overcome 12 years of inadequate training in elementary and high school.

Discrimination in Employment

The Lord spoke to Moses saying: Speak to the Israelite people and say to them: When a man explicitly vows to the Lord the equivalent for a human being, the following scale shall apply: If it is a male from 20 to 60 years of age, the equivalent is fifty shekels of silver by the sanctuary weight; if it is a female, the equivalent is thirty shekels.

Leviticus 27:1–4

There is a great variety of occupations which women have begun to claim as fields for individual effort from which no intelligent, refined man who views things as they really are would seek to exclude them.

Scientific American, September, 1870

More than 2500 years have elapsed since the first quotation above was written. More than a century has elapsed since *Scientific American*'s editorial. Yet there is evidence that women are still a long way from job equality with men. Despite substantial progress, various studies show that women often earn considerably less than men in the same occupational category. (See the table in Exhibit 8.)

Much the same is true of certain minority groups. Blacks, Asians, homosexuals, and members of other groups have long been victims of discrimination in employment. Let us look at some of the effects of job discrimination, and some of the effects that would occur if it were eliminated.

Two-Market Model

An opportunity for discrimination exists when a market can be divided into homogeneous submarkets. Price and quantity can then be established in each submarket through the separate interactions of supply and demand. An illustration of this is shown in the two-market model of Exhibit 8. Figure (a) represents a primary labor market for males. Figure (b) depicts a secondary labor market for females. (The same model could be used to analyze discrimination between whites and blacks, skilled and unskilled, or other competing groups.)

In Figure (a), the demand curve D for labor in the primary market intersects the supply curve of males, S_M. This results in an equilibrium wage rate for males at W_M and an equilibrium quantity of male employment, Q_M.

Because women are to some extent excluded from the primary market, they must seek employment elsewhere — namely, in the secondary market represented by Figure (b). In this market, occupations are less productive than in the primary market. As a result, Figure (b) shows that the demand for women's services is less, and the supply of females looking for jobs is smaller, than the demand for and supply of men's services in Figure (a). The economic consequence of this is that the equilibrium wage rate for females, W_F, and the equilibrium quantity of female employment, Q_F, are less than W_M and Q_M.

How can this situation be corrected? The ideal solution would be to eliminate discrimination by permitting women to compete with men in the primary market. If this were done, the supply curve of females S_F in Figure (b) would be added to the S_M curve in Figure (a). This would yield a new total market supply curve of males and females, S_{M+F}. The secondary market would no longer exist.

Favorable Effects of Eliminating Discrimination

As you can see from Figure (a), the elimination of discrimination would have several major effects.

First, total employment would be raised from the level at Q_M to the level at Q_{M+F}. This would also lead to increased production because women would be employed in more productive jobs than before. Consequently, society would benefit by receiving a larger volume of output.

Exhibit 8
Sex Differences in the Labor Market

Women earn less than men in a number of occupational categories.

In the accompanying diagrams, the total market is divided into a primary market for males and a secondary market for females. Jobs are less productive in the latter. Therefore, the wage rate for females W_F is lower than that for males W_M.

If there were no discrimination, women would enter the primary market. The new total supply curve, S_{M+F}, would lead to a new equilibrium wage, a higher equilibrium level of employment, and thus a larger volume of output. As explained in the text, these changes would occur because of the *gain in productivity* resulting from the elimination of discrimination.

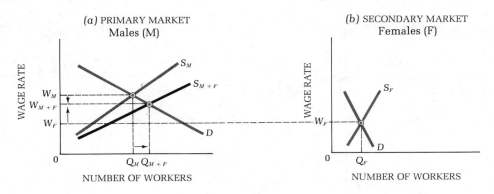

| Occupation | Weekly Median Pay | | | | Occupation | Weekly Median Pay | | |
	Women	Men	Women's pay as a percentage of men's			Women	Men	Women's pay as a percentage of men's
Clerical workers	$220	$328	67%		Nurses	326	344	95
Computer specialists	355	488	73		Physicians	401	495	81
Editors and reporters	324	382	85		Sales workers	190	366	52
Engineers	371	547	68		Teachers (elementary)	311	379	82
Lawyers	407	574	71		Waiters	144	200	72

Second, the equilibrium wage of females would increase, and the equilibrium wage of males would decrease, to the level at W_{M+F}. Further, the increase in wages received by women would more than offset the decrease in wages received by men. Society, therefore, would experience a *net monetary gain*.

Perhaps most important:

The increased wages received by women would not come from the reduced wages received by men. It would come from the *gain in productivity* and the additional output that would result from the elimination of discrimination.

Antidiscrimination Policies

Despite the undesirable economic consequences of discrimination, it nevertheless exists. Although it is unlikely that discrimination will ever be completely eliminated, steps can be taken to reduce it. The chief antidiscrimination measures and policies that currently exist may be identified and discussed briefly.

Equal Employment Opportunity (EEO) and Affirmative Action (AA)

These measures were written into law during the 1960s. EEO legislation prohibits discrimination in employment on the basis of race, religion, sex, or national origin. AA legislation requires firms under federal government contracts to file numerical EEO "goals and timetables." These are compliance reports showing that "good-faith efforts" were made to fill job openings with *target* minorities and females.

These policies have had both positive and negative consequences:

— *EEO Has Reduced Discrimination* On the favorable side, there is substantial evidence that the law has helped to increase the earnings of women and minorities in most occupations. Hiring and promotion opportunities have also improved since the legislation was enacted.

— *AA May Have Increased Discrimination* On the unfavorable side, the evidence is less clear. Some critics contend that the affirmative action program has caused employers to discriminate between two classes of minority applicants — above average and average. "Above-average" applicants are those whose future pay, promotions and discharge patterns, based on their employment records, are likely to be no worse than those of others. "Average" applicants are those who have little or no employment record on which to base a prediction of future performance. Because employers want to minimize risks of discrimination charges, their demand, critics say, has increased for applicants in the above-average category and decreased for all others.

Equal Pay for Equal Work

This standard became law in the 1960s. It is intended to assure male-female equality in pay *within* jobs. Thus, females who perform the same work as males are to be paid the same wages. As a result of this legislation, pay disparities between women and men in many male-dominated occupations such as police, fire, and heavy-industry factory work have declined.

Comparable Worth

The standard of equal pay for equal work does not eliminate wage differences resulting from job segregation. Critics argue that in female-dominated occupations such as elementary-school teaching, nursing, and secretarial work, for example, pay tends to be relatively low. The proposed solution is to pay women as much as men are paid for performing tasks in *other* occupations thought to require comparable (*not identical*) skills, training, responsibilities, hazards, and effort.

What are the consequences of comparable worth as a standard for wage policy? Although it may succeed in reducing wage gaps between females and males, the effects on society must be judged in terms of efficiency and equity:

Efficiency Critics point out that comparable worth neglects labor-market supply-and-demand considerations. It therefore leads to misallocations of society's resources. For example, if wages are raised above the market rate for clerks, secretaries, nurses, librarians, and teachers, women will have a greater incentive to enter these female-dominated occupations. As a result, fewer women will be encouraged to enter traditionally male-dominated occupations such as police work, firefighting, engineering, medicine, and law.

Equity Critics also contend that comparable worth assumes that occupational similarities and differences based on skills, effort, responsibility, and other criteria can be evaluated objectively by *non-market* standards. Attempts by "job evaluators" to do this, however, have often yielded widely different outcomes. Consequently, any wage-setting policy based on comparable worth is bound to create new inequities while trying to correct old ones.

Economics in the News

The Worth of Women's Work

In what is billed as a victory for the concept of "comparable worth," the city of Los Angeles has agreed to raise the pay of workers in municipal jobs traditionally held by women. That probably is a victory for social justice and surely one for common sense.

Los Angeles pays clerks and librarians, who are mostly women, 10 to 15 percent less than workers in a variety of positions mostly filled by men. City officials and the employees' union agreed the pay gap was unfair to women workers. The union might have convinced a court that the city was illegally discriminating against women. But happily, the matter has now been settled without litigation and at modest cost to the city's taxpayers.

What does all this have to do with comparable worth? On average, women employed full time earn about a third less than men. Part of the difference can be explained by the fact that working women tend to be less experienced. But part is certainly the result of discrimination.

One way some employers discriminate is to distinguish between different job categories that demand similar skills — and then channel women into the lower-paying category. For example, the State of Washington paid beauticians who worked in state institutions less than barbers.

To some people, that kind of discrimination is reason enough to demand that employers assess all jobs according to skills and provide equal pay according to comparable worth. But that is just not possible. How, for example, would one decide whether plumbers should be paid more than fire-fighters, male or female? Or carpenters? Or office managers? The idea has turned into a caricature of extremists, defended as moral truth by supporters and ridiculed by the Civil Rights Commission as "loony tunes."

Yet the underlying problem of discrimination linked to job classification endures. The best remedy is the one tried in Los Angeles, where negotiators used common sense to decide there was discrimination and to figure out remedies. It is an example other unions and enlightened employers would do well to follow.

Negotiation is vastly preferable to litigation. Courts are ill-equipped to reshape society's entire wage structure according to some vague standard of comparable worth. But if negotiation fails, pay-classification differences have to play an important part as courts try to sort out inherently messy evidence of discrimination on a case-by-case basis.

Despite these criticisms, unions as well as some other groups have been vocal in supporting comparable worth. Unions in particular see a good opportunity to appeal to white-collar women. These have traditionally been the least organized category of workers, and many of them feel that they are paid too little.

Conclusion: Equal Opportunities Versus Equal Results

The labor market does not make the fullest or best use of human resources. This is due to the market's failure to match the right people with available jobs. Steps that have been taken to correct the situation include:

1. human-resource policies
2. antidiscrimination policies

Some of these have sought to provide equal opportunities; others have sought to provide equal results. The two are not the same:

Legislation requiring equal opportunity does not impede the labor market's function of allocating human resources to their highest-valued use. Indeed, if people are employed solely on the basis of their qualifications, labor-market efficiency will be enhanced.

Exhibit 9
Is Comparable Worth Incomparable?

Should a secretary who can drive a car make as much as a truck driver who can't type? Is the pay in certain jobs low simply because women hold them—not because of supply-and-demand forces? Advocates of comparable worth answer *yes* to both questions.

In response, many state governments have hired job-evaluation experts to identify salary disparities between "comparable" male-dominated and female-dominated occupations. Based on such factors as knowledge, skills, mental demands, accountability, and working conditions, the evaluators came up with their own ideas of jobs that are equivalent. As the table shows, they often disagreed, sometimes by a very wide margin.

Male-dominated Jobs	Monthly Salaries		Comparable Female-dominated Jobs*
Truck driver	$1,600	$1,120	Laundry worker
		$1,235	Pharmacy assistant
Electrician	$1,940	$1,325	Secretary III
		$1,495	Secretarial supervisor
Mechanic	$1,785	$ 950	Medical-records analyst
		$1,450	Supervising counselor
Accountant	$2,500	$1,025	Social worker
		$1,825	Registered nurse
Security officer	$1,130	$ 825	Telephone operator
		$ 800	Office assistant

* Comparability as determined by different job-evaluation experts.

Source: Compiled from various reports on *Commission on the Status of Women,* issued by the states of Illinois, Minnesota, Washington, and Wisconsin. A number of other states issue such reports, some periodically.

In contrast, legislation requiring equal results may impede the labor market's performance. To the extent that people or groups are *unequal* in their productive capabilities, laws that require equal outcomes impair allocative efficiency and create new inequities.

It is easy to understand why employment decisions based on racial or sexual preference goals have been the subject of much controversy. (See Exhibit 9.)

Unions and Management: Collective Bargaining

> **STRIKE THREATENS TO DISRUPT PRODUCTION!**
>
> **UNION WAGE DEMANDS ARE TOP PRIORITY**
>
> **CAN UNIONS AND MANAGEMENT WORK TOGETHER?**

You often encounter headlines like these in the news media. They are indicative of some of today's union-management problems. These problems involve all of us, not only as consumers, employees, or employers, but also as concerned citizens.

What is a **union?** It may be defined as an organization of workers that seeks to gain a degree of monopoly power in the sale of its services. In this way it may be able to secure higher wages, better working conditions, protection from arbitrary treatment by management, and other economic gains for its members.

The chief objective of unions is thus to enhance the status of workers. That goal is largely achieved through **collective bargaining.** This is a process of negotiation between representatives of a company's management and a union. The purpose is to arrive at a set of mutually acceptable wages and working conditions for employees.

Collective bargaining as it is known today came about as a result of the National Labor Relations Act of 1935. This law is the most important piece of labor legislation in American history. It was the culmination of many decades of struggle and hardship by workers to achieve union recognition in labor-management negotiations.

The *National Labor Relations Act* of 1935 (also known as the *Wagner Act*) is the basic labor relations law of the United States. The act contains three major provisions:

1. It guarantees the right of workers to organize and to bargain collectively through representatives of their own choosing.

2. It forbids the employer from engaging in "unfair labor practices." These include:

   (a) Interfering or discriminating against workers who form unions or engage in union activity.

   (b) Establishing a *company union* or organization of workers that is limited to a particular firm.

   (c) Refusing to bargain in good faith with a duly recognized union.

3. It established the *National Labor Relations Board* (NLRB) to enforce the act and to supervise free elections among a company's employees to determine which union, if any, is to represent the workers.

Today's collective-bargaining agreements differ greatly in their scope and content. However, practically all agreements deal with at least three fundamental issues:

— Wages and other benefits

— Industrial relations

— Settlement of labor-management disputes

Wages and Other Benefits

You may read in a newspaper that a labor-management negotiation has resulted in a $2-per-hour "package" increase, consisting of $1.25 in wages and 75 cents in other benefits. Such packages are generally composed of several parts.

Basic Wages

First, there are the payments received by workers for work performed. These payments, called *basic wages,* may consist of time and/or incentive payments.

Time Payments Most workers in American manufacturing are paid on the basis of time—by the hour, day, week, or month. They also receive extra compensation for work done during nights, weekends, and holidays. Two important characteristics of time payments may be noted:

Immeasurability of Workers' Output Time payments tend to be most common in industries where an individual's production cannot be precisely determined. This is because firms' rates of output are substantially influenced by established technology. Examples include the automobile, chemical and machine-tool industries.

Lack of Incentives Time payments provide no incentive for workers to improve productivity. Because earnings are related to time worked rather than to output, workers have nothing to gain by working faster or more efficiently.

Incentive Payments A large minority of American manufacturing workers receive their basic compensation through incentive payments. These may be in the form of wages, commissions, bonuses, etc. They are tied to some measure of company performance such as profit or productivity. Incentive systems of this type are sometimes called *gain-sharing plans.*

Gain-sharing plans offer advantages both to participants and to society:

Improved Efficiency Workers are encouraged to increase their productivity because they stand to benefit from the gains.

Noninflationary Wage Increases Because gain-sharing is dependent on company profits or productivity, there is less pressure on firms to raise prices when wages are increased.

Gain-sharing plans, particularly profit-sharing plans, have become more common in collective bargaining agreements. But the future of the plans remains uncertain. Experience shows that workers will be committed to such a plan only if:

- Management is willing to accept greater worker participation in production-related decisions.
- Payouts are high enough to maintain worker interest.

Fringe Benefits

Another important part of collective bargaining agreements concerns **fringe benefits.** These are monetary advantages other than basic wages that are provided by employers for their employees. Examples include:

Time Off With Pay—the number of nonworking days per year (holidays, sick-leave days, personal-business days, etc.) that workers can take without loss of wages.

Insurance Benefits—the proportion of workers' life- and health-insurance premiums paid by employers.

Pensions—the percentage of payments to retirement plans paid by employers.

Income Maintenance—the proportion, or in some cases the level, of employees' normal pay that they will receive from the company in the event of economic layoffs or job termination.

Are fringe benefits "free"? The answer, of course, is no. Fringe benefits, like wages, are a form of employee compensation. Therefore, fringe benefits are part of total labor costs. Like any other costs, fringe benefits are ultimately paid by someone. This may be consumers in the form of higher prices, workers in the form of lower wages, or stockholders in the form of reduced profits.

Industrial Relations

A second major area of collective bargaining pertains to **industrial relations.** It deals with the rules and regulations governing the relationship between union and management. There are, of course, many aspects of industrial relations. Those that are especially important today from an economic point of view concern (1) restricting membership and output and (2) employment security.

Restriction of Membership and Output

One of the chief goals of unions is to obtain higher incomes for their members. Some unions try to achieve this goal by restricting membership or by restricting output.

If a union can limit its membership, it may be able to create a scarcity of a particular kind of labor. A union can control membership in several ways. These include: (1) varying apprenticeship requirements; (2) sponsoring state licensing for those in the trade (examples are barbers, electricians, and plumbers); and (3) varying initiation fees.

If a union can limit its members' production it can increase the demand for its workers and thereby negotiate higher wages. How might a union restrict output? Three methods are typically used: (1) shortening the working day; (2) limiting output per worker; and (3) resisting the introduction of labor-saving technology.

Thus, on the one hand, management seeks to increase profits by raising productive efficiency. On the other hand, unions seek to improve earnings and working conditions for their members. Sometimes the means used to achieve these objectives may conflict. When they do, the methods of resolving them often play an important role in collective bargaining negotiations.

Employment Security: The New Industrial Relations

Business executives used to believe that because they were dealing with uneducated workers, the only way to improve productivity was through "scientific management." This meant that complex jobs had to be broken down into a number of simple, repetitive operations, and that new equipment had to replace obsolete machinery whenever possible.

Most unions accepted this view and saw their relation with companies as adversarial. The function of union leaders was to protect jobs and wages, even at the cost of imposing restrictive production rules and practices.

Since the 1970s, some of these attitudes have changed. Under the new system, the adversarial relationship in some industries has been de-emphasized. Instead the approach to employment security in these industries consists of developing union-management cooperative agreements. These are designed to accomplish such objectives as the following:

Retraining Workers   Some firms have established special training programs for union members. Laid-off workers have been taught new skills and employed workers have been taught upgraded skills. Several studies report that many of the retrained workers have subsequently found jobs in their own or in other industries.

Encouraging Worker Participation   Workers are becoming more involved with decisions on the plant floor. Committees of workers, called *quality circles,* have been formed within companies to discuss ways of improving production methods, job satisfaction, and productivity. In return, management has agreed to be more open with workers, to share the benefits of participative decision making, and to seek ways of improving job security.

Providing Lifetime Employment   Some union-management negotiations have explored the feasibility of "lifetime" job guarantees. It appears, however, that such policies, when adopted, have usually been limited to select groups of workers with high seniority.

Is this newer approach to industrial relations effective? There is evidence that it is. Studies have shown that in many firms that have adopted employment security programs, improvements in morale, productivity, and therefore in company profitability have been significant. Nevertheless, there are still strong elements of resistance to change.

Some come from managements and some from unions, because both are reluctant to share responsibility and power. It may be years, therefore, before the "new" industrial relations becomes widespread in American industry.

Settling Labor-Management Disputes

Despite efforts at achieving greater cooperation, union-management negotiations sometimes break down. How are they resolved? One possibility is by a **strike.** This is a mutual agreement among workers to stop working, without resigning from their jobs, until their demands are met.

A strike, however, is a costly weapon that unions do not use lightly. Indeed, since 1935, the amount of working time lost on an annual basis because of strikes has averaged less than ½ percent of total labor-days worked. This is far less than the proportion of time lost from work because of the common cold.

Accordingly, unions need alternative means of settling disputes with management. The most common means are arbitration and mediation.

Arbitration is used to resolve union-management differences that sometimes arise over the interpretation of one or more provisions of an *existing* collective-bargaining contract. The two sides select a third party, called an arbitrator, whose decision is legally binding. After hearing the evidence from both sides, the arbitrator issues a decision. It is based not on what the arbitrator believes to be wise and fair but upon how he or she understands the language of the contract to apply to the case at hand. Thus, an arbitrator is like a judge. *An arbitrator relates the case to the contract, just as a judge relates a case to the law.*

Mediation, sometimes also called **conciliation,** is a means by which a third party, the mediator, attempts to reconcile the differences between contesting parties. Mediation is commonly employed to settle labor-management disputes concerning the *negotiation* of a collective-bargaining contract. The mediator attempts to maintain constructive discussions, to search for common areas of agreement, and to suggest compromises. However, the mediator's decisions are not binding, and they need not be accepted by the contesting parties. The federal government provides mediation services through an independent agency called the Federal Mediation and Conciliation Service. In addition, most states and some large municipalities provide similar services.

Conclusion: Economic Impacts of Unions

The growth of unions is not as significant as it once was. As you can see in Exhibit 10, union membership today constitutes approximately 16 percent of the labor force. Nevertheless, unions exert certain economic impacts on the economy. What are they? On the basis of numerous studies that have been done over the years, the main findings can be summarized in the answers to three fundamental questions:

Do Unions Raise Wages?

Here we have to distinguish between unionized firms operating in the union labor market and non-unionized firms operating in the nonunion labor market. Studies have concluded that:

1. *Unions increase total compensation (including wages and fringe benefits) in the union market and decrease it in the nonunion market.* This is because higher labor costs in the union market prompts firms to reduce employment. Some of the unemployed find it necessary to seek jobs in the nonunion market. This causes the supply curve of labor in that market to shift to the right, leading to lower compensation. The result is a significant income differential between union and nonunion workers. How large is the differential? The numbers differ widely across industries, occupations, and individuals. However, as an overall average, it appears that union workers earn roughly 20 percent more in total compensation than nonunion workers.

Exhibit 10
Union Membership Since 1900

The union movement experienced its most rapid growth during the 1930s and 1940s.

Today, union membership constitutes about 16% of the civilian labor force.

THE GROWTH OF UNION MEMBERSHIP

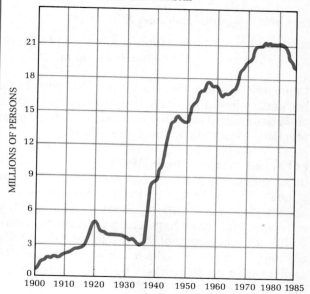

TOTAL UNION MEMBERSHIP AS A PERCENTAGE OF THE CIVILIAN LABOR FORCE

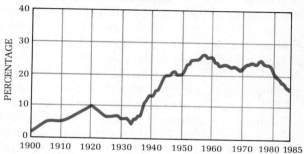

Source: U.S. Department of Labor.

2. *The differential between union and nonunion wages tends to decline during prosperity periods and increase during recessionary periods.* The reason for this is that union wages are relatively fixed in collective bargaining agreements while nonunion wages can fluctuate with economic conditions. Hence, nonunion wages usually rise faster than union wages during business-cycle upswings and decline faster during cyclical downswings.

Do Unions Reduce Business Efficiency?

The answer to this question is not a simple *yes* or *no*. Let us look at three aspects of the matter.

Impaired Worker Productivity As you have learned, some unions have long utilized restrictive policies designed to limit output per worker. These practices have reduced business efficiency.

Enhanced Worker Productivity Although some union practices have held down output per worker, others have increased it. Unions have played an important role in bringing about a safer working environment. They have also greatly reduced the ability of management to discharge employees without "just cause." Such achievements help to explain why union workers have lower quit rates than nonunion workers. These factors have contributed to enhancing productive efficiency in unionized firms.

Improved Plant Management Executives have often countered the negative effects of union behavior by developing more efficient production methods. Indeed, many important advances in production efficiency at the plant level have been due in no small part to efforts aimed at overcoming inefficiencies resulting from some union practices.

Thus, unions have had both negative and positive influences on business efficiency. There is considerable evidence that, on balance, the positive effects have greatly outweighed the negative ones. As a result, *most unionized companies have higher productivity than comparable nonunionized ones.*

Do Unions Cause Inflation?

The answer to this question is not known. There are two schools of thought:

Monopolistic Markets View Many economists believe that much of the economy's markets are not very competitive. Monopolistic labor unions are sometimes able, therefore, to negotiate wage increases in excess of productivity gains. Monopolistic firms, in turn, may agree to union demands if it is believed that wage increases can be simply passed on to consumers in the form of higher prices. The phenomenon thus results in a condition often referred to as *cost-push inflation.*

Competitive Markets View Another substantial group of economists believes that the economy's markets are essentially competitive. Therefore, inflation is not caused by unions, but by government policies. The most important policy consists of erratic increases in the money supply caused by the nation's central bank—the Federal Reserve System. In its efforts to stimulate employment and production the Fed often "pumps" excessive quantities of money into the economy. This practice creates demand-pull inflation—a condition sometimes described as "too much money chasing too few goods."

Both of these points of view contain substantial elements of truth.

Summarizing:

The effects of unions on the economy can be analyzed in terms of their impacts on wages, business efficiency, and inflation. Various studies indicate the following:

Unions Raise Workers' Income Total compensation (including wages and fringe benefits) of union workers is approximately 20 percent higher than for nonunion workers.

Unions Have Had a Net Favorable Effect on Business Efficiency Certain union practices have impaired worker productivity while others have enhanced it. However, the evidence shows that the *net* influence of unions on productivity has been positive.

Unions Do Not Necessarily Cause Inflation There is much disagreement over the extent to which inflation results from unions pushing up wages. Many critics believe that inflation is due to the Federal Reserve creating "too much" money.

What You Have Learned

1. Several aspects of labor supply have been emphasized in this chapter:
    (a) The participation rate of married women in the labor force has increased substantially in recent decades.
    (b) The supply curve of labor to a particular occupation is more elastic in the long run than in the short run because people have time to train for new occupations
    (c) The existence of a backward-bending labor supply curve tells you that people allocate their limited time between work and leisure (i.e., nonwork).

2. This chapter has emphasized several important labor-demand concepts:
    (a) Employers' demand for labor is a derived demand based on the demand for the products that workers help to produce.
    (b) The elasticity of a firm's demand curve for labor depends on several factors. They include the elasticity of demand for the product produced, the percentage of labor costs to total costs, and the ease of substituting other inputs for labor.

3. Unions have employed different methods for enhancing their position in the labor market. The methods include:
    (a) Increasing the demand for labor. This raises both wages and employment.
    (b) Decreasing the supply of labor. This raises wages and decreases employment.

4. Minimum-wage legislation brings higher wages but it also results in some unemployment. In general, the more elastic the labor-demand and labor-supply curves in an industry, the greater the amount of unemployment that is caused by an increase in the minimum-wage rate. This conclusion is affected, however, by various labor-market imperfections. These include qualitative differences among workers, imperfect knowledge about job opportunities, and the existence of segmented labor markets. As a result, both supply-side and demand-side labor policies

have been designed to improve the potential quality and present utilization of human resources.

5. Human-resource development has consisted of policies aimed at improving people's knowledge and skills. Some of these policies have been criticized for being improperly designed, inadequately funded, and inefficiently managed. Because of this, new policies are often formulated—sometimes for political as well as economic reasons.

6. Various remedies for eliminating labor-market discrimination have been adopted. While some of these have reduced discrimination, others may have increased it. In general, any legislation that *requires* equal results among people who are unequal in their productive capabilities interferes with the operation of the market. It therefore impairs efficiency and is likely to create inequities as well.

7. Unions negotiate with managements to arrive at collective bargaining agreements. These contain provisions with respect to such factors as wages and fringe benefits, industrial relations, and the settlement of labor-management disputes. Unions thus exert definite impacts on the economy. Studies show that, in general, unions (a) raise members' wages and (b) have had a net favorable effect on business efficiency. Whether unions cause inflation is a matter of dispute among economists.

Terms and Concepts To Review

labor force	comparable worth
labor-force participation	union
rate	collective bargaining
backward-bending	National Labor
labor-supply curve	Relations Act (1935)
reservation-wage	company union
featherbedding	basic wages
craft union	gain-sharing plans
industrial union	fringe benefits
internal labor market	industrial relations
job-competition market	quality circles
dual labor market	strike
human-resource policies	arbitration
equal employment	mediation
opportunity	cost-push inflation
affirmative action	

For Discussion

1. What factors account for the rapid growth in women's labor-force participation in recent decades?

2. Do individuals (including yourself) have a backward-bending labor-supply curve? Do workers as a whole? Explain.

3. An employer would not be willing to pay someone more than the market value of what that person produces. Do you agree? Give some examples.

4. Which is likely to have a greater degree of monopoly power — a union's monopoly of a labor market or a firm's monopoly of a product market?

5. The minimum-wage law is said to have both harmful and beneficial effects. Can you suggest some of each?

6. Various government-sponsored human-resource policies have been criticized for being largely ineffective and wasteful. Would it be best, therefore, to do away with all such policies? HINT What is the cost of the alternative?

7. Discrimination exists when a worker is paid less than the market value of his or her contribution to production. Do you agree? If so, how can this happen?

8. Unions are usually more interested in raising wages than in increasing employment. Why? SUGGESTION: Think in terms of supply-and-demand models.

Chapter 31

Social Problems: Insecurity, Poverty, Crime, Pollution

Learning Guide

Watch for answers to these important questions

What is the nature of our social security system? What are its problems, and how can the system be improved?

How can we explain the fact that in a country as rich as ours, more than 10 percent of the people are poor? What measures can be adopted to eliminate poverty?

How can economics contribute to a better understanding of crime? Can measures be adopted to reduce crime?

What types of analytical approaches are useful for dealing with environmental problems? What difficulties are encountered in implementing these approaches? Are there policy options for reducing environmental damage?

> I am a conservative in economic affairs, but a liberal in human affairs.
>
> Dwight Eisenhower

This statement by a former American president seems like a contradiction. It implies that economic and social problems are unrelated, and that methods of dealing with them entail separate approaches and policies.

Anyone familiar with the history of social reform in America knows that these implications are false. Since the nineteenth century we have seen the abolition of slavery, the introduction of free public education, and the passage of protective legislation for labor. We have also seen the provision of public charity for the needy, and the enactment of social security legislation providing some protection against the losses that may result from old age, disability, ill health, and unemployment.

All of these measures were designed to implement changes in human affairs. The same is true of legislative reforms today. In this chapter you will find that current social policies are no different in their underlying philosophy from those that were introduced a century or more ago. The differences that do exist are to be found in the details of the specific measures, in the means of implementing them, and in the scope of their objectives.

Understanding Social Security

Insecurity is a fundamental social problem. Most families are insecure in the sense that they stand a chance of suffering from a loss of income. Such losses may occur as a result of unemployment, illness, injury, retirement, or death of the breadwinner. Because of the hardships consequent upon such losses, our present program of social security was instituted during the Great Depression of the 1930s.

The **Social Security Act** of 1935 (with its many subsequent amendments) is the basic comprehensive social security law of the United States. It includes these programs:

1. *Old Age and Survivors Insurance (OASI)* This program, which is the largest of the three, is what most people refer to as "social security." It pays benefits to retired workers and their dependents and survivors.

2. *Disability Insurance (DI)* This program awards benefits to disabled workers and their dependents.

3. *Hospital Insurance (HI)—Medicare* This is a health insurance program providing two sets of benefits:

   (a) Hospital services to those over 65 years of age who are covered by social security—that is, by OASDI.

   (b) Supplementary medical insurance, available on a voluntary basis to the elderly. The benefits are financed partly through monthly premium charges paid by participants and partly through the general tax revenues of the Treasury.

4. *Public Assistance (PA)* This is a *noninsurance* program. It provides public charity in the form of welfare services, institutional care, food, housing, and other forms of assistance to the needy.

Some of the provisions of the social security act are administered by the federal government, some by the state and local governments, and some by all three levels of government. *In the following discus-sion of the social security "system," we shall be referring only to the insured (OASDHI) component, not to the uninsured (PA) one.*

How Does Social Security "Work"?

The social-security system is financed by a payroll tax. This is a tax based on a percentage of wages and salaries up to a specified maximum. The tax is paid both by employers and by employees. (If you are an employee, the amount you pay is shown on your annual withholding statement.) The tax revenues are collected by the U.S. Treasury and deposited in the government's social-security trust funds. Benefit payments are then disbursed from these funds to retirees, survivors, and other social-security recipients mentioned above.

The social-security program thus involves two fundamental ideas:

Pay-As-You-Go-Financing The payroll tax is designed to provide sufficient funds for current and near-future social-security benefits. The tax is not designed to build up large reserves in the trust funds. Therefore it may be said that the system is financed on a "pay-as-you-go" basis.

Intergenerational Transfer of Funds The benefits received by each generation of retirees comes from payroll taxes paid by younger generations. Because of this, the system may be thought of as a social contract, or agreement, to provide a transfer of funds between generations.

What Are Its Problems?

You will hear it said from time to time that our social security system is in trouble. Some observers even say that it could collapse. How can this happen? The answer depends on two major factors that affect the stability of the program. One of these is the magnitudes of inflations and recessions that occur in the short run. The other is the rising average age of the population over the long run.

Short Run: Inflations and Recessions   The social-security system is vulnerable both to inflations and recessions—especially steep ones.   Inflation can cause benefit payments to increase because they are indexed (linked) to cost-of-living changes.   Recession can cause payroll-tax revenues to decrease because people lose their jobs.   Therefore, either inflation or recession can result in a deficit, with the money outflows of the trust funds exceeding the inflows.   This has happened during several severe inflations and recessions in the past and has jeopardized the system.

Long Run: Rising Average Age of the Population
The social-security program is also vulnerable to the consequences of our society growing older.   As the average age rises, the size of the beneficiary group increases relative to the size of the working group.   To the extent that this long-run trend is not taken into account in the financing provisions, the system can face serious difficulties several decades from now.

Of course, inflation accompanied by an aging population also contributes to financing problems for the Hospital Insurance (HI) component of the program.   Numerous studies have projected that hospital costs will rise much faster than taxable wages in the years ahead.   The result will be a massive and growing deficit in the HI fund before the end of this century.

In addition to inherent weaknesses in the social security system, the method of financing social security has been a subject of severe criticisms.   Among them:

Compulsory Participation   Social security "contributions" are not voluntary.   Individuals are not free to select and pay for the particular benefits they wish to receive.

Regressive Payroll Tax   The tax used to finance the social security program is based on a fixed percentage of wages up to specified maximum wage levels.   Therefore, the tax has a regressive effect, because it bears most heavily on low-income and middle-income groups.

Conclusion: How Can It Be Improved?

In view of these weaknesses and criticisms, it is easy to understand why few government programs have aroused more controversy than our social security system.   Can the shortcomings of our social security system be corrected—or at least greatly reduced?   The answer is yes.   However, fundamental policy changes are difficult to achieve because political as well as economic considerations play a role.   Nevertheless, some alternative approaches to reform may be considered:

Privatize the Program   The insurance component (OASDHI) of social security could be removed from government auspices.   Individuals under 40 years of age could be allowed to withdraw from the system and to finance their own protection through *tax-free* private investment and insurance programs.   Several types of tax-free programs, such as Individual Retirement Accounts (IRAs), have existed for a long time.   These programs are offered by financial institutions—banks, brokerage firms, mutual funds, etc.—that invest in stocks, bonds, and other financial instruments.   Various other types of programs would be created if enabling legislation were passed.

Privatization would have two major advantages:

- Retirees would very probably receive a higher rate of return on their investment than has been received on social security.

- The business sector would receive a flow of funds amounting to hundreds of billions of dollars to finance expenditures on new capital goods.

Of course, complete privatization might prove to be too costly for many people in lower-income and middle-income groups.   They may not be able to set aside enough income during their working years to finance retirement.   In that case, a privatized system might be combined with the following approach.

Substitute the Income Tax   The payroll tax, which is the means used to finance social security, is regressive.   Although it could be restructured to be made progressive, a more practical solution is to replace it with the income tax. This would require an increase in income-tax rates in order to produce larger yields. However, the amount of the increase could be modest if the tax rates were restructured annually in small steps. This would permit the full burden of the payroll tax to be transferred gradually to a progressive tax structure.

Some facts and trends pertaining to social security are described and illustrated in Exhibit 1.

Exhibit 1
Social Security: The Costs and Benefits Continue to Rise

The average age of the population is increasing because of reduced birth and death rates. Therefore, the social security system is calling upon fewer workers, ages 20 to 65, to support more retired people. As a result, max-imum annual social security taxes on employee and employer, along with maximum benefits, are expected to soar in the years ahead.

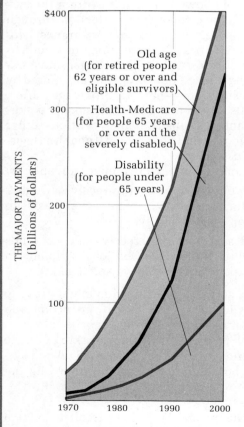

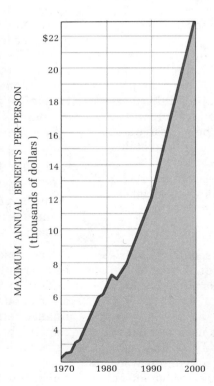

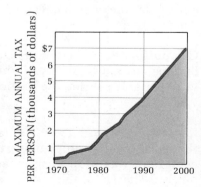

Source: U.S. Department of Health and Human Services.

Affluence and Poverty: America's Underdeveloped Nation

Poverty amidst affluence is another social problem. America's wealth is unmatched by that of any nation in history. Its fields and factories generate a superabundance of goods; most of its families possess automobiles and television sets; and the great majority of families own their homes.

The signs of affluence are everywhere — except among the 25 million Americans who live in poverty and deprivation. This group is larger than the population of many countries. It is composed of men, women, and children of all races who live near or below the bare subsistence level. Some interesting statistics about people living in poverty in the United States are shown in Exhibit 2.

What Is Poverty?

For many years, economists and statisticians have grappled with the problem of defining and measuring poverty. Central to the concept is the ***poverty line*** — a sliding income scale that varies between rural and urban locations according to family size. The poverty line for an urban family of four — which is regarded as fairly typical — was approximately $10,000 annually in the mid-1980s.

Of course, many of the people who fall below the line, such as a married medical-school student or an elderly couple on social security who own their home and car, are poor only by definition. Nor does the poverty line distinguish between costs of living in different areas of the country. A low income goes a lot further in Meridian, Mississippi, than in San Francisco or New York City. Nevertheless, in view of the following facts, a simple income measure of poverty understates the real dimensions of the situation:

- A poverty-line income for a family of four allows for relatively little health care. It permits no movies, newspapers, or books and only very small quantities of clothing, meat, fruits, and vegetables.

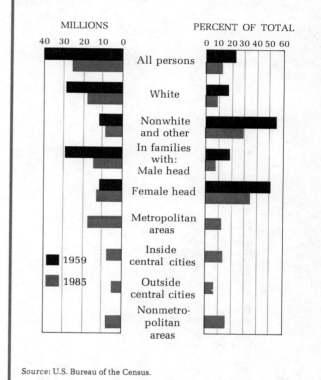

Exhibit 2

Persons Below Low-Income (Poverty) Level, by Family Status, Race, Sex, and Residence

Source: U.S. Bureau of the Census.

- More than 10 percent of the total population is classified as poor. Contrary to a widespread belief, blacks do not constitute a majority in the group. Of 25 million poor Americans, approximately 18 million are white.

- Most of the population lives in cities and towns. Therefore, it is not surprising that the majority of the poor are urban dwellers.

In general, there is no simple and unique definition of poverty — or even of "poorness." It is an economic as well as psychological state of being that varies for different people from time to time and from place to place.

Poverty in America

The Great Paradox

What constitutes poverty? In some of the poorest counties of the nation, the great majority of homes lack baths and inside toilets, and a large minority have no running water. Their inhabitants, by present-day American standards, would be classified as poverty-stricken.

But let us examine the situation more closely.

In the mid-1980s, among households with annual incomes under $10,000, the goods shown in the graph were owned.

The poor in America thus have many of the accoutrements of an affluent society. Most of the American poor are not the same as the starving poor of India or the Far East, but they are poor nevertheless.

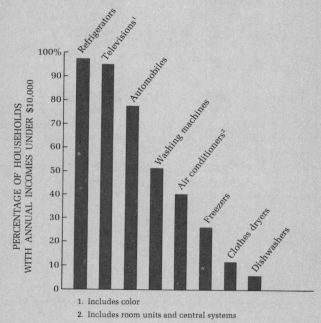

1. Includes color
2. Includes room units and central systems

Source: U.S. Bureau of the Census.

Charles Gatewood/Magnum Photos

The Causes and Costs of Poverty

We may distinguish between two major types of poverty, according to the economic, social, and personal factors that cause them.

Community Poverty   A region may lose its economic base or its major source of income and employment, thereby leaving an entire population in a state of economic deprivation. This has happened to some industrial areas, such as those in the north-central states. They have suffered heavy unemployment, partly because technology has replaced manual labor in their principal industries, and partly because producers have lost markets to lower-cost plants elsewhere. Community poverty can be remedied only through regional economic development programs or outward migration.

Personal Poverty Poverty has always existed among some individuals and families. This is true in times of prosperity as well as in times of depression, in high-income regions and in low-income ones. Poverty is due to personal and social factors, some of which are beyond individual control. For example, there are families that are poverty-stricken because of racial prejudice, inadequate training and job opportunities, physical or mental handicaps, desertion by the breadwinner, and various other causes.

Poverty levies serious social costs. Some sociological studies have concluded that poverty causes ill health and emotional disturbance and helps to spread disease. It also contributes to delinquency, vice, and crime. All these impose heavy costs on the community, which must maintain more police and fire protection, more courts and jails, more public-health and sanitation facilities, and more welfare programs.

Further, there is evidence that poverty breeds poverty. The children of the poor grow up and, in many instances, marry or cohabit with others who are similarly deprived. They tend to have more children than they can provide with an adequate start in life. These children are likewise raised in a poverty environment. In this way the cycle perpetuates itself in a seemingly endless pattern from one generation to the next.

Can We Eliminate Poverty?

Considering the high cost of poverty, what can be done about America's nation of the poor? A number of specific proposals—beyond those involving improvements in the welfare system itself—have been advanced. These proposals fall loosely into three groups:

1. family allowances or guaranteed annual incomes,
2. negative income taxes, and
3. combinations of both.

Family Allowances or Guaranteed Annual Incomes

Many sociologists and social workers have suggested the adoption of a *family-allowance system.* Under this plan, every family in the country, rich or poor, would receive from the government a certain amount of money based exclusively on the number and age of its children. Those families that are above certain designated income levels would return all or part of the money with their income taxes; those below specified income levels would keep it. More than 60 nations, including Canada and all the European countries, give such family allowances.

A modified version of the family-allowance plan is the **guaranteed annual income.** This would award all families under the poverty line a straight allowance for each parent plus specified amounts for each child according to the size of the family. If the family's income were to rise, the payment would be reduced until a break-even level a little higher than the poverty line were reached.

Under both the family-allowance and guaranteed-annual-income plans, families would not be better off, or even as well off, by not working. Nevertheless, there is substantial opposition to these proposals by some political leaders. This is partly because of the fear that the programs would be too costly, and partly because many legislators believe that the plans place more emphasis on governmental paternalism than on providing jobs.

Negative Income Taxes

A scheme that has received widespread interest and support from many liberals as well as conservatives has been the **negative income tax.** This would guarantee the poor a certain minimum income through a kind of reverse income tax. A poor family, depending on its size and private income level, would receive payments from the government. The amount would be enough either to reduce or

Exhibit 3
How the Negative Income Tax Might Work
(annual data — hypothetical)

This is how the negative income tax might work for a family of four, consisting of two adults and two children:

1. As the family's income increases, government payments decrease according to this formula:

$$\frac{\text{government}}{\text{payments}} = \$5,000 - \tfrac{1}{2}(\text{earned income})$$

Thus, you can verify with the formula or from the table or graph that if earned income is zero, the family receives a government payment of $5,000 per year. If earned income rises to $2,000, the family receives a government payment of $4,000. This gives a spendable income of $6,000. Similarly, at an earned income of $4,000, the government payment is $3,000. This makes spendable income $7,000.

2. The break-even point occurs at an earned income of $10,000. At this point, government payments are zero, and at higher income levels the family begins to pay income taxes.

3. Note that the following equation is always true:

$$\frac{\text{spendable}}{\text{income}} = \text{earned income} + \frac{\text{government}}{\text{payments}}$$

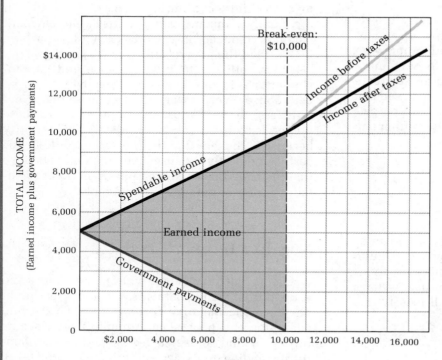

(1) Earned income	(2) Government payments $5,000 − ½(1)	(3) Spendable income (1) + (2)
$ 0	$5,000	$ 5,000
1,000	4,500	5,500
2,000	4,000	6,000
3,000	3,500	6,500
4,000	3,000	7,000
5,000	2,500	7,500
6,000	2,000	8,000
7,000	1,500	8,500
8,000	1,000	9,000
9,000	500	9,500
10,000	0	10,000

close the gap between what the family earned and some explicit minimum level of income. This income "floor" might be equal to, or modestly above, the government's designated poverty line. The size of the payments, of course, would depend on the specific formula adopted. A hypothetical illustration appears in Exhibit 3.

Several major advantages are claimed for this proposal.

Administrative Efficiency The present governmental administrative machinery—the Internal Revenue Service and the Treasury—would handle records and disburse payments, so that a new government agency would not be needed.

Income Criterion Income deficiency would be the sole criterion for establishing eligibility for subsidy. The plethora of criteria that have existed in the past would be eliminated. Many more millions of poor families would thus be eligible. With the resulting expanded coverage, most poor families would have an income "floor" under them and could begin to break the cycle of poverty that has kept some of them on welfare for several generations.

Incentive Maintenance If a family's income were to increase, payments from the government would decrease by some proportion, but not by as much as the increase. Thus, the incentive to work in order to gain more income would not be eliminated.

Despite these advantages, however, there are various difficulties that must also be recognized.

High Cost The negative income tax could not be administered, as many of its proponents claim, with only a small addition to the staff of the Internal Revenue Service. Checks would have to go out monthly or weekly, and the government would have to establish effective controls to prevent abuse. These large tasks would require substantial changes in the administrative structure of the IRS.

Opposition by Middle-Income Groups Workers in the middle-income groups would receive no benefits from the negative income tax, as they would from a family-allowance plan. In addition, they would undoubtedly resent paying taxes to subsidize families whose annual incomes were in some cases only a few hundred dollars less than their own.

Combining the Family-Allowance and the Negative-Income-Tax Plans

Both family allowances and negative income taxes have their advantages and disadvantages. Can a plan be developed that combines the best features of both? One possibility, which may be called an "income-allowance plan," is illustrated for a family of four in Exhibit 4. The same model can be adapted to larger or smaller families.

Look at the table first. The essential feature of the plan is that it grants an annual monetary allowance to each member of a family—regardless of the family's income. (Of course, an upper limit can be set on the total amount granted to any family. Separate allowances can also be provided for those covered by OASDHI insurance.)

Assume that the allowance is $500 for every man, woman, and child and that the tax rate is 30 percent on earned income (income other than the allowance). Then, the way in which the plan would affect a family of four is shown in the table. Note that, at any level of earned income before tax, the family's earned income after the 30 percent tax, plus its fixed income allowance of $2,000, equals it disposable income.

These ideas are also conveyed in the figure. The 45-degree line serves as a benchmark. Along this line, the family's earned income would equal its disposable (spendable) income if there were no taxes or allowances. The influences of taxes and allowances on income are shown by the two remaining lines.

A unique feature of this plan is that it merges the concept of a negative income tax with the existing

Exhibit 4

Income-Allowance Plan for a Family of Four
(annual data — hypothetical)

Assumptions: (1) 30% tax on earned income; (2) income allowance = $2,000 (that is, $500 per person).

Both the table and chart show that, at lower income levels, the family pays less in taxes than it receives in allowances. At higher income levels, the reverse is true. For example, when earned income before tax is $3,000, the family pays $900 in taxes and receives $2,000 in allowances, so it has a net gain of $1,100. When earned income before tax is $8,000, the family pays $2,400 in taxes and still receives $2,000 in allowances — a net loss of $400.

When the family's earned income before tax exceeds $10,000, the income allowance ceases and the present positive tax schedule goes into effect. The rate structure of the tax schedule determines the slope of the line segment *AB* in the figure. Note that the following equation is always true:

$$\frac{\text{disposable}}{\text{income}} = \frac{\text{earned income}}{\text{after tax}} + \frac{\text{income}}{\text{allowance}}$$

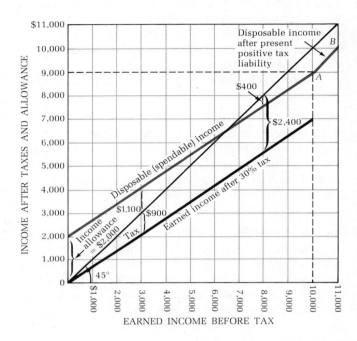

Earned income before tax	Income tax at 30%	Earned income after 30% tax		Income allowance		Disposable (spendable) income
$ 0	$ 0	$ 0	+	$2,000	=	$2,000
1,000	300	700	+	2,000	=	2,700
2,000	600	1,400	+	2,000	=	3,400
3,000	900	2,100	+	2,000	=	4,100
4,000	1,200	2,800	+	2,000	=	4,800
5,000	1,500	3,500	+	2,000	=	5,500
6,000	1,800	4,200	+	2,000	=	6,200
7,000	2,100	4,900	+	2,000	=	6,900
8,000	2,400	5,600	+	2,000	=	7,600
9,000	2,700	6,300	+	2,000	=	8,300
10,000	3,000	7,000	+	2,000	=	9,000

Can Poverty Be Redefined?

The government's definition of poverty is based solely on cash income. The definition does not take into account such noncash benefits as food stamps, medical care, and subsidized housing.

What happens when the dollar value of these benefits is included in poor people's incomes? According to a Census Bureau study, the number of families living below the poverty line declines dramatically. The decrease amounts to about 42% if medical services are included and about 16% if they are not. (The reason for excluding medical services is to avoid the impression that those in the worst health are the best off.)

What does this imply with respect to government antipoverty programs? "People will read into it what they want," says a Census Bureau official. "Conservatives will argue that the poverty problem has been grossly overstated; liberals will say that the figures prove the success of social programs."

Liberals might also argue that the monetary value of government benefits received by low-income families should be compared with those received by middle- and upper-income families. Among the benefits received by the latter groups are tax deductions for mortgage interest and tax exemptions on municipal-bond interest and company-paid benefits.

Conclusion: Income Plans Are Not the Whole Answer

Virtually all income plans have at least three variables in common:

1. An income "floor"—a minimum level of income to be received by every household.

2. A positive "tax" rate, which decreases the government allowance as income increases.

3. A break-even level of income at which the government allowance is zero.

The problem in setting up an income plan, of course, involves the correct selection of these variables while maintaining effective work incentives. The minimum-income and break-even levels should not be set so high as to discourage people from seeking work or to subsidize those who do not need assistance.

All income plans have the same goal—to put money into the hands of the poor. At best, therefore, income plans can only relieve the symptoms of poverty—not its causes. To cure the disease itself, an income plan must be combined with proper work-incentive and job-training programs. But perhaps even more fundamental is the need to develop better methods for defining and measuring poverty.

Attacking Poverty Through the Labor Market

One of the problems encountered in efforts to eliminate poverty is that a very large proportion of the poor constitute a mixed bag of underutilized human resources. They include not only involuntarily unemployed but also large numbers of discouraged jobless people who have given up looking for work. They also include part-time workers who want, but are unable to find, full-time employment; and full-time workers who hold jobs at very low pay.

positive-income-tax schedule. This occurs in the chart where the disposable-income line reaches point A. This point corresponds to an earned income before tax of $10,000 and a disposable income of $9,000. Beyond this point, income allowances are zero and the 30 percent tax no longer exists. In its place, the present positive tax schedule prevails. The rates in this schedule will determine the steepness of the line segment AB. A wide range of rates is possible, and no family need end up paying more taxes than it is now paying.

In view of this, what measures besides family allowances, negative income taxes, and income allowances can be undertaken to improve the lot of America's poor?   There are two approaches that operate directly through the labor market, rather than through income redistribution.   These are (1) minimum-wage adjustments and (2) employment-training programs.

Minimum Wages

Minimum-wage legislation has been in existence since the passage of the **Fair Labor Standards Act** of 1938.   The act has been amended a number of times in order to raise the wage minimum and to provide coverage for broader categories of workers.   Among the chief purposes of the act has been to provide a wage "floor" representing some minimal level of living.

Has minimum-wage legislation contributed to reducing poverty?   The answer appears to be yes.   However, as you learned in some previous chapters, minimum wages are also a cause of unemployment.   (You can refresh your understanding of the reason for this by reviewing the explanation in Exhibit 5.)   Therefore:

Though there is some evidence that minimum-wage legislation has helped reduce poverty, it does *not* unqualifiedly help the poor—as is often believed.   A minimum wage may help some workers, but it is also a cause of unemployment among those whose productivity is not high enough to earn the statutory wage. These are largely the competitively disadvantaged groups in society.   They consist mostly of young people, some racial minorities, and former homemakers who are entering the labor force after raising children.

Employment-Training Policies

A second approach to attacking poverty via the labor market is through **employment-training policies.**   These are deliberate efforts undertaken in the private and public sectors to develop and use the

Exhibit 5
Effect of Minimum Wages in a Competitive Labor Market

In a competitive labor market the equilibrium wage at W and the quantity of labor at N are determined by the intersection of the supply and demand curves for labor.   If a minimum wage is imposed, a surplus of labor (unemployment) results.   Thus, at minimum wage 1, the surplus is JK; at minimum wage 2, the surplus is LM.   In general, the higher the minimum wage, the greater the surplus.

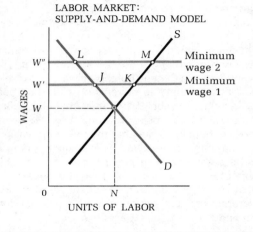

LABOR MARKET: SUPPLY-AND-DEMAND MODEL

capacities of human beings as actual or potential members of the labor force.

Many different groups are involved in formulating and implementing employment-training policies.   They include government agencies at the national and local levels, employers, unions, colleges, and voluntary organizations.   Despite such diversity, however, there is widespread agreement that one of the nation's major employment-training problems is to find adequate jobs for its poor.

Many middle-class Americans believe—because they have been taught to believe—that anyone who really wants to work can find a "good job." The facts indicate that this is not so.   Evidence suggests that there exists what may appropriately be

Economics in the News

Reagan's Job-Training Plan— How It's Working

The Program is Preparing Thousands for Jobs, but Many of the Disadvantaged and Less Educated Feel Left Out

The Reagan administration's Job Training Partnership Act (JTPA) program is winning accolades from many participants who have parlayed their training into jobs. Over all, say Labor Department officials, 115,000 people, or more than 70 percent of those who completed the program in its first six months, found employment—well in excess of expectations. Currently, about half a million people are enrolled.

Despite such enthusiasm, support for JTPA is far from unanimous. In fact, it is drawing heavy fire from critics who argue that its very success is precisely what's wrong with the program.

Their charge: JTPA is working as well as it is only because those who receive the most help already have many of the skills needed to get a job. By deliberately selecting or, as critics term it, "creaming" these applicants for the training, the number of people placed in jobs increases. This way, local agencies that do the training are able to comply with federal guidelines for performance.

Avoiding the Needy?
"The tendency is to take people who are easiest to serve and who probably would have found employment anyway—even without additional training—and steer away from the most needy and hardest to place," says Morton Sklar, director and legal counsel for the Jobs Watch Project of the Center for National Policy Review, Catholic University Law School.

Reagan administration officials call the charges groundless. They counter that, even though the act allows up to 10 percent of enrollees in the basic-training program to be exempt from income-eligibility requirements, 94 percent of those in the program's first six months were economically disadvantaged. More than half were women, nearly half were minorities, a quarter were high-school dropouts and 42 percent were on public assistance.

Reprinted from *U.S. News & World Report* issue of October 22, 1984. Copyright (1984), U.S. News & World Report, Inc.

called a ***dual labor market.*** This is actually *two* markets:

1. A primary labor market, in which jobs are characterized by relatively high wages, favorable working conditions, and employment stability.
2. A secondary labor market, in which jobs, when they are available, pay relatively low wages, often provide poor working conditions, and are highly unstable.

Blue-collar workers, many of whom are union members, and white-collar workers constitute most of the primary market. In contrast, the competitively disadvantaged poor—the unskilled, the undereducated, and the victims of racial prejudice—are largely confined to the secondary market.

In view of this:

Employment-training policies for the disadvantaged should be designed to provide employment opportunities for individuals who want to work but are unable to find a job. More specifically, such policies should seek to accomplish two goals:

1. provide opportunities for those in the secondary market to qualify for primary employment
2. improve the quality of secondary employment.

Many critics contend that employment-training policies by themselves cannot solve the poverty problem. Such policies, they argue, have to be coordinated with other measures—such as a negative-income-tax plan or an income-allowance plan —if significant advances are to be made.

Crime

"Crime doesn't pay!"

If this familiar saying is true, why do so many people engage in crime? The answer must be that certain types of crime do pay. Indeed, such crimes as robbery, theft, arson, commercialized prostitution, drug-law violations, and murder-for-hire, among others, sometimes pay very well. And organized crime, involving such activities as drug dealing, racketeering, and gambling operations, have been estimated by government sources to bring in many billions of dollars annually.

The economics of crime is a vast and complex subject. Consequently, only a portion of it can be examined within the limits of this chapter. For convenience, attention may be focused on the illegal drug market. As you will see, many of the principles and conclusions that are learned can then be applied to a variety of other criminal activities.

To facilitate analysis, the illegal drug market can be viewed as being composed of two markets. One of these is the market for "soft" drugs, such as marijuana. The other is the market for "hard" drugs, such as heroin. Among the questions to be answered are these:

1. Should the market for soft and hard drugs be legalized?

2. Should dealers and distributors of drugs be more severely punished?

The answers to these and other important questions, as you will discover, are sometimes surprising.

Soft Drugs

Supply-and-demand models can often be used to analyze a variety of illegal practices. One illustration depicting the market for marijuana is shown in Exhibit 6.

The curves in the diagram suggest that marijuana can be viewed like any other commodity. Thus the upward-sloping supply curve S tells you that sellers will make more units of the good available at a

Exhibit 6
The "Soft" Drug Market: Marijuana

If the purchase and sale of marijuana were legalized, both demand and supply would increase. That is, the curves would shift to the right—for two reasons:

1. Some people who did not previously purchase the good in an illegal market would now be willing to buy it in the legal one. Therefore, the demand curve would change, say, from D to D'.

2. Producers and sellers (including cigarette companies) who were not previously in the market would now enter because it is legal. Therefore, the supply curve would change, say, from S to S'.

The result of legalization would be a new equilibrium price and quantity, such as P' and Q', respectively. Note that the new, legal price might be lower than the old, illegal one. One reason is that because of the public's growing concern with good health, the increase in demand might be greatly outweighed by the increase in supply.

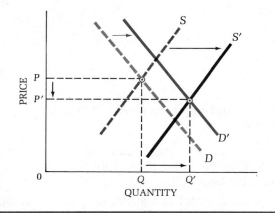

higher price than at a lower one. The downward-sloping demand curve D indicates that buyers will purchase more units of the good at a lower price than at a higher one. The intersection of the two curves determines the equilibrium price at P and the equilibrium quantity at Q.

What would happen if marijuana were now legalized? The answer is that both demand and supply would increase—that is, the demand and supply curves would shift to the right. This is because some people who previously did not buy the good when it was illegal would now do so. Similarly, some sellers (including cigarette companies) that previously neither grew nor distributed the good would now enter the industry as active market participants. The result would be a new equilibrium price and quantity such as the ones at P' and Q', respectively.

In reality, of course, the new equilibrium price and quantity cannot be predicted. They are determined, among other things, by the *relative* shifts of the S and D curves. However, it is quite possible that the new legal equilibrium price would be lower than the previous illegal one, as explained in the diagram.

Hard Drugs

Supply-and-demand models can also be used to analyze the market for hard drugs, such as heroin. This is done in Exhibit 7. Here is how the curves are interpreted:

The Demand Curve D is Relatively Inelastic. That is, percentage changes in quantity demanded respond less-than-proportionately to percentage changes in price. This is because only a small minority of heroin consumers are occasional users. The great majority are physiologically addicted. Hence the total market demand curve reflects the fact that quantity demanded declines very little with increases in price.

The Supply Curve S is Approximately Unit Elastic. That is, percentage changes in quantity supplied respond roughly proportionately to percentage changes in price. This observation is based on government publications (including FBI and U.S. Customs reports) that estimate periodically the amount of heroin smuggled into the country.

Exhibit 7
Heroin Market: Supply Restriction Model

Through increased law-enforcement efforts, government could reduce the supply of heroin from S to S'. But quantity demanded is relatively inelastic. That is, percentage changes in quantity demanded are much smaller than percentage changes in price. Therefore, there would be two effects:

1. The equilibrium quantity will decrease by a relatively small amount, from Q to Q'.

2. The equilibrium price will increase by a relatively large amount, from P to P'.

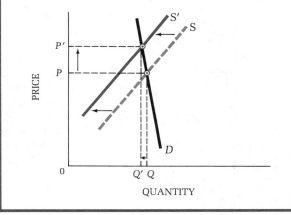

Using this model as a basis, what can be said about various government efforts aimed at controlling the heroin market? Several public-policy options may be considered.

Restrict Supply

One way in which government can reduce the consumption of heroin is to increase law-enforcement efforts. This would shift the supply curve in the market to the left—from S to S'. The result will be an increase in the equilibrium price from P to P', and a decrease in the equilibrium quantity from Q to Q'. As you can see, therefore:

Exhibit 8
Heroin Market: Demand Restriction Model

Through heavier punishment costs in terms of fines and imprisonment, government might reduce the demand for heroin from D to D'. The reduction would be quite limited, however. Most of it would be attributable to occasional users, who constitute only a small proportion of buyers. Addicts, who account for most of the demand, would still purchase nearly as much as before. Therefore, the decrease in demand would result in only modest reductions both in quantity and price. These would be from Q to Q' and from P to P', respectively.

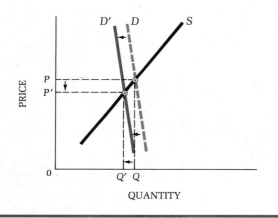

Any enforcement program that reduces supply will have two important social implications:

1. It will result in a relatively small decrease in consumption (mostly by occasional users) and a relatively large increase in price.

2. It is likely to lead to increased crime by addicts who need more money to pay the higher price.

Most government efforts aimed at reducing heroin consumption have focused primarily on restricting supply by preventing the importation of the product. This has resulted in precisely the two social implications predicted by economic analysis.

Restrict Demand

A second way for the government to reduce heroin use is to curb its consumption. This might be done by imposing heavier punishment costs, in the form of fines and imprisonment, on buyers. The result, as you can see in Exhibit 8, would be a decrease in demand from D to D'. The equilibrium price will therefore decline from P to P' and the equilibrium quantity from Q to Q'. Thus:

Any enforcement program that reduces demand will have two important social implications:

1. It will result in a relatively small decrease in consumption (mostly by occasional users) as well as a relatively small decrease in price.

2. It is not likely to lead to decreased crime by those addicts who must steal to support their habit. This is because the decline in price will at best be moderate.

These two implications help explain why government efforts aimed at restricting the demand for heroin have not been particularly successful.

Legalize the Market

A third way in which the government could deal with the heroin market is to legalize it. This would undoubtedly increase both the supply of, and demand for, the good. As a result, the equilibrium quantity would rise, and the equilibrium price would decline.

To illustrate, Exhibit 9 shows that the amounts of the changes in quantity and price depend on the *relative* shifts of the demand and supply curves. The diagram assumes (as explained below) that legalization would lead to the demand curve shifting by a considerably lesser distance than the supply curve. Thus the demand curve shifts from D to D' while the supply curve shifts from S to S'. Consequently, the resulting increase in the equilibrium quantity, from Q to Q', is relatively smaller than the corresponding decrease in the equilibrium price, from P to P'.

The reason for assuming that the increase in demand will be relatively small in relation to the increase in supply is a plausible one. Because of both

Exhibit 9
Heroin Market: Legalization Model

If the market for heroin were legalized, both the supply of the product and the demand for it would increase.

This model *assumes* that the demand curve would shift relatively less than the supply curve. The reason is due to the public's increased awareness of the dangers of drug addiction. Thus the change in demand is from D to D′ and the change in supply is from S to S′. As a result, the increase in the equilibrium quantity, from Q to Q′, is relatively smaller than the decrease in the equilibrium price, from P to P′.

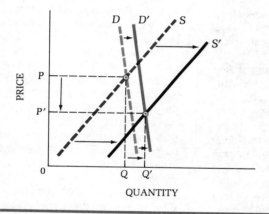

private and governmental educational efforts, people today are much more aware of the dangers of drug addiction than they used to be. This fact suggests some interesting conclusions:

Legalization of the heroin market would have two important social consequences:

1. It would *probably* result in some increase in heroin consumed and in some reduction in its market price. The extent of these changes would depend on the *relative* shifts of the supply and demand curves.

2. It would result in substantial savings in law-enforcement efforts. The money saved could be reallocated to anti-drug educational programs, possibly reducing both present and future demand.

These conclusions can have even wider implications. For example, once the sale of heroin is legalized, steps could be taken to drive organized-crime groups from the market. This could be done in the following way:

Government, working through doctors, clinics, and hospitals, could make heroin available free to certified addicts. This policy would eliminate the huge profits currently realized by heroin dealers and distributors. The result would be the virtual disappearance of the heroin market, or at least its contraction to a small proportion of its current size.

Of course, the government could provide free heroin to addicts without necessarily legalizing the market. But this alternative would be more costly because the government would have to pay a higher price for the drug than would exist in a free market. Nevertheless, even this approach to coping with the problem would be better than the present one, which fosters illegal activity.

Conclusion: Economic and Noneconomic Crimes

Do all types of criminal actions lend themselves to economic analysis and interpretation? The answer is *no*. Those that do are activities undertaken for economic gain—such as drug dealing, gambling, and prostitution. Crimes of violence—such as assault, murder, and rape—fall outside this definition. In view of this distinction between economic and noneconomic crimes, the following conclusion is pertinent:

Our society allocates scarce resources to the prevention of *all* types of crime. Some kinds, however, could be better controlled if they were legalized. Government could then either regulate the activity (as it does with organized gambling in some states) or participate in it to drive out criminal elements (as in the heroin model described above). The result would be a substantial gain in efficiency because much of society's limited law-enforcement resources could be reallocated from economic to noneconomic types of crime.

Controversy Surrounds The Way the Dutch Treat Heroin Addicts

Liberalized Laws Stress Aid Rather Than Penalties; Other Nations Are Irked

By L. Erik Calonius
Staff Reporter of The Wall Street Journal

AMSTERDAM, the Netherlands— Marijuana has ceased to be a big issue in the Netherlands. Pot has been sold freely in cafes and youth centers since 1978, when the government concluded that the substance was "relatively innocuous" and dropped all criminal penalties for using it.

The idea seems to have worked: Fewer young people smoke pot in the Netherlands than in several countries that impose criminal penalties for the activity. In a recent study, more than four-fifths of the young people surveyed said they had no interest in smoking marijuana, although it is as easy to buy here as a bar of chocolate. And less than 2%, according to other studies, say they are "regular" users who smoke pot at least once a week.

(The U.S. does not keep comparable statistics. Its most recent survey classifies 11.5% of youths aged 12 to 17 and 27.4% of youths 18 to 25 as "regular" users but defines regular as having smoked pot within a month of being surveyed.)

Liberalization of marijuana hasn't caused any health problems or criminal problems, Dutch officials say. "Because society hasn't defined it as a problem, it isn't a problem," says Peter Cohen, a psychologist and drug adviser to the government.

The Dutch's liberalized policy toward heroin, however, is controversial. In essence, that policy is to care for heroin addicts, rather than penalize them. A cornerstone of the policy is to allow addicts to remain in methadone-maintenance programs even if they openly continue to use heroin. (In the U.S. and most other countries, addicts have to prove that they aren't supplementing their methadone with heroin.)

The new policy is a radical change from the last decade, when the Netherlands reacted like most neighboring countries to the growing problem of drug addiction. In Amsterdam, where the problem was centered, police with dogs repeatedly swept junkies off the street. Neighborhoods formed vigilante groups that chased addicts out of abandoned houses with baseball bats. One community even installed blue lights over some sidewalks—hoping that junkies wouldn't be able to find their veins in the colored pools of light.

Still, conditions worsened. Dutch policymakers began looking for a fresh way to defuse the problem, one that would cost society less chaos, crime and suffering in the long run.

The new policy rested on several assumptions. The first was that illegal drugs would continue to seep in through the big ports and coastline of the Netherlands. Therefore, a certain percentage of the Dutch population would continue to be addicted to drugs, just as a certain percentage would be alcoholics and others would be chain-smokers. The Dutch policy became one of trying to return addicts to everyday society as much as possible from the criminal world, and to care for them.

Pollution

The Walrus and the Carpenter
Were walking close at hand;
They wept like anything to see
Such quantities of sand:
"If this were only cleared away,"
They said, "it *would* be grand!"

"If seven maids with seven mops
Swept it for half a year,
Do you suppose," the Walrus said,
"That they could get it clear?"
"I doubt it," said the Carpenter,
And shed a bitter tear.

Lewis Caroll, *Through the Looking Glass* (1872)

The penultimate Western man, stalled in the ultimate traffic jam and slowly succumbing to carbon monoxide, will not be cheered to hear from the last survivor that the gross national product went up by a record amount.

John Kenneth Galbraith

As the carpet of increased choice is being unrolled before us by the foot, it is simultaneously being rolled up behind us by the yard.

E. J. Mishan

Suppose that an upstream steel mill discharges its wastes into a river. If by spending a dollar on pollution abatement the mill can save downstream fisheries at least a dollar, it should do so—from the standpoint of society's well-being.

Here we see an example of the fundamental distinction between private costs and spillover costs. The upstream steel mill, for example, disposes of its wastes in a manner that affects others. It does not, however, pay for this disposal. Instead, the mill treats the stream as a free good, and hence the mill's private costs of production are lower than they would be if they included the disposal costs. The downstream fisheries, on the other hand, incur higher private costs because they must absorb the pollutants of the upstream mill.

Therefore, to the extent that prices reflect all production costs, the upstream mill's prices are understated and the downstream fisheries' prices are overstated. This leads to undesirable consequences:

1. Society gets too much steel and not enough fish.

2. Consumers of fish, by paying higher prices, subsidize consumers of steel.

3. Therefore, economic resources are not allocated in the most efficient way.

In this example, the steel mill created private costs for itself as well as *spillover costs* (or externalities) that it imposed on others. Together these costs comprise social costs—the total sacrifice incurred by society.

A similar condition exists in terms of benefits. The steel mill concerned itself only with private benefits of production, not with *spillover benefits* (or externalities) such as those that accrued to the community because of the firm's presence. The sum of private benefits and spillover benefits comprise social benefits—the total gain to society.

Thus:

Social costs = private costs + spillover costs
Social benefits = private benefits + spillover benefits

It is useful to see how these ideas can be applied to environmental policies.

Environmental Policies

How much does it cost to undertake antipollution programs? Who pays for them? These questions are at the heart of environmental policy.

Unfortunately, we do not always know the net gain—the increased benefits relative to the increased costs—of eliminating a particular pollutant from the environment. Hence, we may spend too much money reducing some kinds of pollution that are not very damaging and not enough reducing those forms that are. To minimize the chances of this happening, the following "marginal" principle serves as a guide for policy formulation:

The net gain from any activity is maximized when the marginal cost of that activity is equal to its marginal benefit. Thus, expenditures on pollution abatement will result in added costs as well as added benefits. But the degree of pollution will be at an optimum level from *society*'s point of view when the marginal cost of reducing it further is equal to the marginal benefit derived therefrom.

Thus the socially optimum level of pollution is not necessarily zero. The "best" level for society may be some positive amount, depending on the *incremental* benefits and costs of reducing it.

With this in mind, let us consider five approaches to curbing pollution:

1. Redefine property rights

2. Levy emission fees on polluters

3. Sell pollution "rights"

4. Subsidize pollution-abatement efforts

5. Impose direct regulations

These policy proposals are not mutually exclusive. All have been adopted in varying degrees in the United States and some other countries.

Redefine Property Rights

Pollution occurs most frequently in common-property resources, particularly air, rivers, lakes, and government lands such as forests, parks, and streets. Because common-property resources are public goods, the rights to use them are held by everyone. As a result, "everyone's property is no one's property."

The consequences of this are not hard to understand. People have less incentive to maintain the quality of resources such as air, water, or land when they see no personal advantage in doing so. The resources, therefore, are not put to the uses that are most highly valued by society. Instead they are "overused" or polluted because they are available to everyone either free or at relatively little cost.

If common-property resources were privatized, a free market in property rights would be established. Owners would then have the incentive to protect the quality of their resources because the market would allocate them to those uses (including future uses) most highly valued by society. Of course, not all public goods can be privatized. But many of them can, including large amounts of present government-owned land and water. Our limited efforts in doing so have been, in the opinion of numerous critics, responsible for many of the ills of pollution.

Levy Emission Fees on Polluters

Another way of building the costs of pollution into the price-profit system is to use metering devices to measure the amount of pollution emitted by factories. Fees would then be imposed for every unit of pollutant discharged.

A pollution-control board—a state or federal agency—could determine safe limits of emission. Then the fees it charged could be varied not only by the amount of waste emitted but also by the hour of the day, by the day of the week, and by geographic location. By setting its own multiple-fee schedules on these bases, the board could exert a strong influence on *how much, when,* and *where* pollutants were discharged. And because the emission fees would become part of a firm's costs of operation, the board would be using the price mechanism as a carrot as well as a stick.

Several arguments are offered in favor of this approach:

1. It would permit the imposition of variable charges on the generation of pollutants. Historically, governmental systems for controlling pollutants have often been on a yes-or-no basis. By levying emission fees, it would be possible to impose *degrees* of control as the need arises.

2. It would enable government to distribute the damage caused by pollution more evenly throughout the country. With emission fees lower in sparsely populated areas and higher in the more densely populated regions, more factories would perhaps locate away from the cities, where they could pollute with less social damage.

3. It would cause firms to calculate the costs of waste, as well as the costs and benefits of abatement, and to consider these alternatives in their production and pricing decisions. Businesses would thus be stimulated to seek methods of reducing waste—perhaps by "recycling" it back into production or by developing socially harmless methods of disposal.

The rebuttals to these arguments can be readily anticipated. Essentially, the opponents of emission fees make the following points:

1. Only certain types of pollution can be measured with metering devices.

2. Many factors other than emission fees, such as the availability of a suitable labor supply and access to raw materials and markets, influence the geographic location of firms.

3. Benefits and costs cannot be measured precisely.

For these reasons, those who object to the levying of emission fees argue that such a system would at best have only limited advantages.

Sell Pollution "Rights"

A third proposal for dealing with the problem of pollution is to establish a system of marketable licenses. Each license would give its owner the "right" to pollute—up to a specified amount in a given place during a particular period of time. These licenses or rights could be bought and sold in an organized market—not unlike the stock market or the commodities market. Their prices would fluctuate according to the forces of supply and demand, reflecting the general desire of polluters to dispose of wastes. The basic economic features of the proposal are explained in greater detail in Exhibit 10.

You can see that, at a very low price, any firm that wanted to pollute could do so at relatively little cost. If the price were very high, some form of supplementary rights would have to be issued to financially weaker firms in order to enable them to pollute, while limiting (through special taxes or other means) the opportunities for financially stronger firms to do the same. A similar type of scheme might also be developed for households.

This approach to pollution control would not be adaptable to all forms of pollution. But for those to which it would be suited, its fundamental advantage would be its operation through the free market and the use of the price system as a mechanism for coping with pollution problems.

Subsidize Pollution-Abatement Efforts

A fourth approach to curbing pollution is through government subsidization schemes for firms. This system could take various direct and indirect forms. Among them: outright payments for the reduction of pollution levels, subsidies for particular control devices, and exemptions from local property taxes on pollution-abatement equipment. Also, special fast depreciation allowances and tax credits for the purchase of pollution-control equipment could be granted.

Regardless of the form of subsidy, an important consideration should be kept in mind. Subsidy payments would violate the "benefit principle" of equity if, as is most likely, the subsidies were fi-

---

Exhibit 10
A Market for Pollution "Rights"

One way to attack the pollution problem is through the price system. For each specific type of pollution, the government would determine the maximum amount that is within safe limits—such as the number of tons of organic waste per year that, if dumped into a lake, would disintegrate by normal bacterial processes. It could then sell *rights to pollution* in a free market. Each "right" would permit the owner to dump a specified quantity of sewage per year into the lake.

The supply curve S in this case would therefore be a vertical line. The demand curve D, however, would be downward-sloping. This indicates that some polluters would find it cheaper to buy the pollution rights than to invest in pollution-abatement equipment, while others would not. Hence, the equilibrium price would settle at P and the equilibrium quantity would settle at Q. Note that this quantity is less than the amount at Q', the amount that would prevail if the price of a pollution right were zero.

Over the years, the growth in income and population would cause the demand curve to rise—say to D'. This would bring about a higher equilibrium price, P'.

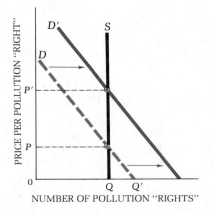

---

nanced out of general tax revenues. According to the benefit principle, consumers who buy products ought to pay the antipollution costs of production just as labor, capital, and other inputs are paid for.

This means that, even though all of society benefits from subsidies to control pollution, consumers who buy the products that cause pollution should pay the costs of reducing it.

Impose Direct Regulations

A fifth method of pollution control would be to invoke the legislative powers of government at all levels. This would involve the use of licenses, permits, zoning regulations, registration, and other controls.

The general objection to direct regulation of pollution is the same as the objection to direct regulation of anything else. Regulation leads to rigidities and, in many cases, unwieldy and inefficient forms of control. A law that sets a limit on pollution levels will cause a greater misallocation of resources than, say, a system of emission fees. This is because the latter can accomplish the same overall reductions in pollution while leaving firms free to adjust to the realities of their own particular production situations.

Does this mean that direct regulations should be avoided at all costs? Not necessarily. In a capitalistic economy, direct regulations may very well be needed. However, they should be adopted, in the opinion of most economists, only after market-oriented mechanisms have been found unsuitable.

Conclusion: Which Policy?

It is impossible to say which approach to pollution control is best. Because there are various sources of pollution, various combinations of policies may be needed. In the meantime, most pollution controls are in the form of direct regulation. This leaves few or no bases for judging the effectiveness of alternative control schemes.

What about technology as a solution? To many critics, technology is the culprit that has been responsible for creating the mess. Cans and bottles accumulate because they cannot be burned. The automobile turns cities into parking lots and landscapes into paved highways. Environmentalists now fear that people will be tempted to turn again to technology — perhaps to the dream of building air-conditioned geodesic domes over the cities, or to visions of colonizing outer space — as an answer to our environmental problems. But these are only fantasies. More realistically:

> Technology will no doubt play a vital role in helping to rescue society from its propensity to create pollution. However, our most fundamental need, if we are to survive on this planet, is to *adopt a value system (of which the price system is one form) that will enable us to make choices about environmental use.* As philosopher Lewis Mumford once stated: "Any square mile of inhabited earth has more significance for man's future than all of the planets in the solar system."

What You Have Learned

1. The U.S. social security system is based primarily on the Social Security Act of 1935 and its many subsequent amendments. Through social insurance, the system provides a measure of protection against old age, unemployment, disability, ill health, and death. Through public charity, the social security system provides welfare services for the needy.

2. The social security system is financed on a "pay-as-you-go" basis. This provides an intergenerational transfer of funds. The system's chief problems are due to (a) its vulnerability to sharp inflations and recessions and (b) the rising average age of the population. In addition, it has been criticized for being compulsory rather than voluntary, and for being financed by a payroll tax that is regressive. Some steps that could be taken to correct these shortcomings include (a) privatization of the system and (b) supplementary financing, if necessary, by the income rather than the payroll tax.

3. Poverty is one of today's most fundamental issues, affecting about 25 million Americans. The basic types of poverty are community poverty and personal poverty. The great social costs of poverty have resulted in many proposals for reform.

4. Various income schemes and assistance plans have been proposed to revise and improve our welfare system. Among the most popular are family allowances, the guaranteed annual income, and the negative income tax. No matter which approach or combination of approaches is adopted, it must be combined with a work-incentive and job-training program if it is to remove people from a lifetime on the dole and make them productive, useful members of society.

5. The problem of poverty can be attacked through the labor market. Two approaches that have been considered are (a) minimum-wage adjustments, and (b) employment-training programs. The preponderance of evidence indicates that minimum wages create adverse employment effects—particularly among competitively "disadvantaged groups"—but the size of the effects are not known. On the other hand, employment-training programs, to be successful, must recognize the existence of a dual labor market and seek to provide opportunities for those in the secondary market to qualify for primary employment.

6. Certain types of crimes are committed for economic gain. Some examples are drug dealing, gambling, and prostitution. It can be argued that such activities could be better controlled if they were legalized. Government could then regulate them and, in some cases such as drug dealing, participate in them by distributing the product free to users. This would greatly reduce the market for the product and, therefore, the need for law-enforcement resources to combat it.

7. Several methods of controlling pollution are possible. Some make use of market mechanisms whereas others rely on governmental regulation. Because no single approach would be suitable in all cases, the challenge of finding the best combination of policies is a continuing one.

Terms and Concepts To Review

Social Security Act (1935)
unemployment benefits
poverty line
family-allowance plan
guaranteed annual income

negative income tax
Fair Labor Standards Act (1938)
monopsony
employment-training policies
dual labor market

For Discussion

1. What are the main features of our social security system? Is the system adequate? Explain.

2. Why not solve the problem of poverty by simply redistributing income equally to everyone?

3. It has been suggested that there is a remarkable inverse relationship between human fertility and "hot baths." The latter represents the reasonable creature comforts of life, such as a basic but adequate amount of food, clothing, housing, and sanitation facilities. If such a relationship exists, it might be better to break the poverty cycle by providing poor people with these goods. What do you think of this argument? (**Note** Do you think the same argument could apply to such underdeveloped, overpopulated regions as India and the Far East?)

4. In contrast to question 3, suppose that providing income allowances to poor families increased their birth rates. What might this imply about the elasticity relationship between the supply of children and family income? Explain the various implications of this.

5. Evaluate the income plans described in the chapter as proposals for attacking the problem of poverty.

6. Two measures have often been advocated by political leaders as means of encouraging employers to provide on-the-job training for the disadvantaged. One of these is tax incentives; the other is contract or employment subsidies. Which measure is likely to be more effective? Discuss.

7. "The effects of legalizing the drug market will depend on the elasticities of the supply and demand curves and on their relative shifts." Illustrate this proposition with graphs.

8. Is it necessary for environmental resources to be privately owned in order to reduce pollution? How else might the market system be invoked while retaining public ownership?

9. Why has privatization of environmental resources not been undertaken on a large scale?

Chapter 32

The Less Developed Countries

Learning Guide

Watch for answers to these important questions

What is meant by "economic development"? Why is the concept difficult to apply?

Are there any fundamental principles of economic development? What must be known about agriculture, population, and capital in order to understand their roles as broad determinants of development?

How do international considerations affect economic development? What roles are played by foreign investment and foreign aid?

While millions of inhabitants of advanced industrial nations worry about eating too much, hundreds of millions of people in dozens of poverty-stricken countries worry about starving. The poverty-stricken countries constitute much of Latin America, Africa, and Asia. It is here that most of the 3 billion citizens of the underdeveloped world live, the majority of them ill fed, poorly housed, and illiterate. Because the poor nations contain three-fourths of the world's population, it is important to understand both the problems they face and the measures that can be taken to help solve these problems.

The Meaning of Economic Development

The poor nations are usually referred to as **less developed countries** (LDCs), underdeveloped countries, or developing countries. They are usually characterized by the following conditions:

− Poverty levels of income and hence little or no saving.

− High rates of population growth.

− Substantial majorities of the labor force employed in agriculture.

– Low rates of adult literacy.

– Extensive **disguised unemployment.** This is a condition in which employed resources (usually labor resources) are not being used in their most efficient ways. The concept is also known as **underemployment.**

– Heavy reliance on one or a few items (mainly agricultural) for export.

– Government control by a wealthy elite, which often opposes any changes that would harm its economic interests.

Among underdeveloped countries, these characteristics are tendencies rather than certainties. Exceptions can be found to all of them.

How many countries of the world are considered to be "less developed"? Which ones are they? From time to time, the United Nations has designated dozens of countries as LDCs. Among them are Indonesia, Burma, India, Pakistan, Egypt, Nigeria, Syria, Morocco, Paraguay, Ecuador, Honduras, Turkey, and Colombia. The map in Exhibit 1 provides a bird's-eye view of the developed and less developed world. The accompanying table shows comparative growth rates of real output for the various regions.

What Is Economic Development?

Economic development is the process by which a nation attains a transformation of its entire socioeconomic system. This means that there are improvements in the quality of resources as well as positive changes in attitudes, institutions, and values of the society.

This characterization of economic development is more of a description than a definition. For economic purposes, a more precise statement is needed:

Economic development is the process whereby a nation's real per-capita output or income (its gross national product, or GNP) increases over a long period of time. A nation's rate of economic development is thus measured by its long-run per-capita rate of economic growth.

The statement that economic development is a long-run process requires emphasis. A short-run spurt in economic growth may be the result of fortuitous circumstances, whereas a long-run expansion in production is generally the result of fundamental change. Thus, it is one thing for a society to experience an increase in real per-capita output over a period of a few years. It is quite another for that society to sustain the increase for perhaps a decade or more.

In addition to increases in real income per capita, there are other objectives of economic development. Among these are greater equality in the distribution of income, a rising minimum level of income, and reduction of disguised unemployment. However, these are generally regarded as secondary goals — mainly because they are strongly influenced in each country by existing social structures and institutions. Therefore, in a developing country, there is some likelihood that these secondary goals will be at least partially attained if the primary goal of a sustained increase in real income per capita is realized.

Economic and "Environmental" Differences

It is useful to compare the gap, at different points in time, between per-capita incomes in the less developed countries and those in the advanced countries. This enables us to see whether the gulf has widened, narrowed, or remained the same. Economists frequently make such comparisons, and the findings portend serious consequences for the world community.

Over the long run, the income gap between the richest countries and the poorest ones has been widening. As a result, an increasing proportion of all goods and services — now more than 80 percent — is produced in countries in which less than 25 percent of the world's people live.

To see clearly why these differences in the economic progress of nations occur, we must first understand the factors determining a nation's economic development. These factors include the quantity and quality of human resources and natural resources, the rate of capital accumulation, the degree of specialization and scale of production, and the rate of technological progress. They also include environmental factors—namely, the political, social, cultural, and economic framework within which growth and development take place. Once we comprehend the significance of these factors, it becomes easy to appreciate why the rich nations are getting richer while the poor ones are getting relatively poorer.

This fact can be illustrated by comparing the United States with most underdeveloped countries. The United States has a large labor force with a relatively high proportion of skilled workers. It has numerous business leaders who are experienced and disciplined. It has a substantial and diversified endowment of natural resources, an extensive system of transportation and power, an efficient and productive technology financed by an adequate supply of savings, and a stable and comparatively uncorrupt government. And, not to be overlooked, it has a culture in which the drive for profit and material gain is generally accepted. These factors in combination have stimulated America's economic development.

In the less developed countries, on the other hand, most of these conditions are absent. The people in the labor force are largely unskilled and inefficient, and many of them are chronically ill or undernourished. Saving is small or even negative,

Exhibit 1
The Developed and Less Developed Countries

Most of the less developed countries are in the tropics —that is, between the Tropic of Cancer and the Tropic of Capricorn. Of course, these countries show various degrees of underdevelopment, ranging from severe to relatively moderate.

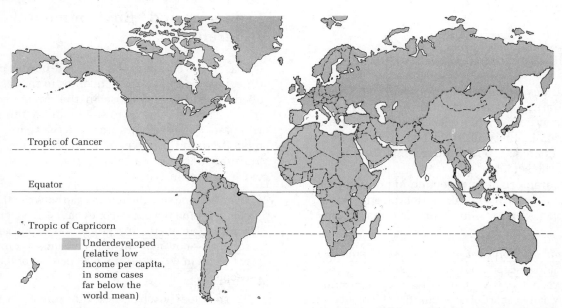

Tropic of Cancer

Equator

Tropic of Capricorn

Underdeveloped (relative low income per capita, in some cases far below the world mean)

resulting in low rates of investment and capital accumulation. Furthermore, government is often either unstable or, if not, dictatorial, corrupt, and inefficient. Paradoxically, many poor countries are rich in natural resources. However, because most of these countries lack the other ingredients, they cannot sustain economic development.

Principles and Strategies of Development

Although there is no single or unified theory of development, various principles and policies would undoubtedly serve as ingredients if such a theory should ever evolve. Moreover, a modern theory would have to embrace several social sciences rather than economics alone. This will become evident as we discuss the following principles and strategies of development theory:

1. The need for agricultural development.

2. Escaping from the "population trap."

3. Investing in physical capital.

4. Investing in human capital.

5. Labor-intensive versus capital-intensive projects.

6. Small versus large projects.

7. Private versus social profitability.

Recent and Projected Rates of Growth in Real Output (GNP)

Region	1985 Total	1985 Per capita	1990 Total	1990 Per capita	1995 Total	1995 Per capita	2000 Total	2000 Per capita
North Africa–Middle East	4.17%	1.5%	3.99%	1.5%	3.62%	1.5%	3.72%	1.5%
Sub-Saharan Africa	2.57	−0.5	2.72	−0.5	3.37	0	3.15	0
European Economic Communities	2.41	2.2	2.50	2.2	2.54	2.2	2.50	2.2
Other Western Europe	3.57	2.5	3.07	2.5	3.04	2.5	2.96	2.5
USSR	3.49	2.5	3.38	2.5	3.23	2.5	3.13	2.5
Eastern Europe	3.21	2.5	3.11	2.5	3.16	2.5	3.04	2.5
South Asia	3.83	1.5	3.64	1.5	3.47	1.5	3.30	1.5
East Asia	5.81	4.0	5.70	4.0	4.59	3.0	4.47	3.0
Asia, centrally planned economies	4.32	2.9	4.80	2.9	4.20	2.9	4.08	2.9
Oceania	3.71	2.5	3.68	2.5	3.60	2.5	3.49	2.5
Latin America	4.64	2.3	4.50	2.3	4.33	2.3	4.13	2.3
North America	3.50	2.7	3.43	2.7	3.30	2.7	3.20	2.7

Source: World Bank, annual reports.

The Need for Agricultural Development

In underdeveloped countries, the great bulk of human resources is devoted to agriculture. These resources tend to be inefficiently employed. As a result, there is a great deal of disguised unemployment or "underemployment."

Agriculture, for the most part, produces the nation's food and raw materials. Therefore, in order for economic development to take place out of domestic resources, agricultural efficiency must improve. This is necessary in order to produce a surplus of output over and above what the agricultural sector itself consumes. As this happens, human and material resources are spared from farming to work in manufacturing. This helps expand the industrial sector while consuming the surplus of the agricultural sector.

These facts suggest a proposition of fundamental importance in economic development:

> In most LDCs there is a close relationship between the agricultural sector and the industrial sector. The relationship is such that the growth of the industrial sector is strongly influenced by prior or simultaneous technical progress in the agricultural sector.

The operation of this important principle has been amply demonstrated in economic history. For example, the development of towns during the Middle Ages was accompanied by, and to a significant extent preceded by, improved methods of agricultural production. Notable was the adoption of the three-field system. Also, the industrial revolution of the eighteenth and nineteenth centuries in Europe and the United States was strongly influenced by an agricultural revolution. This was marked by a number of major innovations, including the introduction of root crops, horse-hoeing husbandry, four-course rotation, and scientific animal breeding. These developments were of such great importance that they actually overshadowed in certain respects the accompanying industrial revolutions. (See Box 1.)

Land Reform

Agricultural development rarely occurs without land reform. In many underdeveloped countries, agricultural land is owned by a small number of rich families but is farmed by large numbers of poor families. Proponents of land reform have almost always advocated the division of land ownership among the families working it. The proponents often argue that the broadening of ownership would yield important psychological and political values as well as economic incentives.

The evidence, however, does not always bear this out. Various studies of land reform have found that the fragmenting of land ownership by itself may actually reduce farm productivity rather than raise it. This is true unless land reform is accompanied by other measures. These include:

− The implementation of new farming techniques, such as improvements in plant strains, irrigation systems, and fertilization programs.

− The increased availability of credit — through the creation of local banks or cooperative credit societies — for investment-minded farmers.

The need for these agricultural reforms is readily seen:

> Legislation that breaks up large landholdings will also eliminate landlords and, therefore, the services they provide. These are mainly tools and credit. Hence, not only must land reform be accompanied by the provision of sufficient technical and financial resources to replace what is lost, it must also provide for the enhancement of agricultural productivity.

Escaping from the "Population Trap"

To solve their economic problems, the less developed countries must either avoid or extricate themselves from the "population trap." That is, their real GNP must continue to increase faster than their population.

Although not all underdeveloped countries are "overpopulated," most of them are. In poor regions

Box 1
Agricultural Development and Economic Growth: A Novel Interpretation

UPI/Bettmann Newsphotos

Terry Qing/FPG

It is an instructive exercise in the interpretation of economic history to consider how far the introduction to agriculture of root crops (such as the turnip) is responsible for the economic development of the past three centuries.

Root crops did two main things: They eliminated the fallow (plowed but unseeded) field and they made scientific animal breeding possible. The fallow field had been necessary to eliminate weeds, but the practice of planting roots in rows between which horses could pull the implements necessary to cultivate the ground made the fallow field unnecessary. Also, the roots enabled the farmer to feed his stock through the winter and thereby eliminate the need for the traditional mass slaughter of farm animals at Christmas. This made selective breeding possible, with astounding results:

1. The increased production of food probably was the principal cause of the amazing fall in mortality, especially infant mortality, in the middle years of the eighteenth century. Most of the rise in population of the Western world has been due to declining mortality.

2. The extra food enabled more babies to live and thus provided the inhabitants for the industrial cities.

3. The new techniques enabled agriculture to produce a large surplus and thus made it possible to feed the hungry people of the new towns.

Thus, even if there had been no startling changes in industrial techniques, it is probable that the agricultural revolution itself would have produced many of the phenomena we usually associate with the industrial revolution. And it is possible that the vast developments in agricultural techniques that have taken place in recent decades may foreshadow a new revolution in economic life as great as that of the last century.

Source: Adapted, with substantial changes, from Kenneth E. Boulding, *Economic Analysis*, 3rd ed., New York, Harper & Row, 1955, p. 719n.

U.S. farming methods, geared to big farms, heavy mechanization, and few farmers, are not easily adaptable to conditions in many of the developing countries. These countries typically have many small farms that are intensively cultivated. More than half the farms in most developing countries are less than 12 acres in size. The type of agricultural revolution that is needed in these countries in order to raise their productivity is to provide farmers with the right incentives and the necessary agricultural inputs.

in Asia, parts of Latin America, and Africa, population presses heavily on physical resources. Accumulation, or saving, is therefore difficult. Why? Because the level of production is low and resources are committed primarily to agriculture in order to produce the bare necessities of consumption. As long as the pressure on food supplies continues, large numbers of people must subsist at the barest survival level. This makes it extremely difficult if not impossible for the nation to extricate itself from the population trap.

What can be done to alleviate the problem? One approach, of course, would be for large numbers of people to emigrate from overpopulated to underpopulated regions. But numerous legal, social, and economic obstacles make this solution unfeasible.

The most practical alternative is to meet the population problem head-on. Various studies have demonstrated quite conclusively that it is cheaper to increase real incomes per capita by slowing population growth than by investing in new factories, irrigation, and so on. Studies have also shown that it is not so much the absolute *size* of the population as the population *growth rate* that holds back improvements in real income per capita. Because of this, a number of developing countries, including China, Indonesia, Taiwan, India, and Pakistan, have instituted family-planning programs. These have ranged from simple counseling services to large-scale voluntary sterilization schemes (usually vasectomies). A chief difficulty is that any population-control scheme may conflict with local religious traditions, which often impede if not prevent the development of effective programs.

An interesting *economic* approach to the problem of overpopulation is proposed in Exhibit 2. It is not likely that such a plan would ever be adopted, but it provides a thought-provoking topic for discussion.

Investing in Physical Capital

Many economists and government officials used to believe that massive infusions of capital were alone sufficient to induce economic development. In-

creases in real output, it was contended, were attributable almost entirely to expansions in the stock of capital rather than to increases in labor employment or improvements in technology.

Where did this assumption come from? It was based on the economic concept of **marginal productivity.** This is defined as the increase in output resulting from a unit change in a variable input while all other inputs are held fixed. The concept is associated with the famous **law of diminishing returns** (the formal meaning of which you can look up in the Dictionary at the back of the book). In simplest terms, the law tells you that the more you have of a particular type of resource, the less productive or useful is any one unit of it.

Now, because most underdeveloped countries have an excess of labor, the marginal productivity of labor in such countries is low or close to zero. And because most underdeveloped countries have an insufficient amount of capital, the marginal productivity of capital is high. Consequently, the infusion of large doses of capital appeared to be the most effective means of raising real GNP per capita.

Recent Findings

This conclusion, although largely correct, has been greatly modified over the years. Research studies and experiences in less developed countries during the past several decades have revealed some interesting findings:

1. There are limits to the amount of new capital that LDCs can "absorb" or utilize effectively in any given period. These limits are set by such factors as the availability of related skilled labor and the level of effective demand for the output of the new capital. It does little good, obviously, to build a railroad if there is not enough skilled labor to operate and maintain it or not enough demand for goods transported by the railroad to support it.

2. The marginal productivity of farm labor may be low because it is employed in densely populated areas where arable land is relatively scarce. Yet in many LDCs large sections of fairly fertile lands

Exhibit 2

Can Population Be Controlled Through the Price System?

Can the price system be used to help influence the size of a nation's population?

Population control might be exercised through the sale of "birth rights." The government, for example, might decide that each married couple should be entitled to two "free births." Beyond that, a couple would have to pay a price if they wanted to have more children. How much would they have to pay? The answer would depend on the current market price of birth-right certificates, each certificate permitting a woman to have one completed pregnancy.

The government would issue a fixed amount of these certificates for a period of time. Hence, the supply curve S would be a vertical line. However, the demand curve D would be normal or downward-sloping. Through the free interaction of supply and demand, the equilibrium price would settle at P; the equilibrium quantity would, of course, be at Q.

Over a period of time, income (and perhaps population) would grow. Therefore, the demand curve would shift rightward to D'. The government might then decide to issue additional certificates, as shown by the new supply curve S'. This would result in a different equilibrium price at P' and an equilibrium quantity at Q'. The additional certificates the government decided to issue would depend on the degree of control it

wished to exercise over the market price and the size of the population.

QUESTION   There are obvious social and economic difficulties in implementing such a system. Can you name them? Can you also suggest ways of overcoming some of the difficulties?

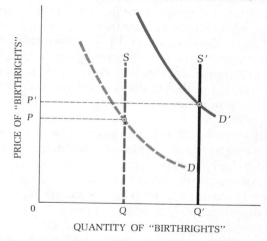

SUPPLY OF, AND DEMAND FOR, "BIRTHRIGHTS"

are underpopulated for cultural or political reasons, or simply because the lands are located in undesirable or inaccessible areas. Of course, some injections of capital may help. But increases in output would be greater if the infusions of capital were accompanied by shifts of farm labor from overpopulated to underpopulated areas.

As a general rule, therefore:

Both extra capital and extra labor of an appropriate type are needed to obtain extra output. The notion that in the LDCs the marginal productivity of capital is high while that of labor is low is undoubtedly correct.

However, it is true only in an overall sense. When used in proper combinations, the marginal productivities of *related* kinds of skilled labor and capital are likely to be quite high.

Investing in Human Capital

Investments in human capital as well as physical capital are needed if increased productivity is to accelerate economic development. The "quality" of a population, as measured by its skills, education, and health, is vitally important in influencing a nation's cultural and economic progress.

Four main areas call for particular attention:

1. Emphasis on Basic Technical Training   Underdeveloped countries usually suffer from a glut of unskilled workers and a shortage of skilled workers.   These nations, therefore, should place more emphasis on vocational instruction and less on academic training.   For example, primary-school and secondary-school curricula should be oriented toward technical education and on-the-job training in such fields as agriculture, commerce, industry, and construction.

2. Development of Middle-Level Skills   Most LDCs suffer from a shortage of people with middle-level skills.   For example, there is usually a much greater need for technicians than for scientists and engineers.   If educational institutions, from elementary schools through universities, were to focus on the development of these middle-level skills, it would enhance productivity.

3. Utilization of Foreign Experts   The LDCs have long suffered from a serious "brain drain."   This results when their talented younger people going to universities in advanced nations remain there instead of returning to their home countries, where they are desperately needed.   Underdeveloped nations may not always be able to eliminate this form of emigration.   However, they can minimize the loss of their trained specialists by making greater use of foreign experts in domestic education and training programs.

4. Investment in Public Health   Large-scale health programs are needed to reduce disease and mortality rates in LDCs.   Of course, reductions in mortality rates result in greater population growth.   This adds to the burden of people pressing against limited resources.   The solution is to supplement public health measures with voluntary birth-control programs.   Only when men and women gain some degree of control over their lives does investment in human capital become a force for cultural as well as economic change.

Labor-Intensive Versus Capital-Intensive Projects

Should an underdeveloped country that is trying to industrialize concentrate on labor-using or capital-using investment projects?   This question can be addressed in terms of what may conveniently be called a "labor-intensity" versus a "capital-intensity" criterion.

Labor-Intensity Criterion   This standard applies when labor is excessive relative to capital.   Emphasis should then be placed on projects that make maximum use of the abundant factor of production, labor, and minimum use of the scarce factor, capital.   Such an approach would tend to reduce the degree of disguised unemployment while increasing industrial output.

Capital-Intensity Criterion   According to this standard, capital-using projects should be favored even if labor is excessive.   The reason is that the potential gains in productivity that are achieved by maximizing the amount of capital per worker will more than offset the loss of output resulting from unemployment.   This is particularly true, it is argued, when the developing country must face competition for its manufactured products from more advanced industrial economies.

To a considerable extent, the controversy over labor-intensive versus capital-intensive investments is academic and irrelevant to modern manufacturing processes.   In most industries there is little room for substitution between capital and labor.   This is because production processes within plants are predetermined by technology.   Combinations of labor and capital are established by engineering rather than according to economic requirements.   A given plant is designed with a predetermined capacity to be operated by a certain number of workers.   Although some variations in output may be made within a single-shift operation, the use of multiple shifts is the only way in which large changes in output can be realized.

These facts suggest the following conclusions:

The labor-intensity versus capital-intensity criterion is usually of little practical value in implementing investment decisions within a particular industry. On the other hand, the criterion assumes greater realism when it is used to compare *interindustry* investments. This is done in order to determine which projects will tend to be more labor-using (or capital-saving) and which more capital-using (or labor-saving). Such comparisons can help in deciding the types of industries that should be promoted by a developing country.

Unfortunately, these economic conclusions are often overshadowed by other considerations. For example, the desire for prestige may often take precedence over logic. The governments of many LDCs often want the most modern and "fashionable" investments. This is true regardless of how well they mesh with domestic economic needs and resources.

Thus, there is hardly an underdeveloped country of any substantial size that does not have an international airline consisting of a fleet of U.S.-built jet aircraft; a modern steel mill, the ore and fuel for which must usually be imported from other countries; and an automobile assembly plant, which turns out new cars at prices two or three times higher than in the advanced countries.

These inefficient industries are protected by high tariffs and low import quotas. But the real costs, of course, are borne by the people at home.

Small Versus Large Projects

Should LDCs try to develop large and complex production operations, or should they concentrate first on small-scale industries? Practical considerations favor the latter approach. In most underdeveloped countries, it is highly probable that one or more of the necessary ingredients of industrialization is lacking. These include adequate capital, transportation facilities, suitable marketing channels, modern technical knowledge, and effective managerial skills.

Small projects demand fewer of the scarce ingredients and, of course, smaller amounts of them. At the same time, they develop needed entrepreneurship, can be instituted more rapidly, and can begin to impart their beneficial economic effects to the community more quickly. Large industrial projects, on the other hand, have less chance of succeeding under these conditions, and their payoffs in terms of economic benefits to the nation are likely to lie far in the future.

The limitations of this conclusion must be recognized, however. The distinction between "small" and "large" projects is not always clear-cut. Moreover, large and small projects are often complementary rather than competitive. A large manufacturing plant, for instance, will frequently stimulate the development of many small plants to provide parts and services. Hence, it cannot be stated as a firm rule that one size or scale of manufacturing is always preferable to another.

As a practical matter, the alternatives must be identified and measured in each case. For certain types of manufacturing, a large, integrated production process may be necessary in order to gain economies that will permit internationally competitive pricing. For other types of manufacturing, differences in scale may hinge on factors other than productive efficiency. Some considerations are size of market and availability of the right type of labor supply. Thus in many LDCs, modern manufacturing plants and paved roads have been provided by foreign aid, while ox-drawn wagons are used to transport the goods. Clearly, therefore, cost is not the only factor to be considered when deciding on the size of the plant to be constructed.

Private Versus Social Profitability

Every real investment yields two kinds of returns. One may be called the "private" rate of return; the other can be referred to as the "social" rate of return. Under certain theoretical conditions they may be identical. In reality, however, they usually differ, sometimes by a wide margin. Let us see why.

The *private rate of return* on an investment is the financial rate. This is the rate that business managers try to anticipate before investing their funds. It is therefore the same as the *marginal efficiency of investment* studied in macroeconomic theory. In simplest terms, the private rate of return on an investment is the expected net profit after taxes in relation to the capital invested. It is usually expressed as a percentage annual return upon the total cost of the project. From the viewpoint of investors, this rate is the most important criterion, because it measures the profitability of the investment.

The *social rate of return* is the net value of the project to the economy. The social rate is estimated on the basis of the net increase in output that a project, such as a new industry, may be expected to bring, directly or indirectly, to the area being developed. The industry's contribution is measured by subtracting the cost to society of the resources used from the value of what the industry produces. Therefore, the concept of a social rate of return is that of a net return.

As a general rule:

A difference usually exists between the private and social rates of return. There are two reasons:

1. The costs of various inputs to the private owner may be different from the cost to the economy.

2. The value of the sales receipts to the private owner may be different from the value to the economy of having the goods produced.

An Illustrative Example

As a practical illustration, you might think in terms of a factory in a certain area. This investment may yield a high private rate of return to its owners. If the factory employs a significant segment of the area's labor force, it may also seem to be yielding a high social rate of return. However, before we can be sure of this, we would have to analyze such offsetting factors as the resources used by the factory and the adverse externalities or spillovers.

After these considerations are taken into account, the difference between the private and social rates

may be quite substantial. Indeed, a project may have a high private rate of return and a low — possibly even negative — social rate. This might be true, for example, if the factory pollutes its environment. Alternatively, a high social rate and a low private rate may also be encountered. This usually happens with certain types of public-works projects.

These two examples are extremes. Between them is a range of projects that are suitable for a particular community in accordance with its stock of human and material resources. This is the range that must be sought out, identified, and developed by the government agencies and organizations that are encouraging industrialization.

Some International Aspects of Development

The fundamental economic task of LDCs is to increase their productivity by improving their methods of production. This requires investment in physical and human capital. Examples are power facilities, factories, machines, education, public health, and the like.

Because the LDCs for the most part are poor, they do not generate enough savings to finance their own capital formation. Therefore, they must acquire the needed investment from abroad by obtaining private foreign investment, foreign aid, or a combination of the two.

Attracting Private Foreign Investment

What economic measures might underdeveloped countries consider in order to attract investment from private foreign sources?

1. Infrastructure Facilities The governments of LDCs might undertake to provide *infrastructure.* This is the economic and social overhead capital needed as a basis for modern production. Examples of infrastructure include roads, telephone lines, power facilities, schools, and public-health services. Many advanced countries as well as international agencies have had a long history of providing less developed countries with generous loans on relatively easy terms for the purpose of building infrastructure facilities.

2. Insurance Protection When considering investment in certain politically volatile LDCs, foreign corporations are concerned with security of life and property. Insurance provisions could help reduce such risks. The governments of LDCs might consider establishing insurance companies, or contracting with foreign insurance companies, for this purpose. The plan could be financed partly by the recipient governments and partly by the governments of the lending countries. An international financing agency of the United Nations, such as the World Bank (discussed later in this chapter), could provide the necessary administrative assistance. Some progress in this direction has, in fact, been made, but observers contend that much remains to be done.

3. Nonnationalization Guarantees Potential investors must be given reasonable assurance that their assets will not be nationalized (that is, expropriated) by the governments of recipient nations. At the very least, investors should be guaranteed "fair compensation" in the event of nationalization. They should also be assured that disputed claims will be settled by the International Court of Justice at The Hague.

4. Profit and Capital Transfers Businesspeople are not likely to invest in LDCs without the knowledge that a certain share of profits can be transferred out of the country each year. In addition, specific provisions are needed to permit capital mobility. For example, laws could be formulated that place minimal restrictions on the transfer of ownership between foreigners, in the event that investors wish to sell their assets.

5. Tax Concessions LDCs can offer a variety of tax inducements to attract foreign capital. As examples, income taxes and property taxes on preferred types of investments can be reduced or postponed for a specific number of years. Several underdeveloped nations have had success with such policies. However, to use tax concessions effectively, governments must take care not to drive out existing firms by giving competitive advantages to new foreign companies.

The foregoing ideas suggest this conclusion:

In order to attract foreign capital, LDCs must create a *favorable climate for investment*. This requires the adoption of economic policies designed to protect property rights, permit capital mobility, and enhance profits.

Foreign Aid

Even under the best of circumstances, some LDCs may not be able to attract sufficient private foreign investment to meet total capital requirements for sustained growth. In that case, help in the form of foreign aid from other nations may be available. *Foreign aid* consists of loans, grants, or assistance by one government to another for the purpose of accelerating economic development in the recipient country.

Among the chief sources of foreign aid are:

1. the World Bank, established by a United Nations charter in 1944.

2. the International Development Cooperation Agency (IDCA), an American organization.

The latter includes the Agency for International Development (AID), the federal government's main foreign-aid unit. In addition, the Soviet Union, China, and other nations have become sources of assistance to underdeveloped countries. This is not surprising because, for any country that provides it, foreign aid may be motivated as much by political considerations as by economic considerations.

Economics in the News

Is the West to Blame for Third World Poverty?

A distinguished economist at the London School of Economics, P. T. Bauer, challenges the conventional wisdom that foreign aid is essential for narrowing the income gap between rich and poor countries. Income statistics, he says, often hide more than they reveal. There is no significant difference between the per-capita income levels of the richest underdeveloped countries and the poorest developed ones.

In a review of Bauer's writings, Edwin McDowell, a member of the editorial staff of the *Wall Street Journal,* paraphrased Bauer this way:

Actually, Western prosperity was generated by its own population, not achieved at anyone's expense. Those countries were already materially much more advanced than the underdeveloped countries when they established contact with the latter in the 18th and 19th centuries. Even now many developed countries, including some of the richest, have few economic contacts with the underdeveloped world.

Moreover, some of the richest Western countries were colonies in their earlier history, notably the U.S., Canada, Australia, and New Zealand. And some were already prosperous while they were still colonies. This certainly does not prove that colonialism is a necessary or admirable precondition of material progress. However, along with the contemporary experience of Hong Kong, it tends to refute the assumption (enunciated as a general principle by the United Nations) that colonial status and economic progress are incompatible.

Nevertheless, belief that Western economic gains were achieved at the expense of the underdeveloped world has led donors to favor economic development assistance as a form of partial restitution and has led recipients to view it as an admission of Western guilt. In part that accounts for what has been described as the "economics of resentment." It consists of the anomaly of donor countries beseeching poor nations not to refuse their aid, combined with recipient governments showing their thanks by pursuing policies hostile to donors.

Bad Economics and Bad Sociology

In a more general sense, Bauer is critical of the social implications of foreign aid. He questions the underlying premise of development—whether it is moral to try to transform human society. "The attitudes and motivations which promote material success are not necessarily or even usually those which confer happiness, dignity, sensitivity, a capacity to love, a sense of harmony, or a reflective mind." Therefore, the attempt to change fundamental attitudes and beliefs for the sake of material progress is not only bad economics, but also bad sociology.

Many people, of course, disagree with these views. Those who support foreign aid argue that the United States should not abandon its tradition of helping needy people. As the critics point out, however, providing food and medicine to nations hit by disasters is one thing, while continuing massive economic transfusions for every country that wants them is quite another.

Issues in Foreign Aid

What are some of the economic issues that arise in the provision of foreign aid? The basic questions involve the kinds, amounts, conditions, and forms of aid that should be given.

1. Projects or Programs? Should the United States confine its aid to specific capital projects, or should it provide aid for general programs? The World Bank, the U.S. Congress, and AID have tended to follow the project approach. This is because specific projects appear more concrete and less wasteful. Economists, however (including those at AID), tend to prefer the program approach. The reason is that it permits greater flexibility, a more general use of the underdeveloped country's resources, and a recognition that capital projects that are really needed will probably be undertaken sooner or later anyhow. This latter view seems to make more sense. In the long run, a nation's economic development is not dependent on single projects. Rather, it depends on a total program whose effectiveness is determined by how it manages its own general resources.

2. How Much Aid Should the United States Give?
Various criteria for granting aid have been proposed. For example:

- Aid should be provided until income per capita in the recipient country has been raised by a certain percentage.

- Sufficient aid should be given to make up a deficit in the recipient country's balance of payments. In simplest terms, this means that, when a nation's outflow of money exceeds the inflow, foreign aid should make up the difference. (This assumes, as is usually the case, that the recipient country tries to maintain a stable world price for its currency.)

- Aid should be provided in proportion to a recipient country's needs as measured by its income per capita.

No matter how rational these and other criteria may seem, they ignore the fact that foreign aid is often more a tool of foreign policy than an application of economic logic. Demonstrations outside an American embassy, the destruction of a U.S. government facility, or the thwarting of a communist coup can influence congressional appropriations for assistance more than the rational dictates of economic experts.

3. Should Conditions Be Imposed on Foreign Aid?
Many political leaders feel that assistance should be provided to any poor country that is trying to improve its economic position. But problems and dilemmas of a political and quasi-political nature tend to cloud this simple criterion. For instance, consider the following questions:

- Should aid be given to some communist countries, such as Poland or Yugoslavia, but not to others, such as China or Cuba?

- Should we confine aid only to the noncommunist countries?

- Should we see to it that the benefits of aid to a given country are spread throughout the society rather than being concentrated in a single socioeconomic class?

- Should aid be given only to countries that accomplish reforms (such as tax, budget, and land reforms), or should it be given without restriction?

4. Should Foreign Aid Take the Form of Loans or Grants?
The answer to this question involves not only economic considerations but moral, ethical, and social ones as well. In many Muslim countries, for instance, charging interest on loans carries an unfavorable connotation because it implies that the lender is taking unfair advantage of the distress of the borrower.

Nevertheless, some guide for policy decisions is needed. Perhaps the most feasible guide is an "international welfare criterion." This might be a standard that provides grants to countries whose per-capita incomes are below a specified level and loans to countries above that level. In the past, our foreign-aid policies have often been inconsistent in the use of this or any other standard.

In conclusion:

Experience shows that average growth rates of many underdeveloped countries have sometimes been extremely impressive for as much as a decade or more. But averages can be deceptive. Actually, there is still a wide disparity in performance among the underdeveloped nations and regions of the world. Studies of the development process indicate that some foreign assistance *in conjunction with* private investment may be necessary if the LDCs are to make the most effective use of their human and material resources.

Newly Industrializing Countries: The Pacific Rim

Among the LDCs are countries that are undergoing rapid economic growth. They are referred to as the *newly industrializing countries* (NICs). Notable examples are the Pacific Rim economies of Hong Kong, Singapore, South Korea, and Taiwan. Known collectively as the "gang of four" and the "four tigers," they have experienced phenomenal growth rates averaging 8% to 11% annually since the 1970s, as the article on the following page illustrates.

What You Have Learned

1. The per-capita income gap between the richest nations and the poorest nations appears to be widening over the long run. This is due to differences in the factors that account for economic development. Among them: the quantity and quality of human and natural resources, the rate of capital accumulation, the degree of specialization and scale of production, the rate of technological progress, and the environmental (political, social, cultural, and economic) framework.

2. The economic process of development can be analyzed within a framework of certain fundamental ideas. Some of the more important are these:

(a) The need for an agricultural revolution to release underemployed resources for industrialization.

(b) The need to reduce birth rates so as to relieve the pressure of population against resources.

(c) The recognition that while investment in physical capital is necessary, that physical capital alone will not stimulate development.

(d) The realization that investment in human capital, as well as in physical capital, is important.

(e) The distinction between labor-intensive and capital-intensive projects.

(f) The possible superiority of small-scale over large-scale projects.

(g) The distinction between private and social profitability, which is a useful guide for judging the desirability of an investment project.

3. One of the ways in which LDCs can acquire capital is by attracting private foreign investment. This requires that LDCs adopt measures that will create a favorable climate for investment. Examples of such measures are provisions for the following:

(a) Infrastructure facilities.

(b) Insurance protection for life and property.

(c) Guarantees against nationalization.

(d) Profit and capital transfers.

(e) Tax concessions.

4. Another way in which LDCs can acquire capital as well as technical assistance is through foreign aid. The World Bank (a United Nations organization established after World War II), with its affiliates, helps to finance loans for investment projects in underdeveloped countries. The United States, through its technical cooperation and assistance programs, has also been a source of foreign aid. So have many other countries, including the Soviet Union and China.

5. A number of problems and dilemmas of foreign aid are of continuous concern to government officials. They involve such issues as these:

(a) The purposes for which aid should be given.

(b) The amount of aid to be provided.

(c) The conditions under which aid should be extended.

(d) The forms that aid may take.

Because political and foreign-policy considerations play a significant role in foreign aid, it is probably impossible to establish a firm set of guidelines that will be applicable in all situations.

Terms and Concepts To Review

less developed countries	foreign aid
disguised unemployment	International Bank for Reconstruction and Development
economic development	
private rate of return	International Development Cooperation Agency
social rate of return	
infrastructure	
newly industrialized country (NIC)	

For Discussion

1. It is sometimes suggested that underdeveloped nations that are seeking to industrialize should simply follow the historical paths taken by the more advanced nations.

Economics in the News

America's New Frontier

Reported from
WASHINGTON, HONG KONG and
SINGAPORE

A new frontier that offers the United States boundless opportunities combined with great hazards is opening up thousands of miles from American shores.

This new frontier lies along a vast rim of the far Pacific, stretching from South Korea in the north to New Zealand in the south.

Dynamic growth is the hallmark of most of the countries in this sweeping Pacific arc, in contrast with the stagnation that plagues America's traditional partners in Western Europe.

East Asian nations, which not long ago were counted among the more backward, are emerging as dramatically expanding markets as well as tough competitors for the United States.

Already, the impact of this phenomenon on the nation's global posture is evident—

— Economically, America's focus internationally is shifting from Western Europe to East Asia. Two-way trade across the Pacific now surpasses transatlantic trade between the U.S. and Europe.

— Politically, the first modest steps are being taken to develop a loose regional grouping to promote cooperation and minimize the dangers of friction among nations of the Pacific basin.

What is transforming America's relationship with the Pacific region is an economic miracle that started in Japan and is spreading to one country after another. South Korea, Taiwan, Hong Kong and Singapore have become mini-Japans, with vigorous growth, rising affluence and modern industries that compete aggressively in world markets.

Since 1978, U.S. trade has expanded on a spectacular scale—by more than 75 percent—with 12 friendly countries that ring the far Pacific.

Nations of the Pacific Rim

	People (millions)	Land (square miles)	Output per person (dollars)	Exports to U.S. (billions of dollars)	Imports from U.S. (billions of dollars)
Australia	15.5	2,969,228	$11,140	$2.2	$4.0
China	1,034.5	3,705,600	310	2.2	2.2
Hong Kong	5.4	400	5,340	6.4	2.6
Indonesia	161.6	735,809	580	5.3	1.5
Japan	119.9	142,963	10,080	41.2	21.9
Malaysia	15.3	128,367	$790	1.0	1.1
New Zealand	3.2	103,555	7,920	0.7	0.6
Phillippines	54.5	115,970	820	2.0	1.8
Singapore	2.5	239	5,910	2.9	3.8
South Korea	42.0	180	1,910	7.1	5.9
Taiwan	19.2	12,452	2,505	11.2	4.7
Thailand	51.7	198,721	790	1.0	1.1

*NOTE: Trade figures are for 1983; output figures for 1982. Population totals are latest 1984 estimates.

After all, why not benefit from the experiences of others?   Evaluate this argument.

2. In the early years of America's post – World War II aid program (1945 – 1955), it was argued by many critics that the provision of health and sanitation facilities to LDCs would worsen their situation rather than improve it. The reason is that health and sanitation programs would *reduce* the LDCs' death rates.   This argument is still heard today.   Can you explain the logic of it?

3. Among the early investments commonly undertaken by LDCs are (a) an international airline and (b) a steel mill.   Does this make sense?   Explain.

4. Rapid economic development requires that a nation save and invest a substantial proportion of its income. What would you advise for the many LDCs whose savings rates are low or virtually zero because the great majority of their population is close to starvation?

5. "Rapid population growth is by far the single most serious obstacle to overcome as far as most LDCs are concerned."   Can you suggest some *economic* approaches to the solution of this problem?

6. Much foreign aid to LDCs is in the form of military aid.   Does this tend to stimulate their economies?   If so, why do some critics object to such aid?   If not, why is such aid given?   Discuss.

Chapter 33

Marxism and Socialism

Learning Guide

Watch for answers to these important questions

Who was Karl Marx? What radical theories did he propose that have become the ideology of more than one-third of the inhabited globe?

What are the strengths and weaknesses of Marx's theories? What can we gain from understanding them?

How do concepts of socialism and radicalism today differ from those developed by Marx in the third quarter of the nineteenth century?

Toward the middle of the nineteenth century, there occurred in Europe a series of events that strongly influenced the future course of the world.

In December 1847, on one of London's typically damp and cold winter days, a small but clamorous group of labor leaders met at a convention of the newly formed Communist League. There were strong currents of anxiety and trepidation in the air, for although England was relatively calm at the time, the Continent was on the verge of an upheaval. Through an almost continuous belt stretching from France to Russia, there was seething discontent over the long-prevailing miseries of poverty, injustice, and political and social intolerance. No one doubted that a series of revolutions would sweep Europe in the coming months.

Marxian Beginnings

Among those who attended this historic meeting were two relatively young and unknown radical intellectuals. One was Karl Marx, aged twenty-nine; the other was his close friend and associate, Friedrich Engels, aged twenty-seven. They had been commissioned by the League to prepare a statement of principles and a program for action that would help incite the masses and foment revolt against the existing order of society. Their tract opened with the following inflammatory, dramatic, and ominous words:

> A spectre is haunting Europe—the spectre of Communism. All the powers of old Europe have entered into a Holy Alliance to exorcise this spectre; Pope and Czar, Metternich and Guizot, French radicals and German police-spies.

After pages of historical analyses and predictions, their treatise ended with the following exhortation:

> The Communists disdain to conceal their views and aims. They openly declare that their ends can be attained only by the forcible overthrow of all existing social conditions. Let the ruling classes tremble at a Communist revolution. The proletarians have nothing to lose but their chains. They have a world to win.
> WORKING MEN OF ALL COUNTRIES, UNITE!

In the following month, January 1848, this statement of principles and objectives was published as a pamphlet under the title *Communist Manifesto*. It is significant not for its economic content, for it had practically none. Its importance lies in the manner in which it presented Marx as a brilliant and forceful revolutionary.

But there is another side to Marx—that of a painstaking scholar and deep philosophical economist—which is of much greater significance. In most of the three decades that followed publication of the *Communist Manifesto*, Marx devoted almost all his working time to developing an extensive and extraordinary "scientific" theory, which was eventually published as a mammoth treatise entitled *Das Kapital* (translated *Capital*) (vol. I, 1867). This was the "Doomsday Book of Capitalism"—a powerfully written work in which Marx predicted the revolutionary overthrow of the capitalistic system and its ultimate replacement by a *classless society*. This society would be composed only of workers, or proletarians, who would own and operate the means of production for the benefit of all.

Marx called this ultimate state "communism." He did this in order to distinguish it from various "unscientific" ideas of socialism, such as *utopian* (voluntary and democratic) *socialism*, that existed during his time. Much of the spirit of his ideas was incorporated in the Russian, Chinese, and Cuban revolutionary versions of communism that were established in the twentieth century.

In some Western nations, by contrast, various evolutionary or moderate Marxian systems were also founded, represented by social-democratic types of political parties. These groups have preferred to retain the title of "socialism" in order to help bridge the gap between certain features of Marxian theory and the rest of the socialist movement.

In general:

> Marxism is by far the most significant and enduring of various radical philosophies that emerged during the nineteenth century as a reaction to capitalism. Indeed, *Marxian views, in one form or another, are the basic ideology of more than one-third of the inhabited globe.*

The Economic Theories of Karl Marx

We can get a good overview of Marx's thinking by examining briefly the fundamental doctrines that appear in his enormous work *Das Kapital*:

1. Economic interpretation of history.

2. Theory of value and wages.

3. Surplus value and capital accumulation.

4. The class struggle.

5. Theory of socialistic and communistic evolution.

These doctrines constitute the framework of Marxian theory. Although they are attributed to Marx, they were formulated during his many years of association with his close friend and intellectual collaborator, Friedrich Engels. Each man had a profound influence on the other.

Economic Interpretation of History

Marx sought to discover the basic principles of history. His method was to construct what he regarded as a completely logical system in which he presented in scientific fashion the laws of historical development, the sources of economic and social power, and a prediction of the inevitable future.

In order to predict future events, Marx had to understand the causal forces that were at work. This, he believed, could only be done by studying the past. Hence, he looked for the fundamental causes of historical events, and he found them in the economic environments in which societies develop.

According to Marx, all great political, social, intellectual, and ethical movements of history are determined by the ways in which societies oganize their social institutions to carry on the basic economic activities of production, exchange, distribution, and consumption of goods. Although economic motives may not always be the sole cause of human behavior, every fundamental historical development is basically the result of changes in the way in which one or more of these economic activities is carried out. This in essence, is the *economic interpretation of history*.

Thus, in the Marxian system, economic forces are the prime cause of change, and they operate with the inevitability of natural laws to determine the development of a society. Even the Protestant Reformation of the sixteenth century, which was a major religious movement in world history, was cloaked in ideological veils, according to Marx. These veils, he argued, concealed its true causes, which were basically economic.

Dialectical Materialism

Marx's philosophy became known as *dialectical materialism*. This expression means that historical change is the result of conflicting forces, which are basically economic or materialistic. Thus in the Marxian view of history, every economic system, based on a set of established production, exchange, distribution, and consumption relationships, grows to a state of maximum efficiency. It then develops internal contradictions or weaknesses that cause it to decay. By this time, the roots of an opposing system have already begun to take hold. Eventually this new system displaces the old one while absorbing its most useful features. This dynamic interaction and reconciliation of opposites continues, with society being propelled from one historical stage to another as each new system triumphs over the old.

Theory of Value and Wages

The second major doctrine in Marxian economics is the theory of value and wages. This was also a fundamental area of concern to the classical economists who preceded Marx—including Smith, Ricardo, and others. But Marx, unlike the classical economists, used these concepts to a different end in explaining the historical development and future course of capitalism.

To Marx, the term "value" had the same meaning as it has had to other orthodox economists both before and since. *Value* is the power of a commodity to command other commodities in exchange for itself. This power is measured by the proportional quantities in which a commodity exchanges with all other commodities. Likewise, to Marx and other economists, the *price* of a commodity is its power to command money in exchange for itself. Price is the "money name" of the value of a commodity.

But what determines the value of a commodity? The answer, said Marx, is labor. In his words:

That which determines the magnitude of the value of any article is the amount of . . . labor-time socially necessary for its production. . . . Commodities, therefore, in which equal quantities of labor are embodied, or which can be produced in the same time, have the same value. The value of one commodity is to the value of another, as the labor-time necessary for the production of one is to that necessary for the production of the other. As values, all commodities are only definite masses of congealed labor-time.

In general terms, therefore, if it takes twice as much labor-time to produce coats as hats, the price of coats will be twice the price of hats. Marx did not restrict his concept of labor-time to direct or current labor spent on the production of commodities. He included indirect or "congealed" labor as well. This consists of the labor-time necessary to construct the factories and machines that are then used to produce other goods.

From Marx's theory of value, it was a short step to his theory of wages. In his view, a mature capitalistic society consists of only two classes. One of these is a capitalist class, which owns and controls the means of production. The other is a working class, which owns and controls nothing and is subservient to the capitalist class. (The land-owning class, at this relatively advanced stage of capitalism's development, had been absorbed by the capitalist class and had declined to a position of minor importance.) This led Marx to the following theory of wages:

> The capitalist class finds, in its competitive struggle to earn profits, that it must pay the lowest possible level of wages to the working class. The wages it will pay, therefore, will be at a subsistence level. This is a wage level that is just high enough for the working population to maintain itself, based primarily on its physical or biological needs and to a lesser extent on its social and customary needs.

This theory of wages, it may be noted, did not originate with Marx. It was a **subsistence theory of wages,** which had been formulated by earlier classical economists, and which Marx adopted from them.

Theory of Surplus Value and Capital Accumulation

When Marx combined his theories of value and wages, the logical outcome was the third feature of his theoretical system: the doctrine of surplus value. From this, there emerged the natural process of capital accumulation.

Surplus Value

In Marx's model, surplus value arises in the following way. When workers are employed in the production of a commodity, it is the capitalist who sets the length of the working day. Thus, on the one hand, the value of what the workers produce is determined by the labor-time embodied in the commodity. On the other hand, the wage that the workers receive is determined by the "subsistence level" of living. The workers do not stop producing when the value of what they create is equal to their subsistence wage. Instead they continue to produce, and the value that they create over and above their subsistence wage represents "surplus value," which goes to the capitalist. In numerical terms, the capitalist may set the working day at 12 hours, but the workers may each produce a value equal to their subsistence wage in 7 hours. The remaining 5 hours of their labor-time is, therefore, surplus value, which is literally appropriated or stolen by the capitalist.

To Marx, surplus value is the driving force of the capitalistic system—the key incentive that prompts capitalists to carry on production. Efforts on the part of capitalists to increase surplus value may take various forms. Among them:

- Increasing the length of the working day.

- Intensifying or speeding up the workers' production (by offering "piece rates" or other incentives).

- Introducing labor-saving machinery, thereby permitting the release of some workers while those who remain are made to work longer hours or more intensively.

Capital Accumulation

What do capitalists do with the surplus value that, according to Marx, has been literally stolen from the labor of workers? Marx's answer is that capitalists use part of the surplus for their personal consumption and part to acquire more labor and machines. They acquire these, of course, because they expect to get back more money than they lay out. The inflow of surpluses, over and above the capitalists' money outlays, continues in an unending series from one production operation to the next, thereby generating a sequence of capital accumulations.

Thus, mainstream classical economists of the nineteenth century contended that capitalists were engaging in "saving" when they acquired funds to hire more labor for production. Marx, on the other hand, argued that the funds which capitalists "saved" were stolen from workers in the form of surplus value.

These ideas, which lie at the heart of the Marxian model of capitalism, may be summarized briefly:

> **Surplus value** is the difference between the value that workers create (as determined by the labor-time embodied in a commodity that they produce) and the value that they receive (as determined by the subsistence level of wages). Surplus value is not created by capitalists; it is appropriated by them through their exploitation of the worker. Hence, capitalists are robbers who steal the fruits of the laborers' toil. The accumulation of capital comes from surplus value and is the key to, as well as the incentive for, the development of a capitalistic system.

It is interesting to note that Marx harbored no particular animosity toward capitalists as such, even though he characterized them as greedy robber barons. In Marx's view, it was the competitive capitalistic system itself that was evil. Capitalists were merely participants in the great race. They had to exploit and accumulate or else they would be exploited and their assets would be accumulated by others.

The Class Struggle

What are the consequences of capitalistic production? In order to answer this question, Marx turned to an examination of the past and again used the method of dialectical analysis — interaction and reconciliation of opposites — to interpret the historical process.

All history, he said, is composed of struggles between classes. In ancient Rome, it was a struggle between patricians and plebeians and between masters and slaves. In the Middle Ages, it was conflict between guildmasters and journeymen and between lords and serfs. And in the modern society that has sprouted from the ruins of feudal society, class antagonisms have narrowed down to a struggle between two opposing groups — the oppressing capitalist class or bourgeoisie and the oppressed working class or proletariat. The former derive their income from *owning* the means of production and from exploiting the labor of workers. The latter own nothing but their labor power and, because they are dependent for a living upon the receipt of a wage, they must sell their labor power in order to exist.

What is the role of the state in this two-class society? Marx's answer was precise: "The state," he said, "is nothing but the organized collective power of the possessing classes." It is an agency controlled by the bourgeoisie to advance its own interests, and its power "grows stronger in proportion as the class antagonisms with the state grow sharper." The state, in short, is an agency of oppression.

The Consequences of Capitalist Production

The class struggle might go on indefinitely, according to Marx, were it not for certain "contradictions" that automatically and inevitably develop within the capitalistic system. Among the more important ones are these:

Increasing Unemployment The capitalists' drive to increase their surplus value and to accumulate capital results in the displacement of labor. This, in modern terminology, is **structural** (including *technological*) **unemployment**. It leads to ever-increasing misery as a "reserve army of the unemployed" builds up.

Declining Rate of Profits As capital accumulates, a growing proportion of it goes into physical capital, such as labor-saving machinery, which yields no surplus value. A declining proportion of it goes into human capital or labor, which is the sole producer of surplus value. Hence, the capitalists' rate of profit — or the surplus value that they appropriate from labor — tends to be a declining percentage of the total capital that is accumulated.

Business Cycles With increasing unemployment, a declining rate of profit, and the tendency for wages to remain at the subsistence level, uncertainty and instability are inevitable. Depressions recur "each time more threateningly" as capitalists find themselves under continual competitive pressure to acquire more capital and to displace workers.

Concentration and Monopolization of Capital Competition among capitalists thus becomes increasingly intense. A dog-eat-dog situation develops as small capitalists are either fatally weakened or absorbed by larger ones. In this way, capital becomes concentrated in large-scale industrial units or monopolies. As Marx put it, "hand in hand with this centralization" of capital goes the "expropriation of many capitalists by the few."

Finance Capitalism and Imperialism Marx implied that a fifth "contradiction" would emerge from the monopoly stage of capitalistic development. The nature of this contradiction was amplified in the early twentieth century by V. I. Lenin, the founder of the USSR. Lenin argued that the growing tendency toward concentration and monopolization of capital would produce an economy dominated by "finance capital." In such a situation, huge business trusts or monopolies, in conjunction with a handful of large banks, control and manipulate the masses. Those who manage finance capital will then reach out beyond their own national boundaries, forming cartels and international combines to dominate and control the markets and resources of other nations. When this happens, the economy has reached the stage of "capitalistic imperialism"—the highest stage of capitalism.

Summary

Marx concluded that these conditions, especially the first, imposed miseries and hardships on workers that they would not tolerate indefinitely. The working class, he said, would eventually revolt against the capitalist class and bring about a system in which economic justice prevails. Before we examine the nature of this change, let us summarize the foregoing Marxian ideas briefly.

The **class struggle** represents an irreconcilable clash of interests between the bourgeoisie or capitalist class and the proletariat or working class. The source of this clash is the surplus value that capitalists steal from workers. This results, over the long run, in increasing unemployment, a declining rate of profit, business cycles, concentration of capital, and finance capitalism and imperialism.

Theory of Socialist and Communist Evolution

According to Marx, the class struggle will eventually be resolved when the proletariat overthrows the bourgeoisie. When this happens, capitalism will be succeeded by socialism, which Marx regarded as a *transitory stage* on the road to communism. This stage will have two major features:

1. "Dictatorship of the Proletariat" This is a state of affairs in Marxian socialism in which the bourgeoisie has been toppled from power and is subject to the control of the working class. In other words, the "expropriators have been expropriated," and capitalists' properties are under the management of the proletariat, who are also in control of the state.

2. Payment According to Work Performed This means that laborers will earn wages, each receiving "for an equal quantity of labor an equal quantity of products," and "he who does not work shall not eat."

Leaders in Economics

Culver Pictures, Inc.

Karl Marx and his family with Friedrich Engels (right).

Karl Marx
1818–1883
Founder of "Scientific Socialism"

If it is true that people are ultimately judged by the influence of their ideas, then Karl Marx surely ranks as one of the most important people who ever lived. His thoughts have shaped the policies of nations and affected the lives of millions.

Born and educated in Germany, Marx spend most of the latter half of his life in England. Here he existed with his wife and children in the depths of poverty, depending for bare survival on two sources. One was the *New York Tribune*, from which he received small and irregular remunerations of $5 to $10 for articles that he submitted. The other was his friend, benefactor, and alter ego, Friedrich Engels. Paradoxically, this man led a double life. He was fully in accord with Marx's anticapitalistic views, yet he also managed his father's factory in Manchester and even held a seat on the Manchester Stock Exchange.

Major Works
Marx sacrificed everything for his research, an activity that engaged his full time and effort from morning until night in the great library of the British Museum. The result, after many years of painstaking work, was the publication, in 1867, of Volume I of his enormous treatise, *Das Kapital*. But his health was never good. In 1883 after a life of extraordinary hardship, intense devotion to family, and a consuming commitment to scholarly research, he died.

Engels labored on Marx's notes for the next several years, thereby making possible the publication of volumes II and III of *Das Kapital* (1885, 1894). Four additional volumes under other titles were published in later years from still other notes. On the basis of these and other writings, Marx has come to be regarded as an economist of major significance.

Keep in mind, however, that it was Lenin, not Marx, who fashioned the content of communism. Marx predicted its eventual occurrence, but it remained for Lenin to design the structure. This he did in his writings and speeches during the first two decades of the present century, and in his founding of the USSR after the Russian Revolution of 1917.

Socialism, in Marxian ideology, may thus be defined as a transitory stage between capitalism and full communism. That is, *Marxian socialism* is a stage in which the means of production are owned by the state, the state in turn is controlled by workers ("dictatorship of the proletariat"), and the economy's social output is distributed by the formula, "From each according to his ability, to each according to his labor."

Communism, in Marxian ideology, is the final, perfect goal of historical development. It means:

1. A classless society in which all people live by earning and no person lives by owning.

2. The state is nonexistent, having been relegated to the museum of antiquities "along with the bronze ax and the spinning wheel."

3. The wage system is abolished and all citizens live and work according to the formula, "From each according to his ability, to each according to his needs."

This last quotation, it may be noted, represents the essence of pure communism.

Evaluation of Marxian Theory

Now that we have sketched the main features of Marxian theory, it is appropriate to discuss its achievements and failures. It is evident that Marx sought to reach three major objectives:

1. To develop a *theory of history* that would explain the causes of capitalistic development.

2. To formulate *theories of value, wages, and surplus value* that would describe the basic processes at work in the capitalistic economy.

3. To establish a foundation for *revolutionary socialism and communism*.

We will evaluate Marx's theories in terms of these objectives.

Theory of History

As you recall, Marx's interpretation of history was based on conflict between opposing *economic* forces. Although he recognized that political, social, and other factors influenced historical development, he regarded them as distinctly subordinate. To him, the basic or causal forces were fundamentally economic, those central to the activities and institutions of production, exchange, distribution, and consumption of goods.

Critics have pointed out that this is a one-sided, oversimplified interpretation. It leaves out, or fails to give sufficient weight to, the many noneconomic forces and institutions in history. Despite this criticism, many distinguished historians through the years have concurred with Marx's view. They have believed that Marx's interpretation of history provided the first deep awareness of the importance of economic forces in the historical process.

In the past several decades, modern historians have increasingly incorporated economic causation in their historical studies. Although it cannot be said that Marx was solely responsible for this trend, there is general agreement that his approach to the study of history played a significant role.

Theories of Value, Wages, and Surplus Value

Marx's theory of value, we have seen, was a *labor* theory of value. In essence, his argument can be stated in the form of a syllogism. This is a type of reasoning in formal logic consisting of two assumptions and a logical conclusion that follows directly from them. Thus, according to Marx:

Labor creates all value.

Labor does not receive all the value it has created.

Therefore, labor is being cheated.

It should be remembered that, according to Marx, the first assumption is true because capital and all other commodities are nothing more than congealed labor. The second assumption is true because labor receives only a subsistence wage, which is less than the value it creates. And the conclusion is true because capitalists appropriate the surplus value of labor for themselves.

Was Marx correct in his assumptions? We can answer this question by offering the following criticisms of his ideas.

Neglect of Entrepreneurial Functions

By attributing all value to labor alone, Marx neglected the functions performed by the entrepreneur as a risk taker and organizer of the factors of production. Without the entrepreneur, labor would be an amorphous mass. It is the entrepreneur who gives "shape and form" to labor by bringing workers together, providing them with capital, and giving them an incentive for working. In a socialistic or communistic society, these functions might be performed by the government or by a committee of workers, but they are functions that must be performed.

Failure to Recognize Demand

Marx's theory of value, based as it was on the labor-time embodied in a commodity, failed to recognize that the normal value of a good is as much a result of demand as of supply. In a competitive capitalistic system, as you already know, the concept of long-run normal value is that of an equilibrium value or price. It reflects diverse consumer demands bidding for the services and products of scarce factors of production. This means that consumers express their preferences through the price system. In that way prices serve the function of inducing both human and nonhuman resources into production. Marx did not fully understand this role of the price system. Hence his theory of value provided an inaccurate and unrealistic measure of the real values at which commodities are exchanged.

Inadequate Analytical Support of Surplus Value

Surplus value, according to Marx, arises because workers are paid a subsistence wage that is less than the value of the commodities that they create. The question we must now ask is whether this theory of surplus value is plausible. The answer appears to be *no*, for the following reasons:

1. Definition of Subsistence Is Vague Marx did not use the concept of subsistence in a consistent manner, nor did he define it as a determinate quantity. At certain times, he employed the term in a biological sense to refer to the goods needed for physical well-being. At other times, he used it to mean the "conventional" goods to which people become "socially accustomed."

2. Competition Will Eliminate the Surplus Marx placed strong emphasis on the competitive forces that exist in a capitalistic society — and in particular on the highly competitive relationships among capitalists themselves. If wages are sufficiently flexible to adjust to the "socially accustomed" level of living, there is every reason to believe that the surplus itself will be eliminated as capitalist employers bid higher and higher wages for the services of employees. This is because, if a worker yields a surplus to a capitalist employer, it will pay for *some other* capitalist employer to hire the worker away at a higher wage. Competition among capitalists will

thus bid wages up to a level at which the surplus no longer exists.

These are among the chief reasons to conclude that Marx's theory of surplus value lacks analytical support. Further, there is no statistical evidence to indicate that there exists in the capitalistic system a fund of value of the type that Marx conceived in his concept of surplus value. Nevertheless, modern radical economists believe in the validity of the concept, as you will see later in this chapter.

Revolutionary Socialism and Communism

Marx predicted that the increasing misery of workers would prompt the proletariat to overthrow capitalism and to replace it first by socialism and then by communism. This, he said, would be the inevitable result of the "internal contradictions" that were inherent in capitalism and that would eventually destroy it.

Was Marx's prediction correct? For the most part, no — at least not in the sense that he meant. But despite the mistakes that exist in the Marxian model, the views of its author have long been accepted by hundreds of millions of people in many nations. In some totalitarian countries, his theory was adopted intact; in many nontotalitarian nations, a brand of "modified" or "revised" Marxism developed. We may refer to the latter as *post-Marxism*. This type of socialism is not necessarily antagonistic to capitalism. However, it seeks to achieve socialistic goals through a much greater degree of government regulation and control than exists in market-oriented capitalistic systems. More will be said about this later.

Conclusions: Two Questions About Marx

We may conclude this evaluation of Marxian theory by answering briefly three fundamental questions that are often asked.

Have Marx's Deductions Been Borne Out?

Some of Marx's deductions of the "economic consequences of capitalist production" have evidently not been realized.

First, the working class, far from experiencing increasing misery, has in fact experienced a long-run growth of real wages and a rising standard of living.

Second, the rate of profits has not declined, nor have business cycles been entirely an overproduction phenomenon, as Marx claimed.

Third, the workers and the capitalists, at least in the United States, have not aligned themselves into two distinct and opposing classes. Indeed, they often overlap to the extent that the great majority of corporation stockholders are also workers. In the United States, most corporate stock is owned by households, either directly or indirectly through pension funds.

There is thus no question that some of Marx's most important theoretical deductions have turned out to be wrong.

Are There Elements of Truth in Marx's Predictions?

Despite his incorrect predictions of economic events, we cannot conclude that Marx was totally wrong. Some of his prophecies contained important truths. For example:

1. It is undeniable that cyclical and structural (including technological) unemployment have continued to plague the capitalistic system.

2. There was certainly a growth in the concentration of capital and monopoly power after the time of Marx's writing during the third quarter of the nineteenth century. However, there is considerable disagreement among economists as to the direction of monopoly trends during most of the present century.

3. Although capitalism has not ended in final collapse, it was certainly dealt a serious blow in 1930. This occurred with the onset of a prolonged and desperate depression that eventually ushered in many new measures of social reform.

Some of Marx's prophecies, in short, were disturbingly accurate.

We are thus led to conclude that Marx put his finger on some of the most important economic problems of our society. Among these problems are unemployment, business cycles, and industrial concentration. Much effort has been devoted to the development of methods for remedying these ills within a framework of capitalism.

It is appropriate that we now turn our attention to examining the ways in which modern socialism — a system rooted in Marxian ideology — seeks to solve these and other economic problems.

Development and Meaning of Socialism

When the nineteenth century drew to a close, Marxism had already become an international movement of considerable significance. But it was a movement whose members had divergent viewpoints. As a result, the followers of Marx began to divide into two factions. One of these consisted of a large and heterogeneous majority called "revisionists." The other was composed of a smaller but more homogeneous minority known as "strict Marxists."

The basic philosophies of these two groups are implied by their names:

The revisionists believe that the theories of Marx must be *revised* in order to accord with conditions of the times. Revisionists argue that socialism should be achieved by peaceful and gradual means through a process of evolution rather than revolution.

The strict Marxists, on the other hand, adhere to a literal interpretation of their master's teachings. They contend that the workers of the world form one great brotherhood that must revolt in order to overthrow the capitalistic system and establish a dictatorship of the proletariat.

Since the early part of this century, the revisionists have been in control of most of the socialist parties of Western nations. Further, since the 1930s, socialistic governments have been in power at one time or another in a number of democratic countries. These include Great Britain, France, Sweden, Norway, Denmark, Australia, and New Zealand. In most of these and various other nations, socialist leaders were placed in office—and subsequently voted out of office—through free elections. This suggests that, when we talk about socialism, we are referring to *democratic* socialism of the liberal reformist type. This is distinguished from *authoritarian* socialism, such as exists in the USSR, eastern Europe, Cuba, and China.

Democratic Socialism

Modern democratic socialism became a major force in political and intellectual life in the period between the two world wars.

During the 1920s and 1930s, peaceful Marxian socialists, both in Europe and in America, launched a renewed and vigorous attack against the shortcomings of capitalism. Expressions like "economic inequality," "chronic unemployment," "private wealth and public poverty," and "degeneration of social and cultural values" became familiar shibboleths. In Europe, social democratic parties were strongly committed to revisionist Marxism, the solidarity of the working class, and the ultimate establishment of socialism by democratic means as a way of correcting the deficiencies of the capitalistic system. This was an era of great ferment in socialist activity.

Lange Model

At the same time, some economists at European and American universities began to grapple with a question that eventually evolved into one of the most interesting controversies in the history of economics. The essence of the controversy can be briefly summarized. Recall that, in the theoretical or pure model of capitalism, there are at least three important features:

1. The means of production are privately owned.
2. Product and resource prices are freely determined by supply and demand in competitive markets.
3. Resources are allocated efficiently in accordance with consumer choice.

Now, if we adopt the classical definition of socialism as an economy in which the means of production are owned by society, two questions arise:

Can a socialistic economic system, seeking to be democratic rather than authoritarian and lacking the prices that are freely established in competitive markets, achieve the same degree of efficiency in resource allocation as the pure model of capitalism? Further, can it do so without destroying the basic economic freedoms of consumer and occupational choice?

These questions, it may be noted, are the fundamental theoretical problems of democratic socialism.

Notice that the issue is complicated by the requirement that the system must remain democratic. It might be easier to achieve greater efficiencies in resource use by *telling* consumers what they can have and by *ordering* workers to their jobs, but such actions would be completely contrary to the basic philosophy of democratic socialism.

This problem became the subject of widespread discussion in the 1930s and was finally resolved in 1938 with the publication of a theoretical model of a socialist economy. The chief architect of the model was a well-known Polish economist, Oskar Lange (pronounced "Lahnga").

According to this theoretical model, a democratic socialist economy could be administered by a Central Planning Board, which would set prices *as if* the competitive market had set them. The Board would, for example, manipulate prices in the product and resource markets with the objective of equating quantities supplied with quantities demanded. This would assure that equilibrium was maintained without surpluses or shortages. In this way the Board, through *trial and error,* would guide the factors of production into their most efficient uses in accordance with the wishes expressed by households. *All this would be done through the operation of a price system that would permit freedom of consumer and occupational choice.*

This type of economy, the socialist theorists contended, would yield a double benefit.

First, it would achieve efficient resource utilization, as in the theoretical competitive model of capitalism.

Second, and simultaneously, it would overcome the major disadvantages of real-world capitalism. It would do so by bringing about (1) a more equitable distribution of income resulting from the elimination of private ownership, (2) an adjustment of production according to consumer demands, and (3) a continuous high level of employment assured by government's stable investment policies.

Conclusion: Recent Developments

After World War II (1939–1945) democratic socialism did not fully recover its prewar vigor — for three major reasons:

1. Mixed capitalistic countries of Western Europe achieved exceptionally high rates of economic growth during the postwar years. These experiences contributed greatly to discrediting the socialistic belief that capitalism was an outmoded economic system.

2. Several conservative governments in Western Europe adopted many far-reaching social-welfare measures that socialist leaders had long advocated.

3. Various nationalization policies (that is, government takeovers of major industries) in some West European nations turned out unsuccessfully. Indeed, they created problems of excessive bureaucratization and inefficiency that were worse then the problems that nationalization had been designed to solve.

These developments led to a substantial change in orthodox socialist thinking. Many social democratic parties abandoned their traditional opposition to private property and their goal of *total* social ownership. They turned their attention instead to "improving the mix" in already mixed economies. The following definition of socialism reflects the modified views of contemporary socialist thinkers:

> **Socialism** is a movement that seeks to improve economic efficiency and equity by establishing (1) public ownership of all important means of production and distribution and (2) some degree of centralized planning to determine what goods to produce, how to produce them, and to whom they should be distributed. (The precise extent of public ownership and centralized planning is not usually specified by today's socialist scholars.)

As you can see, therefore, the core of socialism is *economic.* Socialism's goal is to transform capitalism by altering its most fundamental feature — the institution of private property.

These ideas describe the type of socialism that has existed, in varying degrees, in some mixed economies during recent decades. In contrast, several command economies have adopted a different method of socialist planning that makes deliberate use of market mechanisms:

> **Market socialism** is an economic system characterized by (1) public ownership of land and capital, (2) decentralized decision-making by worker-manager committees, and (3) the use of selective market measures (such as bonuses and profit-sharing) to stimulate productivity and efficiency.

Under market socialism, profits are not viewed in the Marxian sense as evidence of labor exploitation. Instead they serve as a measure of efficiency and thereby help planners allocate the economy's resources. For example, managers use profits as a guide for determining what goods to produce and how to produce them, and government uses profits as a guide for apportioning credit to particular industries. Some of the countries that have adopted different degrees of market socialism include China, Czechoslovakia, Hungary, and Yugoslavia.

Radical Socialism: Another View

In recent decades, a new wave of radical socialism has swept across the major Western democracies. The members of this movement are mostly political and social activists who take an aggressive stand on many fundamental issues. For example, they press for greater social and economic equality, more "worker control" over economic enterprises, nationalization of large firms, and an end to war. Unlike many other socialists, the newer radicals regard centralized authority with disdain. Hence, they are not admirers of the USSR or of any system that suppresses freedom of expression.

The radical socialists have not developed a complete philosophy. However, they have many interesting things to say about economic matters. We can gain an appreciation of some of their main ideas by focusing attention on two fundamental areas: the problem of resource allocation and the nature of surplus value.

Resource Allocation: Free Markets Versus Cooperative Planning

As you have seen in a number of earlier chapters, the free market plays a central role in capitalistic societies. Through the unhampered interaction of supply and demand, the market mechanism accomplishes several major objectives:

- It provides producers with information about consumer preferences.
- It allocates society's resources in accordance with these preferences.
- It encourages the most economical choice of production techniques.
- It synthesizes the individual buying and selling decisions of millions of households and firms.

For these reasons, it is easy to understand why the free market has often been extolled by many distinguished political and economic leaders. (See, for example, Box 1.)

Box 1
The Free Market

Library of Congress   Wide World Photos

Today's radical socialists do not subscribe to the views of President Kennedy or Nobel prize winner Hayek. To the modern Marxists, the market mechanism fosters inequality and oppression rather than equity and freedom.

"The free market is not only a more efficient decision maker than even the wisest central planning body, but even more important, the free market keeps economic power widely dispersed. It is thus a vital underpinning of our democratic system."
John F. Kennedy

"I am convinced that if it were the result of deliberate human design, and if the people guided by the price changes understood that their decisions have significance far beyond their immediate aim, this mechanism would have been acclaimed as one of the greatest triumphs of the human mind. Its misfortune is the double one that it is not the product of human design and that the people guided by it usually do not know why they are made to do what they do."
Friedrich A. Hayek

Despite these apparent virtues, modern radical socialists are not persuaded that the free market is the most desirable device for allocating resources. On the contrary, they believe strongly that the market mechanism is socially and economically objectionable—even evil—for the following reasons:

Inefficiency and Instability   The free market causes unemployment and inflation. Government policies may at times succeed in reducing inefficiency and instability. But history shows that these policies are often ill conceived and improperly administered because they are designed to preserve the market mechanism rather than replace it.

Inequity   The market system perpetuates economic and social inequalities—unjustified disparities in the distribution of income, wealth, and power. Two fundamental institutions of capitalism, private property and inheritance, are among the root causes of economic inequality. In addition, a third institution—the market system—permits inequalities to continue.

Social Imbalance   The free market causes an inefficient distribution of resources between private and social goods—a lack of *social balance*. This happens because the market system, through advertising and promotion, favors the production of private goods (such as automobiles, television sets, and stereos) for which consumers can voluntarily express their preferences by prices offered. At the same time, the free market suppresses the production of social goods (such as schools, libraries, and public hospitals), which come into existence only through compulsory taxes. In other words, as a result of the market system, too much private expenditure goes to satisfy superficial wants artificially created, while many fundamental public needs are neglected because they cannot compete successfully for the same resources.

Today's radical socialists thus conclude:

The market system is inefficient, inequitable, and immoral. It perpetuates a class structure that associates wealth with privilege and poverty with oppression.

These problems cannot be solved within the framework of existing capitalistic institutions. The institutions themselves must be changed before any significant improvements in human welfare can be realized.

In other words, radical socialists believe that the market system should be replaced by some alternative decision-making process that promotes society's economic, moral, and cultural well-being.

Cooperative Planning

If free markets are strongly opposed by modern Marxists, what mechanism do they advocate for providing information and allocating resources? The most obvious answer would appear to be central planning—a method long used in varying degrees by socialistic countries. Under central planning, the government decides *what* goods will be produced, *how* they will be produced, and *to whom* the output will be distributed. At the very least, therefore, central planning requires government to exercise substantial control over most, if not all, important phases of economic activity.

This solution poses a basic problem for radical socialists. Most of them are as strongly opposed to traditional forms of central planning as to free markets. Experiences in socialistic countries show that central planning leads to bureaucracy—excessive multiplication and concentration of power in administrative bureaus—and that this results in inefficiency, waste, and authoritarian decision making.

Modern radical socialists are thus led to the conclusion that a third method of resource allocation—one that avoids what they regard as the undesirable consequences of both the free market and central planning—is needed. The method they advocate may be called "participative decision making" or "cooperative planning."

According to today's radical socialists, cooperative planning is the ideal method of resource allocation. Cooperative planning entails (1) educating people to their "true needs," (2) eliminating "economic waste" caused by unproductive labor, and (3) preserving democratic traditions through worker participation in decision making at both the company and national levels.

Adoption of cooperative planning would lead to "production for use" (rather than for profit) within a social framework oriented toward collaboration (rather than competition) for mutual benefit.

These ideas—particularly the expressions in quotation marks—require some further comment. As you will see, they are directly related to the notion of *surplus value*, a concept of fundamental importance in both Marxian and modern radical thinking.

The Nature of Surplus Value

Marx defined a society's "surplus" as the difference between the value of goods created by workers and the subsistence wage they actually receive. In other words, Marx viewed a capitalistic economy's surplus as consisting of profits, rent, and interest— the sum of which rightfully belongs to workers but is expropriated (or as Marx put it, stolen) by capitalists.

Today's new radicals believe that Marx's definition of surplus was adequate for his time, but that the concept must be broadened to reflect the greater complexity of today's advanced capitalistic economies. Accordingly, modern adherents of Marxism define economic surplus in a capitalistic society as the *difference between the market value of all final goods and services produced during a period and the socially necessary costs of producing them.* Thus, if the total market value of all final goods and services produced in the economy during a given year— called gross national product or GNP—is $1 billion, and the socially necessary costs of producing that output are $400 million, then the society's economic surplus for that year is $600 million.

The question that must be asked, of course, is what is the meaning of "socially necessary costs"? Today's Marxists define this concept for measurement purposes as the sum of three types of expenditures:

1. Replacement Investment This is the value of plant and equipment used up or depreciated each year in producing the nation's final output—its GNP. This amount of investment expenditure is thus necessary to replace that part of GNP that is worn out.

2. Payments for Productive Labor This class of expenditures consists of wages paid to workers producing "socially useful output"—an expression widely employed but not clearly defined by modern radical socialists. They hold that, in a capitalistic economy, a substantial share of the surplus is used to support largely "unproductive" activities— among them excessive advertising and administration (both in business and government). In a socialistic economy, most of these expenditures would be socially unnecessary, leaving a larger proportion of society's resources to be employed in more constructive activities.

3. Minimal Costs of Government This class of expenditures consists of those costs of government needed to provide essential services. These include education, public health, judicial administration, police and fire protection, planning, and perhaps some minimal level of national defense. (The "minimal level," however, is not clearly defined by radicals.) All other expenditures on government in capitalistic societies—such as expenditures for war and "imperialism"—are wasteful. They serve only to absorb a large part of the surplus that could better be used for producing needed social goods.

In summary, therefore:

Modern radical socialists define economic surplus as consisting not only of profits, rent, and interest, as Marx did, but also of socially unnecessary costs in both the private and the public sectors. This concept of economic surplus is, therefore, much broader than the view held by Marx. Thus,

According to Marx:

economic surplus = profits + rent + interest

According to the modern radical socialists:

economic surplus = profits + rents + interest
                          + socially unnecessary costs

What Happens to the Surplus?

Radical socialists believe that, over the long run, the economy's surplus tends to rise—both in absolute terms and as a percentage of GNP. According to some estimates, the surplus today in the United States is more than 60 percent of GNP, having risen from somewhat less than 50 percent since the 1930s.

This growing surplus, the radicals say, exists because of insufficient consumption and investment opportunities available in a mature capitalistic economy. As a result, resources are increasingly utilized in "unproductive" outlets and activities. These include:

Nonprice Competition   This consists of methods of competition that do not involve changes in selling price, such as advertising, product differentiation, superficial model changeovers, and so on.

Bureaucracy   This is the overabundance of administrative bureaus and agencies, especially in government.

War and Imperialism   "War" includes all kinds of military activities. "Imperialism" refers to the exploitation of weaker nations both by government and by large corporations, which may function together in a vast "military–industrial complex."

Radical socialists conclude that these inherent contradictions within capitalism must eventually lead to its collapse—either through revolution or war or through a fundamental transformation of its basic institutions. In fact, according to many radical socialists, the end of capitalism may already be in sight. This is evidenced by the social and economic disruption experienced by today's advanced capitalistic countries, the warlike policies that they pursue, and the growing importance to them of government.

Conclusion: Identifying Fundamental Issues

You can see from the foregoing analysis that radical economists have found much to criticize about capi-
talism's institutions and processes. What solutions to society's ills do these critics offer? The answer is not clear. Although they advocate public ownership of capital, administration by "workers' councils," and cooperative planning, these are only means toward an end. There is much that the radicals do not explain. For example:

− How can resources be allocated without markets?

− How can planning be achieved without bureaucracy?

− How can greater social and economic equality be realized without competition?

− How can collective ownership exist without destroying individual initiative?

− How can national governments of large, complex societies make important social and economic decisions without seriously impairing efficiency and democratic processes?

In view of this, what conclusion can we draw about the merits of radical socialism?

Perhaps the chief contribution of modern radicalism has been its identification of important issues. By pointing to the shortcomings of our economic system, radical socialists have made us more aware of capitalism's failure to achieve desired goals of efficiency and equity.

What You Have Learned

1. There have been a number of major reactions against capitalism. However, the Marxian reaction has had the most significant impact on the political and economic relationships of nations.

2. Karl Marx's theory of history is called "dialectical." This means that history is interpreted as the reconciliation of opposites. The approach provided much of the basis for Marx's (and Engels') theories. There are five major features of Marx's model: (a) economic interpretation of history, (b) theory of value and wages, (c) theory of surplus value and capital accumulation, (d) class struggle, and (e) theory of socialist and communist evolution.

3. Critics of Marx have pointed out major shortcomings: (a) Marx's economic interpretation of history is oversimplified and onesided—although, thanks at least in part to

Economics in the News

Is Capitalism Dying?

In Marxian theory, as well as in modern radical thinking, an advanced capitalistic economy develops certain "contradictions" which lead eventually to the system's collapse. Many of today's radicals believe that these contradictions are already apparent—as evidenced by certain developments in recent history:

Business Cycles

The depression of the early 1980s registered the highest unemployment rate since the depression of the 1930s. In accordance with Marxian logic, the sharp downturn was the result of the growing influence of two long-term trends:

1. The drive for capital accumulation, particularly labor-saving equipment, resulting in the displacement of labor and in an ever-increasing level of unemployment.

2. A declining rate of profit, arising from the inability of physical capital (as distinguished from human capital—that is, labor) to produce surplus value.

Market Concentration

With the worsening of economic conditions—manifested especially by a declining rate of profit—capitalists have sought ways to protect their self-interest by absorbing weaker firms. This has led to the concentration of capital in large-scale industrial units or monopolies.

Imperialistic Multinationalism

The effects of monopolization are ultimately realized on an international scale with the emergence of a new form of business enterprise—the multinational corporation. Operating across national boundaries, the huge multinational organizations dominate markets and control the resources of other countries. This is what Lenin called the stage of "capitalistic imperialism"—the highest and final stage of mature capitalism.

The radicals conclude that the United States entered this last stage in the 1960s, followed shortly thereafter by Japan and West Germany. Therefore, it is only a matter of time, probably not more than a few decades, before these bastions of capitalism either collapse or are drastically transformed by the internal dynamics of their own system.

Radicals base much of their belief in the eventual collapse of capitalism on a declining rate of profit. Do the data in the accompanying table support this contention? Evidently not. There is no apparent *long-term trend* toward a declining rate of profit, although there are considerable fluctuations in the ratios from one year to another.

Sales, Profits, and Stockholders' Equity, in All Manufacturing Corporations

Year	Sales (billions)	Stockholders' equity (billions)	Profit after federal income taxes (billions)	Percentage of Profits After Federal Income Taxes to	
				Sales	Stockholders' equity
1955	$ 278.4	$120.1	$15.1	5.4%	12.6%
1960	345.7	165.4	15.2	4.4	9.2
1965	492.6	211.7	27.5	5.6	13.0
1970	708.8	306.8	28.6	4.0	9.3
1975	1,065.2	423.4	49.1	4.6	11.6
1980	1,912.8	668.1	92.6	4.8	13.9
1985	2,525.1*	902.3*	83.5*	3.3	9.3

* Preliminary data
Source: U.S. Department of Commerce

Marx, there has been a growing emphasis on economic causation in modern historical studies. (b) Marx's theories of value, wages, and surplus value neglected the entrepreneurial functions, failed to recognize the role of demand in the determination of value, and rested on inadequate analytical foundations.

Despite these criticisms, evidence shows that there are some elements of truth in Marx's predictions.

4. Socialism in most of the Western world is conceived as a democratic process — in the sense that socialist leaders may be voted into or out of office in free elections. The goal of the majority of today's democratic socialists is the establishment of the "welfare state" through the electoral process rather than by revolutionary methods.

5. Some command economies have adopted market socialism. This system retains social ownership of land and capital, but makes use of market incentives to stimulate production.

6. Today's radical socialists (as distinguished from conventional democratic socialists) oppose free markets and bureaucratic central planning. They also object to what they contend are social and economic inequities inherent both in market and in command economies. Although many fundamental problems have been identified by modern radical socialists, it is not clear that their proposed methods of solution (public ownership, cooperative planning, and so forth) are superior to those available in present-day mixed economies.

Terms and Concepts To Review

economic interpretation of history	surplus value
dialectical materialism	class struggle
value	Marxian socialism
price	communism
structural unemployment	"dictatorship of the proletariat"
subsistence theory of wages	socialism

For Discussion

1. Why should a student of today be familiar with the nature and origins of radical ideas, some of which are well over a century old?

2. What is meant by an "interpretation of history"? Can you suggest several different types of interpretations? In your previous history courses in high school or college, which interpretations were stressed?

3. Marx was aware that direct labor is only one of several inputs used in production and that raw materials, machines, and other resources were also necessary. How, then, could he argue that labor alone was the basis of value?

4. According to Marx, would there be such a thing as surplus value if capitalists paid workers "what they were worth"? Explain.

5. Do you believe that there is such a thing as a "class struggle" in the Marxian sense? Why or why not? (HINT Can we divide a complex social structure into opposing subclasses? By what criteria?)

6. If we prove that Marx's theory of surplus value is logically incorrect, does this mean that workers *in fact* are not exploited in our capitalistic system? Explain by defining what you mean by "exploitation." (HINT If you were a profit-maximizing employer, would you hire someone to work for you if the added value he or she created were less than the wages you paid?)

7. What major shortcoming do you find in the Marxian model of capitalism?

8. Marxism, it has been said, is like religion: "For those who believe, no explanation is necessary; for those who do not believe, no explanation is possible. Logical arguments, therefore, are not the grounds for acceptance or rejection. It is emotion, not logic, that is the influencing factor. This is why Marxism remains as the basic ideology of several nations and many millions of people throughout the world." Do you agree? Can you add anything to the proposition?

9. Radical socialists have referred to democratic socialists as "coddlers of capitalism." Can you suggest why?

10. Is it possible to have political and social freedom in a command economy? Is it possible to have a market economy without political and social freedom? Explain.

Chapter 34

Economic Planning: The Visible Hand in Mixed and in Command Economies

Learning Guide

Watch for answers to these important questions

What is economic planning? Why do some countries engage in it?

What are econometric models? What is input–output analysis? How do some countries use these tools to facilitate economic planning?

How do the USSR and China engage in economic planning? What means are used to stimulate production? Are economic freedoms in these countries the same as, or different from, those in mixed economies?

As you know, the market system is the basis of capitalism. It is also the fundamental mechanism for allocating resources in mixed economies.

An alternative way in which a society can allocate its scarce resources is by economic planning. An **economic plan** is a detailed scheme for achieving specific objectives by governing the activities and interrelationships of those entities—firms, households, and governments—that have an influence on the desired outcome. This method of resource allocation plays an important role in command economies. However, certain types of economic plans are also employed in many mixed economies.

Why should we study economic planning? There are two reasons.

First, *planned economies*—economic systems in which the government directs resources for the purpose of deciding *what* to produce, *how* to produce it, and possibly *for whom* to produce it—play an important role in the world today.

Second, the problems that economic planning tries to solve are fundamental to every type of economic system. Therefore, an understanding of planning principles and experiences can provide us with guides for evaluating and improving public policies.

Tools of Economic Planning

If economic planning is to be effective, government efforts must be directed toward influencing behavior both at the macroeconomic and at the microeconomic level. What analytical procedures are available for such purposes? There are several, but those that have gained increasing use as tools of economic planning are econometric models and input–output analysis.

Econometric Models

If you were in a high government position responsible for overall economic planning, one of your chief functions would be to identify and analyze relations between important variables that have an influence on the economy's performance. Some examples of such variables are consumption expenditures, investment expenditures, interest rates, prices, production, money supply, employment, and productivity. How would you go about combining these and other factors into a set of meaningful relations that can be used as a guide for forecasting and planning?

One way of attacking the problem is by the use of **econometrics.** This approach integrates economic theory, mathematics, and statistics. That is, it expresses economic relations in the form of mathematical equations and verifies the resulting models by statistical methods. By constructing theoretical models that can be quantified and tested with actual data, econometrics seeks to explain economic behavior.

Econometric models were first introduced on a substantial scale during the 1930s. Among the pioneers in the field were Professors Ragnar Frisch of Norway and Jan Tinbergen of the Netherlands. In recognition of their monumental contributions, both men were honored in 1969 by being made the first recipients of the Alfred Nobel Memorial Prize in Economic Science. Today, as a result of the trailblazing efforts of Frisch and Tinbergen, large-scale econometric models have gained wide use. Consisting of hundreds of equations, they are employed as forecasting and planning devices by some corporations as well as by a number of national governments.

Planning in the Netherlands

The nation that has made the greatest use of econometrics for government planning is the Netherlands. Denmark, Norway, and Sweden have also placed heavy reliance on this planning technique. The approach used by the Dutch, however, may be regarded as typical of the way in which econometric planning procedures can be employed by a government that wishes to use them.

In the Netherlands, a Central Planning Bureau founded by Jan Tinbergen serves as the planning agency for the Dutch economy. The Bureau constructs econometric models that are designed to do two things—*forecast* and *simulate.* Both activities provide the basis for planning.

When used for forecasting, the models are employed to predict the short-term and long-term course of such economic variables as consumption expenditures, investment expenditures, prices, interest rates, and gross national product. These predictions serve the government as a guide for judging future trends in the economy.

When used for simulation, the models are employed to replicate operations within the economy and the outcomes of different policies. The government may want to know, for example, what the effects will be on total output, income, interest rates, and employment if personal income taxes are increased or decreased by specific percentages. The alternative tax rates are fed into the model, and the resulting outcomes are computed. Similarly, alternative raw-materials quantities, factory-utilization rates, and so on, are "plugged" into the model to determine how much production will be available to fulfill expected demands at specified prices.

In these ways, the Central Planning Bureau arrives at numerical estimates of the various inputs needed to reach alternative targets. The Bureau then provides the information to representatives of labor, management, and government, all of whom work together to construct a final plan.

Exhibit 1

Mathematizing the Economy — An Econometric Model

Although an econometric model is usually an elaborate system of mathematical equations, some of the flavor of econometrics can be perceived from a simple model. The following five-equation system describes a national economy:

$$\text{consumption expenditures} = a + b(\text{national income}) \tag{1}$$

$$\text{investment expenditures} = c + d(\text{profits in previous period}) \tag{2}$$

$$\text{taxes} = e(\text{gross national product}) \tag{3}$$

$$\begin{array}{l}\text{gross national} \\ \text{product}\end{array} = \left(\begin{array}{l}\text{consumption} \\ \text{expenditures}\end{array}\right) + \left(\begin{array}{l}\text{investment} \\ \text{expenditures}\end{array}\right) + \left(\begin{array}{l}\text{government} \\ \text{expenditures}\end{array}\right) \tag{4}$$

$$\text{national income} = (\text{gross national product}) - (\text{taxes}) \tag{5}$$

In these equations, each of the letters a, b, c, d, and e are mathematical constants, called parameters. Each represents some particular number derived by statistical procedures. Once the parameters are determined, the model can be "solved" by making various substitutions and calculating the results.

The first three equations in the model are "behavioral." They tell how the dependent variable on the left side behaves in relation to the independent variable on the right. Thus, the first equation states that consumption expenditures depend on — are a function of — national income. The second says that investment expenditures are a function of the previous period's profits. The third states that taxes are a function of — or some proportion of — gross national product.

The last two equations are "definitional." They express identities or truisms about the economy. Equation (4), for example, shows that gross national product is the sum of three classes of expenditures — consumption, investment, and government. Equation (5) says that national income is the difference between gross national product and taxes.

Of course, since the model is intended to be a simplification of reality, the equations necessarily omit certain components that might be included in a more detailed model. [For example, *net exports* could be added as a fourth variable on the right side of equation (4).] Nevertheless, even this basic model could be used reasonably well for forecasting the dependent variables — those on the left sides of the equal signs. First, however, good estimates must be obtained of the five parameters, a through e. It is also necessary to know the values of the two variables, "profits in the previous period," shown in equation (2), and "government expenditures," shown in equation (4). Once the forecasts are made, planning can be facilitated by organizing resources to meet desired goals.

An illustration of an econometric model is presented in Exhibit 1.

Input–Output Analysis

If the demand for automobiles were to increase by 20 percent, how much of an increase could be expected in the sales of rubber, steel, automobiles, and glass to the automobile industry? One way of answering this question would be through the use of input–output analysis.

Input–output analysis is a method of studying the interrelations between industries (or sectors) of an economy. A model in the form of a table is constructed in which each of the economy's industries is listed twice: once down the left side as a seller of outputs and once across the top as a buyer of inputs. Within the body of the table are squares called "cells," which show in numerical terms the sales–purchase relation among the industries portrayed in the model.

A highly simplified illustration of an input–output model for an economy comprising four industries is shown in Exhibit 2. A more realistic model would contain dozens or even hundreds of industries. The model is "read" in the following way:

Interpreting the Rows

Each row (reading across from left to right) shows the value of output sold by each industry at the left to the industries listed across the top of the table.

Exhibit 2
Input–Output Table for an Economy with Four Industries
(millions of dollars; hypothetical data for a given period)

An input–output table shows certain interdependencies between industries in an economy. Reading from left to right, the dollar figure in each cell tells you the *sales* (outputs) that each industry listed at the left made to the industries shown across the top. Similarly, reading down from top to bottom, the dollar figure in each cell tells you the *purchases* (inputs) that each industry shown across the top acquired from the indus-

tries listed at the left. The numbers in parentheses are called *input coefficients*. They indicate the proportions of total inputs (shown at the bottom) that the industries at the top of each column received from the industries at the left. Of course, for each industry at the top of the table, the sum of its input coefficients must equal 1 (or 100 percent).

Output (sellers) \ Input (buyers)	Rubber industry	Steel industry	Automobile industry	Glass industry	Interindustry sales total	Direct consumption*	Total output
Rubber industry	$300 (.27)	$100 (.06)	$500 (.25)		$900	$200	$1,100
Steel industry	$200 (.18)	$400 (.25)	$600 (.30)	$100 (.17)	$1,300	$300	$1,600
Automobile industry	$100 (.09)	$200 (.13)	$400 (.20)	$200 (.33)	$900	$1,100	$2,000
Glass industry			$400 (.20)	$100 (.17)	$500	$100	$600
Other resources	$500 (.45)	$900 (.56)	$100 (.05)	$200 (.33)	$1,700		$1,700
Total input	$1,100	$1,600	$2,000	$600	$5,300	$1,700	$7,000

* Consists of all other sales, including direct sales to households, government, foreign sources, and sales for capital formation (that is, investment goods).

For example, in the period covered, the rubber industry sold $300 million worth of goods to itself for further production, $100 million to the steel industry, $500 million to the automobile industry, and nothing significant to the glass industry. Thus, the interindustry sales total was $900 million. In addition, direct consumption of rubber by other sources amounted to $200 million. The rubber industry's total output was therefore $1,100 million.

The remaining rows for each industry are interpreted similarly. Thus, the dollar figure in each cell tells you how an industry's total output (shown at the right end of the table) was distributed among the various buyers listed across the top.

Interpreting the Columns

Each column (reading down from top to bottom) shows the value of input purchased by each industry at the top from the industries listed along the left side of the table. For example, in the period covered, the steel industry bought $100 million worth of goods from the rubber industry, $400 million worth of steel for its own use, $200 million worth of goods from the automobile industry, and nothing of significance from the glass industry. In addition, it purchased $900 million worth of "other resources." Therefore, the value of total input purchased by the steel industry was $1,600 million.

The remaining columns for each industry are interpreted in the same way. The dollar figure in each cell shows how an industry's total input (shown at the bottom of the table) was distributed among the various sellers listed at the left.

Calculating the Input Coefficients

With this information given, the table enables us to calculate the value of each input needed to produce an additional dollar's worth of output. The resulting numbers, called *input coefficients,* are shown in parentheses in each cell. Each input coefficient is obtained from the formula

$$\text{input coefficient} = \frac{\text{industry's specific input}}{\text{industry's total input}}$$

For example, reading down from the top of the table, the steel industry's specific input from the rubber industry was $100 million, while the steel industry's total input was $1,600 million. Therefore, the steel industry's input coefficient, IC, for rubber is

$$_{\text{STEEL}}IC_{rubber} = \frac{\$100}{\$1,600} = .06$$

Similarly, reading down again from the top of the table, the glass industry's specific input from the automobile industry was $200 million, while the glass industry's total input was $600 million. Hence, the glass industry's input coefficient for autos is

$$_{\text{GLASS}}IC_{autos} = \frac{\$200}{\$600} = .33$$

The remaining input coefficients are calculated similarly. Notice that the sum of the input coefficients in each column must equal 1.

Application to Forecasting and Planning

The input–output table can now be used to answer the question posed at the beginning of this section:

If the demand for automobiles were to increase by 20 percent, how much of an increase could be expected in the sales of rubber, steel, automobiles, and glass to the automobile industry?

A 20 percent increase in the demand for automobiles would increase their direct consumption from $1,100 million to $1,320 million. This additional output of $220 million worth of automobiles would be matched by the following input increases in the automobile industry:

rubber:	0.25 × $220 million =	$ 55 million
steel:	0.30 × $220 million =	66 million
automobiles:	0.20 × $220 million =	44 million
glass:	0.20 × $220 million =	44 million
other resources:	0.05 × $220 million =	11 million
Total value of additional inputs =		$220 million

The total value of additional inputs to the automobile industry thus equals the value of its additional output, $220 million.

As you might guess, there are also numerous secondary, tertiary, and even more remote effects on the automobile and other industries. This is because of the circular repercussions of production decisions among the industries. For example, more automobiles require more steel, rubber, and other inputs, which also require more automobiles, and so on.

You can now appreciate the usefulness of input–output analysis:

An input–output model serves two important planning functions:

1. It indicates the impacts of changes in demand on industry supplies.

2. It suggests where potential bottlenecks may arise in the flow of goods between industries.

For these reasons, input–output analysis permits planners to anticipate changes before they occur. This makes it possible to formulate plans to minimize disruptions in resource use.

Uses and Difficulties

The pioneering work on input–output analysis was done by Wassily Leontief at Harvard University. Leontief devoted most of his professional career to deriving the data needed for compiling massive input–output tables encompassing hundreds of industries. In 1973, in recognition of his scholarship, the Swedish government awarded Leontief the Nobel Prize in Economic Science. As a result of his efforts, many corporations and some governments (including the government of the USSR) today make substantial use of input–output analysis for forecasting and planning their economic activities.

Despite the advances made in input–output analysis, it still suffers from certain problems. Among them:

– The data in input–output tables are based on past relations in the economy. To be more useful for forecasting and planning, the dollar flows and co-

efficients should ideally reflect current, if not future, relations. This will be impossible, however, until more and better information, and improved methods of analyzing it, become available.

– The division of an economy into specific industries raises many problems of definition and classification. Should television production be treated as a separate industry, or should it be grouped with television equipment, electronic equipment, or communications equipment? One classification may be too narrow or refined; another, too broad or aggregated.

These and other difficulties have only retarded, rather than prevented, the implementation of input–output techniques. Much progress has already been made in overcoming these obstacles.

Conclusion: More Scientific Planning

During the past several decades, a growing number of corporations and governments have placed increasing reliance on scientific planning techniques — including econometrics and input–output analysis. The reasons can be attributed to two major factors:

1. Continuing integration of economic theory and mathematics. This makes possible the formulation of complex economic concepts in precise mathematical terms.

2. Rapid advances in computer science. This makes it possible to process and analyze huge quantities of data.

As a result, models of economic systems can now be constructed on much larger scales than was previously possible. This suggests the following conclusion:

In the final analysis, the usefulness of any model depends on the accuracy and completeness of its information. As research and data-collection methods improve, econometrics and input–output analysis will gain wider adoption as scientific planning tools in industry and government.

Leaders in Economics

AP/Wide World Photos

Ragnar Frisch
1895–1973

UPI/Bettmann Newsphotos

Jan Tinbergen
1903–

AP/Wide World Photos

Wassily Leontief
1906–

Econometrics and Input–Output Analysis

Adam Smith and Karl Marx founded systems of economic thought. Yet it is doubtful whether these intellectual giants, if they were students today, could pass a graduate course in economic theory. This is because of the two men's lack of mathematical sophistication in explaining economic ideas. Smith's *The Wealth of Nations* (1776) confines its examples to the use of arithmetic, while Marx's *Das Kapital* (vol. I, 1867) never goes beyond simple algebra. Today the highest status — not only in economics but in all the social and management sciences — is accorded those whose competence in their particular field is buttressed by the ability to use higher mathematics in formulating essential ideas.

Worldwide Recognition

The evidence of this on an international scale became apparent in 1969 when the Swedish Royal Academy of Science bestowed jointly on Norway's Ragnar Frisch and Holland's Jan Tinbergen the first Alfred Nobel Memorial Prize in Economic Science. Both men, the Academy noted, had distinguished themselves since the 1930s by developing pioneering applications of higher mathematics to economic theory and measurement — the integration of which is known as "econometrics."

In 1973 an American economist, Wassily Leontief, became another recipient of the Nobel Prize in Economic Science. Leontief was honored for his outstanding work in developing input–output analysis. This is a highly sophisticated approach to studying complex relationships among industries, regions, and sectors of an economy.

Modern Tools

Today econometrics and input–output analysis are standard tools for forecasting and planning in various countries. As societies become more complex, these tools and other procedures employing advanced mathematical techniques will gain increasing use by governments and corporations.

It is significant to note that econometrics, input–output analysis, and related techniques are more than just analytical tools. As a result of their development and implementation, the nature of economics has changed dramatically in recent decades.

Planning in the USSR

Any study of economic planning would be incomplete without a discussion of the USSR. This nation has been actively engaged in planning longer than any other country.

The USSR came into existence opposed to capitalism. In November 1917, the revolutionary Bolshevik (later known as Communist) party of Russia, under the leadership of V. I. Lenin, overthrew the government and, five years later, established the Union of Soviet Socialist Republics. The ultimate objective of the party, which identified itself with the "dictatorship of the proletariat," was to establish Marxian socialism and eventually full communism in the Soviet Union and throughout the world. This, it was said, would end the "want, misery, and injustice of capitalist society."

Has this goal been achieved? We can answer the question by examining the present structure of the Soviet economy within a framework of three distinguishing features:

1. Soviet economic institutions and organization.
2. Soviet economic planning.
3. Soviet accomplishments and failures.

Soviet Economic Institutions and Organization

Every society is characterized by certain institutions—established ways of doing things based on customs, practices, or laws. Acting in combination, these institutions affect the society's organizational structure. We examine here the more important institutions in the Soviet economy.

Social Ownership of Industry

The Soviet Union defines its economic system as socialist, not communist. Socialism, according to Marxian doctrine, is a preparatory stage in the attainment of full communism. Unlike the United States, therefore, all means of industrial production in the USSR that require the use of hired labor are owned by "society," represented by the government. Although some people, such as professionals and artisans, can work for themselves, they must do so without the help of hired labor. Except for a few special cases (for example, domestic servants), no person may employ another for a wage.

Public ownership in the Soviet Union does not apply to consumer goods. Virtually all consumer goods are privately owned. And, as in the United States, people may own automobiles, houses, furniture, clothing, government bonds, savings deposits, and so on.

Social Ownership of Agriculture

Agriculture in the USSR is organized along somewhat more complex lines. Two types of farms are in operation, both types socially owned:

1. **State Farms** These are agricultural lands owned and operated as state enterprises under government-appointed managing directors. Workers and administrators are hired to run the farms. They are usually paid set wages and, if their work exceeds basic norms of output, they receive bonuses as well.

2. **Collective Farms** These are agricultural cooperatives. They consist of communities of farmers who pool their resources, lease land from the government on a long-term basis, and divide the profits among the members according to the amount and kind of work done by each. Collective farms, which are subject to detailed government regulation, are the dominant form of agriculture in the Soviet Union.

Collective farms were introduced in the late 1920s as a compromise between socialistic principles and political expediency. They were meant to reduce the hostile resistance of the agrarian class (at that time about 80 percent of the Soviet population) to total centralization and control of agriculture. Under the collectivization laws, the farms must sell the bulk of their output to the government at low, pre-set prices. However, they can dipose of the rest of their output as they wish — usually through farmers' markets or bazaars. These are free markets where prices and quality are generally higher than in government stores.

Economic Incentives

A fundamental feature of the Soviet economy is its widespread use of monetary rewards. They are used to induce people to exert the efforts needed to accomplish specific tasks. Two major forms of economic incentive exist:

1. Differential Rewards These are paid to people in occupations requiring different skills. For example, within the high-income groups are research scientists, ballet and opera stars, and university professors of science. In the middle-income groups are engineers, physicians, teachers, and skilled workers. In the lower-income groups are technicians, semi-skilled workers, and unskilled workers.

2. Productivity Incentives These are provided for workers and managers alike. For workers in industry and on state farms, basic pay rates are usually calculated not in relation to the number of hours of work but in relation to the number of units produced. In addition, special graduated rates are paid to those who exceed the norm. (It is interesting to note that, in the United States and other noncommunist countries, piecework payments of this type have long been bitterly criticized by labor unions as exploitative.) Management incentives, on the other hand, consist of bonuses and various types of fringe benefits, including housing and free meals at the plant.

Are economic incentives of this type contrary to Marxian thinking? The Soviets think not:

In a *socialistic* society, the Soviet planners say, people have not yet been prepared for full communism. Therefore, incentives may be needed to persuade individuals to produce at their full potential.

Freedom of Consumer and Occupational Choice

In the competitive model of capitalism, there is *both consumer sovereignty and freedom of consumer choice*. That is, consumers register their demands for goods through the price system, and producers compete with one another to fulfill those demands. In such a system the consumer is theoretically king. This means that consumers not only decide *what* goods are produced but also are free to choose *how much* they want from the supplies that are available.

In the Soviet economy, the state decides which consumer goods, and how much of each good, will be produced (except for the free-market portion of goods produced by collective farms). The state then places these goods in government stores — normally without rationing — at equilibrium prices that it believes will clear the market in a given period of time. Consumers are free to purchase the products or not, as they see fit, at the established prices. Therefore, it is correct to say that, generally speaking, *there is freedom of consumer choice in the Soviet Union, but there is not consumer sovereignty.*

Under normal conditions, there is also *freedom of occupational choice*. As was suggested above, the state sets differential wage and salary structures according to types of occupation, skill, geographic location, and other conditions. Workers are largely free to apply for the kinds of jobs for which they can qualify.

Broadly speaking, therefore:

Soviet households have much the same freedoms of consumer and occupational choice as do households in the United States and most other countries. Although there are exceptions, the Soviet leaders have found through hard experience that the preservation of such freedoms provides for more orderly markets and much greater administrative efficiency.

Taxes

Taxes in the Soviet Union, as a percentage of national income, are much higher than in the United States. They are also higher than in most other countries. This is because the Soviet government does most of the economy's spending. Government expenditures include: military outlays; welfare spending on socialized medicine, free education, and numerous other benefits. Government also operates all state enterprises and finances most new investment in the economy. What are the chief sources of the revenue that pays for these expenditures? In the United States, it would be primarily a graduated personal income tax and to a lesser extent a corporation income tax. In contrast:

The bulk of the Soviet government's revenue comes from a profits tax on state enterprises and a sales tax—called a "turnover" tax—on goods sold to the public. Although the rates vary, the profits tax has tended to bring in about 40 percent of the state's annual revenue and the sales tax about 30 percent. The government's remaining revenue comes from other taxes.

Soviet Economic Planning

The USSR has been a planned economy since the 1920s. However, its economic plans have varied from time to time. Economic plans have taken the form of enormous comprehensive blueprints for coordinating the parts of most or all of the economy. Beginning in 1928, the state embarked on a series of Five-Year Plans (with occasional shorter or longer plans at various times), each with the purpose of achieving certain objectives. There is no need for us to explore the details of each of these plans. However, it will be useful to examine their general features.

Problems of Balance and Flexibility: Input–Output Analysis

Some of the difficulties that arise very early in the planning process involve the problems of achieving appropriate balance and flexibility among the interrelated parts of the economy.

In formulating a five-year plan, for example, production targets are established not only for enterprises and industries but also for geographic regions of the economy. If the plan is to be ideal, it must utilize fully all resources in the most efficient way. This is the task of input–output analysis—a basic tool of planning that has been used in the Soviet Union. Thus, the quantities of inputs to be produced, such as iron, steel, and glass, must be balanced by the quantities of outputs that use those inputs, such as houses, automobiles, and agricultural machinery. Otherwise, there will be excess production of some of these commodities relative to others, with the result that certain resources will be used inefficiently.

These difficulties are further complicated by the fact that the planned balances must be dynamic rather than static. That is, they must allow for growth in the quantities of outputs and inputs to be produced over a period of time. This requires that the plan be sufficiently flexible to permit readjustment of any of its parts at any point during the life of the plan in the event that the desired targets are not being met as originally intended.

Formulation of Objectives

The various five-year plans that have long guided the USSR have emphasized different objectives based on economic, social, political, and military considerations. For the most part, the biggest problem has been deciding on the proportion of the nation's limited resources to be devoted to the production of consumer goods, capital goods, and military goods. In general, the plans have had four major objectives:

1. To attain the highest standard of living in the world by overtaking the advanced capitalistic countries in output per capita as rapidly as possible.

2. To build a major military complex with the most modern nuclear capabilities.

3. To provide for universal health and education so as to further the nation's growth and scientific progress.

4. To achieve a substantial degree of economic independence from the outside world.

On the whole, the effort to attain these goals has made it necessary for the Soviet planners to give high priority to the development of heavy industry, such as steel, machinery, and power, and low priority to the production of consumer goods. The consequences have been painful. Levels of living have remained low compared to the United States.

Progress toward economic goals has also been held back by trouble in agriculture. Output per farm worker is much lower than in the United States, and plans to expand agricultural production have met with repeated failures and setbacks. These have been the cause of serious concern to government leaders.

Details of Planning

A comprehensive economic plan of the type prepared in the USSR is extraordinarily detailed. It includes a number of "subplans," such as an output plan, a capital budget or expenditures plan, a financial plan, a labor-utilization plan, and various regional plans. A few words may be said about the problems of preparing the first two of these plans: the output plan and the capital budget.

Output Plan   In the preparation of the output plan, Soviet leaders must be concerned both with consumer preferences and sacrifices in production.

The Soviets recognize that it would be irrational to produce goods that consumers desire if the production of such goods interfered with the overall objectives of the plan. It would be equally irrational to produce goods that consumers do not desire — that is, would not purchase in sufficient quantities at specified prices. This helps explain why advertising exists in the Soviet Union, although on a much smaller scale than in the United States. Advertising not only seeks to influence the marketing of new products but also helps to clear the market of unsold goods.

Soviet planners must take alternative production costs into account when they set output targets. Labor costs are relatively easy to measure because they are reflected by wage rates. These serve as an indication of the "real costs" of labor — the sacrifices in production that must be made in order to attract labor out of alternative employments. But the means by which the Soviet leaders measure nonlabor costs of production are not always so clear. For example, some experts in the field believe that the Soviet authorities do not attempt to include in their estimates of money costs all the real sacrifices in production resulting from the use of natural resources, capital funds, and land. Nor do they include the costs of distributing goods (such as warehousing and transportation) in their calculation of national income, because they regard distribution activities as unproductive. Thus:

> Soviet attitudes toward alternative costs and distribution are due partly to the difficulties of measurement, partly to the influence of Marxian ideology, and partly to the belief that certan types of price and cost calculations are "capitalistic economics." As a result, there is no doubt that the Soviet planners often sacrifice economic efficiency in order to attain desired objectives.

Capital Budget   How do the Soviet authorities determine the output of specific types of producers' goods? For example, how do they decide between a bulldozer and a power shovel, or between a truck and a railroad flatcar?

Such decisions are governed by the capital budget. This is a list of specific investment projects arranged in decreasing order of priority according to each project's *coefficient of relative effectiveness* (CRE). This technical term, used in the USSR, means the expected payoff or percentage rate of return on a capital investment. It is akin to the concept of "marginal efficiency of investment" used in Western economics. A particular investment project is thus either accepted or rejected by the planning authorities according to whether its CRE is above or below the prescribed minimum.

The CRE is a device for rationing the scarce supply of capital among alternative uses. The method of calculating the CRE is quite similar to procedures used by businesses in the United States. The factors that enter into the calculation include economic costs, interest rates, and the project's expected returns and expenses over its estimated life.

Adoption, Supervision, and Revisions of the Plan

When the Soviet planners complete their plan, it is reviewed by the government, by the representatives of labor and management, and by the Communist party. The advice and suggestions of these groups may then be incorporated by the planners before they submit it to the Politburo — the highest organ of the Communist party — for the resolution of disputes and final approval. Supervision of the plan is then entrusted to various agencies whose responsibility is to see it through to fulfillment. In the process of supervision, however, the plan is revised periodically to correct for unforeseen developments and errors. In effect, therefore, the "plan" is actually a series of plans rather than a rigid once-and-for-all arrangement.

Of course, an effective plan should be responsive to changing needs. In recognition of this, Soviet planners have at times instituted various reforms. For example:

Decision Making This is done at the enterprise level and has been partially decentralized. Company managers are given greater freedom in hiring workers, setting wages, varying product mixes, contracting with suppliers, and making small investments in new equipment.

Incentive Systems These have been introduced in order to encourage greater output. Workers and managers can strive for bonuses and other benefits based on the efficiency of their enterprise. Efficiency is measured by the ratio of a firm's profit to total assets (that is, by a firm's percentage return on assets). This relates the productivity of assets to goods *sold* rather than merely to goods produced.

Marketing Programs These have been instituted in order to stimulate consumer demand. Advertising is employed to help move goods from dealers' shelves, and prices are reduced to promote sales.

What have been the results of these reorganizations and changes? In general:

Soviet reforms have been introduced to encourage greater overall efficiency. However, the reforms in large part have met with limited success — for political as well as economic reasons:

- Central planners have been slow to surrender the real power needed to make decentralization work.

- The economy has not undergone the managerial changes required to permit the introduction of new production and distribution methods.

- Soviet workers have not been sufficiently interested in monetary incentives because of the limited availability of consumer goods on which increased incomes can be spent.

As a consequence, greater pressures are frequently put on the Soviet government to provide more and better consumer goods.

Soviet Accomplishments and Failures

The major economic goal of the USSR has been the attainment of rapid growth. Other objectives — stability, equity, and efficiency — have not been neglected. However, they have been of secondary importance. How successful have the Soviets been in realizing their desired ends?

Growth

Various problems of definition and measurement are encountered in dealing with Soviet data. These difficulties make comparisons with mixed economies much harder. Nevertheless, Exhibit 3 shows some interesting patterns:

1. Since 1971, the growth of real gross national product (GNP) in the Soviet Union has averaged

Exhibit 3
Economic Growth — Mixed Economies and the USSR

The USSR has grown somewhat slower than the average of the major mixed economies. At present, the Soviet economy (measured by real GNP) is roughly half as big as the American economy.

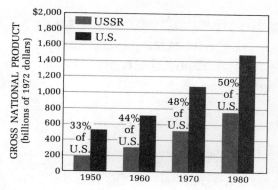

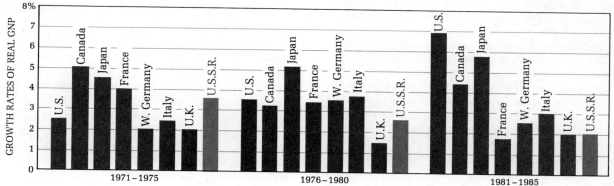

Source: U.S. Department of State and Central Intelligence Agency.

approximately 3 percent per year. This compares with an average of about 4 percent for the major mixed economies.

2. Real GNP in the Soviet Union has increased relative to the United States since 1950, but the rate of increase has been slowing down. In 1950 the USSR's real GNP was one-third that of the United States; in 1960 it was 44 percent, and since 1970 it has averaged close to one-half.

Stability

Fluctuations in investment expenditures are a chief cause of business cycles. In a command system, in which government makes the strategic decisions, it is easier to manage such expenditures than in a capitalistic system, in which decisions are left up to each firm. As a result, the Soviet economy has maintained high employment and stable prices for much longer periods than have mixed economies.

Equity

The distribution of income in the USSR is quite uneven. The highest rewards go to political and military leaders, who constitute an elite group in Soviet society. In addition, enterprise managers not only earn much higher salaries than ordinary workers but also receive substantial fringe benefits in the form of superior housing, longer vacations, and in

Economics in the News

Gorbachev Appoints 3 to Soviet Politburo, Stresses Need for Broad Economic Change

By David Ignatius
Staff Reporter of The Wall Street Journal

MOSCOW — Soviet leader Mikhail Gorbachev added three of his supporters to the ruling Politburo, preparing the way for what he asserted will be a broad program of economic change.

He called for less-rigid economic planning, more independence for Soviet enterprises, improved management techniques, increased emphasis on consumer products and service industries, and a "retooling" of the economy to install advanced technology.

Many Western officials doubt Mr. Gorbachev can achieve such ambitious changes, and nobody expects him to depart from the basic structure of state socialism and tight Communist political control.

But his speech yesterday was a signal to the Soviet party apparatus that he is willing to consider extensive economic experimentation.

some cases a free car. Similarly, as noted earlier, scientists, opera singers, and others in certain preferred occupations (determined by government) are paid considerably more than semiskilled and unskilled workers. Therefore, contrary to Marxian doctrine, *incomes are not generally distributed according to "needs."*

However, there are not the extremes of high and low incomes in the USSR that exist in many mixed economies. Further, all Soviet citizens receive state-subsidized education, health care, housing, and other benefits at relatively little or no direct costs. On the whole, despite some considerable disparities, the distribution of income — both money income and real income — is substantially more equal in the USSR than in most advanced mixed economies.

Efficiency

The Soviet Union has been considerably less successful with respect to efficiency than with its other goals. The factors responsible have been both technical and economic. For example:

The agricultural sector has lagged far behind the industrial sector in productivity. The reasons are due mainly to short growing seasons, inadequate incentives to stimulate productivity, and heavy investment of resources in industry and defense at the expense of agriculture.

Productivity has also suffered in the industrial sector. This is evidenced, as you may recall, by the fact that various reforms designed to increase output — including efforts at management decentralization and the provision of incentives for workers — have not been particularly successful.

On the whole, therefore, it may be said that Soviet planners have failed to achieve technical efficiency — the maximum ratio of physical outputs to available physical inputs.

Nor have the Soviets come anywhere close to attaining economic efficiency — maximum production in accordance with consumers' preferences. This is because a central planning board, rather than a free market, is the mechanism for determining what goods will be produced. Because the central planners have historically given top priority to the production of capital goods (including war goods) relative to consumer goods, the quantities and qualities of the latter have generally fallen far below the levels prevailing in advanced mixed economies.

Conclusion: Better Planning

As a consequence of these experiences, Soviet planners have undertaken instead to improve central

China's Economy Takes Off Like a Rocket

Russia's lackluster economic growth in recent years contrasts sharply with the performance of its chief rival in the Communist world. According to U.S. government estimates, China's GNP expanded at a spectacular 13% annual rate last year, following gains of 9% in 1983 and 7.4% in 1982. And China's economic boom results from the kinds of reforms, particularly in agriculture, that the Soviets have resisted for decades.

China's startling success and its willingness to jettison Marxist doctrines that interfere with economic growth may hold the world's best hope for peace. Economist Sam Nakagama of Nakagama & Wallace Inc. points out that the sharp rise in the Chinese people's standard of living can only increase the pressure for economic reforms within the Soviet bloc, while underscoring the heavy economic costs of a defense-spending burden that consumes 13% to 16% of GNP. In fact, it may have played a part in the Soviet decision to protect consumption last year.

Nakagama says China's rapid growth implies that "competition in world markets will become even more intense in the future and that the arms race must soon give way to the economic race."

Reprinted from March 11, 1985 issue of *Business Week* by special permission, © 1985 by McGraw-Hill, Inc.

planning and management systems in order to reduce inefficiencies and improve productivity.

Soviet emphasis has shifted from more planning to better planning—through the application of modern economic and scientific management principles. Imports from the West, ranging from agricultural goods to advanced equipment and systems, are rising as a result of these efforts. The ultimate goal is to meet the needs of restive consumers, whose living standards are far below those in other industrial nations.

Planning in China: Market Socialism

China, in 1978, made a complete turnaround from its previous thirty years of communist rule and isolation. In an effort to modernize itself and become an economic superpower by the year 2000, it has opened its doors to the advanced nations. Whether the turnaround will continue remains to be seen, for China is still a totalitarian nation with a somewhat divided leadership. Nevertheless, it is a nation that has chosen *market socialism* as a means of achieving faster growth. Thus:

In China, most of the means of production are owned by government. However, as compared with the pre-1978 period:

— Wages more closely match each worker's output, and profit-sharing bonuses are used as incentives for workers and managers.

— Managers make greater use of anticipated profits as a guide for determining what goods to produce and how to produce them.

— Government makes greater use of realized profits as a guide for allocating credit to particular industries.

— Cooperation and trade with foreign nations are recognized as important conditions for growth.

China's political leaders, it is said, are always looking for a quick solution to complex economic problems. At present, they are focusing on rapid modernization in an effort to catch up with the advanced countries by the year 2000. But the difficulties of achieving their desired goals may prove to be much greater than they and their economic planners imagine.

For example, in order to realize its objective, China's real GNP must grow at an exceptionally rapid rate of at least 10 percent annually until the end of the century. In addition, the country must maintain political stability, curb population growth, and greatly improve productive efficiency in agriculture and manufacturing. Otherwise, China will be unable to expand exports enough to earn the funds necessary to import modern plant and equipment.

Although China made an auspicious start toward rapid development in the early 1980s, it remains to be seen how long the economy can maintain its high-growth momentum.

What You Have Learned

1. Countries engage in economic planning to achieve specific economic goals. The chief ones are efficiency, equity, stability, and growth.

2. Econometrics and input–output analysis are gaining increasing use by corporations as well as by governments. Some mixed as well as some command economies use these methods for planning purposes.

3. Since the late 1920s, the Soviet system has been a command economy. Through state ownership of industry and extensive planning, it has become a major industrial and military power. But its citizens have paid a heavy cost in terms of deprivation of consumer goods and lack of political and economic freedoms.

4. Chinese leaders, in their formal planning efforts, have adopted market socialism. They are emphasizing a high rate of investment in heavy industry, accompanied by a reorganization of agriculture to achieve greater efficiency in food and raw-materials production.

Terms and Concepts To Review

economic plan	state farms
planned economy	collective farms
efficiency	coefficient of relative
economic growth	effectiveness (CRE)
econometrics	underemployment
input–output analysis	market socialism

For Discussion

1. In terms of goals, political leaders often place a higher priority on equity than on efficiency, stability, or growth. Can you suggest why?

2. Since the USSR is a centrally directed and collectivist economy, there is no competition as in American capitalism. True or false? Explain.

3. Why would a socialist economy, such as that of the USSR, want to employ the capitalistic device of providing economic incentives? What types of incentives do they use?

4. Is there freedom of consumer choice in the USSR? Is there consumer sovereignty? Explain.

5. Which would you suggest as a better guide for judging the efficiency of firms in the United States and in the USSR—profits or sales? What are some of the assumptions underlying your answer?

6. What criteria would you use in judging whether one nation's economy is "better" than another's? Are there noneconomic criteria, too?

7. Why do the Soviet authorities want to engage in the complex and difficult task of planning? Why do they not simply let a free-market system allocate the resources and distribute the income for them?

8. What are some of the "capitalistic" practices that the USSR has adopted over the years? Do the Soviets view these as a step toward capitalism? Explain.

9. What is the economic function of profits, and of the anticipation of profits, in a market economy? In the Chinese economy?

10. There is considerable evidence that, in advanced Western societies and even in the USSR, the use of material incentives serves to spur worker productivity and thereby to encourage greater output. In view of this, why do you suppose that Chinese leaders under communism (prior to 1978) opposed the use of material incentives?

11. Fill in the required data, including the input coefficients, for the accompanying input–output table.

(a) Suppose that there is a 10 percent increase in foreign demand for manufactured goods. Would any of the numbers in the table be affected? Explain.

(b) Would other sectors of the economy be affected by an increase in foreign demand for manufactured goods? Does it make any difference if the manufacturing sector is operating at full capacity or at less than full capacity? Discuss.

(c) In terms of your answer to part (b), can you explain why an input–output table may serve as a model to depict an economy in general equilibrium?

Input (buyers) / Output (sellers)	Agricultural sector	Manufacturing sector	Service sector	Intersector sales total	All other sales	Total output
Agricultural sector	**$100** ( )	**$200** ( )	**$50** ( )		$150	
Manufacturing sector	**$300** ( )	**$400** ( )	**$200** ( )		$100	
Service sector	**$50** ( )	**$150** ( )	**$100** ( )		$100	
Other resources	**$50** ( )	**$250** ( )	**$50** ( )			
Total input					$350	

Acknowledgments

Part 1
page xxiv
Chicago street scene
Cezus/Click, Chicago

Part 2
page 88
Congressional budget meeting
Dennis Brack/Black Star

Part 3
page 190
The Federal Reserve Building
J. Waring Stinchcomb/F.P.G. International Corp.

Part 4
page 264
Can a computer replace the Fed?
Joel Gordon 1984

Part 5
page 342
The Hope diamond
Lee Bolton

Part 6
page 410
Board room of a major corporation
Marc & Evelyne Bernheim/Woodfin Camp & Associates

Part 7
page 524
The Capitol, Washington, D.C.
Jim Pickerell/Click, Chicago

Index

...of Economic Terms and Concepts

This Dictionary includes the definitions of every technical word, phrase, and concept given in the text, as well as definitions of many other terms of significance in economics. It also presents cross references and brief examples that explain the significance of important terms. Hence the Dictionary will be a convenient and permanent source of reference — not only for this course, but for future courses you may take in economics, other social sciences, and business.

A

ability-to-pay principle: Theory of taxation that holds that the fairest tax is based on the financial means of the taxpayer—regardless of any benefit he or she may receive from the tax. Financial means may be determined by either wealth or income. The U.S. personal income tax is founded on this idea.

absolute advantage, law of: Principle that states that a basis for trade exists between nations or regions when each of them, as a result of natural or acquired superiorities, can provide a good or service that the other wants at a lower cost than if each were to provide it for itself. This law accounts for much of the world's trade.

absolute-income hypothesis: Proposition that states that a family's propensity to consume (that is, the amount it spends on consumption) depends on its *level* of income — the absolute amount available for spending. This concept of the propensity to consume was the one used by Keynes. (*Contrast with* **relative-income hypothesis; permanent-income hypothesis.**)

acceleration curves: Short-run inflation–unemployment relationships showing how the inflation rate speeds up with expansionary fiscal–monetary policies and slows down with contractionary ones. (*See* **Phillips curve.**)

accelerator principle: Proposition that net investment in capital goods depends upon *changes* in the level of output (that is, GNP). This is because capital goods are durable. Therefore, if existing production capacity is adequate, it is possible to produce a constant level of output with existing equipment, replacing it as it wears out. No net investment needs to be undertaken. But if aggregate demand increases, the economy, operating at full capacity, will have to undertake additional investment in order to produce an increase in output. Therefore, net investment is a function of *changes* in the level of output. Thus:

$$\text{net investment} = \text{accelerator} \times \text{change in GNP}$$

and hence

$$\text{accelerator} = \frac{\text{net investment}}{\text{change in GNP}}$$

The accelerator itself is a mathematical constant—a number such as 1.0, 1.5, 2.0, and so on—that is estimated by statistical procedures.

accounts payable: A company's debts to suppliers of goods or services.

accounts receivable: Amounts due to a firm from customers.

accrued expenses payable: Obligations, such as wages and salaries, interest on borrowed funds, and pensions.

additional-worker hypothesis: Theory which holds that, during a period of rising unemployment, the rate of participation in the labor force increases. The reason is that many of the main income-earners of families lose their jobs. Therefore, people who were not previously in the labor force, such as full-time students and homemakers, are forced to seek employment in order to support the family. (*Contrast with* **discouraged-worker hypothesis.**)

adjustable peg: System that permits governmentally controlled changes in the par rate of foreign exchange after a nation has had long-run disequilibrium in its balance of payments. It allows also for short-run variations within a narrow range of a few percent around the par value.

administered pricing: Means by which executives in oligopolistic industries are able to manage ("administer") their firms' prices, instead of permitting them to be determined by the free interactions of market forces. It is based on either of two beliefs about how oligopolies set prices—**cost-plus pricing** and **target-return pricing.**

ad valorem subsidy: Fixed percentage subsidy based on the price or value of a commodity.

ad valorem tax: Fixed percentage tax on the price or value of a commodity. *Examples:* sales taxes, property taxes, and most import duties.

affirmative action: Legislation requiring firms working under contracts with the federal government to file numerical equal-opportunity "goals and timetables." These are compliance reports showing that good-faith efforts were made to fill employment quotas with minority-group members and women. (*See also* **equal employment opportunity.**)

agency shop: Business firm in which workers are required to pay union dues regardless of whether or not they join the union. It is said to be a "compromise" based on two principles: (1) that workers should not be required to join a union against their wishes, and (2) that all workers in a firm (even those who are not union members) benefit from union representation and should therefore pay for it. Agency shops are legal under the National Labor Relations Act, but they can be specifically outlawed by state right-to-work laws.

aggregate concentration ratio: A measure of the relative size of firms within a large segment of the economy. The ratio measures the percentage share of sales, assets, value added, profits, employment (or any other indicator of size) accounted for by the largest firms across entire sectors or subsectors of the economy. The number of "largest firms" may range from a few dozen to several hundred, depending on the size of the sector being measured. (*Contrast with* **concentration ratio.**)

aggregate demand: Total value of real aggregate output that all sectors of the economy are willing to purchase at various average price levels. (*Contrast with* **aggregate expenditure.**)

aggregate expenditure: Total amount of spending on goods and services that all sectors of the economy are willing to undertake at various income levels. Spending and income are usually expressed either in real, or in nominal, terms. (*Contrast with* **aggregate demand.**)

aggregate output: Total value of production of goods and services. It is equivalent in dollars to GNP, and may be expressed either in real or in nominal terms. (*Contrast with* **aggregate supply.**)

aggregate supply: Total value of real aggregate output that will be made available at various average price levels. (*Contrast with* **aggregate output.**)

Agricultural Adjustment Act (1938): Basic farm law (with subsequent amendments) of the United States. It has, at various times, provided for (1) price supports of selected farm products at specified levels; (2) production control through acreage allotments of certain crops; (3) marketing agreements and quotas between the Department of Agriculture and producers in order to control the distribution of selected commodities; (4) payments to farmers and others who follow approved soil conservation practices; and (5) parity payments to farmers for selected agricultural staples.

allocative efficiency: *See* **efficiency.**

Aluminum Company of America (Alcoa) case (1945): Major antitrust case against Alcoa. The company was the dominant firm in aluminum production, accounting for 90 percent of the nation's output. Even though Alcoa did not aggressively seek to attain a monopoly, but rather found that monopoly had been "thrust upon" the company, it was a "passive beneficiary" of monopoly, according to Judge Learned Hand, who therefore found the company in violation of the Sherman Antitrust Act. This stringent interpretation was thus contrary to the traditional *rule of reason* that had prevailed since the Standard Oil case of 1911. As it happened, Judge Hand's rigid interpretation was greatly tempered in subsequent antitrust cases, and has not been strictly applied since 1945.

American Federation of Labor–Congress of Industrial Organizations (AFL–CIO): League of labor unions formed in 1955 by a merger of the AFL and CIO. Its purposes are to improve the wages, hours, and conditions of workers and to realize the benefits of free collective bargaining. It exercises no authority or control over member unions other than requiring them to abide by its constitution and code of ethical practices.

American Tobacco case (1911): Major antitrust case in which the Supreme Court found the "tobacco trust" to be in violation of the Sherman Act. The trust consisted of five major tobacco manufacturers controlling 95 percent of domestic cigarette production. However, the Court did not condemn the trust for that fact. It was the trust's "unreasonable" market behavior, driving competitors out of business, that caused the Court's condemnation.

annually balanced budget: Philosophy that holds that total revenues and expenditures in the government's budget should be balanced or brought into equality every year.

antitrust laws: Acts passed by Congress since 1890 to prevent monopoly and to maintain competition. The chief ones are (1) the Sherman Antitrust Act (1890); (2) the Clayton Antitrust Act (1914); (3) the Federal Trade Commission Act (1914); (4) the Robinson–Patman Act (1936); (5) the Wheeler–Lea Act (1938); and (6) the Celler Antimerger Act (1950).

Aquinas, St. Thomas (1225–1274): Medieval philosopher who wrote on economic problems during the early stages of modern capitalism. He attempted to harmonize reason with faith by applying principles of Aristotelian philosophy to biblical teaching and canonical dogma. Thus he held that the individual's right to private property accords with natural law; commerce is to be condoned to the extent that it maintains the household and benefits the country; fairness and truthfulness in commercial dealings are essential virtues; and so on. In general, these and other ideas of Aquinas make him one of the important leaders in early economic thought.

arbitrage: Act of buying a commodity in one market and simultaneously selling it in a dearer market at a higher price. Arbitrage tends to equalize prices of a commodity in different markets, except for differences in the costs of transportation, risk, and so on.

arbitration: Settlement of differences between parties (such as a union and management) by the use of an impartial third party. The third party is an arbitrator who is acceptable to both sides and whose decision is binding and legally enforceable on the contesting parties. The arbitrator issues a decision based not on what he or she thinks is wise and fair but on how the language of the contract is believed to apply to the case. Arbitration in industrial relations almost always deals with the settlement of union–management disputes over the provisions of an *existing* collective-bargaining contract. (*Contrast with* **mediation.**)

Arrow, Kenneth Joseph (1921–): Leading American economist and Nobel laureate (1972). He is noted for his work in welfare economics, mathematical programming, and growth theory. Arrow served on the President's Council of Economic Advisors in 1962 and has been on the faculties of the University of Chicago, Harvard University, and Stanford University.

Arrow's impossibility theorem: Proposition that proves that no voting system is perfect because group decisions cannot be both rational and fair. The reason is that five conditions are needed to meet all requirements of rationality and fairness: (1) the voter must be able to rank alternatives in a consistent manner; (2) the voter must be free to choose any possible ranking of alternatives; (3) the voting outcome must please as many people as possible while displeasing as few as possible; (4) no individual may dictate a decision to the voting group; and (5) the voting system must preserve the ranking of a given set of alternatives if there is added to it another set of alternatives. Arrow's theorem demonstrates that, because of logical inconsistencies, these conditions cannot be applied simultaneously. Thus, it is impossible to construct a "perfect" voting system—one that is completely rational and fair.

assets: Resources or things of value owned by an economic entity, such as an individual, household, or firm. *Examples:* cash, property, and the rights to property.

automatic fiscal stabilizers: Nondiscretionary or "built-in" features that automatically cushion recession by helping to create a budget deficit and curb inflation by helping to create a budget surplus. *Examples:* (1) income tax receipts; (2) unemployment taxes and benefits; and (3) corporate dividend policies.

automatic transfer services (ATS): A combined interest-bearing savings and zero-balance checking account offered by many banks. When a check written against the account is presented for payment, the bank switches the necessary funds from savings to checking. A more apt description, therefore, would be automatic transfer *of savings* (rather than *services*). ATS accounts are one of several forms of savings-type checkable deposits.

autonomous consumption: Consumption independent of income. It is the part of total consumption that is unrelated to income. (*Compare* **induced consumption.**)

autonomous investment: Investment independent of income, output, and general economic activity. (*Compare* **induced investment.**)

autonomous transactions: Settlements among nations that arise from factors unrelated to the balance of payments as such. The main classes are merchandise trade and services, long-term capital movements, and unilateral transfers.

average-cost price: *See* **full-cost price.**

average fixed cost: Ratio of a firm's total fixed cost to the quantity it produces. Also, the difference between average total cost and average variable cost. Thus,

$$\text{average fixed cost} = \frac{\text{total fixed cost}}{\text{quantity of output}}$$

Also,

$$\text{average fixed cost} = \text{average total cost} - \text{average variable cost}$$

average–marginal relationship: Mathematical relationship between all corresponding average and marginal curves. The relationship is such that: when an average curve is rising, its corresponding marginal curve is above it; when an average curve is falling, its corresponding marginal curve is below it; and when an average curve is either at a maximum or at a minimum, its corresponding marginal curve intersects (is equal to) it.

average product: Ratio of total output or product to the amount of variable input needed to produce that volume of output. Thus,

$$\text{average product} = \frac{\text{total product}}{\text{variable input}}$$

average propensity to consume: Ratio of consumption to income:

$$\text{average propensity to consume} = \frac{\text{consumption}}{\text{income}}$$

It thus reveals the proportion of income that is spent on consumption.

average propensity to save: Ratio of saving to income:

$$\text{average propensity to save} = \frac{\text{saving}}{\text{income}}$$

It thus reveals the proportion of income that is saved (that is, not spent on consumption).

average revenue: Ratio of a firm's total revenue to its quantity of output sold—or, equivalently, its price per unit of quantity sold. Thus,

average revenue

$$= \frac{\text{total revenue}}{\text{quantity}} = \frac{(\text{price})(\cancel{\text{quantity}})}{\cancel{\text{quantity}}} = \text{price}$$

average revenue product: Ratio of total revenue to the quantity of an input employed. Thus,

$$\text{average revenue product} = \frac{\text{total revenue}}{\text{quantity of input employed}}$$

average tax rate: Ratio or percentage of a total tax to the base on which it is imposed. *Example:*

average personal income tax rate

$$= \frac{\text{total personal income tax}}{\text{total taxable income}}$$

average total cost: Ratio of a firm's total cost to the quantity it produces. Also, the sum of average fixed cost and average variable cost. Thus,

$$\text{average total cost} = \frac{\text{total cost}}{\text{quantity of output}}$$

Also,

average total cost

$$= \text{average fixed cost} + \text{average variable cost}$$

average variable cost: Ratio of a firm's total variable cost to the quantity it produces. Also, the difference between a firm's average total cost and average fixed cost. Thus,

$$\text{average variable cost} = \frac{\text{total variable cost}}{\text{quantity of output}}$$

Also,

average variable cost
$$= \text{average total cost} - \text{average fixed cost}$$

B

backward-bending labor-supply curve: Relationship between a worker's real wage rate and the number of labor hours offered. At relatively lower wage levels the relationship is direct: the curve slopes upward over a range of labor hours. However, a point is reached at which the worker is no longer willing to trade additional leisure in return for higher income from working. The relationship then becomes inverse. That is, the curve bends backwards, showing that higher real wage rates result in fewer labor hours offered.

Bain index: Measure of a firm's monopoly power, based on the divergence between price, P, and average total cost, ATC. A modified version of the index in which the divergence is expressed as a proportion of price is

$$\text{Bain index} = \frac{P - ATC}{P}$$

The index will be zero (no monopoly power) when the firm is earning only normal profit (that is, $P = ATC$). On the other hand, the index will be greater than zero when the firm is earning an economic or excess profit (that is, $P > ATC$). Basic shortcomings of the index are that (1) large profits do not necessarily indicate the existence of strong monopoly power, since large profits may be the result of greater efficiency or of different accounting methods used for depreciation and asset valuation; (2) it is a static rather than dynamic measure and therefore cannot be applied to firms that experience rapid changes in technology, demand, and so on.

balanced budget: Budget with total revenues and total expenditures that are equal.

balanced-budget multiplier: Hypothesis that asserts that, if government spending and taxes are increased or decreased simultaneously by equal amounts, GNP will be increased or decreased by the same amount. *Example:*

An equal increase in government spending and taxes of $20 billion will raise GNP by $1 \times \$20$ billion $= \$20$ billion. (Similarly, an equal decrease of $20 billion will lower GNP by $1 \times \$20$ billion $= \$20$ billion.) The reason for this is that the effects of equal increases in government spending and taxes are opposite. Therefore, the two multiplier processes cancel each other out—except on the first round, when the full amount of government spending is added to GNP.

balance of payments: Statement of the money value of all transactions between a nation and the rest of the world during a given period, such as a year. These transactions may consist of imports and exports of goods and services, and movements of short-term and long-term investments, gifts, currency, and gold. The transactions may be classified into several categories, of which the two broadest are the current account and the capital account.

balance-of-payments disequilibrium: Circumstance that exists when, over an unspecified period lasting several years, a nation's autonomous credits do not equal its autonomous debits. A deficit disequilibrium exists when total autonomous debits exceed total autonomous credits. A surplus disequilibrium occurs when total autonomous credits exceed total autonomous debits.

balance of trade: That part of a nation's balance of payments dealing with merchandise imports and exports. A "favorable" balance of trade exists when the value of exports exceeds the value of imports. An "unfavorable" balance exists when the value of imports exceeds the value of exports.

balance sheet: Statement of a firm's financial position on a given date. It shows what the firm owns (its assets), what it owes (its liabilities), and the residual or equity of the owners (the net worth).

Bank of the United States: Chartered for the period 1791 to 1811, the Bank's function was to assist the Treasury in its fiscal activities and to provide an adequate supply of currency to meet the needs of business. The Bank's performance was generally satisfactory, but its charter was not renewed. Primary opposition came from farmers, who felt that the Bank favored urban commercial interests over rural agricultural ones and that the Bank's financial power was too great.

banker's acceptance: Promise by a bank to pay specific bills for one of its customers when the bills become due. It may be thought of as a bank-guaranteed "post-dated" check written by one of its customers and accepted by the bank for payment. The bank thus assumes the customer's debt and guarantees payment on the post-dated day. In the interim, if the bank should need short-term funds, it can sell the check at a discount from face value in the money market. (*See also* **bill of exchange; draft.**)

barter: Simple exchange of one good for another without the use of money.

basic wages: Payments received by workers for work performed, based on time or output.

basing-point pricing: Method of delivered pricing in some industries. Each seller in the industry quotes a given buyer the so-called basing-point price plus the cost of shipping from the basing point to the buyer, regardless of the location from which the product is actually shipped. The basing point is the factory or mill price of the product in a particular city. *Example:* The steel industry, in the early decades of this century, used a basing-point system known as "Pittsburgh plus." All firms in the industry quoted U.S. Steel's mill price at Pittsburgh plus the cost of rail shipment from Pittsburgh to the buyer, regardless of whether the steel came from Pittsburgh or from some other city closer or farther from the buyer. In this way the industry managed to eliminate competition in price, because all sellers quoted the same delivered price to any given buyer. (*Compare* **f.o.b. pricing** *and* **delivered pricing.**)

basis: In the futures market, the difference between the cash and futures price of a commodity:

$$\text{Basis} = \text{futures price} - \text{cash price}$$

The difference is approximately equal to the carrying costs (including freight, insurance, storage, and so forth) of moving the product from local rural markets to major terminal markets, such as Chicago, Omaha, and Kansas City.

"bathtub theorem": A model in the form of a physical analogy—a bathtub. The level of water in the tub represents the economy's output or income. Thus, water flowing into the tub represents "injections." These may consist of investment, government spending, or exports. The effects of these expenditures are to increase aggregate expenditure and thus to raise the water level in the tub (that is, to increase income and employment). Water flowing out of the tub represents "withdrawals." These are "leakages" from total income, which may consist of saving, taxes, and imports. The effects of such leakages are to decrease aggregate expenditure and thus to lower

the water level in the tub (that is, to decrease income and employment). Of course, the level of water in the tub remains constant as long as inflows (injections) equal outflows (withdrawals). Also, at any given level, inflows equal outflows.

benefit–cost analysis: Method of evaluating alternative investment projects by comparing for each the (discounted) present value of all expected benefits or net receipts with the (discounted) present value of all expected costs or sacrifices. Once such comparisons are made, a rational basis exists for choosing one investment project over the other.

benefit–cost (B/C) ratio: Ratio of the present value of benefits (net receipts) of an investment to the present value of costs:

$$B/C = \frac{\text{present value of benefits}}{\text{present value of costs}}$$

The B/C ratio thus gives the present value of net receipts per dollar of investment cost. The ratio must equal at least 1 in order for the investment to be recovered (that is, repaid by its net receipts).

benefit principle: Theory of taxation that holds that a fair tax is one that is levied on people according to the services or benefits they receive from government. The chief difficulties are that: (1) for many goods, benefits cannot be readily determined (for example, national defense, public education, police and fire protection); and (2) those who receive the benefits are not always able to pay for them (for example, recipients of welfare or unemployment compensation).

bilateral monopoly: Market structure in which a monopsonist buyer faces a monopolist seller. The equilibrium quantity may be determinate. However, the price level for that quantity is logically indeterminate. That is, the price will end up somewhere between the minimum price preferred by the monopsonist and the maximum price preferred by the monopolist.

bill of exchange: Draft (or type of "check") used between countries. (*See also* **draft.**)

bimetallic standard: Monetary standard under which the national unit of currency (such as the dollar) is defined in terms of a fixed weight of two metals, usually gold and silver. The United States was on this standard during the nineteenth century, but it usually worked unsatisfactorily because of the operation of Gresham's Law. (*See also* **Gresham's Law; mint ratio.**)

black market: Illegal market in which a good is sold for more than its legal ceiling price. The good may or may not be rationed. If it is, experience indicates that the criteria used for rationing are virtually certain to create skullduggery and inequities. (*Compare* **white market.**)

Board of Governors: Group of seven people that supervises the Federal Reserve System. Members are appointed by the President and confirmed by the Senate for terms of 14 years each, one term expiring every 2 years.

bond: Agreement to pay a certain sum (called the "principal") either at a future date or periodically over the course of a loan. During the period of the loan, a fixed rate of interest may be paid on certain dates. Bonds are issued by corporations and by the federal, state, and local governments. They are typically used for long-term financing.

boycott: Campaign to discourage people from dealing with a particular firm. (Sometimes called a "primary boycott.")

break-even point: Level of output at which a firm's total revenue equals its total cost (or its average revenue equals its average total cost) so that its net revenue is zero. At a break-even point as defined in economics, a firm is normally profitable, since total cost in economics includes normal profit.

Brown Shoe case (1962): Major antitrust case in which the Supreme Court struck down a merger between Brown Shoe and Kinney Shoe as a violation of the Clayton Antitrust Act. Although both companies were shoe manufacturers and retailers with relatively small market shares, the merger, it was held, would nevertheless "foreclose competition from a substantial share of the market for shoes without producing countervailing economic or social advantages." The Court also held that the merger might increase market concentration in a few cities where both companies had retail stores.

budget: Itemized estimate of expected revenues and expenditures for a given period in the future.

budget deficit: Budget in which total expenditures exceed total revenues.

budget surplus: Budget in which total revenues exceed total expenditures.

Burns, Arthur Frank (1904–): American economist and expert on business cycles, fiscal policy, and monetary policy. He served as President of the National Bureau of Economic Research, as a professor of economics at Columbia University, and in various high-level government positions, including head of the President's Council of Economic Advisors and Chairman of the Board of Governors of the Federal Reserve System.

business cycles: Recurrent but nonperiodic fluctuations in general business and economic activity that take place over a period of years. They occur in aggregate variables, such as income, output, employment, and prices, most of which may move at approximately the same time in the same direction, but *at different rates.* Business cycles are thus accelerations and retardations in the rates of growth of important economic variables.

C

cameralism: Form of mercantilism extensively implemented by German governments during the eighteenth century. Its chief objective was to increase the revenue of the state. [The word comes from *Kammer* ("chamber"), the name applied to the royal treasury.]

capital: 1. As a factor of production, capital is a produced means of further production (such as capital goods or investment goods in the form of raw materials, machines, or equipment) for the ultimate purpose of manufacturing consumer goods. Hence human resources are also part of an economy's capital. **2.** As money, capital represents the funds that businesspeople use to purchase capital goods. **3.** In accounting, capital may sometimes represent net worth or the stockholders' equity in a business.

capital consumption allowance: Expression used in national-income accounting to represent the difference between "gross" and "net" private domestic investment. It consists almost entirely of depreciation and is often used as if it were synonymous with it.

capital deepening: Increases in an economy's stock of capital at a faster rate than the growth of its labor force, thus expanding the volume of capital per worker and raising average output per worker.

capitalism: Economic system characterized by private ownership of the factors of production and their operation for profit under predominantly competitive conditions.

capital market: Center where long-term credit and equity instruments, such as bonds, stocks, and mortgages, are bought and sold.

capital–output (or capital/output) ratio: Concept sometimes used in a "total" sense, and sometimes in a "marginal" sense. Thus: **1.** The "total" capital–output ratio is the ratio of an economy's total stock of real capital to the level of its income or output. **2.** The "marginal" capital–

output ratio is the change in an economy's income or output resulting from a unit change in its stock of real capital. Thus a ratio of 3/1 means that three units of additional capital produce one unit of additional output.

capital stock: Unit of ownership in a corporation. It represents the stockholder's proprietary interest. Two major classes are common stock and preferred stock.

capital widening: Increases in an economy's stock of capital at the same rate as the growth of its labor force, thus maintaining the same volume of capital per worker and hence the same average output per worker.

cartel: Association of producers in the same industry, established to increase the profits of its members by adopting common policies affecting production, market allocation, or prices. A cartel may be domestic or international in scope. In the United States, organizations of independent business enterprises established for mutually beneficial purposes are called *trade associations*, not cartels. The latter term has been reserved exclusively for foreign or international associations. However, when a trade association or similar group fixes prices, restricts output, or allocates markets for its members, it behaves *in effect* like a cartel.

Celler Antimerger Act (1950): Major antitrust law. An extension of Section 7 of the Clayton Antitrust Act, it prohibits a corporation from acquiring the stock *or assets* of another corporation if the effect would be a substantial lessening of competition or a tendency toward monopoly. *Note:* Prior to this law, only the acquisition of *stock* by competing corporations was illegal under the Clayton Antitrust Act.

certificate of deposit (CD): *See* **negotiable certificate of deposit.**

Chamberlin, Edward Hastings (1899–1967): American economist who was one of the pioneers in developing the theory of monopolistic competition. His doctoral dissertation, *The Theory of Monopolistic Competition* (Harvard, 1933), became a standard work in the field. In this and in subsequent editions and articles, Chamberlin emphasized the role of product differentiation, advertising, and differences in consumer preferences as factors contributing to the existence of "partial" or "competing monopolists." Chamberlin thus identified a new form of market structure, monopolistic competition, the theory of which has become an essential part of microeconomics.

change in amount consumed: Increase or decrease in the amount of consumption expenditure due to a change in income. It may be represented by a movement along a consumption-function curve.

change in consumption: Increase or decrease in consumption, represented by a shift of the consumption-function curve to a new position. The shift results from a change in any of the factors that were assumed to remain constant when the curve was drawn. These may include (1) the volume of liquid assets owned by households, (2) expectations of future prices and incomes, (3) anticipations of product shortages, and (4) credit conditions.

change in demand: Increase or decrease in demand, represented by a shift of the demand curve to a new position. The shift results from a change in any of the factors that were assumed to remain constant when the curve was drawn. These may include (1) buyers' money incomes, (2) the prices of related goods, (3) buyers' tastes or preferences, (4) the number of buyers in the market, and (5) buyers' expectations about future prices and incomes.

change in quantity demanded: Increase or decrease in the quantity demanded of a good due to a change in its price. It may be represented by a movement along a demand curve.

change in quantity supplied: Increase or decrease in the quantity supplied of a good due to a change in its price. It may be represented by a movement along a supply curve.

change in supply: Increase or decrease in supply shown by a shift of the supply curve to a new position. The shift results from a change in any of the factors that were assumed to remain constant when the curve was drawn. These may include (1) the state of technology, (2) resource prices or the costs of the factors of production, (3) the prices of other goods, (4) the number of sellers in the market, and (5) sellers' expectations regarding future prices.

checkable deposits: Depository-institution accounts that are subject to withdrawals by check. *Examples:* **demand deposits, negotiable orders of withdrawal** (NOW accounts), and credit-union **share-draft** accounts. Checkable deposits are also called **transaction deposits.**

checkoff: Procedure by which an employer, with the written permission of the worker, withholds union dues and other assessments from paychecks and then transfers the funds to the union. This provides an efficient means by which the union can collect dues from its members.

Christian socialism: Movement, since the late nineteenth century, by various church groups to preach the "social gospel"—a type of social legislation and reform that seeks to improve the well-being of the working classes by appealing to Christian ethical and humanitarian principles.

circular flow of economic activity: Model demonstrating the movement of goods, resources, payments, and expenditures among sectors of the economy. A simple model may include the household and business sectors and the product and resource markets—but other models may be constructed that are more complex.

Clark, John Bates (1847–1938): Leading American economist whose major treatise, *The Distribution of Wealth* (1899), was the first American work in pure economic theory. The book developed what is essentially the modern version of the marginal-productivity theory. This theory demonstrates that a (perfectly competitive) capitalistic society distributes incomes to resource owners in proportion to the market values of their contribution to production. The theory was thus used by others to justify capitalism as a fair (equitable) system. Clark, it should be noted, had much in common with his British contemporary, Alfred Marshall. Both used similar methodologies in analyzing economic problems. Clark, however, tended to be more theoretical and abstract.

classical economics: Body of economic thought emphasizing human self-interest and the operation of universal economic laws. These tend automatically to guide the economy toward full-employment, or natural-employment equilibrium, if the government adheres to a policy of laissez-faire or noninterventionism. Among the early chief proponents of classical economics were Adam Smith (1723–1790), Jean Baptiste Say (1767–1832), Jeremy Bentham (1748–1832), Thomas Robert Malthus (1766–1834), David Ricardo (1772–1823), Nassau William Senior (1790–1864), and John Stuart Mill (1806–1873).

class struggle: In the theories of Karl Marx, an irreconcilable clash between the bourgeoisie (or capitalist class) and the proletariat (or working class) arising out of the surplus value that capitalists appropriate from workers. The class struggle will eventually be resolved when the proletariat overthrows the bourgeoisie and establishes a new and equitable economic order.

Clayton Antitrust Act (1914): A major antitrust law aimed at preventing unfair, deceptive, dishonest, or injurious methods of competition. It made the following practices and arrangements illegal, where their effect is a substantial lessening of competition or a tendency toward monopoly: (1) price discrimination, except where there are differences in grade, quality, or quantity sold, or where the lower prices make due allowances for cost differences in selling or transportation, or where the lower prices are offered in good faith to meet competition; (2) tying contracts between sellers and purchasers; and (3) intercorporate stockholdings among competing corporations. It also makes illegal, regardless of the effect on

competition, (4) interlocking directorates, if the corporations involved are competitive and if any one of them has capital, surplus, and undivided profits in excess of $1 million.

closed shop: A firm that agrees that an employee must be a union member before being employed and must remain a union member after becoming employed. It is illegal under the Labor–Management Relations (Taft–Hartley) Act of 1947.

coalition bargaining: Method of bargaining by which a federation of unions (such as the AFL–CIO) tries to coordinate and establish common termination dates for contracts with firms that deal with a number of unions at their plants throughout the economy. Its purpose is to enable the federation to strengthen union bargaining positions by threatening to close down all plants simultaneously.

Coase theorem: Proposition that demonstrates that, if (1) property rights are clearly defined and (2) the number of affected parties is small, individuals seeking to maximize their well-being will negotiate the internalization of their own externalities. The resulting allocation of resources will be efficient and will have been arrived at by private agreement—without a solution imposed by an outside authority (that is, government). Basically, the parties involved will find that, if transactions costs (the costs including time and effort of negotiating contracts) are low because few people are involved, mutual gains will be realized from voluntary agreements. Thus, for example, a farmer whose crops are damaged by the wandering cattle of a neighboring rancher can pay the rancher to reduce his output of cattle. When all costs and benefits are taken into account, an efficient output of crops as well as of cattle is attained without an externally (governmentally) imposed decision.

cobweb theorem: Generic name for a theory of cyclical fluctuations in the prices and quantities of various agricultural commodities—fluctuations that arise because, for certain agricultural products, (1) the quantity demanded of the commodity at any given time depends on its price at that time, whereas (2) the quantity supplied at any given time depends on its price at a previous time when production plans were initially formulated. Hogs and beef cattle have been notable examples.

coefficient of relative effectiveness (CRE): Term used in the Soviet Union to mean the expected payoff or percentage rate of return on a capital investment; akin to the concept of marginal efficiency of investment in Western economics.

coincident indicators: Time series that tend to move approximately "in phase" with the aggregate economy and hence are measures of current economic activity.

collective agreement: A collective-bargaining contract worked out between union and management, describing wages, working conditions, and related matters.

collective bargaining: Negotiation between a company's management and a union for the purpose of agreeing on mutually acceptable wages and working conditions for employees.

collective farms: Agricultural cooperatives in the USSR consisting of communities of farmers who pool their resources, lease land from the government, and divide the profits among the members according to the amount and kind of work done by each. This type of farming, which is subject to detailed government regulation, dominates agriculture in the USSR.

collective good: *See* **public good.**

command economy: Economic system in which an authoritarian government exercises primary control over decisions concerning what and how much to produce; it may also, but does not necessarily, decide for whom to produce. (*Compare* **planned economy.**)

commercial bank: Type of financial depository institution, chartered by federal or state governments. It is primarily engaged in buying and selling money-market instruments and in making business loans by creating demand or checking deposits. It may also engage in certain other financial activities, such as holding time or savings deposits, making long-term mortgage loans, and managing investments.

commercial paper: Unsecured promissory notes, usually in minimum denominations of $10,000, sold by several hundred major corporations. The most familiar example is GMAC paper, sold by General Motors Acceptance Corporation, to finance the purchase of General Motors cars.

common market: Association of trading nations that agrees: (1) to impose no trade restrictions, such as tariffs or quotas, among participants; (2) to establish common external barriers (such as a common external tariff) to non-participants; and (3) to impose no national restrictions on the movement of labor and capital among participants. *Example:* European Economic Community (EEC).

common stock: Shares that have no fixed rate of dividends and hence may receive higher dividends than the fixed rate on preferred stock, if the corporation's earnings are sufficiently high.

Commonwealth (Mass.) v. Hunt (1842): The first case in which a (Massachusetts) court held a trade union to be a lawful organization. It declared that workers could form a union to bargain collectively with employers.

communism: 1. In the theories of Karl Marx, the final and perfect goal of historical development. It is characterized by: (a) a classless society in which all people live by earning and no person lives by owning; (b) the disappearance of the state; and (c) the abolition of the wage system so that all citizens live and work according to the motto: *"From each according to his ability, to each according to his needs."* **2.** In most communist countries today, an economic system based on (a) social ownership of property, including most of the means of production and distribution; (b) government planning and control of the economy; and (c) a scheme of rewards and penalties to achieve maximum productive effort. *Note:* Communist leaders claim that the system that exists in communist countries today is socialism of the type that Marxian ideology holds as being preparatory to the attainment of full communism.

company union: A labor union limited to a particular firm. It is usually unaffiliated with any other union.

comparable worth: Argument that asserts that women should be paid as much as men are paid for performing tasks in other occupations requiring comparable (not identical) skills, training, responsibilities, hazards, and effort. The purpose is to reduce sex discrimination in employment by eliminating the pay gap between female-dominated occupations (e.g., elementary-school teaching, nursing, secretarial work) and most other jobs.

comparative advantage, law of: Principle that states that, if one nation can produce each of two products more efficiently than another nation and can produce one of these commodities more efficiently than the other, it should specialize in the product in whose production it is most efficient and leave production of the alternative product to the other country. Then, by engaging in trade, the two nations will have more of both goods. This principle is applicable to individuals and regions as well as to nations.

comparative statics: Method of analysis in which the effects of a change in one or more of the determining conditions in a static model are evaluated by comparing the results after the change with those before the change. *Example:* Comparing the effects on equilibrium prices and quantities (in a supply-and-demand model) resulting from a shift in supply or demand curves. It is like comparing two "snapshots" of a phenomenon — one taken before the change and one after.

compensatory (accommodating) transactions: Settlements among nations that are a direct response to balance-of-payments considerations. They may be thought of as balancing items that arise to accommodate differences in money inflows and outflows resulting from so-called autonomous transactions. The two main classes are short-term capital movements and shifts in gold holdings.

competition: Rivalry among buyers and sellers of goods or resources. Competition tends to be directly related to the degree of diffusion (as opposed to the concentration) of market power and the freedom with which buyers and sellers can enter or leave particular markets. It is sometimes used to mean perfect (pure) competition, depending on whether it is employed in that context.

complementary goods: Commodities that are related such that at a given level of buyers' incomes, an increase in the price of one good leads to a decrease in the demand for the other, and a decrease in the price of one good leads to an increase in the demand for the other. *Examples:* ham and eggs; hamburgers and buns. (*Compare* **substitute goods.**)

compounding: Process by which a given amount, expressed in dollars, is adjusted at interest to yield a future value. That is, interest when due is added to a principal amount and thereafter earns interest. *Example:* At 6 percent, a principal of $1, plus interest, amounts to a sum of $1.06 after one year, and to an additional 6 percent, for a sum of $1.124, after two years, and so on. Compounding is thus the opposite of **discounting.**

compound interest: Interest computed on a principal sum and also on all the interest earned by that principal sum as of a given date.

Comptroller of the Currency: Federal agency that charters all national banks. It also oversees the operations of national banks and of those state banks that are members of the Federal Reserve System.

concentration ratio: Percentage of an industry's output accounted for by its largest firms—typically, by its four largest. The percentage (or ratio) is usually based either on sales, value added, or value of shipments. Sometimes, however, other measures of size, such as assets or employment, are used.

conglomerate merger: Amalgamation under one ownership of unlike plants producing unrelated products. It reflects a desire by the acquiring company to spread risks, to find outlets for idle capital funds, to add products that can be sold with the firm's merchandising knowledge and skills, or simply to gain economic power on a broader front.

conscious parallel action: A common course of behavior among competing firms. It can consist of identical price behavior (such as price leadership and followership), the sharing of markets, or the calculation of delivered prices according to a common formula. Conscious parallel action may or may not be the result of collusion or prior agreement. Therefore, it may or may not be held illegal by the courts, depending on the circumstances in each case.

consent decree: A means of settling cases in equity among the parties involved (such as a defendant firm and the Department of Justice). The defendant does not admit guilt, but agrees nevertheless to cease and desist from certain practices and to abide by the rules of behavior set down in the decree. This is the chief instrument employed by the Justice Department and by the Federal Trade Commission in the enforcement of the Sherman and Clayton Acts. The majority of antitrust violations are settled in this manner.

conspicuous consumption: Expression originated by Thorstein Veblen (1857–1929) to mean that those above the subsistence level (that is, the so-called "leisure class") are mainly concerned with impressing others through their standard of living, taste, and dress—in Veblen's words, through "pecuniary emulation." ("Keeping up with the Joneses" is a popular expression of this concept.)

constant-cost industry: Industry that experiences no increases in resource prices or in costs of production as it expands, despite new firms entering it. This will happen only when the industry's demand for the resources it employs is an insignificant proportion of the total demand for those resources.

constant dollars: Expression reflecting the actual prices of a previous year or the average of actual prices of a previous period of years. Hence economic data are often quoted in constant dollars. These are also called **real dollars.** (*Compare* **current dollars.**)

Consumer Price Index (CPI): Average of prices of goods and services commonly purchased by families in urban areas. Generally referred to as a "cost-of-living index," the CPI is published by the Bureau of Labor Statistics of the U.S. Department of Labor.

consumer sovereignty: Concept of the consumer as "king"—in the sense that the consumer registers his or her preferences for goods by "dollar votes" in the marketplace. In a highly competitive economy, competition among producers will cause them to adjust their production to the changing patterns of consumer demands. In less competitive circumstances, where monopolistic forces and other imperfections exist, resources will not be allocated in accordance with consumer wishes.

consumer's surplus: Difference between what a consumer pays and the maximum amount he or she would be willing to pay for a given quantity of a commodity.

consumption: Expenditures on consumer goods and services.

consumption function: Relationship between consumption expenditures and income, expressed as a graph or equation. The relationship is such that, as income increases, consumption increases, but not as fast as income. The expression **propensity to consume** is often used synonymously. (*Note:* The word "function" is employed here in its mathematical sense to mean a variable whose value depends on the value of another variable. Therefore, the expression "consumption function" can also be used to designate *any* type of relationship between consumption and income — not necessarily the type defined above. However, the above type is the most common one.)

contestable market: One that is characterized by ease of exit — the ability to leave the market at little cost. Companies already in such a market are under pressure to maintain a low-price policy. This discourages outsiders from entering, capturing some of the industry's profits, and getting out quickly. Airlines and trucking provide good examples of contestable markets because the principal assets — planes and trucks — though expensive, are both mobile and readily resalable.

contribution margin: That portion of a firm's price, above its direct or average variable cost, that contributes to fixed costs (overhead) and the earning of profit. It may be expressed either as an amount or as a percentage markup on average variable cost.

contributive standard: Criterion of income distribution popularly expressed by the phrase, "To each according to his or her contribution." It means that, if the market value of one person's production is twice that of another's, then the first person should be paid twice as much as the second. This is the predominant criterion of income distribution in market-oriented economies. You will consider the contributive standard a just or equitable one only if you believe that each person is entitled to the fruits of his or her labor. (*Compare* **equality standard; needs standard.**)

convergence hypothesis: Conjecture that capitalism and communism, driven by the process of industrialization, will eventually merge to form a new kind of society in which the personal freedoms and profit motive of Western capitalistic democracies blend with the government controls that exist in a communistic (especially Soviet) economy.

corporation: Association of stockholders created under law but regarded by the courts as an artificial person existing only in the contemplation of the law. The chief characteristics of a corporation are (1) limited liability of its stockholders; (2) stability and permanence; and (3) ability to accumulate large sums of capital through the sale of stocks and bonds.

correspondence principle: Proposition that demonstrates that, in order for comparative statics (the comparison of equilibrium positions in static states) to be meaningful, it is first necessary to develop a dynamic analysis of stability.

cost: Sacrifice that must be made to do or to acquire something. What is sacrificed may be money, goods, leisure time, security, prestige, power, or pleasure.

cost–benefit analysis: *See* **benefit–cost analysis.**

cost-effectiveness analysis: Technique of selecting from alternative programs the one that attains a given objective at the lowest cost. It is a type of analysis most useful when benefits cannot be measured in money.

cost-plus pricing: Method of pricing whereby the seller's price (P), at a given level of output, is determined by adding a percentage markup to the direct cost (or average varible cost, AVC) of the product. Thus:

$$P = AVC + \text{\% markup } (AVC)$$

Thus, if a firm's AVC at a given level of output is $100 per unit, a 50 percent markup would result in a price of $150 per unit:

$$P = \$100 + 0.50\ (\$100) = \$150 \text{ per unit}$$

cost-push inflation: Condition of generally rising prices caused by factor payments to one or more groups of resource owners increasing faster than productivity or efficiency. It is usually attributed to monopolistic market power possessed by some resource owners, unions, or business firms. "Wage-push" and "profit-push" are the most common forms of cost-push inflation.

countervailing power: Proposition that the growth of

market power by one group in the United States may tend to stimulate the growth of a counterreaction and somewhat offsetting influence by another group. *Examples:* Big labor unions face big corporations at the bargaining table; chain stores deal with large processing and manufacturing firms; and big government faces big business and big unions.

craft union: Labor union composed of workers in a particular trade, such as bakers, carpenters, or teamsters. It is thus a "horizontally" organized union.

crawling peg: System of foreign-exchange rates that permits the par values of a nation's currency to change automatically by small increments, downward or upward, if in actual daily trading on the foreign exchange markets the price in terms of other currencies persists on the "floor" or "ceiling" of the governmentally established range for a specified period.

credit: 1. A promise by one party to pay another for money borrowed or for goods and services received. Credit may therefore be regarded as an extension of money. **2.** In international economics, any transaction that results in a money inflow or receipt from a foreign country. It may be represented on a balance-of-payments statement by a plus sign.

credit instrument: Written or printed financial document serving as either a promise or an order to transfer funds from one person to another.

creeping inflation: Slow but persistent upward movement in the general level of prices over a long period of years, typically at an average annual rate of up to 3 percent.

cross elasticity of demand: Percentage change in the quantity purchased of a good resulting from a 1 percent change in the price of another good. Thus:

cross elasticity of demand

$$= \frac{\text{percentage change in the quantity purchased of } X}{\text{percentage change in the price of } Y}$$

$$= \frac{(Q_{X2} - Q_{X1})/(Q_{X2} + Q_{X1})}{(P_{Y2} - P_{Y1})/(P_{Y2} + P_{Y1})}$$

in which Q_{X1} and Q_{X2} represent quantities purchased of X before and after the change in the price of Y, and P_{Y1} and P_{Y2} represent the corresponding prices of Y before and after the change. The cross elasticity of demand thus measures the responsiveness of changes in the quantities purchased of a good to changes in the price of another

good. In general, the higher the coefficient of elasticity, the greater the degree of substitutability. (For example, competing brands of goods in the same industry, such as competing brands of television sets, have high positive cross elasticities.) A coefficient of zero indicates goods that are nonsubstitutes or are unrelated. (Examples are lettuce and beer, hats and books.) A negative coefficient indicates goods that are complementary. (Examples are watches and watchbands, cameras and film, shirts and ties.)

crowding out: Proposition that states that large increases in government spending, whether financed by taxing, borrowing, or printing new money, are likely to reduce business investment spending. There are two reasons: (1) Resources that might otherwise be used by the private sector are diverted to public use. (2) Interest rates tend to be pushed up when government spending is financed by borrowing or by printing money. This increases the costs of business borrowing and forces many firms out of the financial markets. For both reasons, therefore, private incentives to work, save, and invest may be diminished, thus reducing productive capital investment.

currency: Paper money. (Coins are not part of currency.)

current assets: Cash and other assets that can be turned quickly into cash.

current dollars: An expression reflecting actual prices of each year. Hence economic data are often quoted in current dollars. These are also called **nominal dollars.** (*Compare* **constant dollars.**)

current liabilities: Debts that fall due within a year.

current yield: Annual return on an investment expressed as a percentage of its present price.

customs union: Agreement among two or more trading nations to abolish trade barriers, such as tariffs and quotas, among themselves and to adopt a common external policy of trade (such as a common external tariff with all nonmember nations). *Example:* Benelux (Belgium, the Netherlands, and Luxembourg).

cyclically balanced budget: Philosophy that holds that total revenues and expenditures in the government's budget should be balanced or brought into equality over the course of a business cycle.

cyclical unemployment: Unemployment that results from business recessions or depressions because aggregate demand falls too far below the full-employment level of aggregate output and income.

D

deadweight loss: The loss in efficiency, measured by the value of output sacrificed, that society incurs as a result of firms practicing monopoly ($MC = MR$) rather than marginal-cost ($MC = P$) pricing.

death taxes: Taxes imposed on the transfer of property after death. They consist of estate and inheritance taxes and are imposed by federal and state governments at progressive rates.

debit: In international economics, any transaction that results in a money outflow or payment to a foreign country. It may be represented on a balance-of-payments statement by a minus sign.

decreasing-cost industry: Industry that experiences decreases in resource prices or in its costs of production as it expands because of new firms entering it. This situation might arise for a while as a result of substantial external economies of scale.

deduction: In logical thinking, a process of reasoning from premises to conclusions. The premises are more general than the conclusions, so deduction is often defined as reasoning from the general to the particular. (Opposite of **induction.**)

deflation: 1. Statistical adjustment of data by which an economic time series expressed in current dollars is converted into a series expressed in constant dollars of a previous period. The purpose of the adjustment is to compensate for the distorting effects of inflation (that is, the long-run upward trend of prices) through a reverse process of "deflation." **2.** Decline in the general price level of all goods and services — or, equivalently, a rise in the purchasing power of a unit of money. (Compare **inflation.**)

delivered pricing: Method of pricing whereby the seller charges the buyer a destination price consisting of both a factory price (called a "mill price") and a shipping charge. However, in order to match the price of a competitor, the factory price may be some other company's mill price rather than the seller's, and the shipping charge may in fact be greater or less than the actual transportation costs that are incurred. When that happens, prices quoted on a delivered basis are discriminatory. They do not reflect the seller's marginal cost of producing and selling the product. (Compare **f.o.b. pricing** and **basing-point pricing.**)

demand: Relation expressing the amounts of a commodity that buyers would be willing and able to purchase at various prices during a given period of time, all other things remaining the same. This relation may be expressed in a table (called a **demand schedule**), in a graph (called a **demand curve**), or in a mathematical equation.

demand curve: Graph of a demand schedule, showing the number of units of a commodity that buyers would be able and willing to purchase at various prices during a given period of time, all other things remaining the same.

demand deposit: Promise by a bank to pay immediately an amount of money specified by the customer who owns the deposit. It is thus "checkbook money" because it permits transactions to be paid for by check rather than with currency. However, unlike other types of checkable deposits, a demand deposit does not pay interest to its owner.

demand, law of: Principle that states that the quantity demanded of a commodity varies inversely with its price, assuming that all other things that may affect demand remain the same. These "all other" things include (1) buyers' money incomes; (2) the prices of related goods in consumption; and (3) tastes and other nonmonetary determinants. Among them: consumer preferences, number of buyers in the market, and characteristics of buyers.

demand price: Highest price a buyer is willing to pay for a given quantity of a commodity.

demand-pull inflation: Condition of generally rising prices caused by increases in aggregate demand at a time when available supplies of goods are becoming more limited. Goods may go into short supply because resources are fully utilized or because production cannot be increased rapidly enough to meet growing demand.

demand schedule: Table showing the number of units of a commodity that buyers would be able and willing to purchase at various possible prices during a given period of time, all other things remaining the same.

demand-side economics: Measures aimed at achieving efficiency through policies designed to regulate purchasing power. Keynesian economics, because it tends to focus on fiscal and monetary policies to control aggregate demand, has been characterized as demand-side economics. (Contrast with **supply-side economics.**)

deposit multiplier: Proposition that states that an increase in the banking system's chackable deposits, D, will be some multiple, m, of the increase in the system's excess reserves, E. Thus,

$$D = mE$$

In the formula, m is the reciprocal of the required-reserve ratio, r. Thus: $m = 1/r$. The above deposit-multiplier formula can, therefore, be written

$$D = 1/r \times E$$

Example: If $r = 10$ percent and $E = \$1,000$, then $D = 1/0.10 \times \$1,000 = \$10,000$. Thus, excess reserves of $\$1,000$ can result in as much as a $\$10,000$ increase in checkable deposits. The formula assumes, however, that the banking system is fully loaned up to begin with — that is, before there is any increase in excess reserves. In reality, there are so-called "leakages" that prevent the deposit-multiplier from exerting its full impact. They include (1) the percentage of checkable deposits that the public withdraws as cash; (2) the percentage of checkable deposits that banks, for one reason or another, hold as excess (idle) reserves; and (3) the percentage of checkable deposits that the public transfers into reservable time deposits.

Depository Institutions Acts (1980, 1982): Legislation consisting of the Depository Institutions Deregulation and Monetary Control Act (1980) and the Depository Institutions Act (1982). Taken together, both laws provided for the following: (1) *Uniform reserve standards:* All depository institutions must meet the same reserve requirements on similar types and sizes of deposits. (2) *Transaction accounts:* All depository institutions may hold interest-bearing checkable deposits. These, along with demand deposits at commercial banks, constitute transaction accounts. (3) *Federal Reserve accessibility:* All depository institutions that issue transaction accounts can borrow on equal terms from their Federal Reserve Bank. Depository institutions can also purchase the Fed's services, such as check clearing and electronic transfer of funds, if desired. (4) *Thrift-institution banking powers:* Savings-and-loan associations and savings banks have limited authority to offer demand deposits and to make commercial loans. (5) *Money-market deposit accounts:* Depository institutions can offer higher-yielding deposit accounts with limited checking privileges at money-market interest rates.

depreciation: Decline in the value of a fixed asset, such as plant or equipment, due to wear and tear, destruction, or obsolescence resulting from the development of new and better techniques.

depression: Lower phase of a business cycle in which the economy is operating with substantial unemployment of its resources and a sluggish rate of capital investment and consumption resulting from little business and consumer optimism.

derived demand: Demand for a product or resource based on its contribution to the product for which it is used. *Examples:* The separate demands for bricks, lumber, and so on, are derived partly from the demand for construction; the demand for steel is derived partly from the demand for automobiles.

devaluation: Official (government) act that makes a domestic currency cheaper in terms of foreign currencies (or in terms of gold under a gold standard). It is typically designed to reduce a nation's balance-of-payments deficits by increasing exports while reducing imports. (*Contrast with* **revaluation.**)

dialectical materialism: Logical method of historical analysis. In particular, it was used by Karl Marx, who employed the philosopher Hegel's idea that historical change is the result of inherently conflicting or opposing forces in society and that the forces are basically economic or materialistic.

"dictatorship of the proletariat": Expression used by Karl Marx to describe a stage of Marxian socialism in which the bourgeoisie (or capitalist class) has been toppled from power and, along with its properties, is under the management of the proletariat (or working class), which is also in control of the state.

diminishing marginal utility, law of: In a given period of time, the consumption of a product while tastes remain constant *may at first* result in increasing marginal (that is, incremental) satisfactions or utilities per unit of the product consumed. However, a point will eventually be reached beyond which further units of consumption of the product will result in decreasing marginal utilities per additional unit of the product consumed. This is the point of diminishing marginal utility. *Note:* Even though marginal utility may rise at first, *it must eventually fall.* It is the diminishing phase of marginal utility that is relevant and serves as the basis for the law.

diminishing returns (variable proportions), law of: In a given state of technology, the addition of a changing or variable factor of production to other fixed factors of production may at first yield increasing marginal (that is, incremental) returns per unit of the variable factor added, but a point will be reached beyond which further additions of the variable factor will yield diminishing marginal returns per unit of the variable factor added. This is the point of diminishing marginal returns. *Note:* Even though marginal returns may rise at first, *they must eventually fall.* It is the diminishing phase of marginal returns that is relevant and serves as the basis for the law.

direct payments: Method of subsidizing sellers while permitting the price of a commodity to be determined in a free market by supply and demand. If the price turns out to be "too low," sellers are compensated by a subsidy from the government for the difference between the market price received and some higher, predetermined target price. If the market price turns out to be equal to or greater than the target price, no subsidized compensation is provided. Under this system, therefore, consumers pay and sellers receive the market price of the commodity, but sellers *may in addition* receive a subsidy. (*Note:* A plan of this type has long existed for certain farm commodities.)

direct tax: Tax that is not shifted—that is, its burden is borne by the persons or firms originally taxed. *Examples:* personal income taxes, social security taxes paid by employees, and death taxes.

discounting: Process by which a given amount, expressed in dollars, is adjusted at interest to yield a present value. *Example:* At 6 percent, $1.06 one year hence has a present value of $1; $1.124 two years hence has a present value one year hence of $1.06, and a present value today of $1. Discounting is thus the opposite of **compounding.**

discount rate: Interest rate charged to depository institutions on their loans from the Federal Reserve Banks. It is called a "discount rate" because the interest on a loan is discounted when the loan is made, rather than collected when the loan is repaid.

discouraged-worker hypothesis: Theory that holds that a rising level of unemployment leads to declining labor-force participation rates. This is because the chances of finding a job diminish during recession. Therefore, many workers stop trying and leave the labor force. (*Contrast with* **additional-worker hypothesis.**)

disequilibrium: State of imbalance or nonequilibrium. *Example:* a situation in which the quantities supplied and demanded of a commodity at a given price are unequal, so there is a tendency for market prices and/or quantities to change. Any economic entity or system, such as a household, a firm, a market, or an economy, that is not in equilibrium is said to be in disequilibrium.

disguised unemployment (underemployment): Situation in which employed resources are not being used in their most efficient ways.

disinvestment: Reduction in the total stock of capital goods caused by failure to replace it as it wears out. *Example:* the consumption or using up of factories, machines, and so forth at a faster rate than they are being replaced so that the productive base is diminishing.

disposable personal income: Income remaining after payment of personal taxes.

dissaving: Expenditure on consumption in excess of income. This may be accomplished by drawing on past savings, borrowing, or receiving help from others.

dividend: Earnings that a corporation pays to its stockholders. Payments are usually in cash, but they may also be in property, securities, or other forms.

division of labor: Specialization in productive activities among workers, resulting in increased production because it (1) permits development and refinement of skills; (2) avoids the time that is wasted in going from one job to another; and (3) simplifies human tasks, thus permitting the introduction of labor-saving machines.

double coincidence of wants: Situation that is necessary in a barter exchange: each party must have what the other wants and must be willing to trade at the exact quantities and terms suitable to both.

double taxation: Taxation of the same base in two different forms. A typical example is the corporate income tax: the corporation pays an income tax on its profits, and the stockholder pays an income tax on the dividends he receives from those profits.

draft: Unconditional written order by one party (the creditor or drawer) on a second party (the debtor or drawee) directing the second party to pay a third party (the bearer or payee) a specified sum of money. An ordinary check, therefore, is an example of a draft.

dual banking system: Expression referring to the fact that all commercial banks in the United States are chartered either as national banks or as state banks. This organizational structure, not found in any other country, is a unique outgrowth of American political history.

dual labor market: Hypothesis that states that the labor market is segmented into two distinct markets. One is a primary labor market, in which jobs are characterized by relatively high wages, favorable working conditions, and employment stability. The other is a secondary labor market, in which jobs, when they are available, pay relatively low wages, provide poor working conditions, and are highly unstable. White-collar and blue-collar workers, many of whom are union members, account for most of the participants in the primary market. In contrast, the competitively "disadvantaged poor"—the unskilled, the undereducated, and the victims of racial prejudice—are confined to the secondary market.

dumping: Sale of the same product in different markets at different prices. *Example:* A monopolist might restrict his output in the domestic market and charge a higher price because demand is relatively inelastic, and "dump" the rest of his output in a foreign market at a lower price because demand there is relatively elastic. He thereby gains the benefit of lower average total costs on his entire output (domestic plus foreign) and earns a larger net profit than if he sold the entire output in the domestic market—which he could do only by charging a lower price per unit on all units sold.

duopoly: Oligopoly consisting of two sellers. Hence it may be either a perfect duopoly or an imperfect one, depending on whether the product is standardized or differentiated.

dynamic model: One in which economic phenomena are studied by relating them to preceding or succeeding events. The influence of time is therefore taken explicitly into account. A dynamic model is thus like a "motion picture" as distinguished from a "snapshot." (*Compare* **static model.**)

E

econometrics: Integration of economic theory, mathematics, and statistics. It consists of expressing economic relationships in the form of mathematical equations and verifying the resulting models by statistical methods.

economic costs: Payments made to the owners of the factors of production to persuade them to supply their resources in a particular activity.

economic development: Process whereby a nation's real per-capita output or income (its GNP) increases over a long period of time. A nation's rate of economic development is thus measured by its long-run per-capita rate of economic growth.

economic efficiency: *See* **efficiency**

economic good: Scarce commodity—that is, any commodity for which the market price is greater than zero at a particular time and place. (*Compare* **free good.**)

economic growth: Rate of increase in an economy's full-employment real output or income over time—that is, the rise in its full-employment output in constant prices. Economic growth may be expressed in either of two ways: (1) as the increase in total full-employment real GNP or NNP over time, or (2) as the increase in per-capita full-employment real GNP or NNP over time. The "total" measure is employed to describe the expansion of a nation's economic output or potential, whereas the "per-capita" measure is used to express its material standard of living and to compare it with other countries.

economic indicators: Time series of economic data, classified as leading, lagging, or coincident indicators. They are used in business-cycle analysis and forecasting.

economic interpretation of history: Proposition advanced by Karl Marx (and others) that the great political, social, intellectual, and ethical movements of history are determined by the ways in which societies organize their social institutions to carry on the basic economic activities of production, exchange, distribution, and consumption of goods. Thus economic forces are the prime cause of fundamental historical change.

economic man: The notion that each individual in a capitalistic society, whether he or she be a worker, businessperson, consumer, or investor, is motivated by economic forces and hence will always act to obtain the greatest satisfaction for the least sacrifice or cost. Satisfaction may take the form of profits to a businessperson, wages or leisure hours to a worker, pleasure to a consumer from the goods that he or she purchases, and so on.

economic plan: Detailed method, formulated beforehand, for achieving specific economic objectives by governing the activities and interrelationships of those economic entities, namely firms, households, and governments, that have an influence on the desired outcome.

economic (pure) profit: Payment to a firm in excess of its economic costs, including normal profit. It is the same as **net revenue.**

economic rent: Payment to an owner of a unit of a factor of production, in an industry in equilibrium, in excess of the factor's supply price or opportunity cost. The payment is thus in excess of the minimum amount necessary to keep the factor in its present occupation. Economic rent is therefore a surplus to the recipient.

economics: Social science concerned chiefly with the way society chooses to employ its limited resources, which have alternative uses, to produce goods and services for present and future consumption.

economic system: Relationships between the components of an economy (such as its households, firms, and government) and the institutional framework of laws and customs within which these organisms operate to determine *what, how,* and *for whom* goods are produced.

economies (diseconomies) of scale: The decreases (increases) in a firm's long-run average costs as the size of its plant is increased. Those factors that give rise to economies of scale are (1) greater specialization of resources; (2) more efficient utilization of equipment; (3) reduced unit costs of inputs; (4) opportunities for economical utilization of by-products; and (5) growth of auxiliary facilities. Diseconomies of scale may eventually set in, however, due to (1) limitations of (or "diminishing returns" to) management in its decision-making function and (2) competition among firms in bidding up prices of limited resources.

efficiency: The best use of what is available to attain a desired result.   Two specific types of efficiency are "technical" and "economic."   **1. Technical efficiency:** Condition that exists when a production system—a firm, an industry, an economy—is achieving maximum output by making the fullest utilization of available inputs.   The system is then producing on its production-possibilities curve.   This means that no change in the combination of resources can be made that will increase the output of one product without decreasing the output of another.   **2. Economic (allocative) efficiency:** Condition that exists when a production system has achieved technical efficiency *and* is fulfilling consumer preferences by producing the combination of goods that people want—are willing and able to buy—with their present incomes.   This means that no change in the combination of resources or of output can be implemented that will make someone better off without making someone else worse off—each in his or her own estimation.   (*Note:* Economic efficiency is synonymous with **Pareto optimality.**)

elasticity: Percentage change in quantity demanded or supplied resulting from a 1 percent change in price. Mathematically, it is the ratio of the percentage change in quantity (demanded or supplied) to the percentage change in price:

$$\text{elasticity, } E = \frac{\text{percentage change in quantity}}{\text{percentage change in price}}$$
$$= \frac{(Q_2 - Q_1)/(Q_2 + Q_1)}{(P_2 - P_1)/(P_2 + P_1)}$$

in which Q_1 and Q_2, and P_1 and P_2, denote the corresponding quantities and prices before and after the change.   This coefficient of elasticity (which is usually stated numerically without regard to algebraic sign) may range from zero to infinity.   It may take any of five forms:

perfectly elastic	$(E = \infty)$
relatively elastic	$(E > 1)$
unit elastic	$(E = 1)$
relatively inelastic	$(E < 1)$
perfectly inelastic	$(E = 0)$

The preceding definition refers to what is known as *price elasticity* of demand or supply.   It is one of several types of elasticities that exist in economics and is the one that is commonly understood unless otherwise specified.   In general, elasticity may be thought of as the responsiveness of changes in one variable to changes in another, where responsiveness is measured in terms of percentage changes.

Employment Act of 1946: Act of Congress that requires the government to maintain high levels of employment, production, and purchasing power.   To assist the President in this task, the act authorizes him to appoint a panel of experts known as the Council of Economic Advisors.

employment ratio: Percentage of the working-age population (16 years of age and older) that is employed.

employment-training policies: Deliberate efforts undertaken in the private and public sectors to develop and use the capacities of human beings as actual or potential members of the labor force.   Employment-training policies are also known as **human-resource policies.**

Engel's Laws: Set of relationships between consumer expenditures and income derived by a nineteenth-century German statistician, Ernst Engel, and based on research into workingmen's purchases in Western Europe during the 1850s.   The relationships state that, as a family's income increases: (1) the percentage it spends on food decreases; (2) the percentage it spends on housing and household operations remains about constant (except for the part spent on fuel, light, and refrigeration, which decreases); and (3) the percentage it spends on all other categories and the amount it saves increase (except for medical care and personal care items, which remain fairly constant).   In general, the *total* amount spent increases as a family's income increases.   *Note:* Strictly speaking, only the first relationship above is attributed to Engel; the other two are modernized versions of his early findings, based on more recent research.

entrepreneurship: Factor of production that is defined as the function performed by those who assemble the other factors of production, raise the necessary money, organize the management, make the basic business policy decisions, and reap the gains of success or the losses of failure.   The entrepreneur is the innovator and the catalyst in a capitalistic system.   He need not be exclusively an owner or a manager; the entrepreneurial function may be performed by either or both, depending on the size and complexity of the firm.

equal advantage, law of: In a market economy, owners of

resources will always transfer them from less desirable to more desirable uses. As this happens, the occupations *out* of which resources are transferred often tend to become more desirable, while the occupations *into* which resources are transferred tend to become less desirable. This transfer process continues until all occupations are equally desirable. At this point, there is no gain to be made by further transfer of resources. Hence the economy is in equilibrium. *Note:* The term "desirable" includes both monetary and nonmonetary considerations. The latter helps explain why permanent differences in monetary rewards may exist between various occupations.

equal employment opportunity: Legislation prohibiting discrimination in employment on the basis of race, religion, sex, or national origin. (*See also* **affirmative action.**)

equality standard: Criterion of income distribution popularly expressed by the phrase, "To each equally." You will regard the equality standard as a just or equitable one only if you assume that all people are alike in the *added* satisfaction or utility they get from an extra dollar of income. If this assumption is false—if an additional dollar of income actually provides a greater gain in utility to some people than to others—then justice is more properly served by distributing most of any increase in society's income to those who will enjoy it more. In reality, there is no conclusive evidence to suggest that people are either alike or unlike in their capacities to enjoy additional income. Therefore, no scientific basis exists for assuming that an equal distribution of income is more equitable than an unequal one. (*Compare* **contributive standard; needs standard.**)

equation of exchange: Expression of the relation between the quantity of money (M), its velocity of circulation (V), the average price (P) of final goods and services, and the physical quantity (Q) of those goods and services:

$$MV = PQ$$

The equation states that the total amount of money spent on goods and services (MV) is equal to the total amount of money received for goods and services (PQ). (*See also* **quantity theory of money.**)

equilibrium: State of balance between opposing forces. An object in equilibrium is in a state of rest and has no tendency to change.

equilibrium conditions: Set of relationships that defines the equilibrium properties of an economic entity such as a household, a firm, or an entire economy.

equilibrium price: 1. Price of a commodity determined in the market by the intersection of a supply curve and a demand curve. (Also called **normal price.**) **2.** Price (and corresponding equilibrium quantity) that maximizes a firm's profit.

equilibrium quantity: 1. Quantity of a commodity determined in the market by the intersection of a supply curve and a demand curve. **2.** Quantity (and corresponding equilibrium price) that maximizes a firm's profit.

equity: Justice or fairness. In economics, equity refers to justice with respect to the distribution of income or of wealth within a society. Because justice is subjective rather than objective, equity may be thought of as a philosophical concept but an economic goal. However, there is no scientific way of concluding that one standard or mechanism for distributing income is just and therefore "good" while another is unjust and therefore "bad." Each society or type of economic system establishes its own standards of distribution. Nevertheless, economics can help to evaluate the material consequences of any standard that a society adopts. (*See also* **contributive standard; equality standard; needs standard.**)

escalator clause: Provision in a contract whereby payments such as wages, insurance or pension benefits, or loan repayments over a stated period are tied to a comprehensive measure of living costs or price-level changes. The consumer price index and the implicit price index (GNP deflator) are the measures most commonly used for this purpose.

estate tax: Progressive (graduated) tax imposed by the federal government and by most state governments on the transfer of all property owned by a decedent at the time of death. Exemptions, deductions, and rates vary widely among the states.

Eurodollars: Dollar deposits in banks outside the United States, mostly in Europe. They are held by American and foreign banks, corporations, and individuals and represent dollar obligations that are constantly being shifted from one country to another in search of the highest return.

European Recovery Program (ERP): Commonly known as the "Marshall Plan" (after Secretary of State George C. Marshall, who proposed it in 1947), this was a comprehensive recovery blueprint for European countries, financed by the United States, for the purposes of (1) increasing their productive capacity, (2) stabilizing their financial systems, (3) promoting their mutual economic cooperation, and (4) reducing their dependence on U.S. assistance. The ERP was terminated in 1951 after considerable success, and its functions were absorbed by other government agencies and programs.

excess reserves: Quantity of a bank's legal reserves over and above its required reserves. Thus:

$$\text{excess reserves} = \text{legal reserves} - \text{required reserves}$$

Excess reserves are the key to a bank's lending power.

excise tax: Tax imposed on the manufacture, sale, or consumption of various commodities, such as liquor, tobacco, and gasoline.

exclusion principle: Basis for distinguishing between nonpublic and public goods. A good is nonpublic if anyone who does not pay for it can be excluded from its use; otherwise, it is a public good.

expenditure multiplier: Principle that states that changes in total spending can bring about magnified changes in real aggregate income. The expenditure multiplier (M_E) is thus the same as the investment multiplier, except that the independent variable is broadened to include total spending rather than investment spending only. (*See* **multiplier.**)

explicit costs: Money outlays of a firm recorded in its books of account. (*Compare* **implicit costs.**)

external economies and diseconomies of scale: Conditions that bring about decreases or increases in a firm's long-run average costs as a result of factors that are entirely outside of the firm as a producing unit. They depend on adjustments of the industry and are related to the firm only to the extent that the firm is a part of the industry. *Example:* External economies may result from improvements in public transportation and marketing facilities as an industry develops in a particular geographic area; however, diseconomies may eventually set in as firms bid up the prices of limited resources in the area.

externalities: External benefits or costs for which no compensation is made. (Externalities are also called **spillovers.**)

F

Fabian socialism: Form of socialism founded in England in 1884. It emerged as an outgrowth of utopian socialism by advocating gradual and evolutionary reform within a democratic framework.

factors of production: Human and nonhuman productive resources of an economy, usually classified into four groups: land, labor, capital, and entrepreneurship.

Fair Labor Standards Act (Wages and Hours Law) of 1938: An act, with subsequent amendments, that specifies minimum hourly wages, overtime rates, and prohibitions against child labor for workers producing goods in interstate commerce.

family-allowance plan: Plan that provides every family, rich or poor, with a certain amount of money based exclusively on the number and age of its children. Families above certain designated income levels return all or a portion of the money with their income taxes, but those below specified income levels keep it. More than 60 countries have family allowance plans.

Fawcett, Millicent Garrett (1847–1919): English economic educator whose book, *Political Economy for Beginners* (1870), was largely a simplification and abridgement of classical economics as expressed by Mill in 1848. (*See* **Mill, John Stuart.**) Her book was highly successful, went through ten editions over a period of forty years, and established her as an outstanding popularizer of classical economic ideas.

featherbedding: Labor union "make-work" rules designed to increase the labor or labor-time on a particular job. Outlawed by the Labor–Management Relations (Taft–Hartley) Act of 1947.

Federal Advisory Council: Committee within the Federal Reserve System that advises the Board of Governors on important current developments.

federal agency discount notes: Short-term credit instruments sold (issued) by certain government agencies. Among these are the Federal Home Loan Bank, the Federal National Mortgage Association, and the Federal Farm Credit Bank System. The money raised by these agencies is used to provide mortgages and other types of loans.

Federal Deposit Insurance Corporation (FDIC): Government agency that insures deposits (demand and time) at commercial and savings banks. Each insured bank pays an annual premium equal to a fraction of its total deposits, in return for which the FDIC insures each account up to $100,000 against loss due to bank failure. In addition to its insurance function, the FDIC supervises insured banks and presides over the liquidation of banks that do fail. Two parallel agencies that perform similar functions are the Federal Savings and Loan Insurance Corporation, which insures deposits in savings and loan associations, and the National Credit Union Administration, which provides deposit insurance for federally chartered credit unions. National banks (chartered by the federal government) are required to be insured by the FDIC, and state-chartered banks may apply if they wish. Since the late 1930s, practically all banks have been covered by insurance, thereby eliminating bank runs and permitting greater bank stability.

federal funds: Unsecured loans that banks and certain other depository institutions make to one another, usually overnight, out of their excess reserves. The purchase and sale of federal funds is limited to banks, savings institutions, and certain government agencies.

federal-funds rate: Interest rate at which banks borrow excess reserves from other banks' accounts at the Fed, usually overnight, to keep required reserves from falling below the legal level. In general, the lower the volume of excess reserves, the higher will be the federal-funds rate. Therefore, the federal-funds rate is an important indicator that the Fed watches to decide whether it should add to banks' reserves or take them away. For short periods of time, the Fed can largely control the federal-funds rate. For example, the rate can be raised by selling Treasury bills to the banking system, thereby pulling out reserves. Conversely, the rate can be lowered by buying bills from the system, thereby putting in reserves. As part of its policy-making function, the Fed tries to maintain a federal-funds rate that is consistent with other monetary goals.

Federal Open Market Committee: The most important policy-making body of the Federal Reserve System. Its chief function is to establish policy for the System's purchase and sale of government and other securities in the open market.

Federal Reserve Bank: One of the 12 banks (plus branches) that make up the Federal Reserve System. Each serves as a "banker's bank" for the member banks in its district by acting as a source of credit and a depository of resources, and by performing other useful functions.

Federal Reserve System: Central banking system created by Congress in 1913. It consists of (1) 12 Federal Reserve Banks — one located in each of 12 districts in the country; (2) a Board of Governors; (3) a Federal Open Market Committee and various other committees; and (4) several thousand member banks, which hold the great majority of all commercial bank deposits in the nation.

Federal Trade Commission: Government agency created in 1914. It is charged with preventing unfair business practices by enforcing the Federal Trade Commission Act and by exercising concurrently with the Justice Department the enforcement of prohibitive provisions of the Clayton Antitrust Act as amended by the Robinson–Patman Act.

Federal Trade Commission Act (1914): A major antitrust law of the U.S. Its chief purpose is to prevent unfair (that is, deceptive, dishonest, or injurious) methods of competition and, as amended by the Wheeler–Lea Act (1938), to safeguard the public by preventing the dissemination of false and misleading advertising of food, drugs, cosmetics, and therapeutic devices.

financial intermediaries: Business firms that serve as middlemen between lenders and borrowers by creating and issuing financial obligations or claims against themselves in order to acquire profitable financial claims against others. Examples of such firms are commercial banks, mutual savings banks, savings and loan associations, credit unions, insurance companies, and all other financial institutions. In general, they are wholesalers and retailers of funds.

financial markets: The money and capital markets. In the former, short-term credit instruments are bought and sold; in the latter, long-term credit and equity instruments are bought and sold.

firm: Business organization that brings together and coordinates factors of production — capital, land, labor, and entrepreneurship — for the purpose of supplying goods or services.

First Bank of the United States: See **Bank of the United States.**

fiscal drag: Tendency of a high-employment economy to be held back from its full growth potential because it is incurring budgetary surpluses. Such surpluses may arise because, other things being equal, a progressive tax system tends to generate increases in revenues relative to expenditures during periods of high employment.

fiscal policy: Deliberate spending and taxing actions undertaken by the federal government in order to achieve price stability, to help dampen the swings of business cycles, and to bring the nation's output and employment to desired levels.

Fisher equation: See **equation of exchange.**

Fisher, Irving (1867–1940): One of America's foremost economists during the first half of the twentieth century. A professor at Yale University, he authored many books and articles on diverse topics, including statistics and monetary theory. Among his many contributions was the "Fisher equation," which he used to explain the cause-and-effect relationship between the money supply and the price level. (See **equation of exchange** and **quantity theory of money**.)

fixed assets: Durable assets of an enterprise used to carry on its business, such as land, buildings, machinery, equipment, office furniture, automobiles, and trucks.

fixed costs: Costs that do not vary with a firm's output. *Examples:* rental payments, interest on debt, property taxes.

floating exchange rates: Foreign-exchange rates determined in a free market by supply and demand.

f.o.b. pricing: Method of pricing whereby the seller charges a buyer the firm's own mill price and places the product "free on board" (or "freight on board") at a nearby shipping site (such as a truck-loading platform, railway station, or dock), with the buyer actually paying the freight costs to the destination point. For many products priced in this way, the buyer is even permitted to pick them up at the mill, if the buyer so chooses. Prices quoted on a strict f.o.b. basis are not discriminatory because they reflect the seller's marginal cost of producing and selling the product. (*Compare* **delivered pricing**.)

"forced" saving: Situation in which consumers are prevented from spending part of their income on consumption. Some examples include: (1) prices rising faster than money wages, causing a decrease in real consumption and hence an increase in real (forced) saving; (2) a corporation that plows back some of its profit instead of distributing it as dividend income to stockholders; and (3) a government that taxes its citizens and uses the funds for investment, thereby preventing the public from utilizing a portion of its income for the purchase of consumer goods.

foreign aid: Loans, grants, or assistance from one government to another for the purpose of accelerating economic development in the recipient country.

foreign exchange: Instruments used for international payments. Such instruments consist not only of currency, but also of checks, drafts, and bills of exchange (which are orders to pay currency).

foreign exchange rate: Price of one currency in terms of another.

foreign-trade multiplier: Principle that states that fluctuations in net exports (that is, imports minus exports) may generate magnified variations in national income. It is based on the idea that a change in exports relative to imports has the same multiplier effect on national income as a change in expenditure "injections" into the income stream. Similarly, a change in imports relative to exports has the same multiplier effect on national income as a change in "withdrawals" from the income stream. In general, an increase in exports tends to raise domestic income, but the increased income also encourages some imports, which act as "leakages." These tend to reduce the full multiplier effect that would exist if imports remained constant.

forward exchange: Foreign exchange bought (or sold) at a given time and at a stipulated current or "spot" price, but payable at a future date. By buying or selling forward exchange, importers and exporters can protect themselves against the risks of fluctuations in the current exchange market.

forward prices: Proposed plan for reducing price uncertainty and encouraging greater stability in agriculture through the use of the price system as an adjustment mechanism. Under the plan, a government-appointed board would predict in advance of breeding or seeding time the equilibrium prices of commodities, based on expected supply and demand. The government would then guarantee those predicted or forward prices in two ways: by storage programs and direct payments to farmers, if actual prices should fall below forward prices, and by a direct tax on farmers, if actual prices should rise above forward prices.

four-firm concentration ratio: See **concentration ratio**.

free good: Good for which the market price is zero at a particular time and place.

free-rider problem: Tendency of people to avoid paying for a good's benefits when they can be obtained free. Public goods (such as national defense, air-traffic control, and so on) provide examples because the benefits of such goods are indivisible and therefore cannot be denied to individuals, whether they pay or not. Those who do not pay are thus "free riders." If many people become free riders, there might be no way of knowing how much of a public good should be provided. In that case, some form of collective action, usually through government, is taken.

free-trade area: Association of trading nations whose participants agree to impose no restrictive devices, such as tariffs or quotas, on one another but are free to impose whatever restrictive devices they wish on nonparticipants. *Example:* The European Free Trade Association (EFTA).

frictional unemployment: Unemployment due to maladjustments in the economic system resulting from imperfect labor mobility, imperfect knowledge of job opportunities, and a general inability of the economy to match people with jobs instantly and smoothly. A common form of frictional unemployment consists of people who are temporarily out of work because they are between jobs.

Friedman, Milton (1912–): A leading American economist and Nobel laureate (1976) who did pioneering work in the study of consumption theory, monetary economics, and other fields. Most of his career was spent as a professor at the University of Chicago, where he was the foremost exponent of the "Chicago School" of economic thought. This approach to economics extolls free markets, a minimal role for government, and other libertarian views. Friedman thus follows in the tradition of Adam Smith and most other classical economists.

fringe benefits: Monetary advantages other than basic wages that are provided by employers for their employees. Examples include supplementary pay, time off with pay, insurance benefits, pensions, and income-maintenance payments for economic layoffs or job termination.

full-cost (average-cost) price: Price for a given volume of output that is at least high enough to cover all of a firm's costs of production — that is, its average total cost for that volume of output. If demand is great enough to enable the firm to sell its entire output at that price, the firm will earn a normal profit. If it can sell its output at a still higher price, it will earn an economic (or pure) profit.

full employment: Level of employment at which (1) everyone who wants to work is working, except for those who are frictionally and structurally unemployed, and (2) the average price level is stable. Full employment is also called **natural employment.**

Full Employment and Balanced Growth (Humphrey–Hawkins) Act (1976): Federal law with three major provisions: (1) Requires the President to set long-term and short-term production and employment goals, including an annual unemployment-rate target of 4 percent, and to identify means for attaining the goals through public-employment programs, employment-training policies, and so on. (2) Requires the Federal Reserve to declare semiannually its monetary policies and their relation to the President's goals. (3) Requires the government to undertake actions that will achieve the goal of full employment while striving for a zero-percent inflation rate.

full-employment (structural) budget: Estimate of annual government expenditures and revenues that would occur at the level of potential real GNP — that is, at full employment. Any resulting surplus (or deficit) is called a full-employment surplus (or deficit).

"functional finance": Philosophy that holds that the government should pursue whatever fiscal measures are needed to achieve noninflationary full employment and economic growth — without regard to budget balancing per se. The federal budget is thus viewed functionally as a flexible fiscal tool for achieving economic objectives rather than as an accounting statement to be balanced periodically.

functional income distribution: Payments in the form of wages, rents, interest, and profits made to the owners of the factors of production in return for supplying their labor, land, capital, and entrepreneurial ability.

G

gains from trade: Net benefits or increases in goods that a country receives as a result of trading with others. This concept also applies to trading between small economic entities, such as regions and individuals.

gain-sharing plans: Incentive compensation systems that tie pay increases to some measure of company performance. Among the measures commonly used are profit, productivity, value-added in manufacturing, or a ratio of labor costs to sales revenues. Profit-sharing plans, in which businesses distribute a share of net profits to workers, are perhaps the best-known examples of gain-sharing plans.

Galbraith, John Kenneth (1908–): American economist whose writing, in the tradition of the "institutionalist school," is perhaps closest to that of Thorstein Veblen. Like Veblen, Galbraith criticized America's capitalistic institutions and processes. Among his chief propositions are these: (1) The market system, dominated by big business, does not perform the way the "conventional wisdom" of traditional economics says that it does. (2) Modern industry is run by a "technostructure" of elite specialists who bamboozle consumers through advertising, thereby insulating big business from the free market. (3) A larger public sector is needed, both economically and politically, to reduce the power of large corporations and to "educate" the people to appreciate "the higher things in life."

General Agreements on Tariffs and Trade (GATT): International commercial agreement signed in 1947 by the United States and many other countries for the purpose of achieving four basic long-run objectives: (1) nondiscrimination in trade through adherence to unconditional most-favored-nation treatment, (2) reduction of tariffs by negotiation, (3) elimination of import quotas (with some exceptions), and (4) resolution of differences through consultation.

general equilibrium theory: Explanation or model of the interrelations between prices and outputs of goods and resources in different markets and the possibility of simultaneous equilibrium among all of them. It is primarily of theoretical interest, but it focuses attention on the fact that, in the real world, markets are often interdependent.

general price level: Expression representing the "average" level of prices in the economy. It is often represented by the **Implicit Price Index,** although no index can accurately reflect all prices.

George, Henry (1839–1897): Prominent American economist whose book, *Progress and Poverty* (1879), ranks as one of the most widely read economic treatises of all time. In the book he advocated a *single tax* on land as the source of all government revenue. In support of his proposal, he argued that, unlike other factors of production, land is provided by nature. Therefore, rent to landlords is an unearned surplus that increases as population grows, depriving the landless of their birthright to a share of the surplus. The solution is government taxation of all land rent. If this were done, no other taxes would be needed. (See **single tax.**)

gift tax: Progressive (graduated) tax imposed by the federal government and by some state governments. It is paid by the donor or person who makes the gift, not the donee or recipient of it. Exemptions, deductions, and rates vary widely among the states.

Gini coefficient of inequality: A measure of the degree of inequality in a distribution. On a Lorenz diagram, it equals the numerical value of the area between the Lorenz curve and the diagonal line divided by the entire area beneath the diagonal line. The ratio may vary between 0 (no inequality) and 1 (complete inequality).

GNP deflator: *See* **Implicit Price Index.**

gold-bullion standard: Monetary standard under which (1) the national unit of currency (such as the dollar, pound, or mark) is defined in terms of a fixed weight of gold; (2) gold is held by the government in the form of bars rather than coin; (3) there is no circulation of gold in any

form within the economy; and (4) gold is available solely to meet the needs of industry (as in jewelry and dentistry) and to settle international transactions among central banks or treasuries. This is the standard that the United States and most advanced nations adopted when they went off the gold-coin standard in the early 1930s.

gold (coin) standard: Monetary standard under which (1) the national unit of currency (such as the dollar, pound, or franc) is defined by law in terms of a fixed weight of gold; (2) there is a free and unrestricted flow of the metal in any form into and out of the country; (3) gold coins are full legal tender for all debts; (4) there is free convertibility between the national currency and gold coins at a defined rate; and (5) there are no restrictions on the coinage of gold. Nearly 50 countries of the world were on this standard in the late nineteenth and early twentieth centuries.

gold-exchange standard: Monetary standard under which a nation's unit of currency is defined in terms of another nation's unit of currency, which in turn is defined in terms of, and is convertible into, gold. This standard prevailed in the noncommunist world from 1944 to 1971 and is primarily of international economic significance. Thus, in this period, the U.S. dollar was defined as equal to $\frac{1}{35}$ of an ounce of gold and was convertible to foreign central banks at this rate. Each foreign central bank, in turn, defined the par value of its own currency in terms of the U.S. dollar and maintained it at that level. The entire system operated by international agreement (under the **International Monetary Fund**).

gold points: Range within which the foreign exchange rates of gold-standard countries will fluctuate. Thus the gold points are equal to the par rate of exchange plus and minus the cost (including insurance) of shipping gold. The upper and lower gold points for a nation are called its "gold-export point" and its "gold-import point," respectively, because gold will be exported when the foreign exchange rate rises above the upper level and will be imported when the rate falls below the lower level. One nation's gold-export point is thus another nation's gold-import point, and vice versa.

goldsmiths' principle: Banks can maintain a fractional— rather than 100 percent—reserve against deposits, because customers will not ordinarily withdraw their funds at the same time. Hence the banks can earn interest by lending out unused or excess reserves. This principle was discovered centuries ago by the English goldsmiths, who held gold in safekeeping for customers.

government monopoly: Monopoly both owned and operated by either a federal or a local government. *Examples:* The U.S. Postal Service, many water and sewer systems, and the central banks of most countries.

grants-in-aid: Financial aid at the intergovernmental level that consists of (1) revenues received by local governments from their states and from the federal government; and (2) revenues received by state governments from the federal government. These revenues are used mainly to help pay for public welfare assistance, highways, and education.

Great Leap Forward: Ambitious economic plan undertaken by China during 1958–1960 to accelerate enormously its rate of economic growth. The plan was unrealistic and forced the country into a major economic crisis.

greenbacks: Paper money (officially called United States Notes) issued by the Treasury to help finance the Civil War, 1861–1865. The currency was not redeemable in specie (gold or silver coins) and was the first official legal-tender money issued by the federal government. (*Note:* The U.S. dollar today is sometimes called a "greenback," but this is a colloquial rather than a literal term.)

Gresham's Law: Principle which asserts that cheap money tends to drive dear money out of circulation. Thus, suppose two kinds of metals, such as gold and silver, circulate with equal legal-tender powers (as happened in the United States under the bimetallic standard during the nineteenth century). Then, the cheaper metal will become the chief circulating medium while the dearer metal will be hoarded, melted down, or exported, thereby disappearing from circulation. The law is named after Sir Thomas Gresham, Master of the Mint under Queen Elizabeth I during the sixteenth century. (*See also* **mint ratio; bimetallic standard.**)

gross national disproduct: Sum of all social costs or reductions in benefits to society that result from producing the gross national product. *Example:* Pollution of the environment is part of gross national disproduct, to the extent that it is caused by production of the gross national product.

gross national income (GNI): The equivalent of gross national product from the "income" viewpoint. It consists of national income at factor cost (that is, the sum of wages, rent, interest, and profit) plus two nonincome or business-expense items: indirect business taxes and capital consumption allowance.

gross national product (GNP): Total market value of all final goods and services produced by an economy during a year.

growth: *See* **economic growth**

guaranteed annual income: Plan that awards all families under a certain "poverty line" level a straight allowance for each parent plus specified amounts for each child according to the size of the family. No family receives less than a designated amount; and, as a family's income rises, the payment from the government is reduced until a break-even level (which is a little higher than the poverty line) is reached.

H

hard-core unemployed: People who are unemployed because they lack the education and skills for today's complex economy. (Discrimination may also be a contributing factor.) They consist mainly of certain minority groups, such as blacks, Chicanos, the "too-old," the "too-young," high-school dropouts, and the permanently displaced (who are victims of technological change).

hedging: Purchase and sale of a commodity in two different markets at the same time and a corresponding offsetting sale and purchase of the same commodity in the two markets at a later time. The markets involved are the cash or spot market, in which a physical commodity is bought and sold, and the futures or forward market, in which contracts for subsequent delivery of the physical commodity are bought and sold. Hedging helps firms to reduce inventory costs, adjust to changing market conditions, and plan future supplies of goods needed for production. Hence it also leads to lower prices.

Herfindahl index: A measure of market concentration. It equals the sum of the squares of the market shares of all the firms in an industry. For example, if an industry has three firms with market shares of 70 percent, 20 percent, and 10 percent, then

$$\text{Herfindahl index} = (.70)^2 + (.20)^2 + (.10)^2 = .54$$

The index can range from 0 to 1. An index of 0 denotes pure competition—the absence of monopoly power. An index of 1 denotes pure monopoly—the absence of competition. An index between these limits denotes the degree of monopoly power. If all firms in a market are of equal size, the index equals the reciprocal of the number (N) of firms—that is, $1/N$. Because of the squaring process, the magnitude of the Herfindahl index is affected more by large firms than by small ones. (For example, a

90 percent market share, when squared, equals .081. A 10 percent market share, when squared, equals .01.) Therefore, it is not necessary to know all of the market shares in an industry in order to estimate a Herfindahl index. The index can be closely approximated simply by using the market shares of the industry's largest firms.

Hicks, John R. (1904–): Leading British economist and Nobel laureate. He contributed significantly to the reconstruction of demand theory through the development of indifference-curve analysis. His work thus follows in the tradition of general equilibrium theory as formulated by Leon Walras and Vilfredo Pareto in the late nineteenth century. Among Hick's other leading contributions have been a refinement of the marginal-productivity theory of wages and an integrated analysis of Keynesian with classical theory.

"high-powered money": See **monetary base.**

hog–corn price ratio: Number of bushels of corn required to buy 100 pounds of live pork:

$$\text{hog–corn price ratio} = \frac{\text{price of live hogs per 100 pounds}}{\text{price of corn per bushel}}$$

When the ratio is relatively low, hog production decreases because farmers find it more profitable to sell their corn in the market than to use it for feeding hogs. Conversely, when the ratio is relatively high, hog production increases because farmers use the corn to feed more hogs and to market them at heavier weights.

horizontal equity: Doctrine that states that "equals should be treated equally." *Example:* Persons with the same income, wealth, or other taxpaying ability should, in order to bear equal tax burdens (or make equal subjective sacrifices), pay the same amount of tax. (*Compare* **vertical equity.**)

horizontal merger: Amalgamation under one ownership of plants engaged in producing similar products. The products might be close substitutes, such as competing brands of cement, or moderate substitutes, such as tin cans and jars. The objective is to round out a product line that is sold through the same distribution channels, thereby offering joint economies in selling and distribution efforts. The result may be an enhancement of market power.

Hotelling's paradox: Proposition that states that monopolistically competitive firms must, in order to attract each other's customers, make their products as similar to existing products as possible without destroying the differ-

ences. Therefore, as a type of market structure, monopolistic competition leads to maximum differentiation of products with minimum differences between them. (This proposition was formulated analytically in 1929 by a distinguished economist and statistician, Harold Hotelling. Because the theory of monopolistic competition had not yet been formulated, Hotelling's model was based on what he called "industries composed of many firms and similar goods.")

household: All persons living in the same home. A household may thus consist of one or more families.

human-resource policies: Deliberate efforts undertaken in the private and public sectors to develop and use the capacities of human beings as actual or potential members of the labor force. (Human resource policies are also known as **employment-training policies.**)

human resources: Productive physical and mental talents of the people who constitute an economy.

Humphrey–Hawkins bill: See **Full Employment and Balanced Growth Act (1978).**

hyperinflation: Situation in which prices are rising with little or no increase in output. It is also sometimes called "runaway" or "galloping" inflation, if prices are rising rapidly.

hypothesis: A working guess about the behavior of things, or an expression about the relationship between variables in the real world. In economics, the "things" may include consumers, workers, business firms, investors, and so on, and the variables may include prices, wages, consumption, production, or other economic quantities.

I

imperfect competition: A classification of market structures that falls between the two extremes of perfect competition and monopoly. It consists of monopolistic competition and oligopoly.

implicit costs: Costs of self-owned or self-employed resources that are not recorded in a company's book of account. *Example:* the alternative interest return, rental receipts, and wages that a self-employed proprietor forgoes by owning and operating his own business.

Implicit Price Index (GNP deflator): Weighted average of the price indexes used to deflate the components of GNP. Thus, for any given year,

$$\text{GNP in constant prices} = \frac{\text{GNP in current prices}}{\text{Implicit Price Index (= IPI)}}$$

Therefore,

$$IPI = \frac{\text{GNP in current prices}}{\text{GNP in constant prices}}$$

Because of its comprehensiveness, the IPI is the best single measure of broad price movements in the economy.

import quota: Law that limits the number of units of a commodity that may be imported during a given period.

impossibility theorem: *See* **Arrow's impossibility theorem.**

incidence: Range of occurrence or influence of an economic act. It is a term used primarily in the study of taxation and refers to the economic entity (such as a household or a firm) that bears the ultimate burden of a tax.

income: Gain derived from the use of human or material resources. A flow of dollars per unit of time. (*Compare* **wealth.**)

income-consumption curve: In indifference-curve analysis, a line showing the amounts of two commodities that a consumer will purchase when his income changes while the prices of the commodities remain the same. Geometrically, it is a line connecting the tangency points of price lines and indifference curves as income changes while prices remain constant.

income distribution: Division of society's output (that is, income society earns) among people. Income distribution thus concerns the matter of who gets how much, or what proportion, of the economy's total production. (*See* **functional income distribution; personal income distribution.**)

income effect: Increased quantity demanded of a good due to a rise in a buyer's real income, resulting from a decrease in the price of a good. *Example:* If you are a consumer of beef, a decrease in its price increases your real income or purchasing power. This enables you to buy more beef, and perhaps more of some other things (such as chicken, pork, and even nonmeat products) as well. The income effect assumes that the consumer's money income, tastes, and the prices of other goods remain constant. It helps explain why a demand curve slopes downward. (*See also* **substitution effect.**)

income elasticity of demand: Percentage change in the quantity purchased of a good resulting from a one-percent change in income. Thus,

income elasticity of demand

$$= \frac{\text{percentage change in quantity purchased}}{\text{percentage change in income}}$$

$$= \frac{(Q_2 - Q_1)/(Q_2 + Q_1)}{(Y_2 - Y_1)/(Y_2 + Y_1)}$$

in which Q_1 and Q_2 represent the quantities purchased before and after the change in income and Y_1 and Y_2 represent the corresponding levels of income before and after the change. Thus the income elasticity of demand denotes the responsiveness of changes in quantity purchased to changes in income, where responsiveness is measured in terms of percentage changes.

income statement: Financial statement of a firm showing its revenues, costs, and profit during a period. Also known as a profit-and-loss statement.

income tax: Tax on the net income, or the residual that remains after certain items are subtracted from gross income. The two types of income taxes are the personal income tax and the corporation income tax.

income velocity of money: Average number of times per year that a dollar is spent on purchasing a part of the economy's annual flow of final goods and services—its GNP. It equals the ratio of GNP to the quantity of money. (*See also* **equation of exchange.**)

incomes policy: Laws aimed at curbing inflation by establishing conditions under which businesses' production costs (especially wages), prices, and profits may be allowed to increase. *Examples:* Wage and price controls.

inconvertible paper standard: Monetary standard under which the nation's unit of currency may or may not be defined in terms of any metal or other precious substance; however, there is no free convertibility into these other forms. Historically, this standard has existed on a domestic basis in all countries since the worldwide abandonment of gold in the 1930s.

increasing-cost industry: Industry that experiences increases in resource prices or in its costs of production as it expands because of new firms entering it. This will happen when the industry's demand for the resources it employs is a significant proportion of the total demand for those resources.

increasing costs, law of: Principle that states that, on an economy's production-possibilities curve relating two kinds of goods, the real cost of acquiring either good is not the money that must be spent for it but the increasing amount of the alternative good that the society must sacrifice or "give up" because it cannot have all it wants of both goods.

Independent Treasury Act (1846): Law that created the Independent Treasury System (1846–1863). During its life, the law enabled the Treasury to act as its own bank, receiving and disbursing its own funds, thus making it independent of the banking system. The Independent Treasury System also engaged in the purchase and sale of government bonds, thus affecting the quantity of money. This procedure, which decades later was called **open-market operations,** became an integral part of the Federal Reserve System after its establishment in 1913.

independent union: Labor union not affiliated with any federation of labor organizations. It may be national or international, and it is not limited to workers in any one firm.

indexation: Assignment of inflation-adjusting escalator clauses to long-term contracts. Thus wages, rents, interest payments, and even the tax system can be readjusted in proportion to price changes so that people's gains due to inflation are not taxed away, thereby reducing real income. *Example:* If your income goes up by 10 percent when prices go up by 10 percent, you have no more purchasing power than before. Yet your income tax will rise because you will be pushed into a higher tax bracket. This situation can be avoided by indexing the income tax, thereby "correcting" it for inflation. (See **escalator clause.**)

index numbers: Figures that disclose the relative changes in a series of numbers, such as prices or production, from a base period. The base period is usually defined as being equal to an index number of 100, and all other numbers in the series both before or after that period are expressed as percentages of that period. Index numbers are widely used in reporting business and economic data.

indifference curve: Graph of an indifference schedule. Every point along the curve represents a different combination of two commodities, and each combination is equally satisfactory to a recipient because each one yields the same total utility.

indifference schedule: Table showing the various combinations of two commodities that would be equally satisfactory or yield the same total utility to a recipient at a given time.

indirect tax: Tax that can be shifted either partially or entirely to someone other than the individual or firm originally taxed. *Examples:* sales taxes, excise taxes, taxes on business and rental properties.

induced consumption: That part of total consumption that is related to income.

induced investment: Tendency of rising income, output, and economic activity to stimulate higher levels of investment. That part of total investment that is related to aggregate income or output. It may also be directly related to induced consumption, which in turn is related to income. (*Compare* **autonomous investment.**)

induction: Process of reasoning from particular observations or cases to general laws or principles. Most human knowledge is inductive or empirical since it is based on the experiences of our senses. (Opposite of **deduction.**)

industrial organization: Branch of applied microeconomics concerned with the ways in which firms direct their production activities in meeting consumer demands. The study of industrial organization is divided into three parts: (1) *Market structure*—the types of competitive environments within which firms operate. (2) *Market conduct*—the practices and policies that firms adopt in their pursuit of profits. (3) *Market performance*—the effect of business behavior on the economy's four goals (efficiency, equity, stability, and growth). A fourth area, *market policy,* deals with the legal environment (such as the antitrust laws) within which firms operate. This is sometimes treated separately, and sometimes integrated with, the study of industrial organization.

industrial relations: Rules and regulations governing the relationship between union and management. It often deals with such matters as union security (for example, the type of recognition that the union is accorded, or its financial arrangement for collecting dues) and methods of controlling the quantity and kind of union membership through apprenticeship requirements, licensing provisions, initiation fees, and seniority rules.

industrial union: Labor union consisting solely of workers from a particular industry. Examples are a union of all workers in the automobile industry or a union of all workers in the steel industry. An industrial union is thus a "vertically" organized union.

industry: Group of firms producing similar or identical products.

infant industry: Underdeveloped industry that, in the face of competition from abroad, may not be able to survive the early years of struggle before reaching maturity.

inferior good: A good whose consumption varies inversely with money income (prices remaining constant) over a certain range of income. *Examples:* potatoes, used clothing, and other "cheap" commodities bought by poor families. The consumption of these commodities declines in favor of fancier foods, new clothing, and the like as the incomes of low-income families rise.

inflation: Rise in the general price level (or average level of prices) of all goods and services over a prolonged period. Equivalently, it is a decline in the purchasing power of a unit of money (such as the dollar) over a prolonged period. The general price level thus varies inversely with the purchasing power of a unit of money. For example, if prices double, purchasing power decreases by one-half; if prices halve, purchasing power doubles.

inflationary gap: Amount by which aggregate expenditure exceeds aggregate output at full employment. Also, the amount by which actual output exceeds potential output at an equilibrium price level. Either condition causes inflationary pressures.

inflation premium: Differential between the market rate of interest and the real rate of interest. The differential may be positive, negative, or zero. Its size is the amount necessary to compensate lenders or borrowers for adverse changes in purchasing power resulting from anticipated inflation or deflation.

infrastructure: A nation's economic and social overhead capital needed as a basis for modern production. *Examples:* roads, telephone lines, power facilities, schools, and public health.

inheritance tax: Tax imposed by most state governments on property received from persons who have died. It is primarily progressive (graduated) in rate structure, but exemptions, deductions, and rates vary widely among the states.

injunction: Court order requiring that a defendant refrain from certain practices or that he take a particular action.

innovation: Adoption of a new or different product or of a new or different method of production, marketing, financing, and so on. It thus establishes a new relation between the output and the various kinds of imputs (capital, land, labor, and so forth) in a production process. In a more formal sense, it is the setting up of a new production function.

innovation theory: Explanation originated by Joseph Schumpeter (1883–1950) that attributes business cycles and economic development to innovations that forward-looking businesspeople adopt in order to reduce costs and increase profits. Once an innovation proves successful, other businesspeople follow with the same or with similar techniques, and these innovations cause fluctuations in investment that result in business cycles. The innovation theory has also been used as a partial explanation of how profits arise in a competitive capitalistic system.

institutions: Those traditions, beliefs, and practices which are well established and widely held as a fundamental part of a culture. *Example:* Institutions of capitalism include private property, economic individualism, laissez-faire, and free markets. (*Note:* In sociology, social systems are often characterized by their institutions. Examples of sociological institutions are marriage, the family, and so on. Institutions are thus the pillars or foundations on which a social system rests.)

interest: 1. Return to those who supply the factor of production known as "capital" (that is, the payment for supplying the funds with which businesspeople buy capital goods). **2.** Price paid for the use of credit or loanable funds over a period of time. It is stated as a rate — that is, as a percentage of the amount borrowed. Thus an interest rate of 10% annually means that the borrower pays 10 cents per $1 borrowed per year, or $10 per $100 borrowed per year, and so on. (*Note:* This definition of interest assumes that borrowers and lenders expect prices to be stable. If they are not, there will be a difference between the actual (or market) rate of interest and the real rate. See **real rate of interest**.)

interest-rate effect: Proposition that states that changes in the average price level result in changes in interest rates in the same direction, thereby affecting the public's spending. For example, when the average price level rises, the public's demand for borrowed funds increases in order to help finance consumption and investment purchases. Interest rates thus rise. This makes spending more costly, thereby reducing people's purchases of goods and services. The reverse happens when the average price level falls. The public's demand for credit decreases because people do not need as much borrowed funds to finance their purchases. Therefore, interest rates decline. This makes spending cheaper, thereby expanding people's purchases of goods and services. *Note:* The interest-rate effect assumes that "all other things," especially the supply of money in the economy, remain constant.

interlocking directorate: Situation in which an individual serves on two or more boards of directors of competing corporations.

internal economies and diseconomies of scale: Conditions that bring about decreases or increases in a firm's long-run average costs or scale of operations as a result of size adjustments within the firm as a producing unit. They occur irrespective of adjustments within the industry and are due mainly to physical economies or diseconomies. *Example:* Internal economies may result from greater specialization and more efficient utilization of the firm's resources as its scale of operations increases, but internal diseconomies may eventually set in because of the limited decision-making abilities of the top management group.

internal labor market: System of procedures and policies that determines the advancement of workers in those firms that adhere to a policy of promotion from within. Each firm's internal market contains its own rules governing job movement within the organization. To the extent that companies rely on such markets, they limit the ability of workers to move from one firm to another. This impedes worker mobility and hence reduces the efficiency of external labor markets.

International Bank for Reconstruction and Development (World Bank): Established by the United Nations in 1945 to provide loans for postwar reconstruction and to promote development of less developed countries. The Bank's chief function is to aid the financing of basic development projects, such as dams, communication and transportation facilities, and health programs, by insuring or otherwise guaranteeing private loans or, when private capital is not available, by providing loans from its own resources and credit. Affiliated agencies also exist to help finance higher-risk investment projects in underdeveloped countries.

International Development Cooperation Agency (IDCA): The most important American organization concerned with foreign aid. Created in 1979, it represents a major restructuring and consolidation of previous development programs operated by different U.S. agencies and various multilateral organizations. IDCA has two major functions. The first is to advise government on development policies. The second is to administer funds voted annually by Congress for the purpose of providing economic, technical, and defense assistance to nations that are identified with the free world. (IDCA includes within its organization the Agency for International Development, the government's chief foreign-aid unit, which was previously part of the U.S. State Department.)

International Monetary Fund (IMF): Established by the United Nations in 1944 for the purpose of eliminating exchange restrictions, encouraging exchange-rate stability, and providing for worldwide convertibility of currencies in order to promote multilateral trade based on inter-

national specialization. More than 100 nations are members of the Fund.

inventory: Stocks of goods that business firms have on hand, including raw materials, supplies, and finished goods.

investment: Spending by business firms on new job-creating and income-producing goods. It consists of replacements of, or additions to, the nation's stock of capital, including its plant, equipment, and inventories (that is, its nonhuman productive assets).

"invisible hand": Expression coined by Adam Smith in *The Wealth of Nations* to convey the idea that each individual, if left to pursue his self-interest without interference by government, would be led, as if by an invisible hand, to achieve the best good for society.

involuntary unemployment: Situation in which people who want work are unable to find jobs at the wage rates prevailing for the skills and experience they have to offer.

isoquant: Curve along which each point represents a different combination of two inputs or factors of production (such as capital and labor) and each combination yields the same level of total output.

J

Jevons, William Stanley (1835–1882): English neoclassical and mathematical economist who made major contributions to value and distribution theory, capital theory, and to statistical research in economics. He is best known as a leading contributor to marginal utility analysis. "Value," he pointed out, "depends entirely upon utility." In equilibrium, marginal utilities are proportionate to prices. "From this, the ordinary laws of supply and demand are a necessary consequence." Jevon's major work in economics was his book, *Theory of Political Economy* (1871).

job classification: Process of describing the duties, responsibilities, and characteristics of jobs, point-rating them (perhaps by established formulas based on engineering time studies of workers in such jobs), and then grouping the jobs into graduated classifications with corresponding wage rates and wage ranges.

job-competition market: Labor market in which the number and types of jobs are determined mainly by prevailing technology. Workers are employed to fill particular job openings associated with existing plant and equipment. (A factory, for example, needs a specific number of operators, maintenance people, supervisors, etc. to run its machines.) Wages for these jobs are established largely by institutional and legislative conditions — industry custom, union–management contracts, minimum-wage laws, etc. — rather than by market forces. The function of job-competition markets, therefore, is to allocate workers to a given number of vacancies at prevailing, relatively fixed, wage rates.

jurisdictional strike: Strike caused by a dispute between two or more craft unions over which shall perform a particular job. Outlawed by the Taft–Hartley Act, 1947.

K

Keynes, John Maynard (1883–1946): British economist and founder of the New Economics. His most widely known work was his book *The General Theory of Employment, Interest and Money* (1936), in which he reorganized thinking about macroeconomic problems. The following chief features characterize the so-called Keynesian "system": (1) the dependency of consumption on income, called the **consumption function;** (2) the **multiplier** relationship between investment expenditures and income; (3) the **marginal efficiency of investment** as a measure of businesses demand for investment; and (4) the use of **fiscal policy** and **monetary policy** to maintain full employment. In contrast to the classical theory, Keynes showed that our economic system could remain in equilibrium at any level of employment, not necessarily full employment. Therefore, he concluded, active fiscal and monetary policies by government are needed to maintain high levels of resource utilization and economic stability. (*See also* **Keynesian economics.**)

Keynesian economics: Body of economic thought that originated with the British economist John Maynard Keynes (1882–1946) in the 1930s. It has since been extended and modified to the point where many of its basic analytical tools and ideas are now an integral part of general economic theory. In contrast to classical economics, which emphasized the automatic tendency of the economy to achieve full-employment equilibrium under a government policy of laissez-faire, Keynesian economics seeks to demonstrate that an economy may be in equilibrium at any level of employment. The theory, therefore, concludes that appropriate government fiscal and monetary policies are needed to maintain full employment and steady economic growth with a minimum rate of inflation.

kinked demand curve: A "bent" demand curve, and a corresponding discontinuous marginal revenue curve, facing an oligopolistic seller. The kinked curve signifies that, if the seller raises the price above the kink, sales will fall off rapidly because other sellers are not likely to follow the price upward. If the seller reduces the price below the kink, sales will expand relatively little because other sellers are likely to follow the price downward. The market price, therefore, tends to stabilize at the kink.

Knights of Labor: National labor organization founded in 1869. It rejected the traditional organizing of workers by crafts, preferring instead the mass unionization of both unskilled and skilled workers. The Knights championed the cause of workers and achieved many liberal improvements and reforms, but began to decline in the late 1880s due to several factors: (1) opposition by craft leaders who preferred organization along craft lines; (2) internal dissension among leading members and groups; and (3) suspicion — unproved — that it was involved in Chicago's Haymarket riot and bombing of 1886. By 1917, it had ceased to exist.

Kuznets, Simon Smith (1901–): Russian-born American economist who made major contributions to the study of national income accounting, economic growth, productivity, and related areas. He is the "father" of national income accounting because much of his efforts toward improving the theory and measurement of national income during the 1930s became a foundation for subsequent methods by the U.S. Department of Commerce. In 1971, at the age of 70, Kuznets was awarded the Nobel Prize in Economic Science.

L

labor: 1. Factor of production that represents those hired workers whose human efforts or activities are directed toward production. 2. All personal services, including the activities of wageworkers, professional people, and independent business-people. "Laborers" may thus receive compensation not only in the form of wages but also as salaries, bonuses, commissions, and the like.

labor force: The employable population, defined for measurement purposes as all people 16 years of age or older who are employed plus all those who are unemployed but actively seeking work.

labor-force participation rate: Percentage of the total population, or of one or more subgroups of the population, that is in the labor force. Subgroups are classified by race, sex, age, marital status, and other demographic characteristics. Thus, some examples of labor-force participation rates are: (1) the percentage of the nation's total white population that is in the labor force; (2) the percentage of the nation's black women, ages 19 to 24, that is in the labor force; and (3) the percentage of the nation's married men that is in the labor force.

Labor–Management Relations (Taft–Hartley) Act (1947): An amendment to the National Labor Relations (Wagner) Act of 1935. It retains the rights given to labor by the 1935 Act but also: (1) outlaws "unfair labor practices" of unions, such as coercion of workers to join unions, failure to bargain in good faith, jurisdictional strikes, secondary boycotts, and featherbedding; (2) outlaws the closed shop but permits the union shop; (3) requires unions to file financial reports with the NLRB and union officials to sign affidavits to the effect that they are not Communists; (4) prohibits strikes called before the end of a 60-day notice period prior to the expiration of a collective-bargaining agreement; and (5) enables the President to obtain an 80-day court injunction against strikes that endanger national health or safety.

Labor–Management Reporting and Disclosure (Landrum–Griffin) Act (1959): Act that amended the National Labor Relations Act of 1935 by (1) requiring detailed financial reports of all unions and union officers; (2) severely tightening restrictions on secondary boycotting and picketing; (3) requiring periodic secret-ballot elections of union officers; and (4) restricting ex-convicts and Communists from holding positions as union officers.

Laffer curve: A hypothetical relationship between tax revenues and the tax rate. The relationship is such that, as the tax rate increases from zero to 100 percent, tax revenues rise correspondingly from zero to some maximum level and then decline to zero. The optimum rate is thus the one that produces the maximum revenue. Rates that are lower than optimum are deemed "normal" because tax revenues can be increased by raising the rate. Rates that are higher than optimum are regarded as prohibitive because they impair personal and business incentives and are thus counterproductive. Therefore, when the tax rate is in the prohibitive range, tax reductions should bring increased economic activity and higher, not lower, tax revenues. (*Note:* There is no concrete evidence to support this assumed relationship between tax revenues and the tax rate.)

lagging indicators: Time series that tend to follow or trail aggregate economic activity.

laissez-faire: "Leave us alone"—an expression, coined in France during the late seventeenth century, that today is interpreted to mean freedom from government intervention in all economic affairs.

land: Factor of production that includes land itself (in the form of real estate) as well as mineral deposits, timber, water, and other nonhuman or "natural" resources.

law: Expression of a relationship between variables, based on a high degree of unvarying uniformity under the same conditions. (Often used synonymously with **principle.**)

leading indicators: Time series that tend to move ahead of aggregate economic activity, thus reaching peaks and troughs before the economy as a whole.

legal monopoly: Privately owned firm that is granted an exclusive right by government to operate in a particular market. In return, government may impose standards and requirements pertaining to the quantity and quality of output, geographic areas of operation, and the prices or rates that are charged. The justification of legal monopoly is that unrestricted competition in the industry is socially undesirable. Public utilities are typical examples of legal monopolies.

legal reserves: Assets that a bank or other depository institution (such as a savings and loan association or credit union) may lawfully use as reserves against its deposit liabilities. For a member bank of the Federal Reserve System, legal reserves consist of deposits held with the district Federal Reserve Bank plus currency held in the vaults of the bank—called "vault cash." Any other highly liquid financial claims, such as government securities, are classified as *nonlegal reserves*. For a nonmember bank or other depository institution, legal reserves include vault cash and deposits held with the district Federal Reserve Bank or with an approved institution. The latter includes any depository institution (such as a member bank) that holds a reserve balance with the Federal Reserve.

Lerner index: Measure of a firm's monopoly power, based on the divergence between price, P, and marginal cost, MC, expressed as a proportion of price. Thus,

$$\text{Lerner index} = \frac{P - MC}{P}$$

When a firm is in equilibrium, the index will range between 0 and 1. It will be zero (no monopoly power) for a firm in perfect competition, since $P = MC$. At the other extreme, the index will be 1 (complete monopoly power) in the rare case of a firm whose marginal costs are zero. Basic shortcomings of the formula are that (1) marginal-cost data for a firm are not generally known and cannot be readily derived; and (2) it is a static rather than dynamic measure.

less developed (underdeveloped) country: A nation that, in comparison with the more developed countries, tends to exhibit such characteristics as (1) poverty level of income and hence little or no saving, (2) high rate of population growth, (3) substantial majority of its labor force employed in agriculture, (4) low proportion of adult literacy, (5) extensive disguised unemployment, and (6) heavy reliance on a few items for export.

liabilities: Monetary debts or things of value owned by an economic entity (such as an individual, household, or business firm) to creditors.

limited liability: Restriction of the liability of an investor, such as a stockholder in a corporation, to the amount of his investment.

liquidity: Ease with which an asset can be converted into cash quickly without loss of purchase price. Liquidity is thus a matter of degree. Money is perfectly liquid, whereas any other asset may possess a lower degree of liquidity—depending on how easily it can be sold without loss.

liquidity preference (theory of interest): Theory formulated by J. M. Keynes (1883–1946). The theory contends that households and businesses would rather hold their assets in the most liquid form—cash or checking accounts. The reason is to satisfy three motives: (1) the "transactions motive," to carry out everyday purchasing needs; (2) the "precautionary motive," to meet possible unforeseen conditions; and (3) the "speculative motive," to take advantage of a change in interest rates. These motives determine the demand for money, whereas the monetary authority determines its supply. The demand for, and supply of, money together determine the equilibrium rate of interest.

liquidity trap: Condition in which an increase in the supply of money will not further reduce the rate of interest, because the total demand for money at that relatively low interest rate (expressed in terms of a liquidity-preference curve) is infinite. This means that, at the low rate of interest, everyone would rather hold money in idle balances than risk the loss of holding long-term securities offering poor yields. (In geometric terms, the liquidity trap exists at that rate of interest where the liquidity-preference curve becomes perfectly horizontal.)

loanable-funds theory of interest: Theory that holds that the interest rate is determined by the demand for, and the supply of, loanable funds. The sources of demand for loanable funds are businesses that want to invest, households that want to finance consumer purchases, and government agencies that want to finance deficits. The sources of supply of loanable funds are the central banking system, which influences the supply of money (and hence the supply of loanable funds) in the economy, and households and businesses that make loanable funds available out of their past or present savings.

lockout: Closing down of a plant by an employer in order to keep workers out of their jobs.

logarithmic scale: Special type of scale used in graphing. The scale is spaced in logarithms. As a result, equal *percentage* changes between numbers are represented by equal distances along the scale. For example, a 100 percent change is always the same distance on the scale whether the change is from 1 to 2, 2 to 4, 3 to 6, 5 to 10, 10 to 20, or 50 to 100. In contrast, a conventional scale is spaced arithmetically. Therefore, equal *amounts* of change between numbers are represented by equal distances along the scale. Thus the changes from 1 to 2, 2 to 3, 6 to 7, 15 to 16, and so on, are all the same distances on an arithmetic scale. A logarithmic scale is useful for comparing *ratios* of change between data. In contrast, an arithmetic scale is used to compare *amounts* of change between data.

long run: Period that is long enough for a firm to enter or leave an industry and to vary its output by varying all its factors of production, including its plant scale.

long-run aggregate supply (LRAS) curve: Straight line depicting the economy's potential real GNP. This is the same as the economy's full-employment (or natural-employment) level of real GNP. The curve indicates that the amount of real output at this level does not vary with changes in the price level.

long-run average cost (LRAC) curve (planning curve): Curve that is tangent to, or envelops, the various short-run average total cost curves of a firm over a range of output representing different scales or sizes of plant. Thus it shows what the level of average costs would be for alternative outputs of different-sized plants.

long-run industry supply curve: Locus or "path" of a competitive industry's long-run equilibrium points. That is, the long-run industry supply curve connects the stable equilibrium points of the industry's supply and demand curves over a period of time, both before and after these curves have adjusted completely to changed market conditions. The long-run industry supply curve may be either upward-sloping, horizontal, or downward-sloping, depending on whether the industry is an increasing-, constant-, or decreasing-cost industry.

long-run Phillips curve (LRPC): Relationship between changing rates of inflation and a constant natural rate of unemployment. Geometrically, the curve is a straight line. It thus emphasizes the idea that there is no long-run trade-off between the rate of unemployment and the rate of inflation.

Lorenz diagram: Graphic device for comparing the actual distribution of a variable with an equal distribution of that variable. It is most often employed to compare a society's actual distribution of income among families with an equal distribution. For example, each axis of the chart is scaled from 0 to 100 percent. Then the cumulative percentage relationships between two variables, such as "percent of income" and "percent of families," are plotted against each other. The resulting (Lorenz) curve of actual income distribution is then compared to a 45° diagonal line representing equal income distribution. The degree of difference between the two curves indicates the extent of income inequality. Similar curves may be constructed to show other types of distributions (such as distribution of wealth or distribution of wages in a factory).

M

macroeconomics: The part of economics that deals with the economy as a whole, or with large subdivisions of it. It analyzes the economic "forest" rather than the "trees."

Malthusian theory of population: First published by Thomas Malthus in 1798 and then revised in 1803, this theory states that population tends to increase as a geometric progression (1, 2, 4, 8, 16, 32, and so forth) while the means of subsistence increase at most only as an arithmetic progression (1, 2, 3, 4, 5, 6, and so forth). This is because a growing population applied to a fixed amount of land results in eventually diminishing returns to workers. Human beings are therefore destined to misery and poverty unless the rate of population growth is retarded. This may be accomplished either by (1) preventive checks, such as moral restraint, late marriages, and celibacy or, if these fail, by (2) positive checks, such as wars, famines, and disease.

Malthus, Thomas Robert (1776–1834): English classical economist. Best known for his theory that held that population would tend to outrun the food supply. The result would be a bare subsistence level of survival for the laboring class. (See **Malthusian theory of population**.)

Malthus, in his book *Principles of Political Economy* (1820), also developed the concept of "effective demand," which he defined as the level of aggregate demand necessary to maintain full employment. If effective demand declined, he said, overpopulation would result. He thus anticipated a fundamental concept in modern macroeconomics.

manpower policies: *See* **employment-training policies.**

Marcet, Jane Haldimand (1769–1858): English economic educator whose book, *Conversations on Political Economy* (1816), conveyed in dialogue form the teachings of her classical-economic predecessors and contemporaries —Smith, Say, Malthus, and Ricardo. She thus contributed significantly to the teaching of economics.

marginal cost: Change in total cost resulting from a unit change in quantity. Marginal cost is thus the additional cost of one more unit of output. It is calculated by a formula:

$$\text{marginal cost} = \frac{\text{change in total cost}}{\text{change in quantity}}$$

Marginal cost is also the change in total variable cost resulting from a unit change in quantity. The reason is that total cost changes because total variable cost changes, whereas total fixed cost remains constant.

marginal-cost price: Price (or production) of output as determined by the point at which a firm's marginal cost equals its average revenue (demand). This is an optimum price for society, because the value of the last unit to the marginal user (measured by the price he pays for the last unit, which is equal to the price he pays for any other unit) is equivalent to the value of the resources used to produce that unit. However, this marginal-cost price will leave the firm suffering a loss if it results in a price below the firm's average total cost.

marginal efficiency of investment (MEI): Expected rate of return on an addition to investment. More precisely, it is the expected rate of return over the cost of an additional unit of a capital good. It is determined by such factors as (1) the demand for the product that the investment will produce; (2) the level of production costs in the economy; (3) technology and innovation; and (4) the stock of capital available to meet existing and future market demands. An *MEI* curve is thus a demand curve for investment. It shows the amount of investment spending that businesses are willing to undertake at each rate of interest (or cost of funds).

marginal (physical) product: Change in total product resulting from a unit change in the quantity of a variable input employed. It is calculated by a formula:

marginal (physical) product

$$= \frac{\text{change in total product}}{\text{change in a variable input}}$$

Marginal product thus measures the gain (or loss) in total product from adding an additional unit of a variable factor of production.

marginal-productivity theory of income distribution: Principle that states that, when there is perfect competition for inputs, a firm will purchase factors of production up to the point at which the price or marginal cost of the factor is equal to its marginal revenue productivity. Therefore, in real terms, each factor of production will be paid a value equal to what it contributes to total output—that is, it will be paid what it is "worth."

marginal propensity to consume: Change in consumption resulting from a unit change in income. It is calculated by a formula:

marginal propensity to consume

$$= \frac{\text{change in consumption}}{\text{change in income}}$$

It thus reveals the fraction of each extra dollar of income that is spent on consumption.

marginal propensity to invest: Change in investment resulting from a unit change in aggregate output. It is calculated by a formula:

marginal propensity to invest

$$= \frac{\text{change in investment}}{\text{change in aggregate output}}$$

marginal propensity to save: Change in saving resulting from a unit change in income. It is calculated by a formula:

$$\text{marginal propensity to save} = \frac{\text{change in saving}}{\text{change in income}}$$

It thus reveals the fraction of each extra dollar of income that is saved.

marginal propensity to spend: Change in total spending on consumption and investment resulting from a unit change in aggregate output or income. The marginal propensity to spend, *MPE*, consists of the marginal propensity to consume, *MPC*, and the marginal propensity to invest, *MPI*. Thus, out of any change in aggregate output or income,

$$MPE = MPC + MPI$$

marginal rate of substitution: 1. In demand theory, the rate at which a consumer is willing to substitute one commodity for another along an indifference curve. It is the amount of change in the holdings of one commodity that will just offset a unit change in the holdings of another commodity, so that the consumer's total utility remains the same. Thus, along an indifference curve,

$$\text{marginal rate of substitution} = \frac{\text{change in commodity } Y}{\text{change in commodity } X}$$

The marginal rate of substitution is always negative because one commodity must be decreased when the other is increased in order to keep total utility the same (that is, to remain on a given indifference curve). **2.** In production theory, the marginal rate of substitution is the change in one type of productive input that will just offset a unit change in another type of productive input, so that the total level of production (along an **isoquant**) remains the same. Some examples of productive inputs are capital and labor, fertilizer and land.

marginal revenue: Change in total revenue resulting from a unit change in quantity. It is calculated by a formula:

$$\text{marginal revenue} = \frac{\text{change in total revenue}}{\text{change in quantity}}$$

Marginal revenue thus measures the gain (or loss) in total revenue that results from producing and selling an additional unit.

marginal revenue product: Change in total revenue resulting from a unit change in the quantity of a variable input employed. It is calculated by a formula:

$$\text{marginal revenue product} = \frac{\text{change in total revenue}}{\text{change in a variable input}}$$

Marginal revenue product thus measures the gain (or loss) in total revenue from adding an additional unit of a variable factor of production.

marginal tax rate: Ratio, expressed as a percentage, of the change in a total tax resulting from a unit change in the base on which it is imposed.   *Example:*

marginal personal income tax rate

$$= \frac{\text{change in total personal income tax}}{\text{change in total taxable income}}$$

$$= \frac{\text{marginal tax}}{\text{marginal income}}$$

marginal utility: Change in total utility resulting from a unit change in the quantity of a commodity consumed.   It is calculated by a formula:

$$\text{marginal utility} = \frac{\text{change in total utility}}{\text{change in quantity consumed}}$$

Marginal utility thus measures the gain (or loss) in satisfaction from an additional unit of a good.

margin requirements: 1. Percentage down payment required of a borrower to finance the purchase of stock. This rate is set by the Federal Reserve System's Board of Governors.   An increase in margin requirements is designed to dampen security purchases; a decrease, to encourage them.   **2.** Percentage down payment required of a borrower to finance the purchase of futures contracts in the futures market.   The rate is set by the exchange's regulatory commission.

market economy: Economic system in which the questions of what to produce, how much to produce, and for whom to produce are decided in an open market through the free operation of supply and demand.   There are no "pure" market economies, but several specialized markets (such as the organized commodity exchanges) closely approximate some of the properties of a pure market system.   (*Compare* **command economy.**)

market failure: Inability of a market, for whatever reason, to allocate resources efficiently.   (The term is usually applied to a competitive market, and the cause of the failure is usually an externality.)

market price: Actual price that prevails in a market at any particular moment.

market rate of interest: Actual or money rate of interest that prevails in the market at any given time.   (*Contrast with* **real rate of interest.**)

market share: Percentage of an industry's output accounted for by an individual firm.   Measures of output usually employed are sales, value added, or value of shipments.

market socialism: Economic system characterized by (1) public ownership of land and capital, (2) decentralized decision-making by worker–manager committees, and (3) the use of selective market measures (such as bonuses and profit-sharing) to stimulate productivity and efficiency.

Marshall, Alfred (1842–1924): English economist who synthesized neoclassical thinking around the turn of the century and made many pioneering contributions as well.   Among these were making a formal distinction between the short run and the long run and describing the equilibrium of price and output resulting from the interaction of supply and demand.   He also formulated the concept of elasticity, made the distinction between money cost and real cost, and framed many other economic concepts.   Much of modern microeconomics stems from Marshall's work.   His best-known book, *Principles of Economics*, went through eight editions and was a standard reference and text in economics from 1890 until the 1930s.

Martineau, Harriet (1802–1876): English economic educator whose book, *Illustrations of Political Economy* (1834), emphasized the teaching of economics through applications and real-life experiences.   She was thus a pioneer in the use of the "case method" of teaching—along the lines used today in many business and in some economics courses.

Marx, Karl Heinrich (1818–1883): Prussian-born and German-educated founder, with Friedrich Engels (1820–1895), of so-called "scientific socialism."   This consists of a body of ideas that were best expressed in Marx's most important economic work, *Das Kapital* (translated *Capital*), the first volume of which was published in 1867. The main concepts rest on five fundamental doctrines: (1) **economic interpretation of history:** Economic forces are the prime cause of fundamental historical change.   (2) **theory of value and wages:** The value of any commodity is determined by the amount of labor-time embodied in its production.   The wages that capitalists pay to labor are held at a subsistence level that is just high enough to allow the working population to sustain itself and to rear children.   (3) **theory of surplus value and capital accumulation:** The value of goods that workers produce is greater than the value, in the form of subsistence wages, that workers receive.   The difference, called "surplus value," rightfully belongs to workers, but it is literally stolen from them by capitalists.   Part of this surplus is used by capitalists for their personal consumption and part to acquire more labor and machines in order to perpetuate and expand the capitalistic system. (4) **class struggle:** The capitalists' drive to increase their surplus value and to accumulate capital results in the displacement of labor and in mounting unemployment. This leads to an irreconcilable clash of interests between the working class and the capitalist class. (5) **theory of socialist and communist evolution:** The working class (called the "proletariat"), experiencing increasing misery, will eventually rise and overthrow the capitalistic system by force. The proletariat will then dictate the establishment of a new system characterized in its early stage by socialism and in its mature stage by full communism. The motto of socialism will be: "From each according to his ability, to each according to his labor." The motto of communism will be: *From each according to his ability, to each according to his needs.*" This last quotation describes the ultimate goal of Marxism and the essence of pure communism.

median: Special type of average that divides a distribution of numbers into two equal parts—one-half of all cases being equal to or greater than the median value, and one-half being equal to or less.

mediation: Method of settling differences between two parties (such as a union and management) by the use of an impartial third party, called a mediator, who is acceptable to both sides but makes no binding decisions. Mediation in industrial relations is commonly employed to settle labor–management disputes concerning the *negotiation* of a collective-bargaining contract. The mediator tries to maintain constructive discussions, search for common areas of agreement, and suggest compromises. Federal, state, and most large local governments provide mediation services for labor–management disputes. Mediation is also sometimes called "conciliation." (*Contrast with* **arbitration.**)

member bank: Bank that belongs to the Federal Reserve System. All national banks (chartered by the federal government) must be members. State banks may join if they meet certain requirements.

mercantilism: Set of doctrines and practices aimed at promoting national prosperity and the power of the state by (1) accumulating precious metals (mainly gold and silver) through the maintenance of favorable trade balances, (2) achieving economic self-sufficiency through imperialism, and (3) exploiting colonies by monopolizing their raw materials and precious metals while reserving them as exclusive markets for exports. Mercantilism

reached its peak in the seventeenth century, serving as a political and economic ideology in England, France, Spain, and Germany.

merger: Amalgamation of two or more firms under one ownership. The three common forms are: (1) *horizontal*, uniting similar plants and products; (2) *vertical*, uniting dissimilar plants in various stages of production; and (3) *conglomerate*, uniting dissimilar plants and products.

merit good: Product provided by government because society deems some minimum amount of the commodity worthy (or meritorious) of production. Merit goods share, in different degrees, some of the properties of both public and private goods. Among numerous examples of merit goods are municipal golf courses, public libraries, national parks, public education, and public hospitals. These and other merit goods are subject to the *exclusion principle*, even though it may not always be invoked. (See **exclusion principle; public good.**)

microeconomics: The part of economics that is concerned with the study of specific economic units or parts of an economic system, such as its firms, industries, and households, and the relationships between these parts. It analyzes the "trees" of the economy as distinct from the "forest."

Mill, John Stuart (1806–1873): Last of the major English classical economists. His two-volume treatise, *Principles of Political Economy* (1848), was a masterful synthesis of classical ideas. Mill advocated laissez-faire, but he was also a strong supporter of social reforms. Among them: worker education, democratic producer cooperatives, redistribution of wealth, shorter working days, taxation of unearned gains from land, and social control of monopoly. Mill supported these measures because he mistrusted government and wanted to guarantee to individual workers the benefits of their contributions to production. Therefore, although Mill was often called a socialist, he was in fact a "moderate conservative" by today's standards. He believed too strongly in individual freedom to advocate major government involvement in the economy.

minimum differences, principle of: See **Hotelling's paradox.**

mint ratio: Under a bimetallic standard, the ratio of the weight of one metal to the other, and their equivalent in terms of the national unit of currency (such as the dollar), as defined by the government. For example, during the nineteenth century, when the United States was on a bimetallic standard, the government defined the mint ratio for many years as

$$15 \text{ grains of silver} = 1 \text{ grain of gold} = \$1$$

The mint ratio was therefore 15:1. Since it remained fixed by law, it resulted in either gold or silver being driven out of circulation, depending on the relative market values of the two metals. (See also **bimetallic standard; Gresham's Law.**)

Mitchell, Wesley Clair (1874–1948): Leading American economist during the first half of the twentieth century. Mitchell was a professor of economics at Columbia University and a founder of the National Bureau of Economic Research, one of the world's major centers for quantitative research in aggregative economic activity. Mitchell's lifework was the study of business cycles, their history, nature, and causes. Much of what is known today about economic fluctuations has grown out of the pioneering research done by Mitchell.

mixed economy: Economic system in which the questions of what to produce, how much to produce, and for whom to produce are decided for some goods by the free market and for other goods by a central government authority. There are varying forms and degrees of mixed economies.

model: Representation of the essential features of a theory or of a real-world situation, expressed in the form of words, diagrams, graphs, mathematical equations, or combinations of these.

monetarism: Macroeconomic theory and policies that follow in the tradition of Irving Fisher. Monetarists contend that an increase in the money supply leads to an increase in prices. This causes the actual or market rate of interest to rise relative to the "real" rate—the rate that would prevail if prices were stable. The difference between the market rate and real rate represents an "inflation premium." This is an amount that lenders require and borrowers are willing to pay because both expect prices to continue rising. Monetarists conclude from their analysis that the effects on aggregate demand of temporary budgetary changes are uncertain. Therefore, steady monetary growth is preferable to discretionary fiscal actions. Thus, stated in concise terms, the monetarist model is characterized by (1) a predominantly monetary theory of the price level, (2) a predominantly nonmonetary theory of the interest rate, and (3) a distinction between market and real rates of interest.

monetary asset: Claim against a fixed quantity of money, the amount of which is unaffected by inflation or defla-

tion. *Examples:* bonds, accounts receivable, savings deposits, promissory notes, and cash. For every monetary asset, there is an equal monetary liability. (See also **monetary liability.**)

monetary base: *Net* monetary liabilities of government—the Fed and the Treasury—held by the public. It equals the sum of currency held by the public plus legal reserves. The monetary base may be called "high-powered" money because it supports the money supply (currency plus checkable deposits), which, because of our fractional-reserve banking system, is a *multiple* of the monetary base. The size of the monetary base thus affects the total monetary assets of the public.

Monetary Control Act: See **Depository Institutions Acts.**

monetary liability: Promise to pay a claim against a fixed quantity of money, the amount of which is unaffected by inflation or deflation. For every monetary liability, there is an equal monetary asset. (See also **monetary asset.**)

monetary policy: Deliberate exercise of the monetary authority's (that is, the Federal Reserve's) power to induce expansions or contractions in the money supply in order to achieve price stability, to help dampen the swings of business cycles, and to bring the nation's output and employment to desired levels.

monetary standard: Laws and practices that define a nation's currency and establish the conditions, if any, under which it is ultimately redeemable.

monetary theory (of business cycle): Explanation of economic fluctuations in terms of financial factors, such as changes in the quantity of money and credit and changes in interest rates. Upswings occur when credit and borrowing conditions become favorable enough for businesspeople to borrow; downswings occur when the banking system begins to restrict its expansion of money and credit.

money: anything that is widely used and freely accepted in payment for goods and services. In modern society, money has at least these four functions: (1) as a medium of exchange for conducting transactions; (2) as a measure of value for expressing the prices of things; (3) as a standard of deferred payments, which permits borrowing or lending for future repayment; and (4) as a store of value, which permits saving for future spending.

money illusion: Situation in which a rise in all prices and incomes by the same proportion leads to an increase in consumption, even though real incomes remain unchanged.

money income: Amount of money received for work

done. It is thus the same as **nominal income**. (*Compare* **real income**.)

money market: Center where short-term credit instruments such as U.S. Treasury bills, corporations' commercial paper or promissory notes, and bankers' acceptances are bought and sold.

money multiplier: Principle that states that the money supply, such as M1, is some multiple, m, of the monetary base, B. Thus,

$$M1 = mB$$

It should be kept in mind that m is not a constant but a variable. It is affected by portfolio decisions of households, financial institutions, and other businesses. These decisions also affect B. Therefore, m and B are *not* independent, and changes in either can influence M1. (*See* **monetary base**.)

money-supply rule: Guide for economic expansion advanced by some economists, especially by Milton Friedman. The "rule" states that the Federal Reserve should expand the nation's money supply at a steady rate in accordance with the economy's long-term real GNP growth trend and capacity to produce. This rate is 3 to 4 percent per year for the United States. More than this would lead to strong inflationary pressures; less would tend to be stagnating if not deflationary.

money wages: Wages received in cash. (*Compare* **real wages**.)

monopolistic competition: Industry or market structure characterized by a large number of firms of different sizes producing heterogeneous (similar but not identical) products, with relatively easy entry into the industry.

monopoly: Industry or market structure characterized by a single firm producing a product for which there are no close substitutes. The firm thus constitutes the entire industry and is a "pure" monopoly.

monopoly price: The profit-maximizing price for an imperfect competitor. It is the price (and the corresponding output) at which $MC = MR$ and $MC < P$. At this price, the value of the last unit to the marginal user (measured by the price he or she pays for the last unit, which is equal to the price paid for any other unit) is greater than the value of the resources used to produce that unit.

monopsony: Market structure characterized by only a single buyer of a good or service. It may be thought of as a "buyer's monopoly."

moral suasion: Oral or written appeals by the Federal Reserve board to member banks, urging them to expand or restrict credit but without requiring them to comply.

most-favored-nation clause: Provision in a trade treaty by which each signatory country agrees to extend to the others the same preferential tariff and trade concessions that it may in the future extend to nonsignatories (that is, the same treatment that each gives to its "most favored nation"). Most trading countries have adhered to this principle since 1948.

multiple expansion of bank deposits: Process by which a loan made by one bank is used to finance business transactions and ends up as a deposit in another bank. Part of this may be used by the second bank as a required reserve, the rest being lent out for business use so that it is eventually deposited in a third bank; and so on. The total amount of credit granted by the banking system as a whole will thus be a multiple of the initial deposit. (*See also* **deposit-expansion multiplier**.)

multiplier: Principle that states that changes in investment can bring about magnified changes in income, as expressed by the equation: multiplier × change in investment = change in income. (The variables are expressed in *real*, not nominal, terms.) The multiplier coefficient is given by the formula

$$\text{multiplier} = \frac{\text{change in income}}{\text{change in investment}}$$
$$= \frac{1}{MPS} = \frac{1}{1 - MPC}$$

in which MPS stands for the marginal propensity to save and MPC the marginal propensity to consume. (*Note:* This multiplier is sometimes called the "simple multiplier," the "investment multiplier," or the "expenditure multiplier." The last expression emphasizes the idea that *any* change in spending, whether by households, businesses, or government, and whether for consumption or for investment, can have a multiplier effect on income. However, the term *investment* is used in this definition because that is the variable that is usually assumed to change.)

multiunit bargaining: Collective-bargaining arrangement covering more than one plant. It may occur between one or more firms in an industry and one or more unions, and it may take place on a national, regional, or local level. It is sometimes called "industry-wide bargaining" — usually inaccurately, because it rarely affects an entire industry.

municipals: Marketable financial obligations — mostly bonds — issued by state and local governmental authorities (the latter including cities, towns, school districts, and so on). Interest income paid to their owners is exempt from federal income taxes and usually also from state income taxes of the state in which they are issued.

N

national bank: Commerical bank chartered by the federal government. Such banks are required to belong to the Federal Reserve System. A minority of banks today are national banks, but they hold considerably more than half the deposits of the banking system and are larger than most state-chartered banks.

National Banking Act (1863): Legislation aimed at standardizing banking practices and reaffirming the existence of our dual banking system. The law contained the following main provisions. (1) Opportunities for banks to be federally chartered, thus making them national banks. (2) Issuance of Treasury currency backed largely by government bonds. (3) Federal taxation of state bank notes, thus forcing them out of existence. (4) Holding of cash reserves against notes and deposits.

national income (at factor cost): 1. Total of all net incomes earned by, or ascribed to, the factors of production — that is, the sum of wages, rent, interest, and profit that accrues to the suppliers of labor, land, capital, and entrepreneurship. [*Note:* It should not be confused with the total income received by people from all sources (that is, personal income). The difference between the two is based on various accounting considerations.] **2.** In general terms and in theoretical discussions, the expression "national income" is often used in a simple generic sense to represent the income or output of an economy.

National Labor Relations (Wagner) Act (1935): Basic labor relations law of the United States. It (1) guarantees the right of workers to organize and bargain collectively through representatives of their own choosing, (2) forbids employers to engage in unfair labor practices, such as discrimination or interference, and (3) authorizes the National Labor Relations Board to enforce the act and supervise free elections among a company's employees.

National Labor Relations Board: Government agency established under the National Labor Relations Act of 1935 to enforce that act, to investigate violations of it, and to supervise free elections among a company's employees in order to determine which union, if any, is to represent them in collective bargaining.

natural employment: Level of employment at which (1) everyone who wants to work is working, except for those who are frictionally and structurally unemployed, and (2) the average price level is stable. Natural employment is also called **full employment.** (*Contrast with* **natural unemployment.**)

Natural Gas Act (1938): Legislation granting the Federal Power Commission (FPC) authority over the interstate transportation of natural gas and empowering the Commission to regulate rates and services.

natural monopoly: Firm that experiences increasing economies of scale (that is, long-run decreasing average costs of production) over a sufficiently wide range of output, enabling it to supply an entire market at a lower unit cost than two or more firms. Electric companies, gas companies, and railroads are classic examples.

natural output level: Amount of real GNP produced when the economy is operating at the natural level of employment (or unemployment). The natural output level is thus the same as the economy's potential real (or full-employment) GNP.

natural rate of employment: Percentage of employment that is consistent with full (or natural) employment and a stable rate of inflation. (A stable rate of inflation is one that is neither increasing nor decreasing, such as 6%, 8%, 10%, or any other percentage.)

natural rate of unemployment: Percentage of unemployment (including frictional and structural) that is consistent with full employment and a stable rate of inflation. (A stable rate of inflation is one that is neither increasing nor decreasing, such as 6%, 8%, 10%, or any other percentage.)

natural unemployment: Level of unemployment (including frictional and structural) that is consistent with full (or natural) employment and a stable price level. In other words, it is the level of unemployment at which (1) there is only frictional and structural unemployment and (2) the average price level is stable. (*Contrast with* **natural employment.**)

near-monies: Assets that are almost, but not quite, money. They can easily be converted into money because their monetary values are known. *Examples:* time or savings deposits, U.S. government bonds, and cash values of insurance policies.

needs standard: Criterion of income distribution popularly expressed by the phrase, "To each according to his or her needs." This is the distributive principle of pure communism and an approximate criterion for apportioning income in most families. If you regard the needs standard as a just or equitable one, you are assuming that a central authority is capable of determining what constitutes your (and everyone else's) needs. (*Compare* **equality standard; contributive standard.**)

negative income tax: Plan for guaranteeing the poor a minimum income through a type of reverse income tax. A poor family, depending on its size and income, would be paid by the government enough either to reduce or to close the gap between what it earns and an explicit minimum level of income. That level might be equal to or above the government's designated "poverty line." As the family's income increases, the government's payment declines to zero.

negotiable certificate of deposit (CD): Large-denomination notes (minimum: $100,000) issued by major banks. They sell these securities to corporations and large individual investors, who buy them for their interest payments. (*Note:* Most banks also issue deposits or savings certificates for smaller investors. However, these are merely special types of time deposits. They are smaller in size and not marketable, unlike negotiable CDs.)

negotiable order of withdrawal (NOW): A check written against an interest-bearing account. NOW accounts are offered by most banks and other depository institutions. Such accounts are one of several forms of savings-type checkable deposits that pay interest to their owners.

neoclassical economics: Approach to economics that flourished in Europe and the United States between 1870 and World War I. Among its leaders were William Stanley Jevons in England, Carl Menger in Austria, Leon Walras in Switzerland, Vilfredo Pareto in Switzerland, Alfred Marshall in England, and John Bates Clark and Irving Fisher in the United States. The neoclassicists were primarily concerned with refining the principles of price and allocation theory, "marginalism," the theory of capital, and related aspects of economics. They made early and extensive use of mathematics, especially differential and integral calculus, in the development of their analyses and models. Much of the structure of modern economic science is built on their pioneering work.

net national product: Total sales value of goods and services available for society's consumption and for adding to its stock of capital equipment. It represents society's net output for the year and may be obtained by deducting a capital-consumption allowance from gross national product.

net-profit ratio: Ratio of a firm's net profit after taxes to its net sales. It is one of several general measures of a company's performance.

net revenue: A firm's "pure" or net profit, which is equal to its total revenue minus its total cost.

net worth: Difference between the total assets or things of value owned by a firm or individual and the liabilities or debts that are owed.

newly industrializing country (NIC): A formerly less developed country that is undergoing rapid economic growth.

nominal dollars: *Same as* **current dollars.**

nominal GNP: GNP expressed in current dollars of each year, thus reflecting the actual prices of each year. (*Compare* **real GNP.**)

nominal income: Amount of money received for work done. It is also known as **money income.** (*Compare* **real income.**)

nonprice competition: Methods of competition that do not involve changes in selling price. *Examples:* advertising, product differentiation, and customer service.

nontariff barriers: Laws or regulations, other than tariffs, used by nations to restrict imports. For instance, in order to "protect" the health and safety of their citizens, many countries establish much higher standards of quality for various kinds of imported goods than for similar goods produced domestically. Food products and automobiles provide some typical examples. Actually, nontariff barriers (other than import quotas) are direct but subtle protective devices that are never publicly identified as such. Hence, they have become major forms of trade protection used by many countries.

normal good: A good whose consumption varies directly with money income, prices remaining constant. Most consumer goods are normal goods. (Same as **superior good.**)

normal price: The dynamic equilibrium price toward which the market price is always tending but may never reach.

normal profit: Least payment that the owner of an enterprise will accept as compensation for his entrepreneurial function, including risk taking and management. Normal profit is part of a firm's total economic costs, since it is a payment that the owner must receive in order to keep him from withdrawing his capital and managerial effort and putting them into an alternative enterprise.

normative economics: Approach to economics that deals with what "ought to be" rather than with what "is."

Because it involves statements that are value judgments, much of it cannot be empirically verified. (*Compare* **positive economics.**)

Norris–La Guardia Act (1932): Act of Congress that outlawed the yellow-dog contract and greatly restricted the conditions under which court injunctions against labor unions could be issued.

notes payable: Promises to pay the holder, such as a bank, a sum of money within the year at a stated rate of interest.

O

Okun's Law: Relationship between changes in unemployment and the rate of economic growth (measured by changes in real GNP). The law, based on long-run trends, states that unemployment (1) decreases less than 1 percent for each percentage point that the annual growth of real GNP exceeds its long-term average and (2) increases less than 1 percent for each percentage point that the annual growth of real GNP falls short of its long-term average. The economy, therefore, must continue to grow considerably faster than its long-term average rate in order to achieve a substantial reduction in the unemployment rate. (The law is attributed to Arthur Okun, chairman of the Council of Economic Advisors under President Lyndon Johnson.)

oligopoly: Industry or market structure characterized by only a few firms selling either (1) a homogeneous or undifferentiated product—the industry is then called a "perfect" or "pure" oligopoly—or (2) heterogeneous or differentiated products—the industry is then called an "imperfect" oligopoly. Some examples of perfect oligopolies are the copper, steel, and cement industries. Some examples of imperfect oligopolies are the automobile, soap, detergent, and household-appliance industries.

oligopsony: Industry or market structure characterized by only a few buyers of a commodity. *Example:* Natural-gas pipeline companies are oligopsonists in that there are only a few of them that purchase gas for transportation from any given field.

open-market operations: Purchases and sales of government securities by the Federal Reserve System. Purchases of securities are expansionary because they add to commercial banks' reserves; sales of securities are contractionary because they reduce commercial banks' reserves.

open shop: Business firm in which the employer is free to hire either union members or nonmembers.

operating profit ratio: Ratio of a firm's operating profit to its net sales.

opportunity cost: Value of the benefit that is forgone by choosing one alternative rather than another. It is also called "alternative cost," because it represents the implicit cost of the forgone alternative to the individual, household, firm, or other decision-making entity. The opportunity cost of any decision is thus the value of the sacrificed alternative. Because it may often be subjective, opportunity cost is not entered in a firm's public accounting records. (*Compare* **outlay costs.**)

outlay costs: Money expended to carry on a particular activity. They are the explicit costs that are entered in a firm's public accounting records, such as its income statement, to arrive at a measure of profit. *Examples:* wages and salaries, rent, and other money expenditures of a firm.

overinvestment theory (of business cycles): Explanation that holds that economic fluctuations are caused by too much investment in the economy as businesspeople try to anticipate rising demands during an upswing, and by sharp cutbacks in investment during a downswing when businesspeople realize they expanded too much in the previous prosperity.

P

paradox of thrift: Proposition that demonstrates that, if people as a group try to increase their saving, they may end up by saving less. The conclusion of the paradox is that an increase in saving may be desirable for an individual or family. However, for an entire economy, it will lead to a reduction in income, employment, and output if it is not offset by an increase in investment. The concept was first introduced by Bernard Mandeville in *The Fable of the Bees* (1714) and was later recognized in the writings of several classical economists. It subsequently became an integral part of Keynesian economics.

Pareto optimality: Condition that exists in a social organization when no change can be implemented that will make someone better off without making someone else worse off—each in his or her own estimation. Because an economic system is a type of social organization, Pareto optimality is synonymous with *economic efficiency*. (*See also* **efficiency.**)

Pareto, Vilfredo (1848–1923): Italian economist and sociologist who developed many elegant mathematical formulations of economic concepts, especially those pertaining to general equilibrium theory. His work provided a foundation for indifference-curve analysis. He showed that a theory of demand could be developed without dependence on utility, by observing consumer purchases of combinations of goods that are equally acceptable. Heavily influenced by Leon Walras, Pareto succeeded him as Professor of Political Economy at the University of Lausanne, Switzerland. (See **Pareto optimality.**)

parity price: Price that yields an equivalence to some defined standard. *Examples:* (1) In agriculture, a price for an agricultural commodity that gives the commodity a purchasing power (in terms of the goods that farmers buy) equivalent to the purchasing power that it had in a previous base period. (2) In international economics, the price or exchange rate between the currencies of two countries that makes the purchasing power of one currency substantially equivalent to the purchasing power of the other.

parity ratio: In agriculture, an index of the prices farmers receive divided by an index of the prices they pay. It is used to measure the economic well-being of agriculture as a whole.

partial-equilibrium theory: Explanation or model of a particular market, assuming that other markets are in balance. It thus ignores the interrelations of prices and quantities that may exist between markets. *Example:* Ordinary supply-and-demand analysis is normally of a partial-equilibrium nature, since it usually focuses on a single market while neglecting others.

participation rate: See **Labor-Force Participation Rate.**

partnership: Association of two or more individuals to carry on, as co-owners, a business for profit. The partners are solely responsible for the activities and liabilities of the business.

patent: Exclusive right conferred by government on an inventor, for a limited time. It authorizes the inventor to make, use, transfer, or withhold an invention (which might be done even without a patent), but it also gives the inventor the right to exclude others or to admit them on his or her own terms (which can be done only with a patent). Patents are thus a method of promoting invention by granting temporary monopolies to inventors.

patent monopoly: Firm that exercises a monopoly because the government has conferred upon it the exclusive right—through issuance of a patent—to make, use, or vend its own invention or discovery.

peak-load pricing: A practice that utilizes the fact that demand elasticities for some products differ at certain times. Therefore, instead of charging the same price at all times, the seller charges a higher price during peak-demand periods, when demand is more inelastic, and a lower price at other times. In this way, the selling firm reallocates its limited facilities during periods of high demand, thus reducing consumption and obtaining a more even use of its facilities at all times. *Example:* Telephone companies charge higher long-distance rates during the daytime (a peak period) and lower rates during the night (an off-peak period). Some electric utilities practice peak-load pricing based on different time periods.

perfect competition: Name given to an industry or market structure characterized by a large number of buyers and sellers all engaged in the purchase and sale of a homogeneous commodity, with perfect knowledge of market prices and quantities, no discrimination in buying or selling, and perfect mobility of resources. (*Note:* The term is usually employed synonymously with **pure competition,** although there is a technical distinction. Pure competition does not require perfect knowledge or perfect resource mobility, and hence it does not produce as smooth or rapid an adjustment to equilibrium as does perfect competition. However, both types of competition lead to essentially the same results in economic theory.)

permanent-income hypothesis: Proposition that states that a family's propensity to consume (that is, the amount it spends on consumption) depends on its anticipated long-run or permanent income—the average income expected to be received over a number of years. In addition, the theory holds that a family's consumption is approximately proportional to its permanent income. This hypothesis is thus an alternative theory of the consumption function. (*Contrast with* **absolute-income hypothesis; relative-income hypothesis.**)

personal income: In national-income accounting, the total income received by persons from all sources.

personal income distributions: Shares of total income received by people. The shares are often expressed in terms of percentages of aggregate income received by each fifth of all families, or in terms of the percentage of families falling within specific income classes.

Phillips curve: Curve that represents a statistical relationship between unemployment and inflation. Every point on the curve denotes a different combination of unemployment and inflation. A movement along the curve reflects the change in one of these associated with a change in the other.

Phillips Petroleum case (1954): Major regulation case in which the Supreme Court authorized the Federal Power Commission to regulate natural-gas prices that producers charge interstate pipeline companies. This was the first time in the nation's history that the Supreme court ordered a regulatory commission to expand the scope of its authority.

physiocrats: Group of French economists of the middle eighteenth century led by François Quesnay. In 1758, Quesnay presented a circular-flow diagram to depict what he called the "natural order" of an economic system. This model was a crude forerunner of general equilibrium theory, which was developed in mathematical precision in the late nineteenth century.

planned economy: Economic system in which the government, according to a preconceived plan, plays a primary role in directing economic resources for the purpose of deciding what to produce, how much, and possibly for whom. A planned economy may or may not be a command economy, depending on whether the government operates within a substantially authoritarian or democratic framework. (*See also* **command economy.**)

planning-program-budgeting system (PPBS): Method of revenue and expenditure management based on (1) determination of goals, (2) assessment of their relative importance to society, and (3) allocation of resources needed to attain the goals at least cost. In more general terms, PPBS is a budgeting method that relates expenditures to specific goals or programs so that the costs of achieving a particular program can be identified, measured, planned, and controlled.

plant: Establishment that produces or distributes goods and services. In economics, a "plant" is usually thought of as a firm, but it may also be one of several plants owned by a firm.

positive economics: An approach to economics that deals with what "is" rather than with what "ought to be." Much of positive economics involves the use of statements that can be verified by empirical research (that is, by an appeal to the facts). (*Compare* **normative economics.**)

potential real GNP: The level of real aggregate output that would exist if the economy were at full or natural employment.

poverty line: Measure of poverty among families, defined in terms of a sliding income scale that varies between rural and urban locations according to family size.

precautionary motive: Desire on the part of households and businesses to hold part of their assets in liquid form so that they can be prepared for unexpected contingencies. This motive is influenced primarily by income levels rather than by changes in the interest rate, and it is one of the chief sources of demand for loanable funds in the modern theory of interest.

preferred stock: shares of stock that receive priority (that is, preference) over common stock at a fixed rate in the distribution of dividends — or in the distribution of assets, if the company is liquidated.

prepayments: Business expenditures made in advance for items that will yield portions of their benefits in the present and in future years. *Examples:* advance premiums on a fire-insurance policy; expenses incurred in marketing a new product.

present value: Discounted value of future sums of money. The discount is taken at a specified interest rate for a specified period of time. Present value is thus a sum of money adjusted for interest over time.

price: The exchange value of a commodity — that is, the power of a commodity to command some other commodity, usually money, in exchange for itself.

price-consumption curve: In indifference-curve analysis, a line that connects the tangency points of price lines and indifference curves by showing the amounts of two commodities that a consumer will purchase when his or her income and the price of one commodity remain constant while the price of the other commodity varies.

price discrimination: Practice by a seller of charging different prices to the same or to different buyers for the same good, without corresponding differences in costs. (It may also consist of charging buyers the same price despite corresponding differences in costs.)

price leadership: Adherence by firms in an oligopolistic industry, often tacitly and without formal agreement, to the pricing policies of one of its members. Frequently, but not always, the price leader will be the largest firm in the industry and other firms will simply go along with the leader by charging the same price.

price line (budget line): In indifference-curve analysis, a line representing all the possible combinations of two commodities that a consumer can purchase at a particular time, given the market prices of the commodities and the consumer's money budget or income.

price system: Mechanism that allocates scarce goods or resources by rationing them among those buyers and sellers in the market place who are willing and able to deal at the going prices. The term is often used to express the way prices are established through the free play of supply and demand in competitive markets composed of many buyers and sellers. In reality, of course, there may be "noncompetitive" price systems in markets where buyers or sellers are relatively few in number.

primary reserves: A bank's legal reserves (consisting of vault cash and demand deposits with the Federal Reserve Bank) and demand deposits with other banks.

prime rate: Interest rate charged by banks on loans to their most credit-worthy customers.

principle: Fundamental law or general truth. It is often stated as an expression of a relationship between two or more variables. (See also **law**.)

private benefit: Utility that accrues to an individual, household, or firm as a result of a particular act. (Compare **social benefit**.)

private cost: Disutility (including dollar cost) that accrues to an individual, household, or firm as a result of a particular act. (Compare **social cost**.)

private property: Basic institution of capitalism that gives each individual the right to acquire economic goods and resources by legitimate means and to use or dispose of them as he or she wishes. This right may be modified by society to the extent that it affects public health, safety, or welfare.

private rate of return: The business or financial rate of return on an investment—that is, the rate that business-people try to anticipate before investing their funds. In financial terms, it is the expected net profit after taxes and all costs, including depreciation, and may typically be expressed as a percentage annual return upon either the total cost of a project or the net worth of the stockholder owners.

private sector: That segment of the total economy consisting of households and businesses, but excluding government.

"process of creative destruction": An expression coined by the economist Joseph Schumpeter (1883–1950) to describe the growth of a capitalistic economy as a process of replacing the old with the new—that is, old methods of production, old sources of supply, and old skills and resources with new ones.

Producer Price Index (PPI): Average of selected items priced in wholesale markets, including raw materials, semifinished products, and finished goods. The PPI is published monthly by the Bureau of Labor Statistics of the U.S. Department of Labor.

production function: Relationship between the number of units of inputs that a firm employs and the corresponding units of output that result.

production-possibilities curve: Curve that depicts all possible combinations of total output for an economy. The curve assumes: (1) a choice between producing either one or both of two kinds or classes of goods; (2) full and efficient employment of all resources (that is, no under-employment); and (3) a fixed supply of resources and a given state of technological knowledge.

productivity: Relationship between the output of goods or services and one or more of the inputs used to produce the output. Productivity is calculated from a ratio:

$$\text{productivity} = \frac{\text{output}}{\text{input}}$$

A distinction is made between two measures of productivity—partial and total-factor. *Partial productivity* uses only one input in the denominator, as in output per worker or yield per acre. *Total-factor productivity* uses a "weighted" sum of all measurable inputs (land, labor, capital) employed in production. Because of the difficulty of measuring *all* inputs in a production process, partial rather than total-factor productivity is the most widely used type of measure.

product markets: Markets in which businesses sell outputs that they produce (in contrast with resource markets in which they buy the inputs they need in order to produce).

profit: 1. Return to those who perform the entrepreneurial function. The residual (if any) after the payment of wages, rent, and interest to the owners of labor, land, and capital. **2.** Difference between total revenue and total cost. It is the same as net revenue, a residual or surplus over and above normal profit that accrues to the entrepreneur-owner after all economic costs, including explicit (outlay) costs and implicit (opportunity) costs, have been deducted from total revenue.

progressive tax: Tax whose percentage rate increases as the tax base increases. The U.S. personal income tax is an example. The tax is graduated so that, other things being equal and assuming no loopholes, a person with a higher income pays a greater percentage of his income and a larger amount of tax than a person with a lower income.

promissory note: Commitment by one person to pay another a specified sum of money by a given date, usually within a year. It is thus an "I.O.U." Such notes are used by individuals, corporations, and government agencies.

propensity to consume: Relationship between consumption expenditures and income such that, as income increases, consumption increases, but not as fast as income. A graph or equation that expresses this relationship is called a **consumption function.**

propensity to save: Relationship between saving and income such that, as income increases, saving increases, but faster than income.

property resources: Nonhuman productive resources of an economy, including its natural resources, raw materials, machinery and equipment, and transportation and communication facilities.

property tax: Tax on any kind of property, whether real property (land and buildings) or personal property (such as stocks, bonds, and home furnishings).

proportional tax: Tax whose percentage rate remains constant as the tax base increases; hence, the amount of the tax paid is proportional to the tax base. The property tax is an example. Thus, if the tax rate remains constant at 10 percent, a taxpayer who owns $10,000 worth of property pays $1,000 in taxes, and a taxpayer who owns $100,000 worth of property pays $10,000 in taxes.

proprietorship: Simplest form of business organization, in which the owner or proprietor is solely responsible for the activities and liabilities of the business.

prosperity: Upper phase of a business cycle, in which the economy is operating at or near full employment and a high degree of business and consumer optimism is reflected by a vigorous rate of capital investment and consumption.

psychological theory (of business cycles): Explanation of economic fluctuations in terms of people's responses to political, social, and economic events. These responses, the theory holds, set off cumulative waves of optimism and pessimism, causing cycles in economic activity.

public choice: Branch of economics concerned with the study of nonmarket collective decision making, or the application of economics to political science. The goal of public choice is to develop ways of improving efficiency in the public sector, particularly in the provision of social goods.

public good: One that is not subject to the exclusion principle. That is, the good's benefits are indivisible and hence no one can be excluded from its consumption for not paying. Therefore, most public goods, but not all, are produced by the public sector because the private sector is usually unable or unwilling to provide them. Other characteristics of a public good are (1) very low (or even zero) incremental or marginal costs and (2) spillover costs to some groups and spillover benefits to others. *Examples:* national defense, fire protection, air-traffic control, radio broadcasting, and most television transmission.

public sector: That segment of the total economy consisting of all levels of government. It is thus exclusive of the household and business segments, which constitute the private sector.

public works: Government-sponsored construction, defense, or development projects that usually (but not always) entail public investment expenditures that would not ordinarily be undertaken by the private sector of the economy.

pure competition: *See* **perfect competition** for similarities and differences.

pure interest rate: Theoretical interest rate on a long-term, riskless loan, where the interest payments are made soley for the use of someone else's money. In practice, this rate is often approximated by the interest rate on long-term negotiable government bonds.

pure market economy: Competitive economic system characterized by many buyers and sellers, so that prices are determined by the free interaction of supply and demand.

Q

quality circles: Committees of a company's workers that meet periodically to discuss ways of improving production methods, job satisfaction, and productivity.

quantity theory of money: Classical theory of the relationship between the price level and the money supply. It holds that the level of prices in the economy is directly proportional to the quantity of money in circulation. The relationship is such that a given percentage change in the stock of money will cause an equal percentage change in the price level in the same direction. The theory assumes that the income velocity of circulation of money remains fairly stable and that the quantity of goods and services is constant because the economy always tends toward full employment. (*See also* **equation of exchange.**)

quasi-public good: *Same as* **merit good.**

R

rate of return: The interest rate that equates the present value of cash returns on an investment with the present value of the cash expenditures relating to the investment. That is, the rate of return on an investment is the interest rate at which the investment is repaid by its net receipts (that is, the difference between total receipts and total costs).

ratio (logarithmic) scale: Scale on a graph on which equal distances represent equal percentage changes. (It is equivalent to plotting the *logarithms* of the same data on an ordinary arithmetic scale.)

rational-expectations theory: Belief that people form expectations about recurring or *systematic* government fiscal–monetary policies and then refer to those expectations in their economic decision-making. Consequently, by the time the government's policies become known, the public has already acted on them, thereby offsetting their effects. This means that, to assure economic stability, government should choose the right policy and stick to it. That is, government should adhere to a policy of balanced budgets and steady growth of the money supply. Failure to do so will lead to public policies that are self-defeating and inflationary. In other words, the theory holds that the only policy moves that causes changes in people's behavior are the ones that are not expected—the surprise moves. Once the public learns to expect a policy, it no longer alters people's behavior.

rationing: Any method of restricting the purchases or use of a good. Government may, for various reasons, institute a system of rationing when, over an extended period of time, the quantity demanded of a good exceeds the quantity supplied at a given price.

real asset: Claim against a fixed amount of a commodity or the right to a commodity, the money value of which is affected by inflation or deflation. *Examples*: house, car, and most other goods and services. (*See also* **real liability.**)

real-balance effect: Proposition that states that changes in the average price level affect the public's real cash balances and hence people's spending behavior. For example, a decline in the average price level causes the real value or purchasing power of the cash balances held by the public to increase. Therefore, people expand their spending on goods and services. Conversely, a rise in the average price level causes the real value of the public's cash balances to decrease. Therefore, people contract their spending on goods and services. (*Note*: The real-balance effect assumes that "all other things," especially the economy's money supply, remain constant.)

real dollars: Nominal dollars adjusted for price changes. (*See* **constant dollars.**)

real GNP: GNP expressed in constant dollars of a previous period, thus reflecting the actual prices of that period. (*Compare* **nominal GNP.**)

real income: Purchasing power of money income or the quantity of goods and services that can be bought with money income. (*Compare* **nominal income.**)

realized investment: Actual investment out of any realized level of income. Equal to the sum of planned and unplanned (inventory) investment.

real liability: Promise to pay a fixed amount of a commodity, or right to a commodity, the money value of which is affected by inflation or deflation. (*See also* **real asset.**)

real output: Value of physical output unaffected by price changes.

real rate of interest: The interest rate measured in terms of goods. It is the rate that would prevail in the market if the general price level remained stable. Factors determining it are "real demand" for funds by businesses and "real supply" of funds by households. The former, in turn, is determined by the productivity of borrowed capital, and the latter by the willingness of consumers to abstain from present consumption. (*Contrast with* **market rate of interest.**)

real wages: Quantity of goods that can be bought with money wages. Real wages thus depend on the prices of the goods bought with money wages.

recession: Downward phase of a business cycle, in which the economy's income, output, and employment are decreasing and a falling off of business and consumer optimism is reflected by a declining rate of business and consumer optimism is reflected by a declining rate of capital investment and consumption.

recessionary gap: Amount by which aggregate output exceeds aggregate expenditure at full (natural) employment. Also, the amount by which potential output exceeds actual output at an equilibrium price level. Either condition exerts downward pressure on production, employment, and prices.

Reciprocal Trade Agreements program: Plan for expanding American exports through legislation that authorizes the President to negotiate U.S. tariff reductions with other nations in return for parallel concessions. The program consists of the Trade Agreements Act of 1934, with subsequent amendments, and related legislation.

recovery: Upward phase of a business cycle, in which the economy's income, output, and employment are rising and a growing degree of business and consumer optimism is reflected by an expanding rate of capital investment and consumption.

refunding: Replacement or repayment of outstanding bonds by the issuance of new bonds. It is thus a method of prolonging a debt by paying off old obligations with new obligations.

regressive tax: Tax whose percentage rate decreases as the tax base increases. In this strict sense, there is no regressive tax in the United States. However, if we compare the rate structure of the tax with the taxpayer's net income rather than with its actual base, the term "regressive" applies to any tax that takes a larger share of income from low-income taxpayers than from high-income taxpayers. Most proportional taxes are thus seen to have regression effects. A sales tax, for instance, is the same for rich people as for poor people. But the latter spend a larger percentage of their incomes on consumer goods. Therefore, the sales taxes they pay — assuming that there are few if any exemptions — are a greater proportion of their incomes.

relative-income hypothesis: Proposition that states that a family's propensity to consume (that is, the amount it spends on consumption) depends on its previous peak level of income or on the relative position that the family occupies along the income scale. A family's spending behavior is thus influenced by the highest past income levels to which it has become accustomed and by the incomes of other families in the same socioeconomic environment. This hypothesis is an alternative theory of the propensity to consume. (*Contrast with* **absolute-income hypothesis; permanent-income hypothesis.**)

rent: Return to those who supply the factor of production known as "land."

repurchase agreement (RP or "repo"): A type of collateralized loan. The borrower sells the lender a credit instrument, usually a government security, and simultaneously agrees to buy it back on a later date at the same price, plus interest at a specified rate. The lender (investor) thus holds a security as collateral for a loan of fixed maturity at a fixed interest rate. Banks, often in need of short-term funds, are major users of RPs. They are sold to

corporations and to large individual customers who have surplus cash balances to lend.

required reserves: Minimum amount of legal reserves that a bank is required by law to keep behind its deposit liabilities. Thus, if the reserve requirement is 10 percent, a bank with demand deposits of $1 million must hold at least $100,000 of required legal reserves.

resale price maintenance: Practice whereby a manufacturer or distributor of a branded product sets the minimum retail price at which that product can be sold, thereby eliminating price competition at the retail level.

reservation price: Lowest price at which a seller will offer a minimum amount of a good. Graphically, the reservation price is the one that corresponds to the lowest point on a supply curve. This price, therefore, determines the *height* of the curve. (*Contrast with* **supply price.** Note that the supply price is the same as the reservation price *only* at the lowest point on a supply curve.)

reservation wage: Lowest wage rate at which a worker will offer a minimum amount of labor. Graphically, the reservation wage is the one that corresponds to the lowest point on a labor-supply curve. This wage rate, therefore, determines the *height* of the curve.

resource markets: Markets in which businesses buy the inputs or factors of production they need to carry on their operations.

restrictive agreement: Conspiracy of firms that restrains trade among separate companies. It may involve a direct or indirect form of price fixing, output control, market sharing, coercion, exclusion of competitors, and so on. It is illegal under the antitrust laws.

restrictive license: Agreement whereby a patentee permits a licensee to sell a patented product under restricted conditions. The restrictions may include the patentee's limiting the geographic area in which the licensee may operate, level of output, or limiting the price the licensee may charge in selling the patented good.

return on net worth: Ratio of a firm's net profit after taxes to its net worth. It provides a measure of the rate of return on stockholders' investment.

return on total assets: Ratio of a firm's net profit after taxes to its total assets. It measures the rate of return on, or the productivity of, total assets.

revaluation: Official (government) act that makes a domestic currency dearer in terms of foreign currencies (or in terms of gold under a gold standard). (*Contrast with* **devaluation.**)

revenue sharing: Plan by which the federal government turns over a portion of its tax revenues to state and local governments each year.

Ricardo, David (1772–1823): English classical economist, generally regarded as the "greatest of the classical economists." Ricardo was responsible for refining and systematizing much of classical economic thinking. He formulated theories of value, rent, wages, and international trade, some of which have since been modified but many of which have endured to the present. In general, Ricardo held a scientific view of the economy; therefore, the task of economists, he believed, was to discover the laws that determine economic behavior. Among Ricardo's chief contributions that are of major relevance today are the **law of diminishing returns**—one of the most fundamental laws of economics; the theory of economic rent (studied in microeconomics); and the **law of comparative advantage** (studied in international economics).

right-to-work laws: State laws that make it illegal to require membership in a union as a condition of employment. These laws exist mostly in southern and midwestern states; their main effect is to outlaw the union shop, but in practice they have been relatively ineffective.

risk: Quantitative measurement of the mathematical probability (or "odds") that a given undesirable outcome (such as a loss) will occur. Because risk is predictable, losses that arise from risk can be estimated in advance and can be "insured" against—either by the firm itself or by an insurance company. *Examples:* The losses resulting from rejects on an assembly line can be "self-insured" by being built into the firm's cost structure; the possibility of fire damage can be externally insured by an insurance company.

Robinson, Joan (1903–1983): English economist who is best known for her distinguished treatise *The Economics of Imperfect Competition*, published in 1933. In this book, she identified and developed the new concept of monopolistic competition (which she called "imperfect competition"). This type of market structure, she emphasized, was characterized by "partial monopolies" producing similar products in order to fulfill diversified consumer preferences. Imperfect competition, she said, was thus a realistic market structure. Therefore, its underlying theory must be understood in order to evaluate the market behavior of a major segment of the private sector.

Robinson–Patman Act (1936): A major antitrust law of the United States, and an amendment to Section 2 of the Clayton Antitrust Act dealing with price discrimination.

Commonly referred to as the "Chain Store Act," it was passed to protect independent retailers and wholesalers from "unfair discriminations" by larger sellers who enjoy "tremendous purchasing power." The act declared the following illegal: (1) payment of brokerage fees when no independent broker is employed; (2) granting of discounts and other concessions to sellers (such as manufacturers) to buyers (such as wholesalers and retailers), unless such concessions are made to all buyers on proportionately equal terms; (3) price discrimination, except where the price differences make "due allowances" for differences in cost or are offered "in good faith to meet an equally low price of a competitor"; and (4) charging lower prices in one locality than in another, or selling at "unreasonably low prices," when either of these practices is aimed at "destroying competition or eliminating a competitor."

rule of reason: Interpretation of the courts (first announced in the Standard Oil case of 1911) that the mere size of a corporation, no matter how impressive, is no offense therefore not contrary to antitrust law. Instead, it requires "unreasonable" behavior in the form of actual exertion of monopoly power, as shown by unfair practices, for a firm to be held in violation of the antitrust laws. This interpretation, also known as the "good-trust-versus-bad-trust" criterion, was largely reversed in the Aluminum Company of America case in 1945. Nevertheless, the "reasonableness" of market behavior is still a factor that is often considered by the courts in antitrust cases.

rule of 72: Approximate formula for expressing the relationship between the number of years, Y, required for a quantity to double if it grows at an annual rate of compound interest, R. Thus, $YR = 72$. Therefore,

$$Y = \frac{72}{R} \text{ and } R = \frac{72}{Y}$$

Example: At 6 percent interest compounded annually, a quantity will double in $Y = {}^{72}\!/_{6} = 12$ years. Similarly, if a quantity doubles in 12 years, the compounded annual rate of growth is $R = {}^{72}\!/_{12} = 6$ percent.

S

sales tax: A flat percentage levy imposed on retail prices of selected items. The rates and the items taxed vary from state to state.

Samuelson, Paul Anthony (1915–): Leading American economist and the first American to receive the Nobel

Prize in Economic Science. Samuelson's publications are extensive. His first treatise, *Foundations of Economic Analysis* (1947), based on his doctoral dissertation, explored the notion of equilibrium in many new and provocative ways. It also developed a concept of economic dynamics that was highly original and sophisticated. His hundreds of articles range through numerous areas of economics. Many of these articles, dealing with both macroeconomic and microeconomic topics, have become classics. In addition, Samuelson authored an introductory text that served as the standard work in the field for several decades.

"satisfice": A concept to convey the idea that, in reality, firms seek not to maximize profit but to achieve certain levels of satiation. *Example:* Firms try to attain a particular target level or rate of profit, and they try to achieve a specific share of the market or a certain level of sales.

saving: That part of income not spent on the consumption of goods and services.

Say, Jean Baptiste (1767–1832): French classical economist. He is best known for his popularization of Adam Smith's *Wealth of Nations* (1776) and for formulating the "Law of Markets"—the classical doctrine that supply creates its own demand. Say's Law thus asserted the impossibility of general overproduction. This idea was central to classical economic thought, because it led to the conclusion that markets were "self-correcting" if left free of government intervention.

Say's Law: An assertion that "supply creates its own demand." That is, the total supply of goods produced must always equal the total demand for them, since goods fundamentally exchange for goods while money serves only as a convenient medium of exchange. Therefore, any general overproduction is impossible. This assertion, named after the French economist Jean Baptiste Say (1767–1832), was fundamental in classical economic thought, for it led to the conclusion that the economy would automatically tend toward full employment equilibrium if the government followed a policy of laissez-faire.

scarcity, law of: Principle that states that, at any given time and place, economic goods, including resources and finished goods, are scarce in the sense that there are not enough to provide all that people want. Therefore, these scarce goods can be increased, if at all, only through sacrifice of other resources or goods.

Schumpeter, Joseph Alois (1883–1950): Leading Austrian-American economist. His theories can be expressed in the form of several fundamental propositions. (1) The entrepreneur (that is, the businessperson) is the central actor—the prime mover of capitalism. (2) In striving for profit, the entrepreneur innovates by introducing new production techniques and new organizational methods. (3) Innovations cause economic growth, but they are also responsible for business cycles, which ultimately lead to the erosion of capitalism. (4) This erosion is already occurring because the capitalistic institutions that encouraged and nurtured entrepreneurship in the nineteenth and early twentieth centuries have either disappeared or undergone substantial change.

scientific method: A disciplined mode of inquiry represented by the processes of induction, deduction, and verification. The essential steps of the scientific method consist of (1) recognition and definition of a problem, (2) observation and collection of relevant data, (3) organization and classification of data, (4) formulation of hypotheses, (5) deductions from the hypotheses, and (6) testing and verification of the hypotheses. All scientific laws may be modified or challenged by alternative theoretical formulations, and hence the entire cycle consisting of these six steps is a self-correcting process.

seasonal fluctuations: Short-term swings in business and economic activity within the year that are due to weather and custom. *Examples:* upswings in retail sales during holiday periods, such as Christmas and Easter; changes between winter and summer buying patterns.

secondary boycott: Attempts by a union, through strikes, picketing, or other methods, to stop one employer from doing business with another employer. Outlawed by the Labor–Management Relations (Taft–Hartley) Act of 1947.

secondary reserves: A bank's earning assets that are near-liquid (that is, readily convertible into cash on short notice without substantial loss). *Examples:* short-term financial obligations, such as U.S. Treasury bills, high-grade commercial paper, bankers' acceptances, and call loans.

Second Bank of the United States: Chartered for the period 1816 to 1836, the Bank's functions were to serve as fiscal agent for the Treasury, issue its own notes, and finance both rural and commercial business interests. However, the Bank's generally conservative policies caused periods of financial strain throughout the economy. When Andrew Jackson, a "hard-money" advocate who opposed the issuance of paper money by banks, became the nation's President in 1828, he undertook measures to weaken the Bank's effectiveness. As a result, when the Bank's federal charter expired in 1836, it was not renewed.

selling costs: Marketing expenditures aimed at adapting the buyer to the product. *Examples:* advertising, sales promotion, and merchandising.

separation of ownership and control: The notion that, in a modern large corporation, there is a distinction between those who own the business (the stockholders) and those who control it (the hired managers). If stock ownership is widely dispersed, the managers may be able to keep themselves in power for their own benefit rather than for the primary benefit of the corporation and its stockholders.

shadow prices: Estimates of a commodity's prices that would prevail in a highly competitive market composed of many buyers and sellers. Shadow prices are established for accounting purposes as a means of valuing goods and resources that are not valued in the desired way by the price mechanism.

share draft: A check written against an interest-bearing account provided by a credit union. Share draft accounts are one of several forms of savings-type checkable deposits.

Sherman Antitrust Act (1890): A major antitrust law of the United States. It prohibits contracts, combinations, and conspiracies in restraint of trade, as well as monopolization or attempts to monopolize in interstate trade or foreign commerce. Violations are punishable by fines, imprisonment, or both.

shortage: The amount by which the quantity demanded of a commodity exceeds the quantity supplied at a given price, as when the given price is below the free-market equilibrium price. (*Compare* **surplus.**)

short run: Period in which a firm can vary its output through a more or less intensive use of its resources but cannot vary production capacity because it has a fixed plant scale.

simple multiplier: *See* **multiplier.**

single tax: Proposal advanced by the American economist Henry George (1839–1897) that the only tax a society should impose is a tax on land, because all rent on land is unearned surplus that increases as a result of natural progress and economic growth. Three major shortcomings leveled against this thesis are that the single tax (1) would not yield enough revenues to meet government's spending needs; (2) would be unjust, because surpluses

would accrue to resource owners other than landlords if the owners were to gain some monopolistic control over the sale of their resources in the marketplace; and (3) would be difficult to administer because it would not distinguish between land and capital — that is, between the proportion of rent that represents a surplus and the proportion that results from improvements made on the land.

slope: Rate of change or steepness of a line as measured by the change (increase or decrease) in its vertical distance per unit of change in its horizontal distance. It may be calculated from a ration:

$$\text{slope} = \frac{\text{change in vertical distance}}{\text{change in horizontal distance}}$$

Hence, a horizontal line has a zero slope, and a vertical line has an "infinite" slope. All straight lines that are upward or positively inclined have a slope greater than zero. (Analogously, all straight lines that are downward or negatively inclined have a slope less than zero.) Parallel lines have equal slopes. The slope of a straight line is the same at every point, but the slope of a curved line differs at every point. Geometrically, the slope of a curve at a particular point can be found by drawing a straight line tangent to the curve at that point. The slope of the line will then be equal to the slope of the curve at the point of tangency. In economics, all "marginals" are slopes or rate of change of their corresponding "totals." *Examples:* The marginal propensity to consume represents the rate of change or slope of its corresponding total propensity to consume; a marginal-cost curve is the slope of its corresponding total-cost curve; a marginal-revenue curve is the slope of its corresponding total-revenue curve; and so on. The concept of slope or rate of change (that is, "marginality") is unquestionably the most powerful and important analytical tool of economics.

Smith, Adam (1723–1790): Scottish philosopher and author of *The Wealth of Nations* (1776). This was the first comprehensive, systematic study of economics. The treatise earned Smith the appellation "Founder of Economics." In the book, he analyzed such concepts as specialization, division of labor, value and price determination, the distribution of income, the accumulation of capital, and taxation. He argued that, if individuals were left alone to pursue their self-interests, their behavior would, as if guided by an "invisible hand," lead to maximum benefits for society. He thus concluded that laissez-faire (that is, nonintervention of government) was essential to a society's economic efficiency. (*Note:* Smith's ideas became the foundation upon which the whole subsequent tradition of classical economics was constructed.)

social balance: Existence of an optimum distribution of society's resources between the private and public sectors. The former is represented by the production of private goods, such as cars, clothing, and television sets. The latter is represented by the production of such social (merit) goods as libraries, public health, and education.

social benefit: Utility that accrues to society as a result of a particular act, such as production or consumption of a commodity. It includes both private and external (or spillover) benefits. Thus:

social benefits = private benefits + spillover benefits

(*Compare* **private benefit.**)

social cost: Disutility that accrues to society as a result of a particular act, such as production or consumption of a commodity. It includes private costs and reductions in incomes or benefits (externalities or spillovers) caused by the act. Thus:

social costs = private costs + spillover costs

(*Compare* **private cost.**).

social goods: Products provided by government, usually because society believes that such goods are not adequately provided by the private sector through the free market. Social goods include (1) *public goods,* such as national defense, public safety, and street lighting, and (2) *merit goods,* such as public education, libraries, and museums. (*See* **public good; merit good.**)

socialism: 1. In the theories of Karl Marx, a transitory stage between capitalism and full communism, in which the means of production are owned by the state, the state in turn is controlled by the workers ("dictatorship of the proletariat"), and the economy's social output is distributed by this formula: From each according to his ability, to each according to his labor. **2.** In its contemporary form, a movement that seeks primarily to improve economic efficiency and equity by establishing (a) public ownership of all important means of production and distribution and (b) some degree of centralized planning to determine what goods to produce, how they should be produced, and to whom they should be distributed.

social rate of return: Net value of a project to an economy

(that is, of a town, city, state, or country). It is estimated on the basis of the net increase in output that a project such as a new industry may be expected to bring, directly or indirectly, to the area being developed. The industry's contribution is determined by subtracting from the value of what it produces the cost to society of the resources used. Hence the measure is intended to reflect all economic and social benefits as well as costs. (*Compare* **private rate of return.**)

Social Security Act (1935): The basic comprehensive social security law of the United States. Its programs include: (1) *Old Age and Survivors Insurance (OASI):* This program, which is the largest of the three, is what most people refer to as "social security." It pays benefits to retired workers and their dependents and survivors. (2) *Disability Insurance (DI):* This program awards benefits to disabled workers and their dependents. (3) *Hospital Insurance (HI)—Medicare:* This is a health-insurance program providing two sets of benefits—(a) hospital services to those over 65 years of age who are covered by social security (that is, by OASDI) and (b) supplementary medical insurance, available on an optional basis to the elderly. The benefits of the supplementary medical insurance are financed partly through monthly premium charges paid by participants and partly through the general tax revenues of the Treasury. (4) *Public Assistance (PA):* This is a noninsurance program. It provides public charity in the form of welfare services, institutional care, food, housing, and other forms of assistance to the needy.

social security tax: Payroll tax that finances the U.S. compulsory social-insurance program covering old-age and unemployment benefits. The taxes are paid both by employees and by employers, based on the incomes of the former.

Special Drawing Rights (SDRs or "paper gold"): Supplementary reserves (established in 1969) in the form of account entries on the books of the International Monetary Fund. SDRs, which are allocated among participating countries in accordance with their quotas, can be drawn upon by governments to help finance balance-of-payments deficits. They are meant to promote an orderly growth of reserves that will help the long-run expanding needs of world trade.

specialization: Division of productive activities among individuals and regions so that no one person or area is self-sufficient. Total production is increased by specialization, thus permitting all participants to share in a greater volume of output through the process of exchange or trade.

specie: Money in the form of gold or silver coins. The nominal or stated value of the coin should equal the market value of the metal contained in the coin, but this does not usually happen. The reason is that the market value of the gold or silver in the coin fluctuates according to supply and demand. Therefore, the metallic value of the coin may be greater or less than the nominal value stated on the coin. (See **mint ratio.**)

specific subsidy: Per-unit subsidy on a commodity. (See also **subsidy.**)

specific tax: Per-unit tax on a commodity. (See also **tax.**)

speculation: 1. In the popular sense, any business transaction involving considerable risk for the chance of receiving large gains. **2.** In the futures market, the purchase or sale of a futures contract without having an offsetting interest in the actual commodity. An increase in the price of the futures contract creates a profit for buyers of the contract (who are called "longs") and a corresponding loss for sellers of the contract (who are called "shorts").

speculative motive: Desire on the part of households and businesses to hold part of their assets in liquid form so that they can take advantage of changes in the interest rate. This motive is thus tied specifically to the interest rate and is one of the chief sources of demand for loanable funds in the modern theory of interest.

spillovers: External benefits or costs for which no compensation is made. (Spillovers are also called **externalities.**)

stable equilibrium: Condition in which an object or system (such as a price, firm, industry, or market) in equilibrium, when subjected to a shock sufficient to disturb its position, returns toward its initial equilibrium as a result of self-restoring forces. (In contrast, an equilibrium that is not stable may be either unstable or neutral.)

stagflation: Combination of *stagnation* and *inflation*. It is a condition characterized by slow economic growth, high unemployment, and rising prices. Stagflation thus combines some of the features of recession and inflation.

Standard Oil case (1911): Major antitrust case in which Standard Oil of New Jersey was ordered broken up by the Supreme Court. The Court held Standard Oil to be in violation of the Sherman Antitrust Act because the company had engaged in "unreasonable market practices, including the attempt to drive others from the field and to exclude them from their right to trade." In this case, the Court introduced an important new criterion for judging monopoly behavior. (See **rule of reason.**)

state bank: Commercial bank chartered by a state government. Such banks may or may not be members of the Federal Reserve System.

state farms: Lands in the Soviet Union that are owned and operated as state enterprises under elected or governmentally appointed managing directors. Workers and technicians are hired to run the farms and are usually paid set wages. They may also be paid bonuses if their work exceeds basic norms of output.

static model: One in which economic phenomena are studied without reference to time—that is without relating them to preceding or succeeding events. Time, in other words, is not permitted to enter the analysis in any matter that will affect the results. A static model is thus like a "snapshot" as distinguished from a "motion picture." (*Compare* **dynamic model.**)

static multiplier: The multiplier without regard to the time required to realize its full effect. (*Compare* **truncated multiplier.**)

stock: Units of ownership interest in a corporation. The kinds of stock include common stock, preferred stock, and capital stock.

strategic-resource monopoly: Firm that has a monopoly because it controls an essential input to a production process. *Example:* DeBeers of South Africa owns most of the world's diamond mines.

strike: Agreement among workers to stop working, without resigning from their jobs, until their demands are met.

structural budget: *see* **full-employment budget.**

structural inflation: Condition of generally rising prices caused by uneven upward demand or cost pressures in some key industries, such as automobiles, construction, or steel. Structural inflation may occur even if aggregate demand is in balance with aggregate supply for the economy as a whole.

structural unemployment: Type of unemployment, usually prolonged, existing because the location and skill requirements of job openings do not always match the location and skills of unemployed workers. It arises from changes in technology, markets, or national priorities. Most types of workers—unskilled, skilled, or professional—are subject to structural unemployment as a result of any of these factors.

subsidy: Payment (usually by government) to businesses or households that enables them to produce or consume a product in larger quantities or at lower prices than they would otherwise.

subsistence theory of wages: Theory developed by some classical economists of the late eighteenth and early nineteenth centuries. It held that wages per worker tend to equal what the worker needs to "subsist"—that is, to maintain himself and to rear children. If wages per worker rose above the subsistence level, people would tend to have more children and the population would increase, thereby lowering real incomes per capita. Similarly, if wages per worker fell below the subsistence level, people would tend to have fewer children and the population would decline, thereby increasing real incomes per capita. Wages per worker would thus tend to remain at the subsistence level over the long run. This theory is also known as the "brazen (or iron) law of wages."

substitute goods: Commodities that are related such that, at a given level of buyers' incomes, an increase in the price of one good leads to an increase in the demand for the other and a decrease in the price of one good leads to a decrease in the demand for the other. *Examples:* gin and vodka; beef and pork. (*Compare* **complementary goods.**)

substitution effect: Increased quantity demanded of a good when its price declines, because the good replaces some other goods that the consumer purchases. *Example:* A decrease in the price of beef may result in it being substituted for chicken, pork, veal, and perhaps some nonmeat products. The substitution effect assumes that the consumer's money income, tastes, and the prices of other goods remain constant. It helps explain why a demand curve slopes downward. (*See also* **income effect.**)

sunspot theory: Theory of business cycles proposed in England during the late nineteenth century. It held that sunspot cycles (disturbances on the surface of the sun) exhibited an extremely high correlation with agricultural cycles for a number of years; therefore, sunspots must affect the weather, the weather influences agricultural crops, and the crops affect business conditions. This theory received worldwide popularity when it was first introduced, but then fell into disrepute because the high correlation between sunspots and agricultural cycles did not endure; it was the result of accidental rather than causal factors.

superior good: A good whose consumption varies directly with money income, prices remaining constant. Most consumer goods are superior goods. (A superior good is also called a **normal good** because it represents the "normal" situation.)

supermultiplier: An enlargement of the simple multiplier, reflecting the inclusion of the marginal propensity to invest, *MPI.* It may be expressed by the formula

$$\text{supermultiplier} = \frac{1}{1-(MPC+MPI)} = \frac{1}{1-MPE}$$

in which *MPE* denotes the marginal propensity to spend.

supplementary (fringe) benefits: Forms of compensation to workers other than basic wages, such as bonuses, pension benefits, and holiday and vacation pay.

supply: A relation expressing the various amounts of a commodity that sellers would be willing and able to make available for sale at various prices during a given period of time, all other things remaining the same. This relation may be expressed as a table (called a supply schedule), as a graph (called a supply curve), or as a mathematical equation.

supply curve: Graph of a supply schedule, showing the number of units of a commodity that sellers would be able and willing to sell at various prices during a given period of time, all other things remaining the same.

supply, law of: Principle that states that the quantity supplied of a commodity usually varies directly with its price, assuming that all other things that may affect supply remain the same. These "all other" things include (1) resource prices, (2) prices of related goods in production, and (3) the state of technology and other nonmonetary determinants, such as the number of sellers in the market.

supply price: Least price necessary to bring forth a given output. Hence it is the lowest price a seller is willing to accept to persuade him to supply a given quantity of a commodity.

supply schedule: Table showing the number of units of a commodity that sellers would be able and willing to sell at various possible prices during a given period of time, all other things remaining the same.

supply-side economics: Measures aimed at achieving efficiency through policies designed to stimulate production. While there are many policies that may encourage increased production, the most fundamental supply-side policies are those that make direct use of *incentives.* For example, reductions in marginal tax rates—the taxes paid on the last few dollars of wages, interest, and dividends—provide direct incentives to work, save, and invest. (*Contrast with* **demand-side economics.**)

surplus: The amount by which the quantity supplied of a

commodity exceeds the quantity demanded at a given price, as when the given price is above the free-market equilibrium price. (*Compare* **shortage.**)

surplus value: In the theories of Karl Marx, the difference between the value that a worker creates (as determined by the labor-time embodied in the commodity that the worker produces) and the value that he or she receives as determined by the subsistence level of wages. This surplus, according to Marx, is appropriated by the capitalist and is the incentive for the development of a capitalist system.

surtax: Tax imposed on a tax base in addition to a so-called normal tax. *Example*: a surtax on income in addition to the normal income tax. Note that a surtax is imposed on an existing tax base; it is not a "tax on a tax" as is popularly believed.

syndicalism: Economic system that demands the abolition of both capitalism and the state as instruments of oppression and, in their place, the reorganization of society into industry-wide associations or syndicates of workers. The syndicates, fundamentally trade unions, would replace the state. Each syndicate would then govern its own members in their activities as producers but leave them free from interference in all other matters. The chief exponent of syndicalism was the French social philosopher Georges Sorel (1847–1922), some of whose views later influenced the growth of fascism.

T

target-return pricing: Method of pricing that seeks to attain a desired (targeted) percentage rate of return on stockholders' equity or ownership at a planned level of output. The target-return price (P) may be expressed by the equation

$$P = \frac{\% \text{ target return (stockholders' equity)}}{\text{planned output quantity, } Q} + AVC_Q$$

in which AVC_Q is the direct or average variable cost of production at the planned output, Q. *Example*: Suppose that a firm plans to produce 10,000 units of output next year at an average variable cost of $50 per unit. If stockholders' equity is $1 million and the firm targets a 20 percent return, it will charge a price of $70 per unit:

$$P = \frac{0.20\ (\$1,000,000)}{10,000} + \$50 = \frac{\$200,000}{10,000} + \$50$$

$$= \$70 \text{ per unit}$$

Two implications are apparent from target-return pricing: (1) Price varies directly with average variable cost and inversely with the quantity produced. (2) Target-return pricing disregards demand considerations and assumes that the firm can sell its planned output quantity at the target-return price.

tariff: Customs duty or tax imposed by a government on the importation (or exportation) of a good. Tariffs may be (1) specific, in the form of a tax per unit of the commodity, or (2) ad valorem, based on the value of the commodity.

tax: A compulsory payment to government. Its purposes may be (1) to influence efficiency through resource allocation (so as to produce more of some commodities and less of others); (2) to influence equity through income and wealth distribution; (3) to influence economic stabilization; and (4) to influence economic growth.

tax avoidance: Legal methods or "loopholes" used by taxpayers to reduce their taxes. (*Compare* **tax evasion.**)

tax base: An object that is being taxed, such as income (in the case of an income tax), the value of property (in the case of a property tax), or the value of goods sold (in the case of a sales tax.)

tax-based incomes policy (TIP): A proposal for curbing inflation. The program provides tax benefits for those workers and firms that keep wage and price increases within established guidelines and tax penalties for those that do not. The guidelines, based on the economy's productivity and the current rate of inflation—perhaps an average of both—would be announced annually by government. In general, TIP is at best a short-run anti-inflation measure because it deals with the symptoms of inflation, not the cause.

tax evasion: Illegal methods of escaping taxes, such as lying about income or expenses. (*Compare* **tax avoidance.**)

tax incidence: Burden of a tax—that is, the economic entities, such as households, consumers, or sellers, that ultimately bear the tax.

tax multiplier: Relation between a change in personal income taxes and the resulting change in aggregate output. For example, an increase in taxes reduces people's disposable income by that amount. Because consumption depends on income, the level of consumption will decrease by MPC multiplied by the change in income (or taxes). This in turn will cause a magnified drop in GNP, depending on the size of the expenditure multiplier, M_E. Thus the tax multiplier, M_T, may be expressed by the formula

$$M_T = MPC \times M_E$$
$$= MPC \times \frac{1}{MPS}$$

tax rate: Amount of tax applied per unit of tax base, expressed as a percentage. *Example:* A tax of $10 on a base of $100 represents a tax rate of 10 percent.

tax shifting: Changing of the burden or incidence of a tax from the economic entity upon which it is initially imposed to some other economic entity. *Example:* Sales and excise taxes are imposed on the products of sellers, but these taxes are shifted in whole or in part through higher prices to buyers of the goods.

technical efficiency: See **efficiency.**

terms of trade: Number of units of goods that must be given up for one unit of goods received by each party (such as a nation) to a transaction. The terms are thus equal to the ratio at which goods are exchanged. In general, the terms of trade are said to move in favor of the party that gives up fewer units of goods for one unit of goods received and against the party that gives up more units of goods for one unit of goods received. In international economics, the concept of terms of trade plays an important role in evaluating exchange relationships between nations.

theory: Set of definitions, assumptions, and hypotheses put together in a manner that expresses apparent relationships or underlying principles of certain observed phenomena in a meaningful way.

time deposit: Money held in a depository-institution account of an individual or firm. Certain types of time deposits have specified maturity dates. For other types, the depository institution may require advance notice of withdrawal.

time preference: Human desire for a good in the present as opposed to the future. The desire is reflected by the price people are willing to pay for immediate possession of the good as opposed to the price they are willing to pay for future possession.

time series: A set of data ordered chronologically. Most of the published data of business and economics are expressed in the form of time series.

time value of money: The notion that dollars at different points in time cannot be made directly comparable unless they are first adjusted by a common factor—the interest rate. For example, if your money can earn 6 percent annually, then $1 today is worth $1.06 to you one year from today. Similarly, $1.06 next year is worth an additional 6 percent, or $1.124, two years from today. Conversely, $1.06 one year from today is worth $1 to you today; $1.124 two years from today is worth $1.06 a year from today, and is worth $1 today. (See *also* **compounding; discounting.**)

TIP: See **tax-based incomes policy.**

Tobin, James (1918–): Leading American economist and professor emeritus at Yale University. Much of his research involved the integration of Keynesian macroeconomic theory with the ways in which people and institutions behave in the market place. His best-known work was on the subject of portfolio-selection theory, for which he was commended when he received the Nobel Prize in 1981.

token money: Any object (usually coins) whose value as money is greater than the market value of the materials of which it is composed. *Example:* pennies, nickels, and so on.

total cost: Sum of a firm's total fixed costs and total variable costs.

total fixed costs: Costs that do not vary with a firm's output. *Examples:* rental payments, interest on debt, property taxes.

total–marginal relationship: Relationship between all corresponding total and marginal curves such that, when a total curve is increasing at an increasing rate, its corresponding marginal curve is rising; when a total curve is increasing at a decreasing rate, its corresponding marginal curve is falling; and when a total curve is increasing at a zero rate, as occurs when it is at a maximum, its corresponding marginal curve is zero. (*Note:* The case of decreasing total curves gives rise to negative marginal curves, but these situations need not be included in the definition because they are not ordinarily relevant or realistic in an economic sense.)

total revenue: A firm's total receipts; equal to price per unit times the number of units sold.

total variable costs: Costs that vary directly with a firm's output, rising as output increases over the full range of production. *Examples:* costs of raw materials, fuel, labor, and so on.

trade association: Organization of independent business enterprises (usually but not always in the same industry) established for mutually beneficial purposes. (*Note:* A trade association that behaves illegally by fixing prices, restricting output, or allocating markets for its members is similar to a cartel.) (See *also* **cartel.**)

Trade Expansion Act (1962): Part of the U.S. Reciprocal Trade Agreements program. This act broadened the powers of the President to (1) negotiate further tariff reductions on broad categories of goods; (2) lower or eliminate tariffs on those goods for which the European Common Market and the United States together account for at least 80 percent of total world exports; (3) lower tariffs by as much as 50 percent on the basis of reciprocal trade agreements, provided that such agreements include most-favored-nation clauses so that the benefits of reduced tariffs are extended to other countries; and (4) grant vocational, technical, and financial assistance to American employees and businesspeople whose industries are adversely affected by tariff reduction.

trade-possibilities curve: Curve that depicts the amounts of goods that countries may exchange with each other. The *slope* of the curve measures the **terms of trade.**

transaction deposit: *See* **checkable deposits.**

transactions motive: Desire on the part of households and businesses to hold some of their assets in liquid form so that they can engage in day-to-day spending activities. This motive is influenced primarily by the level of income rather than by changes in the interest rate, and it is one of the chief sources of demand for loanable funds in the modern theory of interest.

transfer payments: Expenditures within or between sectors of the economy for which there are no corresponding contributions to current production. *Examples:* social security payments, unemployment compensation, relief payments, veterans' bonuses, net interest paid on government bonds and on consumer loans, and business transfers (such as charitable contributions and losses resulting from theft and from debt defaults).

transmission mechanism: Process by which changes in the money supply bring about changes in people's spending behavior, and affect prices, interest rates, and other economic variables. In the Keynesian model, the transmission mechanism or chain of causation is: money $\rightarrow$ interest rates $\rightarrow$ prices. In the monetarist model, the causal chain is: money $\rightarrow$ prices $\rightarrow$ interest rates.

Treasury bills: Marketable financial obligations of the U.S. Treasury. They have minimum denominations of $10,000, and they usually mature in 3 months, 6 months, or 1 year.

Treasury bonds: Marketable financial obligations of the U.S. Treasury, maturing in more than 10 years from the date of issue. (These are *not* U.S. Savings Bonds, with which most people are familiar.)

Treasury notes: Marketable financial obligations of the U.S. Treasury, maturing in 1 to 10 years from date of issue.

trend: Long-run growth or decline of an economic time series over a period of years.

truncated multiplier: The multiplier applicable to a finite number of time periods. Its size approaches that of the static multiplier as the number of periods increases. However, it always realizes more than half the effect of the static multiplier within the first few periods. Thus the truncated multiplier for, say, four periods is:

truncated multiplier for four periods
$$= 1 + MPC + (MPC)^2 = (MPC)^3$$

two-part tariff: Pricing method whereby the buyer pays two different sums: a fixed charge representing an access fee and another charge varying with use. This pricing method is suitable for a product with separable complementary demands. (*Examples:* public utilities charge a minimum fee and then levy an additional charge based on services rendered. An amusement park may charge an entrance fee and then impose separate charges for individual attractions.) In most cases, the fixed fee is intended to recover installation and maintenance costs, while the variable charges are designed to pay for the operation of specific services actually consumed.

tying contract (tie-in sale): Practice whereby a seller requires the buyer to purchase one or more additional or "tied" products as a condition for purchasing the desired or "tying" product. *Examples:* block bookings of motion pictures in which movie theaters are required to take "B" films as a condition for obtaining "A" films; the United Shoe Machinery Co., which once required shoemakers to purchase other materials as a condition for purchasing their shoe machinery.

U

uncertainty: State of knowledge in which the probabilities of outcomes resulting from specific actions are not known and cannot be predicted because they are subjective rather than objective phenomena. Uncertainties, therefore, are not insurable and cannot be integrated into the firm's cost structure.

underconsumption theory (of business cycles): Explanation of economic fluctuations that holds that recessions result from consumer expenditures lagging behind output because too large a proportion of society's income is not spent on consumption. According to the theory, society distributes income too inequitably to enable people to purchase all the goods produced.

underemployment (disguised unemployment): Condition in which employed resources are not being used in their most efficient ways.

unemployment: Situation that exists whenever resources are out of work or are not being used efficiently. There are various types of unemployment, such as technological, frictional, structural, disguised, involuntary, and cyclical. (Each of these is defined separately in this Dictionary.) The type most commonly meant, unless otherwise specified, is **involuntary unemployment.**

unemployment benefits: Weekly payments, administered by state governments, to "covered" workers who are involuntarily unemployed.

unemployment rate: Percentage of the civilian labor force that is not working but is actively seeking work. The figure is based on a monthly survey conducted by the U.S. Department of Labor.

unfair competition: Deceptive, dishonest, or injurious methods of competitive behavior. Such practices are illegal under the antitrust laws.

union: Organization of workers that seeks to gain a degree of monopoly power in the sale of its services so that it may be able to secure higher wages, better working conditions, protection from arbitrary treatment by management, and other economic improvements for its members.

union shop: Business firm that permits a union nonmember to be hired on condition that he or she join the union after being employed.

U.S. Steel case (1920): Major antitrust case against U.S. Steel Corporation. The company, formed from a consolidation of many independent firms in 1901, accounted for nearly half the national output of iron and steel. Nevertheless, the Court found no evidence of wrongdoing and refused to order the breakup of the company. "The law does not make mere size an offense, or the existence of unexerted power an offense," said the Court. This was thus an application of the *rule of reason* by the Court, one of many such applications that have been made.

utility: Ability of a good to satisfy a want. Utility is determined by the satisfaction that one receives from consuming something.

utopian socialism: Philosophy advanced by a group of English and French writers in the early nineteenth century that advocated the creation of model communities, largely self-contained, in which the instruments of production were collectively owned and government was primarily on a voluntary and wholly democratic basis. The leading proponents were Robert Owen (1771–1858) in England and Charles Fourier (1772–1837) in France.

V

value: Power of a commodity to command other commodities in exchange for itself, as measured by the proportional quantities in which a commodity exchanges with all other commodities.

value added: Increment in value at each stage in the production of a good. The sum of the increments for all stages of production gives the total income—the aggregate of wages, rent, interest, and profit—derived from the production of the good.

value-added tax: Type of national sales tax paid by manufacturers and merchants on the value contributed to a product at each stage of its production and distribution.

variable costs: Costs that vary directly with a firm's output, rising as output increases over the full range of production. *Examples:* costs of raw materials, fuel, labor, and so on.

variable proportions, law of: *See* **diminishing returns, law of.**

Veblen, Thorstein Bunde (1857–1929): American institutional economist and critic of neoclassical economics. He emphasized the role of social institutions (that is, customs and practices) as major determinants of economic behavior. Among his many books, his first and best-known one was *The Theory of the Leisure Class* (1899). In this book he coined the famous phrase "conspicuous consumption" as a characteristic of the "leisure class." (*See* **conspicuous consumption.**)

verification: Testing of alternative hypotheses or conclusions by means of actual observation or experimentation—that is, by reference to the facts.

vertical equity: Doctrine that states that "unequals should be treated unequally." *Example:* Persons of different income, wealth, or other taxpaying ability should, in order to bear equal tax burdens (or make equal subjective sacrifices), pay different amounts of tax. (*Compare* **horizontal equity.**)

vertical merger: Amalgamation under one ownership of plants engaged in different stages of production of the same or similar goods, from raw materials to finished products. It may take the form of forward integration into buyer markets or backward integration into supplier markets.   The chief objective is to achieve greater economies by combining different production stages and by regularizing supplies, thereby increasing profit margins. *Example*: A shoe manufacturer may merge with a chain of retail shoe stores, and with a leather-processing firm.

W

wages: 1. Payment to those owners of resources who supply the factor of production known as "labor."   This payment includes wages, salaries, commissions, and the like.   **2.** The price paid for the use of labor.   It is usually expressed as time rates, such as so much per hour, day, or week, or less frequently as rates of so much per unit of work performed.

wages-fund theory: Classical theory of wages best articulated by John Stuart Mill in 1848.   It held that producers set aside a portion of their capital funds for the purpose of hiring workers needed for production.   The amount of the fund depends on the stock of capital relative to the number of workers.   In the long run, however, the accumulation of capital is itself limited or determined by the tendency toward a minimum "subsistence rate" of profits; hence the only effective way to raise real wages is to reduce the number of workers or size of the population.   (*Note:* This theory was a reformulation of the **subsistence theory of wages.**)

Walras, Leon (1834–1910): French economist whose major work, *Elements of Pure Economics* (1874), was done at the University of Lausanne, Switzerland.   He is regarded as one of the greatest economic theorists of all time.   This is due to his mathematical formulations of the theory of general equilibrium "under a system of perfectly free competition."   The model links the various markets of the economy through systems of equations, and shows the conditions needed to determine equilibrium prices and quantities.   The Walrasian system thus represents the perfection of classical and neoclassical economics.

"wastes" of monopolistic competition: Expression used to denote overcrowded "sick" industries of monopolistic competition; the wastes are characterized by chronic excess capacity and inefficient operations.   *Examples:* retail trades; textile manufacturing.

wealth: Anything that has value because it is capable of producing income.   A "stock" of value as compared to a "flow" of income.   (*Compare* **income.**)

welfare economics: Branch of economic theory concerned with the development of principles for maximizing social welfare.

Wheeler–Lea Act (1938): Amendment to the Federal Trade Commission Act.   It was passed primarily to protect consumers, rather than just business competitors, from unfair (deceptive, dishonest, or injurious) methods of competition.   Thus, injured consumers are given equal protection before the law with injured merchants.   The act also prohibits false or misleading advertisements for food, drugs, cosmetics, and therapeutic devices.

white market: Legal market in which ration coupons for a commodity are transferable, permitting people who do not want all their coupons to sell them to those who do.   A white market thus reduces, but does not eliminate, the inequities and skullduggery generally associated with rationing and a black market.   (*Compare* **black market.**)

Y

yellow-dog contract: Contract that requires an employee to promise as a condition of employment that he will not belong to a labor union.   Declared illegal in the Norris–La Guardia Act of 1932.

yield: Effective rate of return on any type of investment. It includes both annual returns and any profit (or loss) that is realized when the investment is terminated.   The yield is expressed as a percentage figure.

yield, current: Annual return on an investment expressed as a percentage of its present price.

yield curve: Graph that shows, at a given time, the relationship between yields and maturities for debt instruments of equal risk (for example, treasury bonds).   The yield curve thus expresses the *term structure of interest rates* for a particular class of debt instruments, which are alike in all respects except their maturity dates.

yield to maturity: Percentage figure reflecting the effective yield on a bond.   The figure is based on the difference between its purchase price and its redemption price, taking into account any returns received by the bondholder in the interim.

El of Demand

$$E_D = \frac{\dfrac{Q_2 - Q_1}{Q_2 + Q_1}}{\dfrac{P_2 - P_1}{P_2 + P_1}}$$

1) $E = \infty$ PERFECT. ELAS.

2) $E > 1$ REL. ELAS.

3) $E = 1$ UNIT ELAS.

4) $E < 1$ REL. INELAS

5) $E = 0$ PER. INELAS

Income el of Dem

$$YE_D = \frac{\dfrac{Q_2 - Q_1}{Q_1 + Q_1}}{\dfrac{Y_2 - Y_1}{Y_2 + Y_1}}$$

General Business and Economic Indicators

Population, Employment, Wages, and Productivity   **Production, Business Activity**   **Prices**

	(28)	(29)	(30)	(31)	(32)	(33)	(34)	(35)	(36)	(37)	(38)	(39)	(40)	(41)	(42)
	Population	Civilian labor force	Unemployment	Unemployment as percent of civilian labor force	Average weekly hours of work	Average gross hourly earnings	Output per hour of all persons	Compensation per hour	Index of industrial production	Total new construction / Value put in place	Business expenditures for new plant and equipment	Manufacturers' new orders	Consumer Price Index	Producer Price Index (total finished goods)	Implicit Price Index (GNP deflator)
					Total non-agricultural private sector		Business sector								
Year	Millions of persons			Percent	Hours	Dollars	1977 = 100		1967 = 100	Billions of dollars	Billions of dollars	Billions of dollars	1967 = 100		1972 = 100
1930	123.2	49.8	4.3	8.7	–	–	–	–	18.0	8.7	–	–	50.0	44.6	33.7
1935	127.4	52.9	10.6	20.1	–	–	–	–	17.3	4.2	–	–	41.1	41.3	29.2
1940	132.1	55.6	8.1	14.6	–	–	–	–	25.4	8.7	–	–	42.0	40.5	30.0
1945	140.0	53.9	1.0	1.9	–	–	–	–	40.6	5.8	–	–	53.9	54.6	40.9
1950	151.7	62.2	3.3	5.3	39.8	1.335	50.3	20.0	44.9	33.6	21.07	20.1	72.1	81.8	53.6
1955	165.3	65.0	2.9	4.4	39.6	1.71	58.2	26.3	58.5	46.5	30.44	27.5	80.2	87.8	61.0
1960	180.7	69.6	3.9	5.5	38.6	2.09	65.1	33.9	66.2	54.7	39.08	30.2	88.7	94.9	68.7
1961	183.8	70.5	4.7	6.7	38.6	2.14	67.2	35.2	66.7	56.4	38.02	31.1	89.6	94.5	69.3
1962	186.7	70.6	3.9	5.5	38.7	2.22	69.8	36.8	72.2	60.2	40.53	33.4	90.6	94.8	70.6
1963	189.4	71.3	4.1	5.7	38.8	2.28	72.4	38.1	76.5	64.8	43.33	35.5	91.7	94.5	71.6
1964	192.1	73.1	3.8	5.2	38.7	2.36	75.5	40.1	81.7	68.0	50.90	38.4	92.9	94.7	72.7
1965	194.6	74.5	3.4	4.5	38.8	2.45	78.2	41.7	89.8	74.1	59.15	42.1	94.5	96.6	74.3
1966	197.0	75.8	2.9	3.8	38.6	2.56	80.6	44.6	97.8	76.8	70.00	46.4	97.2	99.8	76.8
1967	199.1	77.3	3.0	3.8	38.0	2.68	82.4	47.0	100.0	78.5	72.35	47.1	100.0	100.0	79.0
1968	201.2	78.7	2.8	3.6	37.8	2.85	85.2	50.6	106.3	87.5	75.95	50.7	104.2	102.9	82.6
1969	202.7	80.7	2.8	3.5	37.7	3.04	85.4	54.2	111.1	94.3	85.25	54.0	109.8	106.6	86.7
1970	204.9	82.8	4.1	4.9	37.1	3.23	86.1	58.2	107.8	95.2	91.37	52.0	116.3	110.3	91.4
1971	207.1	84.4	5.0	5.9	36.9	3.45	89.2	62.0	109.6	110.3	92.26	56.0	121.3	113.7	96.0
1972	208.9	87.0	4.8	5.6	37.0	3.70	92.4	66.0	119.7	124.4	102.73	64.2	125.3	117.2	100.0
1973	211.9	89.4	4.3	4.9	36.9	3.94	94.8	71.3	129.8	138.4	118.54	76.1	133.1	127.9	105.7
1974	213.9	91.6	5.2	5.6	36.5	4.24	92.7	78.0	129.3	139.2	137.20	87.2	147.7	147.5	114.9
1975	216.0	93.8	7.9	8.5	36.1	4.53	94.8	85.5	117.8	135.9	138.28	85.1	161.2	163.4	125.6
			7.4	7.7	36.1	4.86	97.9	92.9	130.5	151.1	150.91	99.5	170.5	170.6	132.1
									138.2	173.8	174.68	115.0	181.5	181.7	139.8
									146.1	205.6	203.54	131.5	195.4	195.9	150.1
									152.5	230.4	240.22	147.4	217.4	217.7	163.4
									147.0	230.7	264.44	156.2	246.8	247.0	178.4
									151.0	239.1	289.37	167.8	272.4	269.8	195.6
									138.6	230.1	282.71	157.4	289.1	280.7	207.4
									147.6	262.2	269.22	173.4	298.4	285.2	215.3
									163.5	311.9	307.59	191.6	311.1	291.2	223.4